Waterloo County to 1972:
an annotated bibliography of regional history

Waterloo County is a complex region settled by peoples from various ethnic and cultural backgrounds. Its economic activities range from the traditional farms of Old Order Mennonites to the innovative enterprises of "Canada's technology triangle." Compared with neighbouring counties of southern Ontario, Waterloo is also more urbanized and industrialized. A region of great historical interest not only to its own residents but also to researchers across Canada and elsewhere, it is notable for the activity of its local historians and genealogists reflected, for example, in the unbroken publishing record of the Waterloo Historical Society since 1912.

The Waterloo Regional Project has created a bibliographic database with abstracts and detailed indexes for over 4,500 printed items -- books, booklets, theses, reports, journal articles and chapters in books -- that relate to the history of Waterloo County prior to the introduction of regional government in 1973. This reference work has been designed to meet the needs of a wide range of researchers, including amateur historians, genealogists, house history detectives, journalists, neighbourhood groups, landscape architects, museum workers, librarians, archivists, municipal officials and staff, as well as teachers and students at all levels from elementary school children to postgraduates.

Elizabeth Bloomfield is an historical research consultant who uses computer-assisted methods to create information bases and research tools for urban, business and regional history. She has also directed the Guelph Regional Project and the Canadian Industry in 1871 Project. Linda Foster and Jane Forgay are librarian-bibliographers who worked for the Waterloo Regional Project in 1991-92.

The **Waterloo Regional Heritage Foundation** is an organization representing most historical and heritage societies in the Region of Waterloo and supported by the Regional Municipality. The Foundation chose to publish this volume to mark the 20th anniversary of regional government.

WATERLOO COUNTY TO 1972:

an annotated bibliography of regional history

Elizabeth Bloomfield

with Linda Foster and Jane Forgay

waterloo regional heritage foundation

Copyright **C** 1993 by Elizabeth Bloomfield

Printed in Canada on acid-free paper

ISBN 0-9696936-0-5

Canadian Cataloguing in Publication Data

Bloomfield, Elizabeth
Waterloo County to 1972

Includes index.
ISBN 0-9696936-0-5

1. Waterloo (Ont. : County) - History - Bibliography.
I. Foster, Linda, 1949-   . II. Forgay, Jane.
III. Waterloo Regional Heritage Foundation.
IV. Title.

Z1392.W3B56 1993   016.9713'44   C93-093570-5

This book has been published with the help of grants from
the Waterloo Regional Heritage Foundation and The Good Foundation Inc.
The creation of the bibliographic database was supported by generous grants from
the Social Sciences and Humanities Research Council of Canada
(Canadian Studies Research Tools Program) and
the Waterloo Regional Heritage Foundation.

Printed by Cober Printing Limited, Kitchener

DEDICATION

Waterloo County to 1972: an annotated bibliography of regional history
is dedicated to
all who have recorded the history of Waterloo County,
all who care for the historical records,
and all who will use this bibliography
to understand and interpret the region in future.

CONTENTS

FOREWORD

As the 20th anniversary of the Regional Municipality of Waterloo drew near, the Waterloo Regional Heritage Foundation sought a suitable heritage project to recognize the event.

What better legacy could the Foundation leave for this milestone than publication of **Waterloo County to 1972: an annotated bibliography of regional history,** compiled by Dr Elizabeth Bloomfield with Linda Foster and Jane Forgay?

This annotated bibliography with its diverse and cross-referenced subject areas will provide a helpful and convenient tool for regional research. The resource material will assist not only the serious researcher but also the student, businessman or layman.

In research, finding the source of information is often the most difficult task. The indexes of this bibliography volume, along with computer searches of its database, will relieve researchers of hours of work and allow them to concentrate on finding new information.

I commend and praise the work of Dr Bloomfield, Linda and Jane. Their thorough searches of library collections and their concise annotations and detailed indexes of authors, places, topics, persons and organizations will lead users to exact sources of information. From these sources, one can trace our history and lead future historians into new fields perhaps presently ignored or under-researched.

Patricia Wagner, Chair
Waterloo Regional Heritage Foundation

ACKNOWLEDGEMENTS

The production of this bibliography owes a great deal to the Waterloo Regional Project's Research Associates, Linda Foster and Jane Forgay. Funding for the project allowed us to employ qualified librarian-bibliographers who also brought other abilities to the project, Jane in German language and Linda in Scottish history. Both were strongly dedicated to the project's goals and went far beyond their formal job descriptions of searching library holdings, reading the material, writing abstracts, assigning index terms, and entering the data into the computer. Their passion for thoroughness and accuracy is reflected in the pages of this volume. Sharing the challenges of such a project has made us all firm friends.

The interest and support of the project's advisory panel are much appreciated. Two members were very closely involved throughout the project. Thanks are especially due to Susan Saunders Bellingham (Head of Special Collections, University of Waterloo Library) for her constant encouragement and key roles in chairing the advisory group, arranging working space for the team in the Arts Library, and facilitating financial support from the Waterloo Regional Heritage Foundation. And to Susan Hoffman who, with her colleagues in the Grace Schmidt Room, generously accommodated the team for the many months we worked in the local history collections of the Kitchener Public Library and the Waterloo Historical Society.

Other members of the advisory group who advised and encouraged the team were Patricia Wagner (Waterloo Regional Heritage Foundation); Mary Johnston, Kathryn Lamb, Grace Schmidt and Ernst Ritz (Waterloo Historical Society); Erich Schultz (for the Wilfrid Laurier University Library and the Archives of the Eastern Synod, Evangelical Lutheran Church in Canada); James Quantrell (City of Cambridge Archives); Scarlett Janusas (Regional Archaeologist); Mary Anne Kirkness (Elmira Library); Elizabeth Macnaughton (Doon Heritage Crossroads); Janet Seally (Waterloo Public Library); Kenneth McLaughlin and Gary Draper (St Jerome's College); Garry Peters (Emmanuel Bible College); Reg Good (Conrad Grebel College Library); Lorna Bergey (Mennonite Historical Society); Diane Fitzpatrick and Ruth Lamb (Dana Porter Library, University of Waterloo); and Ron Lambert and Ryan Taylor (Waterloo-Wellington Chapter, Ontario Genealogical Society). We greatly appreciate the help given by all these and by others, including Rosemary Willard Ambrose, Tom Arnold, Gerald Bloomfield, Victoria Bloomfield, Jane Britton, Lorna Ferguson, Father John Finn, Virginia Gillham, Marion Hall, Norma Huber, Linda Kearns, Nancy-Lou Patterson, Marie Puddister, Lorraine Roth, Shelley Saunders, Bertha Thompson and Sandra Woolfrey.

We are grateful to all librarians and archivists in more than 40 university, public and special collections for their co-operation and practical help. Ralph Daehn (now in Cataloguing in the University of Guelph Library) consulted on various aspects of the project and provided substantial assistance with data communication, notably in downloading of bibliographic information from the region's three computerized library systems. For this service we thank him and also those who facilitated it, notably Ruth Lamb in the University of Waterloo Library, Herb Schwartz in the Wilfrid Laurier University Library, and Kathy Dutchak of the Kitchener Public Library.

This publication and the Waterloo Regional Project itself were made possible by generous grants from the Social Sciences and Humanities Research Council of Canada (Canadian Studies Research Tools Program), the Waterloo Regional Heritage Foundation, and The Good Foundation Inc. We thank officers and staff of these organizations for their assistance.

INTRODUCTION

Waterloo County (administered as the Regional Municipality of Waterloo since 1973) has several qualities that distinguish it from the rest of southern Ontario. It is a complex region settled by peoples from various ethnic and cultural backgrounds. Its diverse forms of economic activity range from the traditional farms of Old Order Mennonites to the innovative enterprises of "Canada's technology triangle." Compared with neighbouring counties of southern Ontario, Waterloo is also more urbanized and industrialized, its growth for the past century fuelled by manufacturing industry.

Waterloo County is an area of great historical interest, not only to its own residents but also to researchers across Canada and elsewhere. It is notable for the activity of local historians and genealogists, and especially for the unbroken publishing record of the Waterloo Historical Society, founded in 1912. The contents of the Society's annual volumes, as well as other printed materials relating to the history of settlement and development of Waterloo County from about 1800 to 1972, have now been abstracted and indexed, using a sophisticated methodology of creating research tools for local and regional history. The purpose of this bibliography is to provide clear guidance to printed sources of information on the history of Waterloo County so that users with various interests can know what items are likely to be useful and where they may be found.

Here we introduce Waterloo County and the Waterloo Regional Project, outlining how this bibliography has been created and suggesting how it may be used. This reference work has been designed to meet the needs of a wide range of researchers, including amateur historians, genealogists, house history detectives, newspaper reporters, neighbourhood groups, landscape architects, museum workers, librarians, archivists, municipal officials and staff, as well as teachers and students at all levels from elementary school children to postgraduate researchers.

WATERLOO COUNTY

In 1972, Waterloo County had a population of about 260,000 in an area of about 530 square miles (134,000 hectares), occupying the middle section of the Grand River valley in midwestern Ontario. From 1850, Waterloo County comprised Waterloo Township (the largest, with 39,000 ha) in the centre, flanked by the townships of North Dumfries (19,583 ha) to the south, Wilmot (25,833 ha) and Wellesley (27,860 ha) to the west, and Woolwich (24,167 ha) to the north. The county area is surrounded to the east and north by Wellington County, while to the west and south its neighbours are Perth, Oxford and Brant Counties. Though closely connected with Wellington County in location, physiography and hydrography and in early district administration, Waterloo County's history provides many points of contrast.

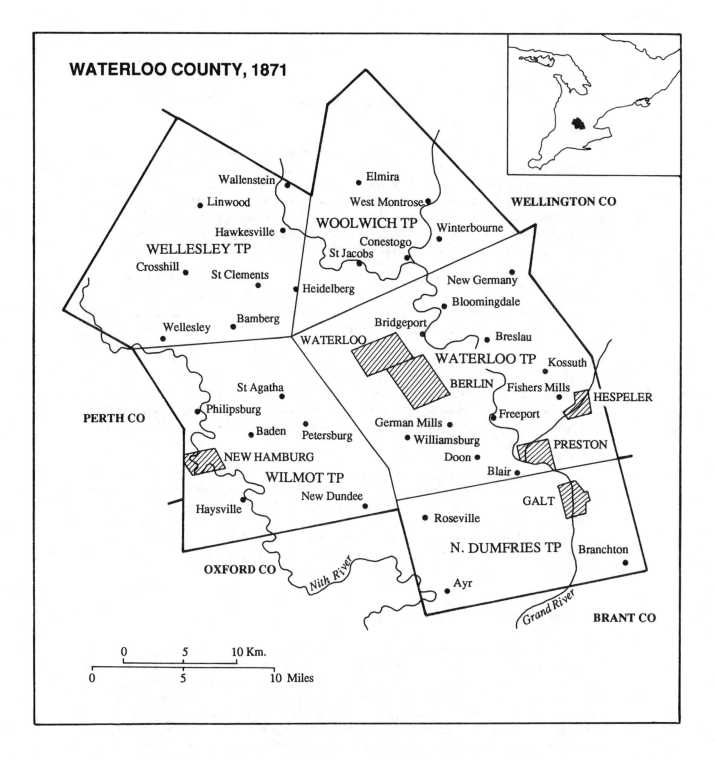

Figure 1: Incorporated municipalities and villages, 1871.
Named places each had at least 100 population in the 1871 census.

During the founding period of white settlement, organized group settlements were significant in and around the Grand River valley lands of the Six Nations Indians. Three important ethnic groups have shaped the history of Waterloo in the nineteenth and twentieth centuries. In the very early years of the nineteenth century, Pennsylvania Mennonites purchased the German Company Tract as the first inland block of land to be settled by whites in Upper Canada; this later became Waterloo Township. Similar groups of Mennonites or Amish settled much of Woolwich Township to the north and Wilmot Township to the west. Still etched in the landscape, particularly of the former townships of Waterloo and Woolwich, is evidence of the distinctive pattern of land subdivision that, among other things, did not provide for surveyed road allowances. As the Mennonite pioneers intended a farm-based culture, townsites were not usually surveyed either. So the small hamlets and villages such as Berlin, Waterloo, Elmira and Hespeler began informally and grew organically at crossroads and millsites. The Mennonite cultural heritage includes many distinctive elements from folk art to food preparation. Those who adhere to the Old Order still maintain a visibly different culture and landscape in the north and northwest of the region.

The well-established Pennsylvania Mennonite settlements attracted some of the thousands of German migrants who came to North America from the 1820s. Generally, those who came between the 1820s to the 1840s were from the southwestern German states and some were Catholics; later migrants tended to be Lutherans from the centre and east of Germany, including Prussia. There were also Polish immigrants from the late nineteenth century and others from central and eastern Europe in the twentieth century. These immigrants from Europe settled throughout the northern and central parts of Waterloo County, but particularly in the villages and towns. Berlin became the centre of an enclave of German language and culture in British Ontario. German newspapers and other printed materials were published and distinctive institutions flourished, such as musical societies and Evangelical, Lutheran and Swedenborgian churches.

Migrants of Lowland Scots origin developed the south of the region, following the initiative of William Dickson in 1816 in founding the town of Galt and the township of North Dumfries. The Dumfries-Galt settlement had more in common with the directed settlements of Guelph, Fergus and Elora in Wellington County. Deliberately founded as a town, Galt was the largest urban centre of Waterloo County till the late 1870s, though Berlin was the administrative and judicial centre from 1854. In town and country, the Scots origin of the settlers was expressed in the styles and stone materials of farm buildings, houses, churches and factories.

In ethnic composition, Waterloo County's population became quite exceptional, compared with Ontario as a whole or with neighbouring counties. By 1871, the peak census year for rural population in most of southern Ontario, the four largest ethnic groups in Waterloo County and in Ontario as a whole were the Irish, English, Scots and Germans. But, in Waterloo County, people of German ethnic origin formed the largest group with nearly 55 per cent of the total, compared with just under 10 per cent in Ontario generally. Germans, including both those of Pennsylvania Mennonite and European German origins, greatly outnumbered the Scots (18 per cent), the English (12.6 per cent) and the Irish (8 per cent).

Table 1
MUNICIPALITIES OF WATERLOO COUNTY/REGION

Municipality pre-1973	Population 1871	Population 1971	Municipality post-1973
North Dumfries Tp	3,951	4,022	NORTH DUMFRIES TP
Ayr V	*	1,272	Amalgamated with N. Dumfries Tp
Galt C	3,827	38,897	CAMBRIDGE CITY (with Preston & Hespeler)
Waterloo Tp	7,838	8,733	Divided between Kitchener, Waterloo, Woolwich and Cambridge.
Bridgeport V	*	2,375	Amalg. with Kitchener
Kitchener C	2,743	111,804	KITCHENER CITY
Waterloo C	1,594	36,677	WATERLOO CITY
Hespeler T	797	6,343	) In CAMBRIDGE CITY
Preston T	1,408	16,723	) with Galt
Wellesley Tp	5,710	5,281	WELLESLEY TP
Wellesley V	*	816	Amalgamated with Wellesley Tp
Wilmot Tp	5,811	7,002	WILMOT TP
New Hamburg T	1,003	3,008	Amalgamated with Wilmot Tp
Woolwich Tp	5,569	6,354	WOOLWICH TP
Elmira T	*	4,730	Amalgamated with Woolwich Tp
WATERLOO COUNTY	40,251	254,037	REGIONAL MUNICIPALITY OF WATERLOO

Notes: * not incorporated by 1871.
Sources: compiled from Census of Canada and Elizabeth and Gerald Bloomfield, **Urban growth and local services: the development of Ontario municipalities to 1981** (Guelph, 1983).

The population of Waterloo County grew quite rapidly from about 26,500 in 1851 to 38,750 in 1861, and then only modestly to reach 42,740 in 1881. In 1901, about 52,600 people were counted in Waterloo County, compared with 55,600 in Wellington County. In the twentieth century, Waterloo County has expanded steadily and on average at least twice as fast as neighbouring areas to reach a population of 126,000 in 1951 and 254,000 in 1971. In the 1991 census, 377,762 people were recorded in the Region of Waterloo.

One factor in the steady growth of Waterloo County was the urban-industrial development that occurred from 1880 mainly around the poles of Berlin-Waterloo in the centre and Galt, Preston and Hespeler in the southeast. Galt was incorporated as a village in 1850, a town in 1857 and a city in 1915. Preston, a village from 1852, gained town status in 1900 while Hespeler, a village from 1859, was declared a town in 1901. Berlin, incorporated as a village in 1854, attained town status in 1871 and cityhood in 1912. Waterloo, a village from 1857, became a town in 1876 and a city in 1948. New Hamburg, a village from 1858, became a town in 1966. Elmira was incorporated as a village in 1887 and a town from 1922. Three other urban centres did not progress beyond village status: Ayr incorporated in 1884, Bridgeport in 1951, and Wellesley in 1962. Six smaller centres in the more rural parts of the county gained the more limited powers of police villages: St Jacobs in 1904; Hawkesville in 1906; Baden, Conestogo and St Clements in 1907; and Linwood in 1917.

Berlin (renamed Kitchener in 1916) is an outstanding example of urban growth driven by manufacturing industry; it made the most spectacular gains in rank and size between 1871 and 1931 of any urban centre in southern Ontario. The proportion of Berlin's population working in factories grew from 11 per cent to 22 per cent in 1881, 28 per cent in 1901 and 36 per cent in 1919. In 1943, the Canadian Chamber of Commerce described Kitchener as a "microcosm of industrial Canada." As recently as 1986, the Kitchener Census Metropolitan Area still had the highest industrial proportion in the labour force of any major urban centre in Canada.

In Waterloo County as a whole, a diversified industrial complex evolved, with large, medium and small enterprises producing a wide range of fabricated and consumer goods. The region's factories employed significant proportions of women and girls as well as men and boys. For longer than in other Canadian centres, entrepreneurs were locals rather than outsiders though this began to change after about 1912. Waterloo County has consistently ranked among the most highly urbanized and industrialized regions of Canada while also maintaining a productive mixed farming system.

The cultural and economic complexities of the region were recognized in the restructuring of its local government in 1973. Waterloo County was reorganized into the Regional Municipality of Waterloo, and fifteen municipal units were subsumed into seven lower-tier municipalities. Most notably, Galt was amalgamated with Preston and Hespeler to form the new City of Cambridge. Kitchener (absorbing Bridgeport) and Waterloo were each enlarged by annexing parts of Waterloo Township, while the remainder of Waterloo Township was split between Cambridge in the south and Woolwich Township in the north and east. Smaller urban centres were amalgamated with their respective townships -- Elmira with Woolwich Township, New Hamburg with Wilmot Township, Ayr with North Dumfries, and Wellesley Village with Wellesley Township. The main effects of regional restructuring on the municipal units of

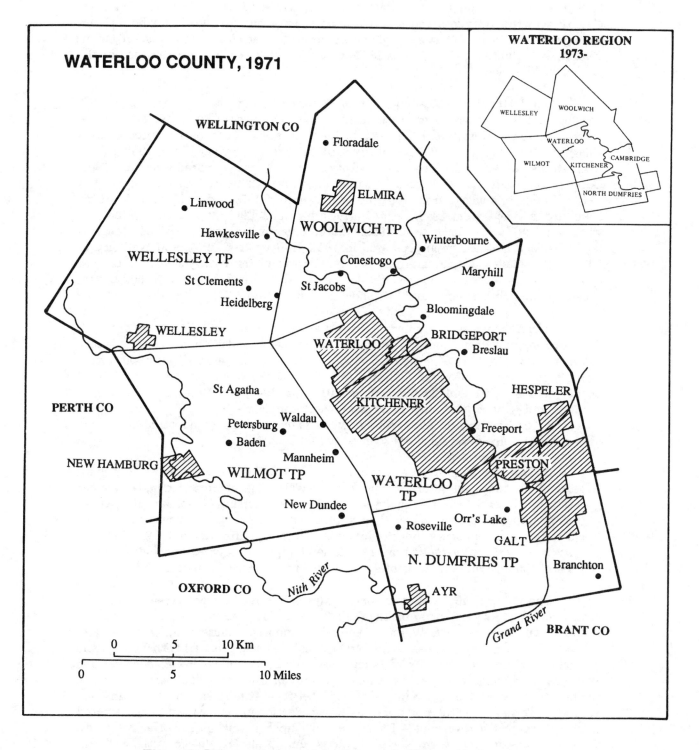

Figure 2: Incorporated municipalities and villages, 1971.
Named places each had at least 100 population in the 1971 census.
The inset shows the effect of restructuring lower-tier municipalities
with the introduction of regional government in 1973.
See also Table 1.

Waterloo County are summarized in Table 1, together with the population data from the censuses of 1871 and 1971.

Though the number of formally incorporated places has been reduced by the regional reorganization of local government, Waterloo County has many villages and hamlets with rich historical associations. The fortunes of small communities have waxed and waned during the past two centuries. Central places with at least 100 population counted in the censuses of 1871 or 1971 are named in Figures 1 and 2.

WATERLOO REGIONAL PROJECT

This volume is one product of a larger project of creating research tools for regional and local history. The Waterloo Regional Project was conceived with the objectives of:

* Increasing access to a large body of print and documentary materials on an important region that has great interest in its own right and can also illuminate larger themes in Canadian studies;

* Supporting research by scholars from various subject backgrounds and the interests of community historians and members of the public and encouraging interaction among these users;

* Facilitating use of computer-based research tools and finding aids by academic and community users by making finding aids available in both print and machine-readable formats and by demonstrating the flexibility and specificity of machine search and retrieval;

* Co-operating with the efforts of local librarians, archivists and heritage groups in promoting awareness of the value of local history materials;

* Refining the methodology of creating the research tools as a model for increasing access to materials on other Canadian regions and themes.

During 1991-92, the Waterloo Regional Project team created a large bibliographic database of references to printed items about Waterloo County history up to the inauguration of regional government in 1973. The project was supported for eight months of 1991 by a Canadian Studies Research Tools grant from the Social Sciences and Humanities Research Council of Canada. For eight months of 1992, a grant from the Waterloo Regional Heritage Foundation subsidized staff costs. These funds made it possible to employ qualified librarian-bibliographers.

Computer-based methods were used to identify, abstract and index the bibliographic records and to make the information accessible in both printed and machine-readable formats. Project procedures were based on those designed for the Guelph Regional Project (1987-1989) which in 1990 won an Award of Merit for its innovative research tools from the American Association for State and Local History. A detailed account of this methodology was published as "Building a better bibliography: computer-aided research tools," **Canadian Library Journal** 46, 4 (1989): 239-249. The research tools that illustrate the project procedures were published as **Guelph and Wellington County: a bibliography of settlement and development since 1800** (1988, 329 p.) and **Inventory of primary and archival sources: Guelph and Wellington County to 1940** (1989, 628 p.).

Between May and August 1991, the Waterloo Regional Project team practised and refined the methodology by indexing and abstracting over 1,250 articles published in the annual reports of the Waterloo Historical Society from 1913 to 1990. These items were described in great detail, to match the interest of historians and genealogists in precise information about places, people, organizations and themes. For example, we indexed names of 12,500 individuals mentioned in the articles and notes in the Waterloo Historical Society's annual volumes, as well as the names of over 2,500 corporate organizations, such as businesses, churches, schools, clubs and societies. The results of the project's first phase were printed in a limited edition for members of the advisory panel and others in the heritage community as **Waterloo Historical Society bibliography** (1991, 390 p).

Next, the project team looked for all books, booklets, theses and reports that are relevant to the history of settlement and development of Waterloo County before 1973. We began with the results of an electronic search of the computerized catalogues of three major libraries in the Region of Waterloo -- the University of Waterloo Library, Wilfrid Laurier University Library and the Kitchener Public Library. Further searching in these and other libraries found other relevant imprints as well as articles in journals and magazines, chapters in books, printed reports, theses, newspapers, directories and gazetteers. Altogether, over 4,530 items are abstracted and indexed in this bibliography. Finally, the whole bibliographic database was edited for accuracy and consistency, in readiness for both print publication and release in computer-searchable formats.

The main features of the project methodology are:

* Inclusion and personal verification of annotated references to most kinds of **printed and secondary literature** relating to Waterloo County up to the introduction of regional government at the end of 1972. Books, booklets, theses, journal articles and shorter notes, chapters in books, special newspaper issues and series, and special reports published right up to the present are all included if they concern the history and development of Waterloo County before 1973. Virtually all items were located and personally examined by a member of the team. As well as the conventional bibliographic details there are abstracts or brief summaries of the scope of each item as index terms for subject headings for people, organizations, places and topics.

* **Computer methods** including use of InMagic software for storing, searching and retrieving the bibliographic data and for formatting them into displayed and printed reports. Portable microcomputers were used in library settings to reduce time and transcription errors.

* A **record structure** that can systematically describe all kinds of printed items relating to the region and is also appropriate for describing primary source materials in any later extension of the project. The record structure includes all the conventional bibliographic fields, a descriptive abstract, and assigned index terms and subject headings. The record structure is designed to be MARC-compatible, to match the

MAchine-Readable Cataloguing systems used extensively in libraries and archives. Because of the computer methodology, items in this bibliography are also known as records.

* Use of **authority lists** for authors, places, personal and corporate names and a **thesaurus** of thematic subject headings relating to regional history, with the assistance of **Instant Authority software** to maintain consistency. The thesaurus of subject headings was based on the National Library of Canada's **Canadian subject headings**, elaborated to describe events, topics and emphases of local and regional history.

* Inclusion of library symbols or location codes for each item, so that the bibliography serves as a **union list** of library holdings within the Region of Waterloo. We have included references to printed items relating to the region held in special library collections, usually only if these items are uniquely accessible in that collection and if their custodians are willing to grant ready access to users. Such special library collections include the Regional Archaeologist's office, the library of Doon Heritage Crossroads, and various denominational archives and collections of rare books. Nearly 50 libraries holding relevant printed materials are listed in the final bibliography and at least one library location (often three or more) is noted for each item. For items not held in a library in the Region of Waterloo, the nearest outside library location is given.

* Design for **accessibility to users** in both machine-readable and print formats. The needs of a wide range of community users have been considered, especially through consultation with the project advisory panel consisting of local archivists, librarians, local historians, and representatives of historical and heritage organizations.

Users should note that this volume is <u>not</u> concerned with what are usually called primary sources -- original manuscripts, papers, or record groups created by individuals or corporate bodies such as businesses, churches, voluntary associations, municipal governments -- that are usually held in archives rather than libraries. The methods used to create the bibliography are appropriate and may be extended to describe these archival resources in future. Meanwhile, researchers may depend on the useful guidance to collections of primary materials provided by Elizabeth Macnaughton and Pat Wagner in **Guide to historical resources in the Regional Municipality of Waterloo** (Wilfrid Laurier University Press, 1989) and by Ryan Taylor in **Family research in Waterloo and Wellington Counties** (Waterloo-Wellington Chapter, Ontario Genealogical Society, 1986). Nor does this bibliography include references to individual maps, as we plan to produce a separate guide later. For maps and plans dating from 1867 or earlier, users may consult Joan Winearls' **Mapping Upper Canada 1780-1867: an annotated bibliography of manuscript and printed maps** (University of Toronto Press, 1991).

A bibliography of secondary literature can only include items that historians, other authors and researchers have written and had printed. Our aim is to provide a clear guide to what has been written and printed on the history of the region, through the thematic arrangement of the references and the abstracts and indexes. We have not set out to appraise the quality of the history or the writing. The omission or scant treatment of some subjects (themes, persons, organizations or places) should not be taken to mean that they were unimportant in the history of Waterloo County. The contents of the bibliography reflect the interests and perceptions of past historians and other writers. There may well be scope for interpreting many new subjects. Users of the bibliography will be able to judge the extent to which some topics of great potential have so far been neglected in the printed literature.

We did try to include references to books, articles and chapters that refer to Waterloo County or its component communities in the context of larger themes or topics. So we searched abstracts, bibliographies, indexes and reviews and asked local authors for references to likely items. Our criteria for inclusion required that there must be specific and fairly detailed references to Waterloo County or one or more of its communities. However, we have probably missed some bibliographic references of this kind. We request details of such items that may be added to the bibliographic database and thus made accessible through electronic search.

References to books, booklets and ephemera printed in Waterloo County before 1901 were included even if they did not specifically discuss local topics and communities. We have included such pre-1901 imprints as a form of co-operation with the Canadian Institute of Historical Microreproductions project, noting which items had been identified and microfilmed by CIHM.

RECORD STRUCTURE

A key feature of the project methodology is the finely indexed record structure which may be used also for describing and indexing primary and archival materials. The main fields used in handling bibliographic materials are listed (with their MARC codes in brackets where applicable):
* unique retrieval key or record number (001)
* main subject code, controlling sequence of records in printed Bibliography
* document type
* personal author/s (100)
* corporate author, (110)
* title of chapter/article etc that is part of a published book/journal
* published title of book/journal/report/thesis   (245)
* series
* names of editors/s of book containing component chapters
* place of publication
* publisher
* year of publication
* details of collation including page length and illustrations, etc (300)
* medium (340) specified if other than paper
* alternate physical form, such as microform as well as paper (530)
* abstract of scope and content in natural language (520)
* library location symbols (535)
* language, if other than English (546)
* personal subject headings (600)
* corporate subject headings (610)
* topical subject headings (650)
* places or geographic subject headings (stressing Waterloo County)
* start date of the time span of subject matter (in relation to Waterloo County)
* end date of the time span of subject matter (in relation to Waterloo County)

The sample computer record presented here illustrates the use of the various indexed fields in the structure of a record for B. Mabel Dunham's **Grand River**. The numbers of subject headings (personal, corporate, topical and geographic) vary from item to item. Articles and notes published in the annual reports and volumes of the Waterloo Historical Society were indexed in great detail, to include names of all persons and organizations mentioned. About 50 other imprints, such as major histories of each municipality, were also indexed very intensively. Examples include Young's **Reminiscences of Galt and North Dumfries**, Eby's **A biographical history of Waterloo Township......**, Uttley's **History of Kitchener**, Taylor's **Our todays and yesterdays**, McLaughlin's histories of Kitchener (with English), Cambridge and Waterloo, **More than a century in Wilmot Township**, Leibbrandt's **Little Paradise, 100 years of progress in Waterloo County: semi-centennial souvenir 1856-1906, Berlin Canada: a self-portrait of Kitchener** (Tiessen reprint), **Confederation number: Diamond jubilee, 1927**, Martin's **The early history of Jakobstettel**, Taylor's **Family research in Waterloo and Wellington Counties**, Macnaughton and Wagner's **Guide to historical resources in the Regional Municipality of Waterloo**, and Stewart, Kitchen and Dietrich's **The Maple Leaf journal: a settlement history of Wellesley Township**. For the remaining 70 per cent of bibliographic items, indexing was somewhat less detailed: persons and organizations had to be more than simply mentioned for their names to be included in the subject indexes.

The simple example of Miss Dunham's book also shows how much of the original record in the database is printed out in the formatted bibliographic reference. The conventional elements of author, title, place of publication, publisher, year of publication and collation are concatenated with library location codes into the first paragraph of each reference. Most punctuation in this part of the entry is formatted in the report program, as is the bolding of the published title. The abstract of scope and content follows in a second paragraph, with the period or time span covered in the work. The various subject heading fields entered in the machine-readable record provide points of access to it through the indexes.

Our bibliographic and typographic conventions are designed for simplicity and clarity of presentation, and generally follow **The Chicago manual of style** (13th edition). They are influenced by some constraints in the process of converting the InMagic record into camera-ready copy. In particular, the computerized sort order depends on the first 59 characters (including punctuation and spaces) of an entry. Thus we had to design the data structure and report formats so that the key bibliographic elements would be included. For this reason (as well as for clarity of presentation), we omit reference to missing bibliographic elements. For items in which the corporate author and publisher are the same, we do not repeat the full name. In some series of related items, such as directories, we insert the year(s) closer to the beginning of the title, to ensure that the references print out in chronological order. We use initial capital letters sparingly, only for proper names and incorporated entities (including titles of newspapers and journals) and the first word of sentences. We use periods to indicate abbreviations only if the final letter of the whole word is not used in the abbreviation. Thus we print "St Jacobs", "Mr Breithaupt", "Mrs Kaufman" or "Dr Vardon". But we abbreviate "Reverend" to "Rev." and "Company" to "Co." All authors' names have surnames and forenames reversed, so that the author index matches the annotated references.

SAMPLE RECORD IN DATABASE AND AS PRINTED IN BIBLIOGRAPHY

a) In Database

```
REC 001    D-0310
CLAS       A
DOC        B
AUT 100    Dunham, B. Mabel
TI  245    Grand River
PL         Toronto
PUB        McClelland and Stewart
YR         1945
COLL 300   299 p. ill., bibl., index
AB 520 A popular account of the history of the valley by the former chief librarian of Kitchener
   Public Library.  The treatment of the Six Nations Indians by land speculators,
   the arrival of the pioneers, and the development of the area into a modern industrial
   society are all vividly described.  The book is illustrated with drawings by Edward Cleghorn.
```

LOC 535 OCCA	SUT 650 Indians, North American	; Transportation
; OCH	; Land surveys	; United Empire Loyalists
; OCP	; Land surveyors	; Drainage
: OKEBC	; Land speculators	; Economic conditions
; OKIT	; Land speculation	; Education
; OWRE	; Land sales	; Writers
; OWT	; Land grants	; Art and artists
; OWTL	; Settlers	; Electricity
; OWTU	; Rivers and streams	; Engineers
; OWTUR	; War, 1812	; Telephone systems
LANG 546 English	; Land patents	; Communications
SUP 600 Dickson, William	; Farm machinery	SUG Grand River Valley
; Beasley, Richard	; Farm making	; Grand River
; Clarke, Thomas	; Land development	; Block Number 1
; Johnson, Pauline	; Mills	; Block Number 2
; Jones, Augustus	; Railways	; Block Number 3
; Shade, Absalom	; Agriculture	; Galt
; Galt, John	; Bridges	; Preston
; Gourlay, Robert	; Dams	; Hespeler
; Beck, Adam	; Industrialization	; Waterloo
; Snider, E.W.B.	; Industries	; Berlin
; Detweiler, D.B.	; Rebellion, 1837-1838	; Dumfries Tp
SUC 610 Six Nations Indians	; Women's Institutes	; Woolwich Tp
; Canada Company	; Government, United Canada	; Huron Road
; German Company	; Government, Provincial	; Waterloo Tp
; Grand River Navigation Co.		DAT1 1800
		DAT2 1910
		$

b) Formatted for Printed Bibliography

14.   Dunham, B. Mabel. **Grand River**. Toronto:
      McClelland and Stewart, 1945. 299 p. ill., bibl.,
      index. Loc: OCCA, OCH, OCP, OKEBC, OKIT,
      OWRE, OWT, OWTL, OWTU, OWTUR.

      A popular account of the history of the valley
      by the former chief librarian of Kitchener
      Public Library. The treatment of the Six Nations
      Indians by land speculators, the arrival of the
      pioneers, and the development of the area into a
      modern industrial society are all vividly described.
      The book is illustrated with drawings by Edward
      Cleghorn. Period: 1800 - 1910

THEMATIC ORGANIZATION

The numbered references in the printed bibliography are arranged by main theme or topic and then presented alphabetically by author, title and year of publication. This order allows the reader to browse among related items in subject areas as one can browse along the shelves of a well-ordered library. The sequence of entries in sections and sub-sections is determined by a special code in the machine-readable record. The number printed in the margin for each entry in the printed bibliography is not part of the machine-readable record. As in any display or printout of references from the database, the sequential numbers are relative to others retrieved according to specific selection criteria. In this bibliography, each reference is printed only once, in one of the following sections set out below. The various index terms provide additional points of access.

Choosing the most appropriate thematic code to control the place of references in this printed volume was far from easy, given the infinite variety of scope and emphasis in the printed materials. Our intent was to assign a code based primarily on the main thematic emphasis of the work. Thus an article about railways across Waterloo County will be found under Transportation and Communications and a thesis about industry in Galt and Preston will be coded to appear with other studies of Manufacturing Industry in the major section on Economic Development. A report on heritage buildings of Bridgeport will be found under Buildings and Architecture under the major on the Landscapes and the Built Environment. Only where an item about a particular community touches on so many topics that it could not be assigned to any one thematic category would it be coded to appear in the final section for specific townships and incorporated urban centres.

* General Surveys and Sources
    General surveys and descriptions of the whole region
    Directories and gazetteers
    Newspapers, including commentaries on their value as historical sources
    Other sources for regional history including bibliographies
        (except those of very specific themes or communities)
* Settlement Processes
    Prehistory, aboriginal people and archaeology (mainly before 1800)
    Pioneer settlement, including travellers' accounts, land surveys
        and land development, studies of place names (mainly
        in the nineteenth century)
    Urbanization and settlement systems (mainly since 1900)
* Demographic and Social Structure
    General demographic studies
    Demographic data sources for genealogy, notably cemetery
        transcriptions and church registers
    Ethnicity, including language, distinctive social features and
        cultural symbols (but not churches and religion)
        Mennonite and Amish
        German
        Scottish
        Other ethnic groups

Family history and genealogy
        Genealogies arranged in order by surname
Social structure, class and elites
        General studies
        Biographies, autobiographies and obituaries of individuals
        arranged in order by surname

* Economic Development
    Economic development processes
    Agriculture and farming
    Finance, land and capital
    Manufacturing industry, including studies of specific businesses
    Transportation and communications, including railways, roads and highways,
        telephone, postal and radio systems
    Trade and commerce
    Trade catalogues

* Landscapes and the Built Environment
    Natural landscapes, including conservation movements
    Buildings and architecture, including conservation and restoration
        efforts for specific buildings and heritage districts
    Urban environments, including planning policies

* Cultural and Social Institutions
    Schools and education
    Colleges and universities
    Literary works
    Libraries
    Music and performing arts
    Visual arts, including folk art and handicrafts
    Folklore, pastimes and festivals
    Food customs and cookbooks
    Churches and religion
        Mennonite, Amish, Brethren in Christ, Missionary
        Baptist
        Catholic
        Anglican
        Evangelical and United Brethren
        Lutheran
        Methodist
        Presbyterian
        Swedenborgian
        Other churches and religions
    Sports and recreation
    Voluntary associations (except historical and heritage)
    Heritage and historical associations and projects

* Government and Politics
    Definition of areas and jurisdictions in 19th century
    Restructuring local government from the 1960s
    Administration of justice: law, order and police
    Local government and services
    Military history
    Politics (municipal, and local aspects of provincial and federal politics)

* Specific Townships and Urban Centres

> Ayr, Bridgeport, Dumfries (North) Township, Elmira, Galt (including some combined studies of Galt, Preston and Hespeler which joined to form Cambridge in 1973), Hespeler, Kitchener (Berlin to 1916; including some studies of both Berlin/Kitchener and Waterloo), New Hamburg, Preston, Waterloo (village, town, city), Waterloo Township, Wellesley Township (and village), Wilmot Township, Woolwich Township

* Local Imprints, published or printed in Waterloo County before 1901, are listed in brief form, with references to the fully annotated references in the body of the bibliography

LIBRARY LOCATIONS

Library location symbols follow the National Library system, and are elaborated for more specialized or branch libraries within the Region of Waterloo. All symbols and libraries are listed below and on the bookmark provided with this volume. For articles and notes in the Waterloo Historical Society annual reports and volumes, we have simply entered the word "all" in the location field. The two university libraries, the Kitchener, Waterloo and Cambridge public libraries, branches of the Waterloo Regional Library system and the City of Cambridge Archives are all believed to hold sets of the Waterloo Historical Society volumes.

OCCA	City of Cambridge Archives
OCH	Cambridge Libraries: Hespeler
OCLG	Cambridge Library and Gallery
OCP	Cambridge Libraries: Preston
OFWCA	Wellington County Archives, Fergus
OG	Guelph Public Library
OGU	University of Guelph Library
OHM	McMaster University Library, Hamilton
OKDHC	Doon Heritage Crossroads, Kitchener
OKEBC	Emmanuel Bible College, Kitchener
OKIT	Kitchener Public Library: Grace Schmidt Room
OKITW	Waterloo Historical Society at Kitchener Public Library
OLU	University of Western Ontario Library
OONL	National Library, Ottawa
OOU	University of Ottawa Library
OPET	Trent University Library, Peterborough
OSTCB	Brock University Library, St Catharines
OTAR	Archives of Ontario
OTMR	Metropolitan Toronto Central Reference Library
OTROM	Royal Ontario Museum
OTU	University of Toronto Library
OTY	York University Library
OWA	University of Windsor Library
OWES	Archives, Eastern Synod, Evangelical Lutheran Church in Canada
OWRA	Waterloo Regional Library: Ayr
OWRB	Waterloo Regional Library: Baden
OWRBL	Waterloo Regional Library: Bloomingdale

OWRBW	Wilmot Township Archives, Baden
OWRE	Waterloo Regional Library: Elmira
OWRL	Waterloo Regional Library: Linwood
OWRMA	Waterloo Regional Municipality: Archaelogist
OWRN	Waterloo Regional Library: New Hamburg
OWRND	Waterloo Regional Library: New Dundee
OWRSC	Waterloo Regional Library: St Clements
OWRSJ	Waterloo Regional Library: St Jacobs
OWRW	Waterloo Regional Library: Wellesley
OWT	Waterloo Public Library
OWTL	Wilfrid Laurier University Library
OWTLA	Wilfrid Laurier University Archives
OWTLR	Wilfrid Laurier University Library: Rare Books
OWTU	University of Waterloo Library: Dana Porter
OWTUCG	Conrad Grebel College Library
OWTUCGR	Conrad Grebel College Library: Rare Books
OWTUCR	Resurrection College
OWTUD	University of Waterloo Library: Davis
OWTUM	University of Waterloo: Map Library, Environmental Studies
OWTUR	University of Waterloo Library: Doris Lewis Rare Book Room
OWTUSJ	St Jerome's College Library

Note: The location "all" is used for articles in the Waterloo Historical Society annual volumes, sets of which are held in virtually all local libraries. A few Mennonite history items are held only in library collections of Bluffton College, Ohio; Goshen College, Indiana; or Lancaster County Historical Society, Lancaster, Pennsylvania.

INDEXES

The various subject headings entered in the **index** fields of the record structure provide additional points of access to bibliographic items according to their alternative and more subtle characteristics and subject areas. These index terms are also important in electronic searching of the bibliographic database. The average article from the Waterloo Historical Society volumes is indexed in the database with at least 20 personal subjects, eight corporate subjects, six places and six topical subject headings. Most other items have fewer personal and corporate subjects and more topical subject headings but about 50 books or reports are indexed in great detail, some having over 500 personal subjects and more than 200 corporate subjects each.

Entries in the **author index**, compiled from all in the AUT field, allow users to find works by any one of over 1,900 personal authors represented in this bibliography. It should be noted that we standardized the forms of authors' names when we knew that slight variants referred to the same individuals.

Compiled from subject headings in the SUT field according to a thesaurus of terms for regional and local history, the **subject heading index** has a controlled vocabulary of nearly 700 terms. This index is particularly useful for gaining additional points of access to the resources of the bibliography. For example, an article primarily concerned with the pioneer period of settlement in Waterloo Township would be programmed to print out among other works on Pioneer Settlement. But in assessing the scope and content of the article, we might have found that it contained important material on the ethnicity of the settlers, the migration process and the establishment of churches and schools. We would then have included in its machine-readable record the subject headings for "Settlers, Pennsylvania", "Migration process", "Churches, Mennonite", "Schools, Rural" and "Landowners". The sequential number of the reference thus appears under each of those index entries in the printed volume.

A **place** index of over 1,000 geographic locations was compiled from the SUG field in the record structure. Urban centres such as Berlin/Kitchener, Galt, Waterloo, Preston, Hespeler, Elmira, New Hamburg and the five townships have at least 300 entries each in the place index. But smaller places have surprisingly large numbers of entries: Ayr (240), Baden (183), Bamberg (183), Blair (146), Breslau (138), Bridgeport (209), Conestogo (138), Doon (186), Erbsville (419), New Dundee (154), St Agatha (148), St Clements (101), St Jacobs (217), and Wellesley (125) all have at least 100 references each. Places located within Waterloo County receive primary emphasis in the index and are not followed by "Ontario", "Ont." or "ON". Places outside the region may be included when apparently significant, as sources of migrants for example. Foreign place names usually begin with the country or national name, then the name of an intermediate province or county, with the locality name last. Thus the place of origin of some of Berlin's pioneer settlers would be expressed as "Germany, Baden" with smaller locality names sometimes added, such as "Wilferdingen" or "Weiler". Locations in the United States are specified by state name first, then county, city or village, such as "Pennsylvania, Lancaster County".

Compiled from entries in the SUC field of the record structure, the index of **corporate subjects** contains about 4,700 names of organizations such as businesses, churches, schools, clubs or municipal governments. Most corporate entries have only one to three references each but the variety of corporate entities and the numbers of citations for some of them are illuminating. About 315 corporate bodies are mentioned in least ten records, 60 of these in at least 25 records. Most commonly mentioned are the Waterloo Historical Society (193), German Company (91), Grand Trunk Railway (79), Doon Pioneer Village (67), University of Waterloo (66), St Jerome's College (63), Six Nations Indians (62), Mutual Life Assurance Co. of Canada (54), Berliner Journal (51), Knox's Presbyterian Church, Galt (47), Central Presbyterian Church, Galt (46), Kitchener Public Library (46), Economical Mutual Fire Insurance Co. (44), Berlin Board of Trade (43), Berlin Town Council (43), Galt Collegiate Institute (42) and Kitchener City Council (42). We tried to standardize the references to these organizations, choosing the most commonly used name if possible. Users should note that rural schools are identified by their School Section number within each township before the reorganization of boards of education in the 1960s. Thus the nine references to the Maple Grove School are given under "Waterloo Township, S.S.#20, Maple Grove".

The **personal subject** index, compiled from the SUP field, lists about 21,500 names of individuals identified as subjects of the works listed in this bibliography. This is an impressive number of people, though we should remember that probably well over 750,000 different individuals lived in Waterloo County at some time before 1972. Most of these persons are mentioned in only one item each. But nearly 500 are mentioned as subjects in at least ten items each, and almost 100 of these in at least 25 items each. The persons mentioned most often are Benjamin Eby (in 149 items), William Dickson

(101), Absalom Shade (94), John Erb (90), E.W.B. Snider (90), Richard Beasley (80), Abraham Erb (64), Jacob Erb (64), Jacob Hespeler (61), Henry William Peterson (60), James Young (59), B. Mabel Dunham (56), L.J. Breithaupt (55), W.D. Euler (55), Jacob Y. Shantz (54), D.B. Detweiler (53), the Rev. Frederick Bindemann (52), Otto Klotz (52), W.H. Breithaupt (51), and Moses Springer (50).

As with the author index, we tried to standardize the form of personal names, but we did so cautiously. For example, only when Mr Eby, B. Eby and Benjamin Eby were positively known to be the same person, did we standardize all citations to the form that appeared most commonly in the literature or was least ambiguous. When we could not be fairly certain, we left the alternative renderings, in the hope that local historians and genealogists will be able to give definitive advice. If at all possible, we have tried to standardize personal names to include at least one full forename and the initial of a middle name.

Women's names can pose problems, especially for researchers who would like to raise the profile of women as historical subjects. In a fair proportion of the references that name women at all, they are identified only as married to their husbands. Where possible, we modified this in the authority list, to include a woman's own name (and often her patronym as well) and to retain a reference to her husband. For example, we expanded "Breithaupt, L.J., Mrs" to "Breithaupt, Emma Devitt (Mrs L.J.)". We were able to do this for several hundred women's names. To implement this convention for all women named in the database would involve considerably more research.

As a result of creating the Waterloo Regional History Bibliography in print and electronic formats, we hope that:
* Groups and individuals can better assess the significance of their subjects and know where to go for the most useful source materials;
* New research on historical themes will be stimulated by the project's very detailed indexing of the published literature;
* The general level of historical awareness in the community will be raised by facilitating access to historical materials; and
* Efficient use of computer-based research tools and finding aids will be encouraged in future studies of the region's history.

We welcome any points of constructive criticism, large or small, which will guide us in revising the bibliographic database.

Elizabeth Bloomfield
December 1992

CHECKLIST OF PERIODICALS REPRESENTED IN THE BIBLIOGRAPHY

Among the annotated references in this volume are articles from the following periodicals. This list does not include local newspapers which produced various special issues featuring local history; nor does it include collections of essays. Periodicals represented by at least five references in this volume are indicated by an asterisk.

American-German Review
APT Bulletin
Architecture Canada
Architecture, Bâtiment, Construction
Birdstone: newsletter of the Grand River/Waterloo Chapter of the Ontario Archaeological Society
Canada Antiques Collector
Canada Quilts
Canadian Antiques and Art Review*
Canadian Architect
Canadian Architect Yearbook
Canadian Business*
Canadian Catholic Historical Association Study Sessions
Canadian Collector*
Canadian Engineer
Canadian Ethnic Studies
Canadian Field Naturalist
Canadian Forum
Canadian Genealogist
Canadian Geographer
Canadian Geographic
Canadian Geographical Journal
Canadian Heritage
Canadian Historical Review
Canadian Journal of Archaeology
Canadian Journal of History of Sport
Canadian Journal of Political Science
Canadian Library Journal
Canadian Literature
Canadian Magazine of Politics, Science, Art and Literature
Canadian National Magazine
Canadian Numismatic Journal
Canadian Papers in Rural History
Canadian Quaker History Newsletter
Canadian Review of Physical Anthropology
Canadian Review of Sociology and Anthropology
Canadian Welfare
Canadian-German Folklore*
Canadiana Germanica
Chatelaine

Christian Monitor
Commerce
Committee on Canadian Labour History Bulletin
Contact
Economic Geography
Environments: a Journal of Interdisciplinary Studies
Executive
Families*
Family Herald
Family Life
Financial Post*
German American Annals
German-Canadian Yearbook /Deutsch-kanadisches Jahrbuch*
Historic Guelph
Historical Geography Newsletter
IA: the Journal of the Society for Industrial Archeology
Imperial Oil Ltd Review
Industrial Canada*
Journal of American Folk-Lore
Journal of Canadian Studies
Journal of Mammalogy
Kentucky Foreign Language Quarterly
Kewa
Labour Gazette
Lancaster Historical Society, Papers and Addresses
Leather World
Macleans Magazine*
Material History Bulletin
Mennogespräch*
Mennonite Historical Bulletin
Mennonite Life
Mennonite Quarterly Review*
Mer Douce*
Modern Language Quarterly
Monatschefte
Monetary Times
Multiculturalism
Newcombe's Monthly Rural Sketches

Office Administration
Ontario Geography
Ontario Historical Society, Papers and
        Records*
Ontario History*
Ontario Library Review*
Ontario Library Review and Book Selection
        Guide
Ontario Library Review and Canadian
        Periodical Index
Ontario Natural Science Bulletin: Journal of
        the Wellington Field Naturalists' Club*
Pennsylvania Folklife
Pennsylvania Mennonite Heritage*
Planning History Bulletin
Police News
Polyphony
Queen's Quarterly
Railway and Marine World
Resurrection Bulletin*
Royal Architectural Institute of Canada Journal
Saturday Night
Scottish Tradition
Shoe and Leather Journal
Small Town
Society for the Study of Architecture in
        Canada Bulletin
Tarot: an illustrated monthly magazine
The Canadian Mennonite
The Dominion
The Pennsylvania German
The United Empire Loyalists' Association of
        Canada Annual Transactions
Town Planning
Town Planning Institute of Canada Journal
Transactions of the Royal Society of Canada,
        3rd series
Transactions of the Royal Canadian Institute
Upper Canadian
Urban Forum: Journal of the Urban Research
        Council of Canada
Urban History Review*
Waterloo Historical Society: annual reports and
        volumes*
Waterloo Review
Western Ontario Historical Notes
Western Ontario Historical Nuggets
York Pioneer and Historical Society

Annotated
Bibliography

GENERAL SURVEYS AND DESCRIPTIONS OF THE WHOLE REGION

1. **100 years of progress in Waterloo County, Canada: semi-centennial souvenir, 1856-1906.** Waterloo: Chronicle-Telegraph, 1906. 94 p. ill. Loc: OWTUCR, OKIT, OWTUR, OWT.

   A portrayal of Waterloo County and its townships, giving some historical background but emphasizing current agricultural and industrial conditions. An article by James Young describes politics in 1850, one by A.C. Hallman describes agriculture, and another describes the Galt, Preston and Hespeler Street Railway Company. There is much information on contemporary municipal officials, businessmen and businesses, and especially the schools and churches of Waterloo. Other communities mentioned are Berlin, Galt, Bridgeport, Hespeler, New Hamburg, Elmira, Preston, Hawkesville, Wellesley, Blair and Baden. The book was published to commemorate the fiftieth anniversary of the newspaper and the centennial of the founding of Waterloo. Names of any company, person or organization described in at least one paragraph have been indexed in the WRP database. Period: 1806 - 1906.

2. Allan, A.S. "Reminiscences of early Waterloo." **Waterloo Historical Society.** 1925. 13: 139-143. ill. Loc: all.

   An historical sketch of Waterloo County during the second half of the nineteenth century, including references to the communities of Freeport, Blair, Ayr, Doon, Preston and Berlin and to community leaders such as Jonathan B. Bowman, James Cowan, Absalom Shade, Jacob Hespeler, Joseph Sherk, John Betzner, George Clemens, the Brickers, the Hilkers, Charles and William Hendry, Frederick Guggisberg, William Dickson and Rev. John Bayne. Period: c1850 - 1924.

3. Boyle, Terry. **Memories of Ontario: the travellers' guide to the towns and cities of western Ontario.** Toronto: Cannonbooks, 1991. 211 p. ill., bibl., map. Loc: OKIT.

   Brief anecdotal histories of 73 locations, including Cambridge (Preston, Galt, and Hespeler), Elmira, Kitchener, St Jacobs and Waterloo. The early settlement, industries, prominent people and tourist attractions are all described for each location, illustrated by historic photographs. Period: 1800 - 1991.

4. Breithaupt, W.H. "Early history of the County of Waterloo." **Waterloo Historical Society.** 1913. 1: 8-9. Loc: all.

   Text of an address outlining the history of Waterloo County and mentioning local historians Ezra Eby, A.B. Sherk, James Young and Gottlieb Bettschen. Period: 1799 - 1913.

5. Breithaupt, W.H. "Historical notes on the Grand River." **Waterloo Historical Society.** 1930. 18: 219-229. ill. Loc: all.

   An address given at Chicopee on August 2, 1930 on the history and prehistory of the river, its geographical characteristics and various inhabitants and explorers since the seventeenth century. Period: 1600 - 1930.

6. Breithaupt, W.H. "History of Waterloo County." **The Province of Ontario: a history 1615-1927.** Edited by Jesse Edgar Middleton and Fred Landon. Toronto: Dominion Publishing Company, 1927. Vol. 2, pp. 991-1001. Loc: OKIT, OWT, OWTL, OWTU.

   An outline history of the county's settlement by various ethnic groups and of industrial development, electrification, publishing and printing, and cultural activities such as music and singing societies. A photocopy of this chapter is also held in the juvenile section of the Kitchener Public Library under the title **History of Waterloo County.** Period: 1798 - 1926.

7. Breithaupt, W.H. "Waterloo County history." **Ontario Historical Society, Papers and Records.** 1919. 17: 43-47. ill. Loc: OWTL, OWT, OWTU.

   A summary history of Waterloo County and its five townships. Topics include local historians, the Attiwandaronk Indians, various groups of settlers, education, newspapers, railways, and Waterloo County men enlisted, killed and decorated in the First World War. Period: 1800 - 1918.

8. Burkholder, Mabel G. "The County of Waterloo." **History of Central Ontario (southwestern).** Edited by H.E. Durant. Montreal: Historical Foundation, 1952. Pp. 178-202. Loc: OWT.

   A concise history of the county with profiles of the communities of Galt, Kitchener, Waterloo, Preston, Hespeler, Elmira and Doon. Short biographies are included for prominent citizens such as Robert Elliott Cowan, William Howard Shaw, J.W. Maus, N.O. Hipel, William Howard Gillespie, Stanley F. Leavine and Mabel Dunham. Period: 1800 - 1951.

9. Byerly, A.E. **The beginning of things in Wellington and Waterloo Counties, with particular reference to Guelph, Galt and Kitchener, illustrated by Leslie Marsh.** Guelph: Guelph Publishing Co., 1935. 106 p. ill. Loc: OCCA, OCLG, OCP, OKIT, OWRE, OWT, OWTL, OWTUR.

   A survey of the history of Wellington and

Waterloo Counties to 1870, highlighting the formation of the municipal governments, the immigration process, and the early settlements. There are brief biographies of some prominent pioneer leaders. Period: 1816 - 1870.

10. "Canada's centennial." **Kitchener-Waterloo Record.** 1967, June 27. Pp. 1-96. ill. Loc: OWT.

A supplement in five sections, presenting a wealth of information about the region's history to commemorate Canada's centennial. The articles mention most communities in Waterloo County but stress the political and social development of the Twin Cities, especially in a section (pp. 50-72) based on the historical writings of Mabel Dunham and Clayton Wells. Many photographs show buildings or street scenes and contemporary advertisements contain historical information on local businesses. Period: 1806 - 1967.

11. **The Canadian Encyclopedia.** Edited by James H. Marsh. Edmonton: Hurtig Publishers, 1985. 59,1: 67-93. Loc: all.

Includes major entries for Germans, Germanic literature, Germanic fraktur and calligraphy, Mennonites, and Kitchener-Waterloo with brief entries for Galt, Hespeler, Cambridge, Elmira, New Hamburg, Homer Watson, the University of Waterloo and Wilfrid Laurier University. There are no entries for Preston, Ayr, any of the townships, the Grand River or the whole Waterloo County or Region. Period: 1800 - 1980.

12. "Celebrating Canada's centennial." **Waterloo Chronicle.** 1967, September 27. Pp. 1-32. Loc: OWT.

A special section presenting historical information about Waterloo County and communities such as St Clements, St Agatha, Waterloo and Bridgeport. Social life, sports, customs and entertainment in the past are compared with conditions in the 1960s. Period: c1800 - 1967.

13. **Confederation number: Diamond Jubilee, July 1st, 1927.** Waterloo Chronicle, 1927. 104 p. ill., ports. Loc: OCCA, OKIT, OKITW, OWRE, OWRW, OWTUCG, OWTUR, OWT.

A history of Waterloo County from the early days to 1927 celebrating "the phenomenal progress of Canada since the federation of the provinces sixty years ago." All areas of Waterloo County are mentioned, but the town of Waterloo and its insurance companies are described in particular detail. There are photographs and short biographies of municipal officials, descriptions of public institutions and private businesses, as well as advertising from many companies. Names of persons and corporations described in at least a

paragraph or shown in a photograph have been indexed in the WRP database. Period: 1867 - 1927.

14. Dunham, B. Mabel. **Grand River.** Toronto: McClelland and Stewart, 1945. 299 p. ill., bibl., index. Loc: OCCA, OCH, OCP, OKEBC, OKIT, OWRE, OWT, OWTL, OWTU, OWTUR.

A popular account of the history of the valley, by the former chief librarian of Kitchener Public Library. The treatment of the Indians of the Six Nations by land speculators, the arrival of the pioneers, and the development of the area into a modern industrial society are all vividly described. The book is illustrated with drawings by Edward Cleghorn. Period: 1800 - 1910.

15. Dunham, B. Mabel. "The history of Waterloo County a story of courage, vision, progress." **Police News.** 1950 - Spring. Pp. 21-25. port. Loc: OKIT.

A brief historical outline to mark a century of county government. The author is most concerned with early settlement by Mennonites, Amish and European Germans before 1850, but she mentions the county town contest, industrialization and hydro-electricity. Period: 1800 - 1950.

16. Hale, Katherine. "Grand River Valley." **This is Ontario.** Toronto: Ryerson Press, 1937. Pp. 32-35. Loc: OCCA.

An account of journeys around Ontario, including observations on Galt, Preston, Breslau, Conestogo and West Montrose. The author describes the contemporary communities and evokes their historical past. Katherine Hale was a pseudonym of Amelia Warnock, a native of Galt, who later became Mrs John Garvin. Period: 1816 - 1937.

17. **Historical atlas of Waterloo & Wellington counties, including: Illustrated Atlas of the County of Waterloo by H. Parsell & Co. (1881), County of Waterloo Directory, 1877-78, by Armstrong & Co., and Illustrated Atlas of the County of Wellington by Walker & Miles (1877).** Port Elgin: Ross Cumming, 1972. 96 p. ill., maps. Loc: OCCA, OCLG, OCP, OKIT, OWRBL, OWRE, OWRN, OWRW, OWT, OWTL, OWTU, OWTUCG, OWTUM.

Waterloo County material in this edition consists of an historical sketch of the county and a description of its geology, drainage, development and government. There is a short account of each municipal unit, outlining its site, situation, pioneer settlers, and general economic and municipal progress. Smaller settlements within each township are described more briefly. Biographical sketches and portraits are included of current reeves and county representatives in the federal parliament and provincial legislature, with briefer entries for all persons who subscribed to the original county atlas. There are maps of the county as a whole, all townships and Berlin, and drawings of various notable farms, town residences and industrial and public buildings. Separate records have been added to the WRP database for each map and municipal profile, and for the reprint of Armstrong's 1877-78 directory. Period: 1800 - 1881.

18. "Historical sketch of the County of Waterloo." **Historical atlas of Waterloo & Wellington counties, including: Illustrated Atlas of the County of Waterloo (1881), County of Waterloo Directory (1877-78) and Illustrated Atlas of the County of Wellington (1877).** Port Elgin: Ross Cumming, 1972 reprint. Pp. 3-5. Loc: OWTU, OWTUM, OWTUCG, OKIT, OWTL, OCCA, OCLG, OCP, OWRBL, OWRE, OWRN, OWRW, OWT.

A general survey of geology, topography and history to about 1880. Leading pioneers and enterprises are named and the importance of early mills, schools and roads is stressed. Though the author notes the general indifference of early Waterloo settlers to politics, he chronicles the background to the 1837 Rebellion, political contests from the 1840s, and the development of municipal government in Wellington District and Waterloo County. All wardens of Waterloo County from 1852 to 1881 and members of the county council in 1881 are named. The value of histories by P.E.W. Moyer and James Young is acknowledged. Period: 1800 - 1881.

19. Jaffray, J.P. **The highly industrialized and strikingly beautiful Grand River Valley: described from Port Dover and Dunnville to Elora and Fergus.** Galt: J.P. Jaffray, 1932. 136 p. ill. Loc: OWTUR, OCCA, OKIT.

A book published under the auspices of the Grand River Valley Boards of Trade to promote tourism. The contemporary valley is described with historical sketches of the towns, including recognition of many "firsts". There are photographs of buildings, street scenes and panoramas and many advertisements for local businesses. Period: 1806 - 1932.

20. Macdonald, D. **Illustrated atlas of the Dominion of Canada: containing maps of all the provinces, the North-West Territories and the Island of Newfoundland, from the latest official surveys and plans, by permission of the general and provincial governments, together with a general descriptive history &c, also maps of Europe, Asia, Africa, North and South America, United States, Oceanica [sic], the world, &c., &c., and local maps.**

Toronto: H. Parsell, 1881. liii, viii [112] p. ill., maps, ports. Also CIHM Microfiche series, no. 27294 (introductory historical sketch). Loc: OCCA, OKIT, OWTLR, OWTUR.

An atlas containing maps of the townships of North Dumfries, Wilmot, Wellesley, Woolwich, Waterloo, and Waterloo County. The second section opens with an historical sketch of the County of Waterloo. There are portraits and brief biographies of Hugo Kranz, Samuel Merner, James Livingston, E.W.B. Snider, William Snider, Lewis Kribs, Otto Pressprich, Isaac Groh, Theron Buchanan, T.B. Snider, James Phin and John Phin. A biographical directory lists Waterloo County subscribers and those from Galt, Preston, Berlin, Hespeler and New Hamburg. Engravings depict Waterloo County farms, residences, livestock and businesses. Period: 1880 - 1881.

21. "Map of the County of Waterloo." **Historical atlas of Waterloo & Wellington counties, including: Illustrated Atlas of the County of Waterloo (1881), County of Waterloo Directory (1877-78) and Illustrated Atlas of the County of Wellington (1877).** Port Elgin: Ross Cumming, 1972 reprint. Pp. 24-5. Loc: OKIT, OWTL, OWTU, OWTUM, OWTUCG, OCCA, OCLG, OCP, OWRBL, OWRE, OWRN, OWRW, OWT.

A general map showing rivers, streams, major roads, railway lines, names of townships, towns, villages and hamlets, and numbers of concessions and lots. Period: 1880 - 1881.

22. **The Maple Leaf: The Canadian Club Magazine.** Sussex, NB: Maple Leaf Publishing Co., 1923. 56 p. ill. Loc: OKIT.

The March 1923 issue of the magazine, containing numerous articles about Waterloo County. Articles by the magazine staff members are entitled "Early settlers of Waterloo," "The Kitchener of today," "Waterloo County Canadian Clubs," "Waterloo, Preston, and Hespeler," "The Hartford of Canada," and "Industrial Kitchener." B. Mabel Dunham's article on "William Wilfred Campbell" is also printed in the Waterloo Historical Society report for 1918. There are articles by N.C. Helmuth on "Kitchener as a sport center" and Owen McGillucuddy on "Boyhood of Canada's Prime Minister." Period: 1800 - 1923.

23. Moyer, William G. **Bill Moyer's Waterloo County diary.** Kitchener: CHYM, 1970. 145 p. ill. Loc: OCCA, OKIT, OWRA, OWRBL, OWRND, OWRN, OWRSJ, OWT, OWTL, OWTUR.

Brief historical sketches about places, industries, prominent people and families. Interesting facts are also described about aspects of daily life from hex signs to weather predictions. Period: 1800 - 1930.

24. Moyer, William G. **This unique heritage: the story of Waterloo County**. Kitchener: Radio Station CHYM, 1971. 143 p. ill. Loc: OCCA, OCH, OCLG, OCP, OKIT, OWRA, OWRE, OWRN, OWRSJ, OWRW, OWT, OWTL, OWTU, OWTUCG.

     A popular history from the Indian period to about 1930, with chapters on the Indians, Richard Beasley, the pioneers, John Galt, the Mennonites, the Scots, the Germans, the County, City of Galt, City of Kitchener, City of Waterloo, the townships and the arts. Period: 1750 - 1930.

25. Noonan, Gerald A. "The local mentality: a history beyond words." **Waterloo Historical Society**. 1980. 68: 43-52. Loc: all.

     An interpretative essay on aspects of the history of the Upper Grand Valley region including the non-verbal evidence of a dominant mentality, visible landscapes and the built environment. The author cites passages from Uttley's history of Kitchener as evidence of a strong bias in favour of industry, frugality and commonsense. Period: 1840 - 1900.

26. Pepper, Paul E. **Name/subject index to Waterloo County diary by Bill Moyer**. Kitchener: The Author, 1986. 11 p. Loc: OKIT.

     Index of nearly 500 entries, mainly persons, mentioned in Moyer's book.

27. Spetz, Theobald, Rev. "The importance of local history." **Waterloo Historical Society**. 1913. 1: 16-18. Loc: all.

     A short address to the Waterloo Historical Society, mentioning Ezra Eby's biographical dictionary of the Mennonite settlers of Waterloo County, the work of Hon. James Young and W.H. Smith's gazetteer of Canada West, and the speaker's own efforts to collect information about the history of the Catholic Church in Waterloo County. Period: 1806 - 1913.

28. **The Waterloo County area: selected geographical essays**. Edited by A.G. McLellan. Waterloo: Department of Geography, University of Waterloo, 1971. 316 p. ill., maps, bibl., tables. Loc: OKIT, OWTL, OWTU, OWTUCG, OWT.

     A collection of 24 essays on varied geographical themes in the county area, sometimes considered as part of a larger region. Topics include landform evolution, settlement and economy before 1900, Mennonites and the Pennsylvania German dialect, demographic features, recreation and tourism, agriculture, urban fringe and urban shadow, the central place system, the central business districts of Kitchener and Waterloo, trends in

industrial employment, climate and weather, water pollution, water supply planning and management, the sand and gravel industry, environmental and ecological planning, urban renewal, regional planning and local government reform. There are individual records in the WRP database for each essay concerned with Waterloo County. Period: 1800 - 1970.

29. **Waterloo County, Ontario, Canada: the record of over a century of progress in the foremost industrial, commercial and agricultural county of the Dominion**. Berlin: Daily Telegraph, 1914, August. 62 p. ill. Also mf. Loc: OCLG, OKIT, OKITW, OWT.

     A special Waterloo County Outlook Edition relating the history of early settlement and pioneer leaders. Contemporary businesses are the primary focus of the publication which contains promotional descriptions of enterprises in Berlin, Waterloo, Galt, Preston, Hespeler and Elmira as well as biographical sketches of their owners and managers. Large advertisements for many of the businesses make up about one-quarter of the issue. Period: 1800 - 1913.

30. Weaver, Emily P. **The story of the counties of Ontario**. Toronto: Bell and Cockburn, 1913. 318 p. ill., index. Loc: OCCA.

     A popular account of all the counties of Ontario, including a brief history of Waterloo County with many references to the Township of Dumfries from James Young's book. Period: 1805 - 1913.

DIRECTORIES AND GAZETTEERS

31. **Buyer's guide and business directory for 1939-1940 for Kitchener-Waterloo and district: street maps, statistical facts and figures, general information**. Waterloo: David Bean and Sons, 1940. 32 p. Loc: OWTUR, OKIT.

     A 1940 guide for Kitchener-Waterloo shoppers, giving a street map, a classified business directory, and some miscellaneous statistical information gathered from the 1939 assessment rolls. Period: 1939 - 1940.

32. **Cairnes' official directory of the city of Kitchener, 1918**. W. Cairnes, 1918. 365 p. Loc: OKIT.

     A 1918 directory of Kitchener in three sections: names of residents with occupations and addresses, a street directory, and a classified business directory. A directory of names for Bridgeport, a street directory and a classified business directory for Waterloo are included. Period: 1917

- 1918.

33. **The Canada directory: containing the names of the professional and business men of every description, in the cities, towns, and principal villages of Canada: together with a complete post office directory of the province; a directory to public offices, officers and institutions; a variety of statistical and commercial tables, exhibiting the population, trade, revenue, expenditure, imports, exports, public works, etc., etc., of Canada, and a variety of other useful information brought down to November, 1851.** Edited by Mackay, Robert W.S. Montreal: John Lovell, 1851. 692 p. ill., indexes. Loc: OCCA.

    A directory including the following Waterloo County centres: Ayr, Berlin, Bridgeport, Galt, Hawkesville, New Hope, Petersburg, Waterloo and Wellesley. Advertisements are included, many from the United States and Montreal. Period: 1850 - 1851.

34. **Canada Kalender.** Berlin and Kitchener: Rittinger and Motz, 1849 - 1920. Also mf. Loc: OKITW, OKDHC, OWTUR.

    An annual publication containing information pertinent to each day of the year such as the time the sun rises and sets, weather predictions, holidays, seasons, astrological and astronomical data, sayings and proverbs, poems, short stories, cartoons, advice for farmers and tips for family members. The information is not specific to Waterloo County but of interest to German-language speakers anywhere. However, each issue contains advertisements by local merchants and professionals, including some trademarks and line drawings. The calendar varies in length from 40 to 104 pages. Printed primarily in the German Gothic script, by the 20th century there are portions in the Latin script and in English. The University of Waterloo Library has the years 1882-1920 on microfiche (1883, 1887, and 1903 are missing) and calendars for the following years can be found in the Doris Lewis Rare Book Room: 1867, 1872, 1874, 1875, 1882, 1902 to 1908, 1911 to 1917, 1919 and 1920. Calendars for 1849, 1850, 1852, 1877, 1882, 1884 to 1886, 1888 to 1894, 1896 to 1900, and each year from 1902 to 1920 are held in the Waterloo Historical Society's collection at the Kitchener Public Library. Doon Heritage Crossroads has calendars for 1847, 1848, 1850, 1852 to 1856, 1858, 1860 to 1862, 1867 to 1874, 1876, 1879, 1884 to 1886, 1889 to 1899, 1901, 1904 to 1920. Period: 1847 - 1920.

35. **Canadian family almanac for the year 1893.** CIHM Microfiche series, no. A00102. Berlin: Berlin Publishing Co., 1892?. 1 fiche. mf. Loc: OWTL, OWTU.

    An English-language edition of the popular annual containing information pertinent to each day of the year such as weather predictions, holidays, astrological and astronomical data, poems, short stories, advice for farmers and family members. For details of German-language versions published at the same time, see: **Canada Kalender and Canadischer Familien Calendar**. Period: 1892 - 1893.

36. **Canadischer Familien Calender auf das Jahr unsers Herrn Jesu Christi.** CIHM Microfiche series, nos. 32376 and A00150. Berlin: Boedecker und Stuebing, 1859 - 1897. mf. Loc: OWTL, OWTU, OKDHC.

    An annual publication containing information pertinent to each day of the year such as weather predictions, holidays, astrological and astronomical data, sayings and proverbs, poems, short stories, advice for farmers and tips for family members. By 1890, the title of the almanac changes to **Canadischer Familien für das Jahr 1890**. Similar in format to the **Canada Kalender**, published during the same period by Rittinger and Motz of Berlin, these booklets also contain advertisements from local merchants and professionals. Calendars for 1859, 1863, 1864 and 1866 were published by Boedecker and Stuebing; those for 1890, 1891 and 1892 by Hett and Eby; and those for 1894 and 1897 by the Berlin Publishing Company, all of Berlin. Doon Heritage Crossroads has copies of the original calendars for all the aforementioned years and for 1867. Period: 1859 - 1897.

37. **The County of Waterloo gazetteer and directory for 1877-8.** Toronto: Armstrong and Co., 1878. 201 p. Loc: OKIT, OWRE, OWTL, OWTUR.

    A compendium of information about the location, population, institutions, societies and especially the businesses of each township and village in the county. Alphabetical lists of all residents state the locations by lot and concession numbers of those on farms, and the occupations of those in towns and villages. Members of parliament and legislative assembly, senators, and county and township officers are named. There are many business advertisements. All businesses and individuals who advertised have been indexed in the WRP database, but not the personal names of residents appearing only in lists. The directory was reprinted by Mark Cumming in 1972 in the **Historical atlas of Waterloo and Wellington Counties** and may be more accessible in that version. Period: 1877 - 1978.

38. **Garden's rural route guide and county directory, 1940-42**. Niagara-on-the-Lake: F.F. Garden, 1942. 2 v. map. Loc: OKIT.

   A list of all persons over 21 years, with address and status as owner or tenant, in all towns, villages, rural routes and post offices in the county. Also included are a county map, lists of members of the county council and municipal officials for 1940, and a classified directory of county businesses. Information for North Waterloo and South Waterloo are presented in separate volumes. Period: 1940 - 1942.

39. **Gazetteer and directory of the County of Waterloo, 1867**. Toronto: W.H. Irwin and George E. Burnham, Publishers, 1867. 167 p. ill. Also CIHM Microfiche series, no. A01171. Loc: OKIT, OWTL, OWTU.

   A directory including brief descriptions of locations, populations, institutions and businesses of all townships and communities. All residents are listed with their addresses and occupations. Other information is presented about county officers, coroners, school superintendents, limits of division courts, banks, agricultural societies, insurance companies, Masonic and Orange lodges, the Berlin Mechanics' Institute, the Berlin Fire Brigade, the 1861 census of population, and post offices and postmasters. Period: 1861 - 1867.

40. **Get the address here: rural mail directory, North Waterloo and district, September 1937**. Kitchener: Commercial Printing, 1937. 42 p. Loc: OWTUR.

   An alphabetical directory of names by rural mail routes from fifteen different places: Baden, Bamberg, Breslau, Elmira, Kitchener, Linwood, New Hamburg, Petersburg, St Agatha, St Clements, St Jacobs, Waterloo, Wallenstein, Wellesley and West Montrose. More than one rural route is given for some centres. There is an index to advertisers as well as a list of post office regulations and rates of postage. Period: 1936 - 1937.

41. **Lovell's 1874 gazetteer of British North America: containing the latest and most authentic descriptions of over six thousand cities, towns and villages in the provinces of Ontario, Quebec, Nova Scotia, New Brunswick, Newfoundland, Prince Edward Island, Manitoba, British Columbia, and the North West Territories; and general information, drawn from official sources, as to the names, locality, extent, etc., of over fifteen hundred lakes and rivers, with a table of routes showing the proximity of the railroad stations, and sea, lake, and river ports, to the cities, towns, villages, etc., in the several provinces**. Montreal: John Lovell, 1874. 1 v. Loc: OKDHC.

   Includes very brief descriptions of 46 towns and villages in Waterloo County and of the Grand, Speed and Conestogo Rivers. Period: 1873 - 1874.

42. National Library of Canada. **Canadian directories, 1790-1987: a bibliography and place-name index**. Ottawa: National Library of Canada, 1989. 3 v. Loc: OWTL, OWTU.

   A guide to Canadian directory holdings of the National Library of Canada and the library of the National Archives of Canada. The first volume presents a bibliography in sections alphabetically arranged by province or territory. Within each province, province-wide directories are listed first, followed by cities, township, counties and districts, alphabetically arranged in one sequence. Within each city, township, county or district, directories are chronologically arranged. The larger second and third volumes contain the place-name indexes for each province and territory. Within each provincial index, the entries for villages, towns, cities, townships or counties are arranged alphabetically, with references in chronological order to all directories in which that place was identified. Waterloo County communities identified with their directory references in this guide include all the townships and incorporated urban centres as well as smaller places, except that Galt, Preston and Hespeler are mentioned only within an entry for Cambridge. The introduction presents a useful explanation of the procedures of directory compilers. Period: 1850 - 1987.

43. **Official telephone directory: including Fergus, Guelph, Preston, Galt, Kitchener, Waterloo and surrounding territory**. Montreal: Bell Telephone Co., 1926. 136, 20 p. Loc: OWTUR.

   A 1926 telephone directory for areas in Waterloo and Wellington Counties, with a small classified section at the end of the book. Period: 1925 - 1926.

44. **Official telephone directory, Western Ontario: January, 1912**. Montreal: Bell Telephone Co., 1912. Loc: OKDHC.

   A directory for exchanges and toll offices west of Hamilton and between Guelph and Palmerston, including Ayr, Berlin, Galt, Hespeler, Linwood, New Dundee, New Hamburg, Preston, St Jacobs, Waterloo and Wellesley. Period: 1912 - 1913.

45. **Ontario directory for 1851: names of professional and business men and other inhabitants in the cities, towns, and villages throughout the province**. Edited by Taylor, L. Joseph. London: Genealogical Research Library, 1984 reprint. 203 p. index. Loc: OCLG, OKIT, OWTUR.

A reprint of the Ontario portion of **The Canada directory** (1851), to which has been added a new index of the cities, towns, and villages. Waterloo County locations include Ayr, Berlin, Bridgeport, Galt, Hawkesville, New Hope, New Aberdeen, Petersburg, Preston, Waterloo and Wellesley. Period: 1850 - 1851.

46. **Province of Ontario blue book and business directory, 1913.** Toronto: Canadian Gazetteer, 1913. 624 p. ill., index. Loc: OKIT.

Directory subtitled "alphabetical and classified list of merchants, manufacturers and professional men, and descriptive matter of each place as to location, population, railroads, water routes, banking, telegraph, express, etc." Waterloo County locations are Ayr, Baden, Bamberg, Berlin, Blair, Bloomingdale, Branchton, Breslau, Bridgeport, Crosshill, Conestogo, Doon, Elmira, Erbsville, Galt, Floradale, Freeport, German Mills, Hawkesville, Haysville, Heidelberg, Hespeler, Josephburg, Kossuth, Linwood, Mannheim, New Dundee, New Germany, New Hamburg, Petersburg, Phillipsburg, Preston, Roseville, St Agatha, St Clements, St Jacobs, Strasburg, Waterloo, Weissenburg, Wellesley, West Montrose, Wellesley and Winterbourne. There is an index to advertisers. Period: 1912 - 1913.

47. **Province of Ontario gazetteer and directory, 1869.** C.E. Anderson and Co., 1869. 719 p. indexes. Loc: OKDHC.

Brief descriptions of towns and villages, including 33 in Waterloo County, with an alphabetical listing of merchants, businessmen, farmers or professionals. Other miscellaneous information is provided on emigration, custom duties, railways, telegraph stations and post offices. Period: 1868 - 1869.

48. **Rural mail route directory North and South Waterloo including rural mail routes.** Brampton: Rural Mail Route Directory Co., 1933. 64 p. Loc: OONL.

Reference from **Canadian directories, 1790-1987: a bibliography and place-name index.** Period: 1932 - 1933.

49. Smith, William Henry. **Canada: past, present and future: being a historical, geographical, geological and statistical account of Canada West; containing ten county maps, and one general map of the province, compiled expressly for the work.** Toronto: T. Maclear, 1851. 2 v. maps. Loc: OCP, OKIT, OWTUR, OWT.

An account of townships and villages, describing land conditions, settlements, roads, schools, acres cultivated and products, with statistics for 1842, 1848 and 1850. Information about Galt and Ayr is included in the first volume (with what was then defined as Halton County), pages 243 to 248. Information about the rest of what became Waterloo County is included in the second volume, pages 90 to 131. A business directory listing merchants, professional men and hotel keepers of Galt and Ayr is printed in the first volume, pages 35 to 44. A similar directory for the rest of the county area is in volume 2, pages 83 to 90. Kitchener Public Library and the Preston Library hold copies of the facsimile reprint produced by Mika of Belleville in 1973. Period: 1850 - 1851.

50. Smith, William Henry. **Smith's Canadian gazetteer comprising statistical and general information respecting all part of the Upper Province or Canada West.** Toronto: H. & W. Rowsell, 1846 reprinted 1970. 285 p. map. Loc: OCLG, OKIT, OWTL, OWTU, OWTUCG, OWTUR.

A compendium of information, including lists of post offices, magistrates, clergymen, hotels, banks and government offices. There are descriptive entries for various communities in what became Waterloo County but was currently part of the Wellington District: Ayr, Berlin, Bridgeport, Dumfries Township, Galt, Little Germany (New Germany, later Maryhill), Glasgow (or Shoemaker's Mills), Grand River, Hamburgh (later New Hamburg), Haysville, New Hope (later Hespeler), Preston, Waterloo Township, Waterloo, Wellesley Township, Wilmot Township and Woolwich Township. The Doris Lewis Rare Book Room has a copy of the original while the Coles facsimile reprint is held in the other collections. Period: 1842 - 1846.

51. Sutherland, James. **Counties of Perth and Waterloo gazetteer and general business directory for 1870-71: containing brief historical and descriptive sketches of the towns, villages and post offices, with the names of residents in each locality, arranged alphabetically.** Ottawa and Toronto: Hunter, Rose, 1869. 282 p. ill., indexes. Also CIHM Microfiche series, no. A01173. Loc: OKIT, OWTL, OWTU.

A directory listing residents by township, concession and lot numbers and noting whether they are householders or freeholders. There are descriptions of each town, village and post office community, with alphabetical lists of residents and their occupations. A general index and an index to advertisements are provided. Period: 1869 - 1871.

52. Sutherland, James. **County of Waterloo gazetteer and general business directory for 1864: containing a brief historical and descriptive**

sketch of the county, townships, towns, villages
and post offices, with the names of residents of
each locality arranged alphabetically and the
local magistracy. Toronto: Mitchell, 1864. 209 p.
ill., indexes. Also CIHM Microfiche series, no.
A00042. Loc: OKIT, OKITW, OWT, OWTL, OWTU.

Introduced by a general description of
education, religion, ethnic groups, agriculture,
judiciary and government officials in the county
and individual descriptions of townships, towns,
villages and post office communities. Township
residents are listed with their lot and concession
numbers and status as householders or freeholders.
Residents of towns are listed with their
occupations. A general index and index to
advertisements are provided. Period: 1863 - 1864.

53. **Town of Galt gazetteer and general business
directory for 1880.** 1880. 43 p. mf. Loc: OCLG.
The earliest known directory for Galt. Period:
1879 - 1880.

54. **Twin-city directory and official guide of the
towns of Berlin and Waterloo.** 1907. 210 p. ill.,
index. Loc: OKDHC.
A classified, street, and alphabetical directory
for each town with interesting facts and figures.
The directory was apparently produced by the town
governments for promotional purposes. Period: 1906
- 1907.

55. **Union Publishing Co. (1884-5) farmers' and
business directory for the counties of Brant,
Halton, Waterloo and Wentworth.** Ingersoll: Union
Publishing, 1884. 1 v. Also CIHM Microfiche
series, no. A01119. Loc: OKDHC.
A directory listing Waterloo County farmers by
township, giving their addresses by concession and
lot numbers and their status as tenants or
freeholders. It includes a business directory
arranged alphabetically by municipality, and a
classified directory. Period: 1884 - 1885.

56. **Union Publishing Co. (1885-6) farmers' and
business directory for the counties of Brant,
Halton, Norfolk, Waterloo and Wellington.**
Ingersoll: Union Publishing, 1885. 1 v. ill.,
indexes. Also CIHM Microfiche series, no. A01195.
Loc: OKIT, OWTL, OWTU, OWTUR.
The first edition, including lists of residents
with post office addresses, concession and lot
numbers, and status as tenants or freeholders.
Waterloo County coverage by township extends from
page 194 to 239. Businesses are listed
alphabetically for each community, beginning on
page 337. These are followed by a classified
business directory and a postal guide. Period:
1885 - 1886.

57. **Union Publishing Co. (1887) farmers' and business
directory for the counties of Waterloo and
Wellington.** St Thomas: The Journal Co., Printers,
1887. 247 p. Also CIHM Microfiche series, no.
A02099. Loc: OWTL, OWTU, OWTUR.
A directory published biennially, including a
list of residents with post office addresses,
concession and lot numbers, and status as tenants
or freeholders. Waterloo County information is
presented by township, starting on page 85.
Businesses are listed alphabetically for each
community, from page 160. Period: 1886 - 1887.

58. **Union Publishing Co. (1888-9) farmers' and
business directory for the counties of Perth,
Waterloo, and Wellington.** Ingersoll: Union
Publishing, 1889. 208, 156 p. ill., indexes. Loc:
OKIT.
A biennial publication including lists of
residents with post office addresses, concession
and lot numbers, and status as tenants or
freeholders. Waterloo County coverage by township
is from page 1 to 52. Businesses are listed
alphabetically for each community, beginning on
page A1. A classified business directory follows
with an index to advertisers. Period: 1888 - 1889.

59. **Union Publishing Co. (1891) farmers' and business
directory for the counties of Halton, Peel,
Waterloo and Wellington.** Ingersoll: Union
Publishing, 1891. 418 p. ill., indexes. Loc: OKIT.
A biennial publication listing residents with
post office addresses, concession and lot numbers,
and status as tenants or freeholders. Waterloo
County coverage by township is from page 176 to
226. Businesses are listed alphabetically for
each community beginning on page 227. A
classified business directory follows with indexes
to the townships, cities, towns and
advertisements. Period: 1890 - 1891.

60. **Union Publishing Co. (1893) farmers' and business
directory for the counties of Peel, Waterloo and
Wellington.** Ingersoll: Union Publishing, 1893.
364 p. Loc: OWTU.
A directory published biennially, including
lists of residents with post office addresses,
concession and lot numbers, and status as tenant
or freeholders. Waterloo County lists, by
township, are presented from page 52 to 103.
Period: 1892 - 1893.

61. **Union Publishing Co. (1895) farmers' and business
directory for the counties of Grey, Waterloo and
Wellington.** Ingersoll: Union Publishing, 1895.
153, 299 p. ill., indexes. Loc: OKIT.
The 9th edition of a biennial publication

listing residents with their post office addresses, concession and lot numbers, and status as tenants or freeholders. Waterloo County coverage by township is from page A145 to A198. Businesses are listed alphabetically under their communities, beginning on page 1. A classified business directory follows, with indexes to the townships, cities, towns and advertisements. Period: 1894 - 1895.

62. **Union Publishing Co. (1896) farmers' and business directory for the counties of Halton, Waterloo and Wellington.** Ingersoll: Union Publishing, 1896. 336 p. ill., indexes. Loc: OKIT.

The 10th edition of a biennial publication listing residents with post office addresses, concession and lot numbers, and status as tenants or freeholders. Waterloo County coverage by township is from page 92 to 146. Businesses are listed alphabetically for each community from page 212. A classified business directory follows with indexes for townships, cities, towns and advertisements. Period: 1895 - 1896.

63. **Union Publishing Co. (1899-1900) farmers' and business directory for the counties of Halton, Waterloo and Wellington.** Ingersoll: Union Publishing, 1899. 529 p. mf. Loc: OG.

Lists of residents including post office addresses, status as tenant or freeholder, and lot and concession numbers. Separate business directories for each town or village list names of proprietor with their types of business. Identified as Volume 12. Period: 1899 - 1900.

64. **Union Publishing Co. (1905) farmers' and business directory for the counties of Huron, Middlesex and Perth.** Ingersoll: Union Publishing, 1905. 535 p. indexes. Loc: OKIT.

A directory including only the township of Wellesley from Waterloo County. Residents are listed from page 359 to 372, with their post office addresses, concession and lot numbers, and whether they were tenants or freeholders. No businesses from Wellesley Township are mentioned. Period: 1904 - 1905.

65. **Union Publishing Co. (1906) farmers' and business directory for the counties of Halton, Waterloo and Wellington.** Ingersoll: Union Publishing, 1906. 331 p. indexes. Loc: OKIT.

Lists of residents with post office addresses, concession and lot numbers, and status as tenants or freeholders. Waterloo County coverage by township is from page 46 to 113. Businesses are listed alphabetically for each community, beginning on page 256. Period: 1905 - 1906.

66. **Union Publishing Co. (1909, 1911) farmers' and business directory for the counties of Dufferin, Halton, Peel, Waterloo and Wellington.** Ingersoll: Union Publishing, 1909. 467 p. mf. Loc: OG, OFWCA.

Lists of residents with concession and lot numbers, post office addresses, and status as tenant or freeholder. Businesses are listed separately for each town or village. Guelph Public Library has a copy of the 1909 directory (identified as Volume 18) and the Wellington County Archives has a copy of the 1911 directory (Volume 19). Period: 1909 - 1911.

67. **Union Publishing Co. Berlin and Waterloo directory, 1893.** CIHM Microfiche series, no. A01423. Ingersoll: Union Publishing, 1893. 154 p. mf. Loc: OWTL, OWTU.

An alphabetical list of businesses and residents, a classified list of businesses and professional men, and a miscellaneous directory of officials, schools, churches, banks and incorporated institutions. From an original in the National Library of Canada. Period: 1892 - 1893.

68. **Vernon's Berlin, Waterloo and Bridgeport street, alphabetical, business and miscellaneous directory.** Hamilton: Henry Vernon, 1897 - 1911. 149 p. Loc: OKIT, OWTUR.

A directory in three main parts. Residents are listed first by street address and then alphabetically by name with some details of occupation and/or employer. A classified business directory provides details about locations, owners and products and there are advertisements by some businesses. Only the University of Waterloo Library's Doris Lewis Rare Book Room is known to have a copy of the 1st edition for 1897-1899 and this copy is missing pages 23-24 and 45-46. The Kitchener Public Library's Grace Schmidt Room of Local History has originals or copies of most editions to the 9th in 1911-12. Period: 1897 - 1911.

69. **Vernon's City of Berlin, Town of Waterloo and Bridgeport street, alphabetical, business and miscellaneous directory.** Hamilton: Henry Vernon and Son, 1912 - 1916?. 273 p. Loc: OKIT.

Alphabetical lists of businesses and residents in each community. Street addresses and occupations are usually specified for each householder and entries often contain telephone numbers. Advertisements by local businesses can be found on every page. The 1912 directory is identified as the first for the City of Berlin and the 10th edition for the Twin Cities, and the 1916 is identified as the 14th edition. Period: 1912 - 1916.

70. **Vernon's City of Kitchener, Town of Waterloo and Bridgeport street, alphabetical, business and miscellaneous directory.** Hamilton: Henry Vernon and Son/Vernon Directories, 1919 - 1991. Also mf. Loc: OKIT, OWT, OWTUR.

Residents are listed first by street address, and then alphabetically by surname with some details of occupation and employer. A classified business directory provides information about locations, owners and products and there are also advertisements by some businesses. The directory published in 1919 is identified as the 15th edition; the 1950 directory is the 45th edition. The University of Waterloo Library's Doris Lewis Rare Book Room has a copy of the 1926 directory, the Kitchener Public Library has copies of all editions, and the Waterloo Public Library has all editions since 1955. Period: 1919 - 1991.

71. **Vernon's farmers' and business directory (1915) for the counties of Dufferin, Halton, Peel, Waterloo and Wellington.** Hamilton: Henry Vernon and Son, 1915. 346 p. indexes. Loc: OKIT.

A list of residents with post office addresses, concession and lot numbers, and status as tenants or freeholders. Waterloo County coverage, by township, is from page 155 to 201. Businesses, their locations and owners are listed alphabetically by community, beginning on page 202. Noted as the 20th edition. Period: 1914 - 1915.

72. **Vernon's farmers' and business directory (1918..) for the counties of Perth, Waterloo and Wellington.** Hamilton: Henry Vernon and Son, 1918, 1924, 1931. Loc: OKIT.

Directories arranged by townships, cities, towns and villages. Residents in townships are listed with their lot and concession numbers, and their status as freeholders, tenants or farmers' sons. A business directory is provided for each city, town and village, with names of enterprises and proprietors. Kitchener Public Library has directories for 1918 (the 21st edition), 1924 (the 22nd edition) and 1931 (the 23rd edition). Period: 1917 - 1931.

73. **Vernon's Galt, Preston and Hespeler street, alphabetical, business and miscellaneous directory.** Hamilton: Henry Vernon/ Henry Vernon and Son/ Vernon Directories, 1898 - 1972. Also mf. Loc: OCCA, OCLG, OKIT, OWTU.

Vernon's street directories for these communities are biennial until the 34th edition of 1962, after which they are annual. The specific titles change from time to time: in 1898 the directory covers Galt and Preston; Hespeler is

included from 1900 to 1912; after 1914 Galt is referred to as a city. In 1973, when the City of Cambridge was formed, the annual Cambridge directory begins. Each volume contains four directories for each town: 1) a miscellaneous directory of city and social institutions, 2) a classified business directory, 3) an alphabetical directory for residents and businesses, including the occupation of the person listed and his address, and 4) a street directory listing buildings in numerical order with the names of their occupants. The Kitchener Public Library has the 1900 and 1910 directories and the University of Waterloo Library has those for 1950, 1952, 1954, 1967, 1970, 1971 and 1972. The City of Cambridge Archives has original hard copies from 1912 to 1972 and the Cambridge Library and Gallery has microfilm copies of the 8th edition (1910) and of all editions from the 10th (1916-17). Period: 1900 - 1972.

74. **Waterloo County gazetteer and directory for 1884-5.** Guelph: William W. Evans, 1884. 271 p. ill., map. Also CIHM Microfiche series, no. A02097. Loc: OKIT, OWTL, OWTU.

Lists of businesses and individuals stating places of residence and type of occupation or business. Information is also provided on county and other municipal officials, monthly cattle fairs, post offices and local court sittings. Period: 1884 - 1885.

NEWSPAPERS, INCLUDING COMMENTARIES ON THEIR VALUE AS HISTORICAL SOURCES

75. **Ayr News.** 1897 -. mf. Loc: OKIT.

A weekly newspaper serving Ayr and its locality, with some national and international news. It covers the spectrum of local events and carries advertisements for local businesses. Older editions serialize short stories and other works. The single issue of 30 January 1897, published by William J. Keyes, is held by Kitchener Public Library on the microfilm reel of Ayr News old editions. The library also holds the issues from 27 October 1904 to December 1989 on microfilm, and has hard copies from 15 November 1962 to the present. The paper was published by R. Constable and Company in October 1904, and from November of that year was published by George W. Dawson. The single issue of 24 July 1952 is held in the Waterloo Historical Society collection at the Kitchener Public Library. Period: 1897 - 1972.

76. **Ayr Observer.** 1856 - 1857. 4 p. mf. Loc: OKIT.

Sometimes entitled the **Ayr Observer, and North Dumfries, Blenheim, Blandford and Waterloo General**

Advertiser, the paper contains mainly local news and advertisements, with some national and international news. Kitchener Public Library has the 17 October 1856 and 2 October 1857 issues on a microfilm reel of Ayr News old editions. Both issues contain articles on the North Dumfries Township fair. Period: 1850 - 1865.

77. **Ayr Recorder**. 1880? - 1892?. 8 p. mf. Loc: OKIT.
     Sometimes entitled **The Recorder**, the paper contains mostly village news and advertising. The Kitchener Public Library holds microfilm copies of the 30 December 1886 and the 24 March 1892 issues, published by G.W. Dennis. Period: 1880 - 1895.

78. Barrie, William C. "History as related by early Canadian newspapers." **Waterloo Historical Society**. 1948. 36: 40-43. Loc: all.
     A short account of the large collection of printed documents of the Johnston family of North Dumfries, including the first volumes of the **Dumfries Courier** (1844-6), the **Dumfries Reformer** (1850) and the **Galt Reporter** (1852), and the minute book of School Section No. 25, West Dumfries, with entries beginning in 1847. Period: 1844 - 1947.

79. **Berlin Chronicle**. 1856 - 1860. mf. Loc: OKIT.
     A Waterloo County newspaper published in the mid 19th century, with articles emphasizing local commerce, politics, and transportation. It was known as the **Berlin Chronicle and Provincial Reformers' Gazette** in January 1856, and by 5 November 1856 was called the **Berlin Chronicle and Waterloo County Reformers' Gazette**. It was originally published in Berlin by William Jaffray and Casper Hett, but in 1860 Jaffray sold the paper to John J. Bowman and Christian Kumpf, who transferred it to Waterloo and renamed it the **Waterloo Chronicle**. The Kitchener Public Library holds most issues on microfilm from 23 January 1856 to 31 January 1860. The Waterloo Historical Society holds original issues for 26 March 1856, 2 April 1856, and 28 September 1858. Period: 1856 - 1860.

80. **Berlin Daily News**. 1878 - 1897. mf. Loc: OKIT.
     The first daily newspaper in Waterloo County, founded in 1878 by P.E.W. Moyer. Following Moyer's death, the paper combined with the **Berlin Daily Record** in late January 1897, becoming the **Berlin News Record**. Microfilm editions held at the Kitchener Public Library include February to December 1878 inclusive, July to December 1879 inclusive, and the editions of 8 June 1892 and 4 July 1889. Original editions held by the Waterloo Historical Society at the library include 3 July 1880, 22 June 1883, 4 December 1883, and 27 December 1883. Period: 1878 - 1897.

81. **Berlin Express**. 1899. 4 p. Loc: OKITW.
     A newspaper for the Berlin-Waterloo area, published by C.E. Moyer. The Waterloo Historical Society holds one issue, for 10 August 1899, at Kitchener Public Library. This was the first edition to be published, and contains a prospectus of the paper, which was to be produced tri-weekly and weekly. Period: 1899 - 1910.

82. **Berliner Journal**. 1859 - 1917. Also mf. Loc: OKIT, OWTL, OWTUR.
     A German-language weekly that carried local, provincial, national and international news. Each issue varied in length from 8 to 12 pages and included advertisements by local merchants, articles on political events, editorials, letters to the editor, a serial story, poetry and humour, dialect writings, as well as announcements of births, marriages and deaths. In July 1904 the paper amalgamated with the **Ontario Glocke** and, on 10 January 1917, its name was changed to **Ontario Journal**. On 2 October 1918, coinciding with an Order-in-Council prohibiting the use of German, the newspaper began publishing in English. The University of Waterloo Library's Doris Lewis Rare Book Room has the issues from 1859 to 1898. The Kitchener Public Library's Grace Schmidt Room has bound volumes and microfilms for the years 1860 to 1909 and 1914 to 1918, as well as a few single issues. The WLU Library reports a microfilm copy for the period from 1859 to 1916. Period: 1859 - 1917.

83. "Berliner Journal." **Waterloo Historical Society**. 1959. 47: 62-70. ill. Loc: all.
     A history commemorating the centennial of the newspaper's founding in 1859, including a discussion of its contents compared with other county newspapers. Period: 1859 - 1959.

84. Breithaupt, W.H. "The **Canada Museum**." **Waterloo Historical Society**. 1939. 27: 62-70. Loc: all.
     A short history of the **Canada Museum und Allgemeine Zeitung**, Kitchener's oldest German newspaper, published from 1835 to 1840. Period: 1835 - 1850.

85. Breithaupt, W.H. "President's address: Waterloo County newspapers." **Waterloo Historical Society**. 1921. 9: 152-159. Loc: all.
     A catalogue of newspapers printed in Waterloo County from 1835 to 1920, with names of their publishers and editors. Period: 1835 - 1918.

86. Burrows, Sandra and Gaudet, Franceen. **Checklist of indexes to Canadian newspapers**. Ottawa: National Library of Canada, 1987. 148 p. index. Loc: OKIT, OWTL, OWTU.

A list of indexes to newspapers in Canada, including partial indexes to **Cambridge Reporter, Galt Evening Reporter, Hespeler Herald, Prestonian, Berlin Telegraph, Berliner Journal, Canada Museum und Allgemeine Zeitung, Der Deutsche Canadier** and **Elmira Independent**. The entries are arranged alphabetically by the name of the town or city of the institution that holds the index. Each entry includes the name and address of institution, name of index, title of newspaper, types of events covered, explanation of how the index is recorded, and conditions of access to researchers. Most indexes concentrate on details of births, marriages and deaths; additional local indexes have been compiled since this report was compiled. Institutions reported as holding indexes are Cambridge Library and Gallery, the Preston Branch of Cambridge Libraries, Kitchener Public Library, University of Waterloo Library, Wilfrid Laurier University Library, and the Waterloo Regional Library. Period: 1830 - 1980.

87. **Canada Museum und Allgemeine Zeitung**. 1835 - 1840. mf. Loc: OKIT.

Founded by H.W. Peterson, this weekly was the first to be published in Waterloo County and among the first German-language newspapers in Canada. It ceased publication when Peterson was appointed Registrar of the Wellington District and moved to Guelph, but was immediately followed by another paper, **Der Deutsch Canadier,** published by Heinrich Eby and edited by Christian Enslin. Kitchener Public Library holds microfilm copies of the following issues: 27 August 1835 to 20 October 1836, 3 November 1836 to 13 December 1838, 22 December 1838 to 18 December 1840. Period: 1835 - 1840.

88. **Canadisches Volksblatt**. 1859 - 1909. mf. Loc: OKIT, OKITW.

A weekly German-language newspaper which was founded in May 1859 by George Reynolds and later absorbed **Der Neu-Hamburger Neutrale**. In 1909 the paper merged with **Der Canadische Kolonist** when it was bought by Rittinger and Motz, owners of the **Berliner Journal**. Microfilmed editions for 1865 to 1866 are available at the Kitchener Public Library. The Waterloo Historical Society holds a set of bound newspapers for 1882, 1884, 1888 and 1889, all the years being incomplete. Period: 1859 - 1909.

89. **Daily Record/ Daily Telegraph/ News-Record/ Kitchener Daily Record/ Kitchener-Waterloo Record**. Berlin and Kitchener: Recordak, 1893 -. 36 reels. mf. Loc: OKIT, OWTL, OWTU.

Microfilmed copies of the major English-language daily which has undergone a number of name changes since first published in 1893. The paper provides coverage of local, regional, provincial, national and international news, with emphasis on local and county-wide current events such as business, politics, sports, social affairs, births, marriages, deaths, letters to the editor and advertisements for the area's businesses and professionals. The sequence of masthead names is: the **Berlin Daily Telegraph** from 30 January to 22 March 1893, the **Berlin Daily Record** from 23 March 1893 to 30 January 1897, the **News-Record** from 1 February 1897 to October 1919, the **Kitchener Daily Record** from October 1919 to 31 December 1947, and the **Kitchener-Waterloo Record** from 1 January 1947. Absorbed by the paper have been the **Berlin Daily News** on 1 February 1897, and the **Daily Telegraph** which was published from 1896 to 1922. Issues missing from the University of Waterloo Library's collection include: 30 January to 22 March 1893, 30 January 1896 to 3 January 1898, January to December 1903, January to June 1911, and all issues in 1914, 1915, 1916, 1917 and 1918. A microfilm copy was made for the Kitchener Public Library and held by the other libraries includes issues for the period from 1893 to the present. Period: 1893 - 1991.

90. **Das Wochenblatt**. 1878. Loc: OKITW.

A short-lived Conservative German-language paper, published and edited in Berlin by P.E.W. Moyer. The Waterloo Historical Society holds issues for 26 February 1878 and 5 March 1878 at the Kitchener Public Library.

91. **Der Canadische Bauernfreund**. 1851 - 1918. Loc: OKITW.

A German-language weekly, first published in Preston by Abraham Erb and edited by Martin Rudolf. The paper moved to Waterloo when it was sold to Moses Springer, and to Berlin in 1903 when it amalgamated with the **Deutsche Zeitung**. It united with the **Canadisches Volksblatt** in 1908, and was absorbed a year later by the **Berliner Journal**. The Waterloo Historical Society holds issues for 27 February 1852, 25 March 1853, 14 May 1868, and 25 December 1890. Period: 1850 - 1918.

92. **Der Canadische Beobachter**. 1848 - 1850?. 4 p. Loc: OKITW.

A German-language weekly, founded by Martin Rudolf and first published in Preston. When Rudolf moved to New Hamburg, the paper continued as the **Hamburger Beobachter**. The 8 February 1849 issue of the paper is held by the Waterloo Historical Society at the Kitchener Public Library. Period: 1848 - 1850.

93. **Der Canadische Kolonist**. 1864 - 1909. 4 p. Loc: OKITW.

    A German-language weekly founded in Stratford by Jacob Teuscher and amalgamated in 1906 with the **Berliner Journal**. The Waterloo Historical Society holds the 4 December 1872 edition at the Kitchener Public Library. Period: 1864 - 1909.

94. **Der Deutsche Canadier und Neuigkeitsbote**. 1841 - 1865. mf. Loc: OKIT, OWTL, OWTU.

    A weekly German-language newspaper, first published by Heinrich Eby and edited by Christian Enslin in January 1841, as the successor to the **Canada Museum**. Kitchener Public Library holds microfilm copies for 5 January 1844 to 25 December 1845; 31 December 1847 to 5 January 1861; 9 January 1862 to 3 July 1862; 21 April 1864 to 11 August 1864. Incomplete holdings are reported by the University of Waterloo Library for the 1842-1864 period and by the Wilfrid Laurier University Library for 1844-62 and 1864. Period: 1841 - 1865.

95. **Der Deutsche Reformer**. 1863. 4 p. Loc: OKITW.

    A political newspaper published and edited in Waterloo by Jakob Teuscher who left for Stratford to found **Der Canadische Kolonist** before the end of 1863. The Waterloo Historical Society holds the first issue of 6 June 1863. Period: 1863 - 1864.

96. **Der Morgenstern**. 1839 - 1841. mf. Loc: OKIT.

    An early German-language weekly published and edited in Waterloo by Benjamin Burkholder. Kitchener Public Library holds microfilm issues from 6 June 1839 to 16 September 1841. Period: 1839 - 1841.

97. **Der Neu-Hamburger Neutrale**. 1855 - 1859?. mf. Loc: OKIT.

    A German weekly paper published by W.H. Boullee and edited by Robert Storch at New Hamburg. The paper was sold to George Reynolds who changed the name to **Canadisches Volksblatt**. The following issues are held on microfilm at Kitchener Public Library: 19 January to 28 December 1855; 2 January to 25 December 1857. Period: 1855 - 1859.

98. **Deutsche Zeitung**. 1891 - 1899, 1915. mf. Loc: OKIT, OWTL, OWTU.

    A weekly German-language newspaper which was published from 1891 to 1899 by the Die Deutsche Druck- und Verlagsgesellschaft von Berlin (German Printing and Publishing Co.), and revived early in the next century with Andrew Weidenhammer as editor. Issues from 3 November 1891 to 27 September 1899 have been microfilmed, and Kitchener Public Library also holds single copies of the issues for 2 February 1892, 23 June 1915, 31 July 1915 and 14 July 1916. Period: 1891 - 1916.

99. **Dumfries Reformer/ Weekly Reformer/ Daily Reformer/ Galt Daily Reformer/ Galt Weekly Reformer**. 1849 - 1912. mf. Loc: OKIT, OCLG.

    A Liberal newspaper founded by James Ainslie in 1849, with Walter Stewart as editor. It was bought in 1853 by James Young, then 18 years old. In 1896 it was published daily as well as weekly, and in 1912 was bought up by the **Galt Reporter**. Another paper by the same title was founded in 1991. The Cambridge Library and Gallery has microfilm copies for the 1849-1892 period. The Kitchener Public Library holds microfilm copies of the **Dumfries Reformer** from 17 September 1849 to 31 December 1897; copies of the **Weekly Reformer** from 29 October 1896 to 31 December 1897, 12 May 1904, 16 March 1905; issues of the **Galt Daily Reformer** for 22 and 23 March 1900, 31 April 1907, 31 October 1899, 21 December 1899; and the **Galt Weekly Reformer** for 1898-1899, 1900 (January and February), 1903-1912 (January-May, June-July). Period: 1849 - 1912.

100. **Elmira Anzeiger**. Elmira: Delion Brothers, 1870 - 1880. 4 p. ill. mf. Loc: OWRE.

    A weekly German-language newspaper, started by the firm of Philip Pfaff and David Wittig but taken over by Frederick and William Delion after one month. The paper covered national and international events with an emphasis on politics, but included notices of local births, marriages, deaths, train times, literary events and entertainments. The Elmira Public Library has the issues of 17 April 1873, 17 June 1875, 3 August 1876, 5 June 1879, 4 March 1880 and 16 September 1880. Period: 1870 - 1880.

101. **The Elmira Signet**. 1893-. Loc: OWRE, OKIT.

    A weekly newspaper reporting local and district news with some provincial and international stories. Local information includes farm news, market prices, editorials, advertisements and notices of births, deaths and marriages. Poetry and short stories are sometimes included. The Elmira Public Library and Kitchener Public Library have holdings on microfilm from February 1893 to February 1894, and 1900 to 1982. The Elmira library also holds a hard copy facsimile of the first newspaper on 18 February 1893. Period: 1893 - 1982.

102. **Freie Presse**. 1886 - 1888?. mf. Loc: OKIT, OWTL.

A weekly German-language newspaper first published by Hett and Buchhaupt in 1886. A year later it was owned by the Freie Presse Actien-Gesellschaft and edited by C. Hartmann. Microfilm copies are available for issues from 6 August 1886 to 5 August 1887. Period: 1886 - 1888.

103. Galt Daily Reporter. **100th anniversary: for 50 years a weekly, for 50 years South Waterloo's daily newspaper**. Galt: Galt Daily Reporter, 1946. 26 p. ill. Loc: OKIT.

An original copy of the commemorative issue on 13 November 1946, in fragile condition. Period: 1846 - 1946.

104. **Galt Reporter/ Galt Weekly Reporter/ Galt Daily Reporter/ The Evening Reporter/ Cambridge Reporter**. 1846 -. mf. Loc: OCCA, OCLG, OKIT.

A paper founded in 1846 by Peter Jaffray and James Ainslie, continuing as the **Cambridge Reporter**. Political differences severed the partnership after three years when Ainslie left to form the **Dumfries Reformer**, leaving the **Reporter** a Conservative paper. The Cambridge Archives and Cambridge Library and Gallery hold microfilm copies for the following years: 1857 to 1876, 1880 to 1889, 1895 to 1898, 1902 to 1904, 1905, 1907 to 1913, 1915 to 1924, and 1925 to 1966 (with the Cambridge Library and Gallery's microfilm collection extending to 1973). The Kitchener Public Library reports microfilm copies for 1857-1859, 1888, 1912-1917, 1919-1922, 1923-1957 and 1967-1971. Period: 1846 - 1992.

105. Gilchrist, J. Brian. **Inventory of Ontario newspapers: 1793-1986**. Toronto: Micromedia Limited, 1987. 74 p. indexes. Loc: OCLG, OKIT, OWTL, OWTU.

A guide to English-language newspapers, including those of Waterloo County. The entries are arranged alphabetically, first by place of publication, then by masthead name. Frequency of publication (such as weekly, semi-weekly or daily) is stated, followed by a summary of the paper's history including name changes, takeovers or mergers, as well as interruptions in printing. In most cases library location codes of the newspaper or microfilmed copies are given. Period: 1844 - 1986.

106. **Hamburger Beobachter**. 1852 - 1856. mf. Loc: OKITW, OWTL.

An early weekly German-language newspaper, founded by Martin Rudolf in 1852. Rudolf was earlier associated with a Preston paper called the **Der Canadische Beobachter**. Microfilm copies are available for issues from 9 February 1855 to 22 February 1856. Period: 1852 - 1856.

107. **Hespeler Herald**. 1895? - 1970. mf. Loc: OCCA, OCLG, OKITW.

A weekly review of local happenings, founded by Oscar Eby and sold in 1918 to George Hudson when Eby was appointed County Registrar. The paper merged in 1970 with one of Walter Baulk's weeklies to become the **Preston-Times-Herald**. The Cambridge Archives and Cambridge Library and Gallery hold microfilm copies for the following years: 1902-1906, 1908-1909, November 1912-December 1918, January 1921-December 1930. The Waterloo Historical Society collection includes bound volumes for 1919 to 1949 and the Cambridge Archives has bound volumes from 1949 to 1969. Period: 1895 - 1970.

108. Kalbfleisch, Herbert Karl. "German literature as represented in two German newspapers of Ontario, Canada." **Kentucky Foreign Language Quarterly**. 1956. 3: 184-191. Loc: OOU.

A case study based on the author's major work on German-language newspapers in Ontario. Period: 1830 - 1920.

109. Kalbfleisch, Herbert Karl. **The history of the German newspapers of Ontario, Canada, 1853-1918**. University of Michigan (Ph.D. thesis), 1953. 1 reel. ill., bibl. mf. Loc: OWTU.

An analysis of the German-language press including numerous newspapers published in Waterloo County. The thesis was later published as a book entitled The history of the pioneer German language press of Ontario, 1835- 1918. The author evaluates the roles of newspapers in providing material of a literary and poetic nature and supplying immigrants with news in German of their homeland and adopted land. Also examined is the response of newspaper publishers to the existing Pennsylvania German culture and their attempts to promote racial and cultural consciousness among all German-speaking people in the area. Newspapers are discussed individually in chronological order, with profiles of their editors and publishers. The work is organized for four eras: 1835-1850, 1850-1900, 1900-1909, and 1909-1918. Appendices include copies of mastheads and excerpts from various newspapers. Period: 1853 - 1918.

110. Kalbfleisch, Herbert Karl. **The history of the pioneer German language press of Ontario, 1835-1918**. Toronto: University of Toronto Press, 1968. 133 p. ill., bibl., index. Loc: OCLG, OKIT, OWT, OWTL, OWTU, OWTUCG.

A comprehensive history of German-language

newspapers in nineteenth-century Ontario, including those published in Waterloo County. The book deals with four periods: the beginning from 1835 to 1850, the flourishing phase from 1850 to 1900, the period of amalgamation from 1900 to 1909, and the critical years from 1909 to 1918. Each section provides information about the people involved in the individual newspapers, including: **Der Deutsche Canadier, Der Morgenstern, Der Canadische Beobachter, Prestoner Express, Der Canadische Bauernfreund, Hamburger Beobachter, Canadisches Volksblatt, Berliner Journal, Elmira Anzeiger, Canada Museum** and **Der Neu-Hamburger Neutrale**. Period: 1835 - 1918.

111. "**Kitchener-Waterloo Record** moves to new building." **Waterloo Historical Society**. 1973. 61: 45. Loc: all.

A short article noting the company's move to Fairway Drive, Kitchener, and mentioning previous names of the newspaper such as **Berlin Daily News, Daily News, News-Record, Daily Record** and **Kitchener Daily Record**. Period: 1853 - 1973.

112. McLaren, Duncan. **Ontario ethno-cultural newspapers, 1835-1972: an annotated checklist**. Toronto: University of Toronto Press, 1977. 234 p. bibl. Loc: OKIT, OWTL, OWTU.

A listing including the German-language press of Waterloo County. Entries include the title of the newspaper as it appears on the masthead, place of publication, frequency, language(s) of publication, founding date, date of last issue (if defunct), names of publishers and editors, and locations of originals and microfilmed copies. Alternate titles are noted and there are chronological and geographic indexes. Period: 1835 - 1972.

113. **New Hamburg Independent**. 1917 -. Loc: OKITW.

A weekly paper, founded in about 1878 by William Dawson, who sold it to Daniel Ritz. Kitchener Public Library holds copies from 1917 to the present. Period: 1878 - 1992.

114. **North Waterloo Protectionist**. 1926 -?. 4 p. Loc: OKITW.

An official organ of the North Waterloo Liberal Conservative Association, published tri-weekly and printed by the Chronicle Press. The first issue of 21 August 1926, held by the Waterloo Historical Society, deals with organized labour and free trade. The paper supported David Gross, the Protectionist candidate. Period: 1926 - 1927.

115. **Preston Progress**. 1885? - 1922. Loc: OKITW.

A weekly paper formed by Preston businessmen about 1885, with E.P. Rice as the first editor.

It was subsequently owned by Thomas H. Sears, G.A. Blackstock, A. Smith, Mark Donald and James Donald. Bound volumes from 1915 to 1917 are held by the Waterloo Historical Society. Period: 1885 - 1922.

116. **Preston Times/Cambridge Times**. 1947? -. Loc: OKITW, OCCA.

A weekly paper begun after the Second World War, printed by Baulk Publishers and first edited by Norman Moeller. In 1969 it was sold to the Kitchener-Waterloo Record Ltd; in 1970 its title changed to the **Times Herald** and later the **Cambridge Times**. The Cambridge Archives holds bound volumes for the years 1948 to 1972. The Waterloo Historical Society holds issues from October 1948 to 28 May 1958 and from 13 July 1966 to 11 June 1969. Period: 1947 - 1992.

117. **Prestonian**. 1912 - 1931. mf. Loc: OCCA, OCLG.

A weekly paper, founded by the Doherty brothers in 1912, reporting on Preston events and containing advertisements for local businesses. The City of Cambridge Archives and Cambridge Library and Gallery hold microfilm copies of the issues from 19 September 1912 to 10 September 1914 and from 23 September 1915 to 10 September 1931. Period: 1912 - 1931.

118. "Retirement of newspaperman Earl Werstine." **Waterloo Historical Society**. 1969. 57: 18. Loc: all.

A profile of Werstine's roles as reporter, editor and columnist for 63 years on the **Galt Evening Reporter**, including references to his coverage of the 1907 and 1947 Old Boys' Reunions and his "Around town" column from 1950. Period: 1907 - 1969.

119. Ritz, Ernst. "The **New Hamburg Independent**'s first century." **Waterloo Historical Society**. 1978. 66: 123-132. ill. Loc: all.

A history of the community's first English-language weekly newspaper which began as a campaign publication for local businessman Samuel Merner. The author describes the involvement of George W. Dawson, Otto Pressprich and the Ritz family and outlines advances in printing technology. Period: 1878 - 1978.

120. Sanders, Constance E. "The **Evening Reporter** celebrates its 125th anniversary, 1846-1871." **Waterloo Historical Society**. 1971. 59: 51-59. Loc: all.

An account of the founding and development of the newspaper, with excerpts of some notable stories. Period: 1846 - 1971.

121. Schmidt, John P. "History of the **Ayr News**."
Waterloo Historical Society. 1979. 67: 20-25.
Loc: all.
    A short history of the founding and development
of the only weekly newspaper in the Waterloo
region to have been independently owned for 125
years. The author describes early printing
processes and presents excerpts from past
editorials and advertisements. Period: 1854 -
1979.

122. "**Waterloo Chronicle**'s century honoured."
Waterloo Historical Society. 1967. 55: 17. Loc:
all.
    A brief account of the newspaper's centennial
celebrations. Period: 1854 - 1967.

123. **Waterloo Chronicle/ Waterloo County Chronicle and
Weekly Telegraph/ Chronicle Telegraph/ Waterloo
County Telegraph.** 1860? -. mf. Loc: OKIT.
    Originally known as the **Berlin Chronicle** or
**Berlin Chronicle and Waterloo County Reformers
Gazette,** the paper became the **Waterloo
Chronicle** when sold by William Jaffray in 1860 to
John J. Bowman and Christian Kumpf, who moved it
to Waterloo. Later owners and editors included
P.E.W. Moyer, Thomas Hilliard and David Bean.
Kitchener Public Library holds microfilm copies
for 1868, 1869, 1922 to 1929, and 1932 to the
present. Period: 1860 - 1992.

124. **Waterloo Sentinel.** 1909 - 1912. mf. Loc: OKIT.
    A weekly and a semi-weekly paper, published
first by Andrew Weidenhammer and then by James
Heveron, and microfilmed from 12 October 1909 to
24 September 1912. Period: 1909 - 1912.

125. **Wellesley Maple Leaf.** 1900 - 1921. mf. Loc:
OKIT.
    A weekly publication, founded and edited by J.G.
Green, and later owned by H.W. Kaufman. Kitchener
Public Library holds microfilm copies for the
years 1900-1904 and 1906-1908. Period: 1900 -
1921.

OTHER SOURCES FOR REGIONAL HISTORY

126. Bellingham, Susan Saunders. "Bowlby family
papers." **Waterloo Historical Society.** 1976. 64:
70-73. ill. Loc: all.
    A short article relating the University of
Waterloo Library's acquisition of a collection of
letters written to D. Shannon Bowlby by members of
his immediate family. The author presents brief
excerpts from the correspondence, with insights
into the lives of a Berlin middle-class family in
1893. Period: 1893 - 1920.

127. Bellingham, Susan Saunders. "Breithaupt papers
return to Waterloo Region." **Waterloo Historical
Society.** 1988. 76: 31-50. ill. Loc: all.
    An account of the discovery in 1987 of
manuscripts, diaries and letters, now part of the
Breithaupt Hewetson Clark Collection in the Doris
Lewis Rare Book Room, University of Waterloo
Library. In reviewing the collection, the author
outlines the history of the Breithaupts and their
extended families and friends including the
Devitts, Anthes and Bowlbys. Excerpts quoted from
Louis Jacob Breithaupt's diary describe the
Friedensfest of 1871, the visit of Marquis of
Lorne and the Princess Louise in 1879, and the
birth of Louis Orville Breithaupt in 1890. Period:
c1850 - c1950.

128. Bellingham, Susan Saunders. **Guide to local
history materials: Doris Lewis Rare Book Room,
University of Waterloo Library.** Waterloo:
University of Waterloo Library, 1981. 1 v.
(unpaged). Loc: OKIT.
    Arranged in three sections: books held in the
collection, books (and other sources) relating to
Waterloo County available in the Genealogical
Society Library of Utah, and archives. References
to books consist of photocopied index cards.
Archival collections include those of David
Shannon Bowlby, William Wilfrid Campbell, John D.
Detwiler, Dumfries Township, Robert Forbes, John
Galt, Jardine Family, Herbert Johnston, the Land
Registration Copy Books for Waterloo County, the
Ontario Historical Collection, Dorothea Palmer,
the Parents' Information Bureau, German Manuscript
Prayer Books, David H. Snyder, John Walter and
Homer Watson. Period: 1830 - 1940.

129. Bellingham, Susan Saunders and Parry, John.
**Opening of the Breithaupt Hewetson Clark
Collection.** Waterloo: University of Waterloo
Library, 1989. 12 p. ill. Loc: OKITW.
    A history and description of family records
including photographs, diaries, correspondence and
account books spanning 150 years. There are
photographs of the donors, H. Spencer and Rosa
Breithaupt Clark, and a programme of the opening
ceremonies. Period: 1843 - 1989.

130. Bellingham, Susan Saunders. **Twenty-five fine
books at the University of Waterloo.** Waterloo:
University of Waterloo Library, 1982. 60 p. ill.
Loc: OKIT, OWTL, OWTU.
    A catalogue celebrating the 25th anniversary of
the University. Items relevant to the history of
Waterloo County are the hymnal and juvenile
instruction book compiled by Benjamin Eby and

printed in Berlin in the 1830s (pp. 24-5) and the set of fire insurance plans depicting the town of Waterloo in 1920 (pp. 46-7). Period: 1836 - 1920.

131. Bishop, Olga B. "Checklist of historical works on western Ontario in the libraries of the University of Western Ontario: Oxford and Waterloo counties." **Western Ontario Historical Notes**. 1958. 14,5: 39-49. Loc: OWTL, OWTU.

An annotated list of directories, major histories, genealogies and atlases, with a summary of early territorial definitions of Waterloo County. Period: 1800 - 1950.

132. Bloomfield, Elizabeth and Forgay, Jane and Foster, Linda. **Waterloo Historical Society bibliography**. Guelph: Waterloo Regional Project, 1991. 390 p. Loc: OKIT, OWTU, OWTUR, OWTUCG, OWTL, OWT, OCCA.

Annotated bibliographic references to all 1,280 articles and notes in the 78 annual reports and volumes published by the society from 1913 to 1990. The numbered references have abstracts of scope and content and are organized in a mainly thematic sequence. There are detailed indexes to authors, places, topical subject headings, corporate subjects and personal subjects, and an introduction to Waterloo County, the Waterloo Historical Society, the Waterloo Regional Project, and procedures of compiling the bibliography. Printed in a limited edition with copies presented to most public and university libraries and heritage groups in the region. Period: 1800 - 1990.

133. Douglas, Robert and Fox, Louise and Percival, Rick. **Oral history of Waterloo County**. Wilfrid Laurier University, 1975. 1 v. (unpaged). Loc: OKIT.

Information derived from interviews of Waterloo County residents about the period from World War I to World War II. The reminiscences have been arranged by topics, including the name change from Berlin to Kitchener, the end of World War I, prohibition, the Depression and birth control in the 1930s. Introductions to each topic contain additional historical information. Period: 1914 - 1945.

134. Fitzpatrick, Diane E. "Canada's written record: pre-1900 Canadian books on microfiche." **Waterloo Historical Society**. 1991. 79: 100-103. Loc: all.

An account of the achievement of the Canadian Institute of Historical Microreproductions (CIHM) in locating and preserving books written by Canadians, about Canada and Canadians or published in Canada. The University of Waterloo Library and Wilfrid Laurier University Library have purchased the collection of over 56,800 items on high-quality microfiche. Period: 1800 - 1900.

135. Fitzpatrick, Diane E. "A window to the past: pre-1901 Canadian journals on microfiche." **Waterloo Historical Society**. 1991. 79: 96-99. Loc: all.

An explanation of the project of the Canadian Institute of Historical Microreproductions (CIHM) in locating and preserving about 1,270 journals published in Canada in the 18th and 19th centuries. The University of Waterloo Library and Wilfrid Laurier University Library have subscriptions to the microfiche collection. Period: 1701 - 1900.

136. Hecht, Alfred. **An index of organizations and agencies which collect statistical data on the Kitchener-Waterloo area, Ontario, Canada**. Working paper no. 4. Waterloo: Wilfrid Laurier University, 1977. 28 l. Loc: OWT.

A guide to various private and governmental service organizations, with a subject index on page 26. A list of area organizations that did not collect statistical data is also included.

137. Hoffman, Susan. **Resources for local history and genealogical research**. Kitchener: Kitchener Public Library, 1983. 10 p. bibl. Loc: OWTUR.

A list of resource materials located in the Kitchener Public Library, including municipal, county, business, church and family histories as well as primary sources such as census records, directories, newspapers, manuscripts, photographs, building inventories and oral histories. Period: c1800 - 1983.

138. Hoffman, Susan. "Tweedsmuir histories on microfilm." **Waterloo Historical Society**. 1983. 71: 14. Loc: all.

A note about the microfilming by the Kitchener Public Library of Tweedsmuir histories for Bridgeport, Centreville, Dorking, Elmdale, Helena Feasby, Lexington, Linwood, Preston (South Waterloo), St Jacobs, Wellesley, Winterbourne and Woolwich Ever Faithful.

139. Hoffman, Susan. "Waterloo County genealogical sources at the Kitchener Public Library." **Families**. 1982. 21,4: 288-294. ill., map. Loc: OKIT, OWTL, OWTU.

A summary of holdings including directories, census records, maps, assessment records, land records, books, marriage records, cemetery records, legal documents, newspapers and the Waterloo Historical Society's collection of local material. Period: 1800 - 1982.

140. Hoffman, Susan. **Your Waterloo County heritage.** Kitchener: Kitchener Public Library, 1982. 6 p. bibl. Loc: OWTUR.

   A short annotated bibliography of local history sources in the Kitchener Public Library, including biographies, historical novels, atlases, guides, ethnic studies and general histories. Period: c1800 - 1982.

141. Kitchener Public Library. **List of oral history tapes in the Kitchener Public Library.** Kitchener: Kitchener Public Library, 1981-. 1 v. (loose-leaf). index. Loc: OCCA, OKIT, OWTUR, OWT.

   An index to a growing collection of oral history tapes, begun by the Kitchener Public Library in 1981 and amounting to more than 700 tapes by 1991. The tapes are listed in numerical order, with brief synopses of content. The names of the people interviewed are listed in alphabetical order. Period: 1981 - 1991.

142. Kitchener Public Library staff. "History of Kitchener, Waterloo and district." **Ontario Library Review.** 1960. 44: 201-202. Loc: OKIT, OGU, OWTL, OWTU.

   A bibliography of 41 titles; no items from the Waterloo Historical Society reports are included. Period: 1800 - 1960.

143. Macnaughton, Elizabeth and Wagner, Pat. **Guide to historical resources in the Regional Municipality of Waterloo.** Waterloo: Wilfrid Laurier University Press and Heritage Resources Department, The Regional Municipality of Waterloo, 1989. 118 p. ill., index. Loc: OCCA, OCLG, OCP, OKIT, OWRA, OWRE, OWRN, OWRW, OWT, OWTL, OWTU, OWTUCG, OWTUR, OWTUSJ.

   A very useful guide to primary source materials on the Waterloo region, compiled mainly from responses to a questionnaire sent to businesses, churches, voluntary organizations of all kinds, educational and social agencies, governmental authorities, heritage organizations, hospitals, libraries, museums and galleries. Each entry usually provides details of founding date, address, phone number, name of head, name and phone number of special contact, statement of mandate, description of holdings and relevant publications, details of accessibility and any restrictions. All organizations are indexed in the WRP database. Period: 1830 - 1987.

144. McKegney, Patricia. **Dickson papers inventory.** 1988. 9 p. Loc: OWTUR, OCCA.

   An inventory of Dickson family records now in the City of Cambridge Archives. Items included are land deeds, land surveys, maps, photographs, books, correspondence, legal records and business records of the founder of Dumfries Township, William Dickson, and his son, William Dickson Jr. The copy of the inventory at the Doris Lewis Rare Book Room, University of Waterloo includes articles about the collection. Period: 1790 - 1926.

145. "More source materials for Ontario Mennonite history." **Mennonite Quarterly Review.** 1931. 5,1: 221-224. Loc: OWTU, OWTUCG.

   Notes on sources including an 1869 affidavit of George Histand of Waterloo Township for militia exemption and an English translation of the **Canada Museum** report about the Mennonite Conference of 1836 in Berlin. Period: 1836 - 1869.

146. Ontario Legislative Assembly Library, Research and Information Services. **Ontario local history.** Microfiche 2011-83. Toronto: The Library, 1983. 137 fiche. ill. mf. Loc: OGU.

   Local history and feature stories dealing with 830 Ontario municipalities and clipped from newspapers mainly of the 1950s and 1960s. Waterloo County communities represented in the collection are Ayr, Breslau, Bridgeport, Elmira, Floradale, Galt, Hespeler, Kitchener, Preston, St Agatha, St Clements, Speedsville, Waterloo, and Waterloo Township. The material on Kitchener businesses is especially detailed. Period: 1950 - 1970.

147. Peters, Diane E. **Roots: genealogical resources in W.L.U. Library.** Waterloo: Wilfrid Laurier University Library, 1990. 161 p. index. Loc: OKIT, OWRE, OWTL, OWTUR, OKEBC.

   A bibliography of Canadian genealogical resources available at Wilfrid Laurier University, including works on heraldry, guides to calligraphy and archives, histories of ethnic groups and local histories for each of the provinces. Period: 1800 - 1990.

148. Peters, Diane E. **Waterloo Region: resources in W.L.U. Library.** Waterloo: Wilfrid Laurier University Library, 1990. 83 p. Loc: OKIT, OWTL, OWTU.

   A bibliography organized by topics such as agriculture, business, education, ethnic groups, health care, history, education, culture, government and religion. The entries include the Wilfrid Laurier University Library call numbers and there is an index to titles. Period: 1800 - 1990.

149. Pinnell, Richard Hugh. "Tremaine's Map of County of Waterloo, Canada West (1861)." **Waterloo Historical Society.** 1986. 74: 23-35. Loc: all.

   A useful account of historical maps of the

Waterloo area, notably the Tremaine map as an example of a commercial type of county map already well developed in the United States. The author discusses the varied information provided by the Tremaine map about Waterloo County just after the 1850s railway boom, especially on land ownership. Period: 1851 - 1861.

150. Roth, Lorraine. "Genealogical resources: census records." **Mennogespräch**. 1985. 3,2: 4-15. ill. Loc: OKIT, OWTUCG.

A guide to Ontario census records with particular reference to Mennonite families. Information available from the records is discussed, using Waterloo County examples. It mentions an index, compiled by Hugh Laurence, of the Mennonite and Amish families in Wilmot and Wellesley Townships according to the 1851-1881 census records, and describes the census records and indexes available at the Kitchener Public Library. Period: 1838 - 1985.

151. Roth, Lorraine. "Genealogical resources: land records." **Mennogespräch**. 1985. 3,1: 6-7. ill. Loc: OWTUCG, OKIT.

An outline of the information available from land deeds and wills at Registry Offices, with a description of the research procedures used at the Kitchener Registry Office. The author also refers to the present locations of early township maps of Waterloo County. Period: 1805 - 1985.

152. Snyder, Bilva Stuhr. **An index to Tremaine's map of 1861**. 1974. 36 p. maps. Loc: OKIT.

Indexes to businesses and landholders of the four townships of North Dumfries, Wellesley, Wilmot and Woolwich, giving their locations by concession and lot numbers. There are sketch maps of each township showing the pattern of concessions and lot numbers. Period: 1860 - 1861.

153. Steiner, Samuel J. and Isaac, Gord. **Conrad Grebel College genealogical resources**. Waterloo: Conrad Grebel College Library, 1989. 28 p. Loc: OKIT.

A list of genealogical resources available at Conrad Grebel College Library which collects materials relating to Mennonites, especially Canadian Mennonites. The bibliography includes books, microfilm records, periodicals, cemetery records and a large section of individual family histories. Period: 1800 - 1989.

154. Steiner, Samuel J. "Genealogical resources at the Conrad Grebel Library and Archives." **Mennogespräch**. 1984. 2,2: 13-16. ill. Loc: OWTUCG, OKIT.

A summary of the material collected at the Mennonite Archives of Ontario at Conrad Grebel College, with a list of genealogical books, microforms, periodicals, family Bibles, archival lists and indexes of interest to genealogists. Period: 1870 - 1984.

155. Steiner, Samuel J. and Arndt, John and Taylor, Ryan. **A representative list of holdings for the use of genealogical workers**. Kitchener: Ontario Genealogical Society, 1981. 32 p. Loc: OWT.

A select bibliography of genealogical works for the Waterloo-Wellington area held by the libraries of Conrad Grebel College, University of Waterloo, Wilfrid Laurier University or University of Guelph, or by Kitchener Public Library or Guelph Public Library. The list includes books, atlases, church records, Tweedsmuir histories, newspapers and periodicals.

156. Taylor, Andrew W. "Galt and Dumfries records on microfilm." **Waterloo Historical Society**. 1971. 59: 73-74. Loc: all.

A report of the microfilming by the Archives of Ontario of records from the Galt Public Library, Doon Pioneer Village, Trinity Anglican Church (Galt) and Wesley United Church (Galt). The records include various assessment and collectors' rolls for North and South Dumfries and the Dickson records (1817-1869, 12 volumes). Period: 1817 - 1916.

157. Taylor, Ryan. **Family research in Waterloo and Wellington Counties**. Kitchener: Waterloo-Wellington Branch, Ontario Genealogical Society, 1986. 106 p. maps, bibl. Loc: OCCA, OCH, OCLG, OCP, OKEBC, OKIT, OWRE, OWRW, OWT, OWTLR, OWTUCG, OWTUR.

A handbook for genealogical researchers, including chapters on libraries and archives, other historical and genealogical organizations, census records, wills, place names and local histories, atlases, maps and directories, land registry offices, assessment records, newspapers, Tweedsmuir histories, cemeteries, church records and other sources. Names of agencies holding relevant records have been fully indexed in the WRP database, as have more than one hundred churches for which at least some records survive. Period: 1800 - 1985.

158. Von Baeyer, Edwinna. **Ontario rural society 1867-1930: a thematic index of selected Ontario agricultural periodicals**. Ottawa: Social Sciences and Humanities Research Council, 1985. 1 v. indexes. Loc: OGU.

A bibliography of Ontario farming journals with an author index and a subject index that is divided into three sections: land, people, and organizations and institutions. It is a valuable

aid to researchers interested in agricultural
subjects but lacks a geographical index making it
difficult for users seeking references on a
specific region. Period: 1867 - 1930.

159. Winearls, Joan. **Mapping Upper Canada, 1780-1867:
an annotated bibliography of manuscript and
printed maps.** Toronto: University of Toronto
Press, 1991. 986 p. Loc: OKIT, OWTL, OWTU.
    A definitive reference work that includes
entries for about 100 maps and plans relating to
Waterloo County. Period: 1800 - 1867.

SETTLEMENT PROCESSES

PREHISTORY, ABORIGINAL PEOPLE AND ARCHAEOLOGY

160. **Archaeological assessment and testing of the Diamond site, AhHc-57, Ayr, Township of North Dumfries, Regional Municipality of Waterloo.** Waterloo: Regional Municipality of Waterloo, Department of Planning and Culture, 1992. 69 p. ill. Loc: OWRMA.

    A report of analysis of prehistoric material dating the site to about 900 to 1000, a transitional period between Middle and Late Woodland. The site occupies part of Lot 37, Concession 8. Period: 900 AD - 1000.

161. **An archaeological assessment of Chimney Hill Estates, Phase 2, 30T-87015, City of Cambridge.** Petersburg: Archaeological Research Associates, 1988. 1 v. ill., maps. Loc: OWRMA.

    Report on 10 findspots in four sites north of Avenue Road and east of Burnett Avenue, registered as: AiHb-64, an early Archaic chipping station; and sites AiHb-65 to 67, Archaic chipping stations. Artifacts include chipping debris, projectile points, scrapers, polished stone tools, and cores or preforms.

162. **An archaeological assessment of Cober Pit 2, Lots 10-14 and 24-26, Registered Plan 585 and part of Lot 149, GCT, City of Kitchener, formerly Waterloo Township.** Petersburg: Archaeological Research Associates, 1992. 1 v. ill., maps. Loc: OWRMA.

    A report on eight findspots in a site licensed for aggregate extraction at Huron and Westmount Roads. The report recommends that the Detzler Site (AiHd-97), described as a Middle Woodland cache or camp, be protected from aggregate extraction.

163. **An archaeological assessment of Pinebush South area, 30T-88051/52/53, City of Cambridge, formerly Waterloo Township, part of Lots 3, 4, 5, Concession 4, Beasley's Lower Block.** Petersburg: Archaeological Research Associates, 1990. 1 v. (various pagings). ill., maps. Loc: OWRMA.

    A report on 51 findspots in the area south of Pinebush Road and west of Town Line Road; 22 of the findspots are identified as sites and 19 of them recommended for further mitigation. The following sites have sufficient data to determine cultural affiliation and temporal sequences: AiHb-131 or Pinebush South 8 is a midden of Historic, Early and Late Archaic periods; AiHb-133 or Pinebush South 10 is an historic residence;

AiHb-144 or Pinebush South 21 is a Late Woodland campsite; AiHb-145 or Pinebush South 22 is a later 19th-century farmstead.

164. **Archaeological assessment of Riverbend Estates Phase III, Ayr.** 30T-88038. Petersburg: Archaeological Research Associates, 1989. 1 v. (various pagings) Loc: OWRMA.

    A report on the prehistoric (Middle Woodland) site on the Nith River flats, which is concluded to have cultural significance and to need careful excavation.

165. **Archaeological assessment of the Lakeview Sand and Gravel Pit, part of Lot 15, Concession 8, and part of Lots 1 and 2 West of the Grand River, Concession 8, North Dumfries Township.** Petersburg: Archaeological Research Associates, 1992. 1 v. ill., maps. Loc: OWRMA.

    A report on 17 findspots located on the property north of Cottrell Lake (formerly Cowan's Lake). Ten sites were registered as sites and given Borden numbers. The most notable (AhHc-92, also known as the Wayward Turtle) consists of an historic midden and is recommended for further mitigation.

166. **An archaeological assessment of the proposed Whistle Bare gravel pit, North Dumfries Township, City of Cambridge.** Petersburg: Archaeological Research Associates, 1991. 1 v. (unpaged). Loc: OWRMA.

    A report on evidence of prehistoric hunting peoples and the site of a mid-19th century house in the former hamlet of Whistlebare. Sic archaeological sites were registered as a result of this assessment. Period: 8000 BC - 1850.

167. **An archaeological assessment of the Warren Cattlelands Pit, Township of Wilmot.** Petersburg: Archaeological Research Associates, 1990. 1 v. ill., maps. Loc: OWRMA.

    A report on four sites and five findspots, located on the property south of Wilmot Township Road 6 and north of Huron Road and recommended for further mitigation or preservation. Site AiHd-84, Warren Cattleland 1, is a Late Archaic campsite; AiHd-86, Warren Cattleland 3, is a Late Woodland small hamlet.

168. **Archaeological assessment, Union Gas Pipeline (NPS 48), Bright to Owen Sound versus preferred route, Oxford County and Regional Municipality of Waterloo.** Petersburg: Archaeological Research Associates, 1991. 1 v. ill., maps. Loc: OWRMA.

    Report of an investigation of a linear strip of land, 18 km by 28 metres wide, where 6 findspots were located but none is considered to warrant further study.

169. **Archaeological mitigative excavation of site AhHc-53, Mill Pond Acres subdivision, Town of Ayr.** 30T-80011. Toronto: Archaeological Services Inc., 1990. 1 v. (various pagings). ill., plans. Loc: OWRMA.

Report on excavation of the site of a hunting camp, identified as significant by the Museum of Indian Archaeology.

170. **Archaeological mitigative monitoring of Black Horse Corners (AhHc-619).** Petersburg: Archaeological Research Associates, 1991. 1 v. (various pagings). Loc: OWRMA.

A report on the archaeological significance of the site and buildings in the Black Horse Inn complex, one of the last remaining, undeveloped historic crossroads settlements, located on the line of the Union Gas pipeline. Period: 1820 - 1880.

171. **An archaeological resource assessment of Black Walnut and Foxpoint subdivisions, Part of Lot 63, City of Waterloo.** Toronto: Archaeological Services Inc., 1989. 13 p. ill., maps. Loc: OWRMA.

A report on four registered sites and several isolated findspots, with artifacts dating from the Middle Archaic period, 5000 to 2500 B.C. Several artifacts were also found relating to the occupation of the Joseph B. Snyder house (AiHd-21). Period: 5000 BC - 2500 BC.

172. **An archaeological resource assessment of draft plan of subdivision 30T-87008, part of Lot 6, Registered Plan 1385, City of Cambridge.** Waterloo: Regional Municipality of Waterloo, Planning and Development Department, Archaeology Division, 1989. 1 v. ill., maps. Loc: OWRMA.

A report on 12 sites and 22 findspots recommended for additional investigation. Sites with an identified culture range from Early Archaic to a Middle Woodland campsite and an historic farmstead.

173. **Archaeological resource assessment of Lincoln Village, City of Waterloo.** 30T-85025. Toronto: Archaeological Services Inc., 1986. 5 p. Loc: OWRMA.

Report on a site in part of Lot 8, German Company Tract, found to contain lithic artifacts probably of the Early Woodland phase. For a more detailed report of excavation, see the article by Williamson in **Kewa** in 1988. Period: 1000 BC - 400 BC.

174. **Archaeological resource assessment of proposed Myers Road subdivision (30T-88044), part of Lots 4 and 5, Concession 9, City of Cambridge.** Toronto: Archaeological Services Inc., 1990. 1 v. ill., maps. Loc: OWRMA.

A report on 10 isolated prehistoric artifacts and one diffuse lithic scatter. Two sites were identified: AiHb-155 or Britpark I, a Middle Archaic/Middle Woodland possible camp; and AiHb-156 or Britpark II, an Early/Middle Archaic possible camp.

175. **An archaeological resource assessment of proposed subdivision 30T-83006, part of Huron Business Park, City of Kitchener.** Toronto: Archaeological Services Inc., 1989. 12 p. ill., maps. Loc: OWRMA.

Of the ten isolated prehistoric artifacts reported, the two with recognizable tools are designated with Borden numbers: AiHc-90 and AiHc-91. The George Israel house (A1Hc-89) is also documented.

176. **Archaeological resource assessment of proposed subdivision, Part of Lots 10-13, Biehn's Tract, Lot 23, 24, Lots 173-180 and Lots 20-31, Registered Plan 640, City of Kitchener.** Toronto: Archaeological Services Inc., 1989. 25 p. ill. Loc: OWRMA.

Report on assessment of a site including parts of both the Van Oordt Site (AiHc-20), a Late Woodland cemetery, and the historic village of New Aberdeen. As well as details of the archaeological excavation, the report presents information about New Aberdeen from its foundation in the 1830s to the 1870s. Further investigation of this site is recommended. Period: 1400 - 1875.

177. **An archaeological resource assessment of proposed West River Road subdivision 30T-90022, part of Lots 2 and 3, Concession 9 West of Grand River, City of Cambridge.** Toronto: Archaeological Services Inc., 1991. 1 v. ill., maps. Loc: OWRMA.

A report on the Blackmere Site (AhHb-39), a camp of the Early Middle Archaic to Early Woodland culture, and a prehistoric findspot.

178. **An archaeological resource assessment of subdivision 30T-76024 (Phase 3), Parts of Lots 20 and 21, South of Bleams Road, Township of Wilmot.** Waterloo: Regional Municipality of Waterloo, Planning and Development Department, Archaeology Division, 1989. 1 v. ill., maps. Loc: OWRMA.

A report on one isolated findspot and a cluster of 13 lithic artifacts, identified as a Middle Archaic campsite and registered as AiHc-34, the Morningside site.

179. **An archaeological resource assessment of the Arriscraft Corporation subdivision (30T-85008) City of Cambridge, Ontario.** London: Mayer, Poulton and Associates Inc., 1989. 48 p. ill. Loc: OWRMA.

A report on analysis of prehistoric lithic tools on three sites (AiHc-73, AiHc-75, and AiHc-76) located on parts of Lots 7, 8, 9, and 10 of Beasley's Lower Block.

180. **An archaeological resource assessment of the Kite site (AiHb-62), subdivision 30T-88048, City of Cambridge.** Toronto: Archaeological Services Inc., 1989. 18 p. ill., maps. Loc: OWRMA.

The site is described as a Middle Archaic chipping station with a low density of artifacts.

181. **An archaeological resource assessment of the proposed subdivision 30T-87024 (M.I. Developments), Township of Woolwich.** Toronto: Archaeological Services Inc., 1 v. ill., maps. Loc: OWRMA.

A report of a prehistoric findspot, a single stone tool fragment, located on parts of Lots 5 and 18 of the German Company Tract.

182. **Archaeological resource assessment survey, draft plans of subdivisions 30T-90024, 30T-89020, and 30T-90024, City of Kitchener.** London: Mayer, Poulton and Associates Inc., 1990. 1 v. ill., maps. Loc: OWRMA.

A report on 18 aboriginal sites and one 19th-century Euro-Canadian house (AiHc-118) in the southwestern portion of Kitchener; further mitigation is recommended.

183. **Archaeological site mitigations, Idylwild subdivision 30T-85008, City of Cambridge.** London: Mayer, Poulton and Associates Inc., 1990. 75 p. ill., maps. Loc: OWRMA.

A report on the detailed excavation of three sites previously recommended for mitigation. At the Archaic campsite AiHc-73, the presence of several projectile points, a hearth and several post moulds support an interpretation that this was a short-term camp used when hunting. Site AiHc-75 yields evidence of chipping detritus, projectile points and post moulds. Site AiHc-76 is found to consist of several isolated findspots.

184. Arnold, Tom and Mayer, Robert G. and Feast, Arnold A.B. "Isolating Late Archaic and Middle Woodland components on the Bertrand Russell, Henry Morgentaler and Agnes McPhail sites, City of Cambridge, Ontario." **Birdstone: Newsletter of the Grand Valley/Waterloo Chapter of the Ontario Archaeological Society.** 1990. 4,1. Loc: OWRMA.

A discussion of techniques used in pre-excavation evaluation of small lithic surface scatters on prehistoric archaeological sites, with reference to a test on the Idylwild housing site, Lots 7 to 10, Concession I, Beasley's Lower Block, Cambridge.

185. Campbell, Dorothy L. "I: Indian and pioneer uses of native plants growing at Doon Pioneer Village." **Waterloo Historical Society.** 1962. 50: 41-45. ill. Loc: all.

A description of tree species and the ways they were used by aboriginals and pioneers. Period: 1600 - 1868.

186. Campbell, Dorothy L. "II: Indian and pioneer uses of native plants growing at Doon Pioneer Village." **Waterloo Historical Society.** 1963. 51: 36-40. ill. Loc: all.

A list of trees, shrubs and woody vines, with notes of how each was used by aboriginals and pioneers. Period: 1600 - 1868.

187. Coyne, James H. "The Indian occupation of southern Ontario." **Waterloo Historical Society.** 1916. 4: 13-23. Loc: all.

A history of the branch of the Huron-Iroquois family, the Attiwandaronk or the Neutrals, from 1616 to 1656. The author reports that smallpox and wars between the Hurons and the Iroquois killed many Neutrals and forced others to leave so that, after the middle of the 17th century, all southern Ontario including Waterloo County was a game preserve of the Iroquois. Period: 1615 - 1790.

188. Cruikshank, E.A. "The reserve of the Six Nations on the Grand River and the Mennonite purchase of Block No. 2." **Waterloo Historical Society.** 1927. 15: 303-350. map. Loc: all.

An account of the land grant to the Six Nations in 1784 by Governor Haldimand on behalf of the Crown and its subsequent sale to Richard Beasley, James Wilson, and John Baptiste Rousseau. In 1798, Wilson and Rousseau transferred their interest to Beasley who sold Block Number 2 to Daniel Erb and Samuel Bricker. The article provides many excerpts from correspondence, agreements and deeds relating to the transactions. Period: 1784 - 1841.

189. Cunningham, Walter. "The legend of Oromocto Spring in Attiwandron Park: Cressman's Woods." **Waterloo Historical Society.** 1937. 25: 264-266. Loc: all.

A recounting of an Indian legend in which two Indian lovers are killed by the Iroquois, resulting in Oromocto Spring near Doon.

190. Fox, William A. "Salvage excavation of Moyer Flats
      site." **Birdstone: newsletter of the Grand
      River/Waterloo Chapter of the Ontario
      Archaeological Society**. 1986. 1,1. Loc: OWRMA.
         An account of the excavation of the Moyer Flats
      village site, with evidence of the early
      agricultural occupation in the 10th century, at a
      time of transition from hunting and gathering to
      gardening. Period: 900 AD - 1000.

191. Good, E. Reginald. **Tour of Kitchener, Ont.:
      featuring sites of aboriginal historical
      interest**. Kitchener: The Author, 1992. 1 folded
      sheet. bibl., map. Loc: OKIT.
         A guide to a six-kilometre walking tour of
      locations relating to the Anishinabe (Ojibwa)
      First Nation, known collectively as Mississaugas
      of the Credit. Sites include Mississauga burial
      grounds thought to be located on the site of First
      Mennonite Church, and Victoria Park where a plaque
      has been erected in memory of Tuhbenahneequay,
      whose extended family wintered in this vicinity at
      the turn of the 19th century. The leaflet
      includes a map, suggested reading, and names and
      phone numbers of local organizations able to
      provide more information. Period: 1784 - 1992.

192. Herriot, William. "Aboriginal agriculture in
      Southwestern Ontario." **Waterloo Historical
      Society**. 1923. 11: 18-21. Loc: all.
         A survey of the Indian cultivation of plants,
      including tobacco for smoking or sniffing and
      American Ginseng and other roots for medicinal
      purposes. Period: 1716 - 1923.

193. Hill, Asa R. "The historical position of the Six
      Nations." **Ontario Historical Society, Papers and
      Records**. 1922. 19: 103-109. Loc: OWTL, OWTU.
         A summary of diplomatic relations between the
      Six Nations Indians and the British government
      from 1717 to 1784, when the Grand River lands were
      granted to the Indians. The nature of the
      alliance between the two parties is discussed, and
      the right of Indian self-government emphasized.
      Period: 1784 - 1922.

194. Horne, Michael. "A preliminary examination of site
      selection criteria for Middleport-Neutral sites in
      Waterloo Region." **Kewa**. 1987. 87,2: 14-24. Loc:
      OHM, OLU, OPET, OWRMA.
         Reference from Regional Archaeologist, Regional
      Municipality of Waterloo.

195. Hunter, A.F. "The trail of the aborigines through
      Waterloo County." **Waterloo Historical Society**.
      1927. 15: 264-267. Loc: all.
         A description of the waterways used by Indians
      before 1800. Period: 1650 - 1800.

196. "Indian collection." **Waterloo Historical
      Society**. 1968. 56: 83. Loc: all.
         A note that Franklin L. Lisso, a North Dumfries
      farmer, had more than 3,000 catalogued Indian
      relics excavated from his own and neighbouring
      farms. Period: 1968 -

197. "Indian dig." **Waterloo Historical Society**. 1970.
      58: 52. Loc: all.
         A note of excavations on the site of an Indian
      village on a farm south of Kitchener by a group of
      students from Waterloo Lutheran University, under
      the direction of Dr Norman Wagner. Period: 1450 -
      1700.

198. "Indian dugout canoe." **Waterloo Historical
      Society**. 1969. 57: 4. ill. Loc: all.
         Photograph of an Indian dugout canoe discovered
      at Puslinch Lake by Michael Hogan and Irvine
      Donald in 1969. The dugout was donated to Doon
      Pioneer Village.

199. Janusas, Scarlett E. **An analysis of the historic
      vegetation of the Regional Municipality of
      Waterloo**. Waterloo: Regional Municipality of
      Waterloo, Planning and Development Department,
      1987. 79 p. ill., bibl. Loc: OWRMA.
         A reconstruction of the historic environment
      from early surveyors' records and pioneer
      journals. Historic vegetation data are used in
      defining archaeological site selection criteria
      for sites dating from the Palaeo-Indian period to
      the historic period. Sources include the survey
      of Dumfries Township in 1816-17 by Adrian Marlet,
      the survey of Wilmot Township by John Goseman in
      1828 and the survey of Wellesley Township by
      William Walker in 1843. The likely vegetation of
      the region during successive periods of occupancy
      is described, from the Palaeo-Indian (9500 to 7800
      BC), the Archaic (7800-900 BC), to the Early
      Woodland (1000 to 400 BC), the Middle Woodland
      (400 BC to 800 AD) and the Late Woodland (800 to
      1650). Period: 9500 BC - 1881.

200. Janusas, Scarlett E. **The cultural implications of
      drainage in the Regional Municipality of
      Waterloo**. Waterloo: Regional Municipality of
      Waterloo, Planning and Development Department,
      1988. 144 p. ill., bibl. Loc: OWRMA.
         An analysis of past and present drainage
      patterns as a framework for a site potential
      model. The main tributaries of the Grand River
      watershed are examined systematically and the
      effects of manmade and natural modifications of
      drainage are discussed. Each cultural period --
      the Palaeo-Indian, the Archaic, the Woodland and
      Historic -- is discussed with respect to the

likely utilization and importance of water resources. Appended tables relate historic sites to their water sources and list dates of floods in the Historic period.

201. Janusas, Scarlett E. and MacDonald, John D.A. **Regional Municipality of Waterloo: archaeological facilities master plan.** Waterloo: Regional Municipality of Waterloo, Planning and Development Department, 1989. 124 p. charts, maps, tables, 21 large folding maps. Loc: OWRMA.

   An account of the purposes and phases of development of the plan and a review of the achievements of the Archaeology Division from 1986 to 1989, including a detailed inventory of 272 known archaeological sites, a synthesis of the history and prehistory of the region, and a series of 76 maps identifying areas of high, moderate and low archaeological potential. Methods of determining archaeological significance are discussed and procedures for assessing and monitoring development sites of high to moderate archaeological potential are recommended. The large maps represent staged development and archaeological potential in each of the seven lower-tier municipal units of the region.

202. Lea, Joanne and Janusas, Scarlett E. **Buried in time.** Kitchener: Doon Heritage Crossroads, Historic Sites Department, Regional Municipality of Waterloo, 1988. 1 v. ill., bibl. Loc: OKDHC.

   Teaching materials on prehistory in the Waterloo area, with references to the Deercrest Site in Cambridge, the Schweitzer Cemetery in Woolwich Township, the Coleman Site near New Dundee, and the Waterloo County Gaol in Kitchener. Archaeological methods and record keeping are demonstrated. Period: 7000 BC - 1978.

203. MacDonald, George F. **Archaeological survey of the Grand River between Paris and Waterloo, Ontario.** Manuscript Report 15. Ottawa: National Museum of Man, 1961. 19 l. map. Loc: OWTL.

   A description of Neutral Indian settlement sites in the Waterloo area. The sites identified are often on farmland, in which case the farmer's name is provided as well as the general geographical location. Numerous existing collections are noted, as well as private collections belonging to local amateurs. The author groups the artifacts by period such as Palaeo-Indian, Archaic, Middle Woodland and Late Woodland, as well as by site. Period: 7000 BC - 1650.

204. MacDonald, John D.A. **Past archaeological research in the Regional Municipality of Waterloo.** Waterloo: Regional Municipality of Waterloo, Planning and Development Department, 1988. 78 p.

ill., bibl. Loc: OWRMA, OWTUR.

   A synthesis of reports of prehistoric sites and artifacts, from those of Boyle and especially Wintemberg, to whose efforts some 30 registered sites and numerous unregistered sites can be attributed, to that of George MacDonald (1961). The author states that, of the total of 216 registered sites located within the region to 1988, 120 have been located by archaeological consultants; these represent 81 per cent of all verified sites. Period: 1896 - 1988.

205. MacDonald, John D.A. "A review of archaeological research in the Regional Municipality of Waterloo." **Birdstone: Newsletter of the Grand River/Waterloo Chapter of the Ontario Archaeological Society.** 1988. 3,1. Loc: OWRMA.

   A survey and evaluation of all previous archaeological research in the region.

206. MacDonald, Robert I. **The Coleman site (AiHd-7): a late prehistoric Iroquoian village in the Waterloo Region.** Trent University (M.A. thesis, Archaeology), 1986. Loc: OWRMA.

   A description of the archaeological investigations of the site at Lot 11, Concession 2, Block A, Wilmot Township. The author reports the discovery of three large longhouses, two with lengths greater than 100 metres, as evidence of a late prehistoric trend. The discovery of semi-subterranean communal sweat lodges may indicate the presence of a male sodality. Period: 1550 - 1600.

207. MacDonald, Robert I. and Ramsden, C. and Williamson, Ronald F. "The Myers Road site: shedding new light on regional diversity in settlement patterns." **Canadian Journal of Archaeology.** 1989. 13: 207-211. Loc: OWRMA, OWTU.

   A comment on the significance of the major archaeological investigation of an Iroquoian site in Dumfries Township. Period: 1275 - 1325.

208. Matheson, Douglas R. **First generations.** Hamilton: Choronomics, 1988. 44 p. ill. Loc: OWT.

   A brief account of prehistory in southern Ontario, including an archaeological record of native habitat and habitation sites before the arrival of European settlers, and descriptions of Indian culture, art and languages. The Algonquians and Iroquoians are identified. Period: 9900 BC - 1800.

209. Mayer, Robert G. **The Julian Baker and Theobald Spetz sites: two nineteenth century pioneer homesteads in southwestern Ontario.** London: Mayer, Pihl, Poulton and Associates, 1988. 70 p. ill., maps, tables, bibl. Loc: OKIT.

A paper presented at the Fifteenth Annual Symposium of the Ontario Archaeological Society, October 22 and 23, 1988. The authors identify similarities in site functions and socioeconomic patterns between the two homesteads and present a detailed record of archaeological evidence from the Spetz site, including Middle Archaic remains from approximately 6000 B.C. as well as ceramic samples probably manufactured at the William Eby Pottery in the 1840s. Period: 6000 BC - 1860.

210. Molto, Joseph E. and Spence, Michael W. and Fox, William A. "The Van Oordt site: a case study in salvage osteology." **Canadian Review of Physical Anthropology**. 1986. 5,2: 49-61. ill. Loc: OWRMA.

Report of a detailed analysis of the remains of between 9 and 13 adult males at a site dating from c.1400 along the Strasburg Creek near Kitchener. The authors conclude that the burial ground was probably reserved for enemy warriors slain by the prehistoric Neutral inhabitants of the area. Period: 1375 - 1425.

211. Montgomery, Malcolm. "The legal status of the Six Nations Indians in Canada." **Ontario History**. 1963. 55,2: 93-105. Loc: OKIT, OWTL, OWTU, OWTUCG.

An examination of the claims made by both the federal government and the Six Nations for the case Logan vs the Attorney-General of Canada. The Indians of the Six Nations argued that they were autonomous, claiming that they were allies, not subjects, and had never been conquered by force of arms. The federal government based its claims on the British North America Act and the Indian Act. The judge ruled that because the Indians settled on the lands and accepted the protection of the government, their status changed from allies to subjects. The implications of this decision are discussed, particularly in relation to the Canadian Bill of Rights. Period: 1784 - 1963.

212. Moses, Elliott. "The long house people." **Waterloo Historical Society**. 1957. 45: 21-22, 25. Loc: all.

An introduction to the National Film Board's production about the Six Nations Indians and their religious customs. The film was shown at the Waterloo Historical Society's 45th annual meeting.

213. Ontario Ministry of Natural Resources: Office of Indian Resource Policy. **The Six Nations Indian land claim to the bed of the Grand River Ontario**. Historical Research Report Series, no. 1. Toronto: Queen's Printer for Ontario, 1986. 25 p. ill., bibl. Loc: OKIT, OWTU.

A review of the background to the land claim submitted to the provincial government in 1981,

including a detailed account of agreements dating from the mid-18th century, a chronology of events and list of documentary sources. Period: 1784 - 1850.

214. **Regional Municipality of Waterloo: archaeological potential maps**. Waterloo: Regional Municipality of Waterloo, Planning and Development Department, Archaeology Division, 1986 - 1989. 76 whiteprint maps. Loc: OWRMA.

A series of maps on which areas of high, moderate, and low archaeological potential are clearly defined, according to Phase II of the Region's Archaeological facilities master plan. Using 1:10,000 base maps produced by the Surveys and Mapping Branch of the Ontario Ministry of Natural Resources (1983), the locations of all areas for which archaeological assessments have been completed are marked, with their development plan numbers. The 76 maps have been generalized from more detailed working maps that may also be consulted in the Archaeology Division by serious researchers. The working maps show probable site information derived from oral history reports, unregistered findspots and literary references, in relation to soil type, historic and present drainage systems, historic site locations, physiography and historic vegetation. The working maps delineate bands of territory along pre-1856 historic roads, within 150 metres of water or within 3 kilometres of historic white pine stands, and locate farmsteads shown on the Tremaine (1861) and Parsell (1881) maps. Period: 9000 BC - 1900.

215. Schmalz, Peter Stanley. **The Ojibwa of southern Ontario**. University of Waterloo (Ph.D. thesis, History), 1985. 6 fiche. bibl. mf. Loc: OKIT, OWTU.

An account of the relationships between the Ojibwa, the largest Indian tribe in Ontario, and the French, British and Canadian governments from 1610 to 1980. The author challenges the belief that the Ojibwa moved into a political vacuum created by the Huron-Iroquois War, and maintains that the Ojibwa decisively defeated the Iroquois. The Ojibwa role in the Pontiac Uprising and in the War of 1812 is recounted, and their loss of power is seen as a result of their acceptance of the United Empire Loyalists. Waterloo County is not specifically mentioned. Period: 1610 - 1980.

216. Seibert, Emily. "Joseph Brant." **Waterloo Historical Society**. 1962. 50: 96-98. Loc: all.

A biography of Brant (1742-1807), leader of the Six Nations Indians and British ally during the American Revolutionary War, who was given land along the Grand River for his people. The article was taken from an address by Emily Seibert at the unveiling ceremony of a Joseph Brant plaque at Doon Pioneer Village. Period: 1775 - 1807.

217. Smith, Allan R.G. "Notes on Indian village site: Wilmot Township." **Waterloo Historical Society.** 1938. 26: 17-20. Loc: all.
A description of artifacts found by local school children. Period: 1000 BC - 1650.

218. Smith, Donald B. "The dispossession of the Mississauga Indians: a missing chapter in the early history of Upper Canada." **Ontario History.** 1981. 73,2: 67-87. ill., maps. Loc: OKIT, OWTL, OWTU.
An account of the process by which the Mississauga Indians (or Anishinabeg) ceded their lands along the north shore of Lake Ontario. A very large tract of hunting grounds, including the valley of the Grand River, was yielded in May 1784. Period: 1680 - 1784.

219. Smith, Donald B. **Sacred Feathers: the Reverend Peter Jones (Kahkewaquonaby) and the Mississauga Indians.** Toronto: University of Toronto Press, 1987. 372 p. ill., maps, index. Loc: OKIT, OWTL, OWTU.
A biography of the son of Augustus Jones the surveyor and Tuhbenahneequay of the Mississauga Indians. The hunting grounds of the Mississaugas (who called themselves the Anishinabeg) included the territory that was later defined as Waterloo County. Period: 1780 - 1810.

220. Stroh, Nathaniel. "Indian relics collected by Jacob Gaukel Stroh." **Waterloo Historical Society.** 1957. 45: 9. Loc: all.
A note about Stroh, the Berlin tanner whose collection of Indian artifacts was given to the Waterloo Historical Society in 1957. Period: 1850 - 1957.

221. Templin, Hugh. "Indians of the Grand River area." **Waterloo Historical Society.** 1964. 52: 8-10. Loc: all.
A brief report of the author's search for a Neutral Indian village near Fergus and of artifacts found in the area along the Grand River. Period: 1626 - 1650.

222. **Test excavations at the Steckle site (AiHc-36), City of Kitchener.** London: Mayer, Poulton and Associates Inc., 1987 revised 1988. 1 v. (various pagings). ill. Loc: OWRMA.
A report on two artifact clusters located within the Huron Business Park development. It concludes that the site probably supported a series of temporary campsites where chipped stone tools were either made or re-sharpened, perhaps during the winter months, in the Archaic period.

223. Trigger, Bruce G. "Northeast." **Handbook of North American Indians.** Edited by William C. Sturtevant. Washington, DC: Smithsonian Institution, 1978. 15, 924 p. ill., bibl., maps, index. Loc: OWTU.
Part of a comprehensive series of scholarly books providing an encyclopedic summary of all aspects of North American Indian history and culture. Volume 15 contains references to the Neutral, Iroquois and Southeastern Ojibway tribes that inhabited Waterloo County, although no specific Waterloo Indian settlement is mentioned. Period: 1600 - 1700.

224. **The valley of the Six Nations: a collection of documents on the Indian lands of the Grand River.** Edited by Charles Murray Johnston. Ontario Series No. 7. Toronto: The Champlain Society and University of Toronto Press, 1964. 344 p. ill., bibl., index. Loc: OKIT, OWRSJ, OWRW, OWTL, OWTU, OWTUCG.
A set of government documents and reports, historical papers, addresses and correspondence, relating to negotiations between the British government and the Six Nations (under the leadership of Joseph Brant) over land along the Grand River, including Blocks 1, 2 and 3. Although almost exclusively devoted to the settlement of land grants since the 1770s, brief mention is made of the Iroquois who previously inhabited the area. Period: 1780 - 1850.

225. Wagner, Norman E. and Toombs, Lawrence E. and Riegert, Eduard R. **The Moyer site: a prehistoric village in Waterloo County.** Waterloo: Wilfrid Laurier University, 1973. 110 p. ill., bibl., maps. Loc: OKIT, OWTL, OWTU.
A report of the excavation of a Neutral Indian village dating from 1400. The site, northeast of New Dundee, was excavated between 1970 and 1972 by a Waterloo Lutheran University team. The site layout and items of bone, stone, pottery and ceramic pipes are described and analyzed. Period: 1400 - 1500.

226. Williamson, Ronald F. **The Myers Road site.** Toronto: Archaeological Services Inc., 1991. 331 p. ill., maps, plates, bibl. Loc: OWRMA.
Final report of a three-year archaeological investigation of a prehistoric Iroquoian site east of Myers Road and east of Highway 24. The report includes chapters by various team members on settlement patterns (with detailed descriptions of 10 longhouses, palisades, sweat lodges, burials and middens), and faunal, floral and artifact analysis. The site is considered to have been

used intermittently over a period of about 50 years in the late 13th century and early 14th century. Period: 1275 - 1325.

227. Williamson, Ronald F. "Report on archaeological investigations of the Cashbrown site (AiHd-42), Lincoln Village subdivision, Waterloo." **Kewa**. 1988. 88,3: 4-13. Loc: OHM, OLU, OPET, OWRMA.

An account of the recovery and documentation of four isolated prehistoric artifact findspots and an Early Woodland site. The author concludes that the number and form of the artifacts might be significant in further studies of long-distance exchange systems between specific regional population groups. Period: 1000 BC - 400 BC.

228. Wintemberg, W.J. "Early names of the Grand River, Ontario." **Transactions of the Royal Society of Canada, 3rd series**. 1929. 23, 2: 125-133. maps, bibl. Loc: OWTU.

An account of seven previous names for the river, Tinaatoua, Riviere Rapide, Urfe (Urse), Grande Riviere, Oswego, Ouse and O-es-shin-ne-gun-ing. Period: 1669 - 1780.

229. Wintemberg, W.J. "Indian village sites in the counties of Oxford and Waterloo." **Annual Archaeological Report of the Ontario Provincial Museum appended to the Report of the Minister of Education**. 1899. Pp. 83-92. Loc: OGU.

Descriptions of Indian sites, including those in North Dumfries Township on the farm of George Elliott near Roseville, in Waterloo Township on John Welsch's farm in the southeast, and around a small lake near Baden in Wilmot Township. Herbert Trussler, L.J. Niebel and H.Z. Smith are mentioned as local collectors of Indian artifacts. Period: 1000 - 1700.

230. Wintemberg, W.J. **Indian village sites in the counties of Oxford and Waterloo**. Annual Archaeological Report of the Ontario Provincial Museum appended to the Report of the Minister of Education. 1900. Pp. 37-40. Loc: OGU.

Reflections based on field evidence of the author's theory of the siting of pre-Neutral and Neutral villages in Blenheim Township (Oxford County) and Waterloo, North Dumfries and Wilmot Townships. Period: 1000 - 1700.

PIONEER SETTLEMENT, TRAVELLERS' ACCOUNTS, LAND SURVEY AND PLACE NAMES

231. Abbott, Joseph. **Memoranda of a settler in Lower Canada; or the emigrant to North America: being a compendium of practical hints to emigrants**. CIHM Microfiche series, no. 48707. Montreal: Lovell and Gibson, 1843. 2 fiche. mf. Loc: OWTL, OWTU.

A guide for emigrants to Canada, in two parts. The second describes Upper Canada through letters by an Ayrshire emigrant to his brother in Glasgow. Letter five contains an optimistic account of the Grand River and a portrayal of the Six Nations Indians, and letter eight describes the area around Waterloo and Galt. The author comments on the large German barns, the Huron Road and the volumes of wheat produced. Period: 1842 - 1843.

232. **An archaeological assessment of the Brill property, part Lot 13, Conc. 3/4, Beasley's Lower Block, City of Cambridge**. Petersburg: Archaeological Research Associates, 1991. 1 v. (unpaged). Loc: OWRMA.

A report on the prehistoric and historic interest of the site, including the small prehistoric campsite near Black Bridge (AiHb-173), the David Panabaker farmstead, the Holm saw mill, and the 19th-century hamlets of Tuck's Hill and Speedslee. Period: 500 AD - 1875.

233. **An archaeological investigation of the side porch, the Shantz site, AiHe-33, Township of Wilmot**. Waterloo: Regional Municipality of Waterloo, Planning and Development Department, Archaeology Division, 1989. 1 v. ill., maps. Loc: OWRMA.

A report on the site, consisting of a Euro-Canadian domestic midden found during renovations of a house located in the southwest quarter of Lot 14, north of Erb Road. Period: 1850 - 1900.

234. **Archaeological investigations of the Ministry of Natural Resources, District Field Office, Cambridge, Ontario**. London: Archaeological Services Inc., 1983. 170 p. ill. Loc: OWRMA.

Report of a study involving test excavations, surface surveys and discussions with an aged descendant of John Groh, the original pioneer settler of Concession 1, Lot 7, Waterloo Township. Included are a history of the Groh family, a description of the property, and a catalogue and analysis of the artifactual remains. Although no significant cultural deposits were found, the study concludes that the whole property has great historical interest and that the original structural details of the buildings deserve further study. Period: 1804 - 1955.

235. **Archaeological mitigation of the Wren site, AiHb-39, the Broomfield site, AiHb-40, and the Mulholland site, AiHb-41**. Waterloo: Regional Municipality of Waterloo, Planning and Development Department, Archaeology Division, 1987. 133 p. ill., plans. Loc: OWRMA.

Report of a detailed study of the site of the proposed Cowan Industrial Business Park, on 170 acres of Beasley's Lower Block, Lots 1, 2 and 3, Concession III. It includes reference to the historic Cowan farm, Clochmohr, on the west side of Franklin Boulevard. Period: 1816 - 1900.

236. **Archaeological mitigative excavation, Joseph Hoffman site (AjHd-27), draft plan of subdivision 30T-87027, town of Heidelberg.** London: Mayer, Poulton and Associates Inc., 1992. 61 p. ill., maps. Loc: OWRMA.

Analysis of artifacts of glass, ceramics, metal and animal bones associated with a mid-1850s homestead site. Period: 1850 - 1870.

237. **Archaeological mitigative excavation of site AjHc-3, part of Lot 80, German Company Tract, village of Maryhill.** 30T-88021. Toronto: Archaeological Services Inc., 1992. 1 v. (various pagings). ill., plans, plates. Loc: OWRMA.

A report on the house site, known to have been occupied by Jacob Bickle between 1841 and 1861. Period: 1841 - 1861.

238. **Archaeological mitigative excavation of the Hammet site (AiHb-57), Melran Estates subdivision, City of Cambridge.** 30T-87013. Toronto: Archaeological Services Inc., 1992. 1 v. (various pagings). ill. plans, plates. Loc: OWRMA.

Report of excavation of a site, part of Lots 10 and 11, Concessions 3 and 4, Beasley's Lower Block in the former Waterloo Township, just north of Hespeler. The property belonged first to Abraham Clemens and was occupied later by Aaron Kribs, Abraham Pannebecker and Thomas Hammet. Though Hammet is known to have been a blacksmith, there is no material evidence of a smithy on this site. Period: 1800 - 1900.

239. **Archaeological resource assessment of a proposed subdivision, Graystone Properties Limited, City of Kitchener.** 30T-85015. Toronto: Archaeological Services Inc., 1988. 4 p. Loc: OWRMA.

Report on Lot 37, German Company Tract, Block F, a property formerly owned by A. Ruby who settled there in 1838 and was an assessor between 1872 and 1878. Period: 1838 - 1878.

240. **An archaeological resource assessment of Hidden Valley, City of Kitchener.** Toronto: Archaeological Services Inc., 1989. 1 v. ill., maps. Loc: OWRMA.

A report on numerous prehistoric artifacts, none of which "point to prolonged or continuous human occupation." The historic farmstead (AiHc-83), identified as that of the Jacob Furtney family in the early 19th century, is recommended for further

mitigation.

241. **Archaeological resource assessment of Hidden Valley, City of Kitchener.** Toronto: Archaeological Services Inc., 1989. 13 p. ill., appendices. Loc: OWRMA.

Report of an assessment of a 42-hectare property of Lot 9, Plan 1519. No prehistoric remains were found, but a farmhouse, ceramic and bone fragments and a tombstone are linked to Jacob and Elisabeth Furtney's occupation of this land from before 1830 to about 1850. Period: 1830 - 1852.

242. **Archaeological resource assessment of Kesmark Estates Ltd, City of Cambridge.** 30T-85016. Toronto: Archaeological Services Inc., 1985. 16 p. Loc: OWRMA.

Report on the property settled by Abraham Pannebecker in 1826, east part of Lot 8, Concession 4, Waterloo Township. The land was sold to Thomas Eskdale in 1856, then to Lewis Kribs in 1869 and to William Shaw in 1890. Four isolated prehistoric artifacts are noted as well as a significant collection of early- to mid-nineteenth-century material from a garden area formerly used for refuse disposal. Period: 1826 - 1890.

243. **An archaeological resource assessment of proposed condominium development at Queen and Margaret Streets, City of Kitchener.** 30 CDM-86013. Toronto: Archaeological Services Inc., 1990. 1 v. (various pagings). ill., plans. Loc: OWRMA.

A report on the Breithaupt property, Sonneck House, including a brief outline of family and business history. Period: 1870 - 1900.

244. **An archaeological resource assessment of subdivision 30T-89005, part of Lot 31, German Company Tract, Township of Woolwich.** Waterloo: Regional Municipality of Waterloo, Planning and Development Department, Archaeology Division, 1989. 1 v. ill., maps. Loc: OWRMA.

A report on site AjHd-17, an historic schoolhouse. Period: 1850 - 1900.

245. **Archaeological resource assessment of the James Markham site (AiHd-40), Doon Village Estates (30T-81027 and 30T-78023) City of Kitchener: Report on excavation.** Toronto: Archaeological Services Inc., 1988. 100 p. ill. Loc: OWRMA.

Report of a detailed investigation of a site that was probably used for a log house occupied by the James Markham family circa 1850, before the construction of a fieldstone house 100 metres to the north. Period: 1840 - 1850.

246. Baird, Sandy. **The story of Waterloo County.** Kitchener: Kitchener-Waterloo Record, 7 p. Loc: OWRA, OWRE, OWRN, OWRND, OWRSC.

A brief history of the settlement and development of the county from the arrival of the pioneer settlers from Pennsylvania and Scotland to about 1900. The achievements of notable persons such as Joseph Schneider, Benjamin Eby, Abraham Erb, John Erb, John Hoffman and D.B. Detweiler are outlined. Period: c1800 - c1900.

247. Bloomfield, G.T. and Bloomfield, Elizabeth and Van Nostrand, Brian. "Waterloo County." **Ontario central places in 1871: a gazetteer compiled from contemporary sources.** Canadian Industry in 1871 Research Report No. 13. Guelph: Department of Geography, University of Guelph, 1990. Pp. 20-21, 118-119, 143. maps. Loc: OWTU, OWT.

A list of the names of Ontario hamlets, villages and towns that were in use at the time of the 1871 Census of Canada. Some 48 named central places are identified in Waterloo County in 1871, with 22 alternate place names. Figure 1 defines boundaries of the 1871 Census Districts and Census Sub-Districts of Waterloo and Wellington Counties and Figure 2 shows the locations of the named central places in the two counties. Period: 1870 - 1871.

248. Bock, Jacob. "Letters from Wilmot: 1840, 1842, 1844." **Waterloo Historical Society.** 1962. 50: 92-93. Loc: all.

Excerpts from Jacob Bock's letters to his brothers in Pennsylvania, describing the difficulties of life in Wilmot Township in the 1840s. Period: 1840 - 1844.

249. Breithaupt, W.H. "Pioneer settlers of Waterloo County [WRP]." **Waterloo Historical Society.** 1926. 14: 220-225. Loc: all.

An address at the dedication of the Memorial Tower in August 1926, listing Waterloo County settlers of German origin. Period: 1800 - 1926.

250. Breithaupt, W.H. "President's address: Early settlement in Upper Canada." **Waterloo Historical Society.** 1923. 11: 11-17. Loc: all.

A survey of pioneer settlement in Waterloo in the context of early Upper Canada. Period: 1800 - 1923.

251. Breithaupt, W.H. "The settlement of Waterloo County." **Ontario Historical Society, Papers and Records.** 1925. 22: 14-17. ill. Loc: OWTL, OWTU.

An account of the early settlement of Block Number 2, Waterloo Township by Pennsylvania Mennonites, with brief mentions of the first pioneers in the other townships. Period: 1800 - 1850.

252. Breithaupt, W.H. "The settlement of Waterloo County." **Waterloo Historical Society.** 1948. 36: 27-31. Loc: all.

A survey of pioneer settlement by Mennonites from Pennsylvania in the early nineteenth century, including the families of Schoerg, Eby, Erb, Betzner, Brubacher, Baumann, Bechtel, Biehn, Bergey, Bingeman, Burkholder, Cressman, Detweiler, Gingrich, Groff, Hallman, Hagey, Honsberger, Hoffman, Kinsie, Kolb, Martin, Moyer, Musselman, Reichert, Schneider (Snyder, Snider), Stauffer, Shantz, Weber and Witmer. The author also mentions the efforts of William Dickson and Absalom Shade in attracting Scottish settlers to Dumfries Township and the work of Christian Nafziger in the Amish settlement of Wilmot Township. Period: 1800 - 1856.

253. Bricker, I.C. "Block number two (Waterloo Township) 1 Sept. 1805." **Waterloo Historical Society.** 1934. 22: 70a. Loc: all.

A manuscript map showing the names of landowners, including original owners of lots in the German Company Tract. Period: 1805.

254. Bricker, I.C. "Block number two (Waterloo Township) 1 Sept. 1805 [reprint]." **Waterloo Historical Society.** 1965. 53: 44-45. ill. Loc: all.

A manuscript map of landowners, previously printed in the Waterloo Historical Society's 22nd Annual Report, 1934, page 70a. Period: 1805.

255. Bricker, I.C. "The first settlement in central western Ontario." **Ontario Historical Society, Papers and Records.** 1934. 30: 58-65. Loc: OWTL, OWTU.

A study of the early land transactions of Waterloo Township, listing original stockholders of the German Company and their farm lots and all properties sold in Bean's Tract in 1800. The author estimates that 32 owners had settled on their own land by July 1805. Period: 1798 - 1810.

256. Bricker, I.C. "The history of Waterloo Township up to 1825." **Waterloo Historical Society.** 1934. 22: 81-122. Loc: all.

An account from the first purchase by Richard Beasley, James Wilson and John Baptiste Rousseau in 1798, to subsequent sales of properties within Blocks 1, 2 and 3. The author lists all properties sold from 1800 to 1825, with the names of purchasers and vendors, acreages, locations and dates of sale. Period: 1798 - 1825.

257. Brydone, James M. **Narrative of a voyage, with a party of emigrants, sent out from Sussex, in 1834, by the Petworth Emigration Committee, to Montreal, thence up the River Ottawa and through the Rideau Canal, to Toronto, Upper Canada.** Petworth: John Phillips, 1834 reprinted 1987. 66 p. maps. Also CIHM Microfiche series, no. 21456. Loc: OWTL, OWTU, OWTUR.

    A reprint by Kelvinprint of James Marr Brydone's account of his expedition with British emigrants through Upper Canada, including a trek through the Waterloo area described on pages 31-33 and 42. He recounts crossing the Grand River, visiting Schneider's Mills and travelling to Wilmot where he meets a Mr Cushman, and mentions Galt and the Speed River. Brydone also comments on the Waterloo area landscape and soil, noting its sandy consistency. A loose map marks the route taken by the travellers. Period: 1833 - 1834.

258. Casselman, A.C. "The settlement of Mennonites and Tunkers." **Canada and its provinces: a history of the Canadian people and their institutions by one hundred associates.** Edited by Adam Shortt and Arthur G. Doughty. Toronto: T. and A. Constable, 1914. 17: 47-49. Loc: OWTUCG, OKIT, OWTU, OWTL.

    A description of the pioneer settlement of Waterloo Township after the American Revolutionary War, the establishment of the German Company and the survey of lots by Augustus Jones, with mention of the founding of the townships of North Dumfries and Wilmot. Period: 1799 - 1835.

259. Casselman, A.C. "The settlement of the Township of Dumfries." **Canada and its provinces: a history of the Canadian people and their institutions by one hundred associates.** Edited by Adam Shortt and Arthur G. Doughty. T. and A. Constable, 1914. 17: 69-71. Loc: OKIT, OWTL, OWTU, OWTUCG.

    A brief account of the transfer of Block Number 1 from Joseph Brant and the Six Nations Indians to William Dickson, with biographical sketches of William Dickson and Absalom Shade and a description of the early Dumfries settlement. Period: 1798 - 1817.

260. Chitwood, Prince and Woolfrey, Sandra. "Archaeological excavation of New Aberdeen." **Waterloo Historical Society.** 1975. 63: 29-31. ill. Loc: all.

    A short history of the community that flourished from the 1840s to the 1870s, with a description of artifacts excavated at the sawyer's house and general store. Period: 1840 - 1875.

261. Coleman, Thelma. **The Canada Company.** Stratford: County of Perth and Cumming Publishers, 1978. 322 p. ill., maps. Loc: OKIT, OWTU, OCCA, OWTL.

    Most of this account of the company's role in the settlement of western Ontario is concerned with the Huron Tract (later organized as the counties of Huron and Perth) immediately to the west of Waterloo. But the Canada Company also owned the three northern and four southern concessions of Wilmot Township. References to Wilmot are all concerned with the building of the Huron Road across the township to link the Company's first town settlement at Guelph with most of its lands to the west. Useful maps on pages 46 and 180 show the Huron Road and the Company lands in the township, in the latter case accompanied by the survey notes of Mahlon Burwell. Period: 1824 - 1830.

262. **Continuation of letters from Sussex emigrants in Upper Canada, written in 1836.** Petworth: John Phillips, 1837. 24 p. Also CIHM Microfiche series, no. 28558. Loc: OWTL, OWTU, OWTUR.

    Letters by immigrants to Ontario, including the Waterloo area, who came under the auspices of the Petworth Emigration Committee. A slip has been inserted stating the intention of the Earl of Egremont under whose sanction the Petworth Emigration Committee was formed. Letters by James Rapson and John and Caroline Dearling refer specifically to a visit to Preston by James Brydone, who was apparently checking on the progress of the various settlers he had brought to Upper Canada a little earlier. Other Petworth settlers are mentioned in Guelph and Eramosa Townships. Period: 1836 - 1837.

263. Cornell, John. "A short sketch of the life and experience of John A. Cornell, author of the preceding articles of faith." **Articles, or confession of faith by the Beverly Reformed Christians, called Dunkerts, with a variety of explanations on different heads of scripture, there is also an appendix subjoined to this work: a short sketch of life and experience of John A. Cornell, the composer of the following confession of faith, also a number of evangelic and variegated poems.** Lewiston, NY: O. Grace, 1825. Pp. 63-82. Loc: OWTUCGR.

    A chapter including Cornell's impressions of a visit to the Waterloo area in the early 19th century. Local references include the lack of English-language religious services, the death of a local man, Cornell's marriage in 1804, and his dream about death and judgement. Period: 1801 - 1825.

264. Cruikshank, E.A. "Statement of losses, Block No. 2 residents, War of 1812." **Waterloo Historical Society**. 1928. 16: 7-9. Loc: all.

A document showing the losses sustained by several of the early inhabitants of Block Number 2, while they were employed in military transport work during the War of 1812. Names of those people and the items they lost are listed. Period: 1812 - 1813.

265. Dickie, D.J. **In pioneer days**. Toronto: J.M. Dent and Sons, 1926 reprinted 1927. 287 p. ill. Loc: OKIT, OWTUCGR.

A Canadian elementary school reader which contains three sections relating to the county. A chapter entitled "Waterloo: the first settlement back from the lake," beginning on page 181, recounts the arrival of the Pennsylvania German Mennonites and includes a Waterloo Historical Society drawing of a Conestoga wagon and a photograph of Samuel Betzner's farm. "Twenty thousand silver dollars," beginning on page 184, explains the establishment of the German Company because of the illegal land dealings of Richard Beasley. The section, "The old log school," has a photograph of the first school in Waterloo on page 250. Period: 1799 - c1830.

266. Dilley, Robert S. "British travellers in early Upper Canada: a content analysis of itineraries and images." **Canadian Papers in Rural History**. 1986. 5: 198-223. maps, tables. Loc: OWTUSJ, OWTU, OWTL.

A survey of the works of ten British travellers in the first half of the 19th century, including John Goldie and Anna Brownell Jameson. Galt is mentioned as a place in the itineraries of Patrick Shirreff and Alexander Graham Dunlop. The author concludes that travellers preferred water routes to overland routes and that, over time, their attention shifted to inland towns farther west, following the pattern of land development. Period: 1800 - 1850.

267. Easton, George. **Travels in America, with special reference to the province of Ontario as a home for working men**. CIHM Microfiche series, no. 02815. Glasgow: J. Marr, 1871. 2 fiche. mf. Loc: OWTU, OWTL.

A Scottish temperance preacher describes six months in rural Ontario in 1869, including a visit to Galt. Many general comments are made about Ontario, but the drinking habits are particularly noted. Period: 1868 - 1869.

268. Eby, Ezra E. **A biographical history of Waterloo Township and other townships of the county: early settlers and their descendants**. Kitchener: Doon Pioneer Village Board of Directors, 1970 reprint. 42 p. ill. Loc: OKIT.

A reprint of the first chapter in Eby's book which is indexed in detail in the WRP database. There is a biographical sketch of Eby as one of the earliest local historians. The Pennsylvania Mennonite settlement in Waterloo Township is related from 1799 to 1835, with many details of individuals, families and farmsteads. The difficulties of pioneering and the formation of the German Company are described, with an account of the part the Waterloo Mennonites played in the War of 1812. Period: 1799 - 1861.

269. **Emigration: the British farmer's and farm labourer's guide to Ontario, the premier province of the Dominion of Canada**. Toronto: Government of Ontario, 1880. 107 p. ill. map. Loc: OKDHC.

A publication encouraging immigration to Ontario with descriptions of each county, including Waterloo. Information is provided on soils, crops, livestock, prices of farm land, and railways. Period: 1879 - 1880.

270. "Excerpts from letters by Abraham Sherk." **Waterloo Historical Society**. 1959. 47: 42-44, 50. Loc: all.

Observations about the roles of Jacob Bechtel and the Sherks in the pioneer settlement of Waterloo Township. Period: 1799 - 1944.

271. Friesen, Leonard. "The early settlement of Waterloo County." **Waterloo Historical Society**. 1979. 67: 10-19. bibl. Loc: all.

An account of the land grant to the Six Nations Indians by the British, the various land transactions including the sale of the large block to Beasley, Wilson and Rousseau and their subsequent dealings with the Pennsylvania Mennonite settlers. Period: 1784 - 1830.

272. Fuller, R.M. "Rewards for settler overshadowed hardships." **Waterloo Historical Society**. 1975. 63: 81-82. Loc: all.

A copy of a letter written by William Daly, an agent for the Canada Company, to the Commissioners in England on 25 April 1842. The letter comments on the success of settler John Ford, who owned a tavern in Wilmot. Period: 1831 - 1842.

273. Gardener, Herbert Frederick. **Nothing but names: an inquiry into the names of counties and townships in Ontario**. CIHM Microfiche series, no. 03289. Toronto: George N. Morang and Company Limited, 1899. 561 p. Loc: OWTL, OWTU.

A brief account of the origins of the names of the five townships in Waterloo County. Period: 1816 - 1840.

274. Gourlay, Robert. **Statistical account of Upper Canada**. London, England: Simpkin and Marshall, Stationers' Court, 1822. 3 v. maps, index. Also CIHM Microfiche series, no. 35936. Loc: OKIT, OWTL, OWTU.

A compendium of information about boundaries, natural resources, agriculture, weather patterns, laws and government, settlement, churches, population, commerce and professional services. Brief township reports from the Gore District include entries for Waterloo and Dumfries Townships. These reports were based on a questionnaire distributed to local landowners. Period: 1815 - 1820.

275. Groh, Ivan. "Pioneers of Waterloo (1799 to 1889)." **Canadian-German Folklore**. 1971. 4: 15-148. bibl. Loc: OKIT, OWT, OWTL, OWTU, OWTUCG.

Fictionalized biographies of Jacob Engle, John Winger, Martin Baer, David Gingrich, Jacob Bechtel, Samuel Bricker, Benjamin Eby, Ephraim Weber and other pioneers. Some of the material on the earliest Pennsylvania settlers to Waterloo was also mentioned in Groh's articles in the 1967 volume of **Canadian-German Folklore**. Reasons for the immigration from Pennsylvania, the hardships endured by the early settlers, and the establishment and later split of the Mennonite Church in Waterloo County during the Great Awakening are all described. Period: 1800 - 1942.

276. Hess, Albert. "The forgotten names and places." **Waterloo Historical Society**. 1974. 62: 46-50. Loc: all.

A short description of lost or renamed villages including Mudge's Mills (renamed Ayr), Jedburgh, Nithvale and Black Horse Corners (at the crossroads of Highway 97 and Ayr Road), Kossuth, Freiburg, Waldau, Oregon, New Aberdeen, Weissenburg, Schindelsteddle, Weimar, Shantz Station, Fisher Mills, Victoriasburg and Cedar Creek. Period: 1816 - 1900.

277. Hess, Albert. "Origin of names in Waterloo County." **Waterloo Historical Society**. 1969. 57: 70-71. Loc: all.

A discussion of place names including Philipsburg, Rummelhardt, Weissenburg and Roseville, with a note on the derivation of some family names such as Eby, Brubacher and Lichty. Period: 1800 - 1900.

278. Hilty, Ann. **The settlement of the German Block in Wilmot Township, Upper Canada**. Toronto: The Author, 1987. 21 l. maps, bibl. Loc: OWTUCGR.

A paper given at the Mennonite Experience in America Conference VI, November 5-7, 1987, at Bluffton, Ohio. The author relates the efforts of Christian Nafziger, and of Canadian Mennonites on his behalf, to purchase the land for the Amish settlement. Brief biographies of many early settlers and information about the lots purchased by each family are also provided. Period: 1820 - c1850.

279. Jaffray, J.P. "Blazing the trail in new Dumfries." **Waterloo Historical Society**. 1926. 14: 234-236. Loc: all.

Text of a speech at the dedication of the Memorial Tower in August 1926, describing the pioneer settlement of Dumfries Township. Period: c1800 - 1926.

280. Jameson, Anna Brownell. **Winter studies and summer rambles**. London, England: Saunders and Otley, 1838. 3 v. map. Also CIHM Microfiche series, no. 35744. Loc: OCCA, OKIT, OWTU, OWTL, OWTUR.

Impressions of Upper Canada by a perceptive woman who travelled to the inland settlements and wrote especially about the wives of immigrants. In the 1852 edition entitled **Sketches in Canada and rambles among the red men**, the author refers to a German-language newspaper being published in Berlin by 1837 and mentions the Grand River, Joseph Brant and his family, and the Kerrs. She also remarks on the "vast number of Dutch and German settlers, favourably distinguished by their industrious, sober and thriving habits. They are always to be distinguished in person and dress from the British settlers; and their houses and church and, above all, their burial-places, have a distinct and characteristic look." The University of Waterloo holds a microfiche copy of the 1838 edition, as well as an original edition in the Doris Lewis Rare Book Room. The City of Cambridge Archives and the Kitchener Public Library have copies of the 1943 reprint edited by James J. Talman and published by Nelson. Kitchener Public Library also has copies of the 1923 and 1965 editions published by McClelland and Stewart while the Wilfrid Laurier University Library has a copy of the 1969 edition by the same publisher. Period: 1800 - 1852.

281. Janusas, Scarlett E. **An archaeological perspective of an historic overview of the Regional Municipality of Waterloo**. Waterloo: Regional Municipality of Waterloo, Planning and Development Department, 1988. 291 p. ill., bibl. Loc: OWRMA, OWTUR, OWT.

A survey of the context for identifying historic properties in both rural and urban areas. Following a general introduction, the report is organized by the seven post-1972 municipalities, the townships of North Dumfries, Wilmot, Wellesley and Woolwich, and the cities of Cambridge, Kitchener and Waterloo. Each section presents a synthesis of earlier studies and usefully reproduces many relevant maps. All known place names of localities are listed and briefly described and all have been indexed in the WRP database. Appendices list historic sites in each municipality with details of location, type of structure and past owner as well as about 160 designated heritage structures with addresses and dates of construction. The Tremaine map of 1861 and the Parsell maps of 1881 are important sources for this study. Period: 1798 - 1972.

282. Johnston, Charles M. "An outline of early settlement in the Grand River Valley." **Ontario History**. 1962. 54,1: 43-67. Loc: OKIT, OWTL, OWTU, OWTUCG.

An account of the Indian tribes living in the Grand River Valley and the land grant to the Six Nations Indians by Governor Haldimand. The author describes how the land was divided into six blocks and sold by the Iroquois to various developers including William Dickson and the German Company. Period: 1600 - 1833.

283. Karcich, Grant. "Augustus Jones, Upper Canada Public Land Surveyor." **Families**. 1983. 22,4: 321-326. map. Loc: OKIT, OWTL, OWTU.

A biographical sketch of one of the earliest surveyors in Upper Canada, who surveyed the Grand River Indian land for Joseph Brant as well as eleven townships between Toronto and the Trent River. Early survey methods and equipment are also described. Period: 1786 - 1836.

284. Klinckhardt, Christian Gottlieb. **C.G. Klinckhardt's Reise nach Nord-Amerika und dessen erste Ansiedelung daselbst, aus Briefen von demselben gezogen und heraugegeben von C.G. Temper, Pastor in Ruppertsgrün.** Edited by C.G. Temper. Leipzig: Carl Andra, 1833. 60 p. (incomplete: pp. vii-viii missing). Loc: OWTUCG.

A photocopy of the published letters from C.G. Klinckhardt to family and friends in Germany. Relating his trip to North America including Upper Canada, he provides one of the earliest accounts of pioneer life in the Waterloo district. Details are given, beginning on page 31, of his arrival in "Willmot, Gore District, Dounschipp Waterloo in Upper Canada." He describes the quality of the land, types of fruit trees, wild nuts and berries, crops and vegetables, and the process of obtaining sap from the maple trees in the spring for making sugar, syrup and cider. Klinckhardt also notes the variety of religious and ethnic groups, particularly the Amish and Mennonite. A letter written by Klinckhardt's son Louis who, with his brother Julius, followed his father to Wilmot in 1831, narrates his experiences as a settler. Period: 1830 - 1833.

285. McKay, Ian A. "Place names in historical geography." **Ontario Geography**. 1987. 1: 40-44. Loc: OWTL, OWTU.

A study of the value of place names as an indicator of ethnicity in the area shown on the Kitchener 1:250,000 topographic map. Period: 1800 - 1900.

286. Morden, Gladys A. "Two pioneers of New Hamburg: William James Scott and Carl Germann." **Waterloo Historical Society**. 1967. 55: 12-15. ill. Loc: all.

Biographical sketches of two early settlers of New Hamburg whose families became related through marriage. Period: 1812 - 1860.

287. Nagel, James. "The Block Line." **Waterloo Historical Society**. 1965. 53: 46. Loc: all.

A short account of the history behind the Block Line boundary. The article was prepared during 1965 in an unsuccessful attempt to preserve the name of Block Line Road. Period: 1784 - 1900.

288. Officer, E.R. "Waterloo County - some aspects of settlement and economy before 1900." **The Waterloo County area: selected geographical essays**. Edited by A.G. McLellan. Waterloo: Department of Geography, University of Waterloo, 1971. Pp. 11-19. map, tabl. Loc: OWTU, OWTL, OWTUCG, OKIT.

A chronological outline of land purchases and pioneer settlement with a discussion of distinctive features of Mennonite land use and the siting of villages at early millsites. A table of populations for each township and urban centre from 1871 to 1911 is included. Period: 1800 - 1900.

289. Panabaker, D.N. "President's address: deserted villages of Waterloo County." **Waterloo Historical Society**. 1930. 18: 164-170. Loc: all.

A discussion of the decline of rural villages such as Fisher's Mills and Kossuth. Period: 1810 - 1930.

290. **A preliminary report on the 1984 Schneider Haus experience: a public program in archaeology.** Thornhill: Foundation for Public Archaeology, 1985. 1 v. (unpaged). ill. Loc: OWRMA.

An account of excavations during the 1984 summer, including historical profiles of the Joseph Schneider family and of the public education programs accompanying the project. Period: 1820 - 1900.

291. Rayburn, Alan. "Place names in the Kitchener-Stratford area as indicators of national origin." **Ontario Geography**. 1968. 2: 82-88. Loc: OWTL, OWTU.

    An article criticizing McKay's attempt to interpret place names in terms of the ethnicity of settlers in the area depicted on the Kitchener 1:250,000 topographic map which includes all of Waterloo County and parts of neighbouring counties. Rayburn explains the origins of several place names. Period: 1800 - 1900.

292. Reaman, G. Elmore. **The trail of the black walnut**. Toronto: McClelland and Stewart, 1957 revised 1965. 267 p. ill., index, maps, tables, bibl. Loc: OKIT, OWRBL, OWRE, OWRN, OWRW, OWT, OWTL, OWTU, OWTUCG, OWTUR, OWTUSJ.

    An account of the migration to North America by ten different European religious groups, notably the Mennonites. The references to Waterloo County (pp. 108-113 and 122-124) relate initial difficulties with land claims, the effect of the War of 1812, and the establishment of early communities and industries. There are brief profiles of early leaders such as Joseph Schoerg, John Biehn, George Bechtel, Sam Betzner Jr, Sam Bricker, John Erb, Benjamin Eby, William Dickson, Absalom Shade, Christian Nafziger and Jacob Hespeler. Period: 1800 - 1830.

293. Sargeant, E.S., Mrs and Goldie, John, Mrs. "Waterloo pioneers' furniture." **Waterloo Historical Society**. 1931. 19: 263-265. ill. Loc: all.

    A brief description of various types with photographs of some original pieces. Period: c1800 - c1900.

294. Sherk, A.B., Rev. "Recollections of early Waterloo." **Waterloo Historical Society**. 1915. 3: 13-19. Loc: all.

    An historical sketch of farm life of the Pennsylvania German pioneers, the Mennonite church, education, German newspapers and bridges over the Grand River. Period: 1800 - 1850.

295. Smith, Allan R.G. "Pioneer settlement of southwest Wilmot." **Waterloo Historical Society**. 1946. 34: 24-33. Loc: all.

    An account of early land clearing practices, crops and the first churches and meeting places. A few references are made to early inhabitants of Wilmot Township including Paddy Darrington, Amos Good and Miss Margaret Allen. Period: 1820 - 1900.

296. Sprung, Dorothea A. **Pioneers of Waterloo County**. Doon Pioneer Village, Historic Sites Department, Regional Municipality of Waterloo, 1984. 48 p. maps, bibl., charts. Loc: OCCA, OKDHC.

    A study of the settlement of the townships in the Waterloo region from the time of the Six Nations Indians to 1850, with an appraisal of the three main ethnic groups, the Scots, the Pennsylvania-Germans and the European Germans. Period: 1800 - 1850.

297. Stark, H. **Salvage archaeology at Woodside National Historic Park**. Ottawa: Parks Canada, 1981. 1 v. ill., maps. Loc: OWRMA.

    A report on the excavation of an exploratory trench along the foundation of the restored Victorian childhood home of W.L. Mackenzie King. The excavation, made necessary by flooding in the basement, allowed artifacts and structural information to be gathered. Period: 1870 - 1900.

298. "Stedman deed, 1795." **Waterloo Historical Society**. 1959. 47: 20-21. Loc: all.

    A photographed copy and brief explanation of the deed by which Dumfries Township and adjoining areas along the Grand River were sold by the Six Nations Indians in 1795. Period: 1784 - 1798.

299. "The Stedman deed." **Waterloo Historical Society**. 1940. 28: 130-135. Loc: all.

    Text of the land grant by the Six Nations Indians to Philip Stedman in 1798, reprinted from an earlier Waterloo Historical Society article in 1919, pp 84-87. The introduction to this article is taken from a 1916 article about William Dickson by James E. Kerr. Period: 1784 - 1798.

300. "Stedman-Indian deed." **Waterloo Historical Society**. 1914. 2: 7-8. ill. Loc: all.

    The text of a deed giving Philip Stedman a 92,160-acre tract of land on the Grand River, by the Sachems of the Six Nations Indians. This tract was later defined as the Townships of North Dumfries and South Dumfries. Period: 1784 - 1798.

301. Taylor, Andrew W. "Galt founders honoured." **Waterloo Historical Society**. 1959. 47: 22-26. Loc: all.

    A survey of early settlement in Galt to mark the unveiling of a commemorative plaque on September 12, 1959. Period: 1816 - 1836.

302. Taylor, Andrew W. "Pioneer days of the East River Road, North Dumfries." **Waterloo Historical Society**. 1946. 34: 7-13. Loc: all.

    An account of the rural area immediately south of Galt, settled by 38 families by 1818. The author describes the role of William Dickson's agent, John Telfer, in recruiting Scottish settlers to come to Dumfries. Reprinted with the article are four letters from John Telfer to Thomas Taylor, dated between 1829 and 1832 and referring to farm making, other pioneer settlers, prices and costs, and events such as the cholera epidemic. Period: 1816 - 1836.

303. "Transcript of Crown grant, confirming previous Indian deed, for Block One Grand River Indians Lands." **Waterloo Historical Society**. 1919. 7: 84-87. map. Loc: all.

Transcript of land grant from the Six Nation Indians to Philip Stedman in 1798. Period: 1784 - 1798.

304. "Transcript of original deed for the German Company Tract, Waterloo Township." **Waterloo Historical Society**. 1919. 7: 87-90. map. Loc: all.

Text of the 1805 deed of sale by Richard and Henrietta Beasley of 60,000 acres of Block Number Two to Daniel and Jacob Erb for 10,000 pounds. Period: 1804 - 1805.

305. Van Dorp, Gerard Francis. **A survey of the place names of Waterloo County**. University of Western Ontario (student essay, Geography), 1962. 71 l. maps, tables, bibl. Loc: OKIT.

A study of the current and former names of communities, including information about location, time of settlement, reasons for adoption of the place name and, in some cases, the first industries. The names of rivers and lakes are also explained. Period: 1800 - 1900.

306. Walker, A.P. "John McDonald, the first surveyor for the Canada Company." **Families**. 1982. 21,4: 275-278. Loc: OKIT, OWTL, OWTU.

A brief biography of McDonald who emigrated from Invernesshire, Scotland via New York to Galt, and then to Guelph. As surveyor for the Canada Company, McDonald directed the survey of the Huron Road between Goderich and Guelph in 1828. Period: 1827 - 1828.

307. Weber, Eldon D. "Some unusual aspects of land surveys in Old Ontario." **Families**. 1976. 15,4: 125-129. Loc: OKIT, OWTU, OWTL.

An account of the haphazard patterns of settlement in southern Ontario, sometimes changing the intended layouts of townships. Waterloo and Wilmot Townships are used as examples, with detailed descriptions of their various tracts and divisions. Period: 1800 - 1850.

308. Wintemberg, W.J. "Origin of the place and stream names of Waterloo County, Ontario." **Waterloo Historical Society**. 1927. 15: 351-380. map, bibl. Loc: all.

A systematic explanation of the probable sources of names of townships, cities, towns, villages, smaller localities, streams, rivers and lakes following the same plan as the author's previous study of Oxford County. The dates when places were named and the persons believed responsible are stated in most cases, and the places are located on a county map. The author mentions the renaming of Berlin as Kitchener during World War I but does not comment on alternative spellings for Conestogo and Hawkesville. Period: 1800 - 1920.

309. Wood, J. David. "The letters of Deputy Surveyor Adrian Marlet to the Surveyor General, 1805-1825." **Waterloo Historical Society**. 1964. 52: 11-15. ill. Loc: all.

A collection of letters by the man who surveyed Dumfries Township for William Dickson in 1816 and 1817. Except for one reference to Absalom Shade, nothing is mentioned of the Dumfries area. Period: 1805 - 1820.

310. Wood, J. David. "The stage is set: Dumfries Township, 1816." **Waterloo Historical Society**. 1960. 48: 40-50. ill. Loc: all.

A description of the survey of Dumfries Township in 1816-1817 by Adrian Marlet who subdivided 465 farm lots, each of approximately 200 acres. The author presents two maps compiled from the rich information on soil texture, surface configuration, drainage, vegetation, existing roads and settlement in Marlet's survey notebooks. The article is illustrated by a reprint of the North Dumfries section of Tremaine's 1861 map, showing all concession and side roads, railways, rivers and streams, lot boundaries, and names of property owners. Period: 1816 - 1861.

311. Wood, J. David. "The woodland-oak plains transition zone in the settlement of western Upper Canada." **Canadian Geographer**. 1961. 51,1: 43-47. bibl., maps. Loc: OKIT, OWTL, OWTU.

An examination of the kind of land settled by Ontario pioneers, using Dumfries Township as a case study. Referring to the land survey notes taken by Adrian Marlet, the author demonstrates that the pioneers preferred a combination of open, flat land with nearby forest. The open oak plains, created by Indian attempts to clear the land by burning, determined the location of the first settlement roads. Period: 1814 - 1818.

312. Woolfrey, Sandra and Chitwood, Prince. **New Aberdeen, a lost village in Waterloo County: an historical and archaeological perspective.** 1980. 317 l. bibl., ill., maps, plans, charts. Loc: OKITW.

A detailed archaeological report of artifacts found in New Aberdeen during excavations in 1974 and 1975. Extensive field work was carried out at the sawmill house and the general store, with more general investigations at Thomas Brydon's house and the flour mill. An introductory history of New Aberdeen including its settlement, industries and social life, provides background information on the village. An article by the same authors, in the Waterloo Historical Society annual report of 1975, gives a short report on the study. Period: 1840 - 1900.

URBANIZATION AND SETTLEMENT SYSTEMS

313. Angst, Garfield. **The changing functions of the village of St Jacobs.** University of Waterloo (B.A. thesis, Geography), 1965. 73 l. maps, bibl. Also mf. Loc: OWTU, OWTUM.

An account of the village's industrial origins, tradition and growth, in relation to the urbanization of the entire county. The author considers the relationship of St Jacobs with its hinterland, particularly the dependence of the Snider Milling Company, St Jacobs Canning Company and Hollinger Hardware Ltd on the farming community. Period: 1848 - 1965.

314. Baird, K.A. "Kitchener-Waterloo, Ontario." **Canadian Geographical Journal.** 1969. 79,3: 90-99. ill. Loc: OKIT, OWTU, OWTL.

An historical and contemporary portrait of the relationship between the two cities. The author reports that the Kitchener metropolitan area (which included Waterloo) had the fastest rate of growth in Canada during the 1960s. Period: 1800 - 1969.

315. Bell, Rose-Marie. **The changing functions of Elmira.** University of Waterloo (B.A. thesis, Geography), 1965. 35 l. maps, tables, bibl. Loc: OWTU.

An historical account of the establishment and growth of the community from a crossroads settlement to an independent centre, in three phases: the pioneer period (1835-1890), diversification and early industrialization (1890-1940), and rapid urban growth (1940-1965). The appendices provide factual information in tabular form. Period: 1835 - 1965.

316. Bloomfield, Elizabeth. **City-building processes in Berlin/Kitchener and Waterloo, 1870-1930.** Guelph: University of Guelph (Ph.D. thesis, History), 1981. 548 l. ill., maps, bibl. Also Canadian theses on microfiche, no. 55516. Loc: OWTUR, OWTU, OWTL, OKIT.

A study in urban history, organized thematically to include chapters on urban-industrial development in southern Ontario between 1870 and 1930, the urban ethos, a prosopographical analysis of community elites, municipal industrial policies, processes shaping the urban environment to 1912, and later efforts to reshape the urban landscape by planning. The thesis includes many maps and graphs, detailed endnotes and a bibliography; appendices present tables summarizing the roles of community leaders and the entrepreneurs who received municipal inducements. Several published articles and chapters in books have made the thesis findings more accessible to users. Period: 1830 - 1930.

317. Bunting, Trudi Elizabeth. **Kitchener-Waterloo: the geography of mainstreet.** Occasional Paper no. 3. Waterloo: Department of Geography, Faculty of Environmental Studies, University of Waterloo, 1984. 117 p. ill., maps, bibl. Loc: OWTU, OWTUCG, OKIT, OWT.

A contemporary survey of the urban economy, municipal government and intra-urban patterns of demography, housing, industry and commerce, with some historical information about industrialization and planning. Three appendices present driving and walking tours of the cities and of the rural-urban fringe. Period: 1961 - 1981.

318. Cowan, Ted. **Galt: the effects of competition in a dispersed city.** University of Waterloo (B.E.S. thesis, Planning), 1971. 2 fiche. maps, tables, bibl. mf. Loc: OWTUM.

An examination of the industrial and commercial interdependence of Galt and neighbouring centres. Following an historical account, the author prescribes policies for downtown Galt and the regional economy. Period: c1820 - 1971.

319. Cox, Kenneth Wayne. **A functional classification of small towns in Waterloo County.** Waterloo Lutheran University (B.A. thesis, Geography), 1969. 66 l. maps, bibl. Loc: OWTL.

A study of 44 dormitory and service towns in relation to large neighbouring centres, based on data for numbers of business establishments or services including churches, schools, post offices, hotels, restaurants, grocery stores, gas stations, automobile repair shops, farm equipment stores and feed mills. Population statistics from the 1961 Census of Canada are given for each community. Period: 1960 - 1969.

320. Dahms, Fredric A. and Forbes, James A. "Central places in the 'Golden Triangle': the Guelph system, 1970." **The Waterloo County area: selected geographical essays**. Edited by A.G. McLellan. Waterloo: Department of Geography, University of Waterloo, 1971. Pp. 113-127. maps, tabl. Loc: OWTU, OWTL, OWTUCG, OKIT.

A study of Guelph's hinterland that incidentally provides useful information on the economic relationships between south Wellington County and the Kitchener-Waterloo urban area. Using data for newspaper circulation, long-distance telephone calls, and retail and service linkages, the authors find that the boundary between the Guelph and Kitchener-Waterloo spheres of influence tends to follow the county boundary between south Wellington and Waterloo. Period: 1969 - 1970.

321. Dahms, Fredric A. "Change and stability within an urban hierarchy: Waterloo County 1864 to 1971." **Urban History Review**. 1991. 20: 38-47. maps, tabl. Loc: OWTL, OWTU.

A research report on numbers of business establishments and functions of all cities, towns, villages and hamlets, based on data from Dun and Bradstreet reference books and the decennial census. The author concludes that, despite some changes in the ranking of specific central places, the settlement hierarchy was very stable throughout the century studied. Period: 1864 - 1971.

322. Dahms, Fredric A. "Economic revitalization in St Jacobs, Ontario." **Small Town**. 1991. 20,1: 12-18. ill., map. Loc: OWTU, OWTL.

A study of the recent transformation of St Jacobs as a tourist attraction, following the village's long decline in business and population from 1881. The author outlines some of the specific agents and circumstances in the original development of St Jacobs, such as the miller E.W.B. Snider, and in its recent "renaissance", notably the entrepreneur Milo Shantz. Period: 1870 - 1990.

323. Dahms, Fredric A. **Functions of settlements in the Waterloo region 1951-1985: with historical background and comparative data for the counties of Bruce, Huron and Wellington**. Occasional Papers in Geography no. 8. Guelph: Department of Geography, University of Guelph, 1986. 88 p. bibl.,tables, maps. Loc: OWTU, OWTL.

An account of economic, demographic and agricultural changes in the smaller settlements of Waterloo County. Using data from Dun and

Bradstreet in Standard Industrial Classification categories, the author concludes that "the picture is one of change and diversification rather than decline." Many maps and statistical tables of businesses and population complement the text. Period: 1864 - 1985.

324. Dahms, Fredric A. "St Jacobs, Ontario: from declining village to thriving tourist community." **Ontario Geography**. 1991. 36: 1-13. ill., map, tables, bibl. Loc: OWTU, OWTL.

A study of the transformation of the village, including a discussion of agents and factors in its original development and recent "renaissance". The case of St Jacobs is set in the more theoretical context of the changing functions of small service centres in Canada and the United States. Data for 1971 and 1986, derived from the Census of Canada and Dun and Bradstreet Reference Books as well as fieldwork and interviews, are used to compare St Jacobs with 42 other small centres in central and eastern Canada. The author concludes that the four most critical factors in economic success are heritage, amenity, access and entrepreneurial effort. Period: 1870 - 1990.

325. Davidson, Jim. **The differential growth rates of urban centres in Waterloo County, 1800-1910**. University of Waterloo (B.E.S. thesis, Geography), 1980. 1 fiche. charts, maps, bibl. mf. Loc: OWTUM.

An assessment of ethnicity, railway systems, technological change and industrialization as factors in the growth of Berlin, Galt, Hespeler, Preston, Ayr, Elmira and New Hamburg. Period: 1800 - 1910.

326. English, John and McLaughlin, Kenneth. **Kitchener: an illustrated history**. Waterloo: Wilfrid Laurier University Press, 1983. 259 p. ill., maps, ports., tables, index. Loc: OCCA, OCLG, OKIT, OWRN, OWT, OWTL, OWTU, OWTUCG, OWTUR, OWTUSJ, OWTUCR.

A study of Berlin/Kitchener in which the themes of economic growth, population and ethnicity, the urban landscape, and social and political life are discussed in six broad eras. These are the early years, the county town period from 1852 to 1880, the coming of age from 1880 to 1912, the trauma of changing Berlin's name to Kitchener during World War I, Kitchener between the two wars, and Kitchener after 1940. All persons and organizations discussed in the text have been indexed in the WRP database, as well as many topical subject headings. Period: 1799 - 1979.

327. Jeffery, John Stephen. **The replacement of Galt by Kitchener as the major centre of the Golden Triangle**. Waterloo Lutheran University (B.A.

thesis, Geography), 1968. 46 l. ill, tables, bibl. Loc: OWTL.

A comparison of the two cities in order to determine the reasons for Galt's relative decline. The factors of location, population size, ethnic composition, transportation and trade links, technological advancement, political strengths and industry are considered. Period: 1881 - 1931.

328. Koebel, Dennis. **New Hamburg: the evolution of historical growth and urban development, 1824-1973.** University of Waterloo (B.E.S. thesis, Geography), 1973. 73 p. ill., maps, tables. Loc: OWTUM.

A survey of the town's development in three phases: 1824-1880, 1880-1940 and 1940-1970, with a description of the contemporary urban setting and services. Period: 1824 - 1973.

329. Lee, Chun-fen. **The middle Grand River Valley of Ontario: a study in regional geography.** University of Toronto (Ph.D. thesis, Geography), 1943. 471 p. ill., maps, tables. Loc: OTU.

A survey of the settlement and agricultural and industrial development of the whole region including Waterloo, Wellington and Brant counties. While the author focuses on current conditions, he outlines the main ethnic groups, traces growth from the pioneer period, and describes the economic and service functions of urban centres in relation to their hinterlands. Period: 1810 - 1943.

330. Lee, Chun-fen. "Twin cities of Waterloo and Kitchener." **Economic Geography.** 1946. 22: 142-147. ill. maps. Loc: OWTL, OWTU.

A geographic discussion of the relation between the cities, initially separated by swamps and sandy hills and later by the main line of the CN railway. Although Kitchener became larger and more industrialized than Waterloo, eventually making the latter a part of greater Kitchener, the distinct location of each city's commercial centre is predicted to ensure continued separation. Period: 1800 - 1946.

331. Maguire, Garth. **Evolution of and conditions within four small regional communities with respect to the regional core, Region of Waterloo.** University of Waterloo (B.E.S. thesis, Geography), 1977. 69 p. maps, tables. Loc: OWTUM.

A short survey of the historical development of the villages of Wellesley, St Clements, Baden and New Dundee as background to a more detailed analysis of their interaction with Kitchener-Waterloo in 1975-76. Period: 1900 - 1975.

332. McLaughlin, Kenneth. **Cambridge: the making of a Canadian city.** Burlington: Windsor Publications, 1987. 208 p. ill., maps, bibl. Loc: OCCA, OCLG, OCH, OCP, OKIT, OWT, OWTL, OWTU, OWTUR.

A popular history of Cambridge to 1987, and of the three separate industrial towns that were amalgamated in 1973: Galt, Preston, and Hespeler. The author presents a general historical overview, emphasizing the economic aspect. Photographs of Cambridge past and present constitute half of the book. The last section, "Partners in Progress" by James Quantrell, gives details of 38 Cambridge corporations and their histories. Any of these existing in Cambridge before 1973 have been indexed in the WRP database. Period: 1775 - 1987.

333. McLaughlin, Kenneth. **Waterloo: an illustrated history.** Burlington: Windsor Publications, 1990. 208 p. ill., maps, index. Loc: OCCA, OCLG, OWRA, OWRE, OWRN, OWRW, OWT, OWTL, OWTU, OWTUR.

A history of what is now the City of Waterloo from its beginnings in 1816 to the late 1980s. The book is very well illustrated with maps, historical photographs and reproductions of works by local artists. Names of persons, businesses, churches and organizations have been thoroughly indexed in the WRP database. Produced in co-operation with the Waterloo Chamber of Commerce, the volume includes profiles of prominent local businesses in a "Partners in Progress" section by Richard Pearce. Period: 1804 - 1988.

334. "Noteworthy neighbor communities - Kitchener and Waterloo: activities and amenities of two cities." **Saturday Night.** 1937. Pp. 26-40. ill., map, tables. Also mf. Loc: OKIT, OWTL, OWTU, OWTUR.

An illustrated account that stresses the prosperity and sophistication of the twin cities by noting the many industries, businesses, services, schools, churches and clubs. Tables summarize debentures, tax assessments and population for the years 1900 through 1937 and there are brief profiles of specific companies and their specialties. The supplement also includes a report by A.R. Kaufman on the Kitchener town plan, advertisements by local businesses and numerous photographs. Period: c1800 - 1937.

335. Rittinger, Glenn R.G. **The changing functions of Ontario urban centres (population 20,000 or more, 1961).** University of Waterloo (B.A. thesis, Geography), 1964. 1 fiche. mf. Loc: OWTUM.

A study of changing economic functions from 1931 to 1961 in 27 middle-sized Ontario urban centres, including Galt and Kitchener. The author concludes that all centres except Oshawa were multifunctional, with the predominant functions being manufacturing, servicing, retailing and construction. Of these four functions, only manufacturing and retailing are classified as stable in the early 1960s. The number of functions performed by the urban centres is generally found to have increased. Period: 1931 - 1961.

336. Russwurm, Lorne H. "Hierarchical and functional stability and change in a strongly urbanizing area of southwestern Ontario, 1871-1971." **Canadian Geographer**. 1981. 25,2: 149-166. maps, tables. Loc: OKIT, OWTL, OWTU.

An analysis of long-term rates of decline, stability and growth of population and commercial functions in central places of the large region comprising Peel, Halton, Wellington, Waterloo, Perth, Oxford, Middlesex, Brant and Wentworth counties. By 1971 "surging" places, growing faster than their long-term mean, are found to be concentrated near larger cities, a pattern similar to 1971. The middle years 1901-41 are found to have been most stable on all measures. "Slowing" places are found on the northern periphery in 1871, from Toronto to Hamilton in 1901-41, and in the rural area west of Kitchener by 1971. Period: 1871 - 1971.

337. Russwurm, Lorne H. **The rural-urban fringe with comparative reference to London, Kitchener-Waterloo and Sarnia**. University of Western Ontario (M.A. thesis, Geography), 1961. 207 l. ill., maps, bibl. Loc: OWTU, OWTL.

An analysis of the interaction in the rural-urban fringe of the factors of physiography and soils, city site, situation and shape, and location of industrial areas. The author discusses problems, such as economic costs and waste, taxation burdens and zoning, and recommends regional planning for each city region. Period: c1930 - 1961.

338. Russwurm, Lorne H. "Urban fringe and urban shadow in the Waterloo-southeast Wellington County area land space matrix." **The Waterloo County area: selected geographical essays**. Edited by A.G. McLellan. Waterloo: Department of Geography, University of Waterloo, 1971. Pp. 97-111. maps, tabl. Loc: OWTU, OWTL, OWTUCG, OKIT.

A study of the impact of rapid urbanization in the region between 1941 and 1966, based on factor analysis of data variables from township assessment rolls. Urban fringe variables measure more concrete phenomena such as non-farm population, land uses and residential assessment. Urban shadow variables reflect urbanization pressures such as non-farm and non-resident land ownership and vacant land. Period: 1941 - 1966.

339. Schnare, Michael L. **Evolution of the urban pattern of Waterloo County**. University of Waterloo (B.E.S. thesis, Geography), 1977. 1 fiche. maps, tables, bibl. mf. Loc: OWTUM.

A description of the technological changes that have affected transportation, communication, manufacturing and agricultural sectors of the county economy. The study is organized in three time periods: 1800-1851, 1852-1931 and 1932-1971. Period: 1800 - 1971.

340. Sellner, James G. **The regional role of Galt in the Grand River urban triangle**. University of Waterloo (M.A. thesis, Geography), 1969. 2 fiche. graphs, maps, tables. mf. Loc: OWTU.

A description and analysis of Galt's development as an urban centre from 1816 to 1969, with a prediction of its future role. Galt was the regional centre in the mid-1850s, but a century later was secondary to Kitchener-Waterloo. The author predicts that Galt will continue to play a strong secondary role in the region, and that its new downtown mall will rejuvenate its central business district. Period: 1816 - 1969.

341. Thakur, Baleshwar. **Changing functional makeup of central place hierarchies in southwestern Ontario between 1871 and 1971**. University of Waterloo (M.A. thesis, Geography), 1972. 2 fiche. maps, tables, bibl. mf. Loc: OWTU.

An examination of functions of each settlement to determine its status as a city, town, village or hamlet. Using Dun and Bradstreet data, the author traces businesses and services over the 100-year period. Patterns in the size of central place systems are identified and discussed, and data on functions and populations are presented in the appendices. Period: 1871 - 1971.

GENERAL DEMOGRAPHIC STUDIES

342. Kozorys, G. **Factorial ecology, Kitchener-Waterloo.** University of Waterloo (B.E.S. thesis, Geography), 1974. 77 l. charts, maps, tables, bibl. Loc: OWTU.

A spatial analysis of socio-economic and demographic factors in familial and ethnic trends, with many of the results presented in tabular form. Period: 1961.

343. Lefevre, Craig. **The spatial variation and spatial distribution of the population age structure of Kitchener-Waterloo, 1961.** University of Waterloo (B.E.S. thesis, Geography), 1974. 113 p. bibl., graphs, tables, maps. Loc: OWTU.

A geographical study of age-groups, as a basis for planning schools and housing. Twenty demographic variables such as ethnic status, sex, occupation, education and income are considered. Period: 1960 - 1961.

344. Lobsinger, Linda. **Elements of population change in Wellesley Township, 1901-1911.** Wilfrid Laurier University (B.A. thesis, Geography), 1983. 69 l. ill., maps, tables, bibl. Loc: OWTL.

A demographic study based on birth, marriage and death records. The author presents statistical information on ethnic origin, gender, religious affiliation, marital and familial trends, births and causes of death. Period: 1901 - 1911.

345. Maloney, M. Christine. **Spatial and social mobility in mid-nineteenth century Galt and Preston.** University of Waterloo (B.E.S. thesis, Geography), 1980. 1 fiche. tables, graphs, bibl. mf. Loc: OWTUM.

An outline of the geographic and social mobility of the adult male population of Galt and Preston from 1851 to 1871, as documented in the manuscript census. In both towns, a high percentage of men left town or died: in Galt 87.2 per cent of men were gone, and in Preston the figure was 93 per cent. Galt had fewer transients and provided for greater upward social mobility than Preston. This can be attributed to the fact that manufacturing in Galt continued to expand during these years, while Preston had reached a peak in 1851. Period: 1851 - 1871.

346. Moyer, Roger L. **A comparative factorial ecology: Kitchener-Waterloo, 1971 and 1981.** Wilfrid Laurier University (B.A. thesis, Geography), 1984. 132 l. maps, bibl. Loc: OWTL.

An examination of socio-economic and demographic characteristics based on census data for ethnic origin, religion, education, mobility, fertility, dwellings, households, employment and income. The author finds that family status, ethnic status, occupational status, tenure, "stock" family, household size and income are the main factors and concludes that the German ethnic group had been virtually assimilated by 1981. Period: 1971 - 1981.

347. Sommerville, E. "Waterloo County: a population profile, 1951-1971." **The Waterloo County area: selected geographical essays.** Edited by A.G. McLellan. Waterloo: Department of Geography, University of Waterloo, 1971. Pp. 40-62. map, tables, graphs. Loc: OWTU, OWTL, OWTUCG, OKIT.

An account of the demographic composition of the county and its component municipalities, based on census data. The author comments on the high degree of urbanization, rapid growth, ethnic background, diversified industries, and wage levels of Waterloo County and the Kitchener Census Metropolitan Area, in relation to national levels. Contrasts are drawn between South Waterloo (Galt, Preston, Hespeler and North Dumfries Township) and North Waterloo over the period from 1881 to 1969. Period: 1881 - 1971.

348. Zimmerman, Idessa and Jennings, Laurie. **Cholera: it swept this area like a scythe.** The Author, 1966?. 4 l. ill., map. Loc: OKITW.

A copy of an article from the **Kitchener-Waterloo Record** of 21 November 1963 by Laurie Jennings, with additional information on members of the Hembling family who were Bridgeport cholera victims, and a description of the burial sites. Period: 1813 - 1895.

DEMOGRAPHIC DATA SOURCES FOR GENEALOGY, NOTABLY CEMETERY TRANSCRIPTIONS

349. Ambrose, Rosemary W. **Births, deaths and marriages in Canada Museum und Allgemeine Zeitung, 1835-1840.** Kitchener Public Library, 1987. 1 v. Loc: OKIT.

A listing of names, dates of events, and dates recorded in the newspaper, prefaced by a brief introduction to the journal and its owner, Henry William Peterson. Period: 1835 - 1840.

350. Ambrose, Rosemary W. **Index to births, deaths and marriages announced in the Deutsche Canadier, Berlin, Canada West.** Kitchener Public Library, 1988. 58 p. Loc: OKIT.

An index to surviving copies of the newspaper for the years 1841 to 1862, held at the Kitchener Public Library. The index includes names, dates of the events, dates recorded in the journal, and brief details. The translation from the German, and an earlier index on which this was based, were prepared by Simone Nieuwolt and Sylvie Kuppek. Period: 1841 - 1862.

351. **An archaeological excavation of the pioneer family Harvie Cemetery, North Dumfries Township.** Waterloo: Regional Municipality of Waterloo, Planning and Development Department, Archaeology Division, 1988. 16 p. map., ill. Loc: OKIT, OWRMA.

A project report, including excerpts from a 1952 newspaper account of the cemetery. Period: 1812 - 1894.

352. Baker, Robert G. **Rosebank Community Cemetery (CC#4565): Block A, Concession 2, Lot 4, Huron Road, Wilmot Township.** Kitchener: Ontario Genealogical Society, Waterloo-Wellington Branch, 1989. 16 p. Loc: OKIT.

Transcriptions with index of about 150 markers. The introduction notes that the cemetery dates from about 1830 and is located on land deeded to the community for use as a cemetery and school. Rosebank was settled in the 1820s by Amish and Tunkers; a large sawmill owned by the Hallman family was located here. The Brethren in Christ Church opposite the cemetery was founded in 1902. Period: 1825 - 1989.

353. Baker, Robert G. and Madill, Dona and Huber, Norma. **Wilmot Mennonite Cemetery (CC#4558): Bleam's Road, South side, Lot 17, Wilmot Township, Waterloo County.** Kitchener: Ontario Genealogical Society, Waterloo-Wellington Branch, 1991. 14 p. index. Loc: OKIT.

Transcriptions with index of about 150 markers in the cemetery that dates from 1846. The introduction notes that the cemetery has always been associated with Geiger Mennonite Church but was also open to members of other denominations. Period: 1846 - 1980.

354. Barnes, Bill and Barnes, Thelma and Hoffman, Frances and Huber, Norma and Lambert, Ronald and Madill, Dona and Taylor, Ryan and Vollmer, Wayne. **Emmanuel Evangelical Lutheran Cemetery (CC#4556): Petersburg, Wilmot Township.** Kitchener: Ontario Genealogical Society, Waterloo-Wellington Branch, 1990. 23 p. Loc: OKIT.

Transcriptions of about 225 stones listed by row and plot, followed by an index. The introduction notes that there have been four church buildings associated with the cemetery, dating from 1844, 1851-3, 1876 and 1915. The cemetery occupies the site of the first village school in the 1830s. The inscriptions show that many children died of diphtheria in 1895-6. Period: 1844 - 1980.

355. Barnes, Thelma. **St James Anglican Church (CC#4571): Huron Road, Wilmot Township, Block A, Concession 2, Lot 27.** Kitchener: Ontario Genealogical Society, Waterloo-Wellington Branch, 1988. 19 p. Loc: OKIT.

Transcriptions with index of about 220 markers in the cemetery adjoining St James Anglican Church. An introduction briefly outlines the history of Anglican places of worship in Haysville and New Hamburg, noting that the nave of the church was built in 1854 and the site was formally deeded by the Canada Company with three acres for a cemetery. The text of the plaque, erected by the Waterloo Historical Society in 1983, is quoted. Period: 1854 - 1987.

356. Bauman, Angus S. **Martin's Mennonite Cemetery: records copied from Angus Bauman's book of information of tombstone inscriptions.** Kitchener: Ontario Genealogical Society, Waterloo-Wellington Branch, 1 v. (various pagings). Loc: OKIT.

Transcriptions, index and plan of about 1000 markers. Interments in the cemetery began in 1831. Period: 1831 - 1980.

357. **Becker family plot (CC#6325): Conc. North Bleams Road, Lot 6, Wilmot Township.** Kitchener: Ontario Genealogical Society, Waterloo-Wellington Branch, 1987. 1 p. Loc: OKIT.

Transcriptions of the two gravestones in the burial plot beside the barn on the Becker family farm on North Bleams Road. Period: 1842 - 1947.

358. Beechey, Marcella and Wall, Donna and Richards, Sharon and Madill, Dona and Huber, Norma. **St Teresa Roman Catholic Cemetery, Elmira (CC#4594): German Company Tract, Lot 92, Woolwich Township, Waterloo County.** Kitchener: Ontario Genealogical Society, Waterloo-Wellington Branch, 1992. 18 p. index. Loc: OKIT.

Transcriptions with index of about 160 markers in the cemetery that was the original churchyard of St Theresa's parish before the church moved into Elmira. The land was originally deeded by Joseph Ruth in 1853. Period: 1853 - 1990.

359. **Beth Jacob Cemetery (CC#4506): Victoria Street, Kitchener.** Kitchener: Ontario Genealogical Society, Waterloo-Wellington Branch, 1987. 26 p. Loc: OKIT.

Transcriptions of the stones, by row and plot, in the two sections of the cemetery located at Victoria Street South and Westmount Road in Kitchener. About 108 stones are transcribed in section A and 150 in Section B; the text of the Holocaust Memorial is also transcribed. An index is included. Period: 1910 - 1987.

360. Bindemann, Frederick W., Rev. **Copy of Pastor Bindemann's records, 1835-1864**. Berlin: St Paul's Evangelical Lutheran Church, 1865. 1 v. (unpaged). Loc: OKIT.

Lists of baptisms, marriages, deaths and confirmations compiled by the pioneer Lutheran pastor who officiated at many early Protestant ceremonies in Waterloo County. Most entries are in English, but some are in German. At the Kitchener Public Library this information has been entered on catalogue cards and the names arranged alphabetically in drawers labelled Bindemann Grooms, Bindemann Brides, Bindemann Baptisms and Bindemann Burials. Period: 1835 - 1864.

361. Bowyer, David G., Rev. **Baptisms performed at St. John the Evangelist Church (Anglican Church of Canada), Berlin, 1858-1872**. Kitchener: Ontario Genealogical Society, Waterloo-Wellington Branch, 1985. 19 p. Loc: OKIT.

Transcriptions, with an index prepared by Sue Mansell, of about 220 baptisms. Details are provided of child's name, date of birth, date of baptism, parents' names, father's trade or profession, place of residence, and names of sponsors and officiating clergy. Period: 1858 - 1872.

362. **Breslau Mennonite Cemetery formerly Cressman Mennonite Cemetery (CC#4579): GCT East of Grand, Lot 115, Woolwich Township (formerly Waterloo Township)**. Mennonite Historical Society of Ontario - Genealogical Committee, 1984. 81 p. Loc: OKIT.

Transcriptions of 596 stones, preceded by an index. The introduction notes that the site was deeded to the Mennonite Church by Christian C. Snyder in 1837. Period: 1834 - 1984.

363. Brubacher, Glenn. **Readings of the tombstones of the cemetery of First Mennonite Church (CC#4507)**. 1985. 65 p. Loc: OKIT.

Transcriptions with plan and index of more than 2,200 markers, including notations of the matching numbers in Ezra Eby's **Biographical history of Waterloo Township**. Period: 1830 - 1983.

364. Buehler, Allan M. **Blair Memorial Cemetery (CC#4501): old and new sections, Waterloo Township Lot #4, Beasley's Old Survey**. Allan Buehler, 1975. 25 p. Loc: OKIT.

Transcriptions and plans of markers in both parts of the cemetery, with an index to about 900 names. The first burial is dated 1804. Period: 1804 - 1975.

365. Buehler, Allan M. **Comments on the Blair Cemetery records**. 1975. 15 p. Loc: OKIT.

Transcription with plan of the old section only of the cemetery. This report replicates part of the report on the Blair Memorial Cemetery described in record D-1057. Period: 1804 - 1920.

366. **Cedar Creek Cemetery records**. 1984. 1 v. (unpaged). map. Loc: OKIT.

Photocopy of the record book begun in 1908 after the earlier records were destroyed in a fire. A plan of the cemetery is in rear pocket. Period: 1908 - 1984.

367. Cemetery Committee. **St James Lutheran Church invites you to their memorial service in the church**. The Church, 1991. 1 folded sheet. ill. Loc: OKIT, OWES.

A list of members of the Lutheran congregation in St Jacobs who died in each year from 1868 to 1991. Period: 1868 - 1991.

368. **Closed St Clement's Cemetery, northeast corner of Duke and Laurel Streets, Cambridge**. Waterloo: Regional Municipality of Waterloo, Planning and Development Department, Archaeology Division, 1989. 1 file folder. Loc: OWRMA.

A report on the excavation of skeletal remains of about 130 individuals found on the site of the former cemetery which had been closed for redevelopment.

369. **Complete Woolwich cemetery records: Elmira Mennonite, St Jacobs Mennonite, Conestogo Old Order, North Woolwich Mennonite, Floradale Mennonite**. 1984. 1 v. (various pagings). ill. Loc: OKIT.

Transcriptions of markers in several Woolwich cemeteries, with indexes, plans and explanatory notes on each. Nearly 800 markers are transcribed and indexed for the West Woolwich or Elmira Mennonite Cemetery which adjoins the Old Order meeting house built in 1854 on the southeast corner of Lot 104. The present red brick Mennonite church was built in about 1923 and the cemetery is also used by members of the Markham-Waterloo Conference who meet in the white meeting house. Over 300 markers are recorded for the burial ground attached to the new Conestogo meeting house which was built in 1894. About 280 burials are noted for the St Jacobs Mennonite Cemetery which includes the Old Conestogo Cemetery dating from the 1850s. The North Woolwich Mennonite Cemetery was associated with the church built in 1872, with about 640 burials recorded since 1875; members of the Floradale Mennonite Church used this cemetery until 1945 before establishing their own. Details of Woolwich residents' burials in the South Peel Mennonite Cemetery, located in Wellington County one mile west of Wallenstein, are included. Period: 1850 - 1980.

370. **Conestogo Old Order Mennonite Cemetery monumental transcriptions (CC#4575): Woolwich Township.** Mennonite Historical Society of Ontario, Genealogical Committee, 1986. 1 v. (unpaged) Loc: OKIT.

Transcriptions of about 300 stones, preceded by an index. There is no introduction.

371. Dettweiler, Allan. **Bloomingdale Mennonite Cemetery (CC#4587), sometime called Snyder's, Road 67A, Woolwich Township, formerly Waterloo Township, Waterloo County, Ontario.** Kitchener: Ontario Genealogical Society, Waterloo-Wellington Branch, 1992. 49 p. Loc: OKIT.

Transcriptions with index of about 500 markers, most of which date from after 1900. Period: 1900 - 1990.

372. **Doon Cemetery (CC#4519): Biehn Tract Lot 1, Waterloo Township (now Mill Park Drive, Kitchener, west of Doon).** Kitchener: Ontario Genealogical Society, Waterloo-Wellington Branch, 1987. 41 p. Loc: OKIT.

Transcriptions of about 260 stones, by row and plot, followed by an index. The introduction notes that the Doon Presbyterian Church was built in 1854 on land given by Robert Ferrie, who also bought part of the Christian Schneider farm for a cemetery. Doon Cemetery adjoins the Kinzie-Biehn Cemetery. Period: 1854 - 1987.

373. Eberhardt, Janet and Huber, Norma. **Doon Pioneer Tower Cemetery (CC#5016): BF East of Grand, Lot 12, Waterloo Township.** Kitchener: Ontario Genealogical Society, Waterloo-Wellington Branch, 1987. 3 p. Loc: OKIT.

Transcriptions of 21 stones, preceded by an index. The introduction notes that the Doon Pioneer Tower was erected on this site (part of the old Betzner homestead) partly because of the existence of the old graveyard. Speaking at the dedication of the tower in 1926, D.N. Panabaker is quoted as referring to seven nameless graves as those of Indians who had been friendly to the early settlers. Period: 1806 - 1875.

374. Eberhardt, Janet and Huber, Norma. **Limerick Cornell Cemetery (CC#5417): Broken Front Concession, East of the Grand, Lot 9, Waterloo Township.** Kitchener: Ontario Genealogical Society, Waterloo-Wellington Branch, 1987. 4 p. Loc: OKIT.

Transcriptions, with an index, of some 31 stones

that were moved in about 1967, from the original location on the west side of Highway 8 about one mile north of Preston, to a location beside Doon Heritage Crossroads on Huron Road at Homer Watson Blvd. At the time of the move, 113 graves were counted but only 45 markers were found; only 31 markers are reported in 1987. Period: 1810 - 1900.

375. Eberhardt, Janet and Huber, Norma. **Pinehill Cemetery (CC#4549): Canada Company Block A, Concession 1, Lot 14 and 15, Wilmot Township, Waterloo County.** Kitchener: Ontario Genealogical Society, Waterloo-Wellington Branch, 1986. 10 p. map. Loc: OKIT.

Transcriptions with plan and index of about one hundred markers in the cemetery located on Huron Road (County Road #2) about four kilometres east of Haysville. The introduction notes that the trustees of the Wilmot Methodist Burial Ground and Chapel bought one-half acre of Lot 14 from Thomas Johnson in 1842 and one-half acre in 1864 from his nephew Samuel Johnson. Chapel services were discontinued around 1900; burials continued until 1939 but the cemetery has since been abandoned, neglected and vandalized. Period: 1841 - 1939.

376. Eberhardt, Janet and Huber, Norma. **St Andrew's Pioneer Pergola (CC#44488): Lansdowne Avenue, Galt.** 1984. 30 p. Loc: OKIT.

Transcriptions with index of the stones from Old St Andrew's and United Presbyterian Cemeteries which were preserved in the rectangular pergola built by the Waterloo Chapter of the IODE in 1907. Period: 1839 - 1869.

377. Eberhardt, Janet and Huber, Norma. **Stauffer Abandoned Cemetery (CC#4547): Canada Company Block A Concession 2, Lot 22, Wilmot Township.** Kitchener: Ontario Genealogical Society, Waterloo-Wellington Branch, 1986. 4 p. map. Loc: OKIT.

Transcription with plan and index of 20 markers in the small cemetery located about one mile south on a winding road from Haysville, at the north corner of the first road to the west. The cemetery, begun as a family burial plot for the John Stauffer family, was later opened to Pennsylvania German neighbours who attended the Biehn Mennonite Church two kilometres west of the cemetery. Period: 1852 - 1908.

378. Elliott, Bruce S. and Kohli, Marjorie. **Index to the 1871 Census of Ontario: Waterloo.** Toronto: Ontario Genealogical Society, 1990. 173 p. map. Loc: OKIT, OWTL, OWTUCGR, OWRE.

An index to 9,513 heads of household and "strays" (persons with surnames different from the surnames of the household in which they were counted) enumerated in Waterloo County in April 1871. The index was created as part of the Ontario Genealogical Society's 25th anniversary project. The tabulation includes details of surname, forename, whether a "stray", age, country or province of birth, religion, ethnic origin, occupation, Census District and Census Sub-District, Census Enumerator's Division and page number in the manuscript census schedules. Period: 1870 - 1871.

379. **Elmira Union Cemetery (CC#4578).** Kitchener: Ontario Genealogical Society, Waterloo-Wellington Branch, 1991. 122 p. Loc: OKIT, OWRE.

Transcriptions with index of nearly 3,000 stones, by row and plot, in the municipal burying ground founded in the 1860s as a non-Lutheran cemetery. Period: 1860 - 1990.

380. Giilck, Helena. **Schmetzer Farm Cemetery (CC#4526), Wellesley Township, Lot 7, Concession X, near Linwood.** Kitchener: Ontario Genealogical Society, Waterloo-Wellington Branch, 1985. 2 p. Loc: OKIT.

Transcriptions with plan of 22 markers in the small, abandoned cemetery west of Linwood. It is on the farm occupied successively by Michael, Georg and Jacob Schmetzer; other family names recorded on the stones are Fleischhauer and Schultheis. Period: 1870 - 1920.

381. Giilck, Helena and Huber, Norma. **Zion United Church Cemetery, Maple Grove, formerly Wesleyan Methodist (CC#4503): Broken Front Concession, Lot 31, Waterloo Township.** Kitchener: Ontario Genealogical Society, Waterloo-Wellington Branch, 1986. 12 p. Loc: OKIT.

Transcriptions with index of more than 100 stones in the cemetery which was associated with the Wesleyan church established by 1855. Period: 1855 - 1975.

382. Groh, Ivan. "The first community cemetery and church." **Waterloo Historical Society.** 1964. 52: 31-33. Loc: all.

A short description of the Hagey Mennonite Church and cemetery where many early residents of Preston are buried. The author lists Clemens family members buried there, with their birth and death dates. Period: 1806 - 1964.

383. Hinds, A. Leone. **Waterloo County marriages, births and burials, 1840-1849, as recorded in Wellington District by the Clerk of the Peace Thomas Saunders.** Kitchener: Ontario Genealogical Society, Waterloo-Wellington Branch, 1992. 30 p. index. Loc: OKIT.

Transcription with index of manuscript records relating to the Waterloo County area before 1850, when it was part of the Wellington District. The entries include ceremonies conducted and recorded by Benjamin Eby, John Oesch and Christian Miller, "ministers of the Mennonist Society." Period: 1840 - 1849.

384. Historical Society of St Boniface and Maryhill Community. **St Boniface's Roman Catholic Cemetery, Maryhill (CC#4580): German Company Tract, Lot 81, Waterloo Township (now Woolwich Township).** Maryhill: The Society, 1985. 1 v. (unpaged). Loc: OKIT.

Transcriptions, with index and plan, of nearly 700 markers, 119 of which are inscribed in German script and 90 of which are crosses. A suggested walking tour is included. Period: 1851 - 1985.

385. Hoffman, Frances and Taylor, Ryan. **Abandoned Baptist Mission Cemetery (CC#4550): Canada Company Block B, Concession I, Lot 19, Wilmot Township.** Kitchener: Ontario Genealogical Society, Waterloo-Wellington Branch, 1988. 4 p. ill. Loc: OKIT.

Transcriptions with index of 25 stones in the small cemetery that lies behind a log house to the left of the Philipsburg-Wellesley road. The log house was first a Baptist church built in 1837, later served as a Pentecostal temple into the 1940s, and is now a private dwelling. The cemetery was most used in the period 1880 to 1920. Period: 1837 - 1942.

386. Hoffman, Frances. **Berlett's Corner Cemetery (CC#4552): Canada Company Block B, Concession III, Lot 13, Wilmot Township.** Kitchener: Ontario Genealogical Society, Waterloo-Wellington Branch, 1988. 5 p. ill. Loc: OKIT.

Transcriptions of grave markers, numbered by rows, with an index of names. The introduction notes that the cemetery occupies the site of the Berlett's Corners Lutheran Church, next to a building previously used as the schoolhouse for Wilmot School Section No. 19. Period: 1862 - 1925.

387. Hoffman, Frances. **Birth, baptismal and marriage registers for the Free Presbyterian Congregation of Chalmers Church, Winterbourne, Ontario.** Kitchener: Ontario Genealogical Society, Waterloo-Wellington Branch, 1987. 17, 86 p. Loc: OKIT, OWRE.

Details of 567 baptisms, each with name, dates of birth and baptism, father's occupation (in about two-thirds of all cases), and the name of the clergyman. Details of some 50 marriages include name, address, place of birth and age of bride and groom, names of parents and witnesses, and date of marriage. The lists are preceded by

an index of names linked to the numbered entries.
Period: 1838 - 1939.

388. Hoffman, Frances and Huber, Norma and Lambert,
Ronald and Robertson, E.A. and Taylor, Ryan.
**Freeborn Cemetery, also known as Zion
Presbyterian Cemetery (CC#4543): West Concession
3, Lot 10, Wellesley Township.** Kitchener: Ontario
Genealogical Society, Waterloo-Wellington Branch,
1988. 10 p. Loc: OKIT, OWRE.

Transcriptions of nearly 100 stones, by row and
plot, followed by an index. The introduction notes
that the cemetery, while located on what was
historically the Freeborn farm, served as a
community cemetery and was also known as the Zion
Presbyterian Cemetery. Period: 1845 - 1988.

389. Hoffman, Frances. **St Clement's Roman Catholic
Cemetery (CC#4499): Speedsville Road, Cambridge,
formerly Waterloo Township.** Kitchener: Ontario
Genealogical Society, Waterloo-Wellington Branch,
1990. 51 p. Loc: OKIT.

Transcriptions with index of nearly 600 markers.
The introduction notes that the parish of St
Clement in Preston dates from about 1847, and that
the Jesuits from Guelph had charge until 1889.
The present church and cemetery date from 1922,
and the stones (but not the graves) in the
churchyard at Duke and Dolph streets were moved to
the new cemetery. Period: 1847 - 1987.

390. Hoffman, Frances. **West Montrose United Church
Cemetery (CC#4596), German Company Tract Lot 71,
Woolwich Township.** Kitchener: Ontario
Genealogical Society, Waterloo-Wellington Branch,
1990. 1 v. (unpaged). ill. Loc: OKIT, OWRE.

Transcriptions with index of some 165 markers.
The introduction notes that the first church was
built in 1862-3, and the present one in 1906-07 at
the time of union into the United Brethren
Association of Congregational Churches. Period:
1862 - 1985.

391. Hoffman, Frances. **Zion Evangelical Lutheran
Cemetery (CC#4576): South Erb's Road, Lot 4,
Wilmot Township (east of St Agatha).** Kitchener:
Ontario Genealogical Society, Waterloo-Wellington
Branch, 1991. 7 p. Loc: OKIT.

Transcriptions with index of some 90 markers.
The introduction notes that the first services
were held in the log schoolhouse on the present
church property in December 1834 by the Rev. F.W.
Bindemann. The present church building dates from
1863. Period: 1834 - 1988.

392. Horst, Isaac R. **Baptismal records, 1842-1980.**
The Author, 198-?. 64 p. Loc: OKIT.

A compilation of all available baptismal records

for Mennonites in Waterloo County to 1889, and
then for Old Order Mennonites to 1980. The
details, presented by year, were apparently
transcribed from the records of Mennonite bishops
-- Benjamin B. Eby (1812-1853), Henry P. Shantz
(1842-1877), Joseph B. Hagey (1851-1876), Abraham
W. Martin (1867-1902), Amos S. Cressman (1875-
1909), Elias E. Weber (1875-1909), Paul S. Martin
(1902-1914), Ezra L. Martin (1914-1939), Jesse B.
Bauman (1933-1939), Daniel G. Brubacher
(1939-1942), Addison M. Gingrich (1942-1961) and
Edward M. Bauman (1961-). Period: 1842 - 1980.

393. Huber, Norma. **1851 Census of Waterloo Township:
alphabetical index by name, with complete
information.** Kitchener: Ontario Genealogical
Society, Waterloo-Wellington Branch, 1988. 1 v.
(various pagings). Loc: OKIT.

An indexed list of persons enumerated in the
1851 Census, with details of surname, given name,
occupation, birthplace, religion, age, division of
the township, page and line. The introduction
notes that the index was first prepared in 1967 as
a project of the Waterloo Historical Society and
then excluded Preston. A team of the OGS Chapter
revised and alphabetized the earlier index with
computer assistance. Period: 1850 - 1851.

394. Huber, Norma and Huber, Doris. **Abandoned
cemetery (CC#4525): Wellesley Township, east
concession VII, lot 8.** 1984. 2 p. map. Loc: OKIT.

Transcriptions with index of 15 markers dating
from between 1860 to 1887. An introduction
explains that Henry and Susannah Ernst in 1864
sold one acre to Daniel Martin, trustee of the
Religious Society of Mennonites, for a meeting
house and burial ground. Most burials were
members of the Ernst, Schmitt and Frey families.
When County Road 15 was relocated and widened, the
cemetery was moved and the stones were salvaged
and reorganized. Period: 1860 - 1887.

395. Huber, Norma and Turnbull, Marjorie. **Anderson
family plot (CC#6336): Concession 10, Lot 4, North
Dumfries Township (formerly Beverly Township,
Wentworth County).** Kitchener: Ontario
Genealogical Society, Waterloo-Wellington Branch,
1987. 1 p. Loc: OKIT.

Transcriptions of two stones in a family plot on
the rear edge of the Cambridge Golf and Country
Club. Two young girls are reported to have died
of cholera. Period: 1834 - 1843.

396. Huber, Norma. **Ayr Cemetery (CC#4489), Ayr
village, North Dumfries Township, Waterloo County,
Ontario,.** Kitchener: Ontario Genealogical
Society, Waterloo-Wellington Branch, 1992. 163 p.
Loc: OKIT.

Transcriptions with index of about 2,000 markers in the cemetery which was established in 1877 to replace various smaller churchyards and rural burial grounds. Period: 1877 - 1989.

397. Huber, Norma and Taylor, Ryan. **The Ayr Cemetery records index.** Kitchener Public Library, 1989. 1 v. (unpaged). Loc: OKIT.

An index to some 3,700 persons whose burials are recorded in the Ayr Cemetery Record book which was microfilmed in the early 1970s, with a copy available at the Kitchener Public Library. The introduction describes the layout of the Record book and appraises the quality of its information. The index includes details only of personal names with their location in the cemetery by lot and range and has no reference to any dates.

398. Huber, Norma. **Bethel United Church Cemetery (CC#4553): Canada Company Block A, Concession 3, Lot 30, Wilmot Township.** Kitchener: Ontario Genealogical Society, Waterloo-Wellington Branch, 1986. 8 p. Loc: OKIT.

Transcriptions of 58 markers by numbered rows, with an index of all names. The introduction summarizes the history of the church which was built in 1861 as part of a circuit based in Bright, Oxford County. The church building was sold in the 1960s to a Mennonite congregation, but the cemetery remains the responsibility of a board of trustees. Period: 1861 - 1986.

399. Huber, Norma. **Bridgeport Free Church Cemetery (CC#5428): Horning's Tract, Bloomingdale Road (now Kitchener) Waterloo Township.** Kitchener: Ontario Genealogical Society, Waterloo-Wellington Branch, 1988. 27 p. maps. Loc: OKIT.

Transcriptions of about 260 markers by row and lot with an index. The introduction notes that land for the Free Church and cemetery was given by John U. Tyson. When plots in this cemetery had all been sold, the Bridgeport Memorial Cemetery next door was developed as an extension. Period: 1848 - 1988.

400. Huber, Norma. **Bridgeport Memorial Cemetery (CC#6259): Horning's Tract, Bloomingdale Road (now Kitchener) Waterloo Township.** Kitchener: Ontario Genealogical Society, Waterloo-Wellington Branch, 1988. 18 p. map. Loc: OKIT.

Transcriptions of some 175 markers in the cemetery created as an extension to the Bridgeport Free Cemetery. Period: 1848 - 1986.

401. Huber, Norma and Kohli, Marjorie. **Calvary Conservative Mennonite Church Cemetery: German Company Tract Lot 124, Regional Road #21, Woolwich Township, Waterloo County.** Kitchener: Ontario

Genealogical Society, Waterloo-Wellington Branch, 1992. 12 p. index. Loc: OKIT.

Transcriptions with index of about 110 markers. An introduction notes that the church to which the cemetery is attached was originally Evangelical when built in 1868 and that it was bought by the Conservative Mennonites in the late 1970s. Period: 1868 - 1990.

402. Huber, Norma. **Cedar Creek Cemetery (CC#4490): Dickie Settlement Cemetery (CC#4491) North Dumfries Township.** Kitchener: Ontario Genealogical Society, Waterloo-Wellington Branch, 1985. 1 v. (unpaged). Loc: OKIT.

Transcriptions of the markers in each cemetery, with an alphabetical index and a list of known burials in Cedar Creek that have no stones. Period: 1834 - 1977.

403. Huber, Norma. **Cedar Grove Amish Mennonite Cemetery (CC#4528): West Concession III, Lot 12, Wellesley Township.** Kitchener: Ontario Genealogical Society, Waterloo-Wellington Branch, 1991. 14 p. Loc: OKIT, OWRE.

Transcriptions with index of about 180 markers. An introduction notes that the older stones bearing only initials are being replaced by plain white stones with more complete information. Period: 1915 - 1988.

404. Huber, Norma. **Evangelical United Brethren Cemetery (CC#4585): now Calvary United Church Cemetery, German Company Tract Lot 37, St Jacobs, Woolwich Township.** Kitchener: Ontario Genealogical Society, Waterloo-Wellington Branch, 1986. 25 p. Loc: OKIT, OWRE.

Transcriptions of about 500 stones with an index. The introduction notes that the Evangelical Association organized its church in St Jacobs in 1848. The cemetery occupies the site of the original log church built on the brow of a hill overlooking the Conestogo River, on land given by Anthony Reitzel. Period: 1848 - 1985.

405. Huber, Norma. **Freeborn Private Cemetery (CC#4527): Wellesley Township, West Concession 3, Lot 7, Waterloo County.** Kitchener: Ontario Genealogical Society, Waterloo-Wellington Branch, 1992. 1 p. index. Loc: OKIT.

Transcriptions with index of the two stones in the private cemetery at the northeast corner of the junction of Township Roads 3 and 16. Period: 1853 - 1858.

406. Huber, Norma and Kohli, Marjorie. **Hallman Mennonite Cemetery (CC#6703): Conc. 11, Lot 31, North Dumfries Township.** Kitchener: Ontario Genealogical Society, Waterloo-Wellington Branch,

1989. 7 p. Loc: OKIT.

Transcriptions of some 62 markers on the one-acre plot originally deeded by Adam Unger in 1847 in trust to Jacob Detweiler for a meeting house and burying ground. The introduction notes that services were conducted in the brick church across the road until 1886. Most stones bear pre-1900 dates. Period: 1847 - 1900.

407. Huber, Norma and Madill, Dona. **Holy Family Roman Catholic Cemetery, New Hamburg (CC#4559): South Bleams Road, Wilmot Township, Waterloo County.** Kitchener: Ontario Genealogical Society, Waterloo-Wellington Branch, 1992. 22 p. index. Loc: OKIT.

Transcriptions with index of about 200 markers. The introduction notes that the cemetery land was bought in 1892, local Catholic burials having previously been in the St Agatha cemetery. Other details of early Catholic churches and schools are also provided. Period: 1892 - 1990.

408. Huber, Norma and Taylor, Ryan and Brown-Kubisch, Linda. **Index to marriages from the record book of Saint Peter's Lutheran Church, Preston, 1839-1847.** Kitchener: Kitchener Public Library, 1991. 1 v. (unpaged). Loc: OKIT.

An index to over 500 marriages, listing names of spouses with dates of the marriages. Period: 1839 - 1847.

409. Huber, Norma. **Kinzie-Bean Cemetery (CC#5425): Biehn Tract Lot 1, Waterloo Township (now Mill Park Drive, Kitchener, west of Doon).** Kitchener: Ontario Genealogical Society, Waterloo-Wellington Branch, 1987. 11 p. Loc: OKIT.

Transcriptions and index of about 80 surviving markers and monuments in the cemetery located on the original farm of John Biehn who came from Montgomery County, PA in 1800. Biehn's son-in-law, Dilman Kinzie of Bucks County, arrived at the same time and settled across the road from the cemetery. The text of a cairn erected in 1974 is also transcribed. Period: 1800 - 1985.

410. Huber, Norma. **Linwood Cemeteries: St Peter's Lutheran Cemetery (CC#4541), Concession XI, Lot 11; Linwood Union Cemetery (CC#4531), Concession X, Lot 10, Wellesley Township, Waterloo County.** Kitchener: Ontario Genealogical Society, Waterloo-Wellington Branch, 1987. 16, 29 p. Loc: OKIT, OWRE.

Transcriptions of about 190 stones in St Peter's Cemetery, founded for the German-speaking people of the community in about 1900, and of the 135 stones in the Linwood Union Cemetery (used from about 1860). There is a consolidated index to names, row and plot numbers and plans of each

cemetery. Period: 1860 - 1986.

411. Huber, Norma. **Marriages of Galt and area inhabitants with some strays.** Kitchener: Ontario Genealogical Society, Waterloo-Wellington Branch, 1986. 33 p. Loc: OKIT.

A computer-generated index with names of both spouses, places of residence, dates of marriage, forenames of father and mother (in a few cases), and the denominations of the churches where the marriages took place. The information is taken from several sources, including Central Presbyterian Church, First United Church, Trinity Anglican Church, Gore District and Waterloo County records, the Alexander MacGregor marriage records and Ezra Eby's **Biographical history of Waterloo Township.** Period: 1841 - 1869.

412. Huber, Norma. **Mount Hope Cemetery (CC#4500), Waterloo City, Roger Street East, Waterloo City (formerly Waterloo Township, Waterloo County, Ontario).** Kitchener: Ontario Genealogical Society, Waterloo-Wellington Branch, 1991. 5 v. Loc: OKIT.

Transcriptions of markers in the municipal cemetery established in 1865. The work is organized in sections A, B, BB, C, D, E, F, H, I, J, K, L, M, N, O, P, New and Old Roman Catholic Sections, with a master index of over 8,000 names. Period: 1865 - 1990.

413. Huber, Norma. **Mount View Cemetery (CC#4495): 80 Blenheim Road, Cambridge, formerly Galt, North Dumfries Township, Waterloo County.** Kitchener: Ontario Genealogical Society, Waterloo-Wellington Branch, 1988 - 1992. 8 v. (various pagings). Loc: OKIT.

Transcriptions with plans and indexes of markers in the large public cemetery that dates from 1867. Originally called the Galt Cemetery, the name was changed in 1886. When the old Strang Burying Ground and St Andrew's Cemetery were closed in 1889, many bodies and monuments were moved to Mount View. In recording the transcriptions, an attempt is made to correlate stone numbers with the cemetery burial map. The transcriptions are reported in seven sections. The reports on 1,100 markers in Section 1 and 1,500 markers in Section 3 appeared in 1988; the report on 2,300 names in Section 4 was published in 1990; the reports on 2,200 names in Sections 5 and 5A, about 6,000 names in Section 6, and 200 markers in the Mausoleum section were published in 1991; and the report on 1,500 markers in Sections 7 and 7A appeared in 1992. Period: 1867 - 1985.

414. Huber, Norma. **New Dundee Cemetery (CC#4561): Block B, Concession III, Lot 6, Wilmot Township.** Kitchener: Ontario Genealogical Society, Waterloo-Wellington Branch, 1987. 41 p. Loc: OKIT.

Transcriptions, with index and plan, of more than 450 markers dating from the 1870s to the present. The introduction notes that the first burial ground was located on the farm of Frederick Lautenschlager on the western side of the mill pond at the north end of the village. In 1914, the village churches decided that the cemetery should be enlarged and adjoining land was purchased for the New Dundee Union Cemetery. The OGS branch also produced an unpaged book showing plans of the cemetery plots in 1986. Period: 1876 - 1986.

415. Huber, Norma. **New Hamburg Reformed Mennonite Cemetery (CC#4562): sometimes called Hostetler's Cemetery, North Snyder's Road, Lot 20, Wilmot Township, Waterloo County.** Kitchener: Ontario Genealogical Society, Waterloo-Wellington Branch, 1992. 16 p. index. Loc: OKIT.

Transcriptions with index of about 150 markers in the cemetery that dates from about 1850. An introduction provides a brief history of the church and school that were originally on the same site and were later moved across the road. Period: 1847 - 1990.

416. Huber, Norma and Huber, Doris. **Newborn Mennonite Cemetery (CC#6439): Woolwich Township, GCT Lot 38.** Kitchener: Ontario Genealogical Society, Waterloo-Wellington Branch, 1986. 1 v. (unpaged). Loc: OKIT, OWRE.

Transcriptions of eight markers in the small cemetery adjoining a large white frame meeting house on the south side of the first road north of County Road 17, about two miles northwest of St Jacobs. Most markers bear post-1950 dates. Period: 1956 - 1986.

417. Huber, Norma. **Nith Valley Mennonite Cemetery, formerly Biehn Mennonite Cemetery (CC#4554): Canada Company Block A, Concession 3, Lot 24, Wilmot Township.** Kitchener: Ontario Genealogical Society, Waterloo-Wellington Branch, 1986. 6 p. Loc: OKIT.

Transcriptions, with index and plan, of about 50 markers. The introduction notes that the Nith Valley Mennonite Church, formerly Biehn Mennonite Church, was originally built in 1870 on land given by John Bean while the cemetery site was bought from Isaac Bean. Period: 1870 - 1986.

418. Huber, Norma. **Saint James Lutheran Cemetery, Elmira.** Kitchener: Ontario Genealogical Society, Waterloo-Wellington Branch, 1991. 41 p. Loc: OKIT, OWRE.

Transcriptions with index of some 480 markers. The introduction notes that Saint James was the first organized congregation in Elmira, being served by the Rev. Jacob Werth who also founded Saint Matthew's in Conestogo during his time at Elmira. During the pastorate of H.W.H. Wichman (1859-1861) a schism led to the founding of St Paul's, Elmira. A brick church was built in 1869 and land for the cemetery was bought in 1884. Period: 1850 - 1990.

419. Huber, Norma and Madill, Dona. **Saint Mark's Lutheran Cemetery (CC#4538): East Concession 2, Lot 13, Wellesley Township.** Kitchener: Ontario Genealogical Society, Waterloo-Wellington Branch, 1991. 16 p. Loc: OKIT.

Transcriptions with index of about 190 markers. The cemetery was begun in association with the Evangelical Lutheran Church which was established in the 1870s and first called St Paul's. The original church building of 1876 was replaced in 1907. Period: 1875 - 1990.

420. Huber, Norma. **Saint Peter's Lutheran Cemetery (CC#4509): Kitchener, Weber Street East.** Kitchener: Ontario Genealogical Society, Waterloo-Wellington Branch, 1991. 3 v. Loc: OKIT.

Transcriptions with indexes of some 2,000 markers in the cemetery established in 1871 by the congregation which organized in 1862. The land was bought from Menno Erb and the cemetery, which adjoins the churchyard of First Mennonite Church, was described in 1950 as the largest Lutheran cemetery in Canada. Each volume contains a plan of the various sections of the cemetery and an introductory history of the church and burial ground. Period: 1862 - 1990.

421. Huber, Norma. **Sheard family monument (CC#4567), Block A, Concession 2, Lot 2, Wilmot Township.** Kitchener: Ontario Genealogical Society, Waterloo-Wellington Branch, 1985. 1 l. Loc: OKIT.

Transcription of text on the spired stone of red-faced granite and on the five small footstones that commemorate Titus and Mary Sheard and family. Period: 1844 - 1890.

422. Huber, Norma and Kohli, Marjorie. **St Mary's Roman Catholic Cemetery (CC#6307): 235 Cooper Street, Hespeler, now Cambridge.** Kitchener: Ontario Genealogical Society, Waterloo-Wellington Branch, 1985. 22 p. Loc: OKIT.

Transcriptions of the stones with an index to all personal names. A preface outlines the history of the Church of St Mary of the Visitation which was built in 1857 and destroyed by fire in 1916. The cemetery was used for interments from 1894 to 1951. Period: 1894 - 1951.

423. Huber, Norma. **St Patrick's Cemetery (CC#4496): Avenue Road, Galt.** Kitchener: Ontario Genealogical Society, Waterloo-Wellington Branch, 1988. 1 v. (various pagings). Loc: OKIT.

Transcriptions with index of some 300 markers. The introduction notes that the cemetery was originally cared for by St Patrick's Roman Catholic Church but then taken over by the Hamilton Diocese. Period: 1866 - 1986.

424. Huber, Norma. **Strang Cemetery and miscellaneous misplaced stones (CC#4): Cambridge (Galt), N. Dumfries Township, Waterloo County.** Kitchener: Ontario Genealogical Society, Waterloo-Wellington Branch, 1992. 1 p. index. Loc: OKIT.

Transcriptions of seven markers, representing a few that have been traced of those that were left at the Old Strang burying ground after most stones were removed to Mount View Cemetery in the early twentieth century. Period: 1840 - 1863.

425. Huber, Norma. **Trinity Anglican Cemetery (CC#4497): Blenheim Road, Galt.** Kitchener: Ontario Genealogical Society, Waterloo-Wellington Branch, 1991. 87 p. Loc: OKIT.

Transcriptions with index of over 1,000 markers. The introduction notes that the cemetery was begun as a traditional Anglican burying ground at a time when each church had its own. Period: 1840 - 1990.

426. Huber, Norma. **Wilhelm Cemetery (CC#4573): Wilmot Township, South Erb's Road, Lot 13.** Kitchener: Ontario Genealogical Society, Waterloo-Wellington Branch, 1987. 6 p. map. Loc: OKIT.

Transcriptions with index of some 50 markers in the cemetery that was founded in the 1830s. The location is described as facing Shantz Mennonite Church and Cemetery across the road, with a school house on the northeast corner. Period: 1833 - 1952.

427. Huber, Norma. **Winterbourne Presbyterian Cemetery (CC#4597) and Winterbourne Pioneer Methodist Cemetery (CC#4587): both Lot 5, Broken Front Concession East of Grand River, Woolwich Township.** Kitchener: Ontario Genealogical Society, Waterloo-Wellington Branch, 1984. 25 p. Loc: OKIT, OWRE.

Transcriptions, with index and plan, of about 580 markers in the Presbyterian cemetery and 81 in the Methodist cemetery. The introduction notes that one acre for Presbyterian cemetery purposes was promised by Luman Woodward in 1836 but not conveyed until 1855. The Chalmers Presbyterian Church bought half an acre in 1915. The Methodist church was built of fieldstone in 1856, closed in 1915 and was demolished in 1927; the site is marked by a plaque erected by the Winterbourne Women's Institute in 1972. Period: 1835 - 1983.

428. Huber, Norma and Giilck, Helena. **Woodland Cemetery, Kitchener (CC#4510): Arlington Boulevard, formerly in Waterloo Township.** Kitchener: Ontario Genealogical Society, Waterloo-Wellington Branch, 1991. 12 v. Loc: OKIT.

Transcriptions with indexes and plans of markers in the various sections of the 50-acre cemetery that contains the Roman Catholic Mausoleum and the Protestant Mausoleum as well as the main administrative office for the City of Kitchener Cemeteries. A special section is for German War Graves of Canadian prisoners of war. The earliest interment was in 1926. Period: 1926 - 1991.

429. Hulford, Sheila. "Waterloo County marriages, 1866." **Families**. 1972. 11,2: 39-54. Loc: OKIT, OWTL, OWTU.

A list of marriages from 1863 to 1869 in two parts, the first by bridegroom's name, the second by bride's name, with details of their ages, places of birth and the names of their parents. The author notes that the original register, at the Public Archives of Ontario, contains more information. Period: 1863 - 1869.

430. Kauk, Patricia J. and Kubisch, Michael. **Genealogical information in the Bibles of the Waterloo Historical Society.** Kitchener Public Library, 1990. 1 v. Loc: OKIT.

Translations from the German, arranged alphabetically by family name and providing information on births, deaths and marriages. Period: 1726 - 1965.

431. **Kingwood Reformed Mennonite Cemetery (CC#4535): West Concession III, Lot 3, Wellesley Township, Waterloo County, Ontario.** Kitchener: Ontario Genealogical Society, Waterloo-Wellington Branch, 1989. 12 p. Loc: OKIT, OWRE.

Transcriptions with index of some 120 stones in the small cemetery located just west of the crossroads hamlet formerly known as Goosetown. The cemetery served the Reformed Mennonites connected with a North Easthope church to the west as well as the community at large. Period: 1860 - 1988.

432. **Kitchener Mount Hope Cemetery walking tours.** Kitchener: City of Kitchener Parks and Recreation Department, 1980. 9 p. ill. Loc: OKIT.

A guide to three suggested walking tours,

following a brief historical sketch of the cemetery administered by the City of Kitchener since 1958. The earliest markers date from 1812. Berlin bought two acres from John Hoffman in 1868 and a further 10 acres in 1871 for what was originally called Greenbush Cemetery, renamed Mount Hope in 1872. At this time, remains from church burial grounds in central Berlin were re-interred at Mount Hope. The guide notes the graves and monuments of prominent people in the history of Berlin/Kitchener. Period: 1812 - 1980.

433. Kohli, Marjorie and Madill, Dona and Wall, Donna and Huber, Norma. **Detweiler Mennonite Cemetery (CC#4493): Roseville: Concession 11, Lot 37, North Dumfries Township**. Kitchener: Ontario Genealogical Society, Waterloo-Wellington Branch, 1990. 28 p. Loc: OKIT.

Transcriptions of some 320 stones, by row and lot, followed by an index. The introduction notes that the Detweiler Mennonite Church dates from 1822 with the arrival of Jacob Detweiler who became the first minister. One acre of ground was registered in 1842 for the sole use of the church and cemetery. The congregation disbanded in 1966. Period: 1822 - 1966.

434. Kohli, Marjorie. **Hawkesville Cemetery (CC#4529): Concession 12, Lot 1, Wellesley Township, Waterloo County**. Kitchener: Ontario Genealogical Society, Waterloo-Wellington Branch, 1986. 1 v. (unpaged). Loc: OKIT, OWRE.

Transcriptions, with index, of at least 500 stones. The 3-page introduction by Grace Ogram summarizes the founding and history of Hawkesville, noting that the cemetery dates from the 1840s and that the early records were destroyed in a fire at the Hawkesville store. Period: 1848 - 1985.

435. Kohli, Marjorie and Huber, Norma. **Sandhills Baptist Cemetery (CC#4598): German Company Tract Lot 63, Woolwich Township**. Kitchener: Ontario Genealogical Society, Waterloo-Wellington Branch, 1991. 5 p. Loc: OKIT.

Transcriptions with index of some 57 markers in the German Baptist churchyard also known as North Woolwich Baptist Church. No other records survive of the church or cemetery. Period: 1860 - 1900.

436. Lamb, Kathryn Hansuld. "The puzzle tombstone and Rushes Cemetery." **Waterloo Historical Society**. 1982. 70: 114-119. ill. Loc: all.

An account of the cryptic tombstone which marks the graves of the two wives of Dr Samuel Bean in the Rushes Cemetery, Wellesley Township. Replicas were placed beside the original weathered markers in a ceremony on 17 October 1982 for Henrietta and Susanna Bean. The author also gives a short history of the cemetery itself. Period: 1848 - 1982.

437. Lambert, Ronald and Kohli, Marjorie and Taylor, Ryan. **Linwood Mennonite Cemetery (CC#4544), West Concession 10, Lot 12, Wellesley Township, Waterloo County**. Kitchener: Ontario Genealogical Society, Waterloo-Wellington Branch, 1986. 2 p. Loc: OKIT.

Transcriptions of 21 markers in a recently opened cemetery beside the yellow brick Mennonite meeting house just east of Linwood. In almost all cases, the family name is Martin. Period: 1965 - 1985.

438. Lambert, Ronald and Kohli, Marjorie and Schmidt, William A. and Taylor, Ryan. **Martin's Mennonite Cemetery (CC#4533): East Concession 12, Lot 7, Wellesley Township, Waterloo County**. Kitchener: Ontario Genealogical Society, Waterloo-Wellington Branch, 1986. 2 p. Loc: OKIT.

Transcriptions with index of 29 stones in a small cemetery adjoining a traditional Mennonite meeting house on the Linwood road. More than half the stones have the family name Martin; other names include Hoover, Bauman/Bowman and Sherk. Period: 1945 - 1985.

439. Madill, Dona and Richards, Sharon and Huber, Norma and Wall, Donna. **First Saint Paul's Lutheran Cemetery, Wellesley (CC#4540): East Concession I, Lot 13, Wellesley Village, Wellesley Township, Waterloo County**. Kitchener: Ontario Genealogical Society, Waterloo-Wellington Branch, 1992. 26 p. index. Loc: OKIT.

Transcriptions with index of nearly 300 markers in the cemetery associated with the church originally established in 1854. An introduction provides additional historical information about Lutheran churches in the area. Period: 1854 - 1990.

440. Madill, Dona. **Hagey Mennonite Cemetery (CC#5431): Beasley's Broken Front Concession, Waterloo Township**. Kitchener: Ontario Genealogical Society, Waterloo-Wellington Branch, 1988. 1 v. (various pagings). Loc: OKIT.

Transcriptions, with plan and index, of some 450 stones. The cemetery dates from 1824 and is now located on Fountain Street North, across from the Preston Cemetery and beside Park Lawn Cemetery. The introduction contains a transcription of the plaque placed at the site in 1970 by the Preston Mennonite Church and the Waterloo Historical Society to mark the original brick church of 1842. Period: 1824 - 1987.

441. Madill, Dona. **Methodist baptisms: Preston Circuit (St Paul's United Church) 1907-1915**. 1987. 13 p. Loc: OKIT.

    Alphabetical and chronological lists of persons baptized between 1907 and 1915 at the German Methodist Church which became St Paul's United Church in 1933. Period: 1907 - 1915.

442. Madill, Dona. **Methodist burials: Preston Circuit (St Paul's United Church), 1908-1929**. 1987. 13 p. Loc: OKIT.

    Alphabetical and chronological lists of persons buried between 1908 to 1929, from the German Methodist Church which became St Paul's United Church in 1933. Period: 1908 - 1929.

443. Madill, Dona. **Methodist marriages: Preston Circuit, part 1: 1897-1912; 1923-1927; part 2: 1912-1923**. 1986. 2 v. Loc: OKIT, OWRE.

    An index and chronological list of marriages performed at the church. Each part is prefaced by a brief historical outline of the church condensed from the booklet, **History of St Paul's United Church 1868-1968** by Mrs Arthur Hipel. Period: 1897 - 1927.

444. Madill, Dona and Barnes, Thelma and Barnes, Bill and Wall, Donna and Madill, Karen and Richards, Sharon and Brown, Sheila. **New Hope Cemetery, Hespeler (CC#4498): 235 Cooper Street, Cambridge, formerly Waterloo Township, Waterloo County, Ontario**. Kitchener: Ontario Genealogical Society, Waterloo-Wellington Branch, 1992. 5 v. Loc: OKIT.

    Transcriptions and indexes of the markers with the cemetery plans. Separate areas for a Potters Field and a Sons of England section are designated. Period: 1867 - 1991.

445. Madill, Dona. **Old Preston Cemetery master index (CC#6335)**. Kitchener: Ontario Genealogical Society, Waterloo-Wellington Branch, 1988. 1 v. (various pagings). Loc: OKIT.

    An index to all transcriptions of markers in all sections of the cemetery. The introduction notes that the oldest tombstone dates from 1846 and that the cemetery was still in use and maintained by the Cambridge Cemetery Board in 1988. Period: 1846 - 1987.

446. Madill, Dona. **Old Preston Cemetery Register of Interments (CC#6570)**. Kitchener: Ontario Genealogical Society, Waterloo-Wellington Branch, 1988. 1 v. (various pagings). ill. Loc: OKIT.

    A transcription with index for the years 1859 to 1901, from the original register held in the City of Cambridge Archives. Some 557 interments are indexed by surname, with details of place of residence, cause of death, marital status, remarks, and number of cemetery lot. Period: 1859 - 1901.

447. Madill, Dona and Huber, Norma. **Trinity Lutheran Cemetery (CC#6477), Floradale, German Company Tract, Lot 117, Woolwich Township**. Kitchener: Ontario Genealogical Society, Waterloo-Wellington Branch, 1991. 13 p. Loc: OKIT, OWRE.

    Transcriptions with index of about 320 markers. The introduction explains that the church at Floradale was one of the earliest local congregations of the Missouri Synod in Canada, in existence by 1852. A new church was built in 1880. For much of its history, the church has been linked with St Paul's, Elmira. Period: 1852 - 1989.

448. Madill, Dona. **United Brethren, Congregational and Methodist marriages 1898-1931**. 1986. 9 p. Loc: OKIT, OWRE.

    Alphabetical and chronological lists of marriages performed at the United Brethren in Christ, Hawkesville from January 1898 to September 1906, the Bloomingdale Congregational Church from March 1909 to December 1924, and the Freeport Methodist Circuit (including West Montrose and Bloomingdale) from 1926 to 1931. All records are contained in the book of marriages held at St Paul's United Church, Preston. Period: 1898 - 1931.

449. Madill, Dona. **Wanner Mennonite Cemetery (CC#6479): Concession B, Lot 11, Beasley's Old Survey, Woolwich Township, Waterloo County (formerly Waterloo Township)**. Kitchener: Ontario Genealogical Society, Waterloo-Wellington Branch, 1990. 49 p. Loc: OKIT, OWRE.

    Transcriptions with index of some 950 names. The cemetery, dating from 1814 on Wanner family land, was enlarged in 1880 to serve the larger community. Period: 1814 - 1988.

450. **Mannheim-Latschar Mennonite Cemetery (CC#4560): Concession North of Bleam's Road, Lot pt 4, Wilmot Township**. 197-?. 12 l. Loc: OKIT.

    Transcriptions with plan and index of 275 markers dating from about 1840. There is no introduction. Period: 1841 - 1976.

451. Mansell, Sue. **Burials from the parish register of St John the Evangelist (Church of England) Berlin, now Kitchener, Ontario, 1859-1890**. Kitchener: Ontario Genealogical Society, Waterloo-Wellington Branch, 1985. 7 l. Loc: OKIT.

    A transcription of details of 94 burials, with name of deceased, age at death, trade or profession, place of birth, disease, date of burial, place of interment, and officiating minister. The information was extracted from two registers and the categories of information are different before and after 1878. Period: 1859 - 1890.

452. Mansell, Sue. **Confirmation lists from the parish registers of the Church of St John the Evangelist, Church of England.** Kitchener: Ontario Genealogical Society, Waterloo-Wellington Branch, 1985. 7 l. Loc: OKIT.

Lists of confirmations for the years 1870, 1873, 1875, 1877, 1880, 1882, 1884 and 1888, with dates and names of Bishops of Huron officiating and incumbent clergyman. Period: 1870 - 1888.

453. Mansell, Sue. **Marriages from the parish register of St John the Evangelist, Church of England, Berlin, now Kitchener, Ontario, 1878-1889.** Kitchener: Ontario Genealogical Society, Waterloo-Wellington Branch, 1985. 18 l. Loc: OKIT.

Details extracted from the original register, including date and place of marriage, age, marital status, profession, residence, denomination, with names of the bride and groom, their parents, witnesses and clergy. 1878.

454. McAndless, J.E. "Dickie Cemetery, North Dumfries Township, Waterloo County." **Families.** 1978. 17,3: 105-108, maps. Loc: OKIT, OWTL, OWTU.

A description of a family cemetery, unusual because it was used by both Scots and Pennsylvania Mennonites, including members of the Bechtel, Dickie and Amos families. Period: 1828 - 1878.

455. **Minute and account book of the burying ground known as Rushes Cemetery, September 25, 1874-.** 197-?. 1 v. (unpaged). Loc: OKIT.

A photocopy of pages relating to the years from 1878 to 1971. According to the records, the earliest burial occurred in 1848. Period: 1848 - 1971.

456. Mitton, Judith A. **Rushes Presbyterian Cemetery (CC#4536): Wellesley Township, East Concession IV Lot 13, with index to minute and account book, 1878-1921.** Kitchener: Ontario Genealogical Society, Waterloo-Wellington Branch, 1987. 1 v. (various pagings). Loc: OKIT.

Transcriptions with index of some 270 markers that date from as early as 1848. The report includes an index to the minute book of Rushes Cemetery, and a facsimile and decoded inscription of the "puzzle stone," Dr Samuel Bean's memorial to his first two wives. Period: 1848 - 1986.

457. Mitton, Judith A. **Wilmot Centre Brenneman Cemetery (CC#4574): South Bleams Road, Lot 13, Wilmot Township.** Kitchener: Ontario Genealogical

Society, Waterloo-Wellington Branch, 1986. 22 p. Loc: OKIT.

Transcriptions with index of some 225 markers in the community burial ground that is locally called "the Section Ten Cemetery." The oldest graves are at the east end, near the school. Period: 1850 - 1986.

458. Moore, George P., Mrs. "Cedar Creek and Dickie Cemeteries." **Waterloo Historical Society.** 1950. 38: 28-30. Loc: all.

An account of two cemeteries in North Dumfries Township, with references to well-known area surnames found on the tombstones, such as Kersell, Cranston, Veitch, Brown, Lee, Wilson, Dalgleish, Johnston, Henderson, Vair, Moore, Dickie, Gehman, Bechtel and Amos. Period: 1834 - 1950.

459. Ogram, Elmer. **Records of Linwood Union Cemetery.** Elmira: Dreisinger Funeral Home, Elmira, 195-?. 16 p. Loc: OKIT.

Photocopy of two indexes of burials, by location and by year of death. The first list includes details of names (including maiden names of married women), dates of birth and death, age at death and precise location. The index relates to the period between 1860 and 1953. Period: 1860 - 1953.

460. Panabaker, D.N. "Historical notes, 1936." **Waterloo Historical Society.** 1936. 24: 234-235. Loc: all.

A note of the removal of graves in the second Preston Roman Catholic cemetery to an area near the Speedsville Road, because of the widening of the highway between Galt and Preston. Period: 1857 - 1936.

461. Peterson, Henry William. "A sample page from the Berlin Lutheran Church records [WRP]." **Waterloo Historical Society.** 1929. 17: 138-139. Loc: all.

A page from the records of births, baptisms, marriages and deaths, kept by Henry William Peterson from 1833 to 1835. Period: 1833 - 1835.

462. Putnam, Robert T. **Erb Street Mennonite Church Cemetery (CC#4512), Waterloo.** Kitchener: Ontario Genealogical Society, Waterloo-Wellington Branch, 1991. 23 p. Loc: OKIT.

Transcriptions with index of some 260 stones in the cemetery located at the corner of Erb Street and Fischer-Hallman Road, in what is now the City of Waterloo. The introduction notes that land for the original church on this site was given by David Eby senior in 1851 and was thus later known as the David Eby Church. In 1902, the church was replaced by a new building closer to the town, but the cemetery continued in use. Period: 1851 -

1989.

463. Putnam, Robert T. **Saint Clement's Roman Catholic Cemetery (CC#4534): St Clements Village, East Concession VIII, Lot 2, Wellesley Township, Waterloo County.** Kitchener: Ontario Genealogical Society, Waterloo-Wellington Branch, 1992. 56 p. index. Loc: OKIT.

Transcriptions with index of nearly 500 markers in the cemetery that has been associated with St Clement's Catholic Church since 1840. The introduction notes that the cemetery was moved in 1885 and expanded in 1973. Period: 1840 - 1990.

464. Putnam, Robert T. **Saint James Lutheran Cemetery (CC#4590): St Jacobs, German Company Tract Lot 8, Woolwich Township.** Kitchener: Ontario Genealogical Society, Waterloo-Wellington Branch, 1991. 21 p. ill., map. Loc: OKIT, OWRE.

Transcriptions of about 190 stones, with an index and plan. The introduction notes that the church was founded in 1866 as an offshoot of the church of the same name in Elmira, and has long been linked to the church at Conestogo. Period: 1866 - 1990.

465. Putnam, Robert T. **Saint Peter's Lutheran Cemetery, Heidelberg (CC#4593): German Company Tract Lot 13, Woolwich Township, Waterloo County.** Kitchener: Ontario Genealogical Society, Waterloo-Wellington Branch, 1992. 41 p. index. Loc: OKIT.

Transcriptions with index of about 450 markers in the cemetery located a little east of Heidelberg. The introduction notes that the cemetery adjoined the original log church erected in 1851 and the present brick church was built at a new location in 1870. Period: 1851 - 1990.

466. Putnam, Robert T. **Shantz Mennonite Church Cemetery (CC #4566): Lot 12, South Erb's Road, Wilmot Township.** Kitchener: Ontario Genealogical Society, Waterloo-Wellington Branch, 1991. 16 p. ill., map. Loc: OKIT.

Transcriptions with plan and index of some 175 markers. The introduction notes that the land was originally part of the farm of George Schmidt, with a schoolhouse in which the first church meetings were held. The church was formerly known as the Upper Street Church, as Erbs Road was originally called the Oberstrasse. In 1853, David Y. and Barbara Shantz conveyed land for the stone church and cemetery. A new church in red brick was erected in 1929. Period: 1853 - 1989.

467. Putnam, Robert T. **St John's Lutheran Cemetery, Bamberg (CC#4537): Concession VI, Lot 6, Eastern Section, Wellesley Township, Waterloo County, Ontario.** Kitchener: Ontario Genealogical Society, Waterloo-Wellington Branch, 1990. 12 p. map. Loc: OKIT, OWRE.

Transcriptions with index and plan of about 130 markers. The introduction notes the association with St John's Lutheran Church (Canada Synod), founded in 1852 with the present stone church built in 1872. When the local population declined, the church was joined with St Peter's Lutheran Church in Linwood from 1907. A campaign to save the church building in 1973 succeeded. Period: 1872 - 1973.

468. Putnam, Robert T. **St Matthew's Evangelical Lutheran Cemetery (CC#4592): Conestogo, German Company Tract Lot 31, Woolwich Township.** Kitchener: Ontario Genealogical Society, Waterloo-Wellington Branch, 1989. 1 v. (various pagings). maps. Loc: OKIT, OWRE.

Transcriptions with index and plan of nearly 400 markers. The introduction notes that the first congregation was formed by F.W. Bindemann and the first church built in 1853. A new church was dedicated in 1892. Period: 1853 - 1986.

469. Putnam, Robert T. **St Paul's Lutheran Cemetery, Erbsville (CC#4539): Concession A, Lot 5, Eastern Section, Wellesley Township.** Kitchener: Ontario Genealogical Society, Waterloo-Wellington Branch, 1990. 22 p. map. Loc: OKIT, OWRE.

Transcriptions with plan and index of some 160 markers. The introduction notes that the church and cemetery are located on the Wellesley-Waterloo line, and not particularly near Erbsville. The original log church of 1852 was replaced in 1877 by the present yellow brick structure with white frame steeple on a new site. Period: 1852 - 1990.

470. Putnam, Robert T. **Zion Evangelical Lutheran Cemetery (CC#6478): Philipsburg, south side of Erb's Road, Lot 19, Wilmot Township at Regional Road #5.** Kitchener: Ontario Genealogical Society, Waterloo-Wellington Branch, 1990. 37 p. Loc: OKIT.

Transcriptions with index of some 400 markers. Period: 1845 - 1988.

471. **Register of interments in the Preston Public Cemetery.** 38 p. Loc: OKIT.

Photocopy of the register from 1858 to 1901, with details of some 575 burials, including date of burial, name, age at death, place of birth and place of death, cause of death, marital status, and lot and block number of grave within the cemetery. A copy of an undated letter from Otto Klotz (for the Cemetery Committee) to the Preston Council is appended. Period: 1858 - 1901.

472. Reist, Agnes. **Baird Family Cemetery (CC#6283):
Block A, Concession 4, Lot 27, Wilmot Township.**
1985. 1 l. Loc: OKIT.

Transcription of the details of seven burials
recorded on the monument, dating from 1848 to
1929. The author notes that the small plot is
located on Prospect Farm, a Baird family farm
since 1841. The Bairds are recorded as migrating
from Kirkintillock, Campsie and Dalkeith in
Scotland. Period: 1848 - 1929.

473. Robertson, E.A. and Schmidt, William A. and Ogram,
Grace. **Early Presbyterian Cemetery (CC#6275):
German Company Tract Lot 86, Woolwich Township.**
Kitchener: Ontario Genealogical Society,
Waterloo-Wellington Branch, 1985. 4 p. ill. Loc:
OKIT, OWRE.

Transcriptions with index of 18 stones from
between 1833 and 1875. The cemetery is described
as located on the corner where Highway 86 turns
west towards Listowel. Period: 1833 - 1875.

474. Roth, Lorraine. **Maple View Amish Mennonite
Cemetery (CC#4532): Wellesley Township, West
Concession II, Lot 11.** Mennonite Historical
Society of Ontario - Genealogical Committee, 1987.
1 v. (unpaged). Loc: OKIT.

Transcriptions of some 336 stones, with index
and plan. The introduction notes that a corner of
the lot was first used by the McKee family as a
burial ground. Half an acre was deeded in 1870 by
Leonard Streicher to the trustees of the "Amisch
Menonist Congregation", Christian S. Erb, Joseph
B. Lichti and John B. Schwartzentruber. A meeting
house was erected in 1886 and replaced in 1928.
The oldest marked grave is dated 1887. Period:
1887 - 1987.

475. Roth, Lorraine and Hammer, Ruby. **Old Baden
Mennonite Burying Ground (CC#4563): Lot 13 North
Snyder's Road Wilmot Township.** Kitchener: Ontario
Genealogical Society, Waterloo-Wellington Branch,
1986. 2 p. Loc: OKIT.

Transcriptions of 12 markers, with index, for
the Genealogical Committee of the Mennonite
Historical Society of Ontario. The introduction
notes that the ground was conveyed to Nicholaus
Klein and Peter Spehnler by the trustees of School
Section 13 in 1866. Some markers date from the
early 1840s. Period: 1840 - 1887.

476. Roth, Lorraine. **Saint Agatha Amish Mennonite
Cemetery (CC#4568), Waterloo County.** Mennonite
Historical Society of Ontario - Genealogical
Committee, 1984. 1 v. (unpaged). Loc: OKIT.

Transcriptions of 192 markers, preceded by a
plan and index. The introduction notes that the
land for a school house and burying ground was
conveyed by Nicholas Lichti in 1845 but that a log
school house already existed and some burials had
already taken place. The log schools here and at
the site of the Lutheran Church at the other side
of St Agatha were removed in 1865 and replaced by
a stone building at the eastern end of the
village. The Wilmot Amish Mennonite Congregation
built its second meeting house at the Lichti
burial ground. The meeting house and cemetery
were thereafter referred to as "Lichti'", "Upper
Street" or "St Agatha". The conference dropped
the term "Amish" from its name in 1964. Period:
1834 - 1984.

477. Saint Boniface-Maryhill Historical Society. **Index
to the Official family register of the belonging
souls of the community of New Germany with
statement of their names and ages: a census of the
Roman Catholic families of Maryhill, written down
in month of February 1866 through Father Francis
Breitkopf, priest.** Maryhill: The Society, 1985.
30 l. Loc: OKIT.

Index to a manuscript register originally
compiled in February 1866. In all, 195 family
names are indexed, with forenames of all persons
recorded; 77 family names, each with at least 8
members recorded in the register, have been
indexed in the WRP database. Period: 1865 - 1866.

478. Saunders, Shelley R. and Lazenby, Richard. **The
links that bind: the Harvie Family
nineteenth-century burying ground.** Occasional
Papers in Northeastern Archaeology. Copetown
Press, 1991. Loc: OWRMA.

An account of the results of an excavation of a
pioneer family cemetery, with reflections on the
ability to trace genealogy through archaeology and
osteology. Period: 1816 - 1900.

479. Saunders, Shelley R. "Skeletal biology in Waterloo
Region." **Waterloo Historical Society.** 1990. 78:
126-138. ill. Loc: all.

Report of an archaeological excavation of the
Harvie Cemetery in North Dumfries Township in
1988. In addition to identifying the skeletal
remains of 15 individuals, the investigators
analyzed their characteristics in relation to
published data on skeletal samples in other places
and periods. This analysis provides clues to the
health, work, lifestyles, and material culture of
pioneer settlers. Period: 1825 - 1894.

480. **St James Lutheran Cemetery, Mannheim (CC#4572):
Wilmot Township, Concession North of Bleam's Road,
Pt Lot 1.** 197-?. 8 l. Loc: OKIT.

Transcriptions with plan and index of 139
markers which date from between 1840 and 1978.
Period: 1840 - 1978.

481. Steinmann, Reuben and Roth, Lorraine. **Steinmann Amish Mennonite Cemetery (CC#4570): Wilmot Township, Waterloo County, Lot 18, South Snyder's Road**. Mennonite Historical Society of Ontario, Genealogical Committee, 1987. 1 v. (unpaged). Loc: OKIT.

Transcriptions of 340 markers preceded by a history and guide to the cemetery, a plan of the cemetery and an index. The introduction explains that the cemetery's origins are obscure but that it probably began as a family plot which later served the community. A land deed makes reference to the burial ground in 1860, but the earliest extant Amish marker is dated 1895. Period: 1860 - 1986.

482. Strickler, Diane. "St Boniface Cemetery, Maryhill." **Waterloo Historical Society**. 1991. 79: 117-119. ill. Loc: all.

An historical sketch and description of the second oldest Roman Catholic cemetery in the region, originally established in 1834 but dating from 1851 in its present location. Period: 1834 - 1990.

483. Taylor, Ryan and Brown-Kubisch, Linda. **Church register of H.W. Peterson, 1833-1835**. Kitchener: Kitchener Public Library, 1991. 17 p. Loc: OKIT.

Transcribed and indexed extracts from the record book kept in Berlin in the early 1830s. Details are provided of about 125 births, baptisms, confirmations and burials conducted by visiting clergymen and by Peterson himself. Period: 1833 - 1835.

484. Taylor, Ryan. **Index to births, deaths and marriages published in the Hamburger Beobachter, 1855-1856, transcribed from the originals in the Kitchener Public Library and translated**. Kitchener: Ontario Genealogical Society, Waterloo-Wellington Branch, 1985. 3 p. Loc: OKIT.

A chronological index prefaced by a brief history and description of the contents of the newspaper. The compiler observes that few notices of family events were placed in this weekly paper. Period: 1855 - 1856.

485. Taylor, Ryan. **An index to the journals of Joseph B. Weber**. Kitchener Public Library, 1990. 1 v. (various pagings). Loc: OKIT.

Alphabetized lists of births, deaths and marriages recorded in the personal journals of Joseph B. Weber. Though the journals run from January 1876 through December 1882, the lists of family events extend from December 1858 to August 1900. For births, the lists include only name, sex and date, with occasional remarks. For marriages, the place and date as well as names of both spouses are recorded. For deaths, the name, date, place, age at death and (frequently) the cause of death are stated. Period: 1858 - 1900.

486. Taylor, Ryan. **Old Christner Cemetery (CC#4548): North Schneider's Road, Lot 23 Wilmot Township**. Kitchener: Ontario Genealogical Society, Waterloo-Wellington Branch, 1987. 3 p. Loc: OKIT.

Transcriptions with index of 23 markers in the long unused cemetery located one mile north of New Hamburg, near the border with Perth County. The introduction notes that the cemetery was used by members of the Christner, Kuntze and Hostetler families and maintained by the Christner family who lived in the stone house across the road. Period: 1841 - 1919.

487. Taylor, Ryan. **Waterloo County naturalisations from the Upper Canada Sessional Records for 1841: extracted from the original document**. 1991. 6 l. tables. Loc: OKIT.

A listing of nearly 200 names of Waterloo County area individuals naturalized between 1829 and 1832. Given in alphabetical order, the entries include details of township of residence, occupation, date of naturalization, and access points in the original Sessional Papers of 1841. Period: 1829 - 1832.

488. Turnbull, Marjorie and Huber, Norma. **Harvie Cemetery (CC#4492): Concession 8, Lot 2, North Dumfries Township**. 1984. 3 p. Loc: OKIT.

Transcriptions with index of 15 markers in the small burial ground on the old Harvie homestead. The introduction notes that the stones were moved to Doon Heritage Crossroads in the early 1980s. Many inscriptions are reported illegible, but those which can be read date from between 1828 and 1894. Period: 1828 - 1894.

489. **A walking tour of Kitchener's Mount Hope Cemetery**. Kitchener: Kitchener Department of Park Management, 1984. 1 v. (unpaged). ill., plans. Loc: OKIT.

A brief historical outline and guide to three suggested tours, with notes on 38 notable community leaders buried in the cemetery. A slightly revised version of the guide was published in 1980. Period: 1812 - 1980.

490. Wall, Donna. **Strasburg Lutheran Cemetery (CC#6480): Waterloo Township**. Kitchener: Ontario Genealogical Society, Waterloo-Wellington Branch, 1990. 3 p. Loc: OKIT, OWES.

Transcriptions of 13 markers with an index. The introduction notes that the first log church was built in 1847-8 and the cemetery was officially established in 1850, though some burials occurred earlier. In 1893, the Strasburg congregation decided to join the St James Lutheran Church in Mannheim. The site was marked as an historic site by the Kitchener LACAC and restored by the City of Kitchener as part of the development of the Huron Business Park. Period: 1845 - 1910.

491. Wall, Donna and Madill, Dona. **Weber Mennonite Cemetery (CC#5426): Biehn Drive, Kitchener.** Kitchener: Ontario Genealogical Society, Waterloo-Wellington Branch, 1990. 15 p. Loc: OKIT.

    Transcriptions with index of some 170 markers in the cemetery that dates from about 1850. Period: 1850 - 1988.

492. Wall, Donna and Madill, Dona and Richards, Sharon and Huber, Norma. **Wellesley and Wilmot Amish Mennonite Cemeteries (CC#4551 and CC#6076): Waterloo County.** Kitchener: Ontario Genealogical Society, Waterloo-Wellington Branch, 1992. 5 p. index. Loc: OKIT.

    Transcriptions with indexes of 19 markers in the Wilmot cemetery and 75 markers in the Wellesley cemetery. The introduction explains that Michael Zehr sold land for the Wilmot cemetery in 1873 to the trustees of the Amish Mennonite Society, and that the Wellesley Amish Cemetery dates from 1929 on land purchased from Nelson McFadden. Period: 1873 - 1990.

493. Weber, Eldon D. **Assessment/Collector's roll 1859, Waterloo Township.** Kitchener: Ontario Genealogical Society, Waterloo-Wellington Branch, 1976. 16 p. maps. Loc: OKIT.

    A roughly alphabetical index to all persons recorded in the Collectors' Rolls. Details are given of the name, occupation, and concession and lot number of each assessed property-owner. Joel Clemens recorded 338 persons in Ward 1, an unnamed Collector recorded 252 persons in Ward 2, Daniel Wismer recorded 220 persons in Ward 3, Adam Rudy recorded 209 in Ward 4, and Abraham Z. Detwiler recorded 254 persons in Ward 5. Period: 1858 - 1859.

494. Weber, Eldon D. **Freeport Pioneer Cemetery (CC#5432): Riverbank Drive, Broken Front Lot 14, Waterloo Township.** Kitchener: Ontario Genealogical Society, Waterloo-Wellington Branch, 1974. 5 l. map. Loc: OKIT.

    Transcriptions with index of about 100 markers in the half-acre burial ground which dates from 1818. Period: 1818 - 1950.

495. Weber, Eldon D. **Waterloo County births as recorded in 1872 and 1873.** Kitchener: Ontario Genealogical Society, Waterloo-Wellington Branch,

1974. 1 v. (unpaged). Loc: OKIT, OWT.

    Transcriptions of all births by townships and villages, with details of date, name of child, names of father and mother, father's occupation, place of residence and accoucheur (doctor or midwife). Names of the registrars of each division are given. The numbers of births in each place were reported to be: Woolwich 94, Galt 118, Berlin 67, Wellesley 158, North Dumfries 54, Wilmot 294, Waterloo Village 23, and Waterloo Township 99. Period: 1872 - 1873.

496. Weber, Eldon D. **Waterloo County deaths as recorded in 1870, 1871 and 1872.** Kitchener: Ontario Genealogical Society, Waterloo-Wellington Branch, 1973. Loc: OKIT, OWT.

    Lists of 304 deaths in 1870, 363 in 1871 and 426 in 1872, transcribed from records in the "Waterloo County Archives". In each case details are provided of name, date of birth, age at death, occupation (of father if a child), place of birth, cause of death, name of informant, and religion (of parent if a child). Names of the registrars for each municipality and of all medical practitioners are given. A consolidated index of all names, apparently produced later with computer assistance, has been added to the report. Period: 1870 - 1872.

497. Weber, Joseph B. **Births, deaths and marriages recorded in the personal journals of Joseph B. Weber.** 1989. 1 v. (unpaged). Loc: OKIT.

    Photocopies of the originals in the collection of Robert Weber in California. Details of family events span the period from 1858 to 1900 and have been indexed by Ryan Taylor. Period: 1858 - 1900.

498. Weicker, Samuel. **Church records of Strasburg Evangelical Lutheran Church, 1844-1893, Waterloo Township, Ontario.** Kitchener: Ontario Genealogical Society, Waterloo-Wellington Branch, 1985. 7 p. Loc: OKIT, OWES.

    Information about baptisms, confirmations, funerals, communicants and pastors during the autonomous life of this congregation from 1844 to 1893. In 1893 the church was joined with St James Lutheran Church in Mannheim. Period: 1844 - 1893.

499. Weicker, Samuel. **Trinity Lutheran Church, Shantz Station Cemetery (CC#4595): German Company Tract Lot 85, Waterloo Township (now Woolwich).** Kitchener: Ontario Genealogical Society, Waterloo-Wellington Branch, 1982. 10 p. map. Loc: OKIT.

    Alphabetical index to about 520 burials since 1862. The author notes that Trinity Lutheran Church was organized in 1860 by the Rev. Immanuel Wurster and that the cemetery was dedicated in

1863. The index notes location of the stones by row and lot and those with German inscriptions are indicated. Period: 1860 - 1982.

500. Witmer, Leslie D. and Hagey, Simon. **Hagey's Cemetery record, 1935.** 1935. 73 p. Loc: OKIT.

Photocopy of a manuscript record noting dates, names of deceased persons with grave numbers and payments received for grave space or perpetual care. A detailed plan of the cemetery is appended. Period: 1831 - 1965.

501. Zimmerman, Idessa. **Transcription from tombstones in the original part of the Free Church Cemetery, Kitchener (Bridgeport).** The Author, 1983. 1 v. (unpaged) Loc: OKIT.

Typed with handwritten additions, in an unexplained order.

ETHNICITY, INCLUDING LANGUAGE, DISTINCTIVE SOCIAL AND CULTURAL FEATURES

502. Brewster, Winfield. **The floodgate: random writings of our ain folk.** Hespeler: T and T Press, 1952. 44 p. facsim. Also mf. Loc: OCCA, OCLG, OKIT, OWTUR.

A collection of anecdotes about the Doon, Hespeler and Galt areas. The author relates personal encounters with artist Homer Watson and describes people from different ethnic and cultural backgrounds including the Mennonites, English, Irish and Scottish. The cover of the work has a print of Watson's painting **The floodgate**. The book has been indexed by Paul Pepper and another index is available at the Cambridge Library and Gallery and the City of Cambridge Archives. Period: c1800 - 1952.

503. "British outnumber Germans in Waterloo County." **Waterloo Historical Society.** 1964. 52: 60. Loc: all.

A report of a finding by the federal immigration office that 38 per cent of the county's population were of British ancestry and 37.3 per cent of German. Period: 1964.

504. Campbell, Elsie and Staal, Helen and Wideman, Herb. **Ethnic communities in Kitchener Waterloo Region.** Kitchener: Kitchener Waterloo Regional Folk Arts Multicultural Centre, 1979. 49 p. ill., bibl. Loc: OCCA, OCLG, OKIT, OWRN, OWT.

A brief survey of the history of the Portuguese, Polish and Greeks, describing family life, social institutions and ethnic organizations. Information is provided about the Kitchener Waterloo Regional Folk Arts Multicultural Centre, established in 1970, and its member groups. Period: 1895 - 1979.

505. Cowan, Jennie F. "Principal immigration groups of Waterloo County: from a display card in the History Tent at the International Plowing Match, 1954." **Waterloo Historical Society.** 1954. 42: 26-27. Loc: all.

Information about the main ethnic groups of Waterloo County (Mennonites, Scots, Germans, English, Native Canadians and Russian Mennonites), arranged chronologically and telling where they settled. Period: 1800 - 1945.

506. Lea, Joanne and Geddy, Hilary. **My mother tongue.** Kitchener: Doon Heritage Crossroads, Historic Sites Department, Regional Municipality of Waterloo, 1987. 1 v. Loc: OKDHC.

Materials for teachers on the four settler groups of the Waterloo area, the Mohawks, the Pennsylvania-Germans, the Germans and the Scots. Printed material, slides and audio cassettes are provided on four different levels from primary to senior, and contain information on the language and heritage of each ethnic group. The kit was also published in French as **Ma langue d'heritage**. Period: 1840 - 1850.

507. McLaughlin, Kenneth. "Waterloo County: a Pennsylvania-German homeland." **From Pennsylvania to Waterloo: Pennsylvania-German folk culture in transition.** Edited by Susan M. Burke and Matthew H. Hill. Kitchener: Friends of the Joseph Schneider Haus, 1991. Pp. 35-45. ill., maps. Loc: OKIT.

An outline of the settlement of Mennonite and Amish pioneers between 1800 and 1835 and the subsequent arrival of German-speaking migrants from Europe. The author compares the main groups of settlers in their occupations, values and culture, and notes the development of strong German nationalism among some Waterloo County Germans from the late nineteenth century. Illustrations include a facsimile and redrawing of what is believed to be the first map of Waterloo Township in 1818. Period: 1800 - 1900.

508. Nicholson, Chris, Jr. **A geographic study of the ethnic composition of Waterloo County.** University of Waterloo (B.E.S. thesis, Geography), 1964. 2 fiche. charts, maps, tables, bibl. mf. Loc: OWTUM.

An examination of ethnic change and diversification, based on analysis of census reports over 90 years, for the nine incorporated communities of Ayr, Berlin (Kitchener), Bridgeport, Elmira, Galt, Hespeler, New Hamburg, Preston and Waterloo. Period: 1871 - 1961.

509. Pepper, Paul E. **Index to The floodgate: random writings of our ain folk.** 1987. 4 p. Loc: OKIT.
An index of about 220 names mentioned in Brewster's book. Period: 1800 - 1952.

MENNONITES & AMISH OF WATERLOO COUNTY

510. Ahrens, Carl. "An Amish wooing." **Tarot: an illustrated monthly magazine.** 1896. 1,2: 12-13. Loc: OWTUCG.
An anecdotal and humorous account by the noted Waterloo County painter. Period: 1896.

511. Bausenhart, Werner A. **The terminology of agronomy of the Pennsylvania German dialect of Waterloo County, Ontario.** University of Waterloo (M.A. thesis, Linguistics), 1966. 135 p. table, bibl. Also mf. Loc: OWTL, OWTU.
A glossary of agricultural terms, based on interviews with 47 local Pennsylvania German Mennonites in 1965. Each farm task or object is described in English and the equivalent Pennsylvania German and standard German word are given. If possible, a comparison with other Pennsylvania German or Continental German dialect forms is made in an attempt to trace the origin of each term. The terms or phrases included in the study relate to farm buildings, tillage, meadows and pastures, haying, grain crops, cultivated crops, land forms, soil and fences. Period: 1965 - 1966.

512. Bausenhart, Werner A. "The Waterloo Pennsylvania German dialect community." **The Waterloo County area: selected geographical essays.** Edited by A.G. McLellan. Waterloo: Department of Geography, University of Waterloo, 1971. Pp. 31-40. maps. Loc: OWTU, OWTL, OWTUCG, OKIT.
Report on a project to compile a linguistic atlas of the dialect in Waterloo County. The information was based on a survey of 164 farm families. The author comments on the importance of church, separate schools and a conservative way of life in protecting usage of the dialect. Period: 1800 - 1970.

513. Bender, Anthony. **Study of rural and urban Mennonites in Waterloo County and their participation in traditional and non-traditional leisure activities.** University of Waterloo (student essay, Recreation), 1978. 1 fiche. mf. Loc: OWTU.
An analysis of responses to a questionnaire developed under the direction of J. Winfield Fretz and sent to 21 Mennonite churches in the county. The author finds little difference in the level of participation in traditional leisure activities between rural and urban Mennonites, but that urban Mennonites participated more in the non-traditional activities as well. Period: 1977 - 1978.

514. Bender, Harold S. "New source material for the history of Mennonites in Ontario." **Mennonite Quarterly Review.** 1929. 3,1: 42-53. Loc: OWTU, OWTUCR.
Transcripts and notes of four relevant documents: a list of claims by Waterloo County Mennonites for losses suffered when employed in military transport during the War of 1812; an outline of several journeys from eastern Pennsylvania to Waterloo Township taken by Joseph Bowman in 1817, 1819 and 1845; statistics regarding Mennonite ministers and population in Ontario about 1825; and a form for the oath of allegiance. Period: 1813 - 1845.

515. Bergey, Lorna L. "Changes in cultural symbols for Ontario Mennonite women of the Swiss tradition during the 1950s and 60s: stories we need to hear." **Mennogespräch.** 1990. 8,2: 9-11. ill. Loc: OWTUCG, OKIT.
Personal observations and experiences of the changing role of Mennonite women. A farm accident necessitated the reversal of traditional roles in the Bergey family, leaving the author in charge of the family cheese business at several farmers' markets. She comments on the changing dress of Mennonite women and their entry into business, describing the development of the sewing circles operating the profit-making Kitchener Cutting Room and the organization of the Women's Mission and Service Auxiliary as examples of the pattern of change. Period: 1935 - 1990.

516. Bergey, Lorna L. "Contribution of the Mennonites to the development of Waterloo County." **The Canadian Mennonite.** 1967. 15,24: 51-54. ill. Loc: OWT, OWTU, OWTUCG.
An essay in the special centennial issue about the role of Mennonites in settling Waterloo County and their subsequent contributions as farmers, entrepreneurs, educators, lawyers, clergy and professionals. About fifty Mennonite men and women are mentioned, with their areas of leadership. Period: 1800 - 1967.

517. Bergey, Lorna L. "Early Mennonite migrations from Pennsylvania and subsequent settlements in Canada." **Pennsylvania Mennonite Heritage.** 1986. 9,2: 2-12. ill., maps. Loc: OKIT, OWTUCG.
A useful summary of settlement in what became Waterloo, Woolwich and Wilmot Townships, in the context of Upper Canada generally. The author recounts the dealings with Richard Beasley and

other Loyalist speculators and names early families and community leaders. She discusses reasons for the Mennonite migrations to Canada and notes continuing family ties and travel between Ontario and Pennsylvania. Period: 1800 - 1900.

518. Bergey, Lorna L. and Hunsberger, Albert and Cooper, Russell. **Three Pennsylvania German pioneer homesteads in Ontario: the families and their way of life.** Canadian-German Folklore, v.10. Pennsylvania German Folklore Society of Ontario, 1986. 80 p. ill., maps, indexes. Loc: OKIT, OWT, OWTL, OWTU, OWTUCG.

Illustrated accounts of three Pennsylvania German pioneer homesteads, including the Shantz family homestead in Wilmot Township. Each family is described with its crops, livestock and farm buildings, and there is a general account of folklife and folklore. Period: 1781 - 1955.

519. Biehn, Donald M. "Mennonite settlement: the Bucks County caravan." **Waterloo Historical Society.** 1990. 78: 69-73. map. Loc: all.

An account of the migration of the families of John Biehn and George Bechtel from Bucks County, Pennsylvania in 1800. The author notes that, contrary to most historical sources, these Mennonite pioneers were actually the first to purchase land in what became Waterloo County. Period: 1798 - 1800.

520. Bowman, Alvah S. **Homestead days and early settlement of the Waterloo District, south-west of Guernsey, Sask..** 12 p. ill. Loc: OWTUCGR.

An account of the land development scheme in the Saskatchewan Valley which attracted settlers from Waterloo County Mennonite families in the early years of the 20th century. Members of the committee that reported on the suitability of the area and those who migrated as homesteaders are named. Period: 1903 - 1916.

521. Breithaupt, W.H. "First settlements of Pennsylvania Mennonites in Upper Canada." **Ontario Historical Society, Papers and Records.** 1926. 23: 8-14. Loc: OWTL, OWTU.

An account of the settlements in the Niagara region, Waterloo County and Markham, with brief references to notable Mennonites and their descendants. There are biographical sketches of Benjamin Eby, Isaac E. Baumann and E.W.B. Snider. Period: 1795 - 1925.

522. Bricker, I.C. "The trek of the Pennsylvanians to Canada in the year 1805." **Waterloo Historical Society.** 1934. 22: 123-131. Loc: all.

A detailed description of the route taken by migrants from Pennsylvania to Waterloo County.

The travellers, mostly Mennonite, came from the counties of Lancaster, Cumberland, York, Berks, Franklin, Bucks, and Montgomery via Harrisburg, PA. No personal or family names are given. Period: 1805.

523. Buehler, Allan M. "The Old-Order Mennonite wedding and highlights of their social life." **Explorations in Canadian folklore.** Edited by Edith Fowke and Carole H. Carpenter. Toronto: McClelland and Stewart, 1985. Pp.76-89. Loc: OKIT.

An account of Old Order Mennonite weddings in Waterloo County, with particular reference to the author's marriage in 1922. Customs include the wedding feast, the hiding of the bride's shoes by children and the shivahree. Other social activities, including visiting on Sundays, harvesting and the various "bees" are also described. Period: 1922 - 1977.

524. Buehler, Allan M. **The Pennsylvania German dialect and the autobiography of an Old Order Mennonite.** Cambridge: The Author, 1977. 227 p. ill. Loc: OCCA, OCLG, OCP, OKIT, OWRE, OWRN, OWT, OWTL, OWTU, OWTUCG.

A book combining the Pennsylvania German dialect of the Waterloo area with reminiscences and stories from the author's youth. Written using English phonetics, the dialect is presented for readers who have been taught to read English but who speak the dialect at home or wish to study its pronunciation. There is a lexicon of common Pennsylvania German words with their standard German equivalents and English meanings. Many aspects of Old Order Mennonite life are described, including schooling, working away from home, youth groups, courtship, weddings, church meetings, dress regulations and excommunication. The book also includes Pennsylvania German proverbs, sayings, folk rhymes and poetry. Period: 1899 - 1977.

525. Burke, Susan M. and Hill, Matthew H. **From Pennsylvania to Waterloo: Pennsylvania-German folk culture in transition.** Kitchener: Friends of the Joseph Schneider Haus, 1991. 148 p. ill., maps, index. Loc: OKIT, OWTUR.

Proceedings of the 10th anniversary symposium, **Continuity and change: Pennsylvania-German folk culture in transition,** richly illustrated with photographs of the accompanying exhibit, **Changes in latitudes,** displayed at the Joseph Schneider Haus. The volume includes eleven essays, usually paired for Lancaster County and Waterloo County, and describing the regions or aspects of their folk culture such as folk art, textiles, gardens and foodways. Each essay relating to Waterloo County has been individually abstracted and indexed in the WRP database. Period: 1750 - 1950.

526. Burkholder, Lewis J. "The early Mennonite settlements in Ontario." **Mennonite Quarterly Review.** 1934. 8,3: 103-122. Loc: OWTU, OWTUCG.

A discussion of the reasons for Mennonite immigration to Ontario following the American Revolutionary War, with details about the Waterloo settlement including family names of early settlers, the difficulties of land titles and the creation of an offshoot colony in Zurich, Ontario. Period: 1795 - 1828.

527. Burridge, Kathryn. **Pennsylvania-German dialect: a localized study within a part of Waterloo County, Ontario.** Canadian-German Folklore v.11. Pennsylvania German Folklore Society of Ontario, 1989. 160 p. ill., maps, bibl. Loc: OWTL, OWTUCG, OKIT.

A study of the dialect, in four sections: a pronunciation guide and explanation of the spelling system, lists of vocabulary and expressions, a description of the grammar, and an example of the written language with an English translation. The appendix contains a dictionary in two parts, Pennsylvania-German dialect to English, and English to Pennsylvania-German, prepared by the editor Eldon Weber. Period: 1800.

528. Clow, Cynthia M. **The Schneider House, Kitchener: a study of 19th century Berlin and Mennonite daily life in 19th century Ontario.** Toronto: Museums Section, Heritage Administration Branch, Ontario Ministry of Culture and Recreation, 1977. 122 l. ill., bibl. Loc: OKIT, OWTUCG.

A report that includes copies of advertisements from local newspapers and directories such as **Smith's Canadian gazetteer** and the **County of Waterloo gazetteer and general business directory for 1864** and early maps of Berlin. Details of the Schneider family of Lot 17, German Company Tract were gathered from assessment rolls, census records, land records, diary entries, church records, wills, correspondence, marriage records, cemetery lists, photographs and reminiscences. Period: c1820 - c1900.

529. Coffman, S.F. "The adventure of faith." **Waterloo Historical Society.** 1926. 14: 228-233. Loc: all.

Text of an address given at the dedication of the Pioneers' Memorial Tower, reflecting on various groups of people who have migrated from their homelands for reasons of faith and conscience.

530. Cressman, Kenneth W. **A descriptive summary and analysis of the changing settlement and occupational patterns of the Mennonites and Amish**

Mennonites of Wilmot Township. University of Waterloo (M.A. thesis, Geography), 1988. 236 p. maps, charts, bibl. Loc: OWTU, OWTUCG.

A study by a Mennonite of settlement patterns and trends in Wilmot Township, the only area of Ontario settled by both Amish and Mennonites. The author surveys the whole township for the period from 1860 to 1980 but comments more specifically on change during the 1980s in the more limited area around New Hamburg, based on data from members of four Mennonite churches, the Steinmann Church, the Hillcrest Church, the Nith Valley Church and the Living Waters Community Fellowship. Period: 1860 - 1980.

531. Crownover, Donald and Wenger, Daniel. **The trail of the black walnut.** Lancaster, PA: Second Penn Institute in Local History, University of Pennsylvania, 1985. 1 v. (unpaged). ill., maps, bibl. Loc: OWTUCG.

A teaching aid intended for high school students learning about the ties between Lancaster County, Pennsylvania, and Waterloo County, Ontario. The kit consists of loose overhead transparencies and printed resource materials, including maps and pictures. Period: c1790 - c1820.

532. Davies, Blodwen. **A string of amber: the heritage of the Mennonites.** Vancouver, BC: Mitchell Press, 1973. 228 p. ill., index. Loc: OCH, OCLG, OKIT, OWTL, OWRN, OWTU, OWTUCG.

A popular account with occasional references to Waterloo County. Topics include the settlement process, charming and divining, and marriage and funeral customs. Personal anecdotes by the author, who lived in the Markham area, are interspersed through the text. Period: 1800 - 1973.

533. Dilley, Robert S. "Migration and the Mennonites: nineteenth-century Waterloo County, Ontario." **Canadian Papers in Rural History.** 1984. 4: 108-129. maps, tables. Loc: OWTL, OWTU, OWTUSJ, OWTUCG.

A study based on information from Ezra Eby's history, concluding that the Mennonite population of Waterloo was very stable, only a small percentage leaving the area for Michigan and northern and western Ontario. Occupation influenced migration (farmers stayed, businessmen and professionals moved), but family size and marital status appear not to have been factors. Period: 1800 - 1984.

534. Dunham, B. Mabel. "Beginnings in Ontario." **Mennonite Life.** 1950. 5,4: 14-16. ill. Loc: OKIT, OWTUCG.

An account of the Mennonite migration to Ontario

from Pennsylvania following the American Revolutionary War, and of the three settlements established in the Niagara, Waterloo and York districts. Period: 1783 - 1924.

535. Dunham, B. Mabel. **Kristli's trees.** Toronto: McClelland and Stewart, 1948. 198 p. ill. Loc: OCLG, OKIT, OWT, OWTL, OWTUR.

A fictional story for children about an Old Order Mennonite boy coming to terms with his uncompromising religion and way of life. The book is illustrated by Selwyn Dewdney. Period: c1940 - 1948.

536. Dunham, B. Mabel. "Mid-European backgrounds of Waterloo County." **Ontario Historical Society, Papers and Records.** 1945. 37: 59-70. bibl. Loc: OWTL, OWTU, OKIT.

An account of the Mennonites and Amish of Waterloo County, including their religious background and the political, economic and religious reasons for emigrating to North America. The settlement process in the first half of the nineteenth century and the emigration of the Russian Mennonites in 1870 and 1923 are recounted. Period: 1800 - 1925.

537. Dunham, B. Mabel. "Mid-European backgrounds of Waterloo County [reprint]." **Waterloo Historical Society.** 1948. 36: 7-20. Loc: all.
Period: 1800 - 1925.

538. Dunham, B. Mabel. "Some 'plain' people of Canada." **Canadian Magazine of Politics, Science, Art and Literature.** 1924. 62: 188-195. Loc: OGU.

A general account of pioneer settlement by Mennonites, Amish and Tunkers, especially in Waterloo and Wilmot Townships but with references to their significance in western Canada. Period: 1800 - 1870.

539. Dunham, B. Mabel. "The story of Conestoga." **Waterloo Historical Society.** 1945. 33: 16-23. Loc: all.

A short history of the word Conestoga. First used to describe "the people of the forked roof poles" in what is now Virginia, the word has also become synonymous with the early migrations of the Mennonites from Pennsylvania to Waterloo County. The names of the wagon, the trail, the river and the community (now spelled Conestogo) all have the same origin. Period: 1800 - 1812.

540. Dunham, B. Mabel. **Toward Sodom.** Toronto: Macmillan, 1927. 336 p. Loc: OKIT, OWT, OWTL, OWTUCGR, OWTUR.

A fictional account of religious and family disruptions caused by the conflict between the

worldly ways of Ebytown and traditional Mennonite values. The novel continues the chronicle of Waterloo County Mennonites begun in **The trail of the Conestoga.** Period: 1850 - 1920.

541. Dunham, B. Mabel. **The trail of the Conestoga.** Toronto: Macmillan, 1924 reprinted 1925. 341 p. Loc: OCCA, OKIT, OWT, OWRE, OWRN, OWRSJ, OWTL, OWTU, OWTUCG, OWTUR.

An historical novel based on fact about the migration of Pennsylvania German Mennonites from Lancaster County to the Waterloo area at the beginning of the 19th century. The 1924 edition contains a foreword written by W.L. Mackenzie King. The book was re-issued by McClelland and Stewart in 1942 (with later reprints). Period: 1800 - 1830.

542. Eby, Aaron, Dr. **Die Ansiedlung und Begründung der Mennoniten Gemeinschaft in Canada.** Milford Square, PA: J.C. Stauffer, 1872. 32 p. Loc: OWTUCG.

An account of the settlement and founding of the Mennonite community in Canada. The author outlines the migration of Pennsylvania Germans to the county from Franklin, Lancaster and Cumberland Counties, the landownership problems between Richard Beasley and the German Company, the roles of Waterloo Mennonites in the War of 1812, the leadership of Benjamin Eby and the subsequent growth of the county. A translation of this work can be found in Daniel K. Cassel's 1888 edition of **History of the Mennonites: historically and bibliographically arranged...**, in the chapter "A sketch of the Mennonite settlement in Canada." Period: 1799 - 1848.

543. Eby, Aaron, Dr. "A sketch of the Mennonite settlement in Canada." **History of the Mennonites: historically and biographically arranged from the time of the Reformation, more particularly from the time of emigration to America, containing sketches of the oldest meeting houses and prominent ministers, also their confession of faith adopted at Dortrecht in 1632.** Edited by Daniel K. Cassel. Philadelphia, PA: Daniel K. Cassel, 1888. Pp. 309-325. Loc: OKIT, OWTUCG, OWTU.

An overview of the settlement of Pennsylvania German Mennonites in Waterloo Township, translated from German by the editor. Migrations of Mennonites are traced from Franklin, Lancaster and Cumberland Counties in Pennsylvania and the leadership of Benjamin Eby in the Mennonite community is described. Appended to Dr Eby's article is a paragraph from Col. W.W.H. Davis' history of Bucks County, Pennsylvania, naming many emigrants to Canada between 1786 and 1823. Period:

1799 - 1848.

544. Epp, Marlene. "Mennonite women slowly gain equality." **Polyphony**. 1986. 8,1-2: 75-76. ill. Loc: OKIT, OWTU.

A general review with no specific references to Waterloo County except that one of the two photographs shows Mennonites picking berries in Berlin, circa 1912. Period: 1800 - 1985.

545. Fleming, Patricia. **Sources for a study of the Mennonites of Waterloo County.** 1969. 42 p. Loc: OKIT.

Apparently a student essay in librarianship that lists and comments on about 100 bibliographic items in the following thematic groups: Mennonite faith and history, life in America, immigration to Canada, and Waterloo County. Almost all the references to Waterloo County are from the annual volumes of the Waterloo Historical Society. The author also comments briefly on primary sources, including newspapers, almanacs and religious literature printed in Berlin. Period: 1800 - 1968.

546. Fleming, Robert G. **The Mennonite home in Waterloo County**. Ontario College of Art (student essay), 1961. 36 l. ill., bibl. Loc: OKIT.

A general description of Old Order Mennonite daily life with sections on the history, life and customs, and architecture and interior design of houses. Period: 1802 - 1961.

547. Flint, Joanne. **The Mennonite Canadians**. Edited by Daniel Hill. Multicultural Canada Series. Toronto: Van Nostrand Reinhold, 1980. 72 p. ill., maps, bibl. Loc: OKIT, OWRE, OWT, OWTUCG.

Textbook for primary school children with questions and activities. Mennonite faith, settlement in Waterloo County, the immigration of the Russian Mennonites and the present way of life are all described and illustrated. Other topics include the Mennonite Central Committee, fraktur, the Kitchener Farmers' Market, quilting and education. Period: 1780 - 1980.

548. Fretz, A.J. "The exodus to Canada: Moyer family history." **Waterloo Historical Society**. 1929. 17: 133-135. Loc: all.

Accounts of three different groups of pioneers journeying from Pennsylvania to Upper Canada at the very end of the 18th century. Period: 1799 - 1868.

549. Fretz, J. Winfield. **The Mennonites in Ontario**. Waterloo: The Mennonite Historical Society of Ontario, 1967 reprinted 1974 1977 1982. 42 p. ill., tables. Loc: OCP, OKIT, OWRE, OWRN, OWRND, OWT, OWTL, OWTU, OWTUCG.

A concise account first published to commemorate Canada's centennial year. There are variations in layout, ink colour, illustrations (including the cover photograph) and tables, but the text in unchanged in the various reprints. One edition includes drawings by Douglas Ratchford and another is illustrated by both Douglas Ratchford and Alan Hildebrand. Period: 1787 - 1967.

550. Fretz, J. Winfield. "The plain and not so plain Mennonites in Waterloo County, Ontario." **Mennonite Quarterly Review**. 1977. 51,1: 377-385, tables. Loc: OWTU, OWTUCG.

A discussion of twelve Mennonite groups, concluding that the differences are more sociological than theological. The author cites statistics showing Old Order Mennonites' responses to economic pressures in gradually accepting the use of farm machinery. The various groups are reported to agree in supporting the Mennonite Central Committee and separate Mennonite schools, in advocating the work programme for conscientious objectors as an alternative to military service, and in maintaining their right not to support the Canada Pension Plan.

551. Fretz, J. Winfield. **The Waterloo Mennonites: a community in paradox**. Waterloo: Wilfrid Laurier University Press for Conrad Grebel College, 1989. 391 p. ill., map, bibl., index. Loc: OCLG, OKIT, OWRE, OWRN, OWT, OWTL, OWTU, OWTUCG.

A scholarly study by a sociologist who was also founding president of Conrad Grebel College of what he calls "the most ethnically and organizationally diverse of any Mennonite community." Information was gathered by fieldwork, including a special census in 1972. The author explains the historical and religious background in the main Swiss, Amish and Dutch-Russian strands of Anabaptists who migrated within and from Europe between the sixteenth and twentieth centuries. Differences among the three original types are shown to have been complicated by subsequent splits in faith, doctrine and practice, and related to the degree of exposure to the mainstream economy and culture. Despite these differences, the Mennonites of the Waterloo region are described as sharing some values, customs and traditions, including a strong sense of community forged during centuries of persecution and migration in search of religious freedom. Other chapters discuss the roles of church, family and school; the importance of farming not only as livelihood but also as "sacred vocation" and ideal environment; distinctive occupational and leisure patterns; traditions of self-sufficiency and mutual aid; and forces of change within the Mennonite community and between Mennonites and the larger society and culture. The book concludes with a useful account of recent changes in Mennonite institutions, including the formation of the Mennonite Conference of Eastern Canada, the Mennonite Credit Union of Ontario, the Mennonite Historical Society of Ontario, and Conrad Grebel College. Period: 1800 - 1988.

552. Gingerich, Orland, Rev. "The service." **Waterloo Historical Society**. 1975. 63: 44-48. ill. Loc: all.

Text of an address about the contribution of the Amish to Wilmot Township, given at the Waterloo Historical Society's meeting in June 1975, on the same day that a plaque was unveiled at Steinman Mennonite Church, Baden, to commemorate Ontario's first Amish settlement. Period: 1824 - 1975.

553. Groh, Ivan. "History or fiction." **Waterloo Historical Society**. 1963. 51: 54-58. Loc: all.

A critical comment on the notion that the Pennsylvania German pioneers of Waterloo County were generally farmers and not interested in manufacturing industries or commerce. Period: 1806 - 1875.

554. Groh, Ivan. **Uncle Hannes and Levi**. Canadian-German Folklore v.3. Pennsylvania German Folklore Society of Ontario, 1970. 162 p. ill. Loc: OKIT, OKITW, OWTU, OWTUCG.

A description of a week's events in the life of a Mennonite boy who lived near Hespeler at the end of the nineteenth century. Two of the main characters and their families are fictitious but most are factual. There is an introductory tribute to Dr George Elmore Reaman by Norman H. High. Period: 1800 - 1900.

555. Groh, Ivan. "Why the Bechtel, Biehn, Betzner and Gingrich families chose the Beasley Tract in 1800." **Canadian-German Folklore**. 1967. 2: 61-92. Loc: OKIT, OWTL, OWTUCG, OWTU.

A partly fictionalized account of how the early Pennsylvania Mennonite and Tunker settlers came to Waterloo Township and paid Richard Beasley forty thousand dollars for sixty thousand acres. The genealogical relationships between the families are noted, along with the difficulties of procuring secure land titles. Period: 1800 - 1804.

556. Hamilton, O.A.F. "The Amish settlement in the Township of Wilmot in the County of Waterloo." **Waterloo Historical Society**. 1944. 32: 15-21. Loc: all.

A short history of the Amish from their beginnings in the late seventeenth century to the migration to Wilmot Township. The leaders of the Amish community are identified, as are the many of

the early settlers. Period: 1820 - 1860.

557. Heintz, Gladys. **German immigration into Upper Canada and Ontario: from 1783 to the present day**. Queen's University (M.A. thesis, History), 1938. 4 fiche. ill., maps, bibl. mf. Loc: OWTU.

An overview of the migration trends, patterns of settlement, and general adaptation of Germans and Pennsylvania Germans. The author examines racial origins, religious backgrounds, land purchases, German contributions to Ontario life, political interests, and federal government immigration programmes. A section entitled "Life in Waterloo District" considers themes such as Pennsylvania Germans as Canadian pioneers, clearing the land, the district in the early days, the district as of 1938, living conditions, economic development, the influence of the Mennonite religion on the character of the settlers, and the development of the Mennonite church. Period: 1800 - 1938.

558. Hill, Matthew H. "Folkways: personal views." **From Pennsylvania to Waterloo: Pennsylvania-German folk culture in transition**. Edited by Susan M. Burke and Matthew H. Hill. Kitchener: Friends of the Joseph Schneider Haus, 1991. Pp. 125-139. Loc: OKIT.

An edited summary of a panel discussion moderated by Clarke Hess and Lorna Bergey and including Donald Martin and Ivan Kraemer of Waterloo County and other Mennonite members from Pennsylvania. Topics included religion, the use of dialect, education, celebrations of festivals such as Easter and Christmas, farming customs and off-farm work, the persistence of cottage industries and crafts, rites of passage such as births and burials, and youth organizations and activities. Period: 1900 - 1990.

559. Hoffman, Susan. "Mennonite genealogical resources: the Grace Schmidt Room, Kitchener Public Library." **Mennogespräch**. 1986. 4,2: 19-20. Loc: OWTUCG, OKIT.

An outline of materials available, including books, periodicals, census and assessment records, naturalization records, Tweedsmuir histories and birth, marriage and death records.

560. Holden, M.L. "Pursuit of Utopia." **Canadian Forum**. 1948. 28: 106-7. Loc: OWTL, OWTU.

Reference from the Canadian Periodical Index. Period: 1948.

561. Horst, Isaac R. **Separate and peculiar**. Mount Forest: Durham Chronicle, 1979 reprinted 1983. 75 p. ill. Loc: OKIT, OWRE, OWRSJ, OWT, OWTUR, OWTUCG.

An account of the Old Order Mennonites in

Woolwich Township. Homes, clothing, customs, religious services and family events are described with simple drawings and a short glossary. Period: 1880 - 1980.

562. Horst, Isaac R. **Up the Conestogo**. Mount Forest: Isaac R. Horst, 1979. 462 p. ill., indexes. Loc: OCCA, OKEBC, OKIT, OWRE, OWT, OWTL, OWTUR, OWTUCG.

An historical account of the lifestyles of the Old Order Mennonites in North America, with particular reference to Waterloo County. Beginning with the settlement years, the author notes events, customs, traditions, family stories, genealogical ties and schisms. Period: 1800 - 1974.

563. Horst, Isaac R. **Why, Grossdaudy?**. Mount Forest: The Author, 1985. 79 p. Loc: OKIT, OWRSJ.

A sequel to **Separate and peculiar**, using the convention of a conversation between grandfather and grandson, supported by biblical texts, to explain differences between Mennonites and the larger society.

564. Horst, Mary Ann. **My Old Order Mennonite heritage**. Kitchener: Pennsylvania Dutch Craft Shop, 1970. 35 p. ill. Loc: OCH, OKIT, OKITW, OWRE, OWRND, OWRSJ, OWT, OWTL.

A brief description of the faith, history and lifestyle of the Old Order Mennonites of Waterloo County. The author describes her own experience, from an Old Order Mennonite upbringing to baptism as a member of the more liberal Ontario Conference Mennonites.

565. Hunsberger, Albert. "Russian Mennonites mark 60th anniversary." **Waterloo Historical Society**. 1984. 72: 161-164. ill. Loc: all.

A description of the arrival in 1924 of 800 Russian Mennonites in the Kitchener-Waterloo area. Period: 1923 - 1924.

566. Hunsberger, David L. and Hertel, James and Lattner, Koni and Fretz, J. Winfield. **People apart: portrait of a Mennonite world in Waterloo County, Ontario**. St Jacobs: Sand Hills Books, 1977. 111 p. ill. Loc: OCH, OCP, OKIT, OWRE, OWTL, OWTU, OWTUCG.

A collection of black-and-white photographs of scenes of everyday life among the Old Order Mennonites of Waterloo County, linked by excerpts of text by the sociologist Winfield Fretz. Period: 1800 - 1975.

567. Hunsberger, Wilson. "Pennsylvania-German rhymes and sayings." **Waterloo Historical Society**. 1976. 64: 26-30. Loc: all.

A collection of about 15 short poems written in dialect with an English translation. The topics of the verses vary from weather predictions to children's nonsense rhymes and a general acceptance of life as it comes. Period: 1800 - 1976.

568. Janzen, William. **On the Mennonites who have come from Mexico to southern Ontario**. 1974. 17 l. Loc: OWTUCG.

A report on the trend since the mid-1950s of seasonal migration from Mexico to Ontario by Old Colony, Evangelical Mennonite Mission Conference, Sommerfelder and Church of God Mennonites. The author comments on the historical roots, values and ideals of the migrants and their desire for economic standards equal to those enjoyed by Canadian Mennonites. Kitchener, Elmira and St Jacobs are noted as the main destinations in Waterloo County. Period: 1955 - 1974.

569. Jeffreys, C.W. "Clothes in history." **Waterloo Historical Society**. 1942. 30: 207-208. Loc: all.

A summary of a talk given by Dr. C.W. Jeffreys that contains introductory remarks about Conestoga wagons, their drivers, and "stogies," the cigars that the drivers smoked. Period: 1800 - 1830.

570. Kaiser, T.E., Dr. "Origins and early Pennsylvania Dutch settlements in Upper Canada." **Waterloo Historical Society**. 1932. 20: 309-314. Loc: all.

A brief historical account of the migrations to North America, including the journey to Canada by some sixty families in the 1790s. Period: 1790 - 1800.

571. Klinckhardt, Christian Gottlieb and Proudfoot, William, Rev. "Amish and Tunkers critiqued ca. 1830." **Mennogespräch**. 1992. 10,1: 6. ill. Loc: OWTUCG, OKIT.

Contemporary descriptions of Waterloo County Amish and Tunkers in the 1830s, taken from a journal of Rev. William Proudfoot and a letter by Christian G. Klinckhardt. Brief introductions by E. Reginald Good give background notes on the excerpts. Period: 1829 - 1834.

572. Klippenstein, Lawrence. **David Klassen and the Mennonites**. Edited by Keith Wilson. We Built Canada. Agincourt: Book Society of Canada, 1982. 75 p. ill. Loc: OCH, OCLG, OCP, OKIT, OWTUCG.

Textbook for primary school children, including biographical notes on William Hespeler and Jacob Y. Shantz of Waterloo County who helped Russian Mennonites to settle in Manitoba in the 1870s. Period: 1813 - 1900.

573. Kratz, Henry and Milnes, Humphrey. "Kitchener German (part 1), a Pennsylvania German dialect: phonology." **Modern Language Quarterly**. 1953. 14,2: 184-198. Loc: OWTL, OWTU.

A detailed comparison of the pronunciation of the Pennsylvania German dialect in Waterloo County with that of Pennsylvania. The authors conclude that the Waterloo dialect is homogeneous except for the Maryhill area, founded by Catholic Alsatians, and that Kitchener German was more influenced by English and possibly Standard German than other dialects of Pennsylvania German. Period: 1800 - 1953.

574. Kratz, Henry and Milnes, Humphrey. "Kitchener German (part 2), a Pennsylvania German dialect: morphology." **Modern Language Quarterly**. 1953. 14,3: 274-283. Loc: OWTL, OWTU.

A detailed comparison of the language structure of the Pennsylvania German dialect of Pennsylvania and that of Waterloo County. Many similarities are noted, but the percentage of English loan words is found to be higher in the Waterloo dialect. Period: 1800 - 1953.

575. Kurogawa, Minako. "Mennonite children in Waterloo County." **Immigrant groups**. Edited by Jean Leonard Elliott. Scarborough: Prentice-Hall, 1971. Pp. 33-46. Loc: OWTL, OWTU.

Reprinted from the **Canadian Journal of Sociology and Anthropology** (1969), a psychosocial study of 460 10-year-olds from traditional, transitional and progressive Mennonite backgrounds. Children from progressive families in rural areas are reported to have the highest overall adjustment profiles. Period: 1967 - 1968.

576. Kurogawa, Minako. "Psycho-social roles of Mennonite children in a changing society." **Canadian Review of Sociology and Anthropology**. 1969. 6: 15-35. bibl., tables. Loc: OKIT, OWTL, OWTU.

Reference from the Canadian Periodical Index. Period: 1967 - 1968.

577. Laurence, Hugh. **Boundary maintenance among Ontario Amish Mennonites**. 1983. 42 p. tables. Loc: OWTUCG.

An analysis of the challenge to the Amish Mennonites' ethnic identity by external economic forces and internal differences in ideology, during the period of increasing prosperity between 1940 and 1970. The author considers mainly the Wellesley Mennonite congregations of Waterloo County, both the Beachy and Western Ontario Mennonite Conference and the Mornington Mennonite community in Perth County. Period: 1940 - 1970.

578. Levitch, Gerald. "Mennonites: the old ways are forever." **Imperial Oil Review**. 1981. 65,3: 22-25. Loc: OWTL, OWTU.

A popular account of the traditional values and customs preserved by the Mennonites. Period: 1800 - 1980.

579. "List of Mennonists, Quakers and Tunkers in Wilmot Township, 1836." **Waterloo Historical Society**. 1983. 71: 46. Loc: all.

A list of those who paid 10 shillings as tax exemption money, including Peter Lammer, Joseph Lichte, Michael Roth, Jacob Miller, John Erb, Christian Moyer, John Lugibihl, David Geiger, Jacob Gingrich, Abraham Bean, Isaiah Geiger, George Levigood and David Richard. Period: 1836.

580. Loewen, Royden. "Diaries as sources for studying Mennonite history." **Mennogespräch**. 1991. 9,2: 9-14. ill. Loc: OKIT, OWTUCG.

A discussion of the cultural values and the seasonal round of farm-based tasks and social interactions revealed in the diaries of four Mennonite men in Waterloo County in the 1880s and 1890s -- Ephraim Cressman of Breslau, Isadore Snyder of Berlin, David Bergey of New Dundee, and Moses Bowman of Mannheim. The author briefly compares these with diaries kept by women, Laura Shantz in 1917-1918 and Susanna Cassel Shantz from 1904 to 1920. Period: 1880 - 1920.

581. Macnaughton, Elizabeth. **The Old Order Mennonite community in the early twentieth century**. Kitchener: Doon Heritage Crossroads, Historic Sites Department, Regional Municipality of Waterloo, 1988. 217 p. ill., maps, bibl. Loc: OKIT, OWRE, OWT, OWTUCG.

A report intended for the use of interpreters at Doon Heritage Crossroads, where the Peter Martin house represents an Old Order Mennonite farm. Information is presented on family and social units, divisions within the faith, courtship, family size, the Pennsylvania German dialect and the use of German in services, education, the use of technology, rites of passage, modes of dress, foodways, farming practices, houses and home furnishings and hobbies. Photographs, drawings and a glossary of household terms illustrate the very detailed research. Period: 1900 - 1920.

582. Mage, Julius A. and Murdie, Robert A. "The Mennonites of Waterloo County." **Canadian Geographical Journal**. 1970. 80: 10-19. ill. map. Loc: OKIT, OWTU, OWTL.

An account of the religion, education, dress, architecture and farming techniques of Old Order Mennonites in Waterloo County. The authors discuss threats to this lifestyle from urbanization and government programmes of health insurance, old age pensions and workman's compensation. Period: 1800 - 1970.

583. Magee, Joan. **The Swiss in Ontario**. Windsor: Electra Books, 1991. 271 p. ill., bibl., index. Loc: OKIT, OWTUCG.

An account of the Swiss experience in Ontario, with chapters on the Pennsylvania Mennonites and European Amish in Waterloo County. The author refers to Waterloo Swiss pioneers including the Bettschen, Guggisburg, and Mürner or Merner families, and mentions David Peter Hunsberger, a Waterloo artist and a Swiss Mennonite. Period: 1800 - 1991.

584. Martin, Cleon, Mrs. **The pineapple quilt**. Aylmer and LaGrange, IN: Pathway Publishers, 1987 reprinted 1989. 240 p. Loc: OWTUCG.

A novel about Nancy Martin and her experiences with family and friends in the Old Order Mennonite community of Waterloo County.

585. Martin, John S., Hon. "Characteristics of the Pennsylvania German in Canada." **Waterloo Historical Society**. 1926. 14: 217-219. Loc: all.

A brief address by the Minister of Agriculture of Ontario at the dedication of the Memorial Tower (28 August 1926), honouring the first settlers in the county. Period: 1800 - 1926.

586. Martin, Maurice and Maust, Miriam and Fretz, Glenn. **Mennonites in Ontario: a Mennonite bicentennial portrait, 1786-1986**. Mennonite Bicentennial Commission, 1986. 175 p. ill., map. Loc: OKIT, OWTUCG.

A contemporary portrait of all the Mennonite, Amish, and Brethren in Christ groups in Ontario, illustrated with many large coloured photographs. Short essays on history, faith, farming, education, mission work and art are included. Charts illustrate the relationships of the Dutch and Swiss Mennonites and a map shows the location of the Swiss Mennonites, Tunkers (Brethren in Christ), Amish and Dutch Mennonites in southern Ontario. Period: 1800 - 1986.

587. Martin, Peter G. **Peter G. Martin letters**. Edited by Isaac R. Horst. 1980. 156 p. ill. Loc: OWTUCGR.

A collection of letters written by Peter G. Martin of St Jacobs to friends in other parts of Canada and the United States. The letters are mainly in German but have been transcribed from the Gothic script by Isaac R. Horst and others. The letters by Martin are addressed to Christian Zimmerman and relate information about family members and neighbours including sicknesses, births, marriages and deaths as well as other community news and weather. Period: 1872 - 1899.

588. Murdie, Robert A. **A geographic study of the Mennonite settlement in Waterloo County**. Waterloo Lutheran University (B.A. thesis, Geography), 1961. 91 l. ill., maps, tables, bibl. Loc: OWTL, OKIT.

A comprehensive study of early history, population, Mennonite churches and Mennonite farmsteads, and the economic and cultural patterns of Mennonite life. Charts, graphs and tables provide concise details on a wide variety of topics. Period: 1800 - 1961.

589. Murdie, Robert A. "The Mennonite communities of Waterloo County." **The Waterloo County area: selected geographical essays**. Edited by A.G. McLellan. Waterloo: Department of Geography, University of Waterloo, 1971. Pp. 21-30. tabl. Loc: OWTU, OWTL, OWTUCG, OKIT.

A summary of early Mennonite history and the founding of settlements in Waterloo and Wilmot Townships, followed by some discussion of differences in farming practices and general way of life between Old Order Mennonites and adherents to the Mennonite Conference of Ontario. A table summarizes numbers of Mennonites in each township and urban centre from 1861 to 1961. Period: 1861 - 1961.

590. Paetkau, Henry. **Separation or integration?: the Russian Mennonite immigrant community in Ontario, 1924-45**. University of Western Ontario (Ph.D. thesis), 1986. 420 p. tables, bibl. Loc: OWTUCG.

An examination of the ethnic identity of Russian Mennonites who came to Ontario in 1924. This identity is seen as consisting primarily of three elements: 1) a separatist, pacifist religious faith, 2) German language and culture, and 3) an agrarian lifestyle. The author concludes that while the New World cultural environment challenged the traditional Russian Mennonite way of life, the strength of their religious values enabled them to survive as a distinct ethnoreligious group in Canada. Period: 1924 - 1945.

591. Paetkau, Henry. **A struggle for survival: the Russian Mennonites in Ontario, 1924-1939**. University of Waterloo (M.A. thesis, History), 1977. 239 p. bibl., glossary. Loc: OWTUCG, OWTU.

A study of the group's difficulties in adjusting from a rural to an urban society and its development of religious, cultural and educational organizations. About half the Russian Mennonites who arrived in 1924 journeyed west, but many stayed in Ontario and the Kitchener-Waterloo area. Period: 1924 - 1939.

592. Panabaker, D.N. "President's address: the Pennsylvania background of early Waterloo settlers." **Waterloo Historical Society**. 1934. 22: 75-80. Loc: all.

An account of the material culture in eighteenth-century Pennsylvania, based on a survey of the "estates of representative families" such as Panabaker, Tyson, Weber, Levering, Keyser, Shuler, Johnson and Schneider. Members of several of these families later migrated to Upper Canada as pioneer settlers of what became Waterloo County. Period: 1701 - 1800.

593. Pennsylvania German Folklore Society of Ontario. **Canadian-German Folklore**. 1961-. Loc: OKIT, OWRE, OWT, OWTL, OWTU, OWTUCG.

A publication series produced irregularly by the society that was founded in 1951 by people such as Mabel Dunham and G.E. Reaman; the society assisted in organizing the Ontario Genealogical Society in 1960. The name of the society as printed on the cover began as The Pennsylvania Folklore Society of Ontario, but between 1977 and 1979 changed to The Pennsylvania German Folklore Society of Ontario. The volumes contain information about the settlement of Pennsylvania German families in Ontario, particularly the York, Vineland and Waterloo areas. Not many articles are written explicitly about Mennonite faith, though the Mennonite background is implicit throughout the volumes. The two first volumes (1961 and 1967) contain collections of articles on miscellaneous topics, as in a journal, but later volumes are monographs on particular topics. Those volumes pertaining specifically to Waterloo County are given separate entries in the WRP database. Period: 1784 - 1991.

594. Peters, John F. and Wentzell, Marlin. **The demographic basis of the Old Order Mennonites**. Research Paper Series no. 8694. Waterloo: Wilfrid Laurier University, 1988. 21 p. charts, bibl. Loc: OWTUCG.

A study of marital patterns, fertility, migration and occupations of Old Order Mennonites in Canada and the United States between 1939 and 1985. Research shows a young population, an increasing number of single females, and an increase in the number of ways in which economic self-sufficiency is achieved. Period: 1939 - 1985.

595. Reaman, G. Elmore. **Some notes on the background of this unique centre, Kitchener, Ontario, Canada: a short series of articles of interest**. Kitchener: Kitchener-Waterloo Record, 15 p. Loc: OWTUR.

A brief account of Pennsylvania German culture in the Waterloo area, including farming, art and cooking. Period: 1800 - c1970.

596. Redekop, Calvin W. **A bibliography of Mennonites in Waterloo County and Ontario**. Waterloo: Conrad Grebel College, Institute of Anabaptist and Mennonite Studies, 1988. 9 l. Loc: OKIT, OWT, OWTUCG.

A list of over 120 monographs, serials, journal articles, newspaper articles and unpublished works, including theses and private papers relating to the Mennonite and Amish. Period: 1800 - 1988.

597. Richter, Manfred Martin. **The phonemic system of the Pennsylvania German dialect in Waterloo County, Ontario**. University of Toronto (Ph.D thesis, Modern Languages), 1969. 2 fiche. bibl. mf. Loc: OWTU, OWTL.

A description of the dialect based on data collected from eleven speakers in the northeastern part of the county. The author identifies the dialect's segmental and suprasegmental phonemic features and their distribution and fluctuation. The thesis included phonetic and phonemic transcriptions of sample interviews, with their English translations. Period: 1968 - 1969.

598. Roth, Lorraine. "150 years of Amish history." **Waterloo Historical Society**. 1972. 60: 52-57. ill., map. Loc: all.

A short history of the Amish in Wilmot Township beginning in the 1820s with the arrival of Christian Nafziger. A map, based on surveyor Samuel S. Wilmot's 1830 report, shows the early settlement of the central part of Wilmot Township. Period: 1822 - 1972.

599. Roth, Lorraine and Grant, Marlene J. "Canadian Amish Mennonite roots in Pennsylvania." **Pennsylvania Mennonite Heritage**. 1986. 9,2: 13-17. Loc: OKIT, OWTUCG.

An account of early settlement by Amish from Pennsylvania between 1785 and 1835, including references to particular families who owned land in or migrated to Woolwich and Wilmot Townships. Period: 1800 - 1835.

600. Rowe, P. "Amish country: a people as unprocessed as their produce." **Financial Post**. 1972. 66: 40-1. mf. Loc: OWTL, OWTU.

Reference from the Canadian Periodical Index. Period: 1972.

601. Saillour, Dominique. **The Mennonites in Waterloo County**. 1984. 101, 70 p. ill., maps, bibl. Loc: OWTUCG.

An student dissertation written in France "sous

la direction de Daniel Gouadec," comparing stereotypes of Waterloo Mennonites with the realities. The author outlines the history of Canadian Mennonites, especially in Waterloo County, and describes Mennonite daily life, customs and attitudes. Period: 1800 - 1984.

602. Sauder, Dorothy M. "Mennonite Central Committee: early days at the Kitchener, Ontario office." **Mennogespräch.** 1989. 7,1: 1-3. ill. Loc: OKIT, OWTUCG.

The history of a Mennonite relief centre in Kitchener, from its opening in 1944 at the home of Dr J. Hett, to 1964. The organization, operation, buildings and personnel are described and illustrated. Period: 1920 - 1964.

603. "Sauerkraut" "Waterloo Mennonites in 1867: some observations." **Mennogespräch.** 1989. 7,1: 7-8. Loc: OWTUCG, OKIT.

A transcript of a letter to the editor of the **Huron Signal,** dated 1 March 1867 from Berlin, humorously describing the Pennsylvania Mennonite settlers of Waterloo Township from an Englishman's viewpoint. It portrays the furnishings of the farmhouse and meeting house, and the food, clothing, church service and farming methods of the Mennonites. Period: 1802 - 1867.

604. Schaefer, Thomas L. **Russian Mennonite immigration and settlement in Waterloo County, 1924-1925.** Wilfrid Laurier University (B.A. thesis, History), 1974. 56 p. maps, bibl. Loc: OWTL.

A description of the efforts of local Waterloo Mennonites and others to help Russian Mennonites adjust to life in Canada. Initially, Waterloo County was seen as a temporary refuge for the overflow of Russian Mennonites heading west. Between 600 and 700 Russian Mennonites settled in Waterloo County in 1924 and 1925, many of them finding factory work in the towns when temporary work on the farms was exhausted. A map based on the immigration lists of 1924 shows the distribution of Russian Mennonite immigrants in Waterloo County, and another shows the Mennonite settlements of southern Ukraine. Period: 1924 - 1925.

605. Seyfert, A.G. "Address delivered at the dedication of the Memorial Tower, August 28, 1926." **Waterloo Historical Society.** 1926. 14: 204-211. Loc: all.

An uplifting address by the representative of the Lancaster County Historical Society, praising the pioneer settlers who came to Waterloo County from Pennsylvania. Period: 1798 - 1830.

606. Seyfert, A.G. "Migrations of Lancaster County Mennonites to Waterloo County, Ontario, Canada, from 1800 to 1825." **Lancaster Historical Society, Papers and Addresses.** 1926. 30: 33-41. Loc: Lancaster.

Content probably similar to article by the same author in the Waterloo Historical Society report for 1926, based on remarks at the dedication of the Pioneers' Memorial Tower. Period: 1800 - 1925.

607. Shank, Robert J. "Mennonite odyssey." **Canadian Genealogist.** 1982. 4,1: 29-37. bibl., maps. Loc: OKIT.

An outline of Mennonite history, with some emphasis on Waterloo County. Period: 1800 - 1982.

608. Shantz, Jacob Y. **Narrative of a journey to Manitoba: together with an abstract of the Dominion Lands Act and an extract from the Government pamphlet on Manitoba.** Ottawa: Department of Agriculture, 1873. 31 p. Also CIHM Microfiche series, no. 30484. Loc: OWTL, OWTU, OWTUCG, OWTUR.

A government publication describing the journey made by Waterloo County native Jacob Y. Shantz to Manitoba, in order to help new Mennonite immigrants from Russia (Ukraine) settle in that province. There are no references to Waterloo County. The Doris Lewis Rare Book Room, University of Waterloo holds an imperfect copy, with loss of print caused by cropping of pages. Period: 1870 - 1873.

609. Shantz, Jacob Y. **Relation d'un voyage a Manitoba: accompagnée d'une analyse de l'Acte concernant les Terres de la Puissance et d'un extrait du pamphlet publié par le gouvernement at [sic] sujet de Manitoba.** Ottawa: Department of Agriculture, 1873. 29 p. Also CIHM Microfiche series, no. 13478. Loc: OKITW, OWTL, OWTU, OWTUCG, OWTUR.

An account of the journey made by Waterloo County native Jacob Y. Shantz to Manitoba, to help new Mennonite immigrants from Russia settle in that province. There are no references to Waterloo County. Period: c1870 - 1873.

610. Sherk, A.B., Rev. "The Pennsylvania-Germans in Canada." **The Pennsylvania German.** 1907. 8: 101-104. map. Loc: OWTUCGR.

An outline of the early Mennonite settlements of Ontario, with references to such pioneer leaders as Benjamin Eby, Henry Eby, Ezra Eby and H.W. Peterson. An introductory editorial note contains some biographical information about the author. Period: 1800 - 1841.

611. Sherk, A.B., Rev. "The Pennsylvania Germans of Waterloo County." **Ontario Historical Society, Papers and Records.** 1906. 7: 98-109. Loc: OWTL, OWTUCGR, OWTU, OWT.

    An account of the Pennsylvania Mennonite migration to and settlement in Waterloo County. Topics includes the leadership of Benjamin Eby, education and the press. This article was reprinted in **The Pennsylvania German,** volume 12 (1911), pp. 280-287. Period: 1799 - 1841.

612. Sherk, M.G. "The Pennsylvania-German in history." **Waterloo Historical Society.** 1926. 14: 237-246. Loc: all.

    A general history of the Mennonite people from their origins in Switzerland, their migration to Pennsylvania and later to Waterloo County. Period: 1775 - 1825.

613. Smith, C. Henry. "Expansion of the Pequea and Germantown settlements." **The story of the Mennonites.** Berne, IN: Mennonite Book Concern, 1941. Pp. 566-567. Loc: OWTUCG.

    A general history that is largely a revised and enlarged version of a book entitled **The Mennonites** by the same author, published in 1920 and included in the WRP database. A section relating to the early settlement of Waterloo is contained in a unit on immigration to Ontario. A fifth edition of the book, edited by Cornelius Krahn in 1981, is also indexed in the WRP database. Period: 1799 - 1827.

614. Smith, C. Henry. **Smith's story of the Mennonites.** Edited by Cornelius Krahn. Newton, Kansas: Faith and Life Press, 1981. 589 p. ill., bibl., index, maps. Loc: OWTUCG.

    The fifth edition of a general history of the Mennonites, including a short history of the early Mennonite settlement of Waterloo County on pages 377-378. Other index entries refer to Kitchener and Waterloo. Period: 1799 - 1827.

615. Smith, George. "The Amishman." **Ontario Historical Society, Papers and Records.** 1919. 17: 40-42. Loc: OWTL, OWTU.

    A brief history of the origins of the Amish religion with reference to the settlement of Wilmot Township by Christian Nafziger and his followers in 1822. Period: 1799 - 1913.

616. Smucker, Barbara C. "They found a home in Canada." **Waterloo Historical Society.** 1974. 62: 16-25. Loc: all.

    A collection of reminiscences of Russian Mennonites who came to Waterloo County in the 1920s. The stories of painter Woldemar Neufeld, Herbert and Marie (Warkentin) Enns, Herman and Agnes (Wiens) Koop, Henry and Katherina (Ewert) Rempel, Mr and Mrs Schoenke, Tina and Anna Wall describe their journeys and early experiences in Canada. Period: c1924 - 1974.

617. Smucker, Donovan E. **The sociology of Canadian Mennonites, Hutterites and Amish: a bibliography with annotations.** Waterloo: Wilfrid Laurier University Press, 1977. 232 p. indexes. Loc: OKIT, OWT, OWTUCGR.

    An 800-item annotated bibliography including references to books, graduate theses, pamphlets, articles and unpublished sources. An introduction discusses sources, methods, scope and leading ideas. Name and subject indexes help users to locate references to Waterloo County. Period: 1926 - 1977.

618. Smucker, Donovan E. **The sociology of Mennonites, Hutterites and Amish: a bibliography with annotations, 1977-1990.** Waterloo: Wilfrid Laurier University Press, 1991. 194 p. indexes. Loc: OKIT, OWT, OWTUCGR.

    A companion volume updating and expanding the 1977 bibliography by the same author. There are critical annotations for bibliographies and encyclopedias, books and pamphlets, articles and theses. An introduction summarizes the trends of recent scholarship in these areas and appendices list other locations of Mennonite, Hutterite and Amish material. References to Waterloo County are listed in the subject index. Period: 1977 - 1990.

619. Snyder, Peter Etril and Herrfort, A.K. **Mennonite country.** St Jacobs: Sand Hills Books, 1978. 87 p. ill. Loc: OCP, OKIT, OWRE, OWTL, OWTU, OWTUCG, OWTUR.

    Thoughts of an Old Order Amishman on farming and his faith, illustrated with pen and ink drawings of Mennonite farm life by Peter Etril Snyder. Period: 1880 - 1978.

620. Staebler, Edna. "How to live without wars and wedding rings." **Macleans Magazine.** 1950. 63: 14-15, 41. ill. Loc: OKIT, OWTL, OWTU.

    Reference from the Canadian Periodical Index. Period: 1950.

621. Staebler, Edna. "Why the Amish want no part of progress." **Macleans Magazine.** 1958. 71: 20-1, 51-6. ill. Loc: OKIT, OWTL, OWTU.

    Reference from the Canadian Periodical Index. Period: 1958.

622. Stauffer, Joseph S. "The family book." **Waterloo Historical Society.** 1967. 55: 16-17. Loc: all.

    A description of the Mennonite tradition of keeping a family book, an account book in which were recorded the expenses of the children once they reached their late teens. Period: 1800 - 1883.

623. Tutton, Diane A. **Dermatoglyphic traits in an Amish-Mennonite population in Ontario**. University of Waterloo (M.A. thesis, Biology), 1978. 2 fiche. charts, ill., tables, bibl. mf. Loc: OWTUD.

A study of the Amish-Mennonite group descended from the immigrants to Ontario from Alsace-Lorraine in the 1820s and 1830s. The author examines the patterns of arches, loops, and whorls found on the fingers and the volar pads of the hand to determine whether increased homozygosity can be associated with any recognizable change in genetic traits of a culturally isolated group. Period: 1820 - 1978.

624. Waite, Gary K. **From separation to assimilation: Mennonites in Berlin, 1800-1880**. Kitchener: Joseph Schneider Haus, 1987. 93 p. ill., map. bibl. Loc: OWTUR.

A discussion of the process by which some Mennonites in 19th-century Berlin accommodated their lifestyles and values to the larger urban society. The author uses statistical methods to describe two generations of Mennonites and their attitudes to intermarriage, business, politics and worship. Period: 1800 - 1880.

625. Weber, M. "The part played by immigrants from Waterloo County to the Didsbury, Alberta, settlement in 1894." **Waterloo Historical Society**. 1950. 38: 13-21. Loc: all.

A short account of the migration which was arranged by Jacob Y. Shantz and included the families of Mr Hunsberger, J.B. Shantz, Ephraim Shantz, M. Weber, Elias Shantz and Rev. J.B. Detwiler. Period: 1893 - 1950.

626. Winland, Daphne N. **A plea for peoplehood: religious and ethnic identity, continuity, and change among the Mennonites of Kitchener-Waterloo, Ontario**. York University (Ph.D. thesis, Sociology), 1989. 312 p. bibl., tables. Loc: OWTUCG.

An analysis of the ethnic identity of the Mennonites, with particular reference to the Kitchener-Waterloo area. Topics include religious divisions, the amalgamation of church conferences, and the sponsoring and conversion of Southeast Asian refugees to the Mennonite faith. The author who attended eleven churches in the Kitchener-Waterloo over a three-year period, concludes that group identity is a "dialectical process involving the simultaneous expression of numerous and often seemingly conflicting expressions of identity." Period: 1800 - 1989.

627. Woodhall, David and Yandt, Carolyn. **The Old Order Mennonite community**. Present Day Cultures in Waterloo County: Environmental Studies Program. Kitchener: Waterloo County Board of Education, 1978. 220 p. ill., maps, music. Loc: OKIT, OWTUCG, OKEBC.

A workbook designed for teachers of Grade Four classes. Rich in information about Old Order customs and traditions, the book has eleven appendices containing historical background, maps, stories, excerpts from Mabel Dunham's **Trail of the conestoga** and Edna Staebler's **Sauerkraut and enterprise**, sketches by Peter Etril Snyder and Marlene Jofriet, photographs by Allen D. Martin, common sayings, recipes and songs. The authors are concerned with pedagogical techniques and provide advice on the use of maps, problem-solving sessions, and how to teach the skills of observation, classification, description and comparison.

628. Zimmerman, Idessa. **History of early Mennonite settlers**. 1963. 21 l. ill. Loc: OKITW.

A summary of the Mennonite European and American background with brief biographical sketches of some early Pennsylvania Mennonite settlers in Waterloo County and a reference to resolution of the land claim with Richard Beasley. Part of this history is taken from Mabel Dunham's chapter on Waterloo in her book about the Grand River. A note on the cover page indicates that the account was compiled for Mr Elliott Moses, Department of Indian Affairs, Six Nations Reserve, Oshwegan. Period: 1800 - 1825.

THE GERMANS OF WATERLOO COUNTY

629. Auburger, Leopold and Kloss, Heinz and Rupp, Heinz. **Deutsch als Muttersprache in Kanada: Berichte zur Gegenwartslage**. Deutsche Sprache in Europa und Übersee, Berichte und Forschungen, Band 1. Wiesbaden: Franz Steiner Verlag, 1977. 175 p. tables, bibl. Loc: OWTU, OWTL.

A collection of essays about German-language enclaves in Canada. Werner Bausenhart, Kurt Nabert, Klaus H. Bongart and others discuss the dialects of Ontario German-speaking communities, especially the Mennonites, Amish and other German-born groups of Waterloo County. Fritz Wieden provides information on German newspapers and periodicals published in Canada since World War II, as well as radio and television broadcasting in German. In addition to bibliographies presented with each essay, the final chapter is an extensive bibliography of the studies of German dialects in Canada, compiled by

Wolfgang Viereck and J. Eichhoff. Period: 1945 - c1975.

630. Bassler, Gerhard P. "Franz Straubinger and the Deutsche Arbeitsgemeinschaft Ontario." **German-Canadian Yearbook / Deutschkanadisches Jahrbuch**. 1984. 8: 225-234. Loc: OKIT, OWTL, OWTUCG.

An account of efforts to unify German secular and religious associations in Ontario in the 1930s by stressing their common heritage and language. The author shows how Straubinger persisted in spite of anti-German tensions in the 1930s and 1940s, maintaining that the events he organized were not pro-Nazi. Though provincial in scope, the article suggests the significance of the Kitchener community in preserving German ethnicity. Period: 1929 - 1939.

631. Bausenhart, Werner A. "The Ontario German language press and its suppression by Order-in-Council in 1918." **Canadian Ethnic Studies**. 1972. 4,1-2: 35-48. Loc: OWTL, OWTU, OWTUCG.

A portrayal of the plight of German-language newspapers during the First World War. Quoting frequently from the **Berliner Journal**, the author suggests that the date of the legislation was connected to the proposed Imperial News Service being considered by the supervisor of the Canada Department of Public Information, N.W. Rowell, in 1918. The legislation is seen also as part of the federal government's support of provincial legislation to discourage bilingual schools. Period: 1914 - 1918.

632. Benjamin, Steven M. **The German-Canadians: a working bibliography**. Occasional Papers of the Society for German-American Studies, no. 1. Morgantown, WV: Society for German-American Studies, 1979. 41 p. Loc: OWTU.

A supplement to two bibliographies published in the **German-Canadian yearbook**, vol. I (1973), pp. 327-44 and vol. III (1976), pp. 291-302. It contains citations for about 440 books, theses and articles, many of which refer to Waterloo County.

633. Boeschenstein, Hermann. "Das Studium der deutschkanadischen Presse - ein fruchtbares Arbeitsfeld." **German-Canadian Yearbook / Deutschkanadisches Jahrbuch**. 1973. 1: 41-46. Loc: OKIT, OWTL, OWTUCG.

A review of the German-language press in Canada before 1918, including analysis of the style and use of "German-Canadianisms" by newspaper editors, and appreciation of historical research by H.K. Kalbfleisch. Period: 1835 - 1918.

634. Brast, Heinz and Kraft, Annemarie. **Kanada, Ihre neue Heimat: Handbuch für Auswanderer**. Stuttgart: Orac Pietsch, 1983. 183 p. ill. Loc: OKIT, OWTUR.

A handbook for German-speaking Europeans intending to emigrate to Canada. Chapter 4 describes the Region of Waterloo, especially the Old Order Mennonites. Period: 1977 - 1983.

635. Breithaupt, W.H. "Presidential address: some German settlers of Waterloo County." **Waterloo Historical Society**. 1913. 1: 11-15. Loc: all.

Brief sketches of some influential European settlers, including Peter N. Tagge, Jacob Beck, Otto Klotz, Jacob Hailer, Jacob Hespeler and John Motz. Period: 1800 - 1911.

636. Brewster, Winfield. **Pine Bush genealogy: something about the German people who came to Canada from 1850 on, and settled in "Pine Bush" a mile south of Hespeler, east of the Back Road and of their descendants**. Hespeler: T and T Press, 1961. 85 p. Loc: OWTUR, OKIT, OWTL, OCCA.

Biographical and historical information about the first German families who settled in the Pine Bush area of Hespeler from about 1850. Most names were found in the records of births and deaths at St James Lutheran Church, Hespeler. All the main family names are indexed in the WRP database. An index is available at the City of Cambridge Archives and the Cambridge Library and Gallery. Period: 1850 - 1960.

637. **Briefe über West-Canada das Runner-Unwesen und die deutsche Gesellschaft in New-York, nebst einem Anhange über die östlichen Townships in Unter Canada und die Passage-Büreaus in Europa und Amerika: ein Wegweiser für Auswanderer**. CIHM Microfiche series, no. 32509. Preston: Jakob Teuscher, printed by Abr.A. Eby, 1854. 3 fiche. mf. Loc: OWTL, OWTU.

A guide to prospective German emigrants and travellers to Canada. Also published by Schabelitz in Basel. Period: 1853 - 1854.

638. Canadian German Society. **German-Canadian Review: quarterly of the Canadian-German Society, Inc..** Galt: Canadian German Society, 1956. 22 p. Loc: OWTUR.

A continuation of the quarterly **German-Review**, published by the Canadian Society for German Relief in Manitoba. The format, place of publication and publisher all changed in 1956 when the Canadian German Society began publishing the review in Galt. Edited by Gottlieb Leibbrandt, the magazine focused on German-Canadian life and its history. There are book reviews and articles in English and German about German settlers in Canada. The University of Waterloo Rare Book Room has the first of these publications, vol. 9, no. 1 (Autumn 1956). Period: 1948 - 1956.

639. Canadian Society for German Relief. **Canadian Society for German Relief Bulletin.** Winnipeg: The Society, 1948 - 1953. Loc: OWTUR.

A bulletin published in co-operation with the Göttingen Research Committee into the Refugee and Expellee Problem, an organization devoted to the alleviation of suffering in Germany and Austria. The serial contains items in both English and German, and most issues contain reports from the Kitchener branch. In 1955 the name of the publication changed to the **German-Canadian Review** and the society's name changed to the Canadian-German Society. The University of Waterloo's Doris Lewis Rare Book Room has vol. 4, nos. 2, 5-7 (1951); vol. 5, nos. 1-5 (1952); and vol. 6, nos. 2 and 3 (1953). Period: 1948 - 1953.

640. Canadian Society for German Relief. **The German-Canadian Review: a quarterly, published in cooperation with the Goettingen Research Committee into the Refugee and Expellee Problem.** King's Park, Manitoba: Canadian Society for German Relief, 1954 - 1956. 8 p. ill. Loc: OWTUR.

A continuation of the monthly bulletin produced by the Canadian Society for German Relief to assist German-speaking immigrants. In 1954 the review was published in Manitoba and focused on the problems of German refugees. It contains articles in German and English which have a worldwide scope. The University of Waterloo Rare Book Room holds vol. 7, nos. 1, 2, and 3 and vol. 8, no. 1. In 1956 the review was published by the Canadian German Society, and the place of publication changed from Manitoba to Galt. Period: 1954 - 1956.

641. **Canadiana Germanica: a journal for German-Canadian Studies and news bulletin of the German-Canadian Historical Association and the Historical Society of Mecklenburg Upper Canada Ont..** Loc: OWTL, OWTU, OWTUCG.

A quarterly publication with articles in both English and German on German-Canadians. Many are transcripts or facsimiles of articles in other periodicals such as the **Kitchener-Waterloo Record.** Although about a tenth of the material concerns the Waterloo area, some issues contain more. For example, nearly half of the March 1992 issue consists of copies of documents, articles and editorials on the proposal to rename Kitchener Berlin. The Conrad Grebel Library has subscribed to the journal since 1988. Users should note that articles from the **Kitchener-Waterloo Record** are systematically clipped and indexed at the Grace Schmidt Room of Kitchener Public Library. Period: 1799 - 1992.

642. Eby, Peter. **Canada's Zustände, Uebersetzung einer Depesche von Sr. Excellenz dem General Gouverneur, an den Right Hon. Sir John Pakington, Baronet.** Berlin: The Author?, 1854. 26 p. Loc: OWTUCGR, OKITW.

A German translation of an 1852 dispatch from the Governor General relating Canada's imports, exports, transportation, population, agriculture and other production. Five thousand copies of this translation were sent to Germany in order to encourage more emigration from Europe. In a brief appendix, Peter Eby stresses the great advantages to German emigrants of choosing such townships as Waterloo, Wellesley, Wilmot and Woolwich, already settled by German-speaking people. He notes the special opportunities for teachers of German to make better salaries than their American counterparts. Period: 1848 - 1854.

643. Eichhoff, Jürgen. "Bibliography of German dialects spoken in the United States and Canada and problems of German-English language contacts especially in North America, 1968-1976, with pre-1968 supplements." **Monatschefte.** 1976. 68,2: 196-208. Loc: OWTL, OWTU.

A bibliography of 150 items, some of which refer to Waterloo County. It is a continuation of a bibliography on the same topic by Wolfgang Viereck. Period: 1968 - 1976.

644. Featherston, Maria. **The Berliner Journal: a study of a German-language newspaper.** Wilfrid Laurier University (M.A. thesis, History), 1977. 88 l. bibl. Loc: OWTL.

An examination of the newspaper's history, founders, policies, community role and contents for the years 1906 to 1915. The author discusses the journal's role in preserving German language and culture and describes editor John A. Rittinger's character, "Joe Klotzkopp," whose humorous letters were written in the Pennsylvania German dialect. Period: 1906 - 1915.

645. Fitzgerald, E. Keith. "The anglicizing of German surnames - a frustrating genealogical experience." **Families.** 1983. 22,2: 97-99. Loc: OKIT, OWTL, OWTU.

A summary of the topics, followed by a discussion of the name Empey, for which the author finds over 65 spellings. Period: 1709 - 1983.

646. Froeschle, Hartmut. "1784-1984: 200 years of German participation in building Ontario: a chronological table." **German-Canadian Yearbook / Deutschkanadisches Jahrbuch.** 1984. 8: 6-23. table. Loc: OKIT, OWTL, OWTUCG.

A summary of the migrations of German-speaking people and the areas they settled in the Waterloo region. Prominent individuals including Benjamin Eby, Christian Nafziger, F.W. Bindemann, George Rebscher, Louis Funcken, Otto Klotz and John A. Rittinger are noted for their roles in the region's religious, political, cultural and industrial development. Period: 1800 - 1984.

647. Froeschle, Hartmut. "Deutschkanadische Bibliographie. Eine Auswahl." **German-Canadian Yearbook / Deutschkanadisches Jahrbuch.** 1973. 1: 327-344. Loc: OKIT, OWTUCG, OWTL.

A select German-Canadian bibliography listing publications in German on literature, the press, education, settlement, travels in Canada by Germans from the late 19th and the 20th centuries, German organizations and other bibliographies. Period: 1800 - 1970.

648. Froeschle, Hartmut and Zimmermann, Lothar. **German Canadiana: a bibliography / Deutsch kanadische Bibliographie.** German-Canadian Yearbook/ Deutschkanadisches Jahrbuch. Toronto: Historical Society of Mecklenburg Upper Canada, 1990. 420 p. index. Loc: OWTUCG, OWTL.

A multidisciplinary listing of titles up to 1987, including monographs, articles from journals and newspapers, theses, and manuscripts and typescripts, arranged under thematic headings such as histories, group life (ethnicity, identity, and acculturation), religious life, language and literature, German language press, and cultural, economic, political and military contributions. This reference work forms the entire eleventh volume of the periodical and lists many sources for Waterloo County. Period: 1800 - 1987.

649. Froeschle, Hartmut. "German immigration into Canada: a survey." **German-Canadian Yearbook / Deutschkanadisches Jahrbuch.** 1981. 6: 16-27. Loc: OKIT, OWTL, OWTUCG.

An overview of German settlement including the waves of migration to the Waterloo area. It is noted that this article is a translation of the original German work by Werner Bausenhart. Period: 1799 - c1835.

650. Froeschle, Hartmut and Zimmermann, Lothar. "The Germans in Ontario: a bibliography." **German-Canadian Yearbook / Deutschkanadisches Jahrbuch.** 1984. 8: 243-279. Loc: OKIT, OWTL, OWTUCG.

A listing of nearly 750 titles of articles appearing in newspapers, periodicals and encyclopedias, as well as of genealogies, biographies, and church, local, and provincial histories, many of which refer to the German-speaking peoples of Waterloo County. Appended to the bibliography is a subject index identifying such themes as architecture, Amish, business, Catholics, customs, Dunkards, folklore, immigration, language, Lutherans, Mennonites, newspapers, clubs, settlement, politics, schools and Swedenborgians. Period: 1800 - 1984.

651. Froeschle, Hartmut and Roger, Dieter and Unruh, Peter. **Globus.** Berlin, Germany: Verein für das Deutschtum im Ausland e.V., 1985. 17,3: Pp. 5-9, 17-19, 24-26. Loc: OWTUR.

A photocopy of an issue containing three articles relating to the achievements of German immigrants in Canada, including those who came to the Waterloo area. The articles are entitled "Die deutsche Volksgruppe im kanadischen Mosaik" = "The German ethnic group in the Canadian mosaic", "Deutsches Bauen und seine Einflüsse in Kanada" = "The German building style and its influences in Canada", and "Die Renaissance des deutschkanadischen Schrifttums" = "The renaissance of German-Canadian literature". Each article touches on the contributions that the German culture has made to the county, through the Pennsylvania German Mennonites, European Germasn or Russian Mennonites. Period: 1800 - 1985.

652. Froeschle, Hartmut. **The history and heritage of German immigration to Canada.** Canadiana Germanica Occasional Papers, No 3. Toronto: German-Canadian Historical Association, 1982. 19 p. bibl. Loc: OKIT.

A brief overview of German groups who settled in Waterloo County, from the Pennsylvania-German Mennonites in the early nineteenth century to the Volksdeutsche in the 1950s. Period: c1800 - c1950.

653. "German Peace Festival 1871." **Waterloo Historical Society.** 1966. 54: 78-80. ill. Loc: all.

An address written at the time of the Friedensfest of 1871 in Berlin by W. Jaffray, G. Davidson and J. King on behalf of the English residents of Berlin. The address was sent to the members of the committee of the German Peace Festival, congratulating them on the German victory in Europe as well as the celebrations in Berlin, Canada. Period: 1871 -

654. Helling, Rudolf A. **A socio-economic history of German-Canadians: they, too, founded Canada: a research report.** Edited by Bernd Hamm. Vierteljahrschrift für Sozial- und Wirtschaftsgeschichte, Nr. 75. Wiesbaden: Franz Steiner Verlag, 1984. 156 p. tables, bibl. Loc: OKIT, OWTL, OWTU, OWTUCG.

A survey of German groups who settled in the

Waterloo County area, including discussion of migration, settlement, war, education, politics, recreation, communications and culture. Period: 1799 - 1984.

655. Hess, Albert. "Deutsche Bräuche und Volkslieder in Maryhill (Waterloo County)." **German-Canadian yearbook / Deutschkanadisches Jahrbuch.** 1976. 3: 221-225. Loc: OKIT, OWTUCG, OWTL.

A brief overview of German customs and folk songs traced back to the settlement of the community (known as New Germany before 1941) by Catholic Alsatians in the 1820s and 1830s. Based on interviews with local residents Marie Scherer and Albert Zinger, the author relates musical, culinary and family traditions which have nearly disappeared from the area. Samples of songs remembered by the two elders are included. An English version of this article was published in the Waterloo Historical Society's 64th annual report in 1976, pages 31-36. Period: c1820 - 1976.

656. Hess, Albert. "From Baden to Baden." **Waterloo Historical Society.** 1970. 58: 35-42. Loc: all.

A discussion of factors in the emigration of German residents of Baden (Sachsens and Schwabens) to Baden, Waterloo County, in 1816-17, the 1840s and the 1920s. The author uses evidence from contemporary family letters. Period: 1816 - 1920.

657. Hess, Albert. "From Strasburg to Strasburg." **Waterloo Historical Society.** 1971. 59: 20-30. ill. Loc: all.

An account of the European background of Waterloo County's village of Strasburg, from the Amish settlers led by Christian Nafziger in the 1820s to Alsatians who came between the 1830s and 1850s. Period: 1820 - 1850.

658. Hess, Albert. "I found Waterloo County in Hesse." **Waterloo Historical Society.** 1972. 60: 63-72. ill. Loc: all.

A short account of life for peasants in Hesse, Germany, from which significant numbers emigrated to Waterloo County in the 1830s and 1840s. The article is based on research done on the author's trip to Hesse in 1972, where he found convincing evidence of ancestors of county families such as Ratz, Euler, Dreger, Ernst, Kaufman, Kranz, Schmalz, Breithaupt, Lautenschlager, Smith (Schmidt), Pfohl, Einwechter, Nahrgang, Hachborn, Stroh, Wettlaufer, Kalbfleisch, Krug, Schaefer, Staebler, Seyler, Wilker, Doerbecker, Doersam, Doering, Hahn, Neeb, Weitzel, Knipfel, Lotz, Doehn and Koch. Period: 1830 - 1850.

659. Hess, Albert. "Impressions of a German immigrant." **Waterloo Historical Society.** 1978. 66: 46-47. Loc: all.

A short article, based on comments made by Waterloo County newcomers in letters to European relatives in the 1830s, about the availability of food, low taxes, free hunting and good pay. Period: 1830 - 1840.

660. Hess, Albert. "The wandering Schwabens." **Waterloo Historical Society.** 1973. 61: 58-63. ill. Loc: all.

A short history of the Schwabens who emigrated from the Banat in Rumania to Waterloo County, mainly the events in Europe that prompted them to move to North America. The author suggests that by 1973 there were over 6,000 Schwabens in the Kitchener-Waterloo area. Very few personal names are provided. Period: c1925 - 1973.

661. Hunsberger, Albert. "Philipp Lautenschlager's letter." **Waterloo Historical Society.** 1978. 66: 41-45. ill. Loc: all.

Translated of a German letter from a new Canadian resident to his family in Herchenrode, Hesse. The letter describes the passage to North America and the way of life, wages and prices in Waterloo Township in the 1830s. Period: 1830 - 1831.

662. Intschert, Michael. **Burghalle remembered: a Saxon village in Transylvania.** Waterloo?: The Author?, 1989. 316 p. ill. map. Loc: OWT.

An account of the people and customs of the Transylvanian village of Burghalle, some of whom came to the Waterloo area following the Second World War. There are recollections of immigrants, such as Georg Hendel and Michael Intschert, and a portrayal of the adaptation to Canadian society. The development of the Transylvania Club of Kitchener is recorded, with photographs of its members and its activities. Names and addresses of immigrants to Canada and the United States from Burghalle are listed. Period: 1945 - 1989.

663. Jakobsh, Frank K. "German and German-Canadian literature as contained in the **Berliner Journal.**" **German-Canadian Yearbook / Deutschkanadisches Jahrbuch.** 1979. 5: 108-120. ill. Loc: OKIT, OWTUCG, OWTL.

An analysis of the literary content of the weekly newspaper published from 1859 to 1918, including its style, quality and purpose. The author considers particularly the Pennsylvania German dialect in the letters to the editor by the fictitious character "Joe Klotzkopp" (John A. Rittinger). Period: 1859 - 1918.

664. Kalbfleisch, Herbert Karl. "Among the editors of Ontario German newspapers, 1835-1918." **Canadian-German Folklore**. 1961. 1: 78-85. Loc: OKIT, OWTL, OWTU, OWTUCG.

A profile of German newspapers and their editors, most of them from Waterloo County. With a few exceptions, the editors are seen as partisan, provocative, libellous and pugnacious: most were involved in court cases, some went bankrupt, and one was jailed. Quotations from the newspapers reflect the editors' uncompromising stands and their rivalry with one another. Period: 1835 - 1918.

665. Kalbfleisch, Herbert Karl. "German or Canadian?." **Waterloo Historical Society**. 1952. 40: 18-29. Loc: all.

An essay about German identity in southwestern Ontario, based on examples from German-language newspapers in Ontario. The author attributes the lack of active political ambition by early German Canadian settlers, their loyalty to the British monarchy from the 1870s, and the events of World War I to the decline of the German language and any strong ties to the Fatherland. Period: c1800 - c1950.

666. Karch, Dieter and Moelleken, Wolfgang Wilfried. **Siedlungspfälzisch im Kreis Waterloo, Ontario, Kanada**. Phonai: Lautbibliothek der europäischen Sprachen und Mundarten: Deutsche Reihe; Bd. 18 Deutsches Spracharchiv. Monographien; Bd. 9. Tübingen: M. Niemeyer, 1977. 201 p. maps, indexes. Loc: OWTU.

A study of the Pennsylvania-German dialect (ideolect) as it was spoken in the county in 1969. The book contains the texts, in phonetic transcription with a translation in High German, of interviews with two native speakers from Woolwich and Wellesley Townships. A phonotape of the interviews is also available. Period: 1968 - 1969.

667. Kurz, Carl Heinz. **Liebeserklärung an das kleine Paradies**. Kleine Plesse Bücherei; Bd. 9. Hann. Münden: Gauke, 1980. 32 p. ill., maps. Loc: OWTU.

A romantic description of Waterloo County's landscape and people, emphasizing the contributions of Germans in farming, music, popular culture, education and industry, and referring briefly to the earlier presence of aboriginal people. Period: 1799 - 1980.

668. Lehmann, Heinz. "Das Deutschtum in der Provinz Ontario." **Zur Geschichte des Deutschtums in Kanada. Band 1: Das Deutschtum in Ostkanada**. Schriften des Deutschen Ausland-Instituts Stuttgart, A. Kulturhistorische Reihe, Band 31. Stuttgart: Ausland und Heimat Verlags-Aktiengesellschaft, 1931. Pp. 48-114. maps, tables, bibl. Loc: OWTL, OWTUCG.

A comprehensive study of German ethnicity in the province, including an outline of the settlement and development of the Waterloo area. Strong German influences on local place names, cultural organizations and the press are emphasized, as are the achievements of German-Canadian community leaders such as Adam Beck, D.B. Detweiler and the Breithaupt family. For an English translation, see **The German Canadians 1750-1937** by Heinz Lehmann. Period: 1800 - 1930.

669. Lehmann, Heinz. **The German Canadians 1750-1937: immigration, settlement and culture**. Edited by Gerhard P. Bassler. St John's, NF: Jesperson Press, 1986. lxii, 541 p. ill., maps, tables, bibl., index. Loc: OKIT, OWTU, OWTUSJ, OWTUCG.

A detailed study organized in chronological and geographical order, with Chapter 3 including a section on Waterloo County. This book is the translation of several of Lehmann's works including **Zur Geschichte des Deutschtums in Kanada** (On the history of German identity in Canada) from which the first three chapters are taken. Period: 1800 - 1937.

670. Leibbrandt, Gottlieb. "Deutsche Ortsgründungen und Ortsnamen in der Grafschaft Waterloo." **German-Canadian Yearbook / Deutschkanadisches Jahrbuch**. 1973. 1: 119-129. bibl. Loc: OKIT, OWTUCG, OWTL.

Brief histories of communities with German names in each township of Waterloo County, with notes of their connections with German-speaking migrants from Europe and Pennsylvania. Period: 1800 - 1916.

671. Leibbrandt, Gottlieb. **Little Paradise: aus Geschichte und Leben der Deutschkanadier in der County Waterloo, Ontario, 1800-1975**. Deutschkanadische Schriften; Bd.1. Kitchener: Allprint, 1977. 416 p. ill., facsims., ports., bibl. Loc: OKIT, OWRN, OWT, OWTL, OWTU, OWTUR, OWTUSJ, OWTUCG.

A history of German-Canadians in the Waterloo region. While all ethnocultural strands are considered, including the Pennsylvania German Mennonites and the Volksdeutsche from east and southeast Europe, the author emphasizes the experience of the European Germans who settled in the Waterloo area from the 1830s. The book is especially rich in details of the distinctive religious, educational, cultural, social and recreational organizations and achievements of people of German origin. The impact of the two world wars on the German-Canadian community is also discussed. An English translation of the book, published in 1980, is also indexed in great detail in the WRP database. Although the translation remains true to the original, some of the photographs, poetry selections, newspaper reproductions and personal profiles have been omitted, resulting in a work that is some 75 pages shorter than the German version. The English edition contains an index while the German does not. Period: 1800 - 1975.

672. Leibbrandt, Gottlieb. **Little paradise: the saga of the Germans of Waterloo County, Ontario, 1800-1975**. Kitchener: Allprint, 1980. 342 p. ill., bibl., index. Loc: OCP, OKIT, OWRE, OWRN, OWRW, OWT, OWTL, OWTU, OWTUR, OWTUSJ, OWTUCG, OWTUCR.

Translated by G.K. Weissenborn and M.G. Weissenborn from the original German edition with the same title. While all ethnocultural strands are considered, including the Pennsylvania German Mennonites and the Volksdeutsche from eastern and southeastern Europe, the author emphasizes the experience of the European Germans. The book is especially rich in details of distinctive religious, educational, cultural, social, and recreational organizations and achievements by people of German background. The impact of the two world wars on the German-Canadian community is also discussed. Period: 1800 - 1975.

673. Nicolay, C.L. "Berlin, a German settlement in Waterloo County, Ontario, Canada." **German American Annals**. 1907. NS 5, OS 9: 105-121. Loc: OWTUCG.

An account of the town's development, outlining land grants, early settlement, industries and transportation and emphasizing its ethnic German characteristics. The author contrasts current cultural vitality and industrial prosperity with the difficulties of earlier pioneer days. Period: 1812 - 1907.

674. Pepper, Paul E. **Index to Pine Bush genealogy (Hespeler, Ontario) by Winfield Brewster**. 1987. 35 p. Loc: OKIT.

An index to some 650 personal names mentioned in Brewster's book.

675. Richardson, Lynn E. **A facile pen: John Motz and the Berliner Journal, 1859-1911**. University of Waterloo (M.A. thesis, History), 1991. 127 p. Loc: OWTUR.

A biographical appraisal of the roles of Motz as writer, editor and business manager of the **Berliner Journal** and of the newspaper's influence in preserving German culture. The author presents a translation of the announcement that launched the **Berliner Journal** in 1859 and

summarizes information on other German newspapers in western Ontario. Period: 1859 - 1911.

676. Sanders, D.M. "Blood ties and war fears draw Germans to Kitchener." **Financial Post**. 1962. 56: 11. mf. Loc: OWTL, OWTU.

Reference from the Canadian Periodical Index. Period: 1962.

677. Schaefer, Thomas L. "Kitchener's Swastika Club." **Waterloo Historical Society**. 1979. 67: 33-42. Loc: all.

An account of the unsuccessful organizational meeting of the Kitchener Swastika Club in 1933 and the efforts by Kitchener City Council and other concerned citizens to discourage any promotion of racial or religious hatred, such as had occurred in Berlin/Kitchener in 1916 when the Concordia Club was destroyed. Period: 1916 - 1933.

678. **Statuten und Nebengesetze des Deutschen Unterstützungs-Vereins in Toronto, Ontario**. Berlin: Rittinger and Motz, 1871. 15 p. Loc: OKITW.

Statutes and by-laws of the German Aid Association in Toronto, printed in Berlin by Rittinger and Motz. Page 15 in the copy owned by the Waterloo Historical Society has been removed. Period: 1870 - 1871.

679. Stoesz, Dennis. **German immigration from Germany to Waterloo County from 1819 to 1840**. University of Waterloo (student essay), 1978. 25 p. bibl., map. Loc: OWTUCG.

A study of the reasons for emigration, the process of migration, and those areas of Germany that produced immigrants to the townships of Waterloo, Wilmot, Woolwich and Wellesley. Period: 1819 - 1840.

680. Teuscher, Jakob. **Briefe über West-Canada: ein Wegweiser für Auswanderer**. CIHM Microfiche series, no. 32509. Preston: Abr. A. Erb, 1854. 176 p. Loc: OWTUCG.

A collection of 18 letters about Canada West, some of which had previously appeared in the Preston newspaper **Der Canadische Bauernfreund**. As a guide to prospective German-speaking immigrants, the author describes the established German settlements with their schools, churches and newspapers, and discusses land prices, farm statistics, government policies and practices, geography, and modes of travel to Canada and the United States. Period: 1853 - 1854.

681. Vey, Waldtraut Elisabeth. **The German immigrants of Waterloo County: 1840-1900**. University of Western Ontario (M.A. thesis, History), 1976. 178 l. bibl. Loc: OWTL, OWTU.

An analysis of the background, places of origin, economic status, possible reasons for emigration, and choice of destination of the European Germans who settled in the county. The author also discusses the roles of Germans in industrial and cultural development and includes short biographical sketches of prominent citizens of German origin. Period: 1840 - 1900.

682. Wagner, Jonathan. "The Deutscher Bund Canada 1934-39." **Canadian Historical Review**. 1977. 58,2: 176-200. Loc: OKIT, OWTL, OWTU, OWTUSJ.

A history of the pro-Nazi German-Canadian organization, founded by five men associated with Waterloo: Ernst Kopf, Otto Geisler, Georg Messer, Paul Lechscheidt and Karl Gerhard. Toronto and Kitchener-Waterloo were the most active Ontario centres, but the real strength of the Bund was in Western Canada. The Kitchener-Waterloo group challenged the leadership of Gerhard, who was forced to resign in 1935. The society's failure is attributed to the strength of the German-Canadians' ties to Canada. Period: 1934 - 1939.

683. Widder, Friederich. **Anleitung für die Emigranten aller Klassen, welche nach Ober Canada auszuwandern beabsichtigen, ganz besonders den kleinern Güterbesitzern der Ackerbau treibenden Klasse gewidmet, die aber auch für solche Klassen von Interesse die im Besitze eines ziemlichen Capitals oder sicheren Einkommens den Entschluß fassen, nebst ihren Familien die alte Heimath zu verlassen.** CIHM Microfiche series, no. 47676. Berlin: Heinrich Eby, 1850. 18 frames. mf. Loc: OWTL, OWTU.

A pamphlet containing a series of questions and answers intended to help Europeans, especially farmers, considering emigration to Upper Canada. The guide was prepared by a commissioner of the Canada Company and gives information about weather, crops, capital needed to settle, the cost of raising cattle and other animals, the standard of living, wages, churches, schools and banking. The CIHM series also has an English version of this document. Period: 1850 - 1855.

684. Woollatt, Margarete. **The German Canadians of Berlin (Kitchener), Ontario in the First World War**. Waterloo Lutheran University (B.A. thesis, History), 1968. 43 l. bibl. Loc: OWTL.

A study of the loyalty to the British Empire generally felt by German Canadian citizens and the perception of that loyalty by the Scottish citizens of Galt. The author discusses material collected from two newspapers, the **Berliner Journal** (**Ontario Journal** from 10 January 1917), and the **Galt Daily Reporter**. The **Berliner Journal** was the only secular German-language paper in the county, and the **Galt Daily Reporter** was the main paper of South Waterloo and was thought best to represent the English Canadian viewpoint. Appendices present information on ethnic groups in Kitchener and Galt for 1911 and 1921. Period: 1914 - 1918.

THE SCOTTISH OF WATERLOO COUNTY

685. Cameron, James M. "An introduction to the study of Scottish settlements of Southern Ontario." **Ontario History**. 1969. 61: 167-172. Loc: OKIT, OWTL, OWTU.

A study of place names of Scottish origin, including brief references to the settlements founded by William Dickson and others in the Upper Grand Valley. Period: 1815 - 1855.

686. Cameron, James M. **A study of the factors that assisted and directed Scottish immigration to Upper Canada, 1815-1855**. University of Glasgow (Ph.D. thesis, Geography), 1970. 615 p. ill., tables, maps. Loc: OGU.

An analysis of eight factors: friends and relatives, periodicals and newspapers and books, Scottish ports, shipping and emigration agents, government, emigration societies and trade unions, landlords, land companies and land speculators, and churches. The author's main focus is Scottish settlement in Wellington County and his references to William Dickson's development of Dumfries Township are incidental rather than detailed. Period: 1815 - 1855.

687. Duncan, Kenneth J. "Patterns of settlement in the east." **The Scottish tradition in Canada**. Edited by W. Stanford Reid. Toronto: McClelland and Stewart, 1976. Pp. 49-75. Loc: OWTU.

An analysis of the Scottish settlement from the 1820s to the 1860s, including a brief description of Dumfries Township, founded by William Dickson, as a successful example of a proprietary settlement. Period: 1826 - 1870.

688. Hess, Albert. "From Ayr to Ayr." **Waterloo Historical Society**. 1975. 63: 63-65. Loc: all.

A general account of factors in the early settlement in North Dumfries Township by immigrants from Dumfriesshire in Scotland. Period: 1816 - 1866.

689. Mackean, William. **Letters home during a trip to America, 1869.** Paisley: The Author?, 1875. 240 p. ill. Loc: OWTUR.

Privately printed letters which describe a trip to Galt on pages 80 to 87. The author describes the town and its Scottish inhabitants, and comments on the food, Presbyterian churches, woodland and the lives of farm women. Period: 1869 - 1870.

690. Taylor, Andrew W. "Dumfries: early settlers in an inland township." **Families.** 1976. 15,4: 130-137. Loc: OKIT, OWTU, OWTL.

A discussion of developers, promoters and early settlers such as William Dickson, John Telfer and James Hogg. Scottish migration from both the Scottish Borders and New York State is mentioned, with a description of the hardships endured by the early pioneers. Period: 1816 - 1976.

691. Vance, William E. "Impressions of a Berlin pioneer: the emigrant letters of Dr John Scott." **Waterloo Historical Society.** 1989. 77: 26-37. ill. Loc: all.

A study of letters written between 1835 and 1845 by Dr John Scott, showing the importance of personal connections in directing further emigration to the region and in providing social networks for the immigrants upon arrival. Period: 1835 - 1845.

692. Whyte, Donald. **A dictionary of Scottish emigrants to Canada before Confederation.** Toronto: Ontario Genealogical Society, 1986. 445 p. Loc: OKIT, OWTU.

A compilation of brief entries for about 12,500 Scottish emigrants to Canada, including details of name, parentage, place of origin, dates of birth and death, destination, date and ship of migration, occupation, wife/husband, parentage, date of marriage and children. Sources include the Public Archives of Canada, Provincial Archives of Nova Scotia, the Scottish Record Office and National Library of Scotland in Edinburgh, the Mitchell Library in Glasgow and the Library of Scottish Genealogy Society in Edinburgh. The volume is not indexed by Canadian province, county or locality in which Scottish emigrants settled, but the basic data could be analyzed to derive details for Waterloo County. Period: 1800 - 1967.

693. Whyte, Donald. "Scottish emigration to Canada before Confederation." **Families.** 1982. 21,4: 197-222. ill. Loc: OKIT, OWTL, OWTU.

A comprehensive article that mentions the establishment of Dumfries Township and refers to the roles of William Dickson, Absalom Shade, John Telfer and the Rev. William Stewart in the settlement of that area. Period: 1815 - 1831.

694. Wood, J. David. "A Scottish note on Dickson of Dumfries." **Waterloo Historical Society.** 1960. 48: 37-39. Loc: all.

A description of the Dumfriesshire countryside from which William Dickson emigrated in 1784, later founding and directing the settlement of Dumfries Township, Upper Canada. The author compares the natural and cultural landscapes of Dumfriesshire and Dumfries Township and comments on the place names which Dickson and other early settlers gave to localities in Dumfries Township. Period: 1784 - 1816.

OTHER ETHNIC GROUPS OF WATERLOO COUNTY

695. Anderson, M. Grace and Higgs, David. **A future to inherit: the Portuguese communities in Canada.** Toronto: McClelland and Stewart, 1976. 202 p. ill., index, bibl. Loc: OCCA, OKIT, OWTU, OWTUCG, OWTUSJ.

A general survey including references to the Galt and Kitchener Portuguese-Canadians. Topics include labour, language education, clubs and organizations, family, religion and cultural identity. Period: 1953 - 1976.

696. Canadian Jewish Congress, Central Region, Research Committee. **The Jewish communities of Galt, Preston and Hespeler, Ontario: a self-survey.** Toronto: The Committee, 1954. 15 l. map, chart, tables. Loc: OTU.

Reference from **Bibliography of Ontario history, 1867-1976** (Bishop et al.). Period: 1951 - 1954.

697. Costa-Pinto, L.A. and de Britto Costa-Pinto, Sulamita. "The Portuguese in Canada: Waterloo Region." **Waterloo Historical Society.** 1987. 75: 5-15. ill. Loc: all.

An account traced from the first immigrant, Manuel Cabral, who arrived in Ayr in 1928, with references to many other Portuguese people who came to the area. Period: 1928 - 1975.

698. de Britto Costa-Pinto, Sulamita. "The Portuguese community of Galt." **Polyphony.** 1987. 9,1: 33-34. ill. Loc: OKIT, OWTU, OWTUSJ.

A brief history of the ethnic community, with a note of the author's proposal to interview pioneer Portuguese immigrants and collect historical material about them. Period: 1928 - 1987.

699. Devitt, A.W. "Blacks celebrate abolition of slavery in Elmira [WRP]." **Waterloo Historical Society.** 1961. 49: 47. Loc: all.

A brief note about the colony of Blacks who

settled in Peel Township between 1860 and 1875 and their annual summer celebration of the abolition of slavery. The last one recalled by the author took place in the summer of 1886. Period: 1860 - 1886.

700. Duncan, Susan J. **Portuguese in Galt: two decades of isolation.** University of Waterloo (B.E.S. thesis), 1977. 1 fiche. maps, tables, bibl. mf. Loc: OWTUM.

A study of postwar development of the community which was the city's largest ethnic group by 1975. The focus is on the current Portuguese population of Galt and their areas of settlement but an historical section presents trends in Portuguese immigration to Galt and mentions the leadership of Manuel Cabral. Period: 1946 - 1976.

701. Enchin, Gerald D. **A locational analysis of the Kitchener-Waterloo Jewish community.** Waterloo Lutheran University (B.A. thesis, Geography), 1971. 76 p. bibl., maps, tables. Loc: OWTL.

A report on the development of the group which grew from 10 people in the 1901 census to 525 in 1961. The author explains changes in Jewish residential location between 1920 and 1970 in terms of proximity to work and to the synagogue. A questionnaire sent to Jewish residents gathered additional socio-economic information. Period: 1901 - 1971.

702. Fyfe, Susan. **The immigrants who came to Kitchener and Waterloo after the Second World War.** University of Waterloo (student essay, History), 197-?. 16 l. bibl., tables. Loc: OKIT.

A study of the experiences of European immigrants, including brief summaries of interviews with Kitchener residents who had emigrated from Germany, Yugoslavia and Austria. Period: 1941 - 1973.

703. "The Hawksville celebration." **Waterloo Historical Society.** 1963. 51: 50. Loc: all.

Transcript of an article from the **Dumfries Reformer** describing an Emancipation celebration held at Hawksville by the Black people of Wellesley and Peel in 1863. Period: 1863 -

704. Lamb, Kathryn Hansuld. "Armenians in Waterloo Region." **Waterloo Historical Society.** 1991. 79: 54-79. ill., map. Loc: all.

A detailed account of the settlement of Armenian refugees in Preston, Guelph, Galt and Kitchener, in two major waves after the First World War and the Second World War. The experience of particular families and the establishment of voluntary associations are described. Period: 1915 - 1988.

705. Radecki, Henry. **Ethnic organizational dynamics: the Polish group in Canada.** Waterloo: Wilfrid Laurier University Press, 1979. Pp. 45-46, 60. Loc: OKIT.

A description of Polish voluntary organizations in Canada, including a note of the earliest group formed in Berlin in 1862. This group was also the first to establish a mutual aid society, with the preservation of Polish customs and traditions as a later objective. The Berlin Polish parish was officially recognized in 1912 and a church was built in 1913. Period: 1862 - 1912.

706. Smith, Claudette Pamela. **West Indian migration to Kitchener-Waterloo, Ontario.** University of Waterloo (M.A. thesis, Geography), 1975. 2 fiche. bibl. mf. Loc: OWTU.

An analysis of the factors which attracted migrants to the area, based on responses to a 1975 questionnaire. The author finds that friends and relatives were the single most important locational factor and that 75 per cent of West Indians sampled came to the area after 1966. Period: 1946 - 1975.

707. Tevlin, M. "How Galt meets an immigration problem." **Canadian Business.** 1949. 24: 54, 86. mf. Loc: OWTL, OWTU.

Reference from the Canadian Periodical Index. Period: 1949.

708. Vuorinen, Saara Sofia. **Ethnic identification of Caribbean immigrants in the Kitchener-Waterloo area.** University of Waterloo (Ph.D. thesis, Psychology), 1973. 2 fiche. tables, bibl. mf. Loc: OWTU.

An analysis of the inter-relationships of ethnic identification, similarity, perceived acceptance and social distance of Caribbean-Canadians. Based on interviews with 120 local immigrants, the author concludes that individuals will identify more with ethnic groups that they see as being similar to themselves, and that the more individuals perceive acceptance by the people of the host country, the more they will identify with that country. Period: 1963 - 1973.

709. Wright, Gerald. "Fugitive negro slaves." **Waterloo Historical Society.** 1979. 67: 26-32. Loc: all.

A short history of Black settlement in the townships of Wellesley and Peel. The author cites census reports, survey maps and reminiscences to support an estimate of between 500 and 900 former slaves from the United States. Period: 1800 - 1860.

710. Wynnyckyj, Iroida. "Ukrainians in Waterloo Region." **Waterloo Historical Society**. 1990. 78: 6-19. Loc: all.

A survey of the distinctive forms of community life resulting from three waves of Ukrainian migration to the region since 1906, when a group of about 70 families began to settle in Preston. The author explains that, as in the homeland, cultural and educational activities in the early years centred around the Prosvita (Enlightenment) halls. She describes various associations formed by Ukrainians, especially the Ukrainian Catholic Church of the Transfiguration in Kitchener, established 1926, of which she has written a 60th anniversary history. Period: 1906 - 1989.

FAMILY HISTORY AND GENEALOGY
GENERAL

711. **Ancestor charts**. Waterloo: Ontario Genealogical Society, Waterloo-Wellington Branch, 1974. 54 p. Loc: OKIT.

Five-generational charts compiled for their families by early members of the branch. Principal family names connected with Waterloo County are Bauman, Blundell, Buehler, Clemmer, Cook, Cornell, Cressman, Doud, Faber, Fairbairn, Farrow, Freeman, Fuller, Greig, Hahn, Howey, Jones, Kieffer, Lednor, Kinzie, Lehman, Lelond, Martin, Mather, McDonald, McKinnon, Near, Norris, Oberholtzer, Robertson, Roth, Rudy, Schneider, Snyder, Schoenhals, Shaver, Smuck, Stroh, Strong, Tindale, Warren, Weber and Weicker. There is also an index of about 400 family names included in the charts in some way. Period: 1800 - 1950.

712. **Ancestor charts, Volume 2**. Waterloo: Ontario Genealogical Society, Waterloo-Wellington Branch, 1974. 37 p. Loc: OKIT.

Five-generational charts compiled for their families by early members of the branch. Principal family names connected with Waterloo County are Brox, Dare/Doerr, Kieffer, Kriesel and Moyer. There is also an index of some 150 family names included in the charts in some way. Period: 1800 - 1970.

713. Eby, Ezra E. **A biographical history of Waterloo Township and other townships of the county: being a history of the early settlers and their descendants, mostly all of Pennsylvania Dutch origin: as also much other unpublished historical information chiefly of a local character**. Berlin: The Author, 1895. 2 v. Also CIHM Microfiche series, nos. 10018-10020. Loc: OCCA, OKIT, OWRE, OWRW, OWT, OWTL, OWTU, OWTUCG, OWTUR.

A collection of biographical sketches of the mainly Pennsylvania German Mennonites who settled in Waterloo Township and adjoining areas in the first half of the nineteenth century. The details for nearly 8,500 pioneers and their descendants are organized alphabetically according to the 142 principal pioneer families identified by the author through exhaustive research. A 44-page introduction outlines the migrations of Mennonite families from Pennsylvania to Upper Canada between 1799 and 1835, the formation of the German Company, and the locations in which families settled. The main family names, all separately indexed in the Waterloo Regional Project's database, are Adolph, Albright, Baumann (also spelled Bauman and Bowman), Bear (formerly Baehr), Bearinger, Bechtel, Benner, Bergey (formerly Birgi), Betzner, Biehn (later spelled Bean), Bingeman, Bliehm (later spelled Bleam), Block, Bock, Bowers, Brech (later Breck), Bretz, Bricker, Brower, Brubacher, Burkhard, Burkholder, Cassel, Christner, Clemens, Clemmer, Cober, Cowan, Cress, Cressman, Detweiler (also spelled Dettweiler and Detwiler), Devitt, Eby, Erb, Ernst, Eshelman, Fordney, Fried, Gehman, Geiger, Gingerich, Gole, Good (formerly spelled Guth), Goudie, Grody, Groff (formerly Graff), Groh, Haas, Hagey, Hallman, Hammacher, Heckedon, Hembling, Herner, Hilborn, Histand, Hoffman, Holm, Honsberger, Horst, Hostetler, Huber, Janzen (later and also spelled Johnson), Jones, Kauffman, Keller, Kinzie (also Kinsey), Kinzinger, Koch, Kolb, Kraft, Latschaw, Levan, Lichty, Livergood, Lutz, Martin, Master (formerly Meschter), McNally, Meyer, Miller, Mohr, Moyer, Mosser, Musselman, Myers, Nahrgang, Oberholtzer, Pannebecker, Quickfall, Reichert, Reist, Reitzel, Rife (formerly Reiff), Ringler, Roat, Rosenberger, Rudell, Rudy, Saltzberger (later Salsberry), Sararas, Sauers, Scheifle (later Scheifley, Shifley or Shyflee), Scheirich (later Shiry), Sherk (formerly Schoerg or Schörg and later also Shirk), Schiedel, Schlichter, Schmidt, Schneider, Schroder, Shuh (formerly Schuh), Schwartz, Seibert, Shantz (formerly Tschantzen then Schantzen, and later also Schantz, Shants, or Shons), Shelly, Shoemaker (formerly Schuhmacher), Shupe, Sitler, Souder (also spelled Sauder), Springer, Stauffer, Stoeckle, Strickler, Strome (formerly Strohm), Thomas, Tohman, Tyson, Unger, Urmy, Wanner, Weber (also Weaver), Winger (also spelled Wenger), Wideman, Wile, Wildfong, Wing, Wismer, Wissler, Witmer, Woolner, Yost, Zeller and Ziegler. Users should note the supplement compiled by Joseph Snyder and published in 1931, and the indexes, notes and maps added by Eldon Weber who reprinted Ezra Eby's volumes in 1971. Period: 1798 - 1895.

714. "Family names in the Kitchener-Waterloo City Directory [WRP]." **Waterloo Historical Society.** 1960. 48: 76. Loc: all.

A report of a survey finding more Schmidts listed than any other name, with Webers in second place and Millers third. Period: 1960.

715. **Genealogies cataloged by the Library of Congress since 1986.** Washington, DC: Library of Congress, 1991. 1349 p. Loc: OWTUCG.

Complete bibliographic data on nearly 9,000 genealogies cataloged between January 1986 and July 1991, with lists of more than 10,000 authorized surname spellings and over 22,000 cross references to variant spellings of those surnames. Subject headings used in cataloging are included.

716. Gingerich, Hugh F. and Kreider, Rachel W. **Amish and Amish Mennonite genealogies.** Gordonville, PA: Pequea Publishers, 1986. 848 p. Loc: OKIT.

A comprehensive list of the first Amish immigrants to North America and their descendants to 1850. For Amish who migrated to Waterloo County between 1815 and 1850, 91 surnames are listed. These family names have been indexed in the WRP database. There are geographic codes identifying immigrants to Wellesley Township, Waterloo Township and Wilmot Township. Period: 1815 - 1850.

717. Graber, Arthur. **Swiss Mennonite ancestors and their relationship from 1775.** Freeman, SD: Pine Hill Press, 1980. 691 p. indexes. Loc: OWTUCGR.

A genealogy referring mainly to the South Dakota Swiss Mennonites. Waterloo County names occurring in this genealogy are indexed in the WRP database. These are the Albrecht, Gerin, Graber, Kaufman, Kramer, Krehbiel, Miller, Ortman, Preheim, Ries, Schmidt, Schrag, Schwartz, Stucky, Straus, Sutter, Tieszen and Waltner families. Period: 1800 - 1980.

718. Peters, Victor and Thiessen, Jack. **Mennonitische Namen / Mennonite names.** Marburg, Germany:

Elwert, 1987. 247 p. ill., bibl., maps. Loc: OKIT.

An alphabetical listing of Mennonite surnames giving their probable derivation and meaning. Mennonite nicknames are discussed, as are the 20 most common Mennonite family names in Canada. There are no specific references to Waterloo County.

719. Snyder, Joseph B. **Supplement to Ezra E. Eby's Biographical history of early settlers and their descendants in Waterloo County.** Waterloo: J.B. Snyder, 1931. 195 p. Loc: OWTUR, OWTL, OKIT, OKEBC, OWT.

An index to supplement Ezra Eby's 1896

compilation, recording 2,800 names of persons (listed and numbered as in Eby's volumes) who died between 1895 and 1931. The spouse of each deceased person is also named. Period: 1895 - 1931.

720. Weber, Eldon D. **A biographical history of early settlers and their descendants in Waterloo Township by Ezra E. Eby 1895 & 1896; a supplement by Joseph P. Snyder 1931; plus an intensive index of all entries of all persons whose names are used throughout the volumes; an ordinal index of geography related to the numbered items; notes about some of the families and individuals; maps and other documents of interest.** Kitchener: AlJon Print-Craft, 1971. 1 v. (various pagings). ill., maps. Loc: OCCA, OKIT, OWRE, OWRN, OWT, OWTL, OWTU, OWTUCG.

An introduction, notes, maps and set of indexes to accompany and update the reprinting of Ezra Eby's **Biographical history** of 1895-6 (qv) and Joseph B. Snyder's **Supplement** of 1931 (qv). Lists are provided of the original owners and acreages of the 130 lots of Woolwich Township and the 160 lots of the German Company Tract in Waterloo Township, as well as of other blocks and tracts in Waterloo Township, such as the James Wilson Upper Block, Beasley's Middle Block, Beasley's Lower Block east and west of the Grand River, Beasley's Old Survey, Beasley's New Survey, Bechtel's Tract, Histand Tract, Bean's Tract, Beasley's Broken Front east of the Grand River, and the four Lower Block concessions. The maps include clear reproductions of each township from the Tremaine Map of Waterloo County (1861). The geographical index is organized according to the numbered family and personal entries in Eby's volumes. Eldon Weber's own meticulous cross-referencing of all persons including spouses, in the Eby and Snyder lists, is reflected in the book's detailed personal index of at least 14,000 entries, each numbered according to the order in Eby's 1895 volumes. Period: 1798 - 1970.

SURNAMES BEGINNING WITH A

721. Shantz, Mary C. **The Ahrens story.** Sudbury: The Author, 1981. 83 p. ill., charts, maps. Loc: OKIT.

A lively narrative of the life and times of the Ahrens family, German immigrants who were prominent in the development of Berlin/Kitchener and related to the J.M. Schneider family by marriage. The paper also contains background information about the community and the Swedenborgian Church. Period: 1803 - 1980.

722. Cowan, Virginia Bollacker. **Catherine Litt and Peter Alles family**. Dacono, CO: The Author, 1987. 61 p. ill., map. Loc: OKIT.

A collection of documents about Peter Alles (1829-1892), a German immigrant to Wilmot Township who became an Evangelical preacher, and his descendants. Peter and his wife Catherine later moved to Michigan. Many of the items are letters from relatives about their family histories; a separate section contains family photographs. Period: 1829 - 1987.

723. Kalbfleisch, Raymond W. **The Pirie book**. Petoskey, MI: The Author, 1980. 37 p. ill., index. Loc: OKIT.

A genealogy with some biographical information on the descendants of John and Janet Anderson, Scottish emigrants who settled near Winterbourne in 1838. Period: 1838 - 1980.

724. Norris, Jacqueline. **Children of John Arnold and Mariah Barnes: Dorset County, England to Markham Township 1841, Wellesley Township, Waterloo County 1847**. Guelph: The Author, 1986. 24 p. ill., index. Loc: OKIT.

The genealogy of an English farmer whose descendants migrated to Michigan, New York and parts of Ontario. Period: 1847 - 1986.

725. Arthaud, John Bradley. **The Emile and Susanna (Ebersol) Arthaud family, 1765-1987: with allied families of Blank/Plank, Lebold, Neuhauser, Schwartzentruber and Zwalter**. Columbia, MO: The Author, 1987. 104 p. index. Loc: OKIT, OWRW, OWTUCGR.

History of the descendants of Emil Arthaud, a French Mennonite who migrated to Canada in 1833 and married Susanna Ebersol of Wilmot Township. The couple bought one hundred acres of land in Zorra Township and later moved to the United States. Information and copied documents on the Ebersol family and their ties with the Zwalder, Neuhauser, Schwartzentruber, Blank and Lebold families are included in the appendices. Period: 1833 - 1987.

726. Hammond, Florence M. Ayres and Ratchford, Douglas. **Little apples growing**. Waterloo: R. Bean, 1972. 136 p. ill. Loc: OCLG, OCP, OKIT, OWTU, OWRA.

Humorous recollections of Ayres family life in Kitchener from the 1930s depression to the 1960s. This is a sequel to the author's book **Little apples will grow again**. Period: 1928 - 1971.

727. Hammond, Florence M. Ayres. **Little apples will grow again**. Kitchener: Reeve Bean Printers, 1970. 63 p. ill. Loc: OCLG, OCP, OKIT, OWRA, OWRBL, OWRE, OWTUR.

A biographical novel based on the settlement of the Ayres family at Doon. Told by the youngest Ayres child, Florence M. Hammond, the story begins in Essex, England in 1911, on the day it was decided to come to Canada. The Doon community is described with the names of many Doon residents and businesses. Period: 1911 - 1961.

SURNAMES BEGINNING WITH B

728. **Ephraim Baer family 1876-**. 1976. 16 p. Loc: OWTUCGR.

A genealogy of the descendants of Ephraim (1876-1953) and Lovina Nahrgang (1881-1956) and their sixteen children. There are minutes of the 1971 reunion and handwritten notes updating the information to 1976. Period: 1876 - 1976.

729. Groh, Ivan. "Aunt Hannah." **Canadian-German Folklore**. 1967. 2: 58-60. Loc: OKIT, OWTL, OWTU, OWTUCG.

Reminiscences of a Groh family visit by wagon to Aunt Hannah Baer, daughter of Levi Snyder, at Owen Reist's farm. There is genealogical information on the Baers, some of whom built bridges at Freeport and West Montrose. Period: 1845 - 1920.

730. Martin, Winston J. **A history of the Baer family**. The Author, 1987. 14 p. ill. Loc: OWTUCGR.

A genealogy of the Bear/Baer family, based on the work of Ezra Eby and Jane Evans Best. Martin Baer came to Preston from Pennsylvania in 1801 and married Catharine Gingrich. Others of the family later moved to Mannheim, West Montrose, New Hamburg, Michigan and further west. Period: 1801 - 1976.

731. Robbins, Elizabeth Luella Eby. **The Henry Baer family history**. Glanworth: The Authors?, 1977. 30 p. ill. Loc: OKIT, OWTUCGR.

A genealogy of the descendants of Henry Baer (1842-1927) and Leah Bowman (1847-1937), Mennonite farmers of Wilmot Township. There is a biographical introduction for each of the fourteen children whose descendants are listed. Period: 1842 - 1977.

732. Bauman, Angus S. **Family records: mostly of three distinct groups and descendants of Joseph, David and Henry Bauman who settled as pioneers in Waterloo Township, Waterloo County, up to the year of 1825, each representing one of the three tribes of Christian, Peter and Jacob, respectively, who are children of the old progenitor Wendel Bauman: also an extensive history and records of family lineages of the early ancestors**. Wallenstein: Angus S. Bauman, 1940. 201 p. index. Loc: OWTUR,

OWTUCG, OKIT, OWRE.

A detailed genealogical study of the members of the Bauman family from their arrival in Waterloo Township at the beginning of the 19th century to 1940. An historical sketch of the family includes transcripts of wills and correspondence, and also descriptions of the journey from Pennsylvania to Waterloo Township. Period: 1800 - 1940.

733. Bauman, David S. and Malloy, Reta Hoffman. **The descendants of Henry S. Bauman.** 1987. 38 p. ill. Loc: OKIT.

The third edition of a 1965 mimeographed report listing the descendants of Henry S. Bauman (1867-1935). It was also revised in 1979. Henry, the fifth son of Martin H. Bauman, first married Judith Martin and later Lavina Steckle. There is a biographical sketch of Henry, an Old Order Mennonite preacher who lived in Woolwich, with family photographs and genealogical charts tracing his descendants to the ninth generation. Period: 1867 - 1987.

734. Bauman, Roy G. and Bauman, Salome. **The Martin H. Bauman family history.** The Authors, 1969. 63 p. ill. Loc: OWRE, OWTUCGR, OKIT.

A genealogical account, based on Eby's history of Waterloo Township, a mimeographed 1932 listing of the descendants of Martin H. Bauman, and the genealogy of the descendants of Joseph Bauman by Sarah Bauman and Erma Freeman (1967). The present authors have added updates in the index format originally used by Ezra Eby. A final section presents humorous anecdotes about the Pennsylvania German way of life. Period: 1800 - 1969.

735. Bauman, Sarah and Freeman, Erna. **Family records of the descendants of pioneer Joseph Bauman, also some records of David and Henry Bauman.** St Jacobs: The Authors, 1967. 308 p. index. Loc: OKIT.

A revised edition of Angus S. Bauman's **Family records** (1940). The genealogical charts and the name index are updated to 1967, but the family history at the front of the book, the essay "Glimpses of the past" and the family information to 1941 are reprinted from Angus Bauman. Period: 1800 - 1967.

736. **The Enos M. Bauman family.** 1989. 12 p. Loc: OKIT.

A genealogical chart of the descendants of Enos M. Bauman and Elizabeth Lichty Martin, to the fourth generation. Period: 1871 - 1989.

737. Schmadl, Elizabeth L. **Index to Bauman family history by Angus Bauman.** 1990. 23 p. Loc: OKIT.

An index to Bauman family members, giving the number of the generation as well as the page on which the name is mentioned. Period: 1800 - 1940.

738. Schmidt, William A. **Simon Beaty and Julie Ann Bascom: a record of their descendants.** Waterloo: The Author, 1988. 1 v. (unpaged). ill., index. Loc: OKIT.

A genealogy of the Waterloo family from 1779 to 1988, including a biographical sketch of Simon's parents, John Beatty and Mary Cress. John Beatty was an Irishman and one of Waterloo's first schoolteachers. Period: 1800 - 1988.

739. Bechtel, Gary and Bechtel, Ruth. **Bechtel family, originator: Hans Jacob Bechtel, 1720.** Brantford: The Authors, 1981. 26 p. Loc: OWTUCGR.

A genealogy of a Pennsylvania Mennonite family, some members of which came to Canada in 1817 and settled in Wilmot Township and Roseville. There are transcripts of 18th century wills and a household inventory. Period: 1817 - 1981.

740. Bowman, Christian and Bowman, Elizabeth. "A letter: 1846." **Waterloo Historical Society.** 1969. 57: 16-18. Loc: all.

A letter written to Samuel and Elizabeth Bechtel of Hespeler from Christian and Elizabeth Bauman (Bowman) of Berks County, Pennsylvania in 1846. Period: 1846.

741. Brubacher, Mable Bechtel and Martin, Winston J. **Descendants of Hans Jacob Bechtel of Pottstown, PA and George III to Ont. 1929, Rev. Joseph to Ont. 1802.** The Authors, 1987. 60 p. Loc: OKIT, OWTUCGR.

Genealogical chart of the descendants of the four members of the Bechtel family who came to Waterloo County from Pennsylvania, Abraham, Joseph, George and George B. Period: 1802 - 1987.

742. Poth, Ruby Bechtel. **Family history of Mervin Bechtel and Adelia Brighton, compiled by their daughter, Ruby Bechtel Poth, copied from the original in her collection, 1983.** The Author, 1983. 1 v. (unpaged). ill. Loc: OKIT.

A collection of copied documents relating to the Bechtel family, including copies of marriage certificates, obituaries, photographs, genealogical charts and newspaper clippings. It also contains information about related families, such as the Brightons, Walkers, Sniders and Bocks. Period: 1803 - 1983.

743. Wenger, George F.P. **Descendants of Hans Jacob Bechtel, better known as Rev. Jacob Bechtel.** Pottstown, PA: The Author?, 1916?. 137 p. Loc: OWTUCGR.

A genealogy which includes Joseph Bechtel, a

Mennonite who moved from Pennsylvania to Waterloo Township with his wife Magdalena Allebach in 1802. Documents such as wills and inventories are transcribed. Period: 1802 - 1916.

744. Yates, G. Kenneth. **Migration of Bechtel family members from Montgomery County, Pennsylvania to Waterloo County, Ontario.** Westford, MA: The Author, 1991. 4 p. charts. Loc: OKIT.
    A comparison of two 1895 genealogies by Henry S. Bower and Ezra E. Eby, making inferences about American Bechtel family relationships in the 18th and early 19th centuries. Period: 1800 - 1847.

745. Pryce, Nona Beck. "The Becks of Doon." **Waterloo Historical Society.** 1966. 54: 59-61. Loc: all.
    A short history of the family, beginning with the birth of Jacob Beck in Baden, Germany in 1816, and mentioning the achievements of later family members including Adam Beck's role in the Hydro Electric Power Commission of Ontario. Period: 1810 - 1880.

746. Beachy, Lucy. **Daniel Bender family history.** Grantsville, MD: Bender Book Revision Committee, 1985. 648 p. ill., charts, indexes. Loc: OWTUCGR.
    A genealogy of the Daniel Bender family, Amish Mennonites who migrated to Pennsylvania from Germany in 1842. One chapter traces descendants of one son, Johannas D., who came to Canada and married Elizabeth Erb of Baden. Descendants of Johannas and Elizabeth remain in Waterloo County. Period: 1856 - 1985.

747. Bender, David M. and Bender, Noah R. **Family register of Jacob and Magdalena Bender and their children to the sixth generation: from the year of our Lord 1832 to 1925.** Tavistock: Gazette Printery, 1925. 61 p. Loc: OWTUCGR.
    The second edition of a genealogy with a brief introduction noting that the Amish Mennonite family settled near New Hamburg about 1832 after first coming to Lancaster County, Pennsylvania from Hessen, Germany. No death dates are given. Period: 1832 - 1925.

748. Bender, Jacob. **Familien-Register von Jakob und Magdalena Bender und ihr Nachkommen bis 1897.** Jakob and David Bender, 1897. 12 p. Loc: OWTUCGR.
    An early genealogy with a brief introduction relating the journey from Hessen, Germany to Lancaster, Pennsylvania, and then to Wilmot Township. Period: 1832 - 1897.

749. Bender, Jacob R. **Genealogy of Jacob and Magdalena Bender: record of descendants until the year of our Lord 1946.** Tavistock: The Author, 1947. 91 p. ill., index. Loc: OWTUCGR.

The third edition of the genealogy, noting addresses and the religion of the head of each family and whether or not he was ordained. Period: 1832 - 1946.

750. Bergey, Barbara G. and Koch, Alice and Bergey, Dorothy M. **Family history of Jacob and Elizabeth Eby Bergey.** D. Douglas and Anne Eby Millar, 1987. 98 p. ill., index. Loc: OWTUR, OWTUCGR.
    An annotated genealogy updating the 1925 work by Dr David Hendricks Bergey and including brief histories of the Bergey and Clemens families. Period: 1818 - 1987.

751. Bergey, David Hendricks. **Genealogy of the Bergey family: a record of the descendants of John Ulrich Bergey and his wife, Mary.** New York: Frederick H. Hitchcock, 1925. 1150 p. ill., index. Loc: OKIT, OWTUCGR.
    An encyclopedic history of the Bergey family in North America from 1719 to 1925. The book is divided by generations, with many details of individuals and places of residence and a comprehensive index of names. Period: 1815 - 1925.

752. Atkinson, Clara Wurster. "The Jacob Bernhardt family history." **Waterloo Historical Society.** 1957. 45: 16-18. Loc: all.
    An account of Philip and Barbara Bernhardt who came from Alsace to Preston in 1855, including details of their ten children. Period: 1817 - 1881.

753. Bettschen, Gottlieb. **Genealogical, biographical and pictorial history of the Bettschen family and its connections.** The Author, 1910. 110 p. ill., maps. Loc: OKIT, OKITW, OWRND.
    An account of many members of the Bettschen family, beginning with David Bettschen in Canton Berne, Switzerland in 1723 and including David's son, Jacob, who settled in Wilmot Township in the early 1820s and Jacob's son, Gottlieb, born in 1841. Photographs and maps accompany the biographical sketches. Period: 1828 - 1910.

754. Schmadl, Elizabeth L. **Index to History of the Bettschen family and its connections, by Gottlieb Bettschen.** 1991. 6 p. Loc: OKIT.
    Index to some 300 personal names mentioned in the volume actually entitled **Genealogical, biographical and pictorial history of the Bettschen family and its connections.** Period: 1828 - 1910.

755. Brown, Harry W. "The second Betzner reunion." **Waterloo Historical Society.** 1920. 8: 133-139. Loc: all.
    An account of Betzner family history, including

the 1920 Betzner reunion. Period: 1800 - 1920.

756. Edworthy, Laura Betzner. **The Betzner family in Canada: genealogical and historical records, 1799-1970.** 1970. 56 p. ill., bibl., map, charts. Loc: OKIT.

A history of the Betzners, some of whom migrated to Waterloo County from Pennsylvania in 1799. It contains biographical information on Samuel D. Betzner, general information about the early Mennonite settlement of Waterloo County, and details of the Betzner Family Reunions of 1917, 1920 and 1967. Genealogical charts show the families of Samuel Betzner, Abram Betzner, Jacob Betzner, David S. Betzner and John Weir Betzner. Period: 1799 - 1970.

757. Kalbfleisch, Raymond W. **The Bickel book, including genealogies of the following main branches: Boettger, Buck, Heipel, Helwig, and Kalbfleisch lines.** Petoskey, MI: The Author, 1982. 189 p. ill., bibl., indexes. Loc: OKIT.

A looseleaf binder containing information about the ancestors, descendants and relations of Mathias Bickel (1822-1906), a pioneer German immigrant who settled near Neustadt, Ontario. Many members of this family settled in Waterloo County; the geographical index has entries for Ayr, Cambridge, Elmira, Galt, Hespeler, Kitchener, Mannheim, New Dundee, New Hamburg, Petersburg, Preston, Roseville, St Jacobs, Waterloo, Waterloo Township, Wellesley, Wilmot, Winterbourne and Woolwich Township. There is also a personal name index. Period: 1850 - 1982.

758. Bean, S.U. **Historical sketch of the Biehn families and the descendants, 1700-1947.** Stratford: The Author?, 1947. 31 p. ill. Loc: OWTUR, OKIT.

A detailed account of the Biehn family, from 1800 when John Biehn Sr migrated to Waterloo County, to 1946. Many descendants are listed, with birth and death dates and some mention of their achievements. Information about the Bean family is also contained in S.U. Bean's article in the Waterloo Historical Society Report of 1947. Period: 1800 - 1947.

759. Bean, S.U. "Historical sketch of the Biehn family." **Waterloo Historical Society.** 1947. 35: 15-18. Loc: all.

A short account of the Biehn (Bean) family, with particular reference to the direct descendants of John Biehn Jr who arrived in the Waterloo area in 1800. Period: 1800 - 1840.

760. Biehn, Donald M. **Biehn/Bean family of Bucks County, Pennsylvania and Ontario, Canada, 1700-1986.** Baltimore: Gateway Press, 1987. 368 p. ill., bibl., maps, index. Loc: OKIT, OWTUCGR.

A family history including a reprint of Samuel U. Bean's work on the Bean family in Canada, with the addition of information from the **Mennonite Quarterly Review** of 1939 and 1929. The genealogical data are updated, and the sequence of descendants is changed to agree with the order of births. Period: 1800 - 1986.

761. Rommel, Hazel Hathaway. **My mother's people: a history of the related families of the Bingamans - Betzners - Bowmans - Clemens and Sniders of Pennsylvania, Ontario and Michigan.** Port Angeles, WA: The Author, 1985. 110 p. ill., charts, maps. Loc: OWTUCGR.

A history of the ancestors and descendants of Elizabeth Betzner of Breslau and Aaron Bingaman, with brief accounts of the early Betzner, Bingeman, Clemens and Snider families in Waterloo County. Many family members later moved to Michigan. Period: 1799 - 1985.

762. Boehm, M.S. "History of the Boehm (Beam) family." **Waterloo Historical Society.** 1936. 24: 213-228. Loc: all.

An account of the migration of ancestors of Charles Adam Boehm to Pennsylvania and later to Canada. Period: 1700 - 1929.

763. Carr, Lucile Boshart and Boshart, Shirley Jantzi and Roth, Lorraine. **Christian E. Boshart and Catherine Buerge family history and genealogy.** Newport, OR: Pioneer Printing, 1978. 300 p. ill., maps, index. Loc: OWTUCGR.

An account of a French Amish Mennonite family who settled in Wilmot and Wellesley Townships in 1834 and later moved to Nebraska and Oregon. Reminiscences and photographs complement the genealogical information. Period: 1834 - 1978.

764. Livingston, James D. **Wilhelm and Augusta Boullee of New Hamburg, Ontario: their descendants.** Schenectady, NY: The Author?, 1981. 8 p. map. Loc: OKIT.

A brief account of the New Hamburg physician/publisher who emigrated from Germany in the 1840s. The research begins with information on Wilhelm and Augusta, and concludes with short entries on their children, grandchildren and great-grandchildren. Period: 1821 - 1981.

765. Bowlby, Raymond E. **Our Bowlby kin, United Empire Loyalists: the Richard Bowlby (7) family.** Chicago: Genealogical Services and Publications, 1978. 21 p. bibl., indexes. Loc: OKIT.

A continuation of the book, **Our Bowlby kin, volume one,** about the branch which migrated to Nova Scotia from the United States during the American Revolutionary War. Waterloo County members of this family, including W.H. Bowlby and D.S. Bowlby, are mentioned and placed in their genealogical context. Period: 1850 - 1904.

766. Bowman, H.M. "The Mennonite settlements in Pennsylvania and Waterloo with special reference to the Bowman Family." **Waterloo Historical Society.** 1922. 10: 225-247. ill. Loc: all.

An account of Mennonite migration, including some references to the settlement of Bowmans in the Blair area of Waterloo Township. Period: 1800 - 1857.

767. Bowman, Jesse. **Detailed history of the Henry B. Bowman descendants.** St Jacobs: The Author?, 1964. 36 p. Loc: OKITW, OWTUR, OWTUCGR.

A genealogy of the Bowman family from Wendel Baumann's emigration to America in the early 18th century, with a general introduction and an index. Period: 1800 - 1963.

768. Bowman, Jesse. **Supplement to Henry B. Bowman descendants.** St Jacobs: The Author, 1980. 20 p. Loc: OWTUCGR.

A supplement to the author's earlier detailed study, listing names and birth and death dates of the descendants and noting the generation of each individual. Period: 1965 - 1979.

769. Brake, Eunice M. **Schnitz and plum pudding: a family history of the Brake-Break-Brech, the Cosens, the Kraft, the Wismer families.** The Author, 1992. 268 p. ill. Loc: OWTUCGR.

A history of a family with Pennsylvania Dutch and English origins. Many of its members came first to Waterloo County, moving on to Michigan. Autobiographical details of the author, reminiscences of her family and descriptions of ancestors are included with genealogical charts and family recipes. Period: 1806 - 1992.

770. Breithaupt, W.H. **Sketch of the life of Catharine Breithaupt, her family and times.** Berlin: R.G. McLean, 1911. 29 l. ill., ports. Loc: OKIT, OWTLR, OWTUR.

A biography of the author's mother, with details and photographs of other family members as well as the family tanning business. Period: 1834 - 1910.

771. Breithaupt, James R. "Breithaupt origins." **Families.** 1976. 15,4: 122-124. Loc: OKIT, OWTL, OWTU.

An account of the family's 1843 migration from Germany to Buffalo, and later to Berlin. The author briefly surveys the generations of Waterloo County Breithaupts and their contributions to the community. Period: 1843 - 1976.

772. Breithaupt, Theodor. **Chronicle of the Breithaupt family in biographies.** Schlüterschen Buchdruckerei, 1899 - 1903. 2 v. ill. ports. Loc: OWTUR.

Translation of **Chronik der Familie Breithaupt in Biographien.** Volume 2 contains detailed profiles of Philipp Ludwig (born 1827, usually called Louis after his migration to North America) and Louis Jacob (born 1855), as well as references to other members of this branch. Period: 1857 - 1929.

773. Breithaupt, Theodor. **Chronik der Familie Breithaupt in Biographien.** Hannover (Germany): Schlüterschen Buchdruckerei, 1899 - 1929. 4 v. ill., ports. Loc: OWTUR.

A genealogy of many branches of the family, including the Kreuzburger line to which the Berlin/Kitchener Breithaupts belong. Volume (Band) 2 contains detailed profiles of Philipp Ludwig (born 1827, usually called Louis after his migration to North America) and his son, Louis Jacob (born 1855). Volume 4 was published by G.J. Pfingsten. Period: 1857 - 1929.

774. Roth, Lorraine. **History and genealogy of Jacob and Lydia (Leonard) Brenneman family, 1843-1963.** Shakespeare: The Author?, 1963. 96 p. index, map. Loc: OWTUCGR.

Jacob Brenneman, the son of an Amish Mennonite pioneer family, grew up in Wilmot Township. He settled in South Easthope Township at the time of his marriage about 1840. An account of each of the ten children is given. Many of them settled just beyond the boundaries of Waterloo County, some of their descendants later moving to Kitchener. Period: 1843 - 1963.

775. Yantzi, Mae. **Family tree of Daniel and Barbara Brenneman up to June 1979.** Glen Allan: The Author, 1979. 45 p. ill., index. Loc: OWTUCGR.

A genealogy of a Mennonite family who farmed south of New Hamburg. Both parents died of tuberculosis, leaving their three children, Peter, Elizabeth and Daniel, orphans at an early age. Biographical information and reminiscences are provided on each child's family. Period: 1835 - 1979.

776. Larson, Elsie Bricker and Baer, Clara Bricker. **The ancestors and descendants of Isaac Bricker, 1718-1973.** The Authors, 1973. 17 p. ill., chart. Loc: OKIT.

A genealogy of Isaac Bricker (1835-1926) who

farmed in Blenheim Township and was a grandson of Samuel Bricker, one of the organizers of the German Company, and the son of Peter and Susannah Erb Bricker. The authors present information about the migration of the Bricker family from Switzerland to Pennsylvania in 1718 and the arrival of Samuel and John Bricker in Waterloo County in 1802. Period: 1802 - 1973.

777. Schmadl, Elizabeth L. **Index to The ancestors and descendants of Isaac Bricker by Elsie Larson and Clara Baer.** Kitchener Public Library, 1991. 6 p. Loc: OKIT.

An index to more than 400 names. Period: 1802 - 1973.

778. Schmidt, William A. **The Bricker connection, part 1: Jacob C. Bricker and Mary Greenfelder, their ancestors and descendants.** Waterloo: The Author, 1985. 1 v. index. Loc: OKIT, OWTUCGR.

Part of a 5-volume genealogy of the children of Peter Bricker and Elizabeth Cress, devoted to their son Jacob. Period: 1800 - 1986.

779. Schmidt, William A. **The Bricker connection, part 2: Nancy Bricker and Jacob Snider, their ancestors and descendants.** Waterloo: The Author, 1985. 1 v. index. Loc: OKIT, OWTUCGR.

A portion of the genealogy of Peter and Elizabeth Cress devoted to their daughter Nancy, her husband Jacob Snider and their four children. Period: 1800 - 1985.

780. Schmidt, William A. **The Bricker connection, part 3: Catherine Bricker and George Brink, their ancestors and descendants.** Waterloo: The Author?, 1986. 1 v. index. Loc: OKIT, OWTUCGR.

A genealogy of the family of Catherine Bricker, daughter of Elizabeth Cress and Peter Bricker, and her husband George Brink. Period: 1800 - 1986.

781. Schmidt, William A. **The Bricker connection, part 4: John C. Bricker and Sallie Wideman (Elizabeth Cress), their ancestors and descendants.** Waterloo: The Author, 1985. 1 v. index. Loc: OKIT, OWTUCGR.

A genealogy of the family of John C. Bricker, son of Elizabeth Cress and Peter Bricker, with his first wife, Sallie Wideman, and his second wife, Elizabeth Cress. Period: 1800 - 1985.

782. Schmidt, William A. **The Bricker connection, part 5: Rachel Bricker and John Martin.** Waterloo: The Author, 1984. 1 v. index. Loc: OKIT, OWTUCGR.

A genealogy of the descendants of Rachel Bricker, daughter of Peter Bricker and Elizabeth Cress, and her husband John Martin. Period: 1800 - 1986.

783. Gray, Marilyn Tone. **And now we are many: a history and genealogy of the Brohman family.** Toronto: Marilyn Tone Gray, 1971. 181 p. ill., index. Loc: OKIT, OWRE, OWTL, OWTUR.

A detailed work, tracing the family from the migration of Gottlieb Brohman to New Germany (Maryhill) from Alsace in the late 1820s. He married Catherine Lauber and the succeeding generations to 1970 are all recorded. There is a brief mention of Joseph Brohman who was noted for his herbal remedies, some of which are included in the appendices. Tremaine's 1861 map of Waterloo Township is reproduced on the front lining paper, and a map of Block Number Two in 1805 is on the back. There is a lengthy index to all personal names and a bibliography. Period: 1833 - 1968.

784. Shantz, Helen. **Descendants of Louis Brox, 1861-1938.** 1985. 46 p. ill. Loc: OWTUCGR.

A genealogy of the ancestors and descendants of Louis Brox, son of Jacob Brox, a German baker in Elmira. Louis and his wife Caroline Randall farmed northeast of Elmira and had twelve children. Period: 1861 - 1985.

785. Bowman, Henry B. **Ancestral record of Henry Martin Brubacher, 1838-1910.** Preston?: The Author?, 1965. 31 p. index. Loc: OKIT.

A chronology of the Brubacher family, tracing ancestors back to 17th-century Switzerland and descendants to 1965. John W. Brubacher, the first member of the family to come to Canada, settled in Woolwich Township in 1825. The history focuses on the family of Henry Martin Brubacher, the fourth son of John W., who continued his father's interests in woollen mills. The text describes a sawmill owned by John W. on the bank of the Conestogo River, and woollen mills in St Jacobs, Chicopee and Baden. An index prepared by Elizabeth L. Schmadl in 1990 includes 861 names. Period: 1825 - 1965.

786. Brubacher, Aden H. **Record of the ancestors and descendants of Jacob Sherk Brubacher (D-67) and his brother Daniel Sherk Brubacher (D-71).** Elmira: The Author, 1974. 150 p. ill., index. Loc: OKIT, OWTUCGR.

A genealogy including the Waterloo families of John Brubacher and Elizabeth Burkhart, John Shelley Brubacher and Anna Edy, Jacob Shelley Brubacher and Anna Martin, and Samuel Kurtz Brubacher and Magdalena Murphy. Period: 1807 - 1974.

787. Brubacher, Benjamin. "Brubacher family history." **Waterloo Historical Society.** 1923. 11: 38-45. Loc: all.

A detailed account of four generations of Brubachers in North America from about 1710, including a family tree, locations of family members in Pennsylvania and Waterloo County, many given names and names of those related by marriage. Period: 1800 - 1923.

788. Brubacher, Jacob N. **The Brubacher genealogy in America**. Elkhart, IN: Mennonite Publishing Co., 1884. 243 p. index. Loc: OWTUCGR.

A pocket-sized genealogy of the descendants of John and Anna, the first American Brubachers, including identification of some family members who came to Waterloo County early in the 19th century. Period: 1807 - 1884.

789. Brubacher, Landis H. **Descendants of John Hess Brubacher D-14, 1782-1862 of Juniata County and his nephew "Cooper" John Sherk Brubacher D-63, 1807-1887 of Ontario, Canada**. Seven Valleys, PA: The Author?, 1977. 309 p. ill., index. Loc: OWTUCGR.

A genealogy including many Waterloo descendants. One of the earliest Brubachers to settle in the Waterloo region was John W. Brubacher who came to Woolwich Township from Pennsylvania in about 1825 and founded a sawmill in 1847 and a woollen mill in 1855, both near Hawkesville. A preface gives some background information and biographical notes. Period: 1825 - 1977.

790. Brubaker, Calvin B. **A brief history and genealogy of the Brubacher families in Waterloo County and Ontario**. Kitchener: The Author, 1990. 1 v. (unpaged). Loc: OKIT, OWTUCGR.

A genealogy tracing the family back to John Weber Brubacher (1803-1886) who arrived in 1825 and settled two miles west of St Jacobs. Period: 1825 - 1895.

791. Brubaker, Calvin B. **Family record of Anson Beeshy Brubacher, 1863-1926**. Kitchener: The Author, 1967. 16 p. Loc: OKITW, OWTUCGR.

A history of the Brubacher family, with particular attention to the families of Anson B. Brubacher and Magdalena Bowman. Period: 1863 - 1967.

792. Brubaker, Calvin B. **The history and genealogy of the Brubacher Brubaker families in Waterloo County and Ontario**. Kitchener: The Author, 1975. 32 p. Loc: OWTU, OWTUCGR, OKIT.

A family history that begins with Hans Brubacher in mid-sixteenth-century Switzerland and traces his descendants to Pennsylvania and Waterloo County. Period: 1807 - 1975.

793. Gibble, Phares Brubaker. **History and genealogy of the Brubaker-Brubacher-Brewbaker family in America**. Eastern Pennsylvania Brubaker Association, 1951. 93 p. ill. Loc: OWTUCGR, OKIT.

A general account including a note of the family reunion at Kitchener in 1923 and references to early Brubachers in Canada, such as Maria Brubacher Eby, Deacon John Brubacher, Elias S. Brubacher and descendants of John Brubacher of Juniata County, Pennsylvania. Period: 1807 - 1951.

794. McKinnon, William A. **Family history of Jacob R. Brubacher**. St Jacobs: The Author?, 1979?. 97 p. ill. Loc: OKIT.

A detailed account of the ancestors and descendants of Jacob B. Brubacher (1855-1937), the oldest son of John Martin Brubacher and grandson of John Weber Brubacher. Jacob B. and his wife, Elizabeth Martin farmed in Woolwich Township, later moving to Iowa and then to Pennsylvania. An index to names mentioned in this book has been compiled by Elizabeth L. Schmadl. Period: 1855 - 1978.

795. Schmadl, Elizabeth L. **Index to Family history of Jacob B. Brubacher by William McKinnon**. Kitchener Public Library, 1990. 21 p. Loc: OKIT.

An index of about 1500 names. Period: 1855 - 1978.

796. Schmadl, Elizabeth L. **Index to History and genealogy of the Brubaker-Brubacher-Brewbaker family in America**. Kitchener Public Library, 1990. 37 p. Loc: OKIT.

A name index to Phares Brubaker Gibble's work. Period: 1807 - 1951.

797. Schmidt, William A. **Julian Beaty and Abraham Z. Buehler: a record of their descendants**. Waterloo: The Author?, 1988. 520 p. index. Loc: OKIT.

A genealogy with brief biographies of John Beaty and Mary Cress, parents of Julian, who settled in Waterloo Township. Descendants of the six surviving children of Julian and Abraham Z. Buehler include many members of the Schallhorn, Biehn and Ringler families. Period: 1800 - 1988.

798. Burkhardt, B. LeRoy. **Descendants of Jacob and Maria Burckhart, a genealogy**. The Author, 1980?. 1 v. bibl., index. Loc: OWTUCGR.

A revised version of a genealogy of a Pennsylvania Mennonite family, including references to Peter Burkhard and Barbara Good Burkhard. Period: 1820 - 1970.

799. Burkhardt, B. LeRoy. **Descendants of Jacob and Maria Burckhart, a genealogy**. The Author, 1970?. 1 v. index. Loc: OWTUCGR.

A genealogy of the Burckhart or Burkhard family of Pennsylvania. Peter Burkhard and his wife, Barbara Good, came in 1820 to Woolwich Township where Peter served the Martin Mennonite Church. Four of their children married four of the children of John and Anna Hackman Gingerich, also Pennsylvania Mennonites who came to Waterloo County. Period: 1820 - 1970.

800. Burkhart, Irvin E. and Burkhart, Emerson and Burkhart, Florence. **Reminiscences and records of the family of Enoch and Hannah (Eby) Burkhart, long-time residents of Peel Township, Wellington County, Rural Route #1, Drayton, Ontario, Canada.** Goshen, IN: The Authors, 1970. 67 p. Loc: OKIT, OWTUCGR.

A genealogical record of the couple's ancestors and descendants. Enoch and Hannah bought a farm on the boundary between Wellington and Waterloo Counties and were members of the Floradale Mennonite Church. Many of their descendants still live in the Waterloo area. A name index for this work was prepared by Elizabeth Schmadl. Period: 1820 - 1970.

801. Schmadl, Elizabeth L. **Index to Reminiscences and records of the family of Enoch and Hannah (Eby) Burkhart, by Irvin E. Burkhart.** Kitchener Public Library, 1990. 5 p. Loc: OKIT.

An index to more than 240 names. Period: 1820 - 1970.

SURNAMES BEGINNING WITH C

802. Christner, H. Walter. **Our immigrants: Christian and Elizabeth Christner's family.** Sarasota, FL: The Author, 1991. 254 p. Loc: OWTUCG.

A family history tracing the descendants of Christian Christner who came to Wilmot Township in the 1820s and served as deacon in the Geiger (now Wilmot) Mennonite Church. An index to spouses and descendants is included. Period: 1825 - 1990.

803. Beirnes, Eileen and Clemens, Lloyd. **Family history of John Strohm Clemens 1833-1991.** 1991. 106 p. ill. Loc: OWTUCGR.

A genealogy of the descendants of the twelve children of John S. and Rebecca Snyder. John was the grandson of Abraham Clemens who came from Pennsylvania to settle in Fisher's Mills in 1818. Notes on the Clemens family in Europe and biographies of early Clemenses in Pennsylvania and Canada are included. Period: 1818 - 1991.

804. Clemens, Gerhard. "Early American Clemenses." **Waterloo Historical Society.** 1929. 17: 120-132. Loc: all.

A history of the Clemens family in America, including excerpts from the notebooks of Hans Stauffer and Gerhard Clemens and the will of Abraham Clemens. Period: 1800 - 1876.

805. Clemens, Jacob Cassel. **Genealogical history of the Clemens family and descendants of the pioneer, Gerhart Clemens.** The Clemens family, 1948. 56 p. ill., charts, index. Loc: OWTUCGR.

A genealogy of a Pennsylvania family, mentioning Abraham S. Clemens and Abraham O. Clemens whose families came to Waterloo Township in 1825 and 1855 respectively. Period: 1825 - 1948.

806. Clemens, Zena. **Clemens.** 1974?. 31 p. bibl. Loc: OWTUCGR.

A family tree containing biographies of two brothers, George and Abraham C. Clemens, who came to Waterloo County from Pennsylvania in the early 19th century. C.A. Panabaker's story of John Strohm Clemens and the horse-thief of Fisher's Mills is retold. Period: 1802 - 1974.

807. Fuller, Gordon H. **Clemens family history [WRP].** Caledonia: The Author, 1977. 58 p. ill., charts, maps. Loc: OKIT.

A genealogy interspersed with reminiscences and articles about the family, including one by D.N. Panabaker. The family emigrated from England to Pennsylvania, then to Waterloo County, and later to Michigan and to other parts of Canada. Period: 1800 - 1977.

808. Gaines, Marjorie Clemens. **The story of George and Salome Clemens: their forebears and descendants.** 1959. 49 p. Loc: OWTUR, OKIT.

A collection of family histories by descendants of the children of George and Salome, describing their lives and communities. Charts trace the Clemens (Clements) family back to 1563. Period: 1800 - 1957.

809. Panabaker, D.N. "Historical sketch of the Clemens family." **Waterloo Historical Society.** 1921. 9: 161-170. Loc: all.

A history of the Clemens family, especially those members who became pioneers of Waterloo Township. Period: 1800 - 1921.

810. Schmadl, Elizabeth L. **Index to The story of George and Salome Clemens: their forebears and descendants by Marjorie Clemens Gaines.** Kitchener Public Library, 1990. 8 p. Loc: OKIT.

An index of over 500 names. Period: 1800 - 1957.

811. Cober, Alvin Alonzo, Rev. **The Cober genealogy of Pennsylvania, Iowa and Canada.** Berlin, PA: Berlin Press, 1933. 289 p. ill., index. Loc: OKIT,

OWTUCGR.

A history of the Cober family, some members of which migrated from Pennsylvania to Ontario. Nicholas Cober Jr, his brother Jacob, and sister Susanna (Mrs Neils Peter Holm) moved to Puslinch Township near Hespeler in about 1832. Genealogical and biographical information is given on their descendants, many of whom became members of the Brethren in Christ or Tunkers. Period: 1832 - 1933.

812. Cober, Peter, Rev. "Cober family history." **Waterloo Historical Society.** 1940. 28: 113-119. Loc: all.

A history of the Cober and Holm families who settled near Puslinch in Wellington County. Some members moved to Waterloo County but this aspect is not emphasized. Period: 1820 - 1914.

813. Houser, John and Houser, Eileen. **A genealogical sketch of the descendants of Andrew and Anna Christina (Palmer) Cook, 1769-1970.** 1970. 581 p. ill., index. Loc: OKITW.

A genealogy including James and Elizabeth Williams Cook, who moved from Beverly Township to Waterloo Township in 1841. They had one son and eleven daughters, some of whom married into the Oberholtzer family. There are references to Bloomingdale and the Cook family on pages 355 to 364 and pages 490 to 493. Other areas settled by descendants include Breslau and Kitchener. Period: 1841 - 1970.

814. Cornell, Thomas V. **The Cornell family of Ontario, Michigan & Ohio.** 1990. 1 v. bibl., index, charts. Loc: OCCA, OKIT.

A revised account of the family, many members of which settled in Beverly Township. Cornells associated with Waterloo County are Daniel, who bought land from Richard Beasley, and Samuel, who owned the North American Hotel in Preston. Separate chapters trace the Cornell descendants in Ontario, with an appendix listing Ontario Cornells and the land they owned. Period: 1800 - 1990.

815. Schmidt, William A. **The Cress connection, part 1: a record of Simon Cress (1764-1851) and his descendants.** Waterloo: The Author, 1982. 1 v. ill., maps, index. Loc: OWRE, OKIT.

A history of the descendants of Simon and Catharine Cress, Mennonites who are thought to have been the first white settlers in the St Jacobs area. Period: 1800 - 1982.

816. Schmidt, William A. **The Cress connection, part 2: a record of Jacob Cress (1804-1881) and Magdalena Eby (1813-1883), their ancestors and descendants.** Waterloo: The Author, 1986. 1 v. index. Loc: OKIT.

Genealogical details on the descendants of Jacob, the eldest son of Simon, who moved with his family from St Jacobs to Port Elgin. There is introductory biographical information about the Eby and Cress antecedents. Period: 1800 - 1986.

817. Schmidt, William A. **Elisha Hewitt and Rachel Cress: a record of their descendants.** Waterloo: The Author, 1989. 385 p. index. Loc: OKIT.

A genealogy of the Cress and Hewitt families, containing biographical information on Elisha (1800-1863) and Rachel (1797-1846) who owned land near Winterbourne. Period: 1800 - 1989.

818. "Seventh generation of Cress family." **Waterloo Historical Society.** 1968. 56: 48. Loc: all.

A brief note stating that John and Lloyd Cress are the only seventh-generation descendants of Simon Cress who came to Woolwich Township in 1819. Period: 1819 - 1968.

819. Arnold, Margaret-Ruth Ramey (Mrs Richard) and Cashatt, Nancy Cressman (Mrs Wesley L.) and Cressman, Paul L. **A partial history of the Crossman-Kressman-Cressman-Crissman-Crisman Family, first edition, by the History Committee, Mechanicsburg, Pennsylvania, 1972.** Mechanicsburg, PA: The Family, 1972. 119 p. bibl., map, charts. Loc: OKIT.

A genealogy with an account of how the material was researched. One chapter gives reasons for the migration to Canada and the names of those who came to Waterloo County. Among those mentioned are Daniel Cressman, John Cressman and Nicholas Cressman. Period: 1800 - 1973.

820. Bowman, Sybilla (Mrs Tobias) **History of Isaac S. Cressman family, 1830-1965.** Kitchener: The Author, 1965?. 40 p. ill. Loc: OKITW.

A genealogy of the fourteen children of Isaac S. Cressman, who was born near Strasburg in 1830. Isaac's first wife was Barbara Schneider; after her death, he married her sister Elizabeth. There are family photographs, a drawing of the Cressman homestead, and a list of dates and locations of the reunions. A second edition of this genealogy, by David Robert Cressman, was published in 1982. Period: 1830 - 1965.

821. Cressman, David Robert. **History of the Isaac S. Cressman family, 1830-1981.** Kitchener: The Author, 1982. 40 p. ill., map. Loc: OWTUCGR.

The second edition of a genealogy of the descendants of Isaac and his wives, Barbara Schneider and her sister Elizabeth. There is a list of the dates and locations of family reunions from 1920 to 1980 and a picture of the Cressman homestead near Strasburg. Period: 1830 - 1981.

822. Cressman, Orpha. **History of Daniel E. Cressman family**. The Author, 1967. 7 p. Loc: OWTUCGR.

A brief account of the ancestors and descendants of a Mennonite farmer, Daniel, (1847-1925) and his wife, Hannah Shantz (1848-1940), who settled in Oxford County. Some of the family later moved to Wilmot Township and Kitchener. Period: 1847 - 1967.

823. Schmadl, Elizabeth L. **Index to A partial history of the Crössman-Kressman-Cressman-Crissman-Crisman family, by the History Committee of Mechanicsburg PA**. Kitchener Public Library, 1990. 16 p. Loc: OKIT.

An index to names mentioned in the Cressman family history. Period: 1800 - 1973.

824. **Parshall Terry family history**. 1956. 1 v. Loc: OKIT.

Extracts from a family history, with information about the family of David and Mary Ann Cunningham of Linwood. David emigrated from New York State and managed John Hawke's grist mill for five years before becoming a farmer. Genealogical data on this family is provided. Period: 1830 - 1956.

825. Domm, J.G. and Domm, E.E. **For friendship sake: a record of the descendants, Johannes A. Damm**. 1929?. 61 p. Loc: OKIT.

A genealogy with biographical notes of the family of a German sawmiller who gave his name to Dammsville, near Heidelberg, in 1855. Most of the family later moved to the Ayton area, but some descendants remain in the Kitchener area. Period: 1826 - 1929.

SURNAMES BEGINNING WITH D

826. Lang, E. Elizabeth Koch. **The family of Barbara Koch, 1831-1910, and Abraham Dettwiler, 1828-1912**. New Dundee: The Author, 1988. 1 v. ill., index. Loc: OWTUCGR.

A genealogy with biographical notes and reminiscences of the descendants of Abraham, ordained a minister of the North Woolwich Mennonite Church in 1858. The family moved to Michigan in 1864, some members later returning to Waterloo County. Period: 1828 - 1988.

827. Shook, Jay L. **The history of the descendants of Heinrich Detweiler**. Caledonia, MI: The Author?, 1981. 111 p. indexes. Loc: OWTUCGR.

A genealogy of a Pennsylvania Mennonite family who came to Waterloo County in 1810. The family first settled in Waterloo and Woolwich Townships, and later in Wilmot and Wellesley. Many Waterloo County Detweilers, descendants of Rudolph and Anna Wanner, are among those listed as the third and fourth generations in this book. Period: 1810 - 1981.

828. **Genealogical chart of the Devitt family and related branches**. 1977. 19 p. bibl. Loc: OWTUR, OKIT.

A detailed genealogical chart of descendants of Dennis Devitt who came to Waterloo County about 1815. Other family branches included are those of John W. Hinchcliffe, Louis J. Breithaupt, Harvey Devitt, Alva E. Devitt and Edward M. Devitt. Some biographical information about family members is included. Period: 1815 - 1977.

829. **Genealogical chart of the Devitt family and related branches, 1780-1980**. 1980?. 21 p. bibl. Loc: OKIT.

A detailed genealogical chart of the descendants of Dennis Devitt, builder of the Union Mills in Waterloo. This report contains biographical information on the fourth and succeeding generations of the Dennis Devitt II branch which was not included in the 1977 genealogy. Period: 1815 - 1980.

830. Stewart, Catharine M. **The Dickies of Dumfries**. Montreal: The Author, 1966. 16 p. bibl., charts. Loc: OCCA, OKITW.

An account of the families and descendants of John and William Dickie, Ayrshire farmers who migrated to Dumfries Township in 1833. The migration process and early settlement are described, with references to the establishment of the Dickie Settlement School. Period: 1833 - 1895.

831. Helwig, Solomon, Mrs and Helwig, John A., Mrs. **A history of the Diebel family, tracing the descendants of Johann Heinrich Diebel, born March 18, 1736, died October 18, 1813, and his wife, Anna Katherine Glebe, born May 5, 1744, died April 20, 1798**. Hanover: The Authors?, 1936. 93 p. index. Loc: OKIT.

A genealogy with biographical information on family members, many of whom moved to Michigan, Wellington and Bruce Counties. Some descendants reside in Waterloo County. Period: 1855 - 1936.

832. Schmadl, Elizabeth L. and Baron, Marilyn. **Diebel Reunion minutes, 1926-1974**. Kitchener: The Authors, 1989?. 63 p. Loc: OKIT.

Minutes containing information on the reunion location, programme, expenses and people who attended. About half the reunions were held in Waterloo County, usually at Waterloo or Victoria Parks. Period: 1926 - 1974.

833. Schmadl, Elizabeth L. and Baron, Marilyn. **A history of the Diebel family, tracing the descendants of Johann Heinrich Diebel, born March 18, 1736, died October 18, 1813, and his wife Anna Katherine Glebe, born May 5, 1744, died April 20, 1798.** Kitchener: The Authors, 1991?. 1 v. ill., index. Loc: OKIT.

An updated version of the 1936 genealogy. John Diebel, a shoemaker, arrived in Bridgeport in 1855 and later moved to Wellington County. While most descendants settled in Wellington County, some resided in Waterloo. Period: 1855 - 1990.

834. Diefenbacher, Karl. **Die Kraichgauer Vorfahren von John George.** Ladenburg, Germany: The Author, 1990?. 19 p. ill. Loc: OKIT.

A genealogy of former Canadian Prime Minister, John George Diefenbaker, whose ancestors are traced back to the Kraichgau region in what is now Baden-Würtemburg, Germany. Diefenbaker's grandfather, Georg Jacob Diefenbacher, settled in Hawkesville in 1853. Period: 1853 - 1979.

835. Schnarr, Wilfrid. **Genealogy of Doering, Lenhardt, Schnarr, Zinkann, Schoen families.** Toronto: The Author, 1972. 35 p. Loc: OKIT.

A record of the author's forebears and relations, some of whom lived in Waterloo County. Period: 1830 - 1972.

836. Schmidt, William A. **The ancestors and descendants of Johann George Doerrbecker.** Waterloo: The Author?, 1991. 653 p. ill., maps, index. Loc: OKIT.

A genealogy of Johann George who arrived in 1841 and settled near Erbsville with his wife, Anna Martha Vetter. Period: 1841 - 1991.

837. Doll, Irene. **Our family history: book one, supplements, and newsletters [WRP].** Lena, IL: The Author?, 1976, 1977. 1 v. (various pagings). ill., maps. Loc: OKIT.

A genealogy of a Waterloo County German Catholic family, written in 1976 with a 1977 supplement. Newsletters from 1979 and 1981 contain additional photographs and information. A reference to Frederick Doll in the 1981 newsletter is of particular interest: he stayed in Canada when other members of the family migrated to the United States. Period: 1799 - 1981.

838. Doll, Irene. **Our family history: book two, supplements and newsletters [WRP].** Lena, IL: The Author?, 1976, 1977. 1 v. (various pagings). ill. Loc: OKIT.

A genealogy of a Waterloo German Catholic family who later settled in Illinois. It contains the original 1976 edition, a 1977 supplement, and newsletters from 1979 and 1981. Period: 1799 - 1981.

839. Doll, Irene. **Our family history compiled by Irene Doll 1976, Book I: Doll, dedicated to the memory of Anthony and Margaret (Wendling) Doll, Book II: Beingess(n)er-Wendling, dedicated to the memory of grandmother Margaret (Wendling) Doll.** Lena, IL: The Author?, 1976. 195 p. ill., index. Loc: OKIT, OWTUCR.

A genealogy of a German Catholic family who came to Waterloo County in the first half of the 19th century and later settled in Illinois. It includes some biographical data on family members. Period: 1799 - 1976.

840. Read, Dorothy J. **Descendants of Jacob Donnenworth (b. 1798 Alsace, Fr.; d. 19.09.1870) and his wife, Catharina Milhausner (b. 1800 Alsace, Fr.; d. 3.5.1872) of Waterloo and Wilmot Townships, Waterloo Co., Ontario.** 1988. 30 p. ill., maps, index. Loc: OKIT.

A family history with biographical sketches of Jacob and Catharina, farmers who settled first in Williamsburg and later Mannheim. It refers to Thomas Woods and Margaret Donnenworth who lived on a farm near Bleams Road, and to the Isaiah Eby Farm that was in the Donnenworth family for three generations, and includes a photograph of Williamsburg School. Period: 1820 - 1988.

841. Barrie, James R. "Dryden descendants unveil plaque in North Dumfries." **Waterloo Historical Society.** 1982. 70: 60-62. ill. Loc: all.

A short account of the Dryden family, especially Andrew and Janet (Cairns) Dryden and their children, honoured by a plaque unveiled on 12 September 1982. The author notes that the Drydens farmed 9000 acres and comments on the accomplishments of some descendants. Period: 1834 - 1982.

842. Gordon, Hugh. **The Dryden family, 1296-1989.** Hamilton: June and Jack Guenther, 1989. 611 p. ill., index, charts. Loc: OKIT.

A comprehensive portrayal of the Canadian Drydens, including their Scottish antecedents. Some family members farmed in the 8th concession of Dumfries Township while others lived in the section of Galt known as Drydensville. The book includes reminiscences, poetry, a Dryden bus tour, an edited version of Earl J. Taylor's **The Drydens of Teviotdale**, photographs and genealogical charts. Period: 1834 - 1989.

843. Gordon, Jean and Gordon, Hugh. **Dryden 1984.** Burlington: The Authors?, 1984. 52 p. ill., map, chart. Loc: OKIT.

A history of the descendants of Andrew Dryden and Janet Cairns, Scottish immigrants who settled in Dumfries Township in 1834. It includes biographical information on some family members and notes the Drydens who settled in Eramosa Township. Period: 1834 - 1984.

844. Taylor, Earl J. **The Drydens of Teviotdale**. Burlington: The Author, 1970?. 34 p. Loc: OCCA.

An account of the author's research into his Scottish ancestry. The Dryden family came from Roxburgh, Scotland to Dumfries Township in 1834. Period: 1834 - 1970.

SURNAMES BEGINNING WITH E

845. Eby, Aden. "Readers' ancestry." **Mennogespräch**. 1988. 6,1: 6-8. ill. Loc: OWTUCG, OKIT.

An illustrated genealogy of the family of Aden Eby and his wife, Ruby Winger. The family is descended from Benjamin Eby, a leading Mennonite of Waterloo Township, and John Winger, founder of the River Brethren Church in Canada. Period: 1806 - 1988.

846. Eby, Allan A. "The Eby family as related to the Brubachers." **Waterloo Historical Society**. 1923. 11: 46-49. Loc: all.

A brief history of the Eby family's migrations from Switzerland to Pennsylvania and then to Waterloo County. The author explains the Ebys' original connection with the Brubachers through the marriages of Bishop Benjamin Eby to Mary Brubacher and Marie Eby to Jacob Brubacher in the early nineteenth century. Period: 1800 - 1923.

847. Eby, Dorothy and Eby, Grace and Coldren, Charles, Mrs. **Notes on the Eby family**. Waterloo: The Authors, 1974. 2 v. Loc: OKIT.

Genealogical notes on the Canadian and United States members of the Eby family. The first volume contains photocopies of the index card file of Eby names, arranged alphabetically by first name with information on vital dates, marriages, children and occupations. The second volume consists of handwritten notes on the Eby family, noting sources of information. Period: 1800 - 1974.

848. Eby, Ezra E. **A biographical history of the Eby family: being a history of their movements in Europe during the Reformation and of their early settlement in America; as also much other unpublished historical information belonging to the family**. Berlin: Hett and Eby, 1889 reprinted 1970. 144 p. ill. Also CIHM Microfiche series, no. 05213. Loc: OCP, OKIT, OWRE, OWTL, OWTU,

OWTUCG, OWTUR, OKEBC.

A detailed genealogy of the descendants of Theodorus Eby, Peter Eby and Nicholas Eby who migrated to Pennsylvania from Europe between 1715 and 1820. Names and vital dates are given of all descendants, with their spouses and children. The author explains the roles of those who took part in the Mennonite migrations to Waterloo County in the early nineteenth century, notably Bishop Benjamin Eby (pp. 26-45), Samuel Eby, Daniel Eby, David Eby, Peter Eby, John Eby, George Eby, Barbara Eby Schneider and Susannah Eby Winger. The book was reprinted in a facsimile edition by Aden Eby in 1970. Period: 1800 - 1889.

849. Groff, Clyde L. and Newman, George F. **The Eby report**. Philadelphia: The Authors, 1975 - 1978. Loc: OKEBC, OKIT.

Articles, charts, illustrations and documents pertaining to the Eby family in America. Three issues were published: volume I, no. 1 in 1975, volume I, no. 2 in the summer of 1976, and volume II, no. 1 in the summer of 1978. Much of the material concentrates on Pennsylvania Ebys, but the 1978 edition reproduces the fraktur from Benjamin Eby's Bible and traces the first four generations in America. All three reports are held at the Kitchener Public Library while the only the first is at the Emmanuel Bible College. Period: 1800 - 1978.

850. Martin, Simeon E. **History of the Eby family**. The Author?, 1972. 89 p. Loc: OKIT.

A sequel to the major work by Ezra E. Eby, continuing the detailed family history from 1889 to 1972. The names and vital dates of all family members are given, with occasional brief notes on residence or occupation. Introductory information about the Mennonite immigration to America is copied from a 1929 issue of the Pennsylvania German Society. Period: 1889 - 1972.

851. Millar, Anne Eby and Millar, D. Douglas. "Jacob Foster Eby, local hero." **Waterloo Historical Society**. 1990. 78: 103-115. ill. Loc: all.

An account of the tragic accident at the Kitchener sewer plant in 1930, in which the engineer, Jacob Eby, died in trying to save other workers overcome by a deadly gas. The authors also provide genealogical details for the Eby family. Period: 1930 - 1931.

852. Robbins, Elizabeth Luella Eby. **David E. Eby - Leah Eby family history**. Glanworth: The Author?, 1978. 79 p. ill., charts, index. Loc: OWTUCGR.

An account of the families of David and Leah and their ten children, with reminiscences and biographical information for each family. David and Leah farmed in Wellington County but they are buried in the Martin Meeting House Cemetery; all their children settled in Waterloo County. Period: 1804 - 1978.

853. Bean, Reta M. and Trask, Mabel Edler and Edler, Margaret (Mrs John) **Family history of Karl Edler and his descendants, 1775-1975**. St Jacobs: St Jacobs Printery, 1976. 49 p. ill. Loc: OKIT, OWTU.

An illustrated chart of the eight generations descended from Karl Edler of Dresden, Germany, whose three sons George, Karl and Frederick emigrated to Canada and the United States. George Edler operated a butcher business in Waterloo, and Frederick owned a farm in North Woolwich before moving to Peel Township. The chart includes birth, marriage and death dates and occupations. Period: 1825 - 1975.

854. Schmadl, Elizabeth L. **Index to Family history of Karl Edler and his descendants**. Kitchener Public Library, 1991. 15 p. Loc: OKIT.

An index of nearly 1000 personal names. Period: 1825 - 1975.

855. Eydt, Ronald and Eydt, John. **The Eidt and Eydt families in Canada, 1835-1985**. Waterloo: The Authors, 1985. 373 p., maps. Loc: OKIT.

A genealogy with an introduction describing the arrival of the Eidt and Eydt families in Woolwich Township from Germany in 1835. The authors explain the connections between the two families, their German roots and numerous descendants. A separate section on the Philipsburg Eidts lists the names and addresses of current family members. Elizabeth Schmadl has compiled an index of names. Period: 1835 - 1985.

856. Schmadl, Elizabeth L. **Index to The Eydt and Eidt families in Canada, 1835-1985**. Kitchener Public Library, 1990. 34 p. Loc: OKIT.

An index to approximately 2,500 personal names. Period: 1835 - 1985.

857. Shewchuk, John P. "The Elliotts and Inglewood Farm." **Waterloo Historical Society**. 1985. 73: 52-56. ill. Loc: all.

An account of the property on the south half of Lot 20, Concession 9, Dumfries Township, taken up in 1832 by William S. Elliott (1806-1881). The stone farmhouse, built in 1856, is described as an example of local vernacular architecture with some Gothic elements. The author describes the farming successes and leadership roles of Elliott and his descendants and refers to the manuscript collection of Hugh C. Elliott, to whom the farm passed in 1929. Period: 1806 - 1970.

858. Dunham, B. Mabel. "Ellis family history." **Waterloo Historical Society**. 1947. 35: 29-32. Loc: all.

An account of some of the adventures of Squire Ellis, an early settler in the southeastern corner of Waterloo Township. Period: 1800 - 1947.

859. Shannon, George D. **The Ellis family**. Chatham: The Author, 1982. 6 p. Loc: OKIT.

An account of William Ellis, an Irish magistrate who came to Hespeler in 1810. His part in the War of 1812 and stories of his dealings with Indians are related and some genealogical details are provided. Period: 1810 - 1982.

860. Hunsberger, Mary. **The family history of Enoch Clemens Erb and Catharine Stauffer Good: their descendants and his ancestors**. Baden: The Author?, 1980. 11 p. Loc: OWTUCGR.

A genealogy of the seven children and a niece who were raised by Enoch Clemens Erb (1842-1917) and his wife Catherine. Background biographical information is included about the Erb family. Period: 1800 - 1980.

861. Martin, Winston J. **Descendants of Christian Erb II, 1734-1810, and Maria Scherch, 1737-1814, (12 children) who came to Ontario, 1808 (bu. at Blair)**. 1984. 103 p., charts. Loc: OKIT, OWTUCGR.

Genealogical charts of the descendants of Christian and Maria Erb, who migrated to Canada to be with their daughter, Elizabeth Erb Schneider. The Erbs married into the Eby, Schneider and Sherk families. Period: 1808 - 1984.

SURNAMES BEGINNING WITH F

862. Fenn, Edward and Fenn, Laura and Everts, Margaret Fenn. **In search of the Fenns and Grahams, our ancestors**. Edward Fenn, 1982. 1 v. ill. Loc: OKIT.

A history tracing descendants of the Fenn, Graham, Ziegler and Ford families, some of whom settled in Elmira and Preston as well as Oxford County. The book combines genealogical information with reminiscences and photographs. Period: 1830 - 1982.

863. Kelly, Maurice. **The Fischer people**. 1981. 1 v. ill. Loc: OKIT, OWTUCR.

A chronicle of six generations of Fischers, the offspring of Philip and Caroline Wilhelm, German emigrants who arrived in Canada about 1835. Philip was a blacksmith who bought farmland near Strasburg. Genealogical information is interspersed with information and reminiscences of family members. Period: 1835 - 1981.

864. Schmadl, Elizabeth L. **Index to A Fischer and Benninger family tree by Helen A. Schroeder.** Kitchener Public Library, 1991. 13 p. Loc: OKIT.

    An index to over 800 personal names. Period: 1821 - 1984.

865. Schroeder, Helen A. **A Fischer and Benninger family tree.** 1984. 131 p. Loc: OKIT.

    A family tree of the descendants of Michael Fischer (1821-1882), his first wife Regina Zettel, and his second wife Catherine Hohenadel. Michael and Regina were married and at least two of their four children were born in New Germany, where they farmed. The couple later moved to Bruce County where Michael was elected Reeve of Carrick Township. A name index has been compiled by Elizabeth Schmadl. Period: 1821 - 1984.

866. Strome, Laurie and Johansen, Millie and Miller, Veronica A. **Another Fischer family history.** 1991. 1 v. ill., maps. Loc: OKIT.

    An illustrated genealogy of the descendants of Michael Fischer (1821-1882) and his two wives, Regina Zettel and Catharine Hohenadel. Michael and Regina were married at Maryhill, and later moved to Carrick Township. The introduction describes Michael's possible motives for leaving Germany and the development of his farm in Bruce County, and gives a transcript of his will. Period: 1821 - 1991.

867. Curtis, Rosina Hass. **Ludwig Foerster and his descendants.** Czar, Alberta: Mrs Rosina (Hass) Curtis, 1971. 111 p. ill. Loc: OKIT.

    An annotated genealogy of the Foerster family who emigrated from Germany to Heidelberg, Wellesley Township, in 1836. Period: 1836 - 1971.

868. Foot, W.W. **What's my line.** The Author?, 1978. 124 p. ill. Loc: OWT.

    A personal account of the Foot family who migrated to Muskoka from Ireland in 1871. The author was appointed City Treasurer of Kitchener in 1927 and retired as chairman of the Economical Mutual Fire Insurance Company in 1974. Period: 1871 - 1978.

869. Deverell, James F. **The Friedrichs of Waterloo.** The Author, 1986. 97 p. ill., index. Loc: OKIT.

    A history of the family (also spelled Friederich or Frederick) and related families: the Deverells, the Baltzers, the Bergeys, the Kehls and the Bortzs. Certificates, census information, photographs and other information are reproduced with the genealogical charts. Period: 1834 - 1986.

SURNAMES BEGINNING WITH G

870. Gascho, Milton. **The descendants of John Ingold Gascho.** Kokomo, IN: The Author, 1987. 192 p. ill., charts, index. Loc: OWTUCGR.

    A chronicle of a German Amish Mennonite family who came from Bavaria to Huron County before 1850. Some descendants settled in Waterloo County and Joseph, son of John, married Barbara Erb of Wilmot Township. Period: 1916 - 1987.

871. Bender, Shelley. **The Gerber family history.** 1985. 81 p. ill. Loc: OWTUCGR.

    A genealogy with an introductory biographical sketch of Michael and Veronica Jantzi, Mennonite farmers near Shingletown. John Gerber, Michael's father, settled in Wilmot Township in 1838. A list of addresses of family members in 1985 concludes the work. Period: 1838 - 1985.

872. **Family records of the Gingrich descendants.** 1969. 94 p. index. Loc: OKIT, OWTUCGR.

    A genealogy of eight generations of descendants of John Gingrich and Anna Hackman, who came from Pennsylvania and settled on a farm south of Elmira. Period: 1800 - 1969.

873. Gingrich, Jacob Cecil. **Gingrich genealogy: addendum to the Ulrich Gingrich family, with limited data of Joseph (Yost) Gingrich.** 1986. 732 p. ill., index. Loc: OKIT.

    An updated and expanded version of John Edmond Gingrich's Ulrich Gingrich genealogy of 1981. Period: 1810 - 1986.

874. Roth, Clara Ann Gingerich and Schrag, Keith G. and Gingerich, Alvin. **Family history and genealogy of Jacob (Wagner) Gingerich and Veronica Litwiller, 1825-1975.** Baden: The Authors?, 1975. 192 p. map, index. Loc: OKIT, OWTUCGR.

    A genealogy of over 2,000 descendants, introduced by a section on the German background, the early Amish Mennonite settlement of Wilmot Township, and the development of the Gingerich family farm in Wilmot from the 1830s. A narrative introduction is given to the families of each of the six children of Jacob and Veronica. Period: 1825 - 1975.

875. Kerr, Jane Easton Clark. **The ancestry of Walter Gladstone and his descendants, 1817-1967.** 1967. 60 p. ill. Loc: OKIT.

    A genealogy with a brief introduction to the Gladstone family, Scots who came to Ayr in 1840. Walter founded the Nithvale Chair Factory, built the Stanley Street and Knox Presbyterian Churches in Ayr and owned a general store on the corner of Stanley and Swan Streets. He and his wife, Jane

Easton, moved their family to Missouri in 1869.
Period: 1840 - 1967.

876. Schmadl, Elizabeth L. **An index to The ancestry of Walter Gladstone and his descendants, 1817-1967.** Kitchener Public Library, 1990. 8 p. Loc: OKIT.
A name index prepared for a genealogy by Jane Easton Clark Kerr. Period: 1840 - 1967.

877. Whitson, Bessie B. "The Gladstone family of Ayr, Ontario." **Waterloo Historical Society.** 1951. 39: 17-22. ill. Loc: all.
A brief history of the family of William, Elizabeth and their seven children who came to Ayr in 1840. Each family member's contributions to the family and the community are noted. Some historical information about Ayr is also given. Period: 1840 - 1951.

878. Bricker, I.C. "History of the Gowdy-Goldie-Goudie family." **Waterloo Historical Society.** 1938. 26: 20-37. Loc: all.
A genealogical account of the Viking and Ayrshire origins of a notable county family. The author recounts the migration of John Goldie (1793-1886) from Ayrshire to Ayr, Ontario in 1844 and the success of his second son, John (1822-1896) in the foundry business of Goldie McCulloch in Galt. The Goudies established a department store in Kitchener while the Gowdy family was active mainly in the Guelph area. Period: 1844 - 1931.

879. Falkner, Theresa Goldie. **The Goldie saga: part one.** The Author?, 1968. 15 p. Loc: OKIT.
A history of the pioneer days of John and Margaret Goldie, with particular reference to the family of their youngest son, David. The difficulties of establishing a farm and mills in Greenfield are recounted, based on the diaries and letters of John Goldie and on family reminiscences. This work is bound with parts two, three and four at the Kitchener Public Library. Period: 1833 - 1968.

880. Falkner, Theresa Goldie. **The Goldie saga: part three.** The Author?, 1982. 11 p. ill. Loc: OKIT.
Personal reminiscences of family life in Ayr at the beginning of the twentieth century, mentioning social events, education, health care, and the church. This portion is bound with parts one, two and four at the Kitchener Public Library. Period: 1890 - 1957.

881. Wrong, George M. **The chronicle of a family: the Goldie saga, part four.** 5 p. Loc: OKIT.
An account of the immigration of a Scottish Highlander, Neil Mackinnon. It contains a letter written in 1833 describing his arrival in Upper Canada in the company of John Goldie, and his impressions of the land. This portion of the work is bound with parts one, two and three in the Kitchener Public Library. Period: 1833 - 1857.

882. Good, Cranson. **The family history of Jonas Good and Elizabeth Snyder Good: their descendants and his ancestors.** Petersburg: The Author?, 1976. 35 p. ill. Loc: OWTUCGR.
Genealogies and tributes to Jonas, Elizabeth and their seven children. Jonas' father, Daniel Good, came from Pennsylvania to Waterloo in 1826. Jonas and Elizabeth began farming south of the Baden Hills in 1868, and their descendants still farm in Wilmot Township. Period: 1826 - 1976.

883. Good, Elias H. **History of the "Good" ancestry.** Kitchener: The Author, 1929. 23 p. Loc: OWTUCGR.
A reprint of a history of the family of John and Magdalena Baumann, Pennsylvania Mennonites who came to Waterloo in 1818. The journey to Waterloo and early pioneer life are described, with biographical notes on John Good, Samuel Good, Dr Joseph Good, and Joel Good who surveyed the northern part of Waterloo County. A short article about Mennonite history and the Good ancestry is included. Period: 1818 - 1929.

884. Good, M.R. **A Good family genealogy: a detailed record of the descendants of Menno Good (1838-1919).** Breslau: M.R. Good, 1979. 16 p. ill., ports. Loc: OKIT, OWT, OWTUCGR.
A history of the Good family, members of which emigrated to North America in the early 18th century. Particular emphasis is given to the descendants of Menno Good and Joanna Martin and their seven children. Elizabeth Schmadl has compiled an index to this work. Period: 1800 - 1979.

885. Schmadl, Elizabeth L. **Index to A Good family genealogy (Menno Good).** Kitchener Public Library, 1991. 6 p. Loc: OKIT.
A name index to the work by M.R. Good. Period: 1800 - 1979.

886. Goodall, Ann. **Goodall family history.** Galt: The Author?, 1964 updated 1968. 7 p. Loc: OWTUCGR.
Genealogical notes on a family who came to Toronto following the Crimean War, their descendants moving to Galt. A chart compiled in 1968 shows the relationship between the McGregor and Johnston families who intermarried with the Goodalls. Period: 1900 - 1968.

887. Grubb, Nathaniel B. **A genealogical history of the Gottschall family: descendants of the Rev. Jacob Gottschall with the complete record of the descendants of William Ziegler Gottschall.** Gottshall Family Association, 1924. 112 p. Loc: OKIT, OWTUCGR.

A genealogy of a Pennsylvania Mennonite family, members of which intermarried with the Clemens, Hunsberger, Bergey, Detweiler, Bean, Ziegler and Reiff families of Waterloo County. A name index to this work was prepared by Elizabeth Schmadl. Period: 1800 - 1924.

888. Schmadl, Elizabeth L. **Index to A genealogical history of the Gottshall family.** Kitchener Public Library, 1991. 40 p. Loc: OKIT.

A name index to the book by Nathaniel B. Grubb. Period: 1800 - 1924.

889. Bauman, Roy G. **Graaf, Graf, Groff, Bale.** 1970. 65 p. ill., map, chart, index. Loc: OKIT, OWTUCGR.

An updated version of a 1932 genealogy of the descendants of Abraham Groff (1829-1885), the fourth son of Andrew Groff and Annie Huber. Andrew and his family migrated to Waterloo County from Pennsylvania in 1822. An introduction gives background information on Groff ancestors and includes the obituary of their mentor, G.E. Reaman. A name index to this work was compiled by Elizabeth Schmadl. Period: 1822 - 1970.

890. Schmadl, Elizabeth L. **Index to Graf-Graaf-Groff: a family history of Abraham Groff by R.G. Bauman.** Kitchener Public Library, 1991. 12 p. Loc: OKIT.

A name index to the Groff genealogy. Period: 1822 - 1970.

891. Groh, Ivan. **My family tree.** 1969. 104 p. Loc: OKEBC, OKIT, OWTUCGR.

A genealogy of the author's eight great-grandparents, of the Groh, Wanner, Bechtel and Clemens families who settled near Preston and Hespeler in the first two decades of the 19th century. Information on family members and names introduces each of the four sections. Period: 1800 - 1969.

892. Nurse, Lorein L. and Schmadl, Elizabeth L. **The family tree of Heinrich (Henry) and Phillipine Grube.** London: The Author, 1986. 343 p. ill., maps, index. Loc: OKIT.

A genealogy of a German emigrant couple who settled in Wilmot Township, and the families of their thirteen children. Henry was a shoemaker in New Hamburg, but later farmed in Logan Township. Photographs and obituaries open each of the fourteen sections. A 37-page supplement by the original author was added in 1989, and a name index by Elizabeth Schmadl was completed in 1991. Period: 1815 - 1986.

SURNAMES BEGINNING WITH H

893. Trueman, Marie. **Greener pastures: pioneer stories of Thomas Haddow, Hannah Robertson and their descendants, 1797-1986.** 1986. 138 p. ill., bibl., maps, charts, index. Loc: OKIT.

The family history of a Scottish family who came to Galt in 1843, later moving to Peel Township near the Wellesley Township boundary. A description of life in contemporary Scotland suggests reasons for the emigration. Period: 1843 - 1986.

894. Dahms, Vera E. Schweitzer. **The family history of John Hahn.** 1952. 27 p. Loc: OWTUCGR.

A genealogy with a brief biographical introduction to two brothers, John and Henry, who left Hesse Darmstadt in Germany in 1853 to settle near Heidelberg in Waterloo County. The genealogy charts the descendants of Elizabeth Sippel and John Hahn, son of Henry, who was apprenticed as a wagon maker to Jacob Wagner of Waterloo. Period: 1853 - 1952.

895. Rogers, Genevieve Hahn. **The family of Johann Georg Hahn and Elizabeth Herber.** Tavares, FL: The Author, 1985. 110 p. ill., index. Loc: OKIT.

A genealogy of the family of George Hahn, a German farmer who settled near Bamberg in 1860. Among his descendants was Lewis Hahn, an entrepreneurial carpenter who founded the Hahn Furniture Company and the Hahn Brass Company of New Hamburg. The family tree is followed by copies of newspaper clippings, letters and biographical sketches. Period: 1860 - 1985.

896. Hallman, E.S., Rev. **The Hallman-Clemens genealogy with a family's reminiscence.** Tuleta, TX: The Family, 1950?. 80 p. ill. Loc: OWTUCGR.

An autobiography of Rev. Eli Schmidtt Hallman, who was born near New Dundee and moved to Saskatchewan in 1905, later moving to Goshen, Indiana and then Texas. He describes the Mennonite revival led by J.S. Coffman at the end of the 19th century and how it affected him personally. He married Melinda Clemens, daughter of M.B. Clemens. Some genealogical information about the Hallman and Clemens families is included; both families came to Waterloo County from Pennsylvania in 1825. Period: 1825 - 1949.

897. Hallman, H.S. **An addition to the history of the Hallman family in Canada.** Berlin: The Author, 1912?. 23 p. ill. Loc: OWT.

A continuation of the work published in 1906, with a drawing of the family crest, information on the names Hallman and Heilman by Dr Bergey, a description of the second Hallman reunion held in Berlin in 1912, and documents concerning the Pennsylvania progenitors Anthony Hallman and his wife. There are also lists of the descendants of Jacob Hallman, Adam Unger, Jacob Bechtel, Joseph Hallman, Abram Bricker, John Hallman, William Hunsberger, Samuel Hunsberger, Benjamin Hallman, Christian Hallman, Enoch Ziegler and Wendell Hallman. Period: 1800 - 1912.

898. Hallman, H.S. **History of the Hallman family in Canada.** Berlin: The Author, 1906. 109 p. ill. Loc: OWTUCGR, OWTL, OKIT.
A genealogical account of the family with photographs of various Hallman homesteads and a description of the family reunion at Schneider Grove, Berlin on June 22, 1905. Period: 1800 - 1906.

899. Hallman, Joan. **Hallman family history in Canada.** Kitchener: Jacob C. Hallman, 1991. 383 p. ill., maps, index. Loc: OKIT, OWTUCGR.
A genealogy containing portions of family histories by H.S. Hallman and Dr Bergey. Biographical data and photographs of family farmsteads precede the genealogical data for each branch of the family. Period: 1825 - 1991.

900. Hallman Reunion Committee. **Twelfth Hallman Reunion.** Waterloo: The Committee, 1966. 16 p. Loc: OWTUCGR.
A 1966 programme containing genealogical information and other material from H.S. Hallman's 1906 and 1912 family histories, a history of earlier family reunions, and the story of Benjamin Hallman and Elizabeth Detweiler's move to Canada from Pennsylvania in 1825. Period: 1825 - 1966.

901. Hunsberger, Vera H. **Abraham Hallman family and descendants.** 1970?. 48 p. ill. Loc: OKEBC.
A genealogy of the descendants of the twelve children of Abraham Hallman (1832-1904) and his wife Mary Schmitt, Mennonites who farmed between New Dundee and Plattsville. Reminiscences and tributes by relatives are included. Period: 1826 - 1969.

902. Hannush, Russell G. **Notes (part 1) on the Hannusch family of Berlin, Ontario.** 1985?. 1 v. (unpaged). Loc: OKIT.
Report on research on five generations of descendants of Johannes Hannusch who migrated from Bohemia to Heidelberg, Waterloo County in the early 1870s. Period: 1870 - 1985.

903. Hannush, Russell G. **Notes (part 2) on the Hannusch family of Berlin, Ontario, Canada.** 1989. 100 p. ill. Loc: OKIT.
An expanded version of the 1985 genealogy, with more illustrations and lists of sources and associated family names. Period: 1870 - 1985.

904. Schmadl, Elizabeth L. **Index to Notes on the Hannusch family of Berlin, Ontario [Canada] by Russell G. Hannush.** 1991. 4 p. Loc: OKIT.
Indexes to both editions of the family genealogy. The Kitchener Public Library holds two versions of the index, one relating to both editions of the Hannusch genealogy, the other to the earlier edition only. Period: 1870 - 1985.

905. Briggs, David A. **Genealogical summary of the Harvie family.** The Author, 1989. 10 p. Loc: OKIT.
A chart of the descendants of Alexander Harvie (1754-1825), one of the first settlers in Dumfries. It was prepared for use in the excavation of the Harvie Cemetery in 1988, when remains were re-interred in Sheffield Cemetery. Period: 1816 - 1976.

906. Jantzi, Bruce W. and Roth, Lorraine. **The family history and genealogy of Andrew and Anna (Sommer) Herrfort.** New Hamburg: Herrfort/Herford Family Book Committee, 1992. 335 p. Loc: OWTUCG.
Period: 1830 - 1980.

907. "Kin of Hespeler." **Waterloo Historical Society.** 1960. 48: 50. Loc: all.
A note of a letter received by the Mayor of Hespeler from Mrs H.B. (Stephanie) Benn, granddaughter of William Hespeler, the younger brother of Jacob. Period: 1840 - 1960.

908. Schmalz, W.H.E. "The Hespeler family." **Waterloo Historical Society.** 1969. 57: 20-29. ill. Loc: all.
An account of the descendants of John George and Anna Wick Hespeler. For each of their nine children (Jacob, Ferdinanda, William, Stephanie, Louis, Marie, Wilhelmina, Anna Barbara and Charlotte), there is a genealogical table as well as biographical information. The Hespelers married into Seagram, Warnock, Chapman and Beck families. Period: 1810 - 1921.

909. Hilborn, Roy H. **Hilborn family.** Drumheller: The Author, 1961. 30 p. Loc: OKIT.
A history of a Pennsylvania Quaker family, with notes on the Ebys and Erbs. Joseph Hilborn owned land in the Waterloo area in 1806. An index to names in this work was prepared by Elizabeth Schmadl. Period: 1806 - 1961.

910. Schmadl, Elizabeth L. **Index to Hilborn family.** Kitchener Public Library, 1991. 5 p. Loc: OKIT.

An index of names in Roy H. Hilborn's family history. Period: 1806 - 1961.

911. Hoch, J. Hampton. **Hoch-High family in America: a record of some Hoch immigrants and their descendants.** Charleston, SC: Hoch-High Family Reunion, 1962. 200 p. Loc: OWTUCGR.

A genealogy of a Pennsylvania Mennonite family, some of whom settled in the Vineland area of the Niagara peninsula. Anna High married Jacob L. Kinzie of Doon in 1854 and her brother, Samuel K. High, married Mary Ann Detweiler of Roseville in 1871. Period: 1854 - 1962.

912. Hoffman, Anna Bauman and Malloy, Reta Hoffman. **The descendants of Samuel B. Hoffman 1839-1904, George B. Hoffman 1842-1927, Joseph B. Hoffman 1845-1938.** 1982. 75 p. index. Loc: OWTUCGR.

A genealogy of the families of three of the five children of Samuel Hoffman and Veronica Bricker, settlers of Woolwich Township. Their daughter Barbara never married, and the descendants of their son Daniel are chronicled separately by Elizabeth D. Wideman. Period: 1802 - 1982.

913. Tiessen, Henry B. **50 Jahre in Canada: damals und heute.** Kitchener: The Author, 1973. 105 p. ill. Loc: OWTUCG.

An account of Jacob Hoffman's family after arrival in Canada from Ukraine in the 1920s. The first 21 pages describe the family's stay in Waterloo County, living on the Burkhart farm or in Kitchener after Jacob took work in a furniture factory, until they left for northern Canada. The work focuses mainly on personal experiences but the Waterloo area is also described, for example in a passage about the Kitchener Farmers' Market. Period: 1923 - 1973.

914. Wideman, Elizabeth D. **Family history of Daniel B. Hoffman 1837-1979.** 1979. 37 p. index. Loc: OWTUCGR.

A genealogy of a son of Samuel and Veronica Bricker of Woolwich Township. Period: 1802 - 1979.

915. Sias, Wilhelmine Ramsay Hogg. **The family and childhood of Wilhelmine Ramsay Hogg Sias.** Edited by Peggy Sias Lantz and Richard Alan Sias. 1981 reprinted 1989. 165 p. Loc: OWT.

An account of the migration of the Hogg family from Scotland in the 1830s, with a description of the Galt community up to 1850. The author also traces the history of her mother's family, the Breimers, who came to Waterloo from Germany in the 1850s and includes brief profiles of immediate family members and childhood reminiscences.

Period: 1835 - 1894.

916. **The Daniel and Annie (Weber) Horst family book, 1876-1955.** Elmira: The Family, 1990. 93 p. ill., charts, map. Loc: OWTUCGR.

Reminiscences and genealogies of Daniel, Annie and their twelve children, Mennonites of North Woolwich Township. Topics include an interlude in Florida for Daniel's health, financial hardships and Mennonite farm life. Period: 1876 - 1990.

917. Hostetler, Harvey and Hostetler, Stanley W. **Ancestors and descendants of Moses Hostetler.** Ottawa: Bookman Press, 1955. 74 p. ill., maps. Loc: OKIT.

An updated version of the 1912 Hostetler family history by Harvey Hostetler, including brief biographical information on the descendants of Moses Hostetler, a Mennonite who settled in Wilmot Township. A name index to this work was prepared by Elizabeth Schmadl. Period: 1820 - 1955.

918. Schmadl, Elizabeth L. **Index to Ancestors and descendants of Moses Hostetler.** Kitchener Public Library, 1991. 11 p. Loc: OKIT.

An index to the family history by Harvey Hostetler and Stanley W. Hostetler. Period: 1820 - 1955.

919. Hunsberger, Byron K. **The Hunsbergers.** Norristown, PA: Hunstberger-Hunsberger Family Association, 1925 - 1926. 2 v. ill., index. Loc: Bluffton, Goshen.

The original version of a comprehensive family history that includes descendants of Abraham and his son Abram who came to the Waterloo area from Pennsylvania in 1801. Period: 1801 - 1920.

920. Hunsberger, Byron K. **The Hunsbergers.** Norristown, PA: Hunsberger Family Association, 1941. 828 p. ill., index. Loc: Goshen.

Most Waterloo County Hunsbergers in this book are descendants of Abraham and his son Abram who settled in Wilmot Towmship after migrating from Pennsylvania in 1801. Period: 1801 - 1940.

921. Hunsberger, George S. **The Hunsbergers: a portion of the genealogy history of a few Swiss Hunspergers (also spelled Hunstsberger, Honsberger, Huntzberger).** Germantown, NY: Hunsberger Family Association, 1969. 1015 p. ill., index. Loc: OKIT.

A revised edition of the 1941 book, with a chapter on Hunsbergers in Canada. Most Waterloo County Hunsbergers in this book, identified in the text by the letters CD, are descendants of Abraham and his son Abram who came to the Waterloo area from Pennsylvania in 1801. Period: 1801 - 1969.

SURNAMES BEGINNING WITH J

922. Eash, Fannie Kauffman and Jantzi, Daniel and Litwiller, Nelson. **Christian B. Jantzi and Anna Lichty.** Goshen, IN: The Authors?, 1974?. 167 p. index. Loc: OWTUCGR.

    A genealogy of the descendants of Christian and Anna, some of whom still live in Waterloo County. Christian was the eldest son of Michael and Marie Boshart who farmed near Baden. Handwritten additions update the book to 1977. Period: 1837 - 1973.

923. Kuepfer, Nancy Jantzi (Mrs Menno W.) and Roth, Lorraine. **Family history and genealogy of John Jantzi and Elizabeth Gerber.** London: The Authors, 1974. 299 p. ill., map, index. Loc: OWTUCGR, OKIT.

    A genealogy of an Amish Mennonite family who migrated from France to New York State and then settled in Wilmot Township. The biographical sketches which introduce the families of each of John and Elizabeth's ten children include detailed lists with values of all the house and farm equipment and animals which each received at the time of marriage. Period: 1832 - 1974.

924. Roth, Lorraine and Ryan, Ruth Y. **The family history and genealogy of Joseph and Catherine (Boshart) Jantzi, Christian and Catherine (Boshart, Jantzi) Riser, John and Anna (Jausi) Ulrich.** Kitchener: The Authors?, 1982. 437 p. ill., maps, index. Loc: OKIT, OWRW.

    A history of an Amish Mennonite family with roots in France and related families in New York State. The family settled in Wilmot and Wellesley Townships from the 1830s. The Lichti, Ulrich, Riser, Jausi and Schweitzer families are also mentioned. A supplement to this book by Lorraine Roth was compiled in 1991. Period: 1830 - 1982.

925. Roth, Lorraine. **Introduction: the Jantzi/Yantzi/Yancey family from Lorraine, France to Lewis County, New York and Ontario, Canada with smaller contingents soon moving on to Iowa and Illinois; Supplement: additions and corrections to Family history and genealogy of John Jantzi and Elizabeth Gerber by Mrs Menno W. Kuepfer and Lorraine Roth, 1974 and to The family history and genealogy of Joseph and Catherine (Boshart) Jantzi, Christian and Catherine (Boshart, Jantzi) Riser, John and Anna (Jausi) Ulrich by Ruth Yantzi Ryan and Lorraine Roth, 1982.** Waterloo: The Author?, 1991. 17 p. ill., map. Loc: OKIT.

    Background material on the French origins of the family with additions and corrected information, though the contemporary genealogy has not been updated. Both books mentioned in the title are indexed in the WRP database. Period: 1830 - 1991.

926. Troyer, Nancy D. Miller. **Family history of Joseph B.S. Jantzi and Magdalene Boshart.** Middlebury, IN: Wakarusa Tribune, 1967. 16 p. Loc: OWTUCGR.

    A genealogy of Joseph (1842-1925) and the descendants of his eleven children for five generations. The family moved to Minnesota for 19 years but returned to Waterloo. Period: 1842 - 1967.

927. Miller, Betty Ann Bixel and Miller, Oscar R. **The Cornelius Jansen family history 1822-1973.** Berlin, OH: The Authors?, 1974. 73 p. ill., maps. Loc: OWTUCGR.

    A history of a Russian Mennonite family who were exiled in 1873 and stayed briefly in Berlin before moving to the United States in 1874. Quotations from Margaretha's diary refer to making maple sugar and doing farm work, to which she was unaccustomed, with the Schantz family. Period: 1873 - 1874.

928. Peters, K. **Genealogy of Johann Janzen family, 1752-1977.** Winnipeg: E.J. Klassen, 1977. 408 p. charts, index. Loc: OWTUCGR.

    A genealogy of a Russian Mennonite family, many of whom settled in Manitoba and Alberta. Among those who settled in Waterloo County were Rev. Jacob H. Janzen, Heinrich Janzen, George Braun and Jacob H. Braun. Period: 1923 - 1977.

929. Rice, Paul L. **Elfriede and company: a tale of two families.** Decatur, Ga.: P.L. Rice, 1988. 227 p. charts, table, maps. Loc: OWTUCG.

    The chronicle of the Janzen family, Russian Mennonites who fled to Waterloo County in 1924. The story includes the Neufeld family, for Eliese Neufeld married Rev. Jacob H. Janzen, and both had children from previous marriages. Although the book contains biographical information about J.H. Janzen, an important Mennonite leader, the focus is on his children and how they coped with the hardships in both Russia and Canada. There are detailed descriptions of the emigration from Russia and of the jobs the girls got in the homes of St Jacobs and the factories of Kitchener. The book is based on the reminiscences of family members and the memoirs of Eliese Janzen. Period: 1903 - 1979.

SURNAMES BEGINNING WITH K

930. Schuler, Wendlin and Kauk, Patricia J. **Kaiser family reunion: February 1854, St. Agatha.** 1854 translated 1989. 8 p. Loc: OKIT.

A description of the Kaiser family reunion of 1854 by the teacher, Wendlin Schuler, including poems dedicated to Anton Kaiser the elder and Anton Kaiser the younger. The poems and description were translated into English by Patricia J. Kauk. Period: 1853 - 1854.

931. Kalbfleisch, Raymond W. **A genealogical record of the descendants of Reinhardt Kalbfleisch, born 12 August 1812 in Germany, died 27 June 1894 near Elmira, Ontario.** Levering, MI: The Author, 1956. 107 p. ill., charts, map, index. Loc: OKIT.

A genealogy with introductions to the families of Reinhardt and each of his eight children. A section on non-related Kalbfleisches indicates that this family is not connected with that of Joachim Kalbfleisch, the Waterloo County printer. Period: 1812 - 1956.

932. Kauffman, Charles F. **A genealogy and history of the Kauffman-Coffman families of North America, 1584-1937: including brief outlines of allied Swiss and Palatinate families who were among the pioneer settlers in Lancaster and York Counties of Pennsylvania from 1717 on; viz., Becker, Baer, Correll, Erisman, Fahs, Kuntz, Kneisley, Hershey, Hiestand, Meyers, Musselman, Neff, Martin, Ruby, Snavely, Shenk, Shirk, Sprenkle, Witmer and others.** York, PA: Lawrence P. Kauffman Jr, 1940 reprinted 1980. 776 p. ill., maps, index. Loc: OKIT, OWTUCGR.

Includes incidental references to several Waterloo County families. Period: 1800 - 1937.

933. Fries, A.J. "The Pennsylvania German family named Kinsey." **Waterloo Historical Society.** 1941. 29: 173-182. Loc: all.

A genealogical account of the Kinsey family whose ancestor, Jacob Kintsing, came from Switzerland to Pennsylvania in 1737. The article deals primarily with family members in Pennsylvania, the Waterloo members being mentioned in a footnote. Many primary source materials are quoted. Period: 1800 - 1867.

934. Kinzie, Lester. **Kinzie family history: study research material, incomplete.** Banning, CA: The Author, 1977. 47 p. bibl. Loc: OWTUCGR.

Working papers including a bibliography, biographies of the American Kinzies, and a genealogy beginning in 1716. Dilman Kinzie and his wife Barbara came to Doon from Pennsylvania in 1800. Dilman died five years later, leaving his wife and five young children to carry on clearing the land and farming. Period: 1800 - 1977.

935. Kinzie, Lester and Schmadl, Elizabeth L. **Kinzie genealogy.** Culver City, CA: The Authors, 1972. 47 p. index. Loc: OKIT.

A revised edition of a genealogy of the ancestors and descendants of Dilman Kinzie, a Pennsylvania Mennonite who died in Doon in 1806. There is biographical information on family members, excerpts from the works of Eby and from the **Bulletin of the Historical Society of Montgomery County.** It includes a name index compiled in 1991 by Elizabeth Schmadl. Period: 1800 - 1972.

936. Kloepfer, C. Victor. **Canadian ancestral roots of Arthur Thomas Kloepfer and Philomena Agnes Gilker.** Whitefish, 1988. 312 p. ill., charts, maps. Loc: OKIT.

A history of the family's progenitors and descendants. Arthur and Philomena came to the Maryhill area from Germany early in the nineteenth century. There are maps of the family farms, located on lots 81, 82, and 83 of the German Company Tract, and biographical information on family members. The family later moved to Bruce County. Period: 1810 - 1988.

937. Kloepfer, C. Victor and Little, Mary Kloepfer. **Kloepfer family data.** The Authors?, 1990. 1 v. (unpaged). Loc: OKIT.

The background to a genealogical study of the Kloepfer family who emigrated to the Maryhill area from Germany in the first half of the 19th century. Lists of the descendants of many branches of the family are included. Period: 1810 - 1990.

938. Knechtel, Valentin and Nechtel, Naomi M. **A partial record of the descendants of Valentin Knechtel and Eva Maria Glück.** Minneapolis, MN: Naomi Margaret Nechtel, 1984. 119 p. Loc: OKIT.

A revised edition of an unpublished genealogy written in the 1930s by Valentin Knechtel. The earlier Valentin and his wife Eva arrived in Preston from Germany with their children in 1831, their descendants settling throughout Waterloo County. Period: 1831 - 1984.

939. Nechtel, Naomi M. **A supplement to the Knechtel family book printed in 1984.** Minneapolis, MN: The Author, 1986. 59 p. Loc: OKIT.

Additions and corrections to a genealogy of the Knechtel family. Period: 1831 - 1986.

940. Schmadl, Elizabeth L. **An index to A partial record of the descendants of Valentine Knechtel and Eva Maria Glück.** Kitchener Public Library, 1990. 41 p. Loc: OKIT.

A name index to Naomi M. Nechtel's family history of 1984 and its 1986 supplement. Period:

1831 - 1986.

941. Lang, E. Elizabeth Koch. **Koch: some ancestors and descendants of David Ludwig Koch, 1801-1889, and Barbara Reist, 1801-1890.** New Dundee: The Author, 1988. 427 p. ill., maps, charts, index. Loc: OWTUCGR, OKIT.

An account of the family of an early settler of Woolwich Township who was ordained a minister for the Conestogo Mennonite Meeting House in 1845. There is information on Ludwig's ancestors and the descendants of his eight children, with facsimiles of correspondence, land deeds and certificates. Period: 1823 - 1988.

942. Cassel, Daniel Kolb. **A genealogical history of the Kolb, Kulp or Culp family, and its branches in America with biographical sketches of their descendants from the earliest available records from 1707 to the present time, including Dielman Kolb in Germany with portraits and other illustrations.** Swarthmore, PA: Glenn H. Landis, 1895 reprinted 1990. 584 p. ill., index. Loc: OWTUCGR.

A genealogy with biographical notes on a Pennsylvania Mennonite family, including Dillman Ziegler and his sister Hetty Detweiler, children of Elizabeth Kolb and Jacob Ziegler, who came to Waterloo County early in the 19th century. Period: 1816 - 1895.

943. Kraemer, William and Graf, Sister Clara and Schmadl, Elizabeth L. **The Kraemer-Spetz families: early settlers in Waterloo County, 1827-1961.** 1961?. 16 p. ill., index. Loc: OKIT, OWTUCR.

Family histories and genealogies of the Kraemer and Spetz families, Catholics of Waterloo County who intermarried. Information about St Jerome's College and early priests of Waterloo County is given, and the work concludes with a name index compiled by Elizabeth Schmadl in 1991. Period: 1827 - 1961.

944. **Kropf family book, 1969.** 1969. 36 p. index. Loc: OKIT.

A genealogy of the descendants of David N. Kropf of Baden and Magdelena Lichty of Wellesley, with a name index by Elizabeth Schmadl. Period: 1845 - 1969.

945. Kuepfer, Nancy Jantzi (Mrs Menno W.) and Roth, Alvin N. and Roth, Lorraine. **Family history and genealogy of Jacob and Marie (Lichti) Kuepfer.** Kitchener: The Author?, 1976. 292 p. ill., map. Loc: OWTUCGR, OWRW, OKIT.

A genealogical summary of the ancestors and descendants of a Swiss Anabaptist farming family in Wilmot Township. Biographical sketches introduce the families of the ten children. The 1861 census description of Jacob's assets is included, with a transcript of his will. Period: 1820 - 1976.

946. Kuepfer, Nancy Jantzi (Mrs Menno W.) **History and genealogy of Andrew and Lydia (Getz or Goetz) Kuepfer.** London: Alvin N. Roth, 1974?. 80 p. Loc: OWTUCGR.

A genealogy of a poor Swiss Amish family who arrived in Wilmot Township about 1850. Andrew was a weaver whose twin brother Jacob migrated to Wilmot before him. The five children of Andrew and Lydia, all born in Switzerland, intermarried with the Kennel, Eiman, Schweitzer, Wagler and Lehman families. Period: 1850 - 1974.

SURNAMES BEGINNING WITH L

947. Laschinger, Russell H. **A genealogical record of the descendants of Joseph Laschinger, Abraham Nash and Gwer Merner.** Gilmer, TX: The Author, 1966. 16 p. ill. Loc: OKIT.

A family history of the author's forebears, the Laschingers of New Hamburg, who intermarried with the Nash and Merner families. Reminiscences of the author's childhood in New Hamburg and memories of family members are included with genealogical and biographical information. A name index was compiled by Elizabeth Schmadl. Period: 1819 - 1966.

948. Schmadl, Elizabeth L. **Index to A genealogical record of the descendants of Joseph Laschinger, Abraham Nash and Gwer Merner.** Kitchener Public Library, 1991. 5 p. Loc: OKIT.

A name index to Russell H. Laschinger's family history. Period: 1819 - 1966.

949. **Lautenschlager family 1618-1929.** 1930. 338 p. ill. Loc: OKIT, OWTUR.

A genealogical record of family members, with birth and death dates and places of residence. Some entries include photographs and more detailed biographical information. Most names are connected with the Waterloo County, but the work includes people who settled in the United States. The book contains newspaper clippings of obituaries which update the original text. Period: 1830 - 1929.

950. Steinman, Gerald. **Christian Lebold history and genealogy.** Cambridge: The Author?, 1991. 156 p. ill., index. Loc: OWTUCGR.

A history of the Lebold family of Wilmot Township whose progenitor, Jacob, arrived from Germany about 1835. Christian (1836-1903) was

Jacob's eldest child who inherited the family farm north of Punkeydoodle's Corner. There are photographs and stories of Christian, Barbara and their seven children, with genealogical information to 1991. Information on the Blank and Roth families is also included. Period: 1835 - 1991.

951. Lebold, Ralph A. **The John B. Leis family history and genealogy.** 1979. 50 p. ill. map. Loc: OWTUCGR.

A history of a family founded by Joseph, a German orphan who came to Canada in 1817 and began farming in Wellesley in 1844. His grandson, John B., was a farmer, an implement dealer, and the owner of a fruit store and harness shop in the Wellesley area. Census information, correspondence and land records have been reproduced, with family photographs, reminiscences and genealogical information. Period: 1844 - 1979.

952. Lichti, Willis. **Nicholas and Barbara (Schmidt) Lichti: ancestors and descendants.** New Hamburg: The Author, 1985. 146 p. ill. Loc: OWTUCGR.

A genealogical account beginning with Johannes Lichti, born in Upper Alsace in 1756, and ending with the ninth generation. An index of personal names of the direct descendants is provided on pages 133-146. Period: 1820 - 1985.

953. Martin, Winston J. **The Lichtys.** 1987. 19 p. Loc: OWTUCGR.

A genealogy of the ancestors and descendants of Johannes W. Lichty who came to Waterloo County in 1822 with his wife Barbara Hoffman, settling where the Conestoga Mall was later built. Period: 1822 - 1987.

954. Schmidt, William A. **The ancestors and descendants of Menno Lichty and Catharine Martin.** Waterloo: The Author, 1984. 1 v. (unpaged). Loc: OWRE, OKIT.

A genealogy of the Swiss Mennonite family, taken mainly from Ezra Eby's **A Biographical History of Waterloo township** (1895). Period: 1822 - 1983.

955. Litwiller, Mary and Litwiller, Earl. **Peter Litwiller and Elizabeth Lichti family history and genealogy.** Petersburg: The Authors?, 1981. 323 p. ill., map, index. Loc: OWTUCGR.

Biographical sketches and genealogies of the parents and their twelve children. Peter came in 1829 from Alsace to Wilmot Township, where he later became a bishop serving the Wilmot Amish Mennonite congregation. He was closely associated with Rev. Eugene Funcken, parish priest at St Agatha. Period: 1829 - 1981.

956. Sanders, Phoebe Litwiller. **Christian Litwiller genealogy 1848-1966.** 1966. 41 p. index. Loc: OWTUCGR.

A genealogy of the descendants of Christian (1848-1924), youngest son of Peter and Elizabeth Lichti of Wilmot Township. Christian was ordained a minister of the Wilmot Amish Mennonite Church in 1877 and farmed north of St Agatha with his wife Maria Miller. Reminiscences of the parents and their nine children introduce each genealogy. Period: 1829 - 1966.

957. Duck, William A. **A Longhouse genealogy.** Toronto: The Author?, 1987. 16 p. bibl., charts, index. Loc: OKIT.

A genealogy of a German family who settled first in the Genesee region of New York State and later in Markham Township. Peter Longhouse, a farmer, moved to Waterloo County where he held land in Woolwich Township and Hespeler. Period: 1820 - 1986.

SURNAMES BEGINNING WITH M

958. Brubacher, Susanna M. Sittler. **The Peter G. Martin family history.** Hawkesville: The Author, 1968?. 91 p. index. Loc: OWTUCGR.

A genealogy of the American forebears and offspring of Peter (1816-1902), a Mennonite who came from Pennsylvania in 1820 with his parents. He later settled on a farm north of St Jacobs with his wife, Maria Bowman. Period: 1820 - 1968.

959. **The family of Amanda Brubacher.** 1973?. 9 p. Loc: OWT.

A list of the descendants of Amanda Brubacher and Oliver S. Martin, including birth, marriage and death dates. Period: 1868 - 1973.

960. Good, M.R. **A Martin family genealogy: a detailed record of the descendants of Isaac D. Martin (1844-1931).** Waterloo: The Author, 1968. 19 p. ill. Loc: OKIT, OWT, OWTUCGR.

The Martin family farmed near Elmira and then near Hawkesville. There are short profiles of Isaac D. Martin's children and a chart naming his grandchildren and great-grandchildren. Period: 1844 - 1968.

961. Hoover, Peter. **A record of the ancestors and descendants of David B. Martin, 1838-1920; supplement: John C. Weber family, the Hoover family.** Wallenstein: The Author, 1973?. 119 p. index. Loc: OWTUCGR.

A genealogy of the family of an Old Order Mennonite who farmed near Wallenstein with his wife, Catherine Weber. There are biographical notes on David's American ancestors, but none on his descendants. Period: 1820 - 1920.

962. Martin, Delton. **Detailed history of the Noah B. Martin descendants.** 1961. 20 p. Loc: OWTUCGR.

A genealogy of Noah (1850-1933) and his wife Catherine Martin (1853-1919), both descendants of David Martin who left Switzerland for Pennsylvania in 1727. Noah and Catherine had nine children whose descendants are listed. Period: 1820 - 1961.

963. Martin, Delton. **Supplement to the 1961 edition of the Noah B. Martin family history.** The Author, 1973. 28 p. Loc: OWTUCGR.

Additions and corrections to the Martin genealogy compiled in 1961. Additional information on the early Martin family in Canada and the United States is included from Isaac W. Martin, Mennonite bishop of Indiana, supplementing and correcting Ezra Eby's book. Also included are a transcript of Peter Martin's will which was used as a land deed, and reminiscences of Noah. Period: 1820 - 1973.

964. Martin, Ezra and Martin, Edith. **History and descendants of Josiah Martin and Sarah Clemmer.** Ephrata, PA: The Authors, 1988. 74 p. ill. Loc: OWTUCGR.

A history of a Mennonite family who first farmed near Floradale, later moving to Iowa with other Stauffer Mennonites from Woolwich Township. Josiah was an ordained minister and the grandson of Peter Martin who came to Woolwich Township in 1819. Period: 1819 - 1988.

965. Martin, Menno. **History of the descendants of Christian B. Martin 1834-1912.** Zurich: The Author, 1964. 56 p. ill., index. Loc: OWTUCGR.

A genealogy of a Woolwich Township Mennonite farmer who married Maria Bauman and had seven children. Both American ancestors and descendants are noted, with an introduction describing Mennonite emigration to America and early life in Waterloo County. Some brief biographical notes accompany the genealogical information. Period: 1834 - 1964.

966. Martin, Peter G. **Peter G. Martin letters - English.** Edited by Isaac R. Horst. 1984. 132 p. ill. Loc: OWTUCG.

A collection of letters from Peter G. Martin of St Jacobs to friends in other parts of Canada and the United States. The letters have been transcribed and, where necessary, translated from German into English by Isaac R. Horst and others. Period: 1872 - 1899.

967. Martin, Winston J. **Christian (1669-1759) and Elizabeth; David (1771-1854) and Maria Martin and their descendants.** Elmira: Bauman Printing, 1983. 200 p. ill., index. Loc: OKIT, OWTUCGR.

A genealogy of the Martin family spanning 300 years, giving special attention to the Waterloo County descendants of David and Peter. 1984.

968. Martin, Winston J. **Martins of Waterloo County: the descendants of David and Peter the pioneers.** Elmira: Bauman Printing, 1983. 211 p. ill., index. Loc: OWT.

An account of the migration of the Martins' ancestors to Pennsylvania and of David and Peter Martin to the Waterloo area in the early nineteenth century, with a comprehensive list of all their descendants. A name index includes the father's name with each entry. Period: 1800 - 1983.

969. Rudy, Aaron, Mrs. **A history of the ancestors and descendants of Peter P. Martin, also a short sketch of the Daniel M. Brubacher family.** 1966. 46 p. index. Loc: OWTUR, OWTUCG.

A record of the two Waterloo County families from 1650 to 1966. Biographical information about some family members is included, and there is an alphabetical index of names. Period: 1800 - 1966.

970. Schmidt, William A. **The ancestors and descendants of Menno Martin and Elizabeth Koenig (King).** Waterloo: The Author, 1984. 11 p. index. Loc: OKIT.

A genealogy of the descendants of Menno, son of John M. Martin and Rachel Bricker. Their Mennonite ancestor, David Martin, came to Waterloo County with his family in 1820. Period: 1820 - 1984.

971. Schmidt, William A. **The ancestors and descendants of Noah B. Martin and Catharine Martin.** Waterloo: The Author, 1984. 77 p. index. Loc: OKIT, OWTUCGR.

A genealogy of members of a Swiss Mennonite family who migrated from Pennsylvania to Waterloo County in 1820. Noah was the son of John M. Martin and Rachel Bricker. Period: 1820 - 1984.

972. Weber, Joan L. and Schmadl, Elizabeth L. **Descendants of Manassah Martin.** The Author, 1974. 23 p. ill., index. Loc: OKIT, OWTUCGR.

A genealogy of the ancestors and descendants of Manassah, son of David and Rebecca Shantz. Manassah and his wife, Magdalena Shantz, had nine children. A name index for this work was added in 1991 by Elizabeth Schmadl. Period: 1800 - 1974.

973. Schmidt, William A. **The Mayer-Moyer family tree (1818-1981): a record of the descendants of Adam Mayer (1818-1895).** Waterloo: The Author, 1981. 241 l. ill., map. Loc: OWRE.

A genealogical account of the family that came to Waterloo County in the 1850s from Niederstetten, Germany. The work is primarily a name index providing birth, marriage, and death dates of the descendants, but more detailed information such as addresses and occupations is provided for some family members. Period: 1855 - 1981.

974. Waldie, F. Jane McIntyre. **A genealogical record of the descendants of Alexander McIntyre and Philip Zeller, John Smith, John Beamer, John Kennedy.** Kitchener: The Author?, 1987. 1 v., index. Loc: OKIT.

A history of a family with combined German and Scottish ancestry. Those who settled in Waterloo County include the families of Philip Zeller who lived near Breslau, Elmer Zeller McIntyre who bred Hereford cattle in Wilmot Township, and George Alexander McIntyre, a teacher and businessman in Kitchener. Period: 1840 - 1987.

975. Pratt, Florence Conway. "Saskatchewan remembers." **Waterloo Historical Society.** 1957. 45: 38-44. ill. Loc: all.

The daughter of Kate (Catherine) McPherson recounts the stories that her mother told her about growing up on a farm near Galt. Period: 1824 - 1957.

976. Connell, Ruth Merner. **Mürner, Muerner, Merner: genealogy and related branches.** Cleveland, OH: The Author, 1976. 586 p. ill., indexes. Loc: OKIT, OWRN.

A genealogy of the Merner family including the descendants of Jacob and Susanna Schluchter Muerner who settled in New Hamburg in 1837 after leaving Kien/Reichenbach, Switzerland. There are biographical sketches of their 13 children including Samuel Merner, noted businessman and politician. Name and picture indexes are provided. Period: 1837 - 1976.

977. Schmidt, William A. **The Milatz, Militz family tree: a record of Frederick Milatz (1837-1917) and his descendants.** Waterloo: The Author, 1984. 107 p. ill., maps, index. Loc: OKIT.

A genealogy with an introductory family history of Germans who came to the Preston area in 1886. Frederick Jr became a stationary engineer in charge of Preston's power supply at Blair and later at the Pattinson Woollen Mill. Photographs, reminiscences and newspaper quotations portray life in Blair at the beginning of the twentieth century. Period: 1886 - 1984.

978. Millar, D. Douglas and Millar, Anne Eby. **Two pine trees: pictorial biographies of the antecedents, descendants and relatives of David Douglas and Anne Eby Millar.** Kitchener: The Authors, 1992. 243 p. ill. Loc: OWTUCGR.

A history of a Waterloo County family with both Scottish and Pennsylvania German ancestors. Some biographical information is given, but most of the material consists of family photographs with explanatory captions. Many photographs were taken by Gordon Eby, father of Anne Eby Millar. Other families related to the Millars are the Bergeys and the Hewitts. Period: 1800 - 1992.

979. Hett, Dorothy. **Behind the hills.** The Author, 1972. 43 p. ill. Loc: OWT.

Recollections of life on a family farm near Doon at the turn of the twentieth century. Family information about Ferdinand Miller, his wife Johanna Wagner, and their descendants is given with facts about the farm property and buildings. The text is interspersed with poetry, drawings and family photographs. Period: 1836 - 1972.

980. Montag, Theresa Lang and Montag, Sister Liguori and Montag, Sister Jeannette. **Family of Karl Montag and Margaret Wenzel.** Hanover: The Authors, 1982. 286 p. index. Loc: OKIT.

An extended genealogical chart of an Alsatian Catholic family who settled in St Agatha early in the 19th century. Period: 1813 - 1982.

981. Moogk, Edward and Moogk, Rose. **The Moogk family history.** The Authors, 1970. 49 p. ill. Loc: OKIT.

A revised and expanded version of the 1965 book, including information on the Lockard family and a description of the second Moogk reunion of 1965. A name index for this work was compiled by Elizabeth Schmadl. Period: 1818 - 1970.

982. Moogk, Peter N. **The ancestors and family of Charles Moogk (1848-1924) of Waterloo, Ontario: the story of ten generations.** Vancouver: The Author, 1988. 19 p. ill., map. Loc: OKIT, OKITW, OWT.

An account of the family's German background and ancestry, with biographies of Balthasar, the first Moogk to emigrate to Waterloo County, and his son, Charles George, Waterloo architect and builder. Genealogical information is included on the children of Josephine and Charles Moogk. A name index was compiled by Elizabeth Schmadl. Period: 1841 - 1988.

983. Moogk, Rose and Moogk, Edward. **The Moogk family history**. The Authors, 1965. 39 p. Loc: OKIT.

Reminiscences and genealogical data on the ancestors and descendants of Balthasar and Salome Schmitt Moogk. Balthasar arrived in Waterloo County from Germany in 1841. A son, Charles, was a Waterloo architect, and a grandson, Frederick, was president of the Waterloo Music Company. The copy at the Kitchener Public Library is incomplete, but the missing information appears in its copy of the 1970 expanded edition. Period: 1841 - 1965.

984. Schmadl, Elizabeth L. **Index to The ancestors and family of Charles Moogk (1848-1924) by Peter N. Moogk**. Kitchener Public Library, 1990. 3 p. Loc: OKIT.

A name index to the family history. Period: 1841 - 1988.

985. Schmadl, Elizabeth L. **Index to The Moogk family history by Rose Moogk and Edward Moogk**. Kitchener Public Library, 1990. 8 p. Loc: OKIT.

A name index to the 1965 and expanded 1970 editions. Period: 1841 - 1970.

986. Martin, Winston J. and Moser, Blanche. **Moser families of Waterloo County**. 1987. 1 v. Loc: OKIT.

Genealogies of several Moser families who settled in Hespeler, Bamberg, Heidelberg and Berlin, and near Paradise Lake. Genealogical information is also given on the Musselmans who intermarried with one of the Moser families. Period: 1800 - 1987.

987. DeKay, George P. **The Moxleys: early pioneers of Waterloo County, Ontario, Canada**. The Author, 1970. 1 v. Loc: OKIT.

A genealogical record of the descendants of a widow, Mrs Delilah Moxley, who married Daniel Eby in 1818 and farmed north of Waterloo. There is a descriptive introduction to each of the genealogies of her seven children. Period: 1818 - 1970.

988. Schmadl, Elizabeth L. **Index to History of the Moxley family by George P. DeKay**. Kitchener Public Library, 1991. 15 p. Loc: OKIT.

An index to more than one thousand personal names mentioned in the genealogy of the Daniel Eby and Delilah Moxley. Period: 1820 - 1970.

989. Buehler, Allan M. **A record of the ancestors and descendants of Isaac Moyer and wife Esther Weber**. Hespeler: The Author, 1970. 22 p. ill., chart. Loc: OWTUCGR, OKEBC, OKIT.

A history and genealogy of a Swiss Mennonite family who settled in Waterloo County. Isaac's grandfather, Samuel Moyer, came to the Vineland district of Ontario from Pennsylvania in 1800. The relationship of the Moyer family to the Shantz, Weber and Martin families is described. Period: 1860 - 1970.

SURNAMES BEGINNING WITH N

990. Nafziger, Cheryl E. **An example of an Amish Mennonite family history**. 1981. 16 p. bibl., charts. Loc: OWTUCGR.

A genealogy of the author's families, the Gaschos who settled east of Baden and in Wellesley and the Nafzigers who farmed in Perth County. Both families were members and clergy of Amish Mennonite churches. Period: 1854 - 1981.

991. Fretz, A.J. **A genealogical record of the descendants of William Nash of Bucks County, Pennsylvania, together with historical and biographical sketches and illustrated with portraits and other illustrations**. Scottdale, PA: Westmoreland-Fayette Historical Society, 1903 reprinted 1985. 88 p. ill., index. Loc: OWTUCGR.

A history of a Pennsylvania Mennonite family, some of whom settled in New Hamburg and others in Lincoln County. Sarah Nash married Jacob Laschinger and Anna Nash married William W. Schweitzer, both of New Hamburg. This reprint of the Nash genealogy is bound with a similar work on the Oberholtzer family by the same author. Period: 1881 - 1903.

992. Neuschwanger, Weldon D. and Neuschwanger, Barbara L. **The genealogy of Henry and Froenika Neuschwanger who arrived in North America from Germany in 1846: organized down to the sixth generation**. Olympia, WA: W. & B. Neuschwanger, 1988. 575 p. ill. Loc: OWTUCGR, OKIT.

A six-generation history of the descendants of Henry and Froenika Neuschwanger and their twelve children. Henry was ordained as a Mennonite bishop in 1867. He and his family led a group of settlers from Hay Township to Kill Creek, Osborne County, Kansas not long after 1871. The family has since settled in many locations in the United States, Canada and Australia. Period: 1846 - 1988.

993. Olde, F. Evelyn Jones. **The genealogy of William John Nugent and his wife Jane Esther Charlotte Currell**. Clinton: The Author, 1984. 121 p. ill., maps, charts. Loc: OKIT.

A history of an English family who came to Canada in 1870. One of the family, Emily Nugent, married William McCormick whose family farmed near Millbank. Data relating to the McCormick family from the 1871 Wellesley Township census and information on the descendants of Emily and William are found on pages 72-90a. Period: 1870 - 1984.

SURNAMES BEGINNING WITH O

994. Roth, Lorraine. **John and Barbara (Schultz) Oesch family history and genealogy.** Kitchener: The Author?, 1964 - 1969. 2 v. Loc: OWTUCGR.

A substantial genealogy of the descendants of John, a Bavarian who bought lot 15 of Wilmot Township and later moved to Huron County. He and his wife Barbara had fourteen children who survived childhood; each has a biographical introduction to a family genealogy. Veronica Oesch married John Gerber and farmed in Wilmot, but some of her siblings farmed in Huron County and others moved to the United States, particularly Missouri. Period: 1820 - 1960.

995. Thayer, Ruth V. Eicher Neesz. **History of John and Barbara Nafziger Oesch and their descendants by a great-granddaughter.** 1986. 24 p. index. Loc: OWTUCGR.

A genealogy of the descendants of John and Barbara who migrated from France in 1857 and settled near Philipsburg. They had three children, John N., Barbara and Anna. This second edition contains additions to the 1982 genealogy. Period: 1857 - 1986.

996. Ogram, Grace. **The Ogram-Milner family history.** Kitchener: The Author, 1974. 155 p. ill., maps, index. Loc: OKIT, OWRW.

A genealogy including a short narrative of the process of compilation. As well as basic biographical information for each descendant of Richard and Mary Milner and Robert and Mary Ogram, the entries often include details of occupation and place of residence. Period: 1800 - 1973.

997. Oppertshauser, Orval and Oppertshauser, Joan. **Oppertshauser family tree, 1837-1988.** Victoria, BC: The Authors?, 1988. 1 v. ill., maps, index. Loc: OKIT.

A chronicle of the descendants of Conrad Oppertshauser, a German emigrant to Waterloo County who became a wagonmaker. He and his wife, Katharine Lippert, were married in Waterloo County, but later moved to Hanover where they spent most of their married life. Period: 1838 - 1988.

998. Klinger, Robert and Klinger, Jacqueline O. (Mrs Robert) and Schmadl, Elizabeth L. **The ancestry in Germany and the descendants in Canada and the**

United States of Caspar Otterbein and his wife Margaret Hahn, and of Jakob Braun and the wife Wilhelmina Pränkert. Ann Arbor, MI: The Authors, 1974. 27 p. index. Loc: OKIT.

Genealogies of two German families who came to Woolwich Township. Other related families include the Strohs, Oswalds, Stefflers and Israels. A name index to this work was produced by Elizabeth Schmadl. Period: 1800 - 1974.

999. Robbins, Elizabeth Luella Eby. **The Otterbein family history, August 1985 update: the descendants of Valentine and Elisabetha Herrman Otterbein.** The Author, 1985. 24 p. Loc: OKIT, OWTUCGR.

A sequel to the author's 1981 genealogy in 1981, with data on family ancestors in Germany, material received from the Joanna Shelly Cram family, and events since the previous printing date. Period: 1840 - 1985.

1000. Robbins, Elizabeth Luella Eby. **The Otterbein family history: the descendants of Valentine and Elisabetha Herrmann Otterbein.** The Author, 1981. 239 p. ill., index. Loc: OKIT, OWTUCGR.

A history of a German family who settled near Breslau in the 1840s, with biographical facts on most family members. A supplement to this work was compiled in 1985. Period: 1840 - 1981.

SURNAMES BEGINNING WITH P

1001. Panabaker, C.A. **Pannabecker - Panabaker: a family history by the late Cornelius Arthur Panabaker about 1960.** 1967. 40 p. Loc: OKIT.

Short biographies of members of the Panabaker family, including the author, descendants of pioneer settlers in the Hespeler area in 1810. Many of the family were farmers and some were later associated with the R. Forbes Company. The role of the single women of the family is also described. Period: 1810 - 1966.

1002. Panabaker, D.N. "Panabaker family history." **Waterloo Historical Society.** 1937. 25: 254-260. Loc: all.

A narrative of the family, from its European origins to the settlement in the Hespeler area of Waterloo Township. The author explains variant spellings of the family name and refers to other pioneer families who are related by marriage. Period: 1800 - 1937.

1003. Peterson, Jean E. **From Norway to North America: the descendants in Canada and the United States of Olaf and Caroline Pederson who came from Norway about 1867 to Manitoba and North Dakota.** Dubuque,

IA: Gorsuch Grace Printers, 1981. 122 p. ill., index. Loc: OCCA.

A genealogy of a family, some of whose members settled in the Galt area about 1940. Related families include the Currys and the Coveretts. Period: 1940 - 1981.

1004. Kelly, James R. **Pepplers and their cousins.** Sacramento, CA: The Author, 1988?. 294 p. ill., maps, charts, index. Loc: OKIT.

A genealogy with some biographical notes about a German family who migrated to North America in about 1840. Among the many Waterloo County descendants are those of George and Ludwig, original immigrants and Waterloo blacksmiths. Period: 1840 - 1985.

1005. Dunham, B. Mabel. "The Pequegnat family." **Waterloo Historical Society.** 1948. 36: 50-55. Loc: all.

A history of the Swiss family who settled in Berlin in 1874 and established clock and jewellery stores around southwestern Ontario. The author notes the family reunion at Eugene's home at Bridgeport in 1924 attended by 145 descendants, many of whom are named. Period: 1874 - 1948.

1006. Varkaris, Jane and Varkaris, Costas. **The Pequegnat story: the family and the clocks.** Dubuque, IA: Kendall/Hunt Publishing, 1982. 187 p. ill., indexes, bibl. Loc: OKIT, OWRE.

A history of the large family of Ulysse and Francoise Pequegnat who arrived in Berlin from Switzerland in 1874. Various family members had clock and jewellery stores in Ontario towns and cities, including Waterloo and New Hamburg, managed in part from the central store in Berlin/Kitchener. Pequegnat family members were very closely involved in school, church and public affairs and intermarried with various other Berlin families, notably those of the Benton Street Baptist Church. Edmond (1884-1963) was secretary of the Berlin Public School Board from 1911 to 1942. Marcel (1886-1963), a professional engineer, played a key role in the developing the waterworks and in the origins of the Grand Valley Conservation Authority. Eugene (1888-1974) worked for Mutual Life from 1908 to 1974. Mathilde (1876-1924) married Fred Boehmer and Angeline (1879-1963) married Benjamin Schulte, who worked for Dominion Rubber for 25 years. Information is presented on about 700 family members and on family businesses including The Arthur Pequegnat Clock Company and the Berlin and Racycle Manufacturing Company. The book also contains descriptions and photographs of the clocks and several of the clocks' workings. General, name and clock indexes are added. Period: 1874 - 1982.

1007. Perrin, Jean. **The story of John Perrin and Charlotte Wingham, the son of William Perrin Sr and Mary Ann Newstead.** 1 v. ill. Loc: OKIT.

An account of a farming family who lived in the Roseville area, including selections from John's diary, and biographical information about his family, particularly the women. A story tells how Charlotte cradled the grain of 36 acres in a day. Period: 1842 - 1942.

1008. Wood, William H. **Remembrance.** The Author, 1925?. 1 v. Loc: OKIT.

A genealogy of the descendants of William Perrin and Mary Ann Newstead, who settled near Roseville. Period: 1817 - 1925?

1009. **The Peterson family tree.** 7 p. Loc: OKIT.

A genealogical chart of the descendants of John Dieter Peterson. A grandson, Henry William Peterson, was one of Berlin's earliest newspaper publishers. Period: 1830 - 1973.

1010. Poth, Ruby Bechtel. **Poth family history: descendants of Andrew Poth and Magdalena Lautenschlager.** The Author, 1983. 1 v. ill., charts. Loc: OKIT.

A scrapbook of photographs, articles, documents and genealogical charts relating to the New Dundee family. Period: 1822 - 1983.

SURNAMES BEGINNING WITH R

1011. Ratz, Herbert C. **The family of Valentine Ratz.** Waterloo: The Author, 1988. 10 l. Loc: OKITW.

A genealogy of the family of John Ratz and Salome Heist of Elmira, and their ten children. Period: 1828 - 1988.

1012. Ratz, Herbert C. "From forge to farm." **Waterloo Historical Society.** 1991. 79: 145-161. ill. Loc: all.

A history of the emigration of Valentin and Anna Gertrude Ratz from Germany in 1828, based largely on the memories and family traditions contained in a 1918 letter by Jacob Ratz, who was an infant when his family arrived in Waterloo. Valentine worked as a blacksmith until 1840, when he moved to a farm in Woolwich Township and developed a sawmill one mile west of St Jacobs. Period: 1828 - 1918.

1013. **Ratz reunion, July 1st, 1909, Martin's Grove, St. Jacobs.** 1909. 6 p. ill. Loc: OKIT.

Programme for the Ratz Family Reunion of 1909, including photographs of family members and the words of English and German songs. The programme included speeches, vocal and instrumental music, and a performance in Pennsylvania German dialect. Period: 1908 - 1909.

1014. Read, Donald Edwin. **Our family history, 1600-1980: ancestors and descendants of Siderick Read (1822-1877)**. Ottawa: The Author, 1980. 444 p. ill., index. Loc: OCCA, OWT.

Siderick Read came to Canada from England in 1872. Members and descendants of his family settled in Elmira, Waterloo, Kitchener and Galt. The volume includes family photographs, information on individuals and an index of names. Period: 1872 - 1980.

1015. Redekop, Freda Pellman. **The Redekop(p) book: the descendants of Benjamin Redekopp (1833-1907) and Anna (Wiebe nee Berg) Redekopp (1819-1899)**. Waterloo: BenAnna Tree Publishers, 1984. 323 p. ill., maps. Loc: OWTUCGR.

A record of a Russian Mennonite family which includes Calvin W. Redekop, a professor of Sociology at Conrad Grebel College, among its descendants. Other members settled in Montana and Saskatchewan. Period: 1920 - 1984.

1016. Reinhart, Eileen and Reinhart, Beatrice. **Family history of Gottfried Reinhart**. Kitchener: The Authors?, 1981?. 39 p. ill., chart. Loc: OKIT.

A genealogy of the descendants of Gottfried Reinhart and Anna Marie Bruder who owned a farm near Berlin, south of the Grand Trunk Railway. A description of their farmhouse and a history of the farm ownership are included. Period: 1824 - 1981.

1017. Reist, Agnes. "Reist family reunion." **Mennogespräch**. 1986. 4,1: 9-10. Loc: OWTUCG, OKIT.

A report on the reunion at St Jacobs, with genealogical notes on this Pennsylvania Mennonite family. Although Abraham Reist owned land in Woolwich Township he never came to Canada, but his son John and daughter-in-law Susannah settled near Kossuth in 1827. Period: 1821 - 1986.

1018. Reist, Henry G. **Peter Reist of Lancaster County, Pennsylvania and some of his descendants**. 1933 reprinted 1977. 118 p. ill., index. Loc: OKIT, OWTUCGR.

An account of a Mennonite family, emphasizing its 18th-century Pennsylvania antecedents. It gives brief biographical information on later Waterloo County descendants, including John Reist who came to Waterloo County in 1826. Kitchener Public Library has the original edition and Conrad Grebel the reprint. Period: 1826 - 1933.

1019. Peters, K. and Stein, A. **Genealogy of Jakob Rempel, 1766-1984**. Winnipeg: E.J. Klassen, 1985. 218 p. ill., index, bibl. Loc: OWTUCGR.

A genealogy of a Russian Mennonite family, many of whom settled in Manitoba after coming to Canada in 1925. Reminiscences by family members include the realization, on arrival in Kitchener-Waterloo, that only the Old Order Mennonites dressed conservatively in black. Some descendants of the Rempel and Willms families were born in Hespeler and Kitchener. Period: 1925 - 1984.

1020. Renwick, Walter. **Renwick family history: detailing the descendants of John Renwick and Janet Middlemus of North Dumfries, by Walter Renwick, copied from the original in the collection of Eleanor Perriman, with her handwritten amendations**. Clifford: The Author, 1970?. 137 p. ill., maps, index. Loc: OKIT.

A history of a family of Scottish emigrants who settled in North Dumfries near Ayr in 1841. Biographical and genealogical information is complemented by photographs, newspaper clippings, obituaries and reminiscences. Period: 1841 - 1970.

1021. Lang, E. Elizabeth Koch. **Riebel: some ancestors and descendants of Georg Riebel (1820-1872) and Theresa Sieffert (1834-1927)**. New Dundee: The Author?, 1988. 168 p. ill., maps, index. Loc: OKIT.

An annotated genealogy of a German family who initially settled in the Roseville and Strasburg areas about 1846, and later moved to Bruce County. A daughter, Josephine Riebel, returned to Elmira and married Conrad Schwindt. An introduction discusses German ancestors and includes biographical information about the early Canadian Riebels. Period: 1846 - 1985.

1022. Krueger, Alice M. **A family history of David Rife, formerly Reiff, beginning about 1751: also a history of Michael Troyer, beginning about 1706**. Sheldon, ND: The Authors, 1980. 1 v. ill., charts. Loc: OKIT.

A combined genealogy of the Rife family, some of whom settled in Waterloo County, and the Troyer family in Vaughan County. Articles, obituaries, wills and photographs relating to the families are collected at the end of the book. Period: 1800 - 1980.

1023. Ritter, Robert P. **A history of the descendants of Philip Ritter of Baden, Germany, 1819-1973**. 1973?. 113 p. map, bibl. Loc: OWT.

Philip Ritter migrated to Woolwich Township from Germany in 1845. Genealogical charts for Ritter, his wife Elizabeth Knechtel and their eleven children are given with introductions for each family chart. Period: 1845 - 1973.

1024. Hoffman, Frances. **Jacob and Johannes Roos**. 1985. 13 p. Loc: OKIT.

Text of a speech to the Waterloo-Wellington Branch of the Ontario Genealogical Society about descendants of two German families who settled in Preston and Wilmot Township. A photocopy of a letter from David M. Jackson contains additional genealogical information. Period: 1813 - 1985.

1025. Rosebrugh, Harold. **1971 supplement to the Rosebrugh family**. Galt: Galt Printers, 1971. 59 p. ill., index. Loc: OKIT.

An addendum to the family history, continuing the pagination of the book written by the same author in 1965. It expands the information on the Rosebrughs and their land purchases in Dumfries Township, and includes a photograph of Thomas's stone farmhouse in Branchton. Period: 1816 - 1971.

1026. Rosebrugh, Harold. **The Rosebrugh family story, also spelled Rosbrugh, Rosebrough, Rosborough, Rossborough, Rosebroock, etc.**. Galt: Galt Printers, 1965. 168 p. ill., map, ports., index. Loc: OCCA, OWTUR, OKIT.

Genealogical study of the Rosebrugh family in the British Isles, the American colonies and Canada. A section on Dumfries Township notes the landholdings of William, Thomas, Robert and Abner Rosebrugh. Details are given of William's land dealings with William Dickson and Robert Rosebrugh's donation of land for the Branchton School. Period: 1816 - 1965.

1027. Roth, Alvin N. **History and a partial genealogy of Michael and Magdalena (Lichti) Roth and history and full genealogy of John and Catherina (Boshart) Roth**. London: The Author?, 1972. 118 p. ill., map. Loc: OWTUCGR.

An account of the family of John and Catherine and the descendants of their five married children. Michael and Magdalena, the parents of John, were French Amish Mennonites who bought land in Wilmot Township in 1835. A facsimile of the Roth coat of arms and a map of Wilmot Township are included. Period: 1835 - 1972.

1028. Roth, Lorraine. **History and genealogy of Joseph and Anna (Kauffman) Roth 1851-1966**. Kitchener: The Author?, 1966. 78 p. maps, index. Loc: OWTUCGR.

A history of an Amish Mennonite family of French origin who settled mainly in Oxford and Perth Counties. Three families are shown on a map as owning land in Wilmot Township: Edwin and Elizabeth Albrecht, Nicholas and Leah Lichti, and Peter S. and Mary Schrag Roth. Other members of

the family settled in the New Hamburg area. Period: 1896 - 1966.

1029. Roth, Olivia and Harloff, Verdella Roth. **Family history and genealogy of Benjamin S. and Barbara (Lichti) Roth, Anna Roth and Christian Lichti, Catherine Roth and Rudolph Schwartzentruber, John E. and Annie (Kropf) Lichti**. New Hamburg: The Authors?, 1984. 63 p. ill., index. Loc: OWTUCGR.

A history of the Roth, Erb, Brenneman and Lichti families. Many of the Roths lived in Perth County, but because John F. Roth married Catherine Brenneman, they had a farm next to the Brennemans' in Wilmot Township. The families of the three children raised by John and Catherine are included in this book. Period: 1827 - 1984.

1030. Roth, Ruth C. and Roth, Roy D. **A genealogical study of the Nicolaus and Veronica (Zimerman) Roth family 1834-1954**. Elkhart, IN: Roth, Ruth C., 1955. 331 p. ill., indexes. Loc: OWTUCGR, OKIT.

An Amish Mennonite family history, in which most Waterloo County connections will be found in the chapter on the family of Barbara Roth Zehr. Barbara and her husband Peter settled in the Wilmot Township-East Zorra area, Peter later becoming the first minister of the East Zorra congregation. Period: 1834 - 1954.

1031. Roth, Sadie and Golay, Alfred and Muller, Emmanuel. **Descendants of Mary Egli (1848-1918) and Joseph Roth (1838-1910)**. Salem, OR: The Author?, 1982. 238 p. ill., index. Loc: OWTUCGR, OKIT.

A history of the ancestors and descendants of a French Mennonite family. Although Mary Egli was born in Waterloo, she and Joseph were married in Iowa, and many of their descendants settled in Oregon. Period: 1838 - 1982.

1032. Bender, Delmer. **The Christian Ruby family**. New Hamburg: The Committee, 1989. 231 p. ill., maps, ports. Loc: OWTUCGR.

A genealogy including biographical articles by Lorraine Roth about Christian Ruby and his son Joseph who emigrated to Wilmot Township in 1838. In 1853 Joseph was ordained bishop of the Amish Mennonite congregation of East Zorra. The book is organized by family branches, with an introductory biographical history and genealogical chart for each. The charts state the occupation of each person, and photographs of some descendants are included. A name index includes addresses of all those listed. This is a second edition of the Ruby genealogy first published in 1952. Period: 1838 - 1989.

1033. Rudy, Ruth E. **William Rudy of Waterloo County, Ont.: his ancestors and his descendants.** Kitchener: The Author, 1991. 118 p. ill., map. Loc: OKIT.

A genealogy of the Rudy family beginning with Daniel and Barbara (Rosenburger) Rudy who purchased land west of Waterloo in 1827. The work includes information in chart form about their descendants, newspaper clippings, certificates, photographs and text with details of occupations, marriage dates and places of residence. Period: 1827 - 1990.

1034. Freiburger, Rose. "The Rummelhardts of Rummelhardt." **Waterloo Historical Society.** 1987. 75: 47-49. ill. Loc: all.

A brief family history beginning with the arrival of stonemason, Franz Joseph Rummelhardt, in Canada in 1833. Bascom, Freiburger, and Schwarz are three family names mentioned among Rummelhardt's descendants. Period: 1833 - 1967.

1035. Ruppel, Lydia A. and Ruppel, Harold and Lossner, Rosetta. **Tracing the descendants of John and Mary Ruppel.** 1975?. 14 p. ill. Loc: OKIT.

A revised edition of a 1971 genealogical chart, tracing the family of a German who came to Berlin in 1852 and settled in Elmira a year later. Period: 1827 - 1975.

1036. Rutherford, Robert. **Pedigree of Rutherfoord, Lord Rutherfoord.** 1978?. 92 p. ill. Loc: OCCA.

A history of a Scottish family including J. Thomas who came to North Dumfries with his wife, Janet Hall in 1829. There are photographs of Janet and the Rutherford farmstead and genealogical information on their descendants. Period: 1829 - 1978.

SURNAMES BEGINNING WITH S

1037. Olaskey, Terry M. "The history of the Sararas family." **Waterloo Historical Society.** 1975. 63: 49-51. Loc: all.

A sketch describing the family's migrations, first from North Carolina to Pennsylvania and then to Waterloo County in 1802. The homestead was situated on Lot 12 of Beasley's Old Survey and remained in the family until it was moved to Doon Pioneer Village in 1970. Period: 1802 - 1975.

1038. Martin, Melinda. **The Jacob N. Sauder genealogy.** 1985. 92 p. Loc: OWTUCGR.

A genealogy of a German Mennonite family who settled in Wellesley Township about 1846. Brief biographies introduce each of the genealogies of their twelve children, many of whom lived near St

Jacobs. Period: 1846 - 1985.

1039. Westfall, Katie and Bauman, Velina. **The Jacob A. Sauder genealogy.** 1973. 74 p. Loc: OKIT, OWTUR, OWTUCGR.

A record of the descendants of Jacob N. Sauder (1809-1875) and Barbara Funk (1822-1899), German Mennonites who settled in Wellesley Township in the mid-nineteenth century. Their twelve children and their descendants are listed, with their dates of birth, marriage and death. A description of the Sauder coat of arms is also given. Period: 1846 - 1973.

1040. Gebert, Narona Kemmerer. **The history and genealogy of the Schantz family.** Red Hill, PA: The Author, 1980. 316 p. ill., index. Loc: OWTUCGR.

A family history with a brief section on Shantzes in Canada and the United States. This portion mentions Christian who settled near Freeport in 1810 and Jacob Yost Shantz, a Berlin industrialist who helped settle Russian Mennonites in Manitoba. Period: 1810 - 1980.

1041. Schaus, Lloyd H., Rev. **The history of the Schaus family in Canada, 1846-1979.** Waterloo: The Author, 1979. 74 p. ill., map. Loc: OKIT, OWTUCGR.

A genealogy of a German family who farmed near Breslau before moving to Normanby Township in 1854. Family reunions have been held in Kitchener, Waterloo and St Jacobs. Period: 1846 - 1979.

1042. Jackson, David Marvin. **The Schenk family of Utzhausen, Hessen, Germany.** Vancouver, BC: The Author?, 1988. 67 p. ill., chart, maps. Loc: OKIT.

A collection of facsimiles of documents relating to the Schenk family. Papers referring to Waterloo County settlers Johann Conrad and his wife, Katherina Siebert, include a dismissal permit, a passenger list and baptism, marriage and death certificates. A genealogical chart indicates that four of their ten children were born in Wilmot Township in the mid-19th century. Period: 1840 - 1941.

1043. Schenk, Alfred J. **A history of the Schenks.** 1973. 163 p. ill., maps. Loc: OKIT.

A genealogy with an historical introduction to the earlier Canadian Schenks who migrated from Germany in 1848 and farmed near Mannheim and Shingletown; other family members moved to Normanby and Egremont Townships. The book contains reminiscences and some traditional family remedies, including one for deafness. Period: 1848 - 1973.

1044. Dettweiler, Allan. "Reunions and anniversaries: the Schiedel reunion." **Mennogespräch**. 1984. 2,2: 12. ill. Loc: OWTUCG, OKIT.

An account of the reunion of the descendants of Martin and Susannah Ries, Mennonites who came to Breslau from Pennsylvania in 1825. Some genealogical notes are included. Period: 1825 - 1984.

1045. Schiedel, Ian H. **The Schiedel book**. Richmond, BC: BC Genealogical Society, 1986. 270 p. ill., maps, charts, indexes. Loc: OKIT, OWTUCGR.

A history of the ancestors and descendants of Martin and Susannah Ries, Mennonites who settled near Breslau in Waterloo Township in 1825. A brother, John Schiedel, and his family settled in Woolwich Township in 1841. Genealogical charts, biographical sketches and information about farmsteads are included. Period: 1825 - 1986.

1046. Yantzi, Henry and Yantzi, Mae and Roth, Lorraine. **The family history and genealogy of Nicolaus and Barbara (Roth) Schlegel**. New Hamburg: Henry and Mae Yantzi, 1986. 246 p. ill., index. Loc: OKIT, OWTUCGR.

A genealogy of the descendants of a French Mennonite family who emigrated to the East Zorra area in 1839, with the main focus on Perth and Oxford Counties. There are introductory biographies of each of the seven children, most of whom farmed in Perth or Oxford Counties. Catherine married John Brenneman of Wilmot and Anna (Nancy) married Christian E. Lichti of St Agatha. Period: 1853 - 1986.

1047. Arndt, Barbara Timm. **Dorothea Schlote and her family: a remembrance**. Cleveland, OH: B. Arndt, 1988. 99 p. ill., facsims., maps, ports. Loc: OWTUCG, OKIT, OWT.

An anecdotal family history celebrating the 100th birthday of Dorothea Herbst Schlote. The book includes descriptions of the family's emigration from Germany, farming in Ontario at the end of the 19th century, and life in Waterloo in the first half of the twentieth century. Genealogical charts, a medical history through three generations, and the German alphabet written by Charles Herbst are among the illustrations. Period: 1830 - 1988.

1048. Schmidt, Nicholas J. **Jacob and Barbara (Boshart) Schmidt genealogy**. 1980. 61 p. Loc: OWTUCGR.

A list of the descendants of Jacob and Barbara of Mornington Township, with an introduction giving background information on the family. Jacob's parents, John and Barbara Schwartzentruber, arrived in Waterloo County about 1835 and gave their name to the settlement of Schmidtsville. Period: 1835 - 1980.

1049. Schmidt, William A. **The Schmidt-Smith family tree, 1787-1981**. St Jacobs: St Jacobs Printery, 1981. 119 p. ill. map, index. Loc: OKIT, OWRE, OWT.

A list of the descendants of Johannes and Maria Catharina Schmidt who came to Waterloo County in the 1860s. Entries are arranged by family and generation and give birth and death dates. There are photographs of family members and a name index. Period: 1860 - 1981.

1050. **History of the Jacob B. Schmitt family**. 1970?. 27 p. Loc: OWTUCGR.

A genealogy of the descendants of Jacob (1845-1925), his first wife, Magdalena Snyder, and his second wife, Catherine Shantz. An introduction gives background information on the Schmitts who came from Germany in 1832 and farmed lots 12 and 13 of Wilmot Township. Period: 1832 - 1970.

1051. Eby, Ezra E. "Genealogy of the Schneider-Snider family." **Waterloo Historical Society**. 1968. 56: 49. Loc: all.

An extract from Ezra Eby's history of Waterloo Township (Volume 2, pp. 266-272) setting out the genealogy of the Schneider and Snider families. Period: 1800 - 1872.

1052. **Herkommen und Geschlechts Register des Schneider Familie**. Berlin: Heinrich Eby, 1849. 8 p. Loc: OTMR.

The earliest genealogy of a Waterloo family, locally printed in Gothic script on small pages. Period: 1800 - 1849.

1053. Martin, Winston J. **Schneider, Snider and Snyders: the descendants of Hannes, 1534 and Catherine (Haus) of Berne Switzerland and Jacob, 1764-1853 (Bloomingdale)**. Milverton: The Author?, 1984. 72 p. ill. Loc: OKIT, OWTUCGR.

A genealogy, based on historical sources, of the ancestors and descendants of the three Schneider brothers, Jacob, Joseph and Christian, who came to Waterloo County early in the 19th century. Jacob bought land near Bloomingdale, Joseph settled on what is now Queen Street in Kitchener, and Christian farmed at Doon. Period: 1800 - 1983.

1054. Snyder, Bilva Stuhr. **Barth and Schneider (Snyder) families: the ancestors and descendants of Michael Barth and his wife, Anna Marie Dittus and Johann Theobald Schneider and his wife, Helene Magdalene Scholl, immigrants to the New World mid-1800's**. Muncie, IN: The Authors, 1978. 239 p. ill., bibl., maps, index, charts. Loc: OKIT.

A family history of the descendants of Johann Theobald Schneider, a shoemaker who came to Wellesley from Alsace. Some of his children later migrated to Nebraska. Period: 1850 - 1970.

1055. Schrag, Keith G. and Roth, Lorraine and Gingerich, Ruby. **The Daniel Schrag family history and genealogy.** Kitchener: The Authors?, 1981. 196 p. ill., index, maps. Loc: OKIT, OWTUCGR.

An expanded revision of an earlier 1964 edition by Keith Schrag. More biographical information on family members is contained in this illustrated version than in the previous book. Daniel was a German emigrant who came to South Easthope Township, some of his descendants settling in the western part of Waterloo County. Period: 1813 - 1981.

1056. Schrag, Keith G. **Daniel Schrag genealogy, 1813-1964.** Goshen, IN: The Author?, 1964. 144 p. index. Loc: OKIT, OWTUCGR.

A genealogy of the family of a German farmer who became the minister of the East Zorra Mennonite Church in 1849. Many of his descendants settled in Wilmot and Wellesley Townships. Introductions to each branch of the family include facts and reminiscences about those members. Period: 1813 - 1964.

1057. Grove, Joseph H. **Noah and Annie (Nafziger) Schultz of Wellesley Township.** Elmwood: The Author, 1988. 37 p. ill., maps, bibl. Loc: OWTUCGR.

An account of the Schultz and Nafziger families, including genealogical charts and an index of nearly 200 names. Period: 1840 - 1988.

1058. Brown, Ruth Schwartz. **Schwartz/Swartz.** The Author, 1974. 11 p. Loc: OKIT.

The history of a German Mennonite family who emigrated to Pennsylvania early in the 18th century. Christian Schwartz and his wife Sophia Ruth moved from Pennsylvania and settled near Preston about 1808. Period: 1800 - 1880.

1059. Roth, Lorraine. **Family history and genealogy of Jacob and Catherine (Roth) Schwartzentruber, 1835-1969.** Kitchener: The Author, 1969. 116 p. ill., maps, index. Loc: OWTUCGR.

A record of an Amish Mennonite couple who were married in Wilmot in 1835 and farmed there and later in Perth County. Biographies of their nine married children are included with genealogies of their descendants. Corrections were added in 1982. Period: 1835 - 1969.

1060. Swartzentruber, Peter. **Christian Schwartzentruber: Magdalena Shoenbeck 1743-1956.** Westmoreland, NY: The Author?, 1956. 136 p. index. Loc: OWTUCGR.

The history of a German couple, two of whose four sons, Jacob and Michael, came to Canada. Jacob married Catherine Schmucker and moved to Waterloo County towards the end of his life, while Michael married Barbara Oswald and settled in Wilmot Township in 1823. Michael and Barbara's immigration and pioneering work are described with a record of their descendants. The index, pages 128 to 136, is not bound with the book. Period: 1823 - 1956.

1061. Swartzentruber, Peter. **History and genealogy of John and Veronica Erb Schwartzentruber 1743-1956.** Westmoreland, NY: The Author?, 1956. 203 p. indexes. Loc: OWTUCGR.

An account of the ancestors and descendants of an Amish Mennonite couple who came from Pennsylvania in 1826 and settled in Wilmot Township. Their children married into the Steinman, Gardner, Gascho, Litwiller and Lichti families. Period: 1826 - 1956.

1062. Swartzentruber, Peter and Arthaud, John Bradley and Arthaud, Gwynneth Charlotte. **John Schwartzentruber, wifw's name unknown, 1727-1957, progenitorial forefather of the descendents of this book [copied verbatim].** Westmoreland, NY: The Authors?, 1957. 129 p. Loc: OWTUCGR.

A genealogy of the ancestors and descendants of John S. Schwartzentruber and his wife Catherine Blank/Katherine Plank, Amish settlers in Wellesley Township. The introduction describes the immigration and settlement processes. An index and addenda to this work, compiled by John Bradley Arthaud and Gwynneth Charlotte Arthaud in 1987, are included in the copy at Conrad Grebel College. Period: 1833 - 1957.

1063. Dahms, Vera E. Schweitzer. **The family history of Jacob (1834-1891) and Catherine Schweitzer (1819-1888): major emphasis on the Michael Schweitzer branch, 1834-1972.** 1972. 36 p. ill. map. Loc: OWTUCGR, OKITW.

A chronicle with biographical sketches of a German family who first settled in the Huron Tract and moved on to Wilmot Township in 1857. Descendants farmed near Mannheim and Erbsville and belonged to the Mennonite and Evangelical churches. Period: 1857 - 1972.

1064. Lang, E. Elizabeth Koch. **Schwind: some ancestors and descendants of Andreas Schwind (1822-1905) and Katharina Miller (1821-1886).** New Dundee: The Author?, 1988. 254 p. ill., maps, index. Loc:

OKIT.

A history of a German family who settled in the Lexington area in the mid-19th century and later moved north of Elmira. Andreas was a farmer and a stonemason who helped build the North Woolwich Evangelical Church. Period: 1840 - 1988.

1065. "New Hamburg visited by descendant of the founder." **Waterloo Historical Society**. 1962. 50: 47. Loc: all.

A note of the visit of William John Scott of New Zealand. His great-grandfather, William Scott, founded New Hamburg. Period: 1857 - 1962.

1066. Axt, Elam and Feick, Leota and Good, Olive. **Family history of Jonas C. Shantz and Hannah Snyder Shantz, 1710-1980**. 1980. 79 p. ill. Loc: OKIT, OKITW, OWTUCGR, OWRN, OWRND.

An account of the progenitors and descendants of Jonas C. Shantz (1813-1898) and Hannah Snyder and their eight children. There is a biography of each of the children, apart from Magdalena who died in infancy, and descendants are listed with birth and death dates. Period: 1813 - 1980.

1067. Cressman, Orpha and Cressman, Barbara and Cressman, Mary Ann Shantz. **Family history of Joseph Y. Shantz and Elizabeth (Stauffer) Shantz**. St Jacobs: The Author?, 1971. 74 p. ill. Loc: OWTUCGR, OKIT.

A genealogy introduced by reminiscences of Joseph and Elizabeth's twelve children. Joseph owned a sawmill on Plum Creek and founded the Haysville Cheese Factory, the first in Waterloo County. The family played a leading role in establishing Wilmot Township's Pine Hill School and the Mennonite Aid Union. Period: 1800 - 1971.

1068. Martin, Almeda. **My grandparents: Tilman B. Martin and Mary Shantz; Henry D. Steckle and Maryann Sitler**. The Author, 1989. 5 p. Loc: OKIT.

Reminiscences of the author's Mennonite grandparents, including the Shantzes who farmed in Woolwich Township. Period: 1866 - 1978.

1069. Martin, Winston J. **Jacob Shantz (c1710-1781) and his descendants**. 1984. 90 p. chart. Loc: OKIT, OWTUCGR.

A genealogy of the three of Jacob's children whose families came to Waterloo County: Isaac who married Barbara Reiff, Esther who married Abraham Bergey, and Christian who married Hannah Paul. Period: 1808 - 1983.

1070. Shantz, E. Clare. **History of the John C. Shantz descendants**. 1971. 19 p. Loc: OKIT.

A genealogy with some biographical notes on a Pennsylvania Mennonite family who migrated to

Waterloo County in 1806. The family farmstead was located where Kitchener's Sunnyside Home now stands. Period: 1806 - 1970.

1071. **The Shantz family: being an outline of family history beginning with Jacob Shantz, in the year of our Lord, seventeen hundred and ten.** Kitchener: The Shantz Family Association, 1930. 31 p. Loc: OWTUCGR.

An genealogical account of the American descendants of Jacob Shantz, mentioning notable members. Members of this Mennonite family came from Pennsylvania to Waterloo Township in 1806. There is a description of the Shantz crest and photographs of some Shantz Reunion officials. Period: 1806 - 1930.

1072. "Shantz family reunion." **Waterloo Historical Society**. 1940. 28: 135-136. Loc: all.

An article reprinted from the **Waterloo Chronicle** giving details about the fourth Shantz family reunion, held in Waterloo Park in 1940. Some information about family members, past and present, is also given. Period: 1805 - 1940.

1073. Shantz, Frederick R. "The Shantz family history." **Waterloo Historical Society**. 1930. 18: 208-212. Loc: all.

A brief account of the emigration of Jacob Tschanz from Switzerland to Pennsylvania in 1737 and the subsequent migration of his children to Waterloo Township in the first years of the nineteenth century. Period: 1800 - 1930.

1074. Shantz, Lorne and Shantz, Doreen. **Memories of yesteryears**. The Author, 1987. 74 p. ill. Loc: OKIT, OWRN, OWRND, OWRW, OWTUCG.

The autobiography of Lorne Shantz, born in 1906 on a farm near Philipsburg, describing his childhood and farm life. There are also genealogical charts and photographs of the Shantz family. Period: 1906 - 1987.

1075. Shantz, Orvie W. **History of the Noah W. Shantz and Rachel Shantz descendants**. 1974. 23 p. index. Loc: OWTUCGR.

A genealogy of Noah (1854-1920) and Rachel (1856-1890), Waterloo County Mennonites who had seven children. An introduction explains that the family is related to Christian who came from Pennsylvania to Freeport in 1810. There are brief biographies of the children of Noah and Rachel who were placed in foster homes, following their mother's early death. Period: 1810 - 1974.

1076. Sherk, J.H. **Sherk record book**. Vermilion, SD: The Author, 1914?. 12 p. ill. Loc: OWTUCGR.

A genealogy of the descendants of John Schereck

of Pennsylvania who settled near Stevensville, Ontario and whose son, Daniel, came to New Dundee about 1836. A report of the 1914 reunion lists descendants of Daniel Sherk who attended. Period: 1836 - 1914.

1077. Sherk, Thomas A. **The Sherk family**. Baltimore: The Author, 1982. 357 p. ill. Loc: OWT.

A well-documented history of the Sherk family from 1635 to 1982. Most of the book refers to members in the United States, but two chapters refer to Canadian descendants. These include: Joseph Sherk who came to Waterloo in 1800 with Samuel Betzner; Peter Sherk who settled in Bridgeport, becoming the owner of a large flour and saw milling business; and Maria Sherk, wife of Christian Erb. Period: 1800 - 1982.

1078. Hallman, Joan. **Family history of Peter Shirk**. 1984. 80 p. ill., index. Loc: OKIT, OWTUCGR.

A record of the ancestors and descendants of Peter Shirk, an Old Order Mennonite who held political appointments and owned the Lancaster Mills at Bridgeport and the Baden Mills. Short biographies preface the genealogies of each of his thirteen children who lived past infancy. Period: 1862 - 1984.

1079. Schürch, René. **Schürch von Sumiswald**. Berne, Switzerland: The Author, 1986. 280 p. ill., maps. Loc: OWTUCGR.

A genealogy of the Schürch (Schuerch, Shirk, Sherk, Sherrick) family from its 16th-century origins in Switzerland. The research contains information on the origin of the family name, heraldry, the Mennonite connection and the migration to North America. Period: 1800 - 1986.

1080. Boehmer, August. **Shoemaker family history from 1676 to 1951**. Kitchener: The Author, 1951. 10 l. chart. Loc: OKITW.

A brief genealogy of a Pennsylvania Mennonite family who settled in Waterloo Township. Jacob S. Shoemaker, founder of Bridgeport, came to the area in 1820, followed eight years later by his grandfather, Jacob Shoemaker and his family. There are biographical sketches of some family members. Period: 1820 - 1950.

1081. Boehmer, August. "Shoemaker family history." **Waterloo Historical Society**. 1951. 39: 32-36. Loc: all.

An account that begins with the migration of Swiss-born Jacob to Pennsylvania in 1737 and traces the family line that came to Waterloo County in 1828. Period: 1828 - 1900.

1082. Shuh, Barbara Ann and Shaw, Jean. **Descendants of John Shuh, 1828-1901, Waterloo, Ont.**. Truro, NS: J. Edward Shuh, 1986. 5, 15 p. ill. Loc: OWTUR, OKIT, OWT.

A genealogy of descendants of John Shuh, a prominent Waterloo businessman. The first part is biographical, including a transcript of his obituary; the second part is a chart of descendants to 1986. Period: 1828 - 1986.

1083. Shantz, Mary C. **John and Elizabeth Shupe and descendants: a family history of certain Shupes in North America from the early 18th century to the present; including notes on families of Dieffenbach, Munson, Overhold, Warner, Fulsom, Ahrens, Hirschy, Shantz & Bock**. Sudbury: The Author, 1985. 1 v. ill., bibl., maps, charts. Loc: OKIT.

The life and times of the Shupe family who bought land near Freeport in 1810. Background information about the early settlement, the Tunkers and the War of 1812 is interwoven with biographical and genealogical details. Period: 1810 - 1984.

1084. Kalbfleisch, Raymond W. **Captain Thomas Smith (born 1767 died 1850) and descendants**. Petoskey, MI: The Author, 1985. 147 p. ill., indexes. Loc: OKIT.

The history of a Vermont family who were among the first settlers in Woolwich Township in 1806. Thomas Smith was wounded at the battle of Lundy's Lane; he later started a stage coach service from Winterbourne via Berlin to Preston. Genealogical and biographical data on Smith's descendants are included and both geographical and name indexes are provided. Period: 1806 - 1985.

1085. Smith, Marvin C. **Scrapbook of Marvin Smith: St Jacobs, Smith family, Cress family**. The Author, 1983. Loc: OKIT.

Documents referring to the Smith and Cress families, collected by Marvin Smith, postmaster of St Jacobs. Many are newspaper clippings, but they include financial reports of St James Lutheran Church, receipts, voting registration certificates, a copy of Ephraim Cress's will, and a list of St Jacobs buildings shown on an 1857 map that were standing and occupied in 1968. Period: 1806 - 1976.

1086. Hunsberger, Albert. "Reminiscences of Grandmother Snider." **Waterloo Historical Society**. 1978. 66: 5-17. ill. Loc: all.

A detailed account of a Mennonite family in Waterloo County over a period of nearly 150 years, based on the recollections of the author's mother-in-law. Births, deaths, marriages, illnesses, religious and cultural traditions, and new technologies are discussed in the article. Period: 1830 - 1967.

1087. Schmidt, William A. **The ancestors and descendants of Solomon Snider and Elizabeth Martin.** Waterloo: The Author, 1984. 1 v. index. Loc: OKIT.

A genealogy relating to the larger family tree of Peter Bricker and Elizabeth Cress, grandparents of Elizabeth Martin. Period: 1846 - 1984.

1088. Snider, Lloyd and Snider, Vera. **History of the Isaac B. Snider family: 1841-1921.** The Authors, 1985. 44 p. ill., map. Loc: OKIT, OWTUCGR.

An annotated list of descendants of Isaac Bingeman Snider and Nancy Sittler who settled near German Mills in about 1861. Birth and death dates for all of their thirteen children are given as well as information on the grandchildren. Period: 1861 - 1985.

1089. Snider, W.W. "The Snider Pioneer Memorial." **Waterloo Historical Society.** 1922. 10: 248-250. Loc: all.

Brief description of the 1922 dedication ceremony for the Snider Pioneer Memorial in Doon Cemetery, including some information about the Snider family. Period: 1800 - 1922.

1090. Pepper, Paul E. **Hannes Schneider: his descendants and times, 1534-1939.** 1988. 1 v. (various pagings). Loc: OKIT, OWTUCGR.

An index to the detailed family history by Miriam H. Snyder and Joseph M. Snyder, including names of people, businesses, organizations, churches, schools, newspapers, communities and events mentioned in the work. Period: 1800 - 1939.

1091. **Snyder family history.** 1958. 12 p. Loc: OWTUCGR.

A genealogy of the family of Joseph B. Snyder (1854-1938) and Veronica Weber (1857-1934) who had twelve children. Joseph's forebears are traced to Joseph E. Schneider and Mary Bauman, who arrived in Waterloo Township in 1806 with their families. Period: 1806 - 1957.

1092. Snyder, Miriam H. and Snyder, Joseph M. **Hannes Schneider and his wife Catharine Haus Schneider: their descendants and times, 1534-1939.** Kitchener: M.H. Snyder, 1937. 17, 12, 346 p. ill., facsims., maps. Loc: OWTUCGR, OKIT, OWTL, OWT.

A history of thirteen generations of Schneiders, including a wide miscellany of information gathered by Joseph M. Snyder. The range of materials is so inclusive that, as the preface indicates, it is also a history of Waterloo County. A twelve-page table of contents summarizes the topics covered. There are photographs, excerpts from Berlin Council proceedings, reminiscences, and extracts from newspapers in English and German. An index of names for this book is available at the Kitchener Public Library. The copyright date is 1937, but some of the materials seem to date from 1943. Period: 1800 - 1943.

1093. Kilmer, Daisy Spain. **The family of Patrick Spain.** Brantford: The Author?, 1974. 164 p. ill., bibl. Loc: OCCA.

A genealogy of an Irish family who settled in Huron County in the 1850s. There are biographical notes on their descendants, some of whom settled in the Galt and Kitchener areas. Period: 1929 - 1974.

1094. Stager, David. **The Stager family in Canada since 1846.** Toronto: The Author, 1980?. 47 p. ill., maps. Loc: OCCA.

A genealogy with biographical notes about a German family who settled near Preston in 1848. Their descendants later moved to farms near Hespeler and New Dundee. The family name was also spelled Stege and Steger. Period: 1848 - 1980.

1095. Bergey, Lorna L. **A history of the Stauffer families who came to Ontario.** 1977. 32 p. ill. Loc: OWTUCGR, OKIT.

A genealogy based on the 1934 work by C.T. Groh. This report includes more information on the European ancestors, the names of all Stauffers who came to Upper Canada before 1867, and a brief biography of Harold Stauffer Bender. Period: 1800 - 1977.

1096. Francis, Willard Z. and Zug, Michael. **Abraham and Elizabeth (Zug) Stauffer.** Kitchener: Ontario Genealogical Society, Waterloo-Wellington Branch, 1974. 10 p. Loc: OKIT.

A genealogy with biographical notes on a family who left Lancaster County, Pennsylvania for Waterloo County in 1805. The family intermarried with many other well-known Waterloo County pioneers. Period: 1805 - 1970.

1097. Groh, C.T. **History of the Canadian Stauffers and ancestors.** 1934. 23 p. ill. Loc: OKIT, OWTUR, OKEBC.

A genealogical account of the Waterloo County family from its Swiss origins in the seventeenth century to the fifth Stauffer Reunion at Waterloo Park in 1934. Period: 1800 - 1934.

1098. Stauffer, Ezra N. **Stauffer genealogy of America and history of the descendants of Jacob Stauffer.** Goshen, IN: The Author, 1917. 180 p. ill., index. Loc: OKIT.

A genealogy of the Stauffers in the United States. It contains an introduction to the Canadian branch and quotes an article from the **Galt Daily Reporter** of 25 August 1904, describing a centennial reunion commemorating the arrival of Abraham Stauffer in Blair and gives the early history of the family in Canada. Period: 1803 - 1917.

1099. Roth, Lorraine and Kipfer, Alfred. **John Steckly family history: David and Magdalena (Ropp) Steckly genealogy.** Waterloo: The Authors, 1990. 59 p. ill., map, index. Loc: OKIT, OWTUCGR.

An illustrated genealogy of the family of John (Hans) Steckly who came to Wilmot Township in the first half of the nineteenth century. The French origins of the Steckly and Ropp families are described and the descendants listed to the third generation, with only the family of David and Magdalena Steckly followed to 1988. Period: 1820 - 1988.

1100. Weber, Eldon D. **From Stambach to Berlin (Ontario) and the descendants of Rev. John W. Stoeckle/Steckle (JJJ4), 1802-1879.** Waterloo: The Author, 1986. 368 p. ill., maps, index. Loc: OKIT, OWTUCG, OWTUCGR.

A family history of the Rev. John W. Steckle, his wife Esther Bleam and their five grown children. Copies of newspaper clippings, wedding announcements, obituaries and family correspondence are appended. Period: 1802 - 1986.

1101. Weber, Eldon D. **The Henry B. Steckle family.** Kitchener: The Author, 1967. 39 p. ill. Loc: OWTUCGR, OKIT.

A genealogy including information on many family members born in the county. Numerical references correspond to Ezra E. Eby's notations in **Biographical History of Waterloo Township and other townships.** A name index on the back cover includes the children, grandchildren and great-grandchildren of Henry B. Steckle. Period: 1820 - 1967.

1102. Roth, Lorraine. "Documents do tell stories." **Mennogespräch.** 1989. 7,1: 6,8. ill. Loc: OWTUCG, OKIT.

An examination of Steinman family's German correspondence and papers dating from 1800 to 1849. They illuminate the relationships and occupations of the Christian Steinman family which settled in Wilmot Township. Period: 1843 - 1989.

1103. Roth, Lorraine. **The family history and genealogy of Christian Steinman(n) and Veronica Eyer.** Baden: Christian Steinman(n) Family Book Committee, 1990. 433 p. ill., maps, index. Loc:

OKIT, OWRW, OWTUCGR.

An account of an Amish family who came to Wilmot Township in 1827. The genealogy of each family is prefaced with biographical information, and illustrations include photographs and facsimiles of documents such as wills, inventories and passenger lists. Period: 1827 - 1990.

1104. Stock, Harold Thompson. **Biographical history of the families of William H. Stock and Emma Cutler Stock, his wife, and John Stock and Laura Bamford (Bumford) Stock, his wife, and their descendants.** 1979. 185 p. ill., chart. Loc: OCCA.

A history of an English family which came to Canada about 1870. Descendants of Richard Bruce Dawson, son of Emma Stock Dawson and Joseph Wellington Dawson, settled in Ayr and Galt. Period: 1924 - 1979.

1105. Stockton, Margaret. **Within our time: the history of Charles Sheldon Stockton and Isabella Young McRae.** 1989. 73 p. ill., index. Loc: OKIT.

A history of a South Dumfries farming family who were associated with Knox United Church in Ayr. George D. Stockton was a director of the Ayr Co-operative. There are biographical sketches of family members and clippings from the **Ayr News.** Period: 1867 - 1989.

1106. Erb, David L. **The Streichers 1812-1970.** 1970. 60 p. Loc: OWTUCGR.

A genealogy of the descendants of the Swiss Leonhardt Streicher and Barbara Kennel, who married in 1845 and later farmed in Wellesley Township; they had eight children. Transcripts of Leonhardt's will and farm purchase of 1878 are included. Period: 1869 - 1970.

SURNAMES BEGINNING WITH T

1107. Thaler, A.F. and Thaler, Ralph H. **History of the Thaler family: tracing the descendants of George Adam Thaler, born September 11, 1785, died December 11, 1865.** Leamington: Widmeyer Press, 1960. 114 p. ill., index. Loc: OKIT.

A genealogy, biographical notes and reunion reports relating to a German family who settled near Breslau about 1820. An expanded second edition was published in 1966. Period: 1820 - 1960.

1108. Thaler, Ralph H. **History of the Thaler family: tracing the descendants of George Adam Thaler, born September 11, 1785, died December 11, 1865, second edition.** 1966. 172 p. ill., index. Loc: OKIT.

A revised and expanded edition of the Thaler

genealogy published in 1960. The family emigrated from Germany about 1820 and farmed near Breslau. Biographical notes and reunion reports are included with genealogical data on the families of Christina, Joseph, David and Adam Thaler. Period: 1820 - 1966.

1109. Thaler, Ralph H. **Name and address supplement to the History of the Thaler family**. Kitchener: The Author, 1966. 23 p. Loc: OKIT.

A list grouped according to the families of Christina, Joseph, David and Adam Thaler, complementing the author's work on the family history. Period: 1965 - 1966.

1110. Arndt, Barbara Timm. **The Timms of Waterloo County: a chronicle**. Cleveland, OH: The Author, 1991. 131 p. ill., bibl., maps. Loc: OKIT.

A history describing the emigration of Ludwig Timm's family from Mecklenberg to Waterloo County in 1869 and the activities of his descendants to 1985. Accounts of life in Kitchener at the end of the 19th century and the first half of the twentieth are recalled through the eyes of family members. Period: 1869 - 1990.

1111. Falkiner, Joan. **Three charts of the Timm family**. 1991. 3 p. Loc: OKIT.

Two genealogical charts and a map of the Timm family's home villages in Germany, produced as a supplement to the family history by Barbara Timm Arndt. Period: 1869 - 1991.

SURNAMES BEGINNING WITH U

1112. **Umbach family history**. 1988. 25 p. Loc: OKIT.

A genealogical chart of the descendants of Johann Umbach (1797-1879) and Katherine Laschinger (1802-1871). Period: 1824 - 1988.

SURNAMES BEGINNING WITH V

1113. Schmadl, Elizabeth L. **Index to Joseph Voisin and descendants**. Kitchener Public Library, 1991. 14 p. Loc: OKIT.

An index to the genealogy by Frank W. Voisin and Clifton E. Voisin. Period: 1856 - 1982.

1114. Voisin, Frank W. and Voisin, Clifton E. **Joseph Voisin and descendants, 1805-1892**. Kitchener: The Author, 1982. 62 p. ill. Loc: OKIT, OWTUCR.

A genealogy of the German family who bought farmland near St Clements, Wellesley Township, in 1856. An index to this work was compiled by Elizabeth Schmadl. Period: 1856 - 1982.

SURNAMES BEGINNING WITH W

1115. Kelly, Maurice. **Descendants of Theobald Waechter**. 1989. 1 v. ill. Loc: OKIT.

A history of a French Catholic family who settled near New Germany in 1829 and moved to Bruce County by 1866. A description of the early Catholic church in New Germany tells how Father Peter Schneider's move to St Agatha can be explained by a dispute over land ownership. Father Anton Waechter, son of Joseph and Mary Ann Schmidt, was a priest at Waterloo and New Hamburg. An index for this book was compiled in 1991 by Elizabeth Schmadl. Period: 1829 - 1989.

1116. Schmadl, Elizabeth L. **Index to Descendants of Theobald Waechter by Maurice Kelly**. Kitchener Public Library, 1991. 20 p. Loc: OKIT.

An index to the family history by Maurice Kelly. Period: 1829 - 1989.

1117. Roth, Lorraine. **Christian Wagler family**. 1983. 366 p. Loc: OWTUCGR.

A manuscript genealogy of the family of Christian and his wife, Anne Marie Wagler, who came from France in 1848 and settled on what later became the Livingston farm in Baden. Period: 1848 - 1975.

1118. Roth, Lorraine and Jantzi, Bruce W. **The family history and genealogy of Jacob Wagler and Magdalena Gardner and Barbara Lebold**. Wellesley: Jacob Wagler Family History Committee, 1989. 422 p. ill., ports., index. Loc: OKIT, OWRE, OWRW, OWTUCGR.

A history of the Wagler family, commemorating the 150th anniversary of the birth of Jacob Wagler, bishop of the Wellesley Amish Mennonite Congregation. Biographical information is provided about Jacob Wagler, his wives, and each of his nine children. A family tree is provided for each of the nine family branches, and they are illustrated by old photographs. There are brief histories of related families such as Gardners, Lebolds, Gerbers and Reschlys and an index of names. Period: 1839 - 1989.

1119. **Aaron Weber family history**. 1977. 20 p. ill. Loc: OKIT, OWTUCGR.

A genealogical chart of the family of Aaron (1833-1916) and Mary Weber who farmed north of Elmira. Aaron was a Deputy Reeve of Woolwich Township from 1890 to 1894 and Reeve in 1895. Period: 1833 - 1977.

1120. Freeman, Leonard. **History of the ancestors and descendants of Daniel H. Weber (1797-1864)**. St Jacobs: The Author, 1971. 94 p. ill., map, index. Loc: OKIT, OKEBC, OWTUCGR.

A genealogy of a Pennsylvania Mennonite who emigrated to Waterloo County with his brothers Abraham, Benjamin and Henry. An introduction briefly explains the reasons for the emigration from Lancaster County and describes the farmstead there. Occupations and places of residence, if known, are noted with the genealogical data. Period: 1797 - 1971.

1121. Hoover, Saloma. **The Weber family: a historical novel [WRP]**. 1 v. (unpaged). Loc: OWTUCGR.

An unpublished historical novel telling of the migrations of the Anabaptists from Switzerland to the Palatinate, then to Pennsylvania and lastly to Canada in 1819. Based on the experiences of the Weber family, the author describes travels, new beginnings and hardships through several generations. The Old Order Mennonite way of life is conveyed through folklore, traditions and Pennsylvania German dialect sayings. This photocopy of the original manuscript is part of the Pennsylvania German Folklore Society of Ontario collection in the Conrad Grebel College Archives. Period: 1819 - 1905.

1122. Kraemer, David M. **Family records of the descendants of Moses M. Weber, 1847-1937**. St Jacobs: The Author, 1972. 67 p. index. Loc: OKEBC, OKIT, OWTUCGR, OWTUR.

A genealogy of a family who moved to Canada from Pennsylvania in 1816. Moses' first wife was Barbara Horst and the second was Lydia Gingrich. Period: 1816 - 1937.

1123. Martin, Winston J. **John Anton Weber (1660-1724) and his sons: George (1693-1772) and Henry (1690-1745)**. 1984. 219 p. charts. Loc: OKIT, OWTUCGR.

A genealogy of the Webers who intermarried with the Horst and Good families. Descendants of all these families emigrated to Waterloo County. An index to this book was compiled by Elizabeth Schmadl. Period: 1818 - 1984.

1124. Martin, Winston J. **Weber families in Waterloo and Bruce Counties (non-Mennonite)**. Milverton: The Author?, 1991. 63 p. Loc: OKIT.

A genealogy with some added handwritten notes, linking this family of Webers to the Mennonite Webers in Martin's earlier work on John Anton Weber. Most families mentioned here were Lutherans or Catholics who settled in the northern and western areas of Waterloo County. Period: 1830 - 1991.

1125. Schmadl, Elizabeth L. **Index to John Anton Weber and his sons (the Webers, Horsts and Goods) by Winston Martin**. Kitchener Public Library, 1991. 56 p. Loc: OKIT.

Period: 1818 - 1984.

1126. Weber, Angus G. **History of the descendants of Daniel M. Weber, 1836-1888**. Elmira: The Author, 1967. 62 p. index. Loc: OWTUR, OWTUCGR.

A genealogy including biographical notes on many family members. Period: 1800 - 1967.

1127. Weber, Eldon D. **Descendants of pioneer HH214 Henry Hershey Weber (1793-1862) and Salome (Baer) Bauman (1791-1868): ordained 1824 as first minister for Martin's Mennonite Church.....** Kitchener: The Author, 1981. 298 p. ill., index. Loc: OKIT, OKITW, OWTUCGR.

A genealogy that uses a numbering system to identify each generation and the order of children's births. The entries are interspersed with short anecdotes and illustrated with photographs and drawings of farms and meetinghouses used by the family. Period: 1800 - 1981.

1128. Weber, Eldon D. "Waterloo Township, German Company Tract lot number 16." **Waterloo Historical Society**. 1970. 58: 8-16. ill. map. Loc: all.

A portrait of the Weber family who settled in Waterloo Township in 1805. The author defines German Company Tract lot 16, owned by various members of the Weber family from 1805 to 1853, as the part of Kitchener bounded by Belmont Avenue, Glasgow and Wilhelm Streets, Duke Street and Victoria Street. Period: 1805 - 1853.

1129. **Weber's write-up: history and heritage, Johannes Weber and Elisabeth Muench: a compilation of papers published on and for the descendants of Johannes Weber and Elisabeth Muench who settled in Ontario in 1854**. Edited by Leslie Herman Weber. Canyon Country, CA: L.H. Weber, 1986. 1 v. (various pagings). ill., tables. Loc: OWRE, OWT, OWTUR.

A collection of issues of a family journal published quarterly in California from 1981 to 1984. The collection contains genealogical information, mostly in charts, about the Weber family who came to Waterloo County from Hessen, Germany. While many entries refer to descendants who moved to the United States, family names such as Pflug, Oberthauser, Kalbfleisch, Raddatz, Hillgartner, Kaufman and Schoch have ties to the Waterloo area. Photographs and family stories are also included in the book, as is a loose map of Mücke, Nieder-Ohmen where Johannes and Elisabeth

Weber lived before emigrating. Period: 1854 - 1984.

1130. Schmadl, Elizabeth L. **Index to John Weicker family: 1830 pioneers of South Easthope and East Zorra by Sam Weicker.** Kitchener Public Library, 1991. 25 p. Loc: OKIT.
Period: 1830 - 1987.

1131. Weicker, Samuel. **John Weicker family: 1830 pioneers of South Easthope Tsp., Perth County, East Zorra Township, Oxford County.** Kitchener: The Author?, 1987?. 299 p. ill., maps, charts. Loc: OKIT.
A compendium of family trees, reunion reports, photographs, biographies and reminiscences relating to the Weicker family, German Lutherans who settled mostly in Perth County. Some of the family settled in Waterloo County and family reunions were held in New Hamburg. An index was compiled by Elizabeth Schmadl. Period: 1830 - 1987.

1132. Weicker, Samuel. **Pioneering with John Weicker.** 1962. 1 v. ill., map, chart. Loc: OKIT.
A history of a German family who settled in Perth, Oxford and Waterloo Counties, with a description of pioneer life in the first half of the 19th century based on Waterloo County historical sources. Period: 1830 - 1962.

1133. Weicker, Samuel. **Weicker family history [WRP].** Kitchener: The Author?, 1966. 1 v. ill., maps, charts. Loc: OKIT.
A compilation, consisting mainly of genealogical charts but including also containing the description of John Weicker's pioneering days by Samuel Weicker. Period: 1830 - 1966.

1134. Weicker, Samuel. **William Weicker family.** Kitchener: The Author, 1987. 1 v. ill. Loc: OKIT.
A collection of photographs, newspapers, songs, correspondence and eulogies, compiled to celebrate the 66th anniversary of the family of William and Emma's Jungblut's return to Kitchener from Edmonton. Period: 1906 - 1987.

1135. O'Neill, Evelyn C. and Schmadl, Elizabeth L. **The Weishar family, 1818-1983.** 1984. 51 p. ill., index. Loc: OKIT.
A history of the ancestors and descendants of Andrew Weishar and Margaretha Zinger. Andrew, a native of Alsace-Lorraine, farmed in Woolwich Township from 1863 to 1871, when he and his family moved to Bruce County. A name index added by Elizabeth Schmadl in 1991 follows the text. Period: 1860 - 1983.

1136. Wenger, Jay V. **The Wenger book index.** Akron, PA: Pennsylvania German Heritage History, 1989. 340 p. Loc: OWTUCGR.
An index to Samuel S. Wenger's 1978 history of the Wenger family. Period: 1825 - 1978.

1137. Wenger, Samuel S. **The Wenger book: a foundation book of American Wengers including variant spellings such as Winger, Wanger, Whanger, Wegner, Wengert, Wengerd, Wingart, Wingard, Wingert, Wangerd, Wengar, Wencker, and names spelled with "V" rather than "W".** Lancaster, PA: Pennsylvania German Heritage History, 1978. 1218 p. ill., bibl., maps, charts. Loc: OWTUCGR.
A history of the family in America, particularly descendants of Christian Wenger and Eve Graybill who came to Pennsylvania in 1727. Among those who came to Waterloo County were Elizabeth Zimmerman with her eleven children shortly after her husband's death in 1825, and Barbara Z. Wenger and John W. Dettwiler. Other Waterloo relations include members of the Weber, Eby, Brubacher, Bowman, Hoffman and Martin families. A separate name index for this work was compiled by Jay V. Wenger. Period: 1825 - 1978.

1138. Hallman, Joan. **Adam Wettlaufer family.** Kitchener: The Author, 1991. 4 p. Loc: OKIT.
A genealogy of the descendants of Adam and Nancy Kaercher of Blyth, some of whom settled in Waterloo County. Period: 1884 - 1990.

1139. Wideman, Norman E. and Wideman, Enoch M. **The Wideman family in Canada and the United States: a genealogical record, 1803-1955.** 1955. 319 p., charts, index. Loc: OKIT, OWTUCGR.
The second chapter lists descendants of Jacob Wideman and Barbara Lichty who settled in Woolwich Township in 1822. Others of the family settled in Markham Township. Period: 1822 - 1955.

1140. **The centennial anniversary of the founding of the Wilhelm family in Canada, 1837-1937.** 1937. 13 p. index. Loc: OKIT.
A pamphlet containing a programme of the Wilhelm Reunion of 1937, a transcript of the centennial anniversary address by W.J. Leinweber, and a genealogy of the descendants of Michael Wilhelm who began farming in Wilmot Township in 1837. Period: 1837 - 1937.

1141. Reinhart, Beatrice. **Family history of Anthony Wilhelm II.** Kitchener: The Author, 1980?. 32 p. ill. Loc: OKIT.
A genealogical chart of seven generations of the Wilhelm family, German farmers who bought portions of Bechtel's Tract and Heistand's Tract in Waterloo County in the mid-19th century. A list

of land transactions involving the Wilhelm family is included. Period: 1850 - 1980.

1142. Schmadl, Elizabeth L. **Index to Michael Wilhelm and Margaret Wettlaufer family history by Elizabeth L. Schmadl.** Kitchener Public Library, 1991. 80 p. Loc: OKIT.
Period: 1837 - 1988.

1143. Schmadl, Elizabeth L. and Baron, Marilyn. **Michael Wilhelm and Margaret Wettlaufer family history.** Kitchener: The Authors?, 1988. 2 v. Loc: OKIT.
A genealogy of a German family with seven children who settled in Wilmot Township in 1837. It includes newspaper clippings, mostly announcements of births, deaths and marriages. One daughter, Elizabeth, married Otto Klotz, a prominent Prestonian and leading educator; biographical information in her chapter includes Otto Klotz, Otto Julius Klotz, Jacob E. Klotz, Oscar Klotz, David Forsyth and Dr George Rudolph Mylius. An index to this work was compiled in 1991 by Elizabeth Schmadl. Period: 1837 - 1988.

1144. Schmadl, Elizabeth L. **Wilhelm alphabet.** Kitchener: The Author, 1988. 1 v. Loc: OKIT.
A list of the descendants of Michael and Margaret Wettlaufer Wilhelm of Wilmot Township, giving the birth date, spouse and generation number of each person. Period: 1837 - 1988.

1145. Watkinson, Alice. **The Wilhelm family in Canada... minutes of the Wilhelm family reunions (Michael Wilhelm and Margaret Wettlaufer), 1927-1987, Elizabeth, Peter, Valentine, Anna Margaret, Jacob.** Carl and Helen Dahmer, 1987. 87 p. Loc: OKIT.
Minutes of 56 Wilhelm family reunions, describing the organization, programmes and finances. Many of the reunions were held in Baden and New Hamburg. Period: 1837 - 1987.

1146. Stager, David. **The Wilkins family: in New England from 1630 and in Ontario from 1868.** Toronto: The Author, 1980. 48 p. ill. Loc: OCCA.
A genealogy, with biographical notes on Charles Perkins Wilkins, a textile man who moved to Hespeler from New England in 1882 to install twelve new looms at the woollen mill. Many of his descendants still live in the Hespeler area. Period: 1882 - 1980.

1147. Ambrose, Rosemary W. **The Willard family of Beverly Township and Galt.** Kitchener: The Author, 1988. 51 p. ill., maps, index. Loc: OCCA, OKIT.
A history of the Willard family, some of whom emigrated from England to Beverly Township in the 1830s and to Galt in the 1880s. Albert Edward and his brother, James Melvin, were both mayors of Galt and successful businessmen. Period: 1830 - 1988.

1148. Parry, Ross and Williams, Sandra L. **The family of Daniel Mills Williams and Margaret Lloyd O'Brien.** Scarborough: The Authors?, 1988?. 57 p. ill., index. Loc: OKIT.
A history of an Irish family who began farming in Wellesley Township in the mid-nineteenth century. References to the family, transcribed from the **Waterloo Chronicle-Telegraph** from 1902 to 1919, are included. Period: 1850 - 1988.

1149. Woolner, Ward, Dr. "The Willsons of Hemlock Grove Farm." **Waterloo Historical Society.** 1949. 37: 39-42. Loc: all.
A brief history of the Willson clan who settled in Waterloo Township in 1837, including names and dates of many descendants of Ephraim Willson. Period: 1837 - 1949.

1150. Smith, Orpha McChesney. **Descendants of John Wismer and his wife Agnes Honsberger of Lincoln County, Ontario, Canada.** Richland, WA: Locust Grove Press, 1974. 110 p. ill., index. Loc: OWTUCGR.
An account concentrating on the history of the family in Pennsylvania and the Vineland area, with biographical notes on descendants who moved to Waterloo County, especially Kitchener. Period: 1907 - 1974.

1151. Wissler, Henry. **The Wissler family record: being a brief account of Andrew Wissler's branch of the Wissler family in the United States and Canada.** Toronto: Bryant, 1904. 95 p. ill., charts. Loc: OKIT.
A family history with biographies of three brothers, John, Levi and Sem, the father of the author. They moved from Pennsylvania to Berlin and founded the Eagle Tannery in 1837. Sem Wissler later founded a tannery in Salem when tan bark became scarce in the Berlin area. Period: 1834 - 1903.

1152. Spaetzel, Roy Clifford. **History and genealogy of the Witmer family.** Kitchener: The Author, 1977. 126, 164 p. ill., bibl., map. Loc: OKIT, OWTUCGR.
A book by the president of Spae-Naur Inc. of Kitchener. The Witmer family came from Pennsylvania to Waterloo Township in 1804 and is connected by marriage with the Groh, Gingerich and Reichert families. It mentions the history of Rosebank including the school, the Brethren in Christ Church and the Huron Road. A genealogy lists descendants of Christian Wittmer of Pennsylvania. Period: 1804 - 1977.

1153. Spaetzel, Roy Clifford. **The Witmer story.**
Kitchener: The Author?, 1962. 15 p. chart. Loc:
OKIT, OWTUCGR.

A brief history of the Witmer family, Tunkers
who came to Preston from Pennsylvania in 1804 and
intermarried with the Grohs and Gingerichs. It
includes reminiscences of the Isaac Witmer family
who settled in Wilmot Township in 1871, written by
Rev. Wesley Witmer in 1956. Period: 1804 - 1910.

1154. Wolfhard, Duretta. **Information on the descendants
of Harry Wolfhard and Duretta Leslie, copied from
the collection of Duretta Wolfhard, 1983.** 1983. 8
p. charts. Loc: OKIT.

Biographical notes on the Wolfhard family.
Peter Wolfhard, a bricklayer, came to Berlin from
Germany in 1854 and married Margretta Besserer.
Related families are the Leggates, Kutts and
Leslies. Period: 1854 - 1983.

1155. Wolfhard, Duretta. **The yesteryears, 1902-1989: a
collection of memories.** Waterloo: The Author,
1990. 42 p. ill. Loc: OKIT.

A family history of Duretta and Harry Wolfhard
who lived in Elmira and Kitchener. Information is
presented about their life together and their
community activities, such as Red Cross
fundraising efforts during World War I. Also
included are some poems addressed by Mrs Wolfhard
to members of her family. Period: 1902 - 1989.

1156. Gimblet, Elwin B., Mrs. **The Woolner family.**
Arthur: The Author, 1965?. 10 p. Loc: OWTUCGR.

A genealogy of the family of William Woolner, an
Englishman who received one hundred acres in
Waterloo County in return for his services during
the War of 1812. William and his family arrived
in 1834, later exchanging the property for land in
Dufferin County. Period: 1834 - 1965.

SURNAMES BEGINNING WITH Y

1157. Yantzi, Henry and Yantzi, Mae and Roth, Lorraine.
**The family history and genealogy of Michael B.
Yantzi and Jacobena (Kennel) Yantzi.** New Hamburg:
Henry and Mae Yantzi, 1991. 183 p. ill., maps,
index. Loc: OKIT, OWTUCGR.

An account of Michael B. Yantzi (also spelled
Jantzi and Yancey) and his wife, with individual
genealogies for each of their children. Family
lists and information about the Kennel and Ruby
Families are provided. Photographs and
photocopies of other materials are reproduced for
the older generations, and there is a name index.
Period: 1823 - 1991.

1158. Duncan, Lois Nickason. **William H. Yost family
tree.** Listowel: The Author, 1983?. 144 p. index.
Loc: OKIT, OWTUCGR.

A genealogy of a German Mennonite family who
settled in the Stratford area in the 1840s;
descendants moved to Waterloo County. An index to
this work was compiled by Elizabeth Schmadl.
Period: 1847 - 1983.

1159. Schmadl, Elizabeth L. **Index to Yost genealogy.**
Kitchener Public Library, 1991. 17 p. Loc: OKIT.
Period: 1847 - 1983.

1160. **From the old land to the new.** 1961?. 14 p. Loc:
OKIT.

A genealogy of the Youngs and the Pringles, two
Scottish families related by marriage who settled
near Ayr. There are brief descriptions of the
Scottish background of both families, their
migration to Canada and early life in Dumfries
Township. Period: 1816 - 1961.

SURNAMES BEGINNING WITH Z

1161. Albrecht, Emanuel and Albrecht, Laurene and Zehr,
Ezra. **Family history and genealogy of Joseph C.
Zehr and Barbara Wutherick, Henry Oakley and
Katherine Yoder, Joseph C. Zehr and Katherine
Yoder.** Kitchener: The Authors?, 1980. 191 p. ill.
charts, index. Loc: OWTUCGR.

A genealogy of a French Amish Mennonite family
who settled in Oxford County about 1860 and later
in Wilmot and Wellesley Townships. Biographical
sketches have been included for the second
generation. Period: 1896 - 1980.

1162. Cressman, Ella M. "Zeller homesteads at Breslau."
Waterloo Historical Society. 1971. 59: 61-63.
ill. Loc: all.

An account of the Zeller family who settled
south of the village of Breslau. Philip Zeller, a
native of Rhein Baierin, Germany, purchased the
farm in 1846 from John Cressman. The last members
of the family to live on the farmstead were Ira
and Seleda Zeller who retired in 1971. Walter P.
Zeller, founder of Zeller's Ltd, was born on this
farmstead in 1891. Period: 1846 - 1971.

1163. Francis, Willard Z. **Descendants of Michael Zug
and Ulric Zug.** Elizabethtown, PA: The Author,
1972. 1 v. Loc: OKIT.

Excerpts from the diary of Michael Zug of
Pennsylvania, recording a trip to Waterloo County
in 1883 and including genealogical information on
the descendants of Elizabeth Zug and Abraham
Stauffer who settled in Waterloo County in 1805.
A name index for this work was compiled by

Elizabeth Schmadl. Period: 1805 - 1904.

1164. Schmadl, Elizabeth L. **Index to Descendants of Michael Zug and of Ulrich Zug by Willard Z. Francis.** Kitchener Public Library, 1991. 6 p. Loc: OKIT.

> Period: 1805 - 1904.

SOCIAL STRUCTURE, CLASS AND ELITES; BIOGRAPHIES OF INDIVIDUALS

1165. "Biographical directory of Waterloo County subscribers." **Historical atlas of Waterloo & Wellington counties, including: Illustrated Atlas of the County of Waterloo (1881), County of Waterloo Directory (1877-78) and Illustrated Atlas of the County of Wellington (1877).** Port Elgin: Ross Cumming, 1972 reprint. Pp. 11-14. Loc: OKIT, OWTL, OWTU, OWTUM, OWTUCG, OCCA, OCLG, OCP, OWRBL, OWRE, OWRN, OWRW, OWT.

> Lists of over 500 subscribers to the atlas, with brief details of occupation, public office, place and date of birth, and value and location of landed property. Some entries refer to businesses rather than individuals. The largest number of subscribers is listed for Waterloo Township with 140. For the other places the numbers are: 76 in Woolwich Township, 72 in Wellesley Township, 59 in Wilmot Township, 33 in Berlin, 32 in each of Galt and Waterloo, 23 in North Dumfries Township, 19 in Preston, 16 in New Hamburg and 6 in Hespeler. All names are been indexed in the WRP database. Period: 1880 - 1881.

1166. "Biographical sketches." **Historical atlas of Waterloo & Wellington counties, including: Illustrated Atlas of the County of Waterloo (1881), County of Waterloo Directory (1877-78) and Illustrated Atlas of the County of Wellington (1877).** Port Elgin: Ross Cumming, 1972 reprint. p.10. Loc: OWTU, OWTUM, OWTUCG, OKIT, OWTL, OCCA, OCLG, OCP, OWRBL, OWRE, OWRN, OWRW, OWT.

> Brief profiles of men who held office as county Warden or Reeve of a township or village, or represented North Waterloo or South Waterloo in the federal parliament or provincial legislature, or held office in local political associations. They are Hugo Kranz, Samuel Merner, James Livingston, E.W.B. Snider, William Snider, Lewis Kribs, Otto Pressprich, Isaac Groh, Theron Buchanan, T.B. Snider, James Phin and John Phin. Period: 1823 - 1881.

1167. Bloomfield, Elizabeth. "Community leadership and decision-making: entrepreneurial elites in two Ontario towns, 1870-1930." **Power and place:**
Canadian urban development in the North American context. Edited by Gilbert A. Stelter and Alan F.J. Artibise. Vancouver: University of British Columbia Press, 1986. Pp. 82-104. graphs, tabl., bibl. Loc: OWTL, OWTU.

> A discussion of the power of community elites in Berlin/Kitchener and Waterloo. The author reports systematic analysis of the economic, political and associational roles of community leaders, based on evidence of wealth, business success, occupation, municipal office-holding, ethnocultural background, church affiliation and participation in boards of trade and other voluntary associations. Two "concrete decisions" are compared to illustrate how community leaders exercised their decision-making power: the municipal "industrial policy" of bonusing manufacturers from the 1870s, and the city planning movement of 1912-14. Period: 1870 - 1930.

1168. Bloomfield, Elizabeth. "Lawyers as members of urban business elites in southern Ontario, 1860 to 1920." **Beyond the law: lawyers and business in Canada, 1830-1930.** Edited by Carol Wilton. Toronto: The Osgoode Society, 1990. Pp. 112-148. maps. tabl., bibl. Loc: OWTU.

> An analysis of the changing distribution and organization of law practices in southern Ontario communities, in relation to the main phases of business activity. Lawyers are described as members of "overlapping elites" who combined leadership in economic, political and associational roles. The main phases and themes are explored in case studies of lawyers in the neighbouring towns of Guelph and Berlin. Names of the Berlin lawyers and business corporations have been indexed in the WRP database. Period: 1860 - 1920.

1169. "Brief biographies." **Waterloo Historical Society.** 1951. 39: 38-41. Loc: all.

> Short profiles of seven county individuals who died in 1951: Alexander Rodgers Goldie, Karl K. Homuth, William J. Pelz, Arthur B. Pollock, Alexander Schaefer, Evelyn L. Breithaupt and John Christian Breithaupt. Period: 1870 - 1951.

1170. Campbell, Alexander D., Dr. **Doctors in Waterloo County: 1852-1925.** 1986. 327 l. Loc: OKIT.

> A collection of short biographies of physicians who practised in the county, including details of year of birth, education, local practice and, if available, other community interests. Period: 1852 - 1925.

1171. Campbell, Alexander D., Dr. "The first physicians in Waterloo County." **Waterloo Historical Society.** 1987. 75: 96-97. Loc: all.

A chart showing 27 communities, the first physicians who practised in them, the year the practices began and, if available, the next locality to which the physicians moved. Period: 1824 - 1914.

1172. Campbell, Alexander D., Dr. **List of doctors who worked in Waterloo County.** 1975. 11 l. Loc: OKIT.

A compilation including names, places of study, dates of graduation, places of local practice and dates of death. More complete biographical information is contained in the same author's work, **Doctors in Waterloo County: 1852-1925.** Period: c1800 - c1960.

1173. "Centenarians." **Waterloo Historical Society.** 1967. 55: 62. Loc: all.

A note of the birthdays of Mrs John Koch and Mrs A.Y. Haist. Period: 1865 - 1967.

1174. "Centenarians." **Waterloo Historical Society.** 1968. 56: 85. Loc: all.

A note of the 100th birthdays of Mrs Meta Wurm and Mrs Emma Maurer. Period: 1868 - 1968.

1175. "Centenarians." **Waterloo Historical Society.** 1970. 58: 73. Loc: all.

A note of the 100th birthdays of Mrs Mena Kinzie, Mrs Agnes (Sarah) Stauffer and Miss Sarah McLellan. Period: 1869 - 1970.

1176. Charlesworth, Hector. **A cyclopedia of Canadian biography: brief biographies of persons distinguished in the professional, military and political life, and the commerce and industry of Canada, in the twentieth century.** Toronto: Hunter, Rose, 1919. 303 p. ill., index. Loc: OCCA.

Short entries for many public figures and community leaders. Men from Waterloo County include C.K. Hagedorn, C.H. Mills, E.J. Beaumont, L.J. Breithaupt, Rev. J.A.R. Dickson, William George Weichel, F. Stewart Scott, J.C. Breithaupt and Noah Bechtel Detwiler. Period: 1855 - 1919.

1177. Cornish, C.R. **Berlin, Ontario, 1916.** University of Waterloo (student essay, History), 197-?. 47 p. bibl., tables. Loc: OKIT.

An analysis of the 1916 Berlin assessment rolls, the first year for which there is a complete assessment record. The author concludes that by 1916 the German entrepreneurial elite was being undermined by the British element which was gradually increasing its power through control of the managerial and professional positions. Information about the occupational categories, residential property assessment, marital status, age, nationality, religious affiliation of heads of household by ward is summarized in appendices.

A list of 1916 Berlin businesses by pecuniary strength is also provided. Period: 1912 - 1916.

1178. "Deaths, 1952." **Waterloo Historical Society.** 1952. 40: 9. Loc: all.

A note of seven prominent individuals who died in 1952: Mrs Lucy McPhail, Mrs Mary Milroy, Dr E.N. Coutts, Mrs Racie Pollock, R.N. Merritt, Edward Schnarr, and John Reidel. Period: 1852 - 1952.

1179. "Deaths, 1955: prominent people die in 1955." **Waterloo Historical Society.** 1955. 43: 54-55. Loc: all.

A note of Waterloo County people who died in 1955: Albert Breithaupt, Milton H. Good, George W. Gordon, Sr, E.G. Heise, James W. Henderson, John Charles Iredale, David Knipfel, Frederick E. Macklin, Norman G. McLeod, Ivan A. Shantz, W.S. Sheppard, Peter A. Snider, H. Leslie Staebler, and Bertram David Turnbull. Period: 1858 - 1955.

1180. "Deaths, 1956." **Waterloo Historical Society.** 1956. 44: 68. Loc: all.

A list of prominent Waterloo County people who died in 1956: Bishop Oscar Burkholder, Amelia Warnock Garvin (who wrote under the pseudonym "Katherine Hale"), Owen A.F. Hamilton Q.C., Joseph A. Huck, Edwin Huehn, John N. MacKendrick and Thomas Yates ("Mr Preston"). Period: 1859 - 1956.

1181. "Died in 1957." **Waterloo Historical Society.** 1957. 45: 64. Loc: all.

A list of some notable people of Waterloo County who died in 1957: Ernest Denton, Enoch Eby, William Henderson, Charles F. McKenzie, Dr James McQueen, E.O. Ritz, and James W. Washburn. Period: 1867 - 1957.

1182. "Died in 1958." **Waterloo Historical Society.** 1958. 46: 58-59. Loc: all.

A note of prominent people of Waterloo County who died in 1958: Sylvia Bock, J.G. (Jack) Brown, Andrew Feick, Mrs John Flynn, Harry Griffin, Mrs Alex F. Hahn, Dr Stanley F. Leavine, Rev. C.H. Little, L. Clare Moyer, Hugh Robert Polson, Ophelia Rife, James S. Webster, and Dr Ward Woolner. Period: 1854 - 1958.

1183. "Died in 1959." **Waterloo Historical Society.** 1959. 47: 70-71. Loc: all.

A list of notable people of Waterloo County who died in 1959: Rev. MacFarlane Bell Davidson, Mrs S.A. Detweiler, Louis Blake Duff, Gordon C.G. Fleming, Harry L. Guy, Alexander F. Hahn, Charles Keith Henderson, Miss Kate Fleury Jaffray, Louis Kaiser, John Alexander Martin, and Mrs Fred H. Schneider. Period: 1869 - 1959.

1184. "Died in 1960." **Waterloo Historical Society**.
1960. 48: 80-84. Loc: all.

A list of 28 notable people of Waterloo County who died in 1960: Dr C.C. Ballantyne, Msgr William Becker, Mrs Samuel B. Cassel, Mrs Sophia Doering, Dr Samuel H. Eckel, G.A.M. Edwards, Msgr William C. Gehl, Arthur Goudie, A.G. Haehnel, Charles C. Hahn, Mrs Mary L. Heist, J.C. Jaimet, Miss Luella Klinck, Ford S. Kumpf, Col W.M.O. Lochead, Dr Hugh MacDonell, Mrs Margaret Madden, George Harding McCormick, James D. Panabaker, Robert M. Phin, Oliver W. Reichard, Frank H. Russ, Miss Susanna Scharlach, Dr Robert Frank Slater, Michael Wagler, Lester Everett Weaver, Mrs James E. (Betsy) Whitson, and Jack Woodhouse. Period: 1856 - 1960.

1185. "Died in 1961." **Waterloo Historical Society**.
1961. 49: 77-80. Loc: all.

A list of notable people of Waterloo County who died in 1961, including William Anderson, Robert E. Cowan, Senator W.D. Euler, Enoch S. Gingrich, Andrew Heipel, Henry Herber Johnson, Mrs Leah Musselman, James Sanderson, Alfred H. Schefter, Mrs Sydney S. Shantz, Mrs Susan B. Slater, Mrs Thomas Taylor, Otto C. Weppler, William S. Wiegand, Mrs E. Langdon Wilks and Mrs Barbara Yirka. Ten members of the Waterloo Historical Society who died in 1961 are listed separately. Period: 1860 - 1961.

1186. "Died in 1962." **Waterloo Historical Society**.
1962. 50: 102-107. Loc: all.

A list of some notable people of Waterloo County who died in 1961-2, including Winfield Brewster, Albert E. Broome, Robert A. Dietrich, Mrs Elizabeth Feick, Mrs Mathilda Hahn, Irvin C. Hallman, Mrs John Manson, William J. Marriott, Joseph Meinzinger, George Pearse Moore, Menno S. Nahrgang, Leo M. Quinn, Franklin A. Shantz, Mrs Catherine Schierholtz, Milton A. Schmidt, Addison S. Snider, Herman A. Sturm, Daniel Beaver, Isaac Cober, Irvin Snyder, Emilea Birnstihl, Clayton Koch and John L. Hammond. A list of eight members of the Waterloo Historical Society who died in 1962 is also given. Period: 1861 - 1962.

1187. "Died in 1963." **Waterloo Historical Society**.
1963. 51: 89-92. Loc: all.

A list of notable people from Waterloo County who died in 1963, including Addison A. Armbrust, T. Marshall Aver, Charles Harry Boehmer, Martha Edna Breithaupt, Ewan Cameron, Roy B. Hemmerich, Charles H. Janzen, Emma Kaatz, Thomas H. Kay, Samuel E. Leis, Arnold T. Panabaker, C.A. Panabaker, Edmond Pequegnat, Mrs Margaret Rieder, Hugh A. Rodgers, Frederic D. Rueffer, Moses B. Shantz, R. Frank Skelly, Martin Milne Todd, Mrs

Elizabeth Turner, Orley S. Uffelman, and Noah Weber. Five members of the Waterloo Historical Society who died in 1963 are also listed. Period: 1864 - 1963.

1188. "Died in 1964." **Waterloo Historical Society**.
1964. 52: 89-91. Loc: all.

A list of 28 county residents who died in 1964: D.A. Bean, Mortimer Bezeau, Leonard Burton, Dr William L. Catherwood, Gordon Chaplin, Harry M. Lackner, Dr Sangster Lederman, J.D. Miller, William Philip, Mrs M.A. Secord, Dr J. Reginald Smith, A.M. Snider, Nathaniel Stroh, Mrs O.T. Ball, Mrs Thomas Ballantyne, Abraham Bowman, Levi Bowman, Mary Buchanan, John Davidson, Lily Dimmock, Robert W. Donaldson, M. Haller, Margaret Heller, Mrs Ephraim High, Mary Janke, John E. Johnson, John Schnaeringer, and Mrs Ephraim Snider. Period: c1860 - 1964.

1189. "Died in 1965." **Waterloo Historical Society**.
1965. 53: 81-86. Loc: all.

Brief notes on Waterloo County residents who died in 1965: Robert Bieth, Mrs William Brown, George Buck, R.H. Dickson, Gordon Eby, Carl Ellis, Charles C. Farnham, Louis Feick, Ray M. Gillespie, Charles Halberstadt, W. Norman Hancock, C. Howard Harding, Adolph Heller, Wilfred L. Hilliard, Moses O. Jantzi, Henry C. Krug, Louis Lacourse Lang, Patrick J. McNulty, I.C. Marritt, John Martin, Walter Renwick, William A. Rife, Susannah Schaefer, T.W. Seagram, Nelson Seibert, Ford Sudden, William C. Turnbull, Alfred W. Watson, T.H. Wholton, Mrs Noel Campbell, Mrs F.W.R. Dickson, Mrs Frank E. Page, Mrs Norman Sipes and Mrs Harold Slee. Period: c1865 - 1965.

1190. "Died in 1966." **Waterloo Historical Society**.
1966. 54: 89-91. Loc: all.

Brief notes on 32 Waterloo County residents, 15 of whom were over 95 years old: Martin Andesian, Jack Bechtel, William D. Brill, H. Milton Cook, Dr John D. Detweiler, Odo Eby, F.S. Forwell, W.L. Hilliard, Charles Iredale, Mrs Roy Luckhardt, R.L. McGill, Jairus W. Maus, Janet Wright Maus, Mrs W.A. Osbourne, Frank E. Page, Edward A. Rieder, Emma Wade, E.G. Warnock, Mrs Frederick Falkinen, William F. Haas, Kate Longhurst, Augustus T. McKenzie, Aaron Mader, Elizabeth Panabaker, Nancy Rae, Addison Reitzel, Leonard Rockel, Elizabeth Scott, Mrs Nelson Shantz, Margaret Shaver, and Charles Spurgeon. Period: c1864 - 1966.

1191. "Died in 1967." **Waterloo Historical Society**.
1967. 55: 90-92. Loc: all.

A list of notable people who died in 1967, including Norman H. Bennett, Armin M. Bitzer, Miss Henrietta Bowman, Bishop Clayton F. Derstine,

George C. Doerr, Mrs Ephraim B. Erb, Mrs Vorwerk Ernst, Mrs Richard Gemmell, Rev. C.N. Good, Bishop Menasseh S. Hallman, Miss Mary H. King, J. Stanley Knapp, Norman R. Morton, Dr. C.G. Powers, Mrs Weston Sararas, Frederick H. Schneider, Charles A.R. Tilt, Frank J. (Snoozer) Trushinski, J. Willard Witmer and Mrs Ward Woolner. Those who were 90 years of age or over are identified. Period: 1870 - 1967.

1192. "Died in 1968." **Waterloo Historical Society**. 1968. 56: 86-87. Loc: all.

A list of notable people who died in 1968, including Miss Sara Elizabeth Barrett, Mrs Frederick Claire, William H. Gillespie, Mrs Louis L. Lang, John D. Murray, John A. Schmidt, R.K. Serviss, William W. Snider, and O.W. (Mike) Weichel. Period: 1868 - 1968.

1193. "Died in 1969." **Waterloo Historical Society**. 1969. 57: 83-84. Loc: all.

A list of notable people who died in 1969: Amos B. Bowman, Miss Isabella C. Deans, Mrs Aaron Y. Haist, Henry H. Johnson, Miss Margaret P. McKenzie, William H. Milroy, Dr Alex O. Potter, Dr G. Elmore Reaman, Mrs. Nancy Schmiedendorf, Robert James Spalding, and Harvey J. Zeller. Period: 1865 - 1969.

1194. "Died in 1970: W.H.S. members and centenarians." **Waterloo Historical Society**. 1970. 58: 87. Loc: all.

A list of six Waterloo Historical Society members and four centenarians who died in 1970. More information is given for Monseigneur Emmett A. Doyle who served St Patrick's Roman Catholic Church in Galt for 54 years. Period: 1868 - 1970.

1195. Dunham, B. Mabel. "Brief biography." **Waterloo Historical Society**. 1948. 36: 21-22. Loc: all.

Notes on 22 Waterloo County residents who died in 1948: Henry Wolfhard, Mrs S.C. Tweed, Charles R. Phelps, Louis D. Merrick, Dr R.L. Shields, John E. Vogt, George Karges, Mary Weber, Mrs Minerva Dart, Henry P. Bingham, Nelson G. Shantz, Percy W. Swartz, J.D.C. Forsyth, Clare S. Snider, Fred Graham, Louis Graham, William R. Bricker, Edward J. Schnarr, William H. Leeson, Harry P. Livingston, Rev. Albert Zinger, and B. Frank Matthews. Most entries state the person's name, age, and occupation, as well as the date of death. Period: 1850 - 1948.

1196. Findlater, Ron. **A short history of Kitchener, Ontario, 1933-1935**. University of Waterloo (student essay, History), 1973. 15 l. tables, bibl. Loc: OKIT.

An examination of the economic and political status of the city's elite, classified as patricians, entrepreneurs or ex-plebes. Tables list members of boards, commissions and political departments. Period: 1933 - 1935.

1197. Forbes, William F. and Dust, Alvin I. and Green, Maurice H. **Present faces of Waterloo past**. Waterloo: Program in Gerontology, University of Waterloo, 1988. 91 p. ill., ports. Loc: OKIT, OWT, OWTUR.

A collection of photographs of nearly 50 county residents over the age of 70, with a brief biography for each person. Period: 1900 - 1988.

1198. Howse, Hannah Erb. **Hannah's albums**. 1923. 1 v. index. Loc: OKIT.

Copies of 95 photographs from two albums of Hannah Erb Howse, with an index of people portrayed, Hannah's captions, and the name of the photographer if known. Among Waterloo County people are Thomas and Hannah Quickfall of Waterloo, Irvine and Almon Devitt of Floradale, and Maria Proudlove of Hawkesville. The names of the Waterloo County photographers and people photographed are indexed in the WRP database. Period: 1857 - 1923.

1199. "Kitchener old-timers [WRP]." **Waterloo Historical Society**. 1956. 44: 62. Loc: all.

Photographs reproduced from the **Kitchener-Waterloo Record** show 96-year-old Andrew Heipel gardening and Mr and Mrs Jacob Oberholtzer celebrating their 73rd wedding anniversary. Period: 1860 - 1956.

1200. Lea, Joanne and Geddy, Hilary. **Persons past**. Kitchener: Doon Heritage Crossroads, Historic Sites Department, Regional Municipality of Waterloo, 1989. 1 v. Loc: OKDHC.

A teachers' guide designed to provide a general history of women, for use from grades 7 to O.A.C., with printed information, slides and audio cassettes. It includes a short history of Waterloo area women and biographical sketches of some of those in the Waterloo Hall of Fame. Period: 1806 - 1989.

1201. MacNaughton, Ian Fraser. **A historical study of political, ethnic and religious composition of Kitchener and Waterloo**. University of Waterloo (student essay, Political Science), 1968. 27 p. ill., tables. Loc: OKIT.

An analysis of the social and occupational characteristics of elected officials in the two cities from 1854 to 1968. The author presents tables on education levels, incomes, professions, club memberships, ethnic composition and religious affiliations. Period: 1854 - 1968.

1202. McNaughton, I.W. "Wedding anniversaries in New Hamburg." **Waterloo Historical Society**. 1964. 52: 78. Loc: all.

A note of the 58th anniversary of Mr and Mrs Edwin F. Scherer and the 59th anniversary of Mr and Mrs A.F. Dorsch. Period: 1905 - 1964.

1203. Morgan, Henry J. **Sketches of celebrated Canadians, and persons connected with Canada, from the earliest period in the history of the province down to the present time.** Quebec: Hunter, Rose, 1862. 779 p. index. Loc: OCCA.

Biographical notes on statesmen, soldiers and professional men including the Rev. John Bayne of Galt. Bayne's entry is a reprint of the Toronto Globe obituary of November 1859. Period: 1806 - 1859.

1204. "Nonagenarians who died in 1965." **Waterloo Historical Society**. 1965. 53: 87. Loc: all.

A list of 17 county residents with their ages and the communities: Frederick William Bartels, Mrs Oscar Bean, Mrs Margaret Brooks, Mrs I. Burton, Mrs Norman Clemens, Louis Feick, George Moser Fischer, Charles Halberstadt, Adolph G. Heller, Miss Isabella Jackson, Isaac Nicholls, Elizabeth Nickason, Mrs Arthur Charles Norman, Ada Elizabeth Ranscombe, Mrs Esther Reist, Mrs Sophia Robb and Miss Susannah Schaefer. Period: 1866 - 1965.

1205. **Prominent people of the Province of Ontario in business and professional life.** Ottawa: Canadian Biographies Limited, 1925. 273 p. ill. indexes. Loc: OWTL, OWTU.

Brief biographical entries for approximately 3,350 public figures and community leaders, with a emphasis on those in professional occupations such as clergymen, dentists, lawyers, physicians and teachers. The 65 persons with addresses in Waterloo County have been indexed in the WRP database. Period: 1850 - 1924.

1206. "Twins celebrate 92nd birthday." **Waterloo Historical Society**. 1965. 53: 78. Loc: all.

A paragraph about 1965 of Mrs Caroline Knechtel and Mrs Katherine Pines of New Hamburg. Period: 1873 - 1965.

SURNAMES BEGINNING WITH A

1207. Ainslie, Adam. **On life's stage: the autobiography of Adam Ainslie.** Cambridge: The Corporation of the City of Cambridge Archives, 1987. 91 p. ill., port., map, index. Loc: OWTUR, OKIT, OWTL, OCCA.

The lively memoirs of Adam Ainslie (1807-1896),

written when he was 82 years of age. Born in Scotland, Ainslie came in 1834 to Galt where he was a busy as a lawyer, land owner, banker, sawmill operator, captain in the militia and Reeve in 1856. In 1857 he moved to Leith, Ontario, near Owen Sound. An account of Ainslie's life in Galt comprises about half the book and includes descriptions of many people and buildings in the early history of the town. Period: 1834 - 1897.

1208. Kerr, James E. "Sheriff A. S. Allan." **Waterloo Historical Society**. 1928. 16: 88-89. Loc: all.

An obituary of the sheriff of Wellington County, recalling his youth in the Preston area and his schooling at the Freeport Academy. Period: 1843 - 1928.

1209. Middleton, Jesse Edgar and Landon, Fred. "Addison Allen Armbrust." **The Province of Ontario: a history, 1615-1927.** Toronto: Dominion Publishing Company, 1927. Vol. 4, pp. 379-380. Loc: OWTL, OWTU.

A profile of the Kitchener shoe manufacturer. Period: 1883 - 1926.

1210. Middleton, Jesse Edgar and Landon, Fred. "Nicholas Asmussen." **The Province of Ontario: a history, 1615-1927.** Toronto: Dominion Publishing Company, 1927. Vol. 3, pp. 243-244. Loc: OWTL, OWTU.

A profile of the building contractor elected to the Ontario Legislature in 1921 and Mayor of Kitchener in 1925. Period: 1876 - 1926.

1211. Middleton, Jesse Edgar and Landon, Fred. "Albert William Augustine." **The Province of Ontario: a history, 1615-1927.** Toronto: Dominion Publishing Company, 1927. Vol. 3, p. 244. Loc: OWTL, OWTU.

A profile of the Waterloo trunk and bag manufacturer whose mother was a sister of L.J. Breithaupt and who married a daughter of Jacob Kaufman. Period: 1890 - 1926.

SURNAMES BEGINNING WITH B

1212. Middleton, Jesse Edgar and Landon, Fred. "Charles Joseph Baetz." **The Province of Ontario: a history, 1615-1927.** Toronto: Dominion Publishing Company, 1927. Vol. 4, p. 579. Loc: OWTL, OWTU.

An account of the business and community activities of the sons of Jacob Baetz, Jacob H. and Charles J., notably in the furniture industry of Kitchener. Period: 1900 - 1926.

1213. Gingerich, Melvin. "An old Ontario letter." **Mennonite Historical Bulletin.** 1967. 28,4: 4-5. Loc: OWTUCG.

Transcript of a letter to Jacob Groff from

Johannes Baer of Preston, written in 1858. Baer tells of receiving the monthly **Mennonitsche Blatter** from Danzig in west Prussia and gives the name and address of the publisher in case Groff is interested in ordering some copies. He also reports attending the Christian Eby meeting on Sunday and "heard no special complaint there." Period: 1857 - 1858.

1214. Middleton, Jesse Edgar and Landon, Fred. "John Bahnsen." **The Province of Ontario: a history, 1615-1927.** Toronto: Dominion Publishing Company, 1927. Vol. 4, pp. 416-417. port. Loc: OWTL, OWTU.
   A profile of the man invited to manage the Globe Furniture factory of Waterloo in 1912. Period: 1912 - 1926.

1215. Barrie, David. "My bells." **Waterloo Historical Society.** 1960. 48: 55. ill. Loc: all.
   A description by David Barrie of his hobby, bell ringing; he was currently the chimer at Central Presbyterian Church, Galt. Period: 1958 - 1960.

1216. Hoover, Muriel I. "James R. Barrie, president 1989-90." **Waterloo Historical Society.** 1990. 78: 4-5. Loc: all.
   A brief biography of Mr Barrie, born 1924, mentioning his various roles and offices in associations. Period: 1924 - 1990.

1217. "W.H.S. salutes Will C. Barrie." **Waterloo Historical Society.** 1960. 48: 6-7. ill. Loc: all.
   A biographical sketch of William Carrick Barrie, particularly noting his contributions to the Waterloo Historical Society. Period: 1884 - 1960.

1218. "Will Barrie receives award." **Waterloo Historical Society.** 1980. 68: 36-37. ill. Loc: all.
   An account of the presentation to Mr Barrie on 25 September 1980 of the Jack Young Civic Award for his involvement in community affairs including the Waterloo Historical Society, the South Waterloo Agricultural Society, the Waterloo County Tree Conservation Committee, the Ontario Plowmen's Association, and the South Waterloo Liberal Association. Period: 1884 - 1980.

1219. "William Carrick Barrie." **Waterloo Historical Society.** 1982. 70: 80. Loc: all.
   A obituary of the longtime member of the Waterloo Historical Society. Will Barrie's other contributions are noted in local history (as a founding director of Doon Pioneer Village), agriculture and church work. Period: 1884 - 1982.

1220. Fraser, Alexander. "Aloyes Bauer." **A history of Ontario: its resources and development.** Toronto: The Canada History Co., 1907. Pp. 1210-1211. Loc: OWTL, OWTU.
   Bauer established the Waterloo Shoddy Mills in 1889 and from 1896 also managed the Kuntz brewery in Waterloo. Period: 1861 - 1906.

1221. Middleton, Jesse Edgar and Landon, Fred. "Aloyes Bauer." **The Province of Ontario: a history, 1615-1927.** Toronto: Dominion Publishing Company, 1927. Vol. 4, pp. 489-490. Loc: OWTL, OWTU.
   A biography of the Waterloo manufacturer and community leader. Period: 1861 - 1926.

1222. Middleton, Jesse Edgar and Landon, Fred. "Edgar Jacob Bauer." **The Province of Ontario: a history, 1615-1927.** Toronto: Dominion Publishing Company, 1927. Vol. 4, p. 490. Loc: OWTL, OWTU.
   A profile of the manager of Bauer's Ltd of Waterloo. Period: 1888 - 1926.

1223. Bauman, Salome. **Glimpses of mother.** The Author, 1952. 20 p. ill. Loc: OWTUCG.
   A spiritual character sketch of Mrs Silas Bauman (Lydia Ann Groff, 1862-1949) written by her daughter. It includes letters, poems and other writings by Lydia Ann. Period: 1862 - 1949.

1224. Moir, John S. "Bayne, John." **Dictionary of Canadian Biography.** Toronto: University of Toronto Press, 1985. 8: 67-69. Also in **Dictionnaire biographique du Canada**, 8: 75-76. Loc: OWTL, OWTU.
   A biography of the Presbyterian minister, born in Greenock in 1805, who came to Galt in 1835 to minister first to St Andrew's Church. The author explains Bayne's leading role in the organization of the Free Church in Canada and his long ministry to the congregation of Knox's Church in Galt until his death in 1859. Period: 1835 - 1859.

1225. "Anna R. Bean." **Waterloo Historical Society.** 1944. 32: 36-37. Loc: all.
   A short biography of the accomplished musician, who died on 6 May 1944. Long a music teacher in Kitchener-Waterloo, Miss Bean was also organist at Zion Evangelical Church and Benton Street Baptist Church in Kitchener. Period: c1900 - 1944.

1226. Bean, Abraham T. "More about Dr Samuel Bean." **Waterloo Historical Society.** 1983. 71: 100-101. ill. Loc: all.
   A short biography of the man who was first a teacher, then a physician, then a minister. Also detailed are names and birth and death dates of his five children. Period: 1842 - 1977.

1227. Fraser, Robert L. "Beasley, Richard." **Dictionary of Canadian Biography.** Toronto: University of Toronto Press, 1988. 7: 56-58. Also in

Dictionnaire biographique du Canada, 7: 61-64. Loc: OWTL, OWTU.

A profile of the Hamilton businessman, politician and office-holder (1761-1842). While his main focus is on Beasley's other interests and political and business reverses, the author refers to Beasley's purchase in 1798 of Block 2 of the Six Nations lands, his sale of the block to the Pennsylvania Mennonites and the tangled legal consequences. Period: 1798 - 1842.

1228. Beattie, Jessie L. **Along the road.** Toronto: Ryerson Press, 1954. 168 p. ill. Loc: OCCA, OKIT, OWRE, OWTL, OWTU.

Reminiscences of farm life in Blair at the beginning of the twentieth century. Many of the chapters describe incidents involving transients such as fiddlers, tramps and peddlers, while others describe events in Jessie's childhood. The illustrations by Jean Cockburn Beattie are of local rural landscapes. Period: 1900 - 1930.

1229. Beattie, Jessie L. **A season past: reminiscences of a Canadian childhood.** Toronto: McClelland and Stewart, 1968. 153 p. ill. Loc: OCCA, OKIT, OWRE, OWTL, OWTUR.

A companion to **Along the road,** continuing the author's recollections of childhood and family life on a farm near Blair in the early twentieth century. There are lively descriptions of family members, farm life, community people and special events such as the appearance of Halley's Comet. Period: 1900 - 1930.

1230. Beattie, Jessie L. **A walk through yesterday: memoirs of Jessie L. Beattie.** Toronto: McClelland and Stewart, 1976. 320 p. ill. Loc: OKIT, OCCA, OWRN, OWTL, OWTU.

Beattie's autobiography, describing her family life on a farm near Blair, her struggle for an education despite ill-health, and her work as librarian, teacher and author. Period: 1896 - 1976.

1231. "Waterloo couple married 65 years." **Waterloo Historical Society.** 1961. 49: 61. Loc: all.

A note of the anniversary of Mr and Mrs Albert Beaupre of Waterloo. Period: 1873 - 1961.

1232. Middleton, Jesse Edgar and Landon, Fred. "Wilson Brower Bechtel." **The Province of Ontario: a history, 1615-1927.** Toronto: Dominion Publishing Company, 1927. Vol. 2, p. 272. Loc: OWTL, OWTU.

A profile of the Kitchener real estate and insurance broker whose family operated brick yards at Waterloo. Period: 1890 - 1926.

1233. Carty, Arthur C. "Sir Adam Beck." **Waterloo Historical Society.** 1925. 13: 159-166. ill. Loc: all.

A profile of the native of Baden, Ontario stressing his achievements in the iron foundry and milling business, politics, and the distribution of hydro-electrical power in southwestern Ontario. The article mentions Beck's early life in Baden and also his father, Jacob Beck, and his uncle, Jacob Hespeler, as notable men of Waterloo County. Period: 1837 - 1925.

1234. Hunsberger, Wilson. "Adam Beck and apple pie." **Waterloo Historical Society.** 1981. 69: 91-94. Loc: all.

An anecdote about how a friendly piece of apple pie given to Adam Beck later resulted in St Agatha's acquiring electricity long before its unincorporated status would have merited. Period: 1867 - 1920.

1235. Plewman, W.R. **Adam Beck and the Ontario Hydro.** Toronto: Ryerson Press, 1947. 494 p. ill., index. Loc: OWT.

A biography of one of the key players in the establishment of the Hydro Electric Power Commission and history of the commission itself. The author describes Beck's early years in Baden, his role in the commission and associations with E.W.B. Snider and D.B. Detweiler as well as his political career. Nine appendices present information about Ontario Hydro's costs, investments and usage. Period: 1902 - 1947.

1236. "Sir Adam Beck plaque." **Waterloo Historical Society.** 1962. 50: 70, 77. Loc: all.

A note of the dedication of a plaque honouring Beck, the Baden native who was the first chairman and organizer of the Hydro Electric Power Commission of Ontario. Period: 1960 -

1237. Weissenborn, Georg K. "Sir Adam Beck - the human dynamo (1857-1925)." **German-Canadian Yearbook / Deutschkanadisches Jahrbuch.** 1976. 3: 234-236. ill., bibl. Loc: OKIT, OWTL, OWTUCG.

A brief biography of the Baden-born organizer of the Hydro Electric Power Commission, noting Beck's other achievements and relating the influence of his father, Jacob Beck, on his interest in water power. Period: 1857 - 1925.

1238. "Lorna L. Bergey." **Waterloo Historical Society.** 1971. 59: 6-7. ill. Loc: all.

A biographical sketch of Lorna L. Bergey, pioneer descendant, historian, archivist, and president of the Waterloo Historical Society from 1970 to 1971. Period: 1959 - 1971.

1239. "Peter Bernhardt." **Waterloo Historical Society**. 1947. 35: 51. Loc: all.

An obituary of the co-founder of the Rock Brewery, president of the Preston Silver Band, generous supporter of the Preston Scout Troop, Mayor of Preston in 1908-09, and member of the Preston Public School Board. Period: 1850 - 1947.

1240. "Samuel Betzner." **Waterloo Historical Society**. 1967. 55: 89. Loc: all.

An obituary for Samuel Betzner (1771-1856), reprinted from the **Berlin Chronicle** of August 27, 1856. Period: 1798 - 1856.

1241. Schmidt, Grace. "Betzner, Samuel D.." **Dictionary of Canadian Biography**. Toronto: University of Toronto Press, 1985. 8: 86-87. Also in **Dictionnaire biographique du Canada**, 8: 96-97. Loc: OWTL, OWTU.

A biography of the pioneer settler who, with Joseph Schörg, explored the valley of the middle and upper Grand River and bought land in 1800 close to the site of Blair. After some years as a Mennonite community leader, Betzner (1771-1856) sold his farm and settled in West Flamborough Township. Period: 1800 - 1816.

1242. "John Edward Bilger." **Waterloo Historical Society**. 1942. 30: 242-243. Loc: all.

A biographical sketch of Bilger (1872-1942), sales manager of the Breithaupt Leather Company and an active member of many community organizations, including the Kitchener-Waterloo Y.M.C.A. Period: 1872 - 1942.

1243. Roberts, C.S., Rev. "Rev. F.W. Bindemann, pioneer and preacher." **Waterloo Historical Society**. 1961. 49: 64-65, 71. ill. Loc: all.

A biography of Bindemann (1790-1865) on the occasion of the demolition of his house. Period: 1830 - 1865.

1244. Schultz, Erich. "Rev. Frederick W. Bindemann, 1790-1865." **Waterloo Historical Society**. 1989. 77: 69-73. ill. Loc: all.

A speech at the unveiling of a plaque in honour of the German preacher who founded many Lutheran churches in the Waterloo area. Period: 1830 - 1865.

1245. "Richard Blain, Galt." **The Canadian biographical dictionary and portrait gallery of eminent and self-made men, Ontario volume**. Toronto: American Biographical Publishing Co., 1880. Pp. 301-302. Loc: OWTL, OWTU.

A biography of the owner of the Dickson Mills who served as Mayor of Galt from 1876 to 1880. Period: 1844 - 1880.

1246. "Where is Jacob Bleam?." **Waterloo Historical Society**. 1965. 53: 53. Loc: all.

A short note from the **Canada Museum** of 9 June 1836, appealing for information on Jacob Bleam (Bliehm), a resident of Preston who disappeared in the Dundas area in February 1836. Period: 1836 -

1247. Middleton, Jesse Edgar and Landon, Fred. "Charles Stoltz Boehmer." **The Province of Ontario: a history, 1615-1927**. Toronto: Dominion Publishing Company, 1927. Vol. 4, pp. 350-351. Loc: OWTL, OWTU.

A biography of the late president of A. and C. Boehmer Paper Box Company of Berlin. Period: 1844 - 1917.

1248. Talman, James J. "Boomer, Michael." **Dictionary of Canadian Biography**. Toronto: University of Toronto Press, 1982. 11: 89-90. Also in **Dictionnaire biographique du Canada**, 11: 98-99. Loc: OWTL, OWTL.

A biography of the Irish-born Anglican clergyman (1810-1888) who came to Galt in 1841 as missionary for the Society for the Propagation of the Gospel in Foreign Parts. During his tenure at Little Trinity Church, the substantial stone church and schoolhouse and brick parsonage were built. Boomer's first and second wives were Galt women, Helen Blair Adams and Isabella Jemima Davidson, widow of Absalom Shade. In 1872 he left for London to be dean of the Diocese of Huron. Period: 1841 - 1872.

1249. Bowlby, W.H. **A voyage from Canada to Egypt and a two months' trip on the River Nile on a houseboat**. Toronto: Copp, Clark Company, 1902. Loc: OWTUR.

An account by Berlin's Crown Attorney of travels with his wife. The book begins with references to the winter weather in Ontario and Buffalo and to meetings with Mrs Bowlby's sister and her husband, Mr and Mrs H.M. Farr in Holyoke, Massachusetts and with Mr and Mrs W.H. Breithaupt in New York. Period: 1900 - 1902.

1250. "David S. Bowlby, M.D., Berlin." **The Canadian biographical dictionary and portrait gallery of eminent and self-made men, Ontario volume**. Toronto: American Biographical Publishing Co., 1880. Pp. 769-770. Loc: OWTL, OWTU.

A profile of Berlin's leading physician and surgeon who came to the village in 1853 and was an active community leader. Period: 1853 - 1880.

1251. "David Shannon Bowlby, K.C.." **Waterloo Historical Society**. 1938. 26: 45-46. ill. Loc: all.

A brief biography of David Shannon Bowlby

(1873-1938), lawyer and Crown Attorney of Waterloo County from 1917 to 1934. Period: 1873 - 1938.

1252. "David Sovereign Bowlby, M.D.." **Waterloo Historical Society**. 1917. 5: 49-50. ill. Loc: all.

An obituary of Bowlby (1826-1903), long the leading physician and surgeon of Waterloo County, with genealogical details of the Bowlby family. Period: 1826 - 1917.

1253. Fraser, Alexander. "Ward H. Bowlby, M.A., K.C.." **A history of Ontario: its resources and development**. Toronto: The Canada History Co., 1907. Pp. 967-969. Loc: OWTL, OWTU.

A short biography of the eminent Berlin lawyer who was appointed Crown Attorney and Clerk of the Peace for Waterloo in 1867. Period: 1834 - 1906.

1254. "Major G.H. Bowlby." **Waterloo Historical Society**. 1916. 4: 37. ill. Loc: all.

An obituary of Bowlby who was a surgeon, Mayor of Berlin in 1901, and Director of Medical Service to the Canadian Expeditionary Forces during the First World War. He died falling from a cliff near Seaford, England. Period: 1865 - 1916.

1255. Rose, George Maclean. "Bowlby, Ward Hamilton." **A cyclopaedia of Canadian biography: being chiefly men of the time**. Rose's National Biographical Series 1. Toronto: Rose Publishing Co., 1886. Pp. 123-124. Loc: OWTL, OWTU.

An outline of the legal career and business and community interests of Waterloo County's Crown Attorney. Period: 1858 - 1886.

1256. "Ward Hamilton Bowlby, M.A., K.C.." **Waterloo Historical Society**. 1917. 5: 50-51. ill. Loc: all.

A obituary of Bowlby (1834-1917), lawyer, investor, Reeve of Berlin, and County Crown Attorney for fifty years. Period: 1834 - 1917.

1257. "Charles Martin Bowman." **Waterloo Historical Society**. 1932. 20: 335-336. ill. Loc: all.

An obituary for the native of St Jacobs, who became an active member of the Kitchener-Waterloo and St Jacobs communities as a businessman, politician, and supporter of local athletics. Period: 1863 - 1932.

1258. "Col. H.J. Bowman." **Waterloo Historical Society**. 1916. 4: 33-45. ill. Loc: all.

A short biography of Herbert Joseph Bowman, civil engineer, manager of the Berlin waterworks, and organizer of the 108th Militia Regiment. Information about other members of the Bowman family is included. Period: 1865 - 1916.

1259. Fraser, Alexander. "Charles Martin Bowman." **A history of Ontario: its resources and development**. Toronto: The Canada History Co., 1907. Pp. 1181-1182. Loc: OWTL, OWTU.

A short biography of Bowman and of his father, Isaac Erb Bowman, the St Jacobs tanner who represented North Waterloo in the Dominion Parliament from 1864 to 1878 and from 1886 to 1896 and was president of the Mutual Life Assurance Co. from its establishment until his death in 1897. Period: 1864 - 1897.

1260. "Isaac Erb Bowman." **Waterloo Historical Society**. 1932. 20: 334-335. ill. Loc: all.

A brief biography of the politician and businessman of St Jacobs, who was the son of John B. Baumann, one of the earliest settlers in Woolwich Township. Period: 1832 - 1897.

1261. Johnston, Mary A. "Henry Brubacher Bowman, 1900-1991." **Waterloo Historical Society**. 1991. 79: 113-114. Loc: all.

A biography of the secretary-treasurer of the Waterloo Historical Society from 1967-1973, including a sketch of his working life as an engineer with various industrial businesses. His excommunication from the Old Order Mennonites for using the Kitchener-Elmira bus service in the 1920s is mentioned. Period: 1900 - 1991.

1262. Rose, George Maclean. "Bowman, Isaac Erb." **A cyclopaedia of Canadian biography: being chiefly men of the time**. Rose's National Biographical Series 1. Toronto: Rose Publishing Co., 1886. P. 108. Loc: OWTL, OWTU.

An outline of the business interests and public service of North Waterloo's representative in the Canadian parliament from 1864 to 1878. Period: 1832 - 1886.

1263. Rose, George Maclean. "Bowman, Israel David." **A cyclopaedia of Canadian biography: being chiefly men of the time**. Rose's National Biographical Series 1. Toronto: Rose Publishing Co., 1886. P. 642. Loc: OWTL, OWTU.

A brief biography of the municipal officer who served as county clerk for Waterloo from 1861. Period: 1835 - 1886.

1264. Uttley, W.V. "Hervey M. Bowman, Ph.D.." **Waterloo Historical Society**. 1931. 19: 288-290. ill. Loc: all.

A short biography of the learned Berliner, who, after receiving his university education in Leipzig, Germany, returned to Canada to live. He was employed at one time by the Canadian Archives in Ottawa, but resided mostly in Berlin. Bowman

contributed many articles to the Waterloo
Historical Society and had papers read before the
Royal Society of Canada. Period: 1873 - 1931.

1265. **Memoir of the Rev. James Boyd of Crosshill,
Ontario.** 1888. 24 p. ill. Loc: OKIT.

Written by the man who ministered to the
Presbyterian congregations of Crosshill and
Wellesley for 29 years and for whom the Boyd
Presbyterian Church of Crosshill was named. Boyd
(1814-1888) was also a school inspector for
Wellesley Township. The Kitchener Public Library
holds other items with the memoir, including an
obituary of Boyd, a history of Boyd Church written
by Rev. A.A. Laing in 1934, and genealogical
information about the family of Robert A.
McCutcheon. Period: 1814 - 1888.

1266. "George Bray, K.C.." **Waterloo Historical
Society.** 1937. 25: 275. ill. Loc: all.

A short biography of George Bray (1873-1937),
Waterloo lawyer, Deputy Judge of Waterloo County,
and City Solicitor for Kitchener. Period: 1873 -
1937.

1267. Boyes, Jeannie-Anne. **A profile of the life and
work of Edna Breithaupt.** University of Waterloo
(student essay, History), 1988. 13 l. bibl. Loc:
OWTUR.

A brief biography of the Berlin-born woman who
devoted much of her life to the promotion of art
and the development of community centres. The
author describes her travels, ranging from visits
to the family properties on the Grand River and at
Penetanguishene to her three-year sojourn in
China. Period: 1885 - 1963.

1268. Cross, Austin F. "Business man on the hill."
Canadian Business. 1947. 21,2: 28-29, 106-108.
Loc: OWTUR.

A biography of Berlin-born Louis O. Breithaupt,
written when he was Member of Parliament for North
Waterloo. The article outlines Breithaupt's
business career with the Breithaupt Leather
Company, role in the Kitchener Chamber of
Commerce and service as Mayor of Kitchener and
stresses his family's traditions and high regard for
company employees. Period: 1890 - 1947.

1269. Fraser, Alexander. "Louis Jacob Breithaupt." **A
history of Ontario: its resources and
development.** Toronto: The Canada History Co.,
1907. Pp. 958-960. Loc: OWTL, OWTU.

A profile of the president of the Breithaupt
Leather Co. of Berlin who was also very active in
business promotion, municipal and provincial
politics, and in church and community causes.
Period: 1855 - 1906.

1270. "Louis Breithaupt, Berlin." **The Canadian
biographical dictionary and portrait gallery of
eminent and self-made men, Ontario volume.**
Toronto: American Biographical Publishing Co.,
1880. Pp. 399-400. Loc: OWTL, OWTU.

A short biography including an account of
Breithaupt's tannery business, property interests
and public service. Period: 1857 - 1880.

1271. "Louis Orville Breithaupt." **Waterloo Historical
Society.** 1960. 48: 78-79. Loc: all.

An obituary for L.O. Breithaupt (1890-1960), the
youngest Mayor of Kitchener and MP for Waterloo
North, and former Lieutenant-Governor of Ontario.
Period: 1890 - 1960.

1272. Middleton, Jesse Edgar and Landon, Fred. "John
Christian Breithaupt." **The Province of Ontario: a
history, 1615-1927.** Toronto: Dominion Publishing
Company, 1927. Vol. 3, pp. 134-135. Loc: OWTL,
OWTU.

A profile of the longtime secretary of the
Breithaupt Leather Co. with details of his other
business interests and community service. Period:
1861 - 1926.

1273. Middleton, Jesse Edgar and Landon, Fred. "Louis J.
Breithaupt." **The Province of Ontario: a history,
1615-1927.** Toronto: Dominion Publishing Company,
1927. Vol. 3, pp. 131-133. Loc: OWTL, OWTU.

A biography of Kitchener's leading businessman,
including summaries of Breithaupt family history
and business interests. Period: 1855 - 1926.

1274. Middleton, Jesse Edgar and Landon, Fred. "Louis
Orville Breithaupt." **The Province of Ontario: a
history, 1615-1927.** Toronto: Dominion Publishing
Company, 1927. Vol. 3, p. 133. Loc: OWTL, OWTU.

A profile of the vice-president and general
manager of the Breithaupt Leather Company,
including details of civic improvements during his
terms as Mayor of Kitchener in 1923-4. Period:
1890 - 1926.

1275. Middleton, Jesse Edgar and Landon, Fred. "William
Henry Breithaupt." **The Province of Ontario: a
history, 1615-1927.** Toronto: Dominion Publishing
Company, 1927. Vol. 3, pp. 133-134. port. Loc:
OWTL, OWTU.

A profile of the engineer who managed the
Breithaupt family interests in public utilities
and promoted the causes of local history, public
libraries, town planning and Grand River
conservation. Period: 1861 - 1926.

1276. Parry, John. "Breithaupt, Ezra Carl." **Dictionary of Canadian Biography**. 1990. 12: 123-124. Also in **Dictionnaire biographique du Canada**, 12: 134-135. Loc: OWTL, OWTU, OWTUSJ.

A profile of engineer and businessman (1866-1897) who was a director of the Breithaupt Leather Co. and managed the Berlin Gas Co. and Berlin and Waterloo Street Railway Co. until his accidental death following an explosion in a gas tank. Period: 1866 - 1897.

1277. Sullivan, Julie. **The dual heritage of Berlin, Ontario**. University of Waterloo (student essay, History), 1988. 35 p. bibl. Loc: OKIT, OWTUR.

A biography of L.J. Breithaupt, based on entries in his diaries spanning 35 years and ranging from his apprenticeship in his father's tannery to his later interests in the Breithaupt Leather Company, in politics on local and provincial levels, and in the German-Canadian identity. The author also notes "L.J.'s" role in the Evangelical Church and his strong Christian commitment to the welfare of Berlin's needy. Period: 1875 - 1910.

1278. "William Henry Breithaupt." **Waterloo Historical Society**. 1944. 32: 31-33. Loc: all.

An obituary of Breithaupt (1857-1944), noting his achievements with the Waterloo Historical Society, Berlin and Waterloo Street Railway, Berlin Gas Works, and Waterloo County Pioneers' Memorial Association. Period: 1857 - 1944.

1279. Brown, Richard. **Rural roots: a life story**. 1990. 102 p. ill., chart. Loc: OKITW.

Reminiscences of the author's farming and working life in the Galt and Fergus areas from 1937 to 1990. Genealogical information on the rest of the family is included, with anecdotes of farming and truck driving. Period: 1937 - 1990.

1280. "Harry W. Brown." **Waterloo Historical Society**. 1943. 31: 46. ill. Loc: all.

A short biography of the educator who taught at Natchez School, Berlin Central School, the Model School and the Berlin Collegiate and was also active in the Kitchener-Waterloo Rotary Club, Kitchener Horticultural Society and Waterloo Historical Society. Period: 1870 - 1943.

1281. Lamb, Kathryn Hansuld. "The Browns of Nith Grove." **Waterloo Historical Society**. 1987. 75: 73-93. ill., bibl. Loc: all.

A biographical account of the family of Charles Davy Brown (1834-1921), artist, farmer, and Sunday School superintendent in the Haysville community. The author comments on the English style of life which the Brown family brought to the area. Period: 1856 - 1951.

1282. "Elizabeth M. Bruce." **Waterloo Historical Society**. 1923. 11: 50-52. Loc: all.

A obituary of Miss Bruce who was active in the Princess of Wales (Kitchener) Chapter of the Imperial Order of the Daughters of the Empire, the Freeport Sanatorium Auxiliary, the Women's Christian Temperance Union and the Waterloo Historical Society. Period: c1855 - 1923.

1283. Middleton, Jesse Edgar and Landon, Fred. "Charles Joseph Bruder." **The Province of Ontario: a history, 1615-1927**. Toronto: Dominion Publishing Company, 1927. Vol. 4, pp. 590-591. port. Loc: OWTL, OWTU.

A profile of the Kitchener hotel-owner and real estate developer. Period: 1888 - 1926.

SURNAMES BEGINNING WITH C

1284. "Hugh Cant." **Waterloo Historical Society**. 1919. 7: 91-92. Loc: all.

A profile of Cant (1833-1917) who came to Galt in 1845 and developed the woodworking machinery business of Cant Brothers Ltd. He served on the Town Council, Board of Trade and Gore Mutual Fire Insurance Company, and was a local historian. Period: 1833 - 1917.

1285. Rose, George Maclean. "Cant, John." **A cyclopaedia of Canadian biography: being chiefly men of the time**. Rose's National Biographical Series 1. Toronto: Rose Publishing Co., 1886. Pp. 737-738. Loc: OWTL, OWTU.

Born to a family who migrated to Galt in 1843, Cant was a partner in an enterprise making wood-working machinery by the mid-1880s. Period: 1843 - 1886.

1286. "John F. Carmichael." **Waterloo Historical Society**. 1949. 37: 42-43. Loc: all.

A brief biography of the former supervising principal of the Kitchener Public Schools who was also involved in Masonic circles and in the Presbyterian Church. Period: 1866 - 1949.

1287. "Thomas Carscadden, M.A.." **Waterloo Historical Society**. 1924. 12: 113-115. Loc: all.

A biography of the principal of the Galt Collegiate Institute from 1881 to 1914. He also served the Galt Collegiate Institute Board as secretary for 25 years and was active in the Wesleyan Methodist Church in Galt. Period: 1837 - 1923.

1288. Dickson, Margaret E. "Eric M. Carter, 1911-1986." **Waterloo Historical Society.** 1986. 74: 96-97. Loc: all.

An obituary that mentions Mr Carter's association with heritage groups in Waterloo County after he joined the staff of the Kitchener-Waterloo Collegiate and Vocational School in 1946 and later taught at the Eastwood Collegiate. He was president of the Waterloo Historical Society in 1967 and 1968. Period: 1946 - 1986.

1289. "Eric M. Carter." **Waterloo Historical Society.** 1970. 58: 6-7. ill. Loc: all.

A biographical sketch of Eric M. Carter, teacher, veteran and president of the Waterloo Historical Society. His illustrative line drawings may be seen in several Waterloo Historical Society reports. Period: 1922 - 1969.

1290. "Miss Janet W. Carter." **Waterloo Historical Society.** 1953. 41: 18. Loc: all.

A short biography of the first woman to graduate from the University of Toronto with a Master of Arts degree, who taught English, French, German and Spanish at Galt Collegiate Institute from 1901 to 1934. Period: c1880 - 1953.

1291. "Samuel B. Cassel." **Waterloo Historical Society.** 1949. 37: 43. Loc: all.

A brief biography of the former Wilmot Township resident who held many positions on the township council including Deputy-Reeve and Clerk/Treasurer. He was the great-grandson of Samuel Bricker, one of the County's first settlers. Period: 1858 - 1949.

1292. Essegern, Rudolf. "John Chapman - merchant." **Waterloo Historical Society.** 1986. 74: 73-77. ill. Loc: all.

A profile of Chapman (1824-1880) who married the sister of Jacob Hespeler and was a member of the business elite in Preston and Hespeler from the 1850s to the late 1870s. The article is based on research in Chapman's papers that are held in the Cambridge Archives. Period: 1847 - 1880.

1293. "John Chapman." **Waterloo Historical Society.** 1938. 26: 43-44. Loc: all.

A biography of the store owner, postmaster, justice of the peace and Reeve of Hespeler. Period: 1824 - 1880.

1294. "Samuel Cherry." **Waterloo Historical Society.** 1917. 5: 55. ill. Loc: all.

A biography of Cherry (1843-1917), owner of the flour mill in Preston from 1879 until his death, and long-time chairman of the Preston Park Board.

Period: 1843 - 1917.

1295. Campbell, Alexander D., Dr. "Waterloo's body snatcher." **Waterloo Historical Society.** 1989. 77: 83-86. ill. Loc: all.

A sketch of Dr Friedrich Christ (c1824-1875), a German immigrant who lived in Waterloo for thirteen years and was jailed for selling skeletons. Period: 1824 - 1875.

1296. Armstrong, Rita. "One hundredth birthday of Mrs Fred Clare, Preston." **Waterloo Historical Society.** 1967. 55: 11. Loc: all.

A brief biographical note of the celebrations. Period: 1867 - 1967.

1297. "William Clark." **Waterloo Historical Society.** 1946. 34: 38. Loc: all.

A short biography of the Elmira lawyer who was a member of the Elmira Horticultural Society, Elmira Musical Society and Elmira Board of Trade. Period: 1886 - 1946.

1298. Middleton, Jesse Edgar and Landon, Fred. "William Gibson Cleghorn." **The Province of Ontario: a history, 1615-1927.** Toronto: Dominion Publishing Company, 1927. Vol. 4, p. 383. Loc: OWTL, OWTU.

A biography of the Berlin trunk and bag manufacturer. Period: 1888 - 1926.

1299. Fraser, Alexander. "His Honor Judge Clement." **A history of Ontario: its resources and development.** Toronto: The Canada History Co., 1907. Pp. 955-956. Loc: OWTL, OWTU.

A short biography of E.P. Clement, the Berlin lawyer who was solicitor for the town of Berlin and director of the Mutual Life Assurance Co. of Canada. Period: 1853 - 1906.

1300. Connor, A.W. "James W. Connor, B.A., 1843-1929." **Waterloo Historical Society.** 1929. 17: 153-158. ill. Loc: all.

A biography of James William Connor, principal of Berlin High School (later the Kitchener and Waterloo Collegiate and Vocational School) from 1871 to 1901 and author of textbooks in high school English. Period: 1843 - 1929.

1301. Mills, Richard E. "John Robert Connon, historian." **Waterloo Historical Society.** 1935. 23: 177-180. ill. Loc: all.

A brief biography of Connon (1862-1931), author of the **History of Elora** which includes information about Woolwich Township. His photographs of scenes along the Grand River are outstanding and he invented the whole-circle panoramic camera. Period: 1862 - 1931.

1302. "Colonel J. Laing Cowan, 1846-1936." **Waterloo Historical Society**. 1936. 24: 242-243. Loc: all.
    A brief biography of the colonel of the Highland Light Infantry of Canada. Period: 1846 - 1936.

1303. Taylor, Ryan. "Jennie F. Cowan, 1896-1986." **Waterloo Historical Society**. 1986. 74: 97-99. Loc: all.
    An obituary of the notable local historian who was descended from the pioneering Ferguson and Turnbull families of North Dumfries and Beverly Townships. The author describes Mrs Cowan's roles in the Waterloo Historical Society, local women's institutes and the Ontario Pioneer Community Foundation, and as official historian for the centennial of Waterloo County in 1952. Period: 1898 - 1986.

1304. "W.H.S. salutes Mrs T.D. Cowan." **Waterloo Historical Society**. 1961. 49: 6-7. ill. Loc: all.
    A tribute to Jennie F. Cowan, president of the Waterloo Historical Society from 1951 to 1953, including her photograph and biographical information. Period: 1926 - 1961.

1305. "Dr James H. Coyne." **Waterloo Historical Society**. 1942. 30: 244-245. Loc: all.
    An obituary of Dr James H. Coyne of St. Thomas, a lawyer, honorary member of the Waterloo Historical Society and authority on the Indians of Canada. Period: 1817 - 1942.

1306. Cranston, J. Herbert. **Ink on my fingers**. Toronto: Ryerson Press, 1953. 188 p. Loc: OCCA, OWTL, OWTUR.
    Memoirs of Galt-born editor of the **Toronto Star Weekly** who recounts his early work with the **Galt Reformer** and the **Galt Reporter** and reminisces about Galt newspapermen Andrew Laidlaw, J.P. Jaffray, Tom Sears and Louis B. Duff. Cranston also recalls the Rev. Robert E. Knowles whom he encouraged to write for the **Toronto Star Weekly**. Period: 1896 - 1952.

1307. Middleton, Jesse Edgar and Landon, Fred. "John G. Cress." **The Province of Ontario: a history, 1615-1927**. Toronto: Dominion Publishing Company, 1927. Vol. 4, pp. 466-467. Loc: OWTL, OWTU.
    A profile of the Waterloo spring manufacturer, including a summary genealogy. Period: 1875 - 1926.

1308. Schmidt, William A. "Simon Cress - the first Mennonite settler in the St Jacobs area." **Waterloo Historical Society**. 1983. 71: 4-6. ill. Loc: all.
    A brief account of Cress who bought Lot 7 in Woolwich Township in 1819 from John Erb. The article provides information on the exact location of the homestead as well as biographical details of Simon's immediate family. Period: 1819 - 1852.

1309. Middleton, Jesse Edgar and Landon, Fred. "Alvin K. Cressman." **The Province of Ontario: a history, 1615-1927**. Toronto: Dominion Publishing Company, 1927. Vol. 3, pp. 207-208. Loc: OWTL, OWTU.
    A profile of the Waterloo insurance and real estate broker, including a summary genealogy. Period: 1881 - 1926.

1310. Crozier, John Beattie. **My inner life, being a chapter in personal evolution and autobiography**. London, England: Longmans, Green, and Co., 1898. 562 p. index. Also CIHM Microfiche series, no. 08407. Loc: OCCA, OWTL, OWTU.
    The first portion of the book portrays Crozier's childhood in Galt, mentioning the churches, members of Galt's black community, the library, Galt Grammar School and the discipline of Dr Tassie. The remainder of the book relates his life in England as a philosopher and author. Period: 1850 - 1898.

1311. "John Beattie Crozier." **Waterloo Historical Society**. 1923. 11: 52-55. Loc: all.
    An obituary of the philosopher and political theorist who was born in Galt in 1849, but who spent most of his life in England. A short supplement to this article was published in the Waterloo Historical Society's 13th Annual Report. Contributed by the Right Hon. T.P. O'Connor, M.P., to the London **Times**, it was republished in the Galt **Reporter** on 12 November 1925. Period: 1849 - 1922.

1312. "Brigadier-General E.A. Cruickshank." **Waterloo Historical Society**. 1942. 30: 245. Loc: all.
    An obituary of E.A. Cruickshank, an honorary member of the Waterloo Historical Society who contributed a paper to the 1927 annual volume and assisted in turning the first sod for the excavation of the Pioneers' Memorial Tower. Period: 1924 - 1939.

1313. Middleton, Jesse Edgar and Landon, Fred. "A. James Cundick." **The Province of Ontario: a history, 1615-1927**. Toronto: Dominion Publishing Company, 1927. Vol. 3, pp. 216-217. Loc: OWTL, OWTU.
    A profile of the manager of the Kitchener branch of the Bank of Nova Scotia. Period: 1916 - 1927.

SURNAMES BEGINNING WITH D

1314. "George Davidson, Berlin." **The Canadian biographical dictionary and portrait gallery of eminent and self-made men, Ontario volume.** Toronto: American Biographical Publishing Co., 1880. Pp. 526-527. Loc: OWTL, OWTU.

A biography of the sheriff of Waterloo County, who migrated from Aberdeen, Scotland to Woolwich Township in 1835. Davidson's many public and community interests in Berlin and New Aberdeen are outlined. Period: 1835 - 1880.

1315. Sims, Florence K. "Sheriff Davidson." **Waterloo Historical Society.** 1928. 16: 84-85. Loc: all.

A short biography of the first sheriff of Waterloo County who died in 1881. Period: 1814 - 1881.

1316. De la Roche, Mazo. **Ringing the changes: an autobiography.** London: Macmillan, 1957. 304 p. ill. Loc: OCCA.

Recollections of a Canadian novelist who spent part of her childhood in Galt. Among the experiences described are the author's first awareness of the beauty of nature, her schooling, her mother's illness and the death of her friend, Mina Sylvestre. Period: 1900?-1904?

1317. "Herbert Denis-Nathan." **Waterloo Historical Society.** 1971. 59: 4-5. ill. Loc: all.

A profile of the veteran, teacher and vice-principal at Galt Collegiate Institute, and president of the Waterloo Historical Society in 1969. Period: 1930 - 1971.

1318. Schmidt, Grace. "Herbert Denis-Nathan." **Waterloo Historical Society.** 1989. 77: 4. Loc: all.

An obituary of the vice-principal of Galt Collegiate Institute and former president of the Waterloo Historical Society. Period: 1930 - 1989.

1319. "D.B. Detweiler." **Waterloo Historical Society.** 1919. 7: 93-94. ill. Loc: all.

Brief biography of Daniel Bechtel Detweiler (1860-1919), Berlin businessman and promoter of the distribution of hydro-electric power from Niagara Falls. Period: 1860 - 1919.

1320. Devitt, E. Blake. "Benjamin Devitt." **Waterloo Historical Society.** 1963. 51: 8-11. Loc: all.

Personal recollections of Benjamin Devitt, Mayor of Waterloo and farmer, by his grandson. Period: 1875 - 1963.

1321. "Edward M. Devitt." **Waterloo Historical Society.** 1938. 26: 46-47. Loc: all.

A short biography of Edward M. Devitt

(1867-1938), Waterloo pharmacist and member of the Waterloo Park Board for thirty-five years. Period: 1867 - 1938.

1322. "F.W.R. Dickson." **Waterloo Historical Society.** 1964. 52: 7. ill. Loc: all.

A short tribute to the teacher and long-time member of the Waterloo Historical Society who was also interested in the Doon Pioneer Village, the Kitchener-Waterloo Field Naturalists, and the F.W.R. Dickson Wilderness Area, an 83-acre wild life area named for him. Period: 1964.

1323. Johnson, Beatrice and Taylor, Andrew W. "Memories of Kirkmichael." **Waterloo Historical Society.** 1973. 61: 42-43. ill. Loc: all.

A short description of the Dickson household by a woman who used to sew for Mrs Julia Rooney, the last descendant of William Dickson to live in the Galt home. Period: 1836 - c1930.

1324. Kerr, James E. "Sketch of the life of Hon. William Dickson." **Waterloo Historical Society.** 1916. 4: 26-32. ill. Loc: all.

An account of the life of Dickson (1769-1846), the Scottish lawyer who developed the Township of Dumfries with Absalom Shade. Information about the early settlement of Galt and other Dickson Family members is also provided. Sources include Janet Carnochan's **History of Niagara**, James Young's **Early history of Galt** and Miss Florence Dickson's collection of her grandfather's letters. Period: 1810 - 1846.

1325. Menary, David. "The story behind Dickson's stone." **Waterloo Historical Society.** 1987. 75: 131-139. Loc: all.

A biography of Dickson, relating his many accomplishments in developing Dumfries Township. Period: 1816 - 1846.

1326. Rose, George Maclean. "Dickson, Rev. James A.R.." **A cyclopaedia of Canadian biography: being chiefly men of the time.** Rose's National Biographical Series 1. Toronto: Rose Publishing Co., 1886. P. 492. Loc: OWTL, OWTU.

A biography of the former Congregationalist clergyman called to Galt's Central Presbyterian Church in 1879. Period: 1879 - 1886.

1327. Schmidt, Grace. "F.W.R. Dickson, 1898-1984." **Waterloo Historical Society.** 1984. 72: 20-21. ill. Loc: all.

A obituary which notes Dickson's associations with Doon Pioneer Village, the Waterloo County Hall of Fame, the Waterloo Historical Society and the Kitchener-Waterloo Collegiate and Vocational School. Period: 1898 - 1984.

1328. Wilson, Bruce G. "Dickson, William." **Dictionary of Canadian Biography**. Toronto: University of Toronto Press, 1988. 7: 250-252. Also in **Dictionnaire biographique du Canada**, 7: 271-273. Loc: OWTL, OWTU.

A biography of the businessman, lawyer, politician and office holder (1769-1846). While the author's main focus is on Dickson's years in Newark (Niagara), he describes the efforts to develop and promote Scottish settlement in Dumfries Township from 1816 and mentions Dickson's residence in Galt from 1825 to 1837. Period: 1808 - 1837.

1329. Hunsberger, Albert and Hunsberger, Wilson. "Theodore Dietrich of St Agatha." **Waterloo Historical Society**. 1980. 68: 17-23. ill. Loc: all.

A short biography of the automobile and airplane enthusiast from St Agatha with an account of his many adventures in Skylark, the plane he built himself. Period: 1896 - 1980.

1330. Middleton, Jesse Edgar and Landon, Fred. "Louis Frederick Dietrich." **The Province of Ontario: a history, 1615-1927**. Toronto: Dominion Publishing Company, 1927. Vol. 4, p. 385. Loc: OWTL, OWTU.

A profile of the Waterloo automobile dealer and town councillor. Period: 1868 - 1926.

1331. Middleton, Jesse Edgar and Landon, Fred. "Robert Arthur Dietrich." **The Province of Ontario: a history, 1615-1927**. Toronto: Dominion Publishing Company, 1927. Vol. 4, pp. 443-444. Loc: OWTL, OWTU.

A biography of Henry A. Dietrich, founder of the Berlin bakery and city councillor. Period: 1864 - 1926.

1332. Campbell, Alexander D., Dr. "Nurse becomes doctor." **Waterloo Historical Society**. 1991. 79: 172. Loc: all.

A brief note about Dr Agnes Isabell Dodds, born in Waterloo in 1873, who graduated in nursing in 1901 and in medicine at the age of 57. Period: 1873 - 1965.

1333. Middleton, Jesse Edgar and Landon, Fred. "Charles Henry Doerr." **The Province of Ontario: a history, 1615-1927**. Toronto: Dominion Publishing Company, 1927. Vol. 4, pp. 420-421. port. Loc: OWTL, OWTU.

A biography of the Kitchener confectionery manufacturer. Period: 1868 - 1926.

1334. Warren, Janet. "Cyrus Dolph, Preston philanthropist." **Waterloo Historical Society**. 1990. 78: 20-29. ill. Loc: all.

A biography of Dolph (1865-1937), a Preston manufacturer of sheet metal building products who had many community interests and roles. The author presents a detailed account of Dolph's promotion of "Preston's own" radio station CKPC from 1923 until 1933 when it was moved to Brantford. Period: 1865 - 1937.

1335. "Marcus Munroe Donald." **Waterloo Historical Society**. 1953. 41: 48. Loc: all.

An obituary of Marcus Munroe Donald (1868-1953), newspaperman and founder of **The Preston Progress**. When this paper closed in 1923, he established the Preston Progress Printing Company. Period: 1868 - 1953.

1336. "Edward F. Donohoe, Jan. 11, 1955." **Waterloo Historical Society**. 1954. 42: 42. Loc: all.

A brief obituary of E.F. Donohoe (1889-1955), journalist and member of the Waterloo Historical Society. Period: 1889 - 1955.

1337. "Monsignor E.A. Doyle." **Waterloo Historical Society**. 1961. 49: 61. Loc: all.

An account of the celebrations to commemorate the sixtieth year that Monsignor Doyle had been a parish priest in the Hamilton diocese. Some biographical information is also given. Period: 1901 - 1961.

1338. Schmalz, W.H.E. "August Drechsler." **Waterloo Historical Society**. 1949. 37: 48-52. Loc: all.

A number of brief anecdotes about the eccentric musician who often performed with the Berlin Musical Society under the direction of Theodore Zoellner. Period: c1870 - c1890.

1339. **Louis Blake Duff: the composite man**. Port Colborne: George H. Smith, 1959. 23 p. ill. Loc: OCCA.

A collection of newspaper tributes to Louis B. Duff (1878-1959), writer and historian who worked on the **Galt Reporter** for four years with J.P. Jaffray. He played soccer with the Galt club from 1900 to 1904 when the club held the intermediate championship of Ontario. Duff later went to Welland to edit the **Telegraph**. It includes an article by William Colgate of the **Globe and Mail** published on 15 August 1959. Period: 1900 - 1904.

1340. Stauch, Warren. "Terrence Clarke Dugan." **Waterloo Historical Society**. 1980. 68: 8-9. ill. Loc: all.

A short biography of the former president of the Waterloo Historical Society. The article recounts Dugan's work in the field of education as well as his contribution to heritage in the area. Period: 1956 - 1980.

1341. Banting, Constance. "Mabel Dunham." **Ontario Library Review and Book Selection Guide**. 1928. 12: 66. Loc: OGU.

A brief profile of the noted librarian and author. Period: 1910 - 1928.

1342. "Honour to whom honour is due." **Waterloo Historical Society**. 1953. 41: 7-8. Loc: all.

A note of a birthday tribute to the noted writer who was the first trained librarian in Ontario and the first woman president of various local organizations, including the Waterloo Historical Society. Period: 1953 -

1343. Middleton, Jesse Edgar and Landon, Fred. "Bertha Mabel Dunham." **The Province of Ontario: a history, 1615-1927**. Toronto: Dominion Publishing Company, 1927. Vol. 3, pp. 303-304. Loc: OWTL, OWTU.

A profile of the chief librarian of the Kitchener Public Library, including details of her leading roles in local associations. Period: 1900 - 1926.

1344. Shoemaker, Dorothy. "B. Mabel Dunham, D.Litt.: a tribute." **Canadian-German Folklore**. 1961. 1: 125. Loc: OKIT, OWTL, OWTUCG, OWTU.

A note of Mabel Dunham's accomplishments as librarian, writer, and leader in many organizations including the Waterloo Historical Society and the Kitchener-Waterloo University Women's Club. Period: 1908 - 1957.

1345. Shoemaker, Dorothy. "Dr B. Mabel Dunham." **Waterloo Historical Society**. 1957. 45: 4-6. ill. Loc: all.

An obituary for the noted librarian, clubwoman, author and historian, with a copy of W.L. Mackenzie King's foreword to Dunham's book **The Trail of the Conestoga**. Period: 1881 - 1957.

1346. Taylor, Ryan. "Mabel Dunham's centenary." **Waterloo Historical Society**. 1981. 69: 13-25. ill. bibl. Loc: all.

A biography commemorating the 100th anniversary of the birth of B. Mabel Dunham and describing her roles as chief librarian of Kitchener Public Library, as leader of various local clubs and societies, and as writer and historian. A bibliography lists works written by and about B. Mabel Dunham. Period: 1881 - 1981.

SURNAMES BEGINNING WITH E

1347. "Benjamin Eby." **Waterloo Historical Society**. 1960. 48: 16-18. ill. Loc: all.

A biography to mark the unveiling of a plaque at First Mennonite Church, Kitchener. Period: 1785 - 1853.

1348. Burkholder, Oscar. "Bishop Benjamin Eby, 1785-1853." **Gospel Herald**. 1929. 22,3: 61-62. Loc: OWTUCG.

A short biography of the Waterloo Township pioneer from Hammer Creek, PA, relating his accomplishments as preacher and teacher at the first Mennonite meeting house in Ebytown (Berlin) in 1813. Burkholder describes Eby's character and appearance and lists his publications including various editions of **Die Gemeinschaftliche Liedersammlung** and the **ABC Buchstabir- und Lesebuch**. Period: 1785 - 1853.

1349. Cressman, J. Boyd. "Benjamin Eby, founder of Kitchener and the spirit of progress." **Canadian-German Folklore**. 1961. 1: 130-133. Loc: OKIT, OWTL, OWTU, OWTUCG.

A biographical sketch of the church and community leader in Waterloo Township who established Berlin's first church, school, newspaper and furniture factory and wrote and published two spelling books and a history of the Mennonites. Period: 1785 - 1855.

1350. Cressman, J. Boyd. "Bishop Benjamin Eby." **Waterloo Historical Society**. 1941. 29: 152-158. Loc: all.

A sketch of the spiritual leader of the early Mennonites in Waterloo County. Period: 1785 - 1855.

1351. Cressman, J. Boyd. "Eby, Benjamin." **The Mennonite encyclopedia**. Edited by Cornelius Krahn and Harold S. Bender and C. Henry Smith. Scottdale, PA: Mennonite Publishing House, 1956. Vol. 2, pp. 138-139. Loc: OWTUCG, OWTU.

A biographical sketch of one of the most influential early Mennonite leaders of Waterloo Township. Eby was a bishop, an author, a teacher and a farmer. He gave financial support to the first newspaper, the **Canada Museum**, donated land for the First Mennonite Church, and helped found one of the earliest schools in Waterloo County. Period: 1815 - 1853.

1352. Eby, Elias and Horst, Isaac R. **Diary of Elias Eby, 1810-1878**. Mount Forest: The Author, 1982. 59 p. ill., facsim. Loc: OWTUCG, OWTUCGR.

Diary of Eby's last six years, 1872 to 1878, translated, edited and annotated by Isaac R. Horst. Second son of Bishop Benjamin Eby and Maria Brubacher, Eby bought Lancaster Mills following Jacob Shoemaker's financial failure in 1851. The diary is in three parts: weather observations, a visiting register, and notes.

Horst samples the first two sections, and has fully translated only the notes which include family information and mention many acquaintances. The diaries record both local gossip and events of wider significance. In July 1873, Eby describes how he and others went to Toronto to meet the Russians on their way to Manitoba. He also comments on Mennonite religious issues. Many entries deal with sickness, death and funerals. Period: 1872 - 1878.

1353. Eby, Ezra E. "Bishop Benjamin Eby." **Mennonite Historical Bulletin**. 1962. 23,1: 1-3. ill. Loc: OWTUCG.

A brief biography of Benjamin Eby, containing a transcript of "A short biography of the venerable old bishop," by one of Eby's parishioners who comments on Eby's character and sermons. The article is illustrated with photographs of Eby's first son, Isaac, and Isaac's wife, Veronica. Period: 1785 - 1834.

1354. Eby, Gordon Christian and Nyce, James M. **The Gordon C. Eby diaries, 1911-13: chronicle of a Mennonite farmer**. Ethnocultural Voices. Toronto: Multicultural History Society of Ontario, 1982. 208 p. ill. Loc: OWTU, OWTUCG, OKIT, OWTL, OWT.

The diary of a Mennonite farmer, Gordon Christian Eby (1890-1965), son of Christian Eby, the well-known healer or charmer. The diaries describe farm life in Waterloo County before the First World War, with detailed information about family life and the family enterprise of market-gardening. Entries also record shows and entertainments, including the cityhood celebrations of 1912. Gordon was an amateur photographer and examples of his work are included in the book, with a chart of the Eby family tree. Period: 1911 - 1913.

1355. Epp, Frank H. "Eby, Benjamin." **Dictionary of Canadian Biography**. Toronto: University of Toronto Press, 1985. 8: 265-266. Also in **Dictionnaire biographique du Canada**, 8: 293-266. Loc: OWTL, OWTU.

A biography of the pioneer farmer, community leader, Mennonite bishop, educator and author. Period: 1810 - 1855.

1356. Gingerich, Melvin. "A Benjamin Eby letter." **Mennonite Historical Bulletin**. 1967. 28,4: 4. Loc: OWTUCG.

Transcript of an letter to Jacob Groff from Benjamin Eby written in 1851. Eby writes that Abraham C. Weber was ordained as preacher and that Joseph E. Schneider, Jacob J. Schneider, and Johannes C. Schantz were ordained as deacons at the Mennonite conference of September 1850 in Berlin. Period: 1850 - 1851.

1357. Luthy, David. "Benjamin Eby: pioneer Ontario bishop-teacher-writer." **Family Life**. 1989, June. Pp. 14-19. ill., map. Loc: OKITW.

A biographical account of Benjamin Eby, focusing on his books, the marriage certificates he signed, and the fraktur inscriptions of the Eby meeting house hymnals. There is a modern transcription of the earliest known map of Waterloo Township dating from 1818. Period: 1785 - 1853.

1358. Roth, Lorraine. "The years of Benjamin Eby, pioneer Mennonite leader in Ontario, Canada." **Pennsylvania Mennonite Heritage**. 1986. 9,2: 18-41. ill., maps. Loc: OKIT, OWTUCG.

A study of the life and times of Benjamin Eby (1785-1853), early community and church leader. A chronological account of Eby's accomplishments as a writer, educator, bishop and patron of new enterprises is interwoven with references to contemporary events. There is much information on the genealogy of the Eby family and the interrelationships of the Pennsylvania Mennonite families who emigrated to Waterloo. Period: 1785 - 1909.

1359. Sherk, A.B., Rev. "Ezra E. Eby: the historian and his work." **The Pennsylvania German**. 1908. 9: 273-277. Loc: OWTUCGR.

A biographical sketch of Ezra E. Eby (1850-1901) and review of Eby's **Biographical history of Waterloo** which consists of two parts. The first recounts the early settlement of Waterloo by the Pennsylvania Mennonites while the second presents genealogical information about Waterloo families. Period: 1800 - 1901.

1360. "John R. Eden." **Waterloo Historical Society**. 1938. 26: 45. ill. Loc: all.

An obituary of Eden (1858-1938), businessman and Mayor of Berlin/Kitchener for five terms. One of the memorable events of his term of office was the municipal takeover of the gas and electric utilities in 1903. Period: 1858 - 1938.

1361. Middleton, Jesse Edgar and Landon, Fred. "John R. Eden." **The Province of Ontario: a history, 1615-1927**. Toronto: Dominion Publishing Company, 1927. Vol. 3, p. 214. Loc: OWTL, OWTU.

A profile of the general manager of the Ott Brick Company, with details of civic improvements during his terms as Mayor of Kitchener, especially between 1899 and 1903. Period: 1858 - 1926.

1362. Middleton, Jesse Edgar and Landon, Fred. "Alexander McKay Edwards." **The Province of Ontario: a history, 1615-1927**. Toronto: Dominion Publishing Company, 1927. Vol. 4, p. 410. Loc: OWTL, OWTU.

A profile of the druggist who organized the Galt Stove and Furnace Company and was active in municipal and federal politics. Period: 1897 - 1926.

1363. "Mrs A.M. Edwards." **Waterloo Historical Society**. 1952. 40: 29. Loc: all.

An obituary of Laura Edwards who was noted for her community service with the Red Cross Society in Galt, the Central Council of Ladies Auxiliaries and the Freeport Sanatorium Auxiliary. Period: 1952 -

1364. Einwechter, Earl. **The history of Earl Einwechter by himself, 1980**. 1980. 7 l. Loc: OKIT.

A short autobiography of the employee of the New Dundee Creamery, including stories about his family and neighbours and reminiscences are his work as a hauler for the creamery and as musician-manager in the local "Pickelheimer" family band. Period: 1902 - 1980.

1365. "Mrs William Elliott." **Waterloo Historical Society**. 1952. 40: 29. Loc: all.

An obituary of Eva Elliott, a prominent citizen of Galt who was noted particularly for her work in Knox's Presbyterian Church, Galt, the Y.W.C.A., and the South Waterloo Agricultural Society. Period: 1900 - 1952.

1366. Eadie, Tom. "Enslin, Christian." **Dictionary of Canadian Biography**. Toronto: University of Toronto Press, 1985. 8: 271. Also in **Dictionnaire biographique du Canada**, 8: 300-301. Loc: OWTL, OWTU.

A biography of the bookbinder, newspaperman, notary and first clerk of the Surrogate Court of Waterloo County. With Heinrich Eby, Enslin founded **Der Deutsche Canadier und Neuigkeitsbote**, the sole German-language newspaper published in British North America from 1841 to 1848. Enslin (1800-1856) was also a leader in the Swedenborgian congregation in Berlin. Period: 1836 - 1856.

1367. Steiner, Samuel J. "Frank H. Epp, 1929-1986." **Mennogespräch**. 1986. 4,1: 3. ill. Loc: OWTUCG, OKIT.

A tribute to the Mennonite historian, writer and president of Conrad Grebel College. Period: 1929 - 1986.

1368. Bird, Michael S. "Erb, Abraham." **Dictionary of Canadian Biography**. Toronto: University of Toronto Press, 1987. 6: 235-236. Also in **Dictionnaire biographique du Canada**, 6: 257-258. Loc: OWTL, OWTU.

A biography of the pioneer settler (1772-1830) who migrated from Pennsylvania to the German Company Tract in 1806. The village of Waterloo eventually developed around the nucleus of Erb's water-powered mills; he also endowed schools in Waterloo Township. Period: 1806 - 1830.

1369. Erb, Abraham. **The will of Abraham Erb**. 5 p., facsim. Loc: OKIT.

A transcript of the 1829 will, the largest legacy being to Erb's wife, Magdalena. Two thousand dollars were bequeathed for the use of four schools, one on Erb's own land, one near Jacob Snider's farmstead, Benjamin Eby's school, and one to be established on Lot 35 in Woolwich Township. Money was left for three trustees to be appointed in each school district. Smaller sums of money were left to other people and the remainder of his estate divided among the families of his brothers and sisters. Period: 1829 - 1830.

1370. "Founder of Preston commemorated." **Waterloo Historical Society**. 1960. 48: 22-23. Loc: all.

A short account of the founding of Preston by John Erb, including biographical information and a description of the unveiling of a plaque in 1960. Period: 1805 - 1960.

1371. Esson, George. **A diary of George Esson, Preston, Ont., 1879**. 1 v. (unpaged). Loc: OKIT.

The diary of one of Canada's first photographers who records the weather, his health and business transactions, generally noting the profit made. The original diary belonged to Mr Esson's nephew, Elliot Law, whose son William allowed Kitchener Public Library to make a photocopy in 1986. Period: 1879 - 1880.

SURNAMES BEGINNING WITH F

1372. Middleton, Jesse Edgar and Landon, Fred. "John Fennell." **The Province of Ontario: a history, 1615-1927**. Toronto: Dominion Publishing Company, 1927. Vol. 3, p. 291. Loc: OWTL, OWTU.

A profile of the Berlin hardware merchant and community leader (1838-1923). Period: 1863 - 1923.

1373. Rose, George Maclean. "Fennell, John." **A cyclopaedia of Canadian biography: being chiefly men of the time**. Rose's National Biographical Series 1. Toronto: Rose Publishing Co., 1886. P. 508. Loc: OWTL, OWTU.

A biography of Berlin hardware merchant and community leader. Period: 1863 - 1886.

1374. Cowan, Jennie F. "Duncan Ferguson and his home." **Waterloo Historical Society**. 1984. 72: 26-33. ill. Loc: all.

A history of the Fergusons who settled on the north half of Lot 5, Concession 12, off Avenue Road in the northeast part of Galt. The author describes Ferguson's role in municipal government and quotes family journals for evidence of farm-making activities, book purchases, the development of the Mill Creek school, and transactions with neighbours. The exterior of the stone house that Ferguson built to replace his original log cabin was designated by Cambridge LACAC in 1983. Period: 1826 - 1884.

1375. Burley, David G. "Ferrie, Adam." **Dictionary of Canadian Biography**. Toronto: University of Toronto Press, 1988. 7: 284-285. Also in **Dictionnaire biographique du Canada**, 7: 307-308. Loc: OWTL, OWTU.

An account of the life and business of Adam Ferrie, Jr (1813-1849), including his direction of the Preston branch of his father's wholesale and retail business and the development of the milling complex at Doon Mills. The author analyzes Ferrie's business difficulties as an example of the strengths and weaknesses of the family as a form of business organization. Period: 1830 - 1849.

1376. Ferrie, Adam. **Autobiography**. 1856. 36 p. Loc: OTMR.

Memoirs of the Hamilton merchant (1777-1863) whose sons Colin and Adam Jr looked after the family's business interests in the Preston and Doon areas in the period from the 1830s to the 1860s. Apparently acquired by the Toronto Public Library in 1927 and bound with a series of other pamphlets. Period: 1830 - 1860.

1377. Weaver, John C. "Ferrie, Colin Campbell." **Dictionary of Canadian Biography**. Toronto: University of Toronto Press, 1985. 8: 293-295. Also in **Dictionnaire biographique du Canada**, 8: 324-327. Loc: OWTL, OWTU.

Colin Ferrie (1808-1856), son of Adam Ferrie and son-in-law of Richard Beasley, established a wholesale and retail store in Hamilton with branches in various locations including Waterloo in the early 1830s. Period: 1830 - 1840.

1378. "Mr Peter Fisher." **Waterloo Historical Society**. 1953. 41: 4. Loc: all.

A tribute to Fisher (1872-1953), Secretary-Treasurer of the Waterloo Historical Society from 1913 to 1951. He was a school teacher and administrator for 26 years and later associated with the Mutual Life Assurance Company. Period: 1872 - 1953.

1379. "Peter Fisher." **Waterloo Historical Society**. 1952. 40: 10. ill. Loc: all.

A note of Fisher's service as secretary-treasurer for the Waterloo Historical Society for 40 years. Period: 1912 - 1952.

1380. Middleton, Jesse Edgar and Landon, Fred. "Walter John Fleischauer." **The Province of Ontario: a history, 1615-1927**. Toronto: Dominion Publishing Company, 1927. Vol. 4, pp. 470-471. Loc: OWTL, OWTU.

A profile of the secretary-treasurer of the Baetz Brothers Furniture Company and of his father, Louis Fleischauer, a Wellesley blacksmith. Period: 1865 - 1926.

1381. "David Forsyth, B.A., 1853-1936." **Waterloo Historical Society**. 1936. 24: 244-246. Loc: all.

An obituary of the Scottish emigrant who came to Galt in 1867 and taught at the Berlin High School from 1876, becoming its principal in 1901. Forsyth also served on various boards and commissions and was a notable sportsman. Period: 1867 - 1936.

1382. "David Forsyth, B.A.." **Waterloo Historical Society**. 1924. 12: 116-119. ill. Loc: all.

A short biography of the Principal Emeritus of the Kitchener-Waterloo Collegiate and Vocational School who retired in June 1921. Forsyth is described as an notable sportsman, in soccer, lacrosse, cricket and cycling, and served on the Berlin Library Board, the Berlin Board of Health and the Royal Commission on Industrial Training and Technical Education. Period: 1852 - 1924.

1383. "J.D. Claude Forsyth." **Waterloo Historical Society**. 1949. 37: 43-44. Loc: all.

An obituary of the Waterloo shirt manufacturer who was also active on the boards of the Kitchener-Waterloo Hospital, the Kitchener Board of Health, the Crippled Children's Foundation and the YMCA. Period: 1885 - 1948.

1384. Middleton, Jesse Edgar and Landon, Fred. "Arthur Foster." **The Province of Ontario: a history, 1615-1927**. Toronto: Dominion Publishing Company, 1927. Vol. 4, p. 368. Loc: OWTL, OWTU.

A profile of the former teacher and managing director of the Mutual Life Assurance Co. of Canada. Period: 1885 - 1926.

1385. "Jonathan William Fraser." **Waterloo Historical Society.** 1947. 35: 48. Loc: all.

An obituary of Kitchener's medical officer who established the first school nursing system and the practice of a fall medical examination of children about to enter school. Period: c1880 - 1947.

1386. "R.M. Fraser." **Waterloo Historical Society.** 1953. 41: 28. Loc: all.

An obituary for Richard Munro Fraser (1882-1953), president of the Fraser Hardware Co., Galt from 1921. Period: 1882 - 1953.

1387. Rose, George Maclean. "Funcken, Very Rev. Louis, D.D.." **A cyclopaedia of Canadian biography: being chiefly men of the time.** Rose's National Biographical Series 1. Toronto: Rose Publishing Co., 1886. Pp. 455-456. Loc: OWTL, OWTU.

A brief profile of the rector of St Jerome's College, Berlin. Period: 1864 - 1886.

SURNAMES BEGINNING WITH G

1388. Stroh, Jacob. "Frederick Gaukel." **Waterloo Historical Society.** 1928. 16: 86-87. Loc: all.

A short biography of the hotel-keeper by his grandson. Period: 1785 - 1853.

1389. Wust, Klaus. "Gaukel, Friedrich." **Dictionary of Canadian Biography.** Toronto: University of Toronto Press, 1985. 8: 314-315. Also in **Dictionnaire biographique du Canada,** 8: 348-350. Loc: OWTL, OWTU.

A biography of the emigrant from Württemberg who came to Waterloo Township in 1820, first farming and operating a distillery near Bridgeport. In 1833 he purchased land in the small settlement of Ebytown, renamed Berlin, and established an inn, later known as the Commercial Hotel. Gaukel (1785-1853) gave the site for the Waterloo Township Hall and campaigned for the organization of Waterloo County, providing land for the construction of the county courthouse in 1852. Period: 1820 - 1853.

1390. Middleton, Jesse Edgar and Landon, Fred. "Dr William Geiger, M.D.." **The Province of Ontario: a history, 1615-1927.** Toronto: Dominion Publishing Company, 1927. Vol. 4, pp. 608-609. Loc: OWTL, OWTU.

A profile of the Waterloo physician, including information about his family in Huron County. Period: 1911 - 1926.

1391. "63rd wedding anniversary." **Waterloo Historical Society.** 1958. 46: 57. Loc: all.

A note of the anniversary of Mr and Mrs John Geisel of Elmira. Period: 1895 - 1958.

1392. Foster, Linda. "Elizabeth Gibson: first superintendent of Galt Hospital." **Waterloo Historical Society.** 1990. 78: 30-38. ill. Loc: all.

An account of the appointment and achievements of Galt Hospital's first Lady Superintendent from 1889 to 1895. The author explains how the Galt community was influenced to accept the value of hospitals, partly through the work of various women's organizations. Miss Gibson (1855-1942) was a Galt native who later became a Presbyterian deaconess. Period: 1855 - 1942.

1393. Rose, George Maclean. "Gilholm, Robert." **A cyclopaedia of Canadian biography: being chiefly men of the time.** Rose's National Biographical Series 1. Toronto: Rose Publishing Co., 1886. Pp. 274-275. Loc: OWTL, OWTU.

A short profile of the business and community interests of the partner in the Galt lumber business of Gilholm and Hogg. Period: 1833 - 1886.

1394. Gillespie, Ruth. **Doctor William Gillespie.** 13 l. Loc: OKIT.

A brief account by the doctor's wife, including anecdotes of his practices in Baden and Kitchener from the First World War to the 1950s and an article from the **Daily Record** of 15 September 1923 entitled "Local physician's experience with tires recalls old days." Period: 1905 - 1959.

1395. Middleton, Jesse Edgar and Landon, Fred. "William Gillespie, M.D.." **The Province of Ontario: a history, 1615-1927.** Toronto: Dominion Publishing Company, 1927. Vol. 4, pp. 548-549. Loc: OWTL, OWTU.

A profile of the Baden and Kitchener physician. Period: 1911 - 1926.

1396. Gingrich, Arthur. "Enoch S. Gingrich, pioneer and contemporary." **Waterloo Historical Society.** 1961. 49: 23-24. Loc: all.

Poetical biography of Enoch S. Gingrich, son of the Mennonite minister Jacob Gingrich, whose life spanned both pioneer and modern times. Period: 1800 - 1961.

1397. Middleton, Jesse Edgar and Landon, Fred. "Henry William Glady." **The Province of Ontario: a history, 1615-1927.** Toronto: Dominion Publishing Company, 1927. Vol. 4, p. 615. Loc: OWTL, OWTU.

A profile of the Kitchener upholstery manufacturer. Period: 1869 - 1926.

1398. Good, E. Reginald. "John Goessman." **Dictionary of Canadian Biography**. Toronto: University of Toronto Press, 1988. 7: 350-351. Also in **Dictionnaire biographique du Canada**, 7: 379-380. Loc: OWTL, OWTU.

A biography of the surveyor of the German Block in Wilmot Township for Christian Nafziger's Amish and Mennonite settlers. Goessman (1776-1841) also surveyed other townships and acted as an agent for German-speaking settlers in Upper Canada. Period: 1820 - 1840.

1399. Goldie, John and Spawn, Willman. **Diary of a journey through Upper Canada and some of the New England States, 1819**. Goldie Family, 1967?. Loc: OKIT, OWRA, OWTL, OWTU, OWTUCG, OWTUR.

The diary of the Scottish botanist John Goldie (1793-1886), describing his travels from Montreal around Lake Ontario to Pittsburgh during the summer of 1819. In this edition, the diary is transcribed as it was written: an earlier, privately printed, edition of 1897 omitted or revised the political and social comments. Goldie and his family moved to Ayr in 1844. Period: 1819 - 1886.

1400. Goldie, Roswell. "John Goldie and descendants." **Waterloo Historical Society**. 1922. 10: 251-257. ill. Loc: all.

A short biography of Goldie (1793-1886), Scottish botanist and builder of the Greenfield Mill near Ayr. Information about other members of the Goldie family is also given, as well as Goldie's first description of a fern that was named after him, Aspidium Goldianum. Period: 1820 - 1886.

1401. "John Goldie Jr." **Waterloo Historical Society**. 1922. 10: 258-260. ill. Loc: all.

A short biography of John Goldie Jr (1822-1896) who with Hugh McCulloch developed James Crombie's foundry into one of the largest machinery-making businesses in Canada. Period: 1822 - 1896.

1402. Suffling, Roger. "John Goldie, early Canadian botanist 1793-1886." **Waterloo Historical Society**. 1987. 75: 98-116. ill., bibl. Loc: all.

A biography relating Goldie's education, immigration to North America, scientific travels, and eventual settlement at Greenfield, near Ayr. As well as his many contributions to botany (he collected at least 14 new Canadian and American plant species) and milling, he wrote **Goldie's 1819 Diary of a Journey through Upper Canada and some of the New England States** and finished the task of landscaping The Gore overlooking the Nith River in Ayr at the age of 91. Period: 1793 -

1886.

1403. Middleton, Jesse Edgar and Landon, Fred. "Arthur R. Goudie." **The Province of Ontario: a history, 1615-1927**. Toronto: Dominion Publishing Company, 1927. Vol. 4, pp. 323-325. port. Loc: OWTL, OWTU.

A profile of the president of Goudie's Limited, the Kitchener department store. Period: 1884 - 1926.

1404. Dunnett, Carol. "An interview with a senior citizen, Mrs J.Y. Graham." **Waterloo Historical Society**. 1957. 45: 23-25. Loc: all.

An account of the life and family of Nellie Lundy Graham (born 1862) with additional information about the Lundy and Graham families of Galt. Period: 1862 - 1857.

1405. Middleton, Jesse Edgar and Landon, Fred. "Charles Greb." **The Province of Ontario: a history, 1615-1927**. Toronto: Dominion Publishing Company, 1927. Vol. 4, pp. 549-595. Loc: OWTL, OWTU.

A profile of the footwear manufacturer and Mayor of Kitchener. Period: 1909 - 1926.

1406. Middleton, Jesse Edgar and Landon, Fred. "David Gross." **The Province of Ontario: a history, 1615-1927**. Toronto: Dominion Publishing Company, 1927. Vol. 4, pp. 545-546. port. Loc: OWTL, OWTU.

A biography of the director of several large Kitchener businesses, notably The Dominion Button Manufacturers. Gross was Mayor of Kitchener in 1917, 1918 and 1919. Period: 1866 - 1926.

1407. "George A. Gruetzner." **Waterloo Historical Society**. 1949. 37: 45. Loc: all.

An obituary of the founder of the Hespeler Furniture Company who was elected Reeve in 1921 and Mayor in 1925. Period: 1855 - 1949.

1408. Kerr, James E. "General Sir Gordon Guggisberg." **Waterloo Historical Society**. 1930. 18: 234. Loc: all.

A short biography of the native of Galt who had a career in the British military and become Governor and Commander-in-Chief, first in the Gold Coast, and later in British Guiana. Period: 1869 - 1930.

1409. Middleton, Jesse Edgar and Landon, Fred. "William Stephen Gurton." **The Province of Ontario: a history, 1615-1927**. Toronto: Dominion Publishing Company, 1927. Vol. 4, pp. 389-390. Loc: OWTL, OWTU.

A profile of the managing director of the Dominion Truck Equipment Company of Kitchener, including an outline of the company's development and connection with the Canadian Regal Motor

Company. Period: 1912 - 1926.

1410. Dunham, B. Mabel. "Sir Casimir Gzowski." **Waterloo Historical Society**. 1948. 36: 31-35. Loc: all.
A short biography of the Polish engineer who became a British citizen in 1846 and did much to promote Canadian railways. The author notes that Gzowski Street in Kitchener is named after Sir Casimir. Period: 1813 - 1879.

1411. Leather, Ted. "Casimir Gzowski." **Waterloo Historical Society**. 1968. 56: 27-32. ill. Loc: all.
A biographical sketch of Gzowski (1813-1898), Polish-born engineer and promoter of the Grand Trunk Railway, with a note that a park in a new Kitchener subdivision was being named for him. Period: 1813 - 1898.

SURNAMES BEGINNING WITH H

1412. Fraser, Alexander. "Charles Kappler Hagedorn." **A history of Ontario: its resources and development.** Toronto: The Canada History Co., 1907. Pp. 956-957. port. Loc: OWTL, OWTU.
Born in Williamsburg into a family of farm labourers, Hagedorn developed the Berlin Suspender & Button Co. by 1895 and became active in public affairs. Period: 1859 - 1906.

1413. Middleton, Jesse Edgar and Landon, Fred. "Lloyd Elmo Hagedorn." **The Province of Ontario: a history, 1615-1927.** Toronto: Dominion Publishing Company, 1927. Vol. 4, pp. 380-381. port. Loc: OWTL, OWTU.
A profile of the Kitchener Suspender Co., founded by Charles K. Hagedorn (1859-1921). Period: 1859 - 1926.

1414. Middleton, Jesse Edgar and Landon, Fred. "John Edwin Hagmeier, M.D. and Louis Gordon Hagmeier, M.D.." **The Province of Ontario: a history, 1615-1927.** Toronto: Dominion Publishing Company, 1927. Vol. 4, pp. 597-598. Loc: OWTL, OWTU.
A profile of the Kitchener medical practice of the brothers, including an account of their development of the Preston Springs sanitarium. Period: 1884 - 1926.

1415. Middleton, Jesse Edgar and Landon, Fred. "Monteith C. Hall." **The Province of Ontario: a history, 1615-1927.** Toronto: Dominion Publishing Company, 1927. Vol. 4, pp. 552-553. Loc: OWTL, OWTU.
A profile of the Berlin lumber yard and planing mill established by H.J. Hall (1837-1901) and continued by his son. Period: 1878 - 1926.

1416. "Twins married to sisters for 50 years." **Waterloo Historical Society**. 1965. 53: 77. Loc: all.
A paragraph noting the 50th wedding anniversary of Mr and Mrs Ezra Hallman and Mr and Mrs Eldon Hallman in November, 1965. Period: 1915 - 1965.

1417. Fehrenbach, John F., Rev. "Edward Halter." **Waterloo Historical Society**. 1917. 5: 59-60. ill. Loc: all.
A biography of Halter (1834-1917), prominent citizen of New Germany, justice of the peace, reeve of Waterloo Township in 1879, and active promoter of the Hopewell Creek Fire Insurance Company. Period: 1834 - 1917.

1418. Middleton, Jesse Edgar and Landon, Fred. "William H. Hamblin." **The Province of Ontario: a history, 1615-1927.** Toronto: Dominion Publishing Company, 1927. Vol. 4, pp. 403-404. Loc: OWTL, OWTU.
A profile of the president of the Metcalfe Candy Co. of Kitchener. Period: 1917 - 1926.

1419. "Reverend A.M. Hamilton, M.A.." **Waterloo Historical Society**. 1940. 28: 137. ill. Loc: all.
An obituary reprinted from the Toronto **Globe and Mail** for Hamilton (1841-1949) who was minister of Chalmers' United Church, Winterbourne, for forty years and a local historian. Period: 1841 - 1940.

1420. "Robert Somerville Hamilton." **Waterloo Historical Society**. 1947. 35: 50-51. Loc: all.
A short biography of the long time science master at the Galt Collegiate Institute. In addition to his teaching career, Mr Hamilton was active in Masonic affairs and had a great knowledge of Galt history. Period: c1860 - 1947.

1421. "Ross Hamilton." **Waterloo Historical Society**. 1952. 40: 49. Loc: all.
A brief obituary of the director of the Doon School of Fine Arts who was also one of the founders of the Kitchener-Waterloo Branch of the Canadian Institute of International Affairs. Period: 1899 - 1952.

1422. Moberly, Denise. "Deborah Glaister Hannay, 1906-1986." **Waterloo Historical Society**. 1991. 79: 86-91. port. Loc: all.
A biography of the Wellesley-born physician who served in the Second World War, had a private practice in Kitchener, and retired as chief of staff at Freeport Hospital in 1977. Period: 1906 - 1986.

1423. Harpe, Ulrich. **Looking back: memoirs of Ulrich Harpe.** Waterloo: The Author, 1971. 88 p. ill. Loc: OWTL.

The autobiography of Ulrich Harpe, who was born in Estonia in 1909, became a seaman, and emigrated to Ontario in 1951 with his family. The Harpes settled in Waterloo, Susanne Harpe finding a job as the matron of the residence of Waterloo Lutheran Seminary. The book emphasizes the Estonian and seafaring experiences. Period: 1909 - 1971.

1424. "John Philip Hauch." **Waterloo Historical Society**. 1944. 32: 36. ill. Loc: all.

A short obituary of the former pastor of Zion Evangelical Church in Kitchener. The article notes his missionary service in Japan and his periods as district superintendent of the Kitchener, Waterloo, and Stratford districts. Period: c1870 - 1944.

1425. Havlik, Jaroslav J. **The other side of freedom!**. Davis & Henderson, 19--. 129 p. ill. Loc: OKIT, OCCA.

The autobiography of a Czechoslovakian engineer who came to Canada in 1951 and established Havlik Enterprises Ltd in Preston. Much of the work describes his life in a Nazi concentration camp during the Second World War. He also expounds his views that everyone has the right to work, and that greater opportunity should be given to young people to learn a trade through apprenticeship. Period: 1931 - 1978.

1426. Rose, George Maclean. "Hay, Peter." **A cyclopaedia of Canadian biography: being chiefly men of the time**. Rose's National Biographical Series 1. Toronto: Rose Publishing Co., 1886. Pp. 299-300. Loc: OWTL, OWTU.

A brief biography of the blacksmith who came to Galt in 1861 and worked for Goldie & McCulloch and James Warnock & Co. before starting his own manufactory of edge tools in 1882. Period: 1861 - 1886.

1427. Hendel, George, Sr. **The life and times of George Hendel Sr**. The Author, 1990. 22 p. Loc: OKIT.

The autobiography of George Hendel Sr who was born in Austria-Hungary in 1904 and came to Kitchener in 1929. He started farming in the 1930s but by the 1950s had changed to construction. He recounts the difficulties of providing a living for his family, as well as the people and faith that sustained him. Period: 1904 - 1990.

1428. Middleton, Jesse Edgar and Landon, Fred. "William Henderson." **The Province of Ontario: a history, 1615-1927**. Toronto: Dominion Publishing Company, 1927. Vol. 4, pp. 374-375. Loc: OWTL, OWTU.

A profile of the bakery proprietor and Mayor of Waterloo. Period: 1910 - 1926.

1429. Rose, George Maclean. "Hendry, William." **A cyclopaedia of Canadian biography: being chiefly men of the time**. Rose's National Biographical Series 1. Toronto: Rose Publishing Co., 1886. Pp. 126-127. Loc: OWTL, OWTU.

An account of the early life and business experience of the manager of the Ontario Mutual Life Assurance Co. Period: 1849 - 1886.

1430. "William Hendry." **Waterloo Historical Society**. 1917. 5: 57. ill. Loc: all.

A brief biography of William Hendry, manager of the Mutual Life Assurance Company from 1870 to 1897. Period: 1834 - 1917.

1431. Kerr, James E. "A Canadian botanist." **Waterloo Historical Society**. 1930. 18: 235. Loc: all.

An obituary for William Herriot, the Galt naturalist and active member of the Waterloo Historical Society who was a skilled machinist and employed at Goldie and McCulloch in Galt for 45 years. Period: 1870 - 1930.

1432. Middleton, Jesse Edgar and Landon, Fred. "John E. Hett, M.B.." **The Province of Ontario: a history, 1615-1927**. Toronto: Dominion Publishing Company, 1927. Vol. 3, pp. 98-99. Loc: OWTL, OWTU.

A profile of the physician and medical researcher who was Mayor of Berlin in 1915 and 1916. Period: 1870 - 1926.

1433. Zimmerman, Idessa. "J.E. Hett, spiritualist." **Waterloo Historical Society**. 1984. 72: 158-160. ill. Loc: all.

A short biography of J.E. Hett, a physician and spiritualist, who was Mayor of Berlin when its name was changed to Kitchener in 1916. Period: 1891 - 1956.

1434. Middleton, Jesse Edgar and Landon, Fred. "Daniel Hibner." **The Province of Ontario: a history, 1615-1927**. Toronto: Dominion Publishing Company, 1927. Vol. 3, pp. 311-312. port. Loc: OWTL, OWTU.

A profile of the Berlin furniture manufacturer who was Mayor in 1902 and 1903, including details of his other business and community interests. Period: 1853 - 1926.

1435. "Norman Hervey High: June 15, 1913-December 4, 1974." **Canadian-German Folklore**. 1975. 5: 5. Loc: OWTU, OWT, OWTL, OWTUCG, OKIT.

A biographical tribute to a Mennonite teacher, born in Lincoln and later the first Dean of Arts at the University of Waterloo. Period: 1913 - 1974.

1436. Hilborn, Richard N. **The public career of P.R. Hilborn: a Waterloo County entrepreneur.** Wilfrid Laurier University (B.A. thesis, History), 1977. 39, 2, 9 p. bibl. Loc: OWTL, OCCA.

A biography of Percy Richard Hilborn (1886-1972) by his grandson, tracing his entrepreneurial rise and fall. Hilborn made his fortune with Canada Sand Papers Ltd and furniture factories but sold his businesses in the 1950s and 1960s, unable to adapt to the trend away from wooden furniture or to come to terms with the demands of the trade union movement. Hilborn was well known for his philanthropy and public service. Period: 1886 - 1972.

1437. **"W.H.S. salutes Gordon Verne Hilborn." Waterloo Historical Society.** 1963. 51: 6-7. ill. Loc: all.

A profile of the Blair osteopath and County Registrar of Deeds, who was president of the Waterloo Historical Society from 1944 to 1946. Period: 1900 - 1962.

1438. Middleton, Jesse Edgar and Landon, Fred. "Thomas Hilliard." **The Province of Ontario: a history, 1615-1927.** Toronto: Dominion Publishing Company, 1927. Vol. 4, pp. 474-475. port. Loc: OWTL, OWTU.

A profile of the former teacher and proprietor of the **Waterloo Chronicle** who founded the Dominion Life Assurance Co. in 1888 and the Waterloo Trust and Savings Co. in 1912. Period: 1880 - 1926.

1439. Middleton, Jesse Edgar and Landon, Fred. "William Louis Hilliard, M.B.." **The Province of Ontario: a history, 1615-1927.** Toronto: Dominion Publishing Company, 1927. Vol. 4, pp. 475-476. port. Loc: OWTL, OWTU.

A profile of the Waterloo physician and community leader. Period: 1969 - 1926.

1440. **"Norman O. Hipel." Waterloo Historical Society.** 1953. 41: 28. Loc: all.

An obituary of Hipel (1850-1953), owner of a Preston contracting business that built barns and skating rinks, and Liberal MPP for Waterloo South for thirteen years. Period: 1850 - 1953.

1441. Weissenborn, Georg K. "Johannes Holzer, the Canisius of Upper Canada (1817-1888)." **German-Canadian Yearbook / Deutschkanadisches Jahrbuch.** 1984. 8: 217-220. ill., bibl. Loc: OKIT, OWTL, OWTUCG.

A biography illustrated with a portrait and including references to the priest's time at St Agatha in the mid-nineteenth century. Period: 1848 - 1850.

1442. **"Dr Jerome F. Honsberger." Waterloo Historical Society.** 1937. 25: 272-274. ill. Loc: all.

A biography of Honsberger (1859-1937), physician, humanitarian and co-founder of the Freeport Sanatorium, who was also active with the Berlin Y.M.C.A. and the Berlin Board of Education. Period: 1859 - 1937.

1443. Horst, Samuel R. **A brief history of Sam R. Horst and his relationship.** 1988. 89 l. Loc: OWTUCGR.

A manuscript autobiography of an Old Order Mennonite farmer in Woolwich Township. As well as describing his working years and activities, the author relates his family's hardships including many illnesses and injuries. Period: 1903 - 1988.

1444. Middleton, Jesse Edgar and Landon, Fred. "Daniel Wesley Houston." **The Province of Ontario: a history, 1615-1927.** Toronto: Dominion Publishing Company, 1927. Vol. 3, pp. 292-293. Loc: OWTL, OWTU.

A profile of the Kitchener teacher and partner in an insurance agency. Period: 1867 - 1926.

1445. Middleton, Jesse Edgar and Landon, Fred. "Henry H. Huehnergard, M.D.." **The Province of Ontario: a history, 1615-1927.** Toronto: Dominion Publishing Company, 1927. Vol. 3, pp. 296-297. Loc: OWTL, OWTU.

A profile of the Kitchener physician and obstetrician. Period: 1884 - 1926.

1446. Kreiner, Leona Bramm. **Biography of Christian Esch Huehn.** Kitchener: The Author, 1973?. 4 p. Loc: OKIT.

A biographical sketch of Huehn (1864-1923), office manager of the Breithaupt Leather Company, builder of the Huehn Block and a founder of the Fischman Spring Company. He presented Kitchener with the site for St Mary's General Hospital. Period: 1864 - 1973.

1447. Fraser, Alexander. "Christopher Nicholas Huether." **A history of Ontario: its resources and development.** Toronto: The Canada History Co., 1907. Pp. 960-961. port. Loc: OWTL, OWTU.

A short biography of the proprietor of the Berlin Lion Brewery. Period: 1867 - 1906.

1448. Hunsberger, Albert. "Wilson A. Hunsberger." **Waterloo Historical Society.** 1982. 70: 4-5. ill. Loc: all.

A profile of the president of the Waterloo Historical Society in 1963-64, noting his contributions in teaching and social work as well as his service with the Mennonite Central Committee and the Waterloo Lung Association. Period: 1919 - 1982.

1449. Hunsberger, Wilson. "Albert I. Hunsberger." **Waterloo Historical Society.** 1982. 70: 6-7. ill. Loc: all.

A biography of the president of the Waterloo Historical Society in 1981-1982, noting his career in education and service on many boards including the Conrad Grebel College, the Fairview Mennonite Homes, the Chesley Lake Camp and the University of Waterloo Senate. Period: 1912 - 1982.

1450. "From the **Galt Reporter** files of 1907." **Waterloo Historical Society.** 1962. 50: 21. Loc: all.

An obituary of William Anthony Husband, early town clerk of Preston. Period: 1823 - 1907.

SURNAMES BEGINNING WITH J

1451. "James P. Jaffray." **Waterloo Historical Society.** 1934. 22: 147-148. Loc: all.

A biographical sketch that notes Jaffray's many accomplishments. Besides being publisher of the **Galt Reporter**, a weekly newspaper started by his grandfather, he was also a typesetter, telegraph operator, Commissioner for British Columbia at Chicago's World Fair, Canadian Government Immigration Inspector in Scotland, politician, and publisher of the magazine **The Cycle Age** which later became **The Motor Age.** Period: 1854 - 1934.

1452. Rose, George Maclean. "Jaffray, William." **A cyclopaedia of Canadian biography: being chiefly men of the time.** Rose's National Biographical Series 1. Toronto: Rose Publishing Co., 1886. Pp. 197-198. Loc: OWTL, OWTU.

A biography of the early editor of the **Galt Reporter** and the **Berlin Chronicle** who was also postmaster for Berlin and held many public offices. Period: 1849 - 1886.

1453. Uttley, W.V. "William Jaffray: publisher and postmaster." **Waterloo Historical Society.** 1929. 17: 149-152. ill. Loc: all.

A biography of the founder of the **Berlin Chronicle and Waterloo Reformers' Gazette** who was postmaster and Mayor of Berlin. Information about other members of the Jaffray family is included. Period: 1844 - 1896.

1454. "Arnold Jansen." **Waterloo Historical Society.** 1949. 37: 44. Loc: all.

A short biography of the owner of the Jansen Optical Company in Elmira, who died on 17 May 1949. Period: 1868 - 1949.

1455. Paetkau, Henry. **Jacob H. Janzen (1878-1950): a man with a mission to his people.** Institute of Anabaptist-Mennonite Studies, Conrad Grebel College, 1977. 33 p., 4 p. bibl. Loc: OWTUCG.

A biographical sketch of Jacob Heinrich Janzen, the Russian Mennonite who became bishop of the Waterloo-Kitchener United Mennonite Church. Janzen's roles as writer, educator and community leader are appraised. Period: 1878 - 1950.

1456. Paetkau, Henry. "Jacob H. Janzen: a minister of rare magnitude." **Mennogespräch.** 1988. 6,1: 1-4. ill. Loc: OWTUCG, OKIT.

A summary of the life, ideas and accomplishments of Jacob Heinrich Janzen (1878-1950). He was a Russian Mennonite preacher, teacher and writer who became bishop of the Waterloo-Kitchener United Mennonite Church. Period: 1924 - 1950.

SURNAMES BEGINNING WITH K

1457. Page, Frank E. "The printer of Roseville." **Waterloo Historical Society.** 1957. 45: 52. Loc: all.

A short article indicating that Louis M. Kaiser at the age of 90 was the oldest active printer in Canada. He had operated his printing business in Roseville for 65 years. Period: 1867 - 1957.

1458. Ham, Mary C. "Grandmother Kaufman: Mary Ratz Kaufman, December 14, 1856 - December 24, 1943." **Waterloo Historical Society.** 1990. 78: 62-68. ill. Loc: all.

Recollections of Mary Kaufman by the youngest of her grandchildren, who describes her practicality in the household and her dedication to her church and to community causes such as the Y.W.C.A. Period: 1931 - 1943.

1459. Middleton, Jesse Edgar and Landon, Fred. "Alvin Ratz Kaufman." **The Province of Ontario: a history, 1615-1927.** Toronto: Dominion Publishing Company, 1927. Vol. 3, pp. 185-187. port. Loc: OWTL, OWTU.

A profile of the Kitchener businessman and city planning advocate, including a summary genealogy and account of the businesses promoted by his father, Jacob Kaufman. Period: 1877 - 1926.

1460. Montonen, Susan and Milroy, Beth Moore and Wismer, Susan. "Community-building in Berlin: Mary Ratz Kaufman, 1856-1943." **Waterloo Historical Society.** 1990. 78: 54-61. ill. Loc: all.

An account of the associational leadership roles of the wife of Jacob Kaufman, who was a successful industrialist and prominent member of the Berlin community elite. Period: 1856 - 1943.

1461. "Mrs Mary Kaufman." **Waterloo Historical Society**. 1943. 31: 47. ill. Loc: all.

An obituary of the woman who contributed significantly to community development in Berlin/Kitchener from the 1870s to the 1940s. In addition to her many accomplishments in the area of hospital voluntary work, Mrs Kaufman was instrumental in the establishment and growth of the local Y.W.C.A. Period: 1856 - 1943.

1462. Tokyo Y.W.C.A. **Emma R. Kaufman and the Tokyo YWCA**. Tokyo: Editorial Committee, 1963. 68 p. ill. Loc: OKITW.

A biography mentioning the Kaufman family background in Berlin, Ontario and emphasizing Emma's life and accomplishments in Japan. Period: 1881 - 1963.

1463. Toole, W.X. "A.R. Kaufman: the man behind the name." **Waterloo Historical Society**. 1983. 71: 102-111. ill. Loc: all.

A brief biography of the Kitchener industrialist by a friend and former employee. The article relates anecdotes about Kaufman's relationships with his workers and his many outside interests, including the Parents' Information Bureau which promoted birth control. Period: 1885 - 1979.

1464. Middleton, Jesse Edgar and Landon, Fred. "J.H. Kennedy." **The Province of Ontario: a history, 1615-1927**. Toronto: Dominion Publishing Company, 1927. Vol. 3, pp. 192-193. Loc: OWTL, OWTU.

A profile of the secretary-treasurer of Malcolm and Hill Ltd, which bought out Daniel Hibner's furniture business in 1920. Period: 1920 - 1926.

1465. "James E. Kerr." **Waterloo Historical Society**. 1934. 22: 149-150. Loc: all.

A short biography of the Galt citizen who was a member of the Waterloo Historical Society from 1915 until his death in 1934. Period: 1848 - 1934.

1466. Nicolson, Murray W. **Woodside and the Victorian family of John King**. Studies in Archaeology, Architecture and History. Ottawa: National Historic Sites and Parks Branch, Parks Canada, 1984. 117 p. ill., bibl. Loc: OKIT, OWT, OWTUR.

An account of the family life of John King, especially during his tenancy of the Woodside estate in Berlin from 1886 to 1893. The purpose of the study was to document the historical significance of the property and its connections with Prime Minister W.L. Mackenzie King, as context for its designation as a National Historic Park. In narrating John King's early life in the household of his uncle, Dougall McDougall, and his Berlin law practice from 1869 to 1893, the author provides some insights into the Berlin community elite from the mid-1850s. He also describes the process by which the dilapidated Woodside property was acquired in the 1940s by members of the North Waterloo Liberal Conservative Association (organized as the Woodside Trust) and Mackenzie King's interest in the early phase of the restoration project. Period: 1850 - 1962.

1467. Pennefather, R.S. **New light on John King: a note**. 1989. 9 p. bibl. Loc: OKIT.

Brief descriptions of various fist fights in which John King, father of W.L.M. King, was involved from 1877 to 1886. The author suggests that John King's image as ineffectual and passive should be reconsidered. Period: 1877 - 1886.

1468. Rose, George Maclean. "King, John." **A cyclopaedia of Canadian biography: being chiefly men of the time**. Rose's National Biographical Series 1. Toronto: Rose Publishing Co., 1886. Pp. 156-158. Loc: OWTL, OWTU.

An account of the family background and legal practice of William Lyon Mackenzie King's father, who lived in Berlin from 1857 in the household of his uncle Dougall McDougall and set up as a lawyer in 1869. Period: 1857 - 1886.

1469. Schmidt, Grace. "Mackenzie King Centennial Colloquium." **Waterloo Historical Society**. 1974. 62: 76. Loc: all.

A short report on the colloquium held in December 1974 at the University of Waterloo. Papers on King's political career were presented by historians and tapes of his speeches were played. Period: 1874 - 1974.

1470. Staebler, H.L. "Mackenzie King." **Waterloo Historical Society**. 1950. 38: 10-13. ill. Loc: all.

A short tribute to the former prime minister by a boyhood friend who recalls King as a student and outlines his achievements. Period: 1874 - 1950.

1471. Middleton, Jesse Edgar and Landon, Fred. "Oliver Kinzie." **The Province of Ontario: a history, 1615-1927**. Toronto: Dominion Publishing Company, 1927. Vol. 4, pp. 384-385. Loc: OWTL, OWTU.

A profile of the president and general manager of the Walker Bin and Store Fixture Co., Kitchener, including an account of the establishment of that business. Period: 1890 - 1926.

1472. Middleton, Jesse Edgar and Landon, Fred. "Oscar Roy Kleinschmidt." **The Province of Ontario: a history, 1615-1927**. Toronto: Dominion Publishing

Company, 1927. Vol. 4, p. 470. Loc: OWTL, OWTU.
A profile of a partner in the Studebaker dealership of Kitchener. Period: 1902 - 1926.

1473. Campbell, Alexander D., Dr. "The search for Dr Klinkert." **Waterloo Historical Society**. 1982. 70: 50-52. Loc: all.
A brief account of the research to identify the man described in Uttley's history of Kitchener as the first doctor. The author provides information on both Dr Edward Klinckhardt and Dr Theodore Klinkhardt. Period: 1809 - 1974.

1474. "George Klinck." **Waterloo Historical Society**. 1944. 32: 33-35. ill. Loc: all.
An obituary of the Elmira-born watchmaker turned grain and seed dealer who also published **The Elmira Signet** and was interested in the Elmira Mechanics' Institute and continuing education. Period: 1862 - 1944.

1475. Landon, Fred. "Otto Julius Klotz." **Waterloo Historical Society**. 1952. 40: 30-32. Loc: all.
An address given at the unveiling of a bronze tablet in Preston Town Hall commemorating the achievements of Dr Otto Julius Klotz, Preston-born surveyor and engineer. Period: 1852 - 1952.

1476. Middleton, Jesse Edgar and Landon, Fred. "Hon. Jacob E. Klotz." **The Province of Ontario: a history, 1615-1927**. Toronto: Dominion Publishing Company, 1927. Vol. 3, pp. 172-173. Loc: OWTL, OWTU.
A biography of the promoter of the Canadian Office and School Furniture Company who was Mayor of Preston in 1901-2. Period: 1840 - 1924.

1477. Middleton, Jesse Edgar and Landon, Fred. "Otto Klotz." **The Province of Ontario: a history, 1615-1927**. Toronto: Dominion Publishing Company, 1927. Vol. 3, pp. 171-172. port. Loc: OWTL, OWTU.
A biography of Preston's leading citizen, including details of his public service especially to education. Period: 1838 - 1900.

1478. "Otto Julius Klotz." **Waterloo Historical Society**. 1914. 2: 50. Loc: all.
A note of the Preston native's appointment as Dominion Astronomer. Period: 1852 - 1914.

1479. Stewart, R. Meldrum. "Dr Otto Klotz: Director of the Dominion Observatory, Ottawa." **Journal of the Royal Astronomical Society of Canada**. 1924. 18, 1-2: 1-8. ill. Loc: OKITW.
An obituary of Otto Julius Klotz (1852-1923), the son of Otto Klotz of Preston, recording his education, scientific achievements and writings.

The article was separately printed in 1924 by the University of Toronto Press. Period: 1852 - 1923.

1480. "S.R. Knechtel." **Waterloo Historical Society**. 1947. 35: 50. Loc: all.
A short obituary of the Evangelical Church minister who served for 64 years in various churches, including the Olivet Evangelical Church, Kitchener. Period: 1880 - 1947.

1481. Middleton, Jesse Edgar and Landon, Fred. "David C. Knipfel." **The Province of Ontario: a history, 1615-1927**. Toronto: Dominion Publishing Company, 1927. Vol. 4, pp. 616-617. Loc: OWTL, OWTU.
A profile of the founder of Berlin's Pearl Laundry. Period: 1889 - 1926.

1482. "Rev. Robert E. Knowles, B.A.." **Waterloo Historical Society**. 1946. 34: 40-41. ill. Loc: all.
An obituary of the minister of Knox's Presbyterian Church, Galt, who was also a writer and lecturer and an active golfer and curler. Period: 1868 - 1946.

1483. Middleton, Jesse Edgar and Landon, Fred. "Bernhard Koehler." **The Province of Ontario: a history, 1615-1927**. Toronto: Dominion Publishing Company, 1927. Vol. 3, pp. 109-111. Loc: OWTL, OWTU.
A profile of the superintendent of Kitchener's parks from 1914 to 1924, including a detailed account of the improvements to the park system and references to the prejudices expressed against German-born Koehler during the First World War. Period: 1914 - 1924.

1484. "Carl Kranz." **Waterloo Historical Society**. 1938. 26: 47-48. ill. Loc: all.
A brief biography of Kranz (c1869-1938) who was Mayor of Berlin in 1904 and 1905 and an advocate of hydro-electric power. Period: c1869 - 1938.

1485. Middleton, Jesse Edgar and Landon, Fred. "Carl Kranz." **The Province of Ontario: a history, 1615-1927**. Toronto: Dominion Publishing Company, 1927. Vol. 3, pp. 215-216. Loc: OWTL, OWTU.
A profile of the insurance broker and Mayor of Berlin in 1904 and 1905, with short biographies of his father, Hugo and his grandfather, Carl. Period: 1869 - 1926.

1486. Rose, George Maclean. "Kranz, Hugo." **A cyclopaedia of Canadian biography: being chiefly men of the time**. Rose's National Biographical Series 1. Toronto: Rose Publishing Co., 1886. Pp. 546-547. Loc: OWTL, OWTU.
A biography of the Berlin community leader and M.P. for North Waterloo. Period: 1851 - 1886.

1487. "Diamond anniversary." **Waterloo Historical Society.** 1967. 55: 11. Loc: all.

A note of the 60th wedding anniversary of Mr and Mrs Lewis Krupp of Galt, married in 1907 in the Galt Methodist Church on Ainslie Street. Period: 1907 - 1967.

SURNAMES BEGINNING WITH L

1488. Fraser, Alexander. "Henry George Lackner, M.P.P.." **A history of Ontario: its resources and development.** Toronto: The Canada History Co., 1907. Pp. 964-966. port. Loc: OWTL, OWTU.

A short biography of the Hawkesville-born physician who was Berlin's first medical officer of health and active in municipal and provincial politics. Period: 1851 - 1906.

1489. Middleton, Jesse Edgar and Landon, Fred. "Harry Mackie Lackner, M.D.." **The Province of Ontario: a history, 1615-1927.** Toronto: Dominion Publishing Company, 1927. Vol. 3, p. 100. Loc: OWTL, OWTU.

A short profile of the Kitchener physician, son of Dr H.G. Lackner. Period: 1883 - 1926.

1490. Middleton, Jesse Edgar and Landon, Fred. "Henry George Lackner, M.D., C.M.." **The Province of Ontario: a history, 1615-1927.** Toronto: Dominion Publishing Company, 1927. Vol. 3, pp. 99-100. port. Loc: OWTL, OWTU.

A profile of the Berlin physician and community leader who was born at Hawkesville in 1851, elected Sheriff of Waterloo County in 1912 and died in 1926. Period: 1851 - 1926.

1491. Rose, George Maclean. "Lackner, Dr Henry G.." **A cyclopaedia of Canadian biography: being chiefly men of the time.** Rose's National Biographical Series 1. Toronto: Rose Publishing Co., 1886. Pp. 148-149. Loc: OWTL, OWTU.

A biography of the Berlin physician and community leader. Period: 1851 - 1886.

1492. "Anthony Lacourse, Berlin." **The Canadian biographical dictionary and portrait gallery of eminent and self-made men, Ontario volume.** Toronto: American Biographical Publishing Co., 1880. Pp. 525-526. Loc: OWTL, OWTU.

A brief biography of the Quebec-born junior judge of Waterloo County. Period: 1873 - 1880.

1493. Reist, Agnes. "Mrs Richard Lamb." **Waterloo Historical Society.** 1972. 60: 7. ill. Loc: all.

A profile of the Waterloo Historical Society president for 1972-1973, noting her contributions in journalism, history, conservation and philately. Period: 1819 - 1972.

1494. "Edward D. Lang." **Waterloo Historical Society.** 1952. 40: 49. Loc: all.

A brief obituary of the Kitchener retailer who served the King Street Baptist Church as Sunday School superintendent for 24 years and was on the board of the Y.M.C.A. for 55 years. Period: 1867 - 1952.

1495. Middleton, Jesse Edgar and Landon, Fred. "Oscar Lauber." **The Province of Ontario: a history, 1615-1927.** Toronto: Dominion Publishing Company, 1927. Vol 4, pp. 619-620. Loc: OWTL, OWTU.

A profile of the vice-president and superintendent of the George J. Lippert Table Co. of Kitchener. Period: 1881 - 1926.

1496. Middleton, Jesse Edgar and Landon, Fred. "Philip S. Lautenschlager." **The Province of Ontario: a history, 1615-1927.** Toronto: Dominion Publishing Company, 1927. Vol. 3, p. 293. port. Loc: OWTL, OWTU.

A profile of the Berlin businessman and community leader. Period: 1840 - 1926.

1497. Bitzer, Irmgard C. "Moritz Lindner, Berlin toymaker." **Waterloo Historical Society.** 1971. 59: 74-76. ill. Loc: all.

A biographical sketch of Moritz Lindner (1816-1898), a German immigrant who came to Berlin with his family in 1867 and became a toymaker. An example of one of the toys he made is the "Weihnachtsmanner," now in Doon Pioneer Village. Period: 1867 - 1898.

1498. Fraser, Alexander. "George Lippert." **A history of Ontario: its resources and development.** Toronto: The Canada History Co., 1907. Pp. 975-6. Loc: OWTL, OWTU.

A short biography of the Waterloo furniture manufacturer. Period: 1850 - 1906.

1499. "James Livingston, Baden." **The Canadian biographical dictionary and portrait gallery of eminent and self-made men, Ontario volume.** Toronto: American Biographical Publishing Co., 1880. Pp. 695-696. Loc: OWTL, OWTU.

A biography of the prominent manufacturer and member of the Ontario Legislature, who came to Conestogo in 1857 and developed a flax-milling empire based in Baden. Period: 1857 - 1880.

1500. Livingston, Harry P. "James Livingston." **Waterloo Historical Society.** 1921. 9: 189-191. ill. Loc: all.

A brief biography of James Livingston (1838-1920), a Baden businessman who manufactured linen cloth and linseed oil. Period: 1838 - 1920.

1501. Longo, Michael D. "Castle Kilbride." **Waterloo Historical Society**. 1985. 73: 38-48. ill. Loc: all.

A description of the grand, mid-Victorian home in Baden with a brief biography of its owner, James Livingston, the industrious entrepreneur who founded and bought out various mills manufacturing flax, carpet yarn, twine, cotton, wool and linseed oil. Livingston was also involved in the fire insurance business and in politics. Period: 1864 - 1949.

1502. Middleton, Jesse Edgar and Landon, Fred. "Dr John Milton Livingston." **The Province of Ontario: a history, 1615-1927**. Toronto: Dominion Publishing Company, 1927. Vol. 3, pp. 294-295. Loc: OWTL, OWTU.

A profile of the Waterloo physician whose great-uncles James and John developed the J. and J. Livingston Flax Mills. Period: 1890 - 1926.

1503. Veitch, Sherry. "James Livingston of Baden." **Waterloo Historical Society**. 1967. 55: 59-60. ill. Loc: all.

A biographical sketch of James Livingston (1838-1921), a Scottish immigrant who developed a flax and linseed oil empire based at Baden. Period: 1838 - 1921.

1504. Middleton, Jesse Edgar and Landon, Fred. "W.M.O. Lochead." **The Province of Ontario: a history, 1615-1927**. Toronto: Dominion Publishing Company, 1927. Vol. 3, pp. 118-119. Loc: OWTL, OWTU.

A profile of the district manager of the Mutual Life Assurance Co. of Canada, including details of his roles in the militia and local associations. Period: 1905 - 1926.

1505. "Rev. John James Lowe." **Waterloo Historical Society**. 1953. 41: 29. Loc: all.

A biographical sketch of Lowe (c1854-1951), known as "the marrying parson," who had charge of St Andrew's Mission in Galt and was first minister of St Andrew's Presbyterian Church. Period: c1854 - 1951.

1506. "Never missed a day's work in 47 years." **Waterloo Historical Society**. 1962. 50: 93. Loc: all.

A note about Fred Luft of Kitchener, who worked at the Dominion Rubber Company for 47 years without a day's absence. Period: 1915 - 1962.

SURNAMES BEGINNING WITH M

1507. Rose, George Maclean. "Macdougall, Dougall." **A cyclopaedia of Canadian biography: being chiefly men of the time**. Rose's National Biographical Series 1. Toronto: Rose Publishing Co., 1886. Pp. 145-147. Loc: OWTL, OWTU.

A biography of the man who came to Berlin in 1857 as editor of the **Berlin Telegraph and German Canadian** and was appointed Registrar of Waterloo County in 1864. Period: 1857 - 1886.

1508. Middleton, Jesse Edgar and Landon, Fred. "Robert Alexander MacGillivray." **The Province of Ontario: a history, 1615-1927**. Toronto: Dominion Publishing Company, 1927. Vol. 3, pp. 261-263. port. Loc: OWTL, OWTU.

A profile of the businessman involved with various furniture companies in Hespeler, Preston, Kitchener and Waterloo. Period: 1902 - 1926.

1509. Klinck, Carl F. "Professor MacMechan, native of western Ontario." **Waterloo Historical Society**. 1952. 40: 38-40. Loc: all.

An address commemorating the achievements of the Berlin-born academic who left the city at the age of four with his family. There are some details about MacMechan's father, the Rev. John MacMechan, minister at St Andrew's Presbyterian Church in Berlin. Period: 1852 - 1952.

1510. "Col. J. Norman MacRae, M.C., V.D.." **Waterloo Historical Society**. 1953. 41: 47. Loc: all.

An obituary of MacRae, Galt osteopath, veteran of the First World War and dog fancier. Period: 1914 - 1953.

1511. "Mrs Margaret Madden." **Waterloo Historical Society**. 1959. 47: 7. ill. Loc: all.

A brief biographical note about Mrs Madden, Waterloo County's oldest resident, who placed the cornerstone of the Kitchener Young Men's Club's housing project for elderly people in 1959. Period: 1855 - 1960.

1512. "North Waterloo's oldest voter [WRP]." **Waterloo Historical Society**. 1958. 46: 57. Loc: all.

A note about Mrs Margaret Madden who voted at the age of 103. Period: 1855 - 1958.

1513. Horst, Isaac R. **Thou art Peter: a story of the pioneer Peter Martin and the Woolwich Mennonites**. Mount Forest: Isaac R. Horst, 1983. 37 p. ill. Loc: OKIT, OWRBL, OWRE, OWRSJ, OWRW, OWTL, OWTUR.

A short history of Peter Martin's family, beginning with his grandfather's birth in Switzerland. The main focus is on Peter Martin himself, his accomplishments, interests, and religious devotion, but family connections with Woolwich Township descendants in the early 1980s are mentioned. Peter Martin's house was moved to Doon Heritage Crossroads and the Martin Meeting House, north of Waterloo, is named after him. Period: 1800 - 1983.

1514. Middleton, Jesse Edgar and Landon, Fred. "Jacob Bachert Martin." **The Province of Ontario: a history, 1615-1927.** Toronto: Dominion Publishing Company, 1927. Vol. 4, pp. 472-473. Loc: OWTL, OWTU.

A profile of the partner in the Waterloo shoe-manufacturing business, Valentine and Martin. Period: 1873 - 1926.

1515. Patterson, Nancy-Lou. "Simeon Eby Martin (1892-1984)." **Waterloo Historical Society.** 1985. 73: 80-90. ill. Loc: all.

A transcript of an interview with the carpenter Simeon Martin about his life before the death of his wife, Barbara (nee Snyder) in 1977. Martin's stories convey his deep feelings for his Mennonite heritage and faith. Details of family names and birth dates are provided in the introduction. Period: 1892 - 1977.

1516. Smalldon, John L. "Allen D. Martin, President 1985-1986." **Waterloo Historical Society.** 1986. 74: 4-5. ill. Loc: all.

A brief profile of the current president, describing his interests and roles in various community organizations. Period: 1961 - 1985.

1517. Taylor, Ryan. **Interview with Matthias Martin.** 1990. 8 l. Loc: OKIT.

A summary of the interview with the Old Order Mennonite on his farm. Topics include Mr Martin's collections of bottles, lanterns and bells; the making of harnesses, horse blankets and rope; life on the farm; school days; charming; and home remedies. Period: 1906 - 1990.

1518. Middleton, Jesse Edgar and Landon, Fred. "Arthur B. McBride." **The Province of Ontario: a history, 1615-1927.** Toronto: Dominion Publishing Company, 1927. Pp. 546-547. Loc: OWTL, OWTU.

A profile of the Waterloo lawyer who began in partnership with Frederick Colquhoun. Period: 1889 - 1926.

1519. Burton, Patricia. "Memoirs of David McCloy, 1832-1917." **Waterloo Historical Society.** 1971. 59: 82-88. Loc: all.

A biographical sketch of David McCloy, an Irish immigrant who settled in Mornington Township in 1857 with his wife Annie Byrens. A personal account of his family's emigration and his early life in Waterloo County is quoted and information about David's eight children is also given. Period: 1832 - 1917.

1520. Fraser, Alexander. "Hugh McCulloch." **A history of Ontario: its resources and development.** Toronto: The Canada History Co., 1907. Loc: OWTL, OWTU.

A short biography of the Galt industrialist, including a description of the major business he founded with James Goldie in 1859. Period: 1826 - 1906.

1521. "Hugh McCulloch." **Waterloo Historical Society.** 1927. 15: 387. Loc: all.

A profile of the co-founder of the large manufacturing firm of Goldie and McCulloch, later Babcock and Wilcox. McCulloch (1826-1910) came to Galt in 1851. Period: 1826 - 1910.

1522. "Robert Osborne McCulloch." **Waterloo Historical Society.** 1943. 31: 48. ill. Loc: all.

An obituary of the businessman who became president of the Goldie-McCulloch Company and of Galt Metal Industries. Active in community affairs, McCulloch served as president of the Progressive Conservative Association for South Waterloo and was a member of the Presbyterian Church. Period: 1864 - 1943.

1523. Fraser, Alexander. "John McDougall." **A history of Ontario: its resources and development.** Toronto: The Canada History Co., 1907. Pp. 961-962. Loc: OWTL, OWTU.

A short biography of the Waterloo hardware merchant who became clerk of the County Court and registrar of the Surrogate Court from 1877 to 1906. Period: 1837 - 1906.

1524. McIlwraith, Andrew. **The diaries of Andrew McIlwraith, 1857-1862.** Roy G. Allan, 366 p. Loc: OKIT.

Diaries of a Scottish draughtsman and patternmaker who lived in Galt and Ayr. Entries describe the 1857 Canadian election, McIlwraith's visits to Mary Goldie whom he later married, and his work with Goldie and McCulloch. There are many references to Galt and Ayr people. Eight copies of this diary were typed by Roy G. Allan for his wife, Dorothy Isobel (Nichol) Allan, who was a granddaughter of Andrew McIlwraith. Period: 1857 - 1862.

1525. "David Graham McIntosh, K.C.." **Waterloo Historical Society.** 1940. 28: 137-139. ill. Loc: all.

A short biography of David Graham McIntosh (1889-1940), lawyer and veteran of the First World

War. He was company commander of the North Waterloo Regiment, later changed to the Scots Fusiliers of Canada in 1927. Period: 1889 - 1940.

1526. Middleton, Jesse Edgar and Landon, Fred. "George McIntyre." **The Province of Ontario: a history, 1615-1927.** Toronto: Dominion Publishing Company, 1927. Vol. 4, pp. 544-545. Loc: OWTL, OWTU.
A profile of the teacher who was a partner with I.S.K. Weaver in the Berlin insurance business. Period: 1850 - 1910.

1527. Middleton, Jesse Edgar and Landon, Fred. "Victor Stanley McIntyre." **The Province of Ontario: a history, 1615-1927.** Toronto: Dominion Publishing Company, 1927. Vol. 3, p. 219. Loc: OWTL, OWTU.
A profile of the manager of the Hydro-Electric Gas and Street Railway Department of Kitchener, who began his career with the Berlin Gas Company in 1898. Period: 1881 - 1926.

1528. "Centenarian." **Waterloo Historical Society.** 1969. 57: 83. Loc: all.
A note of Sarah McLellan's 100th birthday in Galt. She recalls her nursing days, when it was considered a disgrace for married women to work. Period: 1869 - 1969.

1529. Best, John C. **Thomas Baker McQuesten: public works, politics and imagination.** Hamilton: Corinth Press, 1991. Pp. 3-5. Loc: OWTU.
A biography of the Ontario cabinet minister, including a reference to his father Isaac's "fatal fascination with manufacturing", most notably the partnership with John Harvey in a Hespeler knitting mill which failed in 1886. Period: 1881 - 1886.

1530. Devitt, E.H. "Hon. Samuel Merner." **Waterloo Historical Society.** 1940. 28: 139-141. Loc: all.
A short biography of "Honest Sam" Merner (1823-1908), entrepreneur, and politician. Period: 1823 - 1908.

1531. Fraser, Alexander. "Samuel Merner." **A history of Ontario: its resources and development.** Toronto: The Canada History Co., 1907. Pp. 1276-1278. Loc: OWTL, OWTU.
A profile of the entrepreneur who developed an extensive trade in blacksmithing and wagon- and carriage-building in New Hamburg and Waterloo into a wide range of other commercial and industrial enterprises. After eighteen years as Reeve of New Hamburg, Merner represented South Waterloo in the Dominion Parliament from 1878 to 1882 and was made a Senator in 1887. Period: 1823 - 1906.

1532. "Frederick Merner, New Hamburg." **The Canadian biographical dictionary and portrait gallery of eminent and self-made men, Ontario volume.** Toronto: American Biographical Publishing Co., 1880. Pp. 334-335. Loc: OWTL, OWTU.
Brother of Samuel, owner of successful carriage and wagon-making businesses in New Hamburg and Waterloo, and very active in community affairs. Period: 1837 - 1880.

1533. Rose, George Maclean. "Merner, Samuel." **A cyclopaedia of Canadian biography: being chiefly men of the time.** Rose's National Biographical Series 1. Toronto: Rose Publishing Co., 1886. Pp. 418-419. Loc: OWTL, OWTU.
A biography of the prominent citizen of New Hamburg who won the South Waterloo seat in the Dominion Parliament in 1878. Period: 1837 - 1886.

1534. "Samuel Merner, M.P., New Hamburg." **The Canadian biographical dictionary and portrait gallery of eminent and self-made men, Ontario volume.** Toronto: American Biographical Publishing Co., 1880. Pp. 145-146. Loc: OWTL, OWTU.
A biography of New Hamburg's leading businessman and community leader and Member of Parliament for South Waterloo. Period: 1837 - 1880.

1535. Bloomfield, Elizabeth. "Alexander Millar, K.C. (1835-1918), Berlin business lawyer." **Waterloo Historical Society.** 1989. 77: 87-99. ill. Loc: all.
A brief biography and appraisal of the business, political and community roles of an early lawyer who played an important part in the incorporation and development of the Economical Mutual Fire Insurance Company, the Mutual Life Assurance Company, the Berlin Board of Trade and the Berlin Waterworks Company. Millar was also solicitor for the Berlin Town Council and Waterloo County Council. Period: 1861 - 1918.

1536. Fraser, Alexander. "Alexander Millar, K.C.." **A history of Ontario: its resources and development.** Toronto: The Canada History Co., 1907. Pp. 966-967. Loc: OWTL, OWTU.
A short biography of the Berlin lawyer who was very active in municipal politics and the business community. Period: 1835 - 1906.

1537. Kraemer, Marie. "Margaret and Kenneth Millar." **Waterloo Historical Society.** 1972. 60: 98-99. Loc: all.
A short profile of the husband and wife team of mystery writers who grew up in Kitchener. After attending university elsewhere, the couple returned to Kitchener from 1938 to 1941, while Kenneth taught at the Kitchener-Waterloo

Collegiate and Vocational School. They then left for the United States where their writing careers were established. Period: c1915 - 1971.

1538. Rose, George Maclean. "Millar, Alexander." **A cyclopaedia of Canadian biography: being chiefly men of the time.** Rose's National Biographical Series 1. Toronto: Rose Publishing Co., 1886. Pp. 514-515. Loc: OWTL, OWTU.
A brief profile of the Berlin lawyer, including references to his militia service, freemasonry and political ambitions. Period: 1835 - 1886.

1539. "Kitchener's oldest merchant retires." **Waterloo Historical Society.** 1961. 49: 63. Loc: all.
A note of the retirement of Jacob D. Miller from his business, Miller and Hohmeier, founded in 1912. Period: 1912 - 1961.

1540. Rose, George Maclean. "Miller, William." **A cyclopaedia of Canadian biography: being chiefly men of the time.** Rose's National Biographical Series 1. Toronto: Rose Publishing Co., 1886. P. 405. Loc: OWTL, OWTU.
A brief biography of the County Court Judge at Galt. Period: 1853 - 1886.

1541. "William Miller, Galt." **The Canadian biographical dictionary and portrait gallery of eminent and self-made men, Ontario volume.** Toronto: American Biographical Publishing Co., 1880. p. 703. Loc: OWTL, OWTU.
A brief biography of the Waterloo County judge appointed in 1853. Period: 1853 - 1880.

1542. Middleton, Jesse Edgar and Landon, Fred. "Michael H. Montag." **The Province of Ontario: a history, 1615-1927.** Toronto: Dominion Publishing Company, 1927. Vol. 4, pp. 550-551. Loc: OWTL, OWTU.
A profile of the co-founder of The Quality Mattress Co. and the Waterloo Bedding Co. Period: 1903 - 1926.

1543. Fraser, Alexander. "George Moore." **A history of Ontario: its resources and development.** Toronto: The Canada History Co., 1907. Pp. 1274-1276. Loc: OWTL, OWTU.
Livestock breeder and proprietor of Canada's largest hop fields, with interests in produce dealing and several industrial enterprises, Moore also served on the Waterloo Town Council and the Waterloo County Council. Period: 1845 - 1906.

1544. "John Douglas Moore." **Waterloo Historical Society.** 1917. 5: 52. ill. Loc: all.
A short biography of the farmer, promoter of the Galt, Preston and Hespeler Railway, Liberal politician and MPP for South Waterloo from 1891 to 1898. Period: 1843 - 1917.

1545. Motz, W.J. "John Motz." **Waterloo Historical Society.** 1939. 27: 90-91. ill. Loc: all.
A brief biography of John Motz (1830-1911), the German immigrant who published the Liberal newspaper, the **Berliner Journal.** Period: 1830 - 1911.

1546. "William John Motz." **Waterloo Historical Society.** 1946. 34: 39-40. ill. Loc: all.
A short biography of the publisher of the **Kitchener Record** who began his publishing career with his father at the **Berliner Journal.** He served for a long period as president of the Canadian Daily Newspapers Association and the Ontario Provincial Dailies Association and was also active in many community organizations such as the Kitchener Chamber of Commerce, the Westmount Golf and Country Club and the St Mary's Hospital Board. Period: 1870 - 1946.

1547. Moyer, Samuel S. **The autobiography of Samuel S. Moyer.** 1940?. 28 p. ill. Loc: OWRE.
The reminiscences of Samuel S. Moyer, tenth of thirteen children, who managed the Dominion Button Factory in Berlin/Kitchener and later owned his own button works. He relates his financial difficulties, spiritual conversion and family life. Information about descendants of the Moyer family who came from Pennsylvania and settled in Waterloo County is also given. Period: 1850? 1940?

1548. McAndless, J.E. "Ephraim Munson: the Grand River squatter." **Families.** 1977. 16,3: 134-140. Loc: OKIT, OWTL, OWTU.
A narrative of the ancestors and descendants of one of the first settlers of Dumfries Township. Munson began as a squatter who built a small flour mill on the Grand River and later purchased 100 acres in the 6th concession. Period: 1800 - 1919.

1549. Cowan, Jennie F. "Isaac W. Myers who fought to help the American slaves." **Waterloo Historical Society.** 1966. 54: 28-30. ill. Loc: all.
A collection of excerpts from letters written to Thomas Cowan by Waterloo County native Isaac Myers from the United States in the 1860s. There are only passing references to Woolwich Township and the Clochmohr property. Period: 1842 - 1893.

1550. Campbell, Alexander D., Dr. "Dr Mylius and the gunpowder plot." **Waterloo Historical Society.** 1988. 76: 152-155. ill. Loc: all.
A brief biographical sketch of the Berlin physician, including an anecdote about the doctor's wood supply in 1865. Period: 1837 - 1902.

1551. Rose, George Maclean. "Mylius, George Rudolph." **A cyclopaedia of Canadian biography: being chiefly men of the time.** Rose's National Biographical Series 1. Toronto: Rose Publishing Co., 1886. P. 224. Loc: OWTL, OWTU.

A brief profile of the German-born physician who practised in Berlin from 1860, including a reference to his unsuccessful efforts to produce beet sugar. Mylius was a cousin of Hugo Kranz and married Dorothea, eldest daughter of Otto Klotz of Preston. Period: 1860 - 1886.

SURNAMES BEGINNING WITH N

1552. Gingerich, Orland, Rev. "Nafziger, Christian." **Dictionary of Canadian Biography.** Toronto: University of Toronto, 1988. 7: 641-642. Also in **Dictionnaire biographique du Canada,** 7: 696-696. Loc: OWTL, OWTU.

A biography of the leader of the Amish settlement in the German Block of Wilmot Township. The author explains the role of Nafziger (1776-1836) in negotiating land grants for Amish families and the difficulties in the late 1820s caused by the rival claims to the land by King's College. Period: 1820 - 1836.

1553. "Lambert Norman, B.A." **Waterloo Historical Society.** 1953. 41: 48. Loc: all.

A brief biography of a teacher and Inspector of Public Schools in South Waterloo from 1914 to 1941. Period: 1869 - 1953.

SURNAMES BEGINNING WITH O

1554. Weber, Eldon D. "Reuben Snyder Oberholtzer (O.G.S. #1): origin of the Ontario Genealogical Society." **Families.** 1981. 20,3: 159-160. ill. Loc: OKIT, OWTU, OWTL.

A profile of the founder and first member of the Ontario Genealogical Society. He was also a member of the Waterloo Historical Society and a leader in the formation of the Pennsylvania German Folklore Society of Ontario. Period: 1904 - 1981.

1555. "Valentines for 69 years." **Waterloo Historical Society.** 1962. 50: 32. Loc: all.

A note of the anniversary of Mr and Mrs Thomas E. Owens. Period: 1893 - 1962.

SURNAMES BEGINNING WITH P

1556. "W.H.S. salutes Frank E. Page." **Waterloo Historical Society.** 1962. 50: 10-11. ill. Loc: all.

A biographical tribute to the bank manager of the Royal Bank of Canada in New Dundee who was an active member of the Waterloo Historical Society. Period: 1919 - 1962.

1557. Panabaker, J.D. "David Norman Panabaker." **Waterloo Historical Society.** 1939. 27: 86-89. ill. Loc: all.

A short biography of one of Hespeler's prominent citizens who worked his way up to become General Manager of the R. Forbes Co., and was Mayor of Hespeler and an active member of the Waterloo Historical Society. Period: 1874 - 1939.

1558. Pattinson, Frank H. "George Pattinson." **Waterloo Historical Society.** 1933. 21: 61-63. Loc: all.

A sketch of Pattinson's roles in the Preston woollen textile industry, in provincial and municipal politics at the time of the original Hydro Electric Commission, and in the Economical Fire Insurance Company and the Mutual Life Assurance Company of Canada. Period: 1854 - 1931.

1559. "Thomas Pearce." **Waterloo Historical Society.** 1914. 2: 49-50. Loc: all.

A short biography of the Irish-born teacher who was Berlin's first Normal-School trained teacher, first chairman of the Berlin Free Library Board and school inspector for forty-one years. Period: 1832 - 1914.

1560. Middleton, Jesse Edgar and Landon, Fred. "A. Eugene Pequegnat." **The Province of Ontario: a history, 1615-1927.** Toronto: Dominion Publishing Company, 1927. Vol. 3, pp. 281-282. Loc: OWTL, OWTU.

A profile of the comptroller of the Mutual Life Assurance Co. of Canada, including an account of the arrival of the Ulysse Pequegnat family in Berlin in 1874. Period: 1888 - 1926.

1561. Perrin, John. **Journal of John Perrin (1842-1922).** 194-?. 1 v. (unpaged). ill. Loc: OKIT.

Material copied from John Perrin's journal which was lent to the Kitchener Public Library by Jean Perrin. The collection includes newspaper clippings noting the deaths and marriages of various members of the Perrin family and acquaintances. Handwritten entries provide other details on the family as well as information on wages, payments, items purchased, numerous songs and poems, and short treatises on marriage and kissing. Period: 1842 - 1922.

1562. "Andrew Jackson Peterson." **Waterloo Historical Society.** 1935. 23: 181-182. Loc: all.

A note including a quotation from a diary of

Henry William Peterson dated February 5, 1841 and an autobiographical sketch of Andrew Jackson Peterson. Period: 1823 - 1857.

1563. Byerly, A.E. "Henry William Peterson." **Waterloo Historical Society.** 1931. 19: 250-262. Loc: all.
A biography of Peterson (1793-1859), publisher of Canada's first German newspaper and other German works, including a collection of hymns for the Berlin community in 1836 and almanacs in 1838, 1839 and 1840. The author notes that Peterson's second wife, Harriet, was sister to John M. Clayton, U.S. Senator and Secretary of State. Period: 1793 - 1913.

1564. Byerly, A.E. "The Peterson diary." **Canadian-German Folklore.** 1961. 1: 110-113. Loc: OKIT, OWTL, OWTUCG.
A discussion of the diary of Rev. John Peterson of Markham, including a brief reference to the description by his son, Henry William, of a church service conducted by Benjamin Eby. Period: 1819 - 1852.

1565. **Henry William Peterson.** 1931?. 1 v. ill., bibl. Loc: OKIT.
A biographical sketch of the publisher of the first German newspaper in Canada, the **Canada Museum.** There are records of relatives, including excerpts from his father's diary and a profile of his son, who became Mayor of Guelph.

1566. Kalbfleisch, Herbert Karl. "Peterson, Heinrich Wilhelm." **Dictionary of Canadian Biography.** Toronto: University of Toronto Press, 1985. 8: 700-701. Also in **Dictionnaire biographique du Canada,** 8: 777-778. Loc: OWTL, OWTU.
A biography of the Berlin printer, publisher and editor (1793-1859), who published Canada's first German newspaper, the **Canada Museum** from 1835, as well as various secular and religious titles. Appointed registrar of the Wellington District in 1840, Peterson sold his press to Heinrich Eby and Christian Enslin and moved to Guelph. Period: 1834 - 1840.

1567. "Edmund Pugsley." **Waterloo Historical Society.** 1945. 33: 42. ill. Loc: all.
A short biography of the former teacher at the Kitchener-Waterloo Collegiate. Period: 1861 - 1945.

SURNAMES BEGINNING WITH Q

1568. Middleton, Jesse Edgar and Landon, Fred. "A.C. Quickfall." **The Province of Ontario: a history, 1615-1927.** Toronto: Dominion Publishing Company,

1927. Vol. 4, pp. 617-618. Loc: OWTL, OWTU.
A profile of the Berlin ice and coal merchant and building contractor, including a summary genealogy. Period: 1878 - 1926.

SURNAMES BEGINNING WITH R

1569. Ratz, Herbert C. "The four faces of John Ratz, Elmira." **Waterloo Historical Society.** 1989. 77: 54-62. ill., map. Loc: all.
An appraisal of Ratz's roles as Reeve, railway promoter, miller, real estate entrepreneur and family man. Period: 1833 - 1889.

1570. "Two brother mayors died in 1954." **Waterloo Historical Society.** 1954. 42: 42. Loc: all.
A short obituary of Henry F. Ratz (1877-1954) and his brother, Edward E. Ratz (1870-1954). Henry was a Mayor of Waterloo and Edward was Mayor of Kitchener as well as a partner in the Ratz-Bechtel Funeral Service. Period: 1870 - 1954.

1571. High, Norman H. "A tribute." **Canadian-German Folklore.** 1970. 3: 6-7. ill. Loc: OKIT, OWTL, OWTU, OWTUCG.
A eulogy for Dr George Elmore Reaman, author and founder of the Pennsylvania German Folklore Society of Ontario. Period: 1940 - 1969.

1572. "Diamond wedding." **Waterloo Historical Society.** 1966. 54: 85. Loc: all.
A short paragraph noting the anniversary of Mr and Mrs John Reid on January 1967 in Galt. Period: 1916 - 1966.

1573. "Hon. Lieut.-Colonel Richard Reid." **Waterloo Historical Society.** 1918. 6: 50-51. ill. Loc: all.
A obituary of Reid (1862-1918), teacher, farmer and Agent General for Ontario in the British Isles. Period: 1862 - 1918.

1574. Reiner, John George. "John George Reiner: autobiography." **Waterloo Historical Society.** 1917. 5: 62-63. ill. Loc: all.
A short autobiography by the owner of many Wellesley businesses, including the woollen mill, flour mill, saw mill, general store, and a stave and heading plant. Period: 1832 - 1917.

1575. Reist, Moses G. **Der goldene biblische Spiegel.** Elmira: The Author, 1913. 462 p. Loc: OWTUCGR.
An autobiography of the Elmira resident who considered himself to be the Second Moses. The work focuses on events in his life, including his stays at the Homewood Sanitarium in Guelph, but also incorporates passages from the Bible and

Reist's own religious writings. Period: c1868 -
1913.

1576. Reist, Moses G. **The golden Bible looking-glass.**
Elmira: The Author, 1913. 462 p. Loc: OWTUCGR,
OKIT, OKITW.

A translation of the autobiography of the Elmira
resident who considered himself to be the Second
Moses. The work focuses on his life's
experiences, but also includes passages from the
Bible and Reist's own religious writings. Period:
c1868 - 1913.

1577. Rempel, Henry. **Passages out of my life.** Toronto
and New York: Edwin Mellen Press, 1977. 96 p.
port. Loc: OWTUCG.

An autobiography of the Russian-born Mennonite
who immigrated to Canada in 1923. Presented as a
collection of snippets, the work provides insight
into his character through his use of humour.
Rempel was employed at various factories and farms
in the Waterloo County area and in 1948 bought his
own firm, Kitchener Upholstery. Period: 1907 -
1977.

1578. "Samuel Richardson, M.D., Galt." **The Canadian
biographical dictionary and portrait gallery of
eminent and self-made men, Ontario volume.**
Toronto: American Biographical Publishing Co.,
1880. Pp. 498-499. Loc: OWTL, OWTU.

A biography of the physician who set up practice
in Galt in 1839 and served many years on the
municipal council. Period: 1839 - 1880.

1579. Panabaker, D.N. "John G. Richter, F.A.S.."
Waterloo Historical Society. 1928. 16: 92-93.
Loc: all.

A brief biography of the Waterloo County native
who became a prominent figure in the insurance
industry in London, Ontario. Period: 1854 - 1928.

1580. Cook, H. Milton. "Talmon Henry Rieder." **Waterloo
Historical Society.** 1928. 16: 90-91. Loc: all.

A short biography of the entrepreneur who became
president and managing director of the Canadian
Consolidated Rubber Company, the Canadian
Consolidated Felt Company and the
Ames-Holden-McCready Company, and was only 43
when he died in 1922. Rieder was responsible for
establishing two rubber tire factories in
Berlin/Kitchener, the Dominion Tire factory in
1912/13 and what became the B.F. Goodrich factory
in the early 1920s. Period: 1878 - 1922.

1581. Middleton, Jesse Edgar and Landon, Fred. "Talmon
Henry Rieder." **The Province of Ontario: a
history, 1615-1927.** Toronto: Dominion Publishing
Company, 1927. Vol. 3, pp. 48-49. port. Loc: OWTL,

OWTU.

A profile of the entrepreneur who established
two rubber tire companies in Kitchener. Period:
1878 - 1922.

1582. "Waterloo County's oldest citizen." **Waterloo
Historical Society.** 1961. 49: 63. Loc: all.

A note of the 103rd birthday of Mrs Margaret
Rieder of New Hamburg. Period: 1858 - 1961.

1583. Dunnett, Carol. "Mrs Ophelia Rife, a warm and
tender tribute." **Waterloo Historical Society.**
1956. 44: 43-54. ill. Loc: all.

A biography of Ophelia Rife (nee Lochead) aged
103, who with her husband David ran the Sunnyhill
Farm dairy enterprise in Hespeler. The author
provides interesting details about Galt in the
mid-nineteenth century. Period: 1853 - 1950.

1584. Kalbfleisch, Herbert Karl. "John A. Rittinger."
American-German Review. 1957. 23,6: 18-20.

A profile of the Berlin newspaper editor who
wrote a regular series of letters in the
Pennsylvania German dialect under the pseudonym of
Joe Klotzkopp. Period: 1855 - 1915.

1585. Middleton, Jesse Edgar and Landon, Fred. "John
Adam Rittinger." **The Province of Ontario: a
history, 1615-1927.** Toronto: Dominion Publishing
Company, 1927. Vol. 4, pp. 438-439. port. Loc:
OWTL, OWTU.

A profile of Rittinger (1855-1915), proprietor
of the **Berliner Journal** and author of the Joe
Klotzkopp letters, with a biography of his son
Frederick. Period: 1855 - 1915.

1586. Weissenborn, Georg K. "John Adam Rittinger: the
'Glockemann' (1855-1915)." **German-Canadian
Yearbook / Deutschkanadisches Jahrbuch.** 1984. 8:
221-224. ill., bibl. Loc: OKIT, OWTL, OWTUCG.

A short biography of the editor of the **Berliner
Journal** who earlier edited the Walkerton paper,
Ontario Glocke. The author discusses letters to
the editor written by Rittinger in the Pennsylvania
German dialect, using the pseudonym Joe Klotzkopp.
Period: 1855 - 1915.

1587. Middleton, Jesse Edgar and Landon, Fred. "Peter H.
Roos." **The Province of Ontario: a history,
1615-1927.** Toronto: Dominion Publishing Company,
1927. Vol. 4, pp. 368-369. Loc: OWTL, OWTU.

A profile of the Waterloo insurance executive.
Period: 1865 - 1926.

1588. Fraser, Alexander. "Richard Roschman." **A history
of Ontario: its resources and development.**
Toronto: The Canada History Co., 1907. Pp.
974-975. Loc: OWTL, OWTU.

Roschman migrated from Germany to Berlin in 1871 and established a button-making factory at Waterloo in 1878. Period: 1848 - 1906.

1589. Middleton, Jesse Edgar and Landon, Fred. "Rudolph Roschman." **The Province of Ontario: a history, 1615-1927.** Toronto: Dominion Publishing Company, 1927. Vol. 4, p. 438. Loc: OWTL, OWTU.

A profile of the Waterloo button manufacturer. Period: 1878 - 1926.

1590. Fraser, Alexander. "George Rumpel." **A history of Ontario: its resources and development.** Toronto: The Canada History Co., 1907. Pp. 969-970. Loc: OWTL, OWTU.

Rumpel built up the Berlin Felt Boot Co. and was very active in municipal and community affairs. Period: 1850 - 1906.

1591. Middleton, Jesse Edgar and Landon, Fred. "George Rumpel." **The Province of Ontario: a history, 1615-1927.** Toronto: Dominion Publishing Company, 1927. Vol. 4, p. 343. Loc: OWTL, OWTU.

A profile of the Berlin community leader and felt manufacturer. Period: 1871 - 1916.

1592. Middleton, Jesse Edgar and Landon, Fred. "Oscar Rumpel." **The Province of Ontario: a history, 1615-1927.** Toronto: Dominion Publishing Company, 1927. Vol. 4, p. 344. Loc: OWTL, OWTU.

A profile of the Kitchener felt slipper manufacturer who took over the old factory of Williams, Greene and Rome in 1913. Period: 1875 - 1926.

1593. Middleton, Jesse Edgar and Landon, Fred. "Walter George Rumpel." **The Province of Ontario: a history, 1615-1927.** Toronto: Dominion Publishing Company, 1927. Vol. 4, p. 344. Loc: OWTL, OWTU.

A profile of the president of the Rumpel Felt Company of Kitchener, in succession to his father George Rumpel. Period: 1885 - 1926.

1594. "John H. Ruppel." **Waterloo Historical Society.** 1940. 28: 143-144. ill. Loc: all.

An obituary reprinted from the **Elmira Signet** for John H. Ruppel (1857-1940), town clerk and treasurer of Elmira for 53 years, organist of St Paul's Lutheran Church and leader of the Elmira, Conestogo and St Jacobs bands. Period: 1857 - 1940.

1595. Ruppel, C. Percy. **Adventures attitudes revealed.** 1953?. 64 p. ill. Loc: OKITW.

A book of poetry and autobiographical reminiscences of life in Elmira during the first half of the twentieth century. The author was a salesman for National Grocers, a member of the

Happy Cousins Concert Company, a member of St Paul's Lutheran Church and the Elmira Horticultural Society.

SURNAMES BEGINNING WITH S

1596. Middleton, Jesse Edgar and Landon, Fred. "William T. Sass." **The Province of Ontario: a history, 1615-1927.** Toronto: Dominion Publishing Company, 1927. Vol. 3, pp. 295-296. port. Loc: OWTL, OWTU.

A profile of the Kitchener furniture manufacturer. Period: 1866 - 1926.

1597. "Oldster still at job after 71 years." **Waterloo Historical Society.** 1959. 47: 72. Loc: all.

A short account of the long working life of Susan Scharlach who began her 72nd year at the A. and C. Boehmer Box Company, Kitchener in 1959. Period: 1876 - 1959.

1598. "Charles W. Schierholtz." **Waterloo Historical Society.** 1953. 41: 47. Loc: all.

An obituary of Schierholtz (1859-1953) who owned **The Elmira Advertiser** until 1916 when it amalgamated with **The Elmira Signet.** Period: 1859 - 1953.

1599. "Elmira's oldest citizen." **Waterloo Historical Society.** 1960. 48: 50. Loc: all.

Mrs Catherine Schierholtz, celebrating her 100th birthday, recalls the first Elmira school on the site of the present Link Belt factory. Period: 1860 - 1960.

1600. Fraser, Alexander. "William Henry Schmalz." **A history of Ontario: its resources and development.** Toronto: The Canada History Co., 1907. Pp. 963-4. port. Loc: OWTL, OWTU.

Schmalz was employed as secretary and later manager of the Economical Mutual Fire Insurance Co. of Berlin and was very active in municipal, church and cultural activities. Period: 1862 - 1906.

1601. Jaffray, J.P. **W.H. Schmalz, citizen: a tribute to a leading citizen of Kitchener by an admiring friend.** Kitchener: The Author, 1933. 14 p. ill. Loc: OKIT.

A biography of the managing director of the Economical Mutual Fire Insurance Company who was also secretary of St Paul's Lutheran Church for 42 years and Mayor of Berlin in 1912-1913. A brief profile of Schmalz's son, W.H.E. Schmalz, is illustrated with a photograph of the Kitchener City Hall (1927) which he designed. Period: 1862 - 1933.

1602. Lamb, Kathryn Hansuld. "William H.E. Schmalz, 1890-1981." **Waterloo Historical Society**. 1981. 69: 151-152. Loc: all.

A tribute to the architect, community leader and active member of the Waterloo Historical Society. Period: 1890 - 1981.

1603. Middleton, Jesse Edgar and Landon, Fred. "John Albert Schmalz." **The Province of Ontario: a history, 1615-1927**. Toronto: Dominion Publishing Company, 1927. Vol. 3, p. 267. Loc: OWTL, OWTU.

A profile of the real estate promoter of The Kitchener East Lands Ltd. Period: 1887 - 1926.

1604. Middleton, Jesse Edgar and Landon, Fred. "William Henry Schmalz." **The Province of Ontario: a history, 1615-1927**. Toronto: Dominion Publishing Company, 1927. Vol. 3, pp. 177-178. port. Loc: OWTL, OWTU.

A brief biography of the insurance company official and first Mayor of the City of Berlin. Period: 1862 - 1926.

1605. "W.H.S. salutes William H.E. Schmalz." **Waterloo Historical Society**. 1962. 50: 8-9. ill. Loc: all.

Photograph and outline of achievements of Schmalz, architect and active member of the Waterloo Historical Society. Period: 1890 - 1962.

1606. Middleton, Jesse Edgar and Landon, Fred. "Dr Robert Werner Schnarr." **The Province of Ontario: a history, 1615-1927**. Toronto: Dominion Publishing Company, 1927. Vol. 3, p. 217. Loc: OWTL, OWTU.

A profile of the Kitchener homeopathic physician. Period: 1905 - 1926.

1607. Good, E. Reginald and Tiessen, Paul Gerald. "Schneider, Joseph." **Dictionary of Canadian Biography**. Toronto: University of Toronto Press, 1988. 7: 778-779. Also in **Dictionnaire biographique du Canada**, 7: 842-843. Loc: OWTL, OWTU.

A biography of the pioneer settler, sawmill owner and community leader, whose property, Lot 17 of the German Company Tract, became the site of Berlin. The authors explain the church and community roles of Schneider (1772-1843) and refer to the restoration of his house as a museum and to various valuable books and other items. Period: 1820 - 1843.

1608. "John M. Schneider." **Waterloo Historical Society**. 1942. 30: 240-241. Loc: all.

A biography of Schneider (1859-1942), founder and president of one of the largest meat packing firms in Canada. Period: 1859 - 1942.

1609. Middleton, Jesse Edgar and Landon, Fred. "John Metz Schneider." **The Province of Ontario: a history, 1615-1927**. Toronto: Dominion Publishing Company, 1927. Vol. 4, pp. 615-616. port. Loc: OWTL, OWTU.

A brief biography of the Kitchener meat packer and sausage manufacturer, including a summary family history and an account of the growth of his business. Period: 1859 - 1926.

1610. **Norman Christoph Schneider: presented lovingly by his children on the occasion of his 70th birthday, December 9, 1958.**. Kitchener: Kitchener Public Library, 1982. 1 reel. ill. mf. Loc: OKIT, OWTU.

A scrapbook compiled by his family as a tribute to the son of the founder of J.M. Schneider, Ltd. The volume contains copies of personal documents, poems, correspondence, newspaper clippings and photographs, with information about his roles in the family business, in politics as a Liberal Member of Parliament, and in sports. Originally assembled in 1958, the scrapbook was updated to the mid-1970s before being microfilmed by the Kitchener Public Library. Period: 1888 - 1960.

1611. Schweitzer, Vera. "The trail blazer." **Waterloo Historical Society**. 1969. 57: 44-47. Loc: all.

A biography and family history of Jacob (Yoch) Schneider (1764-1853) who came to the Bloomingdale area in 1806. Period: 1806 - 1853.

1612. Uttley, W.V. "Joseph Schneider: founder of the city." **Waterloo Historical Society**. 1929. 17: 111-119. Loc: all.

An account of Schneider's establishment of a sawmill and homestead in what was to become Berlin. Various descendants are also listed. Period: 1800 - 1928.

1613. "Wilfred Schneller honoured [WRP]." **Waterloo Historical Society**. 1983. 71: 99. ill. Loc: all.

A photograph of Wilfred Schneller of Baden receiving a citation from Mayor Ralph Shantz of Wilmot Township for his work with the Waterloo Regional Arboretum near New Hamburg.

1614. Middleton, Jesse Edgar and Landon, Fred. "Alvin George Schreiter." **The Province of Ontario: a history, 1615-1927**. Toronto: Dominion Publishing Company, 1927. Vol. 4, pp. 449-450. port. Loc: OWTL, OWTU.

A profile of the Berlin upholstery manufacturer and furniture merchant. Period: 1885 - 1926.

1615. "Erich R.W. Schultz: President, 1983-1984." **Waterloo Historical Society**. 1984. 72: 4-5. ill. Loc: all.

A short biographical sketch detailing his

degrees, publications and contributions to Wilfrid Laurier University Library and the Kitchener-Waterloo Community Concert Association. Period: 1947 - 1984.

1616. "Peter F. Schummer." **Waterloo Historical Society**. 1942. 30: 241. Loc: all.

A short biography of Peter F. Schummer (1851-1942), Wellesley Township Clerk for forty years and a leading citizen of St Clements. Period: 1851 - 1942.

1617. Breithaupt, W.H. "Dr John Scott." **Waterloo Historical Society**. 1941. 29: 197-199. ill. Loc: all.

A biographical sketch of Scott (1814-1856), physician and Reeve of Berlin, based on contemporary newspaper articles. Period: 1814 - 1856.

1618. Campbell, Alexander D., Dr. "Dr John Scott: Berlin's first licensed physician." **Waterloo Historical Society**. 1984. 72: 114-117. ill. Loc: all.

A brief assessment of the medical career of Dr John Scott, who was educated at Edinburgh University in Scotland and came to Berlin in 1834. Period: 1834 - 1856.

1619. "Robert Scott, Galt." **The Canadian biographical dictionary and portrait gallery of eminent and self-made men, Ontario volume**. Toronto: American Biographical Publishing Co., 1880. Pp. 655-656. Loc: OWTL, OWTU.

A short biography of the proprietor of the Victoria Wheel Works which manufactured hubs, spokes and rims for wheelwrights and the carriage-building industry. Period: 1839 - 1880.

1620. Rose, George Maclean. "Scott, Robert." **A cyclopaedia of Canadian biography: being chiefly men of the time**. Rose's National Biographical Series 1. Toronto: Rose Publishing Co., 1886. Pp. 92-93. Loc: OWTL, OWTU.

A profile of the proprietor of the Victoria Wheel Co. who was Mayor of Galt in 1885. Period: 1839 - 1886.

1621. "Philip Frowde Seagram." **Waterloo Historical Society**. 1941. 29: 199. ill. Loc: all.

A short biography of Seagram (1911-1941), businessman son of Edward Seagram. He was killed in London during an air-raid. Period: 1911 - 1941.

1622. Seagram, J.E. Frowde. "Joseph Emm Seagram (1841-1919)." **Waterloo Historical Society**. 1976. 64: 18-22. ill. Loc: all.

An address at the unveiling of a plaque in front of the Seagram Distillery, Waterloo. Joseph Seagram's grandson outlines his grandfather's roles as entrepreneur, federal politician and sportsman. Period: 1837 - 1976.

1623. Cressman, Ella M. "Emily Seibert." **Waterloo Historical Society**. 1970. 58: 4-5. ill. Loc: all.

A profile of the elementary school teacher for forty years and active member of the Waterloo Historical Society. Period: 1929 - 1969.

1624. Middleton, Jesse Edgar and Landon, Fred. "Levi Erb Seibert." **The Province of Ontario: a history, 1615-1927**. Toronto: Dominion Publishing Company, 1927. Vol. 4, p. 392. Loc: OWTL, OWTU.

A profile of the Berlin embalmer and funeral director, whose business was merged with that of the Schreiter Furniture Company in 1919. Period: 1883 - 1926.

1625. Gardiner, Elizabeth. "Biographies: Absalom Shade (1793-1862)." **Historic Guelph**. 1983. 22: 83-84. Loc: OGU, OKIT.

A brief biography of Shade who came from Buffalo in 1816 to be William Dickson's general agent in Dumfries Township and represented Halton as a Conservative from 1831 to 1841. Period: 1816 - 1841.

1626. Johnson, Leo A. "Shade, Absalom." **Dictionary of Canadian Biography**. Toronto: University of Toronto Press, 1976. 9: 717-718. Also in **Dictionnaire biographique du Canada**, 9: 717-718. Loc: OWTL, OWTU.

A biography of the businessman and politician who managed the settlement of William Dickson's lands in Dumfries Township, around Shade's Mills (later renamed Galt). The author describes the varied mercantile, land and transportation interests of Shade (1793-1862). Period: 1816 - 1862.

1627. Menary, David. "The story behind Shade's stone." **Waterloo Historical Society**. 1987. 75: 139-144. Loc: all.

A biography of Absalom Shade recounting his roles as agent for William Dickson, developer of Shade's Mills which later became Galt, and in politics. Period: 1826 - 1862.

1628. Bowman, H.M. "Jacob Y. Shantz: pioneer of Russian Mennonite immigration to Manitoba." **Waterloo Historical Society**. 1924. 12: 85-100. ill. Loc: all.

An account of Shantz's family background and varied business activities in farming, contracting, milling and manufacturing. His role in the Russian Mennonite migrations to Manitoba in the 1870s is stressed and photographs of the family homestead in Berlin and excerpts from Shantz's official account of his journey to Manitoba are included. Period: 1800 - 1909.

1629. Donald, Mark M. "Frederick Robert Shantz." **Waterloo Historical Society.** 1932. 20: 333. Loc: all.

An obituary of Shantz (1875-1932) who worked for his father's foundry business and presided over the Shantz family reunion at Waterloo in 1930. He also served on the Preston Town Council and was president of the Preston Board of Trade, active in industrial promotion, and interested in the Grand Valley Board of Trade. Period: 1875 - 1932.

1630. Fraser, Alexander. "Dilman Brubacher Shantz." **A history of Ontario: its resources and development.** Toronto: The Canada History Co., 1907. Pp. 951-955. ports. Loc: OWTL, OWTU.

Short biographies of Dilman Shantz, president of the Berlin button-manufacturing business, Jacob Y. Shantz & Son, and of his father Jacob Y. Shantz. Period: 1806 - 1906.

1631. Gingerich, Melvin. "Jacob Y. Shantz, 1822-1909, promoter of the Mennonite settlements in Manitoba." **Mennonite Quarterly Review.** 1950. 24,1: 230-247. Loc: OWTU, OWTUCG.

A biography of the Berlin farmer-businessman and community leader, emphasizing his role in helping Russian Mennonites to migrate to Manitoba in the later nineteenth century. Period: 1822 - 1909.

1632. Middleton, Jesse Edgar and Landon, Fred. "Nelson Goetz Shantz." **The Province of Ontario: a history, 1615-1927.** Toronto: Dominion Publishing Company, 1927. Vol. 3, pp. 267-268. Loc: OWTL, OWTU.

A profile of the proprietor of The Brunswick Garage in Kitchener, including a summary Shantz genealogy. Period: 1866 - 1926.

1633. "Samuel Preston Shantz." **Waterloo Historical Society.** 1952. 40: 40. Loc: all.

A short obituary of the Preston-born businessman with interests in the P.E. Shantz Foundry and also active in community affairs; he helped to organize the Preston Old Boys' Reunion in 1949. Period: 1884 - 1952.

1634. Schmidt, Grace. "Jacob Y. Shantz." **Canadian-German Folklore.** 1961. 1: 126-129. Loc: OKIT, OWTL, OWTU, OWTUCG.

A sketch of the Berlin entrepreneur and businessman, noted for his efforts in helping Russian Mennonites to settle in Manitoba during the 1870s. Period: 1822 - 1909.

1635. Shantz, Moses B. **Adventures in colonization: co-ordinated developments unsurpassed in history, transforming a wilderness into the "greatest golden granary of the world", turning almost insurmountable obstacles into a triumphant success.** The Author, 1930?. 106 p. index. Loc: OKITW.

Typescript biography of Jacob Y. Shantz by his son. Jacob's childhood and his role as a leading businessman of Berlin are described, with his settlement of Russian Mennonites in Manitoba given particular attention. A collection of printed tributes is included in part five. Background information about the settlement of Manitoba and Mennonite history is also provided. Period: 1925 - 1950.

1636. Steiner, Samuel J. "Jacob Y. Shantz: Mennonite businessman." **Mennogespräch.** 1987. 5,1: 1-5. ill., bibl. Loc: OWTUCG, OKIT.

An account of the financial fortunes of Shantz (1822-1909), from his farming and sawmill business enterprises in the 1850s, the founding of the Dominion Button Works and other industries in the 1870s, to financial difficulties in 1884. The article is based on the author's research for his book-length biography of Shantz. Period: 1843 - 1914.

1637. Steiner, Samuel J. **Vicarious pioneer: the life of Jacob Y. Shantz.** Winnipeg: Hyperion Press, 1988. 223 p. ill., maps, bibl., index. Loc: OKIT, OWT, OWTUCG, OWTUSJ.

A biography of the Waterloo County Mennonite who played a significant role in helping Mennonites from Ukraine emigrate to Manitoba in the 1870s. Shantz's life is traced from his farm childhood and activities as a businessman and industrialist in Berlin to his relations with the government of Canada concerning the settlement and welfare of the Mennonites from Russia and his numerous trips to the West. Three appendices contain Shantz's **Narrative of a journey to Manitoba,** his testimony to Parliament regarding the success of the settlers in Manitoba and the repayment of the loan, and articles by Shantz published in the **Gospel Banner.** Period: 1822 - 1909.

1638. "Frederick William Sheppard." **Waterloo Historical Society.** 1945. 33: 42-43. Loc: all.

A short biography of the teacher who became the school inspector for North Waterloo in the 1920s and was also active in the Trinity United Church and an avid soccer enthusiast. Period: c1860 - 1945.

1639. Sherk, M.G. "A memoir of Rev. A.B. Sherk." **Waterloo Historical Society**. 1916. 4: 35-36. ill. Loc: all.

A short biography of Breslau-born Rev. A.B. Sherk, who became a missionary preacher for the United Brethren in Christ. Period: 1832 - 1916.

1640. Capling, F. Mrs. "Peter Shirk." **Waterloo Historical Society**. 1933. 21: 63-65. Loc: all.

A biographical sketch of Shirk (1839-1919), noting his migration from Lancaster County, development of the Bridgeport flour mills, and work for the Berlin-Waterloo Collegiate and Technical Institute. Period: 1832 - 1919.

1641. "Henry Weber Shoemaker, 1878-1953." **Waterloo Historical Society**. 1953. 41: 48. Loc: all.

An obituary of the pharmacist who owned Shoemaker's Drug Store in Kitchener for forty years. Period: 1878 - 1953.

1642. Middleton, Jesse Edgar and Landon, Fred. "A.S. Shoemaker." **The Province of Ontario: a history, 1615-1927**. Toronto: Dominion Publishing Company, 1927. Vol. 4, pp. 377-378. port. Loc: OWTL, OWTU.

A profile of the Kitchener milk dealer, including a summary genealogy. Period: 1871 - 1926.

1643. Middleton, Jesse Edgar and Landon, Fred. "Levi Weber Shuh." **The Province of Ontario: a history, 1615-1927**. Toronto: Dominion Publishing Company, 1927. Vol. 3, pp. 144-146. Loc: OWTL, OWTU.

A profile of the manager and president of the Waterloo Mutual Fire Insurance Company including a summary Shuh genealogy and a chronology of the company. Period: 1861 - 1926.

1644. Shuh, Clayton H. **Wavertree chronicles: the diary of Clayton H. Shuh 1899-1935**. Truro, NS: J. Edward Shuh, 1986. 77 p. ill. Loc: OWTUR, OKIT, OWT.

A collection of entries from his diaries, that were edited and published by his son. The entries present a picture of daily life on the Waterloo farm and in the community. Many family members and friends are mentioned, as are activities undertaken by them. Other information includes farm business and crop prices, meals served on the farm, and weather. Period: 1899 - 1935.

1645. "Harvey J. Sims." **Waterloo Historical Society**. 1945. 33: 41-42. ill. Loc: all.

An obituary of the member of the law firm of Sims, Bray, Schofield, and Lochead who also served as general counsel of the Mutual Life Assurance Company of Canada and was director of both the Waterloo Trust and Savings Company and the Economical Fire Insurance Company. Period: 1871 - 1945.

1646. "Rev. James Sims." **Waterloo Historical Society**. 1941. 29: 193-196. ill. Loc: all.

A biography of Sims (1812-1880), copied from the semi-centennial issue of the **Waterloo Chronicle** of 1906. A Scottish emigrant who became an ordained Baptist minister in 1842 but later joined the Christadelphians, Sims was appointed superintendent of schools for the townships of Woolwich and Wellesley in 1853 and was active in the temperance movement. Period: 1812 - 1880.

1647. Smandych, Mavis. **My best year: when we came to Elmira**. The Author, 1989. 4 p. Loc: OKIT.

Recollections of the author's move to Elmira with her family in 1951. She describes how her husband found a job as a chemical engineer at Naugatuck Chemicals, and the experience of settling in Elmira with two babies in the early 1950s. Period: 1951 - 1952.

1648. Middleton, Jesse Edgar and Landon, Fred. "Otto George Smith." **The Province of Ontario: a history, 1615-1927**. Toronto: Dominion Publishing Company, 1927. Vol. 3, pp. 234-235. Loc: OWTL, OWTU.

A profile of the school principal who joined another teacher, D.W. Houston, in forming the Kitchener insurance agency of Smith and Houston in 1919. Period: 1884 - 1926.

1649. Rose, George Maclean. "Smith, James K.." **A cyclopaedia of Canadian biography: being chiefly men of the time**. Rose's National Biographical Series 1. Toronto: Rose Publishing Co., 1886. Pp. 357-358. Loc: OWTL, OWTU.

A profile of the clergyman who succeeded Dr Bayne and Dr Thomson at Knox's Church, Galt in 1865, returning there in the mid-1870s. Period: 1865 - 1886.

1650. Fraser, Alexander. "Robert Smyth." **A history of Ontario: its resources and development**. Toronto: The Canada History Co., 1907. Pp. 970-971. Loc: OWTL, OWTU.

Robert and Edward Smyth owned a drygoods business in Berlin from 1877; Robert was also active in the Waterloo Board of Trade and in promoting the Ontario Sugar Company from 1902. Period: 1851 - 1906.

1651. Fraser, Alexander. "William Snider." **A history of Ontario: its resources and development**. Toronto: The Canada History Co., 1907. Pp. 1173-1175. Loc: OWTL, OWTU.

A short biography of the proprietor of Snider's

Mill, Waterloo, who was also active in various other business ventures and in municipal government. Period: 1845 - 1906.

1652. "John Bricker Snider." **Waterloo Historical Society**. 1917. 5: 58. ill. Loc: all.

A biography of the business partner of John Shuh in a Waterloo general store and later owner of the Graybill Manufacturing Company which produced office and school furniture. Family information about the Sniders and Schneiders is given. Period: 1840 - 1917.

1653. Middleton, Jesse Edgar and Landon, Fred. "Frederick William Snider." **The Province of Ontario: a history, 1615-1927**. Toronto: Dominion Publishing Company, 1927. Vol. 3, pp. 244-245. Loc: OWTL, OWTU.

A profile of the president and general manager of The William Snider Milling Co. of Waterloo, including a summary genealogy and a chronology of the Waterloo mill property. Period: 1886 - 1926.

1654. Richmond, Elliott. "E.W.B. Snider." **Waterloo Historical Society**. 1921. 9: 183-188. ill. Loc: all.

A biography of Snider (1842-1921), mill owner, promoter of the Waterloo Junction Railway and "father of hydro power" in Ontario. Special mention is made of a German roller machine, the "Walzenstuhle" which Snider used in his flour mill at St Jacobs. Period: 1842 - 1921.

1655. Rose, George Maclean. "Snider, Elias Weber Bingeman." **A cyclopaedia of Canadian biography: being chiefly men of the time**. Rose's National Biographical Series 1. Toronto: Rose Publishing Co., 1886. P. 193. Loc: OWTL, OWTU.

A brief biography of the St Jacobs miller who represented North Waterloo in the Ontario Legislature. Period: 1841 - 1886.

1656. Rose, George Maclean. "Snider, William." **A cyclopaedia of Canadian biography: being chiefly men of the time**. Rose's National Biographical Series 1. Toronto: Rose Publishing Co., 1886. Pp. 165-166. Loc: OWTL, OWTU.

A biography of the Mayor of Waterloo and proprietor of the Waterloo Mill. Period: 1845 - 1886.

1657. Snider, Winifred. "E.W.B. Snider, 1842-1921: an appreciation." **Waterloo Historical Society**. 1956. 44: 8-11. ill. Loc: all.

A biographical sketch of the St Jacobs mill owner and promoter of hydro-electric power, by his granddaughter. On 14 May 1956, a memorial to E.W.B. Snider was erected in St Jacobs by the

Ontario Hydro Electric Power Commission. Period: 1842 - 1921.

1658. "Frederick W. Snyder." **Waterloo Historical Society**. 1946. 34: 38-39. ill. Loc: all.

An obituary of the vice-president of the Economical Mutual Fire Insurance Company who was also active in the Kitchener-Waterloo Rotary Club, the Westmount Golf and Country Club and the Waterloo Historical Society. Period: 1881 - 1946.

1659. "Herbert M. Snyder." **Waterloo Historical Society**. 1942. 30: 241-242. Loc: all.

A brief biography of Snyder (1873-1942), president of Snyder's Ltd, Waterloo, a furniture and upholstering business. Period: 1873 - 1942.

1660. Middleton, Jesse Edgar and Landon, Fred. "Herbert Maplin Snyder." **The Province of Ontario: a history, 1615-1927**. Toronto: Dominion Publishing Company, 1927. Vol. 4, pp. 582-583. Loc: OWTL, OWTU.

A profile of the president of Snyders Ltd, with a summary genealogy and a biography of his father, Simon Snyder. Period: 1806 - 1926.

1661. Bergey, Lorna L. "Miriam Snyder Sokvitne." **Waterloo Historical Society**. 1980. 68: 6-7. ill. Loc: all.

A brief biographical sketch of the descendant of Joseph Schneider, one of the county's first settlers. The author describes Sokvitne's interests in heritage preservation including her service as president of the Waterloo Historical Society and her involvement in establishing the Joseph Schneider House as a museum. Period: 1913 - 1980.

1662. "100th birthday of Archie Spalding." **Waterloo Historical Society**. 1966. 54: 85. Loc: all.

A native of Hawick, Scotland, Spalding came to Galt in 1902 from Guelph and was plant superintendent of Newlands and Company for 40 years. Period: 1866 - 1966.

1663. Fehrenbach, John F., Rev. "The Rev. Theobald Spetz, C.R. D.D.." **Waterloo Historical Society**. 1922. 10: 261-264. Loc: all.

A biography of Spetz (1850-1922), priest, president of St Jerome's College, founder of St Louis Roman Catholic Church in Waterloo, and author of a history of the Catholic Church in Waterloo County. Period: 1850 - 1922.

1664. "David Spiers." **Waterloo Historical Society**. 1917. 5: 53. ill. Loc: all.

An obituary of Spiers (1832-1917), businessman, promoter of the Galt, Preston & Hespeler Railway,

Mayor of Galt from 1880 to 1882 and president of the Galt Hospital Board. Spiers is credited with replacing Galt's timber dam with a concrete one and with negotiating the new building for the Galt Collegiate Institute. Period: 1832 - 1917.

1665. Rose, George Maclean. "Spiers, William." **A cyclopaedia of Canadian biography: being chiefly men of the time.** Rose's National Biographical Series 1. Toronto: Rose Publishing Co., 1886. Pp. 558-559. Loc: OWTL, OWTU.

An account of Spiers' establishment of his Berlin store in 1857, as a branch of the Galt business of Osborne Spiers and Co. Period: 1857 - 1886.

1666. "Moses Springer, M.P.P., Waterloo." **The Canadian biographical dictionary and portrait gallery of eminent and self-made men, Ontario volume.** Toronto: American Biographical Publishing Co., 1880. Pp. 119-120. Loc: OWTL, OWTU.

A biography of the man who was Reeve then Mayor of Waterloo for many years, founded the Waterloo Mutual Fire Insurance Co. and represented North Waterloo in the Ontario Legislature from 1867. Period: 1824 - 1880.

1667. Roos, Hilda G. "Moses Springer." **Waterloo Historical Society.** 1940. 28: 142-143. ill. Loc: all.

A biographical sketch of Moses Springer (1824-1898), emphasizing his political roles. Period: 1824 - 1898.

1668. Rose, George Maclean. "Springer, Moses." **A cyclopaedia of Canadian biography: being chiefly men of the time.** Rose's National Biographical Series 1. Toronto: Rose Publishing Co., 1886. Pp. 315-316. Loc: OWTL, OWTU.

A biography of the man who represented North Waterloo from 1867 to 1881 and then became sheriff of Waterloo County. Period: 1824 - 1886.

1669. Middleton, Jesse Edgar and Landon, Fred. "H. Leslie Staebler." **The Province of Ontario: a history, 1615-1927.** Toronto: Dominion Publishing Company, 1927. Vol. 3, pp. 104-106. Loc: OWTL, OWTU.

A profile of the president of the Staebler insurance agency, including an outline of the life and achievements of his father, J.M. Staebler (1846-1906). Period: 1875 - 1926.

1670. Carter, Eric M. "Warren Donald Stauch." **Waterloo Historical Society.** 1980. 68: 4-5. ill. Loc: all.

A profile of the teacher and former president of the Waterloo Historical Society. Period: 1944 - 1980.

1671. Groh, C.T. "Joseph Stauffer." **Waterloo Historical Society.** 1936. 24: 237-238. ill. Loc: all.

A biography of Stauffer (1852-1936), the salesman who worked his way up to be president of Newlands and Company and, with Andrew Newlands, founded the Galt Robe Company. Family information about the Stauffers is also given. Period: 1852 - 1936.

1672. "Jacob G. Stroh, 1848-1935." **Waterloo Historical Society.** 1935. 23: 180-181. Loc: all.

A short biography of Jacob G. Stroh (1848-1935), owner of a Waterloo tannery, collector of Indian artifacts, and authority on early Berlin history. Period: 1848 - 1935.

1673. Foster, Linda. "Lida B. Pearson Sturdy, 1895-1987." **Waterloo Historical Society.** 1991. 79: 40-53. port. Loc: all.

A biography of the Cambridge's first woman lawyer who was also the first woman member of the Preston School Board and an elder in St Paul's United Church, Preston. The author discusses the balance of family and professional responsibilities with community service. Period: 1921 - 1967.

1674. Sword, Jean Cameron. **The story of my life, Jean (Cameron) Sword: how a young girl's dream came true.** 1984. 295 p. ill. Loc: OKITW.

Autobiographical reminiscences of a woman and her family who came to New Hamburg in 1956 and became involved in local community life, including the Fall Fair horse competitions and the Zion United Church. Period: 1956 - 1984.

SURNAMES BEGINNING WITH T

1675. Rose, George Maclean. "Tait, Rev. Donald." **A cyclopaedia of Canadian biography: being chiefly men of the time.** Rose's National Biographical Series 1. Toronto: Rose Publishing Co., 1886. P. 328. Loc: OWTL, OWTU.

A brief profile of the minister appointed to St Andrew's Presbyterian Church, Berlin, in 1879. Period: 1879 - 1886.

1676. "William Tassie, LL.D., Galt." **The Canadian biographical dictionary and portrait gallery of eminent and self-made men, Ontario volume.** Toronto: American Biographical Publishing Co., 1880. Pp. 478-479. port. Loc: OWTL, OWTU.

A short biography of the principal of the Galt Grammar School which was later merged into the Galt Collegiate Institute. Period: 1853 - 1880.

1677. Wilson, J. Donald. "Tassie, William." **Dictionary of Canadian Biography**. Toronto: University of Toronto Press, 1982. 11: 868-869. Also in **Dictionnaire biographique du Canada**, 11: 962-963. Loc: OWTL, OWTU.

A biography of the Irish-born teacher (1815-1886) appointed in 1853 as headmaster of the Galt Grammar School where he built a national reputation. Though the school was the first in Ontario to be named a collegiate institute in 1871, the introduction of provincial examinations and the new stress on practical rather than classical education led to a decline in standards and enrolments during the 1870s. Tassie resigned under a cloud in 1881 and left Galt. Period: 1853 - 1881.

1678. Epp, Marlene. "Harvey W. Taves: one of Christ's men." **Mennogespräch**. 1989. 7,1: 4-5. ill. Loc: OWTUCG, OKIT.

A biographical tribute to the achievements of Harvey Taves (1926-1965), the last director of the Canadian headquarters of the Mennonite Central Committee in Kitchener which closed in 1964, and one of the individuals instrumental in establishing Conrad Grebel College. Period: 1926 - 1965.

1679. "Andrew Winton Taylor." **Waterloo Historical Society**. 1965. 53: 5. ill. Loc: all.

A short biography of the long-time member of the Waterloo Historical Society, with details of his many contributions to the county in history and agriculture. Period: 1918 - 1965.

1680. Barrie, James R. "Andrew Winton Taylor, 1907-1986." **Waterloo Historical Society**. 1986. 74: 99-100. Loc: all.

An obituary of the local historian and municipal official, noting his publications in local history and his roles in the Waterloo Historical Society, Ontario Historical Society, Waterloo County Crop Improvement Association and Central Dumfries Farmers' Club. Taylor also served as assessor, tax collector and building inspector for North Dumfries Township. Period: 1816 - 1986.

1681. "Thomas W. Taylor." **Waterloo Historical Society**. 1947. 35: 48-49. Loc: all.

An obituary of one of the oldest residents of North Dumfries, including references to his service to the Riverside School Board terms and the Central Dumfries Farmers' Club. Mr Taylor's grandfather built the first mill in Galt. Period: 1816 - 1948.

1682. "C.F. Thiele." **Waterloo Historical Society**. 1954. 42: 42. Loc: all.

A short obituary of C.F. Thiele (1880-1954), one of Canada's leading band promoters, director of the Waterloo Musical Society Band and founder of the Annual Waterloo Band Festival. Period: 1880 - 1954.

1683. "Martin N. Todd." **Waterloo Historical Society**. 1917. 5: 54. ill. Loc: all.

A brief biography of Todd (1858-1917), president of the Galt, Preston & Hespeler Railway, manager of the Lake Erie & Northern Railway, first president of the Waterloo County Golf and Country Club, and connected with the Galt Horse Show. Period: 1858 - 1917.

1684. Middleton, Jesse Edgar and Landon, Fred. "Sydney Charles Tweed." **The Province of Ontario: a history, 1615-1927**. Toronto: Dominion Publishing Company, 1927. Vol. 4, p. 399. port. Loc: OWTL, OWTU.

A profile of the Waterloo insurance company executive and organizer. Period: 1916 - 1926.

SURNAMES BEGINNING WITH U

1685. "William Uffelman." **Waterloo Historical Society**. 1947. 35: 49. Loc: all.

An obituary of the prominent Waterloo citizen who was foreman with the Dominion Rubber Company for fifteen years, president of the Waterloo Board of Trade, and Reeve and Mayor of Waterloo.

1686. "William Valores Uttley." **Waterloo Historical Society**. 1944. 32: 35. ill. Loc: all.

A short biography of the teacher, publisher of the Berlin Publishing Company, editor of **Berlin News Record** and owner of **The Elmira Signet**. Uttley was very active in the Waterloo Historical Society and wrote a notable history of Kitchener. Period: 1865 - 1944.

SURNAMES BEGINNING WITH V

1687. Middleton, Jesse Edgar and Landon, Fred. "James Valentine." **The Province of Ontario: a history, 1615-1927**. Toronto: Dominion Publishing Company, 1927. Vol. 4, p. 425. port. Loc: OWTL, OWTU.

A profile of the Waterloo footwear manufacturer. Period: 1903 - 1926.

1688. Campbell, Alexander D., Dr. "The downfall of Dr Vardon." **Waterloo Historical Society**. 1987. 75: 93-96. Loc: all.

A short account of Hawkesville's Dr William H.

Vardon, including his custody battle with his second wife, Elvina, over their daughter Nellie. Period: 1856 - 1886.

1689. Uttley, W.V. "Dr Augustus Stephen Vogt." **Waterloo Historical Society**. 1926. 14: 190-194. ill. Loc: all.

A biography of the former Dean of the Faculty of Music, University of Toronto, Principal of the Toronto Conservatory of Music, and founder of the Mendelssohn Choir. The article relates Vogt's early life in Elmira and his many accomplishments in music. Period: 1861 - 1926.

SURNAMES BEGINNING WITH W

1690. Rose, George Maclean. "Wagner, Joseph." **A cyclopaedia of Canadian biography: being chiefly men of the time**. Rose's National Biographical Series 1. Toronto: Rose Publishing Co., 1886. P. 144. Loc: OWTL, OWTU.

A profile of the German-born tanner and business partner of Galt's Mayor, David Spiers. Period: 1863 - 1886.

1691. Wagner, Gordon. **From my window**. Courtenay, BC: Flying-W-Publishing Co., 1988. 204 p. ill. Loc: OKIT, OWTUR.

Memoirs including an account of a trip to Kitchener to discover the author's ancestral roots. His great-grandparents were Jacob Wagner of Albany, NY, and Margaret Hailer, daughter of Jacob Hailer of Berlin. The book contains a fictionalized description of the courtship and marriage of his great-grandparents in 1849. Louis Breithaupt, who later married Margaret's sister Catharine, was a good friend of Jacob Wagner, and the Wagner marriage took place in the home of Liborius Breithaupt. A visit to the author's relative, Edna Staebler, is also recounted. Period: 1849 - 1987.

1692. Middleton, Jesse Edgar and Landon, Fred. "John Walter." **The Province of Ontario: a history, 1615-1927**. Toronto: Dominion Publishing Company, 1927. Vol. 4, pp. 405-406. Loc: OWTL, OWTU.

A profile of the father and son of the same name who built up a Kitchener business moulding furniture ornamentation out of wood pulp. Period: 1912 - 1926.

1693. "John Watson of Ayr, 1820-1903." **Waterloo Historical Society**. 1929. 17: 143-148. ill. Loc: all.

A biography of John Watson, whose foundry in Ayr grew into the John Watson Manufacturing Company producing farm machinery. A public-spirited man,

Watson was first Reeve of Ayr in 1884, Warden of the County, and a director of the Gore District Mutual Fire Insurance Company. Family information is also included. Period: 1820 - 1903.

1694. "Miss E.D. Watson." **Waterloo Historical Society**. 1944. 32: 37-38. Loc: all.

An obituary of the Ayr native who was active in that community and a member of the Waterloo Historical Society, contributing many articles to the annual reports. Period: 1900 - 1944.

1695. Shewchuk, John P. **A Canadian tragedy: the story of John Watson of Ayr**. University of Waterloo (student essay, History), 1986. 22 p. Loc: OKIT.

A biography of John Watson (1820-1903) stressing his roles as industrialist and community leader in Ayr. The author refers to Watson's early work experience in the Shotts Iron Works near Glasgow, Scotland, and with Fisher and McQuesten in Hamilton and Fisher and Lutz in Galt before establishing his own business in Ayr in 1847. Period: 1846 - 1903.

1696. Shewchuk, John P. "John Watson of Ayr." **Waterloo Historical Society**. 1986. 74: 145-157. ill. Loc: all.

A biography of Watson (1820-1903), Scots-born manufacturer of agricultural implements and Ayr's leading citizen from 1850 to the 1890s, including details of business practices and successes and a chronology of the industrial property. Sources include reminiscences by a former employee, notes by Watson's daughter who was first principal of the Macdonald Institute in Guelph from 1903 to 1920, and other materials held by Watson's great-grandson. Period: 1820 - 1903.

1697. Groh, Herbert. "A long-neglected son of Waterloo County." **Waterloo Historical Society**. 1961. 49: 32-34. Loc: all.

A short biography of Ephraim Weber (1870-1956), writer, teacher, rancher, and correspondent with L.M. Montgomery. Period: 1870 - 1956.

1698. Groh, Ivan. "Ephraim Weber." **Waterloo Historical Society**. 1962. 50: 98,101. Loc: all.

An account of the family of Ephraim Weber, a writer from Waterloo County who later moved to Alberta. Period: 1895 - 1962.

1699. Middleton, Jesse Edgar and Landon, Fred. "William G. Weichel, M.P.P.." **The Province of Ontario: a history, 1615-1927**. Toronto: Dominion Publishing Company, 1927. Vol. 3, pp. 258-259. port. Loc: OWTL, OWTU.

A profile of the Waterloo hardware merchant and politician, including an account of the family business. Period: 1870 - 1926.

1700. "William G. Weichel." **Waterloo Historical Society**. 1949. 37: 46-47. Loc: all.

A brief biography of the Elmira-born businessman who was elected Mayor of Waterloo in 1911 and a member of the Ontario Legislature in 1923. Period: 1871 - 1949.

1701. "Reverend Anthony Weiler, Ph.D., D.D.." **Waterloo Historical Society**. 1949. 37: 45-46. Loc: all.

An obituary of the senior priest of the Congregation of the Resurrection who died at the age of 94. A graduate of St Jerome's College in 1877, he first served at St Clement's Church, Preston and then at the Holy Family Church, New Hamburg. He was also associate master of novices at the novitiate in Kitchener. Period: 1855 - 1949.

1702. "Alex H. Welker retires from high school board." **Waterloo Historical Society**. 1964. 52: 78. Loc: all.

A note of Welker's retirement from the Kitchener-Waterloo High School Board after 54 years of service. Period: 1910 - 1964.

1703. "Fifty two years on high school board." **Waterloo Historical Society**. 1961. 49: 62-63. ill. Loc: all.

A biographical sketch of Alex Welker, co-founder of Dominion-Electrohome Industries Ltd, founder of Met-Craft Industries Ltd, and for 52 years a member of the Kitchener-Waterloo High School Board. Period: 1907 - 1961.

1704. "Clayton W. Wells." **Waterloo Historical Society**. 1934. 22: 150-151. Loc: all.

An obituary of the dentist Wells (1862-1934) who was an active member of the Waterloo community and author of "A historical sketch of the Town of Waterloo, Ontario," published in the 1928 annual report of the Waterloo Historical Society. The article lists his service to the Town Council, the Independent Order of Oddfellows (Germania Lodge), the local Hive of the Knights of the Maccabees, the Waterloo Musical Society, and the Press Section of the Canadian Wheelmen's Association. Period: 1862 - 1934.

1705. "Augustus Werner." **Waterloo Historical Society**. 1937. 25: 275-276. Loc: all.

A short biography of Werner (1856-1937), Elmira pharmacist, manager of the Elmira branch of Bell Telephone, and a member of the Elmira School Board for many years. Period: 1856 - 1937.

1706. "John Lehman Wideman." **Waterloo Historical Society**. 1917. 5: 61. ill. Loc: all.

A short biography of Wideman (1833-1917), Woolwich Township Clerk for 32 years, postmaster of St Jacobs for 44 years, and a director of the Waterloo Mutual Fire Insurance Company. Period: 1833 - 1917.

1707. "William Wylie Wilkinson." **Waterloo Historical Society**. 1945. 33: 43-44. Loc: all.

A short biography of the Galt businessman, who owned the drygoods firm of Wilkinson and Mickleborough until his retirement in 1929. Active in community affairs, Wilkinson sat on the Public and Collegiate School Boards, as well as the Galt City Council. Period: 1867 - 1945.

1708. Dickson, R.H., Mrs. "Miss Katherine Langdon Wilks: an appreciation." **Waterloo Historical Society**. 1948. 36: 45-49. ill. Loc: all.

A tribute to the owner of Cruickston Park who died at the age of 90. The author describes Miss Wilks' interests in horses, charities (she was president of the Galt Red Cross for 25 years), travelling and family tradition. A photograph of Miss Wilks precedes the article and one of Cruickston Park can be found at the front of the 1948 Waterloo Historical Society's Annual Report. Period: 1858 - 1948.

1709. Fraser, Alexander. "Samuel James Williams." **A history of Ontario: its resources and development**. Toronto: The Canada History Co., 1907. Pp. 972-974. Loc: OWTL, OWTU.

President and general manufacturer of the Berlin shirt manufacturing business, Williams, Greene & Rome, Williams also promoted the Ontario Sugar Co. and served on Town Council and Board of Trade. Period: 1853 - 1906.

1710. "Amasa Winger." **Waterloo Historical Society**. 1953. 41: 47. Loc: all.

An obituary of Winger (1869-1953), leading citizen of Elmira and owner of a dry-goods store for forty years. Period: 1869 - 1953.

1711. Weissenborn, Georg K. "William John Wintemberg, father of Canadian archaeology (1876-1941)." **German-Canadian Yearbook / Deutschkanadisches Jahrbuch**. 1986. 9: 198-202. ill. Loc: OKIT, OWTL, OWTUCG.

A short biography of the New Dundee native, from his early years as an apprentice tailor to his appointment as Assistant Archaeologist at the Victoria Memorial Museum in Ottawa. The author notes Wintemberg's many publications in folklore and archaeology and his work for the Canadian Folk-Lore Society founded in 1908. Period: 1876 -

1941.

1712. Woeller, Richard. "William John Wintemberg." **Waterloo Historical Society.** 1979. 67: 4-9. ill. Loc: all.

A biography of the archaeologist born in New Dundee, including references to his research in Ontario prehistory and his many scholarly papers on folklore and Indian artifacts. Period: 1876 - 1941.

1713. "Father Winter honoured." **Waterloo Historical Society.** 1963. 51: 53. Loc: all.

A biographical sketch of Rev. Simon J. Winter, who in 1963 had been teaching for almost fifty years at St Jerome's College. Period: 1914 - 1963.

1714. "Sixty-sixth wedding anniversary." **Waterloo Historical Society.** 1969. 57: 69. Loc: all.

A note of the anniversary of Mr and Mrs Abraham Wismer of Preston. Period: 1903 - 1969.

1715. Middleton, Jesse Edgar and Landon, Fred. "Edward E. Woelfle and Gustave A. Woelfle." **The Province of Ontario: a history, 1615-1927.** Toronto: Dominion Publishing Company, 1927. Vol. 4, p. 436. Loc: OWTL, OWTU.

A profile of the machine shops of John Jacob Woelfle and his two sons in Berlin/Kitchener. Period: 1845 - 1926.

1716. "W. Ervin Woelfle." **Waterloo Historical Society.** 1949. 37: 47. Loc: all.

A brief biography of the proprietor of the W.E. Woelfle Shoe Company and active member of the Waterloo County Health Association, the Lodge, Rotary, and St John's Anglican Church. Period: 1871 - 1949.

1717. Campbell, Alexander D., Dr. "The lively little saint of St Jacobs." **Waterloo Historical Society.** 1986. 74: 137-140. Loc: all.

A brief sketch of Dr Napoleon Bonaparte Wolfe, born in 1823 in Lancaster County, Pennsylvania, who practised in St Jacobs from 1853 to 1857. He later built up a lucrative practice in Cincinnati and published a book on his belief in spiritualism. Dr Wolfe visited Berlin, Ontario in 1888. Period: 1853 - 1888.

1718. Page, Frank E. "Doctor Ward Woolner." **Waterloo Historical Society.** 1954. 42: 43-44. Loc: all.

An account of various tributes honouring the 75th birthday of Dr Ward Woolner and marking his retirement as Medical Health Officer of Ayr and North Dumfries. Period: 1879 - 1954.

1719. Middleton, Jesse Edgar and Landon, Fred. "Joseph H. Wuest." **The Province of Ontario: a history, 1615-1927.** Toronto: Dominion Publishing Company, 1927. Vol. 4, p. 592. Loc: OWTL, OWTU.

A profile of the president of the Fischmann Spring Co. of Kitchener. Period: 1854 - 1926.

1720. Becker, Janet. "Creek Cottage." **Waterloo Historical Society.** 1986. 74: 63-72. ill. Loc: all.

A biography of Robert Wyllie (1805-1875) who migrated to Galt in about 1835 and pioneered the village of Mudge's Mills, renamed Ayr in 1840. Postmaster, merchant, and Ayr agent for marriage licenses, the **Dumfries Reformer** and various insurance companies, Justice of the Peace, and president of the Ayr Drill Association at the time of the Fenian raids, Wyllie carried on his business in the Wyllie Block on Northumberland Street. Creek Cottage, first historical site to be designated in North Dumfries Township, is a one-storey frame structure in the Regency style, apparently dating from the late 1840s. Family letters sent to relatives in Gladstone, Missouri provide valuable evidence of Ayr life in the nineteenth century. Period: 1835 - 1875.

SURNAMES BEGINNING WITH Y

1721. "James Young, Galt." **The Canadian biographical dictionary and portrait gallery of eminent and self-made men, Ontario volume.** Toronto: American Biographical Publishing Co., 1880. Pp. 701-702. Loc: OWTL, OWTU.

A biography of the newspaper proprietor and editor who represented South Waterloo as a Liberal in the Dominion Parliament from 1867 to 1878. Period: 1835 - 1880.

1722. McNaught, Carlton. "Hon. James Young: Canadian patriot." **Waterloo Historical Society.** 1918. 6: 37-43. ill. Loc: all.

A biography by Young's nephew who notes his uncle's political career as the Liberal MP for South Waterloo from 1867 to 1878 and MPP for North Brant from 1879 to 1887 and his introduction of the regular reporting of parliamentary debates in the Dominion Parliament. The owner of the **Dumfries Reformer** at the age of 18, Young also wrote **Reminiscences of the early history of Galt and the settlement of Dumfries** (1880). Period: 1835 - 1913.

1723. O'Hallarn, Michael. **The political views of James Young: editor of the Dumfries Reformer from 1853 to 1863.** Waterloo Lutheran University (B.A. thesis, History), 1967. 22 p. bibl. Loc: OWTL.

A study of the political philosophy of James Young (1835-1913) through an examination of his newspaper editorials. The author concludes that Young represented the non-Anglican Protestants of western Upper Canada in his support of measures which were anti-Roman Catholic, anti-French and opposed to the privileged position of the Anglican Church. Period: 1853 - 1863.

1724. "Unveiling of plaque to the memory of the Honourable James Young, 1835-1913." **Waterloo Historical Society**. 1961. 49: 25-31. ill. Loc: all.

A short biography of the editor and publisher of the **Dumfries Reformer** who represented the Galt area federally or provincially from 1867 to 1887 and was a prominent community leader and notable local historian. The article quotes remarks made at the unveiling ceremony at Young's Galt home, Thornhill. Period: 1835 - 1913.

SURNAMES BEGINNING WITH Z

1725. Crawford, Sybil Card. "George Henry Ziegler 1889-1981." **Waterloo Historical Society**. 1988. 76: 54-77. ill. Loc: all.

A biography listing Ziegler's accomplishments and referring to his parents and ancestors in Germany. Period: 1889 - 1981.

1726. "Elizabeth Ziegler." **Waterloo Historical Society**. 1942. 30: 243-244. Loc: all.

An obituary of the teacher for whom the Elizabeth Ziegler School in Waterloo is named. Period: c1869 - 1942.

1727. Middleton, Jesse Edgar and Landon, Fred. "George Henry Ziegler." **The Province of Ontario: a history, 1615-1927**. Toronto: Dominion Publishing Company, 1927. Vol. 4, p. 585. port. Loc: OWTL, OWTU.

A profile of the principal of the Kitchener Conservatory of Music who also directed other musical organizations including the Kitchener Ladies' Band, Kitchener Symphony Orchestra and various church choirs. Period: 1885 - 1926.

1728. Middleton, Jesse Edgar and Landon, Fred. "The Rev. Albert Lawrence Zinger, C.R., Ph.D.." **The Province of Ontario: a history, 1615-1927**. Toronto: Dominion Publishing Company, 1927. Vol. 4, p. 386. Loc: OWTL, OWTU.

A profile of the pastor of St Mary's Roman Catholic Church, Kitchener and former head of St Jerome's College. Period: 1901 - 1926.

1729. "John Zryd." **Waterloo Historical Society**. 1917. 5: 56. ill. Loc: all.

A biography of Zryd (1835-1917), one of the last of Hespeler's pioneer businessmen. He had a hardware and tinsmith business and was town clerk for thirteen years. Period: 1835 - 1917.

1730. "Frank F. Zwick." **Waterloo Historical Society**. 1947. 35: 52. Loc: all.

A brief biography of the Waterloo doctor who served as county coroner and in both world wars. Active in community affairs, Dr Zwick sat on the Waterloo Public School Board and was a member of the Westmount Golf and Country Club. Period: 1914 - 1947.

ECONOMIC DEVELOPMENT PROCESSES

1731. Bloomfield, Elizabeth. "Community, ethos and local initiative in urban economic growth: review of a theme in Canadian urban history." **Urban History Yearbook**. Edited by David Reeder. Leicester: Leicester University Press, 1983. Pp. 53-72. Loc: OWTL, OWTU.

An essay on the role of human agency in shaping the economic bases of Canadian towns and cities, especially the individual entrepreneurs and associations of community leaders working through municipal councils and boards of trade. The author discusses concepts of community leadership and urban ethos and surveys such growth strategies as railway promotion, industrial bonusing, advertising and boosterism. The Canada-wide study refers at several points to the importance of human agency in the growth of Berlin/Kitchener. Period: 1850 - 1940.

1732. Cowan, H. **Selected economic material on the Midwestern Ontario Region**. Toronto: Ontario Department of Economics and Development, Regional Development Branch, 1966. 76 p. ill. maps, charts. Loc: OWT.

A report on the economic development of Huron, Perth, Wellington and Waterloo Counties. Population, labour force, education, income, agriculture, manufacturing, construction, retail trade and mining are considered. Some sections refer to specific municipalities such as Kitchener, Galt, and Waterloo. Period: 1951 - 1966.

1733. Dreger, Frederick L. **The economic development of the Grand River Valley**. University of Toronto, 1932. 78 p. bibl. Loc: OKIT.

An historical survey of the settlement and industrial growth of towns and cities along the river, including Galt and Kitchener. Kitchener's industries are classified by product and American companies are identified. Period: 1784 - 1932.

1734. "Getting the facts to provide the jobs: survey of the resources of Kitchener-Waterloo." **Canadian Business**. 1944. 17: 48-9, 136. ill. mf. Loc: OWTL, OWTU.

Reference from the Canadian Periodical Index. Period: 1944.

1735. Kitchener Board of Trade/ Waterloo Board of Trade/ Canadian Chamber of Commerce. **Kitchener-Waterloo survey: a fact-finding survey for post-war planning, part I: the findings**. Montreal: Canadian Chamber of Commerce, 1944. 47 p. ill., maps, tables. Loc: OWTUR, OKIT.

Report of a survey of the potential for economic growth and maximum employment in the twin cities. Topics include the viability of postwar manufacturing, industry, farming, income distribution, and wage and salary levels. Appendices provide statistical information on households, farm communities and businesses and illustrate purchasing trends for goods such as home appliances, automobiles, machinery, farm equipment and travel. Period: 1939 - 1944.

1736. Kitchener Board of Trade/ Waterloo Board of Trade/ Canadian Chamber of Commerce. **Kitchener-Waterloo survey: an approach to post-war planning for boards of trade and chambers of commerce, part II: the procedure**. Montreal: Canadian Chamber of Commerce, 1944. 46 p. charts, map. Loc: OKIT.

A description of the procedures used in the economic survey of the Kitchener-Waterloo area, which was planned as a model for other boards of trade and chambers of commerce. An organization chart, notes on how to organize the survey, sample questionnaires, suggestions for publicity, and advice on tabulating the results are included. Period: 1944 - 1945.

1737. "Kitchener-Waterloo." **Financial Post**. 1965. 39 p. ill. Loc: OKIT, OWTL, OWTU, OWT.

A special section of the newspaper describing current economic conditions and mentioning the universities and local companies in the furniture, engineering, shoe, insurance, textile, rubber, plastics, food and meat-packing sectors. Period: 1964 - 1965.

1738. Myhal, Taras G. **Study of the evolution of Kitchener's labour force structure 1951-1977**. University of Waterloo (B.E.S. thesis), 1979. 2 fiche. tables. mf. Loc: OWTUM.

An analysis of Kitchener as a maturing urban complex, including a brief economic history of the region. The author describes the recent shift of its labour force from manufacturing to more service-oriented functions and discusses reasons for the diversification. Kitchener is compared to other cities in southern Ontario. Period: 1951 - 1977.

1739. Oelschlager, William. **Darlegung der augenblicklichen financiellen Verhältnisse Canada's nebst vergleichenden statistischen Tabellen, als Antwort auf Hrn. Fair Play's Angaben mit Ansichten über die brennende Tagesfrage: "Schutzzoll oder Freihandel."**. Berlin: P.E.W. Moyer, Daily News Printing, 1878. 21 p. tables. Loc: OKITW.

A discussion of the issue of free trade. Period:

1877 - 1878.

1740. Panabaker, D.N. "President's address." **Waterloo Historical Society**. 1927. 15: 256-263. tables. Loc: all.

Remarks on various topics including the Winter School courses in New Hamburg, the Waterloo County census of 1861 (summarized in charts showing ethnic origin and religion), and a list of business advertisements between 1860 and 1880. Period: c1860 - 1927.

1741. Panabaker, D.N. "Presidential address: eighty years ago." **Waterloo Historical Society**. 1936. 24: 190-213. Loc: all.

Remarks on the state of the world in 1853, the year Waterloo County was officially established. Topics include the role of the Grand River in shipping, the effect of the Crimean War on prices, and urban rivalry among Chatham, Brantford and Galt. Period: 1853 - 1858.

1742. Perry, Robert Louis. "So, nationalism: what can it buy?" **Financial Post**. 1971. 65: 1-2. ill. mf. Loc: OWTL, OWTU.

Reference from the Canadian Periodical Index. Period: 1971.

1743. "Preview of post-war purchasing power: some findings of the Kitchener-Waterloo survey." **Canadian Business**. 1944. 17: 30-1. tables. mf. Loc: OWTL, OWTU.

Reference from the Canadian Periodical Index. Period: 1946.

1744. Sutherland, S.H. "Jobs for post-war." **Canadian Business**. 1944. 17: 36-7, 122. tables. mf. Loc: OWTL, OWTU.

A brief account of the survey of the economic resources of Kitchener-Waterloo, undertaken by the Canadian Chamber of Commerce. Reference from the Canadian Periodical Index.

AGRICULTURE AND FARMING

1745. "Agricultural and livestock statistics for Waterloo County 1927." **Waterloo Historical Society**. 1928. 16: 11. Loc: all.

A list of statistics for crop yields and livestock numbers. Period: 1927.

1746. Allen, Frederick George. **The diffusion of artificial insemination of dairy cattle in Waterloo and surrounding counties**. Waterloo Lutheran University (B.A. thesis, Geography), 1971. 54 l. ill., bibl. Loc: OWTL.

A study of the development of the practice,

including a brief history of early organizations and notes of problems and successes associated with standards, costs and administration. Period: 1941 - 1967.

1747. "Apprenticeship of Edward Davis, an abandoned child, by the town wardens of Waterloo to Christian Schwartzentruber, a farmer of Wilmot Township, 1 June 1839." **Waterloo Historical Society**. 1969. 57: 80-82. Loc: all.

Transcript of a 1839 apprenticeship contract of a young boy (aged 5) with a farmer. In return for working for Schwartzentruber, Edward is to have three years of schooling, food and lodging, and tools to set up a farm of his own when he is twenty-one. Period: 1839.

1748. Barrie, James R. "The Hill in North Dumfries in 1841." **Waterloo Historical Society**. 1986. 74: 129-136. ill. Loc: all.

Text of a letter written by James Edgar in 1841, describing various aspects of farm making and pioneer life. Edgar (1798-1873) emigrated from Scotland in 1836 to become blacksmith of the Dickie Settlement and in 1837 bought Lot 38, Concession VII, one mile southwest of Ayr, a property known as The Hill which is still farmed by the fifth generation of his family. The Robert W. Edgar family hosted a family reunion in 1987 to mark 150 years of farming. Period: 1836 - 1841.

1749. Barrie, William C. **Excerpts from farming diaries of Will Barrie, Cedar Creek Road, North Dumfries Township: 1912, 1913, 1914/ Excerpts from farming diaries of Ephriam S. Cressman, Breslau, Waterloo Township: 1905, 1906, 1907**. Kitchener: Doon Heritage Crossroads, 1 v. ill. Loc: OKDHC.

Transcriptions of portions of two diaries giving details on daily farming activities at the beginning of the twentieth century. The Cressman farm was primarily a livestock operation while the Barrie farm exemplified mixed farming. Introductions to the diaries provide background information on the farmsteads and a summary of the diary entries. Period: 1905 - 1914.

1750. Bean, Gordon W. **Hallman farm recollections of 1923**. 1989. 6 p. Loc: OKIT.

A collection of reminiscences including a brief history of the farm, its buildings and farming practices, as well as references to family members. Period: 1842 - 1923.

1751. Bechtel, George. **The 1914 look: landscapes and gardens of Waterloo County**. Kitchener: Doon Heritage Crossroads, Heritage Resources Department, Regional Municipality of Waterloo, 1991. 221 p. ill., bibl. Loc: OCLG, OKIT.

A guide for historical interpreters of Doon Heritage Crossroads, explaining gardening styles and processes from the early 20th century. Topics include attitudes toward gardening, garden design, garden location, seeds and seed dealers, flowers, vegetables, the character of the historical landscape, methods of gardening, garden schools, gardening societies, gardening for profit, and marketing. Period: 1910 - 1914.

1752. "Bend-Wright farm house, Conestogo." **Waterloo Historical Society**. 1968. 56: 84-85. ill. Loc: all.

A history of the Bend-Wright farm, built in 1864, which became the Conestogo Golf and Country Club in 1968. Period: 1864 - 1968.

1753. Bergey, Lorna L. "Wilmot family farms, part 1." **Waterloo Historical Society**. 1962. 50: 62-65. ill. Loc: all.

Information about four Wilmot families who have held their farms since receiving patents from the Canada Company. The families are the Hohls, the Hoerles, the Ditners, and the Koch or Cook Family. Period: 1848 - 1962.

1754. Bergey, Lorna L. "Wilmot family farms, part 2." **Waterloo Historical Society**. 1963. 51: 70-73. ill. Loc: all.

A continuation of an article about Wilmot family farms, with information about the Schwartzentruber family, the Murrays, the Honderichs, the Guenthers, and the Gingerichs. Period: 1825 - 1963.

1755. "Century farmers." **Waterloo Historical Society**. 1962. 50: 11. Loc: all.

A report of a meeting at Vance's School Section #17 of six descendants of farmers who settled in the area a century earlier. Period: 1862 - 1962.

1756. Class, R.E. **Study of the agricultural development in Waterloo County**. Ontario Agricultural College (student essay), 1943. 42 p. charts. Loc: OGU.

A brief survey of early settlement, land clearance, early roads and railways as background to analysis of crop and livestock production trends. Period: 1800 - 1940.

1757. Cooper, Mike. **The Kitchener-Waterloo fluid milkshed, 1937-1965**. University of Waterloo (B.A. thesis, Geography), 1967. 1 fiche. maps, tables, bibl. mf. Loc: OWTUM.

A study of the growth of the territory supplying raw milk for fluid purposes (milk and cream). The author describes the organization of the entire operation, including the roles of the government, the distributor, the transporter and the Ontario Milk Marketing Board. Period: 1937 - 1965.

1758. Cowan, Jennie F. "History at the International Plowing Match." **Waterloo Historical Society**. 1954. 42: 34-42. ill. Loc: all.

A description of the exhibits in the History Tent at the International Plowing Match, 1954. Period: 1954.

1759. **Cruickston Park**. 1973. 1 folded sheet. ill. Loc: OWRA.

A brief history of the large property near Blair and of its past owners, Matthew Wilks Keefer and Katherine Wilks. The estate, noted for the Hereford cattle bred there, became the property of the University of Guelph in 1973. Period: 1824 - 1973.

1760. Curry, John A. **Agriculture on the urban fringe: an exploratory study, Kitchener-Waterloo region**. University of Waterloo (M.A. thesis, Regional Planning), 1978. 2 fiche. mf. Loc: OWTUM.

Some analysis of trends between 1956 and 1971 as background to the main focus on conditions in 1975. Period: 1956 - 1975.

1761. Dominion Sugar Co. **The sugar beet**. Wallaceburg and Berlin: The Company, 1915. 20 p. ill. Loc: OWTUR.

An account of the cultivation and processing of the crop, including short articles by the Department of Agriculture and Prof. R. Harcourt and a 1914 list of local sugar beet growers with their gross returns and returns per acre. An advertisement for the company is attached to the inside front cover. Period: 1914 - 1915.

1762. Elliott, Hugh C. **An outline of the history of agriculture in Waterloo County**. Ontario Agricultural College (student essay), 1923. 41 p. bibl. Loc: OKIT.

A study of pioneer and current farming practices, including crop-livestock combinations, methods of harvesting, labour-saving machinery, farmers' markets, reciprocity with the United States, household economics and labour, social activities and farmers' organizations. Period: 1800 - 1923.

1763. Fielding, Jeffrey A. **Farmland rental in an urbanizing environment: the fringes of Kitchener, Waterloo and Cambridge 1971-1978**. University of Waterloo (M.A. thesis, Geography), 1979. 2 fiche. table, bibl. mf. Loc: OWTU.

An investigation of the significance of land ownership, the farmland rental market, and customized farming as trends and options in farm business practices. Period: 1966 - 1979.

1764. "The first bank barn in Waterloo County."
Waterloo Historical Society. 1972. 60: 94. ill.
Loc: all.
   A short entry accompanying the photographs of
James Barclay's bank barn which was in use from
about 1817 to 1955. Period: 1817 - 1955.

1765. Forsyth, R.A. "The Agricultural Representative
Service in Waterloo County (1907-1957)." **Waterloo
Historical Society**. 1956. 44: 55-62. ill. Loc:
all.
   An account of the origins of the service, the
organization of school fairs, and the work of
Frank Hart, J.S. Knapp, E.I. McLoughry and R.A.
Forsyth. Period: 1907 - 1958.

1766. Frey, Kenneth D. **Comparative occupational
aspirations of Old Order Mennonite and non-Old
Older Mennonite farm youth**. University of Guelph
(M.Sc. thesis), 1971. 106 p., tables. Loc: OWTU.
   A study of young Mennonite men, aged 19 to 24,
living north of Waterloo and west of Elmira. The
author found that all Old Order Mennonite
respondents planned to farm, while non-Old Order
Mennonites aspired to a broad range of
occupations. Recommendations are made to
safeguard the Old Mennonite traditions and farming
methods. Period: 1970 - 1971.

1767. "General abstract of agricultural produce, lands
held, occupiers of land, etc. for the County of
Waterloo." **Waterloo Historical Society**. 1928.
16: 10-11. Loc: all.
   A list of statistics from the 1861 Census,
relating to areas of occupied land, numbers of
livestock and crop production. Period: 1861 -

1768. Griffith, Gary Burton. **An analysis of the
economic factors and changes in land-use
associated with the transition to a beef feedlot
system in Waterloo County**. Waterloo Lutheran
University (M.A. thesis, Geography), 1971. 103 l.
ill., bibl. Loc: OWTL.
   A study, based partly on information from ten
feedlot operators, of factors in the shift from
the family farm to a new, specialized, competitive
form of business, and the need for small-scale
operations to change if they are to be viable.
Period: 1970 - 1971.

1769. Hart, Frank C. "The beginnings of agricultural
extension in Waterloo County." **Waterloo
Historical Society**. 1960. 48: 72-76. Loc: all.
   A transcript of a CBC-TV interview with Frank
Hart, the first Agricultural Representative for
Waterloo County in 1907. Topics include problems
of transportation and winning the confidence of

farmers and the benefits of the Junior Farmers
movement and school fairs. Period: 1907 - 1920.

1770. Hoffman, Susan. "Dawson's golden chaff." **Waterloo
Historical Society**. 1981. 69: 61. Loc: all.
   A note on the selection of a superior strain of
wheat by a Scottish immigrant farmer in Galt in
1881. Developed by the Ontario Agricultural
College, the new variety continued to be popular
for winter wheat cultivation in Ontario. Period:
1881.

1771. Hollands, Mara. "Garden to table: continuity and
change in the gardens of Waterloo's Mennonites."
**From Pennsylvania to Waterloo:
Pennsylvania-German folk culture in transition**.
Edited by Susan M. Burke and Matthew H. Hill.
Kitchener: Friends of the Joseph Schneider Haus,
1991. Pp. 108-115. ill. Loc: OKIT.
   A survey of the crops and herbs raised in
Mennonite kitchen gardens in Waterloo County and
methods of food preservation with comments on
changes over time and comparisons with other areas
of Mennonite settlement. Period: 1850 - 1990.

1772. Hunsberger, Wilson. "Threshing day in the
twenties." **Waterloo Historical Society**. 1976.
64: 4-10. ill. Loc: all.
   A short account of the harvesting season
including descriptions of farm machinery used in
the 1920s. Period: 1920 - 1929.

1773. Junior Farmers' Organization. "Century farms of
Waterloo County." **Waterloo Historical Society**.
1967. 55: 56-58. Loc: all.
   A list of farms owned by the same families for
at least a century, with their rural mail
addresses. Each farm is indexed in the database
by the original family name and the 1967 owner's
name. Period: 1867 - 1967.

1774. Knapp, J.S. and Brubacher, A.B. and Steckle, John.
**Waterloo County Holstein-Friesian history,
1882-1962**. Galt: Waterloo Holstein Breeders
Association, 1962. 56 p. ill. Loc: OKDHC.
   A history of the development of the cattle breed
and the Breeders Association, with articles by
J.S. Knapp, A.B. Brubacher, John Steckle, Fred M.
Snyder, Abner B. Martin and J.E. Powell. There is
a list of Waterloo champion cattle and their
owners from 1942 to 1961 and many advertisements
for local livestock farms with photographs of
their cattle. Period: 1882 - 1962.

1775. Ladell, John and Ladell, Monica. "The Gingerich
family, Oaklot Farm, Wilmot Township, Waterloo
County." **Inheritance: Ontario's century farms,
past and present**. Toronto: Macmillan, 1979. Pp.

143-147. Loc: OKIT.

A brief history of the farm, from its first settlement by the Amish family of Jacob Gingerich in 1825-6, through four generations of Gingerichs. The process of farm making is described, with dates of construction of farm buildings. By 1975, it is noted, there were some 3,420 descendants of the six married children of Jacob Gingerich and his wife, Veronica Litwiller. Period: 1825 - 1975.

1776. Lee, Chun-fen. "Land utilization in the middle Grand River valley of western Ontario." **Economic Geography**. 1944. 20: 130-151. ill., maps. Loc: OWTL, OWTU.

A study of the topography, land types, land use and agricultural characteristics of the region, including Waterloo County. The author's maps show that the Waterloo area is typified by dairy and hog farms, while the sandy soil is said to produce high yields of rye and other grains. Period: 1943 - 1944.

1777. Macnaughton, Elizabeth. "Farming among Old Order Mennonites of Ontario in the early twentieth century." **Pennsylvania Mennonite Heritage**. 1991. 14,3: 10-17. ill., map. Loc: OKIT, OWTUCG.

A description of the crops, livestock, gardens and farming techniques of the Woolwich Township Mennonites, noting particularly the Gingrich farmstead on which the Peter Martin House was located. The author comments on ways in which Old Order Mennonites have continued to update their farming methods. Period: 1889 - 1991.

1778. Macnaughton, Elizabeth. **Life in the rural home: Waterloo County 1900-1914**. Kitchener: Doon Heritage Crossroads, Historic Sites Department, Regional Municipality of Waterloo, 1987. 189 p. ill., bibl. Loc: OCLG, OKIT, OWRA, OWRE, OWRN, OWT.

A guide for historical interpreters at Doon Heritage Crossroads, the report focuses on life in the farm home and mainly features the activities of women and children. Information on foodways and health care practices is included, as well as the physical setting of the typical farm house and garden, water and sewage systems, and power supplies. The study is based directly on correspondence, diaries and photographs of Waterloo County farm families. Period: 1900 - 1914.

1779. Macnaughton, Elizabeth. **The new agriculture in Waterloo County**. Kitchener: Doon Heritage Crossroads, Historic Sites Department, Regional Municipality of Waterloo, 1990. 221 p. ill., bibl. Loc: OCLG, OKIT, OWTUCG.

A guide for planners and interpreters at Doon Heritage Crossroads, the report provides detailed information on farm values, income, labour, soils, waterways, weather, land use, crops and crop rotation, weed and pest controls, livestock, machinery, marketing and agricultural societies in the period between 1900 and 1914. Period: 1900 - 1914.

1780. Mage, Julius A. **Land use - edaphic relationships in two selected areas of Woolwich Township**. McMaster University (M.A. thesis, Geography), 1967. 215 l. ill., maps, tables. Loc: OHM.

A study of the relationship between soil characteristics, land use patterns and agricultural productivity, using computerized statistical analysis and detailed map correlations. The author identified the part-time or full-time status of a farm operation as a factor worthy of further study. Period: 1961 - 1965.

1781. Mage, Julius A. **Part-time farming in Southern Ontario with specific reference to Waterloo County**. University of Waterloo (Ph.D. thesis, Geography), 1974. 4 fiche. mf. Loc: OWTL, OWTU.

An analysis of part-time farming as a response by farmers to urbanization. Using the techniques of factor analysis, discriminant analysis, and hierarchical groups, author concludes that the part-time farmer is a force for stability in areas where agricultural and industrial areas are juxtaposed. Period: 1945 - 1974.

1782. Mage, Julius A. "Selected aspects of the agricultural economy of Waterloo County." **The Waterloo County area: selected geographical essays**. Edited by A.G. McLellan. Waterloo: Department of Geography, University of Waterloo, 1971. Pp. 83-95. maps, tabl. Loc: OWTU, OWTL, OWTUCG, OKIT.

A review of soils, climate, land use patterns, crop-livestock combinations, and contrasts between Mennonite and non-Mennonite farm types, based on a sample of 149 farms. The author reports in more detail on a mixed farming area in Woolwich Township. Period: 1880 - 1970.

1783. May, Edna. "Oxen at the International Plowing Match: a radio interview." **Waterloo Historical Society**. 1959. 47: 60-61. ill. Loc: all.

Transcript of a CBC programme hosted by Edna May who interviewed Andrew and Neil Taylor about a pair of oxen they took to the 1959 International Plowing Match. Period: 1957 - 1959.

1784. Maybee, Muriel. **Agricultural systems of three Mennonite orders**. University of Waterloo (B.E.S. thesis, Geography), 1979. 1 fiche. tables, bibl.

mf. Loc: OWTUM.

A study of the variations in farming practices of Old Order Mennonites, Waterloo Markham Mennonites and Ontario Conference Mennonites in Woolwich Township. The author describes the farming traditions of each group, comparing crop-livestock combinations and use of machinery, artificial fertilizers, pesticides and herbicides. Period: 1800 - 1979.

1785. McClure, Robert John. **A feasibility study of commercial upland game bird farms in Waterloo County, Ontario.** Waterloo Lutheran University (M.A. thesis, Geography), 1972. 114 l. ill., bibl. Loc: OWTL.

A study of the development of game farms, including information on the habits of hunters such as their locations, travel patterns, group outings, preferred types of hunting, knowledge and use of game farms, and willingness to pay for hunting facilities. The author also reviews the market potential for new game farms. Period: 1971 - 1972.

1786. McLoughry, E.I. "Agricultural progress in Waterloo County." **Waterloo Historical Society.** 1962. 50: 36-39. Loc: all.

A review of 40 years' work by the former Waterloo County Agricultural Representative. Period: 1907 - 1960.

1787. Olaskey, Terry M. "The history of threshing machinery in Waterloo County as seen at Doon Pioneer Village." **Waterloo Historical Society.** 1974. 62: 64-70. Loc: all.

A description of machines in the Doon collection including products of the John Watson Manufacturing Co. and the Waterloo Manufacturing Co. Period: 1850 - 1907.

1788. Ontario Agricultural Commission. "County of Waterloo." **Report, volume 2, appendix B, containing returns relating to the soil, climate, topographical features; cultivatable area and products of, and the progress and condition of, husbandry in the Province of Ontario.** Toronto: C. Blackett Robinson, 1881. Pp. 587-599. map. Loc: OWTL, OWTU.

A survey of the state of agriculture in the late 1870s, based on answers to 32 questions sent to each township. Information includes the period of settlement, average prices of farms, state of farmhouses and outbuildings, farmers' markets, crops cultivated and chief products. Period: 1878 - 1881.

1789. Panabaker, C.A. **The barefoot farm boy: boyhood reminiscences of C.A. Panabaker, Hespeler.** Kitchener: Waterloo Historical Society in co-operation with the Kitchener-Waterloo Record, 1955. 44 p. Also mf. Loc: OCCA, OCLG, OKIT, OWTUR, OWTUCG, OWRN, OWRSJ.

Recollections of farm life near Hespeler in the 1880s, prefaced by a biographical sketch and photograph of the author. An index is available at the Cambridge Library and Gallery and the City of Cambridge Archives. Period: 1877 - 1893.

1790. Patterson, Nancy-Lou. "Barn-framer and farmer: traditional patterns govern the orderly world of Mennonite barns and farms." **Canadian Collector.** 1982. 17,5: 39-42. ill. Loc: OWTU.

An account of the construction of a Mennonite framed barn, drawn from the experience of Simeon E. Martin, a Waterloo barn framer for many years. The author discusses the layout of the Pennsylvania banked barn and the function of each part, and outlines the patterns of harvesting, ploughing and seeding. Period: 1892 - 1984.

1791. Pierson, Joan. "Century Farm Fair." **Family Herald.** 1967. 99,23: 32-33. ill. Loc: OKITW.

A mainly illustrated account of the fair organized by the Rummelhardt Women's Institute about farm life in the 1860s. It describes display of antique farm equipment, furniture and cars and demonstrations of quilting and the making of soap and icecream by people in centennial costumes. Period: 1867 - 1967.

1792. "Progress removes 114 year old farm." **Waterloo Historical Society.** 1960. 48: 71. Loc: all.

A brief note of the subdivision of 170-acre Quickfall farm in Waterloo for 149 homes. Richard Quickfall acquired the land in 1846. Period: 1846 - 1960.

1793. **Public sale of farmstock and implements.** Waterloo: Chronicle-Telegraph, 1914. 1 sheet. Loc: OWTUR.

A poster advertising the auction to be held at the Dilman Moyer farm, north of Bridgeport on 4 March 1914. Horses, cattle, implements, and grain and hay and listed for sale. Period: 1913 - 1914.

1794. Reaman, G. Elmore. **A history of agriculture in Ontario.** Toronto: Saunders, 1970. 2 v. 180, 264 p. Loc: OKIT, OWTU, OWTUCG.

A general survey by a professor at the Ontario Agricultural College in Guelph. Among the references to Waterloo County are accounts of rivalries among German-language newspapers that covered agriculture (Vol.1, pp.112-3) and of the Agricultural Representative Service (Vol.2) including recollections by Elliot McLoughry who served Waterloo County from 1924 to 1951. Period: 1800 - 1950.

1795. Schierholtz, C.W. "The Elmira Monthly Fair." **Waterloo Historical Society.** 1947. 35: 32-33. Loc: all.

A brief account of the fair which began in the 1860s and was the chief livestock market in the district. Period: c1860 - 1947.

1796. Schmidt, John T. "International plowing match, 1954: it took a hurricane to stop Waterloo County's largest agricultural event!." **Waterloo Historical Society.** 1954. 42: 28-33. ill. Loc: all.

An account of the match which was sponsored by the Ontario Plowmen's Association and interrupted by Hurricane Hazel. Names are given of farm owners, committee members and winners. Period: 1954.

1797. Scorgie, Ed. **The sugar beet industry in southwestern Ontario 1902-1968.** University of Waterloo (B.A. thesis, Geography), 1970. 2 fiche. ill., maps, tables, bibl. mf. Loc: OWTUM.

An historical account of the industry in the communities of Berlin (Kitchener), Dresden, Wallaceburg, Wiarton and Chatham. The author discusses the roles of farmers, companies and government, the commercial significance of the crop, land and climatic factors, the use of immigrant labour for harvesting and processing, marketing strategies, and the demise of the industry in the region. There are profiles of the Ontario Sugar Company and the Dominion Sugar Company of Berlin (Kitchener). Period: 1902 - 1968.

1798. "Seed growers' award to W.C. Barrie." **Waterloo Historical Society.** 1964. 52: 60. Loc: all.

A short note of the Canadian Seed Growers' long service award to W.C. Barrie at a meeting of the Waterloo County Soil and Crop Improvement Association. Period: 1920 - 1964.

1799. Snyder, O.A., Mrs. "1824 barn boards." **Waterloo Historical Society.** 1974. 62: 31-33. ill. Loc: all.

A short history of the Lyndenbrook Farm, lot 128 of the German Company Tract, with a brief description of the buildings on the property. In 1814 John C. Snyder and his wife Catherine Shantz settled the land which, except for the years 1856 to 1890, remained in the family to 1974. Period: 1814 - 1974.

1800. Soehner, Muriel. **The development of agriculture in the Waterloo area before 1900.** Wilfrid Laurier University (B.A. thesis, Geography), 1978. 77 l. maps, bibl. Loc: OWTL.

A study of factors in the county's first century of agricultural development. Information on settlers, farming practices, trends in technology, industrial growth, crop diversification, market prices and exports is analyzed to determine the extent to which each factor influenced change and improvement. Period: 1800 - 1900.

1801. van der Linde, Robert. **Factors affecting the quality of agriculture in a selected area of Waterloo County: the Erbsville area.** University of Waterloo (B.A. thesis, Geography), 1968. 2 fiche. charts, maps, tables, bibl. mf. Loc: OWTUM.

A study of the physical basis for agriculture and the relationship between land capability and present land use. The author identifies changes in land use and property ownership between 1955 and 1967, and predicts future changes based on current trends. Period: 1955 - 1967.

1802. "Wayne Snyder farm home razed." **Waterloo Historical Society.** 1968. 56: 78-79. ill. Loc: all.

A report of the demolition in 1968 of a home built in 1843 by Jacob Schneider and subsequently occupied by four generations of Snyders. In the second generation Jacob C. Schneider changed his surname to Snyder. Period: 1843 - 1968.

1803. Wellington District Agricultural Society. **Rules of the exhibition, Guelph, July 24, 1851.** Berlin: H. Eby, Printer, 1841. 1 sheet. Loc: OGU.

John Harland's name is on the broadside as secretary of the society. Part of Goodwin-Haines Collection. Period: 1841.

FINANCE, LAND AND CAPITAL

1804. **Constitution of the Mennonite Aid Union.** 1866-. Loc: OWTUCGR.

A series of booklets summarizing the rules and procedures of the organization formed in 1866 by Brethren of the Mennonite Church for mutual assistance in case of fire; coverage was extended to loss by fire, lightning, wind or water in 1893. The Conrad Grebel College Library holds copies of editions dated 1866 (in German), 1876 (in German), 1893, 1909, 1919, 1933, 1949, 1954, 1959, 1964, 1969 and 1974. Each edition since 1900 names officers and directors and contains an historical preface. Conrad Grebel College Library also holds a copy of a translation of the 1876 constitution printed in 1959. Period: 1866 - 1974.

1805. Cowls, W.J. and Hawson, J.B. and Panabaker, J.H. **A century of mutuality.** Waterloo: Mutual Life Assurance Co. of Canada, 1970. 167 p. ill. Loc: OKIT, OWT, OWTL, OWTU.

A history of the establishment and growth of the insurance company which began in 1869 in Waterloo. The work includes brief biographies of the company's first officers. Period: 1868 - 1970.

1806. Cunningham, Roderick K. **The legacy of the Gore.** Toronto: The company, 1989. 84 p. ill. Loc: OCCA.

A history commemorating the company's 150th anniversary. The origin of the company and its development, presidents and managing directors are described within the context of Canadian history. Period: 1839 - 1989.

1807. Dominion Life Assurance Co. **Annual report.** The Company, 1921 - 1984. Loc: OWT.

Reports containing presidents' messages, financial statements, and lists of boards of directors and officers. The Waterloo Public Library has reports for most years since 1921, but is missing reports for 1922, 1923, 1928, 1936, 1937, 1941, 1952 and 1981. Period: 1888 - 1984.

1808. Dominion Life Assurance Co. **Four score years 1889-1969: a brief history of the growth and progress of the company.** Waterloo: The Company, 1969. 19 p. ill. Loc: OKIT.

Brief biographies of the founders and an outline of company history in 20-year periods. There are lists and photographs of the first board of directors and the 1969 board. Period: 1889 - 1969.

1809. Dominion Life Assurance Co. **Profiles in leadership: a concise chronicle of accomplishment to commemorate the seventy-fifth anniversary of the Dominion Life Assurance Company.** Waterloo: The Company, 1964. 34 p. ill., tables. Loc: OWTL, OKIT, OWT.

A record of the company and its prominent founders and employees. The achievements of company notables such as Thomas Hilliard, Ford S. Kumpf, and A.S. Upton are related as well as information on the administration and policies of Dominion Life. There are lists of the company's assets and insurance in force from 1893 to 1963 and of long-time employees and branch trophy winners. Period: 1889 - 1964.

1810. Economical Mutual Fire Insurance Co. **70: 1871-1941: threescore years and ten.** Kitchener: The Company, 1941. 24 p. ill. Loc: OKIT.

A handsomely printed commemorative booklet that contains less historical information than the 1921 company publication but includes photographs of current directors, managers and the office premises. Period: 1871 - 1941.

1811. Economical Mutual Fire Insurance Co. **Industry and enterprise, 1871-1921.** Kitchener: The Company, 1921. 23 p. ill. Loc: OKIT.

A summary of milestones in the company's history, illustrated with facsimiles of the original subscribers' list and early policies, portraits of directors and officers, and exterior and interior views of the company offices. Period: 1871 - 1921.

1812. Foot, W.W. **One hundred economical years.** Economical Mutual Fire Insurance Co., 1971. 26 p. ill. Loc: OKIT, OWTU.

Brief commemorative history of the company, organized by the terms of the various presidents: H.F.J. Jackson, William Oelschlager, Hugo Kranz, John Fennell, W.H. Schmalz, Frederick W. Snyder, George C.H. Lang, Henry Knell, William D. Euler and Henry C. Krug. There are drawings of the various buildings used for company offices and photographs of the board of directors in 1971. Period: 1871 - 1971.

1813. Gnys, Stefan Chester W. **Bank branch location and distribution: a case study.** Waterloo Lutheran University (B.A. thesis, Geography), 1973. 74 l. maps, bibl. Loc: OWTL.

A study of the rationale behind the selection of bank branch locations in communities. The first two chapters deal with branch trends found in Canadian banks generally, while chapters three and four concentrate on bank branch development in Waterloo before 1972. The author concludes that the number of branches in an area depends on the factors of population density, the assurance of measurable economic growth (both residential and industrial) and traffic patterns. Period: 1830 - 1972.

1814. Gore Mutual Fire Insurance Co. **Annual meeting held at Galt on January 23, 1893.** CIHM Microfiche series, no. A00712. The Company, 1893. 1 fiche. mf. Loc: OWTU, OWTL.

The company's 54th annual report, containing statements from the auditors, inspectors and directors. A financial summary for the year is given, with an announcement of the purchase of a site at the corner of Main and Ainslie Streets for a new building. Period: 1892 - 1893.

1815. Jones, R.T. **The Waterloo Trust and Savings Company.** University of Waterloo (student essay, History), 1974. 1 v. (various pagings). ill., tables, bibl. Loc: OKIT.

A study of the company's founders and their

original concept of a trust company, with details of the company's growth. Period: 1913 - 1974.

1816. Mennonite Credit Union (Ontario) Limited. **Working together ... the story of Mennonite Credit Union (Ontario) Limited 1964-1984: an account of beginnings and of growth, of learning and of sharing, of creating a financial organization within and for a particular community "where brothers and sisters in heritage and faith serve each other by working together"**. Waterloo: The Company, 1985. 77 p. ill., tables. Loc: OWTUCG.

A history of the organization's creation, evolution and expectations, including an explanation of its cooperative philosophy. Charts and tables illustrate the success of the credit union and there are photographs and lists of notable individuals. Period: 1964 - 1984.

1817. Mutual Life Assurance Co. of Canada. **Annual report**. Waterloo: The Company, 1954-. Loc: OKIT.

Very brief reports to policyholders, each including a balance sheet, list of directors and officers, and some promotional messages. The Kitchener Public Library has reports for the years 1954 to 1965 (except 1961 and 1964) and for 1982 to 1990. The 85th report for 1954 has 24 pages and is more detailed, including a message from the president, highlights from the addresses to policyholders by the president and general manager, a simplified history of the insurance business, some interesting facts on the business methods, and a list of branch offices. Period: 1954 - 1990.

1818. Mutual Life Assurance Co. of Canada. **An epic of progress**. Waterloo: The Company, 1950. 40 p. ill. Loc: OKIT, OWTLR.

A promotional history marking the company's 82nd year of operation and dedicated to W.H. Somerville. The early years under the direction of its founders, J.B. Hughes, Isaac E. Bowman, Cyrus M. Taylor, Moses Springer, John B. Snyder, J.W. Walden, and John Allchin, are described. The work includes an overview of the company's insurance policies and plans and brief biographical profiles of prominent company leaders from the Waterloo area. Period: 1868 - 1950.

1819. Mutual Life Assurance Co. of Canada. **The men who made the Mutual: some remarkable facts connected with the organization of Canada's only mutual life assurance company**. Waterloo: The Company, 1914. 1 v. (unpaged). Loc: OKIT.

Brief biographies of Cyrus M. Taylor, Moses Springer, I.E. Bowman, Charles Hendry, Robert Melvin (of Guelph), E.P. Clement and George Wegenast. There is a photograph of each man, and

also of the first office and the new head office building in 1914. Period: 1869 - 1914.

1820. "Mutual Life celebrates centennial." **Waterloo Historical Society**. 1970. 58: 67. Loc: all.

A brief note that the Mutual Life Assurance Company of Waterloo was incorporated in 1868 and began business in 1870. The first policy was issued to James W. Dodds, and the first woman policyholder was Sophrana Maria Thompson, a resident of Barrie, Ontario. Period: 1870 - 1970.

1821. "North Dumfries and South Waterloo Farmers' Mutual Fire Insurance Company has centennial [WRP]." **Waterloo Historical Society**. 1956. 44: 42. Loc: all.

A note of the centennial of insurance company, with an outline of factors in its formation. Period: 1856 - 1956.

1822. North Dumfries and South Waterloo Farmers' Mutual Fire Insurance Co. **A century of progress**. The Company, 1956. 19 p. ill. Loc: OKIT.

A commemorative history of the company's development, with references to current directors and to the amalgamations with the Hopewell Creek Farmers' Mutual and Guelph Township Farmers' Mutual companies. Period: 1856 - 1956.

1823. North Waterloo Farmers' Mutual Fire Insurance Co. **100 years of service, 1874-1974: North Waterloo Farmers' Mutual Insurance Company**. The Company, 1974. 13 p. ill., graph. Loc: OKIT.

A brief commemorative history of the company, including biographical information about four of its presidents (Levi Stauffer, Josiah Stauffer, J.H. Woods and Campbell Shantz), photographs of buildings used for company offices, and lists of current officers, directors and staff. A chart shows the company's assets and numbers of policyholders from 1936 to 1974 and there are facsimiles of the 1894 annual report and an insurance policy from 1890. Period: 1874 - 1974.

1824. Oberholtzer, R.S. "Waterloo Mutual: century old." **Waterloo Historical Society**. 1963. 51: 75-79. ill. Loc: all.

A centennial history of the company, including a note that three other insurance firms were based in the same building on King Street North, Waterloo: the Dominion Life Assurance Company, the Equitable Life Insurance Company, and the Mercantile Fire Insurance Company. Period: 1863 - 1963.

1825. **Rules adopted by the Galt Building Society, established 1848 and incorporated by act of parliament.** Galt: Ainslie and Jaffray, 1848. 23 p. Loc: OKITW.

Prospectus and rules for an organization designed to assist members to save money and buy houses. In 1848 officials included Absalom Shade as president, Henry McCrum as treasurer and secretary, and John Miller as the solicitor. Period: 1848 - 1849.

1826. Sinclair, S. "Big insurers still call K-W home." **Financial Post.** 1967. 61: 13, 14. mf. Loc: OWTL, OWTU.

Reference from the Canadian Periodical Index. Period: 1967.

1827. Staebler, Edna. **The Waterloo Trust and Savings Company: a brief history.** Kitchener: Waterloo Trust and Savings Co., 1963. 16 p. ill., tables. Loc: OCCA, OKIT, OWTL, OWTU.

An outline of the development of the company founded in Waterloo in 1913. Tables summarize progress from 1913 to 1962 and current directors and officers are listed. Period: 1913 - 1963.

1828. "Trust company grows steadily on a strong regional reputation." **Financial Post.** 1965. 59: 89. mf. Loc: OWTL, OWTU.

Reference from the Canadian Periodical Index. Period: 1965.

1829. Walker, Hester M. **Ontario Mutual Insurance Association: a century of protective service, 1882-1982.** The Company, 1982. 95 p. ill. Loc: OCCA.

A general history including a facsimile of a receipt from the North Dumfries and South Waterloo Farmers' Mutual Fire Insurance Co., correspondence concerning money sent to help British farmers during the Second World War, and photographs of the old and new (1968) Galt offices. There is a biographical tribute to Walter R. Cross of Galt, secretary-treasurer of the association for many years. A list of mutual companies registered in Ontario from 1881 to 1982 is included. Period: 1882 - 1982.

1830. Waterloo Mutual Fire Insurance Co. **28th financial statement of the company: total assets $280,784.** CIHM Microfiche series, no. 38616. Waterloo: Waterloo Chronicle, 1891?. mf. Loc: OWTL, OWTU. Period: 1890 - 1891.

1831. Waterloo Trust and Savings Co. **44 years of growth built on service.** Waterloo: The Company, 1956. 6 p. charts. Loc: OWT.

A financial statement and list of the company's financial services. Names of the current directors, officers and managers are printed on the back cover. Period: 1931 - 1956.

1832. Waterloo Trust and Savings Co. **46 years of growth through service to the people of Waterloo County.** Waterloo: The Company, 1958. 10 p. ill. Loc: OWT.

An annual report and financial statement, including lists of directors, officers, managers and branch offices and a description of the services. Period: 1957 - 1958.

1833. "William Henry Schmalz and the Economical Mutual Fire Insurance Company." **Waterloo Historical Society.** 1933. 21: 65-67. Loc: all.

A short biography dealing mainly with Schmalz's advancement in the Economical Mutual Fire Insurance Company and mentioning others connected with the company, such as L.J. Breithaupt, James Livingston, Joseph E. Seagram, E.W.B. Snider and William Oelschlager. Period: 1862 - 1933.

1834. Young, James. **History of the Gore Fire Insurance Co., from 1839 to 1895 [microform]: being an address delivered by the Hon. James Young, president of the company: in moving the adoption of the report at the 56th annual meeting of the company, held in their new head office, corner Main and Ainslie streets, Galt, on the 28th January 1895.** Galt: Jaffray Bros, 1895. 15 p. ill. Also CIHM Microfiche series, no. 26164. Loc: OKITW, OWTL, OWTU.

Includes lists of members of the first Board of Directors, annual assets from 1877 to 1894, and names of current agents by place. Period: 1839 - 1895.

MANUFACTURING INDUSTRY, INCLUDING STUDIES OF SPECIFIC BUSINESSES

1835. "50 year anniversary of Hydro celebrated." **Waterloo Historical Society.** 1960. 48: 71. Loc: all.

A note quoted from the **Waterloo Chronicle** about the Waterloo Water and Light Commission's plans to celebrate the anniversary. Period: 1910 - 1960.

1836. "The 50th anniversary of the Hydro-Electric Power Commission of Ontario, 1906-1956." **Waterloo Historical Society.** 1956. 44: 11-12. Loc: all.

An account of the various celebrations of the anniversary in Waterloo County, including the unveiling of a memorial to E.W.B. Snider in St Jacobs. Period: 1906 - 1956.

1837. "75th anniversary in 1960." **Waterloo Historical Society.** 1960. 48: 36. ill. Loc: all.

Sattler's Leather Goods, Kitchener, celebrated its 75th anniversary in 1960. A photograph from 1898 shows the firm's founder, Louis Sattler, and three employees, Edward Foerster, A. Heller, and H. Bender. Period: 1885 - 1960.

1838. Adair, Kim and Pautler, Peter and Strang, David. "The U.R.W.A. and the struggle for union recognition: 1937-1939." **Industrial unionism in Kitchener, 1937-47.** Elora: Cumnock Press, 1976. Pp. 1-29. Loc: OWTU, OWTL, OKIT.

A narrative analysis of the negotiations and strikes in Kitchener's rubber factories, as a result of which employees at Dominion Rubber won an agreement recognizing the union while the management of B.F. Goodrich and Kaufman Rubber successfully opposed any concessions. Period: 1936 - 1939.

1839. "'Alone in his glory': documents on the Kaufman strike of 1946." **Industrial unionism in Kitchener, 1937-47.** Edited by Terry Copp. Elora: Cumnock Press, 1976. Pp. 53-78. Loc: OWTU, OWTL, OKIT.

An outline of the successful unionization of the B.F. Goodrich factory by February 1946, followed by a very detailed documentary survey of negotiations between the U.R.W.A. and the Kaufman Rubber Company in 1945. A.R. Kaufman resisted unionization of his workers and by late 1946 was the only major non-union employer in the Ontario rubber industry. Period: 1945 - 1946.

1840. **Archaeological mitigative monitoring of the Bernhardt Brewery site, River's Crest development, City of Cambridge, Regional Municipality of Waterloo.** Petersburg: Archaeological Research Associates, 1991. 1 v. (unpaged). Loc: OWRMA.

A report on evidence revealed during construction of a condominium in Preston. Once the property of John Erb, the site was used by Isaac Salyerds for a tannery and, from 1866, developed as the Rock (Springs) Brewery. Period: 1806 - 1927.

1841. **Archaeological testing of the Baden Brewery, AiHd-91, Baden, Ontario.** Waterloo: Regional Municipality of Waterloo, Planning and Development Department, Archaeology Division, 1990. 63 p. ill., map, plans, graphs. Loc: OKIT, OWRMA.

Report of an investigation, including results of land title searches and a chronology of the brewery begun by Henry Liersch in the 1850s. Period: 1855 - 1900.

1842. Ascherl, Peter. **"Where there is no vision the people perish".** University of Waterloo (student essay, History), 19--. 34 l. bibl. Loc: OKIT.

A review of the efforts of D.B. Detweiler and E.W.B. Snider in establishing hydro-electric service and of the controversy over public versus private ownership of electric power. Period: 1900 - 1910.

1843. Atwater-Hallatt, Rosanne. "The Braendle Cider Mill: Heidelberg, Ontario." **Waterloo Historical Society.** 1985. 73: 22-37. ill., bibl. Loc: all.

A description of shoemaker Braendle's transformation into a cider maker, with a description of techniques including the machinery driven by horse, wind and steam. The author also discusses the styles of the building and attitudes toward alcoholic liquor. Period: 1855 - 1917.

1844. Atwater-Hallatt, Rosanne. "The smokehouses of Heidelberg, Ontario: an inventory." **Waterloo Historical Society.** 1986. 74: 78-95. ill., map., table. Loc: all.

A detailed study of seventeen traditional smokehouses within a one-mile radius of Heidelberg, as examples of functioning vernacular architecture. The author describes and analyzes both the technology of food preservation and the architectural features of the structures. Period: 1850 - 1986.

1845. Baechler, Glenn D. "Waterloo County's romance with the automobile." **Waterloo Historical Society.** 1971. 59: 8-19. Loc: all.

An historical account of early makes of automobiles manufactured in the region. Period: 1899 - 1936.

1846. Ballantyne, H. **Kitchener, the birthplace of hydro.** Kitchener: Public Utilities Commission, 1967. 20 p. ill., ports., tables. Loc: OKIT, OWTUR.

A brief history of electricity in Kitchener from 1906 to 1967, to commemorate Canada's centennial. The roles of community leaders and regulatory institutions, such as the Kitchener Public Utilities Commission, are discussed. Tables illustrate the growth of consumption and compare power rates of 1922 and 1965. Period: 1906 - 1967.

1847. Bater, James H. and Walker, David F. "Foreign ownership and industrial linkage." **Industrial development in Southern Ontario: selected essays.** Edited by James H. Bater and David F. Walker. Publication Series, no.3. Waterloo: Department of Geography, Faculty of Environmental Studies, University of Waterloo, 1974. Pp. 101-125. Loc: OWTU, OWTL.

Report of an analysis of 166 plants in the Hamilton area and 150 in midwestern Ontario (a 50 per cent sample of plants in each of Guelph, Kitchener, Waterloo, Cambridge and Brantford). The authors find that Canadian-controlled operations tend to be functionally more integrated with the local community than foreign-controlled ones. Period: 1970 - 1971.

1848. Bauer, Gary Brian. **Industrial location in small Ontario municipalities: case study of Elmira, Ontario.** Wilfrid Laurier University (B.A. thesis, Geography), 1976. 125 l. ill., maps, bibl. Loc: OWTL.

A study of local industry as an indicator of the viability of a small community. The author concludes that personal, subjective factors in choosing a location may be as important as transportation, labour, buildings and services. Period: 1940 - 1976.

1849. Becker, Annemarie. **Ownership change and the German family manufacturing firm in Kitchener since 1945.** University of Waterloo (B.A. thesis, Geography), 1982. 1 fiche. maps, tables, bibl. mf. Loc: OWTUM.

A study which begins with a brief history of industrial development in the city before 1945 and after World War II. The second half of the essay discusses the ownership structure of Kitchener's industries and the extent to which German cultural elements influenced the city's development. Period: 1945 - 1981.

1850. Bixby, M.G. **Industries of Canada: historical and commercial sketches: London, Woodstock, Ingersoll, Guelph, Berlin, Waterloo, St Thomas, Windsor, and environs: its prominent places and people, representative merchants and manufactures, its improvements, progress and enterprise illustrated.** CIHM Microfiche series, no. 07189. Toronto: M.G. Bixby, 1887. 2 fiche. ill., indexes. mf. Loc: OWTU.

A compendium of information about businesses and businessmen. Period: 1886 - 1887.

1851. Bixby, M.G. **Industries of Canada: historical sketches: Waterloo, Galt, Dundas, St Catharines, Hamilton, Guelph, Berlin and environs: its prominent places and people, representative merchants and manufacturers: its improvements, progress, and enterprise illustrated.** Toronto: M.G. Bixby, 1886. 114 p. ill. photocopy. Loc: OKIT.

A compendium of information about businesses and businesses in various Ontario towns and villages. Similar to the 1887 publication on CIHM microfiche except that the 1886 publication includes Galt but

not Preston while the 1887 publication includes Preston and not Galt. Period: 1885 - 1886.

1852. "Blacksmith for 59 years." **Waterloo Historical Society.** 1966. 54: 10. ill. Loc: all.

A photograph of William Fritz, 75, with a note that he learned his trade in St Agatha and worked from 1917 to 1967 in Erbsville. Period: 1891 - 1966.

1853. Bloomfield, Elizabeth. "Berlin's last bonus: or how Kitchener became the rubber capital of Canada." **Waterloo Historical Society.** 1986. 74: 6-22. ill., map, bibl. Loc: all.

An account of the development of the rubber products industry in Berlin/Kitchener from its origins in the manufacture of leather and felt footwear and the foundation of rubber footwear businesses such as the Berlin Rubber Company (1900), the Merchant's Rubber Company (1904) and the Kaufman Rubber Company (1908). The author discusses the role of T.H. Rieder in establishing two automobile tire factories in the city. The huge Dominion Tire factory was built in 1912-13 by the Canadian Consolidated Rubber Company (CCR), a subsidiary of U.S. Rubber, with the support of Berlin's last municipal bonus. Though Rieder's efforts to establish a second, all-Canadian tire plant in Kitchener were ended by his early death in 1922, the enterprise survived under the BF Goodrich company of Akron, Ohio. Period: 1900 - 1931.

1854. Bloomfield, Elizabeth. "Bonusing and boosterism: industrial promotion by Ontario municipalities to 1930." **Planning History Bulletin.** 1985. 7,2: 23-29. bibl. Loc: OWTU.

A survey of the activities by which Ontario municipalities tried to promote local industry, by advertising to attract the attention of outside entrepreneurs and by more material inducements. Successive changes in municipal bonusing powers are summarized and the author estimates the total dimensions of bonusing in Ontario. Case studies from several Ontario towns and cities including Berlin/Kitchener are cited to illustrate various municipal policies and experiences. Period: 1870 - 1930.

1855. Bloomfield, Elizabeth. "Building industrial communities: Berlin and Waterloo to 1915." **Manufacturing in Kitchener-Waterloo: a long-term perspective.** Edited by David F. Walker. Waterloo: Department of Geography, University of Waterloo, 1987. Pp. 5-33, 195-197. ill., maps., graphs. Loc: OKIT, OWTL, OWTU, OWTUR.

An analysis of factors and phases in the process of industrialization that was especially rapid in

Berlin. The author emphasizes the role of local entrepreneurs in exploiting opportunities to build up and expand particular product lines and the encouragement of enterprise by municipal industrial policies. Maps identify and locate all factories in 1878, 1897 and 1913 in relation to the railway systems. Period: 1809 - 1915.

1856. Bloomfield, Elizabeth. "Building the city on a foundation of factories: the 'industrial policy' in Berlin, Ontario, 1870-1914." **Ontario History**. 1983. 75,3: 207-243. ill. maps, tabl., bibl. Loc: OKIT, OWTL, OWTU.

A case study of the roles of local entrepreneurs and institutions such as boards of trade and municipal councils in stimulating urban-industrial growth. The author describes Berlin's entrepreneurial elite and urban ethos and explains the powers of inducement used by municipal councils to attract and keep manufacturers in the community. The industrial policy is traced through several phases and its effectiveness is assessed and compared with other Ontario towns and cities. Period: 1870 - 1914.

1857. Bloomfield, Elizabeth. "The maturing industrial economy: Kitchener-Waterloo, 1915-1945." **Manufacturing in Kitchener-Waterloo: a long-term perspective**. Edited by David F. Walker. Waterloo: Department of Geography, University of Waterloo, 1987. Pp. 35-59, 195-197. ill., maps, graphs, tables. Loc: OKIT, OWTL, OWTU, OWTUR.

A survey of industrial growth and change during a period when Kitchener-Waterloo retained a diversified structure and high degree of local ownership and management despite the forces of corporate capitalism, foreign investment and new technology. Maps represent the urban-industrial patterns in 1913, 1927 and 1947 and graphs summarize statistics of production and employment. The effects of industrial growth on urban society and environment are outlined. Period: 1915 - 1945.

1858. Bloomfield, Elizabeth. "Municipal bonusing of industry: the legislative framework in Ontario to 1930." **Urban History Review**. 1981. 9,3: 59-76. tables. Loc: OWTU, OWTL.

A survey and summary of the changing legislative framework within which Ontario cities, towns and villages offered various types of bonuses and tax exemptions to attract or hold manufacturers. The author compares the evidence of bonusing contained in municipal by-laws and in special acts of the Ontario Legislature for several towns including Berlin, Waterloo, Galt, Preston, Hespeler, Guelph and Hamilton. Period: 1867 - 1930.

1859. Bloomfield, Elizabeth and Bloomfield, G.T. "Urban industrial development in central Canada." **Historical atlas of Canada, Volume III, 1891-1961**. Edited by Donald Kerr and Deryck W. Holdsworth. Toronto: University of Toronto Press, 1990. Plates 13 and 40. maps, tabl., bibl. Loc: OWTL, OWTU, OKIT.

A series of maps and graphs showing the remarkable growth of Berlin/Kitchener and Waterloo in relation to other cities and towns of central Canada between 1891 and 1937. Plate 13 includes a case study of the twin cities in 1897 and 1927, depicting the locations of factories by industry type and size, and the patterns of workplaces and residences of employees in five sample factories. Period: 1891 - 1937.

1860. Bloomfield, G.T. and Bloomfield, Elizabeth. **Waterloo County industries: index to 1871 manuscript census**. Canadian Industry in 1871: Ontario County Series. Guelph: Department of Geography, University of Guelph, 1991. 76 p. bibl., chart, indexes, map, tables. Loc: OCCA, OKIT, OWT, OWTU.

A discussion of the status of manufacturing industry in the county, based on data collected in the first Census of Canada and made machine-readable in the CANIND71 project. Summary data are presented in appendix tables for more than 700 industrial establishments, organized by location and industry type. Period: 1870 - 1871.

1861. Bowering, Ian. **The art and mystery of brewing in Ontario**. Burnstown: General Store Publishing House, 1988. 131 p. ill., bibl. Loc: OCCA, OKIT, OWT, OWTL.

Descriptions of Ontario breweries, arranged geographically with entries for Baden, Bamberg, Bridgeport, Galt, Kitchener, New Hamburg, Petersburg, Preston, Waterloo and Wellesley. Entries vary from a mention of the brewer's name and dates to several pages of description. Hop growing and the temperance movement are discussed. Period: 1810 - 1972.

1862. Bowman, Henry B. "Preston's furniture industry and Percy R. Hilborn." **Waterloo Historical Society**. 1972. 60: 78-87. ill. Loc: all.

A detailed account of Percy Hilborn's 50-year career, with references to manufacturers and retailers such as Frederick Guggisberg, Frederick Grove, John and William Werlich, Frank and Austin Moss, Charles and Joseph Daniel, Oliver Kummer, Reg Sears, William Stahlschmidt, Percy Hilborn, Alvin Schlegel, Irvin Merkel, Robert Liptrap, Thomas Fink, J. Mickler, John Dopp, Don McCaffery, Ed Bowman, Ed Merkel, George Gruetzner, James Wildman and the Schmidt family. Period: 1838 -

1972.

1863. "Breithaupt centennial: a century in leather."
Shoe and Leather Journal. 1957. 70,3: 85-97.
ill. Loc: OWTUR.

An historical sketch of the Breithaupt Leather
Co. of Kitchener, including a profile of L.O.
Breithaupt as "industrial leader and public
servant." The feature is illustrated with
photographs of family members who had directed the
business during the previous century, the original
Breithaupt home and various tanneries. Period:
1857 - 1957.

1864. Brenner, Jeff. "The history of the phonograph."
Waterloo Historical Society. 1976. 64: 23-25.
ill. Loc: all.

A short discussion including a profile of the
manufacturing business begun by Arthur B. Pollock
in Berlin in 1907. Originally named the Pollock
Manufacturing Company, it was also known as
Phonola Company of Canada, Pollock-Welker Limited,
and Dominion-Electrohome Limited. Period: 1877 -
1925.

1865. Brewster, Winfield. **Hespeler yarns: odds and ends
about the textile trade at Hespeler, and some of
the people who were concerned therewith.**
Hespeler: The Author, 1953. 46 p. ill. map,
facsims. Loc: OWTUR, OKIT, OCCA.

A history of the mill buildings, their owners
and the various factory tasks, with an appendix
listing over 3,000 people who worked in the
woollen mills. The list indicates the number of
generations a family had worked and whether or not
a family member was a manager. Two pages of
facsimiles show the letterheads of the various
textile companies in Hespeler and signatures of
the mill owners. A map of Hespeler and the
surrounding area is included. An index is
available at the Cambridge Library and Gallery and
the City of Cambridge Archives. Period: 1862 -
1953.

1866. Bryden, Annie Rodd. "History of Forest Mills
(Rodd's Mill)." **Waterloo Historical Society.**
1948. 36: 35-40. Loc: all.

A short history of the flour and grist mill on
Mill Creek about three miles from Galt, with
anecdotes about the various owners. Of particular
interest is the Rodd family who ran the mill and
the surrounding farm from 1879 to 1914. During the
time that the railway was built nearby, Mrs Rodd
took in boarders who worked on the railway. By
1947 the mill had all but disappeared. Period:
1836 - 1947.

1867. Burns and Co. **The story of Burns & Co. Limited,
pioneer meat packers of Canada.** The Company,
1943. 40 p. Loc: OWTUR.

An illustrated account of the development and
growth of the meat processing company that
acquired the Dumarts Meat Packing business of
Kitchener in 1941. Period: 1913 - 1943.

1868. Canada Barrels and Kegs. **Rolling out the barrels
for 70 years, 1872-1942.** The Company, 1942. 21 p.
ill. Loc: OWT.

A promotional booklet describing the
barrel-making process with photographs of past
buildings, employees at work, machinery and
various types of barrels. Information is included
about Charles Mueller who founded the business.
Period: 1872 - 1942.

1869. "Canada Felting closes." **Waterloo Historical
Society.** 1969. 57: 58. Loc: all.

A short note of the closing of Canada Felting,
founded in 1903 by E.W.B. Snider and once St
Jacobs' largest employer. Period: 1903 - 1969.

1870. **Canadian industrial record, descriptive of and
illustrating Brantford, Berlin, Waterloo, Galt,
Stratford and Woodstock.** 1914. 39 p. ill. mf.
Loc: OCLG.

Profiles of leading businesses in each
community. Period: 1900 - 1914.

1871. Carter, John. **War-time labour unrest and
industrial conflict: a case study of Kitchener,
Ontario (1941).** University of Waterloo (student
essay, History), 198-?. 28 l., tables, bibl. Loc:
OKIT.

An analysis of the rise of local union
membership and the reaction of management and
government to workers' demands. The author notes
changes in the workforce in explaining the growth
and strength of organized labour. Period: 1939 -
1945.

1872. "Century-old pottery at Conestogo." **Waterloo
Historical Society.** 1967. 55: 33. Loc: all.

An account of the excavation by Walter Kenyon
and Donald Webster of pottery made by William Eby
and his son in Conestogo. The clay was brought
from Philipsburg and production was mostly crocks
and jugs for home use. Period: 1856 - 1967.

1873. Charboneau, Mark. **D.B. Detweiler and E.W.B.
Snider and the cooperative municipal electric
power movement of Ontario.** Waterloo Lutheran
University (B.A. thesis, History), 1972. 85 l.
bibl. Loc: OKIT, OWTL.

A study of the roles of the two men in the
movement to develop and distribute hydro-electric

power from Niagara Falls. Period: 1888 - 1906.

1874. Christie, R.C. **The development of the furniture industry in the southwestern Ontario furniture manufacturing region.** University of Western Ontario (M.A. thesis, Geography), 1964. 136 l. ill. maps, tables. Loc: OLU.

A study of the industry in the larger region. Period: 1850 - 1960.

1875. Copp, John Terry. "The experience of industrial unionism in four Ontario towns, 1937-1947." **Committee on Canadian Labour History Bulletin.** 1978. 6: 4-10. Loc: OWTL, OWTU.

A report based on a preliminary inventory of source materials for labour history in Kitchener, Brantford, Welland and Galt. The author argues that the experience of the industrial working class in each town was shaped more by local factors than regional or national transformations. Period: 1937 - 1947.

1876. Copp, John Terry. **Industrial unionism in Kitchener, 1937-47.** Elora: Cumnock Press, 1976. 99 p. plates, ill. Loc: OWTU, OWTL, OCCA, OKIT.

A collection of four case studies of labour union activities in the Kitchener rubber and meat-processing industries. Copp introduces the volume with a brief survey of the state of Kitchener's industrial economy at the onset of the depression of the 1930s and of the conditions that may explain industrial unionism that began in the furniture factories. The four essays have separate records in the WRP database. The volume is illustrated with some excellent photographs, and two appendices present the brief of the Twin City Labour Council to the National War Labour Relations Board in 1943 and extracts from the Canadian Chamber of Commerce's Kitchener-Waterloo Survey of 1943. Period: 1931 - 1947.

1877. Cowan, Jennie F. "Extending commercial interests and public services: a brief study of the Adam Ferrie & Co. in Waterloo County, 1832-60." **Waterloo Historical Society.** 1953. 41: 19-28. Loc: all.

An account of the business, including biographies of Adam Ferrie and his brother Robert and based on Robert Ferrie's papers. Period: 1832 - 1860.

1878. Cressman, Ella M. "Breslau millstones." **Waterloo Historical Society.** 1973. 61: 19. Loc: all.

A note of the acquisition by Doon Pioneer Village of the circular stones used for grinding grain that were imported from France by Joseph Erb in 1850. Period: 1850 - 1973.

1879. Cressman, Ella M. "The sugar beet industry." **Waterloo Historical Society.** 1972. 60: 91-93. ill. Loc: all.

A short history of the industry in the Berlin area from 1901, noting the promotional roles of D.B. Detweiler and S.J. Williams and the creation of the business later known as the Dominion Sugar Company which lasted until the 1920s. The author includes her childhood reminiscences of a sugar beet farm. Period: 1901 - 1972.

1880. Crocker, R. **The Baden Brewery.** University of Waterloo (student essay), 1989. 32 p. ill., bibl., maps. Loc: OKIT.

A history of the Baden Brewery and its site, including all land transactions, dwellings and commercial ventures. The author notes that the site was used by the Silver Spring Creamery at the turn of the twentieth century and that it was later a Sunday School church camp. Period: 1850 - 1989.

1881. Davey, George M. **Kitchener: a case study in industrial geography.** University of Waterloo (B.A. thesis, Geography), 1966. 3 fiche. ill., maps, tables, bibl. mf. Loc: OWTUM.

A study of the historical development, nature and pattern of the city's manufacturing industries, mainly since 1945 and with reference to the growth and functions of industrial parks. Period: 1945 - 1965.

1882. "Demolition of Parkway Mill." **Waterloo Historical Society.** 1963. 51: 58. Loc: all.

A short history of the Parkway Feed Mill, formerly German Mills, demolished in 1963. Period: 1806 - 1963.

1883. "Deux nouveaux noms." **Commerce.** 1972. 74: 58-9. Loc: OWTU.

A note about new Galt firms, Waltec Industries Ltd and Galt Brass Works. Reference from the Canadian Periodical Index.

1884. "Dominion Button closes." **Waterloo Historical Society.** 1964. 52: 33. Loc: all.

A short note of the closing of the business, founded by H.S. Huber and Emil Vogelsang and owned by the Gross family from 1912. Period: c1877 - 1964.

1885. Dominion Rubber Co. **The Dominion: special issue.** Montreal: The Company, 1948. 7,6: 4-9, 10-15. ill. Loc: OKIT.

A special issue of the company magazine with two articles about Kitchener. The first, "Kitchener: our town," describes history and landmarks of the area and outlines local company history. The second, "Away from work with our Kitchener people," gives photographs and descriptions of Kitchener employees with their hobbies. Period: 1900 - 1948.

1886. Dominion Woollens and Worsteds. **Production at Dominion Woollens and Worsteds, 1900-1934.** The Company, 1934. 1 v. (unpaged). Loc: OKIT.

A summary of monthly output by the mill from 1900 to 1934, classified as to knitting, weaving, yarns, serges, worsteds and coatings, ladies' coats, busters and bathing suits. Monthly shipments, wages and sales are also reported. Period: 1900 - 1934.

1887. Donaldson, Gordon. **Sausages, schnitzels & public power: a brief history of Ontario Hydro's first 75 years.** Toronto: Hydro Electric Power Commission of Ontario, 1980?. 19 p. ill. Loc: OWT.

A brief account of the establishment of the commission through the efforts of D.B. Detweiler, E.W.B. Snider and Adam Beck, including a reference to the day in October 1910 when Berlin was "turned on." Period: 1902 - 1977.

1888. Dunham, B. Mabel. "Mills and millers in western Ontario." **Western Ontario Historical Nuggets.** 1946. 9: 1-9. Loc: OGU.

An account of flour mills in Waterloo County, previously published in **Northwestern Miller** Vol. 145, no. 5, in February 1926. Period: 1806 - 1920.

1889. Duquette, T. "Auto parts retain export sales." **Financial Post.** 1971. 65: 0-2. mf. Loc: OWTL, OWTU.

Reference from the Canadian Periodical Index. Period: 1971 -

1890. Dyas, John H. and Nichols, C.M. **The Twin-City Berlin and Waterloo and their industries, commercial, financial, manufacturing.** Berlin: Berlin News Record, 1908. 44 p. ill., index. Loc: OWTUR, OKIT, OWT, OWTUCR.

A photocopy of the special promotional souvenir of **The Daily Citizen** of Waterloo and **The News Record** of Berlin, presenting detailed profiles of prominent enterprises and biographical sketches of their owners and managers. Period: 1860 - 1908.

1891. Elliott, M.N. **Kitchener 1940-1945.** University of Waterloo (student essay, History), 1973. 25 p. bibl., charts. Loc: OKIT.

An account of the city's economic development during the Second World War, including an examination of labour disputes. The author finds that strikes in the rubber, button and meat-packing industries for union recognition and higher wages ended in compromise. Period: 1940 -

1945.

1892. "The embarrassment of success." **Industrial Canada.** 1963. 64,5: 61-63. Loc: OGU, OWTU.

An account of the Greb Shoe Company of Kitchener. Period: 1913 - 1963.

1893. Engel, R. "Tax changes help generate high voltage for Electrohome." **Financial Post.** 1972. 66: 21. ill. mf. Loc: OWTL, OWTU.

Reference from the Canadian Periodical Index. Period: 1972.

1894. England, Dan and England, Robert and Stewart, Del. "The 1946 rubber workers strike." **Industrial unionism in Kitchener, 1937-47.** Edited by Terry Copp. Elora: Cumnock Press, 1976. Pp. 79-99. Loc: OWTU, OWTL, OKIT.

A narrative analysis of the strike, considered in the context of other industrial disputes in Canada and the United States. The authors conclude that the strike, though perhaps unduly protracted, established the credibility of the union and was followed by over twenty years of relatively smooth labour-management relations. Period: 1945 - 1947.

1895. "Expansion number, 1835-1929." **Kitchener Daily Record.** 1929, April 2. Pp. 1-24. ill. Loc: OWT.

Newspaper supplement celebrating the move of the **Record** from its old headquarters on King Street to a new building at the corner of Queen and Duke Streets. The names and photographs of many employees are given, from the president, W.D. Euler, and manager, W.J. Motz, to the office and editorial staff, consisting of eleven men and one woman. Articles and photographs depict the new building and many aspects of newspaper production. Period: 1835 - 1929.

1896. Falkner, Theresa Goldie. **The Goldie saga, part two: the Goldie Mill.** The Author, 19--?. 4 p. Loc: OKIT, OWTUR.

A history of the mill from its foundation in 1849 as a flour and oatmeal mill, until 1910 when the mills were sold to the Canadian Cereal and Milling Company Ltd. Most of the history is told by quoting from letters written by John Goldie to his son James in New York State. There are descriptions of machinery, expenses, production and buildings. The author is a grand-daughter of John Goldie, the botanist and mill owner. This work is bound with parts one, three and four at the Kitchener Public Library. Period: 1849 - 1910.

1897. "Fiftieth anniversary of Hydro." **Waterloo Historical Society.** 1953. 41: 9. Loc: all.

A description of the celebrations, including the

naming the transformer station at Petersburg after D.B. Detweiler. Period: 1903 - 1953.

1898. "First cheese factory in Wilmot Township [WRP]." **Waterloo Historical Society**. 1965. 53: 52. Loc: all.

A note from the **Berliner Journal** of 19 July 1866, about the construction of the first cheese factory in the township. Period: 1866.

1899. "First tire produced by Dominion in Kitchener." **Waterloo Historical Society**. 1964. 52: 43. Loc: all.

A note of the first tire made at the Dominion Rubber factory on 6 January 1914 and the 40,000,000th tire produced just 50 years later. Period: 1916 - 1964.

1900. "Five generations in business." **Waterloo Historical Society**. 1969. 57: 30. Loc: all.

A short description of five Warnocks (John, Adam, James, E.G., and James G.) and their Galt businesses: a flour mill and the Galt Knitting Company. Period: 1834 - 1969.

1901. Fountain, Judy. "The growth of a local enterprise: from J.M. Schneider Ltd to The Heritage Group." **Manufacturing in Kitchener-Waterloo: a long-term perspective**. Edited by David F. Walker. Waterloo: Department of Geography, University of Waterloo, 1987. Pp. 83-105, 198-9. maps, tables. Loc: OKIT, OWTL, OWTU, OWTUR.

An analysis of the growth of the firm from a part-time sausage-making operation in 1890 to a national food processor and distributor by 1972 when its shares were first traded on the Toronto Stock Exchange. Renamed The Heritage Group in 1980, it returned to the corporate name, J.M. Schneider Inc., in 1986. The main factors in growth are considered to have been livestock supplies, high-quality product differentiation, consumer preferences and demand, transport and communications technology, and management as a family enterprise. Period: 1890 - 1985.

1902. Fountain, Judy. **Market structure and strategy: a historical analysis of J.M. Schneider Ltd, Kitchener**. University of Waterloo (B.E.S. thesis, Geography), 1980. 1 fiche. mf. Loc: OWTUM.

A study of the factors influencing the market growth of J.M. Schneider from 1890 to 1974, and its methods of market penetration. Some of the areas discussed are company policy, changing consumer preferences, livestock supply, and the technological changes in transportation, production, and communication. The appendices include a chronology of plant expansion from 1890 to 1977, employment figures from 1915 to 1938, and the expansion of sales territories from 1925 to 1965. Period: 1890 - 1977.

1903. Fraser, Frank. "Labor cracks the rubber front." **Canadian Forum**. 1939. 19: 7-8. Loc: OGU.

A contemporary account of strikes by workers at the Kaufman Rubber, Dominion Tire and Merchants Rubber factories in Kitchener. The author considers that the strike committees gained community support for the strikers. Period: 1938 - 1939.

1904. "Galt firms spread names far and wide." **Financial Post**. 1967. 61: 11, 14. mf. Loc: OWTL, OWTU.

Reference from the Canadian Periodical Index. Period: 1967.

1905. "Galt pin factory [WRP]." **Waterloo Historical Society**. 1956. 44: 67. Loc: all.

A note that the Galt factory of Manning, Maxwell and Moore Ltd at the southeast corner of Water and Concession Streets was a pin factory in 1883. Period: 1883 - 1956.

1906. Gerland, Martin Edward. **Industrial location in Galt: a study of the factors of industrial location from the founding of the town to 1958**. University of Toronto (B.A. thesis), 1959. 64 l. ill., maps. Loc: OTU.

Reference from **Bibliography of Ontario history, 1867-1976** (Bishop et al.). Period: 1816 - 1958.

1907. Gillies, Archie. "Municipal industrial development with reference to Kitchener." **Industrial development in Southern Ontario: selected essays**. Edited by James H. Bater and David F. Walker. Publication Series, no.3. Waterloo: Department of Geography, Faculty of Environmental Studies, University of Waterloo, 1974. 306 p. ill. Loc: OWTU, OWTL.

An account of the purposes of Kitchener's Industrial Development Committee, reflecting the city's healthy industrial status in the early 1970s. Period: 1966 - 1973.

1908. **Gordon Klager's confidential file of materials concerning the 1933 strike at Dominion Woollen & Worsteds Company, Hespeler**. 1933. 1 v. (unpaged). Loc: OKIT.

A collection of company bulletins, correspondence by both strike committee and management, and communications with Hespeler's Mayor, James J. Shaw, and the Ontario Minimum Wage Board. Information is given about workers' demands and management responses. Photocopied in June 1987 from originals belonging to Mr Gordon Klager, an employee with the company. Period: 1933 - 1934.

1909. Hebblethwaite, Katherine. **Babcock & Wilcox Canada: a history, 1844-1977**. The Company, 1987. 194 p. ill., charts. Loc: OCCA, OCH, OCLG, OCP, OKIT, OKITW, OWTL, OWTUR.

A history of the company from its origins in 1844 as the Dumfries Foundry and 1859 when it became Goldie McCulloch & Co., to 1923 when it joined with Babcock-Wilcox and finally to 1977. Biographical details of the company's entrepreneurs, engineers, managers and presidents are given with product information about the engines, boilers and pumps manufactured. Appendices include a sales history by product line from 1924 to 1987, a typical set of articles of apprenticeship between R.J. Barrie and Goldie & McCulloch dating from around 1900, and information about Babcock-Wilcox in other countries. Period: 1844 - 1977.

1910. Hilborn, Miriam. "The New Dundee Flour Mills." **Waterloo Historical Society**. 1962. 50: 78-79. Loc: all.

A short history of the mills, built in 1847-48 by Frederick G. Millar. Period: 1847 - 1962.

1911. Hilborn, Miriam. "The Poth Furniture Factory in New Dundee." **Waterloo Historical Society**. 1962. 50: 80. Loc: all.

An account of the factory built by Andrew Poth in 1858 that made wooden sinks and coffins in addition to furniture. Period: 1858 - 1962.

1912. "Holm's Mill." **Waterloo Historical Society**. 1969. 57: 63. ill. Loc: all.

A photograph and brief history of the mill, begun in 1850 by Peter Holm and owned by the Knechtel Milling Company of Hanover by 1969. Period: 1850 - 1969.

1913. Houghton, Douglas H. **An analysis of the location and development of manufacturing industries in Galt-Preston-Hespeler, 1969**. University of Waterloo (B.E.S. thesis, Planning), 1971. 145 l. maps, tables, bibl. Loc: OWTU.

A study of the type and degree of industrial development in the three communities with an analysis of the locational characteristics, trends and spatial patterns of each industry. The author stresses the planning implications and includes an appendix lists all contemporary industries by type, with dates of establishment and numbers of employees. Period: 1800 - 1969.

1914. Hudon, Debbie. "Richard Roschman and brother: button manufacturers." **Waterloo Historical Society**. 1977. 65: 72-77. ill. Loc: all.

A brief history of the Waterloo company that was in business for almost 70 years. The author outlines its origins in 1878, growth in the late 1800s, reminiscences of employee Leonora Walz Marks, styles of buttons manufactured, steps in the production of the buttons, and the decline of the business due to the low cost of imported buttons. Period: 1870 - 1946.

1915. Hunsberger, Albert. "Sattler Leather Goods." **Waterloo Historical Society**. 1977. 65: 18-24. ill. Loc: all.

A short history of the Kitchener family business, started in 1895 by Louis Sattler and closed in 1977 by his son, Rufe Sattler. The author also mentions other businesses which were closely tied to Sattler's Leather Goods, including the tanneries of the Langs and the Breithaupts in Berlin and the Strohs in Waterloo, livery stables, blacksmith shops and luggage stores. Period: 1819 - 1976.

1916. Hydro Electric Power Commission of Ontario. **Ontario Hydro news: golden jubilee issue**. Toronto: The Commission, 1956. 40 p. ill. Loc: OWTUR, OWTUCG, OWTUCR.

A history of the commission, including references to its early connections with Waterloo County and brief profiles of Daniel B. Detweiler and E.W.B. Snider. Period: 1900 - 1956.

1917. "Industrial supplements." **Galt Evening Reporter**. 1952 - 1972. mf. Loc: OCLG.

Special illustrated supplements featuring local businesses in 1952, 1954, 1956, 1960, 1965, 1966, 1968, 1969, 1970, 1971 and 1972. Period: 1952 - 1972.

1918. "The industrial towns of Waterloo County." **Mer Douce**. 1924. 14: 47-52. ill. Loc: OKIT.

Brief summaries of the industrial development of Preston, Waterloo, Elmira and Hespeler, with some historical information and names of specific manufacturers and entrepreneurs. Illustrations include an engraving of Preston in 1856 and photographs of the other towns. Period: 1830 - 1924.

1919. J.M. Schneider Ltd. **J.M. Schneider Inc.: history**. 1979. 19 l. Loc: OKIT.

An unpublished history of the company from its beginnings in 1890 under the direction of John Metz Schneider. The company's philosophy is explained, as well as its products, productivity, expansions, and its direction in the 1970s. The final section discusses the employees and the outside programmes such as the Ex-Servicemen's Club, the Schneider Golden Age Club, and numerous community activities. Period: 1890 - 1979.

1920. Jackman, A. and Ralston, J. and Smith, A.F. **History of Uniroyal waste management at Elmira.** Ministry of the Environment and Grand River Conservation Authority, 1985. 31 p. tables, maps. Loc: OWRE.

A report on Uniroyal's production of pesticides and other products and methods of disposing of chemical wastes. The manufacturing processes, problems arising from waste disposal, and a brief history of municipal waste treatment are discussed. Period: 1942 - 1984.

1921. Janusas, Scarlett E. **Report on the monitoring of the Williamsburg blacksmith shop, City of Kitchener.** 1990. 10 p. ill., bibl. Loc: OKIT.

Archaeological description of one of the last extant blacksmith shops in the region. Located at the northwest corner of Bleams and Westmount Road, the rubblestone smithy was demolished in 1989 despite efforts to conserve it. Period: 1800 - 1990.

1922. Jenkins, Claire M. "The growth of a grist mill." **Waterloo Historical Society.** 1979. 67: 69-85. ill. Loc: all.

A detailed history of the Waterloo mill started by Abraham Erb and continued by the Snider family. The author uses land registry documents, census records and directory evidence. Period: 1806 - 1955.

1923. "John Watson Catalogue, 1868." **Waterloo Historical Society.** 1971. 59: 48-50. ill. Loc: all.

A reproduction of a letter which accompanied a catalogue of farm implements manufactured in Ayr. The letter accompanying the catalogue is addressed "To the Farmers of Canada" and headed "From the / Descriptive Catalogue of Threshing, Mowing & / Reaping Machines, Agricultural Implements / and Stoves / Manufactured by / John Watson / Ayr Foundry / Waterloo Co. / 1868 / Ontario. This material, with more on John Watson's business, was previously printed in the 1929 volume of the Waterloo Historical Society. Period: 1850 - 1868.

1924. Judge, Martin R. "The contribution of Kitchener's rubber industry during the Second World War." **Waterloo Historical Society.** 1984. 72: 6-19. ill. Loc: all.

An account that stresses the Kaufman Rubber Company, the B.F. Goodrich Company of Canada, and the Dominion Rubber System during World War II. Products, techniques, labour relations, and the use of synthetic rubber are discussed. Period: 1900 - 1945.

1925. Kealey, Gregory S. and Palmer, Bryan D. **Dreaming of what might be: the Knights of Labor in Ontario, 1880-1900.** Cambridge: Cambridge University Press, 1982. 487 p. ill., tables. Loc: OWTL, OWTU.

An analysis of the emergence of the labour movement in the 1880s in the context of industrial capitalism. The demise of the organization is related to the failure of the Knights ideologically and organizationally to come to grips with the structural transformation of industrial society to corporate capitalism. There is less information on Berlin and Galt than on industrial centres in Ontario but some local details are presented in tables on pages 62, 63 and 86. The Berlin District Assembly included Local Assemblies in Waterloo, Wellington, Brant and Halton counties. Details of Local Assemblies in the later 1880s are as follows: LAs numbered 7469, 9226, 9690, 9691 (Germania) and 10561 in Berlin, LA 6112 in Galt, LA 5181 in Ayr, LA 6058 in Hespeler, and LA 5652 in New Hamburg. Period: 1885 - 1890.

1926. Kelly, Wayne. **Downright upright: a history of the Canadian piano industry.** Toronto: Natural Heritage/Natural History Inc., 1991. 160 p. ill., facsims. Loc: OKIT.

A general survey of businesses that manufactured pianos. Berlin enterprises include the early craftsman J. Maas in 1852, and the Berlin Piano & Organ Company, established in 1890, later bought by W.H. Snyder & Co., and then by the New York-based Foster-Armstrong Co. to be operated as its Canadian branch from 1906 to 1924. The Berlin and Snyder brands were dropped for the popular US names of Haines Bros and Marshall & Wendell. In Preston, Werlich Bros tried to establish a piano-player business in the former Crown Furniture factory between 1908 and 1912. Period: 1852 - 1924.

1927. Kilgour, Nancy. **The Galt steelworkers' strike, 1943.** Wilfrid Laurier University (B.A. thesis, History), 1978. 43 l. bibl. Loc: OWTL.

An account of the events leading to the less than successful strike of 1943. The author summarizes the organizers' attempts to obtain union recognition, the conflicts over the initial establishment of a Board of Conciliation, the subsequent decisions made by the Board, and the ensuing actions of management and employees. Period: 1940 - 1943.

1928. "Kitchener again! Labor may join C of C." **Financial Post.** 1964. 58: 1. mf. Loc: OWTL, OWTU.

Reference from the Canadian Periodical Index. Period: 1964.

1929. "Kitchener converts to natural gas." **Waterloo Historical Society**. 1958. 46: 53-57. ill. Loc: all.

An illustrated description of the Kitchener gas works before the conversion to natural gas in 1958, with a brief history of the Berlin Gas Company from 1883. Period: 1883 - 1958.

1930. "Kitchener's oldest King Street business sold." **Waterloo Historical Society**. 1960. 48: 54. Loc: all.

A note of the sale of the P. Hymmen Company, established in 1850 by tinsmith Peter Hymmen. Period: 1850 - 1960.

1931. Koch, Edward L. **Kitchener: a meat packing centre; a sample study of the meat packing industry in Kitchener, Ontario, an inductive approach.**. People in Places in Canada. Toronto: Holt, Rinehart and Winston of Canada, 1971. 60 p. ill., maps, graphs. Loc: OWTU, OKIT.

A textbook for elementary school children, describing operations in J.M. Schneider's Kitchener plant in the larger context of suppliers and customers. Photographs, maps and graphs accompany the text which includes exercises, suggested activities and further reading. Period: 1890 - 1971.

1932. Kohli, Marjorie. "The DW & W News." **Waterloo Historical Society**. 1985. 73: 66-70. ill. Loc: all.

An account of the informal company newspaper, begun in 1941 by Dominion Woollens and Worsteds to inform company employees who were away on active service about changes in the company and in the town of Hespeler. The author names many people associated with the company and newspaper. Period: 1941 - c1948.

1933. Kostantos, Alexandra. **The entry of Kitchener women into the labour force during the second world war.** University of Waterloo (student essay, History), 1978. 31 p. bibl. Loc: OKIT.

A study of the ways in which middle-class and working-class women were urged by governments to help the war effort by working outside the home. Types of employment and working conditions are described, based on personal accounts. Period: 1939 - 1945.

1934. Kreiner, Leona Bramm. "John Bramm, Kitchener's first brickmaker." **Waterloo Historical Society**. 1971. 59: 36-37. ill. Loc: all.

An account of the business life of John Bramm, the immigrant from Hessen, Germany, who established Berlin's first brick-making business in 1845. Period: 1845 - 1893.

1935. "Labor - C of C courtship in Kitchener off -- but still pals." **Financial Post**. 1964. 58: 24. mf. Loc: OWTL, OWTU.

Reference from the Canadian Periodical Index. Period: 1964.

1936. Lamb, Kathryn Hansuld. "Cheese traditions in Wellesley Township." **Waterloo Historical Society**. 1991. 79: 135-153. ill. Loc: all.

A detailed report on the owners, suppliers and operations of the cheese factory first established in 1895 west of Wellesley village. Since it closed in 1981, the building has been used for storage, including the Wellesley Township Historical Society's collection of artifacts. Period: 1895 - 1981.

1937. Lamb, Kathryn Hansuld. "From plows to hockey sticks." **Waterloo Historical Society**. 1982. 70: 53-59. ill., bibl. Loc: all.

An account of William Hilborn's purchase of the Ayr Agricultural Works from John Watson in 1882 and his successes in manufacturing and marketing hockey sticks made from rock elm. Period: 1882 - 1931.

1938. Lanier, Barbara A. **Selected industries' perception and attitudes towards dissemination and implementation of environmental legislation in Kitchener-Waterloo.** Wilfrid Laurier University (B.A. thesis, Geography), 1974. 144 p. ill., bibl. Loc: OWTL.

A study of attitudes towards pollution control in the food and beverage industries. The author finds a greater awareness of the legislation on water quality than on air or land pollution, of local legislation than of provincial or federal legislation. She finds a greater degree of acceptance of legislation of which industries are notified quickly. Period: 1960 - 1974.

1939. Lavoie, Paul L. **Clocks made in Canada by the Arthur Pequegnat Clock Co., Berlin - Kitchener, Ontario.** Guelph: The Author, 1973. 52 p. ill. Loc: OWTL, OKIT, OWT.

A retrospective catalogue of the company's clocks between 1904 and 1928. Each entry includes a photograph of the clock, its name, a brief description, and, in some cases, its original retail price. The booklet contains a short history of the company and of members of the Pequegnat family and reprints Arthur's 1927 obituary. Period: 1874 - 1928.

1940. Leung, Felicity Hale. **Grist and flour mills in Ontario: from millstones to rollers, 1780-1880.** Ottawa: National Historic Sites and Parks Branch, Parks Canada, 1981. 293 p. bibl. glossary, charts. Loc: OKIT, OWRE, OWTU.

An examination of milling technologies in the context of contemporary political, economic, social and geographic factors. There are chapters on John Brown's process of gradual reduction, used at Elias Snider's mill at Waterloo, and the roller process introduced at E.W.B. Snider's Pioneer Roller Mills at St Jacobs. Illustrations include a roller mill and a flour-dressing machine produced by Goldie and McCulloch of Galt in the 1880s. Period: 1820 - 1880.

1941. Leung, Felicity Hale. "Grist and flour mills in Ontario: their technological development, 1870-1880." **4th Annual Agricultural History of Ontario Seminar proceedings.** Edited by Alan A. Brookes. Guelph: University of Guelph, 1981. Pp. 6-39. ill. Loc: OWTU, OGU.

An overview of methods of milling wheat in Ontario from 1780 to 1880, including explanations of innovations associated with Waterloo County. These were John Brown's new milling process of gradual reduction developed at Elias Snider's mill at Waterloo from the 1860s, and the roller milling process used at E.W.B. Snider's Pioneer Roller Mills at St Jacobs from 1880. Period: 1860 - 1880.

1942. Leung, Felicity Hale. "Roller milling at the St Jacobs flour mill from 1888-1889." **Waterloo Historical Society.** 1975. 63: 13-28. ill., bibl. Loc: all.

An account of the daily routine at the mill during one year, based in part on a diary kept by a miller employed by E.W.B. Snider. The diary is part of the Waterloo Historical Society's collection of Snider Family Papers. The author explains many aspects of the business including milling techniques and equipment, repairs to the equipment, mill workers' duties, and problems of quality control and the weather. This work was also published as Research Bulletin 29 by the National Historic Sites Branch of Parks Canada in 1976. Period: 1830 - 1889.

1943. Lichty, Wilbur and Cope, Verlin. "The Elmira Brickyard." **Waterloo Historical Society.** 1989. 77: 103-108. ill. Loc: all.

A history of the Elmira Brickyard, begun by David Robertson in 1869, purchased by Henry Dahmer in 1902 and closed in 1916. The authors mention structures built with Elmira bricks, particularly the house of William Dahmer. Period: 1855 - 1916.

1944. "Lion Brewery malt house demolished." **Waterloo Historical Society.** 1965. 53: 77. Loc: all.

A brief note of the hotel-brewery at Princess and King Streets, Waterloo. Period: 1840 - 1965.

1945. Loch, Francis J.P. **The Kitchener rubber industries: a geographic analysis.** Waterloo University College (B.A. thesis, Geography), 1966. 103 p. bibl., maps, tables. Loc: OWTL.

An historical examination of reasons for the location of the industry in Kitchener. Descriptions of three major companies, B.F. Goodrich, Dominion Rubber Co. and Kaufman Rubber Co., include facts about their current problems and prospects. Period: 1899 - 1966.

1946. MacEwen, C.R. "Local conciliation." **Saturday Night.** 1941. 57: 9, 13. Also mf. Loc: OKIT, OWTL, OWTU.

Reference to labour relations in the rubber and meat-packing industries. From the Canadian Periodical Index. Period: 1941.

1947. Macnaughton, Elizabeth. **Electric power in the villages and farms of Waterloo County, 1914.** Kitchener: Doon Heritage Crossroads, Historic Sites Department, Regional Municipality of Waterloo, 1984. 33 l. ill., tables, bibl. Loc: OCCA, OCLG, OKIT, OWT.

An assessment of the extent to which electrification should be represented at Doon Heritage Crossroads. The author reviews patterns of electricity service, the price of electric power, electricity on the farm, and systems of generation and distribution. The appendix presents an excerpt from **History of the Forbes Mill, etc., Hespeler, Ontario** entitled "Lighting and electric power, 1864-1928," as evidence of one business's response to the availability of electricity. Period: 1910 - 1914.

1948. Macnaughton, Elizabeth. **Tailors and tailoring in rural Waterloo County: 1900-1914.** Kitchener: Doon Heritage Crossroads, Historic Sites Department, Regional Municipality of Waterloo, 1986. 109 p. ill., tables, bibl. Loc: OCCA, OCLG, OKIT, OWT.

Written for historical interpreters at Doon Heritage Crossroads, the report focuses on the daily routine of the rural merchant in the county. Chapters include information on making the garment, shop equipment and layout, how Canadian men dressed, tailored clothing for women, and tailors of Waterloo and Perth Counties. Period: 1900 - 1914.

1949. Mahn, Bryan and Schaffner, Ralph. "The packinghouse workers in Kitchener, 1940-1947." **Industrial unionism in Kitchener, 1937-47.**

Edited by Terry Copp. Elora: Cumnock Press, 1976. Pp. 30-52. Loc: OWTU, OWTL, OKIT.

A narrative analysis of the negotiations and strikes at Dumarts and Schneiders, as a result of which the packinghouse unions largely achieved local recognition. Period: 1940 - 1947.

1950. **Manual of the textile industry of Canada, 7th edition.** Montreal: Canadian Textile Journal Publishing Co., 1935. 182 p. ill., indexes. Loc: OCCA.

An account of the current state of the industry, including references to the textile companies of Galt, Preston and Hespeler and their products. Details of numbers of workers and their wages are given for Riverside Silk Mills, the Pattinson plant and Dominion Woollens and Worsteds. Period: 1935 - 1936.

1951. "Manufacturers of Waterloo County 1925 and 1926." **Waterloo Historical Society.** 1928. 16: 12. Loc: all.

A list of statistics for cities and towns in Waterloo County showing numbers of establishments, working capital, numbers of employees, wages and salaries, cost of materials, and value of production for each community. No company names are provided. Period: 1925 - 1926.

1952. Marshall, Alex. "A unique exhibition held at Kitchener." **Industrial Canada.** 1919. 20,4: 57. Loc: OGU.

Reference from **Bibliography of Ontario history, 1867-1976** (Bishop et al.). Period: 1918 - 1919.

1953. Martin, Allen D. "Mills at Floradale, past and present." **Waterloo Historical Society.** 1981. 69: 94-102. ill. Loc: all.

An account of the mills at Floradale and their owners from 1853 to 1981. Period: 1853 - 1981.

1954. Martin, Jim. **Kitchener: the industrial city 1951-1955.** University of Waterloo (student essay, History), 1975. 20 p. bibl. Loc: OKIT.

A survey of industrial growth and the policies of the Kitchener Industrial Commission created in 1951. The mayoral elections, the issues of fluoridation and the site of the new police building are also discussed. The city is summed up as "industrial, stable, and practical." Period: 1951 - 1955.

1955. Martin, Jon B. "The old, old business of shoeing horses." **Waterloo Historical Society.** 1978. 66: 48-54. ill. Loc: all.

Text of an address to the Waterloo Historical Society, relating the experiences as a blacksmith, first in Floradale and then in St Jacobs. As well

as describing the types of work done in his shops, Martin also briefly discusses the rise and fall of the trade over his 50-year career. Period: c1920 - 1978.

1956. McCullough, A.B. **The primary textile industry in Canada: history and heritage.** Studies in Archaeology, Architecture and History. Ottawa: National Historic Sites, Parks Service, Environment Canada, 1992. 314 p. ill., bibl., tables, index. Loc: OCCA, OWTU.

An historical survey of the Canadian textile industry, including technology, labour force and factory buildings, as a basis for assessment of textile mills as historic sites. There are profiles of the R. Forbes Company of Hespeler, George Pattinson and Company of Preston, and Galt Knitting Company and Newlands and Company of Galt. Period: 1863 - 1992.

1957. McCutcheon, James Richard. **Industry's perception and attitudes towards water supply uses, costs and future alternatives in Kitchener-Waterloo.** Waterloo Lutheran University (B.A. thesis, Geography), 1971. 108 l. tables, bibl. Loc: OWTL.

An analysis of the water consumption of 40 Kitchener and 25 Waterloo businesses. The results show a direct correlation between level of interest in future water supplies and total volume of water consumed. Industry spokesmen are reported to prefer more efficient use of current supplies including ground, lake, and river water, to any technological developments in water treatment or production equipment. Period: 1969 - 1970.

1958. McKenzie, Kenneth M. **A manufacturing base analysis of Galt.** University of Western Ontario (B.A. thesis, Geography), 1966. 75 l. ill. maps. graphs. Loc: OLU.

A study of changes in Galt's industrial structure between 1941 and 1961, using factor analysis of responses to a questionnaire. Photographs of some enterprises are included with descriptive captions, and a large map of Galt's industrial establishments is folded in the back pocket. Period: 1941 - 1961.

1959. McLaughlin, Kenneth. **Made in Berlin.** Kitchener: Joseph Schneider Haus, 1989. 32 p. ill. Loc: OKIT, OWRA, OWRE, OWRND, OWT, OWTUR.

A well illustrated commentary on industrial development, enterprises, products and labour before 1914, including information on ethnicity, housing, clubs and social events. Period: 1880 - 1916.

1960. McLellan, A.G. "The predicament of the sand and gravel industry - the provincial and local situations." **The Waterloo County area: selected geographical essays**. Edited by A.G. McLellan. Waterloo: Department of Geography, University of Waterloo, 1971. Pp. 217-227. map. Loc: OWTU, OWTL, OWTUCG, OKIT.

A general survey of the industry's significance, based on a 1970 questionnaire survey of gravel pit operators and including a map of all sites. Period: 1965 - 1970.

1961. Meditskos, Peter. **Analysis of the textile industry in Cambridge and in Canada**. University of Waterloo (B.A. thesis, Geography), 1976. 1 fiche. tables, bibl. mf. Loc: OWTUM.

An historical review of the industry with a case study of Galt, Preston and Hespeler. The author considers economic and social systems, labour force, wages and the effects of World War Two on the industry. Period: c1820 - 1976.

1962. Midwestern Ontario Regional Development Council. **MODA municipal-industrial directory**. Stratford: The Council, 1967. Loc: OKIT.

A compilation of information about industrial businesses in the various municipalities of Waterloo, Wellington, Perth and Huron Counties. Kitchener Public Library has directories for 1967 and 1969. Period: 1967 - 1969.

1963. Mika, Nick and Mika, Helma and Turner, Larry. **Historic mills of Ontario**. Belleville: Mika Publishing, 1987. 208 p. ill., index. Loc: OCLG, OKIT, OWRE, OWTU.

A lavishly illustrated volume that includes details of the history and owners of the Dover Mills, Preston and the Dickson Mill, Galt. Period: 1816 - 1987.

1964. Mitchell, James. "Beginning of the hydro-electric system." **Waterloo Historical Society**. 1919. 7: 94-99. Loc: all.

A compilation of newspaper articles and letters that describe the contributions of E.W.B. Snider and D.B. Detweiler in securing hydro-electric power for Ontario. Period: 1902 - 1906.

1965. Munro, Ross. "The Snider Flour Mills, Waterloo." **Waterloo Historical Society**. 1927. 15: 383-384. ill. Loc: all.

A short account of the mill's origins in 1806, reprinted from **Saturday Night** of 10 September 1927. Period: 1806 - 1927.

1966. New Dundee Co-operative Creamery Ltd. **Financial report**. New Dundee: The Company, 1934. 1 folded sheet. Loc: OWTUR.

The company's balance sheet for 1933. E.B. Hallman is identified as president and J.W. Abra, E.K. Beck and M.B. Snyder as directors. Period: 1933 - 1934.

1967. Newlands, David L. **Early Ontario potters: their craft and trade**. Toronto: McGraw-Hill Ryerson, 1979. 245 p. ill., glossary, bibl., index. Loc: OCLG, OKIT, OWRN, OWTL, OWTU, OWTUCG.

A history and description of Ontario potters and pottery from 1796 to the beginning of the twentieth century. Chapter 10 includes details of 25 potters in eleven locations in Waterloo County. The book also contains information on the care of pottery collections, a glossary of ceramic terms, and a checklist of Ontario pottery marks. Period: 1800 - 1907.

1968. Newlands, David L. "The New Hamburg pottery." **Canadian Collector**. 1977. 12,4: 36-39. ill., map. Loc: OWTU.

A study of the owners, buildings and products of a New Hamburg pottery shop established in the mid-nineteenth century by Xavier Boehler. The author reports findings of an archaeological excavation by members of Wilfrid Laurier University, showing that three different forms of utility bowls were produced, as well as stove tubes and flower pots. Period: 1851 - 1977.

1969. Newlands, David L. **The New Hamburg pottery, New Hamburg, Ontario, 1854-1916**. Waterloo: Wilfrid Laurier University Press, 1978. 53 p. ill., maps, bibl. Loc: OCP, OKIT, OWRN, OWTL, OWTU.

The history of the New Hamburg pottery, founded by Xavier Boehler, with a report of its archaeological excavation. The author reports only a limited range of pottery types, most of which could be designated as three different bowl types. There are drawings and photographs to illustrate the pottery and comparisons with pottery from other shops in Ontario. Period: 1854 - 1916.

1970. "Niagara power in Waterloo." **Waterloo Historical Society**. 1960. 48: 70. ill. Loc: all.

A paragraph quoted from **Chronicle-Telegraph** of 3 November 1910, describing the coming of electricity to Waterloo. There is a 1913 photograph of Waterloo linemen with their horse and wagon. Period: 1910 - 1960.

1971. Oberholtzer, R.S. "Hydro City Shoe Company." **Waterloo Historical Society**. 1970. 58: 79. Loc: all.

A note of the closing of the Hydro City Shoe Company, formerly the G.V. Oberholtzer Shoe Company of Kitchener, which specialized in high-quality work shoes. Period: 1899 - 1970.

1972. "Old office building razed." **Waterloo Historical Society**. 1965. 53: 41. Loc: all.
A brief report of the demolition of the stone office building of Babcock-Wilcox (formerly Goldie and McCulloch) on Grand Avenue South. The company's head office was moved to a major site on Coronation Boulevard in 1955. Period: 1859 - 1965.

1973. "Oregon Pond." **Waterloo Historical Society**. 1963. 51: 35. ill. Loc: all.
A brief note of the reconstruction by George Ayres of the dam that once supplied power for the Perine Flax Mill at Oregon (Doon). Period: 1853 - 1963.

1974. Panabaker, D.N. "Glimpses of the industrial activities of Waterloo County about fifty years ago." **Waterloo Historical Society**. 1933. 21: 32-44. ill. Loc: all.
A summary of industries and their proprietors, based on the Armstrong Company's gazetteer and directory for 1878, with population statistics for all municipalities. Period: 1878.

1975. Panabaker, D.N. "Pioneer woollen mills in Preston, Hespeler and vicinity, Waterloo County, Ontario, and their connection with later textile industries." **Waterloo Historical Society**. 1933. 21: 45-52. Loc: all.
A survey of the woollen textile industry from the 1830s to 1880, including references to the enterprises of Jacob S. Shoemaker, Hiram Kinsman, Robert Hunt, Andrew Elliott, George Pattinson, William Robinson, Mr Hoswell, Jacob Hespeler, Jonathan Schofield, Mr Harvey, Mr McQuesten, Alexander Brodie, Robert Forbes and Marshall H. Farr. Period: c1830 - 1880.

1976. Panabaker, D.N. "President's address: the milling industry within the County etc." **Waterloo Historical Society**. 1929. 17: 100-105. tables. Loc: all.
A tabulated description of the industry in Waterloo County in the mid-nineteenth century, before the introduction of the new roller process. One table summarizes the average yield of wheat per acre and price per bushel received in each year. The second table gives the name, location, founder's name, type of power (steam or water), date, and equipment and capacity of each mill in 1864. Period: 1854 - 1887.

1977. "Parkway Mill closed." **Waterloo Historical Society**. 1961. 49: 59-61. ill. Loc: all.
A history of Parkway Mill on Mill Street, Kitchener from 1800 to its closing in 1961, naming its various owners. Period: 1800 - 1961.

1978. Pepper, Paul E. **Index to Hespeler yarns by Winfield Brewster**. 1986. 7 p. Loc: OKIT.
A list of over 300 personal names and some corporate subjects.

1979. "Pequegnat Clock Company." **Waterloo Historical Society**. 1965. 53: 80. ill. Loc: all.
A brief history of the Kitchener building constructed in 1897 by Arthur Pequegnat as a bicycle factory. Converted to a clock factory in 1910, the building was torn down in 1964 and replaced by the Water Commission Building. Period: 1897 - 1965.

1980. Perry, Robert Louis. **Galt, U.S.A.: the American presence in a Canadian city**. Toronto: Maclean-Hunter, 1971. 137 p. ill., bibl., tables. Loc: OCCA, OCLG, OCP, OKIT, OWTU, OWTL.
A case study of American control of the Canadian economy, earlier published as a series of articles in the **Financial Post**. Galt is described as a "small American city" with more than 60 per cent of manufacturing industry owned by foreigners, mainly Americans. The author reports interviews with Galt townspeople and business managers. Period: 1944 - 1971.

1981. Perry, Robert Louis. "Hard noses, cocacolonization bury a way of life." **Financial Post**. 1971. 65: 1,4. ill. mf. Loc: OWTL, OWTU.
Reference from the Canadian Periodical Index. Period: 1971.

1982. Phillips, Glen C. **The Ontario dairy and creamery list (1900-1950)**. Sarnia: Iron Gate Publishing, 1989. 229 p. Loc: OKIT, OWTU.
A list of companies obtained from a variety of business directories and organized by location. The work notes thirteen communities in Waterloo County that had creameries or dairies before 1950. Each business is classified as to whether it was a company or co-operative. Period: 1900 - 1950.

1983. Phillips, Glen C. **The Ontario soda water manufacturers and brewers gazetteer and business directory**. Sarnia: Clearwater Publishing, 1987. 181 p. indexes. Loc: OKIT, OWTUR.
Two separate lists of brewers and soda water manufacturers, each organized by place. Entries include the name of the person or company, products manufactured and the known years of production. Waterloo localities include Ayr,

Baden, Bamberg, Bridgeport, Elmira, Galt, New Hamburg, Heidelberg, Kitchener, Petersburg, Preston, Waterloo, Wellesley and Winterbourne. Indexes list manufacturers and places. The names of all Waterloo County people and companies are indexed in the WRP database. Period: 1851 - 1930.

1984. "Preston Mill historical tablet." **Waterloo Historical Society**. 1928. 16: 77-80. Loc: all.

A report of the unveiling on December 26, 1928 of a tablet honouring the mill as the oldest place of continuous business in Waterloo County, including the address by W.H. Breithaupt. Period: 1807 - 1928.

1985. "Preston's oldest industries." **Waterloo Historical Society**. 1967. 55: 89. Loc: all.

A brief note of the Cherry Taylor Flour Mills Ltd (established 1807) and Clare Brothers Ltd (established 1853). Period: 1807 - 1853.

1986. Quantrell, James. "The economic development of Cambridge: an overview." **Waterloo Historical Society**. 1987. 75: 60-71. ill., bibl. Loc: all.

An historical account of phases of industrialization in Galt, Preston and Hespeler in the 19th and 20th centuries, including references to particular enterprises, businessmen and industry types. Period: 1816 - c1987.

1987. R.M.C. King, Plant Food Planning Ltd. **Nutrite historical audit: final report**. 1985?. 1 v. (unpaged). Loc: OWRE.

An audit of the Elmira fertilizer and pesticide business from 1946 to 1985, based on interviews with employees and review of company records but with no onsite testing. It includes a copy of the report of a 1972 survey by the Industrial Wastes Branch of the Ministry of the Environment, information on chemical products, company memoranda and a plan of the plant. Period: 1946 - 1985.

1988. Ralph E. Loper & Co. **Consultants' report on Dominion Woollens & Worsteds, 1938**. 1938. 1 v. (unpaged). Loc: OKIT.

A summary of the recent history and current condition of the company, with recommendations for the future. It is noted that the company operated at a loss from 1932 to 1936 but that in 1937 a profit was made. Sales, products, salaries, inventories and company organization are all reported. Period: 1931 - 1938.

1989. **Read Bros, then Brockville and Sulco**. 1946 - 1968. 199 p. ill. Loc: OWRE.

A collection of advertisements and articles from **The Elmira Signet** about the fertilizer company

from its opening in 1946 to 1968 when it was purchased and closed by Brockville Chemical Ltd. Descriptions of the company are taken from the souvenirs of the 1948 and 1973 Old Boys and Girls Reunions. Period: 1946 - 1968.

1990. Reive, T.G. **The industrial background of Waterloo County to 1914**. 1970. 51 l. maps, bibl. Loc: OKIT.

An unpublished student paper showing that the cities of Berlin and Galt were the primary centres of manufacturing while Elmira, New Hamburg, Waterloo, Preston and Hespeler were secondary. The author comments on the extent to which industry in Galt complemented industry in Berlin. Period: 1860 - 1914.

1991. Renzella, Luigi M. **A situation-site analysis of the furniture industry in Ontario and Kitchener-Waterloo**. Waterloo Lutheran University (B.A. thesis, Geography), 1966. 77 p. bibl., tables, maps. Loc: OWTL.

A description of four phases in the organization of the industry: cottage industry, market orientation, area specialization, and big business. The author discusses locational factors and reasons for the industry's current decline, with reference to specific local companies. Period: 1856 - 1966.

1992. Ritz, Ernst. "Ritz Printing Inc. marks 125th anniversary." **Waterloo Historical Society**. 1980. 68: 10-16. Loc: all.

A history of the New Hamburg firm that began in 1855. The author traces the family business from Jacob Ritz who joined the firm as an apprentice, to Ernst and his son William Ritz who owned the company in 1980. Some details on changes in printing technology are also provided. Period: 1855 - 1980.

1993. Roberts, Leslie and Cloutier, Albert. **From three men**. Dominion Rubber Co., 1954. 55 p. ill. Loc: OKIT, OWTL.

An general history of the Dominion Rubber Company, founded in 1854 by Ashley Hibbard, William Brown, and George Bourn of Montreal, including references to the plants in Kitchener. Period: 1854 - 1954.

1994. **Rolling out the barrels: cooperage in Waterloo 1853-1987**. 1987?. 13 l. Loc: OWT.

A manuscript account of Charles Mueller's business, including its associations with the Kuntz Brewery and Seagram's Distillery. The work notes the company's transfer to the Seagram family and the establishment of Canada Barrels and Kegs (Canbar) in 1920 and the transition from wood barrel-making to plastic and fibreglass products and rotational mouldings from the 1950s. Period: 1853 - 1987.

1995. "Rosebank sawmill burns." **Waterloo Historical Society**. 1967. 55: 15. Loc: all.

A note of the fire at the steam-powered sawmill on the Huron Road. The 127-year-old mill was owned by Willard G. Hallman. Period: 1840 - 1967.

1996. Rusling, John R. "Factors influencing the location of manufacturing activity in Cambridge, Ontario." **Industrial development in Southern Ontario: selected essays**. Edited by James H. Bater and David F. Walker. Publication Series, no.3. Waterloo: Department of Geography, Faculty of Environmental Studies, University of Waterloo, 1974. Pp. 145-166. Loc: OWTU, OWTL.

Report of an analysis of 193 industrial establishments in Galt, Preston and Hespeler in 1970. The largest sectors were metal fabricating (62), machinery (18) and textiles (17). The author finds that personal, convenience and social factors are significant in the location decisions of most industries. Period: 1970 - 1971.

1997. Rusling, John R. **Industrial development and the expanding hinterland of Galt, 1820-1900**. University of Waterloo (B.E.S. thesis, Geography), 1970. 55 p. maps, tables, bibl. Loc: OWTU.

An evaluation of the rate and direction of urban-industrial growth as Galt changed from a self-sufficient community to an export economy. The author discusses changes in location patterns and industrial structure as a result of improved transportation and other local improvements. Tables provide concise information about local industries and specific companies. Period: 1820 - 1900.

1998. Sararus, Miriam. "The New Dundee Mill." **Waterloo Historical Society**. 1980. 68: 24-29. ill. Loc: all.

A short history of the business started by Frederick G. Millar in 1847, including details of ownership, renovations, floods and fire. Period: 1847 - 1979.

1999. "Sausage supreme - as business, diet." **Financial Post**. 1965. 59: 85, 87. ill. mf. Loc: OWTL, OWTU. Reference from the Canadian Periodical Index. Period: 1965.

2000. Schmidt, William A. "Power firsts in the Preston area." **Waterloo Historical Society**. 1985. 73: 71-79. ill., bibl. Loc: all.

An account of the beginnings of electricity, including details of power plants, generators,

costs and the formation of the Hydro Electric Power Commission. Period: 1891 - 1912.

2001. Schmidt, William A. "The Waterloo Manufacturing Company Limited." **Waterloo Historical Society**. 1987. 75: 16-23. ill. Loc: all.

A history of the business from its founding by Jacob Bricker in 1851, including references to the roles of Abraham Buehler, Absalom Merner and E.W.B. Snider and to the various corporate names. Period: 1851 - 1984.

2002. Schreiner, J. "Diversity, craftsmanship, stability: on these bases, twin cities flourish." **Financial Post**. 1965. 59: 55, 57. ill., maps. mf. Loc: OWTL, OWTU.

Reference from the Canadian Periodical Index. Period: 1965.

2003. "Scramble for industry: 'competition I fervently deplore'." **Monetary Times**. 1967. 135: 31-2. ill. Loc: OWTL, OWTU.

Reference from the Canadian Periodical Index. Period: 1967.

2004. Shantz, Mary C. "Two industrialists of Berlin/Kitchener, Ontario and their families, 1850-1950." **Waterloo Historical Society**. 1982. 70: 68-80. ill., bibl. Loc: all.

An account of the families and businesses of J.M. Schneider and Charles August Ahrens. Many details are provided about members of these families who remained closely interrelated from the marriage between John M. Schneider and Helena Ahrens in 1883. Period: 1831 - 1981.

2005. Shewchuk, John P. **The development of the textile trade at Galt, Preston and Hespeler, 1832-1914**. 1986. 68 p. bibl. Loc: OCCA, OCLG, OKIT.

A collection of case studies of Galt Knitting Co., George Pattinson and Co. and Dominion Woollens and Worsteds, discussed in their community contexts. Period: 1832 - 1914.

2006. Skene, Angus. **Working in: the story of the Breithaupt Tannery, 1858 to 1990**. Kitchener LACAC, 1990. 247 p. ill., plans. Loc: OKIT.

A preliminary report on the Breithaupt family, the Breithaupt Leather Company, and the Adam Street industrial site in Kitchener. The three main sections are: an account of the leather-tanning process, an outline history of the family and business in Berlin, and site plan drawings of buildings on the Adam Street property. Period: 1858 - 1990.

2007. Snider, C.M. "New machinery for historic mill." **Waterloo Historical Society**. 1951. 39: 22-25. ill. Loc: all.

A short history of the flour mill at St Jacobs which began operation in 1851. The article deals mainly with the mill's technological improvements, such as the Roller Mill in 1875, the Plansifer in 1890 and the pneumatic mill in 1951. Period: 1851 - 1951.

2008. Specht, Michael A. **The organization and locational structure of the garment industry in Kitchener, Waterloo, and Cambridge**. Wilfrid Laurier University (B.A. thesis, Geography), 1986. 67 p. maps, bibl. Loc: OWTL.

A study that presents general information on local garment businesses, with an index of area manufacturers including names, addresses, dates established, numbers of employees, and products. Period: 1868 - 1986.

2009. Spricenieks, Alfred. **Historical geography of industrial development of Kitchener, Waterloo, Bridgeport, 1801-1956**. University of Waterloo (B.A. thesis, Geography), 1961. 87 p. ill., maps, bibl. Loc: OWTUR, OWTL.

The industrial development of Bridgeport, Kitchener and Waterloo described in three eras: the pioneer period, the period of industrial and urban expansion, and the era of modern industrial development. Land use maps of different periods show the stages of industrialization in each community. Period: 1801 - 1956.

2010. Spring, Valerie J. "'Cute as buttons': the experience of women war workers at Dominion Woollens and Worsteds Limited." **Waterloo Historical Society**. 1987. 75: 117-131. ill. Loc: all.

A collection of reminiscences of women hired to work at the Hespeler factory during the Second World War. The author describes working conditions and activities that the company organized for its workers. Period: 1939 - c1950.

2011. "St Jacobs creamery closed." **Waterloo Historical Society**. 1972. 60: 90. Loc: all.

A note of the closing of the 100-year-old business, originally established by Gale and Woodcock to make cheese, and later used by William Brubacher and Alfred Snider for making butter. The industry was last owned by Roy Schlueter. Period: c1872 - 1972.

2012. St John, Ian. **The early history of the URW in Kitchener, 1936-1939**. University of Waterloo (student essay, History), 19--. 45 p. bibl., graphs. Loc: OKIT.

An account of the growth of the rubber workers' union and its relationship with the companies. The many strikes and disputes are described, the author concluding that, although the union's objective to organize was accomplished in four of the six companies, a final consolidation of its position had yet to be achieved by 1939. Period: 1936 - 1939.

2013. Staebler, Edna. **The Electrohome story**. Paris: The Walker Press, 1957. 38 p. ill. Loc: OKIT.

A popular history commemorating the company's 50th anniversary, with information about its founders, development, current products, and management. Period: 1907 - 1957.

2014. Stanton, Raymond. "Kitchener, capital of Canada's shoe manufacturing industry." **Leather World**. 1957. 37,3: 22-27. ill. Loc: OKITW.

A short historical account of shoe manufacturing in Kitchener with profiles of seven companies: Galt Shoe Manufacturing, Greb Shoe Company, Hydro City Shoe Manufacturers, Vetter Shoes, W.E. Woelfle Shoe Company, Breithaupt Leather Company, and John A. Lang and Sons. Kitchener suppliers, such as R.D. Goldsworthy and Bennett Limited, are also mentioned. Period: 1882 - 1957.

2015. Stanton, Raymond. **A legacy of quality: J.M. Schneider Inc., a centennial celebration 1890-1990**. Kitchener: The Company, 1990. 191 p. ill., bibl., map. Loc: OCCA, OKIT, OWRE, OWRN, OWT, OWTL, OWTU, OWTUCG, OWTUR, OWTUSJ.

A commemorative history including information about the Schneider family, the expansion of the company, technological change and the development of advertising techniques. The book contains many photographs, facsimiles and drawings. Period: 1890 - 1990.

2016. Symons, John W. **A summary of the history of the rubber industry**. 1958. 21 p. Loc: OKIT.

Typescript of an address to the Rubber Group of the Chemical Institute of Canada at McGill University. The author, who worked for the Dominion Rubber Company in Kitchener, surveys the entire history of rubber manufacture and refers to key dates and places in the development of the Canadian industry. Another version of the speech, apparently earlier, is also held at the Kitchener Public Library. Period: 1900 - 1958.

2017. Tait, Lynne D. **Industrial development in Waterloo**. University of Waterloo (B.E.S. thesis, Geography), 1978. 1 fiche. maps, tables, bibl. mf. Loc: OWTUM.

A general historical account that suggests

reasons for Waterloo's current attractiveness to industrial enterprises seeking new locations. Period: c1830 - 1978.

2018. Taylor, Ryan. "The William Eby pottery, Conestogo." **Waterloo Historical Society**. 1982. 70: 120-125. ill. Loc: all.

A short account of the potter and his work, based mainly on an interview with his grandson Simeon Martin in 1982. The article relates aspects of Eby's business, including the type of clay and processes, and his work for the Berlin Sugarfest in creating miniature barrels as souvenirs. Period: 1831 - 1982.

2019. Thomson, Andrew McCauley. **The Breithaupts and Breithaupt Leather: building a family business in Berlin, Ontario**. University of Waterloo (Ph.D. thesis, History), 1992. 283 p. bibl. Loc: OWTUR.

A business history of the tanneries established in Buffalo in 1844 by German immigrant, Liborius Breithaupt, and in Berlin from 1857 by his son, Louis Breithaupt. The growth of the Berlin-based enterprise is discussed in detail until its incorporation in 1890 while an epilogue outlines developments to 1926. In examining how Breithaupt family members dealt with the challenges of business life, the author makes extensive use of the L.J.Breithaupt diaries in the Breithaupt Hewetson Clark Collection in the University of Waterloo Library. Period: 1844 - 1926.

2020. Trussler, Karen Poser. **Industrial heritage: definition and developments with special emphasis on the former Silknit Ltd textile mill in Cambridge, Ontario**. University of Waterloo (M.A. thesis, History), 1986. 91 p. Also mf. Loc: OWTU, OCCA.

A case study of the Silknit textile mill (formerly Dominion Woollens and Worsteds) in Hespeler. The author describes the building, concluding that it deserves preservation, and outlines the history of the company. Period: 1863 - 1986.

2021. Turner, Harold S. and Irwin, Ross W. **Ontario's threshing machine industry: a short history of these pioneer companies and their contribution to Ontario agriculture**. University of Guelph School of Engineering, 1974. 29 p. ill. Loc: OKDHC.

A collection of descriptions of individual companies, including the New Hamburg Manufacturing Company, the Waterloo Manufacturing Company and the John Watson Manufacturing Company. There are short biographies of the founders, detailed accounts of the machinery produced, and information on the development of both the products and the companies. Period: 1844 - 1949.

2022. **Uniroyal Chemical Ltd**. Waterloo Regional Library, Elmira Branch, 1941 - 1982. 3 v. Loc: OWRE.

A collection of printed materials about the company, formerly Naugatuck Chemicals, culled from advertisements and articles in the **Elmira Signet**. The items were copied from microfilm and bound in chronological order. Period: 1941 - 1982.

2023. **Uniroyal Ltd: abridged history 1853-1984**. 1984. 11 p. Loc: OKIT.

A brief summary of significant dates in the history of the company, with information about purchases, amalgamations, product lines and labour agreements. Period: 1900 - 1984.

2024. Unitt, Doris and Unitt, Peter. **Arthur Pequegnat clocks with history and price guide**. Peterborough: Clock House Publications, 1973 revised 1985. 80 p. ill. Loc: OCLG, OCP, OKIT, OWT.

An inventory of products of the Berlin business, with estimates of current values of the clocks. Photographs and brief descriptions are included, with short histories of the company and the Pequegnat family. Period: 1874 - 1974.

2025. Waite, Gary K. "Joseph Schneider sawmill operations 1848-1859." **Waterloo Historical Society**. 1985. 73: 57-65. tables. Loc: all.

A detailed history of the mill, including figures of production and sales and a description of its clients in the Berlin community. Period: 1848 - 1859.

2026. Walker, David F. "Expansion and adaptation in the post-war years." **Manufacturing in Kitchener-Waterloo: a long-term perspective**. Edited by David F. Walker. Waterloo: Department of Geography, University of Waterloo, 1987. Pp. 61-82. map. Loc: OKIT, OWTL, OWTU, OWTUR.

A survey of structural and spatial changes including more rapid rates of growth in Waterloo than Kitchener, decentralization from the city core to the periphery, and the expansion of metals, machinery, electrical and electronics, and food and beverage sectors. Changes in ownership and innovations in technology are discussed. Period: 1945 - 1985.

2027. Walker, David F. and Bater, James H. "The industrial structure of midwestern Ontario." **The Waterloo County area: selected geographical essays**. Edited by A.G. McLellan. Waterloo: Department of Geography, University of Waterloo, 1971. Pp. 148-147. map, tabl. Loc: OWTU, OWTL, OWTUCG, OKIT.

An analysis of trends in employment by major industry groups in Kitchener-Waterloo, Galt-Hespeler-Preston, Guelph and Brantford between 1961 and 1970. In Kitchener-Waterloo, most rapid growth is reported in transportation equipment (auto parts), electrical products, leather products and chemicals with the only absolute decline in the rubber industry. Galt-Preston-Hespeler's greatest growth is in metal fabricating, machinery and textiles. Period: 1961 - 1970.

2028. Walker, David F. **Manufacturing in Kitchener-Waterloo: a long-term perspective**. Publication Series No. 26. Waterloo: Department of Geography, University of Waterloo, 1987. 220 p. ill., maps, tables, bibl. Loc: OKIT, OWT, OWTL, OWTU, OWTUR.

A collection of essays on industrial change in the twin cities since the 1850s. Each of the five essays relating to the period before 1973 has a separate record in the WRP database. Period: 1855 - 1985.

2029. Walker, Dean and Pollock, C.A. "Marketing at Electrohome: 'We must be Canadians'." **Executive**. 1972. 14: cover, 57-60. ill. Loc: OWTL, OWTU.

Reference from the Canadian Periodical Index. Period: 1972.

2030. Wallace, Alice. "The Reichard and Hallman sawmills at Rosebank." **Waterloo Historical Society**. 1989. 77: 74-82. ill. Loc: all.

A history of the mill begun in 1828 by Samuel and Jacob Reichard and bought by John S. Hallman in 1878, including information about the mill machinery. Period: 1800 - 1989.

2031. Wallace, James. "Hallman sawmill at Rosebank sold." **Waterloo Historical Society**. 1990. 78: 157. ill. Loc: all.

A captioned photograph noting the sale, after 112 years of operation by the Hallman family, of the Rosebank sawmill and farm property at R.R. #2, Petersburg to David Townsend of Tillsonburg. Period: 1878 - 1990.

2032. Waterloo County Area Research Committee (Subcommittee two - Economics) **Manufacturing industries and products, Village of Bridgeport, City of Kitchener, City of Waterloo, Township of Waterloo**. Kitchener: The Committee, 196-?. 16 l. Loc: OWTU.

A list of over 180 manufacturers and their products. Period: c1960 - c1969.

2033. "Waterloo Glove Manufacturing Company." **Waterloo Historical Society**. 1973. 61: 44-45. ill. Loc: all.

A short history of the company begun by John Schondelmeyer in 1902, taken over in 1920 by Elmer Wahl and Valentine Bernhardt, and then by Robert Putnam in 1966. The author mentions the various locations of the business and its products. Period: 1902 - 1973.

2034. Waterloo Regional Heritage Foundation. **Tabular index of the industries of Waterloo County circa 1850-1910: Industrial Heritage Committee report**. Waterloo: The Foundation, 1984. 80 l. bibl., tables. Loc: OWTUR.

A photocopy of the index compiled by students in the University of Waterloo's Masters Program in Public History. The tables are organized by community and list company names by industry. Period: 1850 - 1910.

2035. Webster, Donald Blake. **The William Eby Pottery, Conestogo, Ontario, 1855-1907**. Royal Ontario Museum: Art and Archaeology Occasional Paper 25. Toronto: Royal Ontario Museum, 1971. 54 p. ill., maps, bibl. Loc: OKIT, OWTL, OWTU.

A brief biography of William Eby with an account of his pottery site and the archaeological excavations undertaken in 1967. There are photographs and drawings from the excavation and an annotated inventory of Eby pottery types. Period: 1855 - 1907.

2036. Weiss, Annemarie. "Ownership change and the German family manufacturing firm in Kitchener since 1945." **Manufacturing in Kitchener-Waterloo: a long-term perspective**. Edited by David F. Walker. Waterloo: Department of Geography, University of Waterloo, 1987. Pp. 107-122, 200-204. tables. Loc: OKIT, OWTL, OWTU, OWTUR.

An examination of the extent to which the earlier predominance of German entrepreneurs in Kitchener's business life persisted after 1945. Directories are used to compile lists of manufacturing companies at 5-year intervals from 1945 to 1980 and to deduce numbers of new business entrants and exits. The author notes that post-1945 German immigrants tended to start new businesses in construction, real estate, insurance, service and repair, and foodstuffs, rather than in manufacturing. Period: 1945 - 1980.

2037. "World-class experience, the Seagram Museum: a warm welcome to Waterloo." **Waterloo Chronicle**. 1984, May 9. 24 p. ill. Loc: OKIT.

A profile of the company museum established in 1972, with a brief account of the Seagram family and the business directed by Joseph E. Seagram from the 1870s. Period: 1857 - 1984.

2038. Yundt, Sheralyn E. **Marketing and transportation in the sand and gravel industry in Waterloo and Wellington Counties.** University of Waterloo (M.A. thesis, Geography), 1973. 112 p. 2 fiche. maps, tables. mf. Loc: OWTU.

A general analysis based partly on a case study of the Preston Sand and Gravel Co. in 1969-70. Period: 1969 - 1970.

2039. Zimmerman, Idessa. "Birth of the button in Canada." **Waterloo Historical Society.** 1958. 46: 17-25. ill. Loc: all.

A history of the button industry in Kitchener from 1866 to 1958, with information about various manufacturing processes and leading entrepreneurs such as Emil Vogelsang, Jacob Y. Shantz, David Gross and Mervin Gross. Period: 1866 - 1958.

2040. Zimmerman, Idessa. "The end of Dominion Buttons." **Waterloo Historical Society.** 1970. 58: 81. Loc: all.

An account of the demolition of Dominion Button Manufacturers Limited on Water Street North, Kitchener, to make way for an apartment building. The author notes that the factory at one time employed almost 1,000 workers and that Kitchener was known as "Buttonville." Period: 1866 - 1970.

TRANSPORTATION AND COMMUNICATIONS, INCLUDING RAILWAYS, ROADS, HIGHWAYS, POSTAL AND TELECOMMUNICATIONS

2041. "100th anniversary edition." **Galt Daily Reporter.** 1946, November 13. 101,1: 1-9. ill. Also mf. Loc: OCCA, OCLG, OKIT.

A special issue celebrating the newspaper's centennial, outlining its history and noting past and current owners, editors and employees. There are articles by Irma Green Parks, the first woman reporter hired in 1915 and by Earl Werstine who worked for the paper for 41 years. Period: 1846 - 1946.

2042. "Airport's future: steady growth." **Financial Post.** 1965. 59: 71. mf. Loc: OWTL, OWTU.

Reference from the Canadian Periodical Index. Period: 1965.

2043. Allen, Gary J. **An analysis of the commuter pattern to a major industrial node in Waterloo, Ontario.** Waterloo Lutheran University (B.A. thesis, Geography), 1967. 71 p. maps, bibl. Loc: OWTL.

A study of the commuting patterns of the different types of workers (sales, clerical, unskilled, semi-skilled and skilled) to an engineering firm in Waterloo. The author reports 75 per cent of employees living within four miles but a few as far as 17 miles from the plant. Within the four-mile zone no differences are found among types of workers, but beyond that point the clerical and unskilled groups commute farthest. It appears that there is an inverse relationship between the distance a person is willing to commute and three factors of age, length of employment and relative wage rates. Period: 1961 - 1967.

2044. Andreae, Christopher A. **A railway atlas of southwestern Ontario.** London: The Author, 1972. 25 p. maps, bibl., index. Loc: OGU.

A preliminary collection of maps tracing the growth of railway networks in the region from the 1850s to the 1870s. Dates of opening are marked on each section of line and the mileage of specific lines (including interurban and street railways) is listed for various years. Period: 1850 - 1970.

2045. Andrews, Mervin G. **Travel characteristics of selected manufacturing industries in Kitchener-Waterloo.** University of Waterloo (M.A. thesis, Civil Engineering), 1972. 1 fiche. maps, bibl., graphs. mf. Loc: OWTUD.

An outline of a forecasting model using readily available sources of information such as city and industrial directories. The study examines characteristics of the transport system and the travel patterns of employees of fifteen firms in the Kitchener-Waterloo area. Income and sex of the worker are found to be the most influential factors. Period: 1969 - 1972.

2046. **An archaeological investigation of the historic corduroy road (Columbia Street, Waterloo) AiHd-80, City of Waterloo.** Waterloo: Regional Municipality of Waterloo, Planning and Development Department, Archaeology Division, 1989. 11 p. ill. Loc: OKIT, OWRMA.

Report of an excavation of the road, including a review of literature on corduroy roads and a comparison with the Huron Road. Period: 1820 - 1900.

2047. **An archaeological investigation of the historic corduroy road (Bleams Road) AiHc-92 and monitoring of topsoil stripping of AiHc-55 and AiHc-56, City of Kitchener.** Waterloo: Regional Municipality of Waterloo, Planning and Development Department, Archaeology Division, 1989. 33 p. ill., diagrams, app. Loc: OKIT, OWRMA.

Report of an 1989 excavation of a section of the road, before the sites were destroyed in the course of constructing the Mannheim Artificial Recharge System. A review of the literature on corduroy roads is included on pp. 3-5. Period: 1820 - 1900.

2048. "Area well served by two papers, TV, competing radio stations." **Financial Post**. 1965. 59: 73. mf. Loc: OWTL, OWTU.
Reference from the Canadian Periodical Index. Period: 1965.

2049. Bergey, Lorna L. "The Huron Road." **Waterloo Historical Society**. 1969. 57: 10-15. ill. Loc: all.
An address given at the unveiling of a commemorative plaque, the text of which is quoted. Period: 1827 - 1840.

2050. Bernhardt, Clara. "CKPC's early years in Preston." **Waterloo Historical Society**. 1969. 57: 64-69. Loc: all.
A history of Preston radio station CKPC from its foundation in 1923 to 1933 when it moved to Brantford. Various programmes and people, including station owner Cyrus Dolph, are described and a typical broadcast schedule from 1933 is reproduced from the weekly **Prestonian**. Period: 1923 - 1933.

2051. Breithaupt, W.H. "Early roads and transportation: Upper Canada." **Waterloo Historical Society**. 1919. 7: 59-66. map. Loc: all.
A general survey with particular reference to the routes used by the Mennonite pioneers in the first half of the nineteenth century. Period: 1800 - 1852.

2052. Breithaupt, W.H. "The Huron Road." **Waterloo Historical Society**. 1935. 23: 168-175. Loc: all.
A history of the Huron Road, especially its early development by John Galt of the Canada Company. Period: 1828 - 1928.

2053. Breithaupt, W.H. "Museum report." **Waterloo Historical Society**. 1928. 16: 81-83. Loc: all.
A short annual report on the Waterloo Historical Society's County Museum, including a note of the donation of the first two telephones installed in Berlin in 1880 and a list of subscribers in the Berlin telephone directory of 1883. Period: 1880 - 1883.

2054. Breithaupt, W.H. "The railways of Ontario." **Ontario Historical Society, Papers and Records**. 1929. 25: 12-25. ill. Loc: OWTL, OWTU.
An account of the first railway companies and their territories. The author mentions the Waterloo Junction Railway, the Berlin to Elmira and Berlin to Galt branches of the Grand Trunk, and the electric lines of the Waterloo, Wellington and Lake Huron Railway and the Lake Erie and Northern Railway. Period: 1833 - 1912.

2055. Breithaupt, W.H. "Waterloo County railway history." **Waterloo Historical Society**. 1917. 5: 14-23. ill. Loc: all.
An account of the development of railways from 1854 to 1916, including the Grand Trunk Railway, the Great Western Railway and the Credit Valley Railway, as well as the electric lines (the Berlin and Northern Railroad, the Galt, Preston and Hespeler Railway, and the Lake Erie and Northern Railway). There are short biographies of H.F.J. Jackson, George Randall and Joseph Hobson. Period: 1854 - 1913.

2056. Brown, Harry W. "The coming of the telephone to Kitchener." **Waterloo Historical Society**. 1940. 28: 98-101. ill. Loc: all.
An account of early events, such as W.H. Breithaupt's installation of the first two telephones in 1880, and Bell Telephone's 1883 system with John S. Hoffman as manager. The article concludes in 1940 when a new telephone building was built on Water Street North for the new dial system. Period: 1880 - 1940.

2057. Brown, Ron. **The train doesn't stop here any more: an illustrated history of railway stations in Canada**. Peterborough: Broadview Press, 1991. 200 p. ill. Loc: OKIT.
A general survey that, among many illustrations, reproduces the original plan for the 1897 Grand Trunk Station at Berlin. Period: 1896 - 1897.

2058. "Buggy bridge." **Waterloo Historical Society**. 1962. 50: 9. Loc: all.
A note of the building by Old Order Mennonites of a low-level bridge over the Conestogo River near St Jacobs to divert buggy traffic from Highway 85. Period: 1962 -

2059. "C.P.R. bridge at Galt demolished." **Waterloo Historical Society**. 1956. 44: 67. Loc: all.
A short account of an accident on 2 May 1956 when two engines on a fast freight train crashed into a standing locomotive at Galt. Period: 1956 -

2060. Cain, Peter F. **The Grand River Railway: a study of a Canadian intercity electric railroad**. Waterloo Lutheran University (B.A. thesis, History), 1972. 66 l. ill., bibl. Loc: OWTL, OKIT.
A history of the interurban electric railway including its precursors, the Galt, Preston and Hespeler Street Railway and the Preston and Berlin Street Railway. The author presents information

on passenger and freight services, rolling stock and finances, and considers the effects on the company of the world wars, the depression and the automobile. Period: 1890 - 1960.

2061. "Crosshill Post Office moved." **Waterloo Historical Society**. 1964. 52: 30. Loc: all.
A note of the move to Lloyd Albrecht's store from Mrs Lorne Rennie's house, where the post office had operated since 1899 when her father, Robert Foster was the community's postmaster and shoemaker. A list of all the Crosshill postmasters is provided, since William Logan who was appointed in 1852. Period: 1846 - 1964.

2062. Cuming, David J. **Discovering heritage bridges on Ontario's roads.** Erin: Boston Mills Press, 1983. 95 p. ill. Loc: OCLG, OKIT, OWTL.
A general history of bridge design and construction, including references to flood threats and damage to Galt's Queen Street bridge in 1912 and the Blair bridge after Hurricane Hazel in October 1954 (pp. 32-3). Efforts to save Ontario's last covered bridge at West Montrose are noted on pages 73 and 77. Period: 1912 - 1980.

2063. Currie, Archibald W. **The Grand Trunk Railway of Canada.** Toronto: University of Toronto, 1957. 556 p. map, index. Loc: OKIT, OWTU.
Comprehensive history of the railway company, including references to the Galt and Guelph Railway, the Preston and Berlin Railway, and the towns of Galt, Preston and Kitchener. Period: 1852 - 1934.

2064. Dahms, Fredric A. **Commuting in Waterloo County.** University of Western Ontario (M.A. thesis, Geography), 1962. 115 p. ill., tables, maps. Loc: OWTU.
A study of the direction, amount and implications of daily commuting. The author's data show the interdependence of Waterloo municipalities. Period: 1961 - 1962.

2065. Damas and Smith Limited. **Traffic planning report, 1965-1985.** Don Mills: Damas and Smith Limited, 1967. 2 v. maps, tables. Loc: OWTL.
A 1967 traffic planning report in two volumes, the first on Galt and the second on Preston. Existing traffic conditions and future demands are described, with details of parking, travel demand, traffic accidents and the physical characteristics of the streets. Recommended improvements are listed. Period: 1965 - 1985.

2066. "Detweiler envisioned St Lawrence Seaway in 1912." **Waterloo Historical Society**. 1959. 47: 18-20. ill. Loc: all.
A description of efforts to promote the construction of a Canadian inland seaway by forming the Berlin-based Great Waterways Union of Canada. Extensive passages are quoted from a pamphlet by Detweiler. Period: 1912 - 1959.

2067. "Diesels take over from electric engines." **Waterloo Historical Society**. 1961. 49: 66-68. ill. Loc: all.
An account of the end of the electric lines of the Grand River Railway and the Lake Erie and Northern Railway, when Canadian Pacific Railway decided that diesels were cheaper to operate. Period: 1894 - 1961.

2068. Donohoe, E.F. "From covered wagon to steam railway: Kitchener's saga of transportation links Conestoga wheel ruts and steel rails in industrial development." **Canadian National Magazine**. 1946. 32,4: 6, 16-17. Loc: OWA.
Reference from **Bibliography of Ontario history, 1867-1976** (Bishop et al.). Period: 1800 - 1900.

2069. Dorman, Robert and Stoltz, D.E. **A statutory history of railways in Canada, 1836-1986.** Kingston: Canadian Institute of Guided Ground Transport, 1987. 496 p. Loc: OWTL, OWTU.
A revised version of Dorman's original work, adding post-1938 statutory citations and the 1986 status of railway companies as well as some revisions and additions to the earlier citations, some of which have been abbreviated or omitted. While the companies are listed in alphabetical order throughout Canada, there is unfortunately no index. The major companies in Waterloo County were the major trunk enterprises of the Grand Trunk Railway, the Great Western Railway and the Canadian Pacific Railway, but some 20 other companies were involved in planning and/or operating railways, including interurban and electric street railways. The new version omits references to some companies relevant to Waterloo County that were cited by Dorman, such as the Guelph and Goderich Railway and the Galt, Preston, and Hespeler Railway. All railways operating in the county have been indexed in the WRP database. Period: 1850 - 1986.

2070. Dorman, Robert. **A statutory history of the steam and electric railways of Canada, 1836-1937.** Ottawa: King's Printer, 1938. 200 p. Loc: OKIT, OWTU.
An alphabetical listing of all railway companies in Canada, including those that planned but never built railway lines, with details of the statutes of incorporation and subsequent amendments. The major companies in Waterloo County were the Grand Trunk Railway, the Great Western Railway and the

Canadian Pacific Railway, but some 20 other companies were involved in planning and/or operating railways, including interurban and electric street railways. All of these have been indexed in the WRP database. Period: 1836 - 1937.

2071. Due, John F. "Lines in the Grand Valley." **The intercity electric railway industry in Canada.** Toronto: University of Toronto Press, 1965. Pp. 78-81. Loc: OWTU, OWTL.

Brief histories of the three electric lines that crossed Waterloo County -- the Grand River Railway Company, the Lake Erie and Northern Railway Company, and the Grand Valley Railway Company -- in the context of a general study of the industry in Canada. The author provides details of changes in corporate names and the frequency of passenger and freight services. Period: 1890 - 1960.

2072. Duff, Louis Blake. "Huron Road centennial." **Waterloo Historical Society.** 1928. 16: 13-21. Loc: all.

The address by the president of the Ontario Historical Society at the celebration on 3 September 1928. Period: 1828 - 1928.

2073. Farmer, Mary H. "The Preston and Berlin Railway Company." **Waterloo Historical Society.** 1961. 49: 16-22. ill. Loc: all.

A history of the ill-fated Preston and Berlin Railway Company that operated for only three months in 1857, reputedly the worst part of the worst year in the history of Canadian railroads. The article is based on the Robert Ferrie Papers in Hamilton Public Library. Period: 1855 - 1873.

2074. Galt and Guelph Railway. **Financial statement of the Galt and Guelph Railway Co., from the 3rd March 1856 to the 28th February 1857 as submitted to the stockholders at the Annual Meeting on the 2nd March.** CIHM Microfiche series, no. 52608. The Company, 1857. 1 frame. mf. Loc: OWTL, OWTU.

A list of the cash, debentures and bonds held by the company. Period: 1856 - 1857.

2075. "Galt, Preston and Hespeler Street Railway." **Railway and Marine World.** 1907. 10: 271. Loc: OTU.

Reference from **Bibliography of Ontario history, 1867-1976** (Bishop et al.). Period: 1890 - 1906.

2076. **Galt, Preston & Hespeler Electric Ry.** Hamilton: Howell Lithographic Co., 1 sheet. ill., map. Loc: OWTUR.

Advertising brochure promoting the Galt, Preston and Hespeler Electric Railway and describing scenic spots and hotels such as Idylwild Park, the Preston mineral springs, Del Monte Hotel of Preston, the Preston Kress Hotel, the Galt Imperial Hotel, and Esson's Photographic Atelier in Preston. A small map shows the location of the railway in relation to the Grand Trunk Railway and various cities and towns. Period: 1894 - 1923.

2077. Grindlay, Thomas. **A history of the independent telephone industry in Ontario.** Toronto: Ontario Telephone Service Commission, 1975. 316 p. ill., append. Loc: OKIT.

A history of the development of independent telephone companies, including lists of dates of operation, numbers of subscribers and changes in ownership of specific companies from 1903 to 1975. Companies in Waterloo County, eventually all taken over by Bell Canada, were the Ayr Rural Telephone Co. (1908-1948), the Wellesley Municipal Telephone System (1919-1963, incorporating the earlier Glaister and McEachern systems), the Waterloo Municipal Telephone System (1912-1958) and the Wilmot Municipal Telephone System (1922-1967, incorporating the earlier New Dundee Rural Telephone Co). The Wilmot system is described in more detail on pp. 245-7. The Mornington Municipal Telephone System, begun in 1908 by a predecessor company, was still operating independently in 1975. Period: 1903 - 1975.

2078. Groh, Ivan. "The Indian trail from Blair to Puslinch Lake." **Canadian-German Folklore.** 1967. 2: 21. Loc: OWTU, OWTL, OKIT, OWT, OWTUCG.

A poem describing the influence of the routes of meandering deer and Indian trails on later roads. Period: 1650 - 1967.

2079. Hett, Laverne J. **History of Kitchener Transit.** Kitchener Department of Transportation Services, 1983. 5 l. Loc: OKIT.

A municipal publication which contains a chronological listing of significant dates in the development of the transit service. Entries begin with 1883 when a charter was granted for a street railway between Berlin and Waterloo and end with a short summary of equipment in use in 1983. Period: 1883 - 1983.

2080. Hett, Laverne J. "Kitchener transit: the first hundred years 1889-1989." **Waterloo Historical Society.** 1988. 76: 6-30. ill., bibl. Loc: all.

A history of the utility from its beginnings as the Berlin and Waterloo Street Railway Co. in the 1880s to its electrification in the 1890s and change to buses from the 1920s. Many details are provided about investment, equipment, depots and routes. Period: 1882 - 1988.

2081. Hilborn, Ivan M. "Independent telephone systems." **Waterloo Historical Society**. 1958. 46: 39-41. Loc: all.

A description of three independent systems still operating in Waterloo County. One of these, the New Dundee Rural Telephone Company, celebrated its 50th anniversary in 1958. Period: 1908 - 1958.

2082. "Historic stamp." **Waterloo Historical Society**. 1963. 51: 16. Loc: all.

A note of the new stamp commemorating Sir Casimir Gzowski, with a reference to Kitchener's Gzowski Street east of the CN station. Period: 1963.

2083. "It happened in 1960." **Waterloo Historical Society**. 1960. 48: 77. ill. Loc: all.

A note of three events in 1960, including the opening of Highway 401 between Milton and Preston and the retirement of the last CNR steam locomotive. Period: 1960 - 1969.

2084. Jantzi, S. and Dickson, F.W.R. "Linwood Post Office closed after 77 years." **Waterloo Historical Society**. 1963. 51: 88. Loc: all.

A report of the closing of the Linwood Post Office in 1963, with an account of its history. Period: 1885 - 1963.

2085. Kernighan, R.K. "The Dundas and Waterloo Road: reflections." **Waterloo Historical Society**. 1920. 8: 111-114. Loc: all.

Comments on the changes along the road between about 1800 and 1875. Period: c1800 - c1875.

2086. Kirk, Wayne. **The development of public transit in Kitchener-Waterloo**. Waterloo Lutheran University (student essay), 1964. 30 p. bibl., tables. Loc: OKIT, OWT.

A history of the origins of the system, the public purchase of the Berlin and Waterloo Street Railway in 1907, the introduction of gasoline buses in 1939, and the lifting of the ban on parking in 1961. Tables give financial information, including profits paid to Kitchener and Waterloo by the transit system from 1913 to 1931. Period: 1886 - 1964.

2087. Kirkwood, M.W. **Historical record: Canadian Pacific electric lines comprising the Grand River Railway Company, the Lake Erie and Northern Rail Company**. 1939. 25 l. Loc: OKIT.

An unpublished history of the two railway lines, from the individuals and companies involved in the initial organization and construction to current power sources, equipment and services. Period: 1890 - 1925.

2088. "Kissing Bridge is 100 years old." **Waterloo Historical Society**. 1981. 69: 72-73. ill. Loc: all.

A brief note about the covered bridge at West Montrose, including two photographs, one of the bridge with a scale model next to it, and one of the new plaque which correctly identifies the Bear brothers who built the bridge. Period: 1881 - 1981.

2089. Kitchener-Waterloo Technical Advisory Committee. **Kitchener-Waterloo Expressway: newsletter 1965-1969**. Kitchener: Expressway Information Office, 1969. folded sheets. maps. Loc: OKIT.

A series of pamphlets reporting the progress of the Kitchener-Waterloo Expressway, later named the Conestoga Parkway, between 1965 and 1969. Bulletins describe the detours, the contractors, traffic, tenders, property purchased, and bridges completed. Period: 1965 - 1969.

2090. Kraemer, James E. "How Kingsdale got its name." **Waterloo Historical Society**. 1980. 68: 38-42. ill. Loc: all.

A short history of the post office which was named for Mackenzie King and operated for 22 years. Period: 1949 - 1971.

2091. Lamb, Kathryn Hansuld. "The Huron Road: a memorable highway." **Waterloo Historical Society**. 1984. 72: 128-130. ill. Loc: all.

A note of the erection by members of Kitchener LACAC of historic markers along sections of the road. Period: 1828 - 1984.

2092. Lamb, Kathryn Hansuld. "The post office at North Woolwich." **Waterloo Historical Society**. 1991. 79: 162-169. ill. Loc: all.

An outline of the brief history of the rural post office which lasted less than five years in the area north of Floradale. Approved by federal MP Mackenzie King in 1908, the office was operated by Conrad Schwindt as mail contractor. His wife, Josephine Riebel, sorted the mail and served patrons. The office closed when rural mail delivery began on Elmira Rural Route #1 in July 1913. The author names local families and describes other services which have all now disappeared from the community of North Woolwich which was earlier known as Sandytown. Period: 1857 - 1913.

2093. Lamb, Kathryn Hansuld. "West Montrose covered bridge." **Waterloo Historical Society**. 1977. 65: 25-36. ill. Loc: all.

A detailed history of the last remaining covered bridge in Ontario. The author quotes from minutes of Woolwich Township Council in 1880, when John

Bear presented plans for the bridge, and traces its construction and maintenance up to 1977. Period: 1881 - 1977.

2094. "Last steam locomotive through Kitchener." **Waterloo Historical Society**. 1971. 59: 78. ill. Loc: all.

A note that the last steam locomotive passed through Kitchener in 1971. The engine was officially retired by CN in 1964 but continued to be available for charter. Period: 1971.

2095. "List of mail contracts in the electoral division of North Waterloo." **Waterloo Historical Society**. 1968. 56: 72-73. Loc: all.

A list of contracts dated 14 October 1896, stating the individual mail route, name of contractor, distance involved, frequency of delivery, amount paid per year, and the expiry date of the contract. The list was found among the papers of E.W.B. Snider. Period: 1896 - 1900.

2096. Little, Ellis. "Corduroy roads in Waterloo County." **Waterloo Historical Society**. 1989. 77: 142-160. ill. Loc: all.

A history and description of roads built to cross swampy terrain by means of using logs placed side by side, with reference to examples such as the Bleams corduroy road excavated in 1989. Period: 1800 - 1989.

2097. Little, Ellis. "Fording places in Waterloo Township during the 1800s." **Waterloo Historical Society**. 1988. 76: 85-112. ill., bibl., maps. Loc: all.

A detailed account of the development and use of seventeen fords. Period: c1800 - c1880.

2098. Martin, Mildred. "Farm radio forums in Woolwich Township." **Waterloo Historical Society**. 1981. 69: 62-72. ill. Loc: all.

A description of a radio programme known as the Farm Radio Forum and its impact in Woolwich Township. Started in the 1930s in cooperation with the Ontario Federation of Agriculture, the programme was aired until 1965. Farmers and their wives gathered to hear it and mailed in their comments. Period: 1939 - 1950.

2099. Mills, John M. **Traction on the Grand: the story of electric railways along Ontario's Grand River Valley**. Montreal: Railfare, 1977. 96 p. ill., maps. Loc: OKIT, OCCA, OWTL, OWTU.

An account of each company that carried passengers and freight from the 1890s. Waterloo County railways include the Galt, Preston and Hespeler Railway, the Grand River Railway, the Grand Valley Railroad, the Berlin and Waterloo

Street Railway, the Kitchener-Waterloo Railways, and the Preston Car and Coach Company. Topics include equipment, routes, electrification, dieselization, expansions, franchises, takeovers, municipal ownership and the advent of bus service. Period: 1886 - 1964.

2100. Niehaus, Charles F. "History of the Berlin Post Office [WRP]." **Waterloo Historical Society**. 1929. 17: 139-140. ill. Loc: all.

A brief sketch from its beginnings in 1842, with George Davidson as the first postmaster, to the new Post Office building in 1885. The author includes a note about his own life. Period: 1842 - 1919.

2101. Oberholtzer, R.S. "One hundred and fifty years of change along the Preston-Kitchener roadway." **Waterloo Historical Society**. 1963. 51: 80-81. ill. Loc: all.

A description of changes on the highway, with particular reference to the successive bridges at Freeport. Period: 1813 - 1963.

2102. "Ontario's last covered bridge." **Waterloo Historical Society**. 1959. 47: 27-28. ill. Loc: all.

A short history of the last covered bridge in Ontario, built in 1881 by John and Sam Baer in West Montrose. A new bridge was built in 1959 to take most of the traffic and relieve the old bridge. Period: 1881 - 1959.

2103. Panabaker, Arnold T. "Retrospect." **Waterloo Historical Society**. 1964. 52: 37-39. Loc: all.

A short account, written in 1941, of the author's first job at George Chapman's telegraph office in Hespeler in 1880. Period: 1880 - 1941.

2104. Panabaker, D.N. "President's address: Indian trails - bridle paths - gravel roads - concrete highways in Waterloo County." **Waterloo Historical Society**. 1935. 23: 160-164. Loc: all.

A brief survey of the main phases of road-building, especially the system of concrete highways commenced in 1918. The provincial government provided a 60 per cent subsidy for the improvement of roads classified as Main County Highways. The author notes that the first section of concrete highway in Waterloo County was laid between St Jacobs and the railway crossing 1.5 miles to the north in 1919. Period: 1800 - 1919.

2105. Peter Barnard Associates/ Read, Voorhees and Associates. **Improving public transit in Kitchener and Waterloo: a report prepared for the Kitchener/Waterloo Transit Study Committee**. Toronto: Peter Barnard Associates, 1972. 56 l.

ill. Loc: OKIT, OWTL, OWTU.

A report recommending a five-year plan for improved bus service in the two cities. The suggestions include new routing, a transit vehicle replacement schedule, alternative maintenance facilities, a cost sharing formula, and an implementation plan. Period: 1971 - 1976.

2106. Pinney, Martin D. **Individual consumer travel behaviour in Kitchener-Waterloo.** University of Waterloo (B.E.S. thesis, Geography), 1973. 100 l. graphs, bibl. Loc: OWTU.

An investigation of consumer shopping patterns, including the factors of trip distance, frequency, age of the traveller, number of accompanying children under 10 years, and number of stores visited in one outing. Period: 1972 - 1973.

2107. "Plaque unveiled at Ontario's last covered bridge, Woolwich Township landmark." **Waterloo Historical Society.** 1961. 49: 8. Loc: all.

A copy of the information given on the 1960 plaque commemorating the covered bridge of West Montrose. A list of dignitaries at the unveiling ceremony is included. Period: 1881 - 1960.

2108. "Postal changes in 1971." **Waterloo Historical Society.** 1971. 59: 92. Loc: all.

Note of postal changes resulting from the 1971 consolidation of Kitchener, Waterloo, and Bridgeport mail services in Kitchener. Bridgeport residents received door-to-door mail delivery, and the postmark "Waterloo" was replaced by "Kitchener-Waterloo." Period: 1971 -

2109. "Postmasters of Waterloo County." **Waterloo Historical Society.** 1940. 28: 122-125. Loc: all.

A list of names and dates of appointment of postmasters of various offices in Waterloo County, including Berlin, Waterloo, Breslau, St Jacobs, Elmira, Preston, Hespeler, Galt, Ayr, Baden, Wellesley and Bridgeport. Period: 1831 - 1940.

2110. "Preparation for Highway 401 [WRP]." **Waterloo Historical Society.** 1959. 47: 50. Loc: all.

A note about bridge construction and the widening of Highway 97, in preparation for the opening of Highway 401. Period: 1959.

2111. Preston, Richard E. "Audit Bureau of Circulation's daily newspaper records as a source in studies of post-1915 settlement patterns in the United States and Canada." **Historical Geography Newsletter.** 1977. 7,1-2: 1-12. tables, maps. Loc: OWTU.

A study using data from Kitchener, Guelph and Toronto as examples. Maps of newspaper circulations from 1930, 1950 and 1971 show the increase in Kitchener's area of dominance. Period: 1915 - 1977.

2112. Read, Voorhees and Associates. **Kitchener Waterloo urban traffic study.** 1967. 105 p. ill., maps. Loc: OWTL, OWTU.

A transportation plan which addresses changing travel patterns and the need for better traffic management. The study includes plans for the completion of the Conestoga Parkway as well as the expansion of arterial and collector streets. Other traffic solutions are recommended for Erb Street, Bridgeport Road, Union Street, Allan Street, Westmount Road, Hallman Road and University Avenue. Future land use, development and regional trends, and population and employment forecasts in the two cities are dealt with in this report. Period: 1965 - 1987.

2113. Reed, Harry R., Jr. **The journey-to-work for manufacturing workers: a case study in Kitchener, Ontario.** University of Waterloo (M.A. thesis, Geography), 1969. 2 fiche. maps, tables, bibl. mf. Loc: OWTU.

An analysis of the factors associated with home-work commuting by wage-earning labourers. Environmental factors, workplace, and personal characteristics such as age and family status were examined and compared with similar studies. Three company locations were considered -- the B.F. Goodrich Company and two of the General Springs Products plants. Period: 1961 - 1969.

2114. "A Road and Bridge Committee report, 1861, Township of Waterloo." **Waterloo Historical Society.** 1957. 45: 35. Loc: all.

Transcript of a letter written in 1861 by Wendell Bowman and S.D. Martin of the Road and Bridge Committee, reporting that the bridge erected by J.W. Martin over the Speed River had passed inspection and making other recommendations concerning Hespeler roads. Period: 1861.

2115. Roth, George and Clack, William. **Canadian Pacific's electric lines: Grand River Railway and the Lake Erie & Northern Railway.** Calgary: British Railway Modellers of North America, 1987. 32 p. ill., maps, tables. Loc: OCCA, OKIT.

A photographic history of the Grand River Railway and the Lake Erie and Northern Railway, with detailed notes on each photograph. Tables of the locomotives and passenger car roster of the electric lines from 1894 to 1961 and a list of Canadian Pacific locomotives assigned to the electric lines are provided. Maps show the railway routes. Period: 1894 - 1983.

2116. Ruppel, Harold. **A history of the post office: Elmira, Ontario**. Elmira?: The Author, 1977?. 12 p. ill. Loc: OWRE.

A history of the staff and post office buildings from 1849 to 1977, with portraits of most postmasters. One postmaster, O.W. (Mike) Weichel, was later a Member of Parliament. Period: 1849 - 1977.

2117. Schmalz, W.H.E. "Addendum to postal history of Waterloo County." **Waterloo Historical Society**. 1969. 57: 82. Loc: all.

Corrections and additions to W.H.E. Schmalz's article in Waterloo Historical Society volume 56, pages 53 to 71. Information is added about German Mills and Mannheim. Period: 1863 - 1969.

2118. Schmalz, W.H.E. "Postal cancellations of Waterloo County." **Waterloo Historical Society**. 1962. 50: 33-35. ill. Loc: all.

Illustrated descriptions of 15 cancellation marks from the period between 1847 and 1903, including pen, squared circle and railway cancellations. Period: 1847 - 1903.

2119. Schmalz, W.H.E. **Postal history of Waterloo County**. 1968. 49 l. ill., maps. Loc: OKITW, OWTU.

A detailed record of the development of the postal service, with dates of establishment of all post offices, earlier place names, and names of postmasters. Several postal cancellations are illustrated, and maps showing post office locations and the railway network are included. This work was also published in the Waterloo Historical Society's annual report for 1968. Period: 1826 - 1949.

2120. Schmalz, W.H.E. "Postal history of Waterloo County." **Waterloo Historical Society**. 1968. 56: 53-71. ill., maps. Loc: all.

An outline of the development of communications, including details of dates of establishment of all post offices, earlier place names and names of postmasters. A table summarizes the establishment of all post offices in chronological order, showing that the first in the region was Galt in 1826, followed by Waterloo in 1831, Preston and Wilmot in 1837, Ayr in 1840 and Berlin in 1842. Several postal cancellations are illustrated, and there are maps of all post office locations and of the railway network. Period: 1826 - 1949.

2121. Schmalz, W.H.E. and Hulet, Marion and Pollard, E. "Preston Post Office." **Waterloo Historical Society**. 1968. 56: 74-77. ill. Loc: all.

A history of Preston's post offices and postmasters, including an interview with Charles Nispel, postmaster from 1883 to 1940. There are photographs of Preston's first post office at King and Lowther Streets and the post office at King and Church Streets (demolished in 1960). Period: 1837 - 1960.

2122. Schmidt, John T. and Taylor, Andrew W. "The electric railways of Waterloo County." **Waterloo Historical Society**. 1956. 44: 23-36. ill., map. Loc: all.

An historical account of the development of the Galt and Preston Street Railway Company (1894-1955), taken over by the Berlin, Waterloo, Wellesley and Lake Huron Railway Company in 1903 and leased to the Canadian Pacific Railway for 99 years from 1908. The line, linking Berlin and Waterloo with Port Dover on Lake Erie via Galt, Paris and Brantford, was renamed the Grand River Railway in 1914. The last passenger train ran in 1955. Period: 1895 - 1955.

2123. Schmidt, William A. "Heidelberg Station." **Waterloo Historical Society**. 1989. 77: 100-102. ill. Loc: all.

A short history of what was possibly the smallest railway depot in Canada, Heidelberg Station, built by the Grand Trunk Railway in 1891 and removed in 1949. Information about a train wreck in 1902 that occurred a mile south of Heidelberg is also given. Period: 1891 - 1949.

2124. Scott, Stephen. **Plain buggies: Amish, Mennonite, and Brethren horse-drawn transportation**. Lancaster, PA: Good Books, 1981. 96 p. ill., index. Loc: OKIT, OWRE.

A general account of reasons for the use of horse-drawn vehicles, their manufacture and the main styles. Waterloo County is mentioned several times. Period: 1840 - 1981.

2125. Shaman, Tony. "Bridgeport Post Office closes." **Waterloo Historical Society**. 1988. 76: 148-151. ill. Loc: all.

A note of the closing of the office in 1988, with reminiscences of its 136-year history. Period: 1864 - 1988.

2126. Shaw, J. Horace. "Postal delivery comes to Hespeler." **Waterloo Historical Society**. 1971. 59: 60. Loc: all.

A note of ceremonies marking the commencement of mail delivery in 1971. The first post office was opened in New Hope in 1851 with Conrad Nahrgang as postmaster. Period: 1851 - 1971.

2127. Smith, Robert C. **Ontario post offices**. Toronto: Unitrade Press, 1988. 2 v. Loc: OKIT.

A directory of past and present post offices in Ontario. Volume I lists all post offices with the names, the dates opened and closed, counties and townships, and alternate names if applicable. The second volume gives the same information, but the offices are listed by county and district: Waterloo County post offices are listed on pages 211-214 in volume II. A map shows the location of Ontario counties and there is a photograph of the Galt Post Office. Period: 1826 - 1988.

2128. Stauffer, Joseph S. "Waterloo County's first railways." **Waterloo Historical Society**. 1961. 49: 54-58. Loc: all.

An account, based on engineers' reports, minutes and company statements, of the Galt Branch of the Great Western Railway (1854), the Galt and Guelph Railway (1857) and the Grand Trunk Railway (1856). The author refers also to railway schemes that were never built. Period: 1850 - 1860.

2129. Stitt, Herbert. **I remember**. Kitchener: McBain, 1983. 102 p. ill. Loc: OKIT.

Autobiography of an Ontario CPR locomotive engineer whose working life extended from 1915 to 1962. Between 1921 and 1923, Stitt was a fireman on the Listowel-Linwood branch line when this line was still busy with passenger and freight traffic. Motor transport gradually eroded the railway traffic and the line, with its intermediate stations at Tralee and Dorking, was closed in 1959. Period: 1921 - 1959.

2130. Taylor, Andrew W. "Pioneer roads in the neighbourhood of Galt." **Waterloo Historical Society**. 1954. 42: 49-56. ill., maps. Loc: all.

An explanation of the road pattern as a composite of Indian and pioneer trails and the systematic grid laid down by William Dickson's survey. Period: 1800 - 1954.

2131. Taylor, Andrew W. "The Union Gas Company pipe line." **Waterloo Historical Society**. 1957. 45: 48-50. ill. Loc: all.

A description of the methods and the machines used in laying the Union Gas line in North Dumfries. Period: 1956 - 1957.

2132. Trout, J.M. and Trout, Edward. **The railways of Canada for 1870-1871, showing the progress, mileage, cost of construction, the stocks, bonds, traffic, earnings, expenses, and organization of the railways of the Dominion**. Toronto: Monetary Times, 1871 reprinted 1970. 213 p. Loc: OCLG, OKIT, OWTL, OWTU.

Accounts of all contemporary railways, including the three built and operating in Waterloo County by 1870: the Galt and Guelph Railway, Grand Trunk Railway and Great Western Railway. Period: 1852 - 1871.

2133. "W-W airport bucks London." **Financial Post**. 1962. 56: 12. mf. Loc: OWTL, OWTU.

Reference from the Canadian Periodical Index. Period: 1962.

2134. Walker, F.N. **Daylight through the mountain: letters and labours of civil engineers Walter and Francis Shanly**. Montreal: Engineering Institute of Canada, 1957. Pp. 253-255. Loc: OWTU.

Letters from Walter Shanly to his brother, discussing progress and problems in the construction of major railway lines. The letter dated 19 August 1852 describes the surveying of the Toronto to Sarnia section of the Grand Trunk Railway through Waterloo County. Period: 1851 - 1871.

2135. Weber, Eldon D. "The Huron Road of the Canada Company." **Waterloo Historical Society**. 1977. 65: 55-59. ill. Loc: all.

A brief account of the development of the road between 1826 and 1836, with a list of the owners of land crossed by the road, including Philip Bleam, Daniel Stauffer, Samuel Liebschuetz, Abraham Cressman and Abraham Biehn. Period: 1827 - 1836.

2136. "Wellesley phone system taken over by Bell." **Waterloo Historical Society**. 1963. 51: 88. Loc: all.

A report of the takeover by Bell of the Wellesley telephone system, consisting of the three exchanges of Linwood, Wellesley and St Clements. A brief history of the system is given. Period: 1963.

2137. Willmot, Elizabeth A. **Meet me at the station**. Kitchener: McBain, 1976 reprinted 1984. 122 p. ill. Loc: OCLG, OCP, OKIT, OWTL, OWTUM.

A social history of the railway station in Ontario, including illustrations of the Kitchener Grand Trunk/CNR station of 1897 (pp. 38-9) and the Galt CNR station originally built for the Great Western line (pp. 80-1), among some 50 others. Readers should note that some of the accompanying information is misleading, especially about the line that ran from Galt to Elmira. Period: 1854 - 1897.

2138. Willmot, Elizabeth A. "Petersburg Railway Station." **Waterloo Historical Society**. 1973. 61: 4-8. ill. Loc: all.

A short history of the station built by the Grand Trunk Railway in 1856. After its closing by Canadian National, the building was moved to Doon Pioneer Village in 1968. The author mentions the Ingles as station agents for 25 years. Period:

1856 - 1973.

2139. Woods, W. George. **Hooves and wheels.** 1980. 27 p. ill. Loc: OKITW.

Reminiscences of the founding and growth of Woods Transport (Hespeler) Ltd from 1922 to 1965, by one of its owners. An account is given of the cartage firm's adaptation to the changes in transportation technology, labour force, legislation and markets. Period: 1922 - 1965.

2140. "Woolwich and Preston mail." **Waterloo Historical Society.** 1961. 49: 47. Loc: all.

Copy of a notice by Thomas Smith in the **Deutsche Canadier** of 1848, explaining the times and cost of carrying letters from Woolwich to Preston. Period: 1848.

2141. "Woolwich mail carrier." **Waterloo Historical Society.** 1968. 56: 50. ill. Loc: all.

An article about Amos B. Bowman who delivered Woolwich Township mail for 27 years in a horse-drawn carriage. Period: 1941 - 1968.

2142. "Woolwich postman uses horse and buggy." **Waterloo Historical Society.** 1961. 49: 46. Loc: all.

A note of Amos Bowman's mail service to 60 Woolwich Township farms, by horse and buggy, since 1942. Period: 1942 - 1961.

TRADE AND COMMERCE

2143. "50th anniversary of Meikleham's Pharmacy." **Waterloo Historical Society.** 1962. 50: 80. Loc: all.

A note about Robert W. Meikleham's pharmacy in Galt which was owned by Alex Edwards before 1912 and known as the White Drug Store. Period: 1912 - 1962.

2144. "The American Hotel." **Waterloo Historical Society.** 1963. 51: 82. ill. Loc: all.

A brief article about the American Hotel, Kitchener, which in 1963 celebrated its 100th anniversary. The various owners are listed, and an 1863 photograph is included. Period: 1863 - 1963.

2145. "Baden Hotel has 100th anniversary." **Waterloo Historical Society.** 1974. 62: 33. Loc: all.

A short note on the hotel's owners to 1974: Christopher Kraus, Werner Bauer, William Witt, Henry Stiefelmeyer, John Stiefelmeyer, George Zimmerman, James Craven, Wes Dunn, Earl Baechler, Walter Bibby, and Edward Bodnerchuk. Period: 1874 - 1974.

2146. Badiuk, Eileen G. **Grocery retailing in Kitchener-Waterloo, 1951 to 1984.** University of Waterloo (M.A. thesis, Geography), 1985. 2 fiche. tables, bibl. mf. Loc: OWTU.

A study of structural and organizational adjustments in the retail food industry, based on analysis of store type and form of business ownership. Using NcNee's models, the author considers the region's distinctive retailing characteristics, particularly the German ethnic market. Period: 1951 - 1984.

2147. Blayney, Fred. "Early pharmacy in Canada." **Waterloo Historical Society.** 1967. 55: 30-33. ill. Loc: all.

An article including a description and illustration of apothecary jars from the A.B. Learn pharmacy of Waterloo, also known as the Zoellner or Devitt store. Period: 1880 - 1886.

2148. Bolender, Margaret. "Clerking at Ruggle's General Store." **Waterloo Historical Society.** 1987. 75: 30-34. ill. Loc: all.

Florence Ziegler's account of working at the general store in Floradale from 1927 to 1942. Period: 1927 - 1942.

2149. Bolender, Margaret. "Five generations at Floradale store." **Waterloo Historical Society.** 1987. 75: 24-30. ill. Loc: all.

A history of the family that ran the Ruggle's general store, beginning with Johann Anton and Louisa Ruggle in 1883. The author notes ways in which the business adapted to the changing needs of the community. Period: 1883 - 1984.

2150. Brewster, Winfield. **La rue de commerce: The street of business, Queen Street, Hespeler, Ontario.** Hespeler: T and T Press, 1954. 94 p. ill., map. Also mf. Loc: OCCA, OCLG, OKIT, OWTU.

An account of early Hespeler, emphasizing various businesses and their owners. Industries and occupations include saw mills, blacksmiths, carpenters, masons, painters, shoemakers, saddlers, doctors, dentists, druggists, handloom weavers, tailors, tinsmiths, coopers, watch makers, barbers, tavern owners, liverymen, artists, peddlers, bakers and butchers. The author describes all Queen Street buildings in detail and presents information about prehistory and early settlers such as Michael Bergey and Joseph Oberholtzer. An index is available at the City of Cambridge Archives and the Cambridge Library and Gallery. Period: 1820 - 1937.

2151. Brown-Kubisch, Linda. "Early photographers in Waterloo County." **Waterloo Historical Society.** 1991. 79: 4-19. ill. Loc: all.

A brief survey of photographic techniques in the nineteenth century, followed by accounts of the businesses of Louis Dessauer, George and James Esson (predecessors of the Law Studio in Cambridge), Charles Schneuker, Henry Albert Huber, George Seiler, Levi Yost, Noah G. Cress and John Lautenschlager. Women photographers are mentioned and there is a list of about 150 photographers who worked in Waterloo County at some time between 1845 and 1920. Period: 1845 - 1920.

2152. "Century-old nail display." **Waterloo Historical Society**. 1966. 54: 19. ill. Loc: all.

A photograph of Earl Coleman in 1966 holding a display of 55 nails. Mr Coleman began his hardware business in New Dundee in 1912. Period: 1912 - 1966.

2153. Clare, John. "Taking the waters." **Waterloo Historical Society**. 1988. 76: 125-134. ill., bibl. Loc: all.

A history of the Preston Springs Garden, including information about the inn's various owners and extensive renovations. Period: 1871 - 1978.

2154. "Conestogo store burns." **Waterloo Historical Society**. 1972. 60: 90. Loc: all.

A note of the fire on 21 May 1972 which badly damaged the general store operated by Oscar and Herbert Huehn. The brothers had run the 119 year old building for 51 years. Period: 1853 - 1972.

2155. Connor, James Thomas Hamilton. "Preservatives of health: mineral water spas of nineteenth century Ontario." **Ontario History**. 1983. 75,2: 135-152. ill., bibl. Loc: OKIT, OWTL, OWTU.

A general account that refers to Preston's mineral springs and associated hotels (the Kress Hotel, Swimming and Mineral Bath House and Del Monte Hotel) in a footnote. The author notes that the formal organization of the Preston spa began just as the popularity of such resorts was waning. Period: 1849 - 1983.

2156. Cowan, Jennie F. "Ice harvest on the Mill Creek in North Dumfries." **Waterloo Historical Society**. 1970. 58: 68-69. Loc: all.

A description of the practice of cutting ice from local creeks and ponds for sale, based on the author's memories of her father's business. The ice was used for cooling purposes in nearby towns before the days of electric refrigeration. Period: 1899 - 1947.

2157. Cressman, Ella M. "Kitchener Market." **Waterloo Historical Society**. 1973. 61: 64-66. ill. Loc: all.

A short history of the market that began in 1869. The author recounts the various locations of the market as well as the types of goods sold. Period: 1869 - 1973.

2158. Darrell, Jennifer. **The effects of the two universities in Waterloo, Waterloo Lutheran University and the University of Waterloo, on retail trade in the city of Waterloo.** Waterloo Lutheran University (B.A. Thesis, Geography), 1966. 92 l. maps, tables, bibl. Loc: OWTL.

A study including a history of retailing in the city and the impact of the two local universities. Questionnaire responses from both retailers and students reveal current patterns of expenditure. Period: 1931 - 1966.

2159. Dooley, J.P. "60 + 60 = 120." **C.N. believe newsletter**. Kitchener: C.N. Weber Ltd, 1983. 3,1-4. Loc: OKIT.

A special edition containing a short history of the business founded and operated by John Fennell until 1923 when Carl N. Weber took over. The newsletter contains photographs of buildings, owners and employees. Period: 1863 - 1983.

2160. "Elmira's maple syrup festival." **Waterloo Historical Society**. 1966. 54: 68. Loc: all.

A short note about the second annual maple syrup festival which included a trip to the sugar bush and craft and bake sales. Period: 1965 - 1966.

2161. English, Bill. "Kitchener Waterloo depression scrip." **Canadian Numismatic Journal**. 1986. 31,1: 9-11. Loc: OLU, OOU.

Reference from **Bibliography of Ontario history, 1976-1986** (Gervais et al.). Period: 1930 - 1935.

2162. Guillet, Edwin C. **Pioneer inns and taverns**. Toronto: Ontario Publishing, 1958?. 2 v. ill. Loc: OCLG, OKIT, OWTL, OWTUR.

The second volume includes illustrations of several Waterloo County hotels, including those in Berlin, Bloomingdale, Maryhill, Petersburg, Preston, Wellesley, St Clements and Heidelberg, as well as the Shoemaker House in Bridgeport, the Queen's Hotel in Wellesley and the Bowman House in Blair. There are lists of Waterloo County hotels in 1851 on page 73, Berlin hotels in 1857-58 on pages 73-4, and Galt hotels and owners in the late 1850s on page 68. Period: 1835 - 1900.

2163. Guttmann, Renee. **The history of the Walper Hotel**. Wilfrid Laurier University (student essay, Archaeology), 1979. 10 l. ill., bibl. Loc: OKIT.

A survey of the property at the intersection of King and Queen Streets in Berlin/Kitchener and the various taverns and inns that occupied the site from the 1820s to the 1890s. Building owners during this period, including Phineas Varnum, the Gaukel family, James Potter, Jacob S. Weaver, John Roat and the Walpers are described with short architectural histories. Period: 1820 - 1892.

2164. Hayes, Judith M.C. **The evolution of the Farmers Market in Kitchener, Ontario: a study examining its development and change.** University of Waterloo (B.E.S. thesis, Geography), 1976. 3 fiche. mf. Loc: OWTUM, OKIT.

A history of the market, including the first built in 1868 by Jacob Y. Shantz, the second built on the same site in 1907, and the referendum in 1971 that determined that the site should be sold to Oxlea Investments for a third new market. Changes in vendors, patrons, and produce are traced and the early problems of the 1974 market are reviewed. Period: 1800 - 1976.

2165. Henderson, Barbara. **Culture as a tourist attraction: the Old Order Amish of Lancaster County, Pennsylvania and the Old Order Mennonites of Waterloo Region, Ontario.** University of Waterloo (B.E.S. thesis, Geography), 1988. 1 fiche. mf. Loc: OWTUM.

A study using the theoretical framework of MacCannell's concept of back and front regions and Butler's concept of a tourist area cycle of evolution. The author concludes that compared to Lancaster County, Waterloo Region's tourism is less substantial, less commercial, and not dominated by the Old Order Mennonite image. Period: 1950 - 1988.

2166. Hergott, Patricia. **Scrapbook of Patricia Hergott: employee of Waterloo Music from 1931 to 1981.** 1 v. (unpaged). ill. Loc: OKIT.

A photocopied collection of photographs, newspaper clippings and correspondence relating to the company, which was started by bandmaster C.F. Thiele after the First World War. Period: 1931 - 1981.

2167. Hewson, Karen and Veevers, Terry. **The rural blacksmith in Waterloo County.** Kitchener: Doon Heritage Crossroads, Heritage Resources Department, Regional Municipality of Waterloo, 1991. 176 p. ill., bibl. Loc: OKDHC.

A report written for interpreters at Doon Heritage Crossroads, relating the development of the trade, tools and smithy. Waterloo County blacksmiths are described generally and individually. There are extracts from the daybooks of John McKay of Linwood and Peter

Kolbrenner of Petersburg, with a list of tools and the cost of setting up a business in 1914. The account is based on assessment rolls, directories, photographs and interviews with older blacksmiths and their apprentices. Period: 1900 - 1914.

2168. Hilborn, Miriam. "The E.T. Coleman Hardware Store in New Dundee." **Waterloo Historical Society.** 1962. 50: 79. Loc: all.

A brief history of the oldest building in New Dundee, the E.T. Coleman Hardware Store, built in 1848. Period: 1848 - 1962.

2169. Hilmo, Wayne Dennis. **Food retailing and consumer behaviour in Waterloo, Ontario.** Waterloo Lutheran University (M.A. thesis, Geography), 1971. 88 l. ill., bibl. Loc: OWTL.

A study which develops a model to predict which stores consumers will choose for their major grocery purchases. Surveying stores in Waterloo and Kitchener, the author identifies travel distance, price, and attractiveness of the store as key variables. Period: 1970 - 1971.

2170. Hore, Philip. **An analysis of the 1967 Kitchener Mall.** University of Waterloo (B.A. thesis, Geography), 1968. 3 fiche. ill., tables, bibl. mf. Loc: OWTUM.

An evaluation of the experimental pedestrian zone project, tested for one week in the summer of 1966 and throughout the summer of 1967. The author describes the central business district before the mall, noting blight and lack of vegetation and amenity, and reports reactions by the Kitchener planning department, area merchants, local politicians and mall users. Period: 1966 - 1968.

2171. Horst, Mary Ann and Hertel, James. **Our wonderful Kitchener Farmers' Market.** Kitchener: Pennsylvania Dutch Craft Shop, 1985. 170 p. ill. Loc: OCH, OCLG, OCP, OKIT, OWRW.

A richly illustrated account including a survey of the market's development from the 1830s to the structure built by J.Y. Shantz in 1869 and subsequent buildings. Photographs of vendors and their wares are combined with short reminiscences by both vendors and visitors. A list of current vendors is included, with details of the year each began selling. Period: c1830 - 1985.

2172. "Inspection of 24 Waterloo Township hotels [WRP]." **Waterloo Historical Society.** 1960. 48: 4. Loc: all.

A brief note of the 1858 by-law passed by the Waterloo Township Council to regulate inns. Period: 1858 - 1859.

2173. "Kitchener and Waterloo market at a glance."
Financial Post. 1965. 59: 61. table. mf. Loc:
OWTL, OWTU.
Reference from the Canadian Periodical Index.
Period: 1965.

2174. Kitchener Chamber of Commerce. **Kitchener's
accommodations directory, 1971.** Kitchener: The
Chamber, 1971. 12 p. Loc: OKIT.
A directory of hotels, inns and campsites in the
area, describing their facilities and location.
Period: 1970 - 1971.

2175. "Kitchener hopes for $1 million convention hotel."
Financial Post. 1961. 55: 18. mf. Loc: OWTL,
OWTU.
Reference from the Canadian Periodical Index.
Period: 1961.

2176. "Kitchener-Tyson's Ice Cream Parlour." **Waterloo
Historical Society**. 1960. 48: 69. Loc: all.
After 55 years, Tyson's Ice Cream Parlour in
Kitchener closed. The land was originally bought
by Abram Tyson, Olive Tyson's great-great
grandfather. Period: 1865 - 1960.

2177. Koebel, Michael. **98 damn near 100: a history of
the Walper Tobacco Shop.** 1989. 7 p. Loc: OKIT.
A fictional history of the Walper Tobacco Shop,
written from the building's point of view by its
current owner. Period: 1891 - 1989.

2178. Koshan, Ernest. **Locational analysis of
supermarkets in Kitchener-Waterloo, Ontario.**
Waterloo Lutheran University (B.A. thesis,
Geography), 1966. 102 l. ill. Loc: OWTL.
Period: 1964 - 1966.

2179. Lamb, Kathryn Hansuld. "Bridgeport's Lancaster
Hotel and its owners 1853-1989." **Waterloo
Historical Society**. 1989. 77: 120-141. ill. Loc:
all.
A history of the hotel, meticulously chronicling
successive owners from 1853 to 1989 and quoting
from the ledger of John Grasser, proprietor from
1896 to 1909. Period: 1853 - 1989.

2180. Lang, E. Elizabeth Koch. "The Herman Kavelman
Store, New Dundee, Ontario." **Waterloo Historical
Society**. 1962. 50: 81-84. ill. Loc: all.
A history and description of the Jubilee Block
built in 1887 by Gottlieb Bettschen. In 1962 it
was owned by Herman Kavelman and used as a
general store. Period: 1887 - 1962.

2181. Macnaughton, Elizabeth. **Preliminary report on the
General Store re-restoration, Doon Pioneer
Village.** Kitchener: Doon Heritage Crossroads,

Historic Sites Department, Regional Municipality
of Waterloo, 1984. 104 p. ill., tables, bibl. Loc:
OCLG, OKIT, OWT.
Written as a guide for planners at the Doon
Pioneer Village (later renamed Doon Heritage
Crossroads), the work summarizes economic and
social conditions in 1914 and outlines the
functions of general stores. More specific topics
are architectural design options for the store on
the museum site, store artifacts, accounts,
facilities and services, packaging and
advertising, and store restoration projects of
other museums. Period: 1900 - 1914.

2182. McCalla, Douglas. **The Upper Canada trade,
1834-1872: a study of the Buchanans' trade.**
Toronto: University of Toronto Press, 1979. 231 p.
maps, bibl. Loc: OKIT, OWTL, OWTU.
An analysis of the Hamilton-based business of
Peter and Isaac Buchanan, importers and wholesale
distributors of British dry goods in Upper Canada.
Maps on pages 111 and 120 identify localities in
which storekeepers had accounts with Buchanans,
including Ayr, Roseville, New Dundee, Haysville,
Baden, New Hamburg, Philipsburg, Wellesley, St
Clements, St Jacobs, Conestoga, Waterloo,
Bridgeport, Berlin, Preston and Galt. Period: 1834
- 1872.

2183. Mills, Graham W. and Hoffman, Randall J. **Consumer
survey on shopping area attitudes.** Waterloo
Lutheran University, 1972. 47 p. tables, map. Loc:
OWTU.
A survey conducted for the Retail Committee of
the Kitchener Chamber of Commerce to determine
locational shopping patterns in the
Kitchener-Waterloo area and identify any
shortcomings in the facilities. Information on
access, availability of products and convenience
was gathered for seven shopping areas and malls.
The authors note that parking is the largest
overall drawback to shopping in the downtown area.
Period: 1971 - 1972.

2184. Mills, Ruth. **Effects of changing medical
knowledge on health resort development: examining
three case studies in Cambridge (Preston).**
University of Waterloo (M.A. thesis, History),
1981. 2 fiche. ill., bibl. mf. Loc: OWTU.
A study of the transformation of Preston spas
from healing to recreation centres, as
contemporary medical practices changed. The
author presents an historical analysis of the
establishment, growth and eventual decline of the
three local spas based on mineral springs, the
Kress Hotel, the Sulphur Springs Hotel and the
Preston Springs Hotel. Period: 1849 - 1981.

2185. Murdie, Robert A. "Cultural differences in consumer travel." **Economic Geography**. 1965. 41,3: 211-233. maps, tables, graphs. Loc: OWTL, OWTU.

A study of changing shopping practices, comparing Old Order Mennonites and ordinary farmers in Waterloo and Wellington Counties. The author reports similarities in travel for modern needs such as appliances, medical, dental and banking services but large differences for traditional goods and services such as food, clothing and shoes. The study concludes that for traditional requirements, Old Order Mennonites treat all centres equally, while modern Canadians use the central place hierarchy. Period: 1964 - 1965.

2186. Pepper, Paul E. **Index to La rue de commerce: the street of business, Queen Street, Hespeler, Ontario, by Winfield Brewster**. 1986. 19 p. Loc: OKIT.

A list of over 800 personal names and a few corporate subjects.

2187. "Philipsburg store demolished." **Waterloo Historical Society**. 1965. 53: 78. ill. Loc: all.

A short history of the store, erected in 1843 and demolished in 1965. Successive storekeepers are identified as Christopher Doering, Daniel Lohr, Edwin D. Eidt and Wilfred Kropf and the building's functions as post office, tannery and general store are noted. Period: 1843 - 1965.

2188. Phillips, Glen C. **The Ontario photographers list, 1851-1900**. Sarnia: Iron Gate Publishing, 1990. 126 p. indexes. Loc: OKIT, OWTUR.

A comprehensive inventory and classification with codes indicating the kind of photography such as daguerreotypes or ambrotypes. Photographers are noted in the following Waterloo County towns and villages: Ayr, Berlin, Crosshill, Elmira, Galt, Hawksville, Haysville, Hespeler, New Hamburg, Preston, St Jacobs, Waterloo and Wellesley. Of the 2,976 indexed photographers, 97 can be identified as female. The photographers are grouped according to location, and there are name and community indexes. Period: 1851 - 1900.

2189. "Play-it-yourself trend results in "high C" business for music company." **Financial Post**. 1965. 59: 89. mf. Loc: OWTL, OWTU.

Reference from the Canadian Periodical Index. Period: 1965.

2190. Priamo, Carol. **The general store**. Toronto: McGraw-Hill Ryerson, 1978. 104 p. ill. Loc: OCLG, OKIT, OWTL, OWTU.

A photographic essay about surviving general stores in Ontario, including views of the general store at Doon Pioneer Village (moved from Delaware, Middlesex County), Brubacher's store at Elmira, and a store in Baden. Period: 1840 - 1900.

2191. Rawls, Hazel. **The Kitchener Market**. University of Waterloo (student essay), 1965. 93 p. ill., bibl., tables, maps. Loc: OKIT, OWTU.

A study of the Kitchener Farmers' Market, with a brief early history, a description of the financial and social aspects in 1965, details of the vendors and their produce, and predictions of the market's future. Graphs and maps show the origins of the produce and a chart summarizes the vendors' reasons for selling at the market. The most popular items are noted and the products are listed alphabetically. 1965.

2192. Riddell, John Barry. **Waterloo County; retail trade in the study of central places**. University of Toronto (B.A. thesis, Geography), 1963. 1 reel. ill., maps, bibl. mf. Loc: OWTU.

A study of the effect of the various urban centres of Waterloo County on the retail trade. The author concludes that the county is divided into two economic units, the northern third dominated by smaller centres and the Mennonite influence, and the southern remainder dominated by Kitchener-Waterloo, the county's major retail centre. Period: 1962 - 1963.

2193. "Ritz Pharmacy." **Waterloo Historical Society**. 1968. 56: 32. ill. Loc: all.

A note of the closing of the Ritz Pharmacy, opened in 1905 by E.O. Ritz at King and Queen Streets in Berlin. Period: 1905 - 1968.

2194. "Sehl Hardware Store, Baden." **Waterloo Historical Society**. 1969. 57: 29. Loc: all.

A note of Frederick Sehl's 60th year in the Baden hardware business established in 1883 by his father. Period: 1883 - 1969.

2195. Seiling, Ken and Stauch, Warren. "The Brubacher grocery store in Elmira." **Waterloo Historical Society**. 1973. 61: 20-23. ill. Loc: all.

A short history of the family business that began in 1891, including notes of changes in the types of items sold. Period: 1891 - 1973.

2196. "Shoemaker's Drug Store closes." **Waterloo Historical Society**. 1964. 52: 88. Loc: all.

A note of the company's closing after 51 years in operation. The six remaining downtown Kitchener retail outlets which began before the First World War are identified as William Knell and Co., Schmidt, Dickey and Co., Ritz Pharmacy, Goudie's Ltd, J.C. Jaimet and Co., Herman Lippert

Men's Wear, and Solomon Sauder Men's Wear. Period: 1906 - 1964.

2197. Smith, M. Ian. **A predictive model of the distribution of automatic carwash customers in Kitchener-Waterloo.** Waterloo Lutheran University (B.A. thesis, Geography), 1971. 33 p. maps, tables, bibl. Loc: OWTL.

A locational analysis of factors influencing order in an urban situation, based on customer distribution patterns of one carwash in Kitchener and another in Waterloo. The results show that residential density is by far the most important single factor. Period: 1970 - 1971.

2198. Soeder, R.R. and Russwurm, Lorne H. and Russwurm, Lola M. "Changing retail functions in the central business districts of Kitchener and Waterloo." **The Waterloo County area: selected geographical essays.** Edited by A.G. McLellan. Waterloo: Department of Geography, University of Waterloo, 1971. Pp. 129-145. ill., tabl. Loc: OWTU, OWTL, OWTUCG, OKIT.

An analysis of the changing retail trade and service functions of central Kitchener between 1951 and 1969 and of central Waterloo between 1957 and 1969. Relative decline in Kitchener's retail functions and a trend to specialization are reported. Period: 1951 - 1969.

2199. Staebler, Edna. "Market day in Kitchener." **Macleans Magazine.** 1965. 78: 15-17, 38-9. ill. Loc: OKIT, OWTL, OWTU.

Reference from the Canadian Periodical Index. Period: 1965.

2200. "Tait and Kitchen Hardware closes its doors [WRP]." **Waterloo Historical Society.** 1955. 43: 36. Loc: all.

A report of the plan, following Mr Tait's death, to renovate his hardware store in Galt's Buchanan Block to become a branch of the Bank of Nova Scotia. Period: 1894 - 1955.

2201. Toye, Beverley. **The Galt Public Market, its internal and external functions.** Waterloo University College (B.A. thesis, Geography), 1965. 116 l. ill., bibl., graphs. Loc: OCCA, OWTL.

A contemporary examination of the market's produce, vendors and buyers, with a summary of its history and comments on its future. The author concludes that the market is typical of small southwestern Ontario markets, making local fruit, vegetables and meat available to local people. Maps, tables and graphs show results of questionnaires given to vendors and buyers. Period: 1816 - 1965.

2202. "Trail's End Hotel." **Waterloo Historical Society.** 1968. 56: 80-81. ill. Loc: all.

A brief history of the Trail's End Hotel in Conestogo, destroyed by fire in 1968. Period: 1841 - 1968.

2203. Trnavskis, Boris. **Waterloo Square: a study of a community shopping centre.** University of Waterloo (B.A. thesis, Geography), 1967. 2 fiche. tables, bibl., maps. mf. Loc: OWTUM.

A critical evaluation of Waterloo Square six years after it was built, discussing reasons for its financial failure. The factors of accessibility and competition are discussed in detail, and previous assumptions about the Square are compared with the results of a survey of shoppers in 1966. Period: 1960 - 1967.

2204. "Waterloo Market closes." **Waterloo Historical Society.** 1965. 53: 70-73. ill. Loc: all.

A short history from the market's origins in the 1850s to its closing in July 1965 to make way for the Waterloo Public Library. Period: 1850 - 1965.

2205. Zander, Hans. **Markets of Ontario: a living tradition.** Toronto: Prentice-Hall, 1983. 112 p. ill., bibl. Loc: OKIT, OWTL, OWTU.

An artist's depiction of about 20 markets in the province including the Waterloo Farmers' Market, the Kitchener-Waterloo Stockyards and the Elmira Maple Syrup Festival. Brief descriptions of the markets include historical details. Period: c1830 - 1983.

2206. Zundel, Lucy. **The Waterloo County Farmers' Market: a case study.** Wilfrid Laurier University (B.A. thesis, Geography), 1982. 74 p. ill., maps, bibl. Loc: OWTL.

A study of the market which opened in 1973 following in a new building on the former site. Questionnaire responses by both vendors and patrons are used to compile statistical profiles of both groups. There are diagrams showing the layout of the market, a map showing the residences of patrons, and a table comparing the Kitchener and Waterloo markets. The author draws conclusions about the value of the market, the reasons for its success, and its future prospects. Period: 1960 - 1982.

TRADE CATALOGUES

2207. Ames-Holden Tire and Rubber Co. **Ames Holden Rubber Boot Co. Ltd: AHM Systems.** Kitchener: The Company, 1920. 27 p. ill. Loc: OKIT.

An annual report on management, distribution, profits, earnings and directors for 1919-1920.

Period: 1919 - 1920.

2208. Ames-Holden Tire and Rubber Co. **Ames Holden Tire Company Ltd: AHM Systems**. Kitchener: The Company, 1920. 23 p. ill. Loc: OKIT.

An annual report on profits, distribution, bonds, stock bonuses, the plant, expansion and directors. Period: 1919 - 1920.

2209. Anchor Bedding Co. **Anchor Bedding Company, catalog no. 14**. Preston: The Company, 1910?. 62 p. ill. Loc: OCCA.

An illustrated catalogue of iron and brass bedsteads, with price lists for mattresses, springs and pillows in addition to the beds. A drawing of the factory is included. Period: 1900 - 1920.

2210. Arthur Pequegnat Clock Co. **The Arthur Pequegnat Clock Company catalogue no. 6, 1928**. Kitchener: Merchants Printing, 1928. 36 p. ill. Loc: OKIT.

An inventory of the company's wares including hall, office, school, parlor, and factory pendulum clocks. The booklet provides photographs of each clock, a brief description, and its price. Period: 1927 - 1928.

2211. Aultman, Miller and Co. **Directions for setting up and operating the Buckeye frameless, chain-drive Binder**. Akron, OH: The Company, 1891, 1892, 1899. Loc: OKDHC.

Illustrated brochures for a binder manufactured by P.E. Shantz Agricultural Works of Preston. Doon Heritage Crossroads holds those for the years 1891, 1892 and 1899. Period: 1891 - 1899.

2212. **The auto-spray**. Cavers Bros.?, 191-?. 6 p. ill. Loc: OCCA, OKIT.

Advertisement and price list for an automatic sprayer, used primarily for spraying insecticides. It was sold by the Cavers Brothers in Galt. Period: 1890 - 1920.

2213. A.B. Jardine Co. **Catalogue no. 16: A.B. Jardine and Co., Hespeler, Ontario, Canada**. Hespeler: The Company, 1917. 72 p. ill. Loc: OCCA, OKIT.

A catalogue which contains drawings and descriptions of the company's products. Size options and prices for 1917 are also included. Period: 1916 - 1917.

2214. Babcock-Wilcox and Goldie-McCulloch Ltd. **Babcock centrifugal pumps bulletin no. 36-5**. Galt: The Company, 1950?. 6 p. ill. Loc: OCCA.

A brochure with sectional views of ball-bearing and sleeve-bearing pumps and a table of their performance. Period: 1950 - 1960.

2215. Babcock-Wilcox and Goldie-McCulloch Ltd. **Babcock centrifugal pumps bulletin no. 36-4**. Galt: The Company, 1950?. 1 folded sheet. ill. Loc: OCCA.

A leaflet containing specifications and cross section drawings. Period: 1930 - 1955.

2216. Babcock-Wilcox and Goldie-McCulloch Ltd. **Babcock pumps bulletin #61 type PR for every paper mill application**. Galt: The Company, 1960?. 1 folded sheet. ill. Loc: OCCA.

A brochure containing a sectional arrangement, a performance chart and overall dimensions. Period: 1955 - 1965.

2217. Babcock-Wilcox and Goldie-McCulloch Ltd. **Babcock single-stage double-suction centrifugal pumps bulletin no. 52**. Galt: The Company, 1958. 7 p. ill. Loc: OCCA.

A leaflet showing performance, sectional arrangement, dimensions, and installation of the pump, with illustrations of other Babcock products. Period: 1958 - 1959.

2218. Babcock-Wilcox and Goldie-McCulloch Ltd. **Babcock-Wilcox and Goldie-McCulloch Limited**. Galt: The Company, 1962. 1 v. ill. Loc: OCCA.

An advertising brochure describing products and facilities, including photographs of the North and South Works at Galt. Period: 1962 - 1963.

2219. Babcock-Wilcox and Goldie-McCulloch Ltd. **Bulletin no. 43 index to stoker parts styles 21 and 22**. Galt: The Company, 1930?. 20 p. ill. Loc: OCCA.

Illustrations and descriptions of chain grate stoker parts. Drawings of the South and North factories in Galt are included. Period: 1930 - 1940.

2220. Babcock-Wilcox and Goldie-McCulloch Ltd. **Bulletin no. 59 B & W paper stock pump type P**. Galt: The Company, 1963. 1 folded sheet. Loc: OCCA.

A brochure showing performance curves, internal arrangement, construction features, and methods of installation. Period: 1963 - 1964.

2221. Babcock-Wilcox and Goldie-McCulloch Ltd. **Instruction book for installation and operation of the Babcock vertical high speed steam engine**. Galt: The Company, 1945?. 23 p. ill. Loc: OCCA.

A loose-leaf booklet containing cross sectional drawings and parts lists. Period: 1930 - 1950.

2222. Babcock-Wilcox and Goldie-McCulloch Ltd. **Instructions for installing and operating B. & W. centrifugal pumps**. Galt: The Company, 1963. 8 p. ill. Loc: OCCA.

A manual including a maintenance schedule and a trouble-shooting guide. Period: 1963 - 1964.

2223. Babcock-Wilcox and Goldie-McCulloch Ltd. **Operating instructions and list of parts for Babcock steam turbines bulletin no. 38-1.** Galt: The Company, 1940?. 11 p. ill. Loc: OCCA.

A brochure with detailed cross section drawings of the single wheel turbine, also showing other Babcock products manufactured at Galt. Period: 1920 - 1960.

2224. Babcock-Wilcox and Goldie-McCulloch Ltd. **Specification booklet no. 31-C horizontal return tubular power boilers.** Galt: The Company, 1930?. 11 p. ill. Loc: OCCA.

A catalogue with general information, cross section drawings and data sheets. Period: 1920 - 1940.

2225. Bechtels Ltd. **1913 catalogue, Bechtels Limited.** Waterloo: The Company, 1913. 47 p. ill. Loc: OKDHC.

A catalogue of machinery for making bricks and tiles. The stiff plastic process is described, and products such as a back-geared screw roll, hoists, cutters, disintegrators, barrows, dump cars and portable track are shown. Period: 1913 - 1914.

2226. Berlin Felt Boot Co. **Price list, 1910: warm footwear manufactured by Berlin Felt Boot Co. Limited.** Berlin: The Company, 1910. 5 p. Loc: OWTUR.

A pamphlet showing the company's product line and prices for men's, women's and children's footwear. Period: 1909 - 1910.

2227. Berlin Piano and Organ Co. **Illustrated catalogue of the Berlin upright and grand pianoforte and cabinet organs manufactured by Berlin Piano and Organ Co. (Limited.), Berlin, Ontario, Canada.** 189-?. 23 p. ill. Loc: OKITW.

A list of products, with prices and instructions for unpacking and care of the instruments. Period: 1890 - 1899.

2228. Canada Machinery Corporation. **Canada Machinery Corporation, Limited, Galt, Ontario.** The Company, 19--. 2 v. ill. Loc: OKIT.

Illustrated catalogues of machine tools produced by the company, including descriptions and specifications. Period: 1900 - 1950.

2229. Canadian Blower/Canada Pumps Ltd. **Canadian Blower/Canada Pumps Limited: 75 years, 1905-1980.** Kitchener: The Company, 1980. 12 p. ill. Loc: OKIT.

An illustrated commemorative brochure, giving a brief history of the firm is given and information about its products, pumps and fans. Period: 1905 - 1980.

2230. Canadian Buffalo Forge Co. **The Canadian Buffalo Forge Company Ltd Berlin, Ontario: general catalog no. 179.** Buffalo, NY: The Company, 1913. 305 p. ill., index. Loc: OKIT.

A complete inventory and description of the company's forges, blowers, fans, drills, punches, shears, tire setters, woodworking machines, steam engines, and apparatus for heating and ventilating. Size options and prices are included with photographs of all items. Also included is a letter dated 16 March 1914 referring to the company's new factory in Berlin. Period: 1913 - 1914.

2231. Clare Brothers and Co.? **The farmer's jewel furnace for wood only.** Clare Brothers and Co.?, 1902?. 4 p. ill. Loc: OKIT.

Advertisement describing and illustrating a wood furnace manufactured by Clare Brothers, Preston. Period: 1890 - 1920.

2232. Clare Brothers and Co. **Illustrated catalogue of the Preston hot-air furnaces and registers manufactured by Clare Bros. and Co..** Guelph: James Hough, 1892?. 122 p. ill. Loc: OWTUR.

Descriptions, specifications, and drawings of the coal- and wood-burning furnaces and registers. Directions on setting and operating the furnaces are included, with many testimonial letters, and lists of schools, churches and homes heated by Clare furnaces. The back cover has an illustration of the factory. Period: 1890 - 1895.

2233. **Clemmer Industries Limited company profile.** Waterloo: Clemmer Industries, 1964. 5 p. ill. Loc: OWT.

An historical sketch of the company with information about its current products, manufacturing capability and personnel. Detailed technical data and a product warranty are shown. Period: 1963 - 1964.

2234. **Commemorating the fiftieth anniversary of J.M. Schneider Limited, Kitchener, Ontario.** Kitchener: The Company, 1940. 31 p. ill. Loc: OKIT.

A commemorative brochure including photographs and descriptions of all sections of the plant, the employees, the products and advertising. Period: 1890 - 1940.

2235. Cowan and Co. **Cowan Woodworking machinery, catalogue B.** Galt: The Company, 19--. 186 p. ill., index. Loc: OCCA.

A catalogue containing drawings and descriptions of products such as saws, sanders, planers, moulders, mortisers and clamps. Period: 1905 - 1950.

2236. Cowan and Co. **Galt Foundry, Engine and Machine Works: post boring machine.** CIHM Microfiche series, no. 58808. The Company, 18--?. 1 fiche. mf. Loc: OWTU, OWTL.

A one-page illustrated description of a machine for woodworking companies, to be bolted to a post or any upright. Period: 1835 - 1899.

2237. Cowan and Co. **The new improved adjustable joint cutter and planer: most complete mitre machine in use.** CIHM Microfiche series, no. 42759. Galt: 18--?. mf. Loc: OWTL, OWTU.

A catalogue describing the new product of the company also known as the Galt Foundry and Machine Works.

2238. D.M. Ferry and Co. **Universal almanac and catalogue garden and flower seeds.** Detroit: The Company, 1886. 48 p. ill., index. Loc: OKDHC.

A seed catalogue from a Michigan company, distributed by William Spiers of Berlin, dealer in groceries, wines, liquors, boots and shoes. Period: 1885 - 1886.

2239. Dare Foods. **Dare.** Kitchener: The Company, 197-?. 11 p. ill. Loc: OKIT.

A brochure describing the history, processes, packaging and plants of Dare Food's manufacture of cookies and candies. Period: 1892 - 1971.

2240. Dare Foods. **The Dare story.** Kitchener: The Company, 198-?. 6 p. ill. Loc: OKIT.

An illustrated advertising brochure describing the company and its management. The addresses of its regional sales offices and head office in Kitchener are also given. Period: 1892 - 1989.

2241. **Descriptive circular of the Bear patent highway bridge, built by a combination of wood and iron, Doon, Ontario.** CIHM Microfiche series, no. 37336. Berlin: Berlin Publishing Co., 18--?. mf. Loc: OWTL, OWTU.

Members of the Bear family are noted also for the construction of the covered bridge at West Montrose.

2242. Dominion Woollens and Worsteds. **Dominion Woollens and Worsteds Ltd.** 1910? - 1930?. 16 p. ill. Loc: OKIT.

A promotional brochure with photographs of managers and staff, buildings and machinery of branches at Hespeler, Peterborough, Orillia, and Milton. There are colour photographs of the suitings, worsteds and yarns produced. Period: 1910 - 1930.

2243. Firth-Brown Tools (Canada) Ltd. **Mitia cemented carbides.** Galt: The Company, 1957. 27 p. ill. Loc: OCCA.

Catalogue number c-57, describing a variety of cutting tools used for turning, milling, and gear cutting. A photograph of the Galt factory is included on the title page. Period: 1957 - 1958.

2244. **Galt Edge Tool Works and Carriage Spring Works manufacture all variety of carriage springs ... which are patented in the United States and Canada.** CIHM Microfiche series, no. 56983. Galt: Warnock and Co., 1880?. mf. Loc: OWTL, OWTU. Period: 1880 - 1889.

2245. Galt Metal Industries, Ltd. **Remember when.** 1945. 14 p. ill. Loc: OKIT.

Brochure subtitled **The work and accomplishments of the management and the employees of the Galt Metal Industries Limited, during the Second World War.** Products produced at this time for army vehicles, aircraft, and ammunition are illustrated, and the processes of stamping heavy metal sheets, painting and welding are described. Period: 1939 - 1945.

2246. Galt Wood Tool and Machine Co. **Galt woodworking machinery and tools.** The Company, 1963. 251 p. ill, index. Loc: OCCA.

Product catalogue A63, containing illustrations and specifications for knives, saws, sanders, clamps and drills, and other items. Period: 1963 - 1964.

2247. Globe Furniture Co. **Globe Furniture Co. Limited, Waterloo Ontario.** The Company, 1900 - 1950. 6 v. (unpaged). Loc: OWT.

Six bound catalogues of mounted photographs of furniture made by the company, including details of item, name and address of buyer, negative number and order number. A wide variety of products is illustrated, including wood carvings and panelling for churches and institutions. One volume shows special furniture and carvings produced for St Mary's Hospital and Sacred Heart Church in Kitchener, and for St Louis Roman Catholic Church and the Church of the Holy Saviour in Waterloo. Period: 1900 - 1950.

2248. Goldie and McCulloch. **Banker's safes. The Goldie & McCulloch Co., Limited, Galt, Ont..** CIHM Microfiche series, no. 46493. Galt: The Company, 18--?. 1 fiche. mf. Loc: OWTU, OWTL.

Descriptions of safes, vaults, and safety deposit boxes in drawings and text. Other products manufactured by Goldie and McCulloch are listed, such as engines, mill machinery and pulleys, with an illustration of the company's works and general offices. Period: 1860 - 1899.

2249. Goldie and McCulloch. **Ideal, tubular and copper coil heaters illustrated bulletin no. 19.** Hamilton: The Reid Press, 1910?. 1 v. ill. Loc: OCCA.

A catalogue of steam heaters, with illustrations of the North and South works of the company in Galt. Period: 1890 - 1920.

2250. Greenfield Tap and Die Corporation. **Small tools catalog no. 49.** The Corporation, 1925. 383 p. ill., index. Loc: OKIT.

A catalogue that presents a short history of the company with a detailed description of all product lines, including size options and prices. Taps, dies, screw plates, twist drills, reamers, screw-slotting cutters, gages, pipe tools, and bolt-threading machines are listed. Period: 1924 - 1925.

2251. H. Boehmer and Company Ltd. **Boehmers.** Kitchener: The Company, 19--. 8 p. ill., map. Loc: OKIT.

A brief history and description of the company's products and services as a supplier of fuel oil, building materials and concrete. Period: 1828 - 1960.

2252. H. Krug Furniture Co. **Office chairs as manufactured by the H. Krug Furniture Company Limited, 1917, Kitchener, Ontario, Canada.** Kitchener: The Company, 1917. 30 p. ill. Loc: OKDHC.

A photocopy of a catalogue of armchairs, benches, stools, and rotary or swivel chairs. Another photocopied portion held by Doon Heritage Crossroads shows hatracks, plant stands and footstools, with diagrams showing details of the construction of the chairs. Period: 1916 - 1917.

2253. Hi-Speed Tools Ltd. **Hi-Speed modern cutting tools, catalogue no. 8.** Galt: The Company, 1937. 141 p. ill., index, tables. Loc: OCCA.

A product catalogue describing taps, dies, chasers, thread gauges, drills, end mills and reamers. There are tables of cutting speeds, tapers, hardness conversion, and metric equivalents. Period: 1937 - 1938.

2254. **Howard heaters manufactured by T.E. Shantz & Co., Berlin, Ontario.** Berlin: H.S. Hallman, 1900. 12 p. Loc: OWTUR.

A catalogue advertising the furnaces for which the Shantz company had recently obtained the Canadian patent. There are quotations from testimonials by local businessmen and school trustees. Period: 1903 - 1904.

2255. **Illustrated catalogue of the Berlin Novelty Works.** Berlin: The Company, 1886. 52 p. ill. Loc: OKITW.

Text and illustrations showing baby carriages, sleds, rocking chairs and high chairs manufactured by J.S. Anthes. Period: 1885 - 1886.

2256. J.A.M. Taylor Tool Co. **Taylor Tool: metal cutting tools.** Hespeler: The Company, 1969. 44 p. ill. Loc: OCCA.

Catalogue of taps, dies, drills, and reamers with specifications and prices. Period: 1969 - 1970.

2257. J.M. Schneider Ltd. **Prize winning sausage recipes.** Kitchener?: The Company?, 1925?. 12 p. ill. Loc: OWTUR.

An advertisement for the company, containing twelve sausage recipes which won prizes at the National Exhibition at Toronto. Period: 1920 - 1930.

2258. J.M. Schneider Ltd. **Schneider, famous for quality, 1890-1965.** Kitchener: The Company, 1965. 24 p. ill. Loc: OWTUR.

A promotional history of the meat-packing company, with chapters on the founding years, the second generation, products and productivity, the company's growth and success, customer service, and contributions to the community. The booklet includes many photographs of the Schneider family members involved in the firm, as well as of other company employees and the physical operations of the plant. Period: 1890 - 1965.

2259. Jackson, Cochrane and Co. **Wood-working machinery, illustrated and descriptive catalogue.** Berlin: Merchants Printing, 191-?. 124 p. ill., index. Loc: OCCA.

A catalogue with the subtitle: Showing improved sanders, tenoners, planers and surfacers, borers. moulders, band and rip saws, glue jointers, shapers, dovetailers, clamps, shafting, pulleys, castings, knife-grinders and other tools. Period: 1900 - 1916.

2260. John Watson Manufacturing Co. **Watson Man'f'g Co Limited, Ayr, Ont., Canada: binders, reapers, mowers, rakes.** Ayr: The Company, 1889. 40 p. ill. Loc: OKITW.

An annual catalogue containing illustrated descriptions of horse-powered farm machinery, a photograph of John Watson, a brief note on the company, and illustrations of the Ayr Foundry and Watson Manufacturing factory. Period: 1888 - 1889.

2261. John Watson Manufacturing Co. **Watson Man'fg. Co.: binders, reapers, mowers, rakes**. Ayr: The Company, 1887?. 32 p. ill. Loc: OKDHC.

An illustrated catalogue comparing the advantages of the company's machinery with competing products, mentioning the adjustable back grain board, the simplified knotter, and the all-steel two-horse binder. There are illustrations of the company's foundry at Ayr and its new factory, two-thirds completed. Period: 1887 - 1888.

2262. John Watson Manufacturing Co. **Watson trucks: materials handling equipment, catalogue no. 9 revised 1958**. Ayr: The Company, 1958. 1 v. ill. Loc: OCCA.

A loose-leaf catalogue and price list for trucks, carts, dollies, barrel drain stands, skids and castors. Period: 1958 - 1959.

2263. Joseph E. Seagram and Sons. **The house of Seagram, 1857-1957: 100 years of integrity, craftsmanship & tradition**. Waterloo: Joseph E. Seagram and Sons, 1957. 32 p. ill. Loc: OWT.

A promotional booklet explaining the process of distilling, with photographs of the Waterloo plant and a brief description of the company's origins. Period: 1857 - 1957.

2264. Kaufman Rubber Co. **1913-1914 Kaufman Life-buoy Rubber Co. rubber footwear**. Berlin: The Company, 1913. 64 p. ill. Loc: OKDHC.

The fifth annual catalogue of rubber footwear for men, women and children, including gum boots, overshoes, and footwear with leather tops. Period: 1913 - 1914.

2265. Kaufman Rubber Co. **1914-1915 Kaufman Life-buoy Rubber Co. rubber footwear**. Berlin: The Company, 1914. 64 p. ill., index. Loc: OKDHC.

A photocopy of the sixth annual catalogue of Life-buoy and Rubber-leaf brands of rubber footwear, including an illustration of the Kaufman factory and a list of branch addresses. Period: 1914 - 1915.

2266. Kaufman Rubber Co. **The Kaufman Rubber Co. Limited rubber footwear 1911-1912 catalogue**. 1911. 65 p. ill. Loc: OKIT.

The third annual catalogue of Kaufman's rubber footwear, describing and illustrating the latest products such as hip boots, button gaiters and tennis shoes. Period: 1911 - 1912.

2267. Kaufman Rubber Co. **March 18th, 1914 current price list, the Kaufman Rubber Co. Limited, Berlin, Canada: Life-buoy, Rubber-leaf**. Berlin: The Company, 1914. 16 p. Loc: OKDHC.

A photocopied list of wholesale and net prices to accompany an illustrated 1914 catalogue of rubber footwear. Period: 1914 - 1915.

2268. Kaufman Rubber Co. **May 4th, 1914 net price list, The Kaufman Rubber Co. Limited, Berlin, Canada: Life-buoy, Rubber-leaf**. Berlin: The Company, 1914. 16 p. Loc: OKDHC.

Photocopy of a price list for Kaufman's rubber footwear, to accompany an illustrated 1914 catalogue and a current price list. The list gives the item number, cost and a brief description of each product. Period: 1914 - 1915.

2269. Kaufman Rubber Co. **Super quality rubber clothing catalogue number two**. Kitchener: The Company, 193-?. 15 p. ill. Loc: OKIT.

A photocopy of the company's catalogue, with drawings and brief descriptions of the men's and women's clothing and footwear. Period: 1930 - 1940.

2270. Kaufman Rubber Co. **Super quality rubber clothing: price list Aug. 29, 1933**. Kitchener: The Company, 1933. 3 p. Loc: OKIT.

A photocopy of the company's product price list, including item number, brief description and cost. Period: 1930 - 1933.

2271. MacDonald Electric Ltd. **Electrical supplies, catalogue no. 152**. The Company, 19--. 238 p. ill., index. Loc: OKIT.

An indexed catalogue of electrical supplies produced by the company, including switches, fuses, connectors and outlets. Period: 1920 - 1950.

2272. MacDonald Electric Ltd. **MacDonald Electric Limited: electrical supplies catalogue no. 152**. Kitchener: The Company, 238 p. ill., index. Loc: OKIT.

A catalogue containing drawings and descriptions of the company's electrical parts and fixtures. No prices are included. Period: c1941 - c1961.

2273. MacGregor, Gourlay Co. **The MacGregor, Gourlay Co. Limited wood-working machinery, 1909**. Galt: The Company, 1909. 176 p. ill., index. Loc: OCCA.

An indexed catalogue of the company's saws, planers and lathes, moulding, boring, shaping, dovetailing and sanding machines. Period: 1908 - 1909.

2274. Machinery and Transmission Co. **Elmira grain grinders and portable saws**. Elmira: The Company, 12 p. ill. Loc: OKIT, OWRE.

A catalogue with drawings and descriptions of the company's portable saws and grain crushers and grinders.

2275. Maple Leaf Saw Works. **Price list of the Maple Leaf Saw Works: Shurly and Dietrich, manufacturers of refined silver and cast steel saws of all kinds, patent ground.**. Galt: The Company, 1881. 40 p. ill. Loc: OKIT.

A catalogue including a drawing and description of each type of saw and its price. Plastering trowels and knives are also included in the company's wares. Period: 1880 - 1881.

2276. Metal Shingle and Siding Co. **Ideal barn plans**. Preston: The Company, 19--. 20 p. ill. Loc: OKIT.

A photocopy of a promotional catalogue advertising various barn plans and building materials, including shingles, siding, troughing, pipe, ventilators, cowbowls, and tank screens. Drawings and photographs of barns in Ontario include one near Haysville. Period: c1920 - c1930.

2277. Metal Shingle and Siding Co. **Stable fixtures**. CIHM Microfiche series, no. 59222. Preston: Preston Print, 18--?. 1 fiche. mf. Loc: OWTU, OWTL.

An illustrated leaflet describing steel cattle stanchions sold by the company, with an explanation of how to install them into cement floors and a wooden framework. Period: 1830 - 1899.

2278. P.E. Shantz Agricultural Works. **25th annual catalog: P.E. Shantz, Preston, Ont., farm implements, light running harvesting machinery**. Galt: H.M. Hunt & Sons, 1900?. 24 p. ill. Loc: OKDHC.

A catalogue illustrating the design features of the Buckeye Binder, the Buckeye Knotter, and the Buckeye Truck, with descriptions of ploughs, mowers, rakes, harrows and other products. The frontispiece is a photograph of P.E. Shantz, and the inside back cover has an illustrated advertisement for the Metal Shingle and Siding Company of Preston. Period: 1895 - 1910.

2279. P.E. Shantz Agricultural Works. **Buckeye Light Binder, Shantz Mower, Preston Mower, Preston Reaper, hay rakes, straw and root cutters, grain crushers, plows, etc.: P.E. Shantz, Preston, Ontario**. Hamilton: Robert Raw and Company, 1886, 1888. Loc: OKDHC.

Catalogues describing the implements and containing lists of parts, their prices, and repair prices. Illustrations of the machinery and individual parts are given, with testimonial correspondence. Doon Heritage Crossroads holds catalogues for 1886 and 1888. Period: 1885 - 1888.

2280. P.E. Shantz Agricultural Works. **Descriptive catalogue: P.E. Shantz, Preston, Ont.**. Preston: Progress Print, 1899?. 24 p. ill. Loc: OKDHC.

Illustrated descriptions of horse-drawn binders, mowers, rakes, plows, harrows, and cultivators, with specifications for straw cutters, grain crushers, turnip pulpers and a knife sharpener. The catalogue includes testimonials by local farmers Joseph Mader and Jacob S. Hallman and a small portrait of P.E. Shantz. Period: 1895 - 1915.

2281. P.E. Shantz Foundry. **Children's sleighs for boys and girls**. Galt: Reformer Press, 1890?. 15 p. ill. Loc: OKDHC.

A catalogue of sleds available at the turn of the twentieth century. In general, the boys' sleds are lower to the ground than the girls'. Period: 1880 - 1915.

2282. P.E. Shantz Foundry. **Howard warm air furnaces**. Preston: The Company, 1927. 12 p. ill. Loc: OKDHC.

A catalogue of a range of coal-fired furnaces, with a chart of specifications of different models. P.E. Shantz manufactured furnaces produced by the Howard Furnace Company of the United States, but the catalogue includes a non-radiator furnace called Preston No.4 which may have been designed by Shantz. Period: 1925 - 1930.

2283. P.E. Shantz Foundry. **Trucks: P.E. Shantz Foundry, Preston, Ont.**. Preston?: The Company, 19??. 28 p. ill. Loc: OKIT.

An illustrated catalogue of warehouse and industrial trucks, with their specifications and constructional details. Casters, wheelbarrows, and steel and cast iron wheels are also shown. Period: 1900 - 1950.

2284. P.W. Gardiner and Son Ltd. **A Gardiner door enhances every entrance**. Galt: The Company, 1920?. 88 p. ill. Loc: OCCA.

A catalogue of wooden doors, sashes and millwork, with an illustration of the factory in Galt. Period: 1915 - 1925.

2285. Preston Springs Garden Hotel. **Preston Springs Hotel and Mineral Baths**. The Hotel?, 1920?. 33 p. ill., map. Loc: OWTUCG.

A promotional brochure illustrating and describing the building, gardens and medical facilities available, including the mineral spring treatment, electro-therapeutic department, x-ray department and dental office. Nearby facilities for sports and recreation, such as the Waterloo County Golf and Country Club and Puslinch Lake, are also mentioned. Period: 1900 - 1925.

2286. Preston Woodworking Machinery Co. **Woodworking machinery: the Preston Woodworking Machinery Company Limited, Preston, Canada.** Preston: The Company, 19--. 1 v. ill. Loc: OCCA.

A loose-leaf catalogue describing in text and illustrations the planers, saws, moulders and sanders produced by the company. Period: 1905 - 1950.

2287. R. McDougall Co. **Illustrated catalogue of hand and power pumps hydraulic rams, service boxes, well points: catalogue no. 21.** Galt: The Company, 19--. 118 p. ill., index. Loc: OKIT.

A photocopy of a catalogue containing drawings and descriptions of items sold by the company, with a statement of the basic principles of pumps. Period: 1905 - 1940.

2288. R. McDougall Co. **Improved hydraulic rams.** Galt: The Company, 19--. 15 p. ill., chart. Loc: OKDHC.

A catalogue describing the mechanical principles, use and installation of a hydraulic ram at a water source. Illustrated instructions show how to set the ram, how to lay the discharge pipes, and how to select the proper size. Period: 1900 - 1940.

2289. Spaetzel, Roy Clifford. **Spae-Naur Inc..** Kitchener: The Company, 1986. 10 p. ill. Loc: OKIT.

A promotional pamphlet which contains a short section on the history of the fastener distribution business that began as a supplier for auto body maintenance parts and trimmings in Kitchener in 1936. The booklet contains photographs of the business and its workers. Period: 1936 - 1986.

2290. St Clair Concrete Machinery Works? **St Clair: Galt, Canada.** Galt?: The Company?, 192-?. 24 p. ill. Loc: OKIT.

Illustrated catalogue of concrete mixers, hoisting engines, contractors' supplies and machinery made by the company that claimed to be "the first people to manufacture concrete mixers in Canada." Period: 1920 - 1929.

2291. Stone, W.C. **Directions for using Stone's experience of 12 years for dressing and dyeing skins for mats, robes, and other purposes, with improvements.** New Hamburg: Dawson and Gould, 1877. 8 p. Loc: OWTUR.

Instructions for tanning hides and dyeing skins in five different colours. Period: 1877 - 1878.

2292. Waterloo Manufacturing Co. **53rd annual catalogue.** Waterloo: The Company, 1903. 40 p. ill. Loc: OWT.

A catalogue of traction engines, pumps, separators, threshing machines and other farm machinery. One of the latest products was a pneumatic stacker. Photographs of the company's executives are included. Period: 1902 - 1903.

2293. Waterloo Manufacturing Co. **60th annual catalogue, our "diamond" jubilee, 1850-1910.** Waterloo: The Company, 1910. 44 p. ill. Loc: OWT.

A catalogue of the company's farm implements, including drawings and descriptions but no prices. Period: 1909 - 1910.

2294. Waterloo Manufacturing Co. **The Waterloo Manufacturing Co. Limited, Waterloo, Ontario, Canada: high-class portable and traction engines, separators, wind stackers, self feeders, etc..** 1916?. 56 p. ill., index. Loc: OKDHC.

A facsimile of the western edition of a catalogue describing steam- powered farm machinery. It has unsolicited testimonials and an illustration of the factory in Waterloo. Period: 1915 - 1916.

2295. Weber Hardware Co. **Weber Hardware Co. Limited, mill supply dept.: tools, factory and mill supplies.** The Company, 19--. 132 p. ill., index. Loc: OKITW.

An illustrated product catalogue of tools, paint and hardware sold by the company. Prices are included, and customers are encouraged to use the telephone to make their orders. Period: 1916 - 1950.

NATURAL LANDSCAPES
INCLUDING CONSERVATION MOVEMENTS

2296. "Arboretum opens." **Waterloo Historical Society.** 1964. 52: 83. Loc: all.

A report of the opening of the Waterloo County Arboretum, situated east of New Hamburg. Period: 1964

2297. Barker, James and Geiger, Marj and Kitchen, Cameron. **Steckle Woods: an evaluation of an undeveloped natural area in the Kitchener-Waterloo region.** University of Waterloo (student essay, Geography and Planning), 1968. 56 l. ill. Loc: OWTUR.

A study of the interrelationships of geological structure, soils, vegetation, animal life and land use as a basis for land management. Sections in the work deal with topics such as the Kitchener Park system, natural resources, and recommended uses for the woods. The authors conclude that the unique area can be retained but also enjoyed by local citizens. Period: 1967 - 1968.

2298. Bergsma, John. **Implications of comprehensive water planning in the Grand Basin - with emphasis on traditional engineering tasks.** University of Waterloo (M.A. thesis, Engineering), 1971. 94 l. ill., bibl., tables. Loc: OKIT, OWTU.

A study of planning problems caused by legal and institutional constraints on the agencies involved. The author proposes an overall water planning scheme for the river system, in a context that combines provincial policy and regulated regional implementation. Period: 1790 - 1971.

2299. Boyd, Gary and Goodfellow, Carolyn and Harvey, Ted. **The flood hazard of the Upper Grand River.** Waterloo: University of Waterloo, 1973. 116 p. ill., maps, tables, bibl. Loc: OWTU.

A study of flooding on the Grand River and its tributaries as far south as its confluence with the Speed River at Preston. Topics include a history of floods from 1680 to 1972, physical hydrology, flood prevention, land use change, and differences in the perception of flood hazard between urban and rural people. An appendix includes copies of regulations about construction, filling, and alteration of waterways. Period: 1680 - 1972.

2300. Campbell, C.A. and Dagg, Anne Innis. **Mammals of Waterloo and South Wellington counties, 1972.** Waterloo: The Authors, 1972. 130 p. ill., maps, bibl. Loc: OCCA, OCH, OCLG, OCP, OKIT, OWRE, OWT, OWTL, OWTU.

A survey modelled on the procedure used by J. Dewey Soper who studied the mammals in the area from 1909 to 1921. Illustrated information is provided on 41 extant species of mammals and there is a section on extinct species. The drawings are by M. Dyer and M.E. Gartshore. Period: 1971 - 1972.

2301. Campbell, C.A. and Rowell, Robert. **A valley of value: a brief on the proposed Montrose Reservoir and the Grand River Valley.** Kitchener: K-W Pollution Probe, 1971. 44 p. ill. maps, bibl. Loc: OKIT.

A study of the proposed Montrose Reservoir and possible Elora Gorge overpass. The two reports review the possible impact of construction on the environment and argue against development. Period: 1970 - 1971.

2302. **Canadian Natural Science News.** Baden: Edgar R. Boniface, 1897- . Loc: OWTUR.

A monthly publication of items relating to mammalogy, herpetology, conchology, geology, mineralogy, anthropology, botany, chemistry, ethnology, archaeology, palaeontology, entomology, ichthyology and ornithology, to which individuals are encouraged to make written contributions. The University of Waterloo's Doris Lewis Rare Book Room holds volume 1, number 2 (1897), containing an essay by W.J. Wintemberg on classification in anthropology. Period: 1897.

2303. Clarke, Michael F. **The general composition of the forest of North Dumfries Township, Waterloo County, Ontario, 1817.** University of Waterloo (M.A. thesis, Geography), 1969. 54 p. maps, tables. Loc: OWTU.

A description of the forests of North Dumfries in 1817, based on the notes of surveyor Adrian Marlet. Three different associations of various species of trees are identified: maple, beech, basswood and elm; white pine, white oak, red oak and thickets; and white cedar, tamarack, black ash and birch. Period: 1816 - 1817.

2304. Cleghorn, Edward. "The beauty of Waterloo County." **Waterloo Historical Society.** 1946. 34: 14-18. Loc: all.

A short description of the natural and built environments of the county, noting distinctive features such as the Homer Watson Memorial Park, Mennonite horse-drawn vehicles and the solid farm buildings. 1945.

2305. Clough, Donald J. and Anderson, R.W.P. **Excerpts from brief on flood control and water conservation for Grand River watershed.** 1963. 5 p. Loc: OWTU.

Excerpts from the 1961 brief presented by the

Grand River Conservation Commission, including background historical information on the Grand River system, floods, and the distinction between the Grand River Conservation Authority and the Grand River Conservation Commission. Period: 1912 - 1963.

2306. **Conserving the waters of the Grand River: a necessary public work.** 1936. 10 p. ill., map. Loc: OKIT.

A summary of recommendations for dams and reservoirs to reduce flood damage and insure water supply. The report concludes that local municipalities have done all they can, and that assistance from the federal or provincial governments is necessary. Also provided are a summary of a 1932 drainage report by the Ontario Department of Lands and Forests and a map of the Grand River drainage basin. Period: 1931 - 1936.

2307. Cooper, Mike. **Association of American Geographers field trip: Middle Grand River Region, August 1966.** Waterloo: University of Waterloo, 1966. 1 v. maps. Loc: OWTU.

The University of Waterloo copy is damaged by the removal of some pages. Period: 1965 - 1966.

2308. Cox, Kenneth Wayne. **Preferred rural recreational landscapes in the counties of Waterloo South-Wellington.** University of Waterloo (M.A. thesis), 1973. 3 fiche. tables. mf. Loc: OWTU.

An analysis of perceptions of landscapes of rural open space, with particular reference to the Baden Hills-Spongy Lake area, the Elora Gorge, an Old Order Mennonite farm area, the Homer Watson-Pioneer Village area, and the Grand River area near West Montrose. The responses of three groups of respondents, naturalists, students and business managers, are analyzed and the most significant differences are reported between the naturalists and the managers. All rank the Elora Gorge first and the farm area last. Period: 1972 - 1973.

2309. Davis, Linda Strath. **Evolving landscape productivities in four rural townships of southern Ontario.** University of Waterloo (Ph.D. thesis, Geography), 1986. 4 fiche. tables, maps, bibl. mf. Loc: OWTU.

A study which measures the net primary productivity (NPP) in remnant and human-altered ecosystems co-existing in the contemporary landscape. The author reconstructs pre-settlement forests, woodland, meadows and marshes, and analyzes changes in the vegetation mixes in the landscape since human settlement. Wellesley Township is one of the four areas measured for its spatial-temporal patterns of soil, terrain, tree

lines, water supply, weather (climate) and agricultural use. Period: 1800 - 1986.

2310. Dawson, Robert N. **The Grand River: a study of stream pollution and water supply on the Grand River.** University of Toronto (M.A.Sc. thesis), 1963. 110 p. maps., bibl., tables. Loc: OWTU.

A study of the water supplies of municipalities in the region, with recommendations for sewage treatment, water quality and future water supply. The author presents a flow history of the river and a physical description of the valley, including geology, climate and geography. Period: 1962 - 1963.

2311. de Visser, John. **Grand River reflections.** Erin: Boston Mills Press, 1989. 155 p. ill., bibl., maps, index. Loc: OCLG, OCP, OKIT, OWRE, OWT, OWTL, OWTU.

A photographic tour of the Grand River Valley from the source of the river near Riverview to Lake Erie at Port Maitland. The photographs show the villages and towns through which the river passes, as well as the river itself. Maps show the climatic regions and the forest zones of the Grand River Watershed. The book was sponsored by the Grand River Conservation Foundation. Period: 1988 - 1989.

2312. Derstine, Clayton F., Rev. "Significance of the Memorial Tower." **Waterloo Historical Society.** 1926. 14: 247-249. Loc: all.

An address at the dedication of the tower, commenting generally on the landscape of Waterloo County after a century of settlement. Period: 1805 - 1925.

2313. Donaldson, Gregory R. and Mutrie, Dean F. **Ecological appraisal of Homer Watson Park, Kitchener, Ontario.** University of Waterloo, 1970. 54 p. ill., bibl. Loc: OWTU.

Period: 1969 - 1970.

2314. Dorney, R.S. and George, M.G. and MacNaughton, Ian Fraser. **An ecological analysis of the Waterloo-South Wellington region.** Waterloo: University of Waterloo, 1970. 202 p. maps, bibl., tables. Loc: OWTU, OWTL, OKIT.

A study by graduate students of the natural resources (water, soil, forestry, and wildlife) likely to be affected by further urbanization. The ecological information is intended for the Regional Land Use Plan being developed by the Waterloo County Area Planning Board. Recommendations are made for wildlife areas, surface water and ground water, urbanization and Mennonite farmers, recreation areas, and noise and air pollution. Period: 1969 - 1970.

2315. Dorney, R.S. and Clark, Cameron and Grainger, Robert. **Hilborn Conservation Area study: resource inventory, development and management of the site, Preston, Ontario, by members of the Ecology and Resource Management Research Group in the School of Urban and Regional Planning, School of Architecture, Department of Geography, and the Department of Biology.** Waterloo: Division of Environmental Studies, University of Waterloo, 1971. 119 p. ill., bibl., maps, tables. Loc: OWTU, OKIT, OWTL.

A description of the 180 acres of land between Galt and Preston, given by Percy R. Hilborn in 1967 to be developed as a park. The geology, history, ecology, vegetation and aquatic resources are discussed and fourteen recommendations are made on developing the parkland for public use. Period: 1967 - 1971.

2316. Geiger, Marj. "The snowbelt of southwestern Ontario." **The Waterloo County area: selected geographical essays.** Edited by A.G. McLellan. Waterloo: Department of Geography, University of Waterloo, 1971. Pp. 175-182. maps. Loc: OWTU, OWTL, OWTUCG, OKIT.

An explanation of the heavy snowfalls received in the larger region to the north and west of Waterloo County.

2317. Grand River Conservation Authority. **Annual report.** Cambridge: The Authority, 1966-. Loc: OWTL, OCCA.

A summary of each year's activities, including information on floods, water supply, forests, wildlife, weather and parks. Wilfrid Laurier Library holds reports for the years 1966, 1968 to 1971, 1974 to 1981, 1984 and 1986. The Cambridge City Archives has issues for 1967, 1968, 1969 and all years since 1970. Period: 1966 - 1986.

2318. Grand River Conservation Authority. **Bannister and Wrigley Lakes, Pinehurst Lake Conservation Area, F.W.R. Dickson Wilderness Area, Fairlake Game Farm.** Times Past to Times Present. Cambridge: The Authority, 1977. 9 p. bibl., maps. Loc: OKIT.

A description of the history, wildlife, vegetation and facilities of the four areas. Maps show the forest and vegetation zones of the Grand River watershed and the forest cover types in the Pinehurst Lake Conservation Area. Period: 1792 - 1977.

2319. Grand River Conservation Authority. "An historical background." **Grand River Conservation Authority: 1968 annual report.** 1968. Pp. 7-15. Loc: OCCA.

A brief history of conservation activities, prompted by concern at the damage done by yearly floods, including the formation of the Grand River Valley Board of Trade in 1930, the Grand River Conservation Commission in 1934, and the opening of the Shand Dam in 1942. In 1946 the commission decided that it would continue to construct and maintain dams, while a newly formed Grand Valley Conservation Authority would be responsible for other conservation work. The authority was renamed the Grand River Conservation Authority in 1968. Period: 1930 - 1946.

2320. Grand River Conservation Commission. **Plan for flood control and water conservation in the Grand River Watershed.** Fergus: The Commission, 1964. 48 p. maps, tables. Loc: OWTU, OKIT.

A report supporting the need for multipurpose reservoirs in the Grand River Watershed. to achieve flood control, water conservation and pollution abatement. The study includes cost estimates for the proposed reservoirs and excerpts from relevant legislation. Period: 1938 - 1964.

2321. Grand River Parkway Conference. **Grand River conference report.** Grimsby: Niagara Regional Development Association, 1963. 30 p. Loc: OWTU, OCCA, OWTL.

Reports on various aspects of the Lower Grand River, presented at a conference sponsored by the Niagara Regional Development Association in October 1962. Topics include historical development, recreation, conservation and urbanization. The conference concludes that all levels of government and appropriate agencies should work together to plan and preserve the Grand River's resource potential. Period: 1962 - 1963.

2322. Grand Valley Conservation Authority. **Report on a plan of ancillary conservation measures for the construction of the Conestogo Dam.** Elora: The Authority, 1953. 6 l. charts, map. Loc: OWT.

A study of swamp forests feeding the headwaters of tributary streams and the main rivers of the Grand Valley, with recommendations from the Advisory Board on Reforestation on the protection of these areas. Period: 1952 - 1953.

2323. Guscott, David W. **Regional hiking trails as a planning issue: a case study of a long-distance hiking trail for the Waterloo-Wellington region.** University of Waterloo (B.E.S. thesis), 1972. 36 p. bibl., maps. Loc: OWTU.

A proposal for a 175-mile hiking trail to be named the Trail of the Five Rivers, in reference to the Grand, Nith, Conestoga, Speed, and Eramosa Rivers. Reasons for the layout of the trail and the land use planning techniques are outlined. Information on trail maintenance, funding, and facilities is provided, with maps of the proposed trail and brief descriptions of its wildlife and landscape features. Period: 1971 - 1972.

2324. Guscott, David W. **The Trail of the Five Rivers: a conceptual hiking trail for the Waterloo-Wellington region.** University of Waterloo, School of Urban and Regional Planning, 1972. 30 p. ill., maps. Loc: OWTU, OWTUM, OKIT.

A proposal of a hiking trail linking the Nith, Conestoga, Grand, Speed and Eramosa Rivers. The trail is described in sections, with maps and particulars of landscape and wildlife. Period: 1971 - 1972.

2325. "Hawks of Waterloo County." **Waterloo Historical Society.** 1964. 52: 28-29. Loc: all.

A list including approximate wing-spans and markings.

2326. Herriot, William. "The compositae of Galt, Ontario and vicinity." **Ontario Natural Science Bulletin: Journal of the Wellington Field Naturalists' Club.** 1910. 6: 55-64. Loc: OGU, OLU.

Period: 1905 - 1913.

2327. Herriot, William. "The crowfoot and poppy families and their allies around Galt, Ontario." **Ontario Natural Science Bulletin: Journal of the Wellington Field Naturalists' Club.** 1913. 9: 40-46. Loc: OGU, OLU.

Period: 1905 - 1913.

2328. Herriot, William. "The cyperaceae of the vicinity of Galt." **Ontario Natural Science Bulletin: Journal of the Wellington Field Naturalists' Club.** 1906. 2:35-38. Loc: OGU, OLU.

Period: 1905 - 1913.

2329. Herriot, William. "The ericaceae and orchidaceae in the vicinity of Galt, Ontario." **Ontario Natural Science Bulletin: Journal of the Wellington Field Naturalists' Club.** 1909. 5: 26-33. Loc: OGU, OLU.

Period: 1905 - 1913.

2330. Herriot, William. "The grasses of Galt, Ontario and vicinity." **Ontario Natural Science Bulletin: Journal of the Wellington Field Naturalists' Club.** 1908. 4: 126-132. Loc: OGU, OLU.

Period: 1905 - 1913.

2331. Herriot, William. "The rosaceae and leguminosae of Galt, Ontario and vicinity." **Ontario Natural Science Bulletin: Journal of the Wellington Field Naturalists' Club.** 1912. 8: 28-34. Loc: OGU, OLU.

Period: 1905 - 1913.

2332. Herriot, William. "The trees of Waterloo County." **Waterloo Historical Society.** 1924. 12: 80-84. Loc: all.

A list of 47 indigenous species that attain a trunk diameter of a foot or more. Each entry contains short description of the tree's habitat.

2333. "The Homer Watson Memorial Park." **Waterloo Historical Society.** 1943. 31: 29-32. Loc: all.

An account of the creation of a park in the tract of land known as Cressman's Bush, including the address by Homer Watson supporting conservation of the tract. Period: 1913 - 1943.

2334. Jackson, Alan D. **The Nith River, a deterministic study.** Waterloo Lutheran University (B.A. thesis, Geography), 1971. 52 p. bibl., tables, maps. Loc: OWTL.

A study of the drainage system of the Nith River explaining the disruption by Pleistocene glaciation of the hierarchical, geometric drainage pattern to which the river may revert. There are maps of the Nith and Grand drainage basins, and schematic diagrams of the Nith River basin. Period: 8700 BC - 1971.

2335. Joanette, Nelson K. "Malaria in the Grand River area in the 19th century." **Waterloo Historical Society.** 1986. 74: 51-62. ill. Loc: all.

A study of the prevalence and possible environmental causes of malaria, a serious problem during the nineteenth century when it was considered to have resulted from the building of dams. Citing newspaper evidence of malaria symptoms and the remedies offered by local druggists, the author concludes that mosquito infestation and malaria were probably endemic in the region and that they were abated by land development from the 1840s. Period: 1800 - 1860.

2336. Karrow, Paul F. "The geology of Waterloo County." **Waterloo Historical Society.** 1972. 60: 8-14. ill. Loc: all.

An address to the 59th annual meeting of the Waterloo Historical Society, describing various land, rock and water features such as the Onondaga Escarpment, the Baden Hills, Doon Pinnacle, Sunfish Lake and Puslinch Lake.

2337. Karrow, Paul F. "Landform evolution in Waterloo/Wellington counties." **The Waterloo County area: selected geographical essays.** Edited by A.G. McLellan. Waterloo: Department of Geography, University of Waterloo, 1971. Pp. 1-10. maps. Loc: OWTU, OWTL, OWTUCG, OKIT.

An outline of the bedrock geology with more detail on the Pleistocene landforms. The author identifies local examples of moraines, till plains, kames and eskers, kettles, outwash fans and plains, and alluvial terraces, and comments on the economic aspects of mineral deposits and soil quality.

2338. Karrow, Paul F. and Warner, B.G. and Ellis, C.J. **What's beneath our feet in Waterloo Region.** University of Waterloo. Quaternary Sciences Institute, 1990. 8 p. ill., map, bibl. Loc: OKIT.

An outline of the geological and biological development and prehistory of the region. Diagrams of bedrock formations and buried valleys, charts of botanical trends, and drawings of artifacts in various prehistoric periods supplement the text.

2339. Keizer, Holly I. **Effect of agricultural land drainage on wetlands in Wellesley Township, Waterloo County.** University of Waterloo (B.E.S. thesis, Geography), 1977. 65 l. maps, tables, bibl. Also mf. Loc: OWTU, OWTUM.

An examination of the beneficial and detrimental effects of the major reduction in the area of wetlands since 1930. Changes in soil characteristics, water quality, wildlife and natural vegetation are the author's main concerns. Period: 1930 - 1972.

2340. Kitchener-Waterloo Field Naturalists, Conservation Committee. **A report on the eastern bluebird.** Kitchener: The Club, 1967. 16 p. ill. Loc: OWTL, OKIT.

A report describing the decline of the species in Waterloo County, and giving possible reasons for the decline and suggestions on how to restore the numbers. Period: 1816 - 1967.

2341. Kitchener-Waterloo Field Naturalists. **Great blue heronries in the Grand River watershed: a report on the decline of Southern Ontario's tallest native bird.** Kitchener: The Club, 1967. 15 l. ill., bibl. Loc: OWTL, OKIT.

A statement of concern for the bird's survival, including reports on various heronries near Bloomingdale, Philipsburg and Ayr. Period: 1954 - 1967.

2342. Kitchener-Waterloo Field Naturalists. **Honour roll of trees found in the Great Tree Hunt of 1990 in the Region of Waterloo.** The Club, 1991. 16 p. Loc: OKIT, OWRA.

Lists of trees that are native to Ontario, exotic trees planted in Waterloo, and trees of special interest due to their special shape, history or rarity in the region. The location, height and diameter of the trees are given. Period: 1800 - 1991.

2343. Kitchener-Waterloo Field Naturalists. **Summary, Christmas bird counts, 1934 to 1978.** Kitchener: The Club, 1978?. 38 p. Loc: OKIT.

A tabulation of sightings of over 100 species of birds over the 45-year period, prefaced by reminiscences by members of the club, especially Gerry Knechtel. Period: 1934 - 1978.

2344. Kummer, Oliver A. "Memories of the Grand." **Waterloo Historical Society.** 1973. 61: 35-39. ill. Loc: all.

Reminiscences of spring floods of the river, artists who have painted along its banks, and its recreational value for fishing and swimming. Period: c1850 - 1973.

2345. MacDonald, John D.A. **Cultural implications of the physiography of the Regional Municipality of Waterloo.** Waterloo: Regional Municipality of Waterloo, Planning and Development, 1988. 118 p. ill., bibl. Loc: OWRMA.

An analysis of the diverse landscape that has resulted from complex glacial advances and retreats and subsequent post-glacial erosion and deposition. Following an account of glacial morphology, drainage systems and soils, the author relates physiography to the main settlement sites in each period of human occupancy.

2346. Mage, Julius A. **The physical basis for a land classification in Woolwich Township.** University of Waterloo (B.A. thesis, Geography), 1965. 1 fiche. ill., maps, tables. mf. Loc: OWTUM.

A development policy proposed for the township, based on analysis of the climate and the capability and physical characteristics of the land. Photographs and maps show the geology, physiography, drainage, soils and land use, and there is a map of proposed land use. The author recommends retention of the rural base, increase in the forested area, creation of a reservoir near West Montrose, and preservation of wetland areas as wildlife reserves. Period: 1964 - 1965.

2347. McBoyle, Geoffrey R. "Some notes on the utility of climatic data in the Waterloo-Wellington area." **The Waterloo County area: selected geographical essays.** Edited by A.G. McLellan. Waterloo: Department of Geography, University of Waterloo, 1971. Pp. 159-173. maps, tabl. Loc: OWTU, OWTL, OWTUCG, OKIT.

A review of the significance for transportation, agriculture, and home heating of data recorded at the Ontario Agricultural College and the Waterloo-Wellington Airport stations.

2348. McCartney, John S. **An investigation of the relationship between the growth of Waterloo, Ontario and streamflow in Laurel Creek**. Wilfrid Laurier University (B.A. thesis, Geography), 1976. 59 p. bibl., maps, charts. Loc: OWTL.

A study of urbanization and hydrology, using the water flow in Laurel Creek in Waterloo between 1960 and 1974 as an example. The author finds that urban development increases runoff and peak discharge and decreases lag time, thus causing flood problems. Period: 1960 - 1974.

2349. McCauley, Robert and Goodchild, Gareth A. "The little lakes of Waterloo Region." **Waterloo Historical Society**. 1983. 71: 112-118. ill., bibl., tables. Loc: all.

A brief overview of the depth, surface area, volume, pH levels and alkalinity of 12 bodies of water, including Paradise Lake, Sunfish Lake, Hofstetter Lake, Little Turnbull Lake and Lakeside Park Lake.

2350. McCauley, Robert. "Preston Springs: water with character." **Waterloo Historical Society**. 1988. 76: 134-138. ill., tables. Loc: all.

A short report on two separate chemical analyses (c1925 and 1988) of the waters in the Preston Springs. Period: c1925 - 1988.

2351. Mitchell, Bruce and Gardner, J. and Cook, R. **Physical adjustments and institutional arrangements for the urban flood hazard: Grand River Watershed**. Publication Series, no. 13. Waterloo: Department of Geography, University of Waterloo, 1978. 142 p. ill., maps, tables, bibl. Loc: OWTU, OWTL, OKIT.

A comprehensive description and evaluation of past floods and efforts to control flooding. Bridgeport, Galt (Cambridge) and New Hamburg are considered in the research, which takes into account the costs of various adjustments as well as local residents' attitudes. In reviewing the wide range of physical and institutional controls, the authors note trends in coping with flood hazards and implications for the affected communities. The report includes a chronology of flood damage, graphs of discharge of the Grand River at Galt from 1914 to 1975, and maps of changes in the flood plains at Galt, Bridgeport and New Hamburg from 1945 to 1976. Period: 1850 - 1978.

2352. "Mockingbird in New Dundee." **Waterloo Historical Society**. 1964. 52: 35. Loc: all.

A note of the sighting of the bird by Earlmont Poth in the winter of 1964. Period: 1964 -

2353. Montgomery, F.H. "A botanical survey of Waterloo County, Ontario." **Transactions of the Royal Canadian Institute**. 1945. 25,2: 217-265. ill., bibl., charts, maps. Loc: OGU, OKIT.

A summary of a Masters thesis concluding that Waterloo County has three overlapping floral zones: the Transcontinental Zone, the Alleghenian Zone, and the Carolinian Zone. The author reports 1,191 species, varieties and forms of plants, 102 of them not previously recorded. Charts classify plants as native or introduced. Period: 1943 - 1944.

2354. Montgomery, F.H. **A botanical survey of Waterloo County, Ontario**. McMaster University (M.A. thesis, Biology), 1944. 171 l. tables, bibl. Loc: OWTL, OKIT.

An inventory of vascular plants, compared with the findings of William Herriot who recorded the flora near Galt in the late nineteenth century. In noting differences, the author discusses the extent to which certain species have become rare or extinct, more prolific or newly introduced. Brief comparisons are made with flora in neighbouring counties and some information is given about the county's soil and climate. Period: 1895 - 1942.

2355. Montgomery, F.H. "Interesting botanical areas of Waterloo County." **Waterloo Historical Society**. 1944. 32: 12-15. Loc: all.

A short report of a lecture, describing selected plants of the total of over 1,200 species identified in the county. Period: 1943 - 1944.

2356. Montgomery, F.H. "Introduced plants of Waterloo and adjacent counties, Ontario." **Canadian Field Naturalist**. 1948. 62,2: 79-95. Loc: OWTL, OWTUD.

An annotated list of 432 plant species, 266 in Waterloo County, forming one quarter of its total plant population. The distribution and localities of each plant are noted, with its place of origin. The first portion of the list refers to plants found in Waterloo County, the second portion gives the plants found in neighbouring counties but not in Waterloo. Period: 1889 - 1948.

2357. Nelson, James G. and O'Neill, Pauline C. **The Grand as a Canadian Heritage River**. Waterloo: Heritage Resources Centre, University of Waterloo, 1989. 246 p. ill., maps, bibl. Loc: OWTU, OWTL, OKIT.

A study sponsored by the Canadian Heritage Rivers Board and the Grand River Conservation Authority. Topics include geology, biology, parks, trail systems, prehistory and archaeology, the Six Nations Indians, industrial development, development stresses and heritage management.

Period: 1000 - 1989.

2358. Nelson, James G. **The Grand River as a possible Heritage River: a background study**. Waterloo: Heritage Resources Centre, University of Waterloo, 1988. 1 v. (various pagings). Loc: OKIT, OCCA.

A preliminary study to determine whether the Grand River should be named a Canadian Heritage River. The report includes information on geology, landscape, cultural heritage, trail systems, recreational possibilities, protected areas, water quality, flood control methods, development stresses and institutional arrangements, and an analysis of the official plans of municipalities and townships.

2359. Nelson, James G. and O'Neill, Pauline C. **Nominating the Grand as a Canadian Heritage River**. Occasional Paper No. 13. Heritage Resources Centre, University of Waterloo, 1990. 344, 14, 13 p. maps, tables. Loc: OWTU.

A report nominating the Grand River as a heritage river on human and recreational grounds. Research reports are included on forests, natural resources, water quality, conservation areas, and individual localities with outstanding features or associations.

2360. "Nith River flood of 1883 [WRP]." **Waterloo Historical Society**. 1983. 71: 118. ill. Loc: all.

A photograph and note of the Nith River flood in 1883. Period: 1883.

2361. "One hundred forty five-acre site donated by P.R. Hilborn and family." **Waterloo Historical Society**. 1967. 55: 10. Loc: all.

A brief article describing the property situated between Galt and Preston and called Tinatowa Provincial Park. Period: 1967.

2362. Ontario Conservation Authorities Branch. **Grand Valley Conservation Authority Nith River: supplementary report on methods of flood protection for the village of New Hamburg**. Toronto: Kilborn Engineering, 1968. 9 p. Loc: OWTU.

A short supplement to a report prepared in 1951 by Kilborn Engineering, **Report on methods of flood prevention on the Nith River for the village of New Hamburg**. The update considers a third scheme, excavation and construction of channel improvements to be carried out in stages not discussed in the original report. Cost estimates and detailed descriptions of each additional stage are included. Period: 1951 - 1968.

2363. Ontario Department of Energy and Resources Management. **Grand River Conservation lands study**. Toronto: The Department, 1964, 1965. 2 v. ill., maps, bibl. Loc: OKIT.

A land use study in two parts. The 1964 report describes physical and cultural features and discusses population growth, settlement patterns, land values and needs, and development strategies. The 1965 report addresses conservation options, recreational possibilities, and erosion and pollution control, and makes recommendations for further study. Period: 1964 - 1965.

2364. Ontario Department of Planning and Development. **Agreement between the Government of the Province of Ontario and the Grand River Conservation Commission for construction of the Conestogo Dam on the Conestogo River, a tributary of the Grand River**. Toronto: The Department, 1953. 10 p. Loc: OWTU.

A contract between the Ontario government and the Grand River Conservation Commission outlining the terms of construction for a dam near Glen Allen for flood control and water conservation. Period: 1952 - 1953.

2365. Ontario Department of Planning and Development, Conservation Branch. **Nith Valley conservation report, 1951**. Toronto: The Department, 1951. 1 v. (various pagings). ill., maps, charts. Loc: OKIT, OWTU.

A report on the geography, forestry, water and wildlife of the valley, with 31 recommendations to the Grand River Conservation Authority. Period: 1949 - 1951.

2366. Ontario Water Resources Commission. **Water resources survey of the county of Waterloo**. Toronto: The Commission, 1966. 253 p. maps, tables. Loc: OKIT.

A report on water supply and pollution control facilities, with recommendations for improvements. Period: 1963 - 1964.

2367. Pequegnat, Marcel. "Grand River conservation." **Waterloo Historical Society**. 1942. 30: 211-224. Loc: all.

An account of the significance of the Grand River system by the Kitchener Waterworks Superintendent and vice-chairman of the Grand River Conservation Commission. The author comments on the problems of flooding and pollution caused by land clearance and industrialization, and outlines events leading to the creation of the Grand River Conservation Commission in 1938 and the building of the Shand Dam at Belwood. Period: 1909 - 1942.

2368. Pickard, Theresa. **Riverine land development: a comparison study of Cambridge, Ontario with San Antonio, Texas and Saskatoon, Saskatchewan.** University of Waterloo (B.E.S. thesis, Geography), 1985. 1 fiche. mf. Loc: OWTUM.

A study of river valley planning in the three centres. Development strategies are evaluated in terms of flood reduction, recreational facilities, economic stimulation, educational opportunities and heritage preservation. The author stresses the need for public awareness and participation programmes to be incorporated in the planning. A history of Grand River flooding is included, with notes of the ten most significant floods since 1790. Period: 1790 - 1985.

2369. Presant, E.W. and Wicklund, R.E. **The soils of Waterloo County.** Ontario Soil Survey Report 44. Ottawa: Canada Department of Agriculture, 1971. 104 p. maps, tables. Loc: OWTU, OKIT, OWRE.

A survey including information on classification, horizon characteristics, chemical and physical properties, and uses and limitations of soil for agricultural and engineering purposes. Period: 1970 - 1971.

2370. Priddle, George B. and Lowry, Mark and Carter, Jim. **The scenic roads of North Dumfries, Wellesley, and Woolwich.** Waterloo: Department of Geography, University of Waterloo, 1974. 29 p. maps. Loc: OWTU, OWTUCG.

An inventory of rural roads in the townships, rating them according to their scenic qualities and recommending improvements. Period: 1973 - 1974.

2371. Priddle, George B. "Water resources alternatives in the Grand River watershed." **The Waterloo County area: selected geographical essays.** Edited by A.G. McLellan. Waterloo: Department of Geography, University of Waterloo, 1971. Pp. 195-203. maps. Loc: OWTU, OWTL, OWTUCG, OKIT.

A survey of the current water management systems in the various municipalities with comments on future planning options. Period: 1965 - 1970.

2372. Richardson, A.H. **Conservation by the people: the history of the conservation movement in Ontario to 1970.** Toronto: University of Toronto Press for the Conservation Authorities of Ontario, 1974. 154 p. ill. Loc: OCCA, OWTU, OWTL.

References in a more general history to the work of conservation agencies in the Grand River Valley. Recurrent floods and agitation by prominent citizens and engineers are noted as factors leading to the McIntosh survey and the Grand River Conservation Commission Act of 1932 (superseded by a new act of the same name in

1938). The commission's functions were redefined in the creation of the Grand Valley Conservation Authority in 1948 (renamed Grand River in 1966 and enlarged in 1968). The author also provides details of the various dams and reservoirs (Columbia, Mill Creek, Victoria Mills, Laurel Creek, Chicopee, Shade's Mill, Floradale and New Dundee), forests, and conservation areas for amenity and recreation. Period: 1912 - 1966.

2373. Roth, Donald M. **Historical ecology of Schneider's Creek and Victoria Park in Kitchener, Ontario.** University of Waterloo (B.A. thesis, Geography), 1976. 2 fiche. mf. Loc: OWTUM.

An examination of the history, present problems and likely future development of the city neighbourhood. The author considers the biological, cultural, human and physical factors that have shaped the area and makes recommendations for future use. Period: 1800 - 1976.

2374. Rowell, Margaret. "Floods on the Grand." **Waterloo Historical Society.** 1974. 62: 34-38. ill. Loc: all.

An historical account of flood problems on the Grand River including photographs of Galt and Ayr during floods. Period: 1800 - 1972.

2375. Rump, P.C. "A history of water pollution in the Grand River watershed, Ontario." **The Waterloo County area: selected geographical essays.** Edited by A.G. McLellan. Waterloo: Department of Geography, University of Waterloo, 1971. Pp. 183-193. tabl. Loc: OWTU, OWTL, OWTUCG, OKIT.

A study, based on government reports, historical sources and newspaper accounts, of the impact on water quality of population growth and economic activities in three main periods: pre-1785, 1785-1855, and 1855-1930. Period: 1750 - 1930.

2376. Schneller, W.J. "Waterloo County Arboretum." **Waterloo Historical Society.** 1972. 60: 75-77. Loc: all.

A short description of the arboretum located east of New Hamburg. The author describes its objectives and identifies W.J Schneller, Sandy Forsyth, Clarence Diamond and Roy Gilbert as prominent organizers of the project. Period: 1972.

2377. Shrubsole, Dan. "The Grand River Conservation Commission: history, activities, and implications for water management." **Canadian Geographer.** 1992. 36,3: 221-236. maps, diagram, tables. Loc: OKIT, OWTL, OWTU.

An evaluation of water resource strategies planned between 1932 and 1966 by the commission and the Grand Valley Conservation Authority which was formed in 1948. The author discusses the factors of local initiative, provincial-municipal partnership, the watershed perspective, and collaboration among public agencies, and notes the absence of a basin-wide administration and the confined nature of financial arrangements as weaknesses. Period: 1932 - 1966.

2378. Smith, Charles R. **The impact of agricultural practices on surface water quality and the bottomland ecosystem of selected watersheds in Waterloo Regional Municipality..** University of Waterloo (M.A. thesis, Geography), 1973. 2 fiche. maps, tables, bibl. mf. Loc: OWTU.

A study of the effects of historical and modern farming practices on water quality and floodplain forest areas, with proposals for rehabilitation of the ecosystem and policy changes for the 1971 agricultural programmes of the Ontario Department of Agriculture and Food. Tables provide data on temperature, water supply, wildlife and vegetation, livestock and crop management, and use of chemicals by farmers in Woolwich Township. Period: 1800 - 1971.

2379. Snider, E.W.B. "Waterloo County forests and primitive economics." **Waterloo Historical Society**. 1918. 6: 14-36. ill. Loc: all.

An examination of the depletion of forests and water power in Waterloo County. For each township (Waterloo, Wilmot, Woolwich, Wellesley and North Dumfries) the water sources such as rivers and creeks and the mills using the water power are listed. Accompanying reference notes give additional information about the mills. Period: 1800 - 1918.

2380. Soper, J. Dewey. "The mammals of Wellington and Waterloo Counties, Ontario." **Journal of Mammalogy**. 1923. 4,4: 244-252. Loc: OWTUD.

An annotated list of 42 species of native mammals, including bats, squirrels, mice and deer. Some, such as beavers and bears, are now extinct in the county; others, like the porcupine, have not been seen but are presumed to be indigenous. Period: 1909 - 1923.

2381. Suffling, Roger and McIntyre, Ronald B. **A study of scenic roads in the region of Waterloo, Ontario.** University of Waterloo, School of Urban and Regional Planning,, 1985. 32 l. Loc: OWTU, OKIT, OKITW.

A survey of the scenic quality of rural roads, following the model of Priddle and Lowry's report to the Waterloo Regional Heritage Foundation in 1974. Topics include criteria for scenic roads, features that enhance or detract from scenic qualities, and the purposes of promoting and

preserving scenic roads. Specific roads are not identified, but the townships of North Dumfries, Woolwich and Wellesley are considered to be the most scenic in the region. Period: 1974 - 1985.

2382. Towndrow, John. "A new woods for Woodside." **APT Bulletin**. 1986. 18,1-2: 95-98. Loc: OPET, OTY.

An account of a project to re-create the landscape of woods and gardens as it would have been in 1890, when it was the boyhood home of W.L. Mackenzie King. Period: 1889 - 1890.

2383. Trafford, Margaret. **Stream changes in Waterloo Region, 1880-1984.** University of Waterloo (B.E.S. thesis, Geography), 1987. 1 fiche. 45 p. maps. mf. Loc: OWTUM.

A survey of the inter-relationships of hydrology, settlement, development and landscape change, with reference to the Conestogo River, Nith River, Laurel Creek, Canagagigue Creek and Hunsberger Creek. Period: 1880 - 1984.

2384. Watson, J.W. "An outline of historical geography." **Waterloo Historical Society**. 1944. 32: 8-12. Loc: all.

A brief article on the geography of southwestern Ontario, discussing rock formations, rivers and streams, and glacial changes, with particular reference to the Niagara Peninsula and the Grand River Valley.

2385. Worden, Ethel Wilfong (Mrs Paul) "The beautiful waters of Doon." **Waterloo Historical Society**. 1971. 59: 31-35. ill. Loc: all.

An appreciation of the rivers and streams, plant and animal life, and water-based recreation in the early twentieth century. Period: 1900 - 1920.

BUILDINGS AND ARCHITECTURE

2386. "108 year old Waterloo County Building." **Waterloo Historical Society**. 1961. 49: 9. ill. Loc: all.

A 1871 photograph of the Waterloo County Courthouse, suggested for preservation by John Martin. Period: 1871 - 1961.

2387. "1848 Free Church, Bridgeport." **Waterloo Historical Society**. 1968. 56: 26. Loc: all.

A note of the request to the Bridgeport Village Council that the 1848 Free Church building should be preserved. Bridgeport Council later had the building repaired and improved. Period: 1848 - 1968.

2388. "1896 home disappears." **Waterloo Historical Society.** 1964. 52: 39. ill. Loc: all.

A photograph of the house built by George Schlee who promoted the first rubber industry in Berlin. The house was rented by Mackenzie King while he was Member of Parliament for North Waterloo. Period: 1896 - 1964.

2389. Alder, Elizabeth. **Heritage planning in the Regional Municipality of Waterloo.** University of Waterloo (student essay, Planning), 1992. 25 l. Loc: OWTUR.

An account of the governmental agencies and procedures set up for heritage planning in the Region of Waterloo since 1973, including the various LACACs and the Regional Archaeologist. Period: 1973 - 1991.

2390. **Archaeological mitigation and monitoring, Phase One excavation for parking garage, Regional Administrative Headquarters, City of Kitchener.** Petersburg: Archaeological Research Associates, 1991. 1 v. (unpaged). Loc: OWRMA.

A detailed report of house foundations and other evidence exposed during development of the site at Frederick and Ahrens East. Period: 1860 - 1960.

2391. Architectural Conservancy of Ontario, North Waterloo Region Branch. **Appraisal of Victoria Public School, Kitchener.** 1988. 1 v. (various pagings). ill. Loc: OKIT.

An illustrated history and architectural appraisal of the building designed by the Hamilton architects Munro and Mead and opened in 1912. The authors, retained by the Save Victoria School Committee, conclude that the school building is in excellent condition and should continue to be used by community organizations. Period: 1912 - 1988.

2392. Armstrong, Rita. "Waterloo County's oldest house: Blair Athol, Blair, Ontario." **Waterloo Historical Society.** 1967. 55: 4-8. ill. Loc: all.

A description of the house built in 1817 by Jacob Bechtel and later owned by the Barclay family. Period: 1817 - 1967.

2393. "Arts III building, University of Waterloo, Ont." **Canadian Architect.** 1968. 13: 45. ill., plans. Loc: OWTL, OWTU.

Reference from the Canadian Periodical Index. Period: 1968.

2394. "Arts: trouble on the campus." **Architecture Canada.** 1970. 47: 2-3. Loc: OWTU.

Reference from the Canadian Periodical Index. Period: 1970.

2395. **Auction catalogue: the important collections and furnishings of Castle Kilbride continuously occupied by the Livingston family since its erection in 1873 by James Livingston, the flax and oil king of Canada.** The Auction Galleries, 1988. 1 v. Loc: OKITW.

A descriptive list of toys, books, artwork and furniture, auctioned at Baden in 1988. Period: 1873 - 1988.

2396. Baird, Sandy. "Even nostalgia isn't what it used to be." **Waterloo Historical Society.** 1973. 61: 67-71. ill. Loc: all.

A brief history of businesses and homes in Kitchener's Scott-King-City Hall block, including Hawke's butcher shop, Opal Cafe, Dietrich's bakery, Herzog's grocery, Zuch's barber shop and Scotchmer's drug store. The article includes photographs dating from between 1910 to 1961. Period: c1935 - c1945.

2397. Beglo, Jo. "English Gothic and the architecture of Lutheranism." **A time for building: essays on Lutherans in Canada.** Edited by Barton Beglo. Kitchener: St Mark's Press, 1988. Pp. 33-40, 80-82. ill. Loc: OKIT, OWTL, OWTUCG, OWTUR, OWTUSJ.

An essay on the style and symbolism of St Mark's Lutheran Church, Kitchener, considered in the tradition of Lutheran church architecture. The author notes that the architect was Bernal A. Jones (who worked with W.H.E. Schmalz on the Kitchener City Hall of 1923), and that the building contractors were Ball Bros Ltd while the interior woodwork was executed by craftsmen of the Interior Hardwood Company of Kitchener. Period: 1935 - 1939.

2398. Bensason, Leon R. **A Heritage Conservation District proposal for the Victoria Park neighbourhood in Kitchener, Ontario.** University of Waterloo (B.A. thesis, Geography), 1986. 3 fiche. mf. Loc: OWTUM.

An historical study of the neighbourhood and explanation of heritage conservation legislation, in support of a three-phase proposal to designate the area as a heritage district. Period: 1807 - 1986.

2399. Bergey, Lorna L. "W.H.S. Council tour of New Dundee." **Waterloo Historical Society.** 1964. 52: 34-35. ill. Loc: all.

A tour guide of sites visited, including Frederick Millar's grist mill (1847), the house adjoining the mill (1860), the James Brown residence (1832), the E.T. Coleman building (1848) which was the first post office, the H. Kavelman store (1877) which housed the first village library, and the Bergey home (1836). Period: 1832 - 1964.

2400. Bickle, Lorene, Mrs and Dickson, F.W.R. "Jacob Kolb home." **Waterloo Historical Society**. 1973. 61: 32-33. ill. Loc: all.

A short description of the home near Preston, renovated in 1973 by descendants of Jacob Kolb. Period: 1830 - 1973.

2401. "Blair Mill used the same water twice." **Waterloo Historical Society**. 1961. 49: 14-15. ill. Loc: all.

A short history of the Blair Mill Tower or Sheave Tower from its construction in 1876 to its restoration in 1962. Period: 1876 - 1962.

2402. Blake, Verschoyle B. and Greenhill, Ralph. **Rural Ontario**. Toronto: University of Toronto Press, 1969. 173 p. ill. Loc: OKIT, OWTL, OWTU, OWTUCG, OWTUM.

An essay illustrated by 90 plates, including three from Waterloo County: St John's Lutheran Church, Wellesley Township (Plate 49); workers' cottages at the Greenfield Mill, North Dumfries (Plate 62); and a stone barn in North Dumfries (Plate 72). The author also comments briefly on the exceptional land survey pattern of Waterloo Township (p.13).

2403. Bloomfield, G.T. "Albert Kahn and industrial architecture." **Society for the Study of Architecture in Canada Bulletin**. 1985. 10,4: 4-10. ill. Loc: OGU, OWTL, OWTU.

A discussion of the Canadian work of a leading industrial architect, based in Detroit in the first half of the twentieth century. Kahn's first Canadian factory was probably the Kaufman Rubber Co. plant in Berlin in 1908, followed by the Dominion Rubber Co. tire plant in 1912-14. Both are excellent examples of Kahn's distinctive design features of reinforced concrete construction with large windows. Period: 1908 - 1930.

2404. Bloomfield, G.T. "Canadian fire insurance plans and industrial archeology." **IA: the Journal of the Society for Industrial Archeology**. 1982. 8,1: 67-80. ill. maps. Loc: OWTU.

A discussion of the value of fire insurance plans as a source of information on industrial sites, structures and buildings. The plan of the Williams, Greene and Rome shirt factory, opened in Berlin in January 1914, is reproduced to illustrate the range of detail provided. Period: 1913 - 1914.

2405. Bloomfield, G.T. **Industrial buildings and vernacular housing**. Guelph: The Author, 1984. 22 p. ill., maps, bibl. Loc: OWTUR.

A guide for a tour of Hespeler, Galt, Preston, Kitchener and Waterloo by architectural historians from across Canada. The economic development of each place is described with reference to specific residential and industrial buildings. Tables show the growth of population, industrial employment and industrial production of Guelph, Hespeler, Preston, Galt, Berlin/Kitchener and Waterloo between 1871 and 1981. A note adds statistical information about the percentage of stone dwellings in various places in Ontario. Period: 1807 - 1984.

2406. "Bridgeport Mill burned October 6, 1970." **Waterloo Historical Society**. 1970. 58: 71. ill. Loc: all.

A note of the destruction of the Bridgeport Mill, listing various mill owners and quoting the description of the mill from the 1851 census. Period: 1851 - 1970.

2407. **Bridgeport survey**. Kitchener LACAC, 1984?. 67 p. ill. Loc: OKIT.

Reports on 23 buildings dating from between 1835 and 1860, including details of plan and lot, architectural description and significance, and summary of title search. An introductory history of the village names the founding businesses and landowners and lists residents with their occupations according to the 1854 assessment rolls. Copies of various maps and plans are also included. Period: 1830 - 1860.

2408. Brown, Richard. "The Crozier Cottages, Colborne Street." **Waterloo Historical Society**. 1975. 63: 66-67. ill. Loc: all.

A pen-and-ink drawing and brief account of the Galt cottages built in the 1840s, probably by the father of John Beattie Crozier, whose autobiography is quoted for memories of the cottages and his early life. The cottages are described as typical of a Scottish lowland village. Period: 1845 - 1850.

2409. Brown, Richard. "Dickson Mill." **Waterloo Historical Society**. 1975. 63: 68. ill. Loc: all.

A pen-and-ink drawing and brief history of the mill planned by Robert Dickson to utilize the water power of the Grand River and Mill Creek. The 1843 building at Park Hill Road and Water Street North later housed Galt's gas plant for street lighting. Period: 1840 - 1900.

2410. Bryant, Susan and Thompson, Bertha K. **Elmira: three walking tours.** Woolwich LACAC, 1985. 27 p. ill., map, glossary. Loc: OWRE.

A guide to three walking tours of Elmira, including information on the history and architectural features of over forty older residences and commercial buildings. The brochure also contains a map, a glossary of architectural terms, some notes on architectural styles and a summary history of Elmira. Period: 1830 - 1985.

2411. **Cambridge local building inventory.** Cambridge LACAC, 1978?. 345 p. ill. Loc: OKIT.

A collection of preliminary reports on 345 buildings, arranged in street address order, on forms with spaces for such details as name and address of building, lot and plan, original owner and significant later owners, present owner, architectural description and significance, and historical importance. The level of detail varies for specific buildings and some information has since been added by hand. More recent reports should be requested from the LACAC Co-ordinator for the City of Cambridge. Period: 1830 - 1900.

2412. Campbell, James and Horne, Malcolm and Kolaritsch, Diane. **An inventory of industrial buildings of architectural/historical significance in the City of Kitchener.** Kitchener LACAC, 1985. 124 p. ill. Loc: OKIT.

Reports on 47 industrial buildings including details of plan and lot, zoning, site dimensions, date, original owner and current owner, architectural description and significance, title search, and history of business. Buildings recommended for immediate designation are the Boehmer Box, Hydro City Shoe, Kem Manufacturing, Lang Tanning A and B, MacDonald Electric, Breithaupt Leather, Krug Furniture, Randall and Roos, and Hibner Furniture, the Perine flax mill and terrace housing and housing for the Bear, Moore brickworks. Another 14 buildings are recommended for future consideration. Period: 1850 - 1900.

2413. Canada National Parks Branch: Department of Northern Affairs and National Resources. **Woodside National Historic Park.** Ottawa: The Department, 1964. 1 v. (unpaged). ill. Loc: OWTUR.

An outline of the King family's occupancy of James Colquhoun's property from 1886, including an imaginative reconstruction of everyday life in such a house circa 1891 by Mrs Nell Donaldson of Galt. The booklet also describes the renovation of Woodside from the 1940s until it was deeded to the federal government in 1954, as a memorial to Prime Minister Mackenzie King. Period: 1886 - 1954.

2414. Canada National Parks Branch: Department of Northern Affairs and National Resources. **Woodside National Historic Park, Kitchener, Ontario, Canada.** Ottawa: The Department, 1976. 9 p. ill., map. Loc: OWTUR, OWT.

A description of the boyhood residence of W.L. Mackenzie King, now a museum. A brief history of the house and the King family is followed by an account of the restoration and furnishings of the house. Period: c1876 - 1976.

2415. "Canadian architect yearbook award '70: Psychology building, University of Waterloo, Ontario." **Canadian Architect Yearbook.** 1970. Pp.30-1. ill., plans. Loc: OWTL, OWTU.

Reference from the Canadian Periodical Index. Period: 1970.

2416. **Catalogue of the contents of the residence of the late Edward F. Seagram, Esq., Bratton House, 22 Willow Street Waterloo, Ontario: compiled by order of the executors.** Toronto and Hamilton: Ward-Price Ltd, Auctioneers, 1938. 46 p. Loc: OWTUR.

Period: 1937 - 1938.

2417. City of Cambridge. **Heritage Conservation District Plan for Main Street (Galt).** 1984. 71 p. ill., plans. Loc: OKIT, OWTUR.

Analysis of features of Galt's historic city centre, the area bounded by Main Street, Ainslie Street, Imperial Lane and Water Street, as a basis for determining policies to ensure its viability, preservation and enhancement. The district is described as one of the outstanding historic streetscapes in Ontario, combining "visual unity and strength [with] a rich variety of architectural style and building age." The text and maps of the document constitute Schedule A for a projected City of Cambridge by-law. Period: 1862 - 1895.

2418. Clare, John. **Cambridge Mills walking tour: Preston walking tour.** Cambridge: Heritage Cambridge, 1982. 8 p. ill., map. Loc: OWTUR, OKIT, OCCA.

A guide including information about the history and architecture of outstanding buildings, in the context of a brief outline of Preston's development. Numbers on the map indicate the locations of the buildings. Period: 1802 - 1982.

2419. Coffey, Brian L. "Factors affecting the use of construction materials in early Ontario." **Ontario History.** 1985. 77,4: 301-318. maps. tables. Loc: OKIT, OWTL, OWTU.

Report of an analysis of the relationships

between ethnicity and the use of specific building materials and of economic conditions and the availability of materials as other significant factors. The examination of ethnic preferences for specific building materials is based on a sample of 11,813 heads of household from the 1851-2 manuscript census. The author notes that a greater proportion of Germans (70 per cent) lived in log houses than any other group. Period: 1851 - 1852.

2420. Coffey, Brian L. **The pioneer house in southern Ontario, Canada: construction material use and resultant forms to 1850.** University of Oregon (Ph.D. thesis, Geography), 1982. 210 p. maps, tables, bibl. Also mf (University Microfilms 8224826)

An analysis of early census and assessment roll data and from the Canadian Inventory of Historic Buildings, with a case-study of Augusta Township, Grenville County and a few references to the Waterloo area. The author refers on p. 84 to trends in round-log versus square-log construction for Wilmot Township in the 1830s, and on p. 110 to evidence suggesting that German settlers retained their log houses longer than other immigrant groups. Period: 1830 - 1851.

2421. Collishaw, Wendy and Williams, Bert. **The heritage homes of Kitchener: a calendar for 1982.** Kitchener: Allprint, 1981. 14 p. ill. Loc: OKIT, OWT.

A calendar with twelve paintings of Berlin homes built in the late nineteenth century. Short paragraphs describe the history and styles of the residences of prominent Berlin citizens, John Dauberger, Samuel Brubacher, Judge Anthony Lacourse, Nicholas Zeiger, Joseph Schneider, John Hoffman, Rev. Franz Herlan, Jacob Shantz, Jacob Staebler, Louis Breithaupt, L.J. Breithaupt and Benjamin Burkholder. Period: 1875 - 1899.

2422. Collishaw, Wendy. **Historic building inventory - Kitchener.** Kitchener LACAC, 1978. 100 p. Loc: OKIT.

An early inventory of 93 older buildings, all but four dating from before 1900. Systematic details are provided of plan and lot number, date of construction, original owner and use, present owner and use, material and condition, sources of information and historic significance. An index summarizes street addresses and dates of construction and there are maps of the districts in which buildings were inventoried. Period: 1838 - 1916.

2423. Cornish, C.R. **An architectural survey of Berlin: the central area.** University of Waterloo (student essay, History), 1979. 1 v. (unpaged). ill. Loc: OKIT.

A study of the architectural styles of pre-1914 houses in Berlin's Centre Ward, bounded by Frederick Street, Gordon Street, Lancaster Street, Victoria Street and King Street. The essay is illustrated by approximately 400 captioned photographs, arranged in geographical order by street address. Period: 1850 - 1914.

2424. Couling, Gordon. **Our heritage in stone: a helpful guide to an increased awareness of stone architecture in the Cambridge area.** Cambridge: Heritage Cambridge, 1978. 20 p. ill. Loc: OWTUR, OKIT, OCCA.

A description of stone buildings in Cambridge, noting types of stone, building techniques, some architectural details, pointing techniques and names of some stonemasons. Some buildings are illustrated. The author notes that most stonework dates from the 19th century though the Gore Mutual Insurance Company Building, built of granite fieldstone, was not completed until 1935. Period: 1816 - 1935.

2425. Couling, Gordon. "Stone masonry in Waterloo County." **Waterloo Historical Society.** 1975. 63: 32-43. Loc: all.

A discussion of the distinctive features of Scottish and Pennsylvania stonemasons, with descriptions of specific houses, churches, schools, mills and shops. Period: 1816 - 1896.

2426. **County of Waterloo Court House dedication ceremony, September 22, 1965.** Kitchener: Waterloo County Council, 1965. 9 p. ill. Loc: OKITW, OWTUR.

A brief history of the first Court House which was erected in 1853 and expanded in 1906, with a description of the new building which replaced the original in 1965 and a list of current councillors. Period: 1852 - 1965.

2427. Currie, L. Charleen. **A study of folk housing and regional architecture and the effects on the landscape of rural Woolwich Township, Waterloo County, Ontario.** University of Waterloo (B.E.S. thesis, Environmental Studies), 1973. 58 p. ill., bibl., maps. Loc: OWTU.

A study of farmhouses and barns, stressing the influence of Pennsylvania-Dutch styles. There are over forty drawings of buildings and architectural details such as fretwork, trellises, colour, eavestroughs and half-timbering, as well as a copy of Tremaine's 1861 map of the township, a physiographic map, and a map showing the locations of buildings described and illustrated in the thesis. Period: 1800 - 1973.

2428. Cutts, Anson Bailey. "The old Scottish architecture of Ontario." **Canadian Geographical Journal.** 1949. 39,5: 202-217. ill., maps. Loc: OKIT, OWTL, OWTU.

An essay that stresses Guelph but includes references to the styles of four Galt buildings: Knox's Presbyterian, Central Presbyterian, Galt Collegiate, and Kirkmichael. Period: 1830 - 1880.

2429. David, Raymond and Dilse, Paul. **Ayr's building heritage: a study of those buildings deserving preservation.** 1979. 56 p. ill., bibl., map. Loc: OCCA, OKIT, OWRE.

A survey and architectural description of the buildings of Ayr, with recommendations about which structures, or groups of buildings, should be preserved. A brief history of Ayr and a glossary of architectural terms are provided. Period: 1800 - 1979.

2430. Delhaise, Catherine and Delhaise, John. **Cornerstones: rural churches of southern Ontario.** Erin: Boston Mills Press, 1988. 100 p. ill. Loc: OKIT, OWRE.

A collection of drawings accompanied by brief histories. St George's Anglican Church, New Hamburg and Zion Lutheran Church, St Agatha represent Waterloo County. Period: 1863 - 1906.

2431. "Demolition of old landmark." **Waterloo Historical Society.** 1966. 54: 85. Loc: all.

A brief paragraph noting the destruction in 1966 of the Senate Building in Galt. It had been used as a weigh-scale office and informal meeting place for cattle buyers and politicians for about 100 years. Period: 1866 - 1966.

2432. **Designated buildings and buildings of historic and/or architectural significance: consolidated list updated August 15, 1991.** Cambridge LACAC, 1991. Loc: OWTUR.

A list of about 300 buildings by street address. Some 80 designated buildings and the 99 described by Dilse (1981) are identified, but with no further details. For the other buildings, the type and building material are stated, with some additional information in nearly half the cases about construction date, function and past owners. Street locations are indexed in the WRP database. Period: 1825 - 1930.

2433. **Designated landmarks in the City of Waterloo 1976-1982.** Waterloo LACAC, 1983. 35 p. ill., map. Loc: OKIT, OWT, OWTL, OWTUCG, OWTUR.

An illustrated description of fifteen designated buildings, mostly residences but including also the Roschman button factory and Molson's Bank. Period: 1850 - 1982.

2434. **Designated landmarks of the City of Waterloo.** Waterloo LACAC, 1987. 26 p. ill., map. Loc: OKIT, OWTUR, OWTL, OWT.

An illustrated description of twenty designated buildings, printed by Johanns Graphics. Period: 1850 - 1987.

2435. Diamond, Florence. "Re-opening of former Wilmot Township Hall at Black Creek Pioneer Village." **Waterloo Historical Society.** 1970. 58: 72-73. ill. Loc: all.

An account of the official re-opening of the old Wilmot Township Hall at Black Creek Pioneer Village near Toronto. The hall was built in 1858 by Jacob Beck in a style known as County Greek Revival. A new township hall, commemorating Canada's centennial, was opened in Baden in 1967. Period: 1858 - 1970.

2436. Dick, Jerry. **Conestogo historical buildings: a walking tour.** Woolwich LACAC, 1982. 1 folded sheet. ill., map. Loc: OWRE.

Architectural descriptions of 18 local residences, churches, blacksmith shops, and other business premises, in some cases accompanied by drawings and information about past owners. Period: 1850 - 1916.

2437. Dick, Jerry and Longo, Michael D. **Heritage driving tour of Wellesley Township.** Linwood: Wellesley LACAC, 1984 revised 1989. 28 p. ill., maps. Loc: OKIT, OWRE, OWRN, OWRSC, OWRW, OWTUCG.

A guide to historic structures including churches and cemeteries and commercial, residential and farm buildings in the communities of Wellesley, Crosshill, Linwood, Hawkesville, Heidelberg, St Clements and Bamberg. Kitchener Public Library holds copies of both original and revised editions. Period: 1832 - 1911.

2438. Dick, Jerry. **Jacob Dunke residence Elmira, Ontario (built circa 1891).** Woolwich LACAC, 1982. 25 l. ill., bibl. Loc: OWRE.

A report on the building situated at 2 William Street, Elmira, lot 21, plan 571, German Company Tract. Information is presented on successive owners, building plan and materials, structural condition, and historical and architectural importance. Architectural drawings of the interior, photographs, results of a title search, and additional biographical details for Jacob Dunke and Oscar H. Vogt are included. Period: 1891 - 1982.

2439. Dick, Jerry. **A study of a Waterloo County Pennsylvania German barn.** University of Waterloo (student essay, Architecture), 1978. 43 l. ill., plans, bibl. Loc: OWTUCGR.

A study of the "bank" or "Schweitzer" type of barn based on the example of the Bauman barn, built near Bloomingdale in 1843. The author identifies characteristics peculiar to this type of structure which is commonly built into the side of a hill. Aspects of building design and construction -- roof rafters and purlin, joints, floor beams and planks, sill, girders, masonry walls, doors and forebay -- are described with drawings and photographs. The role of the "framer", or person in charge of barn construction, is explained and interviews with former framers Amos Martin and Simeon Eby Martin are reported. Period: c1800 - 1978.

2440. Dick, Jerry and Longo, Michael D. **Wellesley: a guide to our historical and architectural heritage.** Wellesley LACAC, 1984 reprinted 1989. 1 folded sheet. ill., map. Loc: OKIT, OWRW.

A guide to 32 buildings including residences, stores, factories, hotels, churches and schools. Period: 1853 - 1927.

2441. Dickson, F.W.R. and Schmalz, W.H.E. and Schmidt, Grace. "Some interesting buildings, sites and plaques in Waterloo County." **Waterloo Historical Society.** 1972. 60: 100-107. map. Loc: all.

An annotated list of historic buildings, sites and plaques in all localities, with all sites marked on a county map. Period: 1800 - 1900.

2442. Dilse, Paul. **A remarkable heritage: programmes and policies for heritage conservation in Cambridge, Ontario.** Heritage Cambridge, 1981. 205 p. ill., maps, tables. Loc: OWTUR, OKIT, OWTL, OCCA.

A review of Cambridge's Official Plan, describing the city's architectural heritage, evaluating priorities for the conservation of buildings, outlining programmes for conservation, and formulating a conservation policy. The history of Cambridge from prehistoric times to the present is given, but the emphasis is on the nineteenth century. Hundreds of individual buildings are described and illustrated. The oldest buildings are identified and a table describes building periods from 1807 to 1910. A substantial bibliography is included, as well as a glossary of architectural terms, a summary of the heritage policies of other places, and lists of conservation contacts and organizations that give financial assistance to heritage projects. Period: 1807 - 1910.

2443. Dobbin, Margaret E. **Dreisinger furniture store, Elmira, Ontario (built circa 1870s).** Woolwich LACAC, 1986. 19 l. ill., maps, bibl. Loc: OWRE.

A report on the building situated at 7 Arthur Street North, Elmira, Lot 1, German Company Tract, plan 558, including a chronology of owners based on a land title search, an assessment of architectural and historical significance, and an account of renovations. Photographs illustrate the building's exterior and interior. Period: 1897 - 1986.

2444. Dobbin, Margaret E. **Fences of the Snider houses, St Jacobs, Ontario.** Woolwich LACAC, 1986. 11 l. ill., bibl. Loc: OWRE.

A report on the ironwork fences at 20 Albert Street and 16 Isabella Street, St Jacobs. The author also discusses cast and wrought ironwork generally and the problems of identifying the maker and age of a fence. Period: c1840 - c1900.

2445. Dobbin, Margaret E. **Klinck Feed Mill, Elmira, Ontario.** Woolwich LACAC, 1986. 25 l. ill., bibl. Loc: OWRE.

A history of the octagonal grist mill which was located at 14 Arthur Street, lot 15, plan 560 (parts 14 to 16), Woolwich Township. The author presents a chronology of owners based on a title search, describes its rare architectural style, and discusses its historical and architectural significance. She also includes a brief biography of George Klinck who built the mill. Period: 1904 - 1986.

2446. Dobbin, Margaret E. **Martin's blacksmith shop, St Jacobs, Ontario (built circa 1889).** Woolwich LACAC, 1986. 22 l. ill., bibl. Loc: OWRE.

Report on the shop building located at 30 King Street South, lot "Y", plan 605, G.W. Eby's Survey, lot 49, plan 1549, Woolwich Township. The author presents a chronology of property owners (based on a land title search) and describes the building's style, construction and significance. Period: 1889 - 1986.

2447. Dobbin, Margaret E. **Old Zuber Hotel, West Montrose, Ontario (built 1886).** Woolwich LACAC, 1987. 15 l. ill., bibl. Loc: OWRE.

Report on the building on R.R. #1, West Montrose, located on part of lot 74, German Company Tract, at the corner of Regional Road 86 and Township Road 55 (Zuber's Corner). The author presents a chronology of owners based on a title search, describes architectural style and significance, and outlines phases of construction and renovations. Period: 1868 - 1987.

2448. Dobbin, Margaret E. **School Section No. 6, West Montrose, Ontario (built 1874).** Woolwich LACAC, 1987. 19 l. ill., bibl. Loc: OWRE.

An architectural and historical profile of the building located at 171 Riverside Dr., West Montrose, German Company Tract Lot 74. The author presents a chronology of owners of the property and the building, describes the building's form and condition, and comments on its historical and architectural significance. Also included are an outline of renovations, a list of teachers since 1873, a class photograph from about 1922 (annotated with names), and other photographs of the building's interior and exterior. Period: 1874 - 1987.

2449. Dobbin, Margaret E. **Winterbourne blacksmith shop, Winterbourne, Ontario (built prior to 1871).** Woolwich LACAC, 1987. 16 l. ill., bibl. Loc: OWRE.

A brief architectural history of the building located at 14 Katherine Street North, Winterbourne, R.R. #2, West Montrose, plan 598, lot 7 in Woolwich Township. The report includes a chronology of ownership, details of the building's construction and architectural style, renovations since construction, photographs, and results of a land title search. Period: c1871 - 1987.

2450. Dobbin, Margaret E. **Winterbourne general store.** Woolwich LACAC, 1987. 16 p. ill. bibl. Loc: OWRE.

An architectural report on the store that was built before 1873 and later converted into a house. The author presents a chronology of property owners and describes the style, site and heritage significance of the building. Period: 1867 - 1987.

2451. "Downtown Waterloo - 1920." **Waterloo Chronicle.** 1979, July 11. Section B1-6. Loc: OWT.

A newspaper supplement that promotes the central business district by emphasizing its past. Photographs of historic buildings illustrate accounts of older businesses such as the Seagram Distillery and Waterloo Manufacturing Company. Period: 1920 - 1979.

2452. Duoba, Lilli. **Local heritage conservation in Cambridge, Guelph and Stratford, Ontario.** University of Waterloo (M.A. thesis, Regional Planning and Resource Development), 1988. 3 fiche. charts. mf. Loc: OWTUM.

A comparative appraisal of heritage conservation procedures, mainly since the passing of the Ontario Heritage Act of 1974 but with some historical background. Period: 1960 - 1988.

2453. "Early building dismantled." **Waterloo Historical Society.** 1958. 46: 12-13. ill. Loc: all.

A short history of the Waterloo Township Hall of 1848 which also served as a newspaper office and a church for three congregations. It was demolished in 1958 to make way for the expansion of Kitchener Public Library. Period: 1848 - 1958.

2454. Ennals, Peter M. **The development of farm barn types in southern Ontario during the nineteenth century.** University of Toronto (M.A. thesis, Geography), 1968. 110 l. ill., maps. Loc: OTU.

A non-circulating copy is held by the University of Toronto Library. Period: 1800 - 1900.

2455. Ennals, Peter M. **The Pennsylvania barn in Ontario.** University of Toronto (B.A. thesis, Geography), 1967. 39 l. ill. Loc: OLU.

Reference from **Bibliography of Ontario history, 1867-1976** (Bishop et al.). Period: 1800 - 1900.

2456. "Faculty Club, University of Waterloo, Ontario." **Canadian Architect.** 1971. 16: 41-5. ill., plans, tables. Loc: OWTL, OWTU.

Reference from the Canadian Periodical Index. Period: 1971.

2457. Faulkner, Louise. **The Cavanagh residence of Elmira, Ontario.** Woolwich LACAC, 1980. 24 p. ill. Loc: OWRE.

An architectural report on the structure believed to be the original farmhouse of the Cavanagh family, early pioneers in Woolwich Township. Located at 4 1/2 William Street, it was probably built in about 1874. The author presents a chronology of owners and a brief history of construction, alterations, condition and significance as a heritage site. There are photographs of the exterior, appendices summarizing land ownership from land records and assessment rolls, and sketch plans of the neighbourhood and interior layout. Period: 1807 - 1980.

2458. Faulkner, Louise and Herlovitch, Alex. **The Jackson residence.** Woolwich LACAC, 1980. 22 l. ill. Loc: OWRE.

A report on the building located on Woolwich Township Road 14, part of lots 89 and 90, German Company Tract. The authors present a brief history of construction, alterations and renovations, and an appraisal of its heritage significance. There are photographs and summaries of a land title search and of municipal assessment data. Period: 1807 - 1980.

2459. **First Woolwich heritage tour**. Woolwich LACAC, 1987. 40 p. ill. Loc: OWRE.

A binder containing descriptions of 15 historical sites included on a driving tour in May 1987. Also attached is the leaflet distributed on the actual tour, with historical and architectural details for a total of 20 sites. Period: 1807 - 1987.

2460. Fletcher, John. **The Burkhardt house: an architectural and historical landmark**. Waterloo LACAC, 1978?. 5 l. Loc: OWT.

A description of structural and architectural details of the building located on part of lot 21, plan 491. Built by Samuel Burkholder in 1849, it served as the area's first Evangelical church. Period: 1849 - 1977.

2461. Fletcher, John. **The Hilliard house: criteria for its designation as an architectural and historic landmark**. Waterloo LACAC, 1976?. 10 p. Loc: OWT.

A report recommending the designation of Thomas Hilliard's house at 88 William Street, Waterloo. It contains an architectural description of the house, biographical sketches of Thomas and W.L. Hilliard, and the results of a title search. Period: 1867 - 1976.

2462. Fletcher, John. **The Martin Mennonite Meeting House: criteria for its preservation**. Waterloo LACAC, 10 p. ill. maps. Loc: OWT.

An architectural description of the Mennonite meeting house on Lot 9 of the German Company Tract. It contains information on its interior layout and history, the results of a title search, a plan of its location, and photographs of the building. Period: 1805 - 1980.

2463. Fletcher, John. **The Wissler house: an architectural and historical landmark**. Waterloo LACAC, 1988?. 11 l. Loc: OWT.

A description of the structure and style of the building situated on part of lot number 62, German Company Tract, with a copy of the City of Waterloo's 1988 approval of a designated property grant and a brief biography of John Wissler who owned the Eagle Tannery. Period: 1842 - 1988.

2464. "Food services building, U of W." **Canadian Architect**. 1970. 15: 15-16. ill., plans. Loc: OWTL, OWTU.

Reference from the Canadian Periodical Index. Period: 1970.

2465. "Galt City Hall." **Waterloo Historical Society**. 1955. 43: 9. ill. Loc: all.

A photograph of Galt City Hall with the text of the inscription on its Diamond Jubilee Clock

(1897) and the names of the committee members responsible. Period: 1857 - 1897.

2466. Goodbody, Margaret. **The Peter Martin house: preliminary report**. Kitchener: Doon Heritage Crossroads, Historic Sites Department, Regional Municipality of Waterloo, 1986. 102 l. ill., tables, bibl. Loc: OKIT, OWT, OWTUCG.

An historical study of the Old Order Mennonite farmhouse which was moved to Doon Heritage Crossroads in 1975. The report provides some details of the Martin family and descendants but is primarily an architectural analysis of the house with photographs of the interior and exterior. Period: 1900 - 1914.

2467. Goodbody, Margaret. **Scottish settlement and farm architecture in Southern Waterloo County**. Doon Heritage Crossroads, Historic Sites Department, Regional Municipality of Waterloo, 1988. 102 p. ill., bibl., maps. Loc: OCLG, OKIT, OWRA, OWT.

A study of the buildings of Scottish settlers in North Dumfries Township before 1914, including farmhouses, barns and outbuildings of log, frame, stone and brick. Case studies of particular buildings describe in detail their history, architecture, and interior layout. The author concludes that the farm life of nineteenth-century Scottish settlers in Waterloo County was not very different from that on a Pennsylvania German farm, and that the Scots were influenced by international trends in their house building. Period: 1816 - 1914.

2468. Goodbody, Margaret. **Streetscapes and landscapes of rural Waterloo County, circa 1910**. Doon Heritage Crossroads, Historic Sites Department, Regional Municipality of Waterloo, 1986. 1 v. ill., bibl. Loc: OKDHC.

A study, based on municipal by-laws and photographs, of the roadways, sidewalks, fences, vegetation and electric and telephone lines that would have been visible in a Waterloo village early in the twentieth century. Period: 1906 - 1915.

2469. "Gore District Mutual Fire Insurance Company." **Royal Architectural Institute of Canada Journal**. 1937. 14: 206-208. ill. plans. mf. Loc: OGU.

A description of plans for the new head office building. Reference from the Canadian Periodical Index. Period: 1937.

2470. **A guide to the historical and architectural heritage of the Doon area of Kitchener**. Kitchener LACAC, 1983?. 1 v. [28 p.] ill., maps. Loc: OKDHC.

Walking and driving tours highlighting the landscape, buildings and architectural features.

The guide includes historical notes on prominent people and industries. Period: 1800 - 1984.

2471. Hale, Katherine and Stevens, Dorothy. **Historic houses of Canada.** Toronto: Ryerson Press, 1952. 152 p. ill. Loc: OKIT.

This book includes short descriptions of two Galt houses: Kirkmichael built for William Dickson, and William Tassie's house on Wellington Street (later owned by David Spiers). Period: 1833 - 1850.

2472. Hebblethwaite, Katherine. "Architecture and history in Galt and the neighbouring countryside." **Waterloo Historical Society.** 1970. 58: 17-20. map. Loc: all.

A report of a lecture sponsored by the Department of Continuing Education at McMaster University to foster a new branch of the Architectural Conservancy of Ontario. The lecture introduced a bus tour of distinctive Galt buildings dating from between 1830 and 1870. Period: 1830 - 1870.

2473. Hebblethwaite, Katherine and Taylor, Andrew W. **Architecture in Galt and countryside.** Waterloo: Waterloo Historical Society, 1970. 12 p. ill., map. Loc: OWTUR, OKIT.

Two articles, reprinted together for the Galt Branch of the Architectural Conservancy of Ontario from the Waterloo Historical Society's 1970 report. The original articles are each abstracted and indexed in the WRP database. Period: 1816 - 1970.

2474. Hebblethwaite, Katherine and Hulet, Marion. "Galt City Hall, 1857-1965." **Waterloo Historical Society.** 1965. 53: 6-10. ill. Loc: all.

An account of the construction and opening of the Town Hall and Market Building in 1856-1858 and its restoration in 1964-1965. Period: 1856 - 1965.

2475. Heritage Cambridge. **An heritage stone cottage, 89 Grand Avenue South, Cambridge, Ontario: conditions of purchase.** Community Heritage Fund of Heritage Cambridge, 1988. 34 l. ill. Loc: OKIT.

A detailed architectural description of John McDougall's Galt cottage, with recommended renovations and areas of reconstruction. Photographs and architectural drawings show the cottage's structure and points needing repair. Period: 1858 - 1988.

2476. Heritage Cambridge. **An historic driving tour of Cambridge: a car or bus tour of buildings in the city of Cambridge that are of historical or architectural interest. Also included: an historic walking tour of downtown Cambridge (Galt).** Heritage Cambridge, 1976. 16 p. ill., maps. Loc: OCCA, OKIT, OWTUR.

A guide to outstanding residential, public and commercial buildings, with numbers on the maps indicating the locations and correspond to descriptions in the text. A similarly planned walking tour of Galt, included in the back pocket, is separately indexed in the WRP database. Period: 1806 - 1976.

2477. Heritage Cambridge. **Historic Hespeler: a walking tour.** Heritage Cambridge, 1984. 1 folded sheet. ill., maps. Loc: OKIT, OCCA.

A guide to historic buildings in downtown Hespeler. Period: 1831 - 1920.

2478. Heritage Cambridge. **An historic walking tour of downtown Cambridge (Galt).** Heritage Cambridge, 1976. 1 folded sheet. Loc: OKIT, OCCA.

A guide to sites and buildings including Trinity Anglican Church, the Galt Public Library, the Market Building and Queen's Square. Historical and architectural descriptions are provided for residential, public and commercial buildings. The numbers of the descriptions correspond to numbers on the map. The walking tour is contained in the back pocket of **An historic driving tour of Cambridge.** Period: 1816 - 1967.

2479. Heritage Cambridge. **Old Galt historical walking tour.** Heritage Cambridge, 1988. 36 p. ill., map. Loc: OWTUR, OKIT, OCCA.

A guide to the history and architecture of various residential and commercial buildings, especially those constructed of stone. The numbers on the map show locations of the buildings and correspond to the descriptions in the guide. Period: 1816 - 1980.

2480. "Heritage edition." **New Hamburg Independent.** 1987-. Loc: OKIT, OWRW, OWRN.

Special editions of the newspaper, with articles on the history of Wilmot Township and Wellesley Township. Many old photographs of township subjects are reproduced and the articles contain varied material. The 1987 edition has an article on Shingletown, the 1989 edition has articles on the Indians of Wilmot Township, the Shrine of the Sorrowful Mother in St Agatha, and the 1990 edition has an article about School Section #17 in Philipsburg. The Kitchener Public Library and New Hamburg Library hold all editions; the Wellesley Library has those for 1991 and 1992. Period: 1800 - 1992.

2481. Herlovitch, Alex. **The Caspar Ruppel residence, Elmira, Ontario.** Woolwich LACAC, 1980. 24 p. ill. Loc: OWRE.

An architectural report on what is thought to be the oldest brick house in Elmira, built in 1856 at 31 Church Street East. The author lists the landowners and presents a history of the building with details of its construction, alteration, condition and significance. There are photographs of the exterior and the appendices include results of a land title search, property boundaries given in land deeds, a rough plan of the interior of the house, and assessment roll information. Period: 1808 - 1980.

2482. Herlovitch, Alex. **The Geisel residence, Elmira, Ontario**. Woolwich LACAC, 1980. 32 l. ill. Loc: OWRE.

An architectural profile of the building located at 80 Arthur Street South, Elmira, part of lots 4 and 5, plan 76 (formerly lot 88, German Company Tract). The author presents information on past owners, construction and architectural details, renovations, and the building's historical significance. There are also photographs of the site from 1923, appendices summarizing a land title search, a copy of the 1883 indenture, and municipal assessment data. Period: 1807 - 1980.

2483. Herlovitch, Alex. **Heritage conservation study for the village of Conestogo, Ontario**. University of Waterloo (B.A. thesis, Geography), 1981. 2 fiche. maps, tables, bibl. Loc: OWTUM.

A comprehensive inventory of the built environment, with brief explanations and photographs of early architectural styles. The author describes the contemporary streetscape and stresses the importance of creating a Heritage Conservation District to preserve landmark structures. Period: 1825 - 1981.

2484. Herlovitch, Alex. **The Martin residence, Elmira, Ontario**. Woolwich LACAC, 1980. 39 p. ill. Loc: OWRE.

A report on one of the region's few remaining log structures, at 103 Arthur Street, Elmira. The author presents a list of owners and a short history of the building with details of its construction, alteration, condition, site and significance. Photographs and drawings show the house, additions and the lot location. Appendices summarize land title information, land surveys, assessment roll data and census information. Period: 1807 - 1980.

2485. Hilborn, G.V. "The Registry Office." **Waterloo Historical Society**. 1939. 27: 84-86. ill. Loc: all.

A short history of Registry Office buildings of Waterloo County, with a detailed description of the new 1939 Kitchener Registry Office and a list of registrars from 1853 to 1939. Period: 1852 - 1939.

2486. Hilderley, Brad. **Designated and researched buildings of architectural and historical significance in the Township of North Dumfries**. North Dumfries LACAC, 1989. 80 p. ill. Loc: OKIT.

Brief illustrated descriptions of some 78 early buildings, with details for each of present owner, address, plan and lot, historical information and architectural description. The inventory is prefaced by an index to the original owners. The eleven properties designated by the LACAC between 1984 and 1989 are identified as owned originally by Mary Bishop, Alexander Cranston, Robert Cranston, Walter Heastie, Charles Johns, Angus McIntosh, Walter I. Reid, Scott's Corners School, Francis Tillie and Robert Wyllie. Period: 1830 - 1910.

2487. Hill, Nicholas. **Cambridge (Galt): a building facade plan**. 1987. 1 v. (unpaged). ill. Loc: OWTUR.

A summary report of the first phase of the Cambridge Building Facade Plan, designed to strengthen and improve Galt's historic building district on the south side of Main Street between Ainslie and Water Streets. A more detailed report was produced in 1984. Period: 1862 - 1895.

2488. Hill, Nicholas. **Cambridge (Galt): a Heritage Conservation District plan**. London: The Author, 1984. 71 p. ill. plans. Loc: OKIT, OWTUR.

A detailed report of the first phase of the Cambridge Building Facade Plan, intended to strengthen and improve Galt's historic building district on the south side of Main Street, between Ainslie and Water Streets. Each of the five business blocks -- the Granite Block, the James Young Block, the first and second Osborne Blocks, and the Buchanan Block -- is illustrated with drawings and discussed in terms of its building date, style and materials, current uses, and needs for renovation and restoration. Period: 1862 - 1895.

2489. Horne, Malcolm and Kolaritsch, Diane and Campbell, James. **An inventory of religious buildings of architectural/historical significance in the City of Kitchener**. Kitchener LACAC, 1985. 1 v. (various pagings). Loc: OKIT.

Reports on 24 buildings, with details of plan and lot, dimensions of site, date, owners, architectural description and significance. Six buildings are recommended for immediate designation: Church of St John the Evangelist, First Church of Christ Scientist, Zion United Church, St Matthews Lutheran, International Gospel

Centre (originally United Brethren in Christ), and St Paul's Evangelical Lutheran Church. Recommended for future consideration are St Mary's Roman Catholic, Bethany United Missionary Church, the Olivet Mission, former Beth Jacob Synagogue and the Ukrainian Catholic Church of the Transfiguration. Period: 1850 - 1920.

2490. "L'Hôtel de ville de Waterloo." **Architecture, Bâtiment, Construction.** 1959. 14: 342-7. ill. plans. Loc: OHM.
Reference from the Canadian Periodical Index.

2491. "House moved to Pioneer Village." **Waterloo Historical Society.** 1964. 52: 10. ill. Loc: all.
A note accompanying the picture of Christian Eby's home, moved from Madison Ave South, Kitchener to the Doon Pioneer Village. Period: 1854 - 1964.

2492. "House of Refuge razed in 1961." **Waterloo Historical Society.** 1961. 49: 34. ill. Loc: all.
A photograph and description of the Waterloo County House of Industry and Refuge, with a note of its demolition to make way for the new Salvation Army Eventide Home for elderly people. Period: 1868 - 1961.

2493. Husband, Susan. "Where the past overlooks the present." **Waterloo Historical Society.** 1962. 50: 18-21. ill. Loc: all.
A personal description of the Titus Shantz farmhouse in Kitchener which in 1962 was being surrounded by new houses. Biographical information about the Shantz family is also given. Period: 1806 - 1962.

2494. Janusas, Scarlett E. and MacDonald, John D.A. **The Waterloo County Gaol (AiHc-18) 1986 excavations.** Waterloo: Regional Municipality of Waterloo, Planning and Development Department, Archaeology Section, 1987. 69 p. ill. Loc: OWRMA.
A report on excavations undertaken to locate the remains of Reginald White, executed and buried at the gaol in 1940. It includes a brief history of the gaol building and various structural modifications since 1852 as well as a detailed account of White's trial. Period: 1852 - 1940.

2495. Junker, Alan W. **Township halls in Waterloo County, 1900-1914.** Kitchener: Doon Heritage Crossroads, Historic Sites Department, Regional Municipality of Waterloo, 1988. 240 p. ill., tables, bibl. Loc: OCLG, OKIT, OWRE, OWT.
An examination of the political and social roles of township halls as a basis for planning the restoration of the replica of the 1868 Waterloo Township Hall at Doon. Topics include the history

of Waterloo township halls from 1838 to 1914, their locations and architectural features, the structure of local municipal politics, and the use of the halls for political meetings and as community centres. Appendices contain lists of Waterloo County politicians and township officials from 1900 to 1914, including members of local boards of health. Period: 1900 - 1914.

2496. Kauk, Patricia J. **Berliner Journal: annual building summaries.** Kitchener Public Library, c1989. 1 file box. Loc: OKIT.
A set of translations of the annual summaries of new buildings and improvements published in the **Berliner Journal** newspaper, that are variously titled "Progress in Berlin," "New buildings in Berlin," and "Berlin's prosperity: new buildings and improvements." As explained in the introduction to the 1899 summary, the compilation of the list became more complicated as the town grew: in 1899 it required the better part of 6 weeks and depended on information provided by named contractors, builders and carpenters. The introductions usually comment on the current status of the building industry as an index to Berlin's business health and sometimes on notable new structures and trends in building materials and designs. Each annual list is usually organized by ward, then street, and presents details of the owner or person responsible for the building, type of structure or improvement, number of storeys, building material, and value. The file also includes translated lists for Elmira in 1887, Preston in 1895 and 1896, and Waterloo in 1900, 1901 and 1902. These translations are a valuable resource in dating individual buildings and city streetscapes. Period: 1873 - 1903.

2497. "Kitchener City Hall demolished." **Waterloo Historical Society.** 1973. 61: 72-73. ill. Loc: all.
A short note of the sale of the city hall to developers to make way for the downtown shopping centre. The author recalls the similar fate of the previous city hall in 1922. Period: 1898 - 1973.

2498. Kitchener LACAC. **A guide to the historical and architectural heritage of downtown Kitchener.** 1982. 34 p. ill. Loc: OKIT, OWTUR.
Three suggested walking tours through the city centre, the Victoria Park neighbourhood, and the market village. Drawings illustrate the brief descriptions of more than 50 sites including residences and business and public buildings. Period: c1820 - 1982.

2499. Kitchener LACAC. **Inventory of buildings: index.**
1991. 1 v. (unpaged). Loc: OKIT.
   An index by street and number to the 640
buildings inventoried and the 65 designated by
1991. Page references are provided to the
building inventories produced for Kitchener LACAC
by Collishaw, Campbell, Kobayashi, Shantz, Shea,
Simpson, Horne, Ryan, Kolaritsch, and Lamb.
Period: 1850 - 1930.

2500. Kitchener LACAC. **Waterloo County Jail: documents
relating to the closing of the jail and its
designation by Kitchener LACAC as a heritage
building, 1978-1981.** 1981. 1 v. (various
pagings). ill. Loc: OKIT.
   A collection of correspondence and reports about
the feasibility of restoring and re-using the jail
and the Governor's residence. Period: 1852 - 1980.

2501. "Kitchener Public Library and Knights of Columbus
Hall." **Waterloo Historical Society.** 1963. 51:
59. ill. Loc: all.
   A 1963 photograph of the old Kitchener Public
Library and the Knights of Columbus Hall in the
midst of demolition. The caption gives a brief
history of the buildings. Period: 1963 -

2502. Knight, Dean H. and Parker, L.R. Bud. **An
archaeological assessment of Cruickston Park Farm,
North Dumfries Township and City of Cambridge.**
Petersburg: Archaeological Research Associates,
1991. 1 v. (unpaged). Loc: OWRMA.
   An account of the development of the estate from
the 1850s by William Ashton and Matthew Wilks,
with a description of the various buildings
including the 3-storey manor and private brewery.
At its greatest extent the property included
nearly 2,000 acres. The estate, which belongs to
the University of Guelph, currently consists of
Lots 15 to 19, Concession 12, North Dumfries
Township; Lots 1,2 and 3 of Beasley's Old Survey;
and Lots 5, 6 and 7 of Beasley's Lower Block,
Period: 1853 - 1970.

2503. Kowalski, David J. "Pinke Street revisited."
Waterloo Historical Society. 1989. 77: 63-68.
ill. Loc: all.
   A history and description of Pinke Street, now
part of Weber Street in Kitchener, with emphasis
on what it was like prior to the Second World War.
Period: 1912 - 1989.

2504. Kyles, Kyles and Garratt, Architects. **The
original Waterloo County Jail.** Stratford: The
Consultants, 1979. 29 p. ill., plans. Loc: OKIT.
   Report of a feasibility study of the exterior
restoration of the original jail building, the
Governor's house and the yard walls. The authors

review suggested uses such as an archives,
restaurant, convention centre, boutiques,
historical display, recreational use, winter
garden, office space or arts workshop. Period:
1852 - 1978.

2505. Lamb, Kathryn Hansuld. "The inn at Rummelhardt."
Waterloo Historical Society. 1987. 75: 50-53.
ill. Loc: all.
   A brief history and description of the inn,
first owned by Charles Schaefer in the mid-1850s.
The author quotes parts of bylaw 30 of 1851, for
the regulation of inns and temperance houses, and
names subsequent owners including Sigmund
Freiburger, Jacob Kress and Casper Mahlman.
Period: c1852 - 1944.

2506. Lamb, Kathryn Hansuld. "Langdon Hall." **Waterloo
Historical Society.** 1990. 78: 117-125. ill. Loc:
all.
   A history of the country house built by E.
Langdon Wilks at Blair between 1898 and 1904, and
opened as hotel and conference centre in 1989.
Information about the Wilks and Langdon families
is provided. Period: 1858 - 1989.

2507. Lamb, Kathryn Hansuld. "Our vanishing heritage:
the 19th century barn." **Waterloo Historical
Society.** 1988. 76: 159-171. ill. Loc: all.
   A description of 19th-century barns in southern
Ontario, classified in six basic types:
Pennsylvania-German, English, Dutch, Central
Ontario, Lake Erie, and Wisconsin. Period: 1800 -
1900.

2508. "Largest house in the twin cities." **Waterloo
Historical Society.** 1960. 48: 50. Loc: all.
   A note of the removal of the 65-room house on
Willow Street, Waterloo, to make way for a new St
John's Lutheran Church. Originally one of the
Seagram family homes, the building was later used
for the K-W Orphanage. Period: 1872 - 1960.

2509. "Lecture building, University of Waterloo, Ont."
Canadian Architect. 1968. 13: 53-6. ill., plans.
Loc: OWTL, OWTU.
   Reference from the Canadian Periodical Index.
Period: 1968.

2510. "Lecture centre, University of Waterloo, Ontario."
Canadian Architect Yearbook. 1966. p.86. plans.
Loc: OWTL, OWTU.
   Reference from the Canadian Periodical Index.
Period: 1966.

2511. "Log house on Bridge Street, Waterloo, near
Lexington Road." **Waterloo Historical Society.**
1970. 58: 40. ill. Loc: all.

A photograph from the **Kitchener-Waterloo Record** showing the log house on Bridge Street, Waterloo. Period: 1970.

2512. Longo, Michael D. "John George Reiner house." **Waterloo Historical Society.** 1984. 72: 153-155. ill. Loc: all.

A description of the Reiner/Schmehl house, the first designated heritage landmark in Wellesley Township, with a brief biography of John G. Reiner. Period: 1832 - 1984.

2513. "Lower Doon inn razed in 1960." **Waterloo Historical Society.** 1960. 48: 54. Loc: all.

A note of the demolition of one of the earliest buildings in Doon, first built as an inn for Michael Wildfong and then used as a barn. Period: 1875 - 1960.

2514. M.M. Dillon, Ltd. **Sheave Tower foundation investigation.** 1988. 14 p. Loc: OKIT.

A report on the condition of the Sheave Tower at Blair, submitted to the Waterloo Regional Heritage Foundation, with estimates of repair costs. Period: 1876 - 1988.

2515. Macnaughton, Elizabeth. **Restoration and interpretation of the Wellesley Post Office: Waterloo County, 1914.** Kitchener: Doon Heritage Crossroads, Historic Sites Department, Regional Municipality of Waterloo, 1986. 66 p. ill., tables, bibl. Loc: OKIT, OWRW, OWT.

A report intended as a guide for historical interpreters and those involved in the restoration of the post office now housed at Doon Heritage Crossroads. It includes information on the early history of mail service in Canada, the postal service from 1851 to 1914, the functions of the post office in 1914, the history and setting of the Wellesley Post Office building, and a profile of George Bellinger who was postmaster at Wellesley at the turn of the century. Period: 1910 - 1914.

2516. Macrae, Marion and Adamson, Anthony. **The ancestral roof: domestic architecture of Upper Canada.** Toronto: Clarke Irwin, 1963. 258 p. ill. Loc: OCLG, OCH, OCP, OKIT, OWTL, OWTU, OWTUR.

An illustrated survey of building styles from 1784 to 1867, including plans of the Allison House in Galt (1855) and of Woodside in Berlin (1853) as examples of picturesque styles. Period: 1853 - 1855.

2517. MacRae, Marion and Adamson, Anthony. **Cornerstones of order: courthouses and town halls in Ontario, 1784-1914.** Toronto: Clarke Irwin, 1983. 283 p. ill. Loc: OCLG, OKIT, OWTL, OWTU.

A general survey of Ontario's early courthouses, township halls and town halls, including illustrations of the Waterloo County Court House of 1852 at Berlin, the Galt Town Hall of 1857, and Berlin's first Town Hall and Market House of 1870. Period: 1852 - 1871.

2518. Mader, Iva and Macnaughton, Sandra. **Breslau historical review: Ontario's bicentennial celebration in Breslau September 1984.** 1984. 26 p. ill., bibl., map. Loc: OKIT.

A history of the first settlers of 1815 and their farmsteads, with an illustrated walking tour and map of Breslau's historic buildings. Family names are all indexed in the WRP database. Period: 1815 - 1984.

2519. Maine, A.E. **Derivation of the essential history of an older property in Kitchener.** Kitchener: The Author, 1986. 1 v. (various pagings). ill., maps., bibl. Loc: OWTUR, OKIT.

A history of the house at 155 Margaret Avenue, Kitchener, that previously belonged to a member of the Breithaupt family. The author, who bought the property in early 1986, relates research conducted in a variety of sources, summarizes Breithaupt family history, and discusses the architectural style of his house in relation to some other houses in the region. Illustrations include sketches of the various houses, details of Italianate architectural styles, an extract of a 1947 fire insurance plan showing the Breithaupt Tannery, and a 1985 plan of the Mount Hope - Huron Park Neighbourhood. Period: 1893 - 1986.

2520. Martin, John. "Architecture in Waterloo County." **Waterloo Historical Society.** 1953. 41: 11-13. ill. Loc: all.

A short survey featuring photographs of six buildings: the house of H. Denis-Nathan in Galt, Amy Snider's house in St Jacobs, the Nelson Doering house and Lantz barn in Baden, the M.W. Keefer barn in Blair, and a road house at Petersburg. Period: 1800 - 1900.

2521. Martin, John. "Castles on the ground: the sign-posts of history." **Waterloo Historical Society.** 1956. 44: 63-64. Loc: all.

An address on the architecture of Waterloo County, emphasizing the need to preserve local architectural landmarks. Period: 1862 - 1956.

2522. Martin, John and Dickson, F.W.R. and Schmidt, Grace. **A guide to pleasant places and journeys of historic interest within the county of Waterloo.** Kitchener: Waterloo Trust and Savings Co., 1962 reprinted 1965,1967. 47 p. ill., index. Loc: OCCA,

OKIT, OWRA, OWRE, OWRN, OWRSC, OWT, OWTU, OWTUCGR, OWTUR, OWTUCR.

Four driving tours of Waterloo County. Concise histories of most towns and villages emphasize their buildings and architecture and are illustrated by John Martin. A second revised edition was produced in 1962 and a third in 1967 (published to commemorate Canada's centennial). Period: 1800 - 1900.

2523. "Maryhill hotel." **Waterloo Historical Society.** 1964. 52: 22. ill. Loc: all.

A photograph of the Commercial Hotel in Maryhill (New Germany), built by Mr Frank in 1864. Period: 1864 - 1964.

2524. McIntyre, Ronald B. **Heritage conservation and its role in urban design: a case study of uptown Waterloo.** University of Waterloo (B.E.S. thesis, Geography), 1985. 3 fiche. ill., maps, table, bibl. mf. Loc: OWTUM.

A reconstruction of the architectural history of the central business district as a basis for clear recommendations for the preservation and restoration of existing buildings and the whole area. The author recommends renovations to non-historic buildings, so that they may contribute to a coherent urban streetscape, as well as strategies for implementing legislation to promote heritage conservation. Period: 1840 - 1985.

2525. Mennonite Historic Interest Centre. **John E. Brubacher House: self guided tour.** Waterloo: Mennonite Historical Centre, 197-?. 7 p. Loc: OKIT.

An account of the John E. Brubacher family, property and farmhouse, with a summary of the restoration project. Period: 1850 - 1970.

2526. "Minota Hagey residence, University of Waterloo." **Canadian Architect Yearbook.** 1967. p. 70. ill. Loc: OWTL, OWTU.

Reference from the Canadian Periodical Index. Period: 1967.

2527. Moffat, Ruth and Plaxton, Beverly Bailey. **Stone houses: stepping stones from the past.** Erin: Boston Mills Press, 1984. 84 p. ill. Loc: OCLG, OCP, OKIT, OWTL, OWTU.

A pictorial history of old stone houses in Ontario, including the Brubacher House of 1850, the Holst Farm, the Ellis House of 1828, a Cambridge cottage, a fieldstone farmhouse at Crosshill, several identified cottages dating from about 1840, William Dickson's house, Kirkmichael (1832). There are also views of the Fisher House (probably in Cambridge) under construction and in completed form. Period: 1850 - 1880.

2528. Neal, Carolyn O. "Ontario barns." **3rd Annual Agricultural History of Ontario Seminar proceedings.** Edited by T.A. Crowley. Guelph: University of Guelph, 1978. Pp. 50-67. ill., map. Loc: OWTL, OWTU.

An analysis of the building styles of barns in Ontario from the 1820s to the late nineteenth century, including a description of the Pennsylvania bank barn type that combined the functions of storage and stabling. Period: 1825 - 1900.

2529. "New Hamburg buildings come down." **Waterloo Historical Society.** 1968. 56: 79. Loc: all.

A brief history of New Hamburg's 97-year-old town hall and 86-year-old fire hall, both replaced by new buildings in 1968. Period: 1871 - 1968.

2530. "New Hamburg houses." **Waterloo Historical Society.** 1972. 60: 14. Loc: all.

A short paragraph noting the publication of the Tweedsmuir history compiled by the New Hamburg Women's Institute as part of an architectural survey of the county. The book includes photographs of houses built before 1855. Period: c1855 - 1972.

2531. "New Waterloo County Building opened." **Waterloo Historical Society.** 1965. 53: 55. ill. Loc: all.

An account of the opening of the new county courthouse on 22 September 1965. Period: 1965.

2532. Oberholtzer, R.S. "Fences in Waterloo County." **Waterloo Historical Society.** 1958. 46: 42-45. ill. Loc: all.

An illustrated description of various kinds of fences, with special mention of Martin Loher who built stone fences in the Galt area in the later nineteenth century. Period: 1840 - 1913.

2533. Olaskey, Terry M. "A history of the Detweiler house: a restored log cabin at Doon Pioneer Village." **Waterloo Historical Society.** 1975. 63: 79-80. Loc: all.

A short history of the family and their property near Blair, with a note that the house was being moved to the Doon Pioneer Village and restored. Period: 1800 - 1975.

2534. "Old Elmira building demolished in 1959." **Waterloo Historical Society.** 1959. 47: 72. Loc: all.

A brief account of the demolition of the Snyder Furniture warehouse, previously a furniture factory owned by Heimbecker and Jung. Before that, it had been the property of Klinck and

Heimbecker. Period: 1859 - 1959.

2535. Page, Frank E. "The old fire hall at New Dundee."
Waterloo Historical Society. 1964. 52: 36. ill.
Loc: all.

A short history of the property once owned by
E.W.B. Snider. The author notes various buildings
on the site, beginning with the structure erected
by the Children of Zion about 1887. Both
Presbyterian and Methodist groups made use of the
property at the turn of the century, and during
the period from 1921 to 1933 it served as a
school, a garage and a residence. Period: 1887 -
1964.

2536. Page, Mary-Jean. "The White House on the river:
its role in the history of Greenfield." **Waterloo
Historical Society**. 1991. 79: 20-34. ill., map.
Loc: all.

A history of the house, first built in the 1830s
and later a part of the Greenfield Mills complex
developed by the family of John Goldie. The
author also provides detailed information about
the Goldie family and other Greenfield buildings.
Period: 1831 - 1991.

2537. Patterson, Nancy-Lou and Burke, Susan M.
"Mennonite Georgian: the Joseph Schneider Haus,
Kitchener, Ontario." **Canadian Collector**. 1983.
18,6: 25-30. Loc: OWTU.

A detailed account of the Joseph Schneider Haus
from cellar to the attic, describing construction
and the colours and furnishings of the rooms, with
their German names. Restored to its 1856
condition, the house was opened as a museum in
1981. Period: 1820 - 1983.

2538. Patterson, Nancy-Lou. "A wire fence around the
house: fencing traditions of Waterloo Region
Swiss-German Mennonite settlers." **Waterloo
Historical Society**. 1983. 71: 120-129. ill. Loc:
all.

An account of Mennonite fence customs, with
examples from recent and historical Mennonite
literature and artwork as well as photographs of
properties in the Waterloo region. Period: 1800 -
1983.

2539. Perrin, Jean. **A historical tour of Roseville**.
198-?. 29 l. ill., map. Loc: OKIT.

A guide for a tour of the Grand River, Orr's
Lake, Dickie Settlement School, Roseville Swamp,
Hallman Cemetery, the east end of Roseville, the
west end of Roseville and Black Horse Corners.
The author presents many details about the history
of buildings, churches, schools and businesses as
well as anecdotes about former residents.
Newspaper cuttings contain further information

about the community. Period: c1800 - c1985.

2540. "Preston house built in 1838." **Waterloo
Historical Society**. 1960. 48: 23. Loc: all.

A note of the demolition of the old Guggisberg
home in Preston in 1960 to make way for a gas
station. Period: 1838 - 1960.

2541. "Preston Town Hall gone." **Waterloo Historical
Society**. 1965. 53: 23. Loc: all.

A short note of the demolition to make way for a
new municipal complex. Period: c1865 - 1956.

2542. Priamo, Carol. **Mills of Canada**. Toronto:
McGraw-Hill Ryerson, 1976. 192 p. ill. Loc: OCLG,
OKIT, OWTL, OWTU.

A photographic essay on old Canadian mills,
surveying their architecture, functions and use of
water power. The two examples in Waterloo County
are Cambridge Mills (on the site first used for a
gristmill in 1807) and the Ferrie Mill at Doon
which, when built in 1834, was the largest
gristmill west of Montreal. Period: 1807 - 1975.

2543. Regional Municipality of Waterloo. **Chief
Administrator's report on the Waterloo County
Jail**. 1980. 1 folder (various pagings). Loc:
OKIT.

A memorandum on the status of the old jail and
some alternative proposals for its adaptive
re-use. Copies of 1978 reports by consulting
restoration architect, Peter John Stokes, are
appended. Period: 1852 - 1980.

2544. Reitz, Thomas A. **Historic building assessment:
Doon Heritage Crossroads**. Kitchener: Doon
Heritage Crossroads, 1989. 13 p. ill. Loc: OKIT.

An assessment of the structural stability and
interpretive integrity of buildings at Doon.
Updating an assessment undertaken in 1984, the
author describes the origin of each building and
comments on necessary repairs or additions.
Period: 1984 - 1989.

2545. Reitz, Thomas A. "The Peter Martin House
restoration: a photographic essay." **Pennsylvania
Mennonite Heritage**. 1991. 14,3: 2-9. ill. Loc:
OKIT, OWTUCG.

An illustrated account of the removal of the Old
Order Mennonite farmhouse to Doon Heritage
Crossroads and of its restoration using modern and
traditional techniques. Floor plans of the house
are included, giving both English and German names
for each room. The house, opened to the public in
1988, was originally located near Waterloo.
Period: 1800 - 1991.

2546. Rempel, John I. "The history and development of early forms of building construction in Ontario, part 2." **Ontario History**. 1961. 53,1: 1-35. ill. Loc: OKIT, OWTL, OWTU, OWTUCG.

A detailed analysis and description of the oldest buildings in Ontario, many of which were built of logs. There are two photographs of the 1820 log schoolhouse of Waterloo, with comments on its construction and design. Period: 1800 - 1850.

2547. Renusz, Linda C. **Conestogo Hotel (Oswald House)**. Woolwich LACAC, 1978. 31 l. ill. Loc: OWRE.

A report outlining the history of the building located at 2 Waterloo Street, Conestogo, lot 27 Kaufman Survey, plan 600. The author outlines the sequence of land ownership and construction and comments on architectural style and significance. The appendices present results of a land title search and photographs of the interior and exterior. Period: 1807 - 1978.

2548. Renusz, Linda C. **Conestogo United Church**. Woolwich LACAC, 1978. 21 l. ill. Loc: OWRE.

A history of the building situated on lot 11, north of King Street, east of Water Street, Conestogo (David Musselman's Survey, plan 601), Regional Road 17. The author outlines the chronology of land ownership, construction, restorations and renovations, and comments on the architectural and historical significance. Appended to the work is a copy of the article from the **Berlin Daily News** of 29 October 1878 (when the church was opened), a land title search, and photographs showing its Gothic style. Period: 1878 - 1978.

2549. Renusz, Linda C. **The Ebel residence, Conestogo, Ontario**. Woolwich LACAC, 1978. 27 l. ill., map. Loc: OWRE.

A profile of the building located on lot 41, German Company Tract, including a chronology of ownership, details of construction and architectural style, a land title search, assessment data, and photographs of the exterior and interior. Period: 1859 - 1978.

2550. Renusz, Linda C. **The former Hendry residence, Conestogo**. Woolwich LACAC, 1978. 37 l. ill., maps. Loc: OWRE.

An architectural and historical profile of the brick house located at 39 King Street West, lots 1 and 2, Kaufman Survey, plan 600. The author presents a chronology of property ownership and describes the construction, architectural style and significance. The appendices contain a biographical sketch of William Hendry, a title search, assessment data, an 1861 map of Conestogo, and photographs of the interior and exterior. Period: 1854 - 1978.

2551. Renusz, Linda C. **St Boniface Church, Maryhill, Ontario**. Woolwich LACAC, 1978. 26 p. ill. Loc: OWRE.

A profile of the Catholic Church of St Boniface of Maryhill, built in 1877. The author presents a chronology of land ownership and a short history and description of architectural details, style and significance as a heritage site. Photographs show many inaccessible interior details such as the inside of the steeple, the attic, the space between the roofs, the church bells, and the basement. Period: 1805 - 1978.

2552. Renusz, Linda C. **The Steiner residence, St Jacobs, Ontario**. Woolwich LACAC, 1978. 21 l. ill. Loc: OWRE.

A profile of the building located at 38 King Street, St Jacobs, Snyder Survey, lot 3, plan 605. The author present a chronology of ownership and describes architectural style, construction and historical significance. Appendices include a summary of a land title search, notes from assessment records, and photographs. Period: 1807 - 1978.

2553. Renusz, Linda C. **The Stroh residence, Conestogo, Ontario**. Woolwich LACAC, 1978. 36 p. ill., map. Loc: OWRE.

An architectural profile of the Stroh farmstead located on lot 7, Regional Road 17. The author outlines the chronology of owners and construction and comments on its architectural significance. Early photographs show the house as it was, and contemporary ones illustrate details of construction. A schematic site plan and land record information are appended. Period: 1820 - 1978.

2554. Renusz, Linda C. **The Wylie residence**. Woolwich LACAC, 1978. 26 l. ill., bibl., plans. Loc: OWRE.

An architectural and historic description of the building located at 75 Arthur Street South, Elmira, Wenger Survey lot 33 and 34, plan 560. The author includes details of ownership, construction, architectural style and historical significance, as well as photographs, a land title search, and assessment data. Period: 1855 - 1978.

2555. **Report on the archaeological excavations (1984) at the Waterloo County Gaol**. Thornhill: Foundation for Public Archaeology, 1988. 1 v. (various pagings). ill. Loc: OWRMA.

Analysis of structures and artifacts excavated at the Gaol complex in Kitchener, including a chronology of dates and events in the Gaol's history and analyses of the remains of the two convicted murderers hanged and buried in the gaol yard. Period: 1852 - 1978.

2556. Rieder and Hymmen, Architects. **The Joseph Schneider House: a feasibility study for restoration.** 1978. 1 v. (various pagings). ill., maps, bibl. Loc: OWTL.

A report recommending the restoration of one of the oldest residences in Kitchener as "a living museum depicting the way of life of Kitchener's Pennsylvania German pioneers." It outlines the social history of the house, lists other historic sites in the city, appraises the architectural features of the building, and estimates the costs of restoration. Period: 1820 - 1977.

2557. Ritz, Ernst and McNaughton, I.W. "New Hydro office in New Hamburg in 1963." **Waterloo Historical Society.** 1963. 51: 40. Loc: all.

The history of a building constructed by Jacob Morley as an electrical generating station, and demolished in 1963 when a new Hydro office was built in New Hamburg. Period: 1902 - 1963.

2558. Ritz, Ernst. "Ritz family home, New Hamburg landmark." **Waterloo Historical Society.** 1963. 51: 41. ill. Loc: all.

The history of a house built in 1853 by Charles Germann, later acquired by the Ritz family and sold in 1962 to the Bell Telephone Company. The building was demolished to make room for the extension of Bell's facilities in New Hamburg. Period: 1854 - 1963.

2559. Roger, Dieter. "From German pioneer building to 'Bauhaus' and beyond." **German-Canadian Yearbook / Deutschkanadische Jahrbuch.** 1978. 4: 135-167. ill. Loc: OKIT, OWTL, OWTUCG.

An historical survey of distinctively German features of architectural design and building technology in Canada between the 1790s and the 1970s. References to pioneer farmsteads in Upper Canada are relevant to Waterloo County though the county itself is seldom mentioned. Period: 1800 - 1970.

2560. Romahn, James. "Waterloo Firehall comes down." **Waterloo Historical Society.** 1966. 54: 86-88. ill. Loc: all.

A brief history of the firehall demolished in July 1966, with some comments on the work and social activities of the Waterloo firemen. Period: c1864 - 1966.

2561. Rosebrugh, Ben and Couling, Gordon and Corbett, John. **Dickson School: a photographic and historical tribute to Dickson School on the occasion of its centennial, 1877-1977.** Heritage

Cambridge, 1977. 1 folded sheet. ill. Loc: OKIT, OWTUR.

A brief commemorative history of the school, emphasizing its architecture. Period: 1877 - 1977.

2562. Rowell, Margaret. **The architectural history of the City of Waterloo, 1806-1914.** University of Waterloo (student essay, History), 1979. 47 p. ill., maps, index. Loc: OKIT.

An illustrated survey of the historical and architectural features of 36 buildings, including homes, schools, churches, and commercial and industrial structures. The family and corporate names of those who owned the buildings are all indexed in the WRP database. Period: 1806 - 1914.

2563. Rowell, Margaret and Rowell, Robert. **Historic tours of Waterloo: walking-driving tours, central residential and commercial area.** Waterloo: Waterloo Downtown Residents' Association, 1977. 18 p. ill., maps. Loc: OKIT, OWT.
Period: 1805 - 1977.

2564. Rowell, Margaret and Rowell, Robert. **Historic Waterloo: walking-driving tours, central residential and commercial area.** Waterloo: Waterloo Chamber of Commerce, 1983. 24 p. ill., maps, bibl. Loc: OWTUR.

The second edition of a brochure prepared by the Waterloo Downtown Residents' Association, describing two walking tours and one driving tour. Buildings of architectural interest are described and marked on a map. There is a short history of Waterloo, with an illustrated description of some local architectural styles and details. Period: 1805 - 1983.

2565. Rowell, Margaret and Rowell, Robert and Tittemore, Thomas. **Presentation of Kumpf House 172 King St. South, Waterloo, Ontario.** Waterloo LACAC, 1979?. 43 l. ill. Loc: OWT.

A comprehensive description of the building style and structure, illustrated by architectural drawings of interior and exterior. Biographical sketches are presented of the house's owners and residents, beginning with Abraham Erb who built the house in 1816. Appendices include a copy of Erb's last will and testament, newspaper stories and photographs relating to the site, assessment data, and excerpts from relevant articles in the Waterloo Historical Society's annual reports. Attached to the report is the brief presented at the review board hearing held in January 1979, documenting the architectural and historical significance of the site. Period: c1816 - 1979.

2566. Rowell, Margaret. "Wellesley Township Hall is restored." **Waterloo Historical Society**. 1973. 61: 30-31. ill. Loc: all.

An account of the successful efforts of the Waterloo Historical Society in restoring the facade of the township hall at Crosshill to its style in 1855. Period: 1855 - 1973.

2567. Rowell, Robert. "The structure of the Kumpf house." **Waterloo Historical Society**. 1974. 62: 71-75. ill. Loc: all.

A brief description of construction and various renovations since 1849, noting style and material clues to dates of additions. Also included is a history of ownership for the property from Abraham Erb's purchase in 1805 to Christian Kumpf's in 1869. Period: 1805 - 1973.

2568. Russell and Babcock, Architects. **Residence for Mr A.L. Breithaupt, Berlin, Ont.**. Tacoma, WA: The Architects, 1910. 20 l. ill., plans. Loc: OKIT.

Plans for a family residence which may never have been built. The drawings include both interior and exterior views and represent a style desired by members of Berlin's elite. Period: 1909 - 1910.

2569. Ryan, Don. **Heritage building inventory: Part 1 - Trussler-Laurentian Neighbourhoods; Part 2 - Huron Park, Brigadoon, Doon South, Pioneer Tower West Neighbourhoods**. Kitchener LACAC, 1991. 1 binder (unpaged). ill. Loc: OKIT.

A copy of the original report held in Kitchener City Hall, describing about 50 structures listed in the Historical Buildings Inventory. In addition to the architectural descriptions of each building, the author discusses such factors as the age of the structure, the urgency of the demolition threat, and the distinctiveness or typicality of the style. Period: 1820 - 1900.

2570. Sararus, Miriam. "New Dundee store is designated." **Waterloo Historical Society**. 1985. 73: 49-51. ill. Loc: all.

Reprinted from the **Ayr News**, an account of the designation of the Emporium on 17 November 1985 as an historic site, the first structure to be designated in Wilmot Township. The author outlines the history of the building, naming past owners and employees. Period: 1887 - 1985.

2571. Sarler, Robert and Schmidt, Paul and Wilson, G.E. Duff. **Photos of buildings in Ayr and area**. 1974. 37 p. ill. Loc: OWRA.

An unpublished album of photographs with accompanying text, compiled at the time of Ayr's 150th anniversary. The collection consists of mainly contemporary views of residential and

commercial buildings but includes old, rare photographs as well. Period: c1824 - 1974.

2572. Schenk, Alfred J. and Good, E. Reginald. "The Bricker barn." **Waterloo Historical Society**. 1977. 65: 93-97. ill. Loc: all.

A detailed description of the barn built by Samuel Bricker in 1839, with an account of its dismantling and removal from its Huron Road location to the Doon Pioneer Village. Period: 1802 - 1977.

2573. "Schnurr Store, Linwood, about 1895." **Waterloo Historical Society**. 1964. 52: 29. ill. Loc: all.

A brief history of the store, built in 1858 and still operating in 1964, with an 1895 photograph and some details about the Schnurr family. Period: 1828 - 1964.

2574. Scott, Alison. **The history of the Kent Hotel**. 1985. 28 p. bibl., map. Loc: OWT.

A well-researched report on the building, owners and managers of the hotel at 59 King Street North, Waterloo. Established as a brewery and inn by William Rebscher in 1842, it was later named the Lion Brewery by the Huether family, and in 1975 became the Kent Hotel owned by Bernard and Sonia Aldys. Period: 1842 - 1985.

2575. Seiling, Ken. **Early buildings in the Bridgeport, Ontario area**. Waterloo Lutheran University (B.A. thesis, History), 1969. 104 l. ill., maps, bibl. Loc: OWTL, OKIT.

An inventory of historically significant buildings in the village of Bridgeport, then in Waterloo Township. In all, 55 locations are listed, four of which are discussed at length: the Klie (Daniel Erb) log house, the Bauer (Peter Erb) house, the Bridgeport Mill, and the Shoemaker house. The buildings exemplify various architectural styles including Georgian, Neo-Classicism, Colonial Regency, Classical Revival, Gothic Revival and Italianate. The author outlines his use of sources such as land titles and deeds, assessment and tax collection records, census reports, maps and surveys, newspapers, photographs and directories, in determining construction dates before 1855. Period: 1807 - 1856.

2576. **A selected index to Kitchener building resources available in the Grace Schmidt Room**. Kitchener Public Library, 1991. 1 v. (unpaged). Loc: OKIT.

An index, by street address, to buildings described in the following inventories -- the Vertical Files on the American Hotel, Bridgeport, Buttons, Doon, K-W YMCA, Historic Buildings - Kitchener, History - Kitchener, LACAC - Kitchener,

Post Office - Kitchener, Waterloo County Jail, Cornish, Lamb on Bridgeport, Seiling on Bridgeport, and the Kitchener LACAC guides to Kitchener. This index has entries for a selection of historic buildings that is similar to that in Kitchener LACAC inventory dated November 1991. Period: 1830 - 1930.

2577. Shantz, Cameron. **Inventory of buildings of historical and/or architectural significance.** Kitchener LACAC, 1980. 201 p. ill. Loc: OKIT.

Systematic descriptions of some 87 buildings on the west side of Kitchener that were considered old, historically or architecturally significant, beautiful or out of context with neighbouring buildings. Most are houses. Eight properties are recommended for immediate designation and 16 for future consideration. Details include date, original and other significant owners, notes on architectural style and historical interest, and summary of title search. Period: 1850 - 1900.

2578. Shantz, Cameron and Campbell, James and Kobayashi, Jack. **Upper Doon building inventory.** Kitchener LACAC, 1980 - 1986. 36 p. Loc: OKIT.

Reports on 18 properties located on or near Doon Village Road. For each property there are details of plan and lot, zoning, frontage, date of construction, original owner, current owner, full architectural description, title search, architectural and historical significance. The properties include industrial buildings and sets of workers' rowhouses related to the flax mill and brickyard, as well as the designated residence of Moses Perine of the Doon Twines Company. Period: 1850 - 1900.

2579. Shea, Patti. **Historic buildings inventory.** Kitchener LACAC, 1989. 70, 88 p. ill. Loc: OKIT.

A collection of reports on 29 properties, including details of address, lot and plan, present owner, date constructed, original owner and significant later owners, title search, architectural description, and usually several illustrations. Volume 1 includes reports on St Jerome's High School, the Cluett Peabody factory on Benton Street, York Apartments, Barra Castle Apartments and Buena Vista, and the Nelson Terrace on Courtland Avenue, as well as several residences on Courtland Avenue East and Queen Street South. Volume 2 includes the Boehmer box factory on Duke Street, a former Berlin Firehall, the Kaufman Rubber factory, the Rumpel Felt factory, several business blocks on King Street West, and various residences on Margaret Avenue, Ahrens West, Church, Courtland West, David, Frederick, Highland West and Oak Streets. Period: 1850 - 1920.

2580. Shea, Patti. **An inventory of historic buildings in the Victoria Park Secondary Plan Area, City of Kitchener.** Kitchener LACAC, 1988. Loc: OKIT.

Detailed descriptions of the architectural features and historical significance of 16 houses, most of which were built between 1896 and 1914. The properties are on Courtland Avenue East, David Street, Heins Avenue, Hilda Place, Linden Avenue, Oak Street, Queen Street South, Roland Avenue, Victoria Street South, Henry Street, and Water Street South. Information is provided on plan and lot number, present owner and use, date constructed, original owner and use, significant later owners, and architectural description including materials and style on each elevation. Title search results and photographs are added in each case and relevant descriptions in earlier inventories are included in an appendix. Period: 1880 - 1914.

2581. Shewchuk, John P. **Historical analysis of the Waterloo Arena property.** Waterloo: City of Waterloo, 1989. 20 p. bibl., maps. Loc: OWT.

A study of land use and development in the Silver Lake area of Waterloo from 1805, when Abraham Erb built sawmills there, to the erection of the arena following the Second World War. Built on a landfill site, the arena was eventually demolished because it was sinking. The site was subsequently considered as the site for the Regional Headquarters. The report is illustrated with maps of eight time periods. Period: 1805 - 1988.

2582. Shoemaker, Dorothy. "Kitchener's new main public library." **Royal Architectural Institute of Canada Journal.** 1959. 36: 115. Loc: OWTU.

Reference from the Canadian Periodical Index. Period: 1959.

2583. Shoemaker, Dorothy. "Random notes on the new Kitchener Public Library building." **Ontario Library Review.** 1962. 46: 152-4. Loc: OKIT, OWTL, OWTU.

Reference from the Canadian Periodical Index. Period: 1962.

2584. "Snyder barn at Ottawa and Franklin Streets, Kitchener levelled [WRP]." **Waterloo Historical Society.** 1965. 53: 79. ill. Loc: all.

A photograph of the barn built in 1830 and razed to make room for St Daniel Separate School, Kitchener. Period: 1830 - 1965.

2585. Sokvitne, Miriam Snyder. "The historic buildings inventory." **Waterloo Historical Society.** 1970. 58: 80-81. Loc: all.

A report of a historic buildings inventory

conducted by the School of Architecture at the University of Toronto in co-operation with the Waterloo Historical Society in Waterloo County. The author remarks on 145 houses built in 1855 or earlier and 52 houses dating from the 1856-1865 period. Information about the kinds of houses described in the assessment rolls of 1833, 1840 and 1848 is summarized. Period: 1855 - 1970.

2586. Sokvitne, Miriam Snyder. "The Joseph Schneider House, 1820." **Waterloo Historical Society**. 1966. 54: 20-27. ill. Loc: all.

A description of the farmhouse on Lot 17 of the German Company Tract, now 466 Queen Street South in Kitchener, including a plan of the house, a detailed account of the workmanship in each room and short profiles of early family members. The author quotes the inscription on the plaque unveiled on 29 July 1966, designating the house as an historic site. Period: 1820 - 1966.

2587. Stauch, Warren. "Preserving Waterloo Region's architectural heritage." **Waterloo Historical Society**. 1980. 68: 61-70. ill. Loc: all.

An account of the efforts to conserve architectural landmarks, including organizations and programmes under the Ontario Heritage Act such as Local Architectural Conservation Advisory Committees (LACACs). Historic sites in the region are identified, including the John E. Brubacher house, the Erb- Kumpf house, the Kuntz house, all in Waterloo, and the Joseph Schneider house in Kitchener. Period: 1974 - 1980.

2588. Stauch, Warren. "Preston Public School." **Waterloo Historical Society**. 1975. 63: 77-78. ill. Loc: all.

A short architectural history of the two school buildings, the first built in 1853 and the second in 1889 (to be demolished according to a decision in 1975). Some information is taken from a manuscript by Otto Klotz who served on the Preston Board of Education from 1847 to 1891. Period: 1847 - 1975.

2589. Stauch, Warren. "Society erects two plaques." **Waterloo Historical Society**. 1974. 62: 44-45. ill. Loc: all.

A short note accompanying photographs of the Waterloo Historical Society plaques unveiled in 1974 at the Wellesley Township Hall at Crosshill and the John Watson Manufacturing Company at Ayr. Period: 1847 - 1974.

2590. "Strasburg School." **Waterloo Historical Society**. 1965. 53: 76. ill. Loc: all.

A photograph of the 95-year old brick school closed in 1965 and burned down in a training

exercise for firemen. Period: 1870 - 1965.

2591. Taylor, Andrew W. "Architectural Conservancy Seminar rural bus tour." **Waterloo Historical Society**. 1970. 58: 21-26. Loc: all.

An itinerary of a bus tour of various architectural landmarks in North Dumfries Township. Period: 1850 - 1970.

2592. Taylor, Andrew W. "Historical plaque for Galt City Hall." **Waterloo Historical Society**. 1971. 59: 79. Loc: all.

A report of the designation of the 1857 building as an historic site. Describing the Town Hall and Market House designed and built by H.B. Sinclair in the Italianate style, the author quotes H.B. Timothy's opinion that Galt's town hall is "an architectural replica of a Border townhall." Period: 1857 - 1971.

2593. Taylor, Andrew W. "Some early history of the Galt Collegiate." **Waterloo Historical Society**. 1958. 46: 14-15. ill. Loc: all.

A history of the structure on North Street, Galt, built in the 1840s as a Methodist chapel. It became the Girls' School Division of the Galt Collegiate Institute in 1872, was later the Galt Armoury and in 1958 became a Lutheran church. Period: 1840 - 1958.

2594. Taylor, Shirley A. **The battle to save Preston Public School: the story of the conversion of Preston Public School to senior citizens' apartments**. Heritage Cambridge, 1985. 1 folded sheet. ill. Loc: OKIT, OCCA.

An account of how the school, scheduled for demolition in 1974, was saved and restored. The author discusses results of this conservation project and outlines the history of the school. Period: 1853 - 1985.

2595. Thompson, Hugh. **Picturesque Cambridge, v.1: a pictorial essay**. Cambridge: The Author, 1990. 1 v. (unpaged). Loc: OKIT, OCCA.

A book of pen-and-ink sketches of buildings and structures in Cambridge, many of them in stone. Some of the buildings no longer exist. No historical information is given about the buildings but their locations are noted. Period: 1820 - 1930.

2596. "Thornhill, historic Galt home: 32 McKenzie Street, Galt." **Waterloo Historical Society**. 1961. 49: 30. ill. Loc: all.

A photograph of James Young's house with a description quoted from an article by Earl Werstine. Period: c1865 - 1961.

2597. Turnbull, William C. "Stone masonry arches for railway culverts." **Waterloo Historical Society**. 1963. 51: 52-53. ill. Loc: all.

A description of the four masonry arches built through an embankment on the Harrisburg-Galt branch line of the Great Western Railway. The author quotes local oral traditions that the stone was quarried in Britain and imported ready to assemble. Period: 1850 - 1860.

2598. "University of Waterloo." **Royal Architectural Institute of Canada Journal.** 1962. 39: 45-54. ill. Loc: OWTU.

Reference from the Canadian Periodical Index. Period: 1962.

2599. "Vogelsang home." **Waterloo Historical Society**. 1963. 51: 69. ill. Loc: all.

A photograph of the Vogelsang home in Kitchener with a note that it was built by Emil Vogelsang about 1873 and demolished in 1963. Period: 1873 - 1963.

2600. Walker, Blair. **Heritage inventory: homes of prominent businessmen and professionals.** Kitchener LACAC, Loc: OKIT.

Descriptions of 27 houses built for Berlin business leaders, with an appendix listing former elite houses that have been demolished. The compiler provides plan and lot numbers, original and present owners, and results of title search. Quite detailed information is given on personal biography and business history, but there are no photographs of the houses or detailed descriptions of their architectural features. Persons featured in this inventory are William P. Clement, Gerald Eastman and John G. Martin of Clement, Eastman, Dreger, Martin and Meunier; Charles H. Doerr, Weybourne E. Doerr and Carl M. Dare of Dare Foods; John A. Vila and Henry Knell of the Economical Mutual Fire Insurance Company; Arthur C. Greb and Harry D. Greb of the Greb Shoe Company; John D.C. Forsyth of John Forsyth & Co.; A.R. Kaufman and J.T.("Sam") Hill of Kaufman Footwear; Paul Motz and John E. Motz of the **Kitchener-Waterloo Record**; Albert E. Ruby, Leonard W. Ruby and Brian J. Ruby of Krug Furniture; Jacob M. Staebler and Keith Staebler of Staebler Insurance. The houses were nearly all built between 1900 and 1940. Period: 1900 - 1940.

2601. "Warehouse houses School of Architecture." **Architecture Canada.** 1969. 46: 22. ill., plans. Loc: OWTU.

Reference from the Canadian Periodical Index. Period: 1969.

2602. Waterloo Chamber of Commerce. **Waterloo walkabout: an historical walking tour**. Waterloo: Waterloo Chamber of Commerce, 1987. 1 p. ill., maps. Loc: OKIT, OWTUR.

Guides for two tours in the older areas of the city, including short descriptions of architectural styles of many residences and commercial buildings. In some cases a brief history of the buildings names their original owners or explains their uses. Period: 1805 - 1914.

2603. "Waterloo churches entrance exchange." **Waterloo Historical Society**. 1960. 48: 71. Loc: all.

A brief statement that the Gothic doorway of the burned-out St John's Lutheran Church, Waterloo was used in the reconstruction of the front of St Louis Roman Catholic Church, Waterloo. Period: 1959 - 1960.

2604. "Waterloo City Hall." **Waterloo Historical Society**. 1969. 57: 30-31. ill. Loc: all.

A report of the demolition of Waterloo City Hall to make way for the Stanley Marsland building, with a brief history of the building and its various municipal functions. Period: 1874 - 1969.

2605. Waterloo Department of Planning and Development. **Snyder Gingrich log house utilization feasibility study**. Waterloo: The Department, 1989 - 1990. 3 v. Loc: OKIT.

Reports of a study of potential uses for the log house located on the northern boundary of the City of Waterloo (formerly Waterloo Township to 1972). Built in 1839 by Joseph Schneider and occupied by successive generations of the Snyder and Gingrich families, the house is believed to be one of the largest log houses in southern Ontario and one of the oldest surviving structures in Waterloo. There is very little information on the history of the house and property, most of each report being concerned with current options for their re-use. Period: 1839 - 1989.

2606. Waterloo Downtown Residents' Association. **Tour Waterloo: downtown Waterloo & Bechtel Parks.** Waterloo: Waterloo Chamber of Commerce, 1980. 22 p. maps, bibl. Loc: OKIT, OWTUM, OWTUR.

Two walking tours and one driving tour, with historical information on the buildings in each city block. A brief explanation of architectural styles is included on pages 6-7. Period: 1812 - 1950.

2607. Waterloo-Wellington Museum and Art Gallery Collaborative. **Waterloo-Wellington driving tour: museums and art galleries.** 1992. 60 p. ill., maps. Loc: OKIT.

A driving tour linking the following Waterloo County museums: Doon Heritage Crossroads, the Library and Gallery of Cambridge, the Kitchener-Waterloo Art Gallery, the Homer Watson House and Gallery, the Seagram Museum, the Joseph Schneider Haus Gallery and Museum, the Kitchener-Waterloo Art Gallery, and Woodside National Historic Park. There are descriptions and photographs of many historic sites and buildings along the route. A walking tour from the Joseph Schneider Haus to the Kitchener-Waterloo Art Gallery is included. Period: 1800 - 1992.

2608. **Wellesley Township heritage buildings: calendar 1985.** Wellesley LACAC, 1984. 24 p. ill. Loc: OKIT.

A calendar of twelve drawings of historical buildings, with brief descriptions of architectural style and ownership history. Period: 1856 - 1910.

2609. "When was this house built?." **Waterloo Historical Society.** 1965. 53: 35. ill. Loc: all.

A brief history of the house at 172 King Street South, Waterloo, beginning with the transfer of the property in 1805 from Daniel and Jacob Erb to Abraham Erb. The article also notes the adoption of Barnabas Devitt by Abraham Erb and provides other details on the Devitt family. Period: 1805 - 1899.

2610. Wightman, W.R. "Construction materials in colonial Ontario, 1831-61." **Aspects of nineteenth century Ontario.** Edited by F.H. Armstrong et al. Toronto: University of Toronto, 1974. Pp. 114-134. maps. Loc: OKIT, OWTL, OWTU.

A study of the mid-nineteenth-century transition in the use of building materials in different parts of the province. Four maps show percentages of frame, log, stone and brick buildings for all townships and urban centres in 1851 and 1861. Period: 1831 - 1861.

2611. Zimmerman, Idessa. "Bridgeport blacksmith shop dismantled in 1962." **Waterloo Historical Society.** 1962. 50: 40, 47. ill. Loc: all.

A short illustrated history of the village blacksmith shop started in Bridgeport by Philip Koeber, with a note that it may have been used originally as a distillery. Period: 1830 - 1962.

2612. Zimmerman, Idessa. "Bridgeport Free Church." **Waterloo Historical Society.** 1970. 58: 26. Loc: all.

A report on the condition of Bridgeport Free Church and cemetery since 1965. The building was badly damaged by fire in 1968, but the Bridgeport Women's Institute decided to make its restoration one of their projects. Period: 1965 - 1970.

2613. Zimmerman, Idessa. "Uncle Tom's Cabin." **Waterloo Historical Society.** 1974. 62: 25. Loc: all.

A drawing of the Bridgeport inn demolished in 1974. Period: 1850 - 1974.

URBAN ENVIRONMENTS, INCLUDING PLANNING STUDIES AND POLICIES

2614. Atcheson, John Peter. **An evaluation of the urban renewal scheme proposed for downtown Kitchener: a regional view.** Waterloo Lutheran University (B.A. thesis, Geography), 1968. 92 l. ill., maps, bibl. Loc: OWTL.

An examination of the city's urban renewal plans and the implications for Waterloo County as a whole. Using an urban renewal planning scheme outlined in the initial chapters, the author finds a lack of understanding on the part of all levels of government of Kitchener's role in relation to the rest of the county. He argues that current planning strategies for the central business district do not reflect actual economic and social needs. Period: 1963 - 1968.

2615. Bloomfield, Elizabeth. "Economy, necessity, political reality: town planning efforts in Kitchener-Waterloo, 1912-1925." **Urban History Review.** 1980. 9,1: 3-48. ill., maps, bibl. Loc: OWTU, OWTUR, OWTL, OKIT.

A detailed analysis of two distinct phases of city planning ideas and proposals. The second, in which Thomas Adams and Horace Seymour were the professional planners, led to the Kitchener's adoption of Canada's first urban zoning by-law. Stages in the planning process are reconstructed mainly from records of the municipal councils and boards of trade and from the daily newspapers. The history of the planning movement is presented in five parts: the background to the formation of the Berlin Civic Association in 1912, the plan by Charles Leavitt in 1913-14, the revival of interest in planning by the Kitchener City Planning Commission from 1917, negotiations for the comprehensive plan by Thomas Adams and Horace Seymour from 1921 to 1924, and an assessment of the lasting significance of these planning efforts. This article was reprinted in a revised version as a chapter in the volume **Shaping the urban landscape: aspects of the Canadian city-building process** in 1982. Xerox copies of the article are held by the University of Waterloo Library's Doris Lewis Rare Book Room and Kitchener Public Library's Grace Schmidt Room of Local History. Period: 1911 - 1930.

2616. Bloomfield, Elizabeth. "Reshaping the urban landscape? Town planning efforts in Kitchener-Waterloo, 1912-1925." **Shaping the urban landscape: aspects of the Canadian city-building process.** Edited by Gilbert A. Stelter and Alan F.J. Artibise. Ottawa: Carleton University Press, 1982. 256-303. ill., maps, bibl. Loc: OWTU, OWTL.

A slightly revised version of the original article in the **Urban History Review**, with more detail on the period prior to 1912. Period: 1900 - 1930.

2617. Bloomfield, Elizabeth. "Ubiquitous town planning missionary: the careers of Horace Seymour, 1882-1940." **Environments: a Journal of Interdisciplinary Studies.** 1985. 7,2: 23-29. ill., maps, bibl. Loc: OWTL, OWTU.

A biographical appraisal of a pioneer planner who practised in all parts of Canada in the interwar years. Seymour was largely responsible, as the associate of Thomas Adams, for the 1922-4 plan and zoning scheme for Kitchener-Waterloo. Period: 1920 - 1940.

2618. Bradley, F.B. **Necrogeography in Kitchener-Waterloo.** University of Waterloo (B.E.S. thesis, Geography), 1979. 1 fiche. 74 p. maps. mf. Loc: OWTUM.

A study of the themes of architecture, cultural landscape, religious segregation and language in the five cemeteries of First Mennonite Church, Beth Jacob, Mount Hope (Kitchener and Waterloo) and Kinzie-Bean Pioneer Memorial (now in Doon Heritage Crossroads). Period: 1806 - 1975.

2619. Breithaupt, W.H. "Some features of town planning, with application to the city of Kitchener." **Town Planning Institute of Canada Journal.** 1921. 1,6: 5-8. map. Loc: OWTU.

A summary of the physical development of Kitchener and the need for various improvements including grade separation of railway crossings, a radial system of main thoroughfares, building line setbacks to allow streets to be widened into parkways, and the development of a civic centre surrounded by public buildings. Period: 1853 - 1920.

2620. Brown, Gregory N. and Corfield, Geoffrey and Hermsen, Bernard. **Development concept and proposals for Doon Pioneer Village, Kitchener, Ontario.** Waterloo: University of Waterloo, School of Urban and Regional Planning, 1974. 26 p. ill., maps. Loc: OWTU, OKIT.

A plan to coordinate the buildings of Doon Pioneer Village into distinct thematic areas such as the museum area, the farm display area, the pioneer village, the Indian village, the Victorian village and the workshop area. There are suggestions for landscaping, planting and enhancements of existing facilities. Period: 1973 - 1974.

2621. Canadian Systems/TRW. **Waterloo development program: recommended alternative.** Toronto: The Company, 1970. 55 p. ill., maps. Loc: OKIT.

A comprehensive development plan for Waterloo Township land purchased in 1968 by the Ontario Housing Corporation southeast of Kitchener and north of Preston. The report includes information on population projections, commercial and industrial potential, housing needs, ground water supply, sewage, road and traffic projections, and natural resources. Period: 1968 - 1970.

2622. Coleman, D. and McNaughton, Ian Fraser. "Environmental planning in Waterloo County." **The Waterloo County area: selected geographical essays.** Edited by A.G. McLellan. Waterloo: Department of Geography, University of Waterloo, 1971. Pp. 241-253. maps. Loc: OWTU, OWTL, OWTUCG, OKIT.

A discussion of factors to be considered in comprehensive planning of a rapidly urbanizing region. For Waterloo County, these include agricultural capability, groundwater recharge, engineering properties of soils, forests, important wildlife and unique natural areas, surface water quality, recreation capability, and the distinctive Mennonite way of life. Period: 1965 - 1970.

2623. Cornell, S.J. **A case study in park planning.** University of Toronto (B.A. thesis, Geography), 1970. 76 p. ill., maps. Loc: OTU.

An examination of the outdoor recreation potential of the 175-acre Hilborn property between Preston and Galt. The author surveys all aspects of the site and develops a formal plan for varied recreational uses, based on responses to a questionnaire. Period: 1960 - 1970.

2624. Deverall-Ross, Diana. **Renovated housing and neighbourhood change: a study of two inner city neighbourhoods in the City of Kitchener.** University of Waterloo (B.E.S. thesis), 1980. 3 fiche. ill., bibl., maps. mf. Loc: OWTUM.

A comparative account of the Victoria Park and Civic Centre neighbourhoods in 1961 and 1976. The author finds that households in 1976 were younger and smaller and had fewer ethnic characteristics. Period: 1961 - 1976.

2625. Dorney, R.S. and Priddle, George B. **Inventory, analysis and assessment of urban environmental quality: a case study of Waterloo, Ontario.** University of Waterloo, Faculty of Environmental Studies, 1973. 88 p. maps, tables. Loc: OWTU.

A study of open space, vegetation, water quality, noise pollution, visual amenities, and design concepts for the City of Waterloo. Maps, findings, and recommendations are given for all of these topics. A summary of this report was presented to the Urban Renewal Committee of the City of Waterloo in December 1972. Period: 1971 - 1972.

2626. Draho, Lawrence E. **The location of blight in downtown Kitchener.** University of Waterloo (B.A. thesis, Geography), 1967. 2 fiche. mf. Loc: OWTUM.

An exercise in defining and delimiting physical and social blight, as a basis for a programme of remedial and preventative action. Indicators of physical blight, found along King Street, are the age of the building, the number of fire calls, and air pollution. Indicators of social blight, found along the inner edge of the residential areas, are the number of people on welfare, the number of old age pensioners, and the number of shared toilets between dwelling units. Period: 1965 - 1967.

2627. Dryden and Smith Planning Consultants. **Conestoga College of Applied Arts and Technology: college location study.** 1967. 50 p. maps, tables. Loc: OWTU.

A preliminary report on possible locations for the college planned to serve the four counties of Huron, Perth, Waterloo and Wellington. The study considers the factors of characteristics of the college, population, transportation, industry and business. Seven site evaluations are reported at Galt, Goderich, Kitchener, Listowel, Seaforth, Stratford and Wingham. The report recommends a site at either Galt or Kitchener with a satellite campus in the northwestern area. Maps and tables show population density, location of industry, and possible college locations. Period: 1965 - 1967.

2628. Dudycha, Douglas J. **An exploratory simulation model of residential development: Kitchener-Waterloo.** University of Waterloo (M.A. thesis, Geography), 1972. 2 fiche. maps, bibl. mf. Loc: OWTU.

An account of a model to predict housing development, tested against the actual pattern of subdivisions in suburban Kitchener-Waterloo from 1964 to 1971. The model is reported unable to predict the trend towards higher housing density or the proportions of each type of development. The locational characteristics of the site are found to be more important than physical characteristics in influencing housing patterns. The most important determinant of location is found to be public policy approving the housing plan and the extension of services. Period: 1964 - 1971.

2629. Durst, Albert. **Urban growth in Waterloo Township.** University of Waterloo (B.A. thesis, Geography), 1963. 1 fiche. maps, bibl. mf. Loc: OWTUM.

A depiction of changes in the urban, agricultural and rural-urban zones from 1952 to 1962, based on data of land use, values, and ownership and subdivision locations. The author finds that the major change was in the spatial extent, not the pattern of development, so that by 1962 the agricultural zone was markedly reduced and the urban and rural-urban fringe zones greatly enlarged. Period: 1952 - 1962.

2630. Ferguson, Martin J. **The pre-development land market and the initiation of the rural-urban land conversion process: a case study in the former Township of Waterloo, 1966-1971.** University of Waterloo (M.A. thesis, Geography), 1975. 3 fiche. graphs, tables. mf. Loc: OWTU.

Explanation of a model, based on a study of local land transactions, to describe the process of urbanization of farmland. The author finds that intermediaries hold land far in excess of foreseeable demand for development, that much of the land is bought by development companies directly from farmers, and that an identifiable price spiral occurs. Period: 1966 - 1971.

2631. Galt and Suburban Planning Board. **The official plan of Galt and suburban planning area, comprising the City of Galt and Township of North Dumfries.** 1958. 1 v. (unpaged). graphs, maps. Loc: OCCA.

A report on the factors of land use, traffic, population, bridges, services, recreation, bridges, agriculture, industry and commerce in designing the plan. The first amendment was made in 1968; the second and third were enacted in 1970. Period: 1955 - 1958.

2632. Good, David A. **The Beechwood residential district - a neighbourhood study.** University of Waterloo (B.A. thesis, Geography), 1969. 124 l. maps, tables, bibl. Loc: OWTU.

A physical and sociological examination of the district in the west sector of the city of Waterloo. The author describes the neighbourhood and analyzes theories underlying current urban planning for this area. Appendices include information gathered from questionnaires given to residents on socio-economic status, education levels, ethnic origins, family size, average age, contact with neighbours, and satisfaction level of the neighbourhood. Period: 1968 - 1969.

2633. Gormley, Stephen P. **The transition of inner city neighbourhoods in Kitchener, Ontario, 1921-1982.** University of Waterloo (M.A. thesis, Planning), 1986. 2 fiche. bibl. mf. Loc: OKIT, OWTU.

A comparative study of the development of the Victoria Park, the Civic Centre and Cedar Hill neighbourhoods. Aspects of population, land use and tenure are described from assessment roll statistics of 1921, 1941, 1961 and 1982. Period: 1921 - 1982.

2634. Green, James S. **Overzoning in multiple residential areas: a case study example in Kitchener.** University of Waterloo (B.E.S. thesis, Planning), 1975. 103 p. bibl., maps, tables. Loc: OWTU.

A study designed to find solutions to the overzoning of the Thaler Avenue area of Kitchener, which in 1975 permitted a population exceeding the capacity of the sewer system. An historical section traces the development of the Thaler Avenue area from its annexation in 1958 from the Township of Waterloo, but focuses on the contemporary situation. It recommends development control by a holding by-law to avoid rezoning the area. Period: 1958 - 1975.

2635. Habl, Linda A. **Kitchener's inner city industrial zones: an analysis and revitalization proposal.** University of Waterloo (B.E.S. thesis, Geography), 1982. 2 fiche. charts, maps, tables, bibl. mf. Loc: OWTUM.

A study of industrial activities in the city's central business district and of options for future policies of urban renewal. Statistical tables summarize various industrial trends from the 1830s to the 1970s. Period: 1830 - 1982.

2636. Hallman, D. and Pando, Robert I. and Hope. S. and Webster, D. **Urban renewal in Kitchener: an examination of economic analyses used as a basis for redevelopment proposals in Kitchener Central Area.** Waterloo: University of Waterloo (student essay, Geography), 1965. 13 p. map. Loc: OKIT.

An assessment of three major city planning reports prepared for the Kitchener Department of Planning and Development: **Economic analysis for downtown planning, Downtown Kitchener: land use analysis** and **Downtown Kitchener: plan to 1980.** Period: 1965 - 1980.

2637. Henkelman, Alan. **Land and house values and the dynamics of residential location.** Wilfrid Laurier University (B.A. thesis, Geography), 1975. 64 p.

bibl., maps. Loc: OWTL.

An analysis of sales data for 300 detached dwellings sold in the Kitchener-Waterloo area between January and July 1971. The author concludes that variance in sale price is largely due to the size of the lot and home, and that amenity factors rather than accessibility factors play the next most significant role. A short chapter describes the local housing market between 1961 and 1971 and maps show socioeconomic status, family status and population mobility. Period: 1961 - 1971.

2638. Hildebrandt, Bruno. **A traffic plan for central business districts.** Waterloo Lutheran University (B.A. thesis, Geography), 1967. 73 l. ill., maps. Loc: OWTL.

A survey of downtown Kitchener, with recommendations for traffic engineering and city planning. Period: 1965 - 1967.

2639. Hrivnak, Larry M. **The small town: scale and image.** Waterloo Lutheran University (B.A. thesis, Geography), 1971. 61 p. ill., bibl., maps. Loc: OWTL.

A study of the townscapes of Elmira and Ingersoll using questionnaires, interviews, and fieldwork. The visual elements and images are described by a trained observer and the inhabitants. The study concludes that as scale decreases, orientation increases. Also, that as scale decreases, spiritual images and not mere landmarks are noted. Period: 1970 - 1971.

2640. Jahan, Sarwar. **Spatial and temporal dynamics of land use changes in the Kitchener-Guelph highway corridor.** University of Waterloo (M.A. thesis, Planning), 1982. 221 p. bibl., tables, maps. Loc: OWTU.

A study of the development of Highway 7 between Kitchener and Guelph from 1955 to 1980. Aerial photographs and land use maps show that the intensity and development along the highway is much greater near the cities, and that the number of subsidiary roads increases significantly. In the Waterloo region, industrial use of land was found to have the highest staying power compared to other uses, while in the Guelph region residential uses persist longer. Period: 1955 - 1980.

2641. Juurand, Priidu. **The influence of perception on orientation in Waterloo.** Waterloo Lutheran University (B.A. thesis, Geography), 1968. 65 l. maps, bibl. Loc: OWTL.

An assessment of the visual cues people use in orientation, depending on their length of residence in the city, and based on the results of questionnaires to six sample groups. Paths, edges, nodes, districts and landmarks are the features considered as focal points in the research which includes the analysis of maps sketched by the participants. Period: 1967 - 1969.

2642. Kaufman, A.R. "Town planning in Kitchener after three years trial." **Town Planning Institute of Canada Journal**. 1928. 7: 134-137. Loc: OWTU.

A retrospective view, by the current chairman of the Kitchener City Planning Commission, of the wisdom of Kitchener's adoption of zoning by-laws. The author gives examples of the efficiencies and savings in costs that resulted from zoning. Period: 1923 - 1928.

2643. Kitchener Planning Department. **Downtown Kitchener: a land use analysis**. Kitchener: The Department, 1964. 1 v. (various pagings). maps, tables. Loc: OKIT, OWTL, OWTU.

A study intended to accompany Larry Smith & Co.'s **Economic analysis for redevelopment planning** (1964). Topics include land use, morphology, traffic patterns and parking, building and development practices, land values, retail establishments and shopping patterns, landscape and population. Period: 1962 - 1964.

2644. Kitchener Planning Department. **Multiple residential zoning in Kitchener**. Research Report No. 4. Kitchener: The Department, 1970. 72 p. tables, bibl. Loc: OKIT, OWTU.

A report supporting recommendations for more flexible zoning in medium and high density residential areas. The material, gathered and analyzed by Mr Ross McPhee, provides alternative theoretical and practical approaches to redesigning zoning policies in the city. Period: 1969 - 1970.

2645. Kitchener Planning Department. **Parking, high rise apartments, medical offices and clinics in Kitchener**. Research Report No. 5. Kitchener: The Department, 1970. 55 p. charts, tables. Loc: OKIT, OWTU.

An assessment of parking facilities for high-rise apartments in the city core compared with newer suburban areas, and of problems of parking near medical and dental buildings. The text and accompanying charts include information regarding traffic flow patterns, peak traffic use, visitor parking needs, and public transit use. Period: 1969 - 1970.

2646. Kitchener Planning Department. **Special development areas in Kitchener reviewed**. Staff Report PD21/71. Kitchener: The Department, 1971. 30 l. Loc: OKIT.

A collection of recommendations regarding building regulations and selling prices of houses and lots, presented to the Planning Department by groups including the K-W Builders' Association, the Urban Development Institute, and the Central Mortgage and Housing Corporation. The director of planning, William E. Thomson, comments on the suggestions. Period: 1970 - 1971.

2647. Kitchener Urban Renewal Committee. **The plan...downtown Kitchener**. Kitchener: The Committee, 1965. 56 p. ill., maps. Loc: OWTU, OWTL, OKIT.

A proposal for renewal of the central business district based on projections of socio-economic activity. Downtown Kitchener is described and recommendations are made for: creation of a pedestrian mall, a more elaborate system of walkways, the addition of small parks and arcades, the enlargement of Victoria Park, alternative traffic patterns involving more one-way street systems, improved public transit, an increase of office and commercial buildings, residential development in the form of high density apartment buildings, more hotel and entertainment facilities, the retention of industry and public services, the renovation of the railway station, and better parking facilities. The ideas put forth in this plan are a response to new legislation providing generous grants from federal and provincial governments for urban renewal projects. Period: 1962 - 1965.

2648. Knowles, Ann. **Towards the preservation of an identity: the development of a distinctive local townscape in Doon, Ontario**. University of Waterloo (B.E.S. thesis, Geography), 1980. 2 fiche. maps, bibl. mf. Loc: OWTUM.

A study of the need for proper architectural and design controls to preserve Doon's character in the face of rapid urban growth. The author discusses definitions of identity, the importance of preserving the built environment, Kitchener's planning policies, and the proposed planning policies for Doon. Period: 1800 - 1980.

2649. Krische, Mark F. **Accessibility to open space in the city of Kitchener, 1971**. Wilfrid Laurier University (B.A. thesis, Geography), 1983. 99 l. maps, tables, bibl. Loc: OWTL.

A study of provincial and civic government guidelines for public recreation facility planning and open space standards. The author measures physical accessibility to open space against socio-economic characteristics of Kitchener's population (based on 1971 census tract data) and concludes that the newer subdivisions lack a full complement of recreational space. Period: 1970 -

1981.

2650. Kropf, Brian J. **Legal aspects of mobile homes in Ontario with reference to the cities of Kitchener and Waterloo.** University of Waterloo (B.E.S. thesis, Planning), 1972. 77 l. tables, bibl. Loc: OWTU.

A study of existing legislation governing mobile homes as dwellings and vehicles, as well as the payment of taxes, mobile home parks, and transportation laws. The author recommends specific changes in the legislation. Period: 1970 - 1971.

2651. Krueger, Ralph R. "Renewal in downtown Kitchener - a community project." **The Waterloo County area: selected geographical essays.** Edited by A.G. McLellan. Waterloo: Department of Geography, University of Waterloo, 1971. Pp. 267-275. Loc: OWTU, OWTL, OWTUCG, OKIT.

An account of the deterioration of the central business district that led to the formation of the Kitchener Urban Renewal Committee in 1963 and the preparation of various plans for urban renewal. Period: 1955 - 1970.

2652. Lam, L.S. **Exploration of urban problems using sequential aerial photography: a study of the City of Waterloo.** University of Waterloo (B.E.S. thesis, Geography), 1978. 1 fiche. 65 p. maps. mf. Loc: OWTUM.

Includes maps of urban expansion from 1955 to 1974 and of urban land use in 1974. Period: 1955 - 1974.

2653. Larry Smith and Company. **Downtown Kitchener, Ontario: economic analysis for redevelopment planning.** Kitchener Urban Renewal Committee, 1964. 132 p. maps, tables. Loc: OKIT, OWTU.

The first part of a three-phase project making recommendations for Kitchener's downtown and central business districts. The study proposes that retail and office space development in the suburbs should be limited, and that hotels, apartments and entertainment facilities in the downtown area should be encouraged. Wholesale and industrial users of land should be urged to locate at suburban locations instead of downtown. Subjects discussed include housing, office space, retailing and Kitchener's economic background. The study presents many tables, including a land use inventory, a description of Kitchener's labour force by industry group, and population distribution trends. Period: 1963 - 1964.

2654. Lim, Jee-Lee. **The pattern of apartment development and planning controls: Kitchener 1960-1974.** University of Waterloo (M.A. thesis, Geography), 1975. 1 fiche. tables. mf. Loc: OWTU.

A study of the pattern of apartment development (including design, location, and rate of construction) in relation to the city planning controls. The author finds apartments being used as buffer zones between single-family dwellings and more highly developed areas, and recommends a more comprehensive housing policy for the city. Period: 1960 - 1974.

2655. Maiers, Gary. **The location of residential urban blight in Kitchener, Ontario 1961.** University of Waterloo (B.A. thesis, Geography), 1964. 1 fiche. mf. Loc: OWTUM.

A study of the location of residential urban blight in Kitchener in 1961, with a summary of its causes and characteristics. The author describes historical changes in land uses and analyzes current patterns. The extent and distribution of the blight is mapped according to six economic factors, and the study concludes that blight is only in pockets, primarily in apartment buildings. Period: 1800 - 1961.

2656. Marshall, Patrick N. **After the architects: a study of community planning and development in the University of Waterloo Student Village One.** University of Waterloo (B.E.S. thesis, Urban and Regional Planning), 1983. 3 fiche. 136 p. plans. mf. Loc: OWTUM.

A planner's appraisal of the built environment of the major student residence complex designed in 1965, including an historical outline. Period: 1965 - 1983.

2657. Mberengwa, Ignatius. **Land-use change and stability in unplanned secondary centres: the case of downtown Waterloo, Ontario.** University of Waterloo (M.A. thesis, Geography), 1982. 4 fiche. maps, tables, bibl. mf. Loc: OWTU.

An analysis of Waterloo's central business district over a period of thirty years. Data from municipal assessment records and fieldwork are presented in tabular form. Period: 1951 - 1981.

2658. Melville, R. Douglas. **Intra-city patterns of office development and location in Kitchener-Waterloo, 1952-1972.** University of Waterloo (M.A. thesis, Geography), 1977. 4 fiche. tables, maps, bibl. mf. Loc: OWTU.

A description of spatial, functional, and dynamic aspects of office activities and an analysis of the changes in location trends over the twenty-year period. The study takes into account factors such as transportation, parking, and accessibility in determining reasons for office location. Period: 1952 - 1972.

2659. Murphy, Charlie. **A comparative evaluation of central core revitalization in Sault Ste. Marie and Kitchener, Ontario.** University of Waterloo (B.E.S. thesis, Geography), 1983. 2 fiche. mf. Loc: OWTUM.

An analysis of the causes of decline in downtown Kitchener, with a brief history of the city's efforts at revitalization from 1963 to 1965 and a description of the Urban Renewal Scheme that began in 1965. Examining its economic, functional, physical and social components, the author concludes that Kitchener's urban renewal programme has been a success. Period: 1963 - 1983.

2660. Oakes, John M. **The Kitchener industrial park: a method for planning industrial growth in urban areas.** Waterloo Lutheran University (B.A. thesis, Geography), 1969. 86 p. bibl., maps, charts. Loc: OWTL.

A study based on questionnaire results showing availability of highway transportation to be the most important factor in a company's decision to locate in an industrial park, with potential for expansion being the second. Planning recommendations are made and the current Kitchener by-law relating to industrial parks is included in an appendix. Period: 1855 - 1969.

2661. Pando, Robert I. **A description and analysis of urban land use expansion in Waterloo's urban fringe.** University of Waterloo (M.A. thesis, Geography), 1969. 1 reel. ill., maps, bibl. mf. Loc: OWTL, OWTU.

A study of changing residential, industrial, commercial, institutional and park uses from 1955 to 1965. With the help of maps, the author describes general location patterns and identifies the most influential factors. Period: 1955 - 1965.

2662. Popovich, M. "How the media withheld the message in Kitchener: for urban developers, silence is golden." **Macleans Magazine.** 1972. 85: 25-6, 64-7. ill. Loc: OKIT, OWTL, OWTU.

Reference from the Canadian Periodical Index. Period: 1972.

2663. Project Planning Associates Ltd. **Central Kitchener urban renewal scheme: Phase 1.** Kitchener: Kitchener Planning Department, 1967. 131 p. maps. Loc: OWTU.

Wide-ranging proposals for the renewal of the central business district, describing present conditions and their effect on renewal and presenting designs for future development. The report covers transportation, zoning, population, utilities, commercial relocation including the Farmer's Market, parking, and recommended design criteria for services. Period: 1967 - 1974.

2664. Project Planning Associates Ltd. **City of Kitchener, Ontario: downtown urban renewal scheme.** Kitchener: Kitchener Planning Department, 1967. 114 l. ill., maps. Loc: OWTL.

A report on the central business district with recommendations for future development to the year 2000. A wide range of topics is considered, including population projections, blight, social conditions, land use, the condition of present buildings, roads and walkways, schools, traffic, parking, public and commercial transportation, public services, planning regulations, and zoning and building by-laws. Period: 1961 - 2000.

2665. Radke, John D. **A study of industrial location decision-making in a developed area, at a micro level: a case study of Waterloo.** Wilfrid Laurier University (B.A. thesis, Geography), 1975. 131 p. map, tables, bibl. Loc: OWTL.

A study of 51 firms in Waterloo, surveyed by questionnaire or interview, to establish whether the factors in the company's location were economic or behavioural. The author concludes that increasing technology has decreased the influence of economic factors such as transportation costs, market areas, raw materials and labour sources, leaving entrepreneurs with more flexibility in their criteria for locational decisions. Period: 1960 - 1975.

2666. Rahman, Abdur. **A study of land use stability and change in Kitchener's central commercial area between 1932 and 1979.** University of Waterloo (M.A. thesis, Geography), 1980. 3 fiche. maps, bibl. mf. Loc: OWTU.

An analysis of changing land uses in downtown Kitchener, from which the author reports an expansion in the size of the central business district, a decrease in residential use, and an increase in retail and service activities. He describes the impact of the Market Square and concludes that, despite the construction of Fairview Mall in 1967, downtown Kitchener is gaining rather than losing commercial functions. Period: 1932 - 1979.

2667. Rempel, Martin C. **The intra-urban migrational process; a case study, the City of Waterloo.** Waterloo: Wilfrid Laurier University (B.A. thesis, Geography), 1975. 108 l. ill., maps. Loc: OWTL.

A study of the factors in residential mobility. Period: 1971 - 1975.

2668. Rovers, Fred. **The impacts of urban development standards on the provision of lower-cost housing: a case study of Kitchener's special development area 1970-1984.** University of Waterloo (B.E.S.

thesis, Planning), 1985. 2 fiche. maps, tables, bibl. mf. Loc: OWTUM.

An overview of the roles of provincial and municipal governments in addressing housing needs, particularly in regard to low-cost housing and decreased development standards. The author analyzes the situation in Pineview Heights, a subdivision in the southwest section of the city, in terms of subdivision design, housing mix breakdown, housing type distribution, area and density relationships, and demography and level of satisfaction of residents. Period: 1939 - 1984.

2669. Schmidt, Kevin M. **The development of Breithaupt Park**. University of Waterloo (B.A. thesis, Geography), 1981. 131 p. maps, tables, bibl. Loc: OKIT, OWTUM.

A comprehensive study of the park named for one of the city's most notable families. The author outlines aboriginal occupation and pioneer settlement and the history of the park since 1912, including its early uses as gravel source and recreational facility. Park management is reviewed from the establishment of the Berlin Park Board in 1894 and information is presented on geology, topography, and plant and animal life. Period: 1650 - 1980.

2670. Seabrook, Janet L. **Amenity land use development in the rural-urban fringe: a case study in the Waterloo Sand Hills**. University of Waterloo (B.E.S. thesis, Geography), 1971. 2 fiche. tables, maps, bibl. mf. Loc: OWTUM.

An investigation of changing land use patterns, stressing the establishment and retention of recreational and attractive locations on urban fringes. The author presents a land use classification system that reflects current conflicts and areas of potential problems. Period: 1951 - 1970.

2671. Searth, Tom. **A quantitative analysis of parks and open space in Kitchener**. University of Waterloo (B.A. thesis, Geography), 1967. 2 fiche. maps. mf. Loc: OWTUM.

An inventory of the city's acreage of parks and open space in relation to the recommended minimal standards. The author finds that minimum standards for developed park and open space are achieved, but the standards for underdeveloped park and open space are not. The city core, especially north of King Street, is found to be deficient in areas of open space. Period: 1966 - 1967.

2672. Seymour, Horace. "A plan for the City of Kitchener." **Town Planning Institute of Canada Journal**. 1925. 4,1: 2-8. Loc: OWTU.

An account of Kitchener's first official plan by one of the planners who discusses its implications (including school consolidation) for the rest of the Waterloo Township. The zoning bylaws defining industrial, business and residential districts are printed in an appendix. Period: 1914 - 1925.

2673. Seymour, Horace. "Planning of Kitchener and Waterloo, Ontario." **Canadian Engineer**. 1924. 47: 125-130. Loc: OGU.

An account, by one of the planners, of the objectives and procedures of preparing plans for Kitchener-Waterloo. Period: 1922 - 1924.

2674. Seymour, Horace. "Report of town planning survey of Waterloo, Ontario." **Town Planning Institute of Canada Journal**. 1924. 3,1: 3-8. Loc: OWTU.

A preliminary submission describing present municipal conditions and making no planning proposals. The author discusses the relationship between Waterloo and Kitchener, the need for a town plan, what it would do, and how to implement it. Period: 1922 - 1924.

2675. Shuttleworth, John M. **The habitability of apartment units and a research theory applied to high-rise apartments in Kitchener-Waterloo**. University of Waterloo (B.E.S. thesis, Planning), 1972. 49 p. tables, bibl. Loc: OWTU.

A study of the significant effects of high-rise dwelling on residents. The author examines the degree of satisfaction obtained from living in apartments compared with that of living in single-family dwellings. Period: 1960 - 1970.

2676. Simpson, Michael. "Thomas Adams in Canada." **Urban History Review**. 1982. 11,2: 1-15. Loc: OWTL, OWTU.

An appraisal of the career of the planning pioneer who was adviser to the Canadian Commission of Conservation from 1914 to 1919 and undertook plans for Kitchener and Waterloo (with Horace Seymour) in the 1920s. This article makes only passing references to urban planning in Kitchener-Waterloo. Period: 1914 - 1924.

2677. Simpson, Raymond John. **The evolution of a central business district: Kitchener, Ontario**. Waterloo Lutheran University (B.A. thesis, Geography), 1968. 71 l. maps, bibl. Loc: OWTL.

A history of the city's downtown core in two periods, before and after 1911. The author reviews the functions of the CBD in meeting social and economic needs before the automobile prompted the growth of shopping centres in outlying areas. Charts, maps and tables classify types of industries and commercial establishments located in the core area at various times, and there is a chronology of five blocks along King Street. Period: 1854 - 1966.

2678. Smith, Terence C. **River valley development: urban growth or a greenbelt? a case study - the City of Galt.** University of Waterloo (B.E.S. thesis, Planning), 1972. 52, 60 p. ill., bibl., maps. Loc: OWTU.

An enthusiastic proposal for a greenbelt area along the Grand River in Galt, based on its physical features and historical development and on opinion surveys carried out in the Galt community. Recommendations included removing buildings, replacing the dam, constructing parking lots and washrooms, and establishing hiking trails and picnic areas.

2679. Somfay, J.C. and Budden, D. **Proposed renovations to Hespeler town centre: for the Hespeler Retail Merchants Association.** Elora: Sephora Incorporated Environmental Design, 1972. 50 p. ill., maps, bibl. Loc: OWTU.

A feasibility study of the "Bavarian theme" suggested by Hespeler merchants as a way of increasing retail business and giving the town a unified appearance. The report includes a physical inventory of the downtown area and proposed renovations and recommendations for long-term improvements. Period: 1971 - 1972.

2680. Sweet, Patrick. **Retail strip development in Kitchener: a case study of King Street East - Conestoga Parkway.** University of Waterloo (B.E.S. thesis), 1970. 2 fiche. maps. mf. Loc: OWTUM.

An analysis of the effect on businesses along King Street of the construction of the Conestoga Parkway, through an examination of business classification, customer linkages and trip classification. The study suggests that the new market pattern will require new zoning and new planning initiatives. Period: 1967 - 1970.

2681. Taylor, Joyce. **The use of industrial parks as a form of community development in Kitchener, Waterloo and Owen Sound.** Wilfrid Laurier University (B.A. thesis, Geography), 1985. 67 p. maps, bibl. Loc: OWTL.

A study of the historical development of industrial parks and their role in each community's economic growth. A map shows the location of the six industrial parks of Kitchener and Waterloo. Period: 1856 - 1985.

2682. Thomson, William E. **Renewal in downtown Kitchener: a community project.** Kitchener: Kitchener Planning Department, 1971. 12 l. Loc: OKIT.

A brief history of the central business district

from its beginnings to its deterioration in the 1960s. The work addresses the problem of blight and stresses the need for new planning approaches to make the downtown area more attractive. Traffic flow, parking, downtown employee needs and the general appeal of the area are recognized as important factors. Period: 1830 - 1971.

2683. Thomson, William E. **A total use of public open space.** Kitchener: Kitchener Planning Department, 1970. 32 l. Loc: OKIT, OWTU.

A working paper about parks and recreation planning in the city, including recommendations of walkways, bikeways, green spaces along streams, the creation or enhancement of scenic easements, and more outdoor facilities such as sports fields and swimming pools. Period: 1969 - 1970.

2684. Uliana, John. **An analysis of land use stability and succession in the zone of transition: the case of Kitchener, Ontario.** University of Waterloo (M.A. thesis, Geography), 1975. 3 fiche. maps, tables, bibl. mf. Loc: OWTU.

A study of changes in downtown Kitchener based on analysis of vacant land, single family homes, and industrial and retail uses. The author examines functional reasons for the changes and presents a descriptive model of the sequence of transition in the area. Period: 1932 - 1970.

2685. Unsoy, Jeelee. **Managing land inventories for residential development in Kitchener Ontario, 1967-1977.** University of Waterloo (Ph.D. thesis, Geography), 1982. 5 fiche. mf. Loc: OWTL, OWTU.

A detailed analysis of the decision-making process in the supply of residential lots. The author proposes an optimal ratio of supply to demand of residential lots and guidelines for management of lots by local government. Period: 1967 - 1977.

2686. Vann, Robert. "Industrial parks in mid-western Ontario." **Industrial development in Southern Ontario: selected essays.** Edited by James H. Bater and David F. Walker. Publication Series, no.3. Waterloo: Department of Geography, Faculty of Environmental Studies, University of Waterloo, 1974. Pp. 167-197. Loc: OWTU, OWTL.

A survey concluding that municipalities such as Kitchener and Stratford, with zoning ordinances written into local bylaws, have more effective control over development than Cambridge and Guelph. Period: 1970 - 1971.

2687. Varga, V.E. **Residential property values, a locational analysis: single family housing, Kitchener, Ontario.** Kitchener Department of Planning and Development, 1973. 175 p. bibl., maps, charts. Loc: OKIT, OWTL.

An analysis of house prices in Kitchener over a ten-year period to determine the effect of developments such as new roads, apartments or shopping centres. Period: 1960 - 1971.

2688. Verburg, K. and Russell, W.E. **A regional study: the Golden Triangle**. University of Guelph, 1965. 226 p. ill., maps. Loc: OGU.

A typescript survey of geology, soils, drainage, forests, agriculture, industry, recreation and population change that mentions historical structures and landscapes as a basis for defining sub-regions and making a long-range physical plan for Waterloo and Wellington Counties. Period: 1800 - 1965.

2689. Waterloo City Planning Board. **Official plan of the City of Waterloo planning area**. Waterloo: The Board, 1969. 30 l. maps. Loc: OWT.

A guide for the Waterloo City Council and other boards and commissions on policies relating to future urban growth and the provision of public services. Topics include public transport, land use, school and park facilities, commercial and industrial development, housing and neighbourhood principles. Period: 1968 - 1969.

2690. Waterloo Engineering, Planning, Building and Works Department. **Annual report**. The Department, 1947-. Loc: OWTL.

A summary of the department's activities in each year, with information on projects of sewerage, street cleaning and construction and details of budget forecasts, capital estimates and equipment purchases. Much information is presented on charts or graphs and later issues contain photographs of projects. The Wilfrid Laurier Library holds reports for the years 1957, 1960, 1962, 1964, 1965, 1969, 1971, 1972 and all years from 1975 to 1983. From 1947 to 1964 the report was published by the department under its earlier name: the Engineering, Building and Works Department. Period: 1947 - 1983.

2691. Waterloo Planning Department. **The City of Waterloo urban renewal study, August 1968**. Waterloo: The City, 1968. 84 l. maps, tables. Loc: OWTL.

A study of the central business district including a survey of history, present land use, population, community services, roads and transportation, public utilities and municipal administration in part one. Part two identifies current problems such as blight, parking and traffic, low employment and industry, crime, and incompatible land use. Part three presents recommendations on housing, administration and citizen participation in urban renewal. Period: 1967 - 1968.

2692. Watson, Charles F. **Corporate policy for the future of the Peel Village Highlands project in Preston**. Brampton: Peel Village Developments Co., 1970. 16 p. Loc: OKIT.

A response by the president of Peel Village Developments Company to the Mayor of Preston's request for a statement of his company's policy on its development in Preston. Watson explains the company's goals, gives a detailed chronology of events from 1967 to 1969 regarding the project, and clarifies some "misunderstandings." Period: 1967 - 1970.

2693. Wealleans, R. Paul. **Defining an urban corridor: case study: Highway 7 between Kitchener and Guelph (1955-1978)**. University of Waterloo (B.E.S. thesis, Geography), 1980. 2 fiche. tables, maps, bibl. mf. Loc: OWTUM.

An examination of land use change, using aerial photographs, population density statistics, and fieldwork to determine the influence of urbanization on the development of the intercity corridor. Period: 1955 - 1978.

2694. Wells, Jean. **Livability of the urban neighbourhood: a study of five neighbourhoods in the City of Kitchener**. University of Waterloo (B.E.S. thesis, Planning), 1971. 1 v. (unpaged). maps, tables, bibl. Loc: OWTU.

An assessment of the quality of urban life, based on the results of extensive questionnaires. The author identifies safety, sanitation, size, open space, privacy, and sentimental attachment as important qualities of a livable neighbourhood. The findings of this study are presented as recommendations to planners. Tables provide a wide variety of demographic information. Period: 1970 - 1971.

2695. Whitney, John R. **Linking open space in the urban environment**. Waterloo Lutheran University (B.A. thesis, Geography), 1973. 93 p. ill., maps, bibl. Loc: OWTL.

A general and mainly contemporary study of the role of greenbelts in urban planning, with references to the planning of Kitchener since 1945. Period: 1945 - 1973.

2696. Wilson, Donald C. **The locational and legal aspects of recreational open space in the urban community**. Waterloo Lutheran University (M.A. thesis, Geography), 1969. 162 p. bibl., ill., maps. Loc: OWTL.

An analysis of a locational model for the open spaces of Kitchener-Waterloo to determine if the

locational and acreage standards legally required
by the Community Programs Division of the Ontario
Department of Education are being met. The author
proposes changes in legislation to acquire
sufficient open space to meet current standards.
Appendices include an inventory of park and open
space facilities in Kitchener and Waterloo, a
population density map, and copies of relevant
municipal and provincial legislation. Period: 1960
- 1969.

2697. Wright, W. **Multiple housing and the structure of
cities.** University of Waterloo (B.A. thesis,
Geography), 1968. 2 fiche. ill., bibl. mf. Loc:
OWTU.
   An analysis of the growing trend in Canadian
cities towards high-density housing since the
1950s, as exemplified by Kitchener-Waterloo.
After examining the demographic, economic and
social reasons for this trend, the author proposes
a conceptual model for the urban growth of
Kitchener-Waterloo, based on the constellation
theory of relatively diversified and integrated
cities. Period: 1948 - 1967.

CULTURE AND SOCIAL INSTITUTIONS

SCHOOLS AND EDUCATION

2698. "50th anniversary: Elmira District Secondary School, 1939-1989." **Elmira Independent**. 1989, May 19. 8 p. ill. Loc: OKIT, OWRE.

A newspaper supplement presenting programmes for the anniversary celebrations. Period: 1939 - 1989.

2699. L'abbe, Bernadette. **The historical development of community schools in Kitchener-Waterloo.** University of Waterloo (B.A. thesis, Recreation), 1980. 2 fiche. tables, bibl. mf. Loc: OWTU.

An account of social and political factors in the establishment and growth of community schools, considered in three time periods: the war years (1914-1945), the postwar years (1946-1968), and the modern era (1968-1980). Period: 1914 - 1980.

2700. Ayers, George, Mrs. "The Doon Public School." **Waterloo Historical Society**. 1957. 45: 45-47. ill. Loc: all.

A history of Doon Public School from 1877 to 1956 when a new school was built. Period: 1877 - 1956.

2701. **Ayr School: 100 years, 1890-1990.** 1988. 96 p. ill. Loc: OKIT, OWRA.

A history consisting mainly of class photographs and reminiscences of former pupils and staff members. Following a summary of the provision for education in Ayr up to the 1880s, the authors recount the disagreements in the community and among the members of the village council over the site of the proposed new school. They explain that from 1911 to 1949, it was possible to attend both elementary and secondary school in Ayr, with grades 1 to 8 referred to as Public School and grades 9 to 12 as Continuation School. There are lists of teachers and students from Ayr School from 1890 to 1990, a list of nicknames, and a poem about schooldays in Ayr written for the 1924 Old Boys' Reunion by "Nibs" MacKay. Period: 1854 - 1988.

2702. Barnett and Rieder-Hymmen. **Second addition to S.S.#10 Wilmot Township School.** Kitchener: The Architects, 1964. 1 v. Loc: OKITW.

Invitations for tenders to build the addition to Wilmot Centre School to specifications prepared by the architects, Barnett and Rieder-Hymmen. Period: 1964 - 1965.

2703. Barrie, James R. "North Dumfries School Fair is 75 years old." **Waterloo Historical Society**. 1984. 72: 56-61. ill. Loc: all.

An account of the system of government-sponsored school fairs introduced to promote instruction in improved farming methods. The North Dumfries School Fair was started in 1909 by Frank C. Hart, one of six pioneer agricultural representatives appointed in rural Ontario in 1907. Held each September, the fair rotated around the seven township schools. Sample fair programmes in 1914, 1947 and 1984 are described and there are photographs of the 1909 fair at the Riverside School and of members of the School Fair Board of 1914. Period: 1909 - 1984.

2704. Bergey, Lorna L. "The effects of Bill 54 in Wilmot Township." **Waterloo Historical Society**. 1966. 54: 69-76. ill. Loc: all.

A summary of seven schools consolidated in January 1965 when the province established the township as the smallest school administrative unit. An historical profile is given of each school and many teachers, pupils and trustees are named. The seven schools are Rosebank S.S.#8, Berlett's Corners S.S.#19, New Prussia S.S.#18, Green's School S.S.#4, St James School S.S.#5, Philipsburg S.S.#17, and Mannheim S.S.#9. Period: 1828 - 1966.

2705. Bergey, Lorna L. "History of Pinehill S.S. No. 7, Wilmot." **Waterloo Historical Society**. 1964. 52: 16-21. Loc: all.

A short history of the school, established in 1857 and closed in 1964. The author describes school life and names many teachers and pupils. Period: 1856 - 1964.

2706. **Berlin Collegiate and Technical Institute: historical sketch and calendar of pupils, 1855-1904.** Berlin: The Institute, 1904. 59 p. ill., ports. Loc: OWTUR, OKIT.

A short history of the Berlin High School, opened in 1855 as the Berlin County Grammar School and renamed Berlin Collegiate and Technical Institute in 1904. Most of the booklet consists of lists of pupils and staff by the year they entered the school. The records are incomplete before 1868, but for the years 1868 to 1904 there are complete lists of students with occupations, married names, and places of residence. Also included are photographs of the school and portraits of D.S. Bowlby, Hugo Kranz, C. Bitzer, J.W. Connor, Adolph Mueller and D. Forsyth. Period: 1855 - 1904.

2707. Berlin New Church School Board. **Minutes of the financial and advisory board of the Berlin New Church School, 1891-1896.** 278 p. Loc: OKIT.

The minutes of financial and advisory board for the first five years of the Berlin New Church School, established in 1891 by the Rev. F.E. Waelchli. Waelchli led one of the Kitchener Swedenborgian Churches which divided in 1891. The minutes describe the founding of the school, its finances and administration, doctrinal matters and worship. Period: 1891 - 1896.

2708. Berlin New Church School Board. **School Board minutes of Berlin New Church, 1897-1900.** 34 p. Loc: OKIT.

A photocopy of minutes of the first board, recording discussions and decisions on expenditures, curricula, library holdings, holidays and awards. Period: 1897 - 1900.

2709. Berlin New Church School Board. **School register for the Berlin New Church School: list of pupils and staff, 1891-1901.** 9 l. Loc: OKIT.

A copy of the register including details of the teachers and pupils for each school year including for each pupil: name, parents' names, birth date and place, place of baptism and the name of the minister who performed the baptism, school last attended, home address and class level. Period: 1891 - 1901.

2710. Boulden, John. "The echoes of history." **Waterloo Historical Society.** 1980. 68: 74-89. ill. Loc: all.

A survey of the 125-year history of the Kitchener-Waterloo Collegiate and Vocational School, considered in its broader community, national and international context. The author mentions notable teachers, administrators, students and programmes. Period: 1855 - 1980.

2711. Bowman, Edna. "Maple Grove school days." **Waterloo Historical Society.** 1990. 78: 152-157. ill. Loc: all.

Recollections of the Waterloo Township S.S.#20 in the 1920s, including descriptions of picnics, special events, sports, the school fair and school drill. Period: 1900 - 1930.

2712. Bowman, Henry B. "Miss Alma Crawforth and the Continuation School in Elmira." **Waterloo Historical Society.** 1973. 61: 24-28. ill. Loc: all.

A short profile of the first teacher at the high school which opened in 1914; Miss Crawforth left teaching in 1918 and died in 1969. Period: 1914 - 1918.

2713. Breithaupt, W.H. "Rockwood Academy and its founder, William Wetherald." **Waterloo Historical Society.** 1942. 30: 208-211. Loc: all.

A history of the Quaker academy opened in Wellington County in 1850 and closed in 1883. The academy was attended by boys from Waterloo County (such as the Rev. A.B. Sherk) while some of its teachers (including Donald McCaig) later taught in Waterloo County. Period: 1850 - 1883.

2714. Brown, Harry W. "The Kitchener and Waterloo Collegiate and Vocational School: its history." **Waterloo Historical Society.** 1927. 15: 268-284. Loc: all.

An article tracing the school's history and explaining its various names. The author mentions teachers and administrators as well as former students and their subsequent occupations. An excerpt from a superintendent's report for 1871-2 presents some statistics about the school that are compared with details for 1926. Period: 1855 - 1927.

2715. Brubacher, Elmer G., Mrs. "Plans for a 1957 Elmdale School reunion [WRP]." **Waterloo Historical Society.** 1958. 46: 51-52. Loc: all.

An account of the organization of the reunion celebrating the school's fiftieth anniversary. Period: 1907 - 1957.

2716. Brunn, Jason. **W.C.B.E. directory of schools.** Waterloo: N.A. MacEachern School, 1982. 118 p. ill. Loc: OWTUR, OWT.

A directory listing 118 elementary schools in the Waterloo County Board of Education system. Each entry gives the school's name, address, the year it opened, its first principal, the grades taught in 1982, and a short history accompanied by a photograph. Period: 1820 - 1982.

2717. Brydon, Margaret. "A teacher's life in Doon, C.W. in 1859." **Waterloo Historical Society.** 1989. 77: 109-111. ill. Loc: all.

A letter written by Margaret Brydon, school teacher at Pine Bush School in 1859, and read at a Waterloo Historical Society meeting by her grand-daughter. Information about the Brydon and Brewster families (Margaret Brydon married Andrew Jackson Brewster) is given in an introduction. Period: 1843 - 1903.

2718. Burkhardt, Ferne. "Rockway Mennonite School: conception and birth." **Mennogespräch.** 1983. 1,2: 9-11, 13. ill., bibl., map. Loc: OWTUCG, OKIT.

An account of the events and committees preceding the opening of the Kitchener Mennonite high school in 1945. There are reminiscences of the early days by the first teacher, Salome

Bauman, descriptions of the school building, and notes on the six students who were the first graduates in 1948. Period: 1943 - 1948.

2719. Cameron Heights Collegiate Institute. **Turus**. Kitchener: The School, 1971 -. 100 p. ill. Loc: OKIT.

A series of yearbooks illustrating school activities and achievements. Kitchener Public Library has yearbooks for 1971 to 1973, 1975 to 1979, and 1981 to date. Period: 1971 - 1991.

2720. Carscadden, Thomas, Dr. "History of the Galt Collegiate Institute, 1881-1914." **Waterloo Historical Society**. 1925. 13: 134-138. ill. Loc: all.

A history of the school from its early days as the Galt Grammar School under the direction of Dr Tassie. The author, who was principal for 30 years, lists the school's teachers, its different locations within Galt, and successive additions and improvements to the buildings. He also describes the admission of girls in 1881, the establishment of Departments of Agriculture, Manual Training and Household Science, and the hiring of a permanent school secretary, Miss K.F. Jaffray. Period: 1853 - 1914.

2721. Celebration Committee. **Galt Collegiate Institute Semi-centennial and Tassie Old Boys' Re-union**. Galt: Galt Collegiate Institute Board, 1902. 44, 53 p. ill. Loc: OKIT, OKITW.

A special issue of the G.C.I. Record (vol. 2, No. 7), presenting a short history of the Galt Grammar School and Galt Collegiate Institute and reporting the 50th anniversary celebrations in mid-July 1902. The Hon. James Young chaired the Celebration Committee. Lists of former pupils who attended the celebration and of all former pupils and masters who could be traced (with their current addresses and occupations) are appended. Period: 1852 - 1902.

2722. "Centennial of St Jerome's College." **Waterloo Historical Society**. 1965. 53: 42-43. ill. Loc: all.

A short history of the college which first opened in St Agatha. No names of students or staff are given. Period: 1865 - 1965.

2723. "Centennial of Suddaby School, Kitchener." **Waterloo Historical Society**. 1957. 45: 15. Loc: all.

An account of the school's celebrations, noting its origins as the Berlin Central School and its renaming in 1910 in honour of Jeremiah Suddaby, first principal of the Model School for training teachers. Period: 1857 - 1957.

2724. Christie, Brian B. **A guide to outdoor education facilities within Waterloo County**. Kitchener: Waterloo County Board of Education, 1972. 103 p. maps, bibl. Loc: OKIT, OWTU.

A inventory of locations suitable for outdoor class visits for classes from kindergarten to grade thirteen. Eight historical tours are described, two geological tours, 35 urban sites and 37 rural sites. For each site there are notes about aquatic resources, geomorphology, biology, human influence, access, support facilities and contact person. Large-scale maps illustrate each site description, and a county map shows locations of the sites and the rural schools. There is a glossary of geological terms, a list of recommended books for teachers, and a form for site evaluation. Period: 1971 - 1972.

2725. "Clearview School, Galt closed after 136 years." **Waterloo Historical Society**. 1965. 53: 10. Loc: all.

A note of the reunion in August 1965, attended by nearly 500 people. Period: 1829 - 1965.

2726. Courtland Public School. **Courtland 1890-1990**. Kitchener: The School, 1990. 1 v. (unpaged). ill. Loc: OKIT.

A booklet celebrating the school's centennial but with almost no historical information beyond older photographs of the main facade on the title page. Period: 1890 - 1990.

2727. Cowan, Jennie F. "Early history of the Mill Creek School Section (S.S.#26, North Dumfries)." **Waterloo Historical Society**. 1937. 25: 260-264. Loc: all.

An account of the school founded in 1837 to serve the area on the northeastern margins of Galt. An outline of the main events between 1847 and 1866 is based on the records kept by the secretary-treasurer, Duncan Ferguson. Period: 1837 - 1866.

2728. Cressman, Eben C. **Farewell Riverbank: a short history of Riverbank School**. Riverbank "Old Boys", 1965. 7 l. Loc: OKITW.

A souvenir booklet for a school reunion on 19 September 1965. Waterloo Township School Section #15 was closed in 1961 and reopened as the Waterloo County Library. There are transcriptions of selected items from the minute book from 1921 to 1943, an account of the development of the building, and lists of teachers and school board members. Period: 1810 - 1965.

2729. Cressman, Zenas, Mrs. **History of Green's School (S.S. No. 4, Wilmot) Reunion, Saturday, September 3rd, 1966**. 1966. 11 p. ill., maps. Loc: OKIT.

A short history with details of founders, buildings (including interior and exterior sketches), teachers and activities. Period: 1833 - 1966.

2730. "Deed for first school site in Waterloo." **Waterloo Historical Society**. 1965. 53: 67-68. ill. Loc: all.

A copy of the indenture between Abraham Erb and the two trustees, Jacob C. Snyder and Jacob S. Shoemaker, of the Common School District in the vicinity of Lot Number 14, 3rd concession of the Upper Block in Waterloo Township. The article includes facsimiles of the signatures of Abraham Erb, John S. Roat and Barnabas Devitt. Period: 1826.

2731. Diamond, Florence. "School system: Wilmot Township." **Waterloo Historical Society**. 1962. 50: 88-92. ill. Loc: all.

A history of schools in Wilmot Township from 1835, when the first school was founded in St Agatha, to 1962. Legislation concerning schools is mentioned, together with information about the Separate schools. Period: 1835 - 1962.

2732. Donohoe, E.F. "St Jerome's College: a historical sketch." **Waterloo Historical Society**. 1940. 28: 101-110. ill. Loc: all.

A history of the Roman Catholic college, from its founding in 1864 by Rev. Louis Funcken, to 1940. Names and some biographical information are given about various principals and some teachers. Period: 1864 - 1940.

2733. Douglass, Hugh. "A brief survey of the history of Ontario Public School texts." **Waterloo Historical Society**. 1963. 51: 12-16. ill. Loc: all.

A history of Ontario school textbooks that discusses Otto Klotz's successful efforts to replace the Irish National Series of readers. J.E. Bryant of the Galt Collegiate Institute was one of the editors of the Ontario Readers which replaced the Irish National Series. The title page of Klotz's German grammar book, published in 1867, is reproduced with an English translation. Period: 1865 - 1884.

2734. Downey, Hilda. "David MacGeorge, 'Dear Old Mac'." **Waterloo Historical Society**. 1980. 68: 53-60. Loc: all.

An anecdotal account by his grand-daughter of Scots-born caretaker at Galt Collegiate from 1884 to 1914, who wrote and published verse about the school and its pupils. Period: 1884 - 1925.

2735. "Dr G.A. Klinck." **Waterloo Historical Society**. 1960. 48: 50. Loc: all.

A note that Dr Klinck, a native of Elmira who taught at North Toronto Collegiate Institute, had received the O.E.A. Centennial Award in 1960 for his work in modern languages. Period: 1959 - 1960.

2736. **Early history of Clearview School, 1829-1909**. 1933. 1 v. ill. Loc: OKITW.

A project on Waterloo Township School Section number 19, submitted to the officials of Waterloo Township East Rural School Fair, held at Riverbank School in 1933. It contains a handwritten history of the school, with photographs and newspaper clippings about teachers, trustees and former pupils. A copy of the 1929 Clearview Centennial Reunion programme is included. Period: 1829 - 1909.

2737. Eastwood Collegiate, Kitchener. **Chips: yearbook of Eastwood Collegiate**. Kitchener: The School, 1957-. 80 p. ill. Loc: OKIT.

A series of yearbooks illustrating school activities and achievements. Kitchener Public Library has volumes for 1957-8, 1958-9, the years 1961 to 1968, 1970, 1975, 1978 to 1982, 1984, and 1986 to 1991. Period: 1957 - 1991.

2738. Eby, Benjamin. **ABC Buchstabir- und Lesebuch, zum Gebrauch für deutsche Schulen in Canada, 2nd ed.**. Berlin: Heinrich Eby, 1842. 144 p. ill. Loc: OKITW, OWTUCGR.

A speller and reader for use in German-language schools in Canada, including general guidelines for pupils, short stories, poems and a glossary. The book was compiled by the teacher and preacher Benjamin Eby, who conducted classes in his meeting house on the site of First Mennonite Church in Berlin. The Waterloo Historical Society also holds copies of the 3rd edition (1847) and the 4th edition (1871). Period: 1842 - 1871.

2739. Eby, Benjamin. **Neues Buchstabir- und Lesebuch, besonderes bearbeitet und eingerichet zum Gebrauch deutscher Schulen, enthalted das ABC, und vielerley Buchstabir- und Leseübungen, 1st ed.**. Berlin: H.W. Peterson, 1839. 144 p. Also CIHM Microfiche series, no. 51199. Loc: OWTL, OWTU, OWTUCGR.

A speller and reader especially designed for use in German-language schools and including general guidelines and exercises for children. Eby taught and preached in his meeting house on the site of what is now the First Mennonite Church in Kitchener. The third and subsequent editions were published in Elkhart, Indiana.

2740. "Education and the **Waterloo Chronicle** in the 1860s [WRP]." **Waterloo Historical Society.** 1965. 53: 64-66. Loc: all.

A collection of three items from the newspaper. The first excerpt, dated 14 January 1869, is an advertisement from Waterloo Central School for a teacher of German. The second, dated 20 May 1869, announces the examination of Common School teachers. The third, dated 20 February 1898, is a small note of gratitude to Mr King, principal of the Waterloo Central School. Period: 1868 - 1869.

2741. Eisenbach, Victor. **A brief history of S.S. No. 1 Woolwich.** 4 l. Loc: OWRE.

A short account of the development of Conestogo village and its school, written by pupils and teacher and including a note of the school's first teacher, I.E. Bowman, and facts about school buildings, particularly the 1904 structure. Period: 1834 - c1960.

2742. Elizabeth Ziegler School 50th Anniversary Committee. **Elizabeth Ziegler School, Waterloo, Ontario 1931-1981, 50th anniversary souvenir booklet.** Waterloo: The Committee, 1981. 12 p. ill. Loc: OWT.

A short history including information on the school building, former teachers, principals and students and a brief biography of the teacher for whom the school was named. Period: 1931 - 1981.

2743. Elliott, Hugh C. "Stone School centennial: June 29th and 30th, 1957." **Waterloo Historical Society.** 1957. 45: 19-20. ill. Loc: all.

A description of the centennial festivities (1857-1957) of School Section #19 in North Dumfries Township. A brief history of the school is quoted from Marion Lake's booklet **Glimpses of the past.** Period: 1857 - 1957.

2744. Elmira District Secondary School. **Oracle.** Elmira: The School, 1946-. Loc: OKDHC, OKIT.

Yearbooks giving pictorial descriptions of curriculum, events, sports, clubs, students and staff. Doon Heritage Crossroads holds Volume 8 (1946-7), containing examples of poems, stories and artwork by the students, while Kitchener Public Library has the yearbook for 1967. Period: 1946 - 1967.

2745. **Erbsville Public School, 1859-1987: S.S. #10.** 1987. 40 p. ill., map. Loc: OKIT.

A history of the school, written when it was closed and replaced by a new school in the Beechwood West subdivision. The book includes class photographs from 1920 to 1987, a list of teachers and principals, recollections by ten different principals, and a map of Erbsville printed on the inside back cover. Period: 1859 - 1987.

2746. Etherington, Frank and Kurisu, Jane. **The General.** Toronto: Annick Press, 1983. 60 p. ill. Loc: OKITW.

A children's story, based on fact, about an eccentric crossing guard who was dismissed from his voluntary job in Bridgeport. The schoolchildren protested until Frank Groff got his job back. Period: 1972 - 1981.

2747. Fewster, Kathy. **A history of Victoria School.** The School, 1989. 3 p. ill. Loc: OKIT.

A short history of the school prepared for the school's Open House in 1989. It describes the construction of the school by Jacob Baetz, its architecture, its opening in 1912, and its operation. Period: 1909 - 1989.

2748. Fisher, P. "Semi-centennial of Courtland Avenue Public School." **Waterloo Historical Society.** 1940. 28: 126-129. ill. Loc: all.

A history of the school and its many expansions from 1890 to 1939. Names of the principals and many members of staff are included. Period: 1886 - 1939.

2749. Forest Heights Collegiate. **Celebrate good times! Forest Heights 25th, 1964-1989.** Kitchener: The School, 1989. 44 p. ill. Loc: OKIT.

Recollections, lists and photographs of staff and students, and sketches of the school's highlights in five-year periods. Period: 1964 - 1989.

2750. Frey, Martin. **The origin of Old Order Mennonite private schools in Woolwich Township and the proceedings leading to it.** 1983. 10 l. Loc: OWTUCGR.

A history of the establishment of parochial schools in the township, written by a former trustee of S.S. #8, St Jacobs and chairman of the Township Area Board. The author outlines the events leading to the removal of Old Order Mennonite children from the public school system. Period: c1920 - 1969.

2751. Funcken, Louis, Rev. **Annual report of St Jerome's College, Berlin, Waterloo County, Ontario, (on the Grand Trunk Railroad), for the scholastic year 1866-1867.** CIHM Microfiche series, no. A01837. Berlin: St Jerome's College, 1866?. 4 frames. mf. Loc: OWTL, OWTU.

A synopsis of courses offered at the college and the teachers responsible for each. Period: 1866 - 1867.

2752. Galt Collegiate Institute and Vocational School. **Prospectus of the Galt Collegiate Institute and Vocational School 1926-1927**. 1926. 35 p. ill., index. Loc: OKITW.

A catalogue containing an introduction to the school with information on accommodation, admission requirements, scholarships and prizes, teaching staff and members of the Board of Education. Courses in the collegiate, commercial, technical, home economics and evening vocational departments are described, accompanied by photographs of the various classrooms. Period: 1926 - 1927.

2753. Galt Collegiate Institute. **Galt Collegiate Institute: announcement for the year 1889-90**. Galt: Galt Reporter, 1889. 25 p. ill. Loc: OKITW.

A report of the school staff, courses, organizations, entry requirements and fees, with a list of pupils in attendance from 1882 to 1889 and their place of residence. The cover has an illustration of the school with boys playing cricket. Period: 1889 - 1890.

2754. Galt Collegiate Institute Literary and Musical Society. **Laws and rules of order of Galt Collegiate Institute Literary and Musical Society**. Galt: Galt Reporter, 1893. 1 v. (unpaged). Loc: OKITW.

The constitution of a club founded in 1882 to promote literary and aesthetic culture, and to acquaint its members with orderly transactions of public business. In 1889 the society was the only school organization other than the football club. Period: 1882 - 1893.

2755. Galt Collegiate Institute. **Unveiling of memorial tablet by Major-General Sir Edward Morrison, Galt Collegiate Institute Friday June 4th, 1920**. 1920. 1 v. (unpaged). Loc: OKITW.

A programme listing teachers and students who served in the First World War and those who died. Members of the 1919 graduating classes are listed with staff and board members and the annual sports winners. Period: 1919 - 1920.

2756. Godin, Mark and Wahl, James A., Rev. "The contribution of St Jerome's College to Busy Berlin." **Waterloo Historical Society**. 1982. 70: 11-24. ill. Loc: all.

A survey of students who attended the college in the 1890s and went on to become prominent business leaders. The authors list many individuals and their businesses, as well as information in letters from students who left the area. Bitzer, Bowlby, Bricker, Eby, Killer, Kuntz, Lang, Motz, Rittinger, Spetz and Weiler are some of the family names of former students of St Jerome's College.

Period: 1857 - 1921.

2757. Grand River Collegiate. **Reminiscing 66-91: 25th anniversary**. Kitchener: The School, 1991. 64 p. ill. Loc: OKIT.

An illustrated outline of the school's origins, annual highlights and notable achievements, with lists of faculty and support staff. Period: 1966 - 1991.

2758. Grand River Collegiate. **Sequoyah**. Kitchener: The School, 1968-. Loc: OKIT.

Yearbooks published by the students and consisting of photographs of students and activities, with messages from principals and vice-principals. The Kitchener Public Library has the years 1968, 1971, 1974, and 1976 to date. Period: 1968 - 1991.

2759. Greenfield, Thomas B. and Ryan, Doris W. and McIntosh, Janet C. **Structure, decision-making, and communication in the Waterloo County school system: an evaluation report**. Toronto: Ontario Institute for Studies in Education, 1974. 94 p. Loc: OWTL.

A report by six consultants evaluating the structure of the Waterloo County Board of Education as it was set up in 1968. Several senior administrators were about to retire, and a body of opinion felt that changes to the present system were necessary. Issues are discussed and two points of view presented, the 1968 approach and an alternative. The organizational implications of various viewpoints are identified, and recommendations made. Period: 1968 - 1974.

2760. Groh, Ivan. **The pioneers of Clearview (and some of their successors), being a brief history of School Section Number Nineteen in the Township of Waterloo from about 1800 to 1960**. The Author, 1960. 26 l. Loc: OKITW.

A guide to a driving tour of Clearview, telling of the first settlers and their farming descendants. The author's family was related to many of them, and reminiscences of his own childhood and relations are combined with facts about the successive property owners. The booklet contains a poem on the Indian trail from Blair to Puslinch Lake, also printed in **Canadian-German Folklore** in 1967. Period: 1800 - 1960.

2761. Groh, Ivan. "School Section No. 19 Waterloo Township." **Canadian-German Folklore**. 1967. 2: 42-43. Loc: OKIT, OWTL, OWTU, OWTUCG.

An outline of the early settlement pattern of part of Waterloo Township, giving the names of the settlers and the location of their farms. Period: 1800 - 1840.

2762. Groh, Ivan. "The teachers of Clearview Park School (1843-1848)." **Canadian-German Folklore**. 1967. 2: 48. Loc: OKIT, OWTL, OWTU, OWTUCG.

A description of the five teachers during this period. The Clearview Park School was first known as the Union Church School and later a new log school was built on the Pine Bush Road. Period: 1843 - 1848.

2763. Groh, Ivan. "The teachers of Pine Bush School (1847-1874)." **Canadian-German Folklore**. 1967. 2: 49-52. Loc: OKIT, OWTL, OWTU, OWTUCG.

Notes about the ten teachers and events during their terms of service. John W. Groh was the last teacher in the log school house and the first in the Red Brick School. Period: 1847 - 1874.

2764. Groh, Ivan. "Teachers of the red brick school renamed Clearview School in 1874." **Canadian-German Folklore**. 1967. 2: 53-55. Loc: OKIT, OWTL, OWTU, OWTUCG.

A list of the eighteen teachers between 1874 and 1913, with brief notes about the school and education in Waterloo County generally during each teacher's term of service. Period: 1873 - 1913.

2765. Groh, Ivan. "The trustees of S.S. No. 19 Waterloo Township (1848-1909)." **Canadian-German Folklore**. 1967. 2: 56-57. Loc: OKIT, OWTL, OWTU, OWTUCG.

A list of 26 trustees with their addresses; all names have been indexed in the WRP database. Period: 1848 - 1909.

2766. Groh, Ivan. "The Union Church School (1830-1843)." **Canadian-German Folklore**. 1967. 2: 44-47. Loc: OKIT, OWTL, OWTU, OWTUCG.

A history of the first school building in what became S.S.#19, describing the building, teachers and curricula. Names and farm locations of the 15 families in the locality are listed. Period: 1830 - 1843.

2767. Hamilton, O.A.F. "History of the New Hamburg Public School." **Waterloo Historical Society**. 1943. 31: 32-39. Loc: all.

A brief history of the school, noting people who were instrumental in its foundation and administration and quoting various anecdotes. Period: 1845 - 1943.

2768. Hamilton, R.S. "The history of secondary education in Galt - Part 1: the Howe regime." **Waterloo Historical Society**. 1941. 29: 158-161. Loc: all.

An account of the first Common School in Galt established in 1832, and the circumstances in which the Galt Grammar School was founded in 1851. The teaching methods of the first teacher, Michael Howe, are recalled by one of his Galt pupils who became a noted educationalist himself. Period: 1850 - 1853.

2769. Hergott, Norbert. **History of combined Separate schools of Wellesley Township**. The Author, 1967. 1 v. (unpaged). Loc: OKITW.

A history based on school minute books from 1855 to 1967 and mentioning many teachers, trustees and inspectors. Much of the information deals with events at S.S.S.#11, St Clements School, including a list of teachers from 1876 to 1967, most of them Sisters. It records the 1967 closure of Separate School Sections 5 and 12. Period: 1855 - 1967.

2770. Hilborn, Miriam. **Historical highlights, New Dundee Continuation School, 1922-1955**. New Dundee: The School, 1967. 12 p. ill. Loc: OKIT, OWRND.

A history published at the time of the school reunion in June 1967, with information on former teachers, students and activities and class pictures from 1923-24, 1935-36 and 1945. Period: 1922 - 1955.

2771. **History of Lexington School**. 16 l. Loc: OKIT, OWT.

A photocopied collection of excerpts of minutes of the school section board from its origins in 1850. The entries include the names, salaries and conditions of employment of teachers as well as names of pupils from 1850 to 1912. Period: 1850 - 1912.

2772. **History of Mackenzie King Public School**. 1985. 1 v. Loc: OKIT.

A compilation of photocopied materials about the school, including notes of the minutes of annual meetings from 1930 to 1933, a floor plan, newspaper clippings, a list of principals from 1944 to 1985, and reunion programmes. Among the newspaper clippings is one describing Prime Minister Mackenzie King's visits to the school in 1922 and 1947. Period: 1925 - 1985.

2773. "Hostetler School reunion." **Waterloo Historical Society**. 1965. 53: 43. Loc: all.

A short account of the rural school located between Baden and New Hamburg which closed in 1965. The article notes the efforts from 1847 of Moses Hostetler and William Bosenberger in getting council aid in order to build the school. Period: 1836 - 1965.

2774. Hunsperger, Edna and Hunsperger, Enan. "Centennial of Maple Grove School." **Waterloo Historical Society**. 1951. 39: 43-45. ill. Loc: all.

A brief history of the school founded in 1848,

including many names of pupils and teachers as well as details of renovations to the school building. Period: 1848 - 1900.

2775. Hunsperger, Edna and Hunsperger, Enan. **Maple Grove centennial reunion.** 1951. 20 p. ill. Loc: OKITW.

A commemorative history of the school and of the Beaverdale area. Pupils, teachers and trustees are noted and there are school photographs from 1889 and 1950, two poetic tributes, a reunion programme of events on 1-2 July 1950, and a list of reunion committee members. All names except those in advertisements have been indexed in the WRP database. Period: 1848 - 1951.

2776. "An institution of historical significance: the new secular training school for girls." **Waterloo Historical Society.** 1933. 21: 59-60. Loc: all.

An account of the opening of a reform school near Galt for "girls between the ages of 10 and 16, who show tendencies towards incorrigibility." Period: 1930 - 1934.

2777. Jaffray, K.F., Miss. "The Galt Collegiate Institute, 1914-1926." **Waterloo Historical Society.** 1926. 14: 179-184. Loc: all.

An account of the school since 1914, when it was hoped that classes could be offered in vocational and technical training. The author discusses the roles of Government and the Board of Trustees in the operation of the school and the contributions of the current principal A.P. Gundry, the caretaker David (Old Mac) MacGeorge, and Dr Carscadden who was principal to 1914. Period: 1914 - 1926.

2778. "James William Connor honoured." **Waterloo Historical Society.** 1963. 51: 73. Loc: all.

A note of the establishment of a Greek prize at the University of Toronto in honour of James W. Connor, principal of the Berlin High School. The donor was W.B. Wiegand, managing director of the Ames Holden Company. Period: 1871 - 1963.

2779. Johnson, Dana. **Going to school in rural Ontario.** Research Bulletin No. 212. Ottawa: Parks Canada, 1983. 40 p. ill. plans, bibl. Loc: OWTU.

A survey of the role and form of the one-room schoolhouse before the school consolidation movement of the 1950s and 1960s. The author stresses the design and quality of the school buildings. Waterloo references include pre-1850 evidence of small, modestly-equipped, log schools in Waterloo Township and a view of Green's School, Wilmot Township (built 1907). Period: 1820 - 1950.

2780. Johnston, Mary A. "A brief history of elementary education in the city of Waterloo." **Waterloo Historical Society.** 1965. 53: 56-64. ill., bibl. Loc: all.

An overview of the development of Waterloo schools since 1820, with reference to the Common School Act of 1843, teacher salaries in the 1890s, special programmes, and new teaching methods. There are brief profiles of individual schools. Period: c1820 - 1965.

2781. Johnston, Mary A. **The history of education in the City of Waterloo.** 1962. 18 l. bibl. Loc: OKITW.

An essay submitted for the University of Toronto's Bachelor of Education degree, profiling the history of Waterloo education from 1820 to 1962. Schooling from the elementary level to the university level is considered, as well as the Catholic schools. The principals, teachers and school buildings are noted, and an appendix contains transcripts of Waterloo newspaper items from 1868 and 1869 referring to education. Period: 1820 - 1962.

2782. Johnston, Mary A. **The trail of the slate: a history of early education in Waterloo County, 1802-1912.** Waterloo: The Author, 1975. 144 p. ill., tables, bibl. Loc: OCCA, OCLG, OCP, OKIT, OWT.

An account of relevant legislation and the important roles of administrators such as Otto Klotz, Thomas Pearce and F.W. Sheppard in shaping education in the county. The author summarizes the early history of elementary schools in Galt, Berlin/Kitchener, Preston and Waterloo, secondary schools in Galt and Berlin, some early Roman Catholic Separate schools, and private and special schools. She also briefly outlines the development of public libraries in Galt, Kitchener, Hespeler and Waterloo and the foundations of the two universities. The book is well illustrated with photographs and facsimiles of certificates and regulations, and Appendix A presents a summary of all the elementary and secondary schools in the county in 1972 -- by name, location, principal, date of original building and dates of additions. Period: 1802 - 1972.

2783. Johnstone, G., Mrs and Rutherford, W.C., Mrs. "History of the school at Wrigley's Corners." **Waterloo Historical Society.** 1955. 43: 45-48. ill. Loc: all.

A brief history with a photograph of the red-brick schoolhouse used from 1854 to 1954, when it was replaced by a new structure. Period: 1854 - 1954.

2784. Junker, Alan W. **Otto Klotz and the implementation of education policy in Waterloo County, 1846-1871**. Wilfrid Laurier University (M.A. thesis, History), 1987. 144 p. bibl. Loc: OWTL.

A study of the role of Otto Klotz in promoting free schooling, teacher qualifications, German-language instruction and school readers. The author considers that local school officials like Klotz had significant power in educational administration in the mid-19th century. Period: 1846 - 1987.

2785. Karges, Todd. **The fifth quarter: a history of St Jerome's**. The Author, 1989. 191 p. ill. Loc: OKIT, OWTUSJ.

A popular history of St Jerome's High School commemorating its 125th anniversary. Both St Jerome's College and St Jerome's High School developed from the Catholic educational institute founded by Rev. Louis Funcken in 1865, although in 1953 they ceased to operate in the same location. There are accounts and memoirs from the administrators of the high school since 1953, with student reminiscences from the 1950s, 1960s, 1970s and 1980s. The appendices include transcripts of documents pertaining to the founding and early curricula of St Jerome's. Period: 1865 - 1990.

2786. Kerr, James E. "The Public Schools of Galt." **Waterloo Historical Society**. 1926. 14: 186-189. Loc: all.

A brief history of the development of elementary schools in Galt, with references to the Common School Acts of 1841, 1843, 1850 and 1871 and to teachers and principals such as John Gowinlock, Mr Kelly, Robert McLean, James Harris, James Baikie, William Carlyle and Robert Alexander. The schools discussed are Central, Dickson, Victoria, St Andrew's and Manchester. Period: 1832 - 1926.

2787. Kerr, James E. "Recollections of my schooldays at Tassie's." **Waterloo Historical Society**. 1915. 3: 20-23. ill. Loc: all.

Reminiscences of the Galt Grammar School, known as Tassie's School. The author describes William Tassie and his wife, school curricula, school sports, discipline, leisure time and the school building itself. Period: 1815 - 1895.

2788. King, Jane. "Dickie Settlement schools." **Waterloo Historical Society**. 1950. 38: 25-28. Loc: all.

A brief history beginning in 1847 with the log building located on Roseville Road. The author names teachers at the schools and, in some cases, the salaries they received. Period: 1847 - 1912.

2789. Kitchener Intermediate Schools Students. **The echo**. Kitchener: The Schools, 1936. 100 p. ill. Loc: OWTUR.

A yearbook compiled by the students of Victora and Suddaby Schools. The Doris Lewis Room, University of Waterloo has volume 3 (1936) which contains an interview with Phoebe Watson about her brother, Homer Watson, as well as numerous samples of literary and art work by students of both schools. School activities and student interests are described, and photographs of teachers and students are interspersed throughout the work. Also included is a list of students who attended Suddaby School in 1914. Period: 1935 - 1936.

2790. Kitchener-Waterloo Collegiate and Vocational School. **1855-1955 Kitchener-Waterloo Collegiate and Vocational School centennial, May 6, 1955**. 1955. 1 folded sheet. ill. Loc: OKITW.

A brochure with biographical notes on J.W. Connor, principal of Berlin High School from 1871 until 1901, and a poem by Ephraim Weber in honour of Mr Connor. Period: 1855 - 1955.

2791. Kitchener-Waterloo Collegiate and Vocational School. **The Grumbler: 125th anniversary**. Kitchener: The School, 1980. Loc: OKIT, OWRN, OWRND, OWRE, OWT.

A lavishly illustrated special edition of the yearbook, surveying the school's activities and achievements from 1855 to 1980. Period: 1855 - 1980.

2792. Kitchener-Waterloo Collegiate and Vocational School. **The Grumbler**. The School, 1924 - 1991. Loc: OKDHC, OKIT, OWTUR.

Yearbooks containing short stories, poems, information on sports teams and other school activities, honour rolls, and a list of graduates. In the 1920s the books are primarily text with the occasional photograph, but by the 1990s the books have more photographs than text. The University of Waterloo Rare Book Room has yearbooks for 1924-5, 1926-7, 1928, 1929, 1929-30 and 1938. The Kitchener Public Library has the volumes for Dec. 1924, Apr. 1925, Dec. 1925, Apr. 1926, Dec. 1926, Apr. 1927, Dec. 1927, Apr. 1928, Mar. 1929, 1929-30, 1931 to 1938, 1939-40, Dec 1939, 1941, 1941-42, 1943-44, 1944-45, 1945-46, 1946-47, 1950-51, 1952 to 1956, 1958, 1959, 1959-60, 1961, 1962, 1964, 1965, 1972 and all years from 1975 to 1991. Doon Heritage Crossroads has the yearbook for 1949. Period: 1924 - 1991.

2793. Kitchener-Waterloo Collegiate and Vocational School. **Kitchener-Waterloo Collegiate-Vocational School: a tradition of innovation**. The School, 198-?. 6 p. ill. Loc: OKIT.

A brochure with the school crest on the cover, briefly describing various innovative programmes from 1855 to 1986. Photographs include views of woodworking and household science classes. Period: 1855 - 1986.

2794. Kitchener-Waterloo High School Board. **Saga: 1960-1985, Waterloo Collegiate Institute.** The Board, 1985. 30 p. ill. Loc: OKITW, OKIT, OWT.
A brief pictorial account of various school activities with a list of all teachers. Period: 1960 - 1985.

2795. Klinck, George. **The development and progress of education in Elmira and vicinity.** Elmira: Elmira Signet, 1938. 69 p. ill. Loc: OKITW, OWTUR, OWRE.
A detailed history of education in the community including reviews of all Elmira's public, union, continuation and night schools, as well as its apprenticeship programmes. The roles of prominent individuals, the churches and the library are also discussed. Period: 1827 - 1939.

2796. Klotz, Otto. **Leitfaden zur deutschen Sprache oder kurz gefasstes Lehrbuch der deutschen Sprache in Fragen und Antworten.** Preston: The Author, 1867. 134 p. Also CIHM Microfiche series, no. 08119. Loc: OKITW, OWTL, OWTU, OWTUCGR.
A grammar entitled **Guide to the German language or summarized textbook of the German language.** The author, school superintendent in Preston and member of the Waterloo County Board of Public Instruction, stresses in the preface the need for a textbook especially designed for Canadian children who experience the German language differently from children in Europe.

2797. Knowles, R.H. "Hespeler Public School." **Waterloo Historical Society.** 1927. 15: 297-299. Loc: all.
An historical sketch of the school founded in 1857, including names of former teachers and principals and descriptions of school activities. Period: 1857 - 1927.

2798. Koch, Alice. **History of Haysville School S.S.#6, Wilmot.** 1974. 1 v. (unpaged). ill., bibl. Loc: OKITW.
An account written for the 1974 school reunion, portraying the school curriculum, teachers, administration and buildings. It includes reminiscences of former students and gives the names of many teachers and school inspectors. Period: 1827 - 1974.

2799. Koebel, Judy. **Parochial school education.** University of Waterloo (student essay, History), 1989. 15 l. bibl. Loc: OWTUCGR.
A history of the private schools for Old Order

Mennonites in the county. The author explains the reasons for separation from the public school system in the mid-1960s and the philosophy behind the choice of curricula. Period: c1800 - 1989.

2800. Lake, Marion A. **Glimpses of the past.** Centennial Historical Committee, 1957. 17 p. ill. Loc: OKIT.
A commemorative history of the Stone School, North Dumfries Township, including information about the school's founders and buildings, especially the stone structure of 1857. It includes a list of teachers and school inspectors since 1857, and class photographs from the years 1908, 1910, 1923, 1924, 1939, 1945, 1947, 1952 and 1956. Period: 1835 - 1957.

2801. Lamb, Kathryn Hansuld. "Rummelhardt School." **Waterloo Historical Society.** 1987. 75: 55-59. ill., tables. Loc: all.
A brief history of School Section Number 9 since 1844, including names of many trustees, teachers and pupils, as well as some enrolment figures. In 1966 the school was renamed the Kitchener-Waterloo Bilingual School. Period: 1844 - 1987.

2802. Lamb, Kathryn Hansuld. "Suddaby School celebrates 125 years." **Waterloo Historical Society.** 1982. 70: 127-129. ill. Loc: all.
An account of the festivities in June 1982, with notes of historical highlights such as Jeremiah Suddaby's appointment as first principal in 1857. Period: 1857 - 1982.

2803. Lawrence, Sylvia. "Centennial celebration: Central School, Galt, 1956." **Waterloo Historical Society.** 1956. 44: 65-66. ill. Loc: all.
A brief account by a Grade VII student of the school's centennial with a photograph of the 1856 building and the 1909 addition. There are also reminiscences by a former pupil, Miss Kate F. Jaffray, and a report by Andrew W. Taylor of the graduates' reunion celebration. Period: 1856 - 1956.

2804. Liedtke, Chris and Bott, Dave. **Eastwood Collegiate, 1956-1981: the way we "wuz": Chips silver anniversary edition.** Kitchener: The School, 1981. 72 p. ill. Loc: OKIT.
A commemorative sketch of the school's history, including photographs and reminiscences of staff and students. Period: 1956 - 1981.

2805. Lynn, J.E., Rev. "President's address." **Waterloo Historical Society.** 1926. 14: 177-178. Loc: all.
A short tribute to Dr Egerton Ryerson, Superintendent of Education of Ontario in 1844 and to Thomas Pearce who gave 54 years of continuous service to education in Waterloo County. Period:

1844 - c1890.

2806. "Maple Grove School receives plaque [WRP]."
Waterloo Historical Society. 1983. 71: 119. ill.
Loc: all.
A note of the unveiling of the plaque
commemorating Waterloo Township S.S.#20 as the
oldest school in continuous use in the region.
Period: 1850 - 1983.

2807. Martin, Mildred. "Training for rural youth."
Waterloo Historical Society. 1982. 70: 130-143.
ill. Loc: all.
An account of the short courses held in rural
centres throughout Waterloo County. Intended for
youths who left school after grade 8, the courses
taught elementary agriculture, animal husbandry,
home economics, English, business and finance and
mechanics. The author describes courses held in
Winterbourne, Elmira, Ayr, Preston and Galt during
the 1930s and 1940s. Period: 1914 - 1947.

2808. McKegney, Patricia. "The German Schools of
Waterloo County, 1851-1913." **Waterloo Historical
Society**. 1970. 58: 54-67. ill. chart. Loc: all.
A detailed history based on an M.Phil. thesis
for the University of Waterloo. The year 1851
marked the beginning of regulation of the German
Schools under the control of the Council of Public
Education. McKegney's research shows that the
number of German Schools declined as publicly
supported schools became more centralized and
regulated. In 1872-3 German-speaking settlers
attempted to extend or at least continue German
instruction. In 1900 a compromise was adopted,
German becoming an additional subject of study
within the school system, but on a voluntary basis
and supervised by parents. A chart shows the
scope of language instruction in Waterloo County
from 1873 to 1881. Period: 1851 - 1913.

2809. "A Mennonite's legacy for educational purposes in
Waterloo." **Waterloo Historical Society**. 1970.
58: 74. Loc: all.
A report that the legacy of Abraham Erb, left to
the first school in 1829, had been transferred to
the Waterloo County Board of Education in 1970.
The interest was used to purchase school supplies.
Period: 1829 - 1970.

2810. "Mill Creek School." **Waterloo Historical
Society**. 1936. 24: 236. ill. Loc: all.
A short note of the centenary celebrations for
the school, organized in 1836 and currently in its
third location on the back road between Galt and
Hespeler. Period: 1836 - 1936.

2811. **Northdale Public School, Waterloo, Ontario,
1959-1984**. Northdale Anniversary Committee, 1984.
1 v. ill. Loc: OKITW.
An anniversary booklet with a history of the
school and lists of principals, original staff,
and officials of the Home and School Association.
Period: 1959 - 1984.

2812. "Notes on Freeport Academy." **Waterloo Historical
Society**. 1924. 12: 109-111. ill. Loc: all.
A short description of the academy, opened in
1867 and closed in 1874. An 1869 photograph of
teachers and students is annotated with their
names and, in some cases, the places to which they
later moved. Period: 1867 - 1874.

2813. Oberholtzer, R.S. "On the closing of Pine Grove
School." **Waterloo Historical Society**. 1979. 67:
86-88. ill. Loc: all.
A short history of the rural school built in
1809, including details of various buildings,
names of members of the board of trustees and a
report of costs for the year 1892. Period: 1809 -
1979.

2814. Oudejans, Annette. "The Parochial Schools of
Wellesley Township." **Waterloo Historical
Society**. 1983. 71: 70-76. ill. Loc: all.
A short account of the development of the
Parochial School system which began in 1966. The
author outlines the efforts of Old Order
Mennonites and Amish to establish their own
curricula and win exemption from Bill 52, which
required all Ontario children to attend school
until age 16. A list of nearly 30 Parochial
Schools is provided, with a map locating old
schools, Parochial Schools, and Parochial Schools
that used to be Public. Period: 1966 - 1983.

2815. Oudejans, Annette. "The Separate Schools of
Wellesley Township." **Waterloo Historical
Society**. 1983. 71: 50-69. ill. Loc: all.
A history of the township's Catholic schools in
Separate School Sections (S.S.S.) 4, 5, 9, 11 and
12, with information on teachers, salaries,
pupils, class sizes, curriculum and school
supplies, and photographs of each school. Period:
c1840 - 1983.

2816. Panabaker, D.N. "The life and work of John
Mickleborough, B.A., LL.B., Ph.D.." **Waterloo
Historical Society**. 1927. 15: 388-389. Loc: all.
A brief biography, with references to his early
life as a student in Preston and Galt and as
teacher at the Mill Creek School and Hespeler
Public School. Period: 1840 - 1920.

2817. Pearce, Thomas and Sheppard, F.W. and Norman, L.
Report of the Public Schools of Waterloo County.
Berlin and Galt and Waterloo: 1875 - 1914. Loc:
OKITW, OKDHC.

Comprehensive annual reports on the rural
schools, giving details of the finances, teachers,
pupils, school buildings and further education
including model schools, continuation schools and
the Teachers' Institute. A table lists the
schools in each township, noting for each the name
and number of the school section, the teacher
(with class of teaching certificate and salary),
the assessed value of the school section, and the
yearly average attendance. Earlier reports list
pupils promoted in every school, provide
information about instruction in German, and make
specific remarks about every school. Later
reports include information about school gardens
and school libraries, with more detailed notes on
the ventilation and lighting provided. Arbor Day
is the only holiday specifically mentioned.
Waterloo Historical Society at Kitchener Public
Library holds reports for the years 1874-1880 and
1886-1913 inclusive. The nominal date is not the
year of publication, which generally was a year
later. Doon Heritage Crossroads is believed to
hold reports for 1880 and 1890. Period: 1874 -
1913.

2818. Pearce, Thomas. "School history, Waterloo County
and Berlin." **Waterloo Historical Society.** 1914.
2: 33-48. ill. Loc: all.

A detailed history of the administration of
education from 1802 to 1914, with some reference
to Roman Catholic schools and instruction in
German. Names of teachers, principals, trustees,
board members and inspectors are given. Period:
1802 - 1914.

2819. Petersburg School Centenary Executive. **Souvenir
of Petersburg school, S.S. No. 14, Wilmot,
centenary, 1836-1936.** Waterloo: Waterloo
Chronicle, 1936. 20 p. ill. Loc: OKIT, OWRN.

A brief history of the school originally located
on New Dundee Road, south of the village, with a
programme for the Centenary Garden Party in July
1936 at Fred Knipfel's picnic ground. The work
describes the three school houses built in 1848,
1868 and 1923, comments on past school expenses
and supplies, and lists teachers, trustees,
ratepayers and visitors to the school. Period:
1836 - 1936.

2820. "The Petersburg School." **Waterloo Historical
Society.** 1936. 24: 235-236. Loc: all.

Description of the centennial celebrations of
Wilmot Township School No.14, first established in
1836. Period: 1836 - 1936.

2821. Potter, Alexander O. "Looking back." **Waterloo
Historical Society.** 1955. 43: 29-35. ill. Loc:
all.

A speech commemorating the 100th anniversary of
Kitchener-Waterloo Collegiate and Vocational
School. A brief history of the school refers to
particular staff members and the various school
buildings. Period: 1855 - 1955.

2822. Preston, Barry. **Berlin Public School Board 1905:
photograph presented by Mr Buller Pequegnat to the
Waterloo County Board of Education 1980.**
Kitchener: Waterloo County Board of Education
Program Division, 1980. 14 p. ill. Loc: OKITW.

An explanation of a photograph showing the
twelve trustees: J. Suddaby, William Hertfelder,
Dr C.L. Pearson, Louis Sattler, John L. Meisner,
Dr J.E. Hett, Arthur Pequegnat, Edmond Pequegnat,
J.R. Schilling, W.D. Euler, Frederick Kress and Dr
W.J. Arnott. Biographical information on each is
given, with an account of the Berlin school system
in 1905 and a description of the Board's work.
Period: 1905 - 1906.

2823. Rier, John E. **Social sciences in the study of the
locality: South Waterloo.** 196-?. 68 p. maps. Loc:
OKIT.

A learning kit designed by a committee of
teachers, pupils and consultants for individual,
project and interdisciplinary studies. It
includes sections on field trips, slides, and
bibliographies on specialized topics. Period: 1969
- 1970.

2824. Ritz, Ernst and McNaughton, I.W. "New Hamburg
School building razed." **Waterloo Historical
Society.** 1958. 46: 38-39. ill. Loc: all.

A short account of successive Public School
buildings in New Hamburg, with particular emphasis
on the third, the white brick building erected in
1874 and demolished in 1958. Period: 1874 - 1958.

2825. "Riverbank reunion." **Waterloo Historical
Society.** 1965. 53: 74. Loc: all.

A note of the reunion held in September 1965 at
Maple Grove School. Aaron Mader, 96, of Breslau
was the oldest person present and Minnie Sauder
was the oldest living teacher who attended.
Period: 1965.

2826. Rockway Mennonite School. **Rockway lighthouse.**
Kitchener: The School, 1954-. 60 p. ill. Loc:
OKIT.

A series of yearbooks illustrating school
activities and achievements. Kitchener Public
Library has the volume for 1954, then for each
year from 1983-84 to 1991-2. Period: 1954 - 1991.

2827. "School-house 1802." **Waterloo Historical Society**. 1959. 47: 4. Loc: all.

A note of the Blair School, believed to be the first schoolhouse in any inland county of Ontario. Period: 1802.

2828. Seibert, Emily. "Elmdale School history: S.S. #8, Waterloo Township." **Waterloo Historical Society**. 1958. 46: 46-51. ill. Loc: all.

A history of the school from 1847 to 1958, commemorating the fiftieth anniversary of the second schoolhouse (built 1907). All teachers since 1862 are listed. Period: 1847 - 1957.

2829. Seibert, Emily and Brubacher, Elmer G., Mrs. **Fiftieth Elmdale School anniversary, 1907-1957: souvenir booklet**. Reunion Committee, 1957?. 23 p. ill. Loc: OKITW.

A programme of events with a list of reunion committee members. The introduction by Mrs Elmer G. Brubacher, describing the events preceding the reunion, was reprinted in the Waterloo Historical Society report of 1958, volume 46, pages 51-52. The history of Elmdale school by Emily Seibert for the souvenir booklet was included in the WHS report of 1958, pages 46-51. The Elmdale history in the booklet contains slightly more information, listing the dates of teachers from 1840 to 1862, but without names; it names 17 notable alumni. Period: 1907 - 1957.

2830. Smith, Allan R.G. "Beginning and progress of school fairs in Ontario." **Waterloo Historical Society**. 1930. 18: 171-174. Loc: all.

An account of the importance, events and organization of school fairs in Waterloo County in 1928. Period: 1909 - 1930.

2831. St Clement School. **St Clement School, Cambridge, 75th Anniversary: November 23rd 1988: 1913-1988**. Cambridge: The School, 1988. 7 l. Loc: OKIT.

A programme of the celebratory mass with the school's crest on the front cover; there is no other historical information. Period: 1913 - 1988.

2832. St Clements Catholic Parent-Teacher Association. **Centennial souvenir, 1867-1967: St Clements School**. 1967. 1 v. (unpaged). ill. Loc: OKITW.

A booklet including a list of the Sisters of Notre Dame who ran the school from 1876 to 1967, illustrations of the development of the schoolhouse, and photographs of the current teachers and school board members. Names of some of the Sisters of Notre Dame are given in both their religious and baptismal forms. Period: 1876 - 1967.

2833. St Jerome's College. **Catalogue of St Jerome's College, Berlin, Ontario, Canada**. Berlin: The College, 1952-. 92 p. ill. Loc: OWTUCR.

Calendars each including an historical sketch with information about admission, courses, facilities, faculty members, students and college organizations. Resurrection College has copies of calendars from 1952-3 to 1962-3. Period: 1952 - 1963.

2834. St Jerome's College. **The Quill**. The College, 1959. Loc: OKIT.

Yearbooks containing photographs and a student directory and brief information about students, alumni, faculty, clubs and sports. The Kitchener Public Library has the yearbook for 1959. Period: 1959.

2835. St Jerome's College. **St Jerome's College, Berlin, Ont. Canada (on the main line of the Grand Trunk Railway) scholastic year 1889-90**. CIHM Microfiche series, no. A01838. Berlin: Rittinger and Motz, 1889?. 1 fiche. mf. Loc: OWTL, OWTU.

A description of courses offered at the college, a list of the teachers for the year and student awards and prizes. An entry by Rev. Theobald Spetz relates the death of the founding director of the college, Rev. Louis Funcken, and includes Funcken's last letter to Spetz. Period: 1889 - 1890.

2836. St Jerome's High School. **The lion: St Jerome's High School**. Kitchener: The School, 1958-. 60 p. ill. Loc: OKIT.

A series of yearbooks illustrating the school's activities and achievements. Kitchener Public Library has Volume 9 for 1958, as well as volumes for 1959, 1964, 1965 and every year since 1976. Period: 1958 - 1991.

2837. St Mary's High School. **St Mary's High School: Kitchener, Ontario**. Kitchener: The School, 1959-. 60 p. Loc: OKIT.

A series of yearbooks illustrating school activities and achievements. Kitchener Public Library has the volumes for 1959, 1960, 1961, 1964, 1967, 1969, 1972, 1973 and each year from 1975 to 1991. Period: 1959 - 1991.

2838. "St Mary's School, Kitchener." **Waterloo Historical Society**. 1965. 53: 34. ill. Loc: all.

A short history of the school, noting the demolition of the old building to make way for a new one. The author refers to the Rev. George Laufhuber, the travelling Jesuit who founded the school in 1858, and John Berberich, the school's first teacher. Period: 1858 - 1965.

2839. St Timothy School. **A history: Waterloo County Catholic Separate School Board.** Kitchener: The School, 1984. 63 p. ill. Loc: OKIT, OWT.

A report of a special project by the Grade Eight class, the book serves as a directory and historical record of all Catholic schools in the region. Each entry, presented in order of the age of the buildings, contains a brief history of the school, a photograph and, in some cases, the names of principals. Period: 1836 - 1981.

2840. Stauch, Warren. "Of the days when Tassie was there." **Waterloo Historical Society.** 1977. 65: 98-110. Loc: all.

Anecdotes of Dr William Tassie's direction of Galt Grammar School (later Galt Collegiate Institute) from 1853 to 1881, based on the recollections of past students who celebrated the first 50 years at the Old Boys' Reunion in 1902. Period: 1853 - 1902.

2841. **Suddaby Public School centennial, 1857-1957.** Kitchener Public School Board, 1957. 16 p. ill. Loc: OKIT.

A brief outline of the school's development, with illustrations of the 1857 and 1957 buildings and of early principals and staff. Names of all principals and 1957 staff members are listed. Period: 1857 - 1957.

2842. **Suddaby Public School centennial, Friday, September 27th, 1957, 8.00 p.m., 1857-1957.** Kitchener Public School Board, 1957. 1 folded sheet. Loc: OKDHC.

A programme for the centennial celebrations containing a brief history of the school, a photograph of Jeremiah Suddaby, a list of the school staff in 1957, and a list of the 1957 members of the Kitchener Public School Board. Period: 1857 - 1957.

2843. "Suddaby School, formerly Central School, Kitchener." **Waterloo Historical Society.** 1942. 30: 228-239. ill. Loc: all.

A history of the school opened in 1857, with references to the locations of other early schools and to teachers, principals and trustees. Period: 1813 - 1942.

2844. Suddaby School. **Suddaby Public School, Kitchener, Ontario: 1857-1982.** Kitchener: The School, 1982. 16 p. ill. Loc: OKIT, OWTUR.

A short history of the building and notable individuals who contributed to the school's development, with photographs and a list of principals from 1857 to 1982. Period: 1855 - 1982.

2845. Sutherland, J.C. "At Dr Tassie's." **Canadian Magazine of Politics, Science, Art and Literature.** 1924. 62: 261-265. ill. Loc: OGU.

A description of the Galt Grammar School in the 1870s, including recollections by a former student of the characters and personalities of Dr Tassie and his staff. Period: 1856 - 1880.

2846. Taylor, Andrew W. "James Milroy, an early Galt schoolmaster." **Waterloo Historical Society.** 1972. 60: 73-74. Loc: all.

A short account of Galt's first teacher in the school built in 1832, with some other information about early education derived mainly from James Young's history. Period: 1816 - 1840.

2847. "Teachers honored." **Waterloo Historical Society.** 1965. 53: 66. Loc: all.

A short account of the Wiegand Memorial Foundation awards given to Emily Seibert and Mabel Ziegler for excellence in elementary school teaching. Period: 1965.

2848. Teuscher, Jakob. **ABC Buchstabir- und Lesebüchlein für Elementar-Schulen in Canada, 2d ed..** Waterloo: Springer and Teuscher, 1855. 46 p. Also CIHM Microfiche series, no. 58587. Loc: OKITW, OWTL, OWTU, OWTUCGR.

A German-language speller and reader for elementary schools in Canada. The book contains short passages of prose and poetry and is based on earlier works by Benjamin Eby.

2849. Undergraduates of the Galt Collegiate. **Specula Galtonia.** Galt: The Institute, 1926 - 1968. Loc: OWTUR, OCCA.

Yearbooks including photographs of students, teachers and staff and information about the school's activities. The University of Waterloo holds the volume for 1926. The City of Cambridge Archives hold the yearbooks for 1930, 1948, 1951, 1965, 1966, 1967 and 1968. Period: 1926 - 1968.

2850. University of St Jerome's College. **St Jerome's Schoolman: Golden jubilee number.** Berlin: The College, 1915. Pp. 154-236. ill., ports. Loc: OKIT, OKITW, OWTUR.

An anniversary issue identified as Volume 17, no. 4 (June 1915), containing a history of the college by Theobald Spetz, a history of the Congregation of the Resurrection by Louis Funcken, and a summary of Louis Funcken's views on Christian education based on his letters. Transcripts of sermons, speeches, and toasts by various clergy members, civic leaders and alumni on the occasion are included. Period: 1865 - 1915.

2851. Victoria School. **Commemorative year book: issued on the occasion of the closing of Victoria Public School 1910-1989.** Kitchener: The School, 1989. 40 p. ill. Loc: OKIT.

A brief history by Catherine Fewster, with an account of the efforts of Arthur Pequegnat who served on the Board of Education for 27 years. The work includes a brief architectural description of the 1911 school building, and recollections by Grace Schmidt, who attended the school from 1921 to 1927, and by H.W. Wildfong, former teacher and principal. Period: 1910 - 1989.

2852. Victoria School. **The Victoria Echo.** Kitchener: The School, 1938, 1939. Loc: OKIT.

Yearbooks including typical reports of activities, samples of student writing and artwork, staff and class photographs, and advertisements. Interviews with Mabel Dunham and J.M. Schneider are reported in the 1938 volume and the 1939 volume has a chronology of current events. The 1938 book is "affectionately dedicated" to Mr J.F. Carmichael, and messages to the graduating class are printed in both volumes from H.J. Prueter and S.E. Hodgins. Kitchener Public Library holds yearbooks for 1938 and 1939. Period: 1934 - 1940.

2853. Walker, Franklin A. **Catholic education and politics in Upper Canada: a study of the documentation relative to origin of Catholic elementary schools in the Ontario school system.** Toronto: J.M. Dent and Sons, 1955. 331 p. Loc: OCLG, OKIT, OWTU, OWTUSJ.

A study by a professor of history of St Jerome's College, written at the request of the Roman Catholic members of the Royal Commission on Education in Ontario in 1950 to re-examine the traditional view of the origin of Separate schools which they felt had been distorted by Rev. Egerton Ryerson. There is only an occasional reference to Waterloo County. Period: 1804 - 1955.

2854. Wallace, W.G. "A Tassie boy." **Ontario History.** 1954. 46,3: 169-178. Loc: OKIT, OWTL, OWTU.

An autobiographical sketch by a Galt native (1858-1949), about his life and education before ordination as a Presbyterian minister. Wallace describes William Tassie as a disciplinarian rather than an educator, and attributes the decline of the school to the introduction of the intermediate examination to which Tassie could not adapt. Period: 1858 - 1949.

2855. Waterloo Collegiate Institute. **Saga: Waterloo Collegiate Institute.** Waterloo: The Institute, 1961-. Loc: OKIT, OKITW, OWT.

Yearbooks illustrating the activities and achievements of students and faculty. The Waterloo Historical Society collection includes most yearbooks since 1961, except for 1962, 1967, 1969, 1971, 1973, 1975, 1981 and 1986. Kitchener Public Library has the volumes for 1968, 1970 and 1980, and Waterloo Public Library those for 1971 and 1972. Period: 1961 - 1988.

2856. Waterloo County Board of Education. **20 years of excellence, 1969-89.** Kitchener: The Board, 1989. 24 p. ill. Loc: OKIT.

An illustrated survey of "highlights and milestones" in the Board's first 20 years. Period: 1969 - 1989.

2857. Waterloo County Board of Public Instruction. **Memorial to the Council of Public Instruction of Upper Canada, from the Board of Public Instruction of the County of Waterloo.** CIHM Microfiche series, no. 55445. Galt: Jaffray Bros, 1865. 1 fiche. mf. Loc: OWTU, OWTL.

A pamphlet written on behalf of Waterloo teachers, requesting that the reading books presently in use, compiled for the Irish National School, be replaced with others. The teachers complain that Canada is terra incognita to the authors of the Irish readers, and that the books are inconsistent, dull and outdated. Period: 1865 - 1866.

2858. Waterloo County Teachers' Association. **The annual meeting of the Waterloo County Teachers' Association will be held in the Model School building, Galt on Thursday and Friday, March 6th and 7th, 1890.** CIHM Microfiche series, no. 54805. 1890?. 1 fiche. mf. Loc: OWTL, OWTU.

A programme of topics and speakers. Period: 1889 - 1890.

2859. Waterloo Planning Department/ Waterloo Public School Board. **City of Waterloo report on present and future elementary school enrolments.** 1966. 15 l. map. Loc: OWTL.

A study based on data obtained from assessment rolls for addresses and ages of preschool children, addresses and numbers of units in apartment and low-density multiple dwellings, and from school board records for names, addresses and grades of children attending elementary schools in Waterloo. The report describes the current distribution of public school pupils and predicts future enrolments by residential district. Period: 1965 - 1966.

2860. Watson, Cicely and Quazi, Saeed. **Future needs for elementary and secondary school classrooms in the County of Waterloo.** Toronto: Department of Educational Planning, Ontario Institute for

Studies in Education, 1970. 120 p. tables, maps. Loc: OWTU.

An exhaustive statistical study of future requirements for new or expanded elementary and secondary schools, prepared for the Waterloo County Board of Education. The report contains much demographic information including school enrolment trends. Period: 1970 - 1990.

2861. Wholton, T.H. "Forty years on." **Waterloo Historical Society**. 1963. 51: 17-18. ill. Loc: all.

A description of extensions to Galt Collegiate Institute when it became Galt Collegiate and Vocational Institute in 1923 and also later in 1963. The author, headmaster of the school from 1925 to 1959, discusses the challenges faced by the 1963 architects, Cameron and Ralston, in choosing a "free treatment of the castellated Scottish Baronial of the Fourth Period (1550-1700)." Period: 1923 - 1963.

2862. Wholton, T.H. **One hundred years: an outline of the history of the Galt Collegiate and Vocational School prepared for presentation at the centenary dinner on Feb. 9, 1952.** Galt: Gore District Mutual Fire Insurance, 1952. 7 p. Loc: OCCA, OKITW.

A short history of prominent individuals, school curriculum and extra-curricular activities. Period: 1851 - 1951.

2863. Wholton, T.H. "One hundred years: an outline of the history of the Galt Collegiate Institute and Vocational School prepared for presentation at the centenary dinner on Feb. 9, 1952." **Waterloo Historical Society**. 1951. 39: 25-32. Loc: all.

A short history, mentioning prominent individuals in the school's development and describing school curriculum and extra-curricular activities. Period: 1851 - 1951.

2864. Wilson, David J. "Community co-operation in education." **Industrial Canada**. 1950. 51,4: 46-48. ill. Loc: OWTU.

An account of a vocational guidance project in which all first-year high school classes studied community occupations. The Galt Board of Education organized student visits to workplaces in Galt, Preston, Kitchener, Waterloo, Guelph and Hamilton. Visits to Dominion Woollens and Worsteds, the Galt Reporter and Newlands are mentioned. Period: 1949 - 1950.

2865. Woodley, Don. "K.C.I.'s 125th anniversary." **Waterloo Historical Society**. 1980. 68: 71-73. Loc: all.

An account of the reunion celebrations held in

May 1980. Period: 1855 - 1980.

COLLEGES AND UNIVERSITIES

2866. "$15 million growth plan at Waterloo." **Financial Post**. 1958. 52: 16. mf. Loc: OWTL, OWTU.

Reference from the Canadian Periodical Index. Period: 1958.

2867. "400 new engineers a year buy Waterloo's unique plan." **Financial Post**. 1957. 51: 13. mf. Loc: OWTL, OWTU.

Reference from the Canadian Periodical Index. Period: 1957.

2868. "Academic look hands region dollar-earning bonus." **Financial Post**. 1967. 61: 14. ill. mf. Loc: OWTL, OWTU.

Reference from the Canadian Periodical Index. Period: 1967.

2869. Allaby, Ian. "The not so hallowed halls of learning." **Canadian Business**. 1984. 57,9: 85-89. ill. Loc: OWTL, OWTU.

An account of the role of the University of Waterloo in combining business and academia, particularly in the fields of electronic engineering and computers. Professorial entrepreneurs are mentioned, as are companies benefiting from the university's expertise. Period: 1957 - 1984.

2870. "Case for the co-operative curriculum." **Labour Gazette**. 1970. 70: 840-5. ill. Loc: OWTL, OWTU.

Reference from the Canadian Periodical Index. Period: 1970.

2871. "Co-operative program accelerates expansion." **Financial Post**. 1965. 59: 59, 61. mf. Loc: OWTL, OWTU.

Reference from the Canadian Periodical Index. Period: 1965.

2872. **College Cord**. 1929 - 1958. Loc: OWTLA.

Published by students of Waterloo College and covering most aspects of college life. Until 1949, it was produced more frequently (usually once every two weeks) in larger format; from 1950 it appeared in booksize format only 5 to 6 times a year. The Wilfrid Laurier University Archives holds a complete set. Period: 1926 - 1958.

2873. "College plans course to ease engineer shortage." **Labour Gazette**. 1956. 56: 1230-1. Loc: OWTL, OWTU.

Reference from the Canadian Periodical Index. Period: 1956.

2874. Conestoga College/ Marani Rounthwaite and Dick Planning Consultants. **Conestoga College of Applied Arts and Technology**. Kitchener: Conestoga College, 1967. 2 v. maps, tables. Loc: OKIT.

A survey of the proposed academic and physical growth of the college from 1968 to 1972, including details of curricula, estimated enrolment and construction programme. Period: 1968 - 1972.

2875. **Cord Weekly**. 1958 -. Loc: OWTLA.

A weekly paper published by students of Waterloo College and Associated Faculties, later Waterloo Lutheran University and Wilfrid Laurier University. Early issues consist of four pages in large format on newsprint; sports news features prominently. Period: 1958.

2876. Dainton, D.G. "Co-operative education at work." **Monetary Times**. 1958. 126: 20-2. ill. Loc: OWTL, OWTU.

Reference from the Canadian Periodical Index. Period: 1958.

2877. Emmanuel Bible College. **50th anniversary, alumni homecoming June 2,3,4 1989: Emmanuel Bible College**. Kitchener: The College, 1989. 1 folded sheet. map. Loc: OKEBC.

A programme of anniversary activities, including class reunions, speeches, music and church services. There are plans of the campus and individual buildings on the back of the programme. Period: 1939 - 1989.

2878. Emmanuel Bible College. **The pilot**. Kitchener: The College, 1944-. Loc: OKEBC.

Yearbooks containing information on school curricula, administration, student organizations and activities, with photographs of many students, staff and the school buildings. Period: 1944 - 1973.

2879. Emmanuel Bible College. **The pilot: twenty-fifth anniversary 1940-1965**. Kitchener: The College, 1965. 1 v. (unpaged). ill. Loc: OKIT.

A commemorative yearbook consisting mainly of illustrations and a short historical outline of the Emmanuel Bible School's origins in Stouffville in 1940, its move to Ahrens Street, Kitchener in 1943, and change of name to Emmanuel Bible College in 1948. The new campus on Fergus Avenue was opened in July 1964. Period: 1940 - 1965.

2880. Euler, W.D. **Berlin Business College**. Berlin: Berlin Business College, 1907. 32 p. ill. Loc: OWTUR.

A promotional brochure including a brief history, descriptions of courses, photographs and some "stories of success." Period: 1906 - 1907.

2881. "The first sixty years of Waterloo Lutheran University." **Waterloo Historical Society**. 1971. 59: 70-72. ill. Loc: all.

A brief history of Waterloo Lutheran Seminary, founded in 1911. Waterloo College, Waterloo Lutheran University and the University of Waterloo later developed from this institution. Period: 1911 - 1971.

2882. "Fledgling engineers already fly a little." **Financial Post**. 1962. 56: 36. mf. Loc: OWTL, OWTU.

Reference from the Canadian Periodical Index. Period: 1962.

2883. G.A. Brakely and Co., Toronto. **New design for higher education**. Kitchener: Waterloo College and Associate Faculties, 1958. 14 p. ill. Loc: OKIT.

Brochure promoting the Waterloo Co-operative Education Fund to establish the future University of Waterloo. It explains the idea of co-operative education for engineering and describes plans and finances. Period: 1925 - 1958.

2884. Galt Business College. **Annual announcement of the Galt Business College**. CIHM Microfiche series, no. A01727. Galt Business College, 1898?. 13 frames. mf. Loc: OWTL, OWTU.

A promotional brochure and college calendar, giving course descriptions and tuition fees. The school was affiliated to the Hamilton Business College. Period: 1890 - 1899.

2885. Greene, Maurice and Thomas, Walter Keith. **Reflections of Waterloo: University of Waterloo, Waterloo, Canada**. Waterloo: University of Waterloo Bookstore, 1980. 65 p. ill. Loc: OKIT, OWT.

A brief history lavishly illustrated with mainly contemporary photographs of the campus buildings, colleges and students. Some local attractions, such as Sheave Tower, Waterloo's first schoolhouse and the Brubacher farmhouse, are also featured. Period: 1957 - 1980.

2886. "How a university operates for business." **Canadian Business**. 1970. 43: 74. Loc: OWTL, OWTU.

Reference from the Canadian Periodical Index. Period: 1970.

2887. "Insurance companies back co-op plan at Waterloo U." **Financial Post**. 1964. 58: 4. mf. Loc: OWTL, OWTU.

Reference from the Canadian Periodical Index.

Period: 1964.

2888. Klinck, Carl F. "Waterloo College library."
Ontario Library Review and Canadian Periodical Index. 1942. 26: 430. Loc: OGU, OWTU.
A brief account by the current librarian, including references to the grant from the Carnegie Corporation in 1932, the new room and shelving, the affiliation of the college with the University of Western Ontario, and the separate library of the Waterloo Lutheran Seminary. Period: 1914 - 1942.

2889. Lyon, Barry. **The first 60 years: a history of Waterloo Lutheran University from the opening of Waterloo Lutheran Seminary in 1911, to the present day.** Waterloo Lutheran University, 1971. 56 p. ill. Loc: OKIT, OWT, OWTL.
A lavishly illustrated history of the university, describing the students, faculty, sports teams and buildings. Period: 1911 - 1971.

2890. Marjoribanks, R.C. "They train on the job in college." **Financial Post.** 1959. 53: 31. mf. Loc: OWTL, OWTU.
Reference from the Canadian Periodical Index. Period: 1959.

2891. Mathews, R.D. and Byrne, Cyril and McKinnon, Kenneth. **The University of Waterloo: a special study.** The Montreal Committee on the de-Canadianization of the Universities: Sub-committee 6, 1969. Loc: OWTU.
A report on the growing number of American citizens appointed as faculty at the university during the 1960s. Non-Canadian curricula in the humanities and social sciences, deterioration of Canadian traditions, and the low proportion of Canadian graduate students are seen as consequences of this trend. The authors propose various recommendations to the Canadian Association of University Teachers and the Minister of University of Affairs in Ontario, William G. Davis, to ensure the promotion of Canadian culture at the University of Waterloo as well as other Canadian universities. Period: 1961 - 1969.

2892. McLean, Celia and Redmond, Chris. **University of Waterloo 1957-1982: twenty-fifth anniversary year begins.** Waterloo: University of Waterloo, 1982. 24 p. ill. Loc: OWRE, OWT.
A commemorative outline of the university's development out of the general arts college that was associated with the Lutheran Church and affiliated with the University of Western Ontario. The authors comment on the co-operative work programme and the establishment of St Jerome's,

Renison, Conrad Grebel and St Paul's Colleges. Photographs of campus buildings and student activities are interspersed through the text. Period: 1957 - 1982.

2893. Mungall, C. "Run university like a business." **Financial Post.** 1967. 61: 19. mf. Loc: OWTL, OWTU.
Reference from the Canadian Periodical Index. Period: 1967.

2894. Mungall, C. "These college students can't help making $$." **Financial Post.** 1967. 61: 9. mf. Loc: OWTL, OWTU.
Reference from the Canadian Periodical Index. Period: 1967.

2895. "New building 'pro' status for Waterloo." **Financial Post.** 1962. 56: 3. mf. Loc: OWTL, OWTU.
Reference from the Canadian Periodical Index. Period: 1962.

2896. "New school of social work." **Canadian Welfare.** 1966. 42: 33. mf. Loc: OWTL, OWTU.
Reference from the Canadian Periodical Index. Period: 1966.

2897. "No 'multiversity' 'dialogue' to continue." **Financial Post.** 1965. 59: 59. mf. Loc: OWTL, OWTU.
Reference from the Canadian Periodical Index. Period: 1965.

2898. "Ontario okays Waterloo plan $25,000 grant." **Financial Post.** 1956. 50: 11. mf. Loc: OWTL, OWTU.
Reference from the Canadian Periodical Index. Period: 1956.

2899. Potter, Alexander O. "Waterloo College." **Waterloo Historical Society.** 1949. 37: 10-14. ill. Loc: all.
A short history of the undergraduate arts college which was developed in association with the Evangelical Lutheran Seminary founded in 1911. The author explains the college's affiliation with the University of Western Ontario and names many important individuals connected with the institution. Period: 1911 - 1949.

2900. **Reflections and visions: 25 years of geography at Waterloo.** Edited by Richard E. Preston and Bruce Mitchell. Publication Series, no. 33. Waterloo: Department of Geography, University of Waterloo, 1990. 312 p. ill. Loc: OKIT, OWTU, OWTL.
A collection of essays on trends in the discipline of geography in Canada and at the

University of Waterloo, with profiles of leading geographers. Appendices include information on courses offered by the Department of Geography at Waterloo and provide lists of faculty and staff members since 1962. Period: 1962 - 1988.

2901. Resurrection College. **Resurrection College Calendar**. Kitchener: The College, 1962 - 1969. Loc: OWTUCR.

A calendar for the institute of the Congregation of the Resurrection, formerly the Pre-Theology Department of St Jerome's College. Information includes a list of faculty, course descriptions, admission regulations and an historical sketch. The Congregation of the Resurrection Archives in Waterloo holds the calendars for the years 1962-1963, 1963-64, 1964-65, 1965-66, 1966-67, 1967-68, 1968-69. Period: 1962 - 1969.

2902. Roger, I. "Training a generation to lead." **Financial Post**. 1968. 62: 21. ill. mf. Loc: OWTL, OWTU.

Reference from the Canadian Periodical Index. Period: 1968.

2903. Sanders, Ann Holm and Donovan, Mary Cochrane and Donovan, Mary Ann. **History of the Kitchener-Waterloo Hospital School of Nursing, 1895-1974**. Kitchener: Kitchener-Waterloo Hospital, 1977. 1 v. (unpaged). ill., bibl. Loc: OKIT.

A brief history of the school including information on early admission requirements, training programmes, uniforms, lectures and courses, residence rules and the Alumnae Association, and reminiscences of former student nurses dating back to 1909. The booklet also includes the names of all graduates since 1898. Period: 1895 - 1974.

2904. Schultz, Erich. "75 years at Wilfrid Laurier University." **Waterloo Historical Society**. 1986. 74: 159-172. ill. Loc: all.

A history of the university's origins as a theological seminary founded in 1911, its affiliation with the University of Western Ontario in 1925, and status as a full degree-granting institution in 1960. Waterloo Lutheran University was renamed Wilfrid Laurier University in 1973. The author relates the establishment of the main programmes of study and describes the expansion of physical facilities, enrolment, student organizations, university administration, finances, sports and publications. The article concludes with an account of the 75th anniversary celebrations. Period: 1911 - 1986.

2905. Scott, James. **Of mud and dreams: University of Waterloo, 1957-1967**. Toronto: Ryerson Press, 1967. 194 p. ill. Loc: OKIT, OWT, OWTL, OWTU, OWTUCG.

A chronology of the university's first decade, including information on the establishment of the university and its church-related colleges, the first students, the faculties of engineering, arts, science, and graduate studies, the co-operative work-study programme, the administration and funding. Period: 1957 - 1967.

2906. Sprung, J.P. "How a progressive university provides computer education." **Office Administration**. 1968. 14: 31-2, 34 ill. Loc: OHM, OLU.

Reference from the Canadian Periodical Index. Period: 1968.

2907. St Jerome's College of Arts. **St Jerome's College: Faculty of Arts announcement**. Kitchener: The College, 1952 - 1960. Loc: OWTUCR.

Calendars for the postsecondary institute of the Congregation of the Resurrection which became affiliated with the University of Ottawa in 1947. Each includes a list of faculty, course descriptions, admission regulations, a brief history of the college and a description of its facilities. The Congregation of the Resurrection Archives in Waterloo holds the calendars for the years 1952-53, 1954-55, 1955-56 and 1959-60. Period: 1952 - 1960.

2908. Steiner, Samuel J. "The birth of Conrad Grebel College." **Mennogespräch**. 1988. 6,2: 16. Loc: OWTUCG, OKIT.

A note of the 25th anniversary of the commencement of teaching by J. Winfield Fretz. The author remarks that the college might be dated from 1959 because in that year Harvey Taves, H.H. Epp and Ross Bender prepared a report that led to its establishment. Period: 1959 - 1988.

2909. Stephen, Arthur and Ratchford, Douglas. **Laurier: a photographic history**. Wilfrid Laurier University, 1988. 167 p. ill. Loc: OKIT, OWTL, OWT, OWTUR, OWTUSJ.

A pictorial account of the establishment and growth of the institution which began with the founding of Waterloo Lutheran Seminary in 1911 and included Waterloo College from 1925, Waterloo Lutheran University in 1959 and Wilfrid Laurier University in 1973. Period: 1911 - 1986.

2910. Taylor, Richard K. "Wilfrid Laurier University." **Waterloo Historical Society**. 1973. 61: 74-75. Loc: all.

A brief history of the university, noting its

change of name from Waterloo Lutheran University and mentioning the residences which are named after those people who have contributed greatly to the institution. Period: 1911 - 1973.

2911. "Two universities now educate 5,000." **Financial Post.** 1965. 59: 59. ill. mf. Loc: OWTL, OWTU.
Reference from the Canadian Periodical Index. Period: 1965 -

2912. "U. of Waterloo launches drive for $3 million." **Financial Post.** 1962. 56: 8. mf. Loc: OWTL, OWTU.
Reference from the Canadian Periodical Index. Period: 1962.

2913. "U. of Waterloo names 11 new faculty." **Financial Post.** 1962. 56: 24. mf. Loc: OWTL, OWTU.
Reference from the Canadian Periodical Index. Period: 1962.

2914. "Unique plan for education at Waterloo." **Financial Post.** 1956. 50: 4. mf. Loc: OWTL, OWTU.
Reference from the Canadian Periodical Index. Period: 1956.

2915. "University expands: editorial." **Industrial Canada.** 1962. 63: 7. mf. Loc: OWTU.
Reference from the Canadian Periodical Index. Period: 1962.

2916. University of St Jerome's College. **Calendar.** Kitchener: The College, 1960 - 1963. Loc: OWTUCR.
Calendar of the postsecondary institute of the Congregation of the Resurrection which became affiliated with the University of Waterloo in 1960. In 1962 the University of St Jerome's College moved from Kitchener and was integrated with the University of Waterloo. Each calendar includes information about admissions, courses, faculty and facilities, with an academic calendar and an historical sketch. The Congregation of the Resurrection Archives in Waterloo holds the calendars for 1960-61, 1961-62 and 1962-63. Period: 1960 - 1963.

2917. University of Waterloo. **Report of the president.** Waterloo: The University, 1967-. 86 p. ill. Loc: OKIT, OWTU.
Brief illustrated surveys of programmes and achievements. Period: 1967 - 1981.

2918. University of Waterloo. **A university of its time.** Kitchener: Bean Printing, 1967. 12 p. ill. Loc: OKIT.
A brief survey of the university's first decade, reporting success in the experiment of a close

working relationship with business and industry. The brochure is illustrated with views of the new campus buildings and presents details of the 10th anniversary fund-raising programme. Period: 1957 - 1967.

2919. Villaume, W.J. "Why they go it alone: excerpts from address." **Financial Post.** 1964. 57: 6. mf. Loc: OWTL, OWTU.
Reference from the Canadian Periodical Index. Period: 1964.

2920. "Watch for 75 unique students. Waterloo University engineers will be looking for jobs soon." **Financial Post.** 1961. 55: 63. ill. mf. Loc: OWTL, OWTU.
Reference from the Canadian Periodical Index. Period: 1961.

2921. Waterloo College and Associated Faculties. **Keystone.** Waterloo: The College, 1950 -. Loc: OKIT, OWTLA.
Yearbooks that give pictorial descriptions of life on the campus of Waterloo College and later Waterloo Lutheran University. There are photographs and brief descriptions of graduates, faculty, school organizations, school publications and athletics. The first yearbook was published to mark the 25th anniversary of the affiliation of Waterloo College with the University of Western Ontario. The Wilfrid Laurier University Archives holds a complete set while the Kitchener Public Library has yearbooks for 1958, 1959 and 1967. Period: 1950 - 1991.

2922. "Waterloo college extends course." **Financial Post.** 1960. 54: 19. mf. Loc: OWTL, OWTU.
Reference from the Canadian Periodical Index. Period: 1960.

2923. "Waterloo forms new division." **Architecture Canada.** 1969. 46: 21. ill. Loc: OWTU.
Reference from the Canadian Periodical Index. Period: 1969.

2924. Waterloo Lutheran Seminary. **50th anniversary catalogue, 1960-1961.** Waterloo: The Seminary, 1961. 20 p. ill. Loc: OKIT, OWTLA.
Includes a brief history and recollections and reflections by the seminary's first graduate, Dr Nils Willison, and the president of the Alumni Association, Albert A. Lorch. Period: 1911 - 1961.

2925. Waterloo Lutheran Seminary. **Waterloo Lutheran Seminary 75th Anniversary fund appeal for the Seminary Endowment Fund: 1911-1986.** Waterloo: The Seminary, 1986. 8 p. ill. Loc: OKIT, OWES.
A booklet which contains a brief historical

summary of the institution. Period: 1911 - 1986.

2926. "Waterloo's engineering students spend six months on the campus, six months on the job." **Industrial Canada**. 1959. 60: 47-8. ill. mf. Loc: OWTU.
Reference from the Canadian Periodical Index. Period: 1959.

2927. "Waterloo School of Architecture." **Architecture Canada**. 1967. 44: 57-9 charts. Loc: OWTU.
Reference from the Canadian Periodical Index. Period: 1967.

2928. "Waterloo teaching investment." **Financial Post**. 1958. 52: 4. mf. Loc: OWTL, OWTU.
Reference from the Canadian Periodical Index. Period: 1958.

2929. "Waterloo: where the action is." **Monetary Times**. 1967. 135: 35. ill. Loc: OWTL, OWTU.
Reference from the Canadian Periodical Index. Period: 1967.

2930. Wilson, L.A. "How engineer plan is meeting tests." **Financial Post**. 1958. 52: 41. tables. mf. Loc: OWTL, OWTU.
Reference from the Canadian Periodical Index. Period: 1958.

2931. Wright, D.T. "Industry welcomes its Waterloo." **Monetary Times**. 1966. 134: 34-6. ill. Loc: OWTL, OWTU.
Reference from the Canadian Periodical Index. Period: 1966.

LITERARY WORKS

2932. Bearinger, N.M. **Among the thorns**. 1955. 36 p. Loc: OWTUCG.
A collection of religious stories and poems by a local Old Order Mennonite woman, dedicated to her grandchildren. Period: c1890 - 1955.

2933. Bunyan, John. **Johann Bunyan's dritter Theil der Pilger Reise aus dieser nach der zukünftigen Welt**. Berlin: Heinrich Eby, 1850. 192 p. Loc: OWTUCGR.
A German edition of John Bunyan's **Pilgrim's progress** part 3, published in Berlin.

2934. Campbell, Ian. "Knowles of Galt (1868-1944)." **Scottish Tradition**. 1981 - 1982. 11-12: 163-176. Loc: OGU.
An appraisal of the literary output of the Rev. Robert E. Knowles, minister of Knox's Church and author of seven successful novels which are mostly set in the Scottish community of Galt and Dumfries Township. The author compares Knowles's treatment of his setting and themes with John Galt's **Bogle Corbet**, set in neighbouring Guelph. Period: 1900 - 1911.

2935. Dilse, Paul. **Grand River people: poem. Engravings, typesetting and printing by G. Brender a Brandis**. Carlisle: Brandstead Press, 1982. 4 p. ill. Loc: OWTUR.
Poem about coming home to the Grand River Valley in June with an Indian friend, and of the poet's love for the land.

2936. **Drei frühe deutschkanadische Dichter: Eugen Funcken, Heinrich Rembe, Emil Querner**. Edited by Hartmut Froeschle. Toronto: German-Canadian Historical Association, 1978. 112 p. Loc: OWTU.
A collection of poems by three early German-Canadians, two of whom, Eugen Funcken (a Catholic priest) and Heinrich Rembe (a Lutheran pastor) lived and wrote in Waterloo County in the late nineteenth and early twentieth centuries. In the introduction, translated into English, the editor provides brief biographical sketches and comments on themes of the poems which range from religious devotion to nature. Period: 1831 - 1904.

2937. Dumas, Gerald. **An afternoon in Waterloo Park: a narrative poem**. Boston: Houghton Mifflin, 1972. 134 p. Loc: OWTUR, OWTL, OKIT, OWT.
A long narrative poem that describes growing up in Conestogo and Detroit in the 1930s and 1940s. Memories of other German family members, particularly the author's mother, are also recalled. Period: 1891 - 1971.

2938. Dunham, B. Mabel. "William Wilfred Campbell, 1861-1918: an appreciation." **Waterloo Historical Society**. 1918. 6: 44-47. ill. Loc: all.
A short biography of the Berlin-born poet with an appraisal of some of his works. Period: 1861 - 1918.

2939. Dyer, Mary Sparks. **Spires aloft**. Galt: Galt Printers, 1938. 39 p. Loc: OCCA, OWTUR.
Collection of verse by a local poet and printed locally, including poems on many topics including Galt. An example is: "Oh, surely the Galt that I see today/ Has a storied past that has slipped away!" Period: 1938 - 1939.

2940. Dyer, Mary Sparks. **Through that bright wood**. Galt: Galt Printers, 194-?. 39 p. Loc: OCCA, OKIT, OWTUR.
Collection of poems by a local author, some of which refer to Waterloo County locations such as the covered bridge at West Montrose and the Grand River valley. Period: 1920 - 1950.

2941. Eby, Malcolm A. and Eby, Elizabeth R. **Sam Bricker and other Pennsylvania Dutch poems.** The Authors, 1981. 1 v. (unpaged). Loc: OCP, OKIT.

A popular account in verse of the Pennsylvania Mennonite migration to the Waterloo Township area, illustrated with fraktur drawings. Period: 1800 - 1850.

2942. Eby, Oscar S. **Red chalk rhymes.** Kitchener: Oscar S. Eby, 1922. 32 p. Loc: OWTUCG.

A locally printed collection of poems dedicated to the members of the Red Chalk Club. Period: 1922.

2943. Edwards, Elin S. **"Something awful happened in Mitchell": Elmira Gothic: "The verandah fell on Mrs. Martin".** 1987. 31 p. ill. Loc: OKIT.

A paper written for a university English course, analyzing news stories and headlines from the **Elmira Signet** between 1893 and 1894 for their Gothic content. The essay presents excerpts from the newspaper illustrating its tendency to sensationalize rather than simply report bizarre, unfortunate, tragic or cruel events. Euphemism and juxtaposition are examined as journalistic techniques. Period: 1893 - 1894.

2944. Erb, Peter C. "The Canadian poems of Eugen Funcken, C.R.." **German-Canadian Yearbook / Deutschkanadische Jahrbuch.** 1978. 4: 225-233. Loc: OKIT, OWTL, OWTUCG.

A biographical appraisal of the verse of the Resurrectionist priest at St Agatha, interpreted in terms of the poet's adaptation to the Canadian milieu. Period: 1860 - 1880.

2945. Fischer, William Joseph. **Child of destiny.** Toronto: William Briggs, 1909. 272 p. ill. Loc: OWT.

A romantic novel involving a stolen child and an orphan, written by Dr William J. Fischer (1879-1912). Fischer was born in Waterloo and later returned there to practise medicine. Period: 1879 - 1912.

2946. Fischer, William Joseph. **The toiler and other poems.** Toronto: William Briggs, 1914. 167 p. ill. Loc: OWT.

The second edition of the 1907 publication of over one hundred poems by the Waterloo writer and physician. Many poems have a Canadian flavour but direct references to Waterloo County are few. Period: 1907 - 1914.

2947. Friesen, Gerhard. **Hier lasst uns Hütten bauen: deutsche Gedichte lutherischer Pfarrer in Ontario 1869-1930.** Deutschkanadische Schriften. Reihe A: Belletristrik v. 7. Toronto: German-Canadian Historical Association, 1984. 173 p. bibl. Loc: OWTL.

A collection of German-language poems by Lutheran pastors who, at some time in their lives, resided in Ontario. Over half the fourteen pastor-poets had ties to Waterloo County. All the poems have religious themes but vary in form and style. The author's introduction (with an English translation) provides some analysis of the works in relation to the time and place in which each was written.

2948. Froeschle, Hartmut. **Nachrichten aus Ontario: deutschsprachige Literatur in Kanada.** Auslandsdeutsche Literatur der Gegenwart; Bd. 6. Hildesheim: Olms Presse, 1981. 290 p. bibl. Loc: OWTU.

A collection of German-language poems, prose, and essays written in Ontario. Works are included by Waterloo County residents Valentin Sawatzky, George von Cardinal, Ben Sauder and Jacob H. Janzen. There are brief references in the section on literary criticism to the Pennsylvania-German dialect and Russian Mennonite literature. Period: 1878 - 1981.

2949. Hale, Horatio. **Was America peopled from Polynesia: a study in comparative philology.** CIHM Microfiche series, no. 06667. Berlin: H.S. Hallman, 1890. 1 fiche. mf. Loc: OWTL, OWTU.

2950. Hess, Gerald. "The unveiling of a plaque to William Wilfred Campbell." **Waterloo Historical Society.** 1946. 34: 33-36. Loc: all.

Report of a gathering at Kitchener-Waterloo Collegiate honouring the Berlin-born poet. Key speakers were Fred Landon, president of the Historic Sites and Monuments Board of Canada and Mabel Dunham, chief librarian of Kitchener Public Library and current president of the Waterloo Historical Society. A letter from Prime Minister W.L. Mackenzie King in memory of W.W. Campbell is included. Period: 1858 - 1946.

2951. Hett, J.E., Dr. **The sexual organs, their use and abuse: the subject on which men and women know the least and ought to know the most.** CIHM Microfiche series, no. 01534. Berlin: The Author, 1899. 2 fiche. mf. Loc: OWTL, OWTU.

By the physician who was Mayor of Berlin in 1915 and 1916. Period: 1899 - 1900.

2952. Klinck, Carl F. **Giving Canada a literary history.** Ottawa: Carleton University Press for the University of Western Ontario, 1991. 228 p. Loc: OWTL, OWTU.

Memoirs of the Canadian literary historian, including his recollections of Elmira where he was born in 1908, and of Waterloo College where he studied and taught until he resigned in 1947 on a question of principle and moved to the University of Western Ontario. His doctoral thesis was a study of the Berlin-born poet, William Wilfred Campbell, and Klinck recalls his role in the dedication of a plaque honouring Campbell at the Kitchener-Waterloo Collegiate in 1947. Klinck pioneered the study of Canadian literature and co-ordinated the writing of the **Literary history of Canada** by a team of scholars. Period: 1908 - 1947.

2953. Knowles, Robert E., Rev. **St Cuthbert's: a novel.** Toronto: Revell, 1905. 339 p. Loc: OCCA.
A parish romance written from the minister's point of view and based on the church and parishioners of Knox's Presbyterian Church, Galt. The author was minister of Knox's at the turn of the century. The book was reissued by McClelland and Stewart in 1933. Period: 1900 - 1905.

2954. Knowles, Robert E., Rev. **The undertow: a tale of both sides of the sea.** Toronto: McClelland and Stewart, 1935. 403 p. Loc: OCCA, OKIT, OWTU.
A novel set in Galt, telling the story of a young clergyman torn between his Scottish homeland and an Ontario town. Minister of Knox's Presbyterian Church, Galt from 1898 to 1915, the author was later a feature writer for the **Toronto Star.** The book was earlier published by Revell in 1905. Period: 1850 - 1900.

2955. MacGeorge, David. **Ae' glint on ither days: being incidents in the history of school life at the famous old G.C.I. for the past thirty-two years and a collection of recent poems.** Galt: Reporter Press, 1917. 100 p. ill., ports. Loc: OCCA, OKITW, OWTUR.
Recollections of Galt Collegiate Institute from 1884 to 1917 by its caretaker, David MacGeorge. The memories are mainly of accidents and mischief of the pupils, but "Old Mac" also gives an account of his being named "Poet Laureate of Galt." Many of the 40 poems are about students, some titles being the names of individuals, and some poems refer to topical events such as the First World War and women's suffrage. Period: 1884 - 1917.

2956. MacGeorge, David. **Bubbles from the boiler room.** Galt: Reformer Press, 1910. 198 p. ill. index. Loc: OCCA.
A second book of poems, written as a memento of "Old Mac's" twenty five years as a caretaker of Galt Collegiate Institute. Most of the poems describe local scenes, local people, or recent events: there are poems about women's institutes, Dickie Settlement, how G.C.I. won the track cup,

and the coming of electricity. Period: 1900 - 1910.

2957. MacGeorge, David. **Original poems.** Galt: Reformer Press, 1904. 144 p. ill., port. Loc: OWTUR, OCCA.
A book of poems written by the caretaker of Galt Collegiate Institute. Many of the poems are written about the school or the students, and some are written in Scottish dialect. The book opens with a photograph of "Old Mac" and ends with an alphabetical listing of the poems by title. Period: 1903 - 1904.

2958. Merz, Philip Paul. **Thesaurus biblicus, or, hand-book of scripture reference.** CIHM Microfiche series, no. 26870. Waterloo: Observer Book Co., 1880. 11 fiche. mf. Loc: OWTL, OWTU.
A local imprint of a standard work.

2959. Noonan, Gerald A. and Linley, Margaret and Mota, Miguel. **Guide to the literary heritage of Waterloo and Wellington counties from 1830 to the mid-20th century: an historical bibliography of authors and poets.** Waterloo: Wilfrid Laurier University, 1985. 152 p. ill., indexes, bibl. Loc: OCLG, OCP, OKIT, OWRE, OWT, OWTL, OWTU, OWTUCG.
A collection of brief biographies of creative writers who had some connection with Waterloo or Wellington counties. There are entries for fourteen writers associated with Waterloo County, though their literary works do not necessarily reflect or depict the region. The novelist James Algie (1857-1928), born at Ayr, wrote under the pseudonym "Wallace Lloyd." William Wilfred Campbell (1861-1918) was a prolific poet and author who was born in Berlin but moved away as a child. Bertha Mabel Dunham (1881-1957), chief librarian of the Kitchener Public Library and very active in community organizations, wrote four novels about the history of the Waterloo region. Oscar S. Eby, founder and editor of the **Hespeler Herald,** published one volume of poetry in 1922. William Joseph Fischer (1879-1912), a Waterloo physician, contributed poems, short stories and essays to magazines and published two collections of verse. Charles Fotheringham (1895-1978) taught music and published a collection of poems about freemasonry in 1970. Henry Spencer Howell (1857-1912) of Galt wrote poems and a travel book. Robert Edward Knowles (1868-1946), minister of Knox Presbyterian Church in Galt, published seven novels depicting life in small-town Ontario. David MacGeorge (1845-1925), caretaker of Galt Collegiate for thirty years, published three volumes of verse. Frank E. Page (1887-1965) lived most of his life as a community leader in New Dundee, and wrote a community history, poetry, a

memoir of Homer Watson and two plays. Janette Somerville of Ayr had poems published in the **Ayr Observer**. Amelia Warnock (1878-1956), born in Galt, became literary editor of the Toronto **Mail and Empire** and wrote at least twelve books under the pseudonym "Katherine Hale." Homer Ransford Watson (1855-1936), noted painter of pioneer life in Ontario, wrote two chapters of an unpublished novel set in pioneer days. Mrs Aaron Weber, born 1893 into the family of a Mennonite preacher, published three volumes of poetry in the 1950s. Period: 1850 - 1970.

2960. "Publication of **The barefoot farm boy** [WRP]." **Waterloo Historical Society**. 1955. 43: 53. Loc: all.

A note of the joint publication by the **Kitchener-Waterloo Record** and the Waterloo Historical Society of C.A. Panabaker's booklet. Period: 1955.

2961. Reed, Raymond. **Jessie L. Beattie, her life and works: a critical study**. The Author, 1974?. 101 p. bibl. Loc: OCCA.

An analysis of Beattie's poems, novels, biographies and autobiographical stories, many of which are set in Ontario and some describe her childhood on a Blair farm. Period: 1896 - 1972.

2962. Sauder, Ben. **Der Nachbar an de Schtroas**. St Jacobs: Pennsylvania German Folklore Society of Ontario, 1955. 35 p. port. Loc: OKIT, OKITW, OWTUR.

A collection of 23 poems in the Pennsylvania-German dialect, reflecting the lifestyle and upbringing of the author. Edited and introduced by Kurt Nabert, with a brief biography of Ben Sauder. Period: c1932 - 1955.

2963. Sawatzky, Valentin. **Glockenläuten: Gedichte**. St Michael, Austria: J.G. Bläschke, 1983. 284 p. Loc: OWTUCG.

A collection of poems with various North American and European themes. References to the county are few and deal with the landscape. Period: c1925 - c1980.

2964. Sims, Rachel. **Under the maples**. Blandford Station: The Author, 1927?. 98 p. Loc: OKIT.

A fictional account based on the experience of pioneer Scottish settlers in the Queen's Bush, including Wellesley Township. Period: 1830 - 1930.

2965. Stewart, Charles. **The harp of Strathnaver: a lay of the Scottish Highland evictions and other poems**. CIHM Microfiche series, no. 33550. Galt: Peter Paul and Bro., Buffalo, 1884. 1 fiche. mf. Loc: OWTL, OWTU.

2966. Williams, Margaret and Gledhill, Robert and Noonan, Gerald A. **Two stories about Waterloo County's puzzle tombstone**. Wilfrid Laurier University, Department of English, 1973. 11 p. ill. Loc: OCCA, OWTL, OWTU, OWTUCG.

Two short stories, "Graveyards are interesting places" by Margaret Williams and "Gone home" by Robert Gledhill, giving fictional explanations for the puzzle tombstone in Rushes Cemetery. The stories were originally published in **From 231**, volume 2, number 1. Period: 1865 - 1973.

2967. Wilson, D. "Dorothy Shoemaker award for literature." **Ontario Library Review**. 1972. 56: 125-6. ill. Loc: OKIT, OWTL, OWTU.

Reference from the Canadian Periodical Index. Period: 1972.

LIBRARIES

2968. "Ayr Public Library centennial [WRP]." **Waterloo Historical Society**. 1956. 44: 62. Loc: all.

A note including a reference to Dr G.E. Duff Wilson's history of the library. Period: 1856 - 1956.

2969. Beckman, Margaret and Langmead, Stephen and Black, John. **The best gift: a record of the Carnegie libraries in Ontario**. Toronto: Dundurn Press, 1984. 192 p. ill. bibl., maps, indexes. Loc: OCLG, OKIT, OWRE, OWT, OWRN, OWTL, OWTU.

An account of the library-building programme in Ontario that was financed by the Carnegie Foundation. It includes information on 111 public libraries, including the seven in Waterloo County at Ayr, Berlin, Elmira, Galt, Hespeler, New Hamburg, Preston and Waterloo. Maps, floor plans, and photographs illustrate the work which is based on library board minutes and the correspondence of Andrew Carnegie and his secretary James Bertram. Period: 1900 - 1917.

2970. Beckman, Margaret. "In the University of Waterloo Library." **Canadian Library Journal**. 1964. 21: 177-178. Loc: OWTL, OWTU.

Reference from the Canadian Periodical Index. Period: 1964

2971. Bergey, Lorna L. "History of New Dundee Library." **Waterloo Historical Society**. 1962. 50: 86-87. Loc: all.

An historical sketch from 1900 to 1962 when the library moved out of Herman Kavelman's general store into a new building. Members of the library boards are listed. Period: 1900 - 1962.

2972. Bergey, Lorna L. "Library facilities of Wilmot Township, 1853-1889." **Waterloo Historical Society**. 1962. 50: 85-86. Loc: all.

A history of the township library from its foundation in 1853 until 1889 when the books were presented to the Mechanics' Institute in Baden. Period: 1853 - 1889.

2973. Berlin Free Library. **Berliner Freibibliothek deutscher Katalog**. Berlin: Rittinger and Motz, 1905. 22 p. Loc: OKITW.

A catalogue of German books available at the Berlin Free Library in 1905, listed by author. Period: 1904 - 1905.

2974. Berlin Public Library. **Berlin Public Library by-laws, rules and regulations**. 1907. 24 p. Loc: OKITW.

An outline of the duties of the Berlin Public Library Board and those of the librarian and assistants, and of borrowing regulations and fines. The rules forbade any work of a controversial or infidel nature in religious matters in the library. Period: 1906 - 1907.

2975. Bowron, Margaret. "A short history of the Galt Public Library, 1835 to 1905." **Waterloo Historical Society**. 1955. 43: 37-44. ill. Loc: all.

A survey of library services from the formation of the Galt Subscription and Circulating Library and the organization of the Galt Mechanics' Institute to the opening of the Carnegie building in 1905. The author notes persons who promoted library services and discusses library finances. Period: 1835 - 1905.

2976. Brisbin, C.E. "Something new in Waterloo." **Ontario Library Review**. 1961. 45: 237-8. ill. Loc: OKIT, OWTL, OWTU.

Reference from the Canadian Periodical Index. Period: 1961.

2977. Bruce, Lorne. "Public libraries in Ontario, 1882-1920." **Ontario History**. 1985. 77,2: 123-149. ill., tabl., index. Loc: OKIT, OWTL, OWTU.

A general survey of libraries in Ontario, outlining the evolution of administrative and financial policies and management at provincial and municipal levels. Berlin is included in a table comparing statistics of free libraries in various cities in 1894. Wilmot Township's library policy is quoted as an example of the way smaller communities adhered to older practices. B. Mabel Dunham is shown as instructor in a group photograph of the first summer library school in 1911. Period: 1882 - 1920.

2978. Buchanan, Rena. **The history of St Jacobs Public Library**. St Jacobs: The Author, 1959. 31 l. Loc: OWRE.

An account by the assistant librarian of the library's origins in a donation by Lola Snider, with a narrative of its early development. The names of library board members and library staff are listed (with an addendum updating this to 1964). Period: 1933 - 1959.

2979. Dunham, B. Mabel. "Co-operation in the libraries of Waterloo County." **Ontario Library Review**. 1937. 21: 120-122. Loc: OKIT, OGU.

Reference from **Bibliography of Ontario history, 1867-1976** (Bishop et al.). Period: 1935 - 1937.

2980. Dunham, B. Mabel. "Waterloo County's library scheme." **Ontario Library Review and Canadian Periodical Index**. 1938. 22: 197-199. Loc: OGU.

Reference from **Bibliography of Ontario history, 1867-1976** (Bishop et al.). Period: 1936 - 1938.

2981. Ettinger, J. "County report: Waterloo County Public Library." **Ontario Library Review**. 1972. 56: 245-7. Loc: OKIT, OWTL, OWTU.

Reference from the Canadian Periodical Index. Period: 1972.

2982. Galt Public Library. **The public library catalogue 1900, Town of Galt**. Galt: Jaffray Bros, 1900. 86 p. Loc: OCCA.

A list of the non-fiction holdings arranged by subject, together with the library regulations. Fiction, children's books, periodicals and reference books are listed separately. Period: 1899 - 1900.

2983. Grigg, Dorothy and Dunham, B. Mabel. "The Kitchener Public Library." **Waterloo Historical Society**. 1928. 16: 68-76. Loc: all.

An historical sketch of the library which began as a Mechanics' Institute in 1854. The authors mention programmes, policies and the names of librarians and members of the library board. Period: 1854 - 1928.

2984. Hebblethwaite, Norman. "Galt builds a new library: with excerpts from Sheila Egoff's opening address." **Ontario Library Review**. 1969. 53: 214-16. Loc: OKIT, OWTL, OWTU.

Reference from the Canadian Periodical Index. Period: 1969.

2985. Hoffman, Susan. "Kitchener Public Library, 1884-1984." **Waterloo Historical Society**. 1984. 72: 34-39. ill. Loc: all.

An account of the celebrations of the library's

100th anniversary, particularly the opening of the Grace Schmidt Room of Local History. Period: 1884 - 1984.

2986. Kerr, James E. "History of the Galt Public Library." **Waterloo Historical Society.** 1914. 2: 17-19. Loc: all.

A brief history of the Galt Public Library, from its beginnings in 1836 as a subscription library to 1853, when the circulating library merged with the Galt Mechanics' Institute, and 1905 when the Carnegie building was opened. Period: 1836 - 1905.

2987. Kirkness, Mary Anne and Miller, Bruce. **The Elmira Library: 100 years of service.** Elmira: Waterloo Regional Library, Elmira Branch, 1990. 11 p. ill. Loc: OKIT, OWRSC, OWT.

A brief commemorative history, noting the library's origins as the Elmira Mechanics' Institute and mentioning librarians, buildings present services. Period: 1888 - 1988.

2988. Kirkness, Mary Anne. "The Elmira Library: 100 years of service." **Waterloo Historical Society.** 1988. 76: 78-81. Loc: all.

A short history from the library's beginnings as a Mechanics' Institute to its present location in the Carnegie building. Period: 1888 - 1988.

2989. Kirkness, Mary Anne. **The Elmira Library: a history, a heritage.** Elmira: Waterloo Regional Library, Elmira Branch, 1988. 21 p. ill. Loc: OKITW, OWRE.

To commemorate its 100th anniversary, one of its staff traces the library's development from its beginnings with the Germania Society and the Elmira Mechanics' Institute, to the Elmira Carnegie Free Library and its current status as a branch of the Waterloo County Library. Topics include the various library buildings, librarians, the fire of 1915, library services and the question of censorship. Period: 1888 - 1988.

2990. Kitchener Daily Record. "Retires after 36 years of library work." **Ontario Library Review and Canadian Periodical Index.** 1944. 28: 313-314. Loc: OGU, OWTU.

An announcement of Miss Dunham's resignation because of ill-health from her post as chief librarian at the Kitchener Public Library. A biographical sketch includes references to the tenfold expansion of the library's circulation and other measures of growth during her years there. Period: 1908 - 1944.

2991. Lewis, D.E. "Lions share." **Ontario Library Review.** 1961. 45: 239-40. Loc: OKIT, OWTL, OWTU.

About the contribution by the Waterloo Lions Club to the Waterloo Public Library. Reference from the Canadian Periodical Index. Period: 1961.

2992. New Dundee Library Board. **Catalogue: New Dundee Public Library.** The Library, 1912?. 51 p. ill. Loc: OKITW.

A list of books for adults and children, divided into subject categories and arranged by title. There is an illustration of the library building on Front Street and a photograph of Gottlieb Bettschen, the original organizer and promoter of the library. The rules of the library are listed, the board of directors and librarians are named, and there are advertisements by local businessmen. Period: 1900 - 1915.

2993. "A new library at Kitchener." **Waterloo Historical Society.** 1962. 50: 22. ill. Loc: all.

A note of the new Kitchener Public Library opened in May 1962. Period: 1962.

2994. Ramsay, J.D. "The Hespeler Mechanics' Institute and Public Library." **Waterloo Historical Society.** 1927. 15: 300-302. Loc: all.

A short history of the Institute from its beginnings in 1871 to the formation of the Hespeler Public Library in 1900. Period: 1871 - 1900.

2995. "Riverbank School becomes Waterloo County Library." **Waterloo Historical Society.** 1965. 53: 74. ill. Loc: all.

A note of the re-opening of the school building in October 1965, with some budget and collection statistics for the Waterloo County Library since its establishment in 1956 under the direction of Walter Gowing. Period: c1865 - 1965.

2996. Schultz, Erich. "Kitchener-Waterloo welcomes the Ontario Library Association." **Ontario Library Review.** 1963. 47: 48-50. Loc: OKIT, OWTL, OWTU.

Reference from the Canadian Periodical Index. Period: 1963.

2997. Shoemaker, Dorothy. "Fifty years of growing." **Waterloo Historical Society.** 1954. 42: 19-20. Loc: all.

A report of celebrations of the 50th anniversary celebrations at the Kitchener Public Library, including some library statistics. Period: 1904 - 1954.

2998. Snider, Lillian. **Thirtieth anniversary of the St Jacobs Public Library, Nov. 23, 1964.** 1964. 4 l. Loc: OKIT.

An unpublished address given at the time of the anniversary. The speech praises libraries in general and mentions the St Jacobs library and the

Kitchener Public under the direction of Dorothy Shoemaker. Period: 1934 - 1964.

2999. Waterloo County Library. **The official opening and dedication of the Waterloo County Library building, October 16, 1965.** The Library, 1965. 8 p. ill. Loc: OKIT, OWRE, OWRND.

A programme for the opening of the headquarters of the county library in the former Riverbank School building. It presents a brief history of the school and of the county library itself, commenced in 1956 by Walter Gowing as chief librarian. Period: 1810 - 1965.

3000. Waterloo County Library. **Report for the year** .... Waterloo County Library, Loc: OKIT.

Annual reports, each containing a statement from the chief librarian, circulation statistics, a financial statement, and a list of schools served by the library. The Kitchener Public Library has reports for the years 1957, 1958, 1959, 1962, 1965 and 1966. Period: 1957 - 1966.

3001. Waterloo Public Library. **Official opening of the new Waterloo Public Library.** Waterloo: The Library, 1966. 1 folded sheet. Loc: OWT.

The programme for the 1966 ceremony, including a drawing of the exterior and a list of members of the library board. Period: 1965 - 1966.

3002. "Waterloo Public Library." **Waterloo Historical Society.** 1966. 54: 88. Loc: all.

A note of the opening of the new library building in June 1966, including a reference to the library's origins as a Mechanics' Institute in 1867. Period: 1867 - 1966.

3003. Waterloo Public Library. **Waterloo Public Library.** 3 v. ill. Loc: OWT.

A continuing scrapbook of the history of the library in three volumes, with material copied from newspapers and organized chronologically. Plans and paper ephemera are included. The first volume contains material from 1876 to 1966, the second materials only for 1965, and the third covers the period from 1966 to 1989. Period: 1876 - 1989.

3004. Waterloo Public Library. **The Waterloo Public Library golden jubilee, 1876-1926.** Waterloo: The Library, 1926. 16 p. ill. Loc: OWT.

A brief history of the institution which began as a Mechanics' Institute and was awarded a Carnegie grant in 1902 to construct a new building. The booklet presents the library's constitution and current with information on the collection. Period: 1876 - 1926.

MUSIC AND PERFORMING ARTS

3005. Baker, George. **A vocabulary of musical terms for the use of the student in harmony, counterpoint and composition, and for the executant, &c., with which is interspersed notices of all modern musical instruments.** CIHM Microfiche series, no. 25719. Galt: Anderson, 1874. mf. Loc: OWTL, OWTU. Included as a local imprint.

3006. Berg, Wesley. **From Russia with music: a study of the Mennonite choral singing tradition in Canada.** Winnipeg: Hyperion Press, 1985. 152 p. ill., index. Loc: OKIT, OWTL, OWTUCG.

A history of choral singing among the Mennonites of Russia and Canada including a description of the tradition of saengerfests and references to Waterloo County choirs and to musicians such as Jacob H. Janzen, Abner Martin and Nicolai Fehderau. Period: 1800 - 1985.

3007. "Berlin Philharmonic Society, 1896." **Waterloo Historical Society.** 1921. 9: 194. Loc: all.

A list of 155 members in 1896, identified on a large group photograph donated to the Waterloo Historical Society during 1921. Only the first initial is usually provided with few indications of gender, so it is difficult to match names with those already in the WRP database. Fourteen that could be matched are indexed with this record. Period: 1896 - 1921.

3008. Bickel, P.W. **Das Singvögelein, oder Melodien und Lieder für Sonntags-Schulen.** Berlin: Oberholtzer and Bowman, 1871. 96 p. music. Also CIHM Microfiche series, no. 58638. Loc: OKDHC, OWTL, OWTU, OWTUR, OWTUCG.

A collection of 22 children's hymns with music. Some are translations of English-language songs or use their melodies. An index lists the hymns by their first lines. Period: 1870 - 1871.

3009. Breithaupt, W.H. "The Saengerfest of 1875." **Waterloo Historical Society.** 1934. 22: 136-137. Loc: all.

A description of the three-day festival held in Berlin in August 1875. Some participating groups were the Concordia of Berlin, Liedertafel of Waterloo, the Orpheus Society of Detroit, the Saengerbund and Orpheus Society of Buffalo, Harmonia of Toronto, Germania of Hamilton, Teutonia Lisbon and Liederkranz of Preston. Period: 1875.

3010. Chadwick, W.R. and Reilly, P.F. **The Berlin Opera House, 1896-1900.** Waterloo: Reilly and Chadwick, 1976. 153 p. ill. Loc: OWTUR, OKIT.

A report describing the building and

performances. Floor plans and a cross-section drawing are presented in the first part, with information about the theatre's operations. The second section names each show, who put it on, the cast, and the price, with comments about each one. There are annual summaries of the productions, with a longer conclusion that spans all four years. Six appendices include a copy of the obituary of the theatre's owner, G.O. Philip. Period: 1896 - 1900.

3011. Chislett, Anne. **Quiet in the land.** Toronto: Coach House Press, 1983. 115 p. ill. Loc: OKIT, OWRE, OWTL, OWTU, OWTUCG.

A two-act play about the dilemma of a young Amish man near Elmira who wishes to enlist in the First World War despite the pacifist stance of his family and community. First performed at the Blyth Summer Festival in 1981, the play became very popular and Anne Chislett won the Governor General's Literary Award in 1983. Period: 1914 - 1983.

3012. Farquharson, Dorothy H. **O, for a thousand tongues to sing: a history of singing schools in early Canada.** The Author, 1983. 114 p. facsims., bibl. Loc: OKIT.

A general survey that refers (pp. 68-70) to schools of the Amish and Old Order Mennonites. The author reports conversations with Harold Schiedel who worked as a coal trucker by day but taught singing school in the evenings from 1930 to 1950. Classes were organized at Strasburg Mennonite Church, the Mennonite Fellowship Groups at Heidelberg and East Flora, and the ladder factory at St Jacobs. Period: 1930 - 1950.

3013. Hill, Harry. **School music: its practice in the class-room.** Waterloo: Waterloo Music Co., 1934. 133 p. music. Loc: OWTUR.

A guide for elementary school teachers of music. At the time of writing, the author was the director of the Department of Music Education of the Kitchener-Waterloo Public Schools and Collegiate Institute. Apart from the author's local connections and publication by the Waterloo Music Co., there are no specific references to the county. Period: 1934.

3014. Hill, Harry. **A study of the voice of the boy.** Canadian Music Education Series. Waterloo: Waterloo Music Co., 1943. 20 p. ill. Loc: OKIT.

A booklet dedicated to C.J. MacGregor, then supervising principal of the Waterloo Public Schools, and the pupils of Elizabeth Ziegler School, Waterloo. The work is theoretical and there are no direct references to the county, but there is a short advertisement promoting C.F.

Thiele's **Pocket dictionary of musical terms,** also published by the Waterloo Music Company. Period: 1942 - 1943.

3015. IODE, Queen Anne Chapter. **For the relief work of the Berlin Red Cross Society, the Daughters of the Empire, Queen Anne Chapter present The Slender Maid, Grand Opera House, January 1916.** Berlin: The Chapter, 1916. 2 p. Loc: OWTUR.

A concert programme from the Clement/Bowlby Family Papers. Period: 1915 - 1916.

3016. Kallmann, Helmut. "The German contribution to music in Canada." **German-Canadian Yearbook / Deutschkanadisches Jahrbuch.** 1975. 2: 152-166. ill. Loc: OKIT, OWTUCG, OWTL.

An historical overview including short profiles of musicians from German-speaking countries and a description of music in Waterloo County at the time of the Saengerfeste and musical societies from the 1870s to about 1914. Period: c1860 - 1958.

3017. Kitchener IODE, Princess of Wales Chapter. **Kenneth Sakos, tenor, with W.P. Clement at the piano.** Kitchener: The Chapter, 1935. 4 p. Loc: OWTUR, OKIT.

Programme of a concert held in October 1935 at the Kitchener-Waterloo Collegiate. From the Clement/Bowlby Family Papers. Period: 1935 - 1936.

3018. Kitchener-Waterloo Community Concert Association. **Kitchener-Waterloo Community Concert Association programmes and season calendars.** Kitchener: The Concert Association, 1931-. Loc: OWTUR.

Three programmes and two season calendars of the association. The three programmes are for: an undated concert by the baritone, Richard Bonelli; a harp recital by John Duncan in 1935; and an undated piano concert by Dalies Frantz. The season calendars are for the years 1931-1932, and for the season 1935-1936. The calendar for 1931-1932 lists all the association's members. Most of the items are single sheets of paper. Period: 1931 - 1936.

3019. Kitchener-Waterloo Community Concert Association. **Six decades of music: 1930-1990.** Kitchener: The Association, 1990. 11 p. ill. Loc: OKIT, OWTU.

An outline history of the association and its performers with a list of local organizers of the association. Period: 1930 - 1990.

3020. Kitchener-Waterloo Kinsmen Club. **Kitchener-Waterloo Kinsmen Club presents.** Kitchener: The Club, 1945. 36 p. Loc: OKIT.

Programme for a concert by the Toronto Symphony Orchestra in November 1945. All but one half-page consists of advertisements for local businesses. Period: 1945 - 1946.

3021. Kitchener-Waterloo Kiwanis Club. **Waterloo County Kiwanis Music Festival.** Kitchener: The Club, 1960-. Loc: OKIT.

Programmes for the annual festivals at which young music students competed. Kitchener Public Library has programmes for 1960, 1965 and 1969. Period: 1960 - 1969.

3022. Kitchener-Waterloo Little Theatre. **The Kitchener-Waterloo Little Theatre journal.** 1935 - 1940. 2 v. (unpaged). ill. Loc: OKIT.

Two bound scrapbooks of notices, advertising, printed programmes, press reports and photographs of the productions staged by the theatre company. The first volume covers 1935 to 1938, and the second 1938 to 1940. Tables of contents list plays presented each season, with names of authors and the dates produced. Plays by local authors Edna Staebler and Clara Bernhardt are included. Information is also given about the organization and members of the theatre group, and other activities such as workshops. Period: 1935 - 1940.

3023. Kitchener-Waterloo Little Theatre. **The Kitchener-Waterloo Little Theatre journal; special volume A: festivals, Western Ontario Drama League, general drama, 1935-1940.** 1940. 1 v. (unpaged). ill. Loc: OKIT.

A bound scrapbook of programmes, playbills, newspaper clippings, regulations and schedules of the plays submitted to the Western Drama League and other festivals from 1935 to 1940. A table of contents lists each year's festival participation. Period: 1935 - 1940.

3024. Kitchener-Waterloo Orchestral Society. **Kitchener-Waterloo Symphony Orchestra: second annual concert.** Kitchener: The Society, 1927. 4 p. Loc: OWTUR.

Programme of the concert conducted by James Galloway in January 1927. From the Clement/Bowlby Family Papers. Period: 1926 - 1927.

3025. Kitchener-Waterloo Philharmonic Choir. **The Kitchener-Waterloo Philharmonic Choir, accompanied by the Kitchener-Waterloo Symphony Orchestra, presents.....** Kitchener: The Choir, 1939 - 1960. Loc: OWTUR, OKIT.

The University of Waterloo Library's Doris Lewis Rare Book Room, as part of the Clement/Bowlby Family Papers, has a collection of seven programmes for concerts presented in March 1946, March 1949, April 1952, December 1952, May 1953, February 1956 and April 1960. Among the works performed were Haydn's **Creation,** Bach's **St**

Matthew's Passion, Handel's **Messiah,** and Verdi's **Requiem.** Some of the programmes are signed by soloists. The Kitchener Public Library holds one programme for 1939. Period: 1939 - 1960.

3026. Kitchener-Waterloo Philharmonic Choir. **Ye Philharmonic Quire of Kitchener and Waterloo presents ye olde tyme concerte on ye nyghte of ye 4th daye of December, MCMXXXIV, whych falleth on a Tuesday, at ye Auditorium of ye Collegiate Institute.** Kitchener: The Choir, 1934. 2 p. Loc: OWTUR.

A programme for a concert presented at the Kitchener-Waterloo Collegiate Institute. Period: 1933 - 1934.

3027. Kitchener-Waterloo Symphony Orchestra. **The Kitchener-Waterloo Symphony Orchestra presents....** Kitchener: The Orchestra, 1948 - 1974. Loc: OKIT, OWTUR.

A collection of 33 concert programmes for performances over a 36-year period. More than half the programmes date from 1954 or earlier, when Glenn Kruspe was conductor. Frederick Pohl was conductor between 1961 and 1967. From the Clement/Bowlby Family Papers in the Doris Lewis Rare Book Room. Several programmes are also held in the Grace Schmidt Room's Rare Collection at the Kitchener Public Library. Period: 1948 - 1974.

3028. **Kiwanis jollies for nineteen thirty-one.** Kitchener: Kitchener-Waterloo Kiwanis Club, 1931. 32 p. Loc: OKIT.

Programme for a concert in the Lyric Theatre in aid of the Kiwanis Summer Camp for children at Paradise Lake. Members and officers of the club are listed with a message from president W.H.E. Schmalz, and all but three of the pages carry advertisements. Period: 1930 - 1931.

3029. Klinck, Carl F. "Early theatres of Waterloo County: an article based upon the **Berliner Journal,** 1859-1899." **Waterloo Historical Society.** 1951. 39: 14-17. Loc: all.

A short account of the roles of the Turnvereine and Little Theatre, including references to some individuals and plays. Period: c1845 - c1900.

3030. Klinck, Otto W. "Concert halls and theatres in Elmira." **Waterloo Historical Society.** 1984. 72: 40-55. ill. Loc: all.

An account of the concert halls and theatres in Elmira, giving their locations, descriptions of the buildings, and information about the owners as well as the performers. Period: 1886 - 1982.

3031. Lamb, Kathryn Hansuld. "Kitchener Ladies' Band." **Waterloo Historical Society**. 1975. 63: 4-10. ill. Loc: all.

A short history of the group that flourished from 1925 to about 1935. The author relates the various functions in which the band participated, and lists members including Evelyn Hofstetter Barrett, Ada Eby, Nora Kaufman, Catherine Holle Gourlay, Betty Ziegler, Dorothy Hughes Tuck, Pauline Hahn Daniell and Helen Sim. Period: 1925 - 1935.

3032. Lamb, Kathryn Hansuld. "William Kaiser's band." **Waterloo Historical Society**. 1982. 70: 144-147. ill. Loc: all.

An account of the Berlin band, organized in 1866, which was the nucleus of the Berlin Musical Society formed in 1876. Band members are listed. Period: 1866 - 1905.

3033. Machan, Claire. **The first 40 years (1945-1985): the history of the Kitchener-Waterloo Symphony Orchestra**. Kitchener: Ainsworth Press, 1986. 75 p. ill. Loc: OKIT.

A detailed history of the musicians, conductors, performers, and managers who were involved with the Kitchener-Waterloo Symphony Orchestra. It includes the programme of the first concert in 1945 and a list of musicians in 1965. Period: 1945 - 1985.

3034. Maves, Dale Paul. **The German Sängerfest in Waterloo during the late nineteenth century**. University of Western Ontario (M.A. thesis, Music), 1981. 248 l. ill., bibl. Loc: OKIT, OWTUCG.

A comprehensive study of the singing societies and festivals (Sängerfeste) in the Berlin area from the 1870s to 1912. The author examines their origins in the Turnvereine (gymnastics clubs) of the 1850s and discusses the influences of this German cultural movement on the community and on later musical associations. The last 150 pages of the thesis comprise nine appendices of programmes, photographs, drawings and newspaper clippings. Period: 1860 - 1920.

3035. Mellor, John. **Music in the park: C.F. Thiele, father of Canadian band music**. Waterloo: Melco History Series, 1988. 139 p. ill., bibl. Loc: OWTL, OKIT, OWT.

A biography of the most famous conductor and composer of the Waterloo Musical Society Band, Charles Frederick Thiele (1884-1954). Originally the author's M.A. thesis, this printed version retains the same text but includes many photographs and illustrations. Period: 1884 - 1954.

3036. Mellor, John. **Professor C.F. Thiele: "father of Canadian band music"**. Wilfrid Laurier University (M.A. thesis, History), 1986. 112 p. ill., bibl. Loc: OWTL.

A biography of Thiele (1884-1954), with an appraisal of his role in the development of band music in Canada. Director of the Waterloo Musical Society Band from 1919 to 1932, Thiele later organized the Waterloo Band Festival and the Waterloo Music Company. An entertainer and showman of international repute, Thiele promoted bands and musicians throughout Canada. Period: 1884 - 1954.

3037. **Mendelssohn's masterpiece "St Paul" at the Skating Rink, Berlin, Ont., on Thursday evening, May 28th, 1896**. Berlin: Record Press, 1896. 5 p. Loc: OKIT.

Text of the oratorio, conducted by Theo. Zoellner, with Emma Specker as pianist, Annie Bean as organist, Detta Ziegler soprano, Clara Specker contralto, S.R. Gains tenor, E.W. Schuch and Charles A. Ruby, bass, and a chorus of 200 voices. Advertisements by local businesses make up half the booklet. Period: 1895 - 1896.

3038. Moore, Karolyn M. **Music at Waterloo College and Waterloo Lutheran University, 1926-1959: with special reference to the work of Ulrich S. Leupold**. Wilfrid Laurier University (B.A. thesis, Music), 1974. 69 p. bibl. Loc: OWTL.

A history of the musical organizations, leaders, and events at Waterloo College and Waterloo Lutheran University, from 1926 until the establishment of a Department of Music in 1965. A section is devoted to the musical accomplishments and influence of Ulrich S. Leupold during his tenure at the university from 1945 to 1970. Musical programmes, choir members, and choir tours are listed, and the music and words for "Waterloo we'll praise thee" and "Alma mater" are included. Period: 1926 - 1970.

3039. **The Navy League of Canada presents Gracie Fields ... assisted by the Waterloo Musical Society Band and the YMCA Chorus**. Kitchener: The Navy League, 1940. 3 p. Loc: OWTUR.

Programme for a performance in September 1940, at the Queen Street Auditorium, Kitchener. From the Clement/Bowlby Family Papers. Period: 1939 - 1940.

3040. **Official souvenir program: golden jubilee and Saengerfest of the Harmonie Singing Society**. Waterloo: Waterloo Chronicle, 1912. 32 p. Loc: OWT, OKITW.

Musical programme for the Saengerfest of 1912,

held in Waterloo to commemorate the 50th anniversary of the Harmonie Singing Society. It includes a brief history of the club in German, photographs of its officers and photographs of the officers of the North American Saengerbund. Photographs show the Waterloo Saengerfest of 1874 and the Waterloo Musical Band. Local businesses placed advertisements, and one by the Waterloo Water and Light Commission has a photograph of Waterloo lit up at night. Period: 1911 - 1912.

3041. Peninsular Saengerfest, 1898. **Official souvenir program of the 13th Peninsular Saengerfest, to be held at Berlin, Ontario, August 10, 11, 12 1898.** Berlin: Record Electric Press, 1898. 32 p. ill. Loc: OKIT.

A programme containing short biographies of some of the performers, a list of participating societies from Canada and the United States, and lists of Berlin's Saengerfest executive and committee members. The German words to some songs are included. There are photographs of Berlin, advertisements by local establishments, and a description of St Jerome's College by Rev. Theobald Spetz. Period: 1897 - 1898.

3042. Peninsular Saengerfest, 1902. **Official souvenir program: International Saengerfest under the auspices of the Lake Erie and Canadian Saengerbunds, Waterloo, Ontario, August 12, 13 and 14, 1902.** 1902. 40 p. ill. Loc: OKIT, OWT, OWTUCR.

Musical programme for the 1902 Saengerfest held in Waterloo, including photographs of performers and the Saengerfest officers. Brief information about the participating societies, advertisements from local merchants, and the words to German songs are provided. Period: 1901 - 1902.

3043. Reaney, James. **I, the parade: the story of Professor C.F. Thiele.** 1982. 39, 29 p. Loc: OWTUR.

Script of a two-act play about Charles Frederick Thiele, conductor of the Waterloo Musical Society Band and founder of the Waterloo Music Company. The premiere was staged at the University of Waterloo Humanities Theatre to celebrate the university's 25th anniversary. Period: 1883 - 1982.

3044. Ronnenberg, Ernest. "Kitchener Musical Society." **Waterloo Historical Society.** 1976. 64: 11-17. ill. Loc: all.

A brief history of the band which began in 1876, naming many people and organizations that contributed to musical life in Berlin/Kitchener. Period: 1876 - 1976.

3045. Ronnenberg, Ernest. **The Waterloo Band.** 1955. 146 l. Loc: OKIT.

A history of the band including numerous anecdotes about influential members such as the Zoellner and Roos families and C.F. Thiele. The author describes tournaments, Saengerfeste, excursions, tattoos, concerts, the Waterloo Band Festival, and the sponsorship by the band of bicycle races in the 1890s. Period: 1882 - 1955.

3046. Schultz, Jane M. **The evolution of singing schools among the Swiss Mennonites of Southern Ontario.** University of Waterloo (B.A. thesis, Music), 1987. 82 p., bibl. Loc: OWTUCGR.

A scholarly study of singing schools from their evolution in New England and Virginia in the 18th century to their spread among southern Ontario Mennonites in the 19th and early 20th century. There are biographical sketches of nine Waterloo Mennonite leaders: Menno Shantz, Peter Shupe, Moses Hunsberger, Titus Kolb, Nelson Bechtel, Harold Schiedel, Joseph Steckley, S.M. Knagey and Aaron C. Kolb. The author describes the organization of the singing schools, texts and voice arrangements, and discusses the controversy that four-part harmony and the singing schools created among the Mennonites. Period: 1800 - 1940.

3047. **Scott's Opera House programmes, 1920-1927.** Galt: 1920 - 1927. 6 sheets. mf. Loc: OCLG.

A collection of theatre programmes for popular entertainments, including the Galt Kiwanis Club's presentation of the Galt Comedy Players in "Adam and Eve." Period: 1920 - 1927.

3048. Staebler, H.L. "Random notes on music of nineteenth-century Berlin, Ontario." **Waterloo Historical Society.** 1949. 37: 14-18. Loc: all.

A sketch that mentions band competitions and festivals, including the Saengerfests of 1886 and 1898, the development of the Berlin Musical Society, and many names of local musicians such as Glebe, Kaiser, Zeller, Zoellner and Bean. Period: c1850 - 1900.

3049. Taylor, Andrew W. "The Galt Maple Leaf Quartette, 1913-1936." **Waterloo Historical Society.** 1949. 37: 18-23. ill. Loc: all.

An account of a very popular entertainment group from Galt and its predecessor, the Manchester Male Quartette, formed in 1905 and engaged by railway and steamer companies for tours. The diary of the leading member, Howard Henselwood, is reported to contain details of all concerts ever given and every number and encore. Period: 1913 - 1936.

3050. Thompson, Bertha K. "Musical merriment in Elmira." **Waterloo Historical Society.** 1985. 73: 119-132. ill. Loc: all.

An historical review of Elmira's musical heritage, including references to many local people and the groups or concerts they organized. Period: 1850 - 1983.

3051. Wall, Geoffrey and Mitchell, Clare. **The Kitchener-Waterloo Symphony Orchestra: community impact.** Toronto: The Association of Canadian Orchestras, 1984. 111 p. maps, bibl. Loc: OWTU.

One of a series of reports examining the community impact of four Canadian symphony orchestras. Using questionnaires and interviews, the authors analyze the socio-economic characteristics of the patrons, the involvement of the musicians in the community, and the socio-cultural and economic impact of the orchestra in the Kitchener-Waterloo area. The study concludes that "the Kitchener-Waterloo Symphony makes positive contributions to the quality of life in Kitchener-Waterloo." Period: 1983.

3052. "Waterloo band marks 90th anniversary." **Waterloo Historical Society.** 1972. 60: 90. Loc: all.

A short note of the anniversary of the Waterloo Concert Band which was formed in 1882, before the Waterloo Musical Society. The article mentions three of the band's most notable directors: Noah Zeller, Charles F. Thiele and John Conrad. Period: 1882 - 1972.

3053. Waterloo Celebration Theatre. **Waterloo Celebration Revue.** Waterloo: University of Waterloo, 1982. 4 p. ill. Loc: OWTUR.

An advertisement for three historical plays set in Waterloo County and produced in celebration of two anniversaries, the 125th of Waterloo as a municipality, the 25th of the University of Waterloo. The plays are **Emma Orr, Quiet in the Land,** and **World Premier.** Period: 1897 - 1982.

3054. Waterloo Musical Society Band. **1882-1932, Golden jubilee 50th anniversary of the Waterloo Musical Society: official syllabus and history of Waterloo Musical Society Band.** The Band, 1932. 44 p. ill. Loc: OKITW, OWT.

A history including details of competitions, performances, music, and band uniforms. There are photographs of the bandmasters, presidents, and an 1867 photograph of the whole band. The second part lists the contest rules for bands and individual instruments, stating the various classes and their test pieces. Period: 1882 - 1932.

VISUAL ARTS, INCLUDING FOLK ART AND HANDICRAFTS

3055. Arts and Crafts Society of Kitchener. **Papers presented at the Arts and Crafts Society of Kitchener, 1937-1941.** 1988. 1 v. (unpaged). Loc: OKIT, OWTUR.

Papers presented on such topics as tapestry, jade, medieval guilds and Gothic architecture, with notes of the names of authors and hostesses. In 1937 the society was known as the Community Centre of Art and met in rooms provided by Mr Janzen the florist. When the war began and Janzen required the rooms, the society continued to meet monthly at members' homes. The Doris Lewis Rare Book Room has a photocopy of the original volumes held by the Kitchener Public Library. Period: 1937 - 1941.

3056. Bice, Clare. "Homer Watson." **Waterloo Historical Society.** 1955. 43: 50-53. ill. Loc: all.

An address at the unveiling of a plaque commemorating the artist. Period: 1856 - 1936.

3057. Bird, Michael S. "Beauty and simplicity: Germanic folk art in Canada." **German-Canadian Yearbook / Deutschkanadisches Jahrbuch.** 1983. 7: 63-81. ill. Loc: OKIT, OWTUCG, OWTL.

A discussion of decorative arts in the categories of furniture design, textiles, ceramics, pottery, woodcarving, fraktur and gravemarkers, including photographs of numerous Waterloo pieces and profiles of artists David B. Horst, Moses Eby, Adam Birnstihl, Mary Snyder and Abraham Latschaw. Period: 1817 - 1965.

3058. Bird, Michael S. **Calligraphy to cabinetmaking: the fraktur and furniture of Abraham Latschaw (1799-1870).** Kitchener: Joseph Schneider Haus, 197-?. 20 p. ill. Loc: OKIT.

A collection of sixteen samples of the artist's work accompanied by a short text describing the background of each. A summary of Latschaw's dual career is provided at the front of the booklet. Period: 1799 - 1870.

3059. Bird, Michael S. **Canadian folk art: old ways in a new land.** Don Mills: Oxford University Press, 1983. 121 p. ill., bibl. Loc: OKIT, OWRE, OWTL, OWTUR, OWTUCG.

A colourful collection including twelve items from Waterloo County. Photographs of paintings, drawings (fraktur), sculptures, textiles, furniture, architecture, gravemarkers, religious objects, household articles and decorated boxes are accompanied by brief descriptions of the cultural, ethnic and historical background of each object. Period: 1823 - c1950.

3060. Bird, Michael S. "Gravestone symbolism: St Boniface Cemetery, Maryhill." **Waterloo Historical Society**. 1991. 79: 120-127. ill. Loc: all.

A discussion of the symbolic significance of the cemetery's arrangement and location and of the decorative motifs on its stone markers, including the cross, angels, birds, lambs, hands, hearts and eyes. Period: 1826 - 1930.

3061. Bird, Michael S. "Jacob Bock (1798-1867): Waterloo County's first potter." **Waterloo Historical Society**. 1982. 70: 63-67. ill. Loc: all.

An account of the man who briefly worked as a potter from 1822 to 1825, with a description of his straight-sided earthenware jars. Period: 1822 - 1825.

3062. Bird, Michael S. "Ontario and Pennsylvania: parallels in the decorative arts." **Canadian Collector**. 1979. 14,5: 48-51. ill. Loc: OWTU.

An account of a 1979 exhibition by the Heritage Center of Lancaster County. The author suggests that the exhibit indicates a new appreciation of Canadian antiques, and gives details of the displays and artists. The article includes photographs of a fraktur drawing by Anna Weber, woodcarvings by David Horst and furniture made in Waterloo County. Period: 1800 - 1979.

3063. Bird, Michael S. **Ontario fraktur: a Pennsylvania-German folk tradition in early Canada**. Toronto: M.F. Feheley, 1977. 144 p. ill., bibl., map. Loc: OCLG, OCP, OKIT, OWTL, OWTU, OWTUCG, OWTUR.

An illustrated history of fraktur in Canada, describing its main elements, its major decorative forms, and its best known artists. A chapter on Waterloo County presents over 100 illustrated examples of fraktur. Period: 1800 - 1890.

3064. Bird, Michael S. "Ontario fraktur art: a decorative tradition in three Germanic settlements." **Ontario History**. 1976. 68,4: 247-272. ill. bibl. Loc: OKIT, OWTL, OWTU.

A general description of fraktur and its uses, with specific reference to work produced in the geographical areas of Niagara, Markham Township and Waterloo County before about 1920. There are biographical notes on Waterloo fraktur artists Abraham Latschaw, Samuel and Daniel Hoffman, Noah Reist, Anna Weber and Joseph Martin. Period: 1800 - 1920.

3065. Bird, Michael S. "The painted furniture of John J. Gerber and Christian O. Gerber." **Waterloo Historical Society**. 1981. 69: 26-31. ill. Loc: all.

An illustrated account of the painted furniture produced by John Gerber (1809-1889) and his son Christian (1845-1928) for the Amish people of Wellesley Township between 1860 and 1928. Information about other members of the Gerber family is also given. Period: 1809 - 1928.

3066. Bird, Michael S. "Pennsylvania-German parallels: decorative arts of Pennsylvania and Ontario." **Canadian Antiques and Art Review**. 1979. 1,2: 20-27. ill. Loc: OWTU.

A discussion of the similarities in furniture, folk art and decorative accessories between Lancaster County and Waterloo County, illustrated by photographs from the 1979 Pennsylvania-German Parallels exhibition at the Heritage Centre of Lancaster County. The author mentions specific artists whose work demonstrates the evolution of the Pennsylvania German tradition. Period: 1800 - 1979.

3067. Bird, Michael S. "A spirit of exuberance: Germanic decorative arts in Nova Scotia and Ontario." **Canadian Antiques and Art Review**. 1979. 1,1: 16-23. ill. Loc: OWTU.

An illustrated discussion of the Germanic influence in the decorative arts in Canada, particularly Nova Scotia and Ontario. Waterloo County examples include the door of the Goetz House of Maryhill, a Mennonite show towel embroidered by Susanna Horst, and a hooked rug with geometric patterns. Period: 1800 - 1979.

3068. Bird, Michael S. and Kobayashi, Teruko. **A splendid harvest: Germanic folk and decorative arts in Canada**. Toronto: Van Nostrand Reinhold, 1981. 240 p. ill., bibl., index. Loc: OCLG, OCP, OKIT, OWTL, OWTUR, OWTUCG, OWRE.

An historical survey, with particular reference to the Waterloo area. The book traces the European and Pennsylvanian roots of fraktur, furniture designs, woodcarvings, building styles, textiles, pottery and gravemarkers, and places them in their Canadian context. Artists are identified with brief biographical sketches. Period: 1800 - c1920.

3069. Bird, Michael S. "Taking it and leaving it: fraktur in Waterloo County." **From Pennsylvania to Waterloo: Pennsylvania-German folk culture in transition**. Edited by Susan M. Burke and Matthew H. Hill. Kitchener: Friends of the Joseph Schneider Haus, 1991. Pp. 55-65. ill. Loc: OKIT.

A review of the process of discovering examples of fraktur in Waterloo County and a discussion of the main types. The author reports that most Waterloo County fraktur art dates from the years between 1822 and 1890 and comes from the small geographical area bounded by Berlin, Breslau, St Jacobs and Hawkesville, in which Abraham Latschaw, Isaac Hunsicker, Anna Weber and Joseph D. Bauman worked. He concludes that the fraktur of Waterloo County was conserving rather than a creative response to its Lancaster County models, and that there was much omission, simplification and copying. Period: 1822 - 1923.

3070. Bird, Michael S. "Three Waterloo County fraktur artists." **Waterloo Historical Society**. 1976. 64: 78-90. ill., bibl. Loc: all.

A detailed analysis of the works of Abraham Latschaw, Isaac Z. Hunsicker and Joseph Bauman. The author notes that the iconographic depictions used by the local artists can be traced to medieval European origins. Period: 1799 - 1889.

3071. Blain, Brad. **Elizabeth Eastman: a quiet inner authority**. Kitchener: Kitchener-Waterloo Art Gallery, 1982. Loc: OKIT.

Catalogue of a 1982 exhibition at the Kitchener-Waterloo Art Gallery, including paintings of West Montrose, Mannheim, Conestoga, Chicopee, Doon, Victoria Park and Hidden Valley. Eastman's roles in the Kitchener-Waterloo Society of Artists and the Kitchener-Waterloo Art Gallery are noted in a brief memoir of her life and work. Period: 1905 - 1982.

3072. Burke, Susan M. "Perpetuation and adaptation: the Germanic textiles of Waterloo County, 1800-1900." **From Pennsylvania to Waterloo: Pennsylvania-German folk culture in transition**. Edited by Susan M. Burke and Matthew H. Hill. Kitchener: Friends of the Joseph Schneider Haus, 1991. Pp. 79-95. ill. Loc: OKIT.

A survey of the extent to which decorative needlework (such as the embroidered towel and sampler), comforters and other quilted items, handwoven and jacquard fabrics, and carpets, in Waterloo County may be related to practices in the source areas of Pennsylvania and continental Europe. The author concludes that a strong traditionalism within the Pennsylvania-German culture, reinforced by textile traditions brought directly from Europe, allowed certain textile arts to flourish longer than elsewhere in Ontario. Period: 1800 - 1900.

3073. Burnham, Dorothy K. **Pieced quilts of Ontario**. Toronto: Royal Ontario Museum, 1975. 64 p. ill. Loc: OKIT.

Photographs and diagrams of quilts and designs from the Royal Ontario Museum's collection, including three examples from Waterloo County. Period: 1875 - 1900.

3074. Burnham, Harold B. and Burnham, Dorothy K. "**Keep me warm one night": early handweaving in eastern Canada**. Toronto: University of Toronto Press, 1972. 387 p. ill., bibl., index. Loc: OKIT.

A scholarly and comprehensive work produced in association with the Royal Ontario Museum. Many examples of Waterloo weaving are shown in the chapters on linens, twill diaper coverlets, doublecloth and jacquard coverlets, with information on the date, place, owner and weaver of each. Waterloo weavers mentioned include Wilhelm Werlich, August Ploethner, Aaron Zelner, Daniel Knechtel, Johan and George Lippert, and John and William Noll. Period: 1799 - 1900.

3075. Conrad Grebel College. **Woldemar Neufeld: an exhibition of paintings of Waterloo County**. Waterloo: The College, 1974. 32 p. ill. Loc: OWTUR, OKIT, OWT.

A description of the works held by Conrad Grebel College, depicting various county scenes including residences, parks, markets, and the Grand and Conestogo Rivers. Period: 1808 - 1974.

3076. Coumans, Camilla C. "Ornamental iron grave markers." **Waterloo Historical Society**. 1961. 49: 72-75. ill. Loc: all.

An account of ornamental iron markers in Waterloo County, most of which were made between 1860 to 1903 and are found in the German Catholic settlements. Period: 1860 - 1903.

3077. Good, E. Reginald. **Anna's art: the fraktur art of Anna Weber, a Waterloo County Mennonite artist, 1814-1888**. Kitchener: Pochauna Publications, 1976. 48 p. ill., map. Loc: OCLG, OCP, OKIT, OWRN, OWT, OWTL, OWTUR, OWTUCG.

A biographical appraisal of Anna Weber, a fraktur artist who was born in Lancaster County, Pennsylvania and came to Waterloo County with her family in 1825. Examples of her work are presented in chronological order to show her artistic development. Period: 1814 - 1888.

3078. Good, E. Reginald. **Fraktur in Waterloo County, Ontario**. University of Waterloo (student essay), 1980. 1 v. bibl. Loc: OWTUCG.

An analysis of the work and biographies of Waterloo County fraktur artists Jacob Schumacher, Isaac Z. Hunsicker, H. William Gerhardt, Abraham Latschaw, Joseph Bauman and Anna Weber. The local information is placed in the larger context of the history of fraktur, from its origins in the Rhine Valley in the 17th century to the changes in Mennonite life that led to its decline at the end of the 19th century. Period: 1800 - 1900.

3079. Good, E. Reginald. "Isaac Ziegler Hunsicker: Ontario schoolmaster and fraktur artist." **Pennsylvania Folklife**. 1977. 26,4: 2-8. Loc: OWTUCG.

A scholarly biography of Hunsicker (1803-1870), describing his works of fraktur and schierschnibble or paper cuttings. Born in Pennsylvania, the artist had moved to Waterloo County by 1830 when he illuminated the family Bible of Jacob Kolb. Many examples of Hunsicker's art are discussed and six are illustrated. Period: 1803 - 1870.

3080. Good, E. Reginald. "Jacob Bock and his folk art." **Mennonite Life**. 1980. 35,4: 20-34. ill. Loc: OKIT, OWTUCG.

An analysis of Jacob Bock's 1825 tobacco jar, Ontario's earliest piece of dated earthenware which is decorated with relief portraits of St Ambrose. The author gives biographical information about Bock and historical information about the 1825 election in Waterloo Township. Period: 1798 - 1825.

3081. Good, E. Reginald. "Johann Michael Stuempfle." **Waterloo Historical Society**. 1978. 66: 55-60. ill. Loc: all.

A biographical sketch of the Preston potter, with English translations of his birth and baptism certificates, a certificate of character, a vaccination certificate, and a record of discharge from his residence in Wuerttemberg. A letter from his sisters in fraktur is reproduced with photographs of a few pieces of his pottery. Period: 1806 - 1879.

3082. Good, E. Reginald. "Joseph Witmer." **Ontario History**. 1979. 71,4: 191-204. Loc: OKIT, OWTL, OWTU, OWTUCG.

A well documented biography of Joseph Witmer, (1812-1896), Tunker cabinetmaker and entrepreneur, with photographs of his work and information on his family, tools, furniture and workshops. Period: 1812 - 1896.

3083. Good, E. Reginald. "Ontario fraktur artist Joseph Bauman (1815-1890)." **Canadian Collector**. 1976. 11,6: 35-37. ill. Loc: OWTU.

A biography of the only known Ontario-born fraktur artist of the nineteenth century. Bauman was a pioneer Mennonite farmer in Woolwich Township and created fraktur as a pastime. Examples of illuminated song sheets and fraktur produced for his many grandchildren illustrate the article. Period: 1815 - 1889.

3084. Good, E. Reginald. **Waterloo County itinerant fraktur artists**. Kitchener: Pochauna Publications, 1977. 9 p. ill. Loc: OWTUR, OWTUCG.

A discussion of artists Jacob Schumacher, Isaac Z. Hunsicker and William Gerhard, with samples of their work including illuminations of bibles and certificates. Period: 1805 - 1913.

3085. Good, E. Reginald. "Weber, Anna." **Dictionary of Canadian Biography**. Toronto: University of Toronto Press, 1982. 11: 913. Also in **Dictionnaire biographique du Canada**, 11: 1011-1012. Loc: OWTL, OWTU.

A profile of the needleworker and fraktur artist, whose family migrated from Pennsylvania in 1825 and settled one mile south of Conestogo. Unusual as a female in this genre, Anna (1814-1888) is described as "the most original and prolific of Ontario's fraktur artists." Period: 1825 - 1888.

3086. Greenspan, Sheila. **Pennsylvania German frakturs in Canada**. University of Toronto (M.A. thesis), 1968. Loc: OTROM.

A non-circulating copy is held by the Royal Ontario Museum's Curatorial Department.

3087. Hamilton, Ross. **Memorial exhibition of original paintings by Homer Watson, R.C.A., LL.D.**. 1937. 12 p. ill. Loc: OKIT.

A catalogue of 90 paintings with a memoir of Homer Watson as artist, a list of his awards and small reproductions of **The flood gate, The sheep pasture, The valley of the ridge** and **The fallen tree**. A similar but mimeographed catalogue listing 217 paintings is dated 1947, apparently marking the death of the artist's sister Phoebe. Period: 1880 - 1947.

3088. Hanks, Carole. **Early Ontario gravestones**. Toronto: McGraw-Hill Ryerson, 1974. 94 p. ill. Loc: OKIT, OWTL, OWTU.

A survey of types of markers, materials used for gravestones, techniques employed in marking the stones, shapes, epitaphs, motifs and modern stones. The author refers to the Kinzie-Bean Pioneer Memorial Cemetery, Rushes Cemetery in Wellesley Township, and Doon Cemetery and includes photographs of many gravestones. Period: c1860 - c1890.

3089. Harper, J. Russell. **Homer Watson, R.C.A., 1855-1936: paintings and drawings**. Ottawa: National Gallery of Canada, 1963. 44 p. ill., bibl. Loc: OKIT, OWT, OWTU, OWTUR.

A illustrated catalogue of Homer Watson's oil paintings, drawings, prints and water colours, exhibited by the National Gallery of Canada in

1963. It also provides biographical information, a chronology of Watson's life and a selected bibliography. Period: 1855 - 1936.

3090. "Homer Ransford Watson." **Waterloo Historical Society.** 1936. 24: 239-241. ill. Loc: all.

A brief biography of the artist whose paintings **The Pioneer Mill** and **Last of the Drought** were bought by Queen Victoria and who produced the panoramic **Valcartier Camp** during World War I. Period: 1855 - 1936.

3091. "Homer Watson sketches sold to National Gallery." **Waterloo Historical Society.** 1962. 50: 11. Loc: all.

A note that about 500 sketches by Homer Watson had been sold to the National Gallery, on condition that six representative sketches were to be donated to the Kitchener-Waterloo Art Gallery. Period: 1961 - 1962.

3092. Johannesen, S.K. "Unknown furniture master of Waterloo County." **Canadian Collector.** 1977. 12,4: 18-23. ill. Loc: OWTU.

Detailed descriptions of cupboards, chests and wardrobes found in Waterloo County and attributable to one craftsman. The furniture is made of hardwood or painted and grained pine and produced in a countrified American Empire style. The author discusses design, construction and ornamentation, and presents photographs of six pieces. Period: 1820 - 1860.

3093. Kaethler, Marjorie and Shantz, Susan D. **Quilts of Waterloo County: a sampling.** Waterloo: Marjorie Kaethler, 1990. 63 p. ill., bibl. Loc: OWTUCG, OKIT.

An illustrated account of quilt-making in three eras: "colonial" in the nineteenth century, "traditional" since World War II, and "contemporary". The accompanying text provides a brief explanation of each work. The authors note the significance of the Waterloo County Quilters' Guild and the annual Ontario Mennonite Relief Sale at New Hamburg. Period: 1850 - 1990.

3094. Kitchener-Waterloo Art Gallery. **Annual report.** Kitchener: The Gallery, 1968 - 1991. Loc: OKIT.

Annual financial statements of the gallery, including reports by the president, director and volunteer committee and lists of supporters. Some issues are bound with the summer issue of **The Calendar**, the gallery's quarterly newsletter. The Kitchener Public Library has all annual reports from 1968 to 1991. Period: 1968 - 1971.

3095. Kobayashi, Teruko and Bird, Michael S. **A compendium of Canadian folk artists.** Erin: Boston Mills Press, 1985. 243 p. ill., bibl. Loc: OCLG, OCP, OKIT, OWTL, OWTU, OWTUCG.

An illustrated dictionary providing biographical information about artists and their art forms, with references to museum collections and books for each entry. Potters, woodcarvers, rug makers, gravestone carver, painters and yard artists are represented. Artists from Waterloo County include Anna Weber (fraktur artist), Rebecca Schweitzer (rug maker), Leah Frey Daum (painter) and Hella Klassen Braun (doll-maker). Period: 1800 - 1985.

3096. Kobayashi, Teruko. "David B. Horst: St Jacobs woodcarver." **Waterloo Historical Society.** 1977. 65: 78-92. ill. Loc: all.

A biographical account of Horst's moves to the United States, his jobs and health problems, with an appraisal of his style. Period: 1873 - 1965.

3097. Kobayashi, Teruko. "Folk art in stone: Pennsylvania German gravemarkers in Ontario." **Waterloo Historical Society.** 1982. 70: 90-113. ill. Loc: all.

A general discussion of the unique types of gravemarkers and their decorative art, including references to local cemeteries such as the Kinzie-Biehn, First Mennonite Church (East End), Martin Meeting House, Hagey and Wanner. Period: c1804 - 1878.

3098. Kobayashi, Teruko and Bird, Michael S. and Price, Elizabeth. **Folk treasures of historic Ontario.** Toronto: Ontario Heritage Foundation, 1985. 128 p. ill. Loc: OKIT, OWTL, OWTU, OWTUCG.

A catalogue of over 200 items of Ontario folk art displayed at an exhibition in 1985. Artifacts from Waterloo County include examples of paper cutting, embroidery, painting and fraktur. Period: 1800 - 1985.

3099. Kobayashi, Teruko. "Fred. G. Hoffman (1845-1926): Waterloo County itinerant woodcarver." **Waterloo Historical Society.** 1981. 69: 111-126. ill. Loc: all.

A biographical appraisal of the folk artist, largely based on interviews with people with whom Hoffman stayed. Period: 1845 - 1926.

3100. Kobayashi, Teruko. "Local paintings tour Canada." **Waterloo Historical Society.** 1974. 62: 26-29. ill. Loc: all.

A short description of the two county paintings chosen for the 1974 National Gallery of Canada exhibition, People's Art: Naive Art in Canada. One, **Birth of a City** by Ora Walper, depicts the corner of Schneider's Lane and the Great Road (now the King-Queen intersection in Kitchener) in 1824. Period: 1824 - 1974.

3101. Lamb, Jennifer A. "Nineteenth century jacquard coverlets by German handweavers in Waterloo County." **Waterloo Historical Society**. 1981. 69: 43-60. ill. Loc: all.

A discussion of the machinery, dyes and patterns used between 1850 and 1914 by notable local weavers including Aaron Zelner, Julius Noll, John Noll, Wilhelm Magnus Werlich, Daniel Knechtel, August Ploethner, and John and Henry Lippert. Period: 1850 - 1914.

3102. Lamb, Kathryn Hansuld. "Wilfred H. Schultz, artist." **Waterloo Historical Society**. 1989. 77: 38-53. ill. Loc: all.

A biography of Schultz (1908-1975) who is best remembered for his floral works but also sketched Waterloo County landscapes. Period: 1908 - 1975.

3103. Lang-Runtz, Heather. "Snyder's Mennonites." **Canadian Heritage**. 1983 - August. 41: 31. ill. Loc: OKIT, OWTL, OWTU.

An interview with Peter Etril Snyder who paints Mennonites engaged in farming activities. The artist explains how he became interested in the subject and talks about his technique and approach. Period: 1966 - 1983.

3104. "Makes iron grave marker." **Waterloo Historical Society**. 1962. 50: 77. Loc: all.

A note that Simon Dentinger of Elmira, retired St Agatha blacksmith, had finished his own grave marker. He made other markers and the iron cross for the St Agatha Roman Catholic Church spire. Period: 1886 - 1962.

3105. McIntosh, Frances R. "Homer Watson House Charitable Foundation formed." **Waterloo Historical Society**. 1982. 70: 125-127. ill. Loc: all.

A short history of the house on Old Mill Road, Kitchener, that served as the Doon School of Fine Arts and as the Homer Watson Art Gallery. The author notes the mandate of the management board, formed in 1982, to maintain the house as a memorial to Homer Watson, one of the first internationally recognized Canadian artists. Period: 1834 - 1982.

3106. McKendry, Ruth. **Quilts and other bed coverings in the Canadian tradition**. Toronto: Van Nostrand Reinhold, 1979. 240 p. ill. bibl., glossary, index. Loc: OKIT.

A general account with specific examples of Waterloo County quilts and jacquard coverings included in the index. Among the artists

represented are Fanny and Lydia Leis and John Noll. Period: 1868 - 1885.

3107. **Memorial exhibition of selected works: Homer Watson R.C.A., LL.D.**. Toronto: Mellors Galleries, 1936. 12 p. ill. Loc: OKIT.

A catalogue of 54 paintings with an appreciation by Sir Wyly Grier and small reproductions of four works. Period: 1880 - 1936.

3108. Miller, Muriel. **Homer Watson, the man of Doon**. Toronto: Ryerson Press, 1938 reprinted 1988. 164 p. ill., index. Loc: OKIT, OWRE, OWT, OWTL, OWTU, OWTUR.

A biography of the landscape artist including copies of several of his paintings. The author discusses phases of Watson's work and notes the individuals who encouraged and influenced him. The 1988 reprint by Summerhill Press, Toronto adds an epilogue as well as an updated list of Watson's works. The Kitchener Public Library, Wilfrid Laurier University Library and the University of Waterloo Library's Doris Lewis Rare Book Room hold copies of the original edition. Period: 1855 - 1936.

3109. Milloy, Cathy. **Waterloo County artists, 1930-1960: research done for an exhibit at the Kitchener-Waterloo Art Gallery to commemorate the 75th anniversary of Wilfrid Laurier University**. 1986. 33 p. Loc: OKIT.

Brief sketches of the art education, exhibitions and affiliations of 33 Waterloo artists, including Ralph Ashton, Dorothea Ashton, Jack Bechtel, Alma Bergman, Jeannette Clarke, Ralph Conner, Elizabeth Eastman, Kathleen Geil, Peter Goetz, Beatrice Hatch, Ralph Hodgson, Alethea Johnston, Ruben Jukes, Jerrine Wells Kinton, Carl Klem, Betty Koch, Mathew Kousal, Jim Kraemer, John Martin, Harold Morrow, Herb Odd, Joseph Pantalony, Lottie Rood, Hilda Ruston, Wilfred Schultz, Don Shaw, Nora Smyth, Marjorie Belle Snyder, John Schlachter, Jane Van Every, Ora Walper, Paul Winchester and Idessa Zimmerman. Period: 1930 - 1960.

3110. Noonan, Gerald A. "Conestogo's picturesque past as a summer art colony." **Waterloo Historical Society**. 1982. 70: 25-31. ill. Loc: all.

A short account of artists who painted in Conestogo around the turn of the century, including C.M. Manly, F.S. Challener and Fred H. Brigden. Period: 1855 - 1981.

3111. Page, Frank E. "Homer Watson: an appreciation." **Waterloo Historical Society**. 1944. 32: 22-25. Loc: all.

A biographical sketch of the "man of Doon" by a

close friend. Period: 1855 - 1936.

3112. Page, Frank E. **Homer Watson, artist and man.**
Kitchener: Commercial Printing, 1939. 182 p. ill.
Loc: OKIT, OWTL.

A biography of the Doon-born landscape artist
written by his friend. Chapters provide
information on Watson's early life, his humour,
painting style and technique, studies and work,
family including his sister Phoebe, associations
with other artists, and the correspondence of his
wife Roxie Watson. Appendices contain criticisms
and tributes and a list of honours and awards.
Period: 1855 - 1936.

3113. Page, Frank E. "Homer Watson plaque." **Waterloo
Historical Society.** 1955. 43: 49. ill. Loc: all.

The transcript of remarks made at the unveiling
of a plaque commemorating Watson's life and work.
Period: 1856 - 1955.

3114. Pain, Howard. **The heritage of Upper Canadian
furniture: a study in the survival of formal and
vernacular styles from Britain, America and
Europe, 1780-1900.** Toronto: Van Nostrand
Reinhold, 1978. 548 p. ill., bibl., glossary,
index. Loc: OKIT.

A well-illustrated book with over 70 Waterloo
County references in the index, many to annotated
photographs of furniture in the chapter on the
Germanic tradition. Period: 1800 - 1900.

3115. Patterson, Nancy-Lou. "Anna Weber hat das gemacht:
Anna Weber (1814-1888), a fraktur painter of
Waterloo County, Ontario." **Mennonite Life.** 1975.
30,4: 15-19. ill. Loc: OKIT, OWTUCG.

A biographical critique of the technique, style
and imagery of Weber's work. Five examples are
illustrated, one on the back page of the magazine.
The article was reprinted in the 1976 spring
edition of the workpapers of the American
Historical Society of Germans from Russia, #20,
pp. 50-54. Period: 1814 - 1888.

3116. Patterson, Nancy-Lou. "Be fruitful and multiply:
Swiss-German Mennonite quilts in Waterloo County,
Ontario, 1875-1975." **Canadian Antiques and Art
Review.** 1980. 1,6: 34-39. ill. Loc: OWTU.

An illustrated survey of styles and symbols used
by local quilt makers. Period: 1875 - 1975.

3117. Patterson, Nancy-Lou. **Christmas characters: text
and illustrations.** Kitchener: Joseph Schneider
Haus, 1983. 6 p. ill. Loc: OWTUR.

An illustrated description of Christmas
personalities, such as Christkindel, Pelznickel,
Santa Claus, St Nicholas, Krampus, Knecht Ruprecht
and Didukh, who have been added to the Canadian

culture by European immigrants. Period: 1800 -
1914.

3118. Patterson, Nancy-Lou. "Crossroads quilts." **Canada
Quilts.** 1990. Issue 86: 28-31. ill. Loc: OKIT.

An account of an exhibition of historic quilts
from Waterloo and Wellington Counties, chosen from
the collection of Doon Heritage Crossroads by the
author. The quilts represent four major ethnic
groups: the Scots, Germans, Pennsylvania Germans,
the English and Irish. The exhibition catalogue
of the same title is also indexed in the WRP
database. Period: 1852 - 1930.

3119. Patterson, Nancy-Lou. **Crossroads quilts: the Doon
Heritage Crossroads collection of historic
quilts.** 1990. 8 p. ill. Loc: OKIT.

An essay on the history, exhibition, and naming
of quilts, showing examples from the 1990
exhibition of Waterloo and Wellington County
quilts in the collection of Doon Heritage
Crossroads. It documents the thirty quilts
exhibited, includes an article on quilt
preservation, and identifies resource materials on
quilting. Period: 1806 - 1990.

3120. Patterson, Nancy-Lou. "The Dutch-German Mennonite
tradition in Waterloo County, Ontario." **Canadian
Antiques and Art Review.** 1980 - 1981. 2,14:
29-32. ill. Loc: OWTU.

A description of the ethnic handicrafts brought
to Waterloo County by Ukrainian Mennonites
following the Russian Revolution and World War II.
Examples of the arts of embroidery, fraktur,
woodworking and cooking are depicted and some
individual artists are mentioned. Period: 1917 -
1981.

3121. Patterson, Nancy-Lou. "The flowering of southern
Ontario Mennonite fraktur." **Multiculturalism.**
1977. 1,3: 9-12. ill., bibl. Loc: OKIT, OWTL,
OWTU.

A description of fraktur and its artists in the
regions of Niagara, Markham and Waterloo. The
techniques of early Waterloo artists such as
Abraham Latschaw and Anna Weber are discussed,
with those of such contemporary artists as
Susannah Shantz and Elizabeth Eby. The author
notes the effects on fraktur of the introduction
of printing in Waterloo County in the 1840s and of
parochial schools. Period: 1799 - 1977.

3122. Patterson, Nancy-Lou. "Gardens, hearts and
distelfinken: symbols in Mennonite folk art speak
of paradise." **Canadian Collector.** 1984. 19,5:
36-39. ill. Loc: OWTU.

A discussion of a nineteenth-century ink drawing
by Judith Hoffman, an Old Order Mennonite child.

The author claims that the symbols of landscape, plants, animals, people and geometric forms, seen in the work of Hoffman and other Mennonites, are images of paradise. Period: 1787 - 1979.

3123. Patterson, Nancy-Lou. "German-Alsatian iron grave markers in southern Ontario Roman Catholic cemeteries." **Material History Bulletin**. 1983. 18: 35-36. ill. Loc: OWTL, OWTU.

A short review including references to the churchyards of St Agatha, St Boniface (Maryhill), St Clements and St Joseph's (Macton) in Waterloo County, as well as seven other cemeteries in Bruce and Huron Counties. Period: 1835 - 1982.

3124. Patterson, Nancy-Lou. **"A great many tramps we had overnight...": Fred Hoffman and the tramp art tradition in Waterloo County**. Kitchener: Joseph Schneider Haus, 1989. 10 p. ill. Loc: OKIT.

A description of the woodcarving work of Fred Hoffman (1845-1926), set in the context of other tramp art in the county. Historical information is given about itinerants, including the Mennonite custom of providing a Trampstub or "tramp's room." Period: 1845 - 1989.

3125. Patterson, Nancy-Lou. **Handschriften: handwritten forms in Germanic Waterloo County**. Kitchener: Joseph Schneider Haus, 1984. 12 p. ill. Loc: OKIT.

A discussion of five types of script identified as fraktur (Gothic), cursive, Roman, round-hand, and public school hand, with reference to examples from the work of printers, gravestone cutters, teachers and amateurs. Period: 1810 - 1897.

3126. Patterson, Nancy-Lou. "Hearts and flowers: paper-cutting and paper-weaving in the Waterloo County Swiss-German Mennonite community." **Canadian Antiques and Art Review**. 1980. 1,8: 33-39. ill. Loc: OWTU.

Descriptions of the various forms of paper art, including paper cutting, paper-weaving, paper-braiding and paper sculpture, Period: 1800 - 1980.

3127. Patterson, Nancy-Lou. "The iconography of the show towel." **Waterloo Historical Society**. 1976. 64: 49-69. ill., bibl. Loc: all.

A detailed article on the history and significance behind the embroidered symbols stitched by Pennsylvania-German women in Waterloo County. Photographs of nineteenth-century needlework illustrate the recurring motifs and messages in the work of various textile artists. Period: 1799 - 1878.

3128. Patterson, Nancy-Lou. "Im Zeichen der Zwillinge." **Waterloo Historical Society**. 1975. 63: 52-62. ill. Loc: all.

An analysis of the birth certificates of Veronica Schumacher Eby and Lidia Kolb as examples of "Fraktur" and "Scherenschnitte", executed by the same unknown artist. The author also explains the astrological significance of the figures in the certificates and makes genealogical connections to family members still living in Waterloo County. Period: 1815 - 1975.

3129. Patterson, Nancy-Lou. "In Thy holy place: a model of the Tabernacle of Israel." **Mennogespräch**. 1985. 3,2: 9-11. ill. Loc: OKIT, OWTUCG.

A discussion of a model made by the students of S.F. Coffman at the Ontario Mennonite Bible School in Berlin, at the beginning of the twentieth century. The author considers the model as a work of art and a symbol, and places it in the context of the life of S.F. Coffman and a hymn that he composed, "In Thy holy place." The model was part of a 1985 exhibition of folk art from Mennonite and other Anabaptist communities of Ontario. Period: 1909 - 1919.

3130. Patterson, Nancy-Lou. "The iron cross and the tree of life: German-Alsatian gravemarkers in Waterloo Region and Bruce County Roman Catholic cemeteries." **Ontario History**. 1976. 68,1: 1-16. Loc: OKIT, OWTL, OWTU, OWTUCG.

An historical account of the iron gravemarkers in the cemeteries of Maryhill (formerly New Germany), St Agatha and St Clements. The author discusses the symbolism of motifs dealing with the affirmation of life, life everlasting and resurrection found in tree of life (Lebensbaum) designs on the cast metal crosses. The work of St Agatha artisan Simon Dentinger is identified. Period: 1858 - 1903.

3131. Patterson, Nancy-Lou. "A laboratory of tradition: a visit to Waterloo County." **Canadian Collector**. 1981. 16,1: 32-34. ill. Loc: OWTU.

An account of a visit to an Old Order Mennonite household in Waterloo County, with a discussion of the furnishings and decorated items as examples of folk art. Period: 1981.

3132. Patterson, Nancy-Lou. "Landscape and meaning: structure and symbolism of the Swiss-German Mennonite farmstead of the Waterloo Region, Ontario." **Canadian Ethnic Studies**. 1984. 16,3: 35-52. ill. Loc: OWTL, OWTU, OWTUCG.

An analysis of the layout of Waterloo Mennonite farmsteads, described in terms of a miniature paradise that reconciles the three polarities of male/female, farmstead/world, and God/humankind.

The imagery of the decorations within the home, on textiles, woodwork, fraktur and tinware, is seen as reflecting this paradise theme.

3133. Patterson, Nancy-Lou. **The language of paradise: folk art from Mennonite and other Anabaptist communities of Ontario.** London: London Regional Art Gallery, 1985. 66 p. ill., bibl. Loc: OWTUR, OKITW, OKIT.

A catalogue of the folk art exhibition organized by Patterson at the gallery in September-October 1985. It provides historical background as well as detailed descriptions and photographs of samples of fraktur, textile arts, quilting, woodcarving, pottery and furnishings. Period: c1800 - 1985.

3134. Patterson, Nancy-Lou. "Meditative hearts: heart symbolism in the Mennonite folk art of Southern Ontario." **Waterloo Historical Society.** 1982. 70: 32-49. ill., bibl. Loc: all.

A detailed study of the significance of the heart as both symbol and ornament in Mennonite art forms. Beginning with examples from 15th-century Europe, the author traces the continuity of the heart motif to the work done by Pennsylvania-Germans in Waterloo County as late as the 1970s. Period: 1800 - 1976.

3135. Patterson, Nancy-Lou. "Mennonite dolls and costumes." **Canadian Collector.** 1979. 14,6: 35-38. ill. Loc: OWTU.

A description of five dolls of Waterloo County, ranging in time from 1900 to 1975. The dolls reflect the changing dress of Mennonite women from their hairstyles and cap to their underwear and shoes. Dress style, fabric and colour are discussed in relation to age, Mennonite church order and season. The author gives the German names for the articles of clothing and related items. Period: 1900 - 1975.

3136. Patterson, Nancy-Lou. **Mennonite folk art of Waterloo County.** Waterloo: University of Waterloo, Gallery of the Theatre of the Arts, 1966. 50 p. ill. Loc: OWTUR, OKIT.

Catalogue of an exhibition held at the university gallery, with photographs and notes on the various exhibits including quilts, towels, baskets, clothing, fraktur and paper cutouts. Period: 1800 - 1966.

3137. Patterson, Nancy-Lou. "Mennonite folk art of Waterloo County." **Ontario History.** 1968. 60,3: 81-104. ill. Loc: OKIT, OWTL, OWTU.

A detailed examination of fraktur, needlework and cut-paper work by Waterloo Mennonite women such as Anna Weber, Mrs Noah Reesor, and Fanny

and Lydia Leis. The embroidery and needlework of the Russian Mennonite artists are also discussed, and other forms of folk art such as basketry, painting, furniture, decorated food and carved wooden items called "treen" are briefly mentioned. Period: 1800 - 1968.

3138. Patterson, Nancy-Lou. "Mennonite gardens." **Canadian Antiques and Art Review.** 1980. 1,9: 36-39. ill. Loc: OWTU.

An illustrated description of the four-square garden, a type of garden brought to Waterloo County by Mennonites from Pennsylvania. The garden is seen as a reflection of the biblical paradise garden, especially when contrasted with the early wilderness. Period: 1800 - 1980.

3139. Patterson, Nancy-Lou. "Mennonite traditional arts." **Canadian Antiques Collector.** 1971. 6,5: 77-80. ill., bibl. Loc: OWTU.

A brief overview of some of the traditional Mennonite arts in Waterloo County. The emphasis is on folk arts still practised in 1972, such as fraktur, needlework and cookery, but tree-carving, pottery, furniture and paper-cutting are also mentioned. Period: 1830 - 1972.

3140. Patterson, Nancy-Lou. **Mennonite traditional arts of the Waterloo Region and Southern Ontario: a historical view.** Kitchener: Kitchener-Waterloo Art Gallery, 1974. 23 p. ill. Loc: OWTU, OKIT.

A catalogue for an exhibition during the summer of 1974 at the gallery. Short paragraphs describe 157 samples of fraktur, woodcarvings, furniture, paper cuttings, pottery, ceramics, textiles, needlework, quilts and paintings. Period: 1800 - 1975.

3141. Patterson, Nancy-Lou. **Minerva Hoffman Martin and Simeon Eby Martin: two Swiss-German Mennonite folk artists of the Waterloo Region, Ontario.** Waterloo: The Author, 1979. 140 l. ill., bibl. Loc: OWTU.

Transcriptions of autobiographical narratives by the two folk artists, with comments by the author on their lives and art. Minerva Martin was chosen for her talents in sewing, knitting, crocheting, rug hooking, quilting and gardening while Simeon Martin was chosen for his skills in woodcarving and designing barns and churches. Photographs of both artists' works are included as well as drawings and plans of their homes and farmyards. Period: 1892 - 1978.

3142. Patterson, Nancy-Lou. "Piece by piece: Anna Shoemaker of Waterloo County (1909-1983)." **Canada Quilts.** 1984. 8,4: 2. ill. Loc: OKIT.

A description of the design and technique used

by a Mennonite quilt maker, with reference to a quilt made of block quilts with different motifs appliqued on them. The author notes that another of Anna's quilts, **Log cabin (straight furrow)** won a prize in the Design Canada Exhibition of 1974. Period: 1909 - 1983.

3143. Patterson, Nancy-Lou. "Settlers in paradise: Mennonite folk art in Waterloo County." **Acts of concealment: Mennonite/s writing in Canada.** Edited by Hildegard Froese Tiessen and Peter Hinchcliffe. University of Waterloo Press, 1992. Pp 152-165. ill. Loc: OWTUCG, OWTU, OWTL.

An essay tracing the development of Waterloo Mennonite traditional arts from early 19th-century Pennsylvania to the early modern, modern and contemporary styles of the twentieth century. The author refers to artists in furniture, fraktur, embroidery, woodcarving and quilting. Period: 1800 - 1990.

3144. Patterson, Nancy-Lou. **Swiss-German and Dutch-German Mennonite traditional art in the Waterloo Region, Ontario.** Mercury Series: Canadian Centre for Folk Culture Studies no. 27. Ottawa: National Museums of Canada, 1979. 216 p. ill., bibl. Loc: OWTU, OWTUCG, OKITW.

A comparison of the two styles of folk art and a discussion of different cultural influences on each group's traditional styles. Art forms include fraktur, paper cutting, textile work, embroidery and other needle work, drawing, woodcarving and other wood work, ribbon work, quilt making, rug hooking, painting, toy making, children's school work, and ornamental cooking. Period: c1800 - c1930.

3145. Patterson, Nancy-Lou. "Waterloo region gardens in the Germanic tradition." **Material History Bulletin.** 1984. 19: 49-52. ill. Loc: OWTL, OWTU.

A review of the ornamental and symbolic features of the Germanic garden, especially its rectangular, enclosed form and four-square composition. The author describes several Waterloo County examples that survive in pure or modified form. Period: 1820 - 1980.

3146. Patterson, Nancy-Lou. "Where one teaches God's Word: image and text in Mennonite folk art." **Mennogespräch.** 1990. 8,1: 1-4, 7-8. ill. Loc: OWTUCG, OKIT.

An analysis of the textiles, woodwork, books and fraktur displayed at an exhibition at the Conrad Grebel Library in 1990, with a list of items and their owners. The purposes of the objects are described, whether for teaching, giving, displaying, identification or recording. Period: 1820 - 1990.

3147. Patterson, Nancy-Lou. **Wreath & bough: decorative arts of Amish-Mennonite settlers in Waterloo County.** Waterloo: Ontario German Folklife Society, 1983. 16 p. ill. Loc: OWTU, OWTUCG, OWTUR.

An appraisal of the recurring motifs of Amish folk art, in relation to the history of the Amish people. Fraktur, embroidery, wreath and quilt making, stone work (for grave markers), rug hooking, woodcarving, and landscape art (the four square garden) are all discussed. Period: c1820 - c1920.

3148. Regional Municipality of Waterloo, Historic Sites Department. **The Canadian Harvest Collection of Terry Kobayashi and Michael Bird.** Waterloo: The Department, 1987?. 6 p. ill. Loc: OKITW.

A description of a collection of over 500 examples of Germanic folk art, many by artists in the Waterloo area. Including pottery, weaving, furniture, woodcarving, fraktur and paintings, the collection was acquired by the Regional Municipality of Waterloo in 1984 for the Joseph Schneider Haus Gallery and Museum. Period: 1850 - 1989.

3149. Shackleton, Philip. **The furniture of old Ontario.** Toronto: Macmillan, 1973. 399 p. Loc: OKIT.

A profusely illustrated book, showing chairs, chests, cupboards, looking-glasses and a dry sink from Waterloo County. Period: 1830 - 1900.

3150. Shantz, Minerva. **Minerva's notebook on spinning and weaving.** Kitchener-Waterloo Weavers' Guild, 1982. 19 p. ill. Loc: OKIT, OWRE.

Minerva Shantz's (1896-1977) notes on how to prepare fleece for spinning and dyeing. Recipes show how to prepare many different plant dyes. Period: 1896 - 1977.

3151. Shea, John G. **The Pennsylvania Dutch and their furniture.** Toronto: Van Nostrand Reinhold, 1980. 284 p. ill., index, bibl. Loc: OKIT.

A study of the wooden furniture made by Mennonites in Pennsylvania, with detailed information on early folk art and artists, the furniture they designed, and how the works were constructed, carved, painted and decorated. Many photographs and drawings illustrate the text. Although no direct reference to Waterloo County is made, the furniture is typical of the pieces brought to the county by settlers from Pennsylvania and later built by Waterloo people. Items include household furniture, clocks and musical instruments. Period: c1800 - c1900.

3152. Sladen, Gib. **Beautiful iron crosses.** The Author, 19--. 6 p. Loc: OKIT.

A description of the iron crosses at the cemeteries of St Agatha, St Clements and Maryhill, made by the German Catholic blacksmiths of those areas in the second half of the nineteenth century. Period: 1850 - 1903.

3153. Snyder, Peter Etril. **A painter's harvest: the works of Peter Etril Snyder.** Toronto: CBC Enterprises, 1986. 170 p. ill. Loc: OCLG, OCP, OKIT, OWTL, OWTU, OWTUCG, OWRE.

A collection of 320 paintings and drawings by the local artist whose work features Old Order Mennonite scenes. Interspersed throughout the book are short paragraphs by Snyder describing his techniques and the scenes. Period: c1960 - 1986.

3154. Tiessen, Hildegard Froese and Tiessen, Paul Gerald. **Waterloo County landscapes 1930-1960: a sense of place.** St Jacobs: Sand Hills Books, 1986. 1 v. ill. Loc: OCLG, OCP, OKIT, OWRE, OWT, OWTL, OWTUR.

A collection of 123 paintings, drawings and block prints, that was published in conjunction with a 1986 exhibition by the Kitchener-Waterloo Art Gallery and to mark the seventy-fifth anniversary of Wilfrid Laurier University. Artists whose works are reproduced include Woldemar Neufeld, Homer Watson, Carl Ahrens, Carl Schaefer, Ralph Conner, George Eitel, Peter Goetz, John Schlachter, Jack Bechtel, H. Eric Bergman, Edward Cleghorn, Elizabeth Eastman, Kathleen Geil, Ralph Hodgson, Alethea Johnston, Carl Klem, Julia E. Koch, John Martin, Harold Morrow, Herbert Odd, Hilda Ruston, Wilfred Schultz, Don Shaw, Nora Smyth, M.B. Snyder, E.J. Mulrooney, Paul Winchester and Idessa Zimmerman. Period: 1875 - 1980.

3155. Urquhart, Jane. **Nancy-Lou Patterson: mythopoeic drawings.** Kitchener: Kitchener-Waterloo Art Gallery, 1984. 4 p. ill. Loc: OWTU.

A catalogue of the exhibition held at the gallery in 1984, including a biographical sketch and appraisal of Patterson's style and the main influences on her art. Period: 1984.

3156. VanEvery, Jane. **With faith, ignorance and delight.** Homer Watson Trust, 1967. 64 p. ill. Loc: OKIT, OWRE, OWTL, OWTUR.

A biography of Homer Watson by his niece, including personal anecdotes about the artist, his family and acquaintances as well as descriptions of his career and travels. Letters and short pieces by Homer Watson are also included with numerous colour and monochrome plates of his work. Period: 1855 - 1936.

3157. **Waterloo portfolio: Woldemar Neufeld's paintings and block prints of Waterloo, Ontario.** Edited by Paul Gerard Tiessen and Hildegard Froese Tiessen. St. Jacobs: Sand Hills Books, 1982. 110 p. ill. Loc: OWTUCG, OWTUCGR, OWTL, OKIT, OWT.

A collection of the painter's works accompanied by brief explanations of each scene, often by Neufeld himself. Many communities within the county/region are featured. Period: 1928 - 1982.

3158. Watson, Jennifer C. **Carl Ahrens as printmaker: a catalogue raisonné.** Kitchener: Kitchener-Waterloo Art Gallery, 1984. 44 p. Loc: OKIT, OWTU.

A catalogue of the landscape artist's works exhibited at the gallery in 1984. It includes a biography of the artist and an appraisal of his paintings, many which depict Waterloo County scenes. Period: 1862 - 1936.

3159. Watson, Jennifer C. **Homer Watson in the Kitchener-Waterloo Art Gallery.** Kitchener: Kitchener-Waterloo Art Gallery, 1987. 24 p. ill., bibl. Loc: OWTU, OKIT.

An illustrated catalogue of twenty-five works by Watson (1855-1936) collected by the gallery. It includes a biographical sketch of the artist ("the Canadian Constable"), with detailed descriptions of the paintings. The article is summarized in French. Period: 1855 - 1936.

3160. "Wayside crosses in or near Waterloo County." **Waterloo Historical Society.** 1939. 27: 83-84. Loc: all.

A brief description of three wayside crosses in the Maryhill-Weissenburg area. Period: 1846 - 1870.

3161. Wilson, Barbara M. "Ontario's first war artist." **Ontario and the First World War, 1914-1918: A collection of documents.** Ontario Series of the Champlain Society: 10. Toronto: University of Toronto Press, 1977. Pp. cxv-cxvii, 176-180. Loc: OWTU, OWTL.

A small selection of documents relating to Homer Watson's patriotic paintings of Canada's First Contingent in training at Valcartier, for which the artist sought a payment of $20,000 from the reluctant Borden Government. The paintings were shown first in Watson's studio in aid of the Doon Patriotic Society. Period: 1914 - 1918.

FOLKLORE, PASTIMES AND FESTIVALS

3162. Arthur, T.S. **Strong drink: the curse and the cure.** Berlin: Oberholtzer and Co., 1877. 676 p. Loc: OKIT, OWTU.

A substantial volume published in Berlin but apparently printed in the United States, with no specific reference to Waterloo County.

3163. Balzlev, R. **Erbauliche Betrachtungen für Kranke.** Berlin: Rittinger and Motz, 1883. 160 p. Loc: OWTUCGR.

A publication of "edifying considerations for the sick", originally written in Danish and translated into German for this edition by Albert Knapp. Apart from being printed in Berlin, the book contains no direct references to the county.

3164. Brubacher, Albert. "The unaffluent society." **Waterloo Historical Society.** 1969. 57: 61-62. Loc: all.

A personal description of life at the turn of the twentieth century in Elmira. The author recounts a mother's work, travelling tradesmen, and the lack of plumbing and electricity. Period: 1900 - 1918.

3165. Campbell, Alexander D., Dr. "Dr H.G. Roberts: a concept of superstition." **Waterloo Historical Society.** 1983. 71: 7-9. Loc: all.

An account of the address given in 1902 by Dr Roberts entitled "The prevalence of superstition in Waterloo County" at a county teachers' convention. The address reported unconventional cures for sicknesses such as insanity, jaundice and heaway, and appealed for proper health education. Period: 1902 -

3166. Campbell, Alexander D., Dr. "Dr H.G. Roberts challenges the oak leaf test." **Waterloo Historical Society.** 1990. 78: 99-102. Loc: all.

An account of a paper presented to the Waterloo County Teachers' Association in 1902 on "The prevalence of superstition in Waterloo County" by a physician who practised at New Germany (later Maryhill) from 1885 to 1903. Period: 1885 - 1903.

3167. Colombo, John R. "Moses in Waterloo County." **Waterloo Review.** 1960. 2,2: 41-9. Loc: OWTU.

A description of the American publication entitled **The 6th and 7th Books of Moses or Moses' Magical Spirit-Art**, valued in the county mainly because of its section dealing with seership, charming, prophecy, miracles and magic. A compendium of prescriptions, recipes, charms, and cures, the book is known to have been used by local charmer Christian Eby (1842-1920), about whom Colombo relates various stories. A photocopy of Christian Eby's personal copy of the book is located in the Conrad Grebel College Archives' Christian Eby Collection. Period: c1890 - 1960.

3168. Connor, James Thomas Hamilton. **Minority medicine in Ontario, 1795 to 1903: a study of medical pluralism and its decline.** Waterloo: University of Waterloo (Ph.D. thesis, History), 1989. 525 p. bibl. Loc: OWTU.

A study of the origins, activities, and fate of eleven medical therapeutic systems or practices in Ontario, namely, domestic medicine, folk medicine, self-help medicine and midwifery, mesmerism, phrenology, hydropathy and mineral water (spa) therapy, Baunscheidtism, Thomsonianism, eclecticism and homeopathy. Physicians George Husband and Charles C. Job of Galt, Henry Yeagsley of Waterloo and William O. Robinson of St Jacobs are noted for their active participation in folk medicine and remedies. Conversely, county physicians John Scott and Hugh G. Roberts are mentioned for their disdain of such methods. Period: c1800 - 1903.

3169. Doering, John F. "More folk customs from western Ontario." **Journal of American Folk-Lore.** 1945. 58: 150-155. Also mf. Loc: OWTU, OWTL.

Descriptions of folklore, folk medicine, and traditional games and folk toys of the Waterloo County area. This supplements a 1938 article by the same author in the same journal. Period: 1800 - 1945.

3170. Doering, John F. "Pennsylvania German folk medicine in Waterloo County, Ontario." **Journal of American Folk-Lore.** 1936. 49: 194-198. Also mf. Loc: OWTU, OWTL.

A list of folk remedies with a note that many Pennsylvania practices were not used in Waterloo. Three notable Waterloo healers, Mr Eby, Mr Yantzi and Mrs Lichty are mentioned, and articles by E.H. Good are cited as sources on folklore. Period: 1800 - 1936.

3171. Doering, John F. and Doering, Eileen E. "Some western Ontario folk beliefs and practices." **Journal of American Folk-Lore.** 1938. 51: 60-68. Also mf. Loc: OWTU, OWTL.

A list of omens, folk remedies, children's rhymes, charms, unusual words, domestic and agricultural tips found among the Pennsylvania German population of Waterloo County. Period: 1800 - 1938.

3172. Fowke, Edith and Henderson, Carole and Brooks, Judith. **A bibliography of Canadian folklore in English.** Downsview: York University, 1976. 146 p. Loc: OKIT, OWTL, OWTU, OWTUSJ.

A bibliography of sources in English on Canadian folklore, arranged by genre, with subdivisions for four ethnic groups: Anglo, French, Native peoples, and Other. The works of W.J. Wintemberg about

Waterloo County are classified with "other cultural groups." Period: 1800 - 1976.

3173. Fowler, Orson Squire. **Creative and sexual science: or, manhood, womanhood, and their mutual interrelations; love, its laws, powers, etc.; selection, or mutual adaptation; courtship, married life, and perfect children; their generation, endowment, paternity, maternity, bearing, nursing and rearing; together with puberty, boyhood, girlhood, etc; sexual impairments restored, male vigor and female health and beauty perpetuated and augmented, etc., as taught by phrenology and physiology.** Berlin: Oberholtzer and Co., 1875 reprint. 1065 p. Loc: OKIT.

A local imprint apparently first registered with the Library of Congress in 1870. Period: 1870 - 1875.

3174. Good, Milton. "Folklore of Waterloo County." **Waterloo Historical Society.** 1981. 69: 103-110. Loc: all.

A personal description of the Pennsylvania-German folklore of Waterloo County, including folk medicine, proverbs, natural phenomena, similes, children's rhymes and festivals. Period: 1807 - 1981.

3175. Hammond, John. "Leap year: girls take your pick and get after the Crosshill boys." **Waterloo Historical Society.** 1988. 76: 156-157. Loc: all.

A poem written in a leap year in the early 1920s calling on the single women of Crosshill to choose a husband from among eleven named bachelors. Period: c1920 - c1924.

3176. Helmuth, Dennis R. **In their own words...Amish folk medicine memories and practices (Western Ontario Mennonite Conference).** Canadian Mennonite Bible College (student essay, Religion), 1984. 43 p. bibl. Loc: OWTUCGR.

A study of alternative health care practices, including charming, infant and childhood remedies, and remedies for sore muscles, bones and joints, colds, flu, pneumonia, internal organ and blood disorders. Based on questionnaires received from congregations including St Agatha, Steinmans, Maple View (Wellesley), and Hillcrest, the findings report folk medicines and practices used by the original Amish settlers of the Wilmot area. Period: 1825 - 1984.

3177. Hess, Albert. "Old customs and traditions of the Alsatians in and around Maryhill." **Waterloo Historical Society.** 1976. 64: 31-36. Loc: all.

A collection of about five German dialect songs from the Alsace region of Europe that have been found in the Maryhill area. The songs tell of the New Year, the three Holy Kings, the Black Forest, weddings and wine. Period: c1820 - 1976.

3178. "Keep polishing steins, Hans, we may yet toast '67 with Bavarian brew." **Financial Post.** 1963. 57: 63. mf. Loc: OWTL, OWTU.

Reference from the Canadian Periodical Index. Period: 1963 - 1967.

3179. Kitchener-Waterloo University Women's Club. **Script used in the Centennial fashion show October 1967.** 1967. 11 l. Loc: OKIT.

A commentary of the fashion show featuring Waterloo County fashions from the 1860s to the 1950s. The setting for each scene is described, as well as the clothing worn by the models. Period: 1867 - 1967.

3180. Kummer, Oliver A. "Idylwild." **Waterloo Historical Society.** 1970. 58: 30-32. ill. Loc: all.

A description and history of Idylwild, a "Coney Island" in Preston that was popular with Waterloo residents from the 1850s to the First World War. The park was accessible by street car and offered facilities for picnics, dancing, swimming and other sports. The development of Riverside Park and the advent of the automobile contributed to the park's demise. Period: 1850 - 1915.

3181. Lamb, Kathryn Hansuld. "Folk artist publishes song book." **Waterloo Historical Society.** 1991. 79: 92-95. port. Loc: all.

A biographical tribute to Alfred Schenk on the launching of **Folk song book in the street-talk of Berlin, Ontario,** published with the assistance of the Waterloo Regional Heritage Foundation, Pennsylvania German Folklore Society of Ontario and Waterloo Historical Society. Period: 1914 - 1991.

3182. Lamb, Kathryn Hansuld. "Lights out!." **Waterloo Historical Society.** 1991. 79: 104-112. ill. Loc: all.

A retrospective survey of the region's last surviving drive-in theatre, the K-W Drive-in, which opened in Bridgeport in 1950 and closed in 1991. The author describes operations and patronage, based on reminiscences and newspaper reports, and refers to the larger context of this form of popular culture. Period: 1950 - 1991.

3183. Litwiller, David. "To the ladies of New Dundee." **Waterloo Historical Society.** 1988. 76: 51-53. Loc: all.

A poem written in a leap year in the early 1920s inviting the women of New Dundee to ask local men to marry them. The verses refer to 19 available men. Period: c1920 - c1924.

3184. McKegney, Patricia. **"Charm for me, Mr. Eby": folk medicine in southern Ontario, 1890- 1920.** Bamberg Heritage Series no. 1. Bamberg: Bamberg Press, 1989. 34 p. ill., map, bibl. Loc: OKIT, OWRSC, OWTL, OWTUR.

An account of herbal medicines and charming, based on the correspondence of Christian Eby with his patients from 1890 to 1920. Waterloo County was the centre of the geographical area from which Eby's patients were drawn. There are drawings of some of the plants used and biographical information about Eby. Period: 1890 - 1920.

3185. Milnes, Humphrey. "German folklore in Canada." **Journal of American Folk-Lore.** 1954. 67: 35-43. Also mf. Loc: OWTU, OWTL.

Illustrations of Pennsylvania German proverbs, anecdotes, poems and songs of Waterloo County. The author notes that, although the German dialect is still spoken in the area, most printed material is in standard German, leaving a mass of unpublished dialect material based on folk tradition. Period: 1800 - 1954.

3186. Nyce, James M. **Convention, power and the self in German Mennonite magic.** Brown University (Ph.D. thesis, Anthropology), 1987. 180 p. Loc: OWTUCG.

A discussion of traditional magic, medicine and witchcraft, focusing on Christian Eby (1842-1920), a Waterloo Mennonite who was well known for his healing powers and witchcraft. Christian's roles as a charmer and an innovative farmer are described. The study is based on interviews, the diaries of Christian's son Gordon, and letters to Christian asking for help and cures. Period: 1842 - 1987.

3187. Panabaker, D.N. "Pastimes among the Pennsylvania Dutch in Waterloo." **Waterloo Historical Society.** 1931. 19: 245-249. Loc: all.

An identification of children's games and rhymes used around the 1870s and 1880s. Gathering after a funeral is also discussed as a social activity of the Pennsylvania Dutch. Period: c1870 - c1880.

3188. Rauchfuss, Julius. **Oktoberfest scrapbook.** 1983. 1 v. (unpaged). Loc: OKIT.

Copy of a scrapbook collection of newspaper clippings, correspondence, pamphlets and advertisements relating to the establishment and growth of the K-W Oktoberfest. Period: 1968 - 1978.

3189. Reaman, G. Elmore. "Folklore, folk art and characteristic foods of the Province of Ontario." **German-Canadian Yearbook / Deutschkanadisches**

Jahrbuch. 1973. 1: 77-80. Loc: OKIT, OWTL, OWTUCG.

A short essay on Mennonite, Amish, Catholic and Lutheran influences originating in the German-speaking areas of Europe and persisting as popular superstitions, tales, traditions, legends, sayings, folk art and food customs in the Waterloo region. The article was first published in 1957 in the **German Canadian Review.** Period: 1800 - 1950.

3190. Rittinger, John A. **The letters of Joe Klotzkopp, Esq..** Kitchener: Kitchener-Waterloo Record, 1967. 40 p. ill. Also mf. Loc: OWTL, OWTU, OWTUR.

A collection of "letters to the editor" which appeared in both **Die Ontario Glocke** and the **Berliner Journal** between 1890 and 1915. Written in the Pennsylvania German dialect by then publisher of **Die Ontario Glocke,** John A. Rittinger (alias Joe and Sarah Klotzkopp), the letters gave readers a humorous view of small-town life in southwestern Ontario. The reprint in the Kitchener-Waterloo Record includes English translations by Herbert K. Kalbfleisch. The Doris Lewis Rare Book Room, University of Waterloo holds a copy of the reprint. Period: 1890 - 1915.

3191. Sangster, D. "Gemütlichkeit! In K-W that means Oktoberfest." **Canadian Geographic.** 1989. 109,5: 52-59. ill. Loc: OKIT, OWTL, OWTU.

A lavishly illustrated description of the popular festival from its origins as a centennial project in 1967. Period: 1967 - 1989.

3192. Schenk, Alfred J. **Folk song book in the street-talk of Berlin, Ontario.** The Author, 1991. 200 p. ill. Loc: OKIT, OWTL, OWTUCG, OWTU.

Illustrated text of songs about birds, flowers, animals and the Berlin market, in both Pennsylvania German and English, with musical scores in most cases. Short introductory chapters outline the various German groups that immigrated to and settled in Waterloo County, as well as their dialects and musical traditions. A basic glossary of some 30 common words is provided in English, High German and dialect. Period: 1800 - 1990.

3193. Staebler, Edna. **Sauerkraut and enterprise.** Kitchener: University Women's Club of Kitchener and Waterloo, 1966 revised 1969. 96 p. ill. Loc: OCP, OKEBC, OKIT, OWRA, OWRE, OWRN, OWRSJ, OWT, OWTL, OWTU, OWTUCG.

A discussion of the ways of life, beliefs and customs of distinctive cultural groups in Waterloo County, such as Old Order Amish and Mennonites and early German entrepreneurs. Copies of the 1966 edition are known to be held by the Kitchener

Public Library, Elmira Public Library, University of Waterloo Library, Wilfrid Laurier University Library, and Conrad Grebel College Library. The 1969 edition, published by McClelland and Stewart, contains an introduction by Pierre Berton. Period: c1800 - 1965.

3194. Thoms, Elise. "Leap year in Haysville 1936." **Waterloo Historical Society**. 1988. 76: 139-140. Loc: all.

A reprinted poem calling upon the single women of Haysville to ask the bachelors. Period: 1936.

3195. Wintemberg, W.J. and Leechman, Douglas. **Folk-lore of Waterloo County, Ontario**. National Museum of Canada Bulletin No.116, Anthropological Series No. 28. Ottawa: Canada Department of Resources and Development, Development Services Branch, 1950. 68 p. bibl. Loc: OCCA, OKIT, OWRND, OWT, OWTU.

A posthumously published collection of Wintemberg's manuscripts on the German folklore of Waterloo County. Parts of these had already been published in the **Journal of American Folk-lore**. Subjects include weather and animal lore, plant and folk medicine, good and bad luck, folk names of native animals, riddles, rhymes, lullabies, games, customs, proverbs and stories. Many phrases and rhymes are given in German. Period: 1876 - 1949.

3196. Wintemberg, W.J. "German-Canadian folk-lore." **Ontario Historical Society, Papers and Records**. 1901. 3: 86-96. Loc: OWTL, OWTU.

A collection of Waterloo County superstitions about the weather, witches, cures, flora and fauna. Halloween and Christmas Eve customs are described, there is a recipe for invisibility, and the author concludes by commenting on the importance of preserving folklore. Period: 1800 - 1901.

FOOD CUSTOMS AND COOKBOOKS

3197. Bergey, Lorna L. "Pennsylvania German Mennonite food." **Canadian Collector**. 1984. 19,5: 47-50. ill. Loc: OWTU.

A description of Ontario Mennonite food with illustrations and recipes. The author explains that the Mennonites' choice of apples, cheese, chicken and pork derived from their experiences in Switzerland and Pennsylvania. Period: 1786 - 1984.

3198. **The Berlin cook book**. 1909. 300 p. Loc: OKIT.

A volume apparently printed and distributed for Geo. E. Potter, hardware and stove merchants, King Street, Berlin, whose advertisement appears on the last page. The recipes seem to be typical of Canadian household cooking at the time rather than particular to Waterloo County. Period: 1908 - 1909.

3199. Calarco, Marcella Wittig. **Waterloo County cook book**. Kitchener: The Author, 1980. 110 p. Loc: OKIT.

A collection of recipes for breads and muffins, cakes and pies, casseroles, cookies and squares, salads, and special occasions, with a final section of Waterloo County specialties. Period: 1979 - 1980.

3200. **Carter's almanac and cook book for 1897**. Berlin: H.R. Carter, 1897. Loc: OKDHC.

A promotional publication including a calendar, recipes, jokes, hints on dyeing and other domestic work. The White Drugstore's name, address and telephone number are prominently displayed on the cover. Period: 1897 - 1898.

3201. Central Ontario Exhibition, Women's Division. **A collection of early Canadian cookery**. Kitchener: The Division, 1967. 48 p. Loc: OKIT.

A modest collection of recipes "gathered from all the good cooks of Waterloo County." Period: 1966 - 1967.

3202. Denny, Frances L. **A century of cooking, Kitchener-Waterloo**. Kitchener: K-W Record, 1978. 48 p. Loc: OKIT.

A commemorative collection of recipes, introduced by household hints and grocery advertisements culled from 100 years of past issues of the newspaper. Period: 1878 - 1978.

3203. "Even in a city full of fine restaurants, Walper House cuisine is outstanding." **Financial Post**. 1965. 58: 75. ill. mf. Loc: OWTL, OWTU.

Reference from the Canadian Periodical Index. Period: 1965.

3204. Horst, Isaac R. **Conestogo Mennonite cookbook: a collection of Waterloo County Mennonite recipes, folklore and Pennsylvania Dutch philosophy**. Mount Forest: The Author, 1983. 252 p. Loc: OKIT.

A revised edition of a collection of recipes, interspersed with titbits on varied topics including Mennonite etiquette, table settings, gardens and weddings. Period: 1950 - 1980.

3205. K-W Quota Club. **K-W Quota Club presents the 1951 Cooking School to all those interested in home, health and philosophy**. Kitchener: The Club, 1951. 12 p. Loc: OKIT.

A collection of basic recipes, with local advertisements and an announcement that proceeds of selling the book are to support community service work in the Twin Cities. Period: 1950 - 1951.

3206. Kitchener IODE, Queen Anne Chapter. **Queen Anne cook-book: tested recipes for housekeepers.** Kitchener: The Chapter, 1925. 80 p. Loc: OWTUR.

A collection of recipes compiled by the chapter, including a list of current officers and advertisements by local businesses. The recipes themselves are standard fare; none can be said to be typically from Waterloo County. Period: 1924 - 1925.

3207. Ladies Aid Society, Central Presbyterian Church, Galt. **The Galt cook book: comprising a large number of tested recipes for the kitchen, dining room and sick room.** Toronto: Robert G. McLean, 1892. 525 p. index. Loc: OWTUR.

A collection of practical recipes contributed by the ladies of Galt and surrounding area. Information is included on simple cures, useful hints, table etiquette, window gardening and serving meals. Period: 1891 - 1892.

3208. Markham-Waterloo Mennonite Conference. **Favorite family foods: recipes compiled by the sisters of the Markham Waterloo Mennonite Conference.** Markham Mennonite Church, 1984. 367 p. ill., index. Loc: OWTUCG.

An indexed collection of homestyle recipes gathered by the women of the Markham-Waterloo Mennonite Conference as a charitable project. Period: 1964 - 1984.

3209. New Dundee Women's Institute. **Homemaker's delight no. 2 - 1964.** New Dundee: The Women's Institute, 1964. 66 p. Loc: OKIT.

A collection of recipes, for a wide range of dishes from breads and meats to pickles and desserts, contributed by members of the local Women's Institute. Period: 1963 - 1964.

3210. Ontario Equitable Life and Accident Insurance Co. **Selected recipes.** Waterloo: The Company, 1930?. 96 p. Loc: OWTUR.

A collection of recipes and household hints contributed by members of St Quentin Chapter of the Imperial Order of Daughters of the Empire. Period: 1920-? 1930-?

3211. Pauls, Pat Gerber and Kaethler, Rita. **Canadian Mennonite cookbook: with recipes in metric and imperial measures.** Toronto: Stoddart Publishing, 1978 reprinted 1981 1985 1989. 267 p. ill., index. Loc: OKIT.

A collection of recipes for beverages, quick breads, yeast breads and rolls, cakes, confections and frostings, cookies, desserts, puddings, sauces, jams, pickles, canning, meats, pies, salads, soups, and vegetables. While generally Canadian in scope, the recipes are typical of those used in Mennonite kitchens in Waterloo County.

3212. Presbyterian Young Women's Club. **Cook book: containing many carefully chosen practical recipes.** Kitchener: Cober Printing Service, 1947. 64 p. Loc: OWTUR.

A collection of recipes and household hints interspersed with advertisements from local businesses. The dishes are standard fare and not peculiar to Waterloo County. Period: 1946 - 1947.

3213. Queen Esther Auxiliary. **Favorite recipes, 1930-31.** Waterloo: First United Church, 1931. 52 p. Loc: OWTUR.

A collection of recipes and household hints with the names of the auxiliary members who contributed them. Advertisements by local businesses are interspersed throughout the book. Period: 1930 - 1931.

3214. Showalter, Mary Emma. **Mennonite community cookbook: favourite family recipes.** Scottdale, PA and Kitchener: Herald Press, 1950 reprinted 1957. 494 p. Loc: OKIT, OWTUCG.

Names of some Waterloo County women who contributed to this large collection are given. Period: 1950 - 1957.

3215. Snyder, Beatrice Miller. **Pennsylvania German customs and cookery.** Pennsylvania German Folklore Society of Ontario, Waterloo Chapter, 1979. 93 p. ill., index. Loc: OWTUCG, OKIT.

A collection of recipes and customs relating to food preparation from the family and friends of the author's grandmother. Breads, soups, potatoes, meats, salads, vegetables, pickles and relishes, pies, puddings and sauces, cakes and icings, cookies and candies, pancakes, waffles, doughnuts, beverages, jams, jellies, cheeses, apples, butter sculpturing, and maple syrup treats are included in 17 chapters. A brief glossary of Pennsylvania German food expressions is provided as well. Period: c1800 - 1979.

3216. Staebler, Edna. **Food that really schmecks: Mennonite country cooking as prepared by my Mennonite friend Bevvy Martin, my mother and other fine cooks.** Toronto: Ryerson Press, 1968. 297 p. Loc: OCLG, OCH, OKIT, OWRE, OWTL, OWTUCG.

A cookbook of local recipes interspersed with anecdotes about Mennonite customs and traditions. Period: 1800 - 1968.

3217. Staebler, Edna. "Foodways of the Waterloo County relatives." **From Pennsylvania to Waterloo: Pennsylvania-German folk culture in transition.** Edited by Susan M. Burke and Matthew H. Hill. Kitchener: Friends of the Joseph Schneider Haus, 1991. Pp. 117-123. Loc: OKIT.
Reflections on distinctive recipes and methods of food preservation and preparation, with anecdotes and reminiscences from her Mennonite friends. Period: 1950 - 1990.

3218. Staebler, Edna. **More food that really schmecks.** Toronto: McClelland and Stewart, 1988. 318 p. ill., index. Loc: OCH, OCLG, OCP, OKIT, OWTUCG.
A collection of recipes from Edna Staebler's Mennonite friends and relations. An introductory chapter describes the Kitchener Farmers' Market. Period: 1800 - 1972.

3219. Staebler, Edna. **Muffins and quick breads with schmecks appeal.** Schmecks Appeal Cookbook Series. Montreal: McGraw-Hill Ryerson, 1990. 88 p. ill., index. Loc: OKIT, OWTUCG.
A compilation of muffin and quick bread recipes from the three "Schmecks" cookbooks, interspersed with anecdotes about the Old Order Mennonites.

3220. Staebler, Edna. **Pies and tarts with schmecks appeal.** Schmecks Appeal Cookbook Series. Montreal and Toronto: McGraw-Hill Ryerson, 1990. 92 p. ill., index. Loc: OKIT, OWTUCG.
A cookbook containing recipes gathered by the Waterloo County author from her Mennonite friends and family in the area. The recipes are accompanied by short anecdotes about customs and traditions found in Mennonite kitchens. Period: c1950 - 1990.

3221. Staebler, Edna. **Schmecks appeal: more Mennonite country cooking.** Toronto: McClelland and Stewart, 1987. 292 p. ill., index. Loc: OCLG, OCP, OKIT, OWRE, OWTUCG.
A collection including local Mennonite recipes. The introduction mentions the "Great Cookie War" when Staebler was approached by corporate lawyers for the recipe for the "Rigglevake" cookie, a crispy and chewy cookie similar to those made by commercial companies in the mid-1980s. Period: c1950 - 1987.

3222. Staebler, Edna. **Soups and salads with schmecks appeal.** Schmecks Appeal Cookbook Series. Montreal and Toronto: McGraw-Hill-Ryerson, 1990. 87 p. ill., index. Loc: OKIT, OWTUCG.
A collection of recipes gathered from the author's Mennonite friends in the Waterloo County area and accompanied by short anecdotes of Mennonite traditions. Period: c1950 - 1990.

3223. Staebler, Edna. **Sweets, sours, and drinks with schmecks appeal.** Schmecks Appeal Cookbook Series. Montreal and Toronto: McGraw-Hill Ryerson, 1990. 86 p. ill., index. Loc: OKIT, OWTUCG.
A collection of recipes from local Mennonite kitchens, interspersed with stories about Old Order Mennonite traditions and customs. Period: c1950 - 1990.

3224. Staebler, Edna. "Those mouth-watering Mennonite meals." **Macleans Magazine.** 1954. 67: 20-1, 60. ill. Loc: OKIT, OWTL, OWTU.
Reference from the Canadian Periodical Index. Period: 1967.

3225. Stauffer, Joseph S. "Pie making developed in Pennsylvania." **Waterloo Historical Society.** 1967. 55: 43. Loc: all.
A short article describing how the Waterloo County tradition of pie making was derived from the practice of early Pennsylvania settlers. Period: 1800 - 1850.

3226. Taylor, Margaret and McNaught, Frances. **The early Canadian Galt cookbook, revised edition, comprising a large number of tested recipes for the kitchen, dining room and sick room.** Toronto: Coles, 1974. 454 p. index. Loc: OCH, OCLG, OCP, OKIT.
Facsimile edition of an 1898 revised edition published by William Briggs in Toronto. The names of the ladies who gave the recipes are included, such as Mrs James Young, Mrs Richard Strong, Mrs R. Barrie, and Mrs George Jaffray. Useful hints and simple cures are included. Period: 1897 - 1898.

3227. Taylor, Margaret and McNaught, Frances. **New Galt cook book.** Toronto: McLeod and Allen, 1898. 454 p. index. Also CIHM Microfiche series, no. 38741. Loc: OCCA, OWTL, OWTU, OWTUR.
A revised edition which omits duplicate recipes, improves others, and adds new ones to the original collection of 1892. The format is the same, including simple cures and useful hints, and the purpose is the same: practical recipes "prepared for the housewife, not for the chef." The 1898 edition in the City of Cambridge Archives differs slightly in being "entirely re-set" and published by George G. McLeod. CCA also has a copy of **The Galt cook book** (revised edition), published by William Briggs in 1902. Period: 1897 - 1898.

CHURCHES AND RELIGION

3228. "1610 Bible donated to Foundation." **Waterloo Historical Society**. 1960. 48: 54. Loc: all.

A note of the gift by Warlaw Vair of Galt of the 1610 Geneva "breeches" Bible to the Ontario Pioneer Community. Period: 1610 - 1960.

3229. **Apocalyptic sketches: being a condensed exposition of the views of the most eminent writers upon the prophecies of Revelation, Daniel, Isaiah, &c. respecting the second coming of Our Lord with all his saints at the first resurrection.** CIHM Microfiche series, no. 48175. Galt: W. March, 1860. mf. Loc: OWTL, OWTU.

Included as a local imprint.

3230. Cowan, Jennie F. "Bibles of historic interest to citizens of Waterloo County." **Waterloo Historical Society**. 1958. 46: 32-37. ill. Loc: all.

A description of the oldest Bibles in Waterloo County, the earliest of which was printed in 1550. Most were printed in Switzerland in the 16th and 17th centuries and brought to Waterloo County via Pennsylvania. Of special interest is the Bible of Benjamin Eby who recorded important events in it. Period: 1550 - 1823.

3231. Esson, Henry. **A plain and popular exposition of the principle of voluntaryism in opposition ot the misapprehensions of those who have imputed to them an infidel tendency: being a humble essay to mediate between the advocates and antagonists of the establishment principle, and to promote generally the catholic unity of the evangelical churches.** CIHM Microfiche series, no. 63135. Galt: Jaffray and Son, 1851. mf. Loc: OWTL, OWTU.

Included as a local imprint.

3232. Groh, Ivan. "Disabilities of the dissenters." **Canadian-German Folklore**. 1967. 2: 22-42. Loc: OKIT, OWTL, OWTU, OWTUCG.

An examination of discrimination against early Canadian nonconformists such as Mennonites, Tunkers and Methodists, in relation to the solemnization of marriages and church property rights. Among Waterloo Mennonite churches discussed are the Union Church on land known as the Gypsy Camp, the Brick meeting house near Preston, and the Union Meeting House at Hagey's Crossing. Period: 1811 - 1967.

3233. Hallman, H.S. **Songs of glad tidings, 2d ed..** Berlin: Gospel Banner Office, 1898. 221 p. Loc: OKIT, OWTUCGR.

A pocket-sized volume of 221 hymns.

3234. Taylor, Ryan. **A checklist of pre-1900 Baptist, Methodist, Presbyterian and United Churches in Waterloo and Wellington Counties.** Kitchener: Ontario Genealogical Society, Waterloo-Wellington Branch, 1985. 5 l. Loc: OKIT.

Brief accounts of the chronologies of church schisms and unions in these denominations, and lists of the congregations noted at specific dates in denominational yearbooks. Localities rather than names of congregations are given. Period: 1800 - 1899.

3235. Weicker, Samuel. **History of congregations in Kitchener-Waterloo from K-W Record 1934-1935.** St Matthews Lutheran Church, Kitchener, Archive Booklet No. 34. 1990. 33 p. ill. Loc: OKIT.

An unpublished collection of photocopied newspaper clippings, containing historical information on many denominations, including the Mennonites, Lutherans, Swedenborgians, Jews, Anglicans and Catholics. Period: 1934 - 1935.

3236. Witmer, Douglas C. **The journey to worship: a case study in Waterloo, Ontario.** Waterloo Lutheran University (M.A. thesis, Geography), 1972. 138 p. bibl., maps, charts. Loc: OWTL.

A study of the geography of religion that concludes that most people in Waterloo attend the closest church of their particular denomination, correlating with the principle of least effort. An appendix contains a list of denominations and churches in Kitchener and Waterloo, including for each the date of establishment in its current location. Period: 1971 - 1972.

MENNONITE, AMISH, BRETHREN IN CHRIST, AND MISSIONARY CHURCHES

3237. Alder, Elizabeth. **The first Mennonite Church of Kitchener.** Wilfrid Laurier University (student essay), 1985. 50 p. ill., bibl., maps. Loc: OKIT.

An attempt to trace the present location of the church first used in 1813 by Benjamin Eby. The author finds that the church stood on Frederick Shaeffer's lot, that his family may have lived in it between 1880 and 1899, and that parts of it may have been used in the construction of the present house at 18 Woolwich Street in Breslau. Biographical information is given about Frederick Shaeffer, his businesses, land dealings and family. Period: 1813 - 1900.

3238. Bauman, Salome. "First Mennonite Church, 1813-1963." **Waterloo Historical Society**. 1963. 51: 19-26, 28. ill. Loc: all.

A history of the Kitchener church, condensed

from the published church history and describing
the ministries of various bishops and pastors and
the church buildings. Period: 1813 - 1963.

3239. Bauman, Salome and Johnston, R.N. and
Swartzentruber, Dorothy. **One hundred fifty years
First Mennonite Church.** Kitchener: The Church,
1963. 24 p. ill. Loc: OWTUCG, OKIT.

A commemorative history of the Kitchener church
which describes the buildings erected in 1813,
1834 and 1902 and additions in 1927 and 1950. The
author note leaders such as the first bishop,
Benjamin Eby, who served for forty-four years, as
well as Christian Eby, Samuel S. Bowman, Urias K.
Weber and C.F. Derstine. All ministers, associate
ministers and deacons from 1804 to 1963 are
listed, as are 75 families who were charter
members of the church. Contemporary church
activities are described, including Bible study
classes, youth groups, Women's Auxiliary,
missionary and children's services. Period: 1804 -
1963.

3240. Bauman, Trevor. **A historical study of the Ontario
Quebec Mennonite Youth Fellowship.** Canadian
Mennonite Bible College (student essay, Religion),
1987. 64 l. facsims. Loc: OWTUCGR.

A study of continuity and change in the group's
organization and activities since the mid-1940s.
Conferences, rallies, sports events and other
social gatherings are reviewed in an effort to
identify a common purpose throughout the group's
history. Appendices include copies of posters,
registration forms, invitations to events and
correspondence. Period: c1945 - 1987.

3241. Bechtel, Ken. "Elmira Mennonite Church: 60th
anniversary." **Mennogespräch.** 1984. 2,2: 17. Loc:
OKIT, OWTUCG.

An account of the anniversary events which
included sessions of reminiscence and music, with
displays of pictures and memorabilia. A
commemorative history, written by Ken Bechtel for
the occasion, is indexed in the WRP database.
Period: 1924 - 1984.

3242. Bechtel, Ken. **Strangers within the gates: Wanner
Mennonite Church, 1837-1987.** Petrolia: The
Church, 1987. 111 p. ill., bibl. Loc: OCCA, OKIT,
OKITW, OWTUCG.

A history of the development of the congregation
with an account of changes from traditional church
practice and biographical sketches of ministers
and active church members. Period: c1800 - 1987.

3243. Bechtel, Ken. **Three score years: Elmira Mennonite
Church, 1924-1984.** Elmira: Bauman Printing, 1984.
67 p. ill. Loc: OWTUCG, OKIT, OWRE.

A history of the church which was founded partly
as a result of an earlier religious division among
the Floradale Mennonites. The building, clergy,
and church activities are described and
illustrated. Differences of opinion among
Mennonites on dress, jewellery, and ceremonies
such as weddings and funerals are also discussed.
Anyone named in a photograph is indexed in the WRP
database. Period: 1924 - 1984.

3244. Bender, Harold S. **Two centuries of American
Mennonite literature, 1727-1928.** Studies in
Anabaptist and Mennonite History. Goshen, IN:
Mennonite Historical Society, 1929 reprinted 1969.
181 p. indexes. Loc: OKIT, OKITW, OWTL, OWTU,
OWTUCGR.

An annotated bibliography of works published in
North America with author and title indexes and
library locations in the United States. Many of
the Berlin imprints (or photocopies thereof)
identified in this book are held in the Conrad
Grebel College Archives. Period: 1836 - 1928.

3245. Bender, John. **Pilgerleben, pilgrims, peregrinos:
sixty years of vision and ministry: Amos and Edna
Swartzentruber, Nelson and Ada Litwiller.**
Waterloo: Western Ontario Mennonite Conference,
1984. 47 p. ill. Loc: OKIT.

A work which provides biographical information
on the Swartzentrubers and the Litwillers who
served with the Western Ontario Mennonite Church
in Argentina as missionaries. There are
references to relatives and friends who were also
born and raised in Waterloo County. Period: 1893 -
1984.

3246. Bender, Urie A. **Four earthen vessels:
biographical profiles of Oscar Burkholder, Samuel
F. Coffman, Clayton F. Derstine, and Jesse B.
Martin.** Kitchener: Herald Press, 1982. 315 p.
ports., bibl. Loc: OKIT, OWRE, OWRN, OWTL,
OWTUCG, OWTU.

Biographical vignettes of the "Ontario Four",
influential Mennonite clergymen who met at the
Ontario Mennonite Bible School in Kitchener and
provided leadership in the "hinge years" following
the Second World War. An introductory section
provides historical context for the biographies,
and appendices give chronological outlines of the
lives of the four men. Period: 1900 - 1981.

3247. Bergey, Lorna L. "Hagey Mennonite Church,
1842-1953." **Waterloo Historical Society.** 1970.
58: 33-34. Loc: all.

Excerpts from an address at the unveiling of a
memorial cairn on the site of the church at
Preston. After fires in 1950 and 1953, the
congregation built a new church, the Preston

Mennonite Church, on Concession Road in 1954. The text of the plaque is quoted. Period: 1815 - 1970.

3248. Bergey, Lorna L. "The Mennonite community at Port Elgin." **Mennogespräch.** 1983. 1,1: 2-3. ill., bibl. Loc: OWTUCG, OKIT.

A history of an offshoot of the Waterloo Mennonite community, mentioning David Wismer and John Bear. Notes in the September 1984 issue provide additional information on Daniel Wismer (1820-1909) and David Wismer (1861-1949), Waterloo Mennonite pastors. Period: 1815 - 1949.

3249. Bergey, Lorna L. "The Mennonites and their faith." **Waterloo Historical Society.** 1959. 47: 8-11, 14-17. Loc: all.

An account of the history of the Mennonite faith which had its origins of the Anabaptist movement of the Reformation. The author recounts the persecution of early leaders and the movement of the Mennonites to the Palatinate, then to Pennsylvania, and finally to Ontario. Period: 1798 - 1828.

3250. **Bethany Mennonite Brethren in Christ Church.** Kitchener: The Church, 1980. 1 folded sheet. Loc: OKEBC.

Programme for the 60th anniversary celebrations of the denomination which was founded in 1883. It notes that Janet Douglass of Kitchener, later Mrs James Hall, became the first Mennonite woman preacher. Period: 1883 - 1943.

3251. "Blenheim Mennonite Church." **Waterloo Historical Society.** 1962. 50: 65. Loc: all.

A brief history of the Blenheim Mennonite Congregation, which used a Wilmot schoolhouse from 1839 until its church was built in 1850. Names of families that appear on Blenheim grave markers in the church cemetery are mentioned, since that cemetery was used before the formation of the Union Cemetery Association in New Dundee. Period: 1839 - 1962.

3252. Boldt, Edward. **When your children shall ask, Joshua 4:6: a history of the Ontario Conference of Mennonite Brethren Churches, 1957-1982.** Ontario Conference of Mennonite Brethren Churches, 1982. 84 p. ill. Loc: OWTUCG.

A history published at the time of the 50th anniversary of the conference. It describes the formation of the conference and its various programmes, and provides information about fifteen churches including the Kitchener Mennonite Brethren Church, the Zion Mennonite Brethren Church in Kitchener and the Waterloo Mennonite Church. Period: 1957 - 1982.

3253. Bowman, Peter M. **Record of ordinations in the Markham-Waterloo Mennonite Conference in Waterloo County and district, 1939-1977.** 1977. 14 p. Loc: OWTUCG.

A list of deacons, ministers, and bishops ordained for the congregations in the Markham-Waterloo Mennonite Conference from 1939 to 1977. The birth and ordination dates of the men are given, as well as a list of the other candidates. Period: 1939 - 1977.

3254. Bowman, Samuel S. "The Christian Eby district: a 1902 history by Samuel S. Bowman." **Mennogespräch.** 1984. 2,1: 4-6. ill. Loc: OWTUCG, OKIT.

A short history and membership list of First Mennonite Church, once called the Christian Eby Church. The piece was written by one of its ministers in 1902, the year the new meeting-house was built and the 1834 building dismantled. Notes on the article and its author are provided by Samuel Steiner. Period: 1809 - 1902.

3255. **Breslau Missionary Church, 1882-1982: 100th anniversary.** Breslau: The Church, 1982. 32 p. ill. Loc: OWTUCG, OKIT, OKEBC.

A programme including an account of the church's origins in the evangelical fervour of the early 1870s which affected Mennonite groups in New Dundee, Berlin and Blair as well as Breslau. Brief biographies of successive preachers are given, with photographs and information from church records about the church building, organizations, missionaries and leading members. General information on the history of Breslau is also provided, with aerial photographs taken in 1942 and 1982 and photographs of Breslau residences. Period: 1882 - 1982.

3256. Brethren in Christ. **Annual report of the United Brethren in Christ, Waterloo Circuit, Ontario.** 1902. 38 p. ill. Loc: OKITW.

A booklet giving the church's articles of belief, with reports on its organizations and the congregations of Hawkesville, Bloomingdale and West Montrose. Short histories of the church in each place are given, with lists of individual contributors from the congregations. Period: 1804 - 1902.

3257. **Briefe an die mennonisten Gemeine, in Ober Canada, mit einer Zugabe.** Berlin: Heinrich Eby, 1840. 47 p. Loc: OWTUCGR, OWTUCG.

A collection of letters written to the Mennonite community in Upper Canada from various people and groups in Pennsylvania and Europe. The letters offer encouragement to settlers including Benjamin Eby and also contain references to the origins of the Mennonite faith in Europe. A letter from Mennonite elders from Bedminster Township, Bucks County, PA grants the Niagara District Mennonites permission to assign their own ministers by votes and lots. The booklet was translated into English and is held in the Conrad Grebel College Archives as **Letters to the Mennonite community in Upper Canada with an addition Berlin, (Upper Canada)**. Period: 1801 - 1840.

3258. Burkhardt, Ferne. **Full circles: Mannheim Mennonite Church, 1836-1986**. Petersburg: Mannheim Mennonite Church, 1986. 74 p. ill., bibl., index. Loc: OKIT, OWTUCG, OWRN.

A commemorative history of the church which was known as Latschar Mennonite Church until 1969. The author describes church members, clergy, buildings and church activities. Period: 1836 - 1986.

3259. Burkholder, Lewis J. **A brief history of the Mennonites in Ontario: giving a description of conditions in early Ontario, the coming of the Mennonites into Canada, settlements, congregations, conferences, other activities and nearly 400 ordinations, written and compiled under the direction of the Mennonite Conference of Ontario**. Waterloo: Mennonite Historical Society of Ontario, 1935 reprinted 1986. 358 p. ill., maps, bibl., index. Loc: OCLG, OKEBC, OKITW, OWRE, OWT, OWTL, OWTU, OWTUCG.

An authoritative study of the Ontario Mennonites, the first covering the period from the beginning of the 19th century to the 1930s. Its scope includes the history of congregations in the Waterloo District, the Russian Mennonite migrations of 1873 and 1923, Tunkers, Quakers, Amish Mennonites, and divisive movements such as the Hoch Division of 1849, the Mennonite Brethren in Christ, the Division of 1889, and the Stirling Avenue Mennonite Church. Also discussed are the Mennonite Aid Union, the Sisters' Sewing Circles, and the issue of military service. Biographical sketches of all bishops, ministers and deacons who served Ontario Mennonite congregations are arranged in alphabetical order and there are 100 photographs of men and churches. An index refers primarily to geographical locations. The author was appointed conference historian at the Mennonite Conference of Ontario in Kitchener in 1928. The text of the 1986 reprint by the Mennonite Historical Society of Ontario is identical to the 1935 original. Period: 1800 - 1935.

3260. Burkholder, Oscar. **Cressman Mennonite Church, Breslau, Ont., 1908-**. Breslau: The Church, 1955. 24 p. ill. Loc: OWTUCG, OKIT, OKITW.

A history of the congregation from 1815 to 1956, with brief biographies of bishops, ministers, deacons and members and an account of the church property and building. The author also comments on preaching in the German language, Sunday Schools and revival meetings at Breslau. Period: 1815 - 1956.

3261. Burkholder, Oscar and Coffman, S.F. and Bergey, Gilbert. **Resolutions: Ontario Mennonite Conference, 1847-1928**. 1929. 1 v. (unpaged). Loc: OWTUCGR.

A summary of resolutions passed at the annual conferences on all aspects of church life and practice, including ministry, missions and funerals. Period: 1847 - 1928.

3262. **Calender für die Versammlungen der mennoniten Gemeinde in Canada West, und im Staat Neu York, auf das Jahr unsers Herrn 1877**. CIHM Microfiche series, no. A01682. Berlin: Rittinger and Motz, 1877. 1 fiche. mf. Loc: OWTL, OWTU.

A list of locations for meetings to be held in the Mennonite community throughout Canada West and New York State in 1877. Names of preachers, many from Waterloo County, are also given. Period: 1876 - 1877.

3263. **Centennial anniversary service, United Brethren in Christ Church, Roseville, Ontario**. 1981. 1 v. (unpaged). ill. Loc: OKIT.

A programme with an historical sketch and a list of pastors. Period: 1881 - 1981.

3264. **Christliche Gemeine im Waldeckischen. Katechismus, oder kurze und einfältige Unterweisung aus der Heiligen Schrift, in Frage und Antwort, für Kinder zum Gebrauch in den Schulen**. Ephrata, PA: The Gemeine, 1824. 68 p. Loc: OWTUCGR.

A catechism or instructional guide, in the form of questions and answers, for children to use in schools. This edition was printed in Pennsylvania by Joseph Bauman but, as the preface indicates, was intended for the use of Waterloo County Mennonites. Period: 1823 - 1824.

3265. Conference of Mennonites in Canada. **Celebration in song: selected hymns for the 70th session of the Conference of Mennonites in Canada, July 5-9, 1972, Waterloo, Ontario**. Waterloo: The Conference, 1972. 32 p. Loc: OWTUCG.

About half the hymns are taken from the **Gesangbuch der Mennoniten** and are in German, the other half from **The Mennonite Hymnal** in English. Composers and dates of most hymns are given. Period: 1971 - 1972.

3266. Conference of the United Mennonite Churches in Ontario. **Information bezueglich der Vereinigten Mennoniten Gemeinden in Ontario: gelegentlich der Konferenz der Mennoniten in Canada.** Niagara-on-the-Lake: The Conference, 1956. 15 p. ill., map. Loc: OWTUCG.

An illustrated booklet published in connection with a denominational conference. The United Mennonite Church, Waterloo is noted as the only member congregation in Waterloo County. Period: 1925 - 1956.

3267. Conservative Mennonite Church of Ontario. **Minutes of the Conservative Mennonite Church of Ontario ministers' meetings.** 1976. Loc: OWTUCGR.

A record of the meetings from November 1959 to January 1976, many of which were held in the Waterloo area. Also included are details of the departure of several members from the congregation, as well as copies of **Constitution and faith and practice of the Conservative Mennonite Church of Ontario** (1962 revised 1973), and **Faith and practice of the Mennonite Fellowship Church.** Period: 1959 - 1976.

3268. **Constitution and by-laws of the Mennonite Mission Board of Ontario.** Elmira: Bauman Printing, 1956. 12 p. Loc: OWTUCGR.

Period: 1956.

3269. Countryside Mennonite Fellowship Church Publishing Committee. **Countryside Mennonite Fellowship Church, Hawkesville, Ontario.** St Jacobs: St Jacobs Printery, 1990. 89 p. ill. Loc: OWTUCG.

A history of the church's formation as the Heidelberg Mennonite Church in 1960 when eleven families of the Woolwich district left the Ontario Mennonite Conference after religious disagreements. The name changes in 1976 to Heidelberg Mennonite Fellowship Church and in 1983 to Countryside Mennonite Fellowship Church are also recorded. Other topics include the clergy, members, church activities and organizations. Deaths, marriages and baptisms of members are recorded. Period: 1960 - 1990.

3270. Cressman, Eben C. "In the beginning: at Hageys and Wanners." **Mennogespräch.** 1983. 1,2: 12-13. ill. Loc: OWTUCG, OKIT.

A summary of the origins and growth of two Mennonite congregations from 1799 to 1983. A map of the Beasley Survey Concessions locates the churches and marks the boundary of each congregation. Period: 1799 - 1983.

3271. Cressman, Eben C. **Wanner Mennonite Church - wilderness to wide world.** 1987. 15 l. Loc: OKIT.

A musical play celebrating the 150th anniversary of the congregation founded in 1837. The historical development of the church is depicted in four scenes set in 1834, 1884, 1952 and 1987. Period: 1837 - 1987.

3272. Cressman, Ella M. "The Seventh Mennonite World Conference." **Waterloo Historical Society.** 1962. 50: 99-101. Loc: all.

An account of the events at the conference held in Kitchener in 1962. Period: 1962.

3273. Cressman, J. Boyd. "History of the First Mennonite Church of Kitchener, Ontario: I. the early period 1800-1859." **Mennonite Quarterly Review.** 1939. 8,3: 159-186. Loc: OKIT, OWTU, OWTUCG.

A comprehensive history including a brief description of early settlement of the Pennsylvania German Mennonites and a study of Mennonite faith and education in the Berlin (Kitchener) area. The influence of teacher and bishop Benjamin Eby is documented, as are the efforts of other community leaders in the establishment of the meeting house which became the First Mennonite Church. Period: 1800 - 1859.

3274. Cressman, J. Boyd. "History of the First Mennonite Church of Kitchener, Ontario: II. the middle period 1859-1902, III. the modern period 1902-." **Mennonite Quarterly Review.** 1939. 8,4: 251-283. Loc: OKIT, OWTU, OWTUCG.

A continuation of Cressman's article published in the July 1939 issue of the journal, with details of the church under the leadership of Daniel Wismer, Moses Erb, John S. Coffman, C.F. Derstine and others. Topics include meeting houses, Sunday schools, baptisms, members, church disputes and, after 1902, the building of the brick structure known as Berlin Mennonite Church, renamed First Mennonite Church in 1917. Period: 1859 - 1939.

3275. Cressman, J. Boyd. "Waterloo County." **The Mennonite encyclopedia.** Scottdale, PA: Mennonite Publishing House, 1959. Vol. 4, pp. 897-899. map. Loc: OKIT, OWTUCG.

A survey of Mennonite settlement in the county, emphasizing the development of the congregations. A map shows many Amish and Mennonite meetinghouses, while the text explains their interrelationships and notes the numbers of their members. Period: 1800 - 1957.

3276. Cressman, Kenneth W. **A descriptive analysis of the Conservative Mennonite schisms in Ontario, 1956-1979.** University of Waterloo (student essay, Sociology), 1979. 104 p. ill., maps., bibl. Loc: OWTUCGR.

An analysis of the causes and effects of the

schism of 1959-60 in the Wilmot District of the Mennonite Conference of Ontario. There are biographical sketches of Curtis Cressman, Moses Roth, Moses Baer, Elmer Grove, Clarence Huber and Andrew Axt. The appendices include the minority report of the Conference Constitutions Revisions Committee, and information and literature about various conservative Mennonite groups and congregations in Ontario. Period: 1956 - 1979.

3277. Cressman, Kenneth W. **The development of the Conservative Mennonite Church of Ontario.** University of Waterloo (student essay), 1976. 70 p. maps, tables, bibl. Loc: OWTUCGR.

An analysis of the split of 1959-60 by members of the Wilmot District of the Mennonite Conference of Ontario, against the background of earlier Mennonite divisions, particularly that of 1870. The initial rift was caused by the denial of communion to anyone wearing a wedding ring, but the author believes that personalities and not biblical issues were the main factor in religious dissension. Biographical details are given for the people involved in the schism. Period: 1870 - 1976.

3278. **Dedication...Evangel United Missionary Church.** Trinity Publishers, 1950. 7 p. ill. Loc: OKEBC.

A programme for the dedication service, including a list of church officers, a brief history, and a song written for the occasion by Everek R. Storms. Period: 1949 - 1950.

3279. Detweiler, John D. "The Detweiler Meetinghouse - the old stone church." **Waterloo Historical Society.** 1965. 53: 36-40. Loc: all.

An anecdotal account of the Mennonite church built in 1855 half a mile west of Roseville and closed in January 1966. Period: 1855 - 1966.

3280. **Die ernsthafte Christenpflicht, enthaltend schöne geistreiche Gebete, das Glaubens Bekenntniß der Mennoniten, mit einem Anhang über die Wehrlosigkeit; und das geistliche Luftgaertlein frommer Seelen.** Berlin: Heinrich Eby, 1846. 240 p. Also CIHM Microfiche series, no. 34879. Loc: OKDHC, OWTL, OWTU.

A book emphasizing the "earnest duties of a Christian" and containing prayers, articles of faith of the Mennonites and a section on pacifism. A original copy of this book is held at Doon Heritage Crossroads. Revised editions were published in Berlin, in 1878 by Oberholtzer and Co., and in 1908.

3281. **Die gemeinschaftliche Lieder-Sammlung, zum allgemeinen Gebrauch des wahren Gottesdienstes, mit einem Inhalt sammt zweifachem Register**

versehen. Edited by Benjamin Eby. Berlin: Boedecker und Stuebing, 1857 reprinted 1883, 1901, 1908, 1918. 388 p. Also CIHM Microfiche series, no. 35959. Loc: OWTL, OWTU, OWTUCGR, OWTUR.

A collection of 222 hymns for use at Mennonite services in Waterloo County. It is assumed that Benjamin Eby originally compiled the book based on the **Unparteyisches Gesangbuch** published in Lancaster, PA. The hymns are organized by themes and indexed by melody and first lines. Fifteen of the 222 hymns were added in a supplement. For a brief history of the hymnal and an explanation of each hymn, see **Lieder-Sammlung Commentary** by Isaac Horst. Also useful is Martin E. Ressler's historical explanation of the printing of the hymnal in **An annotated bibliography of Mennonite hymnals and songbooks: 1742-1986** (Gordonville, 1987). The Doris Lewis Rare Book Room of the University of Waterloo Library has copies dated 1883 and 1892. The 1857 edition has been microfilmed by CIHM. Period: 1857 - 1908.

3282. **Die gemeinschaftliche Lieder-Sammlung, zum allgemeinen Gebrauch des wahren Gottesdienstes, mit einem Inhalt sammt zweyfachem Register versehen.** Edited by Benjamin Eby. Lancaster, PA: Johann Bär's Söhnen, 1860 reprinted 1870. 344 p. Loc: OWTUCGR.

A collection of hymns for use at Mennonite services in Waterloo County. It is assumed that Benjamin Eby originally compiled the book based on the **Unparteyisches Gesangbuch** published in Lancaster, PA. The hymns are organized by themes and indexed by melody and first lines. For a brief history of the hymnal and an explanation of each hymn, see the **Lieder-Sammlung Commentary** by Isaac Horst. See also Martin E. Ressler's historical explanation of the printing of the hymnal in **An annotated bibliography of Mennonite hymnals and songbooks: 1742-1986** (Gordonville, 1987). Period: 1860 - 1870.

3283. **Die gemeinschaftliche Liedersammlung, zum allgemeinen Gebrauch des wahren Gottesdienstes, aus vielen Liedernbüchern gesammelt, und mit einem Inhalt sammt Register versehen. Erste Auflage.** Edited by Benjamin Eby. Berlin: H.W. Peterson, 1836 reprinted 1838. 328 p. Also CIHM Microfiche series, nos. 38605 (1836) and 18500 (1838) Loc: OWTL, OWTU, OWTUCGR, OKEBC.

A collection of hymns used at Mennonite services in Waterloo County. It is assumed that Benjamin Eby originally compiled the book based on the **Unparteyisches Gesangbuch** published in Lancaster, PA. The hymns are organized by themes and indexed by melody and first lines. Conrad Grebel College Archives, University of Waterloo has the 1836 and 1838 editions published in Berlin by H.W. Peterson, as well as subsequent editions indexed in the WRP database. The 1838 edition was enlarged by two hymns and has a slightly altered title: **Die gemeinschaftliche Liedersammlung, zum allgemeinen Gebrauch des wahren Gottesdienstes, aus vielen Liederbüchern gesammelt, und mit einem Inhalt sammt einem zweyfachen Register versehen.** For a brief history of the hymnal and an explanation of each hymn, see Horst's **Lieder-Sammlung Commentary.** Also useful is Martin E. Ressler's historical explanation of the printing of the hymnal in **An annotated bibliography of Mennonite hymnals and songbooks: 1742-1986** (Gordonville, 1987). Period: 1836 - 1838.

3284. **Die gemeinschaftliche Liedersammlung, zum allgemeinen Gebrauch des wahren Gottesdienstes, mit einem Inhalt sammt zweyfachem Register versehen.** Edited by Benjamin Eby. Berlin: Heinrich Eby, 1841 reprinted 1849. 396 p. Loc: OWTUCGR, OWTUR, OKEBC.

A collection of hymns for use at Mennonite services in Waterloo County. First published in 1836 and 1838 in Berlin by H.W. Peterson, it is assumed that Benjamin Eby originally compiled the book based on the **Unparteysches Gesangbuch** published in Lancaster, PA. The hymns are organized by themes and are indexed by melody and first lines. The 1841 (third edition) and the 1849 (fourth edition), as well as subsequent editions contain a supplement (Zugabe). For a brief history of the hymnal and an explanation of each hymn, see the **Lieder-Sammlung Commentary** by Isaac Horst. Also useful is Martin E. Ressler's historical explanation of the printing of the hymnal in **An annotated bibliography of Mennonite hymnals and songbooks: 1742-1986** (Gordonville, 1987). The Doris Lewis Rare Book Room of the University of Waterloo Library has copies dated 1841 and 1849. Period: 1941 - 1949.

3285. Douglass, Janet. **Immanuel hymns for the worship of God.** Berlin: Mennonite Brethren in Christ, 1886. 95 p. Loc: OKDHC.

The words to 130 hymns sung by the Mennonite Brethren in Christ, and published at the Gospel Banner Office in Berlin. The copy at Doon Heritage Crossroads is missing the last page of the index. Period: 1885 - 1886.

3286. Dyck, Cornelius J. **The Lordship of Christ: proceedings of the seventh Mennonite World Conference, Kitchener, Ontario, Canada, August 1-7, 1962.** Elkhart, IN: The Conference, 1963. 702 p. ill. Loc: OKIT, OWTU, OWTUCG.

Proceedings of the Mennonite World Conference held in Kitchener in 1962, including details of all addresses, sermons and reports and lists of exhibits, delegates and authors. The volume is dedicated to the memory of Harold S. Bender. Period: 1961 - 1963.

3287. "Early Mennonite churches." **Waterloo Historical Society.** 1959. 47: 12-13. ill. Loc: all.

Illustrated descriptions of three early Waterloo Mennonite Churches: Benjamin Eby's church of 1813, the Mennonite Church in Berlin of 1834, and the Shantz Church (north of Baden) of 1853. Period: 1813 - 1929.

3288. Eby, Benjamin. **A concise ecclesiastical history and doctrinal theology of the Baptists or Mennonites.** Elkhart, IN: Mennonite Publishing Co., 1901. 171 p. index. Loc: OWTLR, OWTUR, OWTUCGR.

An account written in 1841 of the origin and doctrines of Mennonites and of their migrations to various parts of the world including Canada. The author narrates the arrival in the Waterloo district of both the Pennsylvania German Mennonites and the Amish from Europe. Also included are the **Confessions of faith of the Mennonites** and a translation of **Church regulations**, first published in Berlin by Benjamin Eby in 1841. Period: 1800 - 1841.

3289. Eby, Benjamin. **Confession of faith of the Mennonites, also a translation of church regulations published by Benjamin Eby, Berlin, Canada, Aug. 30, 1841, with a selection of scripture texts suitable for funeral services.** The Committee (Old Order) Mennonites, 1935 revised 1940, 1948. 84 p. Loc: OWTUCG.

A booklet which contains Benjamin Eby's translation of the articles of faith adopted at the Dortrecht Convention in April 1632, entitled **Declaration of the chief articles of our general Christian faith.** Period: 1810 - 1841.

3290. Eby, Benjamin. **Kurzgefasste Kirchen Geschichte und Glaubenslehre der Taufgesinnten-Christen oder Mennoniten.** Berlin: Heinrich Eby, 1841. 240 p. Also CIHM Microfiche series, no. 35039. Loc: OKEBC, OKITW, OWTL, OWTLR, OWTU, OWTUCGR.

A summary of the history and teachings of the Anabaptist Christians or Mennonites, compiled by Benjamin Eby and printed by Heinrich Eby. Pages 150 to 159 describe the migrations of Mennonites and Amish to the Waterloo area. Period: 1801 - 1841.

3291. Enns, Herbert P. **A date to remember: historical reflections.** Waterloo: H.P. Enns, 1987. 6 p. Loc: OWTUCGR.

A history written to commemorate the 60th anniversary of the church building of Waterloo-Kitchener United Mennonite Church. The congregation began in 1925, but moved to its present location in 1927 under the leadership of Rev. J.H. Janzen. The church building had previously been occupied by St Paul's Presbyterian Church. Period: 1927 - 1987.

3292. Enns, Herbert P. and Fast, Jacob. **Jubilee issue of the Waterloo-Kitchener United Mennonite Church, 1924-1974**. Waterloo: The Church, 1974. 136 p. ill., ports. Loc: OWTUCG, OKIT, OWT.

A history of the church which was founded by Russian Mennonites led by Rev. Jacob H. Janzen. The clergy, organizations, building and music are all described, and there are also reminiscences by members of the congregation describing what it was like to come to Waterloo from Russia. Period: 1924 - 1974.

3293. Epp, Frank H. **Mennonites in Canada, 1786-1920: the history of a separate people**. Toronto: Macmillan, 1974. 480 p. ill., maps, tables, bibl., index. Loc: OCH, OCLG, OCP, OKIT, OWRE, OWRN, OWTL, OWTU, OWTUCG, OKEBC.

First volume in a comprehensive history, commemorating the 450th anniversary of the Mennonite faith. There are many references to people and places of Waterloo County (including a map of the region in about 1830) but they are set in the larger context of Canada and are necessarily brief. The book is said to represent "a contribution to a true Canadian multiculturalism and a true religious pluralism." Period: 1786 - 1920.

3294. Epp, Frank H. **Mennonites in Canada, 1920-1940: a people's struggle for survival**. Toronto: Macmillan, 1982. 640 p. ill., tables, charts, bibl., index. Loc: OCH, OCLG, OCP, OKIT, OWRE, OWT, OWTL, OWTU, OWTUCG, OKEBC.

A companion to the author's comprehensive history of Canadian Mennonites before 1920. There are many brief scattered references to Waterloo County Mennonites. Period: 1920 - 1940.

3295. Erb, Peter C. **On being the church: essays in honour of John W. Snyder**. Waterloo: Conrad Press, 1992. 178 p. Loc: OWTUCG.

A collection that includes a history of Rockway Mennonite Church, Kitchener by Eleanor High Good and Peter C. Erb. Snyder was pastor of the church from 1966 to 1991. Period: 1966 - 1991.

3296. **Evangeliums Panier**. Berlin: Mennonite Brethren in Christ, 1887. Loc: OWTUCGR.

The German edition of the **Gospel Banner** (also indexed in the WRP database), a news and devotional journal published by the Mennonite Brethren in Christ. **Evangeliums Panier** was published monthly for the first year, 1879-1880, and then semi-monthly to about 1895. It was first published in Goshen, Indiana, and a year later moved to Berlin. The Conrad Grebel Library holds the 16-page issue, volume 9, number 21, dated 7 November 1887. Period: 1879 - 1896.

3297. Feick, Magdalena. **I will build my church: Conestogo/St Jacobs Mennonite Church, 1844-1986**. St Jacobs: St Jacobs Mennonite Church, 1986. 48 p. ill., ports., bibl. Loc: OWTUCG.

A history celebrating both Roy S. Koch's fifty years in the ministry and the Mennonite Bicentennial. Topics include church buildings, short biographies of clergy, a list of Conestogo members from 1889 to 1915, song books and hymnals, church activities, and women's groups. Memoirs, poems, and extracts from the sermons of Roy S. Koch are quoted at the end of the book. Period: 1844 - 1986.

3298. Felstead, Allan G. **A socio-historical analysis of the sectarian divisions in the Mennonite Church of Waterloo County, 1849-1939**. University of Waterloo (M.A. thesis, Sociology), 1978. 168 p. bibl., tables. Loc: OWTUCG, OWTU.

A study of factors in the Waterloo Mennonite schisms of 1849, 1874, 1889 and 1917. The author concludes that systematic differences in church rank and interpersonal conflicts were significant internal divisive factors, and not economic or age differences. Period: 1849 - 1939.

3299. **Fiftieth anniversary service: commemorating fifty years of service rendered by Bishop E.S. Hallman to the Mennonite Church in Canada and the United States**. Tuleta, TX: E.S. Hallman, 1948. 31 p. ports. Loc: OKITW.

Addresses given by E.S. Hallman, S.F. Coffman, Oscar Burkholder, Curtis C. Cressman and M.C. Cressman at the First Mennonite Church, Kitchener, with a copy of the notice in the **Kitchener Daily Record**. The speeches contain tributes, reminiscences and reflections on evangelical changes. Period: 1897 - 1947.

3300. Fransen, David W. **Canadian Mennonites and conscientious objection in World War II**. University of Waterloo (M.A. thesis, History), 1977. 3 fiche. tables, bibl. mf. Loc: OWTU, OWTUCG.

An examination of the divisions among Mennonite churches and the their struggle with the Canadian government regarding participation in the war. Mennonites who figure significantly in the study include Jacob H. Janzen, S.F. Coffman and J.B. Martin. Tables summarize various groups of conscientious objectors and types of alternative service they performed. Period: 1938 - 1945.

3301. Fretz, J. Winfield. **The MEDA experiment 1953-1978: twenty-five years of experience in helping "little people" to get established in their own businesses in over twenty countries around the world.** Waterloo: Conrad Press, 1978. 118 p. ill. Loc: OKIT, OWTU, OWTUCG.

A record of the goals and achievements of the service agency, the Mennonite Economic Development Associates, started by the Mennonite Central Committee with Waterloo Mennonite support for its programmes of development assistance in Latin America, Asia and Africa. The contributions of local Mennonite leaders Edward G. Snyder and Milo Shantz are noted. Period: 1953 - 1978.

3302. Garland, G. Elwin. **The Old Order Mennonites and the movement to Mount Forest.** University of Waterloo (student essay, Geography), 1974. 75 l. maps, bibl. Loc: OWTUM, OWTUCG.

A paper that includes information on Mennonite schisms that affected Waterloo County from 1889 to 1958. Charts and maps provide an overview of the sizes of the various congregations in the 1960s. Period: 1889 - 1964.

3303. General Conference Mennonite Church: Commission on Home Ministries. **Major papers presented at the war tax conference in Kitchener, Ont., October 30 to November 1, 1975.** Newton, Kansas: Home Ministries, 1976. 140 p. bibl. Loc: OWTUCG.

A compilation of the papers presented at the inter-Mennonite/Brethren in Christ War Tax Conference, assembled for personal or group discussion or action. Topics include tax resistance, militarism, and Christian attitude to the payment of war taxes. There is also a conference summary statement. Period: 1975 -

3304. **Geschichte der Waterloo-Kitchener Vereinigten Mennonitegemeinde, 1925-1953.** 1953. 1 v. ill. Loc: OKITW.

A history of the church that was founded by Russian Mennonites led by Rev. Jacob H. Janzen. The clergy, church organizations, building and music are described. Period: 1925 - 1953.

3305. Gingerich, Mary Etta. "Hagey Mennonite Church, Preston, Ont." **Christian Monitor.** 1932. 24,2: 48-50. ill. Loc: OWTUCG.

An historical account of the congregation, clergy and church building, mentioning church organizations such as the Sunday School, the Alpine Literary Society and the Young People's Meetings. Period: 1799 - 1932.

3306. Gingerich, Melvin. "Joseph Hagey writes to Jacob Groff." **Mennonite Historical Bulletin.** 1967. 28,4: 5. Loc: OWTUCG.

Transcript of a letter written in 1856 by Joseph Hagey to Jacob Groff, noting that he has "seen what Jacob Krehbil writes about the trouble in their congregation but I could not make much out of it," and concluding with expressions of faith in God. Period: 1855 - 1856.

3307. Gingerich, Orland, Rev. **The Amish of Canada.** Waterloo: Conrad Press, 1972. 244 p. ill., bibl., index. Loc: OCH, OCP, OKIT, OKITW, OWRN, OWTU, OWTL, OWTUCG.

A scholarly account of the Amish of Canada from their Reformation origins to 1972. The author describes the migration from Europe, particularly the pioneer settlement established by Christian Nafziger, and explains Amish faith and congregational life including the divisions between various churches. Individual congregations named are those of Wilmot, St Agatha, Wellesley, Crosshill and the Steinmann Church at Baden. Appendices include a list of congregations and ordained leaders of the Western Ontario Mennonite Conference from 1824 to 1970, and copies of important constitutional documents of the conference. Period: 1800 - 1972.

3308. Gingerich, Orland, Rev. **Early Amish settlements and their development: a paper prepared for the Mennonite Historical Society, November 5, 1966.** 1966. 5 p. Loc: OWTUR.

An historical sketch of the Amish in Ontario, from the arrival of Christian Nafziger in Wilmot Township in 1822. The expansion and divisions of the Amish are recounted, including such events as the organization of a Fire and Storm Aid Union in 1872 and the organization of Sunday schools in 1903. In 1966 there were fourteen Amish congregations in the Western Ontario Conference, four of them Old Order congregations. Period: 1822 - 1966.

3309. Gingrich, Newton L. **Mission completed: history of the Ontario Mennonite Bible School and Ontario Mennonite Bible Institute.** St Jacobs: St Jacobs Printery, 1969. 157 p. ill., bibl. Loc: OWTUCGR.

A history of the school by its last principal who describes its establishment and growth, explains its constitution and lists former teachers and students. Photographs of many staff are included. Period: 1907 - 1968.

3310. Good, E. Reginald. **Frontier community to urban congregation: First Mennonite Church, Kitchener 1813-1988**. Kitchener: The Church, 1988. 160 p. ill., maps, ports, bibl., index. Loc: OKIT, OWTL, OWTU, OWTUR, OWTUCG.

A history of the church, considered in the larger context of the settlement and development of Waterloo County and with a chapter on the displacement of the aboriginal inhabitants. The author outlines changes in Mennonite faith and practice and the leading role of Berlin Mennonite Church in the Waterloo District Conference. He stresses the leadership of Benjamin Eby and issues on which the congregation was later divided such as unauthorized prayer meetings, dress, Sunday Schools and the use of English in services. Period: 1813 - 1988.

3311. Good, E. Reginald. "Jacob Moyer's Mennonite church records: an interpretive sketch." **Mennogespräch**. 1985. 3,1: 1-3. ill., bibl. Loc: OKIT, OWTUCG.

A study of handwritten entries found in Bishop Moyer's Bible, including details about the Moyer family and Mennonite annual conferences and council meetings. Most significant to Waterloo researchers is the section on the ordination list, as it sheds new light on the ordination of Benjamin Eby as preacher and his confirmation as bishop and on the purported tension between Lancaster and Franconia conferences at that time. Appended to this article is an English translation by Isaac R. Horst of some of these handwritten notes (pages 4-5). Period: 1767 - 1833.

3312. Good, E. Reginald. "A review of Aaron Eby's 'Geschichte der Mennoniten in Canada,' published in 1872." **Mennonite Quarterly Review**. 1990. 64,4: 362-370. Loc: OWTU, OWTUCG.

An analysis of an essay on the early settlement of Mennonites in Ontario, first published by **Der Mennonitische Friedensbote** of Pennsylvania. Good's study adds biographical information on Eby (1838-1899) of Berlin who studied medicine and later became a publisher. Eby's sources and content are found to provide new information while demonstrating the point of view of New and Reforming/Reformed Mennonites. Part of Eby's essay was translated into English by Daniel K. Cassel in his history of the Mennonites. Period: 1838 - 1899.

3313. Good, E. Reginald. **War as a factor in Mennonite economic policy: a case study of insurance institutions sponsored by the Ontario Conference, 1864-1954**. University of Waterloo (M.A. thesis, History), 1984. 172 p. bibl. Loc: OWTUCG, OWTU.

An investigation of the interrelationship between economics and the Mennonite religion, using the development of insurance institutions sponsored by the Ontario Conference of the Mennonite Church between 1864 and 1954 as a case study. After examining the reaction of the Mennonite insurance company to three wars, the American Civil War, World War I and World War II, Good concludes that the Mennonites safeguarded their pacifist convictions by providing an alternative to commercial insurance and government welfare. Period: 1864 - 1954.

3314. Good, Margaret and Steiner, Samuel J. "The Breslau Mennonite Church: a brief history." **Mennogespräch**. 1984. 2,1: 1-3. ill., bibl. Loc: OKIT, OWTUCG.

An article commemorating the sesquicentennial of the congregation's first meeting house. The log building was originally the Benjamin Eby meeting house and was brought from Berlin. Significant people and events in the development of the congregation from 1815 to 1984 are described, with an account of the early landowners of the church site. The name Kressman or Cressman Mennonite Church was changed in 1968 to Breslau Mennonite Church. Period: 1815 - 1984.

3315. **Gospel Banner**. 1877 - 1969. Loc: OKEBC, OWTUCG.

A publication of the Mennonite Brethren in Christ, later the United Missionary Church, of the United States and Canada, recounting the work of missionaries abroad and congregations at home. Inspirational articles and testimonials are included, with notes from pastors, reports on conferences, marriage and death notices. A German edition of the paper, the **Evangeliums Panier**, was published by Benjamin B. Bowman of Waterloo from 1880 to 1896. From 1885 to 1908 the **Gospel Banner** was edited by Joseph Bingeman and published in Berlin. Everek R. Storms, a newspaper reporter and former school teacher from Kitchener, became editor in 1952. Many references concern churches and clergy in Breslau, Blair, New Dundee, Berlin and Hespeler, particularly in the earlier volumes. The Conrad Grebel College Library holds a complete set of newspapers; the Emmanuel Bible College Library has most of the volumes from 1909 onwards. The name of the paper was changed in 1969 to **Emphasis on Faith and Living**, and is indexed at the Emmanuel Bible College Library. Period: 1877 - 1969.

3316. Hartzler, J.S. and Kauffman, Daniel. "The Canada Conference." **Mennonite Church History**. Scottsdale, PA: 1905. Pp. 237-246. Loc: OWTUCG, OKIT.

A summary of the early settlement of Mennonites in Waterloo, noting the religious schisms. A table compiled by S.S. Bowman lists the Mennonite congregations in Ontario, fifteen of which were in Waterloo County. The table shows the first settlers, the first ministers, the present ministers, the present deacon, when the first meeting house was built, and the number of members. Period: 1799 - 1905.

3317. Hiebert, Victor. "Waterloo Mennonite Brethren Church: twenty-five years of service." **Mennogespräch**. 1985. 3,1: 8. Loc: OWTUCG, OKIT.

A history of the formation and development of the congregation, started in 1960 as a mission Sunday-school project by the Kitchener Mennonite Brethren Church. A church building was opened in 1973 on Lexington Road. Period: 1960 - 1986.

3318. Hoch, Daniel. **Kurz gefasste Kirchen-Ordnung der Mennoniten oder Wehrlosen Christen in Canada.** Preston: Martin Rudolf, 1850. 25 p. Loc: OWTUCG.

A copy of the summary of the church ordinances for rites and ceremonies of the Mennonites or the "unarmed Christians in Canada." The committee responsible for this compilation included also Jacob Albrecht, Henry Bechtel, David Weber, Peter Huber, Abraham Bechtel, Abraham Kinsey, Jacob Hoch and William Hoch.

3319. Hoover, Amos B. **The Jonas Martin era: presented in a collection of essays, letters and documents that shed light on the Mennonite churches during the 50 year ministry (1875-1925) of Bishop Jonas H. Martin, collected, arranged, edited, interpreted and published by Amos B. Hoover.** Denver, PA: The Author, 1982. 1128 p. ill. indexes. Loc: OWTUCG.

A compilation of documents in English and German, pertaining to an Old Order Mennonite bishop from Pennsylvania. Many of the papers refer to Waterloo Mennonite people indexed in the WRP database. The letters are introduced with summaries of the contents and information about the writers. The book contains a lengthy annotated Old Order Mennonite bibliography with Ontario references in appendix N. There are indexes to people, places, and subjects, as well as a list of correspondents, photographs, maps, graphs showing the division of the Old Order Mennonites, and a chronological list of all the dated letters and documents in the book. Period: 1875 - 1925.

3320. Hoover, Muriel I. **Bethel, house of God: a history of Bethel Missionary Church, New Dundee, Ontario, 1878-1978.** Centennial Committee, 1978. 76 p. ill. Loc: OKEBC.

An account of the church's ministers, members, organizations, women's activities, music, and outreach ministries, with photographs of a camp meeting and a baptismal service at New Dundee in 1934. Period: 1878 - 1978.

3321. Horst, Isaac R. **Canada-Iowa Stauffer letters.** Mount Forest: The Author, 1991. 28 p. map. Loc: OWTUCG.

Translations of letters written to David Stauffer between 1881 and 1888 with annotations by the editor, Isaac Horst. They deal with the organization of a Stauffer Old Older Mennonite church in Waterloo County in 1882 and the establishment of a community in Osceola County, Iowa in 1887. Some of the letters are written by Jesse Bowman/Bauman, the leader of the Iowa group, and shed light on the formation of that community. Period: 1881 - 1888.

3322. Horst, Isaac R. **Close ups of the great awakening.** Mount Forest: Isaac R. Horst, 1985. 331 p. bibl. Loc: OKEBC, OWTUCG, OWTL, OKIT.

A compilation by an Old Order Mennonite of primary sources relating to the Mennonite divisions of 1889 and 1893. Some sources are fully translated for the first time into English in this book, and include correspondence, diaries, memoirs and conference proceedings. The material is briefly introduced by the author in "as impartial and unprejudiced way as possible." Period: 1847 - 1920.

3323. Horst, Isaac R. **Conference records: minutes of semi-annual sessions of the Waterloo District of the Ontario Conference of the Mennonite Church, 1842-1890 [WRP].** Mount Forest: Isaac R. Horst, 1984. 16 p. Loc: OWTUCGR.

A record of "discussions of the preachers and deacons of the Mennonite parishes in the County of Waterloo containing the resolutions passed at the semi-annual conferences," translated by Isaac Horst. This is said to be the only surviving official record from the period between 1842 and the church division of 1889. Period: 1842 - 1890.

3324. Horst, Isaac R. and Oberholtzer, John H. and Bauman, Samuel B. **Disclosure of the persecutions against Daniel Hoch, preacher of the Mennonite Church in Upper Canada.** Mount Forest: The Author, 1982. 47 p. Loc: OWTUCG.

Translation and annotation by Horst of a work first published in Pennsylvania in 1853. It is in two parts: the first written by Oberholtzer entitled, "Disclosure of the persecutions against Daniel Hoch," the second entitled, "An illustration written by Samuel B. Bauman to Benjamin Eby about the disturbances in the Mennonite churches of Canada." The material gives insights into the Mennonite division of 1849 and information about Benjamin Eby. Period: 1849 - 1853.

3325. Horst, Isaac R. **Discussions of the preachers and deacons of the Mennonite parishes in the County of Waterloo containing the resolutions passed at the semi-annual conferences.** 17 p. Loc: OWTUCGR.

An unpublished collection of incomplete records compiled by Isaac R. Horst about ministers of the Mennonite community before the church division in 1889. Discussions and resolutions concern entertainment, temperance, participation in livestock exhibitions, clothing and insurance. Period: 1842 - 1890.

3326. Horst, Isaac R. **Lieder-Sammlung commentary: self-helps for the Gemeinschaftliche Lieder-Sammlung.** Mount Forest: Isaac R. Horst, 198-?. 64, 24 p. facsims. Loc: OWTUCG.

A guide to the Old Order Mennonite hymnal for Waterloo County. The author explains the meaning of each of the 222 German hymns and translates some of them. He notes that the hymnal was adapted from the **Unpartheyisches Gesangbuch,** published in Lancaster County, PA. Biographical information is given on some composers, ranging from a date to fuller details.

3327. Horst, Isaac R. "The Markham Waterloo-Old Order Mennonite division." **Mennogespräch.** 1988. 6,2: 9-12. ill. Loc: OWTUCG, OKIT.

A study of the division among Woolwich Old Order Mennonites in the 1930s that caused the creation of the Markham Waterloo Mennonites, led originally by Jesse Bauman and Urias Martin. The issues involved differences over the use of the telephone and automobile, and a doctrinal dispute which led to the establishment of a church known as the Bible Chapel. Period: 1930 - 1988.

3328. Huffman, Jasper A. **History of the Mennonite Brethren in Christ Church.** New Carlisle, OH: Bethel Publishing, 1920. 283 p. ill., bibl., map, chart. Loc: OKEBC, OWTUCG.

A general history, published by order of the Executive Board of the church, referring to many Waterloo County people, places and events. For example, there are photographs of a typical camp meeting scene in the 1890s at Berlin and more than 150 biographical sketches of ministers and editors, many of whom were natives of Waterloo County. Period: 1806 - 1920.

3329. Hunsberger, Albert and Hunsberger, Greta. **A brief history of the David Eby Church and Erb Street Mennonite at Waterloo, Ontario from 1851-1976.** Waterloo: The Church, 1976. 23 p. ill., ports. Loc: OKEBC, OWTUCG, OKIT, OWT.

A commemorative history of church buildings and organizations and the Russian Mennonites who were

a particular care of this church, with biographical sketches of all ministers and deacons. Period: 1851 - 1976.

3330. Hunsicker, M.Z. and Hunsicker, Johannes C. **Kleine Sammlung geistiger Gedichte gewidmet von M.Z. Hunsicker und J.C. Hunsicker ihrer verstorbenen Gattin und Mutter.** Berlin: The Authors, 1868. 55 p. Loc: OWTUCG.

A small collection of spiritual poems and hymns dedicated to the memory of the wife and mother of the authors. Intended to help readers who have lost close members of their family, the work contains poems of comfort and hope, often with a clue to the melody of the works. Although published in Berlin, the book was printed in Elkhart, Indiana by J.F Funk and contains no direct references to the county. Period: 1867 - 1868.

3331. The Hymn Book Committee. **A choice collection of spiritual hymns, adapted to public, social, and family devotion, and designed for the use of the Mennonite Brethren in Christ and all lovers of Zion.** Berlin: Gospel Banner, 1893. 63 p. indexes. Loc: OKEBC.

The revised edition of a Mennonite hymn book, arranged by topic. The committee was organized after the 1879 general conference held in Blair, and the first edition was published two years later. Period: 1879 - 1893.

3332. **Jährliche Conferenz der mennoniten Gemeinde von Ontario: abgehalten am 25 und 26 Mai, 1893 zu Berlin, Ontario.** CIHM Microfiche series, no. 15676. 1893?. mf. Loc: OWTL, OWTU.

Programme for the annual conference of the Mennonite churches to be held in Berlin, at the Christian Eby meeting house. Period: 1892 - 1893.

3333. Jantzi, Johannes and Roth, Lorraine. **Record book of the Wellesley-Wilmot congregation, 1861-1921.** Mennonite Archives, 1977. 22 p. index. Loc: OKIT.

Transcription of the Wellesley-Wilmot Mennonite Congregation's record book begun by bishop Johannes Jantzi in 1861. The book contains records of births, marriages, deaths, baptisms, and an index of names. Period: 1861 - 1921.

3334. Kennel, Lillian. **History of the Wilmot Amish Mennonite congregation: Steinmann and St Agatha Mennonite churches, 1824-1984.** Baden: Steinmann Mennonite Church, 1984. 49 p. ill., ports., bibl. Loc: OWTUCG, OKIT.

A history of the churches which began as one congregation with two meetinghouses but separated in 1939. There are descriptions of the early Amish and Mennonite settlements in Wilmot

Township and of church leaders, members, buildings, activities, music and the role of women. The appendix includes lists of leaders in both congregations and copies of the first recorded minutes of a business meeting in 1906 and of various church programmes. Period: 1824 - 1984.

3335. Koch, Alice. "Biehn Mennonite Church." **Waterloo Historical Society**. 1964. 52: 61-62. ill. Loc: all.

A short history of the old church which was in use from 1865 to 1963. Period: 1865 - 1964.

3336. Koch, Alice and Good, Edward and Cressman, Irvin W., Rev. **Dedication of Biehn Mennonite Church**. The Church, 1964. 1 v. (unpaged). ill. Loc: OKITW.

A booklet commemorating the opening of the new building in 1964. It contains an historical sketch of the church from 1870 to 1964, a report from the Building Committee Chairman, a message from the pastor, and a programme of the service of dedication. Period: 1870 - 1964.

3337. Lageer, Eileen. **Merging streams: story of the Missionary Church**. Elkhart, IN: Bethel Publishing, 1979. 374 p. ill., bibl., map, charts, index. Loc: OKEBC.

A general history of the development of this Mennonite denomination and its component churches, ministers and missionary accomplishments. There are many Waterloo County references, including accounts of the establishment of Bethany Mennonite Church in Berlin in the 1870s and the dedication of Emmanuel Bible School in 1943. Period: 1807 - 1979.

3338. Landers, Bertha. **History of the Stirling Avenue Mennonite Church**. Kitchener: The Church, 1979. 200 p. Loc: OWTUCG.

A history of the church since 1924 when a new constitution was drawn up and land bought for the church building. There are annual historian's reports on church activities from 1925 up to and including 1977. Also included are a list of charter members, a tribute to Rev. Urias K. Weber, a capsule history of significant dates, and historical sketches commemorating the 50th anniversary in 1974. This copy is a photoreproduction of a typescript held at the church office. Period: 1924 - 1979.

3339. Laurence, Hugh. **Change in religion, economics, and boundary conditions among Amish Mennonites in Southwestern Ontario**. McGill University (Ph.D. thesis, Anthropology), 1980. 303 p. bibl., tables, charts. Loc: OWTUCG.

An adaptation of Kuhn's model of scientific change through the interaction of theory and independent phenomena, to explain the social change of Ontario Amish through the interaction of internal and external forces. Nineteenth- century revivalism challenged ethnic distinctions by allowing for individual salvation rather than community discipline. The economic prosperity of the 1950s led to increased contact with individualization through mechanization and wage labour. Both forces resulted in a new conception of Amish Mennonite identity. Period: 1820 - 1975.

3340. Laurence, Hugh and Roth, Lorraine. **Daniel S. Iutzi, Jacob R. Bender: servants of God and the church**. Waterloo: Historical Committee of the Western Ontario Mennonite Conference, 1984. 66 p. ill., maps. Loc: OWTUCG.

Biographies of those who led the East Zorra Amish Mennonite Congregation between 1917 and 1947 and were instrumental in forming the Ontario Amish Mennonite Conference in 1924 from congregations in Wilmot, Wellesley, Mornington and Hay Townships. The Bender family settled west of New Hamburg in 1832; some members of the Iutzi family stayed in Wilmot after others moved on to East Zorra and Michigan. Period: 1917 - 1947.

3341. Martin, Delton. **History of the Floradale Mennonite Church: witnessing to the faith in the Floradale community, Woolwich Township, Waterloo County**. Floradale: Floradale Mennonite Church, 1971. 28 p. ill. 1 folded map, ports. Loc: OWTUCG, OKIT.

A history of church from 1857 to 1971, with information about the various church buildings, church leaders, church members, and congregational activities. A short description of the Mennonite division of 1889 is given, as well as a chronology of the church. A map of the Floradale community shows individual buildings and lists owners from 1857 to 1971. Period: 1857 - 1971.

3342. Martin, Isaac G. **The story of Waterloo-Markham Mennonite Conference**. 1953. 125 l. Loc: OWTUCGR.

An unpublished account of divisions in the church, Mennonite meeting places in Ontario, the Bible as poetry, and bishops, ministers and deacons. The author lists Canadian ministers for 1825 and 1853, birth dates of members from 1855 to 1900 and ordinations in the Markham-Waterloo Conference. Period: 1847 - 1953.

3343. Martin, Jacob. **Ein Büchlein, namlich ein Auszug aus der Heiligen Schrift über einige Religions= Fragen unserer Zeit**. Waterloo: The Author, 1875. 226 p. Loc: OWTUCGR.

A unique copy of a book that was censored by the Ontario Mennonite Conference (then called the Canada Conference) in 1880. A supplement in the book, entitled "Beilage für die Belesenen der heiligen Schrift," is dated April 1879. Copies of the book were presumed to have been destroyed, but the Conrad Grebel College Library obtained a copy in 1992. A second edition of the book, published in 1883, was widely distributed and is separately abstracted in the WRP database. Period: 1875 - 1883.

3344. Martin, Jacob. **Ein Schifflein gegen den Wind gerichtet, nämlich ein Auszug aus der Heiligen Schrift über einige Religions Fragen unserer Zeit.** Berlin: The Author, 1883. 210 p. Loc: OWTUCGR.

A local imprint, the title of which may be translated as **A ship directed against the wind, taken from the Holy Scriptures about certain questions of religion of our time.** The author's writings were found to be unscriptural at the semi-annual Mennonite conference held in Berlin in 1880 and this edition is believed to be a revised version of one which was not accepted by church elders. A translated and abridged version by Isaac R. Horst was completed in 1984 and is held by the Conrad Grebel College Library. Period: 1880 - 1883.

3345. Martin, Jacob. **A ship directed against the wind.** Edited by Isaac R. Horst. 1984. 37 p. Loc: OWTUCG.

An unpublished translation and abridgement of **Ein Schifflein gegen den Wind gerichtet,** published in Berlin in 1883, two copies of which can be found in the Conrad Grebel College Archives. In the original introduction, Martin states that the 1883 edition was the second version, and Isaac Horst offers the information that a resolution had been passed by the church elders in 1880 confirming that Martin's writings were "unscriptural" and should be recalled. It seems likely that the 1883 text represents a revision of the original work. A unique copy of an earlier version of Martin's book, dated 1875 with the title **Ein Büchlein, namlich ein Auszug aus der Heiligen Schrift über einige Religions= Fragen unserer Zeit,** is held by the Conrad Grebel College Library and is separately abstracted. Period: 1880 - 1983.

3346. Mennonite Conference of Ontario. **Constitution and discipline of the Mennonite Conference of Ontario.** The Conference, 1909-. Loc: OWTUCG.

A series of handbooks, published irregularly and setting out the constitution of the Mennonite Conference of Ontario and the code of conduct of church members. They show the development of the Mennonite church government over the years. For instance, the 1949 constitution considered "the wearing of a plain bonnet as the approved head dress of our sisters." The language also changes

from a simple to a more legalistic form. The Conrad Grebel Library has the **Constitution and discipline** for the years 1909, 1940, 1948 and 1958. Period: 1909 - 1958.

3347. **The Mennonite encyclopedia: a comprehensive reference work on the Anabaptist-Mennonite movement.** Scottdale, PA: Mennonite Publishing House, 1955 - 1990. 5 v. ill., charts, maps. Loc: OKIT, OWTUCG, OWTUSJ, OWTU.

A compendium of information on all aspects of Anabaptist Mennonite history, theology, ethics, migrations and congregations throughout the world. Written by notable scholars in the field, the entries include many references to Waterloo County and often provide bibliographies. Volumes 1 to 4 were published between 1955 and 1959 and compiled under the direction of editor Harold S. Bender. Volume 5, edited by Cornelius J. Dyck and Dennis D. Martin, was published in 1990 by Herald Press and is a continuation of the previous four volumes with over 900 additional entries, as well as updates for articles in the previous volumes. Period: 1800 - 1990.

3348. **Mennonite meeting calendars: condensed form.** 1980?. 60 p. Loc: OKDHC.

A history of the Ontario Mennonite calendars from 1836 to 1980, including photocopied reproductions. The calendars list the meeting houses and their clergy, with some printed in German and others in English. Annotations explain the formation of new Mennonite churches, and there is a list of places given as appointments, many of them in Waterloo County. Period: 1836 - 1980.

3349. Mennoniten Gemeinde. **Kleiner Katechismus, oder kurzgefasste Unterweisung aus der Heiligen Schrift, in Fragen und Antworten zum Gebrauch für Kinder.** Berlin: Heinrich Eby, 1844. 64 p. Loc: OWTUCGR.

A "catechism, or short summary of instruction from the holy scriptures, in the form of questions and answers for the use of children."

3350. Millar, Anne Eby. "Stirling Avenue Mennonite Camp." **Mennogespräch.** 1990. 8,1: 5-6. ill. Loc: OWTUCG, OKIT.

A history of the congregation's summer youth camps, from the 1943 Thayandanega Camp near Paris to the Silver Lake Camp in the 1960s. Period: 1943 - 1975.

3351. Miller, John W. **Jesus and the growing use of alcohol among Ontario Mennonites.** 1976. 8 l. Loc: OWTUCG.

A talk about the developing pattern of alcohol use among the Ontario Mennonites, first given to the quarterly meeting of Ontario Mennonite ministers at Breslau in 1976. After a Biblical examination of the topic, the author concludes that Jesus practised a "cautious" use of wine and recognized the dangers in the use of alcohol. Period: 1972 - 1976.

3352. "'New Mennonites' in Waterloo County." **Mennogespräch.** 1987. 5,2: 14,16. Loc: OWTUCG, OKIT.

The first of a two-part transcript of the early minute books of the Blair New Mennonite congregation in 1869-1870. The minutes record the conference meetings and mention the behaviour of pastor John McCauley, and the selling of the Mennonite share of the Baptist church at New Dundee. The New Mennonites joined the Reforming Mennonites in 1875, later becoming the Mennonite Brethren in Christ, now the Missionary Church. The transcript is continued in the March 1988 edition of **Mennogespräch.** Period: 1869 - 1870.

3353. "'New Mennonites' in Waterloo County, part 2." **Mennogespräch.** 1988. 6,1: 5-6. Loc: OWTUCG, OKIT.

Continuation of a transcript of the minute book of the New Mennonite congregation at Blair from 1869 to 1874, begun in the September 1987 issue of **Mennogespräch.** It includes a list of members in 1869, the year the church was founded. Period: 1869 - 1874.

3354. Nissly, Heinrich. **Geistliches Sendschreiben des christlichen Lehrers und Predigers Heinrich Nissly.** Berlin: Heinrich Eby, 1842. 20 p. Loc: OWTUCGR.

A spiritual circular letter of the Christian teacher and preacher Heinrich Nissly. Part of the L.J. Burkholder collection in the Conrad Grebel College Archives, the work has no direct reference to the Waterloo area other than its publication by Heinrich Eby in Berlin.

3355. Pannabecker, S. Floyd. **Origin and growth of the Mennonite Brethren in Christ.** Bluffton, OH: Bluffton College (M.A. thesis, Church History), 1918. 96 p. bibl., map. Loc: OKEBC, OWTUCG.

A survey of the evangelical Mennonites from 1500 to 1917. Two groups, the New Mennonites and the Reformed Mennonites, joined to form the United Mennonites in 1875 at the Snyder Meeting House at Bloomingdale. The Evangelical Mennonites from the United States joined with the United Mennonites in 1879, forming the Evangelical United Mennonites. This group in turn united with the Swankite portion of the Brethren in Christ movement or Tunkers, forming the Mennonite Brethren in Christ in 1883. An account is given of the doctrines and beliefs of the Mennonite Brethren in Christ. Period: 1800 - 1917.

3356. "Records of ordination of Old Order Mennonites of Waterloo County, Ontario, Canada from 1804 to 1962." **Records of ordination of the Old Order Mennonites from 1750 to 1963.** Edited by Ervin Shantz and Orvie Shantz. Pennsylvania: 1964. Pp. 15-24. Loc: OWTUR, OWTUCGR.

A chapter listing the names of men ordained, with the year and place of their ordination and the year they died as well as their age. Handwritten entries have been added for ordinations from 1964 to 1977. Period: 1804 - 1977.

3357. Regehr, T.D. and Sawatzky, Rodney J. and Epp, Marlene. **Symposium on Mennonites in Canada: the influence of World War II, 1939-1955.** 1987. Loc: OWTUCG.

A collection of papers with occasional references to Waterloo County subjects. These include: the position of Rev. J.H. Janzen on military alternatives; the difference in attitude towards Mennonite and Jehovah's Witness conscientious objectors discussed at a meeting in Galt; and a "cutting room" established in 1942 by Mennonite women of Kitchener to produce clothing for overseas relief. Period: 1939 - 1955.

3358. Reimer, Margaret Loewen. **One quilt, many pieces: a concise reference guide to Mennonite groups in Canada.** Waterloo: Mennonite Publishing Service, 1983 reprinted 1984. 60 p. ill., tables, bibl. Loc: OKIT, OWTL, OWTU, OWTUCG.

A brief survey of the general philosophy, background and geographical location of various Mennonite groups, including those of the Waterloo area. Period: 1800 - 1982.

3359. Reist, Moses G. **The Christian's religious voice of warning.** Elmira: The Author, 1915. 32 p. Loc: OKITW, OWTUCGR.

Written by the Elmira resident who called himself the Second Moses and claimed that his words came directly from God, the tract pleads with other Mennonites in the area to believe in him.

3360. Ressler, Martin E. **An annotated bibliography of Mennonite hymnals and songbooks, 1742-1986.** Gordonville, PA: The Author, 1987. 117 p. ill. Loc: OWTLR, OWTUCGR.

A collection of references to mainly American sources which also includes hymnals and sheet music published in Waterloo County, such as Benjamin Eby's **Gemeinschaftliche Liedersammlung** and C.F. Derstine's **The sheet music of heaven.**

Annotations include a brief description of each item, the number of editions published, and name of the publisher. Period: 1838 - 1986.

3361. Rich, Elaine Sommers. **Mennonite women: a story of God's faithfulness, 1683-1983.** Kitchener: Herald Press, 1983. 257 p. ill., bibl., index. Loc: OWTUCG, OWTU.

A study of North American Mennonite women of Swiss, South German and Alsatian backgrounds, including Old Order and Amish. It does not refer to women from the General Conference or Mennonite Brethren of Dutch, Prussian and Russian backgrounds. The book was commissioned by the Women's Missionary and Service Commission of the Mennonite Church to mark the 300th anniversary of the arrival of Mennonites in North America. There are several references to women of Waterloo County, among them the pioneer Barbara Schultz Oesch, missionary Mabel Groh, school teacher Amelia Bergey Nahrgang, and deaconess Louida Bauman. The first women's groups to be organized in the Ontario Mennonite Conference were the Waterloo Charity Circle in March 1908, and the Sisters' Aid Sewing Circle in July 1908 at Berlin Mennonite Church. Period: 1800 - 1983.

3362. Risser, Johannes. **Glaube und Lehre von der Taufe der Mennoniten in Deutschland.** Berlin: Heinrich Eby, 1845. 128 p. Loc: OWTUCGR.

An edition of **Belief and teachings of the baptism of Mennonites in Germany.** Other than being printed in Berlin, the work has no direct references to Waterloo County. Period: 1843 - 1845.

3363. Roosen, Gerhard. **Christliches Gemüths Gespräch vom seligmachenden Glauben, für die Jugend, in Fragen und Antworten; und ein Glaubens Bekenntniß der Mennonisten, nebst einem Anhang.** Berlin: H.W. Peterson, 1839. 340 p. Also CIHM Microfiche series, no. 38684. Loc: OWTL, OWTU, OWTUR, OWTUCGR.

A catechism for young people entitled **A Christian spiritual conversation on saving faith for the young, in questions and answers; and a confession of faith of the Mennonites, with an appendix.** This is a reprinted version of previous editions published in Pennsylvania, and contains a brief note by Benjamin Eby. A later edition, also published in Berlin (Kitchener) by Hett and Eby in 1891, can be found in the Conrad Grebel College Rare Book Collection.

3364. Roth, Lorraine. "Goldsmith, Brenneman, Kropf: first Amish ordinations in Canada." **Mennogespräch.** 1984. 2,2: 9-11. ill., bibl. Loc: OWTUCG, OKIT.

Details on the ministry and families of the first Amish Mennonites ordained in Canada in 1824, Joseph Goldsmith and John Brenneman as ministers and Jacob Kropf as a deacon. Joseph Goldsmith left Ontario for Ohio in 1831, but the others remained in Wilmot Township. Period: 1824 - 1984.

3365. Roth, Lorraine. **Willing service: stories of Ontario Mennonite women.** Waterloo: Mennonite Historical Society of Ontario with Women's Missionary and Service Commission of Eastern Canada, 1982. 275 p. ports., bibl., index. Loc: OWTUCG.

Short biographies of more than 60 women who were active in Mennonite church life in Waterloo County at some time between 1800 and the 1970s. Names of the women and of churches and other organizations are indexed in the WRP database. An appendix lists officers of successive Ontario Mennonite women's organizations: the Ontario Branch of the Mennonite Woman's Missionary Society, 1917-1927; the Ontario District Sewing Circle, under the General Sewing Circle Committee of the Mennonite Board of Missions and Charities, 1927-1955; the Ontario Women's Missionary and Service Auxiliary, 1955-1974; and the Ontario Women's Missionary and Service Commission since 1974. Period: 1850 - 1979.

3366. Sauder, Dorothy M. "First Mennonite anniversary." **Mennogespräch.** 1988. 6,2: 15. ill. Loc: OWTUCG, OKIT.

A report of the events commemorating the 175th anniversary of the church, including a seminar on peace and justice, a weekend return of previous pastors, a picnic, and the publication of a church history. Period: 1813 - 1988.

3367. Sauder, Dorothy M. **Trail's end: the Oxbow.** 1972. 18 l. ill. Loc: OKIT.

An unpublished history of the Bloomingdale Mennonite Church, formerly known as Schneider's Mennonite Meeting House. The author presents information on the establishment and development of the congregation under the direction of Jacob "Yoch" Schneider who gave land for the church in 1826. Photographs of church leaders are included. Period: 1805 - 1972.

3368. Schultz, Beatrice and Knechtel, Brenda Lichti and Lebold, Fran. **Maple View Mennonite Church, 1859-1984.** Wellesley: Maple View Mennonite Church, 1984. 54 p. ill., bibl. Loc: OKIT.

A commemorative history of the congregation, with biographies of church leaders, descriptions of land deeds and church buildings, and an account of church organizations and activities. The Fire and Storm Aid Union, the issue of conscription during the First and Second World Wars, and church music are all discussed. Period: 1859 - 1984.

3369. Schultz, Beatrice. "Maple View Mennonite Church, Wellesley." **Mennogespräch**. 1984. 2,2: 17. Loc: OWTUCG, OKIT.

A short history of the congregation, founded in 1859, with a description of events planned to celebrate its 125th anniversary. Period: 1859 - 1984.

3370. **Seventy-first anniversary of the founding of Bethany United Missionary Church, 1877-1948, Sunday, June 6th, 1948.** Kitchener: The Church, 1948. 2 folded sheets. map. Loc: OKEBC.

An anniversary programme including historical notes on the church and congregation, and a separate map showing the location of the church. Period: 1877 - 1948.

3371. Shantz, Elven. "Mennonite groups in Waterloo County and adjacent area." **Waterloo Historical Society**. 1967. 55: 18-29. ill. Loc: all.

An outline of the beliefs and practices of 15 groups including: the House Amish, the David Martin Mennonites, the Reformed Mennonite Church, the Waterloo-Markham Mennonite Church, the Conservative Mennonite Fellowship, the Cedar Grove Amish Mennonite Church, the Mornington Amish Mennonite Church, the Mennonite Conference of Ontario, the Western Ontario Mennonite Conference, the Ontario Conference of Mennonite Brethren Churches and the Stirling Avenue Mennonite Church. There are two photographs of Mennonite houses, those of Soloman Gehman and of Joshua Y. Shantz. Period: 1800 - 1967.

3372. Shantz, Ervin and Shantz, Orvie W. "Records of ordinations of Old Order Mennonites of Waterloo County, Ontario, Canada from 1804 to 1975." **Records of ordinations of the Old Order Mennonite, Groffdale Conference Churches, 1750 to 1975.** Edited by Joseph H. Shirk and Ezra S. Zimmerman. Adamstown, PA: Ensinger Printing Service, 1975. Pp. 46-67. Loc: OWTUCG.

Ordination records of deacons, ministers and bishops, beginning with Joseph Bechtel and ending with Elam Weber, and including birth, death and ordination dates and name of the church for which the man was ordained. Ordination records from several locations in the United States are also given in this book. Period: 1804 - 1975.

3373. Shantz, Mary C. "Discovering the Tunkers." **Waterloo Historical Society**. 1984. 72: 62-73. ill., bibl. Loc: all.

A brief history of the Anabaptist or Pietist sect that began in Germany and arrived in Upper Canada from Pennsylvania. Names of some of the Tunkers in Waterloo Township are included. Period: 1800 - 1988.

3374. Shantz, Norman. "The Detweiler Mennonite congregation near Roseville, Ontario: 1830-1966." **Mennogespräch**. 1984. 2,2: 18-19. ill., bibl. Loc: OWTUCG, OKIT.

A history especially of the clergy and the church property, with illustrated descriptions of the interior and exterior of the building. The congregation was founded by one of Roseville's earliest settlers, Jacob Detweiler, and was disbanded in 1966. Period: 1822 - 1966.

3375. Shantz, Ward M. **A history of Bethany Missionary Church, Kitchener, Ontario, Canada, 1877-1977.** Kitchener: The Church, 1977. 68 p. ill., map, chart. Loc: OKEBC, OWTUCG.

An commemorative account of the church building, clergy, members and activities with particular details of evangelical revivals. Period: 1877 - 1977.

3376. Shantz, Winnie Goldsworthy. **A history of Bethany Missionary Church.** 1991?. 12 p. ill. Loc: OKEBC.

A short account commemorating the 115th anniversary of the Kitchener church with descriptions of the building, members, organizations and activities. Period: 1877 - 1991.

3377. Sherk, A.B., Rev. "The Tunkers." **The United Empire Loyalists' Association of Canada Annual Transactions**. 1914. Pp. 62-68. ill. Loc: OWTUCGR.

A history of the Tunkers by a Waterloo historian who was also a missionary preacher for the United Brethren in Christ. The doctrines and rituals of the Tunkers or River Brethren are described, including a Love Feast held on the banks of the Grand River near Preston. There is information about the founders of the Tunker Church in Upper Canada, John Winger and Andrew Hensler, and the dress customs of early Tunkers in Ontario. Period: 1800 - 1914.

3378. Sherk, J. Harold. **Conference record; proceedings of the Ontario Conference of the Mennonite Brethren in Christ.** Toronto: Ontario Conference of the Mennonite Brethren in Christ, 1937. 72 p. ill., tables. Loc: OWTU.

A transcript of the proceedings of the fifty-fourth Annual Session of the Ontario Conference of the Mennonite Brethren in Christ, held at Kitchener in 1937. There are reports of all committees, a directory of pastors, financial statistics and missionary news. Period: 1937 - 1938.

3379. Sherk, Mary Ann and Hoover, Sarah. **The origins of the Orthodox Mennonite Church at Wallenstein.** 1975?. 24 l. Loc: OWTUCGR.

A record of the establishment of the Elam S. Martin church which broke away from the David Martin group in 1957. The manuscript account contains the names of individuals and the dates they joined, as well as information on births, baptisms, marriages and deaths of members. The authors also note a further division in 1974. Period: 1957 - 1974.

3380. Sherrick, David. **Letter by David Sherrick of Preston, Canada, 1859, and letter by Christian Schmutz, Ulrich Hege, and Heinrich Landes of Baden, Europe, 1862 [WRP].** 24 p. Loc: OWTUCGR.

A booklet with no title or other bibliographic information but a foreword describing the acquaintance between local Mennonite, Elias Eby and a European Mennonite with whom he discussed Mennonite practices. The letters consist of questions put by elders from the Duchy of Baden to which David Sherrick provides answers and then asks questions on behalf of Canadian Mennonites. These are replied to by Christian Schmutz, Ulrich Hege, and Heinrich Landes. The pamphlet is part of the L.J. Burkholder collection, Conrad Grebel College, and a translation can be found in **Herald of Truth**, 1866. Period: 1859 - 1862.

3381. Sider, E. Morris. "The early years of the Tunkers in Upper Canada." **Ontario History.** 1959. 51,2: 121-129. Loc: OKIT, OWTL, OWTU, OWTUCG.

A study which mentions the founding of a Tunker congregation in the Waterloo area in 1801 by George Shupe and David Gingrich. A.B. Sherk's description of a Tunker love feast on the banks of the Grand River near Preston is quoted, as is his description of the appearance and dress of the Tunkers in the earlier years of the church. In 1933 the name Tunker was officially changed to Brethren in Christ. Period: 1800 - 1933.

3382. Sider, E. Morris. **History of the Brethren in Christ (Tunker) Church in Canada.** University of Western Ontario (M.A. thesis, History), 1955. 308 l. ill., bibl. Loc: OWTUCG.

A study of the denomination, including the Waterloo-Howick District to which the Waterloo (Rosebank) congregation belongs. The author discusses doctrine, social attitudes, education, religious services and organization. Period: 1801 - 1955.

3383. Smith, C. Henry. **The Mennonites: a brief history of their origin and later development in both Europe and America.** Berne, IN: Mennonite Book Concern, 1920. 340 p. ill., bibl. Loc: OKIT, OWTUCG.

A general history containing several Waterloo County references: the Amish leader, Christian Nafziger is mentioned on page 217, the early settlement is portrayed in chapter XIV on Ontario (pp. 229-233), and nineteenth-century religious dissensions and unions specifically relating to the county are discussed in pp. 246-249. Period: 1799 - 1920.

3384. Snider, Esther. **135th anniversary, 1842-1977: to the glory of God.** Kitchener: Pioneer Park Christian Fellowship, 1977. 19 p. ill., ports. Loc: OWTUCG.

A commemorative history of the congregation, formerly the Weber Mennonite Church, Strasburg, including brief biographies of all ministers and mentions of deacons and bishops. Church organizations such as the Sunday School and mission programmes are described, with a chronological list of historical events. There is a photographic directory of all church members in 1977, with names and addresses listed in an index. Period: 1842 - 1977.

3385. Snyder, Lorne W., Mrs. "A House Amish wedding." **Waterloo Historical Society.** 1976. 64: 74-77. Loc: all.

A brief account of the service held in an Amish family home in 1976. The day-long proceedings are detailed including the roles played by family, friends, and the bishop. Food and song are described as important parts of the festivities.

3386. Snyder, Mabel. **25th anniversary, Hawkesville Mennonite Church.** Hawkesville: The Church, 1974. 32 p. ill., ports. Loc: OWTUCG, OWRE.

A commemorative history that includes brief biographies of the church leaders, information about the church building, a description of the congregational activities, and a list of the charter members. Period: 1949 - 1974.

3387. Snyder, O.A., Mrs. "The first Mennonite Sunday School." **Waterloo Historical Society.** 1963. 51: 27-28. ill. Loc: all.

A description of the unveiling of a plaque at Wanner Mennonite Church to commemorate the first Mennonite Sunday School in North America. A short history of the school is also given. Period: 1840 - 1963.

3388. Southgate, H. Jane. **An examination of the position of the Mennonites in Ontario under the jurisdiction of the Military Service Act, 1917.** Wilfrid Laurier University (M.A. thesis, History), 1976. 116 l. bibl. Loc: OWTL, OWTUCG.

A study of the Mennonite principle of

non-resistance and problems with the Canadian military during the 1914-1918 war. The author examines the treatment of Mennonites by Military Tribunals, established under the Military Services Act of 1917. The author does not discuss Waterloo County specifically but considers all Mennonites in the province as one group. Period: 1917 - 1918.

3389. Springer, Nelson P. and Klassen, A.J. **Mennonite bibliography, 1631-1961.** Kitchener: Herald Press, 1977. 2 v. indexes. Loc: OWTL, OWTU, OWTUCG.

A listing of publications relating to all aspects of Mennonite religion and culture, arranged by place of publication, with sub-categories for periodicals, history and description, doctrine and miscellanea. Volume II lists the North American publications and has indexes of authors, subjects and "books reviewed." Period: 1800 - 1961.

3390. Stirling Avenue Mennonite Church. **Stirling Avenue Mennonite Church: sixtieth anniversary.** Kitchener: The Church, 1984. 8 p. ill. Loc: OKIT.

A brief history including details of pastors, charter members and church buildings. Period: 1924 - 1984.

3391. Storms, Everek R. **History of the United Missionary Church.** Elkhart, IN: Bethel Publishing, 1958. 309 p. ill., maps, charts, bibl., index. Loc: OKEBC, OWTUCG.

A history commemorating the denomination's 75th anniversary with descriptions of the schools, missions and publications of various districts of the church, including Ontario. The index contains many references to Waterloo County people and places. There are also a chronology of important events, a directory of churches and a list of superintendents for the Ontario district from 1874 to 1958. Period: 1883 - 1958.

3392. Thiessen, Jack. "Canadian Mennonite literature." **Canadian Literature.** 1972. 51: 65-72. bibl. Loc: OKIT, OWTL, OWTU.

Reference from the Canadian Periodical Index.

3393. van der Smissen, Carl Justus and Roosen, Berend Karl. **Sammlung von Predigten von Carl J. van der Smissen, Prediger der mennoniten Gemeinde in Friedrichstadt, Dänemark, und Berend Karl Roosen, Prediger der mennoniten Gemeinde zu Hamburg und Altona.** Berlin: Peter Eby, 1852. 163 p. Loc: OWTUR, OWTUCGR.

A collection of sermons given in Europe by Mennonite elders, van der Smissen of Denmark and Roosen of Hamburg, and sent to North America. Apart from being published in Berlin, there are no direct references to the area.

3394. van der Smissen, Carl Justus. **Zweyter Brief aus Dänemark an die mennonisten Gemeine.** Berlin: Heinrich Eby, 1841. 23 p. Loc: OWTUCG.

The second letter by fellow Mennonite van der Smissen to Benjamin Eby in 1840, expressing interest in Mennonite life and practices in North America. The first letter may be found in **Briefe an die mennonisten Gemeine in Ober Canada.** Period: 1838 - 1840.

3395. Vereinigten Mennoniten Gemeinden in Ontario, Canada. **Jubilaeums Jahrbuch der Vereinigten Mennoniten Gemeinden in Ontario, Canada, 1954.** Publikationskomitee der Konferenz der Vereinigten Mennoniten Gemeinden in Ontario, 1954. 136, xiv p. ill. Loc: OWTUCG.

A book published to mark the jubilee held in Waterloo on 13-14 November 1954 by the United Mennonite Churches of Ontario. Historical information is provided on the denomination and its activities and programmes, such as the Mennonite Central Committee, the Mennonite Provincial Relief Committee and education. Various Ontario localities and Mennonite leaders are mentioned and there are short chapters on such topics as the immigration to Ontario by the Mennonites from Russia, occupations of Mennonites, poetry, and the conference agenda. Period: 1924 - 1954.

3396. Wambold, Isaac A. **Scriptural admonitions.** Mennonite Conference of Ontario, 1947. 12 p. Loc: OWTUCG.

A sermon read to the Mennonite Conference of Ontario at St Jacobs in 1947 by Isaac Wambold, who recounts his own conversion at a revival meeting in Breslau in 1885 and the first Mennonite Conference he attended in 1891, and stresses the continuing need for conformity and simplicity of dress. Isaac Wambold was ordained to the Gospel Ministry in the Mennonite Church, Ontario Conference, at Breslau in 1890. Period: 1947 - 1948.

3397. Weaver, Edward N. and Weaver, Landis M. and Hoover, Amos B. **The Old-Order Mennonite directory including the Weaverland Conference of Pennsylvania, Virginia and Missouri, and the Markham-Waterloo Conference of Ontario, Canada, and the Ohio-Indiana Conference of Ohio and Indiana.** Ephrata, PA: The Home Messenger, 1976. 78 p. maps, index. Loc: OWTUCG.

A directory including all the congregations in the Markham-Waterloo Conference, including those of Elmira, Martins, North Woolwich and West Montrose. Names and addresses of all the bishops, ministers, deacons and caretakers of the churches are given, as well as the date the church was built. Maps show the location of each church. Although the title conveys the impression that these churches are "Old Order", the Markham-Waterloo Conference members drive cars, not horses.

3398. Weber, Alson. "Stirling Avenue Mennonite Church, Kitchener." **Mennogespräch**. 1984. 2,2: 17. Loc: OWTUCG, OKIT.

A summary of the congregation's history from 1924 to 1984, taken from the anniversary brochure. Period: 1924 - 1984.

3399. Weber, John S. **A history of Samuel Frederick Coffman 1872-1954: the Mennonite churchman**. University of Waterloo (M.A. thesis, History), 1975. 231 p. bibl. Loc: OWTUCG.

A biographical essay of S.F. Coffman that identifies and interprets his influences on the Mennonite Church. Coffman was a spokesman for the Mennonite position of non-resistance during both world wars, a catalyst for the Russian Mennonite immigration in the 1920s, a church historian, composer and teacher. A pastor of a Mennonite congregation in Vineland, he was ordained in 1903 Bishop of the Niagara District Churches of the Mennonite Conference of Ontario. Coffman's part in attempting to resolve the schism at Kitchener's First Mennonite Church that later led to the creation of the Stirling Avenue Mennonite Church, is recounted in a chapter entitled, "A moderate amidst conflict: 1921-1935." Period: 1872 - 1954.

3400. Wideman, Ernie and Frey, Clare and Weber, Amsey. **Record of ordinations leading to and including the Markham-Waterloo Mennonite Conference, 1891-1986**. The Conference, 1988. 28 p. Loc: OWTUCGR.

Biographical information is provided on the ordinands, as well as lists of the other candidates and the names of bishops involved in the ordinations. Period: 1891 - 1986.

3401. Wiebe, Anne. "The Mennonite Brethren in Ontario: a short history." **Mennogespräch**. 1986. 4,1: 4-8. ill. Loc: OWTUCG, OKIT.

A record of the development of the Mennonite Brethren, the Ontario group of which was founded in 1924 with the arrival of many Russian immigrants at the Erb Street Church, Waterloo. The Kitchener Mennonite Brethren Church was founded the following year. The experiences of the Russian Mennonites are quoted, the expansion of the church described, and brief biographical sketches of influential clergy are included. Period: 1924 - 1980.

3402. Witmer, Leslie D. **Pioneers of Christendom in Waterloo County, 1800-1967: history of Hagey-Preston Mennonite Church**. Preston: The Church, 1967. 64 p. ill., bibl., map. Loc: OKIT, OCCA, OKITW, OKEBC.

A scholarly study of the establishment of the church, early pioneer families, church leaders and church buildings. Religious divisions, the Sunday School, missionaries and other church activities are described. The appendix contains a translation of the earliest portion of the Hagey Deacon's Book which gives information about the churches finances, as well as plans of part of Block Number Two (showing landowners) and Hagey's Cemetery. Period: 1800 - 1967.

BAPTIST CHURCHES

3403. Benton Street Baptist Church. **113th annual financial statement for the year 1964: Benton Street Baptist Church**. Kitchener: The Church, 1964. 20 p. Loc: OKITW.

The annual church report, including financial information, a membership list, and a list of committees and their members. Period: 1964 - 1965.

3404. Benton Street Baptist Church Building Committee. **The proposed Benton Street Baptist Church edifice**. 1964. 8 p. plans, ill. Loc: OKITW.

An outline of requirements for music, fellowship and Christian education, including an auditorium and offices. There are floor plans and illustrations of the new church submitted by the architectural firm of Barnett and Rieder-Hymmen.

3405. Benton Street Baptist Church. **Dedication of the new Benton Street Baptist Church, September 18, 1966**. The Church, 1966. 12 p. ill. Loc: OKIT.

A booklet commemorating the new church which replaced the old building destroyed in the fire of 1964. An illustrated historical sketch of church buildings from 1851 to 1966 is provided, as well as a description of the new church and a list of clergy. Period: 1851 - 1966.

3406. Benton Street Baptist Church. **History of Benton Street Baptist Church, Kitchener, Ontario**. Kitchener: The Church, 1926. 12 l. ill. Loc: OKIT.

A programme of the 75th anniversary celebrations, with a history of the growth of the German Baptist community, clergy, church members and various church buildings. Period: 1851 - 1926.

3407. "Benton Street Baptist Church, Kitchener." **Waterloo Historical Society**. 1964. 52: 82-83. Loc: all.

A brief history of the first German Baptist

church in Canada which was organized in 1851. The article relates the church's separation from the Eastern Conference of German Baptists in the 1930s and its union with the Ontario and Quebec Conference. The church's radio ministry after 1929 is also discussed. Period: 1851 - 1964.

3408. "Blair building rededicated." **Waterloo Historical Society.** 1960. 48: 33. Loc: all.

A note of the rededication as the Blair Evangelical Baptist Chapel of a church which served Blair 100 years earlier and was then used for many years as a school. Period: 1860 - 1960.

3409. Buehler, Allan M. **Hespeler Baptist Church, 75th anniversary souvenir, 1889-1964.** Hespeler: The Church, 1964. 12 p. Loc: OKIT.

An account of the church's beginnings and early administration, including quotations of historically significant entries from the church minute book. Period: 1889 - 1964.

3410. **The celebration of the Diamond Jubilee: Preston Baptist Church with recollections of former days, 1895-1955.** The Church, 1955. 17 p. ill. Loc: OCCA.

A programme of jubilee activities, with greetings from former pastors and members, an historical chronology, and a list of clergy. Rev. P.P.W. Ziemann mentions two former slaves who were members, Philip Smith and Mrs Maloney. Period: 1895 - 1955.

3411. Clubine, Robert. **Benton Street Baptist Church, Kitchener, Ontario: 125 years of God's faithfulness.** Kitchener: Benton Street Baptist Church, 1976. 32 p. ill. Loc: OKIT.

A chronology of significant events with a photographic directory of current church members and staff in 1976. Period: 1851 - 1976.

3412. **How the Avenue Road Baptist Church came to be.** 1984?. 2 l. Loc: OKIT.

A short account of the 1984 union of South Water Street Baptist Church with the Delta Park Baptist Church (Bremner Baptist Church) to form the Avenue Road Church in Cambridge. The changes of name and location of the congregations are emphasized. Period: 1870 - 1984.

3413. McDonald, Mary Margaret. "Wellesley Baptist Church." **Waterloo Historical Society.** 1985. 73: 91-95. Loc: all.

An historical sketch of the church presented at a meeting of the Guelph Association in Hespeler in about 1938, with names of various church leaders from 1850 to 1875. The author provides a few details on church finances and membership. Period:

c1850 - 1875.

3414. Poth, Ruby Bechtel. **History of New Dundee Baptist Church.** New Dundee: The Author, 1983. 87 p. ill. Loc: OKIT.

A scrapbook history of the church which was founded in 1848, to celebrate its 125th anniversary. There are photographs of clergy and church members, newspaper clippings of events at the church, and lists of clergy, deacons, organists, and other church officials. Programmes, an historical sketch of the church and information about the church building and parsonage are included. The use of the German language in the early years is noted and the 100th anniversary celebrations are reported. Period: 1848 - 1977.

3415. Poth, Ruby Bechtel. "The New Dundee Baptist Church, 1852-1962." **Waterloo Historical Society.** 1962. 50: 87. Loc: all.

A history of the New Dundee Baptist Church from 1852 to 1962. The first minister was the Rev. H. Schneider and services were conducted in German until 1910. Period: 1852 - 1962.

3416. Schulte, Ben C. and Schade, H.F., Rev. **Benton Street Baptist Church, Kitchener, Ontario: one hundredth anniversary, 1851-1951, a century of gospel testimony.** Kitchener: The Church, 1951. 23 p. ill. Loc: OKITW.

An account of the founding of the congregation, the clergy, members, missionaries and church buildings. Financial statistics from 1896 to 1950 are given, with statistics of baptisms and membership and a list of current church officers. Period: 1851 - 1951.

3417. Wright, Gerald. **Still going forward.** Cambridge: Forward Baptist Church, 1984. 84 p. ill. Loc: OCCA.

A history of the congregation, clergy and buildings of the Forward Baptist Church, to commemorate its fiftieth anniversary. Most of the book consists of brief personal reminiscences and testimonials by church members and missionaries. Period: 1934 - 1984.

CATHOLIC CHURCHES

3418. **1900-1950: St Mary's Church, Kitchener, Ontario.** Kitchener: The Church, 1950. 16 p. ill. Loc: OKITW.

A history of the church of Our Lady of Seven Sorrows, with biographical sketches of the pastors, a description of the building, and reference to the School Sisters of Notre Dame.

Period: 1900 - 1950.

3419. Borho, William, Rev. "The founder." **Resurrection Bulletin.** 1959 - 1961. 1,1: 2-3; 1,2: 2-3; 1,3: 2-3; 2,1: 2-3; 2,2: 2-3; 2,3: 2-3; 3,1: 2-3. Loc: OWTUCR.

A seven-part biography of Louis Funcken (1833-1890), priest of the Congregation of the Resurrection who founded St Jerome's College in St Agatha in 1864. The author relates the removal of the college from St Agatha to Berlin, its financial difficulties in the 1870s and expansion in the 1880s and 1890s. The last section is a character sketch of Louis by "J.F.", from **The Bee** of April 1905. Period: 1833 - 1907.

3420. Borho, William, Rev. "The pioneer." **Resurrection Bulletin.** 1959. 1,1: 2-3. ill. Loc: OWTUCR.

A brief account of the life of Eugene Funcken, priest of the Congregation of the Resurrection who came to Waterloo County in 1857. Eugene later became Provincial Superior in charge of the four parishes of St Agatha, St Boniface, St Clements and Berlin, and the seven missions at Preston, New Hamburg, Elmira, Shakespeare, Mornington, New Prussia and Bamberg. Period: 1831 - 1888.

3421. Borho, William, Rev. "St Louis Parish, Waterloo." **Resurrection Bulletin.** 1966. 8,2: 2-3. Loc: OWTUCR.

An article commemorating the church's 75th anniversary and honouring its first pastor, the Rev. Theobald Spetz. It gives a brief history of the Catholic church in Waterloo from the appointment of Father Wiriath in 1834 to the dedication of the church of St Louis in 1891. Period: 1834 - 1891.

3422. Brenner, Nancy. **The Holy Family Church: the Roman Catholic Church in New Hamburg and district.** The Church, 1983. 39 p. ill., bibl. Loc: OKIT, OKITW.

A history published to commemorate the centennial of the church building, built in 1883. It includes descriptions of both German and Italian settlements, a detailed account of the construction of the church, and information about clergy and the Holy Family Separate School. Period: 1883 - 1983.

3423. **Centennial 1857-1957: St Mary's Church, Kitchener, Ontario.** Bishop of Hamilton, 1957. 79 p. ill. Loc: OKITW.

A history with biographies of pastors, descriptions of the building, and accounts of the church's contributions to education and health care. A substantial section reports on contemporary church organizations and Kitchener's separate schools, with photographs of each class.

It mentions church services that were provided in Polish, Assyrian, German and Slovak. Period: 1857 - 1957.

3424. "Centennial of Kitchener's first Roman Catholic parish." **Waterloo Historical Society.** 1957. 45: 36-37. ill. Loc: all.

An historical sketch of St Mary's Church. Period: 1857 - 1957.

3425. "Father Andrew Spetz CR, biographical sketch." **Resurrection Bulletin.** 1972. 14,2: 2-3; 14,3: 2-3. Loc: OWTUCR.

A two-part biography of a member of the Congregation of the Resurrection who was a missionary in Italy, Turkey, Bulgaria and the United States. Andrew was the brother of Theobald and grew up in Waterloo County. Period: 1858 - 1918.

3426. "Father Edward Glowacki, CR." **Resurrection Bulletin.** 1960. 2,3: 10-11. ill. Loc: OWTUCR.

A biographical sketch of the first Catholic priest to be ordained in Waterloo County. As a member of the Congregation of the Resurrection, Glowacki accompanied Eugene Funcken to St Agatha in 1857, and was later priest of several congregations in Waterloo County. Period: 1830 - 1919.

3427. "Father Peter Graf, CR, 1902-1960." **Resurrection Bulletin.** 1960. 3,2: 12-13. ill. Loc: OWTUCR.

An obituary for a member of the Congregation of the Resurrection, who taught Industrial Arts at St Jerome's High School and died in a canoeing accident. Period: 1902 - 1960.

3428. Foyster, Ken. **Anniversary reflections: 1856-1981, a history of the Hamilton diocese.** Hamilton: The Diocese, 1981. 128 p. ill. Loc: OCLG, OKIT, OWTL, OWTUSJ.

The section on Waterloo County (pp. 83-89) outlines the early German Catholic settlements at St Agatha and New Germany (Maryhill), the establishment of Redemptorist and Jesuit missions at St Agatha in 1834 and New Germany in 1847, the subsequent work of priests of the Congregation of the Resurrection from the 1860s, and the history of St Jerome's College and the School Sisters of Notre Dame. The author depends mainly on Spetz's history of the Catholic Church for the period before 1916, but adds new information on priests and parishes in the twentieth century. Period: 1825 - 1981.

3429. Funcken, Eugene, Rev. **Gedichte von Pater Eugen Funcken, apostol. Missionär in Ober Canada, zum Besten eines deutschen Waisenhauses in Ober Canada.** CIHM Microfiche series, no. 05926. Einsiedeln, NY: Benziger Brothers, 1868. 3 fiche. mf. Loc: OWTL, OWTU.

A collection of the priest's poems, dedicated to the success of "an orphanage in Upper Canada." The poems are about relationships, nature, emotions, rites of passage, and various religious themes. Period: 1853 - 1868.

3430. Girodat, Edmund. "Rev. Theobald Spetz, CR, D.D.." **Resurrection Bulletin.** 1972. 14,1: 2-3. ill. Loc: OWTUCR.

A brief biography of the founder of St Louis Roman Catholic Church, Waterloo. He was also the second president of St Jerome's College and author of a book on the history of the Catholic Church in Waterloo County. Period: 1850 - 1921.

3431. Iwicki, John. "The first province of the congregation." **Resurrectionist charism: a history of the Congregation of the Resurrection, volume II, 1887-1932.** Rome: Congregation of the Resurrection, 1992. Pp. 69-90; 341-344; 388-389. Loc: OWTUCR, OWTUSJ.

An international history of the Congregation that mentions the deaths of the Funcken brothers and the development of their work in the parishes of St Agatha, St Mary and St Louis, and at the New Hamburg Mission and St Jerome's College. The erection of new churches and the achievements of the School Sisters of Notre Dame are recounted. Period: 1887 - 1932.

3432. Iwicki, John and Wahl, James A., Rev. "Resurrectionists in Canada." **Resurrectionist charism: a history of the Congregation of the Resurrection, 150 years, volume 1, 1836-1886.** Rome: Congregation of the Resurrection, 1986. Pp. 231-255; 370-374. Loc: OWTUCR, OWTUSJ.

An account of the founding of St Jerome's College and the orphanage at St Agatha. The authors discuss the curriculum and pedagogy of St Jerome's and the dispute between German and Polish clerical factions over college administration. Period: 1864 - 1871.

3433. Mahler, Louis J. **History of St Patrick's Parish, Galt, as a mission and parish, 1827-1962.** Galt: The Church, 1962. 16 p. ill. Loc: OCCA, OKIT.

A history of the congregation, clergy, buildings, and schools of the parish of Galt, noting the successive dioceses to which the parish belonged. There is a biography of Monsignor E.A. Doyle, parish priest for nearly fifty years, and photographs of the Galt Separate Schools. Period:

1867 - 1962.

3434. "Monsignor Doyle honoured." **Waterloo Historical Society.** 1964. 52: 88. Loc: all.

A brief reference to the 50th anniversary of the arrival of the Right Rev. E.A. Doyle, pastor of St Patrick's Roman Catholic Church in Galt. Period: 1914 - 1964.

3435. Resurrection College. **Fishermen.** Resurrection College, 1965 - 1968. Loc: OWTUCR.

Yearbooks with photographs of the staff, students and activities of Resurrection College, opened in 1962. A directory lists names and addresses of students. Period: 1965 - 1968.

3436. Resurrection College. **Resurrection College, 1963.** Resurrection College, 1963. 1 v. ill. Loc: OWTUCR.

The first yearbook of Resurrection College including a student directory, with photographs of staff, students and student activities. The college continued the work previously conducted by the Pre-Theology Department of St Jerome's College. Period: 1962 - 1963.

3437. Sacred Heart Catholic Church. **Sacred Heart Parish: 75th jubilee, 1912-1987 = Parafia Najswietszego serca Pana Jezusa: 75-letni jubileusz.** Sacred Heart Parish, 1987. 240 p. ill., bibl. Loc: OKIT.

A history of the parish, including a brief account of early Polish immigration to and settlement in the city. The book provides a detailed chronology (in both Polish and English) of the Polish Mission at St Joseph's Chapel, the establishment of Sacred Heart Parish, the parish between the world wars, the effects of the Second World War on the parish, the growth of the parish from 1950 to 1968, the parish after Vatican II, and the parish's jubilee year in 1987. The work includes details on church activities such as the mutual aid societies, choirs, youth groups, the Holy Name Society, missionaries, and the Altar and Rosary Society. Also included are many photographs of buildings, parishioners and clergy, as well as lists of baptisms, marriages and funerals in the congregation. Period: 1861 - 1987.

3438. Schenk, Alfred J. "Wayside crosses." **Waterloo Historical Society.** 1977. 65: 44-54. ill. Loc: all.

An historical account of three roadside shrines near Maryhill, the Klein Crucifix, the Keleher Crucifix and the Drexler Cross, which were erected by German and Irish Catholics between 1846 and 1860. Period: c1820 - 1977.

3439. Schumilas, Catherine. "The Shrine of the Sorrowful Mother, at St Agatha." **Waterloo Historical Society.** 1975. 63: 11-12. ill. Loc: all.

A brief history of the brick chapel erected in the 1860s. The author mentions the relics collected by Rev. Eugene Funcken and Rev. John Fehrenbach for the shrine as well as the later renovations in the 1920s. Period: 1849 - 1950.

3440. Smolikowski, Paul, Rev. and Wahl, James A., Rev. **Excerpts from the History of the Congregation of the Resurrection of our Lord Jesus Christ by Paul Smolikowski, C.R.** 1980. 93 p. ill. Loc: OWTUCR, OWTUSJ.

A translated history of early Resurrectionist missionaries in Canada, based on correspondence and church records. The achievements of the missionaries, especially the founding and development of St Jerome's College by Eugene and Louis Funcken, are described in detail. The Congregation's missions in Chicago and Kentucky are also discussed. Period: 1857 - 1871.

3441. Smolikowski, Paul, Rev. "Father Eugene Funcken." **Resurrection Bulletin.** 1973. 13,1: 2-3; 13,2: 2-3; 13,3: 2-3. Loc: OWTUCR.

A biographical sketch, taken from a history of the Congregation of the Resurrection and published in three parts. The author describes St Agatha's Catholic Church in 1857, the warm welcome given the priests by the people of St Agatha, and parish work during the first year. Period: 1857 - 1858.

3442. Spetz, Theobald, Rev. **The Catholic Church in Waterloo County, book I: with a summary history of the Diocese of Hamilton, book II, and a list of the clergy who labored in its district from the beginning to the present, book III.** Toronto: Catholic Register and Extension, 1916. 262 p. ill. Loc: OKIT, OWTL, OWTUR, OWTUCR.

An authoritative history from the arrival of the first Catholic settlers of Waterloo Township in 1827. There are biographies of many pioneer clergymen, often with photographs and descriptions of the churches, schools and societies they established. The volume concludes with alphabetical, annotated lists of parishes and current clergy. Period: 1856 - 1916.

3443. "Spire of St Clements Roman Catholic church removed for safety." **Waterloo Historical Society.** 1961. 49: 76. ill. Loc: all.

Photograph of a worker climbing the steeple of the Preston church which was built in 1858, with the spire rebuilt about 1900. Period: 1858 - 1900.

3444. "St Agatha: our pioneer mission." **Resurrection Bulletin.** 1963 - 1966. 5,3: 2-3; 6,1: 2-3; 6,2: 2-3; 6,3: 2-3; 7,1: 2-3; 7,2: 2-3; 8,1: 2-3. Loc: OWTUCR.

An article in seven parts, usually of two pages each, published between November 1963 and March 1966 and summarizing the history of the Catholic Church at St Agatha from 1834 to 1928. Notable church members, clergy, buildings and institutions are described, particularly St Jerome's College and the orphanage at St Agatha. Period: 1827 - 1928.

3445. St Francis of Assisi Roman Catholic Church. **St Francis of Assisi Parish: 25th anniversary, 1959-1984.** Kitchener: The Church, 1984. 16 p. ill. Loc: OKIT, OWTUCR.

A short history of the parish which began under the direction of Bishop Joseph F. Ryan. Period: 1959 - 1984.

3446. St Joseph's Roman Catholic Church. **St Joseph's Parish Community, Kitchener, Ont. 1930-1990.** Hamilton: A.J. Photographic Industries, 1990. 36 p. ill. Loc: OKIT.

A photographic directory of the parishioners, with a brief history of the church in which significant events are listed for each year. Period: 1930 - 1990.

3447. St Louis Roman Catholic Church. **The spirit lives 1890-1990: a history of St Louis Parish, Waterloo.** Waterloo: The Church, 1990. 218 p. ill., bibl. Loc: OKIT, OWTUCR, OWTUR, OWTUSJ.

A brief survey of the establishment of Catholicism in the county by Fathers Funcken, Kloepfer and Spetz, with more detail on the work of Theobald Spetz in St Louis Parish from 1889. Information on the various parish priests, church members and activities is placed in the context of local and world events, including epidemics, depressions and wars. Period: 1889 - 1990.

3448. "St Mary's Parish, Kitchener." **Resurrection Bulletin.** 1966 - 1969. 8,3: 2-3; 9,1: 2-3; 9,2: 2-3; 9,3: 2-3; 10,1: 2-3; 10,2: 2-3; 10,3: 2-3; 11,1: 2-3. ill. Loc: OWTUCR.

A history published in eight parts, recounting the clergy, buildings and events from the time of the first pastor, George Laufhuber, to the death of Rev. William Kloepfer. Particular attention is paid to Louis Funcken, pastor of St Mary's from 1866 to 1889 and founder of St Jerome's College. It is noted that Funcken was unable to follow his first choice of vocation to be a physician, owing to a hearing impairment. Period: 1827 - 1910.

3449. **St Michael's Parish, Waterloo, Ontario, 1962-1987, 25th anniversary.** Waterloo: The Parish, 1978. 18 p. ill. Loc: OKITW, OWT.

A brief history of the church which began under the direction of Rev. Bernard Hogan. There are photographs of the building and of former clergy. Period: 1962 - 1987.

3450. St Teresa of Avila Roman Catholic Church Centennial Book Committee. **St Teresa of Avila Parish: the first 100 years in Elmira 1889-1989.** St Jacobs: The Committee, 1990. 116 p. ill. Loc: OKIT, OWRE.

A history of the parish with information on clergy, members and activities. Although the early years are described, the book deals mainly with the period starting in the 1930s. Period: 1889 - 1989.

3451. **Translation of the chronicles of the beginnings of the work of the School Sisters of Notre Dame in St Boniface Parish/School, New Germany, Ontario.** 7 p. Loc: OKIT.

Translation of a manuscript history of the mission of St Boniface by one of the Sisters, recounting events from the cold January of their arrival in 1882, to the construction of a new school in 1898, and 1919 when a well and windpump were constructed. Period: 1882 - 1919.

3452. Wahl, James A., Rev. "Father Louis Funcken's contribution to German Catholicism in Waterloo County." **Canadian Catholic Historical Association Study Sessions.** 1983. 50,2: 513-531. Loc: OWTL, OWTUSJ.

An account of the founding of St Jerome's College by the Catholic order of the Congregation of the Resurrection. The author discusses the school's goals and curriculum and its impact on the community. Period: 1857 - 1890.

3453. Wahl, James A., Rev. **The letters of Eugene Funcken, v.1: 1857-1862.** Resurrection Studies. Waterloo: Resurrection College, 1981. 92 p. Loc: OWTUCR, OWTUSJ.

Translated letters beginning with Funcken's arrival in St Agatha with Edward Glowacki and ending with his departure for Rome with the Bishops of Hamilton and Montreal. Most of the letters are addressed to Rev. Jerome Kajsiewicz, co-founder of the Congregation of the Resurrection. An introduction by the editor notes that ten volumes of letters are planned, corresponding to the volumes of Funcken's diary. Period: 1857 - 1862.

3454. Wahl, James A., Rev. **The letters of Eugene Funcken, v.2, no.1: 1862-1864.** Resurrection Studies. Waterloo: Resurrection College, 1981. 61 p. ill. Loc: OWTUCR, OWTUSJ.

Correspondence mostly to Rev. Jerome Kajsiewicz, co-founder of the Congregation of the Resurrection. The letters include poetry, descriptions of travels abroad, and attempts to convince Louis Funcken to come to St Agatha. Period: 1862 - 1864.

3455. Wahl, James A., Rev. **The letters of Eugene Funcken, v.2, no.2: 1864-1868.** Resurrection Studies. Waterloo: Resurrection College, 1982. 72 p. Loc: OWTUCR, OWTUSJ.

Correspondence to Rev. Jerome Kajsiewsicz pertaining to the founding of St Jerome's College in 1865 and of the orphanage at St Agatha in 1868, and the first mission of the Resurrectionists in the United States by the Rev. Francis Breitkopf. Period: 1864 - 1868.

3456. Wahl, James A., Rev. **The letters of Eugene Funcken, v.2, no.3: 1869-1871.** Resurrection Studies. Waterloo: Resurrection College, 1983. 78 p. ill. Loc: OWTUCR, OWTUSJ.

Correspondence reflecting the difficulties and development of St Jerome's College and other projects of the Congregation of the Resurrection. The 1871 Friedensfest of 1871 in Berlin is mentioned, with Funcken's comment that he does not intend to join the celebrations. Period: 1869 - 1871.

3457. Wahl, James A., Rev. **The letters of Eugene Funcken, v.3: 1871-1873.** Resurrection Studies. Waterloo: Resurrection College, 1985. 82 p. Loc: OWTUCR, OWTUSJ.

Letters describing Theobald Spetz, a graduate of St Jerome's College who went to Rome to study theology and then returned to his alma mater. Funcken comments on his own trips abroad and on the affairs of the Congregation of the Resurrection in North America. Period: 1871 - 1873.

3458. Wahl, James A., Rev. **The letters of Eugene Funcken, v.4: 1873-1875.** Resurrection Studies. Waterloo: Resurrection College, 1986. 79 p. Loc: OWTUCR, OWTUSJ.

Details of the ecclesiastical politics of the Congregation of the Resurrection in North America, addressed to Rev. Jerome Kajsiewsicz. Period: 1873 - 1875.

3459. Wahl, James A., Rev. **The letters of Eugene Funcken, v.5: 1875-1877**. Resurrection Studies. Waterloo: Resurrection College, 1988. 41 p. Loc: OWTUCR, OWTUSJ.

Observations on the difficulties and developments of the Congregation of the Resurrection at St Agatha, mentioning an attack on Catholics by Orangemen and young Britons. Period: 1875 - 1877.

3460. Wahl, James A., Rev. **The letters of Eugene Funcken, v.6: 1877-1878**. Resurrection Studies. Waterloo: Resurrection College, 1989. 38 p. ill. Loc: OWTUCR, OWTUSJ.

An account of the work of the Congregation of the Resurrection in Waterloo County, addressed to Louis Funcken and Jerome Kajsiewicz, with particular mention of church work in Preston. Period: 1877 - 1878.

3461. Wahl, James A., Rev. **The letters of Eugene Funcken, v.7: 1879-1880**. Resurrection Studies. Waterloo: Resurrection College, 1989. 65 p. ill. Loc: OWTUCR, OWTUSJ.

A collection of letters to Louis Funcken and the Father General of the Congregation of the Resurrection, including a report on the missionary work based in Waterloo County from 1866 to 1879 and requests to maintain the mission at St Agatha. Period: 1879 - 1880.

3462. Wahl, James A., Rev. **The letters of Eugene Funcken, v.8: 1880-1881**. Resurrection Studies. Waterloo: Resurrection College, 1991. 63 p. ill. Loc: OWTUCR, OWTUSJ.

Letters referring to the administration of St Jerome's College. A comment is found to the effect that the bishops' advice not to serve beer at the college might be interpreted to mean not imbibing in excess. Despite divisions in the Congregation of the Resurrection caused by the revelations of Mother Marcelline, the future of St Jerome is noted to be secure. Period: 1880 - 1881.

3463. Wahl, James A., Rev. "Looking back: the early days of Louis Funcken and St Jerome's College." **Resurrection Bulletin**. 1977 - 1979. 19,3: 2-3; 20,1: 2-3; 20,2: 2-3; 20,3: 2-3; 21,1: 2-3. ill. Loc: OWTUCR.

A five-part history of the college, discussing its educational ideals, the internal arguments by members of the Congregation over matters of discipline and curricula, and its final success. Louis Funcken's advice to the administrators of St Mary's College in Kentucky, based on his experience at St Jerome's, is quoted. Period: 1865.

3464. White, Patty and Lienhardt, Janet. **125 years: St Clement's Church: St Clements, Ontario, 1858-1983**. St Clements: St Clement's Church, 1983. 96 p. ill. Loc: OKIT.

A history of the church in its community setting, including an account of the development of separate schools from the founding work of the School Sisters of Notre Dame in 1876. There are brief biographies of parish priests, bishops of the Diocese of Hamilton, and persons from the parish with religious vocations. Teachers and sisters are named and there are many illustrations of individuals, groups and buildings, including several of the church interior. Period: 1858 - 1983.

3465. Winter, Simon J., Rev. "New Hamburg Parish." **Resurrection Bulletin**. 1969 - 1971. 11,3: 2-3; 12,1: 2-3; 12,2: 2-3; 12,3: 2-3; 13,1: 2-3. Loc: OWTUCR.

An article printed in five parts between July 1969 and March 1971, summarizing Catholic history in the village from 1827 to 1969. Buildings, prominent clergy and members are described by the author who was parish priest from 1930 to 1955. Period: 1827 - 1969.

3466. Wynnyckyj, Iroida. **Milestones: a history of the Ukrainian Catholic Church of the Transfiguration, Kitchener, Ontario, 1926-1986 = Litopys: Ukraïns'koï Katolyts'koï Tserkvi Preobrazhennia Hospodn'oho, Kitchener, Ontario, 1926-1986**. Kitchener: Ukrainian Catholic Church of the Transfiguration, 1987. 109 p. ill., bibl., index. Loc: OWTUSJ, OKIT.

An account, written in Ukrainian and English, of the establishment and growth of the Ukrainian Catholic community in the city. The first record of a local Ukrainian organization is noted as the formation of a literary fellowship (Prosvita) in 1917. From this society grew the Ukrainian Catholic Church, whose history is chronicled year by year in this comprehensive overview of the congregation's many activities. Reminiscences from members of the congregation are included, as are many photographs dating back to 1917. Church groups and their leaders are listed at the end of the book, with an index of individuals, groups and important gatherings. Period: 1926 - 1986.

3467. Zinger, Joseph A. **St Boniface, 1877-1977, Maryhill, Ontario**. Maryhill: St Boniface Roman Catholic Church, 1988. 59 p. ill. Loc: OKIT.

A photocopy of the booklet published for the church's centennial. The author surveys the establishment and development of the parish and the community of Maryhill (formerly named New Germany), and describes past church leaders and various church buildings including the first log church and school, the first stone church, the convent and the chapels. Period: 1877 - 1977.

ANGLICAN CHURCHES

3468. Bowyer, David G., Rev. **The Church of St John the Evangelist, Kitchener.** The Church, 1980. 59 p. ill. Loc: OKIT.

A history commemorating the church's 125th anniversary, with information about the clergy, members, building, activities and organizations. Lists of priests, curates, church wardens and of donors of memorials and gifts are provided, and there is an illustrated description of the ceiling panels which portray Christian symbols. Period: 1855 - 1980.

3469. "A brief history of Trinity Church, Galt, Cambridge." **Waterloo Historical Society.** 1980. 68: 90-91. Loc: all.

An historical sketch of the church founded in 1844; the nave of the original building survives making it the oldest stone church in the Region of Waterloo. Period: 1844 - 1967.

3470. Cassel, Winifred M. "The parish of Wilmot." **Waterloo Historical Society.** 1962. 50: 71-77. ill. Loc: all.

A history of the Anglican Church in Wilmot Township from 1852 to 1952, including Christ Church (Haysville), St George's Church (New Hamburg) and St James Anglican Church. There are lists of rectors of Christ Church, charter members of the Women's Auxiliary, and organists in the three churches. Period: 1852 - 1952.

3471. Christ Anglican Church. **Christ Anglican Church 1912-1987, Ayr, Ontario.** Ayr: The Church, 1987. 7 p. ill. Loc: OKIT.

A photographic directory of the 22 families or individuals, currently members of the church, with their addresses and telephone numbers. The introduction includes a brief history of the church by the Rev. Roy Shepherd. Period: 1912 - 1987.

3472. Cornell, Paul. **Church of the Holy Saviour: seventy-fifth anniversary.** Waterloo: The Church, 1974. 12 p. ill. Loc: OKIT.

A history of the Waterloo Anglican congregation from 1876 to 1974, including a chronology, a list of clergy, and notes on the memorials and their donors. The author describes church organizations and the building, mentioning the names of many members and noting the Seagram family's association with the church and the role of James

W. Connor, principal of Berlin and Waterloo High School, as father of the parish. Period: 1876 - 1974.

3473. Denis-Nathan, H. "A short history of Trinity Church, Galt." **Waterloo Historical Society.** 1970. 58: 27-29. Loc: all.

A brief account of the founding and development of the Anglican church in Galt, noting interior alterations of original 1844 building and the addition of the Norman Tower in 1885-6. Period: 1840 - 1956.

3474. Fox, Charles James and Cassel, Winifred M. **The Parish of Wilmot.** New Hamburg: St George's Anglican Church?, 1913. 70 p. Loc: OKITW.

A history of three Anglican churches in Wilmot Township: St George's, Christ Church, and St James. There are over forty biographies of members associated with St James Church, a section by Winifred Cassel on the Wilmot Branch of the Woman's Auxiliary to the Missionary Association, and a section comparing the locations of New Hamburg businesses in 1913 to locations in the 1850s. Hundreds of names are quoted from the records of all three churches and some information on early settlement of the areas is given. The history was written to commemorate the sixtieth anniversary of St George's Church. Period: 1828 - 1913.

3475. "Henrietta Annie Smith." **Waterloo Historical Society.** 1986. 74: 158. ill. Loc: all.

A photograph of the missionary from Wilmot Township who died at Yang-chau, China in 1892. Period: 1892.

3476. **A historical pageant celebrating 150 years of Anglican worship in Wilmot Township: St James, Wilmot; St George's, New Hamburg, presented on September 17, 1988.** 1988. 14 l. Loc: OKIT.

A history written in the form of a stage presentation. The narrator sets each scene and explains the participants' clothing and actions as the pageant progresses chronologically from the 1830s to 1988. Names of prominent township inhabitants and church members are mentioned in relating the histories of the two parishes. Names of the actors are also given in the script. Period: 1830 - 1988.

3477. Jaegers, Mary. **A history of Anglican worship in Wilmot Township.** 1988. 33 p. ill. Loc: OKIT.

A survey of 150 years, including brief profiles of the three parishes of St James, St George's in New Hamburg, and Christ Church in Haysville. Information is given on early families, clergy church activities such as the Sunday school, young people's associations, the women's auxiliaries and choirs. Period: 1820 - 1988.

3478. Lamb, Kathryn Hansuld. "Wilmot missionaries die in China." **Waterloo Historical Society**. 1985. 73: 96-107. ill., map. Loc: all.

An account of the adventures of sisters Margaret and Annie Smith with the China Inland Mission from 1891 to 1900. Period: 1890 - 1900.

3479. Shepherd, Audrey. **A history of Christ Anglican Church in Ayr, Ontario.** Ayr: The Church, 1987. 19 p. ill. Loc: OKIT.

An account of buildings, activities, members, gifts and significant events, marking the church's 75th anniversary. Period: 1912 - 1987.

3480. Smith, Elaine. "The Church of St John the Evangelist (Anglican), Kitchener, 1856-1956." **Waterloo Historical Society**. 1956. 44: 13. ill. Loc: all.

A note of the centennial of the first Anglican church in Berlin (Kitchener), including names of the clergymen. Period: 1856 - 1956.

3481. **Souvenir of Trinity Church Galt commemorating the twenty-fifth anniversary of Rev. Canon Ridley, as rector, and the erection of the new parish hall.** Galt: Jaffray Bros, 1912?. 34 p. ill. Loc: OKITW.

A church history containing a report of the anniversary celebrations of Canon Ridley's incumbency from 1886 to 1911, memories of the old Sunday School building and an account of the laying of the new parish hall's cornerstone. Other topics are the clergy, the oldest parishioners, gifts and their donors, the cemetery, and contemporary church organizations and their members. Period: 1840 - 1912.

3482. Thomas, A.B., Rev. **Trinity Church, Galt, Ontario: centenary souvenir, 1844-1944.** Galt: C.E. Knowles, 1944. 28 p. ill., ports. Loc: OCCA, OKIT, OKITW, OWTUR.

A history by one of the church rectors, with brief biographies of all clergy from Rev. Michael Boomer to Rev. A.B. Thomas, who was inducted in 1937. Leading laymen are also noted. Various changes to the church building, both interior and exterior, are chronicled and the activities of nine church societies are reported. Current leaders of church societies, officers and members of the Centenary Celebration Committee are listed. Period: 1844 - 1944.

3483. **Trinity Church, Galt, Ontario: souvenir commemorating the twenty-fifth anniversary of the Reverend Canon A.B. Thomas, 1937-1962.** Galt: The Church, 1962. 25 p. ill., ports. Loc: OKITW,

OWTUR, OCCA.

A tribute to the Rev. Aelwynn Brant Thomas, detailing his contributions to Trinity Church and giving a chronology of his ecclesiastical life. Church organizations of 1962 are described and church officials are listed. Period: 1937 - 1962.

EVANGELICAL & UNITED BRETHREN CHURCHES

3484. "Anniversary of St Jacobs church." **Waterloo Historical Society**. 1973. 61: 23. Loc: all.

A note of the 125th anniversary of Calvary United Church. Founded by German Evangelical preachers, it became part of the Evangelical Association in 1864 and the United Church of Canada in 1968. Period: 1847 - 1973.

3485. Bowman, C.D. "Reminiscences of the West Montrose Church." **Waterloo Historical Society**. 1946. 34: 18-20. Loc: all.

A short history, naming many members and ministers and based on an address given at the church reunion in September 1946. Period: 1857 - 1946.

3486. "Church union." **Waterloo Historical Society**. 1968. 56: 81. ill. Loc: all.

A note about the church service in 1968 that marked the union between the Canadian Conference of the Evangelical United Brethren Church and the United Church of Canada. The service was held in Zion Church, Kitchener, the oldest E.U.B. congregation in Canada. Period: 1890 - 1968.

3487. **Emmanuel and Calvary United Churches: a historical overview.** 1987?. 14 p. Loc: OKIT.

A study of the Evangelical Church in the Kitchener-Waterloo area from 1800 to 1970, with particular reference to the Emmanuel, Zion and Calvary congregations. This local history is placed in the social and economic context of Canadian history. In 1946 the Evangelical Church joined the United Brethren Church, becoming the Evangelical United Brethren Church, which in 1968 joined the United Church of Canada. Period: 1800 - 1970.

3488. Evangelical Association. **Journal der Canada Conferenz der evangelischer Gemeinschaft von Nord Amerika, enthaltend die Verhandlung der ... Jahressitzung gehalten zu ....** CIHM Microfiche series, nos. 64339 and A01711. Berlin: Berlin Publishing Co., 1890 - 1899. mf. Loc: OWTL, OWTU.

Booklets containing the events of the association's annual conferences beginning with the 26th gathering in Mildmay, Ontario. The conferences were held in various locations throughout North America, but primarily in southwestern Ontario. The publications contain information about active ministers (many from Waterloo County), including years of service, birth dates and places of residence. There are advertisements by local merchants and professionals. Missing from this series is the programme for 1891. The booklet for 1890 was published by Hett and Eby in Berlin and the one for 1899 was published in Stratford (the publisher is not given). Period: 1890 - 1899.

3489. Evangelical Association of Berlin - Young People's Alliance. **Constitution.** 1900?. 7 p. Loc: OKDHC.

Rules and regulations governing the organization, outlining its purposes and describing the duties of its officers and departments. Period: 1875 - 1916.

3490. Evangelical Association of North America. **Forward Movement Convention, Zion Church, Berlin, Ont., November 11th to 14th, 1909.** Berlin: Evangelical Association, 1909. 3 p. Loc: OWTUR.

A programme for a four-day convention in Berlin in 1909, sponsored by the Board of Control for the Young People's Alliance and the Sunday School Departments of the Evangelical Association. The front cover shows the Zion Evangelical Church, and A.L. Breithaupt is listed as one of the officers and members of the Board of Control. Period: 1908 - 1909.

3491. "Evangelical United Brethren camp meeting site." **Waterloo Historical Society.** 1964. 52: 84-86. ill. Loc: all.

An account of the unveiling of a plaque marking the site of a camp meeting in August 1839 that resulted in the formation of the Zion Evangelical Church in Berlin in 1841. Period: 1839 - 1964.

3492. "Freeport United Church, 1861-1961." **Waterloo Historical Society.** 1961. 49: 69-71. ill. Loc: all.

A short history of the church, listing the clergy and mentioning the centenary celebrations. Period: 1861 - 1961.

3493. Getz, J. Henry. **The Evangelical United Brethren Church: a century in Canada.** Kitchener: Historical Society of the Canada Conference of the Evangelical United Brethren Church, 1964. 52 p. ill. Loc: OKIT.

A general church history that mentions significant leaders from Waterloo County, including John Hoffman, Jacob Hailer, Rev. J.P. Hauch, L.H. Wagner and L.J. Breithaupt. Camp meetings, missionary service and children, youth and women's groups are described, with short

sketches of all churches belonging to the Canada Conference in 1964. Period: 1864 - 1964.

3494. Hauch, J.P., Rev. **Historical data of Emmanuel Evangelical Church, Waterloo, Ont..** The Church, 1925. 25 p. Loc: OWT.

A history of the church from the first Evangelical missionaries to Canada in 1812, to 1865 when Waterloo was supplied with its own pastor, and 1906 when the third church was built. Detailed information is presented about the cost, construction, architecture and dedication ceremony of the 1906 church, and all pastors and ministers are listed. Period: 1812 - 1925.

3495. Hirschman, Carl A., Rev. **100th anniversary: 1839-1939, Zion Evangelical Church, Kitchener, Ontario.** Waterloo: Chronicle Press, 1939. 120 p. ill., bibl. Loc: OKIT, OWTUCG, OWTUR, OKITW.

A scholarly history by the current minister, organized chronologically through biographical sketches of successive clergymen. Some church members were among Berlin's prominent businessmen and social elite, notably the Breithaupts and Kaufmans. The establishment of the Calvary and Olivet mission churches in newer parts of the city is noted and there is an account of the Zion Church Choir. The appendix lists all members of the quarterly conference from 1867, as well as presiding elders, preachers recommended for license, lay delegates to annual conference, superintendents and teachers in the Zion Bible School, and presidents of the Ladies' Aid and Women's Missionary Society. The volume is illustrated with many photographs of church groups in the centennial year and earlier pictures of the church and its ministers. Period: 1839 - 1939.

3496. **The history of Grace.** 1980?. 1 v. (unpaged). ill. Loc: OKIT.

A brief account of Roseville's Grace United Church, from its foundation in 1852 as the Evangelical United Brethren Church, through its 1968 amalgamation with the United Church, to 1980. A list of current members and their addresses is given, with a list of the clergy and the years they began their ministries. Period: 1852 - 1980.

3497. "New church in Elmira." **Waterloo Historical Society.** 1964. 52: 86. Loc: all.

A note of the dedication of the new Zion Evangelical United Brethren Church. Period: 1854 - 1964.

3498. Roedding, Wilfrid W. **Local history of Emmanuel Evangelical United Brethren Church, Bridgeport congregation, Emmanuel United Church as of Jan. 1, 1968: history, notes, and comments.** 1967. 57 p.

ill., map. Loc: OWTUR.

An historical account of the congregation which was established in 1879 and joined the United Church of Canada in 1968. Period: 1879 - 1967.

3499. Schweitzer, Vera and Schweitzer, Olive and Weber, Irene. **Bloomingdale United Church Centennial, 1879-1979**. The Church, 1979. 30 l. ill. Loc: OKITW.

A church history taken from the Bloomingdale Women's Institute Tweedsmuir volume compiled by Vera and Olive Schweitzer, and updated from 1969 by Irene Weber. The church began as a United Brethren Church, associated with the United Brethren Association Congregation Churches as the Bloomingdale Congregation Church in 1907. It later became part of the United Church. The authors list pastors and circuits from 1861 and draw on primary sources to describe church organizations, significant events and the building. Period: 1879 - 1979.

3500. **Souvenir programme of the dedication service of the new Evangelical Church, St Jacobs**. St Jacobs: The Church, 1915. 1 v. (unpaged). Loc: OKITW.

A programme containing photographs of the old and new churches and of Rev. W.O. Hehn, and listing Building Committee members. Period: 1915 - 1916.

3501. Taylor, Richard K. **Historical sketch of Emmanuel United Church, Waterloo, Ontario on the occasion of 125th anniversary of Emmanuel Church and 50th anniversary of the United Church of Canada on Sunday, May 4th, 1975**. 1975. 3 p. Loc: OWT.

A brief history of the Waterloo congregation from the 1836 visit of the first Evangelical minister, Rev. Carl Hammer, to the union with the United Church of Canada in 1968. The growth of the congregation, the clergy, the church buildings and church activities are all described. Period: 1812 - 1975.

3502. Thomas and Mattill. **Evangelisches Album: Prämie des christlichen Botschafters und Evangelical Messenger**. Cleveland, OH: Evangelischen Gemeinschaft, 1894. 111 p. ill., port. Loc: OWTUR.

An explanation of the structure of the Evangelical Church in North America, including its publishing houses, missionary service and educational organizations. L.J. Breithaupt is noted as the publications lay member at annual general conferences, the Evangelical Association meeting in Berlin in 1894 is reported, and photographs of Mr Breithaupt and the Berlin churches are included. Period: 1893 - 1894.

3503. Wagner, L.H., Rev. "The Evangelical Church in Upper Canada from 1837 to 1865." **Waterloo Historical Society**. 1939. 27: 75-80. Loc: all.

An early history of the church with particular reference to Waterloo County. It begins with the camp meeting on David Erb's farm in 1839 and ends when the Canadian Conference was organized in 1864. The author mentions Sunday Schools at Berlin and Waterloo and preachers who visited Canada before 1864. Period: 1837 - 1865.

3504. Zion Evangelical Church: Junior Young People's Alliance. **Programme, 1916-1917**. Kitchener: The Alliance, 1916. 1 folded sheet. Loc: OWTUR.

A plan of topics for meetings of the group, with names of members of the organizing committee. From the Breithaupt Hewetson Clark Collection. Period: 1916 - 1917.

3505. Zion United Church, Kitchener. **Consummation of union: the Canada Conference, the Evangelical United Brethren Church with the United Church of Canada**. Kitchener: The Church, 1968. 8 p. Loc: OKIT.

An order of service to mark the formal act of union at the Zion United Church, Kitchener, on 10 January 1968. Period: 1968 -

3506. Zion United Church, Kitchener. **Zion United Church, 1839-1989**. Kitchener: The Church, 1989. 28 p. ill. Loc: OKIT.

A collection of reminiscences by fourteen parishioners who attended the church at various times from about 1910 to 1989. The short entries provide information on church activities such as choirs, Sunday School, C.G.I.T., other youth organizations, missionary service and outreach programmes. Many anecdotes of former church leaders and members are recounted. A list of "interesting notes from Zion's history" contains a chronology account of significant dates. Period: 1839 - 1989.

LUTHERAN CHURCHES

3507. **100th anniversary souvenir of First St Paul's Lutheran Church, Wellesley, Ontario**. 1952. 1 v. ill. Loc: OKIT.

A centennial history which is organized by the ministries of successive clergymen. The photocopy at Kitchener Public Library also contains a chronology and newspaper articles relating to the cemetery which is attached to the church. Period: 1852 - 1952.

3508. **125th anniversary, 1835-1960: St Paul's Evangelical Lutheran Church, Kitchener, Ontario.** Kitchener: The Church, 1960. 30 p. ill. Loc: OKIT, OWES.

An historical account of the congregation for the period 1935-1960 that complements the earlier centennial history. Church groups, and buildings and furnishings are described and illustrated, and all elders, trustees and church officers are named with their periods of service. Period: 1935 - 1960.

3509. **125th anniversary services, 1834-1959: St Peter's Evangelical Lutheran Church, Preston, Ontario, the Rev. J.S. Dauphinee, pastor.** The Church, 1959. 8 p. Loc: OCCA.

A programme for three different jubilee celebrations held in November 1959, with a chronology of the church's history. Period: 1834 - 1959.

3510. "1878 St Peter's Lutheran Church replaced by $980,000 complex." **Waterloo Historical Society.** 1966. 54: 77. ill. Loc: all.

A brief note about the Berlin church organized in 1863. The building was replaced first in 1878 and again in 1966. Period: 1863 - 1966.

3511. **Anfangverein Harmonia, Neu-Hamburg, Ontario.** 1902. 1 v. (unpaged). Loc: OKIT.

A photocopy of the original in the possession of Elena Ritz of New Hamburg in April 1984. Minutes of the choir recorded by its secretary Lillie Ritz from January 1902 to 1904, with details of subsequent gatherings and performances by singers and seniors connected with St Peter's Lutheran Church, New Hamburg. Period: 1902 - 1983.

3512. Anniversary Booklet Committee. **The one hundredth anniversary of St James Evangelical Lutheran Church, Hespeler, Ontario, 1860-1960.** 1960. 1 v. (unpaged). ill. Loc: OCCA, OKIT.

An account of the development of the congregation, clergy and buildings. A separate section is devoted to church organizations, giving a brief history of each and mentioning contemporary members. Period: 1860 - 1960.

3513. Arnal, Oscar. **Heeding the call: St Peter's Lutheran Church, 1863-1988.** Kitchener: St Peter's Lutheran Church History Committee, 1989. 154 p. ill., bibl., index. Loc: OKIT.

A comprehensive history of the church in the broader context of the community. Buildings, activities, organizations and clergy are described, and appendices include a list of pastors, a transcript of Rev. Herman A. Sperling's letter from prison in 1917, and a calendar of

events for celebrating the 125th anniversary. Period: 1863 - 1988.

3514. Becker, George, Mrs and Schmidt, Conradine and Roberts, C.S., Rev. **100th anniversary, 1837-1937: St John's Evangelical Lutheran Church.** Waterloo: St John's Congregation, 1987. 61 p. ill. Loc: OKIT, OKITW, OWES.

A history of pastors, the building and organizations such as the choirs and Luther League. It includes a programme of festival services commemorating the centennial and photographs of pastors and current members. Period: 1837 - 1937.

3515. Beglo, Barton. **A time for building: essays on Lutherans in Canada.** Kitchener: St Mark's Press, 1988. 90 p. ill. Loc: OKIT, OWTL, OWTUCG, OWTUSJ, OWTUR.

A collection commemorating the 75th anniversary of St Mark's Lutheran Church, founded in 1913 as Berlin's first English-language Lutheran church. Six of the eleven essays that discuss the history of St Mark's Church are described in separate records. Erich Schultz surveys early Lutheranism in Ontario, Otto Reble discusses the transition from German to English, and Jo Beglo comments on the church building as an expression of Lutheran architecture. The other essays are by Roy Grosz on the church from 1918 to 1953, Evelyn Vogt on the congregation through three generations, and Delton Glebe on the relationship between the church and Waterloo Lutheran Seminary. Period: 1913 - 1988.

3516. Buehlow, Arthur F., Rev. **One hundredth anniversary of the official organization of Trinity Lutheran Church, New Hamburg, 1834-1934.** The Church, 1934. 16 p. ill. Loc: OWES.

A history of the congregation including a list of all pastors, views of old and new church buildings, and programmes for the services of thanksgiving. Period: 1834 - 1934.

3517. **Canada Lutheran.** 1910 -. Also mf. Loc: OWES.

A Lutheran newspaper in English, published monthly in succession to the **Kirchen-Blatt.** Contents include leading articles and devotions for seasons of the Christian year, news of various congregations, advertisements, and wider Lutheran church news. Samuel Weicker has compiled a card index of references to congregations and pastors. Period: 1910 - 1992.

3518. **Centennial booklet, St James Evangelical Lutheran Church, Elmira, 1850-1950.** Elmira: Elmira Signet, 1950. 52 p. ill. Loc: OKITW.

An historical account of the clergy and

buildings, with descriptions of contemporary organizations and photographs of members. One half of the booklet comprises advertisements by local businesses. Period: 1850 - 1950.

3519. Centennial Committee. **100th anniversary of Emmanuel Lutheran Church.** Petersburg: The Church, 1951. 16 p. ill. Loc: OKITW.

A booklet commemorating the centennial of the congregation and the 35th anniversary of the church building. It combines an historical sketch and descriptions of contemporary organizations with photographs of members. Period: 1851 - 1951.

3520. "Centennial of St James Evangelical Lutheran Church, St Jacobs, Ontario 1966." **Waterloo Historical Society.** 1966. 54: 35. Loc: all.

A brief history of the congregation, first organized in 1864, with references to the rebuilding of the church in 1916 and the new church of the early 1960s. Period: 1864 - 1966.

3521. Christ Lutheran Church, Waterloo. **Dedication, 1974.** The Church, 1974. Loc: OWES.

Orders of service for the dedication ceremonies including a brief outline of the organization of the congregation since 1967. Period: 1967 - 1974.

3522. Christ Lutheran Church, Waterloo. **Tenth anniversary, 1977.** The Church, 1977. 1 v. (unpaged). ill. Loc: OWES.

A history of the organization of the congregation and its early years based at the Waterloo Lutheran Seminary, followed by the building of a church at Lexington and Anndale Roads. Period: 1967 - 1977.

3523. Church of Our Redeemer. **The twenty-fifth anniversary of the Evangelical Lutheran Church of Our Redeemer, 1935-1960.** Waterloo: The Church, 1960. 8 p. ill. Loc: OKITW, OWT.

A programme of the anniversary service, including a brief history of the church buildings, activities and pastors. Period: 1935 - 1960.

3524. "Church organist for fifty years." **Waterloo Historical Society.** 1961. 49: 71. Loc: all.

A note about Mrs Elena Ritz, organist of Trinity Lutheran Church, New Hamburg. Period: 1911 - 1961.

3525. Cronmiller, Carl Raymond. **A history of the Lutheran Church in Canada, vol. 1.** Evangelical Lutheran Synod of Canada, 1961. 288 p. ill. Loc: OWES.

The official history commissioned by the Synod to mark its centennial. Chapter 7 describes the founding of the first Lutheran congregations in the German settlements of Upper Canada before 1861 and includes a translation of the description of the Waterloo area in 1835 from the missionary journal of Pastor John H. Bernheim. Chapters 9 and 10 present an account of the Synod organized in 1861, including details of congregations and clergymen until 1961. The author recounts the establishment of the Waterloo Seminary and explains the relationship of the Synod to other Lutheran bodies in Canada. Period: 1832 - 1961.

3526. Eastern Synod, Evangelical Lutheran Church in Canada. **Verhandlungen/Minutes.** The Church, 1861 - . Also mf. Loc: OWES.

A record of proceedings and resolutions of the governing body of the Evangelical Lutheran Church in Canada, known as:
1. Evangelisch-Lutherischen Synode von Canada from 1861 to 1918;
2. Evangelical Lutheran Synod of Canada, United Lutheran Church in America from 1918 to 1959;
3. Eastern Canada Synod, United Lutheran Church in America from 1960 to 1985.
Period: 1861 - 1991.

3527. Edwards, Henry E. and Edwards, Elin S. **Die evangelische lutherische St Matthäus Gemeinde zu Canestoge: ein Neubau, 1892: a new building for St Matthew's Evangelical Lutheran Church in 1892.** Conestogo: The Church, 1992. 84 p. ill., plans. Loc: OKIT, OWTL.

A history based on church records, emphasizing the construction of the 1892 building and intended to update and supplement histories published for the 90th and 100th anniversaries of the church. It includes a cut-out model of the church as designed in 1892 by Charles Moogk. A list of pastors and early church members, with brief biographical notes, is taken from the 1855 record book. Period: 1892 - 1942.

3528. **Einweihung der evangelisch-lutherischen St Matthäuskirche, Berlin den 7-9 März 1915.** 1915. 22 p. ill. Loc: OKITW, OWES.

A programme in German and English for the bilingual opening ceremonies of St Matthews Lutheran Church, Berlin in March 1915. There is a short history of the church with photographs of the old and new buildings. Period: 1914 - 1915.

3529. Glebe, Delton J., Rev. "Partnership in seminary education." **A time for building: essays on Lutherans in Canada.** Edited by Barton Beglo. Kitchener: St Mark's Press, 1988. Pp. 59-66. Loc: OKIT, OWTL, OWTUCG, OWTUR, OWTUSJ.

An essay on the long tradition of strong links between St Mark's Lutheran Church, Kitchener and the Waterloo Lutheran Seminary. Most of the church's pastors served the seminary in some role, and theological students preached in the church or undertook supervised assignments in pastoral work. The author is a retired Principal-Dean of the seminary. Period: 1913 - 1988.

3530. Grace Lutheran Church, Kitchener. **Grace Lutheran Church: 1944-1984**. Kitchener: The Church, 1984. 18 p. ill. Loc: OKIT.
A directory of current members, with a short history that includes the names of former pastors and comments on the changes that have taken place in the church neighbourhood. Period: 1944 - 1984.

3531. Graupner, Paul, Rev. **Geschichte der deutschen evangelisch-lutherischen St Pauls Gemeinde zu Elmira, Ont., vom Jahr 1860 bis 1910. Zum fünfzigjährigen Jubiläum der Gemeinde**. Elmira: Signet Druck, 1910. 15 p. ill. Loc: OKITW.
A history of St Paul's German Lutheran Church, Elmira from 1860 to 1910, commemorating its fiftieth anniversary. The author describes clergymen and church members, organizations and buildings. Period: 1860 - 1910.

3532. Grosz, Roy N. "The Maurer-Jacobi years, 1918-1953." **A time for building: essays on Lutherans in Canada**. Edited by Barton Beglo. Kitchener: St Mark's Press, 1988. Pp. 41-47. Loc: OKIT, OWTL, OWTUCG, OWTUR, OWTUSJ.
Reminiscences of the ministries of Dr Jacob Maurer and Dr Albert Jacobi by a "son of St Mark's" who became secretary of the Eastern Synod of the Evangelical Lutheran Church in Canada. Period: 1918 - 1953.

3533. Haag, George. **The service areas of the Lutheran churches in Kitchener-Waterloo**. University of Waterloo (B.A. thesis, Geography), 1963. 2 fiche. maps, graphs. mf. Loc: OWTUM.
A description of the locational patterns of members of fourteen Lutheran churches, with maps and graphs. The author finds that the age of the church and individual preference are the most important factors. Period: 1962 - 1963.

3534. Heick, W.H. **Anniversary St John's Evangelical Lutheran Church Waterloo, Ontario: historical supplement 10th, 1972, 135th**. The Church, 1972. 1 folded sheet. Loc: OWT, OWES.
An historical sketch from the move to the new church in 1962 following the 1959 fire. This continues the longer church history published in 1962. Period: 1962 - 1972.

3535. Heick, W.H. "Becoming an indigenous church: the Lutheran Church in Waterloo County, Ontario." **Ontario History**. 1964. 56,4: 249-260. Loc: OKIT, OWTL, OWTU, OWTUCG.

A study of the informal beginnings of Lutheranism in Ontario, the division in 1860 with the Missouri Synod, and the reaction of the German Lutheran clergy and members to both world wars. The author discusses the puritanical tendencies of Waterloo Lutheran clergy, the increasing use of the English language in church services, the attitudes of Lutherans towards the use of alcohol, and the church's reaction to the "social gospel." Period: 1835 - 1964.

3536. Heick, W.H. "The Lutherans of Waterloo County during World War I." **Waterloo Historical Society**. 1962. 50: 23-32. Loc: all.
A scholarly account based on the author's M.A. thesis for Queen's University. Period: 1914 - 1918.

3537. Heick, W.H. **The Lutherans of Waterloo County, Ontario, 1810-1959: a historical study**. Queen's University (Ph.D. thesis, History), 1959. 219 p. bibl., map, charts. Loc: OWTL.
A history of the church and of the role of Lutherans in the county's development. The establishment of Waterloo College is seen as the most important Lutheran contribution to the educational life of the county, but the author concludes that "no distinctive Lutheran pattern of life permeates the community." Appendices include the missionary journal of Pastor John H. Bernheim and a list of the Lutheran congregations in Waterloo County with their dates of foundation and first pastors. Period: 1810 - 1959.

3538. History Committee. **Grace and blessing: a history of the Ontario District of the Lutheran Church, Missouri Synod**. The Church, 1954. 103 p. ill. Loc: OKITW, OWRE.
A history commemorating the District's 75th anniversary. The first section mentions pioneer clergy such as the Rev. F.W. Bindemann and the Rev. A. Ernst, the work of Rev. W.C. Boese in founding the Mission Treasury, the founding of **Das Lutherische Volksblatt** and the effects of the two world wars. The second section presents individual congregational histories, including twelve from Waterloo County: Trinity Lutheran of Floradale, St Paul's of Elmira, St Paul's of Kitchener, Evangelical Lutheran Church of Our Redeemer, Waterloo, Grace Lutheran Church of Kitchener, Holy Cross of Kitchener, Bethel Lutheran Church of Kitchener, St Paul's of Wellesley, Emmanuel Congregation of Petersburg, Linwood Lutheran Church, New Hamburg Lutheran Church, and the Baden Lutheran Congregation. Period: 1879 - 1954.

3539. **A history of St Peter's Lutheran Church, New Hamburg, Ontario**. The Church, 1986. 104 p. ill., bibl. Loc: OKIT, OWRN.

An account of the first 75 years of the church from its founding and growth under the direction of Rev. F.E. Oberlander. Photographs of parishioners and the church and statistical tables are included. Period: 1910 - 1985.

3540. Hollatz, David. **Die Heils und Gnaden Ordnung nach dem Evangelium in vier Gesprächen vorgestellt.** Berlin: Heinrich Eby, 1844. 160 p. Also CIHM Microfiche series, no. 35777. Loc: OKITW, OWTL, OWTU, OWTUR, OWTUCGR.

A didactic interpretation of the Gospel meaning of salvation and mercy through four conversations between student and teacher. Apart from being printed in Berlin, the book has no references to Waterloo County. Period: 1843 - 1844.

3541. Holy Cross Lutheran Church, Kitchener. **35th anniversary: Holy Cross Evangelical Lutheran Church, 1948-1983.** Kitchener: The Church, 1983. 44 p. ill. Loc: OKIT.

A history of the congregation, founded in 1948 as a mission church by members of St Paul's Lutheran Church in Kitchener. The book lists officers, elders, teachers and presidents of societies. Period: 1948 - 1983.

3542. Holy Cross Lutheran Church, Kitchener. **The constitution and the by-laws**. The Church, 1948. 18 p. Loc: OKIT.

The constitution and by-laws of the church, detailing its organization, the duties of the pastor and congregation, and election procedures for officers and administrative boards. Period: 1947 - 1948.

3543. Hulet, Marion. "Preston's first church." **Waterloo Historical Society**. 1968. 56: 52. ill. Loc: all.

A note of the church first built in 1839 and replaced in 1889 by the stone building of St Peter's Lutheran Church. Period: 1834 - 1889.

3544. **In nomine Jesu: the dedication services, the Evangelical Lutheran Church of Our Redeemer, Waterloo.** Waterloo: The Church, 1951. 12 p. ill. Loc: OKITW.

A programme for the dedication service, with a chronology of historical events and a list of memorials and gifts. Period: 1934 - 1951.

3545. **Jahrbuch der evangelisch-lutherischen St Petri Gemeinde zu Berlin, Canada**. Berlin: The Church, 1899 - 1900. Loc: OKITW.

Yearbooks of St Peter's Evangelical Lutheran Church, with information on activities, members,

administration and finances. The 1900 yearbook has a photograph of the pastor, Rev. R. von Pirch, and members of the church session. The Waterloo Historical Society holds yearbooks for 1899 and 1900. Period: 1899 - 1900.

3546. Kalbfleisch, L.H., Rev. "History of St James Evangelical Lutheran Congregation, Elmira, Ontario." **Waterloo Historical Society**. 1950. 38: 38-41. Loc: all.

A short history of the first organized congregation in Elmira which began in 1850. The author describes the building of the first church and lists names of ministers. Period: 1850 - 1950.

3547. Keffer, N.A., Rev. **Seventy-fifth anniversary, 1860-1936: St James' Evangelical Lutheran Church Hespeler, Ontario.** 1935. 26 p. ill. Loc: OKITW, OWES.

A history of the congregation with photographs of many of the pastors and a summary of their achievements. It includes a review of the various organizations with photographs of contemporary members, a list of church members in 1935, and photographs of the church buildings. Period: 1860 - 1936.

3548. **Kirchen-Blatt der evangelisch-lutherischen Synode von Canada**. 1868 - 1910. Also mf. Loc: OWES.

A Lutheran newspaper in German, published twice a month until 1890 and weekly from March 1890 to 1910. The places of publication changed with the editors and include New Hamburg, Elmira, New Dundee and Conestogo. Contents include leading articles and devotions for seasons of the Christian year, news of various congregations, advertisements, and world news of interest to people of German origin. Samuel Weicker has compiled a card index of references to congregations and pastors. From 1910, the monthly **Canada Lutheran** was published with the same purposes. Period: 1868 - 1910.

3549. Klinck, Luella and Graupner, Paul, Rev. and Malinsky, Frank, Rev. **Grace abounding: a history of St Paul's Evangelical Lutheran Church, Elmira, Ontario**. The Church, 1960. 18 p. ill. Loc: OWRE, OKITW.

An historical sketch commemorating the church's centennial, with information about clergy, the church building, members, organizations and activities. Earlier portions are direct quotations from a booklet prepared by the Rev. Paul Graupner for the 50th anniversary. There are photographs of the teachers, pastors and members of contemporary church organizations. A chronology of church history and a programme of centennial events are also provided. Period: 1860

- 1960.

3550. Knauff, W.H., Rev. **Centennial booklet, St Peter's Lutheran Church, Preston, 1834-1934**. The Church, 1934. 60 p. ill. Loc: OKITW, OCCA, OWES.

An historical account of the clergy, building and organizations, with a list of church members, a commemorative sonnet by Clara Bernhardt, and advertisements by Preston businesses. Period: 1834 - 1934.

3551. Koegler, J.B. "St Peter's Church - Berlin's first Lutheran church." **Waterloo Historical Society**. 1950. 38: 41-45. ill. Loc: all.

A short history of the church which was organized in 1863. The author notes the formation of the Sunday school, describes the buildings, and names Sunday school teachers, members of the first church council and all full-time pastors from C.F.A. Kaessemann in 1863 to A.W. Lotz in 1950. Period: 1825 - 1950.

3552. Kraehling, Homer, Mrs. "Zion Lutheran Church, St Agatha." **Waterloo Historical Society**. 1963. 51: 42-43. ill. Loc: all.

A history marking the church's centennial and naming all clergymen and some early church members. Period: 1863 - 1963.

3553. Kraehling, Jean and Kraehling, Myrta, Mrs and Kraehling, Katherine, Mrs. **A history of Zion Evangelical Lutheran Church, St Agatha, Ontario**. St Agatha: The Church, 1963. 1 v. ill. Loc: OKITW, OWES.

A history commemorating the centenary of the church building in 1963, based on the church records. It provides information on the formation of the church, its pastors, members and the building. Period: 1834 - 1963.

3554. Krafft, U., Pastor. **In der Filiale: eine Erzählung für das Luth. Volksblatt**. Elmira: Luth. Volksblatt, 1890. 88 p. Also CIHM Microfiche series, no. 07966. Loc: OWTL, OWTU, OWTUR.

A fictional narrative from the **Lutherisches Volksblatt**. Apart from being published in Elmira by the church newspaper and printed by H. Delion, there are no direct references to the county.

3555. Mount Zion Lutheran Church, Waterloo. **10th anniversary, 1957-1967**. The Church, 1967. 15 p. ill. Loc: OWES.

A programme of the anniversary celebrations with a brief history of the congregation's growth on the west side of suburban Waterloo. Period: 1957 - 1967.

3556. Mount Zion Lutheran Church, Waterloo. **20th anniversary, 1957-1977**. The Church, 1977. 1 v. (unpaged). ill. Loc: OWES.

A souvenir booklet consisting mainly of a photo directory of church members, with a brief chronology of milestones and an aerial view of the church site. Period: 1957 - 1977.

3557. Mount Zion Lutheran Church, Waterloo. **Dedication, first unit, May 14th, 1961**. The Church, 1961. 1 v. (unpaged). ill. Loc: OWES.

Orders of service celebrating the completion of the first phase of the church building, with a brief history of the congregation formed in 1957 and details of the building committee and architect and contractors. Period: 1957 - 1961.

3558. Nabert, Kurt. **In commemoration of the 150th anniversary of St John's Evangelical Lutheran Church, Waterloo, Ontario, 1837-1987**. Waterloo: The Church, 1987. 36 p. ill. Loc: OKDHC, OWES.

A general history, emphasizing the church's German cultural background, affiliation with Waterloo Lutheran Seminary, and the aid to Volksdeutsche following the Second World War. A statue of St John made by William Pfeffer of the Globe Furniture Company is described, with accounts of contemporary church organizations and activities. Period: 1837 - 1987.

3559. Opperman, Henry W., Rev. and Koegler, John. **St Peter's Evangelical Lutheran Church, 1863-1963**. Waterloo: The Church, 1963. 15 p. ill. Loc: OKIT, OWES.

A commemorative history of clergy, building and activities of the Kitchener congregation. Topics include Paster Oberlander's work as founder of tuberculosis treatment in Waterloo County, the weekly radio ministry "Thus it is written," and church services provided to refugees in their own language following the Second World War. Period: 1863 - 1963.

3560. Orzen, Albert, Rev. **100th anniversary, 1835-1935: St Paul's Evangelical Lutheran Church, Kitchener, Ontario**. Kitchener: Merchants Printing, 1935. 71 p. ill. Loc: OKIT, OKITW, OWES.

A centennial history beginning with an account of the dissension between the founding minister, the Rev. F.W. Bindemann and other Lutheran clergy. The contributions of later ministers are discussed and various church organizations are described and illustrated with views of the church interior and church groups such as the Ladies' Aid Society, St Paul's Choir, the Senior and Junior Walther Leagues, the Men's Club, the Swing Bowling Club and the Tennis Club. Elders, trustees and other church officers are listed. The development of

the Church of Our Redeemer in Waterloo as a
daughter congregation is also described. The
authorship of this history is not clear in the
imprint itself, but is stated in the 125th
anniversary history of 1960. Period: 1835 - 1935.

3561. Reformation Lutheran Church, Kitchener.
Dedication services of the first unit, 1960. The
Church, 1960. 1 v. (unpaged). ill. Loc: OWES.
Orders of service for several dedication
ceremonies, with details of members of church
council and building committee and a message from
the pastor. A brief history of the congregation
notes its origins in a survey of Kitchener's East
Ward in 1954 by the Board of American Missions.
Period: 1954 - 1960.

3562. Ronnenberg, Ernest. **The fiftieth anniversary of
Redeemer Lutheran Church, 1935-1985**. Waterloo:
The Church, 1985. 12 p. ill. Loc: OKITW, OWT.
A programme for the anniversary service, with a
brief history of the church describing its clergy,
organizations and building. Period: 1935 - 1985.

3563. Schmidt, William A. "First English Lutheran
Church, 1913-1938." **Waterloo Historical Society**.
1991. 79: 166-169. ill. Loc: all.
An historical sketch of the congregation which
used the former Waterloo Township Hall for
services until 1938, when its name was changed to
St Mark's Lutheran Church and a new building was
erected at the corner of King and Green Streets,
Kitchener. The author describes the original
township hall, built in 1848 on Queen Street
North, and notes its earlier uses by publishers of
the newspapers **Der Deutsche Canadier** and the
Telegraph, and then by the Trinity Methodist
Church from 1875 to 1904 and St Matthews Lutheran
Church from 1904 to 1914. Period: 1848 - 1938.

3564. Schultz, Erich. "Early Lutheranism in Ontario." **A
time for building: essays on Lutherans in Canada**.
Edited by Barton Beglo. Kitchener: St Mark's
Press, 1988. Pp. 5-11. Loc: OKIT, OWTL, OWTUCG,
OWTUR, OWTUSJ.
A brief survey of Lutheran settlements and
church organization in Nova Scotia and Ontario
including Waterloo County. The author describes
the roles of early pastors, the distinctions
between the various major church synods, and the
effects of major mergers and reorganizations in
1925 and 1962. Period: 1830 - 1986.

3565. Spring, Christian F., Rev. **Katechetische
Unterweisung zur Seligkeit über den lutherischen
Katechismus**. Berlin: M.S. Hallman, 1887. 232 p.
Loc: OKDHC.
A collection of guidelines for understanding the

Lutheran catechism, compiled by the Lutheran
pastor in New Dundee and published in Berlin as a
special jubilee issue. Period: 1868 - 1887.

3566. St James Lutheran Church, Elmira. **125th
anniversary: May 11, 1850 to 1975**. St Jacobs: St
Jacobs Printery, 1975. 8 p. ill. Loc: OKIT, OWRE.
A brief history organized by the terms of
pastors who have served the parish since 1850,
with some details of church policies and politics.
Period: 1850 - 1975.

3567. St James Lutheran Church, Elmira. **Dedication
services of Educational Unit and Church House,
Pentecost Sunday, June 2nd, 1963**. The Church,
1963. 8 p. ill. Loc: OWES.
Order of service with details of gifts, and
names of members of the building committee and
church council and of architect, contractors and
sub-contractors. Period: 1963 -

3568. St James Lutheran Church, Hespeler. **Dedication of
parish hall, December 14th, 1947**. The Church,
1947. 1 v. (unpaged). ill. Loc: OWES.
Programmes for several special services with a
church directory; photographs of pastor, church
building, church council and building committee;
advertisements by local businesses; brief history
of the congregation and the church erected in
1868; and an account of the difficulties of
building projects at a time of postwar shortages.
Period: 1854 - 1947.

3569. **St James Lutheran Church, Hespeler, November 12,
1967: the birth of a church**. The Church, 1967. 3
p. ill. Loc: OKITW, OCCA.
An account of the founding of the church,
largely taken from the church minutes, with
details of the work of the church members,
finances and the construction work. A chronology
of improvements to the church building from 1876
to 1967 is appended. Period: 1867 - 1967.

3570. St James Lutheran Church, New Dundee. **Dedication
festivities, July 12 to 17, 1953**. The Church,
1953. 1 v. (unpaged). Loc: OWES.
A booklet including a brief history of the
congregation formed in 1859, its first church
dedicated in 1863, and efforts to build the new
church. It includes illustrations of both
churches, a directory of church officers, and
names of architect and builders and contractors.
Period: 1859 - 1953.

3571. St James Lutheran Church, New Dundee. **One
hundred years of grace, 1859-1959**. The Church, 1959.
1 v. (unpaged). ill. Loc: OWES.
A commemorative booklet including a brief

history, photographs of old and new church buildings and all church organizations, and a list of pastors. Period: 1859 - 1959.

3572. St James Lutheran Church, St Jacobs. **75th anniversary booklet, 1866-1941.** The Church, 1941. 1 v. (unpaged). Loc: OWES.

A commemorative history of the congregation, with a chronology of structural changes including the rebuilding of the church in 1916, and accounts with photographs of various church societies and activities such as the Sunday School, choir, Luther League, Sewing Circle, Brotherhood and Boys' Club. Period: 1866 - 1941.

3573. St James Lutheran Church, St Jacobs. **Centennial: 1866-1966.** St Jacobs: Centennial Booklet Committee, 1966. 32 p. ill. Loc: OKIT, OWES.

A commemorative booklet including historical sketches of the Indians, Woolwich Township, St Jacobs, and other churches in the village, as well as an account of the origins, building, clergy and organizations of the church. A programme of centennial services is also given. Period: 1866 - 1966.

3574. "St James Lutheran Church." **Waterloo Historical Society.** 1962. 50: 94,107. Loc: all.

A brief history of the church in New Dundee, based on the centennial booklet and listing all pastors. Period: 1859 - 1959.

3575. "St John Evangelical Lutheran Church 100 years old." **Waterloo Historical Society.** 1972. 60: 77. Loc: all.

A short history of the rural church located between St Clements and Wellesley. The article mentions Rev. F.A. Pfeiffer and Rev. Daniel Stahlschmidt as the first pastors of the German-speaking congregation. Period: 1852 - 1972.

3576. St John's Lutheran Church, Waterloo. **Gedenkbuechlein zur Erinnerung an das 75 jaehrige Jubilaeum der evangelisch-lutherischen St Johannis-Gemeinde in Waterloo, Ont., August 25-26, 1912.** Waterloo: Sentinel Print, 1912. 24 p. ill. Loc: OWT, OWES.

A commemorative history printed for the 75th jubilee of St John's Evangelical Lutheran Church in Waterloo in 1912. It chronicles the development of the church founded by Pastor F.W. Bindemann, referring to clergy, prominent church members and organizations such as the council of elders, the women's group, Sunday school, youth and children's groups, and the choir. There are photographs of these groups and former pastors and views of the church buildings in 1837 and 1882. Period: 1837 - 1912.

3577. St John's Lutheran Church, Waterloo. **In commemoration of the dedication and 125th anniversary of St John's Evangelical Lutheran Church Waterloo, Ontario, 1837-1962.** Waterloo: The Church, 1962. 52 p. ill. Loc: OWT, OKIT, OWES.

An account of the church and congregation, mentioning the 1959 fire that destroyed the old church and describing in detail the interior and exterior of the new church built on the site of the Kitchener-Waterloo Orphanage's Willow Hall. Programmes for the dedication services of the new church are included, with lists of gifts to the church. Period: 1837 - 1962.

3578. St John's Lutheran Church, Waterloo. **Kirchen-Ordnung der deutschen evangelisch-lutherischen St Johannes-gemeinde in Waterloo, Waterloo Co., Ont., Canada.** Waterloo: Bauernfreund Dampf-Druck, 1888. 12 p. Loc: OWTUR.

A summary of church discipline and ritual. Period: 1887 - 1888.

3579. St John's Lutheran Church, Waterloo. **Rededication, February 1st to 8th, 1953.** The Church, 1953. 24 p. ill. Loc: OWES.

Orders of service with a church directory, history of the congregation and its church buildings, and description of the renovations being dedicated. Period: 1837 - 1953.

3580. St Luke's Lutheran Church, Kitchener. **Dedication, May 26, 1963.** The Church, 1963. 1 v. (unpaged). ill. Loc: OWES.

Programmes for the various services, with names of church leaders and building committee members. A brief history notes the origins of the congregation in 1939 and the construction of the first church on King East during the Second World War to serve the Shantz, Sunnyside, Centreville and Freeport areas. Part of the congregation formed the nucleus of St Philip's in the Parkway Heights area in 1958. When St Luke's relocated to the site on Franklin Avenue, the old church was dismantled and reassembled as St George's Anglican Church on Fischer Drive. Period: 1939 - 1963.

3581. St Luke's Lutheran Church, Kitchener. **Souvenir booklet commemorating the Dedication Day, November 30, 1941, Sunnyside, Kitchener.** The Church, 1941. 16 p. ill. Loc: OKITW, OWES.

Programmes for the various services, with names and photographs of church leaders and building committee members, and details of contractors and supplies. A brief history notes the origins of the congregation in 1939 and the construction of the first church on King Street East to serve the Shantz, Sunnyside, Centreville and Freeport areas.

Period: 1939 - 1941.

3582. St Luke's Lutheran Church, Kitchener. **St Luke's Lutheran Church, Kitchener.** 1982. 28 p. ill. Loc: OKIT.

A photographic directory of the congregation including a brief history. The names of former pastors are given as well as statistical information and descriptions of church buildings and additions. Period: 1939 - 1982.

3583. St Mark's Lutheran Church, Kitchener. **Golden anniversary, 1913-1963.** The Church, 1963. 1 v. (unpaged). Loc: OWES.

A commemorative booklet, with a history of the first English-language Lutheran congregation in Kitchener-Waterloo which used the former St Matthews Lutheran Church building until a new church was completed in 1938. Photographs and names are included of the buildings, clergy, church officials and various church organizations including the choirs, Sunday School, Luther League and Lutheran Church Women. Period: 1913 - 1963.

3584. St Mark's Lutheran Church, Wellesley. **100th anniversary, 1876-1976.** The Church, 1976. 1 v. (unpaged). ill. Loc: OWES.

A souvenir booklet including an historical summary with details of all pastors and accounts with photographs of church groups such as Sunday School, Luther League, Lutheran Church Women, and choirs. Originally known as St Paul's, the congregation was renamed in 1957. Period: 1876 - 1976.

3585. St Matthews Lutheran Brotherhood. **Kirche Daheim: church at home, a souvenir booklet.** Kitchener: The Church, 1930?. 32 p. ill. Loc: OKITW, OWES.

An account of the Sunday radio programme, Kirche Daheim, broadcast by CKCR of Waterloo from St Matthews Lutheran Church, Kitchener. It contains a programme schedule, fan letters, and articles on the broadcasting process, the church bell, and the St Matthews Lutheran Brotherhood. Some articles are in German. Period: 1930 - 1931.

3586. St Matthews Lutheran Church, Berlin. **Kirchenordnung der deutschen evangelish-lutherischen St Matthaus-Gemeinde zu Berlin, Ontario.** Berlin: Rittinger and Motz, 1904. 14 p. Loc: OWTUR.

Rules of order of the church of which the Rev. F. Hoffman is identified as pastor. Period: 1903 - 1904.

3587. St Matthews Lutheran Church, Kitchener. **Dedication of Church House, 1952.** The Church, 1952. 1 v. (unpaged). ill. Loc: OWES.

Order of service, with names of members of church council and building committee, and architect and contractors. Period: 1951 - 1952.

3588. St Matthews Lutheran Church, Kitchener. **Diamond jubilee, 1904-1964.** The Church, 1964. Loc: OWES.

Several programmes for commemorative services, each with a brief history of the congregation founded in 1904. Period: 1904 - 1964.

3589. St Matthews Lutheran Church, Kitchener. **Golden hours: 30th anniversary, Sunday, February 8th, 1960.** Kitchener: The Church, 1960. 1 folded sheet. Loc: OWES.

An order of service and photograph commemorating 30 years of the church's tradition of broadcasting its Sunday morning worship. Period: 1930 - 1960.

3590. St Matthews Lutheran Church, Kitchener. **Golden hours: 50th anniversary 1930-1980.** Kitchener: The Church, 1980. 1 v. (unpaged). ill. Loc: OKIT, OWES.

A souvenir booklet commemorating the 2,600 hours of broadcast worship services, including statistics compiled by Samuel Weicker and the text, in both German and English, of the first radio sermon broadcast by the Rev. John Schmieder on 23 February 1930. Period: 1930 - 1980.

3591. St Matthews Lutheran Church, Kitchener. **Souvenir of the Golden Jubilee: St Matthews Lutheran Church.** Kitchener: The Church, 1988. 48 p. ill. Loc: OKIT, OWES.

A commemorative history containing information about pastors, church members, activities and organizations, as well as details of the various church buildings. A directory of current church members begins on page 31. The booklet also provides a brief account of the development of Lutheranism in the county, including the roles of Rev. John H. Bernheim, Rev. F.W. Bindemann and C.F.A. Kaessmann. Period: 1904 - 1954.

3592. St Matthews Lutheran Church, Kitchener. **St Matthews Evangelical Lutheran Church: anniversary report, 1904-1929.** Kitchener: The Church, 1929. 60 p. ill. Loc: OKIT, OWES.

An outline of the development of the Lutheran Church in Waterloo County and the establishment of the parish of St Matthews in Kitchener. Pastors, other church leaders, members and activities are briefly described. Some entries are written in German by parishioners and are accompanied by photographs of the church members and building. A directory of current members begins on page 39.

Period: 1904 - 1929.

3593. St Matthews Lutheran Church, Kitchener. **St Matthews Evangelical Lutheran Church: annual report**. Kitchener: The Church, 1920 -. Loc: OKITW, OWES.

Each report contains a directory of church members, a financial statement and pastor's report. The first report of 1920 had more German text than English, but by 1935 there were no German articles. The 1920 volume contains only one photograph of the church, but following reports have many more with articles on church activities such as the radio station, Kirche Daheim, and biographical profiles of church members. The special 1929 anniversary report contains an historical account of the church and is indexed separately in the WRP database. The Waterloo Historical Society holds annual reports for the all years from 1920 to 1935 except 1922, 1928 and 1931. The Archives of the Eastern Synod, Evangelical Lutheran Church in Canada (located in the Wilfrid Laurier University Library) hold annual reports for 1932, 1935, 1938 and 1944. Period: 1920 - 1944.

3594. St Paul's Lutheran Church, Bridgeport. **Centennial, 1861-1961**. The Church, 1961. 4 p. Loc: OWES.

The order of the centennial service on 18 June 1961, with a brief history and photographs of the church buildings of 1889 and 1956. Details are provided of successive pastors and of the organization of Bridgeport within the Elmira parish to 1889, the Conestogo-Breslau parish to 1948, and St Stephen's, Kitchener to 1952. Period: 1861 - 1961.

3595. St Paul's Lutheran Church, Bridgeport. **Dedication, 1957**. The Church, 1957. 20 p. ill. Loc: OWES.

Orders of worship for three services held on 31 March 1957, with a brief history, description of the new church building, details of gifts and donations and names of committee members and church officials. Period: 1861 - 1957.

3596. St Paul's Lutheran Church, Erbsville. **Dedication 1968**. The Church, 1968. Loc: OWES.

A leaflet containing the order of service and a brief history of the church building and its improvements and renovations. Period: 1852 - 1968.

3597. St Paul's Lutheran Church, Erbsville. **One hundredth anniversary booklet, 1852-1952**. The Church, 1952. 1 v. (unpaged). ill. Loc: OWES.

A commemorative history of the founding of the original log "Allemang Kirche" church in Wellesley

Township and the move to the new building in 1877. It includes details of cornerstone contents, a church directory, photographs and histories of organizations such as the Ladies' Aid, Luther League and Sunday School. An interesting section describes the transition from the use of the German language for Sunday School, worship services and record-keeping. Period: 1852 - 1952.

3598. St Paul's Lutheran Church, Galt. **Dedication services, December 4th and 5th, 1960**. The Church, 1960. 16 p. ill. Loc: OWES.

Programmes for several services, with photographs of old and new buildings, the pastor and church leaders, and a brief history and an account of the design of the new church. The history notes that the congregation was formed in 1907 and used a former Methodist church on North Street. Period: 1907 - 1960.

3599. St Paul's Lutheran Church, Kitchener. **Lift high the cross: St Paul's Lutheran Church, Kitchener, 150th anniversary, 1835-1985**. Kitchener: The Church, 1985. 22 p. ill. Loc: OKIT, OWES.

A commemorative booklet that draws upon material in the 1935 and 1960 histories but emphasizes current church activities and the dedication of the addition to the church building in April 1985. There are reminiscences by James Huras (whose family belonged to the church through five generations) and Esther Boese Brown (whose father, the Rev. W.C. Boese, was minister from 1896). Period: 1835 - 1985.

3600. St Paul's Lutheran Church, Kitchener. **Serve the Lord with gladness: St Paul's Evangelical Lutheran Church 1860-1985**. Elmira: The Church, 1985. 1 v. (unpaged). ill. Loc: OKIT, OWES.

A history which is well illustrated with photographs of church buildings, activities, former pastors and members. The book also includes information about the Christian Day School and other activities and programmes such as the Braille Centre, the social ministry, the adult society, the Sunday School and youth groups. Period: 1860 - 1985.

3601. "St Peter's Lutheran Church, Heidelberg." **Waterloo Historical Society**. 1970. 58: 53. ill. Loc: all.

A photograph of the church to mark the 125th anniversary of the congregation and the 100th anniversary of the building. Period: 1845 - 1970.

3602. St Peter's Lutheran Church, Kitchener. **St Peter's history 1863-1956: the church with the revolving cross**. The Church, 1956. Loc: OWES.

A brochure summarizing the church's history as

the "oldest distinctively Lutheran congregation" in Kitchener. Details are given of pastors and the two church structures of 1863 and 1878. Period: 1863 - 1956.

3603. St Peter's Lutheran Church, Kitchener. **St Peter's Lutheran Church, Kitchener, Ontario.** Toronto: Church Directories of Canada, 1968. 60 p. ill. Loc: OKIT, OWES.

A photographic directory of the congregation with a short history of the parish which was first organized in 1863 under the leadership of the Rev. C.F.A. Kaessmann. The history includes information on past buildings, clergy, activities and contributions to the larger community. Period: 1863 - 1968.

3604. St Peter's Lutheran Church, Linwood. **100th anniversary, 1873-1973.** The Church, 1973. 1 v. (unpaged). ill. Loc: OWES.

A brief history including names of all pastors, a list of baptized members and photographs of contemporary church activities and organizations. Period: 1873 - 1973.

3605. St Peter's Lutheran Church, Preston. **75jährige Geschichte der deutsch evang.-lutherischen St Peter's Gemeinde in Preston und umgegend, 1834-1909.** Preston: Preston Progress, 1909. 1 v. (unpaged). ill. Loc: OWES.

A commemorative history with a chronology of events, statistics of membership, list of pastors, and accounts with photographs of church officers, organizations and buildings. Period: 1834 - 1909.

3606. St Stephen's Lutheran Church, Kitchener. **25th anniversary, 1952-1977.** The Church, 1977. 1 v. (unpaged). ill. Loc: OWES.

A brochure including a brief history of the congregation founded in 1949 in the Highland Road area of Kitchener's South Ward. Period: 1952 - 1977.

3607. St Stephen's Lutheran Church, Kitchener. **Dedication, September 14, 1952.** The Church, 1952. 1 v. (unpaged). ill. Loc: OWES.

A brochure including a brief account of the organization of the church in 1949 to serve Kitchener's South Ward. It includes details of gifts and memorials and a directory of church officers. Period: 1949 - 1952.

3608. Stroh, Walter. "St Matthew's Evangelical Lutheran Church, Conestogo, 1853-1953." **Waterloo Historical Society.** 1953. 41: 41-46. Loc: all.

A history and programme of the centennial worship services. Pastors and some members are named and changes in the church building are described. Period: 1853 - 1953.

3609. Trinity Lutheran Church, New Hamburg. **A history of Trinity Lutheran Church, New Hamburg, Ontario, 1834-1984.** New Hamburg: Ritz Printing, 1984. 48 p. ill. bibl. Loc: OKIT, OWES.

A commemorative history of the founding of the church with information on past clergy, members and activities. Period: 1834 - 1984.

3610. Trinity Lutheran Church, Shantz Station. **100th anniversary, 1860-1960.** The Church, 1965. 1 v. (unpaged). ill. Loc: OWES.

A brief history including a list of pastors, a copy of the original deed granted by John Galt (son of Guelph's founder), old and recent photographs of the building, and a list of charter members. The church was affiliated with St Paul's Lutheran in Guelph in 1937. Period: 1860 - 1960.

3611. Trinity Lutheran Church, Shantz Station. **Dedication service, October 3, 1965.** The Church, 1960. Loc: OWES.

A leaflet containing an order of service and notes of the new addition, renovation and furnishings. Period: 1860 - 1965.

3612. Trinity Lutheran Church, Shantz Station. **Trinity Evangelical Lutheran Church, Shantz Station, Ontario: 125th anniversary, 1860-1985.** The Church, 1985. 12 p. ill. Loc: OKIT, OWES.

A brief history of the congregation which began under the leadership of the Rev. Immanuel Wurster. Information is presented on the various church buildings, with lists of former pastors and founding members. Period: 1860 - 1985.

3613. Vogt, Evelyn. "St Mark's in three generations." **A time for building: essays on Lutherans in Canada.** Edited by Barton Beglo. Kitchener: St Mark's Press, 1988. Pp. 49-58. Loc: OKIT, OWTL, OWTUCG, OWTUR, OWTUSJ.

An historical sketch and reminiscences of St Mark's Lutheran Church, Kitchener from 1913 to 1988 by one of the church secretaries. Period: 1913 - 1988.

3614. Weicker, Samuel. **CKCR Radio comes to Kitchener-Waterloo and St Matthews begins its Golden Hour broadcast of its Sunday morning service.** 1985. 6 l. Loc: OKIT.

A transcript of an interview with Arthur W. Sandrock about the church's beginning of broadcast services in the Kitchener-Waterloo area. Mr Sandrock names those who organized the services and comments on the support given by the community. Originally called "Kirche Daheim", the programme was renamed "Golden Hours" in 1940.

Period: 1930 - 1980.

3615. Weicker, Samuel. **Golden hours: 60th anniversary 1930-1990.** Kitchener: St Matthews Lutheran Church, 1990. Loc: OKIT, OWES.

An outline of key dates in the church's tradition of broadcasting its Sunday morning worship service from 1930. The order of service for the 60th anniversary broadcast is included. Period: 1930 - 1990.

3616. Weicker, Samuel. **Lutheranism in Kitchener and Waterloo.** The Author, 1985. 6 p. graphs. Loc: OKIT, OWES.

A short history with brief sketches of some Lutheran clergymen between 1833 to 1943. Information on 1985 Lutheran congregations in Waterloo and Kitchener includes addresses, dates founded, numbers of members and names of clergy. There are also statistics of the Sunday School enrolment and baptized memberships in Kitchener and Waterloo churches from 1920 to 1984. Period: 1833 - 1985.

3617. Weicker, Samuel. **St Matthews Lutheran Church.** Kitchener: The Church, 1990. 103 p. ill. Loc: OKIT, OWES.

A collection of excerpts from annual church reports from 1929, 1954, 1974, 1979 and 1988, providing a history of the parish, its pastors and members. The history is illustrated with photographs of past buildings and their interiors and lists church members in various years. Appended to the excerpts are a number of newspaper stories about the Rev. F.W. Bindemann and his influence of Lutheranism in the county. Period: 1904 - 1990.

3618. Welker, Ron. **A historical study of the Lutheran Church in Kitchener 1910-1937.** University of Waterloo (student essay, History), 1974. 1 v. (various pagings). bibl. Loc: OKIT.

A study of the impact of the Lutheran Church during a period that included the First World War and the depression of the 1930s. Notable Lutherans in the community are examined for their actions on issues such as the city name change, military conscription and education. The author stresses the connection of German ethnicity and culture with the Lutheran faith and the role this played in the development of Kitchener. An appendix summarizes numbers of politicians who were of German/Lutheran origin. Period: 1910 - 1937.

3619. Wittig, S.J., Rev. **90th anniversary booklet: St Matthew's Evangelical Lutheran Church, Conestogo, Ontario.** The Church, 1942. 7 p. ill. Loc: OKIT, OWES.

A brief commemorative history including information on the clergy, building and organizations. Period: 1852 - 1942.

3620. Zimmerman, Idessa. "St Paul's Lutheran Church, Bridgeport." **Waterloo Historical Society.** 1964. 52: 40-43. ill. Loc: all.

A brief history of the church built in 1889, with details of the Lutheran community in Bridgeport and names of former pastors and many members. Period: 1889 - 1964.

3621. Zion Lutheran Church, St Agatha. **Zion Evangelical Lutheran Church 1834-1984, St Agatha, Ontario.** St Agatha: The Church, 1984. 16 p. ill. Loc: OKIT, OWES.

A short history of the church founded by F.W. Bindemann in 1834, with an account of Bindemann's influence on Lutheranism in the region. Details are provided on the first baptisms and marriages, and on later pastors and youth and women's organizations. Period: 1834 - 1984.

METHODIST CHURCHES

3622. Baird, James. **One hundred years of Christian witness, 1854-1954, Wesley United Church, Galt, Ont.: a brief history.** Galt: The Church, 1954. 1 v. ill. Loc: OKITW, OCCA.

A transcript of a speech by James Baird on the history of Methodism in Galt, given at a congregational gathering in 1938. It is printed together with a list of ministers of the church and the centennial programme of services. Period: 1854 - 1954.

3623. Bean, Isaac and Bean, Alfred E. and Bean, Ellworth. "Three generations tell of Bethel Church." **Waterloo Historical Society.** 1983. 71: 90-99. ill. Loc: all.

A collection of three essays written by members of the Bean family who were members of the church in Wilmot Township from 1861 to the early 1970s. Period: 1855 - 1971.

3624. "Branchton church closes." **Waterloo Historical Society.** 1970. 58: 70. Loc: all.

A note of the closing of Branchton United Church, a stone church was originally built by the Methodists in 1859 as part of the St George Circuit. Period: 1859 - 1970.

3625. Campbell, James Arthur. **History of the Galt Free Methodist Church.** The Author, 1956. 2 l. Loc: OKIT.

A brief history of the church since 1875,

describing its beginnings, prominent members, clergy, buildings and Sunday School. Period: 1875 - 1956.

3626. "Cornerstone opened." **Waterloo Historical Society**. 1965. 53: 40. Loc: all.

An account of the contents of a Gem preserving jar, placed in the cornerstone of First United Church, Waterloo, in 1890. The **Waterloo Chronicle** from 1890 as well as a poster announcing the opening of the New Methodist Church on 26 May 1890 were among the items. Period: 1890 - 1965.

3627. Cressman, Eben C. **Breslau Bible Society: organized November 19th, 1885**. Breslau: The Society, 1985. 8 p. Loc: OKIT.

A history of the local branch of the British and Foreign Bible Society, commemorating its 100th anniversary. Lists of officers, speakers, memorable events, and rules and regulations are given. Period: 1885 - 1985.

3628. Davis, E.C., Mrs and Rahn, Edgar, Mrs. **Milestones: historical narrative of Wesley United Church 1848-1948**. Elmira: The Church, 1948. 32 p. ill. Loc: OWRE, OKIT.

An account of the establishment and growth of the Elmira Methodist congregation, including information on church buildings, former ministers, officers and prominent members, as well as organizations such as the Young People's Society, Sunday School, the Woman's Missionary Society, the Women's Association, choirs and bands. Period: 1848 - 1948.

3629. Deller, Howard F., Rev. **A message to the people of Trinity United Church**. Kitchener: The Author, 1927. 8 p. port. Loc: OWTUR.

A statement by the departing minister, in an effort to clarify what he considered to be misunderstandings and inaccurate statements by the Church Board. Salary and duties are the chief issues. Period: 1926 - 1927.

3630. Duff, Daniel S. **Journey of faith 1837 to 1987: a history of Saint Luke's United Church Cambridge (Hespeler) Ontario**. Cambridge: The Author, 1987. 113 p. ill. Loc: OKIT.

An account of the congregation first known as Hespeler Methodist Church, including information on its founding and names of ministers and leading members since the 1840s. Period: 1837 - 1987.

3631. Dunham, B. Mabel. "The centenary of Trinity United Church, Kitchener, formerly Berlin." **Waterloo Historical Society**. 1941. 29: 182-193. ill. Loc: all.

An article condensed from the author's published history of the church (previously Trinity Methodist Church, Berlin), giving a chronology of the various church buildings from 1841 to 1941 and also information about some ministers and church members. Period: 1841 - 1941.

3632. Dunham, B. Mabel. **So great a heritage: historical narrative of Trinity United Church 1841-1941**. Kitchener: Cober Printing Service, 1941. 70 p. ill. Loc: OWTUR, OWTL, OKIT.

A centennial history of church buildings, ministers, members and organizations. Until the formation of the United Church in 1925, Trinity was the only Methodist church in Berlin/Kitchener. A condensed version of this work can be found in the Waterloo Historical Society's report for 1941. Period: 1841 - 1941.

3633. Dunham, B. Mabel and Dunford, James Ross. **Trinity United Church, Kitchener, Ontario 1841-1991 - 150th anniversary**. Kitchener: Cober Printing Service, 1990. 146 p. ill. Loc: OKIT.

A history of the church which began as a Methodist congregation. The first seventy pages of the book are reprinted from Mabel Dunham's history published in 1941. Ross Dunford compiled the history of the later period, including information on church buildings and activities as well as many illustrations. Period: 1841 - 1991.

3634. "First United Church, Galt, 1863-1963." **Waterloo Historical Society**. 1963. 51: 11. Loc: all.

A brief description of the centenary celebrations. Period: 1863 - 1963.

3635. **First United Church, Waterloo, Ontario: 71st anniversary services, dedication of Hilliard Hall and the enlarged and renovated sanctuary, December 12th, 1954**. Waterloo: First United Church, 1954. 12 p. ill. Loc: OWT.

A short history of the union of local Presbyterian and Methodist congregations and the later growth of the parish. Information is presented on building renovations including the addition of 1954. Period: 1871 - 1954.

3636. Fowler, Maude Scott. "The church at Branchton." **Waterloo Historical Society**. 1952. 40: 45-49. Loc: all.

A short history of the Branchton Methodist Church, built in 1859. The author describes church activities and names early leaders, all ministers and many members. Period: 1859 - 1952.

3637. Freshman, Charles. **The autobiography of the Rev. Charles Freshman, late rabbi of the Jewish Synagogue at Quebec, and graduate of the Jewish Theological Seminary at Prague, at present German Wesleyan minister at Preston, Ontario.** Toronto: Samuel Rose, 1868. 316 p. port. Also CIHM Microfiche series, no. 03258. Loc: OKITW, OWTU, OWTL.

The autobiography of "the father of German Methodism in Canada," Charles Freshman (1819-1875), who describes his conversion and the establishment of Wesleyan missions in Preston, Erbsville (Berlin), St George, Paris, Conestogo and Heidelberg. Jacob Hespeler, who gave land in Preston for a Wesleyan church, is mentioned. An original copy is held in the Waterloo Historical Society's collection at the Kitchener Public Library. Period: 1819 - 1868.

3638. Hipel, Arthur, Mrs. **History of St Paul's United Church, 1868-1968.** Preston: Preston Printers, 1968. 40 p. ill. Loc: OKIT.

A history of the Preston church which began under the direction of Methodist minister E.W. Frazee in 1861. The booklet provides details on past members and leaders as well as church activities. There are photographs of ministers from 1929 to 1968 and of church buildings and their interiors. A list of ministers from 1868 to 1968 can be found on page 40. Period: 1861 - 1968.

3639. Knox United Church Centenary Committee. **Knox United Church 130th anniversary, 1834-1964.** The Church, 1964. 16 p. ill. Loc: OWRA, OWTUR, OKITW.

A history of Methodism in Ayr researched from church minutes, commemorating its 100th anniversary of the Ayr Methodist Church and the 130th anniversary of Knox Presbyterian Church. Both congregations joined in 1926 to form Knox United Church. Period: 1864 - 1964.

3640. **Lincoln Avenue Church history.** 1991. 2 l. Loc: OKIT.

A centennial history of a congregation that was started as a Methodist Sunday School by A.E. Mullet and J.B. Lobb in 1891 and joined the United Church in 1925. It notes clergy members and describes the construction of the building in 1911. Period: 1891 - 1991.

3641. "Memorial windows at Wesley United Church, Galt." **Waterloo Historical Society.** 1964. 52: 43. Loc: all.

A note of the dedication of two stained glass windows in memory of church members Mr and Mrs Emerson Roelofson and Mr and Mrs T.A. Rutherford. Period: 1963.

3642. Miller, Elizabeth. "Conestogo United Church." **Waterloo Historical Society.** 1981. 69: 146-150. ill. Loc: all.

A history of the church, built in 1878, which was the first building designated by the Local Architectural Conservation Advisory Committee of Woolwich Township. Period: 1878 - 1981.

3643. Nahrgang, Ruth. **History of Zion United Church, Maple Grove, Ontario [WRP].** 1976?. 3 p. Loc: OKIT.

A history of the church, originally the Zion Methodist Church, from 1843 to 1992. It lists the clergy and gives details of the circuits to which the church belonged. Period: 1843 - 1925.

3644. Panabaker, Arnold T. and Hauch, J.P., Rev. **One hundred years of United Church, Hespeler: being a historical sketch from the commencement of the congregation of the Hespeler United Church and associate appointments of the old New Hope Circuit.** 1937. 46 p. ill. Loc: OKITW.

A detailed history with short biographies and photographs of the clergy and leading members, with descriptions of its organizations and buildings. The church began as a Methodist Church in 1837, joining the United Church in 1925. It includes an historical sketch by Rev. J.P. Hauch of the Hespeler Evangelical Church, most members of which joined the Methodist Church in 1922. Period: 1837 - 1937.

3645. Panabaker, C.A. **The United Church of Canada in Hespeler, Ontario, 1837-1957.** 1956. 115 l. ill. Loc: OKIT.

A photocopy of the unpublished manuscript prepared for the 120th anniversary of the church. The author begins with a general history of Methodism in the area before church union in 1925, and then provides more specific information on the clergy and their salaries, recording stewards, church membership, music, Sunday School, the Ladies' Aid Society, young peoples' groups and church buildings. Period: 1837 - 1957.

3646. Trinity United Church, Kitchener. **Annual report.** Kitchener: The Church, 1928 -. Loc: OKIT.

An official church publication with changes in title and format. The Kitchener Public Library holds: **Financial statement of Trinity United Church** (1928); **Statistical statement of Trinity United Church** (1929 and 1930); **Trinity United Church annual report** (1940 to 1945); **Our year book** (1947 to 1951, 1953 to 1957, 1961, 1963 to 1965); **Trinity year book: The church on the market place** (1966 to 1967); **Directory** (1979); and **Annual report** (1980 to 1990). Prior to

1976-77 the reports contain both financial statements and directories. Issues from 1976 to 1990 are directories only and financial statements are published separately. Period: 1928 - 1990.

3647. Trinity United Church, Kitchener. **Letters to Mabel Dunham concerning Trinity United Church, Kitchener, 1941.** 1941. 1 v. (unpaged). Loc: OKIT.

Letters and archival material collected by Miss Dunham during her research for a history of Trinity United Church. Much of the material was sent from Victoria University Library, includes extracts from the diary of Rev. George Ferguson and information about the Dumfries Circuit of the Methodist Church. Reminiscences from Ada Stein of Stratford about the early Methodist Church are part of this collection. Period: 1940 - 1941.

3648. Trinity United Church, Kitchener. **Trinity United Church builds for today and tomorrow.** Kitchener: The Church, 1948. 6 p. Loc: OWTUR.

Prospectus for the church's programme of expansion in 1949-50, estimated to cost $125,000. Plans for the new Fellowship Recreation Hall, Trinity Memorial Chapel and a complete new heating system are outlined, with a brief history of the church. Members are invited to pledge a day's pay per month through 1949 and 1950. From the Clement/Bowlby Family Papers. Period: 1945 - 1948.

3649. Trinity United Church, Kitchener. **Trinity United Church of Canada: the dedication of the Memorial Chapel and the opening of the Fellowship Hall.** Kitchener: Cober Printing Service, 1949. 16 p. ill., map. Loc: OKIT.

A programme for the dedication services, including information on the building and church memorials to past members. On page nine there is a chronology of the church's buildings since 1841, when a Methodist chapel was built at the corner of Church and Benton Streets, Berlin. Period: 1841 - 1949.

PRESBYTERIAN CHURCHES

3650. **128th anniversary services, Sunday, October 21st, 1962: Knox United Church, Ayr, Ontario.** Ayr: The Church, 1962. 1 v. (unpaged). Loc: OKITW.

A programme of events commemorating the 75th anniversary of the laying of the cornerstone in 1887, with a short history of the building. A section is devoted to early music at the church. The cover design reproduces the first page of the 1892 annual report, incorporating an illustration of the church. Period: 1834 - 1962.

3651. Barrie, James R. "Central Presbyterian Church, Cambridge, celebrates its centennial." **Waterloo Historical Society.** 1982. 70: 8-10. Loc: all.

A short history of the church (mentioning its predecessor churches) and a report of the anniversary celebrations. Period: 1882 - 1982.

3652. Barrie, James R. **A century at Central, 1882-1982: Central Presbyterian Church, Cambridge, Ontario.** Ayr: Ayr News for the Church, 1982. 48 p. ill. bibl. Loc: OKIT, OCCA.

A centennial history containing information about ministers, notable members, activities and organizations. The author outlines religious dissensions among Galt's Presbyterian churches and includes annual reports for the years 1882 and 1982, a chronology of significant events and a programme of centennial celebrations. Period: 1882 - 1982.

3653. Bayne, John, Rev. **Is man responsible for his belief?: a lecture delivered before members of the Hamilton Mercantile Library Association on the evening of the 18th February,1851 and now published at their request.** CIHM Microfiche series, no. 41610. Galt: J. Ainslie, 1851. mf. Loc: OWTL, OWTU.

Period: 1850 - 1851.

3654. Bayne, John, Rev. **Was the recent disruption of the Synod of Canada, in connection with the Church of Scotland, called for?: an address to the Presbyterians of Canada who still support the Synod in Connection with the Church of Scotland, published at the request of the Commission of the Synod of the Presbyterian Church of Scotland.** Galt: James Ainslie, 1846 reprinted 1873. 83 p. Also CIHM Microfiche series, no. 54130 (1846); no. 32113 (1873). Loc: OCCA, OWTL, OWTU.

A persuasive argument in favour of the Canadian disruption of the Presbyterian Church in 1845, by the minister of St Andrew's Presbyterian Church, Galt. Issues include the Veto Law (relating to the calling of pastors) and patronage which in Bayne's view undermined the church's power. Bayne and his followers were forced out in 1849 and formed their own church, Knox's Presbyterian Church, Galt. Reprinted by A. Hudson of Brantford in 1873. Period: 1844 - 1846.

3655. Blake, John R. "The history of Knox's Church, Galt, Ontario." **Waterloo Historical Society.** 1937. 25: 266-272. Loc: all.

An account marking the church's diamond anniversary in 1930. The author notes that first minister, John Bayne, was among the founders of the Free Presbyterian Church in Canada and of Knox College, Toronto. Ministers who served the church

after Bayne's early death in 1859 are named.
Period: 1834 - 1937.

3656. Carmichael, J.F. "History of St Andrew's Church,
Kitchener." **Waterloo Historical Society**. 1945.
33: 23-29. Loc: all.

A short history of the church since its founding
in 1854, when the Rev. W. Pirie conducted services
in an old school house in Berlin. The author
recounts stages in the church's development,
noting the controversial issue of church union in
1925 the St Andrew's congregation voted to remain
Presbyterian. Ministers and many parishioners are
named. Period: 1854 - 1945.

3657. **Central Presbyterian Church Galt, Ontario: these
fifty years 1882-1932**. C.E. Knowles, 1932. 11 p.
ill. Loc: OKITW.

A programme of the jubilee services, with a list
of church officials, a chronology of the history
of the church, and a list of those people still
living who were connected with the congregation
fifty years before. Period: 1882 - 1932.

3658. Clare, Elisabeth and McKie, Dorothy. **Knox Preston
Presbyterian Church: the first one hundred years,
1891 to 1991**. Preston: Knox Preston Presbyterian
Church, 1991. 35 p. ill. Loc: OKIT.

A centennial history including information on
clergy, activities and members and a list of
church families in 1991. Period: 1891 - 1991.

3659. Clark, A.J. "Notes on the Galt churches." **Ontario
Historical Society, Papers and Records**. 1925. 22:
18-19. ill. Loc: OWTL, OWTU.

Reminiscences of two Galt ministers, Rev. John
Bayne of Knox's Presbyterian Church and Rev. John
Dyer of St Andrew's Presbyterian Church. The
author's mother recalls crossing an unfinished
bridge to hear a sermon by Bayne and the painting
of the church steeple by Dyer who was afterwards
discovered to be an ex-sailor and not a clergyman.
Period: 1835 - 1922.

3660. Cleghorn, H.G., Rev. "History of Doon Presbyterian
Church." **Waterloo Historical Society**. 1953. 41:
15-18. Loc: all.

An historical sketch of the church founded in
1853, quoting from the church records and
including the programme of the 100th anniversary
service and a list of all ministers. Period: 1853
- 1953.

3661. Cochrane, Charles C. **Knox Presbyterian Church,
Waterloo, Ontario: one hundred years of life and
witness in the community**. 1988. 22 p. ill. Loc:
OKIT.

A chronological account of a congregation that

began as St Paul's Presbyterian Church, becoming
Knox Presbyterian after 1925. Photographs
illustrate events, organizations and the edifice.
Period: 1888 - 1988.

3662. Cowan, Jennie F. and Elliott, Hugh C. and King,
J.L., Dr. **Knox's for the extension of the
Redeemer's kingdom: the story of the congregation
of Knox's Presbyterian Church of Galt, 1844-1969**.
The Church, 1969. 32, 63 p. ill., map, index. Loc:
OKIT, OCCA.

A history compiled for the centennial of the
laying of the cornerstone on 18 June 1869, with
biographies of clergy, descriptions of
congregational activities and church buildings,
and photographs of the church, members of session,
choir, school, women's associations and other
organizations. Period: 1844 - 1969.

3663. Cowan, Jennie F. "Knox's Presbyterian Church,
Galt, 1969 - an anniversary year." **Waterloo
Historical Society**. 1969. 57: 49-58. Loc: all.

An account of the establishment of the
congregation and the building of a new church in
1870, after an earlier church was split by
religious dissension. Names of farmers and Galt
citizens who each gave $200 and members of the
building committee are listed and there are brief
biographies of ten ministers. Period: 1870 - 1958.

3664. **Diamond jubilee, 1855-1915: St Andrew's
Presbyterian Church, Hespeler, Ontario, Canada**.
The Church, 1915. 17 p. ill. Loc: OCCA, OKIT.

A history of the clergy, members and buildings,
with photographs of all ministers and many
prominent church members. Hespeler's congregation
was associated with Doon until 1892, while their
association with Preston had ended a few years
earlier. A programme for the jubilee services is
included. Period: 1855 - 1915.

3665. Dickson, J.A.R., Rev. **Ebenezer: a history of the
Central Presbyterian Church, Galt, Ontario: with
brief sketches of some of its members who have
passed on to the other side**. Toronto: William
Briggs, 1904. 394 p. ill., ports., index. Loc:
OWTUR, OKIT, OWTL, OCCA.

A comprehensive history of the church from 1857
to 1904, by one of its ministers. The formation
of the church in 1857 under Rev. John M. King, its
establishment as the Melville Church, and its
union with the Bayne Church (formed from part of
Knox's Presbyterian Church) as the Union Church in
1870 are all recorded. Various Presbyterian
schisms, including the Disruption of 1844, are
noted and there is a chapter on the history of St
Andrew's Presbyterian Church. The clergy, session
members, buildings and organizations are described

in detail. The second half of the book presents biographical sketches of more than one hundred members. There is an index to the sketches and all names are indexed in the WRP database. Period: 1857 - 1904.

3666. Elliott, T.G., Mrs and Fraser, Margaret. **Central Presbyterian Church.** Galt: The Church, 1967. 16 p. Loc: OCCA, OKITW.

A history compiled from church records to commemorate the 85th anniversary. The authors recount the early development of the Presbyterian Church in Galt as well as the various ministers and buildings of Central Church. Period: 1831 - 1967.

3667. Galt Reporter. "A short history of the First Presbyterian Church of Galt, now the First United Church [WRP]." **Waterloo Historical Society.** 1929. 17: 140-142. ill. Loc: all.

A brief account of the church which in 1929 celebrated its 100th anniversary and dedicated the new Sunday School building. Period: 1829 - 1929.

3668. Gemmell, Bessie D. "One hundred and twenty-fifth church anniversary: Knox United, Ayr, October 1959." **Waterloo Historical Society.** 1960. 48: 65-69. Loc: all.

An address given at the anniversary service, recounting the founding of the Ayr's first church, the Presbyterian congregation of West Dumfries, later renamed the Stanley Street Church, Ayr. There is a photograph of the second church, used from 1843 until 1914 when the Stanley Street Church and Knox Presbyterian united to become Knox Presbyterian Church. Period: 1834 - 1959.

3669. Hamilton, A.M., Rev. "A few notes on the early history of Chalmers' Church, Winterbourne." **Waterloo Historical Society.** 1919. 7: 73-83. Loc: all.

A history of the congregation giving details about its formation, the division during the Disruption, and its eventual reunification. Clergy and elders are named and schools, schoolmasters, early settlers and the Methodist Church in Winterbourne are also mentioned. Period: 1834 - 1919.

3670. Hemphill, John O. and White, A. David and Bruce, Hattie. **The Presbyterian Church, Waterloo Ontario, 1888-1974: St Paul's Knox.** 1974. 15 p. ill. Loc: OKIT.

An account of a Presbyterian church in Waterloo, commemorating the centennial of Canadian Presbyterianism. The Waterloo church was originally known as St Paul's, but in 1925 the congregation divided on the issue of church union.

Those members who decided to remain Presbyterian founded Knox Presbyterian Church in 1927. Period: 1888 - 1974.

3671. **History of Knox's Presbyterian Church, Galt, Ontario.** 1946?. 24 p. Loc: OKITW.

An account emphasizing the more controversial aspects of the church's history such as debates, lawsuits, religious divisions and revivals. There are historical sketches of church organizations such as the Sunday school, missionary society and the choir, with biographical notes on the clergy. Notes from an 1857 sermon by Rev. John Bayne and extracts from a sermon by Rev. J. Keir Fraser are included. Period: 1831 - 1946.

3672. Huber, Norma and Taylor, Ryan. "The Reverend James Strang and his family." **Waterloo Historical Society.** 1990. 78: 143-151. ill. Loc: all.

A biographical account of Strang who served the United Presbyterian Church, Galt (now First United Church, Cambridge) from 1833 to his death in 1857 and was also a prominent community leader. Details of Strang's family are provided. Period: 1833 - 1919.

3673. Kauk, Patricia J. **Church register of the German Reformed Presbyterian Congregation in New Hamburg, Ont., 1875.** 1987. 18 p. Loc: OKIT.

A transcription and translation of the 1875 German Reformed Presbyterian Congregation's constitution in both German and English, with lists of the church members, baptisms, marriages, and deaths from 1875 to 1881. The pastors for those years were Rev. A. Schroeder and Rev. Carl Becker. Period: 1875 - 1881.

3674. **Kirchen Buch der deutschen Reformirten Presbyterianer Gemeinde, New Hamburg, Ontario im Jahr 1875.** 1881. 1 v. (various pagings). Loc: OKIT.

A record of the German Reformed Presbyterian Church in New Hamburg, established in 1875. The volume contains the church's constitution, names of members, and records of baptisms, marriages and burials. Period: 1875 - 1881.

3675. Klager, Gordon. Arrowhead Bible Class. **Scrapbook of the Arrowhead Bible Class, Hespeler.** 198 p. ill. Loc: OKIT.

A photocopy of the class records in Gordon Klager's collection. The binder contains newsletters, minutes, newspaper clippings, and correspondence relating to the class which was open to boys of all denominations and led by Mr Klager. Period: 1932 - 1937.

3676. Knox Centennial Committee. **125th anniversary: Knox United Church, Ayr, Ontario**. Knox United Church, 1959. 8 p. ill. Loc: OWRA.

A programme of the anniversary services. It mentions an historical exhibit and includes photographs of the three churches which combined in 1926 to form Knox United Church: Knox Presbyterian Church, Ayr; Stanley Street Presbyterian Church, Ayr; and Ayr Methodist Church. Period: 1834 - 1959.

3677. Knox Centennial Committee. **Early history of Knox United Church, Ayr**. Ayr: Knox United Church, 1959?. 1 folded sheet. Loc: OWRA.

A description of records relating to the early history of Knox United Church, including a notice calling the first congregational meeting, letters from Robert Gillespie to the trustees of the Scottish Church at Ayr, and financial records. Period: 1834 - c1959.

3678. Knox United Church. **Centenary celebration of the establishing of religious worship in this community**. Ayr: The Church, 1934. 53 p. ill. Loc: OKITW, OWRA.

A history of three churches which united to form Knox United Church in Ayr -- Stanley Street Presbyterian Church, Ayr Methodist Church and Knox Presbyterian Church -- with descriptions of clergy, buildings, organizations and activities. Period: 1834 - 1934.

3679. Kuhn, Grace M. **A history of Livingston Presbyterian Church, Baden, Ontario, Canada**. 1990. 33 p. Loc: OKIT.

A short history of the church, based on various primary sources and including brief descriptions of the community in the early 1890s. Church elders such as James Livingston, Henry Miller, and Richard Bean figure prominently in the initial years and names of clergy and visiting theologians are also given. Period: 1890 - 1990.

3680. Liddell, Thomas, Rev. **Report of the discussion on the late disruption in the Presbyterian Church which took place in St Andrew's Church, Galt between Rev. President Liddell and the Rev. John Bayne**. CIHM Microfiche series, no. 22007. Galt: Dumfries Courier, 1845. 1 fiche. 60 frames. mf. Loc: OWTL, OWTU.

A record of the debate on Tuesday, May 27, 1845 which was taken in shorthand and reviewed by the speakers before being printed. Period: 1844 - 1845.

3681. Plumtree, Laura. "The history of Doon Presbyterian Church 1953-1982." **Waterloo Historical Society**. 1982. 70: 148-155. ill. Loc: all.

A short history of the church since its 100th anniversary in 1953, noting ministers and prominent members and the commemorative plaque unveiled in June 1982. Period: 1953 - 1982.

3682. Quantrell, James. "Rev. John Bayne and the Presbyterian Church in Galt." **Waterloo Historical Society**. 1988. 76: 113-124. ill. Loc: all.

A biography of Bayne, appraising his accomplishments within the Presbyterian Church generally and at Knox's Presbyterian Church in Galt in the 1840s and 1850s. Period: 1806 - 1859.

3683. Riedstra, Lutzen. **111 years: Gale Presbyterian Church, Elmira, 1868-1979**. Elmira: The Church, 1979. 1 v. (unpaged). ill. Loc: OKIT, OWRE.

A history marking the church's 111th anniversary. Presbyterians in the district were associated in the earlier congregations of St Andrew's and Chalmers' Free Presbyterian, Winterbourne that first split in 1844 and then united in 1876. Chalmers' members who lived in Elmira decided to form a separate church and erected a simple white brick church in 1868. The author narrates the main events in the church's development, mentioning all ministers and links with Presbyterian churches in neighbouring communities and explaining the difficulties of surviving as a separate church until Elmira's population began to grow again in the 1970s. Period: 1868 - 1979.

3684. Smellie, George, Rev. **Memoir of the Rev. John Bayne, D.D., of Galt**. Toronto: James Campbell and Son, 1871. 139 p. ill. Also CIHM Microfiche series, no. 13692. Loc: OKIT, OWTL, OWTU, OWTUR.

Biography of Rev. John Bayne (1806-1859) who was instrumental in establishing the Free Church in Canada during the Presbyterian Disruption of 1845. Material was gathered from people who knew Bayne, including his sister, and from obituaries. The book contains a poem by Bayne entitled "A mother's lament for her withered flower" and a lecture delivered before the members of the Hamilton Mercantile Library Association entitled "Is man responsible for his belief?" Period: 1806 - 1859.

3685. **St Andrew's Presbyterian Church, 1979-1980, Kitchener, Ont.**. Kitchener: The Church, 1979. 1 v. (unpaged). ill., map. Loc: OKIT.

A current directory of parishioners with a short history of clergy, members and buildings by John L. Rennie. The early leadership of Sheriff George Davidson is noted. Period: 1854 - 1979.

3686. Stanley Street Presbyterian Church Session. **The sixtieth anniversary of Stanley Street Presbyterian Church, Ayr Ontario, from 1834 to 1894.** Toronto: The Author, 1894. 68 p. ill. Loc: OWRA.

A commemorative history describing the foundation of the church, its ministers, building and organizations, and naming past and present elders. Period: 1834 - 1894.

3687. Taylor, Andrew W. **Banners unfurled: the history of First United Church, Galt, Canada, 1824-1949.** Galt: Galt Printers, 1949. 60 p. ill. Loc: OKIT, OCCA.

A commemorative history that sets the church's development in the wider context of the history of Galt and Canada. Detailed information is provided about clergy, building, organizations and church members. Period: 1824 - 1949.

3688. Taylor, Andrew W. "First United Church, Galt, 1824-1874." **Waterloo Historical Society.** 1974. 62: 30. ill. Loc: all.

A brief note of the church, originally established by Presbyterians in 1824, including an outline of later changes in organization and buildings. Period: 1819 - 1874.

3689. Taylor, Andrew W. "First United Church, Galt." **Waterloo Historical Society.** 1947. 35: 7-15. Loc: all.

A history of the church relating its periods of division and growth up to the time of the union in 1925 and including various interesting anecdotes. Period: 1816 - 1925.

3690. Taylor, Andrew W. "History of St Andrew's Church, Galt." **Waterloo Historical Society.** 1950. 38: 37-38. Loc: all.

A short history of the church which began as a mission school in 1891. Originally part of the Central Presbyterian Church in Galt, St Andrew's became independent in 1917. Names of ministers are mentioned. Period: 1891 - 1950.

3691. Thomas, Walter Keith. **Down-to-earth cherub: the life and legend of Finlay Stewart.** Burlington: Welch Publishing Co., 1983. 270 p. ill., ports., bibl. Loc: OCLG, OKIT, OWTUR, OWTL, OWT.

A biography of the Rev. Finlay Gordon Stewart who was minister at St Andrew's Presbyterian Church, Kitchener, from 1938 to 1974. Period: 1937 - 1983.

3692. "To Frederick G. Millar, Esquire, Most Respected Sir!." **Waterloo Historical Society.** 1962. 50: 46. Loc: all.

Transcript of an 1863 petition to Frederick G. Millar of New Dundee asking that the word "Presbyterian" be added to his deed for the site of the new church, which was being monopolized by the Lutherans. Period: 1863.

3693. "Treasurer for half a century." **Waterloo Historical Society.** 1965. 53: 40. Loc: all.

A note of the long service of Mrs George Buck to the St Andrew's Presbyterian Women's Missionary Society. Period: 1910 - 1965.

3694. **A tribute to a noble effort.** Ayr: News Press, 1896. 6 p. Loc: OWTUR.

A poem honouring the resourcefulness and ingenuity of the women of Stanley Church in paying off the church debt. The unnamed author is described as the Poet Laureate of Stanley Street Church. Period: 1895 - 1896.

3695. Wilson, G.E. Duff and Hall, Andrew C., Mrs. **Knox United Church, Ayr, Ontario, 1834-1984.** Ayr: Ayr News, 1984. 80 p. ill. Loc: OKIT, OWRA.

A scholarly history of Knox United Church and its three constituent churches: Stanley Street United Presbyterian Church, Knox Presbyterian Church, and Wesleyan Methodist Church. Commemorating the 150th anniversary of the first church, it describes the church buildings, clergy, members, activities, internal dissensions and financial difficulties. Period: 1834 - 1984.

SWEDENBORGIAN CHURCHES

3696. Bird, Michael S. "The Swedenborgian community in Waterloo County: two religious approaches to culture." **Waterloo Historical Society.** 1975. 63: 69-74. Loc: all.

A discussion of concepts of exclusive Christianity and cultural Christianity in relation to the Swedenborgian faith and sense of community. Period: 1830 - 1975.

3697. "Carmel Church of the New Jerusalem." **Waterloo Historical Society.** 1963. 51: 74, 79. ill. Loc: all.

The account of the demolition of the 1892 Swedenborgian Church on King Street, Kitchener and the building of a new church at Caryndale, near Strasburg. Period: 1892 - 1963.

3698. Church of the Good Shepherd. **The Church of the Good Shepherd (Swedenborgian) Kitchener, Ontario.** 1978. 5 p. Loc: OKIT.

A brief history that also includes a list of church records such as microfilmed minutes, registers and land deeds, as well as church histories and photographs. Period: 1833 - 1978.

3699. Church of the New Jerusalem. **Constitution of the association of the New Jerusalem Church of Canada, and minutes of its first meeting, held at Berlin, C.W., June 20-23 A.D. 1862**. CIHM Microfiche series, no. 33689. Berlin: Rittinger and Motz, 1862. 1 fiche. mf. Loc: OWTU, OWTL.

A record of the formation and establishment of the Swedenborgian church in Canada, one of the leaders being Rev. F.W. Tuerk of Berlin. Period: 1862 - 1863.

3700. Church of the New Jerusalem. **Minutes of the Seventh Conference of the Association of the New Jerusalem Church in Canada, held in the church in Albert Street, Toronto, Ont., from Friday June 19th, to Tuesday, June 23, 1868**. CIHM Microfiche series, no. A01661. Berlin: Rittinger and Motz, 1868. 1 fiche. mf. Loc: OWTU, OWTL.

A report printed in Berlin, providing an account of the activities and speeches during the Swedenborgian church conference. Rev. F.W. Tuerk of Berlin was the president. Period: 1868 - 1869.

3701. **The history of the New Church in Canada: the Swedenborgians 1830-c1960**. 1960. 13 l. Loc: OKIT.

An account of the development of the Church of New Jerusalem in Berlin/Kitchener, emphasizing early leaders such as Christian Enslin, F.W. Tuerk and F.E. Waelchli. New Church education and the establishment of the Berlin school are also discussed. Period: 1841 - 1910.

3702. Johnson, D., Rev. "The Church of the Good Shepherd." **Waterloo Historical Society**. 1943. 31: 39-43. ill. Loc: all.

A short history of the Swedenborgian church in Kitchener which was built on its current site in 1929 but is linked to a congregation first established in Berlin in the 1840s. Many church members and ministers are named. Period: c1840 - 1943.

3703. Schnarr, Philip B. **A church divided: the story of the split in the Berlin Society of the New Jerusalem, 1891**. University of Waterloo (student essay), 1978. 31 p. bibl. Loc: OKIT.

A history of the Swedenborgian Church in Berlin and of the division between the congregations of the Academy and the General Church when supporters of the Rev. F.E. Waelchli broke away from the Church of the Good Shepherd and formed the Carmel Church of New Jerusalem. The author discusses the religious issues, the leadership of the clergy and the effect of the division on church members. Period: 1832 - 1902.

3704. Zacharias, Paul. **The Swedenborgian presence in Berlin-Kitchener, 1833-1983**. Kitchener: Church of the Good Shepherd, 1983. 11 p. ill. Loc: OKIT.

A brief history of the Church of the Good Shepherd which mentions early church ministers and leaders as well as more recent church members and activities. The author notes the division of the congregation in 1891 and the formation of the Carmel Church of the New Jerusalem. Period: 1833 - 1983.

OTHER CHURCHES AND RELIGIONS

3705. "Century-old church closed." **Waterloo Historical Society**. 1965. 53: 23. Loc: all.

A note of the closing of Wellesley United Church which was an interdenominational church called the Union Church until 1925. Period: c1865 - 1965.

3706. de Bock, Hazel. **The miracle of Gospel Centre: a concise history of International Gospel Centre, Kitchener, Canada**. Kitchener: International Gospel Centre, 1985. 17 p. bibl. Loc: OKITW.

A history commemorating the 25th anniversary of the founding in 1961 of the Pentecostal church, and describing its growth, activities, clergy and buildings. A list of the original church members is included. Period: 1961 - 1985.

3707. First Christian Reformed Church. **First Christian Reformed Church, Kitchener, Ontario 1948-1988, forty years**. The Church, 1988. 13 p. ill. Loc: OKIT.

A history of the Dutch Reformed congregation which was formed in 1947. Church members, the building, clergy and church activities are described. Period: 1948 - 1988.

3708. Highland Road United Church Historical Booklet Committee. **Highland Road United Church, Kitchener, Ontario: historical booklet, 1925-1990, 65th anniversary**. Kitchener: The Church, 1990. 28 p. ill. Loc: OKIT.

An historical sketch of significant events including the renaming from Knox United Church to Highland Road East United Church in 1949. All ministers since 1932 and some church members are listed. Period: 1925 - 1990.

3709. **History of Cambridge (Galt) Citadel Corps, 1884-1984**. 1984. 6 l. ill. Loc: OKIT.

A short history of the Salvation Army in Galt, including a photograph of the first permanent Galt Citadel on Mill Street and a list of the officers from 1884 to 1942. Period: 1884 - 1984.

3710. Kitchener Gospel Temple. **75th anniversary, 1909-1984: celebration of praise, June 8, 9, 10 1984.** 1984. 26 p. ill. Loc: OWTUCG.

A commemorative booklet that includes a six-page historical outline, programmes of the special services of worship, and an honour roll of deceased former pastors, missionaries, members and adherents. Period: 1909 - 1984.

3711. "A memorial of conveyance." **Waterloo Historical Society.** 1965. 53: 20-23. Loc: all.

A facsimile of the indenture made in November 1848 between John U. Tyson and trustees Peter N. Tagge, Isaac Tyson and George Kraft, for the site of the Free Meeting House in Bridgeport. Period: 1848 - 1849.

3712. "Plaque unveiled at Bridgeport 1848 Free Church." **Waterloo Historical Society.** 1972. 60: 50-51. ill. Loc: all.

A report of the unveiling in October 1972 of the plaque given by the Waterloo Historical Society. The inscription notes that the land was purchased to "be kept for the sole purpose of a Free Meeting House for Divine Worship and Burying Ground of all denominations." Period: 1848 - 1972.

3713. **The Salvation Army Kitchener Citadel 100th anniversary souvenir booklet.** 1 v. (unpaged). ill. Loc: OKIT.

A history album with a chronology, list of corps locations, quotations from newspapers, list of officers, band photographs, and calendar of events for the year. An article on the early growth of the Army recounts the difficulties encountered -- the Corps closed in 1904 and reopened in 1907 -- and another short article describes the life of Edward Gnaedinger, one of the early officers. Period: 1886 - 1986.

3714. Sotiroff, Irene. "A short history of the Kitchener area monthly meeting." **Canadian Quaker History Newsletter.** 1983. 34: 20-22. Loc: OSTCB.

Reference from **Bibliography of Ontario history, 1976-1986** (Gervais et al.). Period: 1880 - 1980.

3715. Spaetzel, Roy Clifford. **History of the Kitchener Gospel Temple, 1909-1974.** Kitchener: Kitchener Gospel Temple, 1974. 47 p. ill., bibl. Loc: OKIT.

An account of the church that has been known at different times as the Pentecostal Mission at Berlin, the Berlin Pentecostal Assembly, the Kitchener Pentecostal Assembly, the Pentecostal Tabernacle and the Kitchener Gospel Temple. The author describes former pastors, members of the congregation, and church buildings, and outlines

activities such as the missionary service, Sunday school, music programmes and the young people's society. Period: 1909 - 1974.

3716. Springer, Margaret. **A meeting home.** Canadian Quaker Pamphlet no. 31. Argenta, BC: Argenta Friends Press, 1989. 40 p. ill. Loc: OKIT.

A short history of the Kitchener and area Society of Friends (Quakers) which was formed in 1968. The work provides information on the group's first meeting places in the city and the activities and events of the early years. Period: 1969 - 1989.

3717. Staebler, H.L. "First Church of Christ, Scientist, Kitchener, Ontario." **Waterloo Historical Society.** 1949. 37: 37-38. Loc: all.

A commemorative account of important milestones in the first half-century of the church. Period: c1890 - 1949.

3718. Steinhouse, Nettie and Bergstein, Eve. **Beth Jacob.** Beth Jacob Synagogue, 1983. 102 p. ill. Loc: OKIT.

A history published to commemorate the synagogue's 75th anniversary. Organizations and activities are described, and there are tributes by public figures and reminiscences by members. The book is illustrated with photographs of founding members, Jewish community leaders and members who had celebrated their golden wedding anniversaries. Period: 1903 - 1983.

3719. Van de Kamer, Paul. **Forest Hill United Church: 1960-1985.** The Church, 1988. 25 p. table. Loc: OKIT.

An anniversary history of the clergy, members, activities and building. Charter members are listed, a table shows the growth in membership and budgets, and an article about Rev. Samuel Soper by Gordon Sinclair is reprinted. Period: 1960 - 1985.

3720. Wagner, George P. **Christian Science not the second coming of Christ: Mrs Eddy not his representative for that occasion: a warning.** CIHM Microfiche series, no. 40504. Berlin: Record, 187-?. mf. Loc: OWTL, OWTU.

Included as a local imprint.

3721. Zimmerman, Idessa. "Bridgeport Cemetery and Free Church." **Waterloo Historical Society.** 1965. 53: 18-20. ill. Loc: all.

A short history of the interdenominational church built in 1848 and of the adjoining cemetery. John U. Tyson is mentioned as a key figure in organizing the church. Period: 1842 - 1965.

SPORTS AND RECREATION

3722. "125 years of sporting tradition." **Waterloo Chronicle**. 1982, May 26. Pp. 29-52. ill. Loc: OWT.

Articles and photographs of Waterloo sports teams and athletes, in volleyball, lawn bowling, hockey, horse racing, swimming, ringette and golf. Period: 1857 - 1982.

3723. Barrie, David. "Cedardale (Blair) Youth Hostel." **Waterloo Historical Society**. 1971. 59: 80-81. ill. Loc: all.

A description of the hostel which was opened in 1942 by Janie King as one of 36 youth hostels in Canada. Period: 1942 - 1971.

3724. Barrie, William C. "A bicycle trip to Buffalo." **Waterloo Historical Society**. 1968. 56: 4-5. ill. Loc: all.

An account of a bicycle trip taken after the harvest of 1904 by Will Barrie and his elder brother. There is a photograph of a bicycle used by D.B. Detweiler when he traversed Waterloo County promoting the idea of hydro-electric power from Niagara Falls. Period: 1904.

3725. **Canadian Sporting Chronicle**. 1859. 4 p. Loc: OKITW.

A weekly paper subtitled **A faithful record of the turf, field sports, literature, and the news of the day** and published in Berlin by Robert M. Longan. The Waterloo Historical Society holds one issue for 28 October 1859. Few of the articles in that issue relate specifically to Waterloo County, although it carries local railway timetables and advertisements for local businesses. Period: 1859 - 1860.

3726. Chicopee Ski Club. **The Chicopee skier**. Kitchener: The Club, 1938-. 8 p. Loc: OKIT.

Newsletter of the club established in 1934, giving details of activities such as competitions and skiing trips and of membership and organization. The Kitchener Public Library holds Vol.4, no.6 (December 1938), which includes an organization chart with details of directors, officers and committees, and Vol. 6, no.5 (February 1941). Period: 1934 - 1941.

3727. Crozier, Leif D. **The New Hamburg Memorial Community Centre: a case study in the development of a community institution, 1947-1968**. Waterloo Lutheran University (B.A. thesis, History), 1968. 36 p. bibl. Loc: OWTL, OKIT.

A case study of the postwar "community centre

movement" which was supported by the Ontario government. The author explains how the centre was built in 1948-49 through the fund-raising efforts of the Board of Trade, following the destruction of the old wooden arena by fire in 1947. Only after a recreation director was appointed in 1967 was it possible to offer social, cultural and educational recreation. Period: 1947 - 1968.

3728. "Curling at Ayr and Reidsville." **Waterloo Historical Society**. 1971. 59: 77-78. ill. Loc: all.

A short account of the activities of two early curling clubs. Period: 1875 - 1876.

3729. "Galt Terriers souvenir edition, 1961 Allan Cup champions." **Galt Evening Reporter**. 1961, May 2. Pp. 1A-24A. ill. Loc: OCCA.

A newspaper supplement celebrating the 1961 victory of the Galt hockey team, with photographs and articles on the players and coaching staff. Congratulations from local businesses are printed. Period: 1960 - 1961.

3730. Grand River Country Club. **Ladies' golf fixtures 1915**. Berlin: The Club, 1915. 3 p. Loc: OWTUR.

A booklet which notes the women's golf competitions and tournaments to be held at the club during the year. A letter from Martha C. Breithaupt, secretary of the Ladies' Committee, is enclosed announcing that the club had joined the Canadian Ladies' Golf Union. Period: 1914 - 1915.

3731. Hall, John E. and McCulloch, R.O. **Sixty years of Canadian cricket**. Toronto: Bryant, 1895. 572 p. ill. Also CIHM Microfiche series, no. 50845. Loc: OCCA, OWTL, OWTU.

Accounts of cricket matches from 1834 to 1891, listing the scores of various team members, and reporting locations of the games and the final scores. Matches played by the Galt Cricket Club are mentioned on pages 43, 48, 52, 108, 160, 165, 189, 227 and 243. The Berlin Cricket Club is mentioned on page 248. Period: 1834 - 1891.

3732. Head, John A. and Knowles, Robert E., Rev. **Centennial year 1838-1938: commemoration program of the Galt Curling Club from Nov. 15th to Nov. 19th 1937**. Galt: C.E. Knowles, 1937. 20 p. ill. Loc: OKITW.

A history of the club and its buildings, with references to members, including a biography of David Nairn, a member for thirty-five years. A programme of the anniversary bonspiel and banquet is included. There are lists of past presidents of the Galt Curling Club and the Galt Granite Club: the club divided in 1881 and reunited as the

Curlers of Galt in 1930. Period: 1838 - 1938.

3733. Hearn, Mary Elizabeth. **Waterloo tennis: a history of the Waterloo Tennis Club.** Kitchener: MEH Company, 1977. 84 p. ill. Loc: OWTU, OKIT, OWTUR, OWT.

An historical sketch of the club's first 60 years. The author examines the social and economic conditions which brought about changes in the popularity and image of tennis in the community. There are photographs and lists of the club's patrons and many members. Period: c1914 - 1977.

3734. Hulet, Marion. "Opening of Churchill Park, Galt." **Waterloo Historical Society.** 1968. 56: 86. Loc: all.

A description of the ceremonies marking the opening of the park which was once the farm of James Tutton. Period: 1968.

3735. Johns, Bill and Plomske, Nel. **Rockway Golfer 50th anniversary special edition.** 1985. 1 v. Loc: OKIT, OKITW.

Reflections and comments on the Rockway Golf Club's history by charter members, with lists of trophy winners and champions from 1936. Period: 1935 - 1985.

3736. Kitchener-Waterloo Figure Skating Club. **Kitchener-Waterloo Skating Follies of 1951.** 1951. 10 p. ill. Loc: OKIT.

Programme of the club's 8th annual carnival held at the Waterloo Memorial Arena in April 1951. It includes photographs and names of the performers and a list of the club's directors and executive. Period: 1950 - 1951.

3737. Kitchener-Waterloo Granite Club. **Souvenir program: K-W Granite Club diamond jubilee Saturday, November 7, 1987.** Kitchener: The Club, 1987. 40 p. ill. Loc: OKIT.

An account of various club activities such as the men's, women's and mixed curling and badminton teams. Competitions held and attended by Granite Club members are described and club officials from 1927 to 1987 are listed. Period: 1927 - 1987.

3738. Kitchener-Waterloo Lawn Bowling Association. **Kitchener-Waterloo Lawn Bowling Association souvenir programme, first annual men's rinks tournament, Wednesday, July 11th, 1945.** Kitchener: The Association, 1945. 32 p. ill. Loc: OWT.

A booklet promoting the competition and including brief descriptions of the five lawn bowling clubs in the area, Rockway Lawn Bowling Club, Kitchener Lawn Bowling Club, Beaver Lawn

Bowling Club, Waterloo Bowling Club, and the Mutual Life Bowling Club. Photographs of these organizations' bowling greens are presented with the names of the tournament's administrators and other key local figures in the sport. Period: 1945.

3739. Kitchener Y.W.C.A. **Industrial Girls Basketball League: beginning September 1947.** Kitchener: The Association, 1965. 1 v. (unpaged). Loc: OKIT.

A binder of reports and programmes for the period 1947 to 1965. The league is noted to have begun in 1938. Teams taking part in the matches represented various local businesses including Equitable Life, Mutual Life, Dominion Life, Dominion Tire, Merchant's Rubber, J.M. Schneider, Forsyth, Cluett Peabody, Goodrich, Doon Twines and Electrohome. Period: 1938 - 1965.

3740. Kroekker, Wendy. **Mennonites and their use of leisure time: a comparison study 1945-1981.** University of Waterloo (student essay, Recreation), 1982. 1 fiche. bibl. mf. Loc: OWTU.

Results of a 1981 survey on how Waterloo County Mennonites use and view their leisure time compared with a 1945 study. The most popular 1981 activities involved the family and other Mennonites: visiting, walking, reading, and gardening, much the same in 1945. The biggest difference was that in 1945 most Mennonites felt it was wrong for those older than children to engage in play, and in 1981 the opinion was reversed. Mennonite youth were also participating in more activities, such as retreats, school sports and dancing. Period: 1945 - 1981.

3741. Lamb, Kathryn Hansuld. "Barreling down the Grand River." **Waterloo Historical Society.** 1990. 78: 139-142. ill. Loc: all.

The story of Maggie Moyer who, in 1921, built and paddled an oak barrel boat called the "Grand Sport" from Bloomingdale to Bridgeport. Miss Moyer (1882-1952), also an artist and quilter, lived with her brother on the family farm, boarded local school teachers and sold produce at the Kitchener Farmers' Market. Period: 1900 - 1952.

3742. "Let's go Terriers: all Canadian sports enthusiasts wish you luck in your bid for world hockey supremacy at the 1962 World Hockey Championship Colorado Springs, Colorado." **Galt Evening Reporter.** 1962, February 13. Pp. 1A-24A. ill. Loc: OCCA.

A special edition supporting the Galt hockey team as Canadian representatives in the world championship. There are articles and photographs of all team members, with a schedule of Terrier games and broadcast dates. Period: 1961 - 1962.

3743. Lewis, John E. "Recreation and tourism in Waterloo County." **The Waterloo County area: selected geographical essays.** Edited by A.G. McLellan. Waterloo: Department of Geography, University of Waterloo, 1971. Pp. 63-74. tabl. Loc: OWTU, OWTL, OWTUCG, OKIT.

A description of the county's resources and facilities for leisure activities, with suggestions of how these should be planned and administered. Period: 1969 - 1971.

3744. "Official opening of the Brewster Auditorium and the W.G. Johnson Swimming Pool at Hespeler." **Waterloo Historical Society.** 1969. 57: 48. Loc: all.

A description of the ceremonies that opened Hespeler's new gymnasium-pool complex, with some information about the Brewster family. Period: 1969.

3745. Reist, Agnes. "Ayr Curling Club." **Waterloo Historical Society.** 1985. 73: 133-140. Loc: all.

An historical sketch of the club's activities, describing its Scottish associations, facilities, equipment and notable curlers. All club officers and members in 1876 and all life members are listed. Period: 1845 - 1967.

3746. Renson, Roland and DeKegel, Danielle and Smulders, Herman. "The folk roots of games: games and ethnic identity among Flemish-Canadian immigrants." **Canadian Journal of History of Sport.** 1983. 14,2: 69-79. Loc: OWTL, OWTU.

A study of Flemish immigrants in the London-Kitchener-Dunnville area. The authors conclude that Flemish-Canadians have preserved some of their typical folk games such as popinjay shooting, pigeon racing and "rolle bolle" as expressions of ethnic identity. Period: 1830 - 1983.

3747. Royal Canadian Legion - Kitchener Branch #50. **Kitchener Legionaires baseball magazine official programme, 1950.** Kitchener: The Legion, 1950. 28 p. ill. Loc: OWT.

A game schedule for the local senior intercounty baseball club sponsored by the Legion. The booklet includes photographs and short biographies of the players and of the Legion's executive, many of whom served in the First World War. Advertisements from Kitchener and Waterloo firms make up nearly half of the programme. Period: 1914 - 1950.

3748. Schlotzhauer, Margrete. **25 years: Kitchener-Waterloo Power Squadron commemorative edition.** Kitchener-Waterloo Power Squadron, 1985. 54 p. ill. Loc: OKIT.

An illustrated history of the organization, founded in 1959 by Rance Bricker and Ellis Batson, and dedicated to helping others learn safe boating. There are details of club presidents, members and activities in each year. Period: 1959 - 1984.

3749. Schmidt, Carl B. (Cully) **History of the Kitchener-Waterloo Granite Club.** 1977. 37 l. Loc: OKIT.

A history of the organization's contributions to curling, badminton and other sports. Using newspaper articles and club minutes, the author chronicles significant events in the club's history including the purchase of the property on Agnes Street from A.R. Kaufman, the first club house, subsequent additions, the formation of the Granite Business Girls Curling Club, the fire of 1955, and the hosting of competitions. The names of successful athletes are provided as well as references to changes in club rules. Period: 1927 - 1977.

3750. Shewchuk, John P. **The social implications of sports in Galt 1830-1930.** The Author, 198-?. 55 l. bibl. Loc: OCCA, OCLG.

An examination of how the older, more ethnic and elitist games of curling and cricket were replaced by the more popular sports of baseball and hockey in Galt. There are histories of Galt's curling, cricket and baseball clubs with mention of the Terriers and the establishment of the Galt Arena. Particular winning seasons and leading athletes and sportsmen are mentioned. Period: 1830 - 1930.

3751. Stevenson, John A. **Curling in Ontario, 1846-1946.** Toronto: Ontario Curling Association, 1950. 272 p. ill., index. Loc: OCCA, OKIT, OWTU.

An official survey of the Scottish origins of the game and its development in Canada, with reference to the Ontario Curling Association. There are chapters on each of the "famous clubs" such as the Galt Curling Club formed in 1838 (pp. 175-179, including a facsimile of the club emblem). The Ayr Curling Club, Ayr Union Club, New Dominion Club and Kitchener-Waterloo Granite Club are other Waterloo County clubs mentioned. Period: 1837 - 1946.

3752. Taylor, Len. "Kitchener-Waterloo at the Winter Olympics 1956." **Waterloo Historical Society.** 1956. 44: 14. Loc: all.

The Kitchener-Waterloo Dutchmen senior hockey club finished third in the 1956 Winter Olympics. The Dutchmen were the 1955 Allan Cup champions of Canada. Period: 1955 - 1956.

3753. **Twin City Skating Club, 1911-1912**. Berlin: The Club, 1911. 7 p. Loc: OWTUR.

Report on the club's first year presented to the annual meeting on November 16, 1911 with a prospectus for the second year. Membership was limited to "125 active lady members and 100 active gentleman members." Members of the executive and patrons and patronesses were apparently from community elite families. From the Clement/Bowlby Family Papers. Period: 1911 - 1912.

3754. Waterloo Bicycle Club. **"Willkommen Alle" 13th annual C.W.A. bicycle meet: Waterloo July 1st and 2nd, 1895**. Toronto: Bingham Printing, 1895. 65 p. ill. Loc: OKIT, OWT.

A programme of events for the competition, with short descriptions of local attractions in Waterloo and Berlin and advertisements by local businesses. Period: 1894 - 1895.

3755. Waterloo Memorial Arena. **"Twin Cities" Kitchener-Waterloo and district O.H.A. hockey, season 1948-49: official program**. 1948. 1 v. (unpaged). ill. Loc: OWT.

A sports magazine featuring the Flying Dutchmen hockey club, with sketches of past and current officers, coaches, managers and team players, including the manager and operator of the Waterloo Memorial Arena, Jim McCormick. Nearly half the programme consists of advertisements by local sponsors. Period: 1918 - 1949.

3756. Willetts, Richard John. **Chicopee Ski Conservation Area: an analysis of a recreational ski area within an urban environment**. Waterloo Lutheran University (B.A. thesis, Geography), 1972. 83 l. ill., bibl. Loc: OWTL.

A study of the clientele of the Chicopee Ski area. By analyzing questionnaires distributed to skiers at the site, the author determines whether the facility is used primarily as a weekday or short term ski area rather than a weekend or long term recreational resource, and whether distance from the skiers' residences and their ages are the dominant factors in identifying the user group. Period: 1971 - 1972.

3757. Williams, Peter Wilder. **A case study of industrial recreation in Kitchener-Waterloo and its role in urban recreational planning**. University of Waterloo (M.A. thesis, Geography), 1971. 2 fiche. graphs, maps, tables, bibl. mf. Loc: OWTU.

An examination of cooperation between corporations and city planners in creating recreational facilities and programmes. The author describes existing sport and fitness options and the types of individual likely to

participate in them, and presents a model designed to establish better communication between industry and government departments in planning optimal facilities. Period: 1970 - 1971.

VOLUNTARY ASSOCIATIONS
(except historical and heritage)

3758. Ancient Order of United Workmen. **Nebengesetze der Berliner Loge, No. 154**. Berlin: Deutsche Zeitung, 1888?. 15 p. Loc: OWTUR.

Constitution and by-laws of the Berlin Lodge, dated 11 August 1888. Adam Treusch and H. Zapfe are named as officers. Period: 1888 - 1889.

3759. Ancient Order of United Workmen. **A.O.U.W. Berlin Lodge No. 154, Welcome Lodge No. 334**. Berlin: Journal Print, 189-?. 1 v. (unpaged). Loc: OWTUR.

Lists of members of each lodge with advertisements for local businesses. The Berlin Lodge apparently had about 260 members and the Welcome Lodge about 90 members. Among the businesses and professionals advertising were Dr Honsberger, Dr Hett, H.L. Janzen, E.P. Cornell, P. Hymmen, Berlin & Racycle, C.H. Doerr and G.M. DeBus. Period: 1891 - 1899.

3760. Barrie, James R. "75th anniversary of Central Dumfries Farmers' Club." **Waterloo Historical Society**. 1983. 71: 47-49. Loc: all.

A report on the anniversary celebrations, with some details of the club's founding and notable dates. Period: 1908 - 1983.

3761. Barrie, James R. "North Dumfries Plowmen's Association is 75 years old." **Waterloo Historical Society**. 1983. 71: 130-134. Loc: all.

A description of the first plowing match held by the club in 1908, with shorter accounts of matches in 1912, 1917, 1925, 1958 and 1983. Period: 1908 - 1983.

3762. Bell, Nancy and Hoefert, Teresa and Williams, Dorcas. **Builders and boosters: Kitchener Chamber of Commerce 100th anniversary 1886-1986**. Kitchener: Kitchener Chamber of Commerce, 1986. 140 p. ill., ports., bibl., index. Loc: OWTUR, OWTU, OWTL, OKEBC, OKIT.

A centennial survey of the elite businessmen's organization that urged the municipal council to promote industry and improve urban services. The authors were students associated with the Public History Masters Program at the University of Waterloo, and the volume is introduced by Professor K.M. McLaughlin. Period: 1886 - 1986.

3763. Berlin Board of Trade. **Annual report**. 1905 - 1911. Loc: OKIT.

Reports that each provide a financial statement and an address by the president, with lists of leading industries, officers and members. A general description of Berlin is also given. The Kitchener Public Library has reports for the years 1905 and 1911. Period: 1886 - 1916.

3764. Bernhardt, Clara. **The story of an old stable... and how it became Preston Scout House**. 1945?. 1 v. Loc: OCCA.

A description of the conversion of the building and its many uses, including its function as headquarters for the Preston Scout House Bugle Band. The material was first published in **Saturday Night**. Period: 1895 - 1945.

3765. Biesenthal, Linda. **A rural legacy: the history of the Junior Farmers' Association of Ontario**. The Association, 1981. 221 p. ill. Loc: OKIT, OWTL, OWTU.

A commemorative history that makes few references to Waterloo County. The author notes that the first Junior Farmers' Association was organized in Elmira in 1915, with the encouragement of Agricultural Representative Stan Knapp, and that there were five clubs active when the county association was formed in 1919. When the Waterloo County Association affiliated with the Provincial Association in 1944, it had one of the largest memberships (over 400), but by 1980 there was only one club with 160 members. Period: 1915 - 1980.

3766. Bloomfield, Elizabeth. "Boards of trade and Canadian urban development." **Urban History Review**. 1983. 12,1: 77-99. ill., tabl., bibl. Loc: OWTU, OWTL.

An assessment and comprehensive listing of the boards of trade and chambers of commerce formed in over 600 Canadian communities between the 1840s and 1950. There are details, compiled from legislation and the Secretary of State's register of boards of trade, for Ayr (1906), Berlin (1886), Galt (1889), Hespeler (1910), Preston (1904) and Waterloo (1890). Illustrations include a copy of part of the Berlin Board of Trade's booklet, **Busy Berlin will just suit you** in 1910. Period: 1886 - 1950.

3767. Bolduc, N.G. "The Waterloo Horticultural Society." **Waterloo Historical Society**. 1938. 26: 12-16. Loc: all.

A brief history of the achievements of the Waterloo Horticultural Society, founded in 1895. Period: 1895 - 1938.

3768. Borth, Asher R. "Collecting postage stamps can be historically valuable." **Waterloo Historical Society**. 1949. 37: 23-25. Loc: all.

A very short account of the first stamps issued in Canada in 1851. Brief mention is made of the Kitchener Philatelists but no names of local individuals are provided. Period: 1851 - 1927.

3769. Boston, Susan A. **An historical analysis of the growth, origin and development of the Kitchener Young Women's Christian Association from its inception to the present day**. University of Waterloo (M.A. thesis, Recreation), 1980. 1 fiche. bibl. mf. Loc: OWTU.

A study of six distinctive stages and turning points in the development of the organization, stressing the types of programmes, the shift from Christian education to physical recreation, and the persistent financial problems. Period: 1906 - 1980.

3770. Bowman, Edna. "The Maple Grove Farmers' Club." **Waterloo Historical Society**. 1986. 74: 141-144. Loc: all.

An outline of the club's 50-year history, based on accounts and minute books in the Waterloo Historical Society collection. When first formed in 1908, the club was named the Preston Farmers' Institute Club, affiliated with the South Waterloo Farmers' Institutes, but changed its name in 1911. Period: 1908 - 1958.

3771. Brown, Dorothy. "The Silver Star Society, 1891-1991." **Waterloo Historical Society**. 1991. 79: 35-39. ill. Loc: all.

A history of the Galt philanthropic society founded by Mina Sylvestre and Mazo de la Roche and limited to 30 women members. Among the society's good causes have been the Galt General Hospital, the Old Ladies' Home, Victorian Order of Nurses, Young Men's Christian Association, Young Women's Christian Association, Red Cross, Freeport Sanatorium, Isolation Hospital, Hespeler Coombe Home for Orphans and the Galt Family Service Bureau. Period: 1891 - 1991.

3772. Brown, Harry W. "History of the Kitchener Horticultural Society." **Waterloo Historical Society**. 1938. 26: 6-12. Loc: all.

A short history of the accomplishments of the society, established in 1911. Period: 1911 - 1938.

3773. Bruce, Elizabeth M. "The Daughters of the Empire." **Waterloo Historical Society**. 1920. 8: 123-132. Loc: all.

An article describing the Imperial Order of the Daughters of the Empire, founded in 1900. The chapters in Kitchener, Waterloo, Preston and Galt are mentioned, as well as their officers. Period: 1900 - 1920.

3774. Burkhardt, Ferne. **A mighty flood: the House of Friendship story**. Kitchener: House of Friendship, 1989. 219 p. ill., bibl., index. Loc: OWTUCG, OWTL, OWTUSJ, OKIT, OWT.

A detailed chronicle of the Kitchener-based interdenominational organization which began as a hostel for transient men in the late 1930s, founded by Joseph Cramer, the Kiev-born son of Jewish immigrants. The author traces the organization's growth into a multifaceted community service for people in need, under leaders such as C.F. Derstine, Ross and Shirley Goodall, Orval Jantzi, Gerry Vandeworp and Martin Buhr. In addition to the original Charles Street Home, many other programmes are also described and four appendices provide information on board members, executive officers, staff and finances. Period: 1939 - 1989.

3775. Canadian Association of Stationary Engineers. **Official souvenir of the annual convention of the Canadian Association of Stationary Engineers at Berlin, Canada**. Berlin: The Association, 1899. 48 p. ill. Loc: OKIT.

Programme for the convention held August 15th, 16th and 17th, 1899, including information on the association and its Berlin Branch, founded in 1891. There are photographs of Berlin factories, with local advertisements featuring hotels, boilers and pumps. Period: 1898 - 1899.

3776. Canadian Club of Waterloo County. **Annual report**. Berlin: The Club, 1910-. Loc: OKIT.

Reports that indicate the strength of the organization which had nearly 300 members in 1910. Officers and members of the executive committee are named and the dates and subjects of meetings are reported, with abstracts of some of the addresses. Kitchener Public Library has three reports, for 1910-11, 1911-12 and 1914-15. Period: 1910 - 1915.

3777. Children's Aid Society of Waterloo County. **Annual report**. 1954-. Loc: OKIT.

The organization, founded in 1894, was renamed Family and Children's Services of Waterloo Region in 1978. Kitchener Public Library has all annual reports from 1954 to 1986 except for 1957, 1967 and 1979. Period: 1954 - 1986.

3778. Cook, H. Milton. **The Kitchener Waterloo Rotary Club presents its history from 1922 to 1955 on the golden anniversary of Rotary, founded 1905-1955**. Kitchener: The Club, 1955. 71 p. ill. Loc: OWTU, OKIT.

A history from the club's foundation in 1922 to 1955, written by one of its earliest presidents. The Rotary's development and contributions are described in detail, based on the yearly speeches of the incoming and outgoing presidents, the club minutes, and the author's reminiscences. There are photographs of past presidents, and lists of club officials and members. Period: 1922 - 1955.

3779. Cooper, W. Fred. "The Kitchener-Waterloo Field Naturalists: 50 years of change, 1934-1984." **Waterloo Historical Society**. 1984. 72: 22-25. Loc: all.

A short history of the club, including an account of its founding by F.W.R. Dickson and its conservation efforts such as purchases of land, in cooperation with the GRCA, of the Dickson Wilderness Area, the F.H. Montgomery Wilderness Area, Bannister's Marsh, Wrigley Lake, and land in the Roseville Swamp area. Period: 1934 - 1984.

3780. Crooks, Adam. **Special report of the Minister of Education on the Mechanics' Institutes (Ontario)**. Toronto: Legislative Assembly, 1881. 208 p. tables. Loc: OCCA.

An examination of the Mechanics' Institutes of Ontario with regard to provincial legislation and grants. A history of the organization's British origins in 1780 is given, with yearly synopses of its development in Ontario from 1849 to 1881. General recommendations for improvement are discussed, with summaries of the activities of each Ontario branch in 1880. Waterloo County institutes mentioned are those of Ayr, Berlin, Galt, Hespeler, Preston and Waterloo. Period: 1853 - 1881.

3781. "Elmira and Woolwich Fall Exhibition." **Waterloo Historical Society**. 1962. 50: 93. Loc: all.

A note of the record attendance of 23,000 people at the Elmira and Woolwich Fall Fair of 1962. Period: 1962.

3782. Elmira Germania Society. **Elmira Germania Society's minute book = Elmira Germania Verein Protocol Buch**. 1887 - 1889. 64 p. Loc: OWRE.

A manuscript record of the society's business over a two-year period. Activities such as readings, debates, lectures, concerts and plays are reported in both English and German. The last two pages contain lists of members, many of whom were prominent in the Elmira community during the 1880s. Period: 1887 - 1889.

3783. Epp, Frank H. **Partners in service: the story of Mennonite Central Committee Canada, prepared on the occasion of the twentieth anniversary, 1963-1982**. Mennonite Central Committee Canada,

1983. 76 p. ill., charts, graphs, bibl. Loc: OKIT, OWTUCG.

A history of the relief agency created in 1963 by members of the Mennonite and Brethren in Christ churches. Background information is given about predecessor organizations such as the Canadian Aid Committee headed by Jacob Y. Shantz in the 1870s and the Non-Resistant Relief Organization organized by S.F. Coffman. Statistics of personnel, income and projects of the agency are provided. Period: 1800 - 1982.

3784. "An evening in history: circa 1886." **Contact.** 1986, May. Pp. 1-6. ill. Loc: OKIT.

Special edition of the Kitchener Chamber of Commerce newsletter describing centennial celebrations which included a costume party, the publication of **Builders and boosters** and the donation of the organization's records to the Kitchener Public Library. Period: 1886 - 1986.

3785. Federal Union No. 17. **By-laws of the Federal Union No. 17, Berlin, Ont., under the jurisdiction of the Trades and Labour Congress of Canada.** Berlin: H. Rittinger, 1906. 35 p. Loc: OWTUR. Period: 1906 - 1907.

3786. Felka, Sandra. **Kitchener's four German clubs: European origins and current operations.** University of Waterloo (B.E.S. thesis, Geography), 1987. 2 fiche. mf. Loc: OWTUM, OKIT.

A comparative study of the Concordia Club, the Schwaben Club, the Transylvania Club, and the Alpine Club, with respect to their historical development, their current operation and facilities, and their members' origins. Period: 1873 - 1987.

3787. "Fifty years with the Ontario Plowmen's Association." **Waterloo Historical Society.** 1963. 51: 51. ill. Loc: all.

A note of the long service of W.C. Barrie as a director of the association. Period: 1913 - 1963.

3788. Fruit-growers' Association of Ontario. **Twenty-eighth annual report of the Fruit-growers' Association of Ontario.** Toronto: Ontario Department of Agriculture, 1897. 142 p. ill., index. Also CIHM Microfiche series, no. A00658 (1889) and A00332 (1871-1888) Loc: OKDHC, OWTL, OWTU.

Doon Heritage Crossroads has a copy of the original report for 1897, which includes an account of the second annual meeting of the Waterloo Horticultural Society, listing the officers for the next year and noting that the good attendance included a number of ladies. Some earlier reports are on microfiche through the Canadian Institute of Historical Microreproductions. Period: 1895 - 1896.

3789. Hart, Jean M. and McLaughlin, Marion. **65 years of North Waterloo District Women's Institute, 1902-1967.** 1967. 51 p. ill. Loc: OWRA, OWRE, OKIT.

A history of the North Waterloo District of the Women's Institute, including individual accounts of the fifteen branches in Winterbourne, Wellesley, Linwood, West Montrose, Centreville, St Jacobs, Sunnyside, Bridgeport, Dorking, Bloomingdale, Woolwich, Elmdale, Lexington, Rummelhardt and Williamsburg. Photographs of past presidents and secretary-treasurers are included. Period: 1902 - 1967.

3790. Harvey, William H., Dr. **Kitchener-Waterloo Academy of Medicine.** Kitchener: The Academy, 1950. 38 p. Loc: OKIT.

Charter, constitution, and lists of charter officers and members of the academy that was founded in 1950. A foreword provides historical information on earlier medical societies in Waterloo County, such as the South Waterloo Medical Society formed by a group of Galt physicians in 1887. Period: 1887 - 1950.

3791. Hearn, Mary Elizabeth. **The Canadian Federation of University Women: Kitchener-Waterloo Branch 1922-1972.** University of Waterloo (student essay, History), 1975. 1 v. (unpaged). charts, bibl. Loc: OKIT.

A study of the club's members, in terms of their ethnic background and employment, and of the club's changing role in the community as this reflected changes in women's roles. Period: 1922 - 1972.

3792. House of Friendship. **The story of House of Friendship for All Nations.** Kitchener: The Advisory Board, 194-?. 15 p. ill. Loc: OWTUCG.

A booklet explaining the purpose of the Christian interdenominational centre in downtown Kitchener. During its early days in the latter 1930s and 1940s, the House of Friendship provided food, shelter and the Gospel message mainly to immigrant and transient men. Directed by Joseph Cramer, the hostel had a chapel, a reading room, a dining room, and beds for 33 men. Period: 1938 - 1948.

3793. Kitchener Chamber of Commerce. **Annual report.** Kitchener: The Chamber, 1954-. Loc: OKIT.

A report of each year's accomplishments and activities. Names of presidents are indexed in the WRP database from reports available. Kitchener Public Library has reports for the years from 1954 to 1972/3, 1975/76, 1979/80, 1982 to 1984, and 1986 to 1989. Period: 1954 - 1989.

3794. Kitchener Chamber of Commerce. **Kitchener Chamber of Commerce membership roster**. Kitchener: The Chamber, 1965-. Loc: OKIT.

Biennial publication also sometimes entitled **Kitchener Chamber of Commerce membership roster: constitution and by-laws** and **Kitchener Chamber of Commerce membership directory and buyer's guide**. The directories list members, usually by business classification. Kitchener Public Library has directories for the years 1965, 1970/71, 1973/74, 1974, 1976, 1978/79, 1980, 1982, 1988, 1989, 1990 and 1991/92. Only the 1973/74 directory includes Waterloo businesses. Period: 1965 - 1992.

3795. Kitchener Horticultural Society. **A history of the Kitchener Horticultural Society**. Kitchener: The Society, 1969. 6 l. Loc: OKIT.

An overview of the society's formation and activities since 1910, including details of early members, officers and efforts to live up to its motto: "community beauty a civic duty." Period: 1872 - 1969.

3796. Kitchener Horticultural Society. **Kitchener Horticultural Society year book**. 1930, 1931. Loc: OKIT.

Volumes containing lists of club officers, reprints of articles about the society, announcements of flower shows, and articles about growing and arranging flowers. Kitchener Public Library has the books for the years 1930 and 1931. Period: 1930 - 1931.

3797. Kitchener Horticultural Society. **Kitchener Horticultural Society prize list and garden guide**. The Society, 1928. 48 p. ill. Loc: OKIT.

A list of prizes with rules and regulations governing the exhibition organized by the society in 1928, with descriptions of the 1927 exhibition. There are also articles about gardening. Period: 1927 - 1928.

3798. **Kitchener Local Council of Women: references in the National Council of Women of Canada Yearbook**. Ottawa: National Council of Women, 1921 - 1951. Loc: OWTUR.

Excerpts from the yearbooks of the Annual Meeting of the National Council of Women of Canada, concerning the Kitchener-Waterloo branch which was formed in 1920 and reorganized as the Kitchener branch in 1932. Officers and affiliated societies are listed with summaries of the year's activities. From 1946 on, activities are described in reports of standing committees, such

as arts and letters, natural resources and industries, and child and family welfare. Period: 1921 - 1951.

3799. Kitchener-Waterloo and District Labour Council. **Kitchener-Waterloo and District Labour Council: Labour Day 1963 souvenir program**. Guelph: Guelph Printing Service, 1963. 1 v. (unpaged). ill. Loc: OKITW.

A programme listing the events and times of the Labour Day celebrations, with photographs of the members of the Labour Day Committee. There are messages from labour officials, as well as from the mayors of Kitchener and Waterloo, Kieth Hymmen and James Bauer. Many union locals placed advertisements. Period: 1962 - 1963.

3800. **Kitchener-Waterloo Centre of Community Arts**. The Centre, 192-?. 1 folded sheet. Loc: OKIT, OWTUR.

An advertising brochure for the arts centre, established to encourage interest in painting, music, literature and other arts by offering classes, exhibitions and lectures. Period: 1920 - 1929.

3801. Kitchener-Waterloo Kiwanis Club. **The Kiwanis Club of the Twin Cities, Kitchener-Waterloo: the first 30 years, 1957-1987**. 1987. 42 p. ill., ports. Loc: OWTUR, OKIT, OWT.

An historical account, noting past members and mentioning various fundraising events such as the Oktoberfest and the Sugar Express. Period: 1957 - 1987.

3802. Kitchener-Waterloo Rotary Club. **1922-1972: 50th anniversary club history**. Kitchener: The Club, 1972. 48 p. Loc: OKIT.

A short history of the club which includes brief profiles of club presidents from 1922 to 1972 as well as a list of the charter members and subsequent members. Period: 1922 - 1972.

3803. Kitchener-Waterloo Y.W.C.A. **Annual report**. 1946-. 16 p. Loc: OKIT.

Reports on current activities, staff and directors. Kitchener Public Library has reports for 1946 and 1948. Period: 1946 - 1948.

3804. Kitchener Y.M.C.A. **Annual report**. 1953-. Loc: OKIT.

Reports on the organization's current activities, staff and directors. Kitchener Public Library has reports for 1953, 1960, 1961 and 1989. Period: 1953 - 1989.

3805. Kitchener Y.W.C.A. **To-morrow's YW for to-day's young women.** 1961. 8 p. ill. Loc: OKIT.

A promotional brochure that presents some historical information as part of an appeal for $350,000 to permit expansion and renovation. Members of the campaign committee and other community supporters are named. Period: 1960 - 1961.

3806. Klotz, Otto. **Resolutions of Grand Lodge and ruling of Grand Masters of the Grand Lodge A.F. & A.M., of Canada that have the force of law: and which appear in the Grand Lodge proceedings from the year 1855, being from the formation of this Grand Lodge, to its twentieth annual communication (inclusive) July 1875.** CIHM Microfiche series, no. 37727. Hamilton: Ennis and Stirton, 1875. mf. Loc: OWTL, OWTU.

Included because of the link with Otto Klotz of Preston and the strength of the Lodge in Waterloo County. Period: 1855 - 1875.

3807. Knights of the Maccabees of the World. **Nebengezetze der Berlin Tent No. 21, K.O.T.M. von Berlin, Ont..** Berlin: Berlin Tent No. 21, 1898?. 8 p. Loc: OWTUR.

Constitution and by-laws of the fraternal society, signed by R.E. Hartmann and C. Stein. Period: 1897 - 1898.

3808. Kummer, Oliver A. "Preston Horticultural Society." **Waterloo Historical Society.** 1971. 59: 64-70. ill. Loc: all.

A history of the society's achievements since its foundation in 1878. Period: 1878 - 1972.

3809. Lamb, Kathryn Hansuld. "Mabel McArthur's garden." **Waterloo Historical Society.** 1986. 74: 36-42. ill. Loc: all.

A description of the original model for the garden proposed by the Kitchener-Waterloo Garden Club to surround Peter McArthur's log house that was moved from Middlesex County in 1963 to Doon Pioneer Village (now Doon Heritage Crossroads). The author quotes a letter on the subject from James F. McArthur, son of Peter and Mabel McArthur. Period: 1963 - 1964.

3810. Lamb, Kathryn Hansuld. **The quiet hobby: a history of organized philately in the Grand River Valley 1895-1985.** New Hamburg: Ritz Printing, 1985. 48. p. ill. Loc: OKIT, OWT.

An account of the establishment and development of stamp collecting in the county, including lists of local members of the Dominion Philatelic Association in 1900 and of subsequent county societies. The author clarifies club name changes and describes exhibitions and other meetings.

Period: 1895 - 1985.

3811. Lamb, Kathryn Hansuld. "Waterloo County's oldest Women's Institute." **Waterloo Historical Society.** 1972. 60: 25. Loc: all.

A note of the Winterbourne Women's Institute's 70th anniversary. Period: 1921 - 1972.

3812. Lamb, Kathryn Hansuld. **Women's organizations in Kitchener.** 1979. Loc: OKIT.

A record of 35 clubs, associations, auxiliaries and other organizations. Listed alphabetically, each entry includes a brief history stating the purpose of the group, its starting date, and names of many of its principal members. This collection was the basis of the research for an article appearing in the **Kitchener-Waterloo Record** on 21 June 1979. Period: 1899 - 1979.

3813. Landon, Fred. "The Preston Debating Society 1842-43." **Waterloo Historical Society.** 1988. 76: 82-84. Loc: all.

A brief account of the society's most active year, with a list of founding members. Period: 1842 - 1844.

3814. Leibbrandt, Gottlieb. **Jubiläums Ausgabe: 100 jahre / Centennial issue: 100 years, 1872- 1973.** Kitchener: Concordia Club, 1973. 194 p. ill. Loc: OWTUR, OKIT.

A comprehensive history of the Concordia Club, which grew out of the success of the 1871 Friedensfest in Berlin. The author recounts the club's activities and sub-groups such as the choirs, the Women's Auxiliary, the soccer club, the folkdance group, the Mardi Gras Society and the German Language School. Photographs dating back to the early years of the club provide additional details about past members and activities, and newspaper excerpts show the community's reactions to the local German society in the light of concurrent world events. The book was published as the Club's **Nachrichten** no. 57 in August 1973. Period: 1873 - 1973.

3815. Leibbrandt, Gottlieb. "One hundred years of Concordia." **Waterloo Historical Society.** 1973. 61: 46-57. ill. Loc: all.

An historical sketch of the club formed in 1873 and of German cultural activities generally in Berlin/Kitchener, including references to prominent individuals and notable events. Period: 1873 - 1973.

3816. Light, Frank G. "The Galt Club Limited." **Waterloo Historical Society.** 1964. 52: 87-88. Loc: all.

A short account of the club from its founding in 1910 to the surrender of its charter in 1960, with lists of directors in 1911-12 and 1921-22. The author notes that the club's records were given to the archives of the Waterloo Historical Society. Period: 1910 - 1960.

3817. Lougheed, Lloyd G. **Reflections of the Kiwanis Club of Kitchener-Waterloo chartered March 7, 1921.** Kitchener: The Club, 1991. 47 p. ill. Loc: OKIT, OWTUR.

A brief history of the local organization with details of past activities and members. Included are lists of presidents as well as the text of an address by W.H.E. Schmalz in 1966 to a club meeting. Period: 1921 - 1991.

3818. MacLeod, Barry. **Tailspinner: celebration 60.** 1992. 28 p. ill. Loc: OKIT.

A souvenir edition of the club newsletter commemorating the 60th anniversary of the Waterloo Wellington Flying Club. Facsimiles of club records and newspaper articles provide a decade-by-decade history of the club. Lists of past presidents and current directors and photographs of the club's training airplanes are included. Period: 1931 - 1992.

3819. Malcolm, John and Sanderson, Pete and Schmidt, Bryan. **Magic on the march: the 50 year history of Canada's famous Preston Scout House Bugle Band.** Toronto: Gagne Printing, 1989. 123, 19 p. ill. Loc: OCCA, OCLG, OCH, OCP, OKIT.

A history of the bugle and drum corps and its accomplishments, written by five former members of the band and including biographical information about Wilf Blum, the pharmacist who began the band in 1938. It contains photographs, reminiscences and quotations, as well as lists of members from 1939 to 1966, music played, and performances outside Preston from 1947 to 1966. Period: 1938 - 1988.

3820. Mogilski, Helen. "Canada's oldest Polish organization: the St Joseph and St John Society." **Waterloo Historical Society.** 1986. 74: 43-50. ill. Loc: all.

A history of the fraternal organizations that developed in Berlin/Kitchener to provide mutual assistance to migrants from Poland. The St Joseph Society (1886) evolved around the nucleus of St Mary's Church to provide death benefits, while the St John Society (1913) had its origins in a branch of the Catholic Order of Foresters that provided sickness assistance. The two groups united in 1949. The article is reprinted from the book celebrating the Society's centennial. Period: 1886 - 1986.

3821. Montonen, Susan and Milroy, Beth Moore and Wismer, Susan. "Siting the Berlin Y.W.C.A." **Waterloo Historical Society.** 1990. 78: 39-53. map. Loc: all.

An account of the tortuous negotiations from 1912 to 1914 over potential sites for the Berlin building, interpreted as a struggle between the private business interests of major landowners and employers of women factory workers on the one hand and general community interests on the other. Mary and Jacob Kaufman, influential figures in the early history of the Berlin association, were defeated on this issue by a consensus of other community leaders. Period: 1905 - 1914.

3822. National Council of Women of Canada. **Complimentary dinner in honor of Miss Winnifred Kydd M.A., President National Council of Women of Canada, Canadian Delegate to Disarmament Conference at Geneva: Thursday, Nov. 3rd, 1932, Crystal Ball Room, Walper House, Kitchener, Ont..** 1932. 3 p. ill. Loc: OWTUR.

A programme of a dinner held in Kitchener for Winnifred Kydd, in 1932. Miss Kydd, Canadian delegate to the Disarmament Conference at Geneva, gave a speech, and Mrs Jacob Kaufman was presented with a life membership to the National Council of Women. Period: 1931 - 1932.

3823. Nixon, Nancy. **An historical analysis of the development of the Young Men's Christian Association of Kitchener-Waterloo.** University of Waterloo (B.A. thesis, History), 1974. 2 fiche. bibl. mf. Loc: OWTU.

An examination of the origins and development of the association, including a discussion of its change in focus from Christian education to socialization and physical recreation. Period: 1895 - 1974.

3824. North Waterloo Exhibition Committee. **Programme: the North Waterloo fall exhibition, 1882.** Berlin: Telegraph Office, 1882. 13 p. Loc: OKIT.

Includes rules and prize list for the event to be held in the Berlin Town Park in October 1882. Moses Springer was secretary and John Moffat president of the committee. Period: 1882 - 1883.

3825. Ontario Association of Agricultural Societies. **The story of Ontario agricultural fairs and exhibitions, 1792-1967.** Picton: Picton Gazette Publishing Co., 1967. 212 p. ill. Loc: OKIT, OWTL, OWTU.

A brief history of the founding of early agricultural societies and locations of agricultural fairs. The author presents historical information on the Dumfries Society organized in 1838 and renamed Waterloo County

Agricultural Society in 1852, the Wilmot Agricultural Society first organized in 1854, the Woolwich branch of the Waterloo County Society in existence by 1854, the Wellesley Society dating from 1854 (later including North Easthope), and the Kitchener-Waterloo Agricultural Society organized in 1960. Period: 1836 - 1967.

3826. Order of the Eastern Star, Waterloo Chapter, No. 232. **By-laws of Waterloo Chapter, No. 232 O.E.S., instituted October 6th, 1945, Waterloo, Ontario.** 1945. 8 p. Loc: OWTUR.

A pocket-size, printed copy of the 1945 by-laws of the Waterloo Order of the Eastern Star. Period: 1944 - 1945.

3827. Patrons of Husbandry, Dominion Grange. **Journal of the proceedings of the annual session of the Dominion Grange, Patrons of Husbandry.** CIHM Microfiche series, no. A01477. Preston: T.H. Sears, 1888? - 1890. mf. Loc: OWTL, OWTU. Period: 1888 - 1890.

3828. Patterson, Nancy-Lou. "The gavel of death: Masonic and Orange Lodge markers in Rushes Cemetery near Crosshill, Ontario, 1864-1983." **Waterloo Historical Society.** 1984. 72: 131-149. ill., bibl. Loc: all.

A description of the Masonic and Orange Lodge motifs on the tombstones in Rushes Cemetery, with some historical information on these two organizations. Period: 1864 - 1983.

3829. Pequegnat, C.D. "The Waterloo County Hall of Fame." **Waterloo Historical Society.** 1972. 60: 88-89. ill. Loc: all.

A short account of the project that was commenced in 1965 and opened in 1972 at Doon Pioneer Village. The author describes the planning of the hall by the Kitchener Sports Association and notes that the original sports hall idea was later expanded to honour "any Waterloo County individual and group whose achievements brought fame and recognition." Period: 1950 - 1972.

3830. **The Philatelic Advocate: a monthly journal devoted to stamp collecting.** Berlin: Starnaman Bros, 1896 - 1901. 1 v. Loc: OKIT.

Apparently a full set of the journal edited and published in Berlin. Issues vary in length, for an annual subscription fixed at 25 cents. Period: 1896 - 1901.

3831. Piotrowski, Tadeusz and Mogilski, Helen. **St Joseph and St John Society, 1886-1986: Towarzystwo Wzajemnej Pomocy Sw. Josefa i Sw. Jana Kantego.** Kitchener: Sacred Heart Catholic Church, 1986. 1

v. (various pagings). ill. Loc: OKIT.

A commemorative history of the two Polish organizations, the St Joseph Fraternal Aid Society (1886) and the St John Kanty Brotherly Assistance Society (1913) that united in 1949. Written mainly in Polish, the book names the organization's leaders and officers and presents a summary in English on pp. 86-8. Period: 1886 - 1986.

3832. Preston Horticultural Society. **Prize lists of the Preston Horticultural Society.** 1880 - 1905. Loc: OKITW.

Booklets containing the rules for the society's annual competition with lists of prizes given for flowers, fruits and vegetables. The prize lists of 1880 and 1885 also contain the society's constitution and a list of members while the 1905 editions contains advertisements from local businesses. The Waterloo Historical Society holds prize lists for the years 1880, 1885 and 1905. Period: 1880 - 1905.

3833. Preston Mechanics' Institute. **Constitution, by-laws, rules and regulations.** Galt: Reformer Press, 1871. 17 p. Loc: OWTUR.

A record that includes rules for use of the library and reading room. Period: 1870 - 1871.

3834. Ritz, Orval. "Rockway Gardens' first 50 years 1933-1983." **Waterloo Historical Society.** 1983. 71: 77-81. ill. Loc: all.

A short history including references to members of the Kitchener Horticultural Society who were involved in design and construction of the gardens. Period: c1929 - 1983.

3835. Rooke, Elizabeth A. and Sprung, Dorothea A. **Growth of a legend: a history of CFUW-KW's book sale.** Kitchener: Kitchener-Waterloo Canadian Federation of University Women, 1989. 23 p. ill. Loc: OKIT, OWRE, OWT, OWTL, OWTUR.

An account of the main fundraising event of the Kitchener-Waterloo branch of the Canadian Federation of University Women since 1965. The brochure, illustrated by Jeff Bowlby, lists scholarships and organizations that have benefitted, with names of committee members. Period: 1965 - 1989.

3836. Rotary Club of Kitchener. **Annual rotary review.** Kitchener: The Club, 1957-. Loc: OKIT.

A summary of the year's activities with messages from the outgoing and incoming presidents and a roster of all members with snapshots and facts of their professional and business activities. Kitchener Public Library has Vol. 34 (1957-58) and Vol. 47 (1972-73). Period: 1957 - 1973.

3837. Rudy, Norma I. **A vision and a need: a history of Fairview Mennonite Home, 1943- 1983**. Toronto: Goodhoofd/Fretz, 1983. 16 p. ill. Loc: OKIT, OCCA.

An account of the establishment and growth of the home. The history provides information on the people involved in the creation and administration of the facility which began at Braeside in Preston in 1943. Photographs are included of many of these individuals, as well as of subsequent properties that became known as Fairview. Period: 1943 - 1983.

3838. Sanders, Constance E. "The Red Cross Society celebrates its 60th anniversary in Cambridge, 1914-1974." **Waterloo Historical Society**. 1974. 62: 51-63. Loc: all.

An account of the founding and development of the society in the Galt area, including lists of officers and descriptions of fund-raising projects. Period: 1914 - 1974.

3839. Scott, Grace. **Royal Canadian Legion: Elmira Branch 469**. 1989. 28 p. ill. Loc: OWRE.

A booklet commemorating the branch's 40th anniversary in 1989. The history of the legion is outlined, with information on its members, activities and building. Reminiscences, poetry and photographs of some of the veterans are included. Period: 1914 - 1989.

3840. "Silver Star Society of Galt." **Waterloo Historical Society**. 1967. 55: 40. Loc: all.

A brief note of the oldest philanthropic organization in Galt, founded in 1891. In the 1960s, the society continued to support the Family Service Bureau and the Welfare Department. Period: 1891 - 1967.

3841. South Waterloo Agricultural Society. **South Waterloo Agricultural Society Fall Fair prize list**. The Society, 1970. Loc: OKDHC.

A list of rules and regulations for exhibitors, with an outline of the various competitions for livestock, vegetables, flowers, cookery and handicrafts. An entry blank is included, and there is a list of the society's officers and directors. Period: 1969 - 1970.

3842. South Waterloo District Women's Institute. **South Waterloo District Women's Institute and its 15 branches: 50 years of achievement, 1903-1953**. 1953. 48 p. ill. Loc: OWTUR.

An account of the history of the South Waterloo District, with individual histories of its branches: Branchton, Preston, the Jubilee Women's Institute at Glen Christie, Ayr, Haysville, New Hamburg, Little's Corners, Mill Creek, Maple Grove, Central Dumfries, New Dundee, Grand River of Doon and Blair, and the Laura Rose Young Women's Institute. Each club's members and activities are described, and there is a photograph of all the club officers in 1952. Period: 1903 - 1953.

3843. St Mary's Literary and Dramatic Society. **Social dance: Saengerbund Hall, Wednesday, Feb. 7, 1900**. Berlin: The Society, 1900. 12 p. ill. Loc: OWTUR.

A programme of the evening's events including music by Ziegler's Opera House Orchestra. The names of the dance committee members are printed as well as many advertisements by local merchants. Period: 1900.

3844. Stanbury, Robert. **Notes for a speech: Hon. Robert Stanbury, Minister of Communications at the 25th anniversary of the Canadian German Society at the Schwabenklub, Kitchener, Ontario, 2:00 p.m., September 24, 1972**. Ottawa: Canada Department of Communications, 1972. 9 l. Loc: OWTU.

A brief speech which recognizes the importance of multiculturalism in Canada and praises the efforts of the German-Canadian community in the promotion of its culture. Little mention is made of Waterloo County. Period: 1947 - 1972.

3845. Stephenson, Roy. **The House of Friendship for All Nations, Kitchener, Ontario (1939-1978)**. University of Waterloo (student essay), 1988. 50 p. ill., bibl. Loc: OWTUCG.

A study of the theological impetus behind the founding of the House of Friendship, established in 1939 by Mennonites to preach the gospel to foreign nations (particularly the Jews) and feed the hungry. The visions and goals of the various directors of the House are described, as well as the tension between supporters of professionally run institution and those who favoured a small, theologically motivated service. An annual report or series of "program overviews" for 1987 is included in an appendix. Period: 1939 - 1987.

3846. Waterloo Chamber of Commerce. **Welcome to the party: a salute to Waterloo Chamber's 100th anniversary**. Kitchener: Fairway Group, 1990. 38 p. ill. Loc: OKIT.

A supplement to the **Waterloo Chronicle** on 15 August 1990. In addition to speeches and stories about the 100th anniversary, the booklet includes a section by Ken Magor on the history of the chamber and its relationship with local business and trade. Page 32 includes a list of all presidents of the chamber since Christian Kumpf in 1890. Period: 1890 - 1990.

3847. Waterloo County Federation of Agriculture. **Annual field day programme and year book.** The Federation, 1945-. 44 p. ill. Loc: OKIT.

Programmes for the annual events organized as "rural field days" or "conservation days" from 1944. The Kitchener Public Library holds programmes for the events held 6 June 1945 and 12 June 1946 at Waterloo Park and on 28 July 1948 at Baden. The programmes also include reports of the federation's activities and lists of officers, committee members and affiliated organizations. Period: 1944 - 1948.

3848. Waterloo County Federation of Agriculture. **Annual meeting.** The Federation, 1969. 48 p. ill. Loc: OKIT.

Reports prepared for the annual meeting held at the Breslau Hotel on 30 December 1969. Leaders of the various committees and affiliated organizations are named and there are articles by E.I. McLoughry on farm organizations in Waterloo County since 1900 and by G.H. Thompson on agricultural data from the 1966 census. Affiliated organizations are indexed in the WRP database. Period: 1800 - 1969.

3849. Waterloo County Federation of Agriculture. **Annual report.** The Federation, 1945-. Loc: OKDHC, OKIT, OKITW.

Yearbooks containing reports from federation officials and other items of interest to Waterloo farmers. Some yearbooks contain programmes for Field Days or Conservation Days. The Kitchener Public Library holds the yearbooks for 1945, 1946, 1948 and 1969, Doon Heritage Crossroads has the 1971 yearbook, and the Waterloo Historical Society the centennial yearbook for 1967. Period: 1945 - 1971.

3850. Waterloo County Medical Association. **Constitution and by-laws of the Waterloo County Medical Association, adopted December 10, 1872.** Waterloo: The Association, 1872. 20 p. Loc: OKIT.

A statement of the goals and organization of the Waterloo County Medical Association, setting out a code of medical ethics and a tariff of fees. Doctors who signed the document are named. Period: 1871 - 1872.

3851. Waterloo Horticultural Society. **Waterloo Horticultural Society yearbook.** Waterloo: The Society, 1950-. 1 v. (various pagings). ill. Loc: OKIT, OWT.

An annual account of activities by the society established in 1895. Gardening tips, lists of members, and advertisements from local companies are included. The Kitchener Public Library holds copies for the years 1950, 1960, 1961, and 1966 to 1989. Period: 1895 - 1989.

3852. Waterloo South District Women's Institute. **Waterloo South District Women's Institute.** 1990?. 2 v. ill. Loc: OCCA.

An illustrated record of the Institute in two parts. The branches, officers, administration and activities of the organization from 1903 to 1960 are described in the first volume, and those from 1960 to 1990 in the second volume. An outline of both books is provided in the table of contents. The names of all district officers and anyone given a biographical sketch have been indexed in the WRP database. Period: 1903 - 1990.

3853. Weicker, Samuel. **Waterloo Horticultural Society: history and information.** 1988. 78 p. ill. Loc: OKIT, OWT.

A compilation of excerpts from the society's yearbooks and secretary's and treasurer's reports, as well as information from other sources. The society was established in 1895. Period: 1895 - 1988.

3854. Weiler, Bob and Bauer, Bob. **...The Scout House Band story.** Preston: Scout House Band, 19--. 12 p. ill. Loc: OKIT.

A promotional brochure for the Preston Scout House Bugle Band, describing its history, achievements, the Scout House, and what it is like to be a member of the band. Period: 1957 - 1969.

3855. Wilmot Agricultural Society. **Wilmot Agricultural Society prize list.** 1921, 1963. Loc: OWRBW, OKITW.

Rules and regulations for the Fall Exhibition in New Hamburg, listing the prizes in categories of livestock, fruit, vegetables, flowers, domestic work and school competitions. The Wilmot Township Archives holds the prize list for 1921 and the Waterloo Historical Society holds the list for 1963. Period: 1921 - 1963.

3856. Witmer, Leslie D. **Fairview Mennonite home: a history of homes for the aged: Mennonite Conference of Ontario.** Elmira: Bauman Printing, 1963. 30 p. ill. Loc: OKITW, OWTUR.

An account of the founding of two Mennonite homes in Preston: Braeside Nursing Home in 1943, and Fairview Mennonite Home opened in 1956. The buildings and staff are described and statistics of admissions and deaths are given. There is a short history of Braeside Lodge, formerly the home of Abram Erb and his family. Period: 1943 - 1963.

3857. Women's Canadian Club of Kitchener and Waterloo. **Silver anniversary, 1910-1935.** Kitchener: The Club, 1935. 1 folded sheet. Loc: OWTUR.

Menu and programme for a dinner on 3 October 1935 to commemorate the club's 25th anniversary. Racie Boehmer Pollock sang and Mabel Dunham was the speaker. Names of all presidents are listed, with the officers for 1935. From the Clement/Bowlby Family Papers. Period: 1910 - 1935.

3858. Woolwich Township Agricultural Society. **Annual exhibition programmes.** Elmira: The Society, 1886, 1897. 20 p. Loc: OWRE.

Programmes for the exhibitions held in Elmira on 5-6 October 1886 and 14-15 October 1897, listing the competition classes for horses, cattle, sheep, hogs, crops, fruits, flowers, dairy, poultry, farm implements, fine arts and ladies' work. Rules governing the event and the prize money are also stated. Period: 1886 - 1897.

HERITAGE AND HISTORICAL ASSOCIATIONS AND PROJECTS

3859. "1964 at the Pioneer Village." **Waterloo Historical Society.** 1964. 52: 72. Loc: all.

A note of current activities such as new acquisitions and renovations. Period: 1964 - 1965.

3860. "Artifacts for Doon Pioneer Village [WRP]." **Waterloo Historical Society.** 1965. 53: 54. ill. Loc: all.

A photograph of two old-fashioned coffins and a butter churn discovered in Baden and given to the Doon Pioneer Village in 1965. Period: 1965.

3861. "Assistance of volunteers acknowledged [WRP]." **Waterloo Historical Society.** 1963. 51: 40, 79. Loc: all.

A note of appreciation for those who helped produce the Waterloo Historical Society's 1963 volume, particularly F.W.R. Dickson. Period: 1963 - 1964.

3862. Barnett, John. "The national importance of local history (with particular reference to Waterloo County)." **Waterloo Historical Society.** 1949. 37: 7-10. Loc: all.

A short tribute to the Mennonites of Waterloo and their local historians. Period: 1897 - 1949.

3863. Barrie, William C. and Cowan, Jennie F. and Dickson, F.W.R. "65th anniversary of the Waterloo Historical Society." **Waterloo Historical Society.** 1977. 65: 4-18. ill. Loc: all.

Transcribed addresses presented by three long-serving members. Barrie comments on early schools and the founders of the Dickie Settlement in North Dumfries in 1830 quotes a satirical poem about Farmers' Institutes. Mrs Cowan recalls her long association with the Society, remarking on individuals who had advocated heritage conservation. Dickson discusses milestones in the Society's history, especially the publication of its annual volumes. Period: 1830 - 1977.

3864. Bergey, Lorna L. **The new commandment: centennial pageant 1867-1967, presented by the Mennonite Historical Society of Ontario.** Mennonite Historical Society of Ontario, 1967. 15 p. ill. Loc: OKIT.

A programme for a four part play by Barbara Coffman, recounting the history of the Ontario Mennonites, Amish, and Brethren in Christ. The programme supplements the pageant with illustrations and historical notes on Ontario Mennonite experiences. Period: 1800 - 1967.

3865. Bernhardt, Clara. "Pennsylvania German folklore to the fore." **Ontario History.** 1953. 45,1: 45-46. Loc: OKIT, OWTL, OWTU, OWT.

A profile of the society, formed in 1952 under the leadership of G. Elmore Reaman. The author lists officers for 1953 and describes goals and activities. Period: 1952 - 1953.

3866. Boylen, J.C. "York Pioneer and Historical Society visits Galt." **Waterloo Historical Society.** 1956. 44: 54. Loc: all.

An account of a bus tour to Galt and through Dumfries at the invitation of the Waterloo Historical Society. Period: 1956 - 1957.

3867. Bradshaw, Marion. "Ontario Heritage Foundation plaque unveiled." **Waterloo Historical Society.** 1976. 64: 37-38. Loc: all.

An address at the unveiling of the plaque commemorating the founding of New Hamburg. The author comments on the roles of the Ontario Heritage Foundation, the Waterloo Historical Society, the municipal councils, and Women's Institutes in promoting community heritage. Period: 1840 - 1976.

3868. Breithaupt, W.H. "The crest of the Waterloo Historical Society." **Waterloo Historical Society.** 1953. 41: 29. ill. Loc: all.

A description and explanation of the crest designed by E.M. Chadwick for the Waterloo Historical Society, quoted from W.H. Breithaupt's address of 1922. Period: 1922 - 1953.

3869. Breithaupt, W.H. "Museum and Publication Committee report." **Waterloo Historical Society.** 1931. 19: 285-287. Loc: all.

Reflections and comments on the current state of local history in the county. More particularly, the author remarks on milestones in the history of Preston and the formative roles of Jacob Hespeler and Otto Klotz. Artifacts and buildings associated with E.W.B. Snider and his ancestors are noted, and also the finding of the remains of a large Indian dug-out canoe in Puslinch Lake. W.H. Breithaupt looks forward to an "adequate Waterloo County Museum" to house these and other artifacts as well as archival materials such as 400 volumes of county newspapers. Period: 1930 - 1931.

3870. Breithaupt, W.H. "Museum report and general historical notes and items." **Waterloo Historical Society.** 1929. 17: 137, 159. Loc: all.

An account of recent acquisitions for exhibition in the Society's Museum, including a chime of horsebells brought by Samuel Bricker in 1802, two volumes of the **Der Deutsche Canadier** for 1844 and 1845, and Bishop Benjamin Eby's family Bible. Period: 1802 - 1845.

3871. Breithaupt, W.H. "President's address, 1914." **Waterloo Historical Society.** 1914. 2: 14-16. Loc: all.

A brief summary of the year's accomplishments of the Waterloo Historical Society, mentioning the various papers given, the celebration of the 100th anniversary of Lundy's Lane, and local reactions to the First World War. Period: 1913 - 1914.

3872. Breithaupt, W.H. "President's address, 1916." **Waterloo Historical Society.** 1916. 4: 7-10. Loc: all.

A summary of the year's events, mentioning the participation of Waterloo County in the First World War, the change of name from Berlin to Kitchener, the centenary of the founding of Abraham Erb's grist mill in Waterloo and the centenary of the founding of Galt in 1816. A brief sketch of the early history of Galt is presented. Period: 1816 - 1916.

3873. Breithaupt, W.H. "President's address, 1918." **Waterloo Historical Society.** 1918. 6: 11-12. Loc: all.

A review of the year's activities, with a note that the annual meeting was postponed by the local Board of Health, with all other public meetings, because of an epidemic of Spanish influenza. Facts about the Guelph-Goderich extension of the Canadian Pacific Railway, omitted in a previous article, are included. Period: 1906 - 1917.

3874. Breithaupt, W.H. "President's address, 1920." **Waterloo Historical Society.** 1920. 8: 108-110. Loc: all.

A summary of the society's activities and donations received. Breithaupt presents family information about Daniel Snyder, first postmaster of Waterloo. Period: 1833 - 1884.

3875. "Brightening the corner." **Waterloo Historical Society.** 1958. 46: 5. Loc: all.

A report by the society's Museum Committee, with a note of the appointment of Nathaniel Stroh as Saturday custodian. Period: 1958 - 1959.

3876. Broome, A.E., Dr. "Ontario Pioneer Community Foundation." **Waterloo Historical Society.** 1960. 48: 51-54. ill. Loc: all.

An address at the opening of the Ontario Pioneer Community Foundation Museum and Administration Building, outlining the planning and development of the project. Period: 1952 - 1960.

3877. Broome, A.E., Dr. "Provincial rural life museum." **Waterloo Historical Society.** 1953. 41: 31-40. ill. Loc: all.

Proposal for an Ontario rural life museum in Waterloo County presented to the Minister of Agriculture by a committee of the Waterloo Historical Society. The paper proposes the Homer Watson Memorial Park as the location, and outlines the contents of the collection. A map and aerial photograph are included, with appendices pertaining to the Huron Road and the Grand River. Period: 1953.

3878. **Canada's Diamond Jubilee 1867-1927: joint celebration in Kitchener- Waterloo Collegiate Institute campus, Friday, July 1st 1927.** 1927. 3 p. Loc: OWTUR.

A programme of the celebrations organized jointly by Kitchener and Waterloo. Special events included concerts, athletic events and speeches. Period: 1867 - 1927.

3879. "Catalog of Waterloo Historical Society museum [1917]." **Waterloo Historical Society.** 1917. 5: 65-67. Loc: all.

A systematic list of the articles, books, documents, maps, newspapers and pictures that had been donated to the Society's museum during its first five years. Period: 1800 - 1916.

3880. "Catalog of Waterloo Historical Society museum: additions 1918-1922." **Waterloo Historical Society.** 1922. 10: 267-269. Loc: all.

A systematic list of artifacts, books, documents, maps, newspapers and pictures that had been added to the Society's museum during the previous five years. Period: 1918 - 1922.

3881. "Catalog of Waterloo Historical Society museum: additions 1923-1927." **Waterloo Historical Society**. 1927. 15: 393-394. Loc: all.

A systematic list of artifacts, books, documents, maps, newspapers and pictures that had been given to the Society's museum during the previous five years. Period: 1923 - 1927.

3882. "Catalog of Waterloo Historical Society museum [to 1932]." **Waterloo Historical Society**. 1932. 20: 339-348. Loc: all.

A full list of artifacts, books, documents, maps, newspapers, and photographs that had been given to or acquired by the Society's museum over the previous 20 years. Period: 1913 - 1932.

3883. "Charter members for half a century." **Waterloo Historical Society**. 1962. 50: 7. Loc: all.

Brief biographies of the three charter members of the society still living in 1962: W.W. Snider, D.A. Bean and Louis L. Lang. Period: 1912 - 1962.

3884. "Church, school, and burying ground." **Waterloo Historical Society**. 1969. 57: 19. ill. Loc: all.

A photograph of Henry Bowman examining the Waterloo Historical Society plaque that marks the site of a community meeting house, school, and burial ground at the southern edge of Hespeler. The land for the buildings was donated in 1829 by Samuel Bechtel. Period: 1829 - 1929.

3885. "Clansmen donate landmark to Doon Pioneer Village." **Waterloo Historical Society**. 1969. 57: 60. Loc: all.

A note of the donation by the Grand River Branch of Clan Donald of a log cabin built by Scottish settlers in 1859 and originally situated near Puslinch Lake. Period: 1859 - 1969.

3886. "Constitution and by-laws of the Waterloo Historical Society." **Waterloo Historical Society**. 1914. 2: 9-11. Loc: all.

The constitution and by-laws adopted in 1914, stating one of the society's objectives to be the "collection, preservation, exhibition and publication of material pertaining to the history of the County of Waterloo." Period: 1914.

3887. Coulthard, Elizabeth. "Historical tour of south Waterloo." **York Pioneer and Historical Society**. 1970. Pp. 14-21. ill., map. Loc: OGU, OWTU.

Report of a bus tour of Galt and North Dumfries taken by members of the Toronto group and led by Andrew Taylor, a past president of the Waterloo Historical Society. Period: 1816 - 1969.

3888. Cranston, W.H. "Compulsory rearview mirrors." **Waterloo Historical Society**. 1955. 43: 10-22. Loc: all.

Reflections on the need for awareness of the past in understanding the present, with comments on the current state of libraries, museums, archaeological research and historical societies. The author refers to anecdotes about his ancestor Robert Cranston, a pioneer settler in Dumfries, and later generations of his family. Period: 1831 - 1931.

3889. Cranston, W.H. "Publicizing Ontario's history." **Waterloo Historical Society**. 1960. 48: 56-64. ill. Loc: all.

An address meditating on the pleasures and problems of local history, with particular reference to Waterloo County.

3890. Cruikshank, E.A. "An address on turning the first sod of the Pioneer Monument, Waterloo County Pioneers' Memorial, Schoerg Farm, near Kitchener, Ontario, 24th June, 1924." **Ontario Historical Society, Papers and Records**. 1925. 22: 89-91. Loc: OWTL, OWTU.

Text of a speech about the qualities of the first Mennonite settlers of Waterloo County, and announcing that the Department of the Interior would provide a tablet for the Pioneer Monument. Period: 1800 - 1924.

3891. "Dedication of the Young Memorial Chapel [WRP]." **Waterloo Historical Society**. 1929. 17: 140. ill. Loc: all.

A note of the formal presentation to the City of Galt of the Young Memorial Chapel in Galt Cemetery, in memory of the late Hon. James Young and his wife. Period: 1929.

3892. Dickson, F.W.R. "Waterloo 1857-1957." **Waterloo Historical Society**. 1957. 45: 53-63. ill. Loc: all.

A detailed account of the festivities marking the centennial of incorporation as a village, including the unveiling of a plaque honouring Abraham Erb as founder of the community. Period: 1857 - 1957.

3893. "Donations received in 1913." **Waterloo Historical Society**. 1913. 1: 19. ill. Loc: all.

A list of donations received in 1913, including a settlers' wagon driven by Abraham Weber from Lancaster County, Pennsylvania. Period: 1804 - 1913.

3894. "Donations received in 1914." **Waterloo Historical Society**. 1914. 2: 51. Loc: all.

A list of donations received in 1914, including Indian objects, mounted animals and birds, photographs, some Lovell's Directories and various newspaper volumes. Period: 1841 - 1913.

3895. "Donations received in 1915." **Waterloo Historical Society**. 1915. 3: 31. Loc: all.

A list of newspapers, photographs and artifacts donated in 1915, including the Galines 1670 map and shells manufactured by Goldie-McCulloch and Canadian Buffalo Forge Company. Period: 1835 - 1915.

3896. "Donations received in 1916." **Waterloo Historical Society**. 1916. 4: 38. ill. Loc: all.

List of newspapers, photographs, maps, and a lithograph donated in 1916. Of special interest is the first volume of the **Canada Museum**, loaned by Alexander Peterson of Hawkesville. The donated lithograph of Preston in 1856 is reproduced at the front of the 1917 volume. Period: 1835 - 1916.

3897. "Donations received in 1917." **Waterloo Historical Society**. 1917. 5: 64. Loc: all.

List of donations received in 1917, including newspapers, books, photographs, a retting tool for flax and old-style dentist tools. Period: 1819 - 1916.

3898. "Doon Pioneer Village 1968." **Waterloo Historical Society**. 1968. 56: 82-83. Loc: all.

A report on current acquisitions including the Petersburg Railway Station and the frame building that had served as a Wellesley Post Office. Period: 1967 - 1968.

3899. "Doon Pioneer Village 1970." **Waterloo Historical Society**. 1970. 58: 82-84. ill. Loc: all.

A report of programmes and exhibits, including photographs of a display of stoves and of a telephone switchboard. Period: 1969 - 1970.

3900. "First citizen: Doon Pioneer Village." **Waterloo Historical Society**. 1961. 49: 49. ill. Loc: all.

A photograph of Frank E. Page and Dr and Mrs Albert E. Broome examining the certificate that honours Dr Broome as the first citizen of Doon Pioneer Village.

3901. Fisher, P. "The Waterloo Historical Society Museum." **Western Ontario Historical Notes**. 1944. 2: 11-13. Loc: OWTL, OWTU.

A description of the museum in the fireproof room of Kitchener Public Library. The author, secretary of the Society for about 30 years, refers to the large collections of Waterloo County

newspapers, maps and plans, family bibles in German, deeds, and artifacts including Indian relics. Period: 1912 - 1944.

3902. "The formation of the Waterloo Historical Society [WRP]." **Waterloo Historical Society**. 1913. 1: 5-7. Loc: all.

Report of the public meeting in Berlin on 13 November 1912, establishing the society for the purpose of studying and preserving local history. W.H. Breithaupt was elected President, Rev. Theobald Spetz Vice-President, and R.G. Wood Secretary-Treasurer. Period: 1912 - 1913.

3903. "The fortieth annual meeting, November 7, 1952." **Waterloo Historical Society**. 1952. 40: 8-9. Loc: all.

A brief review of the society's achievements during the previous 40 years. The president, Mrs T.D. Cowan, notes the need for more members and a greater interest in the welfare of the museum. Period: 1912 - 1952.

3904. Groh, Anson. "Address at unveiling of memorial tablet." **Waterloo Historical Society**. 1929. 17: 137-138. Loc: all.

A brief account of the establishment of the first meeting house, school and cemetery in the Hespeler-Preston area in 1829, and the marking of this event 100 years later by the Waterloo Historical Society. Period: 1829 - 1929.

3905. Groh, Howard. "Progress at the Pioneer Village in 1963." **Waterloo Historical Society**. 1963. 51: 86. Loc: all.

A progress report on the past year's events at Doon Pioneer Village, describing the increase in attendance and revenue. New buildings erected and new displays are also mentioned. Period: 1963 - 1964.

3906. Hagler, Ronald. "Waterloo Historical Society Museum." **Waterloo Historical Society**. 1954. 42: 18. Loc: all.

A report on the state of the museum by its curator, noting that was still housed in the Kitchener Public Library but might move to the proposed Ontario Pioneer Museum. Period: 1954 - 1955.

3907. Hansuld, Kathryn. "Waterloo County centennial." **Ontario History**. 1953. 45,1: 43-44. ill. Loc: OKIT, OWTL, OWTU.

An account of the re-enactment of the 500-mile trek by conestoga wagon from Lancaster County to Waterloo and the historical pageant by B. Mabel Dunham entitled **The trail of the Conestoga**. Period: 1800 - 1953.

3908. Hebblethwaite, Katherine. "Pioneer Pergola, Galt." **Waterloo Historical Society**. 1964. 52: 79-82. Loc: all.

A report of research on the 207 headstones dating from 1835 to 1873 and incorporated in the pergola raised by the Waterloo Chapter of the I.O.D.E. in 1907. The pergola is set in a small park on the site of St Andrew's Kirk, the second church built in Galt. Period: 1835 - 1873.

3909. High, Norman H. and Bergey, Lorna L. and Coffman, Barbara F. "Brief histories of the society and its chapters." **Canadian-German Folklore**. 1971. 4: 6-13. ill. Loc: OKIT, OWTL, OWTU, OWTUCG.

A short history of the society, founded in 1951 to promote understanding of Ontario's Pennsylvania German heritage, with reports from the Niagara, York and Waterloo chapters. Period: 1951 - 1971.

3910. High, Norman H. "A point of view of history." **Waterloo Historical Society**. 1960. 48: 24-33. ill. Loc: all.

An address on the role and importance of local history, with reference to the Waterloo Historical Society. It includes two photographs, one of the society's museum in the Kitchener Public Library, the other showing the move from the library in 1960. Period: 1960.

3911. Hoffman, Bob. "Conestoga history repeats itself." **Waterloo Historical Society**. 1970. 58: 75-78. ill. Loc: all.

A description of the making of an identical replica of a conestoga wagon in the Wood Products Technician Course of Conestoga College of Applied Arts and Technology. Period: 1968 - 1970.

3912. Hoffman, Susan. "Historical research workshop." **Waterloo Historical Society**. 1982. 70: 52. Loc: all.

A short account of the workshop on the basics of historical research, sponsored by the Waterloo Historical Society and the Ontario Historical Society. Period: 1982.

3913. Hughes, Paul and Hughes, Marie. "Museums of Ontario." **Waterloo Historical Society**. 1956. 44: 37-42. ill. Loc: all.

Text of an address describing some local museums in Ontario and mentioning the Waterloo County Museum in the Kitchener Library. Period: 1956.

3914. Jackson, Alison. "Progress at Doon continues." **Waterloo Historical Society**. 1983. 71: 10-14. Loc: all.

A review of the administration of Doon Pioneer Village since its conception in 1952, including

responsibility for funding, upkeep and development. The author refers to the Waterloo Region Review Commission Report (1978), the Doon Master Plan Study (1979) and the Scott Report (1981). Period: 1952 - 1983.

3915. Janzen, Elizabeth. "The Ontario Pioneer Community Foundation." **Waterloo Historical Society**. 1954. 42: 44-46. Loc: all.

The minutes of the inaugural meeting of the foundation, naming officers, directors and committee chairmen. Period: 1954.

3916. Jones, Louis C. "Ontario Pioneer Community Foundation." **Waterloo Historical Society**. 1959. 47: 51-59. Loc: all.

An address delivered to members of the foundation, with observations and advice on their museum. Period: 1953 - 1959.

3917. Lamb, Kathryn Hansuld and Taylor, Andrew W. and Stauch, Warren. "Ontario Historical Society meets in Waterloo." **Waterloo Historical Society**. 1972. 60: 95-97. Loc: all.

A report of the meeting held in June 1972 at the University of Waterloo. The conference programme included bus tours of the county, slide presentations and lectures on such topics as historic buildings, the temperance movement, and ancestors in Ontario. Period: 1972.

3918. Lamb, Kathryn Hansuld. "Waterloo Regional Heritage Foundation, 1974." **Waterloo Historical Society**. 1974. 62: 4-6. ill. Loc: all.

A report of the first annual meeting of the foundation in February 1975. Projects supported by the foundation are noted: the addition to Wellesley Township Hall at Crosshill; the colloquium celebrating the 100th anniversary of the birth of William Lyon Mackenzie in 1974; the scenic roads study; and the purchase of the Joseph Schneider house (1820), the Peter Martin house (1820), the Brubacher house (1850) and the Meyer house (1852). Period: 1974.

3919. Lamb, Kathryn Hansuld. "Waterloo Regional Heritage Foundation, 1977." **Waterloo Historical Society**. 1977. 65: 111-112. Loc: all.

A report of the foundation's annual meeting in April 1978 at the John E. Brubacher House, Waterloo. Items included the award to Mr and Mrs David Hysinger for restoring the farmhouse on West River Road in Cambridge, the Joseph Schneider House Committee feasibility study of 1977, the Historic Building Inventory project, and sharing the cost of plaques with local LACACs. Period: 1977.

3920. Lamb, Kathryn Hansuld. "Waterloo Regional Heritage Foundation, 1973." **Waterloo Historical Society.** 1973. 61: 34. Loc: all.

A description of the non-profit foundation, formed in 1973 to assist in the preservation of the region's heritage, including landmarks, historic sites, material culture and traditions. Period: 1973.

3921. Lamb, Kathryn Hansuld. "Waterloo Regional Heritage Foundation, 1975." **Waterloo Historical Society.** 1975. 63: 75-76. ill. Loc: all.

A report of the annual meeting in February 1976. Among the items discussed are the restoration of the University of Waterloo's John E. Brubacher house, efforts to stop the demolition of the Preston Public School, and the use of the Joseph Schneider house as an educational museum. Period: 1975.

3922. Lamb, Kathryn Hansuld. "The Women's Institute's priceless gift: community histories." **Canadian-German Folklore.** 1975. 5: 11-12. ill. Loc: OKIT, OWT, OWTL, OWTU, OWTUCG.

An article reprinted from the **Kitchener-Waterloo Record** of 17 May 1966, highlighting the value to local, provincial and national history of the Tweedsmuir books compiled by branches of the Women's Institutes. Period: 1946 - 1966.

3923. "Life members of the Waterloo Historical Society." **Waterloo Historical Society.** 1962. 50: 108. Loc: all.

A list of over one hundred life members of the society. Period: 1961 - 1962.

3924. "Membership fee increase [WRP]." **Waterloo Historical Society.** 1963. 51: 82. Loc: all.

A notice that the annual fee of the Waterloo Historical Society was increasing to two dollars in 1965, and that the life membership was increasing to fifty dollars in 1963. Period: 1963 - 1965.

3925. "Memorial cairn unveiled in Blair Cemetery." **Waterloo Historical Society.** 1970. 58: 34. Loc: all.

A note of the cairn unveiled on the site of the cemetery's first grave, that of eight-year-old John Bricker, son of John and Annie Erb Bricker, who died in 1804. Period: 1804 - 1970.

3926. "New buildings at Doon Pioneer Village." **Waterloo Historical Society.** 1969. 57: 58-59. ill. Loc: all.

A report of the move to Doon of the Petersburg Railway Station and the Wellesley Post Office and Library. Period: 1856 - 1969.

3927. Oberholtzer, R.S. "At the Doon Pioneer Village in 1967." **Waterloo Historical Society.** 1967. 55: 41-43. ill. Loc: all.

A note of the dedication of a replica of the 1857 Waterloo Township Hall, the presentation of a sawmill by the Pannill Veneer Co. Ltd, and the moving of Limerick Cemetery to an adjoining site. Period: 1897 - 1967.

3928. "Ontario Historical Society, 1960." **Waterloo Historical Society.** 1960. 48: 16. Loc: all.

A report on the annual meeting of the society which took place in Preston. Two plaques were unveiled, one to commemorate John Erb, the founder of Preston, and the other in memory of Benjamin Eby, a founder of Berlin. Period: 1959 - 1960.

3929. "The Ontario Pioneer Community: an outdoor museum." **Waterloo Historical Society.** 1957. 45: 13-15. ill. Loc: all.

A report on the progress of construction of the Ontario Pioneer Community at Doon. Period: 1957.

3930. "Organization of the Waterloo County Pioneers' Memorial Association." **Waterloo Historical Society.** 1926. 14: 202-203. Loc: all.

An appendix to the annual report noting the organization of the Pioneers' Memorial Association and the planning of the Memorial Tower at the site of the old Betzner homestead. The inscription on the Memorial Tower is quoted. Period: 1800 - 1926.

3931. Panabaker, D.N. "Address of the President, Waterloo County Pioneers' Memorial Association, turning-the-sod exercises, June 24, 1924." **Ontario Historical Society, Papers and Records.** 1925. 22: 182-185. Loc: OWTL, OWTU.

A speech delivered to officers of the Ontario Historical Society by the Mayor of Hespeler, describing plans for the monument to be erected on the farm of Samuel Betzner Sr, the Mennonite pioneer who came to Waterloo Township in 1800. Period: 1799 - 1924.

3932. Panabaker, D.N. "Ontario and Michigan Historical Societies." **Waterloo Historical Society.** 1938. 26: 38-40. Loc: all.

A brief report of the joint meeting of the societies that the author attended with W.H. Breithaupt on behalf of the Waterloo Historical Society. He reflects that anyone perusing the printed reports of the Waterloo Historical Society over the previous 25 years "will be impressed with the fact that ... this effort has been to pursue the history of our own and other sections of Canada with a spirit of intimacy and living over again the experiences of our forbears ... [and to] make it possible for the younger generations ... to extend their imaginative powers ... and sense the significance of the historic background out of which the present has come and from which the future will undoubtedly take shape." Period: 1913 - 1937.

3933. Panabaker, D.N. "A tribute to the pioneers." **Waterloo Historical Society**. 1926. 14: 212-216. Loc: all.

A speech at the dedication of the Memorial Tower in honour of the first settlers of the county, Joseph Schoerg and Samuel Betzner, Jr. The author also refers to the people involved in planning the memorial, W.H. Breithaupt, Allan A. Eby, David B. Betzner, Allan C. Hallman, John Fox and W.A. Langton (Architect). Period: 1800 - 1926.

3934. "Peter McArthur Cabin, Doon Pioneer Village." **Waterloo Historical Society**. 1963. 51: 87. ill. Loc: all.

An illustrated description of the Peter McArthur House, a log cabin reconstructed at Doon Pioneer Village. Period: 1963.

3935. "Philatelic covers of the 1952 trek." **Waterloo Historical Society**. 1952. 40: 17. ill. Loc: all.

A short account of the six special envelopes with a cancellation commemorating the Waterloo County Centennial. Period: 1952.

3936. Pitcher, Rosemary. "Waterloo County Centennial." **Waterloo Historical Society**. 1952. 40: 11-12. ill. Loc: all.

An account of the celebrations which took place early July 1952, including the trip made from Pennsylvania by Lorne Weber and Amzie Martin in a conestoga wagon, a revived Saengerfest, and re-enactments of the past based on Mabel Dunham's book **The Grand River**. The author names many people involved in organizing the festival. Period: 1852 - 1952.

3937. "Progress at the Pioneer Village in 1962." **Waterloo Historical Society**. 1962. 50: 95. ill. Loc: all.

A note of the unveiling of a plaque in honour of Joseph Brant, chief of the Six Nations Indians. Period: 1962.

3938. "Progress continues at Pioneer Village." **Waterloo Historical Society**. 1965. 53: 10-11. Loc: all.

A note of the pioneer butcher shop donated by J.M. Schneider Ltd to Doon Pioneer Village in 1965, with photographs showing the shop's fireplace and the exterior of the building as it was being reconstructed at the village. Period:

1890 - 1965.

3939. "Publication Committee acknowledges help [WRP]." **Waterloo Historical Society**. 1962. 50: 22. Loc: all.

Various volunteers and the **Kitchener-Waterloo Record** are thanked for helping to prepare the 1962 report. Period: 1962.

3940. Roddick, Madaline. "A bus trip to Waterloo County." **Waterloo Historical Society**. 1962. 50: 6. Loc: all.

A note of a field trip to Galt and Doon arranged by Andrew W. Taylor for the London and Middlesex Historical Society. Period: 1961 - 1962.

3941. Roy, Flora. "Imagination in history." **Waterloo Historical Society**. 1952. 40: 33-37. Loc: all.

An address by the head of the English Department, Waterloo College on the need to interweave literature and history in order to make history come alive for the future generations. Dr Donalda Dickie, a native of the county, is praised as a writer who has accomplished this in her work. Period: 1852 - 1952.

3942. Schmalz, W.H.E. **A dream come true: a chronological story of Doon Pioneer Village**. 197-?. 20 p. Loc: OKIT, OWTUR.

A narrative of the process of realizing the dream of Dr A.E. Broome to establish a pioneer village, on the model of one he visited in Arnhem, Holland. Organizations instrumental in creating the Ontario Pioneer Community Foundation included the Waterloo Historical Society, the Doon School of Fine Arts, the Waterloo County Council, Kitchener City Council, Federation of Agriculture, Ministry of Agriculture. The plans, donations, acquisitions and exhibits are described, and all officers are listed for the years 1952 to 1974. The text of Dr Broome's speech at the opening of the museum in 1960 is also included. Period: 1952 - 1974.

3943. Schmalz, W.H.E. and Stokes, Peter and Broome, A.E., Dr. **The Ontario Pioneer Community Foundation and Doon Pioneer Village**. 1978. 1 v. (unpaged). Loc: OKIT.

Collected material about the Ontario Pioneer Community Foundation which operated the Doon Pioneer Village, subsequently known as Doon Heritage Crossroads. Items include a speech given by Dr A.E. Broome in 1960 at the opening of the Administration Building, a chronological history of the foundation from 1952 to 1974 by W.H.E. Schmalz entitled **A Dream come true**, the by-law enacting the foundation, and a report by Peter Stokes in 1978 that makes particular reference to the Erb House, the Martin House and the Bricker Barn. Period: 1952 - 1978.

3944. Schmalz, W.H.E. "Ontario Pioneer Community Foundation." **Waterloo Historical Society**. 1963. 51: 83-86. ill. Loc: all.

A brief history of the foundation from 1953 to 1963, listing the first board members and all presidents and naming the various societies represented at the original meeting. Period: 1953 - 1963.

3945. Schmidt, Grace. "Half-a-century with the Waterloo Historical Society." **Waterloo Historical Society**. 1962. 50: 12-16. Loc: all.

A history of the first fifty years of the Waterloo Historical Society, describing its foundation in 1912 and listing all presidents and secretaries. Period: 1912 - 1962.

3946. Schmidt, Grace. "Joseph Schneider House opened." **Waterloo Historical Society**. 1981. 69: 88-90. ill. Loc: all.

An account of the opening of the living museum portraying the life of a Pennsylvania-German family in Berlin in the 1850s. Background information is also given about the Schneider family and the creation of the museum. Period: 1850 - 1981.

3947. **Sesquicentennial of the Amish Mennonites of Ontario: programme [and] 150 years**. Edited by Dorothy M. Sauder. Western Ontario Mennonite Conference, 1972. 50 p. ill., maps. Loc: OKIT, OKITW, OWRND, OWTL, OWTU, OWTUCG, OWTUR, OKEBC.

A souvenir of the sesquicentennial events held in New Hamburg, celebrating the settlement and development of the Amish in the region. Lifestyles, customs, religion, language and dress are surveyed in the main section by Lorraine Roth. The item includes the text for the pageant, **This land is ours** by Urie Bender and the oratorio, **Martyrs mirror Ontario** by Alice Parker and John Ruth. Period: 1822 - 1972.

3948. Silcox, A. Phillips. "Three days in a squirrel cage! (impressions of the August Institute and seminar)." **The Ontario Genealogical Society**. 1966. 5,3: 76-77. ill. Loc: OWTU.

A report on the society's first conference, held at the University of Waterloo's Student Village which was still under contruction. Period: 1965 - 1966.

3949. "The St Agatha Memorial." **Waterloo Historical Society**. 1935. 23: 175-176. ill. Loc: all.

Description of the dedication of the St Agatha Memorial, marking the site of the log cabin in which St Jerome's College was started by Father Louis Funcken. Period: 1864 - 1935.

3950. "Steam fire engine loaned to Pioneer Village." **Waterloo Historical Society**. 1964. 52: 71-72. ill. Loc: all.

A short description of the horse-drawn machine built about 1867 and used in New Hamburg until the 1930s. Period: 1867 - 1964.

3951. "Thresher donated to Doon Pioneer Village [WRP]." **Waterloo Historical Society**. 1962. 50: 9. Loc: all.

A note of the donation by F.C. Taylor of the Waterloo Manufacturing Company Ltd of an 1885 thresher and an 1895 ensilage chopper. Period: 1961 - 1962.

3952. "The trail of the Conestoga." **Waterloo Historical Society**. 1969. 57: 31. Loc: all.

A note that, during the Twin Cities Heritage Festival in June 1969, the Mennonite Historical Society of Ontario presented a dramatization of B. Mabel Dunham's book. Period: 1969.

3953. "Wanted." **Waterloo Historical Society**. 1962. 50: 16. Loc: all.

A note reminding members that the Archives Committee of the Waterloo Historical Society is always eager for material. Period: 1962.

3954. Waterloo County Centennial Committee. **The trail of the Conestoga: Waterloo County centennial 1852-1952**. The Committee, 1952. 20 p. ill., map. Loc: OWTUR, OWTL, OCCA, OWRE, OWTUCR.

A programme published for the county's centennial event, an outdoor musical show based on Mabel Dunham's story **The Grand River**. Featured throughout the booklet is the work of artist Selwyn Dewdney, whose murals depict the history, settlement and development of the county. The county's insurance industry is briefly described. Period: 1852 - 1952.

3955. "Waterloo County Centennial projects." **Waterloo Historical Society**. 1967. 55: 86-88. ill. Loc: all.

A list of publishing projects and special events planned in the county to celebrate Canada's centennial. Period: 1966 - 1967.

3956. Waterloo County Pioneers' Memorial Association. **1800-1926: Souvenir programme, Pioneer Memorial Monument, erected to the memory of the early pioneers of Waterloo County, dedicated August 28, 1926.** Kitchener: The Association, 1926. 1 folded sheet. ill. Loc: OWTUR, OKITW.

A programme giving a short history of the Waterloo County Pioneers' Memorial Association, the text of the inscription on the tablet at the Memorial Tower, and a summary of the day's events. Period: 1800 - 1926.

3957. "The Waterloo County Pioneers' Memorial Tower." **Waterloo Historical Society.** 1926. 14: 185. Loc: all.

A short description of the dedication of the tower in August 1926, on the Grand River opposite the village of Doon. Period: 1924 - 1926.

3958. "Waterloo Historical Society acknowledges help [WRP]." **Waterloo Historical Society.** 1961. 49: 63. Loc: all.

A brief note of thanks to all those who helped prepare the 1961 report. Period: 1961.

3959. "Waterloo Historical Society: annual members." **Waterloo Historical Society.** 1913. 1: 20. Loc: all.

A list of 57 founding members of the Society, with their places of residence. Forty-one resided in Berlin, eight in Conestogo, four in Galt, and one in each of Elmira, Baden, New Dundee and Toronto. All names have been indexed in the WRP database. Period: 1912 - 1913.

3960. "Waterloo Historical Society: annual members." **Waterloo Historical Society.** 1914. 2: 52-53. Loc: all.

A list of 79 members of the Society, with their places of residence. The 25 new members (not listed as founding members in 1913) have been indexed in the WRP database. Period: 1913 - 1914.

3961. Waterloo Historical Society. **Annual report: 1st (1913) - 44th (1956); continued by Annual volume, 45th (1957) - .** 1913- . Loc: all.

A record of the society's activities in collecting, preserving, exhibiting and publishing material relating to Waterloo County. This source provides detailed information about all localities in Waterloo County and includes many photographs and maps. Early reports print the text of addresses to general meetings, while later volumes consist of articles and notes requested or submitted for publication. From a 20-page booklet in 1913, the annual report has an average of 60 pages in the 1920s. Cut back by the 1930s depression, the average length is around 50 pages

each year until the 1950s. Annual volumes grow in size from 80 pages in 1960 to 90 pages in the mid-1960s and over 150 pages during the 1980s. Nearly 1,300 articles and notes published between 1913 and 1990 have been fully abstracted and indexed in the Waterloo Regional Project's database. The project's **Waterloo Historical Society Bibliography,** printed in a limited first edition in 1991, provides annotated references to all these items, as well as indexes of authors, subject headings, places, personal subjects and corporate subjects, and a cumulative table of contents, 1913-1990. Period: 1913 - 1990.

3962. "Waterloo Historical Society constitution and by-laws." **Waterloo Historical Society.** 1971. 59: 89-92. Loc: all.

The constitution of the society, adopted in November 1971. An earlier constitution was printed in the 1914 annual report. Period: 1971.

3963. "Waterloo Historical Society: list of members." **Waterloo Historical Society.** 1915. 3: 32-33. Loc: all.

A list of the 94 annual members with their places of residence, together with the names of the mayors and county councillors who received copies of the annual report. Period: 1914 - 1915.

3964. "Waterloo Historical Society: list of members." **Waterloo Historical Society.** 1916. 4: 39-40. Loc: all.

A list of the 104 annual members with their places of residence, together with names of mayors and county councillors who were members ex officio. Of the annual members, 49 had Kitchener addresses, 16 lived in Galt, 10 in Waterloo, 7 in Elmira, 6 in St Jacobs, 4 in Preston, 3 in each of Hespeler and New Hamburg, 2 in Ayr and one each in Conestogo and Haysville. Period: 1915 - 1916.

3965. "Waterloo Historical Society: list of members." **Waterloo Historical Society.** 1919. 7: 102-104. Loc: all.

A list of the annual members, with their places of residence, together with the names of mayors and county councillors who were members ex officio. Of the 108 annual members, 56 were listed as Kitchener residents, 12 lived in Galt, 13 in Waterloo, 5 in Elmira, 3 in St Jacobs, 4 in Hespeler, 5 in New Hamburg, 3 in Preston, 2 in Ayr and one each in Conestogo, Hawkesville and Wellesley. Period: 1918 - 1919.

3966. "Waterloo Historical Society Reports: corrections." **Waterloo Historical Society.** 1970. 58: 87. Loc: all.

A list of corrections from volume 35 (1947) to

volume 57 (1969). Three volumes are reported to
have been incorrectly dated: volume 35 should be
dated 1947, volume 36 should be 1948, and volume
53 should be 1965. Period: 1947 - 1970.

3967. Watson, Elizabeth Dolman. "Exhibition of pioneer
articles: Ayr, October 20th, 1933." **Waterloo
Historical Society**. 1933. 21: 8-10. Loc: all.
A brief description of the over 700 items
exhibited at the Ayr Public Library in connection
with the annual meeting of the Waterloo Historical
Society. The pieces included furniture, bibles
(English, German and Gaelic), shawls, woven
quilts, tools of all kinds, guns, laundry irons,
candle-sticks, brass and copper pots and kettles,
glass, china, silver, jewellery, snuff-boxes and
old pictures. Period: 1800 - 1900.

3968. Weber, Lorne B. "The trek of the conestoga, 1952."
Waterloo Historical Society. 1952. 40: 13-16.
Loc: all.
An account of the trip made by Lorne Weber and
Amzie Martin on a conestoga wagon to commemorate
the coming of the Mennonites from Pennsylvania in
the early 1800s. Period: 1952.

GOVERNMENT AND POLITICS

DEFINITION OF AREAS AND JURISDICTIONS IN FIRST HALF OF 19TH CENTURY

3969. Armstrong, Frederick H. **Handbook of Upper Canadian chronology**. Toronto: Dundurn Press, 1985. 278 p. index. Loc: OCH, OKIT, OWTL, OWTU.

A compilation of dates, legislation, names and statistics relating to the organization and administration of Upper Canada before about 1850. Part V provides information on the formation and functions of townships, counties, districts, towns and cities while Part VII includes details of corporate legislation and ecclesiastical organization. All counties are listed with their dates of creation and all townships with dates of Indian alienation, first survey, first legal settler and area in acres. For the Gore and Wellington Districts which included the Waterloo County area before 1852, there are lists of clerks of peace, sheriffs, treasurers, district court judges, surrogate court judges, inspectors of licences, schoolmasters, wardens and clerks of the district council. All post offices of Upper Canada are listed with their opening dates and all provincial land surveyors with their appointment dates. Five maps show the original districts of 1788, 1802, 1836 and 1841 and the formation of the county system in 1851. Period: 1788 - 1867.

3970. Cowan, Jennie F. "The grateful hearts of 1852." **Waterloo Historical Society**. 1952. 40: 50-53. Loc: all.

An address by the president of the Waterloo Historical Society commemorating the first meeting of the Waterloo County Council on 3 May 1852. The author surveys events leading to the formation of Waterloo County and the election of Dr John Scott of Berlin as the first Warden. Period: 1852 - 1952.

3971. Cowan, Jennie F. "The year 1852 in the history of Ontario, (Upper Canada) and of Waterloo County." **Waterloo Historical Society**. 1951. 39: 7-11. Loc: all.

A short history of the territorial divisions of Upper Canada and the events leading to the formation of Waterloo County in 1852. Period: 1837 - 1852.

3972. Dickson, F.W.R. "Waterloo County before 1852." **Waterloo Historical Society**. 1963. 51: 44-50. map. Loc: all.

A summary of the early geographical and political divisions of the territory that later became Waterloo County. W.H. Smith's gazetteer is quoted for descriptions of the stage of development of some communities in 1851. Period: 1800 - 1852.

3973. Fisher, P. "First meeting of Waterloo County Council, copied from **Deutsche Canadien** [sic]." **Waterloo Historical Society**. 1951. 39: 11-14. ill. Loc: all.

An account of the meeting on 3 May 1852, from **Der Deutsche Canadier**, with a list of those who attended the meeting, and a summary of the address by Dr John Scott, newly elected Warden. Period: 1852.

3974. Hillman, Thomas A. "A statutory chronology of southwestern Ontario, 1792 to 1981: Waterloo County." **Canadian Papers in Rural History**. Edited by Donald H. Akenson. Gananoque: Langdale Press, 1988. Pp. 343-350. Loc: OWTL, OWTU, OWTUSJ.

An outline of the evolution of the boundaries and dates of incorporation of various counties, townships, villages, towns, cities, and police villages, with details of all relevant statutes and proclamations. The chronology begins in 1838 when County of Waterloo was separated from the County of Halton for electoral and militia purposes but was within the Wellington District for judicial and administrative functions. In 1850, Waterloo County was defined to include most of the townships that had previously been grouped in Wellington District, but the county town remained in Guelph. In 1852, the five townships of Waterloo County were separated from what became Wellington and Grey counties. The main provisions of the Act to establish the Regional Municipality of Waterloo in 1973 and to restructure local government by amalgamating some of the smaller municipal units are also summarized. Period: 1838 - 1973.

3975. Johansson, Eric. "Districts and counties of Southern Ontario, 1777-1979." **Families**. 1981. 20: 91-102. ill., maps. Loc: OKIT, OWTL, OWTU.

A useful summary, well illustrated with maps, of changes in the territorial organization of southern Ontario since the first white settlement. Period: 1777 - 1979.

3976. Newcombe, Hiram K. "June 29, 1852! Forty-ninth anniversary of the corner stone laying of our court house and jail: a hot time in the old town forty-nine years ago, a memorable day of feasting, speech making, toast, societies, marching, etc.." **Newcombe's Monthly Rural Sketches**. 1900, June. Pp. 23-25. Loc: OKITW.

A reprint of a newspaper article by the author,

describing the events leading up to the construction of the Waterloo County Court House, and the opening celebrations. Period: 1852 - 1900.

3977. Panabaker, D.N. "Organization and early political history of what is now Waterloo County." **Waterloo Historical Society**. 1930. 18: 213-218. Loc: all.

A short account of early political organization. Period: 1825 - c1865.

3978. Panabaker, D.N. "President's address: Waterloo County eighty years ago." **Waterloo Historical Society**. 1932. 20: 298-308. Loc: all.

A brief account of the county at the time of its incorporation in 1853, including a list of members of the first county council and a note of their administrative duties. Period: 1853.

3979. Waterloo County Council. **By-laws of the County of Waterloo from the date of its incorporation in 1852 to the year 1900**. Berlin: Gospel Banner Office, 1900. 107 p. Loc: OWTLR, OKITW.

A compilation including lists of wardens and their addresses, county councillors and the years they served, a schedule of 502 by-laws, by-laws printed in full with an index, notes on county council divisions, and a list of 29 bridges (stating lengths, building materials, locations and names). Period: 1852 - 1900.

3980. Waterloo County Council. **Journal of proceedings and by-laws of the municipal council of the County of Waterloo**. 1851 - 1972. Loc: OKITW, OWRE, OWTUR.

Annual printed copies of Waterloo County Council minutes, by-laws, lists of officials, and the reports of various committees such as Education, Roads and Bridges, Finance, and Standing Rules and Regulations. The length of the journal varies from year to year, as does the number of committees reporting. The University of Waterloo has journals for 1851, 1853, 1857, 1875, 1879, 1882, 1892, 1893, 1894 and 1900. Journals for the years 1852 to 1857, 1861, 1864 to 1867, 1869, 1870, 1872, 1873, 1875 to 1879, 1881 to 1889, 1891, 1893 to 1917, 1920 to 1923 and all years from 1926 to 1972 are held in the Waterloo Historical Society collection at the Kitchener Public Library. The Elmira Library has a microfilm copy. Period: 1851 - 1900.

3981. Waterloo County Council. **Standing rules and regulations of the Council of the Corporation of the County of Waterloo, as revised and adopted by the Council, January 28th, 1880**. Berlin: The Council, 1880. 14 p. Loc: OKIT, OWTUR.

A set of rules on meeting procedures including adjournments, recording of minutes, motions and questions, the mode of introducing by-laws and routine business of the council. Period: 1879 - 1880.

3982. Young, James. "The formation and early days of Waterloo County: a reprint, in part, of the sketch prepared on the subject by the late Hon. James Young." **Mer Douce**. 1924. 14: 44-46. ill. Loc: OKIT.

An account of the politics surrounding the Hincks Act of 1851, which divided Dumfries Township into northern and southern portions, and which resulted in Berlin being the county seat of Waterloo. It reflects on the differences and developments in Waterloo County since the arrival of the earliest settlers around 1800. Period: 1800 - 1924.

RESTRUCTURING LOCAL GOVERNMENT FROM THE 1960S

3983. Area Planning and Development Technical Coordinating Committee. **Waterloo-South Wellington area study**. 1968 - 1969. 5 v. Loc: OWTL, OWT.

A prospectus in five volumes, with the goal of preparing for a "comprehensive planning and development study that will estimate the future socio-economic data and develop the optimum land use plan" for Waterloo and South Wellington Counties. The first report describes the components, organization and objectives of the entire study while the others describe the functions of transportation, economic development, planning advisory and public works committees. Period: 1965 - 1969.

3984. Bissell, Brian and Sharpe, Ken. **Is fifty-six percent a majority?: an analysis of the proposed amalgamation of Kitchener-Waterloo**. Waterloo Lutheran University, 1970. 48 l. ill., maps. Loc: OWTL.

A study undertaken by geography students based on the results of a questionnaire circulated among citizens of the two cities. As well as a thorough presentation of the method and results of the research, the work also includes a brief historical account of views of local politicians on the issue of amalgamation. Period: 1969 - 1970.

3985. Canadian Urban Economics Limited. **Waterloo-South Wellington area economic base study**. 1969. 1 v. ill., maps, bibl. Loc: OCCA, OKIT, OWTL, OWTU, OWT.

Explanation of a plan for future regional development, including a brief review of the region's economic history and an assessment of economic prospects and land use requirements in eight zones. Retailing, manufacturing, agriculture, recreation, tourism, health care facilities, industries, schools and churches are considered and statistical information is summarized in 18 appendices. Period: 1951 - 2001.

3986. Department of Municipal Affairs, Community Planning Branch. **Waterloo area.** Toronto: The Department, 1964. 37 p. maps. Loc: OWRA, OWT.

A provincial government report on the growing urbanization in the Waterloo area. Maps show patterns of primary and secondary shopping by place of residence, existing land uses, population density, places of work, changes in municipal boundaries, planning areas and proposed land use zones. Period: 1963 - 1964.

3987. Dryden and Smith Planning Consultants. **Waterloo area local government review: summary [of] reports and studies, Waterloo area, 1960-1968.** Kitchener: The Consultants, 1968. 36 l. map. Loc: OWTU.

A listing of the major studies and reports pertaining to the restructuring of local government. Topics include transportation, sewage treatment, park development, conservation, housing, public utilities, water supply, agricultural land use, and population projections. Period: 1960 - 1968.

3988. Forrest, R. "The Waterloo County area - towards an area official plan." **The Waterloo County area: selected geographical essays.** Edited by A.G. McLellan. Waterloo: Department of Geography, University of Waterloo, 1971. Pp. 278-293. maps, diags. Loc: OWTU, OWTL, OWTUCG, OKIT.

A review of the efforts of the Waterloo County Area Planning Board from 1965 to co-ordinate comprehensive planning of development and services for the region. Period: 1965 - 1970.

3989. "From Waterloo County to the Regional Municipality of Waterloo." **Waterloo Historical Society.** 1973. 61: 38-41. ill. Loc: all.

A short explanation of the restructuring of municipal government that took effect in 1973. Period: 1852 - 1973.

3990. Fyfe, Stewart and Farrow, Ron M. **Waterloo area local government review: report of findings and recommendations.** Toronto: Ontario Department of Municipal Affairs, 1970. 205 p. maps. Loc: OCCA, OCLG, OKIT, OWRND, OWRSC, OWT, OWTL.

A discussion of the implications of regional restructuring of municipal government, including costs, annexation procedures and the current state of municipal services such as public housing and sewerage. The report is based on more than 70 briefs from townships, towns, villages, planning

boards, boards of education, chambers of commerce, service organizations and individuals. Not all briefs are held by all libraries, 40 being held by the City of Cambridge Archives, for example. Period: 1968 - 1970.

3991. Horton, John T. **Recommended programme for the Midwestern Ontario Development Area 1969-1973.** Waterloo: Planning and Resources Institute, University of Waterloo, 1968. 170 p. maps, tables. Loc: OKIT, OWTU.

A regional plan for the counties of Waterloo, Huron, Perth and Wellington, including discussion of agriculture, mineral resources and mining, conservation, recreation and tourism, medical and legal services, education, housing, transportation, public utilities, industrial and commercial development, land use planning and controls and urban centres. Period: 1969 - 1973.

3992. Kitchener Planning Board. **A brief to the Local Government Review Commission, Waterloo County Area.** 1967. 101 p. graphs, maps. Loc: OKIT.

A report on planning strategies for Kitchener to the year 2000, recommending regional government as likely to be efficient and effective in dealing with the city's physical growth. The authors point out problems of duplication and inconsistencies in the existing municipal government system, and describe how regional government would improve services and administration. Some previous planning documents are mentioned and summarized, and comments are quoted from officials in areas with regional government. Eleven maps illustrate drainage, land use, delivery areas, and composite spheres of influence. Period: 1967 - 2000.

3993. Kitchener Planning Board/ Kitchener Planning Department. **Local government review of Waterloo County: a brief to the Council of the City of Kitchener and the Honourable W. Darcy McKeough.** 1970. 36 l. loose maps. Loc: OWTU, OKIT.

A summary of recommendations for future planning policies and government administration, based on population, land use, and economic projections, as well as suggestions obtained from the Fyfe Report. The report contains charts of statistical projections to the year 1991. Period: 1970 - 1991.

3994. Krueger, Ralph R. "Towards regional planning and regional government in Waterloo County." **The Waterloo County area: selected geographical essays.** Edited by A.G. McLellan. Waterloo: Department of Geography, University of Waterloo, 1971. Pp. 295-307. maps. Loc: OWTU, OWTL, OWTUCG, OKIT.

A survey of various initiatives, from the formation of the Kitchener-Waterloo and Suburban Planning Board in 1947 to plans for regional government and restructuring in 1971. Period: 1947 - 1971.

3995. McKeough, W. Darcy. **Address by the Honourable W. Darcy McKeough, Minister of Municipal Affairs in presenting the report of the Commissioner, Waterloo area local government review, Waterloo, Tuesday, March 10, 1970.** Ontario Department of Municipal Affairs, 1970. 19 p. Loc: OWTU.

A summary of the recommendations of the Fyfe Commission on the reorganization of local government. Period: 1969 - 1970.

3996. Milburn, Maurice W. **Regional systemic planning and the Waterloo-South Wellington area study.** University of Waterloo (M.A. thesis, Geography), 1975. 2 fiche. charts, maps, tables, bibl. mf. Loc: OWTU.

An evaluation of the long-range value of the regional systemic planning model used in the area study of 1967-1972. Appendices contain a history of municipal government in the area from 1968 to 1973 and a description of the objectives and policies of the area study. Period: 1967 - 1973.

3997. Nixon, G. Peter and Campbell, Maurice A. "The Waterloo-South Wellington area: a study in regional planning." **Four cities: studies in urban and regional planning.** Toronto: McClelland and Stewart, 1971. 95-120. maps. Loc: OWTU, OWTL.

A useful account of the Waterloo-South Wellington Area Planning and Development Study from the first meeting in March 1967 of representatives of the Waterloo County Area Planning Board, the Department of Highways and the Department of Municipal Affairs. Other agencies later joined what became known as the Area Planning and Development Technical Co-ordinating Committee -- the Regional Development Branch of the Treasury Department, the Midwestern Ontario Development Council, the Ontario Water Resources Commission, the City of Guelph and Wellington County. The authors discuss the purposes and procedures of collecting and analyzing data on development, population and traffic as a basis for the preparation of official plans. They also show how future development might occur in four possible conceptual models of urban growth. Period: 1951 - 1971.

3998. O'Neill, Allan J. **Regionalization of southwestern Ontario.** Waterloo Lutheran University (M.A. thesis, Geography), 1973. 92 p. bibl., tables, maps. Loc: OWTL.

A systems approach to the regionalization of southwestern Ontario that synthesizes homogeneous and nodal regions through mathematical formulation. The data matrices of structure and behaviour were combined to form regions. It is recognized that these artificially derived regions do not address the conflict between Ontario's economic regions and the city-centred economic regions. Period: 1961 - 1972.

3999. Ontario Department of Economics and Development, Special Research and Surveys Branch. **Economic survey of the Mid-western Ontario Region.** Toronto: The Department, 1965. 146 p. ill., maps, graphs, tables. Loc: OKIT, OWTL, OWTU.

Report of a study analyzing major sections of economic activity and reviewing directions of change in the period from the late 1940s to the early 1960s. The region includes Huron, Perth and Wellington counties in addition to Waterloo. There are chapters on the physical base, population, employment and income, agriculture and fur farming, mining, forestry, fishing and conservation, energy, manufacturing, transportation and communications, construction and housing, trade and tourism. Individual counties and municipalities are described and there is a substantial statistical appendix. Period: 1949 - 1963.

4000. Ontario Department of Treasury and Economics: Regional Development Branch. **Design for development: Midwestern Ontario region.** Toronto: The Department, 1970. 175 p. maps, tables. Loc: OCLG, OWTU, OWTL.

Report on an initial analysis of the social, economic and physical resources and trends and problems of the region including Huron, Perth and Wellington counties in addition to Waterloo. There are chapters on the physical and geographic setting, economic base, transportation, physical land capability, potential centres of opportunity, and a summary of goals, needs and priorities. Maps and tables summarize data on land use, population density and urban/rural character, migration (including daily commuting patterns), employment, household income, recreation, agricultural production, land capability, recreation facilities, manufacturing output, accessibility, trends in population growth and the functional hierarchy of urban centres. Period: 1946 - 1968.

4001. Palmer, W.H. **Waterloo Region Review Commission.** Regional Municipality of Waterloo, 1977 - 1979. Loc: OWTL, OCCA, OWRN, OWT, OWRE.

A series of reports reviewing the effects of the regional restructuring of local government. Individual titles are: **Prospectus; Decision** makers in local government; Purchasing in Waterloo local governments; Representation and the electoral system in the Region of Waterloo; An analysis of computer use in Waterloo local governments; Public attitude survey; Financial data base; Planning series 1, perspectives; Municipal services in Cambridge and Woolwich, 1969-1976; Roads and transportation in the Region of Waterloo; Space-saving: an examination of a regional headquarters; Water management on the Grand River: a provincial/municipal dilemma; Report of the Waterloo Region Review Commission, March 1979; Collection of perspectives on municipal planning control in the Region of Waterloo; Planning administration and development control in the Region of Waterloo; Effects of electing municipal councils by ward or at-large: a preliminary comparison in Ontario cities; Operational summary: a summary of the costs and benefits of regional government in Waterloo; Organization of social services in Waterloo Region; Police governance in Waterloo Region; Issues in municipal finance; Environmental services. The report concludes that regional government had generally been beneficial in the Waterloo area. All these titles are held at Wilfrid Laurier University, New Hamburg Public Library and Waterloo Public Library. The other libraries have only some of the reports. Period: 1969 - 1976.

4002. Planning Technical Advisory Committee. **Waterloo-South Wellington area study planning prospectus.** 1969. 29 p. ill., maps. Loc: OWTU, OWT.

A report on planning strategies for land use, transportation, public works and economic development. Period: 1968 - 1969.

4003. Regional Human Resources Development Conference. **Social, health and welfare programs - regional possibilities?.** 1971. 1 v. Loc: OWTU.

A collection of material prepared for participants in the conference at the University of Waterloo in 1971. Short excerpts from papers provide a preview of such topics as income security, health services, and approaches to public assistance. Also included is a 1970 directory of community resources and services for Galt, Preston, Hespeler, Ayr and North Dumfries. Period: 1966 - 1971.

4004. Social Planning Council of Kitchener-Waterloo. **A brief to the Local Government Review Commission, Waterloo County Area.** Kitchener: The Council, 1968. 1 v. (various pagings). Loc: OWTL, OKIT.

A report outlining the council's concerns on health, education, welfare, recreation, and

physical planning for special populations such as disturbed and deprived children, adults who are not accepted socially, lonely or ill old people, people with inadequate housing, children with nowhere to play, and youths in need of direction. The document contains proposals for a county-wide social planning council, the creation of a grants division in the provincial government, and the formation of an association within the Ontario Welfare Council of all social planning councils in Ontario. An appendix lists all current social service agencies and clubs. Period: 1967 - 1968.

4005. Waterloo County Area Planning Board. **Strategy for growth: Waterloo South-Wellington area study. Final report - part one.** Kitchener: The Board, 1972. 49 p. tables, maps. Loc: OKIT, OWRE, OWT, OWTU.

A report summarizing recommendations to all levels of government on the future development of the area. Three guiding principles are endorsed: improvement of the quality of life, economic viability, and careful use of the natural environment. The report includes recommendations for the private sector as well as public policies. Period: 1967 - 1991.

4006. Williams, Robert J. **Papers on local politics in Waterloo Region and two adjacent communities: papers prepared by students in Political Science 344 at the University of Waterloo, Winter Term 1977.** University of Waterloo, 1977. 108 p. ill., maps. Loc: OKIT.

The only paper dealing with information from 1972 or earlier is one entitled "Waterloo Regional Government Review: the Cambridge perspective," which gives background information about the Fyfe Report and Palmer Review. People interviewed on this topic include Claudette Millar, Robert Kerr, D. Collins, Monty Davidson, Alex Lawson and Jack Young. Period: 1972 - 1977.

ADMINISTRATION OF JUSTICE: LAW, ORDER AND POLICE

4007. "Division Courts." **Waterloo Historical Society.** 1970. 58: 32. Loc: all.

A brief note that in 1970 Waterloo County's First Division Court moved to 575 King Street West in Kitchener. The locations of the Second, Third, Fourth, and Fifth Division Courts are also given. Period: 1970.

4008. Fraser, Margaret. "Galt policewoman M.E. Keachie." **Waterloo Historical Society.** 1990. 78: 178-180. Loc: all.

A brief account of the role of Galt's first

policewoman between 1921 and 1927. Margaret Keachie was most concerned with domestic disputes, desertion, and morality issues. In 1927, in spite of support for Mrs Keachie from churches and women's groups, the Galt Police Commission terminated her appointment and bought an automobile instead. Period: 1921 - 1928.

4009. **Further adventures of the great detective: incidents in the life of John Wilson Murray.** Toronto: Collins, 1980. 223 p. Loc: OKIT.

Selections from the original memoirs published in 1904 by Murray, appointed Provincial Detective of Ontario in 1874. Three of the 40 cases relate to Waterloo County: the fraud by J.K. Herres against the Imperial Bank in Galt in 1887, James Little the horse thief caught in 1888, and the unsolved case of strychnine-poisoned chocolates in Galt in 1888. Waterloo County's chief constable, John Klippert, is vividly described in these stories. Period: 1874 - 1890.

4010. **Investigation into the Registrar of Waterloo County, Dougall McDougall.** 1890. 57 l. Loc: OKIT.

A collection of photocopied material relating to the investigation of the Registrar of Waterloo County for incorrect returns concerning fees. Included are statements from all the individuals involved in the investigation, as well as office correspondence between Dougall McDougall and James E. Stanton. See also the official government report on this investigation, **Report of the Inspector of Registry Offices** (1891). Period: 1888 - 1890.

4011. Lamb, Kathryn Hansuld. "The sheriffs of Waterloo." **Waterloo Historical Society.** 1984. 72: 118-127. ill. Loc: all.

A history of the sheriffs of Waterloo, with brief biographies of all ten: George Davidson, Moses Springer, John Motz, Dr Henry George Lackner, William A. Kribs, Edward H. Scully, G.H. Gillies, John A. Seamark, Art Schmitt and Shirley Lincoln. Shirley Lincoln is noted as Ontario's first full-time female sheriff. Period: 1833 - 1984.

4012. McRuer, J.C. "Some historical aspects of the rules by which we live together in organized society." **Waterloo Historical Society.** 1960. 48: 8-15. ill. Loc: all.

A philosophical address given to members of the Waterloo Historical Society and illustrated with a sketch of Waterloo County Court House.

4013. Ontario Inspector of Registry Offices. **Report of the Inspector of Registry Offices in the matter of the official enquiry into certain charges preferred against the late Registrar of the County of Waterloo and also the Reports of the Executive Council on the same.** Toronto: Government of Ontario, 1891. 23 p. Loc: OWTUR, OKITW.

A report of the enquiry into Dougall McDougall's alleged theft of fees from the Registry Office while he was the Registrar of Deeds. Period: 1888 - 1891.

4014. Pike, Roland. "Policing in Waterloo County, 1850-1973, part 1." **Waterloo Historical Society.** 1989. 77: 5-25. ill. Loc: all.

A detailed history of policing in Waterloo County, with special emphasis on the police forces of Kitchener, Waterloo and Bridgeport. Period: 1850 - 1973.

4015. Pike, Roland. "Policing in Waterloo County, 1850-1973, part 2." **Waterloo Historical Society.** 1990. 78: 158-177. ill. Loc: all.

The second part of a history of police services in the county, with reference to the police forces of Galt (since 1851), Hespeler (since 1859) and Preston (since 1867). Period: 1851 - 1973.

4016. Ritz, Ernst. "Policing in Waterloo County, 1850-1973, part 3." **Waterloo Historical Society.** 1991. 79: 128-134. ill. A survey of police services in New Hamburg since 1858, including anecdotes about local officers, crimes and mysteries. Loc: all.
Period: 1858 - 1973.

4017. Sokvitne, Miriam Snyder. "The Waterloo County Gaol." **Waterloo Historical Society.** 1977. 65: 60-71. ill. Loc: all.

A short history of the jail, with emphasis on the period before 1900 and including information on repairs and renovations to the building and on crimes committed by earlier inmates. Period: 1852 - 1978.

4018. Taylor, Ryan. "A breach of promise case of 1874." **Families.** 1989. 28,1: 43-47. ill. Loc: OWTU, OKIT, OWTL.

An extract from the **Dumfries Reformer**, detailing a court case brought against George Washington Ray by Robert Hall, both of Ayr. Ray was charged with failing to marry Margaret, Robert Hall's daughter, and marrying her cousin, Catherine Rose, instead. Courting customs and social attitudes are vividly portrayed. Period: 1871 - 1942.

4019. Urquhart, Duncan. "Crime in Waterloo County 1865-1867." **Waterloo Historical Society.** 1985. 73: 4-16. ill., tables, bibl. Loc: all.

An overview of criminal trends within cultural

and occupational groups, including comparisons of Waterloo County with other Ontario counties. Data are derived from the gaol registers held at the Archives of Ontario. Period: 1865 - 1867.

4020. Weaver, John C. "Crime, public order, and repression: the Gore District in upheaval, 1832-1851." **Ontario History**. 1986. 78,3: 175-207. ill., tables. Loc: OKIT, OWTU, OWTL.

An analysis of local jail records in the Gore District which included the Waterloo County area until the completion of the Guelph jail in 1841. Most examples are drawn from Hamilton, Dundas, Brantford and Paris. The author surveys changes in criminal justice and finds that fluctuations of the economy influenced the incidence of crime. Period: 1832 - 1851.

4021. Ziegler, Noah. "An excuse." **Waterloo Historical Society**. 1991. 79: 19. Loc: all.

An excerpt from **Der Deutsche Canadier** of 31 January 1851, in which Ziegler refers to his conviction on a charge of assault and battery. He justifies his action and his rights in giving "a good whipping" to several unruly children, including one of his own. Period: 1850 - 1851.

LOCAL GOVERNMENT AND SERVICES

4022. "Addition to nurses' residence at K-W Hospital." **Waterloo Historical Society**. 1964. 52: 60. Loc: all.

A short note of the opening of the School of Nursing and Residence at the hospital. Period: 1964.

4023. Badgley, Janice A. **Public decision making on water supply planning and management: a case study of the Waterloo Region, 1846 to 1988**. University of Waterloo (M.A. thesis, Planning), 1991. 487 p. maps., bibl. Loc: OWTUR.

A very detailed history of political decisions regarding the water supply for the urban centres of Waterloo County (Kitchener, Waterloo, Preston, Galt and Hespeler). The author identifies the key factors as institutional arrangements, financial factors and individual entrepreneurs. She discusses the three primary options for long-term water supply: the Grand River, further ground water supplies, and a Great Lakes pipeline. Period: 1846 - 1988.

4024. Baltaduonis, Irena. **Elmira: industrial versus residential assessment**. University of Waterloo (B.E.S. thesis, Planning), 1974. 33 l. maps, tables, bibl. Loc: OWTU.

A study of the financial advantage of the community based on assessment per acre. By analyzing data from industries, expenditures and residential assessment for Elmira, the author shows that residential assessment is more than twice as much as industrial assessment. Period: 1952 - 1971.

4025. Bloomfield, Elizabeth and Bloomfield, G.T. **Urban growth and local services: the development of Ontario municipalities to 1981**. Guelph: Department of Geography, University of Guelph, 1983. 179 p. ill., tables. Loc: OCLG, OKIT, OWT, OWTL, OWTU.

A compilation of key dates and short essays on the development of services in urban centres. There are chapters on incorporation history, local newspapers, boards of trade, railways, gas and electricity, street railways and interurban lines, waterworks and sewerage systems, public libraries, and hospitals. Populations of all urban municipalities are listed for every census from 1851 to 1981. Period: 1830 - 1981.

4026. Borovilos, George A. **The evolution of the Town of Berlin into the City of Kitchener: a period of growth, change, and response to urban industrialization, 1890-1925**. University of Waterloo (B.E.S. thesis, Geography), 1979. 2 fiche. maps, tables, bibl. mf. Loc: OWTUM.

An analysis of the problems associated with urban-industrial growth, such as inadequate sewerage and public health hazards, and the need for better municipal services. The author examines the response of municipal governments to these problems in a case study of Berlin/Kitchener, and emphasizes critical transitional periods in social, political and economic affairs and the co-operative efforts of local entrepreneurs and elected officials. Appendices include tables of local industries, occupations, elected officials and zoning by-laws. Period: 1870 - 1925.

4027. Brillinger, Bruce A. and Adams, Donald W. **Day care: guidelines for action**. Kitchener: The Authors?, 1968. 39 l. maps, bibl. Loc: OWTL.

A study undertaken when the Ontario Government decided to subsidize municipally approved pre-school day care centres. The report provides information on day care needs in Kitchener-Waterloo and perceptions of day care needs by working mothers and makes recommendations on setting up day care facilities and hiring staff. Short profiles of existing centres are contained in the appendix. Period: 1967 - 1968.

4028. Chipman, Willis. **Town of Galt, province of Ontario: report on a proposed system of sewerage and sewage disposal.** Galt: Reformer Press, 1895. 29 p. map. Loc: OKITW.

Report recommending a separate sewerage system with land filtration that would extend 8 miles. Estimated costs and increases in the general tax rate are calculated, and a plan of Galt showing the proposed system is included. Fieldwork for the report was done by A.J. McPherson, superintendent of Galt Water Works. Period: 1894 - 1895.

4029. Conrad, Peter. **Caring on the Grand: a history of the Freeport Hospital.** Kitchener: Freeport Hospital, 1987. 168 p. ill., bibl., index. Loc: OKIT, OWT, OWTL, OWTUCG.

A comprehensive account of the hospital created through the efforts of the anti-tuberculosis movement. Topics include the search for a proper site from 1908, use of the new building by the Military Hospitals Commission from 1916 to 1920, its functioning as a sanatorium between 1920 and 1936, and the eradication of the disease by 1957. The final chapter describes the transformation of the Freeport Sanatorium to a chronic and rehabilitative care hospital during the 1960s. The author mentions physicians, politicians and women's auxiliaries who contributed to the welfare of the hospital, and includes reminiscences by patients as well as numerous photographs. Period: 1908 - 1987.

4030. Coumans, Camilla C. "St Agatha Orphanage." **Waterloo Historical Society.** 1966. 54: 31-32. ill. Loc: all.

A short history of the orphanage, founded in 1858 by Father Eugene Funcken and Miss Margaret Dietrich and renamed Notre Dame of St Agatha Children's Village in 1966. Period: 1858 - 1967.

4031. Coutts, Edgar N., Dr. "History of Freeport Sanatorium." **Waterloo Historical Society.** 1943. 31: 11-28. tables. Loc: all.

An account of the institution's doctors, politicians and women of the Freeport Sanatorium Auxiliary. The author discusses the importance of health education and the X-ray in combatting tuberculosis and presents a table showing changing death rates per 100,000 for Canada, Ontario and Waterloo County since 1901. Period: 1882 - 1943.

4032. Curtis, Kevin R. **Role of municipal government in municipal industrial development - Kitchener: a case study.** University of Waterloo (B.E.S. thesis), 1980. 1 fiche. mf. Loc: OWTUM.

A critical examination of Kitchener's municipal government from 1958 to 1980, concluding that the city's policies and actions had been ineffective in determining its industrial development. A survey of manufacturers showed that 84 per cent were uninfluenced by the City of Kitchener in choosing their location. Period: 1958 - 1980.

4033. Davock, Paul W. **The creation of a social service setting: a description of the history and theoretical considerations.** Wilfrid Laurier University (M.A. thesis, Psychology), 1974. 178 l. bibl. Loc: OWTL.

A review by its first director of the process of setting up the Developmental Centre in Waterloo, a service opened in 1972 for pre-school retarded children. The author outlines the preparations, from writing initial proposals and creating an administrative structure to hiring staff, as well as the first few months in operation. Period: 1971 - 1972.

4034. Dunham, B. Mabel. "Waterloo County House of Industry and Refuge." **Waterloo Historical Society.** 1947. 35: 19-28. Loc: all.

An account of the institution which began in 1866 to house the poor and the infirm. The author describes its establishment and management, how the residents were treated and the rules by which they had to live. Period: 1867 - 1947.

4035. "End of an era." **Waterloo Historical Society.** 1965. 53: 69. ill. Loc: all.

A photograph showing the replacement of the last of Waterloo's globe-cluster street lights by fluorescent lamps. Period: 1965.

4036. "Fires in Kitchener." **Waterloo Historical Society.** 1960. 48: 76. Loc: all.

A note of five fires between December 1959 and July 1960. One of these, described as the worst fire in Kitchener's history, destroyed two commercial buildings on King Street East. Period: 1959 - 1960.

4037. Galt Hospital. **The Galt Hospital, Galt, Ont.: golden jubilee, 1890-1940.** Galt: Galt Hospital, 1940. 15 p. ill. Loc: OKIT, OCCA.

A short history of the hospital and its training school beginning with the first meeting of the Hospital Board of Trustees in 1888. The booklet provides details on the efforts of the first superintendent, Elizabeth Gibson, and others in the early years, as well as the development of the institution and hospital programmes. Lists of Galt Hospital Training School graduates from 1893 to 1934, medical staff in 1940, and past physicians are also included. Period: 1890 - 1940.

4038. "Goudie Home gift totalled $200,000." **Waterloo Historical Society**. 1962. 50: 84. Loc: all.

A note of the opening of the Salvation Army's Eventide Home. A.R. Goudie gave $200,000 towards the construction of this building. Period: 1962.

4039. "Governor-General opens St Mary's General Hospital [WRP]." **Waterloo Historical Society**. 1962. 50: 22. Loc: all.

A note of the vice-regal visit to Kitchener and Waterloo. Period: 1962.

4040. Haner, Vonnie. "Dog days and summer complaints." **Waterloo Historical Society**. 1985. 73: 108-118. Loc: all.

A history of health and welfare services in Wellesley Township from 1849 to 1950, including information on the first Board of Health and its enforcement of Public Health Acts; sanitary regulations in schools, factories and on farms; and quarantine laws. Specific references are made to typhoid, smallpox and diphtheria outbreaks, but other concerns included veterinary-related problems, weed control and the conditions of pioneer graveyards. Period: 1849 - 1927.

4041. Hulet, Marion and Hebblethwaite, Katherine. "Blair Athol." **Waterloo Historical Society**. 1966. 54: 33-35. Loc: all.

An account of the Galt Boys' Home established in 1872 by Miss MacPherson to receive Dr Barnardo's English orphans for adoption or apprenticing in Canada. Period: 1872 - 1883.

4042. Humphrey, E.T., Mrs. **A historical sketch of the Freeport Hospital and the auxiliaries**. 1985. 11 l. Loc: OKIT.

A brief account of the members and activities of the women's auxiliary which began in 1921. Period: 1921 - 1984.

4043. Jaffray, William. "A day at the Waterloo Poor House and what I learned there." **Waterloo Historical Society**. 1969. 57: 72-78. ill. Loc: all.

A lecture by William Jaffray at the Berlin Town Hall in 1870, as reported in the **Journal of proceedings and by-laws of the Municipal Council of the County of Waterloo, 1871**. After a day observing life at the Poor House, the author describes what he saw and makes some recommendations. He concludes that Poor House is a good and benevolent institution. Period: 1869 - 1870.

4044. Johnston, Edward A. **The Berlin-Kitchener Fire Department**. The Author, 1979. 5 p. Loc: OKIT.

A brief history of the Kitchener Fire Department from 1840 to 1967, written by its fire chief in commemoration of Kitchener's 125th anniversary. It provides information about fire-fighting equipment, and a list of fire chiefs from 1854 to 1967. Period: 1840 - 1967.

4045. "Kitchener Fire Department moved." **Waterloo Historical Society**. 1960. 48: 69. Loc: all.

A note of the department's move from the fire station built in 1857 to new headquarters on Highland Road. Period: 1857 - 1960.

4046. Kitchener Light Commission. **The origin of the Ontario hydro-electric power movement**. Kitchener: Quality Printers, 1919. 14 p. ill. Loc: OKIT.

A history of electric power in the province and the efforts of D.B. Detweiler, E.W.B. Snider and Adam Beck in bringing public hydro to the area. The booklet includes an account of the day in October 1910 when electric power was first turned on in Berlin. Photographs are included of members of the Kitchener Light Commission from 1917 to 1919. Period: 1902 - 1919.

4047. Kitchener-Waterloo Hospital. **Kitchener-Waterloo Hospital: our 60th year of community service, 1895-1955**. The Hospital, 1955. 13 p. ill. Loc: OKIT.

A commemorative history and description of current services. Photographs show the Kitchener-Waterloo Hospital graduation class of 1955 and the members of the 1955 Hospital Commission. There are lists of current hospital officers and staff. Period: 1895 - 1955.

4048. Kitchener-Waterloo Hospital. **Official opening of the School of Nursing**. 1964. 1 folded sheet. ill. Loc: OKITW.

A programme including an historical sketch and list of the current faculty and Board of Commissioners. The copy held by the Waterloo Historical Society contains a separate 15-page brochure entitled **School of Nursing and Residence addition**, describing the new building in detail with floor plans. This brochure may have been handed out in a tour of the hospital. Period: 1898 - 1964.

4049. Lamb, Kathryn Hansuld. "Ambulance service gets first home." **Waterloo Historical Society**. 1984. 72: 150-152. ill. Loc: all.

A brief history of Kitchener's ambulance service from 1903 until 1984 when a permanent ambulance station was opened. There are photographs of ambulances in 1903, 1927 and 1951. Period: 1903 - 1984.

4050. Lamb, Kathryn Hansuld. "Firehall bell is rescued."
Waterloo Historical Society. 1984. 72: 156-157.
ill. Loc: all.
The Kitchener Fire Department's bell was
replaced in 1984, after having been placed in the
old city hall building and in storage for more
than 60 years. Period: c1880 - 1984.

4051. MacIver, Ian. **Urban water supply alternatives:
perception and choice in the Grand Basin Ontario**.
University of Chicago, Department of Geography,
Research paper no. 126. Department of Geography,
University of Chicago, 1970. 178 p. ill., maps,
tables, bibl. Loc: OCLG, OKIT, OWTL, OWTU.
An historical survey of past and proposed
solutions to water supply problems, with an
analysis of both community and official government
perceptions and preferences on supply
alternatives. Period: 1969 - 1970.

4052. McMillen, Janet E. **A qualitative analysis of
sewage treatment in Kitchener and Waterloo**.
Wilfrid Laurier University (B.A. thesis,
Geography), 1974. 144 p. bibl., tables. Loc: OWTL.
An historical and contemporary study from which
the author concludes that Kitchener has met
increasing demands for sewage treatment better
than Waterloo. Charts and tables summarize the
sewage flow from Kitchener and Waterloo treatment
plants from 1960 to 1974. Period: 1857 - 1972.

4053. "Members of the Berlin Fire Company No. 1,
January, 1849." **Waterloo Historical Society**.
1983. 71: 6. Loc: all.
A list of 25 firemen reported by Henry Eby to
Thomas Saunders, Clerk of the Peace at the
district capital of Guelph. Period: 1849.

4054. Mitchell, Bruce. "Public participation and
education programs for water management in
Waterloo County." **The Waterloo County area:
selected geographical essays**. Edited by A.G.
McLellan. Waterloo: Department of Geography,
University of Waterloo, 1971. Pp. 206-215. tabl.
Loc: OWTU, OWTL, OWTUCG, OKIT.
Report of a 1970 survey to test the feasibility
of citizen participation in the process of
planning policies for future water management.
Period: 1968 - 1970.

4055. Oliver, Clifford A. **A geographical analysis of
the location factors of fire stations: Kitchener
and London**. Waterloo Lutheran University (B.A.
thesis, Geography), 1966. 134 l. maps, bibl. Loc:
OWTL.
A study of key factors based on population
density, land use and topographic maps, and field
observations. Period: 1957 - 1966.

4056. Ontario Department of Health: Hospitals Division.
The hospitals of Ontario: a short history.
Toronto: Herbert H. Ball, 1934. 289 p. ill. Loc:
OCCA.
A collection of illustrated descriptions of
hospitals including Galt General Hospital,
Kitchener-Waterloo Hospital, St Mary's Hospital
and Freeport Sanatorium. Period: 1890 - 1934.

4057. Peter Barnard Associates. **Waterloo area regional
transit study: Phase 1 report**. Toronto: Peter
Barnard Associates, 1971. 53 p. graphs, maps. Loc:
OWTU.
An assessment of public transport with
recommendations for general improvements and
methods of integrating the various systems. Most
transit riders are found to be women, most without
a driver's licence. Work and school trips account
for over half the journeys. The report recommends
that Kitchener replace its trolleys with diesel
buses, and that re-routing be carried out in the
Kitchener/Waterloo and the Galt/Preston/Hespeler
areas. It also recommends that school buses be
re-routed and that contracts be re-negotiated.
Period: 1970 - 1971.

4058. Quantrell, James. **The history of the Cambridge
Fire Department**. Cambridge: Ditner Printing,
1992. 65 p. ill., bibl. Loc: OCCA.
A pictorial history of the Galt, Hespeler,
Preston and Cambridge fire departments,
commemorating the 150th anniversary of the first
fire service. The text and photographs portray the
firemen, machines, fire halls, notable fires and
accidents. Period: 1842 - 1991.

4059. Roth, Ken. **Comprehensive health planning - a case
study: Kitchener-Waterloo**. University of Waterloo
(B.E.S. thesis, Urban and Regional Planning),
1972. 73 p. maps, tables. Loc: OWTU.
A methodology for health service provision
applied to Kitchener-Waterloo Hospital, including
a brief outline of the hospital's founding and
development, a description of its services in 1971
and an appraisal of its potential to meet local
health care needs to 1981. Period: 1895 - 1981.

4060. Rudy, Norma I. **For such a time as this: L. Earl
Ludlow and a history of homes for the aged in
Ontario 1837-1961**. Toronto: Ontario Association
of Homes for the Aged, 1987. 305 p. ill. Loc:
OKIT, OWRE, OWTL, OWTU, OWTUCG.
A history including short descriptions of
Waterloo County homes and services for the aged.
Period: 1837 - 1961.

4061. Schnarr, Judy. "The early history of optometry and vision care in Kitchener-Waterloo." **Waterloo Historical Society.** 1982. 70: 81-87. ill. Loc: all.

A short account of the development of local services and of individuals such as Henry Knell, A. Chatfield, Arnold Jansen, the Hellers, the Clarkes, John Hett, George Gordon and John Price. Period: c1857 - 1982.

4062. Smith, J. Reginald, Dr. **Galt Board of Health, 1854-1963.** The Author, 1964. 9 p. Loc: OKIT, OCCA.

A history of public health in Galt, from the cholera epidemic of 1834, to the creation of the Board of Health in 1854, to 1963 when the Waterloo County Health Unit became responsible for public health work. The medical officers, epidemics, sanitation, isolation hospitals, and the incident of 1939 when three men died of sewer gas are all mentioned. The author, Dr Smith, was Galt's Medical Officer of Health from 1940 to 1963. Period: 1834 - 1963.

4063. Social Planning Council of Kitchener-Waterloo. **The geographic distribution of users of selected social, health and welfare services in Kitchener-Waterloo: a research report.** Kitchener: The Council, 1973. 27 p. map, tables. Loc: OWTL.

A study of the provision of financial, health, correctional, psychiatric, counselling, occupational training, and housing services. Period: 1966 - 1972.

4064. **St Mary's School of Nursing, Kitchener, Ontario.** Kitchener: The School, 194-?. 1 v. (unpaged). ill. Loc: OKIT.

A brochure designed to attract student nurses, prefaced by a sketch of the establishment of St Mary's Hospital and the School of Nursing, Kitchener. The hospital was officially opened by the Sisters of St Joseph in 1924 and the School of Nursing began in 1931. Period: 1924 - 1931.

4065. Taylor, Ryan. "The Kitchener isolation hospitals." **Waterloo Historical Society.** 1990. 78: 74-82. ill. Loc: all.

A detailed account, based mainly on Board of Health records, of arrangements made in the early twentieth century to segregate patients suffering from infectious diseases such as diphtheria, scarlet fever, consumption and smallpox. The author describes the building on Highland Road East of four houses that were used from 1913 until the early 1940s. Period: 1899 - 1947.

4066. Tompkins, George. **A history of the Kitchener-Waterloo Hospital.** Waterloo Lutheran University (research paper), 1964. 28 l. Loc: OKITW.

An outline of the founding, expansion and financial history of the hospital. A short history of the ambulance service is also given. Period: 1894 - 1964.

4067. Tompkins, George. "A history of the Kitchener-Waterloo Hospital." **Waterloo Historical Society.** 1964. 52: 44-60. ill., bibl. Loc: all.

A concise history of the hospital including topics its founding and opening, the ladies' auxiliary, expansions and the ambulance service. Many names are included of the people who were involved in the hospital's development, administration and promotion. Period: 1893 - 1964.

4068. Tresidder, Marion. **A study of the needs of cancer patients in Waterloo County, 1956-7: a joint project of the Ontario Cancer Treatment and Research Foundation and the Ontario Division, Canadian Cancer Society.** Toronto: The Foundation, 1957. 25 l. tables. Loc: OTU.

Reference from **Bibliography of Ontario history, 1867-1976** (Bishop et al.). Period: 1956 - 1957.

4069. **Victoria Park: 90th celebration: 1896 Berlin - 1986 Kitchener.** 1986. 1 v. (unpaged). ill. Loc: OKIT.

A programme and brief history to mark the celebration on Sunday, 24 August 1986. Topics include the creation of the lake, the erection of busts of Kaiser Wilhelm and Queen Victoria, the building of the Pavilion in 1902 and its destruction by fire in 1916. Period: 1896 - 1986.

4070. **Victoria Park souvenir, 1901: Berlin's beautiful park.** Berlin: H.S. Hallman, 1901. 16 p. Loc: OKIT.

Ten views of the park and portraits of members of the Berlin Park Board in 1894 and 1901. Period: 1894 - 1901.

4071. Vrooman, Paul C. and Morgenson, Donald F. **The day care of children in Kitchener-Waterloo: a research report.** Kitchener: Social Planning Council of Kitchener-Waterloo, 1970. 111 l. ill., bibl. Loc: OWTL.

A statement of the need for quality care that is educational, recreational and social, rather than merely custodial. The authors discuss factors such as maternal employment, neighbourhood considerations, the auspices of day care programmes, and legislation. Numerous recommendations are made, including the provision of more centres in logical locations, more government subsidies and involvement, and the implementation of legislation. Period: 1969 - 1970.

4072. Waterloo County Board of Health. **The health of the County of Waterloo: annual report of the Medical Officer of Health.** The Board, 1972. Loc: OWTL.

A report on the year's activities by divisions including School Health, Public Health, the Community Nutritionist, the Health Inspector, Dentistry Division, and the Environmental Hygiene Division. Statistics of births, infant mortality, deaths and causes of deaths are included. From 1973, the annual report continues as **The health of Waterloo Region: annual report of the Medical Officer of Health** issued by the Board under its later name, Waterloo Regional Health Unit. Period: 1972.

4073. Waterloo County House of Industry and Refuge. **Annual report of the Inspector of the House of Industry and Refuge for the County of Waterloo.** CIHM Microfiche series, no. A00710. 1869 - 1882. 3 fiche. mf. Loc: OWTU, OWTL.

Reports including an account of the causes of pauperism and statistics on the inmates: where they were born, their age, sex, disability, how many had died, and how many had fled the institution. A financial statement sums up the money earned by the inmates through farming and goods manufactured, and the money spent maintaining the institution. Three reports are on microfiche: the 2nd for 1869, the 5th for 1872, and the 15th for 1882. Period: 1869 - 1883.

4074. "Waterloo gets new street lights [WRP]." **Waterloo Historical Society.** 1955. 43: 53. Loc: all.

A note of the installation of fluorescent lights on King Street, Waterloo. Period: 1919 - 1955.

4075. Weiler, Jo-Anne. **One more battle: Kitchener fights influenza, October 1918.** Wilfrid Laurier University (B.A. thesis, History), 1988. 48 p. charts, bibl. Loc: OWTL.

A study from which the author concludes that the severity of the epidemic made the public turn from individual doctors to a broader authority, the Kitchener Board of Health. This resulted in a more bureaucratic public health service and more interaction between physicians and lay people. Statistics and graphs document when and how the disease struck the community. Period: 1918 - 1919.

4076. Wilmot Wellesley Community Inventory Committee. **The Wilmot-Wellesley community inventory: data presentation and report.** The Committee, 1972. 314 l. tables, bibl. Loc: OWT.

A registry of social services with descriptions of the communities of St Agatha, Philipsburg, Petersburg, and Baden in Wilmot Township and Heidelberg, Crosshill, St Clements, Linwood, and Wellesley in Wellesley Township. Topics include population trends, location, climate, soils, water supplies, communications, housing, education, recreation, social structure, municipal services, economic base and regional government. Period: 1825 - 1972.

4077. Wright, Gary W. **Public utilities and regional government in Waterloo County.** Waterloo Lutheran University (B.A. thesis, Geography), 1968. 41 p. maps, tables, bibl. Loc: OWTL.

A study on the basis of which the author recommends that separate regional utility commissions be established for electricity, water, natural gas, and transportation. Street maps of Elmira, Waterloo, Kitchener, Preston, Galt and Hespeler show streets with natural gas lines. Other maps show bus routes in Kitchener, Galt and Waterloo and the land annexed to various towns and cities in the Waterloo County area up to 1964. Period: 1945 - 1968.

4078. Zavaros, Margaret. "Waterloo Park, 1890-1990." **Waterloo Historical Society.** 1990. 78: 83-99. ill. Loc: all.

A well-illustrated account of the planning and development of the park, to mark its centennial. The author provides details of many persons, organizations, and recreational activities associated with the history of the park. Period: 1880 - 1990.

MILITARY HISTORY

4079. Barrie, E.G. "History of the militia in Waterloo County." **Waterloo Historical Society.** 1931. 19: 266-273. Loc: all.

An account of the militia from 1866 to 1931 based on the official **History of the Scots Fusiliers of Canada** by E.C. Shelley. The author explains that, prior to 1914, the militia was drawn from all parts of the county and organized in eight companies but in that year it was divided into northern and southern units. Details of whether drills and training were undertaken are presented for each year between 1866 and 1931. The **Volksblatt** of 12 January 1865 is quoted for the 800 men drafted in the county in response to the Fenian raids, 15 from Berlin being named. A two-page list of officers and men of the Seventh Company of the First Waterloo Battalion for 1857 (for the 7th, 8th and 9th Concessions of Dumfries Township) is appended. Period: 1866 - 1931.

4080. Breithaupt, W.H. "President's address, 1915."
Waterloo Historical Society. 1915. 3: 7-12. ill.
Loc: all.
    An account of the military efforts of Waterloo
County in the First World War, including lists of
battalions, officers, and the dead and missing.
Mention is made of the new fireproof room for the
Society's records in the Berlin Public Library.
Period: 1912 - 1915.

4081. Breithaupt, W.H. "President's address, 1917."
Waterloo Historical Society. 1917. 5: 13-14.
Loc: all.
    A brief account of the war relief efforts in
Waterloo County, with a particular note of the
conversion of the Freeport Tuberculosis Hospital
into a military hospital in 1916. Period: 1916 -
1917.

4082. Bruce, Elizabeth M. "Waterloo County Great War
memorials." **Waterloo Historical Society**. 1923.
11: 22-37. Loc: all.
    An account of various memorials including the
monument in Ayr, the Soldiers' Memorial Home in
Galt, tablets in various churches and schools, and
monuments in cemeteries. Names of all the
soldiers commemorated are given, with a note that
lists previously published in the WHS Reports for
1917 and 1918 were incomplete. Period: 1918 -
1923.

4083. "Dedication of H.L.I. Cairn in France." **Waterloo
Historical Society**. 1969. 57: 69. Loc: all.
    A note of the unveiling of a memorial cairn near
Caen, France in honour of the Highland Light
Infantry and the 25th anniversary of a Second
World War battle in which James P. Kelly won a
medal for destroying two heavy Nazi tanks. Period:
1944 - 1969.

4084. Denis-Nathan, H. "The Highland Fusiliers of
Canada." **Waterloo Historical Society**. 1972. 60:
60-62. Loc: all.
    A history of the regiment from its beginnings as
the Galt Rifle Company in the Rebellion of 1837,
with details of many changes in name of the
various military units until 1965 when Waterloo
County again had a single infantry regiment.
Period: 1837 - 1972.

4085. Donohoe, E.F. "Corvette Kitchener: deposit of bell
in Kitchener City Hall." **Waterloo Historical
Society**. 1946. 34: 36-37. Loc: all.
    A brief description of the work done by the
Local Council of Women for the corvette during the
Second World War, including raising money for
various comforts. In recognition, the Canadian

Government presented the City of Kitchener with
the ship's bell. Period: 1941 - 1945.

4086. Durward, D.N., Lt-Col. "The Highland Light
Infantry of Canada." **Waterloo Historical
Society**. 1945. 33: 8-16. Loc: all.
    A brief account of the overseas service of
"Waterloo County's own" battalion during the
Second World War, including names of the
lieutenant-colonels. Period: 1940 - 1945.

4087. Forbes, Alexander S. **Volunteer recruiting in
Waterloo County during the Great War, 1914-1918**.
University of Waterloo (M.A. thesis, History),
1977. 3 fiche. bibl. mf. Loc: OWTU.
    A study of Galt and Berlin from which the author
concludes that the main difference in recruitment
was not between Germans and other Canadians but
between Canadian-born and British-born males. The
turmoil in Berlin caused by recruiting techniques,
the conflicts among local army units, and the fate
of deserters are all discussed. Period: 1914 -
1918.

4088. "Galt War Memorial." **Waterloo Historical
Society**. 1930. 18: 230-233. Loc: all.
    An account, based on the **Galt Evening Reporter**
of 11 November 1930, of the first remembrance
service at the Galt War Memorial which was
attended by about 9,000 people, including military
and civic officials and veterans. The newly
completed Memorial and Garden of Remembrance, on
the lot formerly occupied by the Galt Opera House
and donated by the Gore Mutual Fire Insurance
Company, were presented to the city by H.F.
MacKendrick, chairman of the War Memorial
Committee. Period: 1914 - 1930.

4089. Glanville, R. and Bartlett, Jack F. **1st
Battalion, the Highland Light Infantry of Canada,
1940-1945**. Galt: Highland Light Infantry
Association of Canada, 1951. 126 p. ill., maps.
Loc: OCCA, OCLG, OKIT, OKITW.
    An illustrated history of Galt's Highland Light
Infantry from May 1940, when the regiment was
ordered to mobilize for active service, until the
end of the Second World War. There are maps of
Normandy, Germany and the Netherlands showing the
regiment's movements and a list of honours awarded
to members of the infantry during the Second World
War. Period: 1940 - 1945.

4090. Green, David. "Waterloo County's militia."
Waterloo Historical Society. 1966. 54: 62-68.
Loc: all.
    A history of the local militia from the early
rifle companies and the formation of the Highland
Fusiliers of Canada and 29th Battalion of Infantry

in 1866 as a defence against Fenian raids. In 1920, the 29th Regiment was permitted to adopt the name, The Highland Light Infantry of Canada. The roles of local militia units in World War I and World War II are described. Period: 1812 - 1965.

4091. Greer, Rosamond. "All aboard!!." **The girls of the King's navy**. Victoria, BC: Sono Nis Press, 1983. 160 p. ill., bibl. Loc: OCCA.

Personal recollections of the author's training at H.M.S.C. **Conestoga**, Galt in 1943. Isabel J. Macneill of Galt was the only woman in command of a naval establishment in the British Empire. Photographs show the Wrens parading through Galt, Wrens working at H.M.S.C. **Conestoga**, and a statue in Galt commemorating the Women's Royal Canadian Naval Service. Period: 1942 - 1943.

4092. "The Highland Light Infantry of Canada presentation of colours by ... H.R.H. the Princess Margaret C.I., G.C.V.O. Friday August 1st, 1958 Civic Stadium, Hamilton." **Galt Evening Reporter**. 1958, July 29. Pp. 1A-28A. ill. Loc: OCCA.

A souvenir edition with articles on the history of the regiment focusing on the Second World War, with photographs and information on its commanders from 1837 to the present. Period: 1837 - 1958.

4093. K-W Naval Association. **K-W Naval Association 25 years**. The Association, 1985. 1 v. (unpaged). ill. Loc: OKIT.

An anniversary history of the association and its activities, including the Ladies Auxiliary. Information about the corvette Kitchener is also given. Period: 1960 - 1985.

4094. Lautenschlager, Harold. **New Hamburg cenotaph**. The Author, 1990. 26 p. Loc: OKIT, OWRN.

A history of the New Hamburg cenotaph, erected in 1929, with brief biographical notes of the thirty Wilmot Township men who died in the two world wars. It lists streets in New Hamburg, Baden, New Dundee, St Agatha and Mannheim named after veterans. Period: 1914 - 1945.

4095. Lautenschlager, Harold. "New Hamburg cenotaphs." **Waterloo Historical Society**. 1991. 79: 80-85. ill. Loc: all.

An account of the planning and erection of the three successive war memorials of 1922, 1928 and 1991. Community leaders who organized these projects and all who died in both world wars and the Korean War are named. Period: 1921 - 1991.

4096. Lea, Joanne. **The great war**. Kitchener: Doon Heritage Crossroads, Historic Sites Department, Regional Municipality of Waterloo, 1987. 1 v. ill., bibl. Loc: OKDHC.

A teacher's kit of printed material, slides and audio cassettes pertaining to Waterloo County during the First World War, including a transcript of an interview with veteran William Green of Galt and his autobiography. Period: 1914 - 1918.

4097. "Lieutenant Willard Ewart Clemens." **Waterloo Historical Society**. 1918. 6: 49. ill. Loc: all.

A note in memory of Willard Ewart Clemens (1898-1917) of the Royal Air Force. Period: 1898 - 1917.

4098. McCallum, Fred H. "Experiences of a Queen's Own Rifleman at Ridgeway." **Waterloo Historical Society**. 1915. 3: 24-39. Loc: all.

An account of the adventures of Fred McCallum of Waterloo County at the Battle of Ridgeway in 1866, during the Fenian Raids. Period: 1866 - 1916.

4099. "Our glorious dead: Kitchener-Waterloo and district war casualties in 1944." **Waterloo Historical Society**. 1944. 32: 25-31. Loc: all.

A list of nearly 200 who died on war service to the end of 1944. Each entry gives details of name, rank, home town, next of kin, and date of death. Period: 1939 - 1944.

4100. "Our glorious dead: Kitchener-Waterloo and district war casualties in 1945." **Waterloo Historical Society**. 1945. 33: 39-40. Loc: all.

A list of about 50 soldiers, including details of name, rank, home town, next of kin, and date of death. Period: 1945.

4101. **Peace souvenir: activities of Waterloo County in the Great War, 1914-1918**. Kitchener: Kitchener Daily Telegraph, 1919. 70 p. ill. Loc: OWTUR, OKIT, OCCA.

A book honouring the efforts of community members who served in the war or at home. Lists of soldiers who fought overseas are provided as are entries on organizations such as the IODE and the Red Cross. Also included are articles by W.H Breithaupt and Mabel Dunham on the war effort. Thirty-six pages of advertisements from local businesses are indexed on page 3. Period: 1914 - 1919.

4102. "Roll of honour, 1916: officers and men of Waterloo County who have made the supreme sacrifice for king and country." **Waterloo Historical Society**. 1916. 4: 24-25. Loc: all.

List compiled in 1916 of men from Galt, Kitchener, Preston, Waterloo and Hespeler who died in the First World War. Period: 1914 - 1916.

4103. "Roll of honour: additions, 1917." **Waterloo Historical Society**. 1917. 5: 41-42. Loc: all.
List of men from Waterloo County killed in the First World War. Period: 1917.

4104. "Roll of honour: additions, 1918." **Waterloo Historical Society**. 1918. 6: 9-10. Loc: all.
List of men of Waterloo County who died in the First World War. Period: 1917 - 1918.

4105. Sherk, A.B., Rev. "Early militia matters in Upper Canada, 1808-1842." **Ontario Historical Society, Papers and Records**. 1915. 13: 67-73. Loc: OWTL, OWTU.
An account of the military exemption of the Quakers, Tunkers and Mennonites, derived from the papers of Jacob Gonder, a pioneer of the Niagara area. Period: 1808 - 1842.

4106. Snowie, J. Allan. **Bloody Buron: the Battle of Buron, Normandy, 08 July 1944**. Erin: Boston Mills Press, 1984. 120 p. ill., bibl., maps. Loc: OCCA, OKIT.
A lavishly illustrated account of the role of the Highland Light Infantry of Canada and its many men from Waterloo County. The names of those who participated in the battle are listed, ten citations are described, and interviews with soldiers are quoted. A family tree of the Highland Fusiliers of Canada outlines Waterloo County military history from 1812 to 1965. Period: 1944 - 1945.

4107. Sykes, C.A., Rev. "Aviation gunner David Ward Clement." **Waterloo Historical Society**. 1918. 6: 48-49. ill. Loc: all.
A short biography of David Ward Clement (1897-1917), a young aviation gunner and observer who was killed during the First World War. Period: 1897 - 1917.

4108. Trinity Methodist Church, Kitchener. **Roll of honor: enlisted men to date, July 1st, 1917, 50th anniversary of Confederation**. Kitchener: The Church, 1917. 1 sheet. Loc: OWTUR.
From the Clement/Bowlby Family Papers. Period: 1914 - 1917.

4109. Waterloo Town Council. **Thanksgiving for victory, Waterloo Ontario Canada**. Waterloo: The Council, 1945. 15 p. Loc: OWTUR, OWT.
A programme of the service in Waterloo Park on Sunday, 20 May 1945, marking the end of World War Two. As well as listing the events of the day, the programme includes names and photographs of many Waterloo men killed in the war. Period: 1939 - 1945.

4110. Wert, Michael. **From enlistment to the grave: a case study of the 34th Battalion's experience with the Great War**. Wilfrid Laurier University (B.A. thesis, History), 1990. 52 p. tables, bibl. Loc: OKIT, OWTU.
A study of the experience of war by fifty-two named recruits from Kitchener who were selected randomly. Using personnel records from the National Archives, pension records from the Department of Veterans Affairs and local sources, the author examines the lives of the soldiers during the war and later. Information is provided about injuries received in the war and the care and compensation the men received as a result. Period: 1914 - 1957.

4111. Wilder, T.A. "The history of the militia in Waterloo County." **Waterloo Historical Society**. 1978. 66: 61-70. Loc: all.
An account of the founding and development of various militia units, with descriptions of typical activities such as the week-long training camps. Period: 1837 - 1878.

POLITICS: MUNICIPAL, AND LOCAL ASPECTS OF PROVINCIAL AND FEDERAL POLITICS

4112. Armstrong, L. **Kitchener's pro-labour council 1940-41**. University of Waterloo (student essay), 1974. 28 p. bibl. Loc: OKIT.
A study of the pro-labour stance of Mayor Meinzinger and the Kitchener City Council in 1940-1941. The author concludes that the council's campaign against some low wages in the city was motivated by concern for the reputation of the city and its industries and a desire to prevent damaging strikes. Period: 1940 - 1941.

4113. Avery, Donald H. "British born 'radicals' in North America, 1900-1941: the case of Sam Scarlett." **Canadian Ethnic Studies**. 1978. 10,2: 65-85. Loc: OWTL, OWTU, OWTUCG.
Biography of a Scottish machinist who emigrated to Canada in 1903 and became a labour organizer involved with the Industrial Workers of the World and the Communist Party of Canada. Scarlett emigrated to work at the firm of Goldie-McCulloch in Galt, becoming a member of its soccer team which won the Canadian championship in 1904 and also the Association Football title at the Olympic games in St Louis. However, Scarlett stayed in Galt for only a year and soon left Canada for the United States. Period: 1903 - 1944.

4114. Boehm, Peter M. "Saw-off! Political turbulence in Waterloo North in 1900." **Waterloo Historical Society**. 1977. 65: 37-43. Loc: all.

An analysis of the compromise to ensure that the federal Conservative candidate, Joseph E. Seagram, would not be opposed by the Liberals in the federal election and that the Liberal, L.J. Breithaupt, would not face opposition by the Tories in the provincial by-election. Period: 1896 - 1900.

4115. Boudreau, Joseph A. **The enemy alien problem in Canada, 1914-1921.** University of California - Los Angeles (Ph.D. thesis, History), 1965. 211 l. ill.

A study concerned mainly with western Canada, with some references on pp. 143-8 to the situation in Kitchener during the 1917 federal election. Period: 1916 - 1917.

4116. Bowman, I.E. and Cowan, James. "Confederation debated in 1865." **Waterloo Historical Society.** 1966. 54: 4-7. ill. Loc: all.

Speeches made during the 3rd session, 8th Provincial Parliament in March 1865 on the subject of Confederation by Isaac Erb Bowman, Liberal member for North Waterloo, and James Cowan, Reform member for South Waterloo. Period: 1865.

4117. Breithaupt, James R. "Legislative Assembly members 1867-1967." **Waterloo Historical Society.** 1982. 70: 30-31. Loc: all.

A list of those who represented Waterloo North in the Ontario Legislature, with their dates of service and political parties. Period: 1867 - 1967.

4118. Calvin, Douglas G. **Labour and municipal politics 1935-1969; Kitchener: a case study.** Wilfrid Laurier University (M.A. thesis, History), 1981. 118 p. maps, tables, bibl. Loc: OWTL.

An examination of Kitchener's labour movement through an analysis of the municipal election results from 1935 to 1969. The author concludes that labour's most successful political activities took place between 1940 to 1946, with Alfred Mustin and William Kartechner being elected to city council. Following the 1946 rubber strike, the labour movement became divided and lost public support. The author suggests that labour's decline was also caused by the conciliatory response of city council to labour's specific demands. Tables of election results and maps showing the areas of labour support in Kitchener are included. Period: 1935 - 1969.

4119. Carter, John. "The reciprocity election of 1911: Waterloo North, a case study." **Waterloo Historical Society.** 1974. 62: 77-91. ill., tables. Loc: all.

An account of the free trade issue in the 1911 federal election in which Mackenzie King, Liberal Member of Parliament, was opposed by W.G. Weichel. The author analyzes coverage of the issue by the **Berlin Daily Telegraph** and the **Berlin News Record.** Four appendices give more details, including names of members of the 1911 Berlin Board of Trade and how each voted, voting figures from the Berlin polling stations, and statistics of how the urban and rural vote was split compared with the federal election in 1901. Period: 1901 - 1911.

4120. Carter, John. **Who governs Berlin-Kitchener, 1910-1917.** University of Waterloo (student essay, History), 1973. 1 v. (various pagings). ill., tables, bibl. Loc: OKIT.

An analysis of the city's leaders, in which occupation, social status and ethnic background are discussed as factors influencing political decisions. The author examines the specific issues of reciprocity in the 1911 federal election and the name change in 1916. Period: 1910 - 1917.

4121. Chadwick, W.R. **The battle for Berlin, Ontario: an historical drama.** Waterloo: Wilfrid Laurier University Press, 1992. 176 p. ill., map, bibl.,index. Loc: OKIT, OWTL, OWTU, OWTUR.

A detailed narrative of the events during the First World War that culminated in the renaming of Berlin as Kitchener in 1916. Period: 1914 - 1919.

4122. "Conestogo election fourth in 51 years." **Waterloo Historical Society.** 1965. 53: 34. Loc: all.

A note of the forthcoming election in the police village. Period: 1914 - 1965.

4123. Day, Cindy. **Anti-German sentiment in Berlin during the First World War.** University of Waterloo (student essay, History), 1988. 20 p. bibl. Loc: OKIT.

A study of how the English reaction to Berlin's German population in the 1914-1918 war destroyed the city's dual English-German nature. The author's sources include newspaper reports, L.J. Breithaupt's diaries, and the letters of William Walter Breithaupt who served with the 108th Battalion. Period: 1914 - 1918.

4124. Donohoe, E.F. "Resolutions passed by Twin City citizens upon the death of President Lincoln." **Waterloo Historical Society.** 1943. 31: 43-45. Loc: all.

An account of the 1865 resolution to send a message of sympathy to Mrs Lincoln and to the United States on behalf of the towns of Berlin and Waterloo. Individuals noted as involved in the decision were Ward H. Bowlby (then Reeve of Berlin), Louis Breithaupt, Israel D. Bowman, William Jaffray, Dougall McDougall, the Rev. John

Armstrong and the Rev. D. Schulte. Period: 1865.

4125. Dunford, James Ross. **Political opinion in South Waterloo 1857-1873.** University of Toronto (M.A. thesis), 1955. 1 reel. mf. Loc: OWTL, OWTU.

A study of the attitudes of the people of Galt to major political events of the period, as recorded in its two newspapers, Jaffray's conservative **Galt Reporter**, and Young's liberal **Dumfries Reformer**. Following an introductory chapter on the early settlement, the political and economic issues of the day at all levels of government are recounted. Special attention is given to the problems of Confederation and to Canada's relations with Britain and the United States. Period: 1857 - 1873.

4126. Edwards, John D. **The Kitchener coalition: a study of urban politics, decision-making and the role of the planner.** University of Waterloo (B.E.S. thesis, Planning), 1972. 203 l. maps, tables, bibl. Loc: OWTU.

An examination of policy planning for urban development and redevelopment with particular reference to the Civic Centre site. The author stresses the roles of the politicians, their use of political power, and the patterns and structures of political influence. The efforts of groups such as the Kitchener Taxpayers' Association, the residents of the site, the Chamber of Commerce, and the Kitchener Coalition are discussed. Period: 1951 - 1971.

4127. English, John and McLaughlin, Kenneth. "Allen Huber: Berlin's strangest mayor." **Waterloo Historical Society.** 1981. 69: 4-12. ill. Loc: all.

A detailed account of the political career of Huber (1847-1915), the maverick Mayor in 1908 who literally punched a member of the Berlin elite on the nose. Period: 1847 - 1915.

4128. Enns, Gerhard. "Waterloo North and conscription 1917." **Waterloo Historical Society.** 1963. 51: 60-69. bibl. Loc: all.

A scholarly account of the 1917 federal election contest in Waterloo North between W.D. Euler and W.G. Weichel in which the key issue was the Conscription Bill. Period: 1917.

4129. Essex, J. "Great Kit-Wat name game." **Macleans Magazine.** 1965. 78: 3. Loc: OKIT, OWTL, OWTU.

Reference from the Canadian Periodical Index. Period: 1965.

4130. Fisher, P. "The royal visit." **Waterloo Historical Society.** 1939. 27: 59-62. ill. Loc: all.

A description of the visit of King George VI and Queen Elizabeth. Period: 1939.

4131. Galt, Alexander Tilloch. **Canada, von 1849 bis 1859.** CIHM Microfiche series, no. 39289. Preston: W. Schlueter, 1860. mf. Loc: OWTL, OWTU.

A locally published translation of a book by the noted Canadian politician. Period: 1849 - 1859.

4132. Heick, W.H. "'If we lose the war, nothing else matters': the 1917 federal election in North Waterloo." **Ontario History.** 1980. 72,2: 67-92. ill. Loc: OKIT, OWTL, OWTU, OWTUCG.

An analysis of the election won by W.D. Euler, a Laurier Liberal who campaigned against conscription. The political issues and campaigns of Euler and his main opponent, the Unionist candidate W.G. Weichel, are presented from both a local and national point of view. The study shows that the election was more complicated than a confrontation between English and French Canada. Period: 1914 - 1918.

4133. Hungler, John Joseph. **The problems and reactions of the German-Canadian community in Kitchener-Waterloo, Ontario, caused by the Military Service Act and Wartime Franchise Act of 1917.** University of Windsor (M.A. thesis, History), 1967. 79 l. tabl. Loc: OWA.

Reference from **Bibliography of Ontario history, 1867-1976** (Bishop et al.). Period: 1916 - 1917.

4134. Hunsberger, Albert. "Biographical sketches of Legislative Assembly Members, 1792-1867." **Waterloo Historical Society.** 1981. 69: 127-145. Loc: all.

Short biographies of those who represented the Waterloo North and then the Kitchener riding, from 1792 to 1867. The original version, available in the Kitchener Public Library and elsewhere, was prepared for James R. Breithaupt, M.P.P. Kitchener, by Mr. James O'Mara of the Legislative Research Service. Biographies are included for: Nathaniel Pettitt, Richard Beasley, Robert Nelles (or Nellis), Joseph Willcocks, John Wilson (or Willson), Abraham (Abram) Markle, James Durand, Moses Gamble, Richard Hatt, James Crooks, George Rolph, Caleb Hopkins, Absalom Shade, James Webster, Adam Johnston Fergusson (later A.J. Fergusson-Blair), Michael Hamilton Foley and Isaac E. Bowman. Insufficient details were available for S. Hill, W. Chisholm and W. Scollick. Period: 1792 - 1867.

4135. Krueger, Ralph R. "The Kitchener Market fight: another view." **Urban Forum: Journal of the Urban Research Council of Canada.** 1976. 2,2: 40-47. ill. Loc: OWTU.

A response to the negative reactions to the

Kitchener urban renewal plan, with critical reference to Jack Pasternak's book on the Farmers' Market-City Hall redevelopment project. The author, geography professor at the University of Waterloo and member of the Kitchener Urban Renewal Committee in 1971, maintains that the process was both democratic and justified by the success of the project. Period: 1960 - 1976.

4136. McIntosh, Frances R. "Our man in Ottawa." **Waterloo Historical Society**. 1967. 55: 63-85. ill. Loc: all.

Biographical sketches of Waterloo North's ten representatives in the Canadian Parliament since 1867: Isaac Erb Bowman, Hugo Kranz, Joseph E. Seagram, William Lyon Mackenzie King, William G. Weichel, William D. Euler, Louis O. Breithaupt, Norman C. Schneider, O.W. Weichel and Kieth R. Hymmen. This essay won first prize in the 1967 Kitchener Public Library Centennial Essay Competition. Period: 1867 - 1967.

4137. McKegney, Patricia. **Germanism, industrialism, and propaganda in Berlin, Ontario during World War I**. University of Waterloo (M.A. thesis, History), 1979. 461 p. ill., map, bibl. Loc: OWTUR.

A study concluding that the general reaction of Berlin citizens to World War I was dominated by three main factors named in the title. The author examines Berlin's institutions such as the City Council, Board of Trade, School Board and churches as well as the various federal and municipal elections, the recruiting campaigns for the 118th Battalion, and the campaign to change the name of the city of Berlin to Kitchener. Period: 1914 - 1918.

4138. McKegney, Patricia. **The Kaiser's bust: a study of war-time propaganda in Berlin, Ontario 1914-1918**. Bamberg Heritage Series no.2. Wellesley: Bamberg Press, 1991. 279 p. ill., bibl., map. Loc: OCP, OKIT, OWRL, OWRW, OWTL, OWTU.

An illustrated history of how government propaganda, Berlin's industrialism and Germanism affected the inhabitants of the city during the First World War. The work is largely based on the author's Masters thesis at the University of Waterloo. A fully indexed record appears in the WRP database under the thesis title, **Germanism, industrialism, and propaganda in Berlin, Ontario during World War I**. Period: 1914 - 1918.

4139. McMahen, Janice A. **Berlin becomes Kitchener: a breach in the German tradition of an Ontario city**. Waterloo Lutheran University (B.A. thesis, History), 1973. 75 l. bibl. Loc: OWTL.

A study of the tension in Berlin/Kitchener during the First World War, especially on the

issues of German-language instruction in public schools and business attitudes to the German name of the city. The work includes excerpts from newspapers reporting the throwing of Kaiser Wilhelm's bust into the lake in 1914, the Concordia Club raid in 1916, and the vote to change the city's name. The author also notes Berlin's contributions to the war effort and impressions of the city by outsiders during the war. Period: 1913 - 1920.

4140. McPhedran, Greta. **A study of Kitchener during the period 1935-1937**. University of Waterloo (student essay, History), 197-?. 1 v. (various pagings). tables. Loc: OKIT.

An analysis of the social and economic status of Kitchener's politicians who tended to be businessmen and entrepreneurs. Tables provide statistical data on the city's industrial growth from 1914 to 1939. Period: 1935 - 1937.

4141. Myers, Pat. **Prohibition as a political issue in Berlin: 1898, 1911, 1914, 1919**. University of Waterloo (student essay, History), 197-?. 35 p. Loc: OKIT.

A study, based on newspaper editorials and church records, showing that prohibition was favoured only by a small, organized lobby identified with the Liberal Party and some churches by the end of the study period. Period: 1898 - 1919.

4142. Norcliffe, G.B. "Territorial influences in urban political space: a study of perception in Kitchener-Waterloo." **Canadian Geographer**. 1974. 18: 311-329. bibl., map, tables. Loc: OKIT, OWTL, OWTU.

A quantitative description of how citizens of Kitchener and Waterloo perceived themselves and each other. The differences are attributed to territoriality operating on an urban scale. The author concludes that his study of local loyalties confirms the correctness of the decision not to amalgamate the two cities as proposed in the Fyfe Report of 1970. Period: 1970 - 1974.

4143. O'Grady, John. **Political power in Kitchener**. University of Waterloo (B.E.S. thesis), 1973. 170 p. bibl. Loc: OWTU.

A analysis of those who governed Kitchener in 1973, following a chapter on the past history of the city's changing political elite. The roles of 30 named community leaders are examined in four specific issues: the Oktoberfest, the Federated Appeal, urban renewal, and City Council. The author concludes that the business community has the decisive voice in community affairs. Period: 1912 - 1973.

4144. O'Mara, James. **Kitchener Legislative Assembly members, 1792-1867.** Toronto: Queen's Park, Legislative Library, Research and Information Services, 1981. 69 p. bibl. Loc: OKIT.

Biographical sketches of those who represented the Berlin district in the provincial legislature, with an explanation of changing definitions of the constituencies. Period: 1800 - 1867.

4145. Offenbeck, John. **The Nazi Movement and German Canadians, 1933-1939.** University of Western Ontario (M.A. thesis, History), 1970. 195 p. bibl. Loc: OLU.

A study of the spread of Nazi propaganda through the Deutsche Bund, the **Deutsche Zeitung** newspaper, the promotion of German-language instruction and the annual German Day celebrations. The author focuses mainly on larger centres and Western Canada but notes the establishment of the Deutsche Bund of Canada at Waterloo in January 1934 and the early leadership of Karl Gerhard who was attached to Waterloo College. The Kitchener-Waterloo branch of the Bund, led by Ernst Woelfle, was the only permanent one in Ontario, though it failed to convince most members of the traditional German social clubs such as the Concordia. Period: 1933 - 1939.

4146. Oswald, Marie C. **The zenith of tension: Waterloo North and the wartime general election of 1917.** University of Waterloo (student essay, History), 1978. 93 l. tables, bibl. Loc: OKIT.

An analysis of the issues of compulsory military service, local anti-conscription political campaigns, local and national anti-German sentiment, the name change from Berlin to Kitchener, and contributions to patriotic and war-relief funds. Tables include statistical information on voters' ethnic origins and religion, as well as changes of business name in the county in 1916. Period: 1914 - 1917.

4147. **The other side: an appeal for British fair play.** 1916. 2 sheets. Loc: OWTLR.

A propaganda pamphlet endorsed by the Citizens' League of Berlin, advocating retention of the city's name. The authors claim that the initial meeting to change the name was packed, that the raid on the Concordia Club was unprovoked, that the Mennonite faith prevented many descendants of Pennsylvania Germans from enlisting, and that the name change was being promoted for commercial reasons by manufacturers. Period: 1915 - 1916.

4148. Pasternak, Jack. **The Kitchener Market fight.** Toronto: S. Stevens, Hakkert, 1975. 236 p. ill., bibl., index. Loc: OWTU, OWTL, OKIT, OWRN.

A strongly partisan account of alleged machinations behind Kitchener's urban development by a member of the Citizens Committee for a Better County Core, an organization which tried to save the old market and the city hall in Kitchener in 1971. Among the organizations criticized are the Kitchener Urban Renewal Committee, the **Kitchener-Waterloo Record**, Oxlea Investments Ltd, and the Ontario Municipal Board. Period: 1962 - 1971.

4149. Penny, Andrew. **The governors of Berlin (1910-13).** University of Waterloo (student essay, History), 197-?. 25 l. tables, bibl. Loc: OKIT, OWTL.

A study of key issues in order to determine how civic decisions were made, which groups and individuals possessed the greatest resources and exercised the greatest influence, and what kind of relationship existed between the decision-makers and the mass of voters. The author presents brief profiles of Berlin politicians and current issues such as cityhood, public ownership of hydro-electricity, and reciprocity. Period: 1910 - 1913.

4150. "Preston's 10th Warden in 103 years." **Waterloo Historical Society.** 1960. 48: 23. Loc: all.

A note of the election of James Sanderson of Preston as Warden of Waterloo County for 1960. His nine predecessors from Preston were Jacob Hespeler, Abraham A. Erb, William C. Scheuter, George A. Clare, S.L. Cherry, Dr Anthony Oaks, Mark M. Donald, William J. Pelz and Ford I. Willson. Period: 1856 - 1960.

4151. **Proclamation! nördlicher Wahlbezirk des County Waterloo.** CIHM Microfiche series, no. 46866, 58274. Berlin: Canadier Druck, 1862 - 1863. mf. Loc: OWTL, OWTU.

An electoral announcement for the north riding of Waterloo County. Period: 1862 - 1863.

4152. **Proclamation! north riding of the County of Waterloo to wit: public notice is hereby given to the electors of the north riding of Waterloo.** CIHM Microfiche series, no. 56145, 55650, 58725, 58286. Berlin: Telegraph, 1861 - 1864. mf. Loc: OWTL, OWTU.

Election proclamations dated 1861, 1862, 1863 and 1864. Period: 1861 - 1864.

4153. **Proclamation! south riding of the county of Waterloo! to wit: public notice is hereby given to the electors of the south riding of the county of Waterloo ... for the purpose of electing a person to represent them in the Legislative Assembly.** CIHM Microfiche series, no. 57196, 58277. Berlin:

Telegraph, 1857, 1863. mf. Loc: OWTL, OWTU. Period: 1857 - 1863.

4154. Proclamation! südlicher Wahlbezirk des County Waterloo. CIHM Microfiche series, no. 58273. Berlin: Canadier Druck, 1863. mf. Loc: OWTL, OWTU.

An electoral announcement for the south riding of Waterloo County. Period: 1863.

4155. Stewart, Rod. "Federal elections in Waterloo South (1867-1963)." **Waterloo Historical Society.** 1963. 51: 29-34. Loc: all.

An analysis based on files of the **Galt Reporter** and **Galt Reformer**, showing that in nearly all elections local voters were against the national trend, electing Liberals in the nineteenth century and Conservatives since 1900. A table summarizes the votes for all candidates in 29 elections or by-elections. Period: 1867 - 1963.

4156. Stovel, Rob. **A spatial analysis of voter turnout in Kitchener, 1972-1985.** Wilfrid Laurier University (B.A. thesis, Geography), 1986. 103 p. maps, bibl., tables. Loc: OWTL.

A study of voter lists and census data from which the author finds that voter turnout is not significantly related to ethnicity, but positively related to high socio-economic status. Voter turnout is found to have been unaffected by increase in population or the change to the ward system after the election of 1976. Controversy and competition are concluded to be the best stimuli to voter participation. Period: 1972 - 1985.

4157. Tessaro, Annamaria. **Mackenzie King and the 1911 election in North Waterloo.** University of Waterloo (student essay, History), 1978. 51 p. bibl., tables. Loc: OKIT.

An analysis of the federal election when the Liberal Minister of Labour, W.L. Mackenzie King, lost to W.G. Weichel of the Conservative Party. The author concludes that the working class vote was instrumental in defeating King, perhaps because of his poor handling of the Grand Trunk Railway strike, or because of fears of the economic threat of free trade to local manufacturers. Period: 1864 - 1911.

4158. Tessaro, Annamaria. "Mackenzie King in North Waterloo." **Waterloo Historical Society.** 1978. 66: 18-40. bibl., tables. Loc: all.

An historical account of the 1911 federal election in which King lost to Conservative W.G. Weichel on the issue of reciprocity with the United States. The author quotes from King's correspondence and diaries and presents tables showing results in the 1908 and the 1911 elections from polling stations in the riding of North Waterloo. Period: 1908 - 1911.

4159. Thomson, Andrew McCauley. "The Berlin scandal of 1866." **Waterloo Historical Society.** 1991. 79: 115-116. Loc: all.

An account of the resignation of Louis Breithaupt as Deputy Reeve of the Waterloo County Council, following exposure of the plan to pad the Berlin assessment roll in order to obtain a second seat for the village on the county council. Period: 1865 - 1866.

4160. Thomson, Georgina H. "A nonagenarian remembers." **Waterloo Historical Society.** 1951. 39: 36-38. Loc: all.

A short account of a political debate between James Young and Samuel Merner, the two candidates for South Waterloo in the 1878 federal election. Period: 1878.

4161. "Tomecko heads Waterloo Council." **Financial Post.** 1961. 55: 3. ill. mf. Loc: OWTL, OWTU.

Reference from the Canadian Periodical Index. Period: 1961.

4162. Tough, Bonnie. **Who governed? Berlin 1900-1905.** University of Waterloo (student essay, History), 197-?. 25 p. bibl. Loc: OKIT.

A study of the city's political leaders and the factors of occupation, social status, and ethnic background in political decision-making. Period: 1900 - 1905.

4163. Trowbridge, Robert W. **War time rural discontent and the rise of the United Farmers of Ontario 1914-1919.** University of Waterloo (M.A. thesis, History), 1966. 3 fiche. bibl. mf. Loc: OWTU.

A study of the party's origins including the desire to keep young farmers at home during World War One. Although the work is broad in scope and deals with issues at the provincial level, the author mentions briefly the stance taken by North Waterloo farmers on the cancellation of exemptions from military service. Period: 1914 - 1919.

4164. Wilson, Barbara M. "Loyalty in question." **Ontario and the First World War, 1914-1918: a collection of documents.** Ontario Series No. 10. Toronto: The Champlain Society, 1977. Pp.lxx-lxxxiv, 75-100. Loc: OWTU, OKIT, OWTL.

A review of the events that expressed anti-German sentiment in Berlin/Kitchener. Pages lxx to lxxxiv describe incidents such as the raiding of the Concordia Club in Berlin and the Acadian Club in Waterloo, the attack on the Rev. C.R. Tappert, the name change issue, the conscription controversy, the unrest associated with the municipal election of January 1917, and the findings of a court of inquiry into the disturbances. Pages 75 to 100 include documents reflecting ethnic and political divisions in the city (including letters to the editor of the **Berlin News Record** by W.H. Breithaupt and W.G. Cleghorn). Period: 1914 - 1918.

4165. Wilson, J.M. "The myth of candidate partisanship: the case of Waterloo South." **Journal of Canadian Studies.** 1968. 3,4: 21-31. Loc: OWTL, OWTU.

An analysis of the 1964 by-election won by Max Saltsman for the New Democratic Party. Period: 1960 - 1964.

4166. Wilson, J.M. "Politics and social class in Canada: the case of Waterloo South." **Canadian Journal of Political Science.** 1968. 1: 288-309. tables. Loc: OKIT, OWTL, OWTU.

A detailed analysis of the 1964 Waterloo South federal by-election won by Max Saltsman, the NDP candidate. The author interprets the result as indicating a growth in class politics and a lessening of the importance of religion and ethnicity in determining the outcome of Canadian elections. Period: 1921 - 1968.

4167. Wilson, J.M. "Waterloo South breakthrough for the NDP?." **Canadian Forum.** 1964. 44,527: 196-198. Loc: OWTL, OWTU, OWTUSJ.

A report of the NDP victory in the 1964 federal by-election in Waterloo South. While the author credits the personality of Max Saltsman for the election win, he suggests that the NDP's ability to collect votes from both the Liberal and Conservative parties could be replicated elsewhere. Period: 1963 - 1964.

4168. Winn, Conrad and McMenemy, John. "Political alignment in a polarized city: electoral cleavages in Kitchener, Ontario." **Canadian Journal of Political Science.** 1973. 6: 230-242, tables. Loc: OKIT, OWTL, OWTU.

A study of the debate over the redevelopment of the Kitchener Farmers' Market, based on data from the 1967, 1969 and 1971 municipal elections, the 1971 referendum ballots and the 1971 provincial election. The authors conclude that the voters split into right and left political wings, as well as dividing along religious lines which isolated the Catholic population. Similarities between provincial and local patterns of voting are also demonstrated. Period: 1967 - 1973.

4169. Winn, Conrad. "The secret life of Kitchener's parties." **Canadian Forum.** 1972. 52,623: 10. Loc: OWTL, OWTU, OWTUSJ.

A portrayal of Kitchener's municipal politics as outwardly discreet and pragmatic but contradicted by partisan voting, as shown in the election following the Farmers' Market controversy. Period: 1970 - 1972.

4170. Young, James. **Our national future!: being four letters by James Young in opposition to commercial union (as proposed) and imperial federation! and pointing out what the writer believes to be the true future of Canada as a part of North America.** CIHM Microfiche series, no. 26165. Galt: Collie and McGiverin, 1887. mf. Loc: OWTL, OWTU.

A political pamphlet by the long-time newspaper proprietor and editor of the **Dumfries Reformer**, who also represented South Waterloo as a Liberal in the Dominion Parliament from 1867 to 1878. Period: 1887 - 1888.

STUDIES OF SPECIFIC TOWNSHIPS AND URBAN CENTRES

AYR

4171. Ayr and District Chamber of Commerce. **Ayr, 1824-1972: "the village beautiful"**. Ayr: The Chamber, 1974. 56 p. ill., map. Loc: OWTU, OWRA.
A commemorative book containing brief notes and photographs of fifty businesses, photographs of public buildings and prominent residents, an index of services, and a zoning map. Period: 1824 - 1972.

4172. Ayr and District Chamber of Commerce. **Ayr, 1986: "the village beautiful"**. The Chamber, 1986. 16 p. ill., maps. Loc: OKIT, OWRA.
A directory of current businesses with a one-page history of the village, a map showing points of interest, and a list of clubs and organizations. Period: 1824 - 1986.

4173. Ayr Boosters' Association. **Our growing Ayr**. Ayr: Ayr News, 197-?. 16 p. ill. Loc: OWRA.
A promotional brochure for the village, with sections on its business district, homes, churches, schools, transportation, communications and recreational facilities. Period: 1824 - c1975.

4174. Ayr Centennial Committee. **Historical pageant presented by Ayr Centennial Committee**. Ayr: The Committee, 1924. 8 p. Loc: OWRA.
The programme of the pageant produced in Victoria Park by F.P. Gorman. The various scenes and characters are explained and there is a list of contemporary businesses. Period: 1824 - 1924.

4175. "Ayr news of 1885." **Waterloo Historical Society**. 1961. 49: 31. Loc: all.
A note of some old municipal records found during renovation of the village council chamber. Period: 1885 - 1961.

4176. Ayr News. **A warm welcome awaits you: 150th anniversary and reunion 1824-1974**. 1974. Loc: OWRA.
A collection of special issues, of which the Ayr Public Library has those of 28 February, 4 July and 29 July 1974. Each issue includes articles on Ayr's history with profiles of various sports teams, local services and businesses, as well as reminiscences of residents and former residents and historical photographs of community buildings. Period: 1824 - 1974.

4177. "Ayr notes." **Waterloo Historical Society**. 1948. 36: 43-44. Loc: all.
A short note of the deaths of two local businessmen: Alexander C. Gillies, druggist and sports enthusiast and James G. Fair, jeweller and active community leader. The article also mentions the sale of two historic buildings, Reid's Hall and The Gore (the Goldie family home). Period: 1855 - 1948.

4178. Ayr Women's Institute. **Tweedsmuir history, Ayr Women's Institute, South Waterloo**. 4 v. ill. Also mf. Loc: OWRA, OKIT.
A scrapbook history of Ayr, with Institute members adding to it from time to time. Topics include schools, industries, outstanding people, churches, century farms, cemeteries, houses and special events such as golden weddings. Photographs and newspaper clippings illustrate the work. Kitchener Public Library has a microfilm copy made by the Archives of Ontario. Period: 1790 - 1990.

4179. Campbell, Alexander D., Dr. "Lincoln's death has repercussions in Ayr." **Waterloo Historical Society**. 1985. 73: 17-21. ill. Loc: all.
A short anecdotal account of Dr Merritt's links with Abraham Lincoln. Period: 1864 - 1865.

4180. North Dumfries Pre-School Co-operative Inc. **The Ayr of days gone by**. Ayr: Ayr News, 1986. 1 v. Loc: OKIT.
A calendar showing twelve photographs of people and places, dating mainly from the early twentieth century, with brief captions of historical information. Period: 1900 - 1940.

4181. North Dumfries Pre-School Co-operative Inc. **A day at Ayr**. Ayr News, 1989. 1 v. Loc: OKIT.
A calendar featuring twelve engravings of Ayr buildings and scenes, reprinted from the Saturday Globe of October 12, 1889. The middle page is a reprint of the article, "A day at Ayr" from the same article. Period: 1889 - 1890.

4182. Schmidt, John P. "Ayr's old boys and girls welcomed home." **Waterloo Historical Society**. 1974. 62: 39-44. Loc: all.
A report of a community reunion to celebrate Ayr's 150th anniversary. Period: 1824 - 1974.

4183. Schmidt, Robert A. **Ayr, 1824-1964: "the village beautiful"**. Ayr: Ayr Boosters' Association, 1964. 52 p. ill., indexes. Loc: OKIT, OWRA.
A promotional account of recreational facilities, housing, public buildings, municipal services and scenery, with photographs and descriptions of 40 businesses, an index of Ayr

services and a telephone index. Period: 1824 - 1964.

4184. Schmidt, Robert A. "Uncover document signed at Ayr in 1826." **Waterloo Historical Society**. 1954. 42: 47-48. Loc: all.

An account from **The Ayr News** of the discovery of an 1826 petition signed by Abel Mudge and others asking for a new road to connect Ayr and Roseville. The document mentions Mudge's mill, establishing the date of the founding of Ayr as 1824. Additional confirmation found in William Dickson's journal is referred to in the 1955 volume, page 53. Period: 1824 - 1954.

4185. Simpson, Gillian. **Historical geography of the village of Ayr**. University of Waterloo (B.E.S. thesis, Geography), 1975. 1 fiche. maps, tables, bibl. mf. Loc: OWTUM.

A study of development through four functional stages: as agricultural service centre in the early nineteenth century, industrial community based on the John Watson company to the turn of the century, subsequent decline, and commuter community beginning in the 1970s. The author also describes the physical environment, including geology, soils, topography, vegetation, and hydrography. Period: 1824 - 1975.

4186. Smith, Murray E. **Ayr's 150th anniversary and reunion: a walking tour of Ayr**. Ayr: Ayr Sesquicentennial Committee, 1974, 1974. 3 p. Loc: OWRA.

A guide to a walking tour, describing the architecture and history of 25 notable structures including residences, churches, dams and bridges. Period: 1824 - 1974.

4187. Taylor, Andrew W. "A walking tour of Ayr." **Waterloo Historical Society**. 1971. 59: 38-47. Loc: all.

An itinerary commenting on places of historical interest in the village. Period: 1850 - 1950.

4188. Watson, Elizabeth Dolman. "Early days in Ayr." **Waterloo Historical Society**. 1924. 12: 72-79. Loc: all.

A short history of the settlement of the village which began as the three separate communities of Ayr, Jedburgh and Nithvale. The author relates many anecdotes about prominent inhabitants including Abel Mudge, John Hall and Mr Colcleugh (all millers), James Jackson and Robert Wyllie (both postmasters), Daniel Manley, William Baker, Mr Laidlaw, John Watson, the Goldies and the Guthries. Period: 1816 - 1867.

4189. Wilson, G.E. Duff. **A walking tour through Ayr**. Ayr: Knox United Church, 1985. 3 p. Loc: OWRA.

A guide to a tour of Greenfield and Ayr, describing the architecture and historical associations of various residential and public buildings. The tour starts at Knox United Church, proceeds along Hall Street, then follows Main Street to Northumberland Street. Period: 1850 - 1985.

BRIDGEPORT

4190. Bridgeport Women's Institute. **Tweedsmuir history, Bridgeport Women's Institute, North Waterloo**. Kitchener: Kitchener Public Library, 1982. 3 reels. ill., map. mf. Loc: OKIT, OWTU, OWRE.

A scrapbook history containing newspaper clippings and text on many topics including schools, churches, organizations, memorable community events, industries, family farms, notable buildings, hotels, the postal service and other businesses. Also included is a history of the Bridgeport Women's Institute itself. Period: 1829 - 1981.

4191. Dickson, F.W.R. "Bridgeport." **Waterloo Historical Society**. 1965. 53: 12-18. ill., bibl. Loc: all.

An account of the community in the nineteenth century, including references to Peter Erb, John U. Tyson, Elias Eby and Jacob S. Shoemaker and their businesses. Period: 1800 - 1965.

4192. Eichler, Idessa. "Bridgeport, a history." **Waterloo Historical Society**. 1950. 38: 30-37. Loc: all.

An historical sketch including details of first residents, hotels, churches, schools, the bridge, the cemetery, the street railway, the sugar factory, the casino and the country club. Period: 1829 - 1950.

4193. Featherston, C. "A history of Bridgeport." **Waterloo Historical Society**. 1939. 27: 80-83. Loc: all.

An historical sketch that emphasizes the earlier years and mentions industries, hotels, schools, bridges and churches. Period: 1807 - 1934.

4194. Hunsberger, Albert. **Nineteen nineteen**. Kitchener: Ainsworth Press, 1980. 244 p. ill. Loc: OKIT, OWT, OWTL, OWTU, OWTUCG.

The events of 1919 seen through the eyes of a young Mennonite boy from Bridgeport. A flood, gathering maple sap, travelling to Markham on the train, going to church and school, and harvesting sugar beets are some of the episodes described. The book is presented as a work of fiction although many events are historically accurate. Period: 1918 - 1920.

4195. Lamb, Kathryn Hansuld. "Bridgeport's first 50 years 1829-1879." **Waterloo Historical Society**. 1979. 67: 43-68. ill., map. Loc: all.

A history of the community known earlier as Shoemaker's Mills, Glasgow Mills, Glasgow and Lancaster. The author presents a detailed account of businesses, churches, the school and of two prominent inhabitants, Jacob S. Shoemaker and John U. Tyson. Period: 1829 - 1879.

4196. "Plan of the village of Bridgeport in the Township and County of Waterloo, C.W. as surveyed for Messrs Shoemaker, Tagge, Devitt and Ferrier by Schofield and Hobson, P.L.S. Berlin, C.W. 1856." **Waterloo Historical Society**. 1965. 53: 24-25. ill. Loc: all.

A plan with a key to 39 numbered buildings noting businesses and residences, to which some 1965 details have been added. Period: 1856 - 1965.

4197. Zimmerman, Idessa. **Bridgeport, Ont.**. Bridgeport: The Author, 1967. 23 p. ill., maps. Loc: OWTUR, OKIT.

A history of the village from 1807 to 1967, illustrated with sketches by the author and by maps of both east and west sides of the town in 1856. Early settlers, industries, hotels, churches and schools are described. Period: 1807 - 1967.

DUMFRIES (NORTH) TOWNSHIP

4198. Barrie, E.G. "North Dumfries Centennial address." **Waterloo Historical Society**. 1952. 40: 42-44. Loc: all.

Remarks about the pioneer era, with names of many settlers and early organizations. Period: 1852 - 1952.

4199. Barrie, William C. "The Dickie Settlement, then and now." **Waterloo Historical Society**. 1950. 38: 21-25. Loc: all.

An account of the area settled by the Dickie family in 1834, with profiles of many family members and others and notes on local schools and farmers' organizations. Period: 1816 - 1950.

4200. Branchton Women's Institute. **Tweedsmuir history, Branchton Women's Institute, South Waterloo**. 1 reel. ill. Loc: OKIT.

A microfilm copy of the community history compiled by the Institute which was formed in the early 1920s. Topics include farm families, businesses, churches, Branchton United Church,

North Dumfries S.S.#17, and the development of the Branchton Women's Institute itself. Microfilmed by the Archives of Ontario, on the same reel as the Mount Healy Tweedsmuir history. Period: 1904 - 1972.

4201. Elliott, Hugh C. "North Dumfries administration building." **Waterloo Historical Society**. 1967. 55: 61-62. Loc: all.

A report by the township's secretary-treasurer of the restoration for municipal office space of the former Stone School of School Section Number 19. Period: 1857 - 1967.

4202. "Galt and North Dumfries." **Historical atlas of Waterloo & Wellington counties, including: Illustrated Atlas of the County of Waterloo (1881), County of Waterloo Directory (1877-78) and Illustrated Atlas of the County of Wellington (1877)**. Port Elgin: Ross Cumming, 1972 reprint. Pp. 8-9. Loc: OWTU, OWTUM, OWTUCG, OKIT, OWTL, OCCA, OCLG, OCP, OWRBL, OWRE, OWRN, OWRW, OWT.

An historical sketch of topography, early settlement, the development of economic activities, municipal government and services, and social institutions such as churches and schools. It is interesting as an early statement of what was to become a widely accepted version of the early history of the region. About half the space is devoted to the period before 1821, and most of the rest to an account of Galt's development with brief notes on Ayr, Roseville and Branchton. Period: 1798 - 1881.

4203. Kinzie, Ira. "Roseville." **Waterloo Historical Society**. 1951. 39: 41-43. Loc: all.

A short history which mentions early inhabitants and businesses. The village's development began in 1805 when Christian Shantz bought a tract of land from Robert Beasley. Period: 1805 - 1951.

4204. Little's Corners Women's Institute. **Tweedsmuir history, Little's Corners Women's Institute, South Waterloo**. 1972. 1 v. ill. Also mf. Loc: OCCA, OKIT.

An illustrated history with sections on farms, landowners, local businesses, schools, churches, roads, veterans, and the Women's Institute itself which was formed in 1927. The histories of the farms give genealogical details of the families who lived there and notes on the changing patterns of farming. A microfilm copy, made by the Archives of Ontario and on the same reel as the Thorndale Tweedsmuir history, is held by the Kitchener Public Library. Period: 1820 - 1972.

4205. MacKenzie, Marilyn Beatty. **A geographical study of North Dumfries Township**. McMaster University (B.A. thesis, Geography), 1958. 111 l. ill., maps. Loc: OHM.

A comprehensive report on the physical environment (landforms, soils, climate, drainage and vegetation), history of settlement and development, contemporary rural land use patterns, and the urban functions of Galt and smaller centres. There are many excellent maps, graphs and photographs. Period: 1816 - 1957.

4206. "Map of North Dumfries Township." **Historical atlas of Waterloo & Wellington counties, including: Illustrated Atlas of the County of Waterloo (1881), County of Waterloo Directory (1877-78) and Illustrated Atlas of the County of Wellington (1877)**. Port Elgin: Ross Cumming, 1972 reprint. p. 19. Loc: OWTU, OWTUM, OWTUCG, OKIT, OWTL, OCCA, OCLG, OCP, OWRBL, OWRE, OWRN, OWRW, OWT.

A map at a scale of 60 chains to the inch that shows rivers and streams, major roads and railway lines, names townships, towns, villages and hamlets, and numbers concessions and lots. Properties of subscribers to the atlas and some rural industries, post offices and churches are also identified. Period: 1880 - 1881.

4207. Mill Creek Women's Institute. **Tweedsmuir history, Mill Creek Women's Institute, South Waterloo**. Mill Creek Women's Institute, 1 v. Loc: OCCA.

A miscellany of information and documents on the history of the locality. Among the documents are a history of Mill Creek W.I. from 1931 to 1936, information on rationing in Canada during the Second World War, and a Mill Creek school reunion programme from 1910. There is also a copy of the 1954 winter issue of the **Home and Country** magazine containing a prize winning essay by Jennie F. Cowan, entitled "The rural home." It includes pieces by Jennie Cowan on humorous incidents in Mill Creek and on Clochmohr farm. The institution disbanded in 1970. Period: 1828 - 1970.

4208. North Dumfries Township Council. **By-laws of the municipal council of North Dumfries for 1852**. Galt: Dumfries Reformer, 1852. 48 p. Loc: OKITW.

By-laws 1 to 17, following the Upper Canada Municipal Corporations Act of 1849 and regulating roads, fences, hotels and inns, and division into wards. Period: 1849 - 1852.

4209. North Dumfries Township Council. **Voters' lists: Township of North Dumfries**. 1925, 1964. Loc: OKITW, OWRBW.

List of people eligible to vote in municipal and provincial elections arranged by polling subdivisions. Other information includes lot, concession, post office and rural route number of the voter, status as tenant or freeholder and whether eligible for jury service. Wilmot Township Archives holds the list for 1925 and the Waterloo Historical Society the list for 1964. Period: 1925 - 1964.

4210. Perrin, George and Perrin, Jean. **History of Roseville village and its school S.S. no. 22, North Dumfries**. Roseville: The Authors, 1967. 15 p. ill. Loc: OKIT, OWTUCG.

A brief history of the community to mark the school's centennial. It provides details on early settlement, prominent inhabitants, churches, war service, agriculture and the former village of Black Horse Corners. A history of the school is based on the reports of Inspector Thomas Pearce and gives the names of many former teachers and pupils. Period: 1822 - 1967.

4211. Taylor, Andrew W. "North Dumfries centennial, 1852-1952." **Waterloo Historical Society**. 1952. 40: 41. Loc: all.

An brief account of the festivities held in August 1952 in Ayr and Galt in recognition of the township's centennial. The author's history of the township, **Our Yesterdays**, was published. Period: 1852 - 1952.

4212. Taylor, Andrew W. **Our todays and yesterdays: a history of the Township of North Dumfries and the Village of Ayr**. Preston: Progress Printing for the North Dumfries and Ayr Centennial Committee, 1970. 344 p. ill., maps. Loc: OCCA, OCLG, OKIT, OWRA, OWT, OWTL, OWTU, OWTUCG.

A new edition of Andrew Taylor's book, **Our yesterdays**, updated for the Canadian centenary. Apart from the first two chapters on prehistory and early settlement, the book is arranged according to subject, not chronology. Topics include municipal administration, organizations, schools, railways, roads and agricultural machinery. One chapter is a reprint of an article by Robert E. Knowles about the Presbyterian churches of Galt. Separate chapters are devoted to Galt, Ayr (based in part on a 1924 Waterloo Historical Society article by Elizabeth Watson), Branchton and Roseville, and other hamlets and subdivisions. The last chapter lists prominent farm families, with lot and concession numbers and names of successive owners. The latter part of the book reproduces several documents, including a transcript of a shortened version of the Crown deed of 1798, confirming a grant of land to Philip Stedman. There are also facsimiles of the Township of Dumfries assessment of 1834 and the portion of Tremaine's map of 1861 showing the individual land holdings of North Dumfries. Councillors and municipal officials of North Dumfries are listed for the years 1852 to 1969 and those of Ayr for the years 1884 to 1969. Period: 1816 - 1969.

4213. Taylor, Andrew W. **Our yesterdays: a history of the Township of North Dumfries, Ontario, Canada, 1816-1952.** Galt: Galt Printers, 1952. 128 p. ill., maps. Loc: OCCA, OCLG, OCP, OKIT, OWTU, OWTUCG.

A detailed history commemorating the township's centennial. Topics include prehistory, municipal organization, agricultural organizations, schools, railways, agricultural machinery and roads. The localities of Galt, Ayr, Branchton and Roseville are given special attention, and township officials from 1852 to 1952 are listed. There is no index or table of contents, and the information given in this book is reprinted in the more detailed edition, **Our todays and yesterdays** (1970), which does contain an index. Period: 1816 - 1952.

4214. "Township of North Dumfries." **Waterloo Historical Society.** 1960. 48: 34-36. Loc: all.

A brief history of the survey and subdivision of the township, its organization as a municipality in 1819, and the division into North and South Dumfries in 1852. Various early settlers and municipal settlers are named and all township reeves from 1852 to 1960 are listed. Period: 1816 - 1860.

4215. Turnbull, William C. "Reminiscences from the East River Road, North Dumfries." **Waterloo Historical Society.** 1949. 37: 25-37. Loc: all.

A description of buildings and topography in the area just south of Galt, with anecdotes about various subjects including early families and smallpox epidemics. Period: 1848 - 1949.

4216. Wood, J. David. **The historical geography of Dumfries Township, Upper Canada, 1816 to 1852.** University of Toronto (M.A. thesis, Geography), 1958. 142 p. ill., bibl., maps. Loc: OWTU.

A description of the natural environment and how it was altered by three distinct groups of settlers: the German Mennonites, the Presbyterian Scots, and the English-Dutch-Irish from the United States who were generally Methodists. The differing patterns of settlement from 1816 to 1852 are analyzed for each ethnic group. Period: 1816 - 1852.

ELMIRA

4217. Anniversary Booklet Committee. **Elmira: 50th anniversary.** St Jacobs: St Jacobs Printery, 1973. 98 p. ill. Loc: OKIT, OWRE.

A history commemorating the 50th anniversary of the Elmira Old Boys' and Girls' Reunion, with biographies of recent mayors, clerks, reeves, educators and eminent citizens, and sketches of churches, schools, sports, cultural activities, organizations, transportation, and current businesses and industries. Personal and corporate subjects are thoroughly indexed in the WRP database. Period: 1923 - 1973.

4218. **Elmira, Ontario: souvenir of inauguration and Old Boys and Girls Reunion.** Elmira: G.C. Hacking, 1923. 66 p. ill. Loc: OKITW, OWTUR, OWRE.

A publication marking Elmira's incorporation as a town, with brief descriptions of industries and services such as schools, churches, public utilities and library as well as a history of the community. There are photographs of homes, streets, commercial buildings and landscapes, and advertisements by local businesses. Period: 1840 - 1923.

4219. "Elmira's town hall." **Waterloo Historical Society.** 1967. 55: 55. Loc: all.

A note of the conversion of the old Elmira Post Office into a Town Hall. Period: 1900 - 1967.

4220. "History of Elmira." **Waterloo Historical Society.** 1973. 61: 9-18. ill. Loc: all.

An historical account of the community's businesses, industries, clubs, and organizations since the 1830s, with brief profiles of Edward Bristow, Peter Winger, Samuel Weaver, the Ruppels, the Klincks and the Brubachers, and descriptions of special events such as Pig Day and the Maple Syrup Festival. Period: 1830 - 1972.

4221. Klinck, George. "The early days of Elmira." **Waterloo Historical Society.** 1927. 15: 285-296. Loc: all.

An account of pioneer settlers and businesses, with references to schools and churches built since the village was named in 1853. Period: 1830 - 1870.

4222. Klinck, George. **Enterprising Elmira: an historical, descriptive, and illustrated book of the village of Elmira, Waterloo County, Ontario, Canada.** Elmira: George Klinck, 1903. 1 v. (unpaged). ill. Loc: OKITW, OWRE.

A compendium of detailed information on businesses, industries, clubs, residents, societies, schools and churches, with photographs of prominent individuals, buildings and streetscapes. Period: 1840 - 1903.

4223. Klinck, George. "Enterprising Elmira." **Waterloo Historical Society**. 1945. 33: 35-38. Loc: all.

A sketch of the contemporary community, including descriptions of businesses, clubs and services such as the Elmira Shirt and Overall Company, the Elmira Furniture Company, the Link Belt Company, Silverwood Dairies, the Horticultural Society, the Elmira Monthly Fair and the Public Library. There are lists of members of the Board of Trade and of the village council of 1895. Period: 1895 - 1945.

4224. Lamb, Kathryn Hansuld. "Elmira, 1886-1986." **Waterloo Historical Society**. 1986. 74: 72. Loc: all.

A brief note of preparations to celebrate Elmira's centennial, including publication of a book by the Woolwich Historical Foundation. Period: 1886 - 1986.

4225. Lamb, Kathryn Hansuld. **Elmira Centennial, 1886-1986**. Elmira Independent, 1986, August 5. 128 p. ill., map, index. Loc: OKIT, OWT, OWRE, OWTU.

A special supplement, celebrating the town's centennial with a wealth of detailed information about industries, businesses, theatres, fairs, parks and organizations. Articles by Otto W. Klinck and Bertha Thompson on theatres and music in Elmira are reprinted from annual reports of the Waterloo Historical Society. Persons and organizations are thoroughly indexed in the WRP database. Period: 1886 - 1986.

4226. Leipnik, Mary. "Elmira: our town." **The Dominion**. 1948. 7,4: 3-10. ill. Loc: OKITW.

An historical and contemporary description of Elmira, featuring the Naugatuck Chemical company and its employees and printed in the house magazine of the Dominion Rubber Company of Montreal. Photographs show Elmira streets, houses and churches, with Naugatuck employees at work and play. Period: 1800 - 1948.

4227. Souvenir Booklet Committee. **Souvenir of the Elmira Old Boys and Girls Reunion, 1948**. Elmira: The Committee, 1948. 52 p. ill. Loc: OKITW, OWRE.

A portrait of contemporary Elmira, with photographs and brief descriptions of industries, services, town officials, schools, sports, churches and organizations, as well as advertisements for many businesses. Period: 1940 - 1948.

GALT (CAMBRIDGE FROM 1973)

4228. "1867-1967...and the years between: Canada's first hundred years." **Galt Evening Reporter**. 1967, June 30. Pp. 1A-48A. ill. Loc: OCCA.

A centennial edition in three sections, with articles and photographs describing the development of Galt and Preston. Emphasis is placed on social and political aspects, though industrial growth is reflected in the advertisements placed by local businesses. Among the many and varied topics are: a list of Preston firsts, the text of a letter describing Galt in 1884 written by Robert Murray, photographs of a 1920 Galt roadway crew getting limestone from the Grand River area, and a brief biographical sketch of Midwife Gress of Preston. Period: 1867 - 1967.

4229. Cant, Hugh. **Historical reminiscences of Galt and other writings**. 1915. 112 p. ill. Also mf. Loc: OCCA, OCLG, OKIT.

A history of early Galt, including information about the first school and its founder John Gowinlock, all local churches, the Galt Y.M.C.A. and the Galt Public Library. An account by William Veitch of his trip from Galt to California in 1857 is also included. An index is available at the City of Cambridge Archives and the Cambridge Library and Gallery. Period: 1802 - 1915.

4230. "Centennial edition." **Galt Evening Reporter**. 1927. Also mf. Loc: OCCA.

A six-part series published to promote the 1927 reunion. There are reminiscences of well-known Galt residents, letters from old boys and girls recounting their past and present lives, and a programme of events including a description of the Made-in-Galt Exhibition. A wide variety of local topics and events are covered by the articles, such as Tassie's School, the explosion of the Crimean cannon, and the sinking of the Empress of India. The Cambridge Archives has microfilm copies of the first edition on March 21, the second on April 11, the third on May 2, the fifth on May 30th and the sixth on June 13th. The fourth edition is missing. Period: 1816 - 1927.

4231. Cowan, Hugh, Rev. "Galt, founded in 1816." **Mer Douce**. 1924. 14: 42-43. ill. Loc: OKIT.

Biographical information on three of Galt's founders: William Dickson, Absalom Shade and John Telfer. The portrait of William Dickson held by the Niagara Historical Society is reproduced, and the information on Shade is quoted from James Young. Period: 1816 - 1870.

4232. Galt Board of Trade. **Galt: central point of a great Canadian market**. Galt: The Board of Trade, 1954. 11 p. ill. Loc: OCCA.

A brochure extolling the advantages of living and working in Galt, including photographs of new industries that had recently moved there. The diverse nature of Galt's industrial base is particularly emphasized. Brief information is given about history, transportation, work force, municipal services and city government. Period: 1950 - 1954.

4233. **Galt Centennial and Old Home Week, Galt, Ontario, Canada, June 29-July 4, 1927**. 1927. 50 p. ill., ports., ads. Also mf. Loc: OCCA, OCLG, OKITW.

A souvenir programme with illustrated information on municipal services, education, parks, newspapers, streets and sports, and some details of city officials and organizers of Centennial Week. Period: 1926 - 1927.

4234. **Galt Kiwanis present their fifth annual show: "World's Fair Follies"**. 1939?. 46 p. ill. Loc: OKITW.

A programme of vaudeville entertainment, including juggling, acrobatics, dancing and music, with advertisements by many Galt industries, businesses and professionals. Period: 1930 - 1940.

4235. Galt-Preston-Hespeler Centennial Committee. **Galt, 1867-1967**. Galt: Galt Printers, 1967. 28 p. ill. Loc: OKIT, OCCA.

A booklet printed on the occasion of Canada's centennial, including historical sketches of Galt and its Public Utilities Commission and of North Dumfries Township. Some articles are contributed by Andrew W. Taylor, E.I. McLoughry and Earl Werstine. In addition to major special events during the centennial year such as Calypso '67, efforts by groups including the Galt Little Theatre, the Galt Kiltie Band, and the Galt Public Schools Choir are mentioned. Period: 1867 - 1967.

4236. Galt Reporter. **The Galt Reporter almanack, for 1847**. CIHM Microfiche series, no. 43233. Ainslie and Jaffray, 1846?. 1 fiche. mf. Loc: OWTU, OWTL.

An 1847 calendar with a directory to local services, including the destinations and times of departure and arrival stages from Galt, names of elected officials and local clergy, dates of fairs and District Council meetings, the post office hours, and a list of banks. Period: 1847 - 1848.

4237. **Galt Summer Carnival, Thursday & Friday, June 12th & 13th, 1890**. 1890. 28 p. ill. Also CIHM Microfiche series, no. 53027. Loc: OCCA, OKITW, OWTL, OWTU.

An illustrated programme of activities including a parade, musical competitions, races, a baseball game and displays by fire departments, with descriptions of the amenities and industries of contemporary Galt and Preston. The names of many local companies which placed advertisements have been indexed in the WRP database. Period: 1889 - 1890.

4238. **Galt: the gem city of the famous Grand River Valley**. Galt: Galt Board of Trade, 1920. 67 p. ill., map. Also mf. Loc: OCCA, OCLG, OKITW.

A promotional statement of Galt's advantages as a manufacturing and residential community, stressing the town's location as a hub of railways, highways and the proposed "hydro radial." More than half the volume consists of advertisements by local banks, hotels and other businesses. Period: 1919 - 1920.

4239. Galt Town Council. **Voters' list: municipality of the Town of Galt**. 1896. mf. Loc: OCLG.

A list of people eligible to vote in provincial and municipal elections, noting name, address, whether an owner or tenant, if qualified to be a juror, and if male and over 21 years of age. Period: 1896.

4240. Hamilton, R.S. and Osbourne, W.A., Mrs and Taylor, Andrew W. **The early history of Galt, 1816-1866**. Galt: The Authors?, 1941 reprinted 1956. 89 p. ill. Loc: OCCA, OCLG.

An account of the first fifty years of Galt by a former science master at Galt Collegiate Institute. The book is divided into five chapters, each devoted to a decade of Galt's history. The material covers a wide range of topics and was gathered from many sources, including newspapers and reminiscences. The book was originally published in 1941 and reissued in 1956, edited by Mrs W.A. Osbourne with the help of Andrew W. Taylor. Period: 1816 - 1866.

4241. "History of Galt: a selected list." **Ontario Library Review**. 1949. 33: 117. Loc: OKIT, OGU, OWTU.

Reference from the Canadian Periodical Index. Period: 1800 - 1949.

4242. Hulet, Marion. "Origin of the corporate seal of Galt." **Waterloo Historical Society**. 1968. 56: 51. ill. Loc: all.

An illustrated explanation of Galt's corporate seal that was adopted in January 1857. Period: 1857 - 1968.

4243. Index to Cant's Historical reminiscences of Galt. 19 l. Also mf. Loc: OCCA, OCLG.

An index to personal and corporate names mentioned in Hugh Cant's book on Galt, also included in the WRP database. A typed copy of the index is available at the City of Cambridge Archives, and a microform copy is available at the Library and Gallery. Period: 1802 - 1915.

4244. Index to Jubilee souvenir of Galt 1897. 6 l. Also mf. Loc: OCCA, OCLG.

An index noting people, businesses and institutions mentioned in the jubilee souvenir by Cornelius Wilson, also included in the WRP database. A typed copy of the index is available at the City of Cambridge Archives, and a microform copy is available at the Library and Gallery. Period: 1896 - 1897.

4245. Index to Picturesque and industrial Galt. 10 l. Also mf. Loc: OCCA, OCLG.

An index to the articles and illustrations in Jaffray's booklet published in 1902 and included in the WRP database. The City of Cambridge Archives has a typed copy of the index, the Library and Gallery has a microfilm copy. Period: 1816 - 1902.

4246. Jaffray Bros. Picturesque and industrial Galt. Galt: Jaffray Bros, 1902. 154 p. ill., ports. Also mf. Loc: OCCA, OCLG, OKIT.

A portrait of Galt at the beginning of the twentieth century, derived in part from Cornelius Wilson's **Jubilee history of Galt**, featuring schools, clubs, churches, local services, streets, transportation, parks and large houses. Manufacturers and businesses are indexed in the WRP database. Products of Galt manufacturers, primarily machinery, are illustrated with advertisements by local companies. There are portraits of clergy, civic officials, entrepreneurs and some of Galt Collegiate Institute's "old boys", many of whom were no longer living in Galt. An index to the articles and illustrations is available at the City of Cambridge Archives and the Cambridge Library and Gallery. Period: 1816 - 1902.

4247. Jaffray, J.P. Picturesque and industrial city of Galt, Ont.. 1928. 90 p. ill. Also mf. Loc: OCCA, OCLG, OKIT.

A promotional description of Galt's history, attractions, industries, transportation and civic facilities. Statistical information for the year 1928 is given, with lists of municipal officials and of members of the Galt School Board and Galt Hospital. Period: 1816 - 1928.

4248. Kerr, James E. "Early days in Galt [original]." **Waterloo Historical Society**. 1920. 8: 115-122. Loc: all.

An historical sketch of the town from its founding by William Dickson and Absalom Shade. The author quotes details from a census of 1834, and mentions such topics as the building of early roads, John Gowinlock's school, the Queen's Arms Hotel, and the ministry of the Rev. John Bayne. A letter written by Alexander Burnett is quoted for its graphic account of the cholera scourge of 1834. Period: 1816 - 1859.

4249. Kerr, James E. "Early days in Galt [reprint]." **Waterloo Historical Society**. 1972. 60: 26-35. ill. Loc: all.

An historical sketch reprinted from the 1920 volume, with illustrations of the Queen's Hotel (originally the King's Arms, 1835), the Post Office and Customs Building, Galt Collegiate Institute (originally Tassie's School) and Galt City Hall building (1857). Andrew W. Taylor has added notes explaining references in terms of 1972 locations. Period: 1816 - 1859.

4250. MacKendrick, J.N. "Local history in the street names of Galt." **Waterloo Historical Society**. 1919. 7: 67-72. Loc: all.

An account of the town's history and physical growth, including mentions of land developers and other persons after whom streets were named. Period: 1816 - 1880.

4251. Meikleham, R.W. and Mahler, Louis J. "Highlights of Galt's history." **Waterloo Historical Society**. 1966. 54: 81-85. Loc: all.

An historical sketch of 150 years since William Dickson's purchase of Dumfries Township, with a brief biography of Adam Ker as miller, municipal official and Mayor of Galt. Period: 1810 - 1879.

4252. Official programme and souvenir number: events to be held in Dickson Park, Galt on Labor Day, September 7, 1908. Galt: Jaffray Bros, 1908. 35 p. ill. Loc: OKITW.

A programme including photographs of people and buildings in Galt and many advertisements by local businesses. Period: 1907 - 1908.

4253. Peck, Thomas. "Galt: sixty years ago." **Waterloo Historical Society**. 1925. 13: 144-153. Loc: all.

Reminiscences of Galt in the 1850s and 1860s, including references to leading enterprises, a burglary at the Gore Bank branch, celebration of the Queen's Birthday, and the founding of the estate and livestock-breeding enterprise at Cruickston Park. Period: 1850 - 1865.

4254. Peck, Thomas. **Stories of an old regime harking back from 1924 to 1860**. 1924?. 1 v. (unpaged). Loc: OKITW.

A corrected typescript containing comic and romantic stories based on life in Galt in the 19th century. Among the stories are the founding of Cruickston Park, how William Dickson got lost in his own cedar swamp, how Absalom Shade gave a ball, education at Tassie's School, and how grand opera played in Galt under adverse circumstances. Period: 1860 - 1865.

4255. Quantrell, James. **A part of our past: essays on Cambridge's history**. Cambridge: City of Cambridge Archives, 1992. 168 p. Loc: OCCA.

A collection of articles originally published in the **Cambridge Reporter** between 1985 and 1989, and revised in 1992. Compiled for teachers and students, the articles cover a wide range of topics, including a postal history of Cambridge, the Preston Kirmess, women politicians, and the wreck of the steam launch **Empress of India**. Period: 1800 - 1992.

4256. Quantrell, James. **Time frames: historical chronologies of Galt, Preston, and Hespeler**. Cambridge: City of Cambridge Archives, 1992. 156 p. bibl., indexes. Loc: OCCA.

An indexed list of dates and events from 1784 to 1972 for each of the three towns comprising Cambridge. It includes population figures for the towns from 1851 to 1972, and for Cambridge from 1973 to 1991. Period: 1784 - 1972.

4257. Robertson, Robert R. **Hume: a novel about a Southern Ontario town that has lost its character and its name**. Cobalt: Highway Book Shop, 1981. 123 p. Loc: OCCA.

A book about the investigations of a young newspaperman into the political intrigues of his community. The novel, describing the rigid social structure of Galt in 1938, was written by a former **Galt Daily Reporter** newspaperman. Period: 1937 - 1938.

4258. "Special Old Boys' editions." **Galt Daily Reporter**. 1946 - 1947. Also mf. Loc: OCCA.

A series of special editions promoting the 1947 Galt Old Boys' Reunion. Most consist of personal recollections of people and places of Galt, with an article by R.S. Hamilton on the history of Galt. Illustrated advertisements for local companies are also included. Editions number one (18 December 1946) and number two (28 January 1947) are available at the City of Cambridge Archives on microfilm, while editions six (28 May 1947) and seven (18 June 1946) are available in printed format. Period: 1816 - 1947.

4259. "Special souvenir centennial edition." **Galt Evening Reporter**. 1967, June 30. mf. Loc: OCLG.

An illustrated survey of the community's development during the century since Confederation. Period: 1867 - 1967.

4260. Stevenson, John A. "The founder of Galt." **Queen's Quarterly**. 1947. 54,3: 336-342. Loc: OWTL, OWTU.

A biographical sketch of William Dickson (1769-1846), with an account of the origins and early settlement of Galt. There are brief biographies of Dickson's associates, including Absalom Shade, James Hogg, John Telfer and Dickson's three sons. Period: 1769 - 1846.

4261. "The story of Galt: city on the go." **Galt Evening Reporter**. 1967, March 28. Pp. 1A-31A, 1B-36B, 1C-12C. ill. Loc: OCCA.

A business review and forecast in five sections, mentioning trends in local population, housing, wages and industrial growth. Many local businesses are featured in text and advertisements. Over 100 Galt plants listed in a directory on pages A27 and A29 are indexed in the WRP database. The directory lists name of establishment, address, officers, number of workers, and products. There are also articles on municipal government, social services, and clubs and societies providing amenities for Galt residents. Period: 1966 - 1967.

4262. Truss, Jean and Hebblethwaite, Katherine. **A short history of Galt, 1816-1916**. Galt Public Library, 1967. 17 p. bibl. Loc: OCCA, OKIT.

A brief history of Galt by two librarians at Galt Public Library. Information is organized chronologically on politics, railways, the market, schools and daily life. Period: 1816 - 1916.

4263. Wilson, Cornelius. **Jubilee souvenir of Galt**. Galt: Galt Town Council, 1897. 1 v. (unpaged). ill., ports. Also mf. Loc: OCCA, OCLG.

A book promoting Galt's businesses, industries and community services, with illustrated descriptions of specific businesses, businessmen and prominent people. Photographs of street scenes, houses, schools and churches are also included. An index is available at the Cambridge Library and Gallery and the City of Cambridge Archives. Period: 1896 - 1897.

4264. Wilson, Ethel. "Letter from an Alberta member." **Waterloo Historical Society**. 1965. 53: 75-77. Loc: all.

Text of a letter written in 1965 to Mrs Paul Worden by Ethel Wilson who was born in Galt in 1883 and recalls her childhood memories of Galt,

Doon and Strasburg. Period: 1883 - 1965.

4265. Young, James. "Laying the corner stone of Galt City Hall." **Waterloo Historical Society**. 1957. 45: 26-28. ill. Loc: all.

A quotation and photograph of Galt's City Hall of 1857 from James Young's history of Galt, and a quotation and photograph of the old township hall from **Picturesque and industrial Galt**, 1902. Period: 1857 - 1957.

4266. Young, James. **Reminiscences of the early history of Galt and the settlement of Dumfries, in the Province of Ontario**. Galt: Galt Public Library, 1967. 272 p. plates, ill. Loc: OCCA, OCLG, OCP, OKIT, OWTU, OWTL, OWRA.

A facsimile of the 1880 original, reprinted by the Galt Public Library to mark the Canadian centennial, and including an index of about 720 names. The history of Galt from its beginnings as Indian land to its incorporation as a town in 1857 is based on the reminiscences of older settlers. Government and politics are emphasized and there are biographies of early notable citizens such as Absalom Shade, Rev. John Bayne and Alexander Burnett. Period: 1800 - 1879.

4267. Young, James. **Reminiscences of the early history of Galt and the settlement of Dumfries, in the province of Ontario**. Toronto: Hunter, Rose, 1880. 272 p. plates, ill., ports., bibl., index. Also CIHM Microfiche series, no. 26166. Loc: OCCA, OCLG, OKIT, OWTL, OWTLR, OWTU, OWTUR.

A history including information on a wide variety of topics, with particular detail on political issues and developments and biographical sketches of early community leaders. This original edition does not include an index as does the 1967 facsimile reproduction, also abstracted in the WRP database. Period: 1816 - 1879.

HESPELER

4268. Brewster, Winfield. **Hespeler, New Hope, C.W.**. Hespeler: T and T Press, 1951. 34 p. Loc: OWTUR, OKIT, OCCA.

An eclectic history of Hespeler including biographical details of its founder Jacob Hespeler, genealogical facts about the Hespeler family, and a list of Jacob's land holdings and buildings in New Hope. Among other topics are Indians, early buildings, local personalities, bridges, hotels, the fire brigade and the rifle range. An index is available at the Cambridge Library and Gallery and the City of Cambridge Archives. Period: 1830 - 1881.

4269. Corporation of the Town of Hespeler. **Hespeler: a brief municipal report**. Hespeler: Hespeler Town Council, 1969. 7 p. ill. map. Loc: OCCA.

A promotional publication including an introductory letter describing the community, a list of industries, a street map, and a fact sheet about population, transportation, industries, utilities, municipal services and housing. Period: 1968 - 1969.

4270. Eby, Oscar S. **Hespeler Canada: a souvenir of the factory town**. Hespeler: Oscar S. Eby, 1901. 1 v. ill. Also mf. Loc: OCCA, OCLG, OKIT, OKITW.

A collection of photographs of commercial blocks, mills and factories, public buildings, schools, churches and residences, and portraits of local businessmen and politicians. The introduction presents a brief history of the community. Period: 1830 - 1901.

4271. Harvey, Percy T. and Franks, H. and Nichols, B. **Hespeler Corporation**. Hespeler: T and T Press, 1966. 94 p. ill. Loc: OCCA, OKITW.

Souvenir booklet commemorating the Hespeler Old Boys' Reunion of 1966. There are photographs and brief historical descriptions of Hespeler's churches, schools, clubs, lodges, library, town hall, fire brigade and sports teams, and illustrated biographies of notable citizens such as Andrew J. Brewster, Winfield Brewster and Robert M. Phin. All reeves and mayors from 1859 to 1966 are noted and there are many advertisements by local businesses. Period: 1859 - 1966.

4272. Hebblethwaite, Katherine. **Index to Brewster**. Galt: Galt Public Library, 20 l. Also mf. Loc: OCCA, OCLG.

An index of personal and corporate names, with some subject references, to Winfield Brewster's books and C.A. Panabaker's **Barefoot farm boy**. Titles of Brewster's works included are the **Floodgate, Pine bush genealogy, La rue de commerce, Hespeler yarns, Lot six in Waterloo Township**, and **Hespeler, New Hope, C.W.**, all of which are included in the WRP database. A typed copy of the index is available at the City of Cambridge Archives, and a microfilm copy is available at the Library and Gallery. Period: 1800 - 1952.

4273. "Hespeler Centennial: souvenir edition, volume 1." **Galt Evening Reporter**. 1959, June 15. Pp. A1-A15. ill. Loc: OCCA, OKIT.

A special edition largely devoted to the centennial of Hespeler's incorporation, with articles on its government, services, clubs and people. Articles mention the decline of Dominion

Woollens and Worsteds after the Second World War, and the imminent closing of passenger service on the radial and the Canadian National Railways lines to Hespeler. The Kitchener Public Library has a copy in the Waterloo Historical Society vertical file. Period: 1859 - 1959.

4274. "Hespeler incorporated in 1859." **Waterloo Historical Society**. 1959. 47: 45-50. ill. Loc: all.

An historical sketch marking the centennial of municipal incorporation, including excerpts from the official proclamation and from the minutes of the first council meeting, a description of the centennial festivities, and three photographs of early Hespeler. Period: 1818 - 1959.

4275. "Hespeler incorporation souvenir number." **Galt Reporter**. Galt Reporter, 1901, January 1. Pp 1-8. ill. Loc: OCCA.

A newspaper supplement containing a brief history of the early period and a description of the contemporary town, with sections on its churches, industries, businesses, and fraternal and benefit societies. There is an article on schools by R.H. Knowles, principal of Hespeler Public School for many years, as well as short biographies and photographs of some of Hespeler's prominent citizens. Individual articles and photographs highlight some of Hespeler's major companies, including R. Forbes, A.B. Jardine, and Canada Woollen Mills, and advertisements for many Hespeler and Preston. A municipal roll of honour lists the reeves, members of council, and other officials from 1859 to 1900. The names of people and places in the photographs have been indexed in the WRP database. Period: 1830 - 1901.

4276. "Hespeler Old Boys' edition." **Galt Evening Reporter**. 1966, June 29. Pp. 1A-16A. Loc: OCCA, OKIT.

A souvenir section for the 1966 reunion, including reminiscences and photographs to illustrate past and present Hespeler. There are profiles of churches, schools, sports teams and clubs, and Hespeler's population growth and new housing are emphasized. The Kitchener Public Library holds a copy in the Waterloo Historical Society vertical file. Period: 1831 - 1966.

4277. Hespeler Old Boys' Reunion Committee. **The busy town of Hespeler, Canada: Old Boys' Reunion, June 30, July 1, 2 and 3, 1906.** Hespeler: Herald Print, 1906. 62 p. ill. Loc: OCCA, OKITW.

The official souvenir programme, profusely illustrated with photographs of scenery, street scenes and eminent Hespelerites and with advertisements for businesses in Hespeler and surrounding towns. Period: 1905 - 1906.

4278. "Hespeler Old Boys' special edition." **Galt Reporter**. 1947, May 6. 14 p. ill. Loc: OCCA.

A special edition marking the 1947 Hespeler Old Boys' Reunion, billed as the most elaborate ever undertaken. Articles describe the Reunion events, including a Made-in-Hespeler exhibition. Industries, veterans, sports teams, churches and clubs are given special attention. Period: 1831 - 1947.

4279. "Hespeler progress 1966." **Galt Evening Reporter**. 1966, March 18. Pp. 1A-14A. Loc: OCCA.

A special section promoting business development, with articles on the town's amenities and municipal services. Period: 1831 - 1966.

4280. "Hespeler Reunion special edition." **Galt Evening Reporter**. 1926, May 29. Pp. 1-8, 9-16. ill. Loc: OCCA.

A Saturday special edition in two sections, describing the history, people, amenities and industries of Hespeler, and presenting a programme of the reunion events. Municipal services and institutions, churches and clubs are given particular attention. The names of people in the photographs are indexed in the WRP database. Period: 1831 - 1926.

4281. Hespeler Town Clerk's Office. **Voters' list: town of Hespeler, 1949.** 1948. 56 p. Loc: OWTU.

A list of voters eligible for provincial and municipal elections, noting name, occupation, place of residence, whether public or separate school supporter, and whether owner or tenant. Period: 1948 - 1949.

4282. Hespeler Women's Institute. **Tweedsmuir history: Hespeler Women's Institute, South Waterloo.** 1 v. Loc: OCCA.

A scrapbook history of Hespeler from 1830 to 1973, with articles on its government, churches, schools, industries and prominent individuals. There are snapshots of the 1926 Old Boys' Reunion, newspaper articles on events such as the 1954 flood, and descriptions of Beaverdale and Puslinch Lake. Period: 1830 - 1980.

4283. **Hustling Hespeler: the town with a future.** Hespeler: Hespeler Board of Trade?, 1915?. 24 p. ill. Loc: OKITW, OCCA.

An illustrated booklet promoting Hespeler and depicting its industries, municipal services, public buildings, education, electricity, clubs, sports and recreational facilities. A list of products manufactured within a ten-mile radius of Hespeler is given. Period: 1900 - 1915.

4284. **Hustling Hespeler: the town with a future.**
Hespeler: Hespeler Board of Trade?, 1922. 27 p.
ill. Also mf. Loc: OCCA, OCLG, OKITW.

An updated and expanded version of the earlier
1915 boosterist publication. The community, its
industries and amenities are described and
illustrated with photographs not contained in the
earlier edition. Particular attention is given to
the R. Forbes Company and its products. Period:
1921 - 1922.

4285. James, F. Treve. **Hespeler, Ont. Old Boys'
Reunion, 1947.** Hespeler: T and T Press, 1947. 68
p. ill. Also mf. Loc: OCCA, OCLG, OKITW.

A souvenir programme with an account of
contemporary Hespeler, including photographs of
churches, public buildings and industries, and
descriptions of the war effort, the corvette
H.M.C.S. Hespeler, and Winston Hall which was
built to house women workers at Dominion Woollens
and Worsteds. Period: 1946 - 1947.

4286. Panabaker, D.N. "The town of Hespeler [original]."
Waterloo Historical Society. 1922. 10: 213-224.
ill. Loc: all.

A sketch of the community's early development,
including references to pioneer settlers and
industries. Period: 1840 - 1920.

4287. Panabaker, D.N. "The town of Hespeler [reprint]."
Waterloo Historical Society. 1972. 60: 36-49.
ill. Loc: all.

An article reprinted from the Waterloo
Historical Society's annual report for 1922.
Period: 1840 - 1922.

4288. Pepper, Paul E. **Index to Hespeler: New Hope,
C.W.: Hespeler, Ontario by Winfield Brewster.**
1986. 4 p. Loc: OKIT.

An index to some 300 personal subjects mentioned
in Brewster's 1951 history.

4289. "'There's no place like home': Old Boys' Reunion,
June 30th to July 6th." **Hespeler Herald.** 1947,
June 17. Pp. 1-24. ill. Loc: OCCA.

A special edition giving details of the
attractions and events for the 1947 Old Boys'
Reunion, with photographs of the Reunion
committees. Articles describe Hespeler's new
memorial arena and Hespeler's postwar industrial
expansion. The emphasis is on the reunion, other
aspects of life in Hespeler being mentioned only
briefly. There are many advertisements for
Hespeler businesses. Period: 1831 - 1947.

4290. "Welcome home: Hespeler Centennial, 1859-1959."
Hespeler Herald. 1959, June 25. 62,25: 1-32.
ill. Loc: OCCA.

A special edition focusing on Hespeler clubs and
organizations such as the Community Senior
Citizens' Club and the Hespeler Kinettes. Other
miscellaneous articles related to Hespeler include
one on "C" Company of the 111th Battalion, one on
the telephone system, and another on the aquatic
Speed Monster. Period: 1858 - 1959.

4291. "Winfield Brewster." **Waterloo Historical
Society.** 1954. 42: 46. Loc: all.

A short paragraph commending Brewster for
recording the history of Hespeler in his various
booklets. Period: 1954.

KITCHENER (BERLIN TO 1916)

4292. **At Berlin: reprinted from the Saturday Globe of
August 31, 1889.** Kitchener: Joseph Schneider Haus
Gallery and Museum, 198-?. 3 p. ill. Loc: OKIT.

A brief history of Berlin since 1800 is followed
by information about contemporary businesses and
businessmen. There are portraits of prominent
community leaders including Reeve Janzen, George
Lang, Mayor Breithaupt and Sheriff Springer, and
drawings of buildings such as the post office, the
first school, the court house, the high school,
the Swedenborgian and St Peter's Lutheran
Churches, and the residences of C.F. Brown, W.H.
Bowlby, Mr Roos, P.E.W. Moyer and George Rumpel.
Advertisements from Berlin companies and
industries are featured on page 3. Reprinted from
a special feature in the Toronto newspaper which
was part of a series on the smaller cities and
towns of Ontario. Period: 1800 - 1889.

4293. Berlin Board of Commissioners of Police. **License
by-laws nos. 2, 3, and 4.** Berlin: City of Berlin,
1912. 32 p. Loc: OWTUR.

Text of by-laws for the licensing of owners of
livery stables and of vehicles used for conveying
goods and persons. These by-laws are signed by
W.D. Euler, then chairman of the Board. The
booklet contains sample license forms. Period:
1903 - 1912.

4294. Berlin Board of Trade. **Busy Berlin will just suit
you.** Berlin: The Board of Trade, 1910. 16 p. ill.
Loc: OTU, OTAR.

A booklet promoting Berlin's advantages for
manufacturers seeking locations for new factories.
Period: 1909 - 1910.

4295. Berlin Daily News Record. **Twentieth century souvenir of busy Berlin: the best town in Canada.** Berlin: News Record, 1901. 13, 115 p. plates. ill. Loc: OWTUR, OKIT, OWT.

A photographic account of Berlin, including a brief description with illustrations of buildings (residences, factories and public institutions) and portraits of doctors, lawyers, businessmen and municipal officials. Period: 1900 - 1901.

4296. "Berlin." **Historical atlas of Waterloo & Wellington counties, including: Illustrated Atlas of the County of Waterloo (1881), County of Waterloo Directory (1877-78) and Illustrated Atlas of the County of Wellington (1877).** Port Elgin: Ross Cumming, 1972 reprint. p. 30. Loc: OWTU, OWTUM, OWTUCG, OKIT, OWTL, OCCA, OCLG, OCP, OWRBL, OWRE, OWRN, OWRW, OWT.

A simple map at a scale of 15 chains to the inch that shows ward boundaries, surveyed lots, streets, railway lines, schools, churches, public buildings, cemeteries and the town park. Period: 1880 - 1881.

4297. "Berlin-Kitchener dates." **Waterloo Historical Society.** 1962. 50: 17. Loc: all.

A list of seven significant dates, from 1852 when Berlin became Waterloo's county town to 1962 when Kitchener celebrated its 50th anniversary as a city. Period: 1852 - 1962.

4298. "Berlin, Ontario: a progressive manufacturing town; a great industrial centre; its rise and progress." **Canadian Trade Review.** 1901. 31,25: 1a-12a. ill. Loc: OKITW.

A feature article with about fifty entries on Berlin's industries, hotels, stores and professional people, as well as shorter references to six Waterloo industries and twenty pages of photographs of people and places in the two towns. Any person or place shown in a photograph is indexed in the WRP database, as well as any commercial establishment or person noted. Period: 1900 - 1901.

4299. **Berlin today: centennial number in celebration of the Old Boys' and Girls' Reunion, August 6th, 7th, 8th, 1906.** Berlin: News Record, 1906. 1 v. (unpaged). ill. Loc: OWTUR, OKIT.

A centennial souvenir programme describing contemporary Berlin and especially its light and power and sewage disposal plants. An article by J.W. Connor presents an historical sketch of the community since 1806. Also included are photographs of notable citizens and their residences, factories and public buildings, as well as biographical sketches of prominent individuals and advertisements for local

businesses. Kitchener Public Library holds a bound photocopy and a card index to names. The work is thoroughly indexed in the WRP database. Period: 1806 - 1906.

4300. Berlin Town Council. **Assessment roll of the Town of Berlin of 1897.** 1897. 82 p. Loc: OKITW.

An alphabetical listing of townspeople by ward, giving addresses, whether owner or tenant, and the property assessment. Berlin was divided into North, South, East, West and Centre Wards. Period: 1896 - 1897.

4301. Berlin Town Council. **Consolidated by-laws of the Town of Berlin.** Berlin: C. Hett, 1886. 134 p. index. Loc: OKITW.

The text of all current town by-laws with a subject index and a list of all member of the Village Council and Town Council from 1854 to 1886. A table on pages 120 to 128 lists every by-law by date, with its status as effete, repealed, consolidated, amended or superseded. Period: 1854 - 1886.

4302. Berlin Town Council. **The consolidated by-laws of the Town of Berlin.** Berlin News-Record, 1902. 232 p. index. Loc: OKIT, OKITW.

Text of all by-laws in force on July 1, 1902. A table on pages 206-232 lists all by-laws passed by the Village Council or Town Council from 1854, stating if they were still in force, amended or repealed. There are also a subject index and a list of Council members from 1854 to 1902. Period: 1854 - 1902.

4303. Berlin Town Council. **Voters' lists: municipality of the Town of Berlin.** 1879 - 1901. Loc: OKITW.

A list of people eligible to vote in provincial and municipal elections, noting name, address, whether an owner or tenant, if qualified to be a juror, and if male and over 21 years of age. The Waterloo Historical Society Collection housed at the Kitchener Public Library has the lists for 1879, 1893 and 1901. Period: 1879 - 1901.

4304. Berlin Village Council. **The consolidated by-laws of the Municipal Corporation of the Village of Berlin, to the 31st day of December, 1868.** Berlin: Telegraph Office, 1868. 54 p. Loc: OWTUR.

A consolidated list of the by-laws in numerical order, with lists of council members and Berlin Grammar School Trustees. Period: 1867 - 1868.

4305. "Birds eye view of Berlin, 1875." **Waterloo Historical Society.** 1930. 18: 160a. Loc: all.

A drawing of Berlin in 1875 showing streets, railway tracks, and an inset illustration of the courthouse. Period: 1875.

4306. Breithaupt, W.H. "President's address: Early local municipal history." **Waterloo Historical Society.** 1922. 10: 205-211. ill. Loc: all.

A history of Berlin from its incorporation as a village in 1854 to 1870 when it was incorporated as a town, including references to municipal officials, issues and buildings. Period: 1854 - 1870.

4307. **Busy Berlin: jubilee souvenir, 1897.** Berlin: Berlin News-Record, 1897. 190 p. ill. Also CIHM Microfiche series, no. 02113. Loc: OWTUR, OWTL, OKIT.

An illustrated volume promoting the attractions of Berlin and including general information about education, recreation, health and parks. There are many photographs of commercial, public and residential buildings and of various sports teams and other organizations. Period: 1896 - 1897.

4308. **Busy Berlin, Ontario: one of the greatest industrial centres of Ontario: a city of gigantic enterprises, manufactories, foundries, mills, substantial banks, beautiful homes, schools and churches.** Berlin: Berlin Board of Trade?, 1907. 17 p. ill. Loc: OWTUR, OKIT.

A promotional description of the town, followed by profiles of 45 businesses. There are many photographs of public buildings, parks, factories and street scenes. The Kitchener Public Library holds a bound photocopy of this publication, from the original presented by W.H.E. Schmalz to the Waterloo Historical Society. Period: 1906 - 1907.

4309. Canadian Broadcasting Corporation. **Kitchener.** Kitchener: Kitchener Chamber of Commerce, 1945. 9 p. ill., maps. Loc: OKIT.

Transcript of a CBC address on a Trans-Canada network, describing Kitchener's German and Mennonite heritage as an example of Canada's cultural mosaic. The phrase "clean as a kitchen" is used and statistical information and maps are included. Period: 1800 - 1945.

4310. Centennial Booklet Committee. **Kitchener Centennial, 1854-1954.** Kitchener: Cober Printing Service, 1954. 106 p. ill., ports. Loc: OKIT, OWT, OWTUR.

A book commemorating the 100th anniversary of Kitchener's incorporation as the Village of Berlin, with historical accounts of industry, services, medical services, education, arts, sports, religion and the armed services. There are many photographs of school buildings, street scenes, and organizations such as sports teams. A programme of the celebrations from 27 June to 3 July 1954 is included. Period: 1854 - 1954.

4311. City of Kitchener. **Activities of public bodies.** 1923. 34 p. index. Loc: OKITW.

A municipal yearbook reporting the work of the various city departments in 1923. Diagrams chart the structure of Kitchener's city government and its expenditures for 1923, with notes on the new city hall. Period: 1922 - 1923.

4312. City of Kitchener. **Auditor's financial statement for the City of Kitchener December 31, 1922, population 23,571.** Kitchener: The City, 1923. 96 p. Loc: OWTUR.

A record of the city's receipts and disbursements, assets and liabilities, submitted by the Municipal Auditor, J.M. Scully, to the Council of which L.O. Breithaupt was Mayor. A complete list of the municipal council can be found on the second page. Period: 1921 - 1922.

4313. City of Kitchener. **By-law no. 1956, regulating the erection and to provide for the safety of buildings in the City of Kitchener.** Kitchener: Commercial Printing, 1927. 73 p. index. Loc: OKITW.

A building code classifying buildings and zones, and specifying construction requirements. Fire prevention measures are noted separately; building inspectors and a permit system are established to administer the by-law. Period: 1926 - 1927.

4314. **The City of Kitchener, Ontario, Canada: the unique center of the fascinating Grand River Valley.** Kitchener: Kitchener Chamber of Commerce, 1958. 1 folded page. ill., maps. Loc: OWTUR.

Promotional brochure including a map of the city, a pioneer map of Waterloo County, and notes on places of interest. Period: 1957 - 1958.

4315. Clarke, Mavis M. "Kitchener's century firms honored." **Waterloo Historical Society.** 1987. 75: 35-46. ill., bibl. Loc: all.

A collection of short histories of 18 Kitchener firms in business since 1887 or earlier and honoured at the Valhalla Inn, Kitchener on 19 November 1987. Period: 1835 - 1987.

4316. Cockman, W.V. and Breen, M. "Kitchener-Waterloo: twins and the county." **Saturday Night.** 1950. 65: 8-10, 36. ill. Also mf. Loc: OKIT, OWTL, OWTU.

Reference from the Canadian Periodical Index. Period: 1950.

4317. Collishaw, Wendy and Preston, Barry. **Recollections of 125 years.** Kitchener: Committee for the 125th, 1979. 28 p. ill., map. Loc: OCCA, OKIT, OWRE, OWRN, OWRND, OWRSJ, OWRW, OWT, OWTL, OWTUCGR, OWTUR, OWTUCR.

An illustrated survey in a large format, commemorating the 125th anniversary of municipal government in Berlin/Kitchener. The main topics are early settlers, industrialization, architecture, the fire and police departments, public health, politics, culinary traditions and recipes, newspapers and telecommunications, schools, sports, churches, music, entertainment and leisure. Period: 1854 - 1979.

4318. "Diamond Jubilee, Dominion Day: a review of the Dominion showing the progress since Confederation, with reference particularly to the twin city of Kitchener and Waterloo." **Daily Telegraph and Daily News Record**. 1927, July 2. Pp. 1-64. ill. Loc: OWTUCR.

A special section largely devoted to the history of Kitchener, with articles by J.P. Jaffray and others reprinted from early issues of the **Berliner Journal**. Some articles discuss changes in lifestyles between 1867 and 1927, for example in the status of women in public life and in the home. Large advertisements by local businesses make up about one quarter of the issue. Period: 1867 - 1927.

4319. Dunham, B. Mabel. "Kitchener, an historical sketch." **Mer Douce**. 1924. 14: 36-38. ill. Loc: OKIT.

A brief narrative of the founding of the community and its subsequent growth and industrialization. The author mentions the impact of the First World War and the fact that Berlin was the first Canadian city to use hydro-electric power transmitted from Niagara Falls. Period: 1800 - 1924.

4320. Eby, Allan A. "The Kitchener of to-day." **Mer Douce**. 1924. 14: 39-41. ill. Loc: OKIT.

A description of contemporary Kitchener, referring to the public utilities, health and the city plan supervised by Thomas Adams, and including biographical information on Mayor Louis O. Breithaupt. Period: 1923 - 1924.

4321. Edwards, F. "Kitchener-Waterloo." **Macleans Magazine**. 1940. 53: 12-14, 32-4. ill. Loc: OKIT, OWTL, OWTU.

Reference from the Canadian Periodical Index. Period: 1940.

4322. German Printing and Publishing Co. **Official souvenir of the celebration of cityhood, July 17th 1912: preliminary announcement**. Berlin: German Printing and Publishing Co., 1912. 8 p. Loc: OKIT.

An advertisement by the printing company, listing special features to be included in the souvenir publication and giving the advertising

rates. Among the features announced are a "Who's who" in Berlin in 1912 and descriptions of businesses and municipal government. Period: 1912 - 1913.

4323. "How Berlin became Kitchener." **Waterloo Historical Society**. 1966. 54: 68. Loc: all.

A brief article on the decision of May 1916 to change the name of Berlin to Kitchener. Period: 1916 - 1956.

4324. Jaffray, J.P. **Kitchener the industrial city**. Kitchener: J.P. Jaffray, 1930. 96 p. ill. Loc: OKIT, OWTUCR.

A promotional booklet that emphasizes the city's amenities and varied industries and presents information about municipal government, with a list of industries established between 1900 and 1929. Period: 1854 - 1931.

4325. Jaffray, J.P. **Kitchener, "the industrial city": the birthplace of the great Niagara power movement**. Kitchener: J.P. Jaffray, 1928. 95 p. ill. Loc: OWTUR, OWTL.

A promotional publication including historical information, current municipal statistics, lists of members of boards and commissions for 1928 and 1929, and names of many clubs and organizations. Short biographical summaries are provided for the more notable industrialists such as the Breithaupts, the Sniders (Snyders) and the Kaufmans. Advertisements for local businesses are a prominent feature. Period: 1882 - 1929.

4326. **Kirmes**. Berlin: The Committee, 1896. 52 p. ill., index. Loc: OKIT.

A programme, in English and German, for the fair held October 1-7, 1896, describing the attractions and containing local advertisements. A short history of the Berlin Kirmes notes that the first was held in 1894. Period: 1894 - 1896.

4327. "Kitchener, 125 years." **Kitchener-Waterloo Record**. 1979, June 21. 84 p. ill. Loc: OWTUR, OWT.

A special edition of the newspaper, in four sections, commemorating the 125th anniversary of municipal incorporation. Topics include industries, economic development, the arts, institutions, municipal government, prominent women, municipal services and sports. There are some "now and then" photographs and articles forecasting the economic future, but generally the focus of these papers is on Kitchener's past. Many companies and institutions placed advertisements in these pages. Period: 1854 - 1979.

4328. Kitchener Board of Trade. **Industrial Kitchener.**
Kitchener: The Board, 1931. 16 p. ill. Loc: OKIT.
    A promotional brochure with brief descriptions
of industries and services such as transportation
facilities, public utilities, local government,
educational institutions, clubs, churches and the
commercial district. Period: 1930 - 1931.

4329. Kitchener Board of Trade. **Key to Kitchener,
Canada.** Kitchener: The Board, 1929. 12 p. ill.,
map. Loc: OWTUR.
    A brochure promoting Kitchener as a place to
live and work, with brief information on
industries, municipal services, schools, public
buildings, hospitals, sports and city government.
Pertinent statistics are given, and a map locating
Kitchener in southern Ontario is on the back
cover. Period: 1928 - 1929.

4330. Kitchener Board of Trade. **Kitchener: a Canadian
industrial city.** Kitchener: The Board, 1935. 24
p. ill., map. Loc: OKITW, OWTUR.
    A promotional brochure with information and some
statistics on municipal services, labour force,
manufacturing facilities, financial institutions,
factory sites, transportation, health and
recreation. A map shows Kitchener's central
location. Period: 1930 - 1940.

4331. Kitchener Board of Trade. **Kitchener, the
industrial city.** Kitchener: The Board, 1927. 12
p. ill. Loc: OWTUR.
    A small booklet of facts about population,
assessments, institutions, clubs and public
utilities. A list of over 140 local industries is
appended. Period: 1893 - 1927.

4332. "The Kitchener centennial." **Ontario History.**
1954. 46: 196-197. Loc: OKIT, OWTL, OWTU.
    Reference from the Canadian Periodical Index.
Period: 1854 - 1954.

4333. Kitchener Chamber of Commerce: Business
Development Branch. **Kitchener factual data.** The
Chamber, 1945-. Loc: OKIT.
    Also entitled **Facts you should know about
Kitchener** and **Kitchener Facts,** these reports
contain statistical information to encourage
business and industrial development. Kitchener
Public Library has reports for 1945, 1962, 1965,
1969, 1970, 1974 and 1975. Period: 1945 - 1975.

4334. Kitchener Chamber of Commerce: Economic Planning
and Industrial Development Committee. **Kitchener
information: summary book.** Kitchener: The
Chamber, 1971-. Loc: OKIT.
    Summaries of current statistical information.
Kitchener Public Library has the reports for the

years 1971, 1977, 1978 and 1980. Period: 1971 -
1980.

4335. Kitchener Chamber of Commerce. **Kitchener
industries.** Kitchener: The Chamber, 1956-. 13 p.
Loc: OKIT.
    Directories of the city's manufacturing
businesses, including names and addresses of
contacts and descriptions of products. Kitchener
Public Library has copies for 1956 and 1962.
Period: 1956 - 1962.

4336. Kitchener Chamber of Commerce. **Manufacturers'
index for the City of Kitchener.** Kitchener: The
Chamber, 1968. 19 p. Loc: OKIT.
    A list of industrial businesses located in
Kitchener, including names and phone numbers of
persons and descriptions of products manufactured.
Period: 1967 - 1968.

4337. Kitchener Chamber of Commerce/ Waterloo Chamber
of Commerce. **Where to go - what to do in
Kitchener-Waterloo, Ontario, Canada, June 1959.**
Kitchener: The Chambers, 1959. 10 p. ill., maps.
Loc: OKIT.
    A promotional account of services,
organizations, industries, and recreational
facilities, with advertisements by local
businesses. Period: 1958 - 1959.

4338. Kitchener City Clerk's Office. **City of Kitchener
municipal manual.** 1945-. Loc: OKIT.
    A series of pocket-sized, annual guides to the
municipal government of Kitchener. Contents
include the text of by-laws governing municipal
procedures, statistics, lists of city officials,
and information on boards, commissions and
committees. Kitchener Public Library has the
manuals for the years 1945, 1946, 1949, 1951 to
1953, 1957, 1958, 1960 to 1962, and 1964 to 1972.
Period: 1945 - 1972.

4339. Kitchener City Council. **The City of Kitchener.**
Kitchener: The Council, 1962. 4 p. Loc: OWTUR.
    Programme for the city's 50th anniversary
celebrations, including parades by naval,
military, legion, boy scouts, girl guides and
ethnic groups with the Kitchener Musical Society
Band, and an evening performance by the
Kitchener-Waterloo Symphony Orchestra and the
Concordia Chorus. From the Clement/Bowlby Family
Papers. Period: 1912 - 1962.

4340. Kitchener City Council. **Zoning ordinance, City of
Kitchener.** 1925. 40 p. map. Loc: OKITW.
    A compilation of by-laws 1823, 1834 and 1835,
establishing land use areas and regulating the
height, bulk, location and spacing of buildings.

Kitchener's zoning by-laws were the first to be approved by the Ontario Railway and Municipal Board in 1924. Period: 1924 - 1925.

4341. Kitchener Manufacturers' Association. **A message from Kitchener, Canada**. Kitchener: The Association, 1917. 64 p. ill. Loc: OKIT.

A photocopy of a promotional publication produced shortly after the city was renamed Kitchener. The introduction explains the desire of "loyal citizens to disassociate themselves from any odium which the name Berlin might suggest." Each page features a full-size advertisement of a local company. Period: 1916 - 1917.

4342. **Kitchener Ontario Old Boys' Re-Union August 1st to 8th, 1925: the industrial city bids you welcome**. Ottawa: Photogelatine Engraving Co., 1925. 1 v. ill. Loc: OKITW.

A booklet of 24 sepia photographs of buildings and parks, prefaced by a brief description. Period: 1924 - 1925.

4343. "Kitchener's 50th anniversary of cityhood." **Waterloo Historical Society**. 1962. 50: 17. ill. Loc: all.

A note of the anniversary celebrations of Kitchener's incorporation as a city in 1912. Period: 1912 - 1962.

4344. Kitchener Water Commission. **Annual report of the Water Commissioners of the City of Kitchener, Canada**. 1933 - 1944. Loc: OKITW.

An account of the year's water supply and consumption, machinery and equipment, first published in 1898. A financial report is given, the members of the commission are listed, and chemical tests by the Ontario Board of Health are reported. Kitchener Public Library holds reports for the years 1933, 1935, 1938, 1939, 1940, 1941, 1943 and 1944. Period: 1933 - 1944.

4345. "Kitchener-Waterloo: a capsule cope-kit." **Chatelaine**. 1971. 44: 24. ill. mf. Loc: OKIT, OWTU.

Reference from the Canadian Periodical Index. Period: 1971 -

4346. **Kitchener-Waterloo, Ontario, Canada**. Woodland Hills, CA: Windsor Publications, 1975. 44 p. ill., map. Loc: OKIT, OWTL.

A promotional booklet, published for the Kitchener and Waterloo chambers of commerce, with photographs of many contemporary businesses and references to community services, historic sites and tourist attractions. Period: 1970 - 1975.

4347. Lamb, Kathryn Hansuld. **Kitchener's business heritage, 1987**. Kitchener: Ainsworth Press, 1987. 8 p. ill. Loc: OKIT.

Profiles of the eighteen businesses and industries of Kitchener which were 100 or more years old in 1987. These were: the Valhalla Inn, the Walper Terrace Hotel, the Lancaster Tavern, Canada Cordage Inc., the law firm of Clement Eastman Dreger Martin & Meunier, C.N. Weber Ltd, The Grand Tavern, Economical Mutual Insurance Company, Boehmer Box Corp., Boehmers, the Rumpel Felt Co. Ltd, Hogg Fuel and Supply Ltd, H.L. Staebler Co., Ltd, **Kitchener-Waterloo Record**, Kissner Milling Co. Ltd, Krug Furniture Inc., the Arrow Company, and Schreiter-Sandrock Funeral Home and Chapel. A programme describing the celebrations to recognize these companies is included, with a list of other Kitchener businesses established for over 75 years. Period: 1887 - 1987.

4348. Lamb, Kathryn Hansuld. **Kitchener's business heritage, 1989**. 1989. 8 p. ill. Loc: OKIT.

Brochure describing four Kitchener businesses which were more than 100 years old in 1989 (the American Hotel; Sims, McKinnon, Varey, Griggs & Trafford; Gowling & Henderson; and the Station Hotel) and four which were 90 years or more (the Walper Tobacco Shop, Weston Bakeries Ltd, Uniroyal Goodrich Canada Inc., and Schreiter's Furniture Store Ltd). A programme describes the celebrations recognizing these companies and includes a list of the 100-year award recipients in 1987. Period: 1889 - 1989.

4349. Lamb, Kathryn Hansuld. **Kitchener's business heritage, 1991**. 1991. 8 p. ill. Loc: OKIT.

Brochure describing four companies which were over 100 years old in 1991, and eight companies established for at least 85 years. The companies over 100 years old were: Joseph and Co., Ltd, Huck Glove Company Inc., J.M. Schneider Inc., and the Walper Tobacco Shop. The companies 85 years and older were: John Forsyth Co., Ltd, Bullas Glass Co., Paul A. Bender General Insurance Broker, Brodey-Draimin Furs, William Knell & Co., Ltd, Nelco Mechanical Ltd, Cressman Meats and Cheese, and Onward Multi-Corp Inc. A programme describing the celebrations recognizing these companies is included, with lists of other companies recognized in 1987 and 1989. Period: 1881 - 1991.

4350. Lamb, Kathryn Hansuld. "Kitchener's business heritage celebration." **Waterloo Historical Society**. 1991. 79: 170-172. Loc: all.

Historical sketches or mentions of 12 firms, recognized for being in business for 85 years or more. The 100-year award recipients include

Joseph and Co. (1880), Huck Glove Co. (1880), J.M. Schneider (1890) and the Walper Tobacco Shop (1891). Period: 1880 - 1991.

4351. Maxwell Publicity Service. **Berlin Ontario, issued in commemoration of its celebration of cityhood July 17th 1912.** Berlin: German Printing and Publishing Co., 1912. 1 v. (unpaged). ill., map. Loc: OWTUR, OKIT, OWTUCG, OWTUCR.

A record of municipal achievements and industrial development. Photographs of prominent Berlin men are included in the "Who's who in Berlin" section and advertisements provide additional photographs and information about businesses. There is a special section on the Berlin sewerage system, as well as a map of the telephone lines in the Waterloo District. Period: 1820 - 1912.

4352. McLaughlin, Kenneth. "Cows and town life: Berlin in the 1870s." **Waterloo Historical Society.** 1987. 75: 144-145. Loc: all.

Two items from the **Berlin Daily News.** The first is a letter dated June 1878 in which a concerned citizen laments the dangers of stray cattle that are allowed to roam freely along King Street. In the second item, dated July 1879, the editor criticizes the employment of young girls in factories until they are married when they should be learning how to run households. Period: 1878 - 1879.

4353. McLaughlin, Kenneth. "Memories of Berlin." **Canadian Heritage.** 1983. 41: 30-31. ill. Loc: OKIT, OWTL, OWTU.

A discussion of the German influences on the community's architecture, noting the Pennsylvania Mennonite farmsteads and German aspects of Berlin's nineteenth-century brick houses. Period: 1800 - 1918.

4354. Moyer, William G. **Kitchener, yesterday revisited: an illustrated history.** Kitchener: Kitchener Chamber of Commerce, 1979. 150 p. ill., bibl., index. Loc: OWTU, OWTL, OKIT, OWTUCG, OWT, OKEBC.

A general history of the town's development, stressing the early period and well illustrated with period and modern photographs. A valuable addition is the "Partners in Progress" section with profiles of city businesses (all indexed in the WRP database). Lists of mayors of Berlin/Kitchener and reeves of Waterloo Township are appended. Period: 1807 - 1979.

4355. **Official program and visitors' service directory: Kitchener Old Boys' Re-Union, August 1 to 8, 1925.** Kitchener: Merchants Printing, 1925. 1 v. (unpaged). ill., map. Loc: OKITW.

A programme of the reunion activities, listing civic and reunion officials and providing a service directory, information on Kitchener, and travel information with timetables of the local railways. Events included parades, pageants, receptions and flying machine tours of Kitchener. Period: 1924 - 1925.

4356. "Official programme: Kitchener's Old Boys' Reunion, August 1st to 8th, 1925." **Kitchener Daily Record.** 1925, August 1. Pp. 1-64. ill. Loc: OWT.

Illustrated supplements honouring the 1925 Old Boys' Reunions of Waterloo and Kitchener with articles on the development of the twin cities, many of them by J.P. Jaffray. The first half deals mainly with Kitchener; the second is entitled "Waterloo section" but Kitchener material resumes on page 42. Many topics are covered and numerous individuals and businesses are mentioned. There are "then" and "now" photographs of street scenes, local anecdotes and poetry, as well as advertisements for local businesses. Period: 1800 - 1925.

4357. Pepper, Paul E. **Name index to Let's reminisce by Alex O. Potter.** 1986. 10 p. Loc: OKIT.

Index to about 450 personal names.

4358. Portlock, Rosa. **Twenty-five years of Canadian life: with a study on Bible prophecy.** Toronto: William Briggs, 1901. Loc: OWTUR, OKIT.

Includes a brief description of the town of Berlin through the eyes of a traveller on pp. 7-13. Period: 1899 - 1901.

4359. Potter, Alexander O. "The Kitchener centennial celebration." **Waterloo Historical Society.** 1954. 42: 21-25. ill. Loc: all.

An account of the celebrations commemorating the centennial of Kitchener's incorporation as a village in 1854. Period: 1854 - 1954.

4360. Potter, Alexander O. **Let's reminisce.** Kitchener: Kitchener-Waterloo Record, 1954. 32 p. Loc: OKIT, OWT, OWTUR.

A collection of articles describing events and people in the history of Berlin/Kitchener, including incorporation as a village, notable citizens, streets and residences, the Berlin Opera House, the Theatorium and Berlin Central School. The booklet was published to mark Kitchener's centennial. Period: 1854 - 1954.

4361. Reed, Mildred. **Bibliography of the history of Kitchener to 1930.** 1973. 18 p. Loc: OKIT.

A course assignment by a teacher-librarian providing an annotated list of 57 printed items held in the Kitchener Public Library. Theses and student research papers on local historical topics are included but not newspapers or histories of individual churches. Period: 1800 - 1930.

4362. Seiling, Ken. "Kitchener's business heritage celebration." **Waterloo Historical Society.** 1989. 77: 112-119. ill. Loc: all.

Speech at the Business Heritage Celebration awards ceremony in 1989, on the role of business history in understanding community history. Kitchener's century firms are briefly described, including the American Hotel; the legal firm of Sims, McKinnon, Varey, Griggs and Trafford; Gowling & Henderson; and the Station Hotel. Period: 1863 - 1989.

4363. **Select community digest: Kitchener-Waterloo edition.** Toronto: Select Publications, 1951. 50 p. ill. Loc: OKIT.

A publication promoting the stability and diversity of the two cities. Current industries and services such as hospitals and schools are described. Messages from Mayors S.F. Leavine of Kitchener and V.J. Bauman of Waterloo are included, with a short article by Ernie Ronnenberg on the Waterloo Band Festival. Period: 1950 - 1951.

4364. Shain, M. "Kitchener-Waterloo: could you live there?." **Chatelaine.** 1971. 44: 22-24, 40. ill. mf. Loc: OKIT, OWTU.

Reference from the Canadian Periodical Index. Period: 1971.

4365. **Souvenir of Berlin.** Valentine's Series. 1913?. 31 p. ill. Loc: OKITW.

Thirty-one coloured views of buildings, parks, and streets. Brief facts on the city are given in an introductory section entitled "Breezes about Berlin." Period: 1912 - 1916.

4366. **Souvenir of Berlin.** 19--. 5 l. ill. Loc: OWTUR, OWTL, OKIT.

A tiny booklet consisting entirely of photographs. Views include the Court House, Central School, Margaret Avenue School and Victoria Park. Period: c1900 - c1915.

4367. **Souvenir of Berlin Ontario: photo-gravures.** CIHM Microfiche series, no. 39259. Berlin: F.I. Weaver & Co., 189-?. 18 frames. mf. Loc: OWTL, OWTU.

Photographs mainly of Berlin, including views of public buildings, King Street, schools and Victoria Park. Some photographs are of Bridgeport and its casino. Period: 1890 - 1900.

4368. Staebler, Edna. "Happily married cities." **Macleans Magazine.** 1952. 65: 16-17, 50-3. ill. Loc: OKIT, OWTL, OWTU.

Reference from the Canadian Periodical Index. Period: 1952.

4369. Staebler, Edna. **The story of Kitchener.** Kitchener: Kitchener-Waterloo Record, 1962. 13 p. Loc: OWTUR, OKIT.

A short history of the city from the early nineteenth century, including sketches of industries and profiles of prominent individuals and families. The author comments on German and Mennonite influences in social and economic development and describes the effects of the First World War on the community. Period: 1800 - 1920.

4370. Stanton, Raymond and Pearce, Richard. **Kitchener: a tradition of excellence.** Windsor: Windsor Publications, 1991. 136 p. ill., index, bibl. Loc: OCH, OCLG, OCP, OKIT.

An overview of the city's contemporary industrial, social, cultural and ethnic character. The author also traces various enterprises back to their origins and includes historic photographs of buildings and colourful anecdotes of former community leaders. Period: 1854 - 1990.

4371. Stroh, Jacob. "Reminiscences of Berlin (now Kitchener), Part I." **Waterloo Historical Society.** 1930. 18: 175-207. ill. Loc: all.

A detailed description of life in the early days of the community. Street by street, the author gives a tour of Berlin, referring to former buildings, residents and businesses. Period: 1854 - 1930.

4372. Stroh, Jacob. "Reminiscences of Berlin (now Kitchener), Part II: churches, roads, miscellaneous." **Waterloo Historical Society.** 1931. 19: 274-284. Loc: all.

A short history of early churches and clergy, streets, the windmill on Mecklenburg Hill, fire-fighting companies, and other clubs and societies. Period: 1854 - 1900.

4373. Stroh, Jacob and Snyder, Joseph M. "Reminiscences of Berlin (now Kitchener), reprinted." **Waterloo Historical Society.** 1978. 66: 71-123. ill. Loc: all.

A detailed description of the early development of the community, reprinted from the annual reports of 1930 and 1931. Personal and corporate names and all subject headings are fully indexed in the WRP database for the original articles.

Period: c1800 - 1930.

4374. Tiessen, Paul Gerald and Hunsberger, David Peter. **Berlin Canada: a self-portrait of Kitchener, Ontario before World War One: being a printing of the complete text of Berlin: Celebration of Cityhood, a volume published in 1912 by The German Printing & Publishing Co. of Berlin Limited, and of various other documents**. St Jacobs: Sand Hills Books, 1979. 1 v. (various pagings). ill., ports, index. Loc: OCH, OCLG, OCP, OKIT, OWRE, OWRN, OWRW, OWT, OWTL, OWTUR, OWTUCR.

A reprint of the 1912 book, preceded by an introduction based mainly on excerpts from the diaries and letters of Gordon C. Eby. Also reprinted in the 1979 volume are the City of Berlin Street Directory, the City of Berlin Miscellaneous Directory, and the Berlin and Waterloo Classified Business Directory from **Vernon's directory** for 1912-13. The illustration on the dust jacket of this limited edition of 2000 copies is reproduced from a painting of Victoria Park by David Peter Hunsberger. Reprinted handsomely on art paper as in the original, it is a superb example of civic boosterism. Contents include a chronology of municipal milestones for Berlin from 1854 to 1912 and portraits of all reeves and mayors and members of the first city council in 1912. There are profiles of William Henry Schmalz (first Mayor of the City of Berlin) and of Berlin's public utilities, the Berlin Light Commission, the Assessment Department, the Fire Department, the Street Railway, the Sewerage System, Victoria Park and the Berlin Board of Trade. The volume is illustrated by many photographs of community leaders and their homes, and by advertisements for their businesses. Persons mentioned at least twice are indexed in the WRP database, as are businesses that placed advertisements. Period: 1912 - 1913.

4375. Town of Berlin. **Practical by-laws of the Town of Berlin**. Berlin: Record Job Office, 1894. 99 p. index. Loc: OKITW.

The text of by-laws passed since the consolidation of 1886 and in force on 31 December 1893. A table of all Berlin by-laws passed from 1886 to 1893 gives the dates passed and their current status. Also included is a list of members of the Berlin Town Council from 1886 to 1894. Period: 1893 - 1894.

4376. Town of Berlin. **Town of Berlin by-laws I. respecting frontage assessment for sewers. II. to license and regulate plumbers. III. to regulate plumbing and to secure the sanitary condition of buildings**. 1892. 19 p. Loc: OKITW.

By-laws with an introduction describing the origins of Berlin's current sewerage system. The main outfall sewer down the valley of Schneider's Creek was built in 1891, and work was begun on the sewerage farm in 1892. Period: 1891 - 1892.

4377. Uttley, W.V. "Berlin, now Kitchener in the beginning." **Waterloo Historical Society**. 1932. 20: 314-320. ill. Loc: all.

A short account of the development of the community, mainly before its selection as county town in 1853. The author refers to early settlers such as Abraham Weber, Joseph Schneider, Benjamin Eby, Jacob Erb and Samuel Eby as well as other people and local businesses. Period: 1807 - 1900.

4378. Uttley, W.V. **A history of Kitchener, Ontario**. Kitchener: The Chronicle Press, 1937. 433 p. ill. Loc: OCCA, OKIT, OWT, OWRA, OWRN, OWTL, OWTU, OWTUCG, OWTUR, OWTUSJ.

An encyclopedic survey of most aspects of the community's development from first settlement by Pennsylvania German Mennonites around 1800 to Berlin's selection as county town in 1852 and its subsequent urban-industrial growth to the mid-1930s. The organization of the volume is complex, being broadly chronological but with self-contained vignettes of particular topics or corporate bodies. There are about 150 illustrations, mainly of buildings or of individuals or groups, and especially detailed histories of the churches of Berlin/Kitchener. Uttley was a newspaper editor and publisher who also took a prominent part in public life, being Mayor of Berlin for a few weeks in 1908. A very detailed index of persons, organizations, places and topical subject headings, based in part on the index compiled by Joyce Lorimer for the 1975 reprinting of Uttley's book, is part of the machine-readable record for the 1975 reprint in the WRP database. Period: 1793 - 1936.

4379. Uttley, W.V. **A history of Kitchener, Ontario, from 1807 to 1916: volume I (busy Berlin period)**. Kitchener: The Author, 1937. 9 p. ill. Loc: OKITW.

A prospectus for W.V. Uttley's book on Kitchener, giving the table of contents and describing illustrations, size, binding and cost. Period: 1936 - 1937.

4380. Uttley, W.V. **A history of Kitchener, Ontario, reissued with an introduction by Gerald Noonan**. Waterloo: Wilfrid Laurier University Press, 1975. 454 p. ill., index. Loc: OCH, OCLG, OCP, OKIT, OWTU, OWTL, OWT, OWRA, OWRBL, OWRN, OWRW, OWTUCR.

An encyclopedic survey of most aspects of the community's development from first settlement to selection as county town in 1852 and subsequent urban-industrial growth to the mid-1930s. The organization of the volume is complex, being broadly chronological but with self-contained vignettes of particular topics or corporate bodies. There are especially detailed histories of churches and about 150 illustrations, mainly of buildings, individuals and groups of people. This reprint of the original 1937 edition has a new introduction and biography of W.V. Uttley (1865-1944) by Gerald Noonan. Uttley was a newspaper editor and publisher who also took a prominent part in public life, being Mayor of Berlin for a few weeks in 1908. The index, compiled by Joyce Lorimer and published with the 1975 reprint, has been supplemented by a new index in the WRP database, adding more corporate, personal and geographical terms as well as topical subject headings. Neither index includes persons named only in lists. Period: 1793 - 1936.

4381. Webber, Bernard F. **Economic conditions in Kitchener during the Great Depression, 1930 to 1935.** Waterloo Lutheran University (student essay, History), 1966. 27 p. bibl., tables. Loc: OKIT.

An analysis of Kitchener's economy during the Depression concluding that in general, Kitchener mirrored the national economy during these years, although its relief costs were more than the national average. Tables show Canadian economic fluctuations from 1919 to 1939, Kitchener relief payments from January 1931 to June 1936, and food prices in Kitchener from 1929 to 1935. Period: 1930 - 1935.

NEW HAMBURG

4382. Berlin News Record. **Enterprising Hamburg and her industries: souvenir industrial number of the News Record of Berlin, Canada.** Berlin: Berlin News Record, 1908. 22 p. ill., index. Loc: OKIT, OWRN.

"A comprehensive review of the natural advantages and resources of the village of New Hamburg, together with historical reviews of those representative concerns and biographical sketches of prominent men that have materially assisted in placing this community in a high position in the industrial, commercial and social world." Period: 1834 - 1908.

4383. **Clippings of New Hamburg and area history.** 1 v. (unpaged). ill. Loc: OWRN.

A collection of printed material about the New Hamburg area, including a programme for the 93rd anniversary of St James Church, Wilmot (1945), 1957 newspaper clippings about the centennial of

New Hamburg's incorporation, articles on the flood of 1883 and the demolition of the New Hamburg town hall and firehall in 1968, and a copy of a 1987 supplement to the **Elmira Independent** sponsored by the Woolwich Historical Foundation. Period: 1835 - 1987.

4384. Diamond, Florence. "The history of New Hamburg." **Waterloo Historical Society.** 1976. 64: 39-48. ill. Loc: all.

A short history of the town which grew around Josiah Cushman's grist mill from 1834. The author mentions many early industries and residents. Part of the 1854 plan of New Hamburg, showing lots and streets, is reprinted. Period: 1834 - 1976.

4385. Hamilton, O.A.F. "New Hamburg historical notes." **Waterloo Historical Society.** 1936. 24: 229-234. Loc: all.

A short history of the community from the founding of Cushman's sawmill to the great flood of 1883, based on an outline by F.H. McCallum. Period: 1820 - 1883.

4386. Mannen, Douglas. **New Hamburg: images and reflections.** 1989. 290 p. ill., maps, bibl. Loc: OKIT, OWRA, OWRE, OWRN, OWRW.

A history of the community from the 1830s to the late 1950s. The book is organized thematically in chapters on the following topics: inns and hotels; merchants and shopkeepers; industrial establishments; dairies, liveries and coal dealers; automobile and implement dealers and garages; the trades; the professions; the press; and public buildings. Historical photographs and the 1885 (revised 1904) fire insurance plans are reproduced, but there is no index to personal or corporate names. Period: 1838 - 1958.

4387. "New Hamburg Centennial." **Waterloo Historical Society.** 1957. 45: 12. Loc: all.

A note of the 100th anniversary of incorporation as a village, including references to articles previously published in the Waterloo Historical Society volumes of 1936 and 1943. Period: 1857 - 1957.

4388. Ritz, Ernst. "New Hamburg 1850-1860: a period of rapid growth." **Waterloo Historical Society.** 1981. 69: 74-87. ill. Loc: all.

A detailed description of the decade when the arrival of the Grand Trunk Railway stimulated the fastest growth in the village's history. The author refers to the 1854 plan by M.C. Schofield, showing about seventy houses and many businesses, and presents information about newspapers, churches, schools, municipal incorporation and services, as well as biographical sketches of village leaders. Period: 1850 - 1860.

PRESTON

4389. Brodie, Phyllis. **A historical geography of Preston.** University of Waterloo (B.E.S. thesis, Geography), 1976. 3 fiche. ill., maps, tables, bibl. mf. Loc: OWTUM.
   A comprehensive survey of economic, political and social changes in the community from its first settlement. Period: 1800 - 1975.

4390. Byerly, A.E. "Preston in 1866." **Waterloo Historical Society.** 1933. 21: 53-56. Loc: all.
   An description of the village, including its architectural styles and landscape, with brief references to the oil industry, S. Cornell's hotel, A.A. Erb and Brothers' mill, F. Guggisberg's cabinet factory, the Preston Linen Factory, Wright and Co.'s cloth factory, and the hopyard of Abbey, Risley and Co. Period: 1865 - 1866.

4391. Cowan, Jennie F. "Preston in early Canada." **Waterloo Historical Society.** 1960. 48: 19-21. Loc: all.
   A summary of the history of Preston from its founding by John Erb in 1806 to 1852. Period: 1806 - 1852.

4392. Klotz, Otto Julius. "Preston: reminiscences." **Waterloo Historical Society.** 1921. 9: 171-182. Loc: all.
   Recollections by the Director of the Dominion Observatory of his home town in about 1860. Listing all the business establishments of that time, he reflects on how self-contained the community had been. Of special interest is his description of sports, pastimes and holidays in a mid-nineteenth century village, notably the annual Turn Fest of athletics usually combined with theatricals, music and dances. Period: 1860 - c1900.

4393. Klotz, Otto. "Sketch of the history of the village of Preston [original]." **Waterloo Historical Society.** 1917. 5: 24-40. ill. Loc: all.
   An industrial history of Preston from its beginnings with John Erb's grist mill to the 1880s. Early entrepreneurs who moved elsewhere are mentioned, including Samuel Liebschuetz who founded German Mills, Adam Ferrie Jr who founded Doon, Jacob Beck who founded Baden, and Jacob Hespeler who founded Hespeler. Other topics are the Preston railway debt, aid to manufacturers by the village of Preston, the Grand River Bridge, schools, the fire department and the Preston

Mechanics Institute. Period: 1800 - 1885.

4394. Klotz, Otto. "Sketch of the history of the village of Preston [reprint]." **Waterloo Historical Society.** 1972. 60: 16-25. ill. Loc: all.
   A history of the village from its beginnings to about 1880, recalling early inhabitants, businesses and industries and presenting profiles of John Erb, Henry Bernhardt, Adam Ferrie, Samuel Liebschuetz, Frederick and John Guggisberg, Jacob Beck and John Clare. Part of a longer article printed in the Waterloo Historical Society's 5th Annual Report 1917, pages 24-40, the 1972 reprint lacks eight pages of the 1917 version, concerning aid to manufacturers, the Preston railway debt, schools, the Preston Fire Department and the Preston Mechanics' Institute. Different photographs from those printed in 1917 are used in 1972. The article was originally published in the **Preston Progress** newspaper, but exact details are not provided. Period: 1800 - 1885.

4395. Nichols, C.M. and Dyas, John H. **Industrial Preston.** Preston: Preston Progress, 1908. 28 p. ill., index. Loc: OKIT, OCCA.
   A "special souvenir number of the Preston Progress newspaper, descriptive of and illustrating Preston and vicinity, an epitome of her commercial supremacy, manufacturing resources and residential advantages, with reviews of the representative establishments, and biographical sketches of the leading business and profession men who have contributed to place them in a pre-eminent position in the business world." Period: 1900 - 1908.

4396. Pautler, Alfred. **Preston: a friendly welcome awaits you.** Preston: Golden Jubilee and Old Boys' Reunion, 1949. 1 v. (unpaged). ill., map, ports. Loc: OKITW, OCCA.
   An illustrated souvenir booklet containing the official programme of the Golden Jubilee and Old Boys' Reunion, with descriptions of businesses, sports, parks, transportation, hotels, clubs, banks, churches and civic government. Period: 1940 - 1949.

4397. "Preston: 1969." **Waterloo Historical Society.** 1969. 57: 48. Loc: all.
   A note of three items of local news: Oliver A. Kummer named Preston's Citizen of the Year, Mrs Claudette Millar elected Preston's first woman Mayor, and three women given forty-year pins for service as members of the Ladies' Auxiliary to the Preston Royal Canadian Legion. Period: 1968 - 1969.

4398. "Preston...holds the key to opportunity." **Galt Evening Reporter**. 1964, February 18. Pp. 13A-24A. ill. Loc: OCCA.

A supplement promoting Preston's industries and local services. Articles give facts on companies and organizations, there are photographs of the Kirmes and other past Preston events, and local businesses have placed large advertisements. Period: 1964 - 1965.

4399. "Preston's Municipal Complex." **Waterloo Historical Society**. 1966. 54: 58. Loc: all.

A short note of the opening. Period: 1966.

4400. Preston Women's Institute. **Tweedsmuir history, Preston Women's Institute, South Waterloo**. Kitchener: Kitchener Public Library, 1983. 1 reel. ill., map. mf. Loc: OCCA, OKIT, OWRE, OWTU.

A scrapbook history of Preston from 1806 to 1972, including details of churches, mayors, pioneers, industries, businesses, hotels and organizations. There is also information about the Preston Kirmessen of 1904 and 1912, the hop fields, the parks, the bands, the early telephone system, and the various municipal services such as the fire and police department. Period: 1806 - 1972.

WATERLOO (VILLAGE, TOWN, CITY)

4401. Centennial Advertising Committee. **Waterloo Centennial Jubilee band and folk festival, June 26 - July 1, 1957: the history of our city's growth, 1857-1957**. Waterloo: The Committee, 1957. 98 p. ill. Loc: OWTUR, OWTL, OKITW, OWT.

An illustrated account of the city's industrial and commercial growth, including its insurance, distilling and brewery, manufacturing, farming, woodworking, clothing and service industries as well as descriptions of churches, schools and entertainment. A detailed programme for the events at the Waterloo Centennial Jubilee begins on page 43 and lists many individuals who were involved in the festivities. There are many advertisements by businesses in Waterloo and Kitchener. Period: 1857 - 1957.

4402. "Century firms in Waterloo." **Waterloo Historical Society**. 1967. 55: 29. Loc: all.

A list of seven companies presented with centennial plaques by the Waterloo Chamber of Commerce on completing 100 years in business. The companies were Kuntz Brewery (Carling Breweries Ltd), Waterloo Manufacturing Co. Ltd, the **Waterloo Chronicle**, Joseph E. Seagram and Sons Ltd, C.A. Boehm Insurance Ltd, McGibbon Harper and Haney, and the Waterloo Mutual Insurance

Company. Period: 1867 - 1967.

4403. Cowls, W.J. **These eventful years: a pageant of the history of the city of Waterloo, Ontario**. 1957. 20 l. Loc: OKIT.

Text of a pageant in 20 scenes, performed in Waterloo on 2 July 1957 during the city's centennial celebrations. Featuring the community's development until 1945 and its leading citizens and businesses, the pageant is mentioned in F.W.R. Dickson's article on Waterloo's centennial in the Waterloo Historical Society's 45th annual report. Period: 1799 - 1946.

4404. Dunham, B. Mabel. "A short history of the new City of Waterloo." **Kitchener-Waterloo Record**. 1948, January 2. p. 3. Loc: OWTUR.

An article marking Waterloo's incorporation as a city. The author outlines the settlement and development of the community, noting individuals who became prominent in business, industry and politics. The article was also printed in the Waterloo Historical Society's 35th annual report and is fully indexed with that record in the WRP database. Period: 1800 - 1947.

4405. Dunham, B. Mabel. "A short history of the new City of Waterloo." **Waterloo Historical Society**. 1947. 35: 34-38. Loc: all.

An historical sketch marking the proclamation of city status. Period: 1800 - 1947.

4406. Dunham, B. Mabel. "The story of Waterloo." **Kitchener-Waterloo Record**. 1948. 5 p. Loc: OWT, OWTUR.

An historical sketch of the community marking its incorporation as a city. It outlines settlement and development, noting prominent citizens such as Abraham Erb, Elias Snider, John Hoffman and Cyrus M. Taylor. Similar accounts were published in the **Kitchener-Waterloo Record** on 2 January 1948 and the Waterloo Historical Society's Annual Report for 1948. Period: 1857 - 1948.

4407. "History of Waterloo, 1806-1961." **Waterloo Chronicle**. 1961, June 8. Pp. 1-28. ill. Loc: OWT, OKITW.

A newspaper supplement commemorating the history of the town of Waterloo with references to its industries, insurance companies, street railway and the 1895 reunion of Waterloo Public School students. Articles are reprinted from earlier editions of the newspaper. Period: 1806 - 1961.

4408. "History of Waterloo, 1806-1962: 156 years of industry." **Waterloo Chronicle**. 1962, July 12. Pp. 1-8. ill. Loc: OWT.

A newspaper supplement containing general articles about the development of industry in Waterloo and advertisements by local businesses. Period: 1806 - 1962.

4409. "Marking 100 years of progress with stability: Waterloo 1857-1957." **Waterloo Chronicle**. 1957, June 20. Pp. 1-40. ill. Loc: OWT.

A special edition of the newspaper celebrating Waterloo's history and reporting the centennial celebrations. Articles are reprinted from past newspapers and advertisements. Period: 1857 - 1957.

4410. Reaman, G. Elmore. "From Waterloo to Waterloo." **Waterloo Historical Society**. 1958. 46: 7-11. ill. Loc: all.

A description of a cultural exchange in 1958 between the cities of Waterloo, Belgium, and Waterloo, Ontario. Period: 1958.

4411. Rowell, Margaret. **Waterloo, the village, 1806-1876 and the development of the central business district of Waterloo between 1861 and 1981**. University of Waterloo (student essay, History), 1981?. 1 v. (unpaged). ill., bibl. Loc: OWT.

An essay in two parts, the first outlining early settlement and development from the German Company and the first mill established by Abraham Erb to the growth of industries, businesses and services in the village. The second section describes the growth of Waterloo since 1861 with particular reference to its strong commercial and industrial base, built environment and architectural history. Period: 1806 - 1981.

4412. Rowell, Margaret and Devitt, Edward and McKegney, Patricia. **Welcome to Waterloo: an illustrated history of Waterloo, Ontario, in celebration of its 125th anniversary, 1867-1982**. Waterloo: Waterloo Printing Co., 1982. 132 p. ill., maps, bibl. Loc: OKIT, OWRA, OWRE, OWRW, OWT, OWTL, OWTU, OWTUCG, OWTUR.

A survey of the village to 1876, the town from 1876 to 1947, and the city since 1947, outlining pioneer settlement, municipal government, transportation and communications, industry and commerce, hotels and inns, financial institutions, schools, churches, and recreation. There are profiles of most organizations and illustrations of industrial and commercial buildings and special events. One appendix presents sports highlights, and another lists the names of municipal politicians and officials. Period: 1857 - 1982.

4413. "Souvenir edition commemorating the 125th anniversary of the city of Waterloo." **Waterloo Chronicle**. 1982, May 26. 80 p. ill. Loc: OWTUR, OKITW, OWT, OWTUCR.

A history of the community's settlement and growth, including information on industries, schools, churches, entertainment, government programmes, universities, notable people and landmarks, with historic and current advertisements by local businesses and many photographs. The final pages are devoted to the history of the **Waterloo Chronicle** itself. Period: 1857 - 1982.

4414. "Story of Waterloo's first hundred years." **Kitchener-Waterloo Record**. 1957, June 25. Pp. 25-44. ill. Loc: OWT.

A newspaper supplement commemorating the centenary of Waterloo's incorporation as a village. The lead article by Mabel Dunham is reprinted from the **Record** of 2 January 1948. Many articles are historical but some concern contemporary issues such as the increase in taxes and urbanization. Numerous people, organizations and businesses are mentioned. Period: 1806 - 1957.

4415. Voelker, Marion. **Waterloo centennial: June 26-July 1**. Waterloo: The Author, 1957. 42 p. ill. Loc: OWT.

An unpublished scrapbook of newspaper clippings, programmes, buttons, posters and items about the centennial celebrations in 1957. It includes a description of the first school house and a list of Waterloo mayors. Period: 1857 - 1957.

4416. "Waterloo 1857-1982." **Kitchener-Waterloo Record**. 1982, June 18. Pp. 53-72. ill. Loc: OWT.

A newspaper supplement commemorating the 125th anniversary of incorporation as a village. There are articles and photographs on many subjects including the University of Waterloo, sports, a walking tour of the city, life as a city employee in 1948, and reminiscences of city seniors. Period: 1806 - 1982.

4417. Waterloo Board of Trade. **The Town of Waterloo, Ontario: the Hartford of Canada**. Waterloo: The Board, 1927. 16 p. ill. Loc: OKIT.

A promotional booklet with brief accounts of contemporary business, education, recreation and services. There are photographs of the Waterloo College and Seminary, the Waterloo Mutual Fire Insurance Co., the Public Library, Mutual Life of Canada building, and Waterloo's first log school house. The title on the cover is "What's this about Waterloo?" Period: 1926 - 1927.

4418. Waterloo Board of Trade. **Welcome to Waterloo, Ontario, Canada: industrially and financially unique.** Waterloo: The Board, 1947. 12 p. ill., map. Loc: OKIT.

A promotional booklet including many photographs of local industries, businesses and services and a list of 1947 Waterloo enterprises, organized by type. Period: 1946 - 1947.

4419. Waterloo Chamber of Commerce. **A good location for your industry: Waterloo, Ontario, Canada: progress with stability.** Waterloo: Waterloo Chamber of Commerce, 1956. 20 p. ill. Loc: OWTUR.

Promotional brochure presenting a general description and history of the city and its municipal services and listing over 60 Waterloo firms and their products. Period: 1956 - 1958.

4420. Waterloo Chamber of Commerce. **Growth with stability in beautiful Waterloo.** Waterloo: The Chamber, 1964. 16 p. ill., maps. Loc: OKIT.

A promotional booklet describing the city's main commercial and residential areas and listing local industries and businesses. In includes statistics relating to local politics, civic tax structure, services and transportation. Period: 1963 - 1964.

4421. Waterloo Town Council. **Records and by-laws of the Town of Waterloo.** Waterloo: Bauernfreund Publishing House, 1904. 144 p. index. Loc: OKITW.

The text of by-laws in force in 1904, with a table giving the title, date passed, and status of each. The names of all Waterloo councillors, reeves, mayors and clerks from 1857 to 1904 are listed. Period: 1857 - 1904.

4422. Wells, Clayton W. and Hilliard, Thomas. "A historical sketch of the town of Waterloo, Ontario." **Waterloo Historical Society.** 1928. 16: 22-67. Loc: all.

A detailed historical account of the town, including aboriginal occupation, settlers from Pennsylvania and Germany, early businesses, churches, the library, local government, the Board of Trade and musical organizations. Many citizens and Waterloo men who died in the First World War are named. Period: 1800 - 1928.

WATERLOO TOWNSHIP

4423. Bean, Clive S. "History of Doon." **Waterloo Historical Society.** 1941. 29: 164-172. Loc: all.

A brief account of the communities of Upper and Lower Doon, from their origins in 1834 with the enterprises of Adam Ferrie and the Perine Brothers to 1941. The author notes that the Grand Trunk Railway diverted traffic and commerce to Berlin.

Period: 1834 - 1941.

4424. "Bloomingdale's Tweedsmuir book." **Waterloo Historical Society.** 1971. 59: 35. Loc: all.

A note of the completion of the Tweedsmuir history of Bloomingdale, edited by Olive and Vera Schweitzer. Period: 1971.

4425. Brewster, Winfield. **Lot six in the third of Waterloo.** Hespeler: T and T Press, 1950. 21 p. ill., maps. Also mf. Loc: OCCA, OCLG, OKIT, OWTUR.

A collection of notes and reminiscences about Lot 6 of Concession 3 in Waterloo Township. Names and anecdotes are presented about many landowners, tenants and workers, especially the Brewster, Brydon and Bergey families. An index is available at the City of Cambridge Archives and the Cambridge Library and Gallery. Period: 1847 - 1950.

4426. Centreville Women's Institute. **Tweedsmuir history, Centreville Women's Institute, North Waterloo.** Kitchener: Kitchener Public Library, 1983. 1 reel. ill., maps. mf. Loc: OKIT, OWTU, OWRE.

A history of the community, presented in scrapbook form with newspaper articles, photographs, handwritten and typed entries relating to such topics as farms, schools, churches, landscapes, roads, services and organizations. Biographical sketches, as well as reminiscences of many local residents, are included. The Kitchener Public Library also holds the original volume. Period: c1800 - 1983.

4427. "Clergy Reserve Fund ended in Waterloo Township." **Waterloo Historical Society.** 1969. 57: 79. Loc: all.

A note of the abolition in 1969 by the Waterloo Township Council of its Clergy Reserve Fund and the transfer of $40,000 to the Waterloo Public School Boards. Period: 1791 - 1969.

4428. Cressman, Ella M. "History of the village of Breslau." **Waterloo Historical Society.** 1969. 57: 32-43. ill. map. Loc: all.

A history of the community from its foundation in 1850 by Joseph Erb, including descriptions of various points located on a 1858 village map surveyed by James Pollock and Joseph Hobson and reproduced in the article. The shops, schools, churches, railway, hotels, and the telephone and electrical systems are all mentioned. Period: 1818 - 1969.

4429. Eby, Marguerite Bechtel. "Doon 1867: before and after." **Waterloo Historical Society**. 1966. 54: 36-58. ill. Loc: all.

A community history that mentions early settlers, businesses and organizations. Family names such as Watson, Tilt, Hamacher, Kinzie, Beck, Peddar, Perine, Schneider and Ferrie figure prominently. Period: c1800 - 1967.

4430. Elmdale Women's Institute. **Tweedsmuir history, Elmdale Women's Institute, North Waterloo**. Kitchener: Kitchener Public Library, 1982. 1 reel. ill., maps. mf. Loc: OKIT, OWTU, OWRE.

A microfilm copy of the Tweedsmuir history which relates the beginnings of the Elmdale Women's Institute in 1952 as well as the settlement and development of its community. Topics include local landowners and the fiftieth anniversary of the Elmdale School House (1907-1957) and its Old Boys' Reunion held June 22, 1957. A programme of the reunion provides a brief history of the school with budgets and lists of school board members and teachers. Period: c1800 - 1957.

4431. "Freeport." **Waterloo Historical Society**. 1956. 44: 42. Loc: all.

A brief description of Freeport's origins, from Parsell's **Atlas of the Dominion of Canada** of 1881. Period: 1820 - 1881.

4432. Haldane, Elizabeth Anne. **The historical geography of Waterloo Township, 1800-1855**. McMaster University (M.A. thesis, Geography), 1963. 199 l. ill., maps, plates, bibl. Loc: OWTU, OWTUR, OKIT.

A useful account of the development of the township from first white settlement to the coming of the railway. The thesis is organized in two main parts: the years 1800-1835, when the main agents of landscape change were the Pennsylvania Mennonite pioneers; and the period from 1835 to 1855, when German migrants from Europe established themselves especially in the villages of Preston and Berlin, but also in Waterloo, Hespeler and smaller centres. The author uses varied primary sources to document the changing economy, society and landscape, and presents many maps and other illustrations to show land sales and surveys, changes in rural land use and productivity, and the growth of hamlets and villages. Period: 1800 - 1855.

4433. Helena Feasby Women's Institute. **Tweedsmuir history, Helena Feasby Women's Institute, North Waterloo**. Kitchener: Kitchener Public Library, 1981. 1 reel. ill., maps. mf. Loc: OKIT, OWTU, OWRE.

A history of the Williamsburg locality of the former Waterloo Township southwest of Kitchener,

beginning with an account of the Tweedsmuir histories project and of the Helena Feasby Branch, named for its founder who was a long-time teacher at the Williamsburg School. Presented as a scrapbook containing newspaper clippings, correspondence, photographs, and handwritten or typed contributions of members, the document provides an eclectic record of local personalities, landownership (including century farms), volunteer services, and numerous community and rural activities from soap-making and syrup-making to stamp-collecting. Period: 1800 - 1981.

4434. Historical Society of St Boniface and Maryhill Community. **The Historical Society of St Boniface and Maryhill Community Calendar**. Maryhill: The Society, 1988-. Loc: OKIT.

A photocopy of the annual calendar including reprints of family portraits, buildings, wayside shrines and activities. Birth dates of pioneer residents are noted each month. The Kitchener Public Library holds calendars for the years 1988 to date. Period: 1820 - 1951.

4435. Johannes, James. "History of Blair." **Waterloo Historical Society**. 1941. 29: 162-164. Loc: all.

An historical sketch of the earlier pioneer years, including references to various mills and industries, the Blair School and Blair Cemetery. Period: 1800 - 1940.

4436. Jubilee Women's Institute. **Tweedsmuir history, Jubilee Women's Institute, South Waterloo, 1947-1988**. 1988. 3 v. ill., maps. mf. Loc: OCCA.

A three-part history of the Glen Christie area, of which the first volume has facts and photographs about families, farmsteads, churches and schools. The second volume contains newspaper clippings, photographs on the area and the institute from 1947 to 1988. The third has photographs of club members and programmes of activities from the same period. Period: 1820 - 1988.

4437. Kinzie, Harry S. "History of Blair." **Waterloo Historical Society**. 1954. 42: 7-10. ill. Loc: all.

A description of Blair, emphasizing the earlier settlement that began in 1800 and the development of its many mills. Period: 1800 - 1955.

4438. Kinzie, Ira. "New Aberdeen." **Waterloo Historical Society**. 1951. 39: 41. Loc: all.

A short description of the village founded in 1824, including names of early inhabitants and businesses. Period: 1824 - c1880.

4439. Kummer, Oliver A. "Reminiscences of A.O. [sic] Kummer, early settler: Doon." **Waterloo Historical Society**. 1964. 52: 63-70. ill. Loc: all.

An historical sketch of early businesses, industries, organizations and activities, including references to Adam Ferrie, John Tilt, William Morrison, Moses Wismer, Jacob Cluthe, James Huber, James Jones, James Card, William Thoms and Charles Ahrens. Period: c1800 - 1965.

4440. Lamb, Kathryn Hansuld. "Maryhill is 50 years old." **Waterloo Historical Society**. 1991. 79: 116. Loc: all.

A note of the anniversary of the community's change of name from New Germany during the Second World War. Period: 1941 - 1991.

4441. Lexington Women's Institute. **Tweedsmuir history, Lexington Women's Institute, North Waterloo.** Kitchener: Kitchener Public Library, 1983. 2 reels. ill., ports. mf. Loc: OKIT, OWTU, OWRE.

A microfilmed scrapbook history of the community northeast of Kitchener-Waterloo. Topics in the first book include schools, industries, personalities, farms and churches. The second book contains information on current events in a wider area, such as Fred Shinn's series of articles in the **Waterloo Chronicle**. The Lexington Institute was founded in 1962, and much of the history records the contemporary urbanization of farmland. Period: 1834 - 1986.

4442. "Map of Waterloo Township." **Historical atlas of Waterloo & Wellington counties, including: Illustrated Atlas of the County of Waterloo (1881), County of Waterloo Directory (1877-78) and Illustrated Atlas of the County of Wellington (1877).** Port Elgin: Ross Cumming, 1972 reprint. p. 23. Loc: OWTU, OWTUM, OWTUCG, OKIT, OWTL, OCCA, OCLG, OCP, OWRBL, OWRE, OWRN, OWRW, OWT.

A map at a scale of 80 chains to the inch, showing rivers and streams, major roads, railway lines, townships, towns, villages, hamlets, concessions and lots. The complicated pattern of land surveys is well illustrated. Properties of subscribers to the atlas are also identified. Period: 1880 - 1881.

4443. Moyer, Helen A. and Reinhart, Sheila. **A journal of New Germany.** Historical Society of St Boniface and Maryhill Community, 1991. 1 v. ill., index. Loc: OKIT.

A selection of interesting items on New Germany from 1850 to 1941 taken from local newspapers and arranged chronologically. The articles provide rich detail on local people and events, while a name index provides access to the death notices,

wedding announcements and other items. Names of the Sisters of Notre Dame and pastors of St. Boniface who served in the community are listed. Period: 1850 - 1941.

4444. Newcombe, Hiram K. "Village of Breslau: its beginning, sketches of its business men and nearby farmers." **Newcombe's Monthly Rural Sketches.** 1900 - June. Pp. 1-22. Loc: OKITW.

Biographical sketches of 34 prominent men and businesses in 1900, with a village history and a glowing contemporary description. Many people, commercial enterprises and farmsteads are noted in this detailed account. Period: 1818 - 1900.

4445. Pepper, Paul E. **Index to Lot six in the third of Waterloo: by Winfield Brewster.** 1987. 3 p. Loc: OKIT.

An index to nearly 150 persons.

4446. "Rummelhardt." **Waterloo Historical Society**. 1970. 58: 74. Loc: all.

A note that Mrs Carl Boettger, while working on the history of Rummelhardt for the Women's Institute Tweedsmuir history, had found records showing the purchase of land in 1842 by Francis Joseph Rummelhardt from Benjamin Eby. Period: 1842 - 1970.

4447. "Rummelhardt." **Waterloo Historical Society**. 1978. 66: 47. Loc: all.

A note about the origin of the name of the small community located west of Waterloo. Period: 1969 - 1978.

4448. Schweitzer, Olive and Schweitzer, Vera. **Bloomingdale Tweedsmuir history, part 1.** Canadian-German Folklore v.5. Pennsylvania Folklore Society of Ontario, 1975. 292 p. ill. Loc: OWTU, OKIT, OKITW, OWTUCG, OWT.

A printed version of most of the first volume of the Bloomingdale Tweedsmuir history, dealing with the early settlement of the families, their farms, and a genealogy of the owners from 1805 to 1968. Persons mentioned in this volume have been indexed in detail in the WRP database. The entire Tweedsmuir history to 1965 is available on microfilm and separately abstracted. Period: 1805 - 1968.

4449. Schweitzer, Olive and Schweitzer, Vera. **Tweedsmuir history of the community of Bloomingdale, 1801-1965.** Toronto: Archives of Ontario, 1969. 2 reels. 274, 320 p. ill. mf. Loc: OKIT.

A comprehensive and well-organized history of the community which was part of Waterloo Township until 1972. The first volume, also printed in

1975 by the Pennsylvania Folklore Society of Ontario, deals with Indian lands, the German Company Tract, pioneer settlement, early government, transportation, agriculture and century farms, and genealogies of pioneer settlers and landowners. Persons named in the printed volume are indexed in detail with the separate record in the WRP database. The microfilmed first volume also includes a 40-page history of Rosendale. The second volume describes the actual village of Bloomingdale, its founders, churches, schools, shops, industries and voluntary organizations. Period: 1805 - 1965.

4450. Sherk, M.G. "Reminiscences of Freeport, Waterloo County from 1867 to 1873." **Waterloo Historical Society**. 1924. 12: 101-108. Loc: all.

An historical sketch that describes the Freeport Academy, the United Brethren in Christ Church, Cornell's Corners and various homesteads. The author mentions early inhabitants such as Abraham B. Sherk, Elias Snyder, Jacob Gingerich, Henry Hilker, Bishop Weaver, Rev. George Plowman, Samuel S. Detweiler, Wesley Meriam, Adam Shupe, Mr Allison and Henry Lutz. Period: 1850 - 1873.

4451. Snyder, O.A., Mrs. "Fisher Mills." **Waterloo Historical Society**. 1957. 45: 29-35. ill. Loc: all.

A history of the village from 1835 when Christian Strome built a saw mill. Period: 1835 - 1957.

4452. Snyder, O.A., Mrs. "Speedsville." **Waterloo Historical Society**. 1955. 43: 24-27. Loc: all.

A brief historical sketch of early settlers and industries and the community's gradual incorporation into Preston. Period: 1801 - 1955.

4453. Steckle, John. "John Steckle recollects." **Waterloo Historical Society**. 1965. 53: 47-52. Loc: all.

A collection of anecdotes about early settlers of Waterloo Township, including references to land transactions and the unsolved disappearance of Jacob Bliehm (Bleam) in 1836. Period: c1800 - 1965.

4454. Ternant, Vera Mavis and Tilt, Millicent and Worden, Ethel Wilfong (Mrs Paul) **Tweedsmuir history, Grand River (Doon-Blair), South Waterloo**. Kitchener: Kitchener Public Library, 1984. 1 reel. maps, ports. mf. Loc: OWTU, OKIT.

A portrait of the community, covering varied topics and drawn from many sources. Major sections deal with churches, schools, industries, family histories and farmsteads. The club's own members and activities are given prominence, but other community activities and clubs are also described. Also included are biographies of notable local people such as Homer Watson and Jessie Beattie, a walking tour of Blair and a discussion of industrial sources of water pollution. The Kitchener Public Library also holds the original volume. Period: 1800 - 1984.

4455. "Township of Waterloo embracing the towns of Berlin and Waterloo and the villages of Preston and Hespeler." **Historical atlas of Waterloo & Wellington counties, including: Illustrated Atlas of the County of Waterloo (1881), County of Waterloo Directory (1877-78) and Illustrated Atlas of the County of Wellington (1877)**. Port Elgin: Ross Cumming, 1972 reprint. Pp. 5-8. Loc: OWTU, OWTUM, OWTUCG, OKIT, OWTL, OCCA, OCLG, OCP, OWRBL, OWRE, OWRN, OWRW, OWT.

An historical sketch of topography, early settlement, the development of economic activities, municipal government and services, and social institutions such as churches and schools. It is interesting as an early statement of what was to become a widely accepted version of the early history of the region. The story of the Mennonite migrations, from Europe to Pennsylvania and thence to Upper Canada, is recounted in considerable detail for the period before 1816. About half consists of accounts of the early settlement and municipal incorporation of Waterloo, Berlin, Preston and Hespeler, with brief notes on the smaller hamlets and villages of Blair, Bloomingdale, Breslau, Bridgeport, Centreville, Doon, Freeport, Freiburg, German Mills, Kossuth and Strasburg. Period: 1800 - 1881.

4456. "Township of Waterloo: the first far-inland settlement in Upper Canada." **Waterloo Historical Society**. 1959. 47: 29-41. map. Loc: all.

Text of the historical sketch from Parsell's Atlas of 1881. Tremaine's 1861 map, naming landowners and listing various merchants, is reproduced and a table summarizes information about houses and livestock from the assessment rolls of 1833, 1840 and 1848. All reeves from 1850 to 1960 are listed. Period: 1800 - 1960.

4457. Waterloo Township Council. **Consolidated by-laws of the Township of Waterloo up to the year 1913: to which is appended an historical sketch of the early settlement and subsequent development of the township, and other interesting matter**. Preston: Preston Progress, 1913. 148 p. Loc: OCCA, OKIT, OWTUR, OKITW.

Synopses of Waterloo Township by-laws in force in 1913, with a list of all bylaws passed by the Township Council between 1850 and 1912. A brief history of Waterloo Township is given, with a list of the municipal officers (reeves, deputy reeves, councillors, clerks and treasurers) from 1850 to 1913. Also included are a list of Gore District by-laws affecting roads in Waterloo Township and a description of road divisions in relation to electoral boundaries. Period: 1850 - 1912.

4458. Waterloo Township Council. **Journal of proceedings and by-laws of the municipal council of the Township of Waterloo in the County of Waterloo.** Berlin: Daily Telegraph and Daily News Record Office, 1855. 42 p. Also CIHM Microfiche series, no. 41869. Loc: OKITW.

Minutes of the 34th to 40th sessions held in 1854, with copies of the by-laws passed. The names of the councillors, reeves, tavern inspectors, assessors, town wardens, fence viewers, pound keepers, collectors and highway overseers are given. Many by-laws deal with roads and highways; by-law no. 91 redefines the school sections. Period: 1854 - 1855.

4459. Waterloo Township Council. **Journal of proceedings and reports of the municipal council of the Township of Waterloo for the year 1942.** Waterloo Township Council, 1942. 16 p. Loc: OKITW.

An account of the year's business, with a report from the medical officer and a financial summary of receipts and disbursements. Many of the accounts presented during the individual sessions are noted as relief payments. Period: 1942 - 1943.

4460. Waterloo Township Council. **Voters' lists: South and North Divisions of the Township of Waterloo.** 1890, 1893, 1925. Loc: OKITW.

Lists of people eligible to vote in municipal and provincial elections arranged by polling subdivisions. Other information includes the lot and concession, name, post office and rural route number of the voter, status as a tenant or freeholder, and whether eligible for jury service. The Waterloo Historical Society holds lists for 1890, 1893 and 1925. Period: 1890 - 1925.

4461. "Waterloo Township Hall." **Waterloo Historical Society.** 1970. 58: 85-86. Loc: all.

Transcript of a petition for the erection of a township hall in Berlin. A competing request from Preston is mentioned in the document. Every third name on the petition is noted at the end of the transcript, about 100 names in all. A short preface describes the petition itself and gives a history of the township hall. Period: 1848 - 1958.

4462. Wendland, Dennis. **Historical articles on Blair.** Waterloo County Board of Education, 1976. 105 p. ill. Loc: OWRE.

A compilation of materials from many sources,

including newspapers, the Waterloo Society's annual reports and Eby's biographical history of early settlers, about the history of Blair and its mills. The book is designed for the use of students and contains questions and suggestions for further activities. General information about the settlement and industrialization of Waterloo County is also given. Period: 1800 - 1976.

4463. Woolwich Historical Foundation. "The heritage of Maryhill." **Elmira Independent.** 1989, June 27. 8 p. ill. Loc: OKIT, OWRE.

A newspaper supplement presenting a short history of the community's early development, the role of religion and education, the cemetery, the Feast of Corpus Christi, wayside shrines and the activities of the Historical Society of St Boniface and Maryhill Community. Names of early settlers and prominent individuals are given as well as information about "con men and bumblers." Period: 1820 - 1989.

4464. Zinger, Joseph A. **Maryhill Historical Society, 1977-1982, Ontario Canada.** Maryhill: The Society, 1982. 66 p. ill. Loc: OKIT.

A transcript of the minutes of the Historical Society of St Boniface and Maryhill Community for its first five years, 1977 to 1982, with historical notes on Maryhill. The minutes report improvements to the Edward Halter house where the society met, and describe the centennial celebrations of the School Sisters of Notre Dame to Maryhill in 1982. There are brief biographies of Edward Halter and other early pioneers and of priests and pastors of St Boniface Church. Period: 1828 - 1982.

4465. Zinger, Joseph A. and Sister Carola and Reinhart, Jerome. **New Germany: Maryhill, 1867-1967.** 1967. 16 p. Loc: OKIT, OWT.

A history of New Germany, later Maryhill, commemorating Canada's centennial. Topics include early industries and pioneers, the School Sisters of Notre Dame, the Corpus Christi processions, St Boniface Roman Catholic Church and its clergy. A list is given of Maryhill century farms with their past and present owners. Period: 1820 - 1967.

WELLESLEY TOWNSHIP AND VILLAGE

4466. Dewar, Florence R. "Wellesley Village." **Waterloo Historical Society.** 1967. 55: 44-55. ill., map. Loc: all.

A history of the village since 1842, with a map and references to other sources. Period: 1842 - 1967.

4467. Dorking Women's Institute. **Tweedsmuir history, Dorking Women's Institute, North Waterloo.**
Kitchener: Kitchener Public Library, 1983. 1 reel.
ill., maps. mf. Loc: OKIT, OWRE, OWRL, OWTU.
An historical account of pioneer settlement, farms, schools, churches, landscapes, services, organizations and community activities. Biographical sketches are included for many individuals and there are newspaper clippings describing the lifestyles of Old Order Mennonites. Period: c1800 - 1983.

4468. Haner, Vonnie. "Licensing houses of entertainment in Wellesley Township 1853-1877." **Waterloo Historical Society.** 1988. 76: 141-147. ill., tables. Loc: all.
An examination of the regulations which governed auctioneers, shopkeepers, tavern and inn keepers, as well as those who kept billiard tables. The article includes a list of tavern and shopkeepers who received licences in 1875. Period: 1853 - 1877.

4469. Herchenrader, Mary Pat, Mrs and Squirrell, L., Mrs. **Hawkesville: the town and the family.** 1991. 24 l. maps. Loc: OWRW.
A history and genealogy of the Hawke and Lount families, United Empire Loyalists who fled from Simcoe County to Wellesley Township following their participation in the Rebellion of 1837. The Hawkes were prominent citizens of the village that bears their name and their contributions to it are described. Period: 1838 - 1991.

4470. Linwood Women's Institute. **Tweedsmuir history, Linwood Women's Institute, North Waterloo.**
Kitchener: Kitchener Public Library, 1982. 1 reel.
ill. mf. Loc: OWTU, OKIT, OWRE.
A scrapbook of newspaper clippings and miscellaneous materials on community history from 1939 to 1982, including accounts of the Linwood, Crosshill and Wellesley schools and churches. A great deal of genealogical information about Linwood residents is contained in the newspaper articles and announcements. Period: 1939 - 1982.

4471. "Map of Wellesley Township." **Historical atlas of Waterloo & Wellington counties, including: Illustrated Atlas of the County of Waterloo (1881), County of Waterloo Directory (1877-78) and Illustrated Atlas of the County of Wellington (1877).** Port Elgin: Ross Cumming, 1972 reprint.
p. 20. Loc: OWTU, OWTUM, OWTUCG, OKIT, OWTL, OCCA, OCLG, OCP, OWRBL, OWRE, OWRN, OWRW, OWT.
A map at a scale of 70 chains to the inch that shows rivers, streams and major roads, names townships, towns, villages and hamlets, and

numbers concessions and lots. Properties of subscribers to the atlas and some rural industries and churches are also identified. Period: 1880 - 1881.

4472. "Marking the 150th anniversary of the settlement of Wellesley Township." **Elmira Independent.** 1982. 16 p. ill. Loc: OWRE, OWRSC.
A newspaper supplement on the history of industries, businesses, sports teams and churches, including reprints of an 1882 historical sketch of Wellesley Township, an early history of Wellesley Village and a biographical directory of subscribers to the 1881 county atlas. Activities planned to celebrate the 150th anniversary are also described. Period: 1832 - 1982.

4473. Ogram, Grace. "Hawksville/Hawkesville on the Conestogo River." **Waterloo Historical Society.** 1986. 74: 101-128. ill., map. Loc: all.
A survey of the community from the first formal settlement by a group of Quakers including the Hawke family (also spelled Hawk) in the 1840s. Archival documents are quoted on the prior land claims by black, ex-slave squatters in the Queen's Bush (part of which became Wellesley Township) and on other disputes over the land developed by John Hawk as a millsite. Information from a wide variety of sources is also cited on prominent families, doctors, churches and the school. The author explains that the community's name was spelled Hawksville until 1881, and then Hawkesville. Period: 1830 - 1980.

4474. Oudejans, Annette. "History of the village of St Clements." **Waterloo Historical Society.** 1984. 72: 74-113. ill., map. Loc: all.
A detailed survey of all commercial and industrial businesses and local services. All persons and organizations mentioned are indexed in the WRP database. Period: 1833 - 1983.

4475. Pepper Paul E. **Index to the Maple Leaf journal.** Kitchener: Ontario Genealogical Society, Waterloo-Wellington Branch, 1985. 39 p. Loc: OKIT, OWT.
Index to nearly 1,500 subjects, mainly personal names mentioned in the history of Wellesley Township.

4476. "The prince and princesses of Wellesley Township." **Waterloo Historical Society.** 1982. 70: 88-89. ill. Loc: all.
A list of the children who participated in Founders' Day celebrations during 1982. The twelve girls and one boy represent fifth, sixth and seventh generation descendants of the original settlers. Frey, Koebel, Forrest, Oesch, Straus,

Hahn, Deckert, Ryan, Kieswetter, Roth, Boshart and Bender are names of some of the first inhabitants of the township. Period: 1840 - 1982.

4477. Schantz, Orpheus Moyer. "Hawkesville, a pioneer village of Waterloo County." **Waterloo Historical Society**. 1934. 22: 138-146. Loc: all.

A sketch of the community's history, with details of early inhabitants and their occupations as well as references to local buildings. Period: 1870 - 1934.

4478. Stewart, Barbara J. and Kitchen, Phyllis Leleu and Dietrich, Debbie. **The Maple Leaf journal: a settlement history of Wellesley Township**. Waterloo: Corporation of the Township of Wellesley, 1983. 148 p. ill., maps. Loc: OKIT, OWRL, OWRSC, OWT, OWTUR, OWTUCG.

A collection of reminiscences, letters, excerpts from newspapers and articles, richly illustrated with excellent photographs and handsomely produced. William Walker's 1843 map and Tremaine's map of 1861 are reprinted. The volume has no index, but the WRP database indexes all corporate subjects, topical subject headings and places. The names of over 125 families or persons mentioned more than twice or the subjects of photographs or the sources of reminiscences are also indexed in the WRP database. An index to 1,500 personal names has been prepared by Paul Pepper. Period: 1800 - 1983.

4479. "Welcome to Wellesley: 15th annual apple butter & cheese festival." **The Elmira Independent**. The Elmira Independent, 1990, September 29. 23 p. ill. Loc: OWRW.

A visitor's guide containing a programme of events, articles about Wellesley people and places, advertisements, and recipes for apple butter and cheese. One article is a history of Wellesley School Section #16 and there is a profile of Ruth Leis. Period: 1848 - 1990.

4480. "Wellesley Township and its early settlement." **Waterloo Historical Society**. 1942. 30: 224-228. Loc: all.

A sketch of the early settlement of the township, with information about place names and community leaders and a list of all reeves from 1852 to 1942. Period: 1837 - 1942.

4481. "Wellesley Township and village." **Historical atlas of Waterloo & Wellington counties, including: Illustrated Atlas of the County of Waterloo (1881), County of Waterloo Directory (1877-78) and Illustrated Atlas of the County of Wellington (1877)**. Port Elgin: Ross Cumming, 1972

reprint. p. 9. Loc: OWTU, OWTUM, OWTUCG, OKIT, OWTL, OCCA, OCLG, OCP, OWRBL, OWRE, OWRN, OWRW, OWT.

An historical sketch of topography, early settlement, the development of economic activities, municipal government and services, and social institutions such as churches and schools. It is interesting as an early statement of what was to become a widely accepted version of the early history of the region. The author describes the arrival of the first pioneers between 1832 and 1842, before the township survey, and briefly outlines the founding and functions of the villages and hamlets of Heidelberg, St Clements, Hawkesville, Linwood, Crosshill, Bamberg and Wellesley. The varied ethnic character of the township's original settlers is noted, from the French and German Catholics around St Clements and those of English extraction around Hawkesville, Linwood and Crosshill, to the Irish in the northwest corner, Amish in the southeast, and Hessian Lutherans along the Fifth Line. Period: 1832 - 1881.

4482. Wellesley Township Council. **Voters' lists: Township of Wellesley**. 1894 - 1966. Loc: OKITW, OWRBW.

Lists of people eligible to vote in municipal and provincial elections arranged by polling subdivisions. Other information includes the lot, concession, post office and rural route of the voter, status as tenant or freeholder and whether eligible for jury service. The Waterloo Historical Society holds a photocopy of the list for 1894 and the Wilmot Township Archives hold lists for the years 1922, 1923, 1924, 1962 and 1966. Period: 1894 - 1966.

4483. "Wellesley Township." **Waterloo Historical Society**. 1958. 46: 26-31. ill., map. Loc: all.

An account of the early history of the last township in Waterloo County to be opened for settlement, with details of the founding of each village or hamlet. Tremaine's map of 1861 is reproduced, showing every landowner's plot in Wellesley Township and listing the major businesses in each village (Wellesley, Crosshill, Heidelberg, St Clements, and Hawkesville). Period: 1832 - 1958.

4484. Wellesley Women's Institute. **Tweedsmuir history, Wellesley Women's Institute, North Waterloo**. Kitchener: Kitchener Public Library, 1982. 1 reel. ill. mf. Loc: OKIT, OWRE, OWTU.

An account of churches, schools, industries, businesses, parks, parades, royal visits, prominent local people and sports teams, with a history of the Wellesley Women's Institute since its founding in 1902. Period: 1806 - 1977.

WILMOT TOWNSHIP

4485. Bauer, H., Mrs. "New Dundee: its history and development." **Waterloo Historical Society.** 1939. 27: 70-74. Loc: all.
   A brief history of New Dundee from 1826 to 1928, mentioning founding families such as the Millars, Bettschens, Halls and Reicherts, as well as the schools, churches and fruit farms. Period: 1826 - 1928.

4486. Bergey, Lorna L. "Haysville District pioneers: a pictorial review of their families and homes." **Waterloo Historical Society.** 1983. 71: 15-46. ill. Loc: all.
   A history of the Smith, Kerr, Illingworth, Mark, Cassel, Bean (Biehn), Puddicombe, Eichler, Christner, Tye, Laird, Somerville, Walker and Shantz families and their properties. Period: 1828 - 1980.

4487. Bergey, Lorna L. "A history of Wilmot Township." **Waterloo Historical Society.** 1962. 50: 48-61. ill., map. Loc: all.
   An historical account that quotes from A.R.G. Smith's report on an Indian village site, the **History of the Bettschen family** by Gottlieb Bettschen, and an 1881 survey of Wilmot by the Ontario Agricultural Commission. Tremaine's 1861 map of Wilmot Township is reproduced, showing landowners and a list of merchants. Period: 1600 - 1960.

4488. Bergey, Lorna L. and Diamond, Florence. "Interesting notations from the minutes of Wilmot Township Council meetings, 1850-1900." **Waterloo Historical Society.** 1962. 50: 66-70. Loc: all.
   A collection of excerpts from the council minutes. Period: 1850 - 1900.

4489. Hallman, D. **The geography of Wilmot Township.** McMaster University (B.A. thesis, Geography), 1964. 65 p. ill., maps. Loc: OHM.
   A comprehensive report on the physical environment (geology, climate, vegetation, drainage and soils), history of settlement and development, agricultural land use, and functions of urban centres. The thesis is very well illustrated with photographs, maps and graphs. Period: 1830 - 1961.

4490. Hilborn, Ivan M. "Historical sketch of New Dundee." **Waterloo Historical Society.** 1970. 58: 43-52. ill. map. Loc: all.
   A history of New Dundee from its foundation in

1830 by John Millar. The author makes many references to a map drawn by Michael Myers in 1856 and updated by W.H.E. Schmalz to show more recent buildings. Many aspects of village life are covered, such as sports, businesses, churches, banks and organizations. Period: 1830 - 1970.

4491. Lamb, Kathryn Hansuld. "Punkeydoodle's Corner." **Waterloo Historical Society.** 1983. 71: 82-89. ill. Loc: all.
   An account of the origin of the name Punkeydoodle's Corner and of the Zurbuchen and Zurbrigg families who settled there. The author notes the celebrations in June 1982 in honour of the community. Period: 1845 - 1983.

4492. "Map of Wilmot Township." **Historical atlas of Waterloo & Wellington counties, including: Illustrated Atlas of the County of Waterloo (1881), County of Waterloo Directory (1877-78) and Illustrated Atlas of the County of Wellington (1877).** Port Elgin: Ross Cumming, 1972 reprint. p. 21. Loc: OWTU, OWTUM, OWTUCG, OKIT, OWTL, OCCA, OCLG, OCP, OWRBL, OWRE, OWRN, OWRW, OWT.
   A map that shows rivers and streams, major roads and railway lines, as well as names of townships, towns, villages and hamlets and numbers of concessions and lots. Properties of subscribers to the atlas and some rural industries and churches are also identified. Period: 1880 - 1881.

4493. Morden, Gladys A. **Petersburg, Ontario and its first pioneer.** 1968. 12 p. ill. Loc: OWTUR, OWTL, OKIT.
   A short biography of Peter Wilker, for whom the village is named, with an outline of early community history. The author describes the main buildings and services from the beginning to the 1930s, including Wilker's blacksmith shop, the Blue Moon Hotel, the railway station and the school. Many early settlers are named. Period: 1809 - 1935.

4494. Morden, Gladys A. "Petersburg, Ontario and its first pioneer." **Waterloo Historical Society.** 1968. 56: 6-18. ill. Loc: all.
   A history of the community including a biography of its first settler, John Peter Wilker (1809-1889) and his family. The author describes schools, churches, recreation and domestic activities in the mid-nineteenth century and quotes the inscription on the Wilker Monument in the Petersburg Cemetery. Period: 1809 - 1899.

4495. New Dundee 150th Anniversary Committee. **150 years New Dundee: 1830-1980.** The Committee, 1980. 68 p. ill. Loc: OKIT, OWRND, OWRA, OWRE, OWRN, OWRW.

A history of the community founded by John Millar in 1830, especially the businesses and organizations that still existed in the 1970s. Period: 1830 - 1980.

4496. New Dundee Public School. **Walking tour of New Dundee.** New Dundee: The School, 1987. 1 sheet. ill., map. Loc: OKIT.

A guide to 20 sites of historical significance. The buildings include schools, stores, residences and factories in various architectural styles. Period: 1824 - 1987.

4497. New Dundee Women's Institute. **Tweedsmuir history, New Dundee Women's Institute, South Waterloo.** 1984. 1 reel. ill. maps. mf. Loc: OKIT.

A scrapbook compilation of material on the history of the community in Wilmot Township, including such topics as Indian encampments, early settlers, farming families, businesses, churches, schools, clubs and societies, and the development of the Women's Institute itself. Period: 1830 - 1978.

4498. "New Hamburg and Wilmot." **Historical atlas of Waterloo & Wellington counties, including: Illustrated Atlas of the County of Waterloo (1881), County of Waterloo Directory (1877-78) and Illustrated Atlas of the County of Wellington (1877).** Port Elgin: Ross Cumming, 1972 reprint. p. 9. Loc: OWTU, OWTUM, OWTUCG, OKIT, OWTL, OCCA, OCLG, OCP, OWRBL, OWRE, OWRN, OWRW, OWT.

An historical sketch of topography, early settlement, the development of economic activities, municipal government and services, and social institutions such as churches and schools. It is interesting as an early statement of what was to become a widely accepted version of the early history of the region. Nearly half is a narrative of Christian Nafziger's settlements in the mid-1820s and a description of Amish beliefs and customs. The rest consists of brief histories of the villages of New Hamburg and Baden, with a short explanation of the Canada Company's settlement of Block A and the development of the villages of Haysville and New Dundee. Period: 1824 - 1881.

4499. New Hamburg-Wilmot Township Centennial Committee. **More than a century in Wilmot Township.** New Hamburg: The Committee, 1967. 123 p. ill., map. Loc: OKIT, OWRA, OWRB, OWRE, OWRN, OWRND, OWRSC, OWT, OWTL, OWTUR.

A comprehensive history of the entire township, including chapters on municipal history, the school system, ethnicity and library facilities. Individual communities are described as to their settlement, schools, churches, industries, services, historical events and century farms. Many personal names and businesses are included in the work and all are indexed in the WRP database. Period: 1800 - 1967.

4500. Newton, James. "New Dundee's Golden Centennial." **Waterloo Historical Society.** 1980. 68: 30-35. ill. Loc: all.

A short account of the celebrations of the 150th anniversary of the community in August 1980. Period: 1830 - 1980.

4501. Pepper, Paul E. **Index to More than a century in Wilmot Township.** 1986. 39 p. Loc: OKIT.

A index to some 800 subjects, mainly persons mentioned in the centennial volume. Period: 1840 - 1967.

4502. Sararus, Miriam and Baldwin, Michael. **New Dundee: building and growing together.** New Dundee: New Dundee Community Center Building Committee, 1988. 12 p. ill. Loc: OKIT.

An outline history of the community, prepared as part of a fund-raising campaign. Plans for the proposed new community centre are described, with a financial statement of costs and fund-raising. Period: 1830 - 1988.

4503. Sauder, Dorothy M. "Amish Mennonite sesquicentennial." **Waterloo Historical Society.** 1972. 60: 58-59. Loc: all.

An account of festivities held in Wilmot Township, including demonstrations, displays, concerts, church homecomings and a pageant written by Baden native, Urie Bender. Period: 1822 - 1972.

4504. Schumilas, Catherine and Williams, Joan. **St Agatha, 1867-1967.** 1967. 24 p. ill. Loc: OWTU, OWTUCGR, OKIT.

A short history of the community, especially its early businesses, schools, churches, prominent inhabitants, centennial farms, and war dead. The authors mention individuals active in the Notre Dame of St Agatha Children's Village and Carmel of St Joseph, as well as all residents of St Agatha and district in 1967. Period: c1830 - 1967.

4505. Smith, Allan R.G. "Early history of Haysville and vicinity." **Waterloo Historical Society.** 1916. 4: 10-12. Loc: all.

A brief history of Haysville, from its origins as one of the chief stage coach stops between Hamilton and Goderich, to its decline after the

Grand Trunk Railway diverted trade to New Hamburg. Period: 1818 - 1900.

4506. Smith, Allan R.G. "Haysville." **Waterloo Historical Society**. 1948. 36: 22-26. ill. Loc: all.

An historical sketch of the village and location on the Huron Road, with particular reference to early settlers such as William Hobson, William Puddicombe, Horn Stevens, Robert Hays, William Illingworth and William Anderson. Period: 1818 - 1883.

4507. Stock, Fred W. "Punkey Doodle's Corners." **Waterloo Historical Society**. 1967. 55: 9-10. Loc: all.

A discussion of the name of the hamlet that is usually spelled Punkeydoodle's Corner. Period: 1836 - 1967.

4508. Thoms, Elise. **The family four**. New Hamburg: Ritz Printing, 1977. 456 p. ill., tables, map. Loc: OKIT, OWRN, OWTUR.

A history of the Marlton, Tye, Macdonald, and Thoms families, written to update the account by Charles James Fox and Winnifred Cassel published in **The Parish of Wilmot**. There are photographs, recipes, transcripts of wills, local histories, newspaper articles and correspondence and two genealogical tables, one showing the interrelationship between the Thoms and Tye families, and the other tracing the Marlton and Puddicombe descendants. A map of Wilmot Township, showing the locations of the Puddicombe and Tye farms, and a plot plan of St James Cemetery are included. Period: 1832 - 1977.

4509. Waltz, Jacob and Roth, Lorraine. "A glimpse of the Amish settlement in Wilmot in 1843." **Mennogespräch**. 1988. 6,2: 14. Loc: OWTUCG, OKIT.

Translation of a letter from Jacob Waltz to his relatives in Germany, describing the difficulties of making a living by farming in Wilmot Township. The cold climate, divisions in the church, and lack of buyers for wheat, are among the problems mentioned. The family later moved to Tennessee. An introduction by Lorraine Roth comments on the persons mentioned in the letter and on the early settlement of Wilmot. Period: 1843 - 1844.

4510. Wilmot Township Council. **The consolidated by-laws of the Township of Wilmot to the 1st December, 1888**. New Hamburg: Jacob Ritz and Co., 1888. 75 p. index. Also CIHM Microfiche series, no. 15689. Loc: OWTUCGR, OWTL, OWTU.

Township laws, including those concerned with roads, animal control, wire fences, school sections, public health and public morals. All

by-laws from 1850 to 1888 are listed by title, with a note of whether they are in force, effete, repealed, consolidated, amended or superseded. A list of township officials for that period is given. Period: 1850 - 1888.

4511. Wilmot Township Council. **Voters' lists: Township of Wilmot**. 1897 - 1966. Loc: OWRBW, OKITW.

Lists of people eligible to vote in municipal and provincial elections arranged by polling subdivisions. Other information includes the lot, concession number and post office of the voter, and whether he is a tenant or freeholder and eligible for jury service. Some lists include occupations. The Wilmot Township Archives hold lists for 1897, 1905, 1917 up to and including 1927, 1930, 1931, 1932, and 1936 up to and including 1966. The Waterloo Historical Society holds lists for 1963 and 1964. Period: 1897 - 1966.

WOOLWICH TOWNSHIP

4512. Boshart, Ruth Anne. "The hamlet of St Jacobs, Ontario." **Waterloo Historical Society**. 1964. 52: 73-78. ill. Loc: all.

A short history of the community, including its early settlers, industries and organizations. The author stresses the role of the Snider family. Period: c1807 - 1964.

4513. Devitt, A.W. "Notes on the pioneer days of Woolwich Township." **Waterloo Historical Society**. 1947. 35: 38-47. Loc: all.

An account of the early development of the township, including names of prominent early settlers and enterprises, churches and schools, with a list of reeves from 1850 to 1947. Period: 1800 - 1947.

4514. Devitt, A.W. "West Montrose and district." **Waterloo Historical Society**. 1946. 34: 20-24. Loc: all.

A brief history of the community, including references to the covered bridge, general store, post office and first school and anecdotes about various early residents. Period: 1865 - c1890.

4515. "Floradale." **Waterloo Historical Society**. 1961. 49: 47-48. Loc: all.

A brief history of Floradale from 1809 to 1890, including names of early settlers and industries. Names of tradespeople are listed from Sutherland's 1864 directory. Period: 1809 - 1890.

4516. "Map of Woolwich Township." **Historical atlas of Waterloo & Wellington counties, including: Illustrated Atlas of the County of Waterloo (1881), County of Waterloo Directory (1877-78) and Illustrated Atlas of the County of Wellington (1877).** Port Elgin: Ross Cumming, 1972 reprint. p. 22. Loc: OWTU, OWTUM, OWTUCG, OKIT, OWTL, OCCA, OCLG, OCP, OWRBL, OWRE, OWRN, OWRW, OWT.

A map at a scale of 70 chains to the inch that shows rivers, streams and major roads, with names of townships, towns, villages and hamlets and numbers of concessions and lots. Properties of subscribers to the atlas and some rural industries and churches are also identified. Period: 1880 - 1881.

4517. Martin, Virgil Emerson. **The early history of Jakobstettel: an account of the people and the land in and around St Jacobs, Ontario ... to the beginning of the 20th century.** St Jacobs: V.E. Martin, 1979. 102 p. ill., maps., index. Loc: OCLG, OKIT, OWRSJ, OWT, OWTU, OWTUCG.

A popular history of St Jacobs from prehistory to 1900, illustrated with many photographs. Topics include geology, Joseph Brant and the Six Nations Indians, the arrival of Pennsylvania Mennonites in Block Number Three in 1813, the establishment of Jacob Snider's mills in the early 1850s, and the development of businesses, professions, and industries in St Jacobs towards the end of the 19th century. Many local businessmen and townspeople are mentioned, notably E.W.B. Snider and John L. Wideman. The names of all persons and corporations are indexed in the WRP database. Period: 1800 - 1900.

4518. **People who put my community on the map.** 1 v. (unpaged). ill. Loc: OWRE.

An unpublished essay written for a North Woolwich Ever Faithful Women's Institute Tweedsmuir History competition on personalities from the North Woolwich - Floradale area. Four families in Woolwich Township are featured in detail: the Bowmans, Seilings, Broxes and Cleghorns. Period: 1877 - c1983.

4519. "Salute to family business in Woolwich Township." **Elmira Independent.** 1991, June 17. 20 p. ill. Loc: OWRE.

A scrapbook of clippings from a supplement to the **Elmira Independent.** The articles present short histories of many family firms in the township including those that have been in business for over 20 years. Period: 1892 - 1971.

4520. Schmidt, William A. "The blind printer of St Jacobs." **Waterloo Historical Society.** 1985. 73: 141-144. ill. Loc: all.

A short biography of John Theodore Schmidt (1870-1948), a typesetter who lost his sight but continued to work in his own printing shop with the help of his wife Ellanora and later his children. Period: 1870 - 1948.

4521. Smith, Marvin C. "St Jacobs: its early history." **Waterloo Historical Society.** 1968. 56: 33-48. ill. Loc: all.

A history of St Jacobs, emphasizing the various businesses and their owners. A map, drawn by W.H.E. Schmalz from a plan surveyed by Schofield and Hobson, shows individual residences and commercial buildings. Period: 1807 - 1966.

4522. St Jacobs Friendly Women's Institute. **Tweedsmuir history, St Jacobs Friendly Women's Institute, North Waterloo.** Kitchener: Kitchener Public Library, 1982. 1 reel. ill. maps. mf. Loc: OKIT, OWTU, OWRE.

A microfilmed community history including information on prehistory and early settlement, churches, schools, organizations and local services such as the telephone system, the railway, the postal service (including Amos Bowman's pony express) and the library. Details about many area residents are provided as is an extensive genealogy of the Jacob and Catherine (Weber) Schweitzer family. It should be noted that this Tweedsmuir history is on the same microfilm as the Elmdale Women's Institute history and is catalogued under that title in the University of Waterloo system. Period: c1800 - c1960.

4523. "Township of Woolwich." **Historical atlas of Waterloo & Wellington counties, including: Illustrated Atlas of the County of Waterloo (1881), County of Waterloo Directory (1877-78) and Illustrated Atlas of the County of Wellington (1877).** Port Elgin: Ross Cumming, 1972 reprint. Pp. 9-10. Loc: OWTU, OWTUM, OWTUCG, OKIT, OWTL, OCCA, OCLG, OCP, OWRBL, OWRE, OWRN, OWRW, OWT.

An historical sketch of topography, early settlement, the development of economic activities, municipal government and services, and social institutions such as churches and schools. It is interesting as an early statement of what was to become a widely accepted version of the early history of the region. Following a reference to the original grant of the township, with Pilkington, from the Six Nations Indians to George Wallace, the author recounts the pioneer settlers and enterprises in the various localities and villages, such as Conestogo, St Jacobs, Heidelberg and Elmira. Period: 1810 - 1881.

4524. "Township of Woolwich." **Waterloo Historical Society.** 1961. 49: 35-46. map. Loc: all.

A history of the township based on information in special newspaper supplements, early directories and maps, and excerpts from municipal records for 1850 and 1861. All reeves from 1852 to 1905 are listed. Period: 1800 - 1905.

4525. Uttley, W.V. "Woolwich Township: its early settlement." **Waterloo Historical Society.** 1933. 21: 10-32. Loc: all.

A detailed account of early landowners (including William Wallace, Richard Beasley, Augustus Jones, John and Jacob Erb, and George and Benjamin Eby), municipal government, the first schools and churches, and the communities of Conestogo and Snider's Woods, Winterbourne, West Montrose, Floradale, Heidelberg, Weissenburg, St Jacobs and Elmira. The author quotes a poem written in the Mennonite dialect about "Die alt Heemet" ("The old home"). Period: 1797 - c1919.

4526. Winterbourne Women's Institute. **Tweedsmuir history, Winterbourne Women's Institute, North Waterloo.** Kitchener: Kitchener Public Library, 1982. 1 reel. ill., maps. mf. Loc: OKIT, OWTU, OWRE.

A history of the Winterbourne area including such topics as churches, schools, farms and organizations, as well as information on many local notables. Presented as a scrapbook, the work is made up of newspaper clippings, programmes and typed contributions by members of the Women's Institute or area residents. The same microfilm reel also contains the Woolwich Ever Faithful Women's Institute's Tweedsmuir history. A second reel, containing a 1989 update to the first Winterbourne work, is held by the Elmira Public Library and the Kitchener Public Library. The Kitchener Public Library also holds the original volume. Period: c1820 - 1982.

4527. Woolwich Ever Faithful Women's Institute. **Tweedsmuir history, Woolwich Ever Faithful Women's Institute, North Waterloo.** Kitchener: Kitchener Public Library, 1982. 1 reel. ill., map. mf. Loc: OKIT, OWRE, OWTU.

A history of the northern part of Woolwich Township around Elmira and Floradale, including information on local personalities, farms, organizations, schools, churches and fairs. Presented as a scrapbook, the history contains newspaper clippings, programmes and typed contributions by members of the institutes. It should be noted that this history is on the same

microfilm reel as the Winterbourne Women's Institute's Tweedsmuir history and is entered under that title in the University of Waterloo catalogue. Period: c1820 - 1982.

4528. Woolwich Historical Foundation. "The heritage of Conestogo." **Elmira Independent.** 1988, May 31. 8 p. ill. Loc: OKIT.

A newspaper supplement containing a short history of early settlers, churches, businesses and the school, with photographs of early buildings. Period: 1807 - 1988.

4529. Woolwich Historical Foundation. "The history of St Jacobs." **Elmira Independent.** 1990, June 26. 12 p. ill. Loc: OKIT, OWRE.

A newspaper supplement presenting a short history of early settlement, the first mills, the first school, the first physician (Napoleon Bonaparte Wolfe), the first church and the library. Photographs of past streetscapes and advertisements by older businesses are included. Period: 1800 - 1990.

4530. Woolwich Township Council. **Journal of proceedings and by-laws of the municipal council of the Township of Woolwich.** 1850 - 1905. Loc: OKITW.

Annual reports of the minutes and by-laws, with financial statements by the Treasurer. The Waterloo Historical Society holds proceedings from the first council meeting in 1850 to 1905. The Society holds some of the proceedings in German only **Journal der Verhandlungen und Neben-Aeleke des Munizipal Raths von Township Woolwich,** while it holds both German and English copies for 1896. Period: 1850 - 1905.

4531. Woolwich Township Council. **Voters' lists: Township of Woolwich.** 1925, 1939. Loc: OWRBW.

Lists of people eligible to vote in municipal and provincial elections, arranged by polling subdivisions. Other information includes the lot, concession number and post office of the voter, status as tenant or freeholder, and whether eligible for jury service. Some lists include occupations. The Wilmot Township Archives holds lists for the years 1925 and 1939. Period: 1925 - 1939.

LOCAL IMPRINTS TO 1900

About 170 imprints, apparently printed in Waterloo County, are listed chronologically here in summary form. For abstracts of scope and content and for library locations, see the full annotated entries for which numbers are given.

1835

Canada Museum und Allgemeine Zeitung. 1835 - 1840. mf. See: #87

1836

Die gemeinschaftliche Liedersammlung, zum allgemeinen Gebrauch des wahren Gottesdienstes, aus vielen Liedernbüchern gesammelt, und mit einem Inhalt sammt Register versehen. Erste Auflage. Edited by Benjamin Eby. Berlin: H.W. Peterson, 1836 reprinted 1838. 328 p. Also CIHM Microfiche series, nos. 38605 (1836) and 18500 (1838). See: #3283

1839

Der Morgenstern. 1839 - 1841. mf. See: #96

Eby, Benjamin. Neues Buchstabir- und Lesebuch, besonderes bearbeitet und eingerichet zum Gebrauch deutscher Schulen, enthalted das ABC, und vielerley Buchstabir- und Leseübungen, 1st ed.. Berlin: H.W. Peterson, 1839. 144 p. Also: CIHM Microfiche series, no. 51199. See: #2739

Roosen, Gerhard. Christliches Gemüths Gespräch vom seligmachenden Glauben, für die Jugend, in Fragen und Antworten; und ein Glaubens Bekenntniß der Mennonisten, nebst einem Anhang. Berlin: H.W. Peterson, 1839. 340 p. Also CIHM Microfiche series, no. 38684. See: #3363

1840

Briefe an die mennonisten Gemeine, in Ober Canada, mit einer Zugabe. Berlin: Heinrich Eby, 1840. 47 p. See: #3257

1841

Der Deutsche Canadier und Neuigkeitsbote. 1841 - 1865. mf. See: #94

Eby, Benjamin. Kurzgefasste Kirchen Geschichte und Glaubenslehre der Taufgesinnten-Christen oder Mennoniten. Berlin: Heinrich Eby, 1841. 240 p. Also: CIHM Microfiche series, no. 35039. See: #3290

van der Smissen, Carl Justus. Zweyter Brief aus Dänemark an die mennonisten Gemeine. Berlin: Heinrich Eby, 1841. 23 p. See: #3394

Wellington District Agricultural Society. Rules of the exhibition, Guelph, July 24, 1851. Berlin: H. Eby, Printer, 1841. 1 sheet. See: #1803

Die gemeinschaftliche Liedersammlung, zum allgemeinen Gebrauch des wahren Gottesdienstes, mit einem Inhalt sammt zweyfachem Register versehen. Edited by Benjamin Eby. Berlin: Heinrich Eby, 1841 reprinted 1849. 396 p. See: #3284

1842

Eby, Benjamin. ABC Buchstabir- und Lesebuch, zum Gebrauch für deutsche Schulen in Canada, 2nd ed.. Berlin: Heinrich Eby, 1842. 144 p. ill. See: #2738

Nissly, Heinrich. Geistliches Sendschreiben des christlichen Lehrers und Predigers Heinrich Nissly. Berlin: Heinrich Eby, 1842. 20 p. See: #3354

1844

Hollatz, David. Die Heils und Gnaden Ordnung nach dem Evangelium in vier Gesprächen vorgestellt. Berlin: Heinrich Eby, 1844. 160 p. Also: CIHM Microfiche series, no. 35777. See: #3540

Mennoniten Gemeinde. Kleiner Katechismus, oder kurzgefasste Unterweisung aus der Heiligen Schrift, in Fragen und Antworten zum Gebrauch für Kinder. Berlin: Heinrich Eby, 1844. 64 p. See: #3359

1845

Liddell, Thomas, Rev. Report of the discussion on the late disruption in the Presbyterian Church which took place in St Andrew's Church, Galt between Rev. President Liddell and the Rev. John Bayne. CIHM Microfiche series, no. 22007. Galt: Dumfries Courier, 1845. 1 fiche. 60 frames. mf. See: #3680

Risser, Johannes. Glaube und Lehre von der Taufe der Mennoniten in Deutschland. Berlin: Heinrich Eby, 1845. 128 p. See: #3362

1846

Bayne, John, Rev. Was the recent disruption of the Synod of Canada, in connection with the Church of Scotland, called for?: an address to the Presbyterians of Canada who still support the Synod in Connection with the Church of Scotland, published at the request of the Commission of the Synod of the Presbyterian Church of Scotland. Galt: James Ainslie, 1846 reprinted 1873. 83 p. Also: CIHM Microfiche series. See: #3654

Die ernsthafte Christenpflicht, enthaltend schöne geistreiche Gebete, das Glaubens Bekenntniß der Mennoniten, mit einem Anhang über die Wehrlosigkeit; und das geistliche Luftgaertlein frommer Seelen. Berlin: Heinrich Eby, 1846. 240 p. Also CIHM Microfiche series, no. 34879. See: #3280

Galt Reporter. **The Galt Reporter almanack, for 1847.** CIHM Microfiche series, no. 43233. Ainslie and Jaffray, 1846? 1 fiche. mf. See: #4236

Galt Reporter/ Galt Weekly Reporter/ Galt Daily Reporter/ The Evening Reporter/ Cambridge Reporter. 1846 - mf. See: #104

1848

Der Canadische Beobachter. 1848 - 1850? 4 p. See: #92

Rules adopted by the Galt Building Society, established 1848 and incorporated by act of parliament. Galt: Ainslie and Jaffray, 1848. 23 p. See: #1825

1849

Canada Kalender. Berlin Kitchener: Rittinger and Motz, 1849 - 1920. Also: mf. See: #34

Dumfries Reformer/ Weekly Reformer/ Daily Reformer/ Galt Daily Reformer/ Galt Weekly Reformer. 1849 - 1912. mf. See: #99

Herkommen und Geschlechts Register des Schneider Familie. Berlin: Heinrich Eby, 1849. 8 p. See: #1052

1850

Bunyan, John. **Johann Bunyan's dritter Theil der Pilger Reise aus dieser nach der zukünftigen Welt.** Berlin: Heinrich Eby, 1850. 192 p. See: #2933

Hoch, Daniel. **Kurz gefasste Kirchen-Ordnung der Mennoniten oder Wehrlosen Christen in Canada.** Preston: Martin Rudolf, 1850. 25 p. See: #3318

Widder, Friederich. **Anleitung für die Emigranten aller Klassen, welche nach Ober Canada auszuwandern beabsichtigen, ganz besonders den kleinern Güterbesitzern der Ackerbau treibenden Klasse gewidmet, die aber auch für solche Klassen von Interesse die im Besitze eines ziemlichen Capitals oder sicheren Einkommens den Entschluß fassen, nebst ihren Familien die alte Heimath zu verlassen.** CIHM Microfiche series, no. 47676. Berlin: Heinrich Eby, 1850. 18 frames. mf. See: #683

Woolwich Township Council. **Journal of proceedings and by-laws of the municipal council of the Township of Woolwich.** 1850 - 1905. See: #4530

1851

Bayne, John, Rev. **Is man responsible for his belief?: a lecture delivered before members of the Hamilton Mercantile Library Association on the evening of the 18th February, 1851 and now published at their request.** CIHM Microfiche series, no. 41610. Galt: J. Ainslie, 1851. mf. See: #3653

Der Canadische Bauernfreund. 1851 - 1918. See: #92

Esson, Henry. **A plain and popular exposition of the principle of voluntaryism in opposition ot the misapprehensions of those who have imputed to them an infidel tendency: being a humble essay to mediate between the advocates and antagonists of the establishment principle, and to promote generally the catholic unity of the evangelical churches.** CIHM Microfiche series, no. 63135. Galt: Jaffray and Son, 1851. mf. See: #3231

Waterloo County Council. **Journal of proceedings and by-laws of the municipal council of the County of Waterloo.** 1851 - 1972. See: #3980

1852

Hamburger Beobachter. 1852 - 1856. mf. See: #106

North Dumfries Township Council. **By-laws of the municipal council of North Dumfries for 1852.** Galt: Dumfries Reformer, 1852. 48 p. See: #4208

van der Smissen, Carl Justus and Roosen, Berend Karl. **Sammlung von Predigten von Carl J. van der Smissen, Prediger der mennoniten Gemeinde in Friedrichstadt, Dänemark, und Berend Karl Roosen, Prediger der mennoniten Gemeinde zu Hamburg und Altona.** Berlin: Peter Eby, 1852. 163 p. See: #3394

1854

Briefe über West-Canada das Runner-Unwesen und die deutsche Gesellschaft in New-York, nebst einem Anhange über die östlichen Townships in Unter Canada und die Passage-Büreaus in Europa und Amerika: ein Wegweiser für Auswanderer. CIHM Microfiche series, no. 32509. Preston: Jakob Teuscher, printed by Abr.A. Eby, 1854. 3 fiche. mf. See: #637

Eby, Peter. **Canada's Zustände, Uebersetzung einer Depesche von Sr. Excellenz dem General Gouverneur, an den Right Hon. Sir John Pakington, Baronet.** Berlin: The Author?, 1854. 26 p. See: #642

Teuscher, Jakob. **Briefe über West-Canada: ein Wegweiser für Auswanderer.** CIHM Microfiche series, no. 32509. Preston: Abr. A. Erb, 1854. 176 p. See: #680

1855

Der Neu-Hamburger Neutrale. 1855 - 1859? mf. See: #97

Teuscher, Jakob. **ABC Buchstabir- und Lesebüchlein für Elementar-Schulen in Canada, 2d ed.** Waterloo: Springer and Teuscher, 1855. 46 p. Also: CIHM Microfiche series, no. 58587. See: #2848

Waterloo Township Council. **Journal of proceedings and by-laws of the municipal council of the Township of Waterloo in the County of Waterloo.** Berlin: Daily Telegraph and Daily News Record Office, 1855. 42 p. Also: CIHM Microfiche series, no. 41869. See: #4458

1856

Ayr Observer. 1856 - 1857. 4 p. mf. See: #76

Berlin Chronicle. 1856 - 1860. mf. See: #79

1857 Die gemeinschaftliche Lieder-Sammlung, zum allgemeinen Gebrauch des wahren Gottesdienstes, mit einem Inhalt sammt zweifachem Register versehen. Edited by Benjamin Eby. Berlin: Boedecker und Stuebing, 1857 reprinted 1883, 1901, 1908, 1918. 388 p. Also: CIHM Microfiche series, no. 35959. See: #3281

Galt and Guelph Railway. **Financial statement of the Galt and Guelph Railway Co., from the 3rd March 1856 to the 28th February 1857 as submitted to the stockholders at the Annual Meeting on the 2nd March.** CIHM Microfiche series, no. 52608. The Company, 1857. 1 frame. mf. See: #2074

Proclamation! south riding of the county of Waterloo! to wit: public notice is hereby given to the electors of the south riding of the county of Waterloo ... for the purpose of electing a person to represent them in the Legislative Assembly. CIHM Microfiche series, no. 57196, 58277. Berlin: Telegraph, 1857, 1863. mf. See: #4153

1859

Berliner Journal. 1859 - 1917. Also: mf. See: #82

Canadian Sporting Chronicle. 1859. 4 p. See: #3725

Canadischer Familien Calender auf das Jahr unsers Herrn Jesu Christi. CIHM Microfiche series, nos. 32376 and A00150. Berlin: Boedecker und Stuebing, 1859 - 1897. mf. See: #36

Canadisches Volksblatt. 1859 - 1909. mf. See: #88

1860

Apocalyptic sketches: being a condensed exposition of the views of the most eminent writers upon the prophecies of Revelation, Daniel, Isaiah, &c. respecting the second coming of Our Lord with all his saints at the first resurrection. CIHM Microfiche series, no. 48175. Galt: W. March, 1860. mf. See: #3229

Die gemeinschaftliche Lieder-Sammlung, zum allgemeinen Gebrauch des wahren Gottesdienstes, mit einem Inhalt sammt zweyfachem Register versehen. Edited by Benjamin Eby. Lancaster, PA: Johann Br's Söhnen, 1860 reprinted 1870. 344 p. See: #3282

Galt, Alexander Tilloch. **Canada, von 1849 bis 1859.** CIHM Microfiche series, no. 39289. Preston: W. Schlueter, 1860. mf. See: #4131

Waterloo Chronicle/ Waterloo County Chronicle and Weekly Telegraph/ Chronicle Telegraph/ Waterloo County Telegraph. 1860? - mf. See: #123

1861

Eastern Synod, Evangelical Lutheran Church in Canada. **Verhandlungen/Minutes.** The Church, 1861 - Also: mf. See: #3526

Proclamation! north riding of the County of Waterloo to wit: public notice is hereby given to the electors of the north riding of Waterloo. CIHM Microfiche series, no. 56145, 55650, 58725, 58286. Berlin: Telegraph, 1861 - 1864. mf. See: #4152

1862

Church of the New Jerusalem. **Constitution of the association of the New Jerusalem Church of Canada, and minutes of its first meeting, held at Berlin, C.W., June 20-23 A.D. 1862.** CIHM Microfiche series, no. 33689. Berlin: Rittinger and Motz, 1862. 1 fiche. mf. See: s-5344

Proclamation! nördlicher Wahlbezirk des County Waterloo. CIHM Microfiche series, no. 46866, 58274. Berlin: Canadier Druck, 1862 - 1863. mf. See: #4151

1863

Der Deutsche Reformer. 1863. 4 p. See: s-5522

Proclamation! südlicher Wahlbezirk des County Waterloo. CIHM Microfiche series, no. 58273. Berlin: Canadier Druck, 1863. mf. See: #4154

1864

Der Canadische Kolonist. 1864 - 1909. 4 p. See: #93

1865

Waterloo County Board of Public Instruction. Memorial to the Council of Public Instruction of Upper Canada, from the Board of Public Instruction of the County of Waterloo. CIHM Microfiche series, no. 55445. Galt: Jaffray Bros, 1865. 1 fiche. mf. See: #2857

1866

Constitution of the Mennonite Aid Union. 1866. See: #1804

Funcken, Louis, Rev. Annual report of St Jerome's College, Berlin, Waterloo County, Ontario, (on the Grand Trunk Railroad), for the scholastic year 1866-1867. CIHM Microfiche series, no. A01837. Berlin: St Jerome's College, 1866? 4 frames. mf. See: #2751

1867

Klotz, Otto. Leitfaden zur deutschen Sprache oder kurz gefasstes Lehrbuch der deutschen Sprache in Fragen und Antworten. Preston: The Author, 1867. 134 p. Also: CIHM Microfiche series, no. 08119. See: #2796

1868

Berlin Village Council. The consolidated by-laws of the Municipal Corporation of the Village of Berlin, to the 31st day of December, 1868. Berlin: Telegraph Office, 1868. 54 p. See: #4304

Church of the New Jerusalem. Minutes of the Seventh Conference of the Association of the New Jerusalem Church in Canada, held in the church in Albert Street, Toronto, Ont., from Friday June 19th, to Tuesday, June 23, 1868. CIHM Microfiche series, no. A01661. Berlin: Rittinger and Motz, 1868. 1 fiche. mf. See: #3700

Kirchen-Blatt der evangelisch-lutherischen Synode von Canada. 1868 - 1910. Also: mf. See: #3548

1869

Waterloo County House of Industry and Refuge. Annual report of the Inspector of the House of Industry and Refuge for the County of Waterloo. CIHM Microfiche series, no. A00710. 1869 - 1882. 3

fiche. mf. See: #4073

1870

Elmira Anzeiger. Elmira: Delion Brothers, 1870 - 1880. 4 p. ill. mf. See: #100

1871

Bickel, P.W. Das Singvögelein, oder Melodien und Lieder für Sonntags-Schulen. Berlin: Oberholtzer and Bowman, 1871. 96 p. music. Also: CIHM Microfiche series, no. 58638. See: #3008

Preston Mechanics' Institute. Constitution, by-laws, rules and regulations. Galt: Reformer Press, 1871. 17 p. See: #3833

Statuten und Nebengesetze des Deutschen Unterstützungs-Vereins in Toronto, Ontario. Berlin: Rittinger and Motz, 1871. 15 p. See: #678

1872

Waterloo County Medical Association. Constitution and by-laws of the Waterloo County Medical Association, adopted December 10, 1872. Waterloo: The Association, 1872. 20 p. See: #3850

1874

Baker, George. A vocabulary of musical terms for the use of the student in harmony, counterpoint and composition, and for the executant, &c., with which is interspersed notices of all modern musical instruments. CIHM Microfiche series, no. 25719. Galt: Anderson, 1874. mf. See: #3005

1875

Martin, Jacob. Ein Büchlein, nämlich ein Auszug aus der Heiligen Schrift über einige Religions= Fragen unserer Zeit. Waterloo: The Author, 1875. 226 p. See: #3343

Pearce, Thomas and Sheppard, F.W. and Norman, L. Report of the Public Schools of Waterloo County. Berlin Galt Waterloo: 1875 - 1914. See: #2817

Fowler, Orson Squire. Creative and sexual science: or, manhood, womanhood, and their mutual interrelations; love, its laws, powers, etc.; selection, or mutual adaptation; courtship, married life, and perfect children; their generation, endowment, paternity, maternity, bearing, nursing and rearing; together with puberty, boyhood, girlhood, etc; sexual impairments restored, male vigor and female health and beauty perpetuated and augmented, etc., as taught by phrenology and physiology. Berlin: Oberholtzer and Co., 1875 reprint. 1065 p. See: #3173

1877

Arthur, T.S. **Strong drink: the curse and the cure.** Berlin: Oberholtzer and Co., 1877. 676 p. See: #3162

Calender für die Versammlungen der mennoniten Gemeinde in Canada West, und im Staat Neu York, auf das Jahr unsers Herrn 1877. CIHM Microfiche series, no. A01682. Berlin: Rittinger and Motz, 1877. 1 fiche. mf. See: #3262

Gospel Banner. 1877 - 1969. See: #3315

Stone, W.C. **Directions for using Stone's experience of 12 years for dressing and dyeing skins for mats, robes, and other purposes, with improvements.** New Hamburg: Dawson and Gould, 1877. 8 p. See: #2291

1878

Berlin Daily News. 1878 - 1897. mf. See: #80

Das Wochenblatt. 1878. See: #90

Oelschlager, William. **Darlegung der augenblicklichen financiellen Verhältnisse Canada's nebst vergleichenden statistischen Tabellen, als Antwort auf Hrn. Fair Play's Angaben mit Ansichten ber die brennende Tagesfrage: "Schutzzoll oder Freihandel.".** Berlin: P.E.W. Moyer, Daily News Printing, 1878. 21 p. tables. See: #1739

1879

Berlin Town Council. **Voters' lists: municipality of the Town of Berlin.** 1879 - 1901. See: #4303

187-?

Wagner, George P. **Christian Science not the second coming of Christ: Mrs Eddy not his representative for that occasion: a warning.** CIHM Microfiche series, no. 40504. Berlin: Record, 187-? mf. See: #1320

1880

Ayr Recorder. 1880? - 1892? 8 p. mf. See: s-5507

Galt Edge Tool Works and Carriage Spring Works manufacture all variety of carriage springs ... which are patented in the United States and Canada. CIHM Microfiche series, no. 56983. Galt: Warnock and Co., 1880? mf. See: #2244

Merz, Philip Paul. **Thesaurus biblicus, or, hand-book of scripture reference.** CIHM Microfiche series, no. 26870. Waterloo: Observer Book Co., 1880. 11 fiche. mf. See: #2958

Preston Horticultural Society. **Prize lists of the Preston Horticultural Society.** 1880 - 1905. See: #3832

Town of Galt gazetteer and general business directory for 1880. 1880. 43 p. mf. See: #53

Waterloo County Council. **Standing rules and regulations of the Council of the Corporation of the County of Waterloo, as revised and adopted by the Council, January 28th, 1880.** Berlin: The Council, 1880. 14 p. See: #3981

1881

Maple Leaf Saw Works. **Price list of the Maple Leaf Saw Works: Shurly and Dietrich, manufacturers of refined silver and cast steel saws of all kinds, patent ground..** Galt: The Company, 1881. 40 p. ill. See: #2275

1882

North Waterloo Exhibition Committee. **Programme: the North Waterloo fall exhibition, 1882.** Berlin: Telegraph Office, 1882. 13 p. See: #3824

1883

Balzlev, R. **Erbauliche Betrachtungen für Kranke.** Berlin: Rittinger and Motz, 1883. 160 p. See: #3163

Martin, Jacob. **Ein Schifflein gegen den Wind gerichtet, nämlich ein Auszug aus der Heiligen Schrift ber einige Religions=Fragen unserer Zeit.** Berlin: The Author, 1883. 210 p. See: #3344

1884

Stewart, Charles. **The harp of Strathnaver: a lay of the Scottish Highland evictions and other poems.** CIHM Microfiche series, no. 33550. Galt: Peter Paul and Bro., Buffalo, 1884. 1 fiche. mf. See: #2965

1885?

Preston Progress. 1885? - 1922. See: #115

1886

Berlin Town Council. **Consolidated by-laws of the Town of Berlin.** Berlin: C. Hett, 1886. 134 p. index. See: #4301

Douglass, Janet. **Immanuel hymns for the worship of God.** Berlin: Mennonite Brethren in Christ, 1886. 95 p. See: #3285

Freie Presse. 1886 - 1888? mf. See: #102

Illustrated catalogue of the Berlin Novelty
Works. Berlin: The Company, 1886. 52 p. ill.
See: #2255

Woolwich Township Agricultural Society. **Annual
exhibition programmes.** Elmira: The Society, 1886,
1897. 20 p. See: p-5062

1887

Evangeliums Panier. Berlin: Mennonite Brethren
in Christ, 1887. See: #3296

John Watson Manufacturing Co. **Watson Man'fg. Co.:
binders, reapers, mowers, rakes.** Ayr: The
Company, 1887? 32 p. ill. See: #2261

Spring, Christian F., Rev. **Katechetische
Unterweisung zur Seligkeit über den lutherischen
Katechismus.** Berlin: M.S. Hallman, 1887. 232 p.
See: #3565

Young, James. **Our national future!: being four
letters by James Young in opposition to commercial
union (as proposed) and imperial federation! and
pointing out what the writer believes to be the
true future of Canada as a part of North America.**
CIHM Microfiche series, no. 26165. Galt: Collie
and McGiverin, 1887. mf. See: #4170

1888

Ancient Order of United Workmen. **Nebengesetze der
Berliner Loge, No. 154.** Berlin: Deutsche Zeitung,
1888? 15 p. See: #3758

Patrons of Husbandry, Dominion Grange. **Journal of
the proceedings of the annual session of the
Dominion Grange, Patrons of Husbandry.** CIHM
Microfiche series, no. A01477. Preston: T.H.
Sears, 1888? - 1890. mf. See: #3827

St John's Lutheran Church, Waterloo.
**Kirchen-Ordnung der deutschen evangelisch-
lutherischen St Johannes-gemeinde in Waterloo,
Waterloo Co., Ont., Canada.** Waterloo:
Bauernfreund Dampf-Druck, 1888. 12 p. See: #3578

Wilmot Township Council. **The consolidated by-laws
of the Township of Wilmot to the 1st December,
1888.** New Hamburg: Jacob Ritz and Co., 1888. 75
p. index. Also: CIHM Microfiche series, no. 15689.
See: #3510

1889

Galt Collegiate Institute. **Galt Collegiate
Institute: announcement for the year 1889-90.**
Galt: Galt Reporter, 1889. 25 p. ill. See: #2753

John Watson Manufacturing Co. **Watson Man'f'g Co
Limited, Ayr, Ont., Canada: binders, reapers,
mowers, rakes.** Ayr: The Company, 1889. 40 p. ill.
See: #2260

St Jerome's College. **St Jerome's College, Berlin,
Ont. Canada (on the main line of the Grand Trunk
Railway) scholastic year 1889-90.** CIHM Microfiche
series, no. A01838. Berlin: Rittinger and Motz,
1889? 1 fiche. mf. See: #2835

1889

Eby, Ezra E. **A biographical history of the Eby
family: being a history of their movements in
Europe during the Reformation and of their early
settlement in America; as also much other
unpublished historical information belonging to
the family.** Berlin: Hett and Eby, 1889 reprinted
1970. 144 p. ill. Also: CIHM Microfiche series,
no. 05213. See: #848

1890

Evangelical Association. **Journal der Canada
Conferenz der evangelischer Gemeinschaft von Nord
Amerika, enthaltend die Verhandlung der ...
Jahressitzung gehalten zu ....** CIHM Microfiche
series, nos. 64339 and A01711. Berlin: Berlin
Publishing Co., 1890 - 1899. mf. See: #3488

**Galt Summer Carnival, Thursday & Friday, June
12th & 13th, 1890.** 1890. 28 p. ill. Also: CIHM
Microfiche series, no. 53027. See: #4237

Hale, Horatio. **Was America peopled from
Polynesia: a study in comparative philology.** CIHM
Microfiche series, no. 06667. Berlin: H.S.
Hallman, 1890. 1 fiche. mf. See: #2949

Krafft, U., Pastor. **In der Filiale: eine
Erzhlung für das Luth. Volksblatt.** Elmira: Luth.
Volksblatt, 1890. 88 p. Also: CIHM Microfiche
series, no. 07966. See: #3554

P.E. Shantz Foundry. **Children's sleighs for boys
and girls.** Galt: Reformer Press, 1890? 15 p. ill.
See: #2281

Waterloo County Teachers' Association. **The annual
meeting of the Waterloo County Teachers'
Association will be held in the Model School
building, Galt on Thursday and Friday, March 6th
and 7th, 1890.** CIHM Microfiche series, no. 54805.
1890? 1 fiche. mf. See: #3858

Waterloo Township Council. **Voters' lists: South
and North Divisions of the Township of Waterloo.**
1890, 1893, 1925. See: #4460

1891

Deutsche Zeitung. 1891 - 1899, 1915. mf. See: #98

Waterloo Mutual Fire Insurance Co. **28th financial statement of the company: total assets $280,784.** CIHM Microfiche series, no. 38616. Waterloo: Waterloo Chronicle, 1891? mf. See: #1830

1892

Canadian family almanac for the year 1893. CIHM Microfiche series, no. A00102. Berlin: Berlin Publishing Co., 1892? 1 fiche. mf. See: #35

Town of Berlin. **Town of Berlin by-laws I. respecting frontage assessment for sewers. II. to license and regulate plumbers. III. to regulate plumbing and to secure the sanitary condition of buildings.** 1892. 19 p. See: #4376

1893

Daily Record/ Daily Telegraph/ News-Record/ Kitchener Daily Record/ Kitchener-Waterloo Record. Berlin Kitchener: Recordak, 1893 - 36 reels. mf. See: #89

The Elmira Signet. 1893- See: #101

Galt Collegiate Institute Literary and Musical Society. **Laws and rules of order of Galt Collegiate Institute Literary and Musical Society.** Galt: Galt Reporter, 1893. 1 v. (unpaged). See: #2754

Gore Mutual Fire Insurance Co. **Annual meeting held at Galt on January 23, 1893.** CIHM Microfiche series, no. A00712. The Company, 1893. 1 fiche. mf. See: #1814

The Hymn Book Committee. **A choice collection of spiritual hymns, adapted to public, social, and family devotion, and designed for the use of the Mennonite Brethren in Christ and all lovers of Zion.** Berlin: Gospel Banner, 1893. 63 p. indexes. See: #3331

Jährliche Conferenz der mennoniten Gemeinde von Ontario: abgehalten am 25 und 26 Mai, 1893 zu Berlin, Ontario. CIHM Microfiche series, no. 15676. 1893? mf. See: #3332

1894

Town of Berlin. **Practical by-laws of the Town of Berlin.** Berlin: Record Job Office, 1894. 99 p. index. See: #4375

Wellesley Township Council. **Voters' lists: Township of Wellesley.** 1894 - 1966. See: #4482

1895

Chipman, Willis. **Town of Galt, province of Ontario: report on a proposed system of sewerage and sewage disposal.** Galt: Reformer Press, 1895. 29 p. map. See: #4028

Eby, Ezra E. **A biographical history of Waterloo Township and other townships of the county: being a history of the early settlers and their descendants, mostly all of Pennsylvania Dutch origin: as also much other unpublished historical information chiefly of a local character.** Berlin: The Author, 1895. 2 v. Also: CIHM Microfiche series, nos. 10018-10020. See: #713

Hespeler Herald. 1895? - 1970. mf. See: #107

Young, James. **History of the Gore Fire Insurance Co., from 1839 to 1895 [microform]: being an address delivered by the Hon. James Young, president of the company: in moving the adoption of the report at the 56th annual meeting of the company, held in their new head office, corner Main and Ainslie streets, Galt, on the 28th January 1895.** Galt: Jaffray Bros, 1895. 15 p. ill. Also: CIHM Microfiche series, no. 26164. See: #1834

1896

Galt Town Council. **Voters' list: municipality of the Town of Galt.** 1896. mf. See: #4239

Kirmes. Berlin: The Committee, 1896. 52 p. ill., index. See: #4326

Mendelssohn's masterpiece "St Paul" at the Skating Rink, Berlin, Ont., on Thursday evening, May 28th, 1896. Berlin: Record Press, 1896. 5 p. See: #3037

The Philatelic Advocate: a monthly journal devoted to stamp collecting. Berlin: Starnaman Bros, 1896 - 1901. 1 v. See: #3830

A tribute to a noble effort. Ayr: News Press, 1896. 6 p. See: #3694

1897 -

Ayr News. 1897 - mf. See: #75

Bender, Jacob. **Familien-Register von Jakob und Magdalena Bender und ihr Nachkommen bis 1897.** Jakob and David Bender, 1897. 12 p. See: #748

Berlin Town Council. **Assessment roll of the Town of Berlin of 1897.** 1897. 82 p. See: #4300

Busy Berlin: jubilee souvenir, 1897. Berlin:
Berlin News-Record, 1897. 190 p. ill. Also: CIHM
Microfiche series, no. 02113. See: #4307

Canadian Natural Science News. Baden: Edgar R.
Boniface, 1897- See: #2302

Carter's almanac and cook book for 1897. Berlin:
H.R. Carter, 1897. See: #3200

Wilmot Township Council. **Voters' lists: Township
of Wilmot.** 1897 - 1966. See: #4511

Wilson, Cornelius. **Jubilee souvenir of Galt.**
Galt: Galt Town Council, 1897. 1 v. (unpaged).
ill., ports. Also: mf. See: #4263

1898

Galt Business College. **Annual announcement of the
Galt Business College.** CIHM Microfiche series,
no. A01727. Galt Business College, 1898? 13
frames. mf. See: #2884

Hallman, H.S. **Songs of glad tidings, 2d ed.** Berlin:
Gospel Banner Office, 1898. 221 p. See: #3233

Knights of the Maccabees of the World.
**Nebengezetze der Berlin Tent No. 21, K.O.T.M. von
Berlin, Ont..** Berlin: Berlin Tent No. 21, 1898? 8
p. See: #3807

Peninsular Saengerfest, 1898. **Official souvenir
program of the 13th Peninsular Saengerfest, to be
held at Berlin, Ontario, August 10, 11, 12 1898.**
Berlin: Record Electric Press, 1898. 32 p. ill.
See: #3041

1899

Berlin Express. 1899. 4 p. See: #81

Canadian Association of Stationary Engineers.
**Official souvenir of the annual convention of the
Canadian Association of Stationary Engineers at
Berlin, Canada.** Berlin: The Association, 1899. 48
p. ill. See: #3775

Hett, J.E., Dr. **The sexual organs, their use and
abuse: the subject on which men and women know
the least and ought to know the most.** CIHM
Microfiche series, no. 01534. Berlin: The Author, 1899.
2 fiche. mf. See: #2951

**Jahrbuch der evangelisch-lutherischen St Petri
Gemeinde zu Berlin, Canada.** Berlin: The Church,
1899 - 1900. See: #3545

P.E. Shantz Agricultural Works. **Descriptive
catalogue: P.E. Shantz, Preston, Ont..** Preston:
Progress Print, 1899? 24 p. ill. See: #2280

189-?

Ancient Order of United Workmen. **A.O.U.W. Berlin
Lodge No. 154, Welcome Lodge No. 334.** Berlin:
Journal Print, 189-? 1 v. (unpaged). See: #3759

Berlin Piano and Organ Co. **Illustrated catalogue
of the Berlin upright and grand pianoforte and
cabinet organs manufactured by Berlin Piano and
Organ Co. (Limited.), Berlin, Ontario, Canada.**
189-? 23 p. ill. See: #2227

Souvenir of Berlin Ontario: photo-gravures. CIHM
Microfiche series, no. 39259. Berlin: F.I. Weaver
& Co., 189-? 18 frames. mf. See: #4367

1900

Evangelical Association of Berlin - Young People's
Alliance. **Constitution.** 1900? 7 p. See: #3489

Galt Public Library. **The public library catalogue
1900, Town of Galt.** Galt: Jaffray Bros, 1900. 86
p. See: #2982

**Howard heaters manufactured by T.E. Shantz & Co.,
Berlin, Ontario.** Berlin: H.S. Hallman, 1900. 12
p. See: #2254

P.E. Shantz Agricultural Works. **25th annual
catalog: P.E. Shantz, Preston, Ont., farm
implements, light running harvesting machinery.**
Galt: H.M. Hunt & Sons, 1900? 24 p. ill. See:
#2278

St Mary's Literary and Dramatic Society. **Social
dance: Saengerbund Hall, Wednesday, Feb. 7, 1900.**
Berlin: The Society, 1900. 12 p. ill. See: #3843

Waterloo County Council. **By-laws of the County of
Waterloo from the date of its incorporation in
1852 to the year 1900.** Berlin: Gospel Banner
Office, 1900. 107 p. See: #3979

Wellesley Maple Leaf. 1900 - 1921. mf. See:
#125

Indexes

Author Index

Subject Heading Index

Place Index

Corporate Subject Index

Personal Subject Index

Clemens, Zena: 806.
Clough, Donald J.: 2305.
Cloutier, Albert: 1993.
Clow, Cynthia M.: 528.
Clubine, Robert: 3411.
Cober, Alvin Alonzo, Rev.: 811.
Cober, Peter, Rev.: 812.
Cochrane, Charles C.: 3661.
Cockman, W.V.: 4316.
Coffey, Brian L.: 2419, 2420.
Coffman, Barbara F.: 3909.
Coffman, S.F.: 529, 3261.
Coldren, Charles, Mrs: 847.
Coleman, D.: 2622.
Coleman, Thelma: 261.
Collishaw, Wendy: 2421, 2422, 4317.
Colombo, John R.: 3167.
Connell, Ruth Merner: 976.
Connor, A.W.: 1300.
Connor, James Thomas Hamilton: 2155, 3168.
Conrad, Peter: 4029.
Cook, H. Milton: 1580, 3778.
Cook, R.: 2351.
Cooper, Mike: 1757, 2307.
Cooper, Russell: 518.
Cooper, W. Fred: 3779.
Cope, Verlin: 1943.
Copp, John Terry: 1875, 1876.
Corbett, John: 2561.
Corfield, Geoffrey: 2620.
Cornell, John: 263.
Cornell, Paul: 3472.
Cornell, S.J.: 2623.
Cornell, Thomas V.: 814.
Cornish, C.R.: 1177, 2423.
Costa-Pinto, L.A.: 697.
Couling, Gordon: 2424, 2425, 2561.
Coulthard, Elizabeth: 3887.
Coumans, Camilla C.: 3076, 4030.
Coutts, Edgar N., Dr: 4031.
Cowan, H.: 1732.
Cowan, Hugh, Rev.: 4231.
Cowan, James: 4116.
Cowan, Jennie F.: 505, 1374, 1549, 1758, 1877, 2156, 2727, 3230, 3662, 3663, 3863, 3970, 3971, 4391.
Cowan, Ted: 318.
Cowan, Virginia Bollacker: 722.
Cowls, W.J.: 1805, 4403.
Cox, Kenneth Wayne: 319, 2308.
Coyne, James H.: 187.
Cranston, J. Herbert: 1306.
Cranston, W.H.: 3888, 3889.
Crawford, Sybil Card: 1725.
Cressman, Barbara: 1067.

Cressman, David Robert: 821.
Cressman, Eben C.: 2728, 3270, 3271, 3627.
Cressman, Ella M.: 1162, 1623, 1878, 1879, 2157, 3272, 4428.
Cressman, Irvin W., Rev.: 3336.
Cressman, J. Boyd: 1349, 1350, 1351, 3273, 3274, 3275.
Cressman, Kenneth W.: 530, 3276, 3277.
Cressman, Mary Ann Shantz: 1067.
Cressman, Orpha: 822, 1067.
Cressman, Paul L.: 819.
Cressman, Zenas, Mrs: 2729.
Crocker, R.: 1880.
Cronmiller, Carl Raymond: 3525.
Crooks, Adam: 3780.
Cross, Austin F.: 1268.
Crownover, Donald: 531.
Crozier, John Beattie: 1310.
Crozier, Leif D.: 3727.
Cruikshank, E.A.: 188, 264, 3890.
Cuming, David J.: 2062.
Cunningham, Roderick K.: 1806.
Cunningham, Walter: 189.
Currie, Archibald W.: 2063.
Currie, L. Charleen: 2427.
Curry, John A.: 1760.
Curtis, Kevin R.: 4032.
Curtis, Rosina Hass: 867.
Cutts, Anson Bailey: 2428.

Dagg, Anne Innis: 2300.
Dahms, Fredric A.: 320, 321, 322, 323, 324, 2064.
Dahms, Vera E. Schweitzer: 894, 1063.
Dainton, D.G.: 2876.
Darrell, Jennifer: 2158.
Davey, George M.: 1881.
David, Raymond: 2429.
Davidson, Jim: 325.
Davies, Blodwen: 532.
Davis, E.C., Mrs: 3628.
Davis, Linda Strath: 2309.
Davock, Paul W.: 4033.
Dawson, Robert N.: 2310.
Day, Cindy: 4123.
de Bock, Hazel: 3706.
de Britto Costa-Pinto, Sulamita: 697, 698.
De la Roche, Mazo: 1316.
de Visser, John: 2311.
DeKay, George P.: 987.
DeKegel, Danielle: 3746.
Delhaise, Catherine: 2430.

Delhaise, John: 2430.
Deller, Howard F., Rev.: 3629.
Denis-Nathan, H.: 3473, 4084.
Denny, Frances L.: 3202.
Derstine, Clayton F., Rev.: 2312.
Dettweiler, Allan: 371, 1044.
Detweiler, John D.: 3279.
Deverall-Ross, Diana: 2624.
Deverell, James F.: 869.
Devitt, A.W.: 699, 4513, 4514.
Devitt, E. Blake: 1320.
Devitt, E.H.: 1530.
Devitt, Edward: 4412.
Dewar, Florence R.: 4466.
Diamond, Florence: 2435, 2731, 4384, 4488.
Dick, Jerry: 2436, 2437, 2438, 2439, 2440.
Dickie, D.J.: 265.
Dickson, F.W.R.: 2084, 2400, 2441, 2522, 3863, 3892, 3972, 4191.
Dickson, J.A.R., Rev.: 3665.
Dickson, Margaret E.: 1288.
Dickson, R.H., Mrs: 1708.
Diefenbacher, Karl: 834.
Dietrich, Debbie: 4478.
Dilley, Robert S.: 266, 533.
Dilse, Paul: 2429, 2442, 2935.
Dobbin, Margaret E.: 2443, 2444, 2445, 2446, 2447, 2448, 2449, 2450.
Doering, Eileen E.: 3171.
Doering, John F.: 3169, 3170, 3171.
Doll, Irene: 837, 838, 839.
Domm, E.E.: 825.
Domm, J.G.: 825.
Donald, Mark M.: 1629.
Donaldson, Gordon: 1887.
Donaldson, Gregory R.: 2313.
Donohoe, E.F.: 2068, 2732, 4085, 4124.
Donovan, Mary Ann: 2903.
Donovan, Mary Cochrane: 2903.
Dooley, J.P.: 2159.
Dorman, Robert: 2069, 2070.
Dorney, R.S.: 2314, 2315, 2625.
Douglas, Robert: 133.
Douglass, Hugh: 2733.
Douglass, Janet: 3285.
Downey, Hilda: 2734.
Draho, Lawrence E.: 2626.
Dreger, Frederick L.: 1733.
Duck, William A.: 957.
Dudycha, Douglas J.: 2628.
Due, John F.: 2071.
Duff, Daniel S.: 3630.
Duff, Louis Blake: 2072.

Kelly, Maurice: 863, 1115.

Kelly, Wayne: 1926.

Kennel, Lillian: 3334.

Kernighan, R.K.: 2085.

Kerr, James E.: 1208, 1324, 1408, 1431, 2786, 2787, 2986, 4248, 4249.

Kerr, Jane Easton Clark: 875.

Kilgour, Nancy: 1927.

Kilmer, Daisy Spain: 1093.

King, J.L., Dr: 3662.

King, Jane: 2788.

Kinzie, Harry S.: 4437.

Kinzie, Ira: 4203, 4438.

Kinzie, Lester: 934, 935.

Kipfer, Alfred: 1099.

Kirk, Wayne: 2086.

Kirkness, Mary Anne: 2987, 2988, 2989.

Kirkwood, M.W.: 2087.

Kitchen, Cameron: 2297.

Kitchen, Phyllis Leleu: 4478.

Klager, Gordon: 3675.

Klassen, A.J.: 3389.

Klinck, Carl F.: 1509, 2888, 2952, 3029.

Klinck, George: 2795, 4221, 4222, 4223.

Klinck, Luella: 3549.

Klinck, Otto W.: 3030.

Klinckhardt, Christian Gottlieb: 284, 571.

Klinger, Jacqueline O. (Mrs Robert): 998.

Klinger, Robert: 998.

Klippenstein, Lawrence: 572.

Kloepfer, C. Victor: 936, 937.

Kloss, Heinz: 629.

Klotz, Otto: 2796, 3806, 4393, 4394.

Klotz, Otto Julius: 4392.

Knapp, J.S.: 1774.

Knauff, W.H., Rev.: 3550.

Knechtel, Brenda Lichti: 3368.

Knechtel, Valentin: 938.

Knight, Dean H.: 2502.

Knowles, Ann: 2648.

Knowles, R.H.: 2797.

Knowles, Robert E., Rev.: 2953, 2954, 3732.

Kobayashi, Jack: 2578.

Kobayashi, Teruko: 3068, 3095, 3096, 3097, 3098, 3099, 3100.

Koch, Alice: 750, 2798, 3335, 3336.

Koch, Edward L.: 1931.

Koebel, Dennis: 328.

Koebel, Judy: 2799.

Koebel, Michael: 2177.

Koegler, J.B.: 3551.

Koegler, John: 3559.

Kohli, Marjorie: 378, 401, 406, 422, 433, 434, 435, 437, 438, 1932.

Kolaritsch, Diane: 2412, 2489.

Koshan, Ernest: 2178.

Kostantos, Alexandra: 1933.

Kowalski, David J.: 2503.

Kozorys, G.: 342.

Kraehling, Homer, Mrs: 3552.

Kraehling, Jean: 3553.

Kraehling, Katherine, Mrs: 3553.

Kraehling, Myrta, Mrs: 3553.

Kraemer, David M.: 1122.

Kraemer, James E.: 2090.

Kraemer, Marie: 1537.

Kraemer, William: 943.

Krafft, U., Pastor: 3554.

Kraft, Annemarie: 634.

Kratz, Henry: 573, 574.

Kreider, Rachel W.: 716.

Kreiner, Leona Bramm: 1446, 1934.

Krische, Mark F.: 2649.

Kroekker, Wendy: 3740.

Kropf, Brian J.: 2650.

Krueger, Alice M.: 1022.

Krueger, Ralph R.: 2651, 3994, 4135.

Kubisch, Michael: 430.

Kuepfer, Nancy Jantzi (Mrs Menno W.): 923, 945, 946.

Kuhn, Grace M.: 3679.

Kummer, Oliver A.: 2344, 3180, 3808, 4439.

Kurisu, Jane: 2746.

Kurogawa, Minako: 575, 576.

Kurz, Carl Heinz: 667.

Ladell, John: 1775.

Ladell, Monica: 1775.

Lageer, Eileen: 3337.

Lake, Marion A.: 2800.

Lam, L.S.: 2652.

Lamb, Jennifer A.: 3101.

Lamb, Kathryn Hansuld: 436, 704, 1281, 1602, 1936, 1937, 2091, 2092, 2093, 2179, 2505, 2506, 2507, 2801, 2802, 3031, 3032, 3102, 3181, 3182, 3478, 3741, 3809, 3810, 3811, 3812, 3917, 3918, 3919, 3920, 3921, 3922, 4011, 4049, 4050, 4195, 4224, 4225, 4347, 4348, 4349, 4350, 4440, 4491.

Lambert, Ronald: 354, 388, 437, 438.

Landers, Bertha: 3338.

Landon, Fred: 1209, 1210, 1211, 1212, 1214, 1221, 1222, 1232, 1247, 1272, 1273, 1274, 1275, 1283, 1298, 1307, 1309, 1313, 1330, 1331, 1333, 1343, 1361, 1362, 1372, 1380, 1384, 1390, 1395, 1397, 1403, 1405, 1406, 1409, 1413, 1414, 1415, 1418, 1428, 1432, 1434, 1438, 1439, 1444, 1445, 1459, 1464, 1471, 1472, 1475, 1476, 1477, 1481, 1483, 1485, 1489, 1490, 1495, 1496, 1502, 1504, 1508, 1514, 1518, 1526, 1527, 1542, 1560, 1568, 1581, 1585, 1587, 1589, 1591, 1592, 1593, 1596, 1603, 1604, 1606, 1609, 1614, 1624, 1632, 1642, 1643, 1648, 1653, 1660, 1669, 1684, 1687, 1692, 1699, 1715, 1719, 1727, 1728, 3813.

Lang, E. Elizabeth Koch: 826, 941, 1021, 1064, 2180.

Lang-Runtz, Heather: 3103.

Langmead, Stephen: 2969.

Lanier, Barbara A.: 1938.

Larson, Elsie Bricker: 776.

Laschinger, Russell H.: 947.

Lattner, Koni: 566.

Laurence, Hugh: 577, 3339, 3340.

Lautenschlager, Harold: 4094, 4095.

Lavoie, Paul L.: 1939.

Lawrence, Sylvia: 2803.

Lazenby, Richard: 478.

Lea, Joanne: 202, 506, 1200, 4096.

Leather, Ted: 1411.

Lebold, Fran: 3368.

Lebold, Ralph A.: 951.

Lee, Chun-fen: 329, 330, 1776.

Leechman, Douglas: 3195.

Lefevre, Craig: 343.

Lehmann, Heinz: 668, 669.

Leibbrandt, Gottlieb: 670, 671, 672, 3814, 3815.

Leipnik, Mary: 4226.

Leung, Felicity Hale: 1940, 1941, 1942.

Levitch, Gerald: 578.

Lewis, D.E.: 2991.

Lewis, John E.: 3743.

Lichti, Willis: 952.

Lichty, Wilbur: 1943.

Liddell, Thomas, Rev.: 3680.

Liedtke, Chris: 2804.

Lienhardt, Janet: 3464.

Light, Frank G.: 3816.

Lim, Jee-Lee: 2654.

Linley, Margaret: 2959.

SUBJECT HEADING INDEX

Conestogo, Waterloo Street: 2483.

The Coombe, Hespeler: 908, 4277, 4280, 4285, 4290.

Corktown: 4277.

Cornell's Corners: 281, 4450.

Cottrell Lake: 165.

Cox Creek: 157, 305, 308, 2120, 3669, 4525.

Creek Cottage, Ayr: 1720.

Cressman: 1358.

Cressman Industrial Park, Kitchener: 2660, 2681.

Cressman's Woods, Doon: 185, 186, 189, 1334, 2285, 2312, 2333, 2353, 2354, 2441, 4342, 4429.

Crooks' Tract: 2553.

Crosshill: 37, 38, 39, 41, 46, 47, 51, 52, 55, 56, 58, 59, 61, 62, 65, 71, 72, 74, 132, 143, 149, 157, 159, 247, 281, 305, 308, 319, 321, 341, 671, 672, 1186, 1265, 1422, 1740, 1936, 2061, 2117, 2120, 2136, 2188, 2369, 2437, 2441, 2522, 2527, 2566, 2589, 2608, 3175, 3307, 3365, 3828, 3918, 3927, 4076, 4079, 4090, 4111, 4468, 4470, 4471, 4472, 4473, 4478, 4480, 4481, 4483, 4484.

Crowsfoot Corners: 281.

Cruickston Park, Blair: 8, 16, 149, 275, 555, 766, 1324, 1561, 1708, 1759, 2502, 2506, 2522, 2532, 2591, 2607, 4247, 4253, 4254, 4255, 4437, 4454.

Crystal Springs: 4473.

Dammsville: 825.

Deans Lake: 4212.

Dearborn Industrial Park, Waterloo: 2681.

Delview: 281.

Denmark, Schleswig: 3257.

Desjardins Canal: 1051, 1652, 1975.

Dickie Settlement: 1544, 1583, 1748, 2591, 2703, 2788, 2956, 3863, 4199, 4212.

Dickson Estate: 2787.

Dickson Park, Galt: 332, 1708, 3841, 4212, 4233, 4246, 4252.

Dickson's Dam, Galt: 2374.

Dodge's Fording, Grand River: 2097.

Doon: 2, 4, 8, 21, 28, 37, 38, 39, 41, 46, 47, 51, 52, 56, 58, 59, 61, 62, 65, 71, 72, 74, 132, 143, 149, 157, 159, 189, 247, 256, 270, 275, 281, 294, 305, 308, 319, 321, 338, 372, 373, 409, 502, 509, 555, 671, 672, 713, 719, 720, 727, 745, 755, 758, 759, 851, 911, 934, 935, 979, 1053, 1089, 1098, 1165, 1171, 1185, 1191, 1216, 1312, 1375, 1376, 1377, 1421, 1499, 1623, 1646, 1652, 1654, 1667, 1668, 1671, 1783, 1787, 1799, 1877, 1973, 1974, 1976, 2096, 2120, 2138, 2172, 2190, 2241, 2304, 2312, 2333, 2336, 2344, 2354, 2379, 2385, 2412, 2441, 2470, 2491, 2493, 2522, 2533, 2542, 2544, 2545, 2569, 2576, 2578, 2607, 2618, 2620, 2648, 2700, 2717, 2782, 2787, 2817, 2818, 2874, 3056, 3071, 3087, 3088, 3089, 3090, 3091, 3097, 3105, 3108, 3111, 3112, 3113, 3156, 3159, 3161, 3383, 3655, 3660, 3664, 3681, 3829, 3842, 3852, 3859, 3876, 3885, 3889, 3898, 3899, 3900, 3911, 3914, 3916, 3918, 3926, 3937, 3938, 3940, 3942, 3943, 3945, 3950, 3951, 3957, 3978, 4264, 4391, 4393, 4423, 4429, 4432, 4437, 4439, 4442, 4450, 4454, 4455, 4456, 4473.

Doon Mills: 49, 157, 247, 281, 671, 672, 1375, 1377, 2073, 2120, 2374, 3972, 4423.

Doon Pinnacle: 2336, 2648.

Dorking: 21, 138, 157, 281, 319, 321, 341, 2129, 4467, 4471.

Dryden Tract: 841, 842.

Drydensville: 842, 843, 1974.

Dumfries Mills: 157, 4266.

Dumfries N Township: 1, 2, 4, 6, 7, 8, 13, 17, 18, 20, 21, 28, 29, 37, 38, 39, 51, 52, 55, 56, 57, 58, 59, 60, 61, 62, 63, 65, 66, 71, 72, 74, 76, 78, 99, 132, 143, 149, 152, 156, 157, 159, 160, 164, 165, 166, 169, 170, 174, 177, 196, 199, 200, 202, 203, 207, 224, 226, 229, 230, 258, 268, 276, 277, 281, 285, 291, 302, 305, 308, 310, 319, 321, 323, 325, 338, 341, 347, 351, 366, 378, 395, 396, 397, 402, 406, 411, 413, 424, 433, 454, 458, 478, 479, 488, 495, 496, 508, 542, 543, 648, 652, 668, 669, 670, 671, 672, 688, 690, 692, 694, 713, 719, 720, 841, 842, 857, 877, 898, 899, 905, 1020, 1036, 1089, 1160, 1165, 1166, 1170, 1172, 1178, 1179, 1183, 1185, 1193, 1216, 1217, 1303, 1304, 1319, 1325, 1358, 1392, 1393, 1457, 1465, 1524, 1544, 1561, 1679, 1680, 1693, 1712, 1718, 1740, 1748, 1749, 1758, 1762, 1765, 1769, 1770, 1773, 1779, 1782, 1788, 1821, 1822, 1829, 1860, 1897, 1932, 1947, 1974, 1976, 1982, 1983, 1990, 2000, 2034, 2039, 2069, 2070, 2087, 2120, 2130, 2131, 2156, 2181, 2303, 2326, 2327, 2328, 2329, 2330, 2331, 2350, 2366, 2369, 2370, 2379, 2381, 2383, 2389, 2402, 2425, 2441, 2467, 2472, 2473, 2486, 2495, 2502, 2522, 2536, 2539, 2591, 2597, 2610, 2631, 2670, 2701, 2703, 2716, 2727, 2743, 2776, 2782, 2783, 2788, 2796, 2800, 2817, 2818, 3101, 3262, 3279, 3374, 3624, 3636, 3639, 3663, 3668, 3682, 3743, 3760, 3761, 3787, 3825, 3838, 3842, 3847, 3848, 3852, 3863, 3887, 3888, 3955, 3974, 3979, 3985, 3986, 3989, 3994, 4001, 4003, 4023, 4054, 4077, 4079, 4155, 4163, 4166, 4184, 4185, 4188, 4198 - 4216, 4229, 4230, 4235, 4240, 4263, 4264, 4267.

Dumfries S Township: 156, 1325, 2783, 4202.

Dumfries Township: 1, 4, 9, 13, 14, 15, 17, 19, 23, 24, 27, 28, 29, 30, 37, 45, 49, 50, 85, 103, 120, 128, 143, 144, 156, 157, 159, 250, 251, 252, 257, 259, 273, 274, 275, 276, 279, 284, 294, 296, 298, 299, 300, 301, 303, 305, 308, 310, 311, 326, 329, 332, 376, 402, 411, 425, 458, 487, 514, 553, 671, 672, 685, 686, 687, 688, 690, 691, 693, 694, 713, 719, 720, 809, 830, 843, 844, 878, 879, 898, 975, 1008, 1025, 1026, 1147, 1171, 1207, 1284, 1287, 1311, 1315, 1323, 1324, 1325, 1328, 1374, 1399, 1400, 1401, 1453, 1465, 1521, 1543, 1544, 1548, 1561, 1617, 1625, 1626, 1627, 1664, 1680, 1681, 1693, 1695, 1696, 1720, 1724, 1733, 1748, 1776, 1834, 1861, 1877, 1900, 1909, 1923, 1963, 1986, 2005, 2051, 2052, 2069, 2070, 2085, 2109, 2118, 2120, 2130, 2162, 2188, 2351, 2368, 2374, 2379, 2405, 2408, 2409, 2424,

Salem: 1151, 2179.
Sand Hills: 157, 308, 2120, 2670, 4380, 4485.
Sandytown: 2092.
Saugeen River: 671, 672.
Saw Mill Creek: 2134.
Schantz: 670, 2128.
Scherer Dam: 4435.
Schindelsteddle: 157, 276, 308.
Schleswig, Denmark: 3394.
Schmidt's Creek: 4466.
Schmidtsville: 157, 308, 1048, 2120, 4466.
Schneider Road: 2586, 4372, 4380.
Schneider's Creek: 28, 191, 270, 305, 308, 330, 1882, 1973, 1977, 2039, 2096, 2313, 2373, 2375, 2379, 2385, 2470, 4372, 4376, 4380, 4454.
Schumacker Mills: 247.
Schweitzer Farm, Bridgeport: 202, 1573.
Scotland, Aberdeen: 2, 1430.
Scotland, Aberdeenshire: 286, 1646, 1770.
Scotland, Aberdeenshire, Udny: 1301.
Scotland, Arbroath: 1392.
Scotland, Argyllshire: 1374.
Scotland, Ayrshire: 688, 1400, 1401, 4188.
Scotland, Ayrshire, Galston: 878.
Scotland, Ayrshire, Kilmarnock: 479.
Scotland, Ayrshire, Kirkoswald: 878, 1402.
Scotland, Ayrshire, Sorn: 1521.
Scotland, Begbie: 1207.
Scotland, Bewlie Mains: 1617.
Scotland, Darvel: 1664.
Scotland, Dumfries: 1324, 1325, 2592, 2717.
Scotland, Dumfriesshire: 688, 694, 4480.
Scotland, Dundee: 4485.
Scotland, Dunlop: 1748.
Scotland, Glasgow: 1451.
Scotland, Greenock: 3655, 3682.
Scotland, Invernesshire: 306.
Scotland, Jedburgh: 857.
Scotland, Kilwinning: 1720.
Scotland, Lanarkshire: 1503.
Scotland, Lanarkshire, East Kilbride: 1500, 1501.
Scotland, Melrose: 1722, 1724.
Scotland, Perthshire: 1374, 1381, 1943.
Scotland, Ross-shire, Calcairn Mills: 1284.

Scotland, Roxburghshire: 688, 691, 841, 1036, 1523, 1544.
Scotland, Selkirkshire: 302, 915.
Scotland, Stirling: 1453.
Scotland, Stirlingshire, Kippen: 3672.
Scotland, The Shotts: 1693.
Scott's Corners: 2486.
Scrimger's Mill: 694.
Seagram Memorial Field, Waterloo: 2889.
Second Concession, Waterloo Township: 253.
Shade's Mills: 157, 279, 301, 302, 308, 332, 1324, 1325, 1626, 1627, 2120, 2372, 4202, 4240, 4385.
Shakespeare: 3420.
Shand Dam: 2305, 2320, 2344, 2367, 2374.
Shantz: 37, 149, 157, 281, 305, 308, 2120, 3580, 3581, 4442.
Shantz Dam: 1631, 2039, 4356.
Shantz Hill, Preston: 281, 908, 1185.
Shantz Lane: 281.
Shantz Station: 157, 276, 281, 499, 1175, 1378, 2711, 2782, 3525, 3610, 3611, 3612, 3770, 4451.
Sheave Tower, Blair: 977, 1556, 2000, 2401, 2441, 2591, 2607, 2885, 4454, 4462.
Shediac: 4505.
Shinglebridge: 157, 247, 4435, 4437.
Shingletown: 871, 1043, 2480, 3181, 3365, 3422.
Shoemaker's Creek: 305, 308, 2379.
Shoemaker's Ford, Grand River: 2097.
Shoemaker's Lake: 4023.
Shoemaker's Mills: 157, 247, 308, 2120, 2179, 3972, 4190, 4193, 4195.
Silver Heights, Hespeler: 4268.
Silver Lake: 1, 2348, 2581, 3075, 4078, 4416.
Slabtown: 4212.
Slask, Poland: 3820.
Slovenia, Gottschee: 671.
Smith's Creek: 286, 3972, 4188, 4385, 4387, 4388, 4480, 4487, 4488.
Smithville: 157, 247, 2120, 2512, 2959, 3462, 4466, 4478.
Snyder Road: 2134.
Snyders Corner: 281, 1611.
Snyders Road: 307, 598, 1061.
Sonneck, Berlin: 2421.
Soper Park, Galt: 8, 332, 3888, 4232, 4233.
South Waterloo: 48, 809, 1500, 1722,

1821, 2485, 4151, 4153, 4154, 4155, 4160, 4423, 4452.
Speed Dam: 4396.
Speed River: 41, 200, 232, 257, 305, 308, 332, 671, 672, 766, 809, 812, 1002, 1370, 1912, 1918, 1963, 1975, 2000, 2005, 2055, 2097, 2104, 2305, 2323, 2324, 2336, 2341, 2353, 2369, 2372, 2374, 2375, 2379, 2711, 2760, 3082, 3180, 3808, 3982, 4023, 4246, 4255, 4270, 4271, 4274, 4275, 4277, 4283, 4284, 4391, 4392, 4393, 4395, 4396, 4432, 4451, 4452, 4456, 4462.
Speedslee: 232, 281.
Speedsville: 146, 281, 305, 308, 348, 809, 1294, 1974, 1975, 2379, 2442, 2711, 2760, 2774, 3082, 3904, 4452.
Speedsville Road Ford, Speed River: 2097.
Spongy Lake: 2308, 2324, 2336, 2349, 2354, 2670, 4478.
Sprague's Road, North Dumfries: 1160, 2130, 2703, 2743, 4212, 4266.
Spring Creek: 2379, 3082, 4487, 4525.
Spring Creek Hamlet: 2085.
Spring Valley Farm: 1430, 1573.
Spruce Farm, Haysville: 4486.
St Agatha: 12, 28, 37, 38, 39, 40, 41, 46, 47, 51, 52, 55, 56, 58, 59, 61, 62, 65, 71, 72, 74, 132, 133, 143, 146, 149, 157, 247, 281, 305, 308, 321, 338, 341, 391, 407, 476, 556, 670, 671, 672, 763, 775, 839, 863, 871, 924, 930, 943, 952, 955, 956, 980, 1029, 1034, 1046, 1061, 1115, 1169, 1171, 1234, 1244, 1329, 1330, 1331, 1441, 1753, 1845, 1852, 1936, 2095, 2120, 2425, 2430, 2441, 2480, 2505, 2522, 2722, 2731, 2732, 2756, 2782, 2785, 2817, 2818, 2839, 2850, 2936, 2944, 3074, 3076, 3104, 3123, 3130, 3152, 3176, 3192, 3259, 3275, 3307, 3334, 3340, 3365, 3419, 3420, 3424, 3426, 3428, 3429, 3431, 3432, 3439, 3440, 3441, 3442, 3444, 3448, 3452, 3453, 3454, 3455, 3456, 3457, 3458, 3459, 3460, 3461, 3462, 3463, 3525, 3552, 3553, 3564, 3621, 3949, 3955, 4023, 4030, 4076, 4094, 4128, 4380,

Berlin Public School: 1278, 1451, 2782, 4380.

Berlin Public School Board: 1006, 1269, 1273, 1280, 1372, 1373, 1432, 1442, 1550, 1559, 1669, 2747, 2818, 2822, 2843, 4380.

Berlin Publishing Co.: 85, 1686.

Berlin Pumping Station: 3775.

Berlin Railway Station: 673, 2055, 2095, 4365.

Berlin Rangers Football Team: 4380.

Berlin Red Cross Society: 3015.

Berlin Reformer and Waterloo County Reformers Gazette: 122.

Berlin Rifle Association: 126, 1250.

Berlin Rink and Auditorium Co.: 1333.

Berlin Robe and Clothing Co.: 326, 1543, 1544, 4371.

Berlin Rubber Co.: 326, 671, 672, 1269, 1459, 1580, 1581, 1716, 1853, 1855, 1856, 1924, 1993, 2023, 2388, 4380.

Berlin Sanatorium Association: 4029.

Berlin School Board: 2805.

Berlin Schuetzenverein: 4380.

Berlin Separate School: 2782, 2818, 2843, 3442, 4380.

Berlin Separate School Board of Trustees: 2818, 3431, 3448, 4374, 4380.

Berlin Shirt Co.: 4380.

Berlin Skating Rink: 3037, 4326.

Berlin Soda Water Works: 1983.

Berlin Steam Mill: 4517.

Berlin Suspender and Button Co.: 1, 1412, 1413, 4298.

Berlin Swedenborgian Church: 1617, 2039, 3696.

Berlin Table Co.: 29, 4011, 4380.

Berlin Tannery: 127.

Berlin Telegraph: 25, 86, 105, 111, 157, 1295, 1507, 1964, 2453, 2843, 3893, 3897, 3978, 4380, 4517.

Berlin Theatorium: 326.

Berlin Tobacco Co.: 2055.

Berlin Town Council: 316, 1167, 1168, 1247, 1256, 1269, 1270, 1272, 1273, 1361, 1373, 1432, 1434, 1486, 1490, 1496, 1535, 1536, 1590, 1591, 1600, 1637, 1669, 1709, 1853, 1855, 1856, 2019, 2843, 3775, 3974, 4023, 4025, 4124, 4143, 4298, 4301, 4302, 4303, 4374, 4375, 4376, 4380.

Berlin Town Hall: 326, 673, 2517, 4299, 4306, 4327, 4367, 4380.

Berlin Town Park: 3824.

Berlin Town Park Association: 4380.

Berlin Trunk and Bag Co.: 4374.

Berlin Turnverein: 326, 671, 672, 3029, 3034, 3815, 4372, 4380.

Berlin Village Council: 316, 1250, 2019, 3974, 4025, 4159, 4301, 4302, 4304, 4374, 4380.

Berlin Water Commission: 1459, 1591, 4299.

Berlin-Waterloo Collegiate and Technical Institute: 1382, 1444, 1640, 2714, 2782, 4380.

Berlin-Waterloo Hospital: 333, 1269, 1460, 2903, 3754, 3790, 4066, 4380, 4412.

Berlin-Waterloo Hospital Board: 1272, 1273, 1600, 1604, 1833, 4066, 4380.

Berlin, Waterloo, Wellesley and Lake Huron Railway Co.: 2060, 2069, 2070, 2071, 2087, 2122, 2581, 4484.

Berlin Waterworks Co.: 1168, 1272, 1535, 4023, 4299, 4375, 4380.

Berlin Woodenware Co.: 4298, 4374.

Berlin Y.M.C.A.: 143, 1269, 1442, 1897, 3823, 4380.

Berlin Y.W.C.A.: 143, 1460, 3821, 4380.

Berlin Y.W.C.A. Advisory Committee (Men's Committee): 3821.

Berlin Y.W.C.A. Building and Site Committee: 3821.

Berliner Journal: 37, 82, 83, 85, 86, 91, 93, 109, 110, 111, 112, 157, 249, 316, 326, 631, 635, 644, 651, 663, 664, 665, 671, 672, 675, 684, 1295, 1545, 1546, 1550, 1584, 1585, 1586, 1637, 1688, 1794, 1855, 1898, 2149, 2756, 3537, 3893, 3894, 3895, 3973, 4011, 4298, 4318, 4371, 4443, 4520.

Bernal Jones, Architect, Kitchener: 1261.

Bernardo Terazzo and Tile Co., Kitchener: 1895.

Berner and Forwell, builders and contractors, Berlin: 2496.

Bernhardt and Gies, Preston: 4395.

Bernhardt's Brewery, Preston: 1, 1840, 4392, 4394.

Bernhardt's Tavern, Preston: 752.

Bert Meyer's Store, St Clements: 4474.

Bert's Lawnmower Service Ltd,

Elmira: 4217.

Beth Jacob Cemetery, Kitchener: 359, 2618.

Beth Jacob Sisterhood: 3718.

Beth Jacob Synagogue, Kitchener: 143, 326, 2489, 3718.

Bethany Mennonite Church, Berlin: 1637, 2489, 3310, 3337, 3375, 3376, 3391, 4380.

Bethany Mennonite Church, Kitchener: 3250, 3370, 3401, 3774.

Bethel Lutheran Church, Kitchener: 3533, 3538, 3616.

Bethel Methodist Church: 3478, 3623, 4499.

Bethel Missionary Church, New Dundee: 3320, 4495, 4496.

Bethel Primitive Methodist Church, Wilmot Township: 398.

Bethel United Church Cemetery, Wilmot Township: 398.

Bethel United Church, Wilmot Township: 157, 398, 3623, 4499.

Bethel United Missionary Church: 4497.

Bettinger's Hotel, Bridgeport: 2179.

Beverly Township, S.S.# 13, Scott's Corners: 2486.

Bibby Ste. Croix Foundries Inc., Galt: 332, 4261.

Biehn Mennonite Church, Wilmot Township: 377, 417, 1186, 2729, 3259, 3275, 3277, 3316, 3335, 3336, 3342, 3365, 4407, 4486, 4499.

Big Four singing quartet, Waterloo: 1704.

Bijou (movie theatre), Preston: 4255.

Bill Ludwig Movie Hall, Elmira: 3030, 4225.

Black Bear Hotel, Preston: 635, 2184, 4393, 4394.

Black Creek Pioneer Village: 2435, 2507.

Black Horse Inn, Dumfries N. Township: 170.

Black Horse Inn, Wellesley: 37, 2379.

Blackhawk Indians: 195.

Blair Baptist Church: 157, 1646.

Blair Cemetery, Waterloo Township: 157, 365, 3097, 3402, 3925, 4435, 4462.

Blair Christadelphians: 1646, 4454.

Blair Evangelical Baptist Chapel: 3408, 4454.

Blair Hotel: 4228, 4435, 4437.

Blair Literary Society: 977.

Galt Methodist Church: 4266.

Galt Militia: 4230.

Galt Milk Producers: 3847.

Galt Motor Co.: 1845, 4228.

Galt Old Boys' Reunion, 1902: 2840.

Galt Old Boys' Reunion, 1907: 118.

Galt Old Boys' Reunion, 1947: 118.

Galt Old Ladies' Home: 3771.

Galt Opera House: 4088.

Galt Paper Box Factory: 4246, 4261.

Galt Park Board: 1187.

Galt Police Commission: 4008.

Galt Police Force: 4015.

Galt Pop Works: 1983.

Galt Post Office: 2424, 2478, 3982, 4237, 4246, 4249, 4252, 4263.

Galt, Preston and Hespeler Railway: 1, 332, 1521, 1544, 1664, 1683, 2055, 2060, 2067, 2070, 2071, 2075, 2076, 2087, 2099, 2122, 3180, 4238, 4246, 4255, 4276.

Galt, Preston, and Hespeler Railway Station, Preston: 4252.

Galt-Preston-Hespeler Centennial Committee: 4235.

Galt Printers: 2940.

Galt Public Library: 143, 156, 332, 1401, 1465, 2478, 2969, 2975, 2982, 2984, 2986, 3773, 3838, 4229, 4230, 4238, 4247, 4252, 4261, 4262, 4263, 4266.

Galt Public Library Board: 1290, 1465, 2975.

Galt Public Library Board Building Committee: 2975.

Galt Public School Board: 1707, 1722, 1724, 1765, 2593.

Galt Public Services Commission: 4057.

Galt Public Utilities Commission: 1147, 4023, 4228, 4235, 4255, 4261.

Galt Public Utilities Commission Building: 4228, 4230, 4233.

Galt Publishers Ltd: 120.

Galt Quadrille Band: 2474.

Galt Railway Station: 2595, 4246.

Galt Red Cross and Patriotic Fund: 143, 1708, 2777.

Galt Red Cross Society: 143, 1184, 1185, 3838.

Galt Reformer: 83, 99, 1306, 4255.

Galt Regular Baptist Church: 3417.

Galt Relief Committee: 3771.

Galt Reporter: 37, 78, 83, 85, 86, 103, 104, 105, 143, 157, 326, 332, 1165, 1180, 1306, 1339, 1450, 1451, 1452, 1453, 1457, 2041, 2843, 2864, 3872, 3893, 4125, 4188, 4212, 4236, 4255, 4257, 4266.

Galt Reporter and General Advertiser: 105, 120, 3888.

Galt Rifle Company: 332, 4084, 4087, 4090, 4230, 4265.

Galt Robe Co.: 1671, 1956, 2005.

Galt Roofing and Sheet Metal Co.: 4261.

Galt Rotary Club: 4261.

Galt Salvation Army Band: 4088.

Galt Scientific, Historical and Literary Society: 2975.

Galt Separate School: 2782, 3442.

Galt Shoe Manufacturing Co., Kitchener: 2014.

Galt Stove and Furnace Co.: 1362.

Galt Subscription and Circulating Library: 2975, 2986.

Galt Suburban Planning Board: 2631.

Galt Suburban Roads Commission: 1217, 1218, 4215.

Galt Summer Carnival 1893: 3870.

Galt Terriers (baseball team): 332, 1334, 2050, 3750, 4233, 4255.

Galt Terriers (hockey): 3729, 3742.

Galt Theatre Co.: 1522.

Galt Thespian Amateurs: 4240, 4255, 4266.

Galt Town Council: 1245, 1284, 1285, 1362, 1393, 1520, 1521, 1578, 1619, 1620, 1664, 1690, 1721, 2374, 2975, 2986, 3974, 4015, 4023, 4025, 4239, 4242, 4246, 4251, 4263.

Galt Town Hall: 332, 1302, 2425, 2517, 2975, 4237, 4251, 4252, 4266.

Galt Town Hall and Market: 149, 2474, 2478, 2592, 4246.

Galt Training School for Girls: 2776, 2782.

Galt Union Church: 3666.

Galt Village Council: 3974, 4025.

Galt Volunteers: 4084, 4087, 4125, 4266.

Galt War Memorial Committee: 4088.

Galt Ward School: 4251.

Galt Waterworks Committee: 4023, 4028.

Galt Waterworks Pumping Station: 4023, 4246.

Galt Weekly Reporter: 105, 157, 1306, 3896, 4255.

Galt Welding Co.: 4261.

Galt Women's Institute: 3852.

Galt Wood Heel Ltd: 4261.

Galt Wood Tool and Machine Company: 2246.

Galt Woollen Mills: 1956, 4263.

Galt Y.M.C.A.: 1722, 2478, 3771, 4229, 4230, 4233, 4238, 4261.

Galt Y.W.C.A.: 4261.

Galtex Co., Galt: 4261.

Gardiners of Galt: 4261.

Gaukel's Hotel, Berlin: 326, 1388, 1389, 4315, 4371, 4380.

Geiger Mennonite Church, Haysville: 353, 802, 3259, 3275, 3277, 3316, 3342, 4486, 4499.

Geiger's Tavern: 4477.

Gem Crib and Cradle Co., Kitchener: 2503.

General Conference Mennonites: 3324.

General Instrument of Canada Ltd, Kitchener: 1737.

General Springs Products, Kitchener: 1446, 1737, 1881, 2113.

Geo. C. Kaitting and Sons, Galt: 4261.

Geo. H. Thomas and Son, Galt: 2994.

Geo. R. Tremaine and G.M. Tremaine, Toronto: 149.

George J. Lippert Table Co., Kitchener: 1495.

George Pattinson and Co., Preston: 13, 332, 977, 1558, 1950, 1956, 1975, 2005, 2153, 2379, 4395, 4396.

George Randall and Co., Waterloo: 37, 1974.

George Street United Mennonite Church: 3292.

George W. Robinson, Dry Goods, Galt: 4246.

German Baptist Church, Berlin: 671, 672, 3406, 4195, 4299, 4377, 4380.

German-Canadian Alliance: 326.

German-Canadian Business and Professional Men's Association of K-W: 671, 672.

German-Canadian Business Council for the Arts: 671, 672.

German-Canadian Review: 671, 672.

German-Canadian Yearbook: 671, 672.

German Catholic Settlement Society: 3453.

German Company: 4, 14, 23, 149, 151, 224, 251, 252, 253, 254, 255, 258, 265, 268, 271, 275, 282, 292,

Hydro Electric Power Commission of Ontario: 8, 256, 316, 635, 671, 745, 1233, 1235, 1236, 1237, 1558, 1654, 1657, 1836, 1842, 1856, 1873, 1887, 1916, 1964, 2000, 2122, 3869, 4046, 4320, 4380, 4414, 4422, 4525.

Hymmen Bros, Berlin: 671, 672, 1850, 4380.

I.E. Shantz and Co., Berlin: 3775, 4298.

I.S.B. Market, Elmira: 4217.

I.W. Wilson, Waterloo: 1198.

Ikey Club, Galt: 4246.

Imperial Bank of Canada, Galt: 4009, 4237, 4246.

Imperial Bank of Canada, Kitchener: 4380.

Imperial Bank of Canada, Preston: 4396.

Imperial Hotel, Galt: 2076, 4228, 4230, 4237, 4246, 4252, 4253, 4263.

Imperial Hotel, New Hamburg: 1, 4382, 4386.

Imperial Knitting Co., Galt: 4237.

Imperial Order of the Daughters of the Empire: 143, 1178, 3015, 3773, 4029.

Implement Day, Wilmot: 2480.

Inca Heat Ltd, Galt: 4261.

Independent Labour Party: 4146.

Independent Order of Foresters: 143, 1729, 4275.

Independent Order of Oddfellows: 1453, 4222, 4265, 4275.

Independent Order of Oddfellows, Germania Lodge: 1704.

Independent Order of Oddfellows, Grand Union Lodge: 1484.

Industrial Disputes Investigation Act: 1927.

Ingo Originals Ltd, Waterloo: 1737.

Inn of the Black Walnut, Kitchener: 4315, 4354.

Inter-Mennonite Conference: 626.

Interior Hardwood Co., Berlin: 1596, 4380.

Interior Hardwood Co., Kitchener: 1596, 2397.

International Association of Machinists, Lodge 120, Galt: 1875.

International Gospel Centre, Kitchener: 3706.

International Moulders Union, Galt Local: 1875.

Iroquois Hotel, Galt: 332, 1718, 4246, 4263.

Iroquois Indians: 164, 173, 202, 203, 206, 207, 215, 223, 224, 226, 227, 250, 282, 673, 1325, 2669, 2760.

Irving Steel Ltd, Galt: 4261.

J.A.M. Taylor Tool Co., Galt: 1927.

J.A.M. Taylor Tool Co., Hespeler: 2256, 4269.

J. and J. Livingston, Baden: 37, 1499, 1500, 1501, 1502, 1503, 1974.

J. and J. Livingston Flax Mills, Wellesley: 1499, 4478.

J. and J. Rau, New Hamburg: 326, 1165, 1974, 4386.

J.B. Snider, Waterloo: 1.

J. Bingeman and Co., Berlin: 1914.

J.C. Jaimet and Co., Kitchener: 2196.

J.C. Klaehn Industrial Engineering: 1261.

J.D. Miller and Sons, Bridgeport: 37, 1974, 4195, 4196.

J.E. Hett Memorial Art Gallery and Museum: 1433.

J.E. Neally, New Hamburg: 1198.

J.E. Turner, Jeweller, Hespeler: 4275.

J.E. Weigand and Co., Berlin: 4380.

J.F. Carmichael School, Kitchener: 1286, 2782, 4380.

J.F. Slee Lumber Co., Galt: 4261.

J.G. Mowat and Co.: 1165.

J.M. Schneider Ltd, Berlin: 4298, 4299, 4350.

J.M. Schneider Ltd, Kitchener: 143, 908, 1191, 1608, 1609, 1610, 1737, 1857, 1881, 1895, 1901, 1902, 1919, 1931, 1949, 2004, 2015, 2026, 2234, 2257, 2258, 3739, 4136, 4349, 4354, 4380.

J.M. Schneider Printing Division, Kitchener: 2503.

J.M. Staebler, Berlin: 1914.

J. Martin and Co., Preston: 1861, 1983.

J.P. Starnaman and Co., Berlin: 4380.

J.R. Phin Drug Store, Hespeler: 4275.

J.R. Stouffer and Co., Berlin: 1412, 3775.

J.S. Roos Shoe Co., Waterloo: 1.

J.T. Huber and Co., Doon: 2385, 4454.

J.U. Clemens and Co., Berlin: 4298.

J.W. Christman's Dry Goods Emporium, Hespeler: 4275.

J.W. Fear and Co., Waterloo: 1699, 1700.

J. Wagner and Co., Galt: 1974.

J.Y. Shantz and Sons, Berlin: 1471, 1630, 1914, 4298, 4380.

J.Y. Shantz Mennonite Congregation, Waterloo Township: 3259.

Jackson Bros, Galt: 4237.

Jackson, Cochrane and Co., Berlin: 1856, 2259, 4298.

Jackson Hall, Elmira: 3030, 4225.

Jackson's Fox Ranch, Elmira: 4223.

Jackson's T.V., Radio Sales and Service, New Dundee: 4499.

Jacob Hespeler and Son, Hespeler: 908.

Jacob Hoffman's Saw Mill: 1640.

Jacob Ritz and Co., New Hamburg: 85, 1992.

Jaffray Bros, Galt: 1165.

Jaimet's Bookstore, Kitchener: 83, 1184.

James Crombie and Co., Galt: 1521, 1558, 2379.

James Warnock and Co., Galt: 908, 1426, 4246.

James Young Block, Galt: 332, 2417, 2487, 2488.

Jansen Optical Co., Elmira: 1454.

Jantzi's Cider Mill, Wellesley: 1953, 4472, 4484.

Janzen Realty Co., Kitchener: 3772.

Jardine Brothers, blacksmiths, Galt: 37, 4253.

Jay Bee's Cafeteria, Kingsdale: 2090.

Jerry's Auto Body Shop, St Agatha: 4499.

Jesuit Fathers of Upper Canada: 187, 635, 671, 672.

John A. Lang and Sons, Kitchener: 2014.

John Ballantine and Co., Ltd, Preston: 4395.

John Brubacher House, Waterloo: 3918.

John Forsyth Ltd, Berlin: 143, 929, 2008, 4299, 4349, 4350, 4374, 4380.

John Forsyth Ltd, Kitchener: 3739.

John Forsyth Ltd, Waterloo: 22, 1195, 1737, 1871.

John Hoffman Co., Berlin: 2025.

John Hoodless Furniture Warehouse,

Waterloo: 1530.

John Kostigian's Ochestra: 704.

John Mahood School, Elmira: 4217.

John Walter and Sons, Kitchener: 1692.

John Watson Manufacturing Co., Ayr: 37, 1693, 1695, 1696, 1787, 1860, 1923, 2021, 2260, 2261, 2262, 2441, 2589, 3745, 4173, 4176, 4181, 4185, 4187, 4212.

Johnston's Library, Galt: 2986.

Johnstone's Furniture, Conestogo: 4519.

Joint Stock Co., Preston: 4390.

Jones' Feed Mill, Linwood: 4470.

Joseph and Co., Kitchener: 2080, 4349, 4350.

Joseph E. Seagram and Sons: 10, 333, 908, 1855, 1857, 1994, 2001, 2037, 2263, 3892, 4136, 4298, 4402.

Joseph Hilborn Flour Mill, Blair: 4454.

Joseph Schneider Haus Gallery and Museum, Kitchener: 3, 143, 191, 290, 516, 1607, 1661, 2537, 2556, 2562, 2587, 2607, 3093, 3117, 3124, 3132, 3148, 3914, 3918, 3919, 3921, 3946, 4327.

Joseph Schneider Sawmill: 2025.

Josslin Insurance Co., New Hamburg: 2480.

Joy Manufacturing Co., Galt: 4232, 4261.

Jubilee Block, New Dundee: 2180, 4490.

Jubilee Women's Institute: 3842, 3848, 3852, 4436.

Jugenbund of Canada Synod: 3525.

Junior Farmers' Association of Ontario: 1191, 1216, 1758, 1765, 1769, 2807, 3765, 3770, 4198, 4199.

Jutzi Store, Wellesley: 2608.

K-Vet Laboratories Ltd, Hespeler: 4269.

K-W Drive-in, Bridgeport: 3182.

K-W Habilitation Services for the Retarded: 4033.

K-W Musical Productions: 326.

K-W Naval Association: 4093.

K-W Oktoberfest: 3, 143, 326, 671, 672, 3178, 3188, 3191, 3743, 4143.

K-W Pollution Probe: 2301.

K-W Social Planning Council: 143.

K-W Women's Club: 2959.

Kanadisch-Schwaebische Kranken-Unterstuetzungs-Vereinigung: 671, 672.

Karch Foundry, Hespeler: 4278, 4283.

Kasper's Kaserne, Berlin: 1915.

Katie Foundry, Galt: 2379.

Katzenmeier and Wing, New Hamburg: 4382.

Kaufman Footwear, Kitchener: 143, 616, 2026, 2600, 2635.

Kaufman Lumber Co., Berlin: 316, 326, 1459, 1460, 1703, 1787, 1845, 3821.

Kaufman Rubber Co., Berlin: 143, 316, 1459, 1462, 1463, 1853, 1855, 1856, 2264, 2265, 2266, 2267, 2268, 2403, 3821, 4370, 4371, 4374.

Kaufman Rubber Co., Kitchener: 326, 929, 1463, 1716, 1838, 1839, 1857, 1875, 1894, 1903, 1924, 1945, 2012, 2016, 2269, 2270, 4370.

Kavelman's Hall, New Dundee: 4490, 4495.

Kaybee Shoppe, Preston: 4396.

Kayson Rubber and Plastics Ltd, Preston: 1153.

Keffer's Tinsmithing, Plumbing and Heating Shop, New Dundee: 4499.

Kenebuc (Galt) Ltd: 4261.

Kennedy Motor Car Co.: 1845, 4398.

Kent Hotel, Waterloo: 1944, 2574, 4407.

Kerr Bros, Berlin: 4299.

Keystone Mennonite Youth Fellowship: 4522.

Kimmel Felt Co., Berlin: 1924.

King Edward Hotel, New Hamburg: 4382.

King Edward School, Berlin: 143, 1573, 1648, 2782, 2818, 4299, 4329, 4380.

King's Arms Hotel, Galt: 144, 332, 2975, 4212, 4248, 4249.

King Street Baptist Church, Berlin: 4380.

King Street Baptist Church, Kitchener: 157, 1494, 1560.

Kingdom Hall, Elmira: 4217.

Kingsdale Post Office: 2090.

Kingwood Reformed Mennonite Cemetery, Wellesley Township: 431.

Kingwood Reformed Mennonite Church, Wellesley Township: 3275.

Kinzie-Bean Pioneer Memorial Cemetery, Doon: 157, 372, 409, 759, 935, 2470, 2618, 3088, 3097, 4423, 4429, 4454.

Kirche Daheim: 3585, 3593.

Kirkwood Property, Preston: 2000.

Kiss Beverages Co., Kitchener: 1983.

Kissner Milling Co., Berlin: 1934, 4315, 4347.

Kitchener and Waterloo Building and Construction Trades Council: 3799.

Kitchener and Waterloo Medical Society: 1432.

Kitchener Area Monthly Meeting, Society of Friends (Quakers): 3714, 3716.

Kitchener Board of Education: 1445.

Kitchener Board of Health: 1383, 1385, 4065, 4075, 4311, 4320.

Kitchener Board of Park Management: 1182, 1273, 1602, 1605, 2333, 4311, 4380.

Kitchener Board of Trade: 143, 316, 1273, 1313, 1360, 1504, 1596, 1608, 1735, 1736, 1857, 1891, 2039, 3766, 4128, 4132, 4136, 4311, 4330, 4331, 4356, 4380.

Kitchener Board of Works: 4311.

Kitchener Boys' Band: 1725, 4380.

Kitchener Branch, Ontario Registered Music Teachers Association: 1725.

Kitchener Business and Professional Women's Club: 1344, 1346.

Kitchener Business Association: 2170.

Kitchener Business Development Department: 4362.

Kitchener Button Co.: 326, 1891, 2039, 2388.

Kitchener Carbonating Co.: 1983.

Kitchener Chamber of Commerce: 143, 316, 1546, 1602, 1605, 1907, 1928, 1935, 2026, 2498, 2681, 3762, 3766, 3784, 3793, 3794, 4032, 4126, 4136, 4143, 4148, 4314, 4333, 4334, 4335, 4354, 4380.

Kitchener Chapter, R.A.M.: 1251.

Kitchener Citadel Corps: 3713.

Kitchener Citizens' League: 684, 4139.

Kitchener City Council: 143, 287, 316, 1169, 1209, 1210, 1274, 1333, 1361, 1405, 1406, 1413, 1445, 1592, 1596, 1608, 1853, 1857, 1891, 1907, 1954, 2615, 2616, 2672, 3942, 3974, 3989, 4025,

Conference: 550, 1784, 3208, 3253, 3298, 3327, 3342, 3358, 3365, 3371, 3397, 3400.

Marshall Milling Co., Galt: 4246.

Marsland Engineering, Waterloo: 333, 1737, 2026.

Martin Feed Mills, Elmira: 1922, 4217, 4223, 4225.

Martin Luther Lutheran Church, Kitchener: 3616.

Martin Meeting House Cemetery, St Jacobs: 157, 356, 438, 852, 872, 2018, 3097.

Martin Meeting House, St Jacobs: 798, 799, 964, 1068, 1075, 1086, 1127, 1513, 2441, 2462, 2562, 2818, 3232, 3302, 3319, 3342, 3365, 3397, 3573, 4441, 4522.

Martin's Book Store, Elmira: 4217.

Martin-Weber Ltd, Elmira: 4217.

Martini Sand and Gravel, Preston: 2766.

Maryhill Cemetery: 4464.

Maryhill Hotel: 2441.

Massey Harris Co., Waterloo: 4469.

Master Feeds, Baden: 1501, 4499.

Master Milling Co., Berlin: 4380.

Material Processing Division, Preston: 1425.

Mathematical Association of Canada: 1382.

Mattel's Grand Central Hotel, Waterloo: 333.

Mattell and Bierwagen, Kitchener: 2748.

Maude Foundry, Berlin: 2039.

Max's Food Market, St Clements: 4474.

Mayfair Hotel, Kitchener: 1128.

McArthur Plumbing and Heating, Hespeler: 4279.

McBrine Luggage Co., Berlin: 1298, 1915, 4011.

McBrine Luggage Co., Kitchener: 616, 1361, 1737, 1871, 1891, 4374.

McCargar and Hachborn Ltd, Kitchener: 1737.

McEachren Heating and Ventilation Co., Galt: 4263.

McFatridge Steel Equipment, Galt: 4261.

McGarvin Trunk Co., Berlin: 326, 1298, 1856, 4380.

McGibbon, Harper and Haney: 4402.

McKay's Carding Mill, Galt: 4246.

McKee Brothers Ltd, Elmira: 4217, 4225.

McKellar Shoe Co., Berlin: 4374.

McLellan's Pharmacy, Kitchener: 2090.

McMurtry Hardware, Ayr: 3761.

McNally and Clemens, Blair: 1974.

McNaught's Service Station, Galt: 4233.

McNeil Auto Supply, Galt: 2478.

Mechanics' Institutes and Public Library Association: 2994.

Medical Society of Waterloo and Wellington: 3790.

Meeting Place, St Jacobs: 2165.

Meikleham's Pharmacy, Galt: 2143.

Meisel's Chopping Mill, Wilmot Township: 4499.

Melville Presbyterian Church, Galt: 157, 332, 3651, 3652, 3665, 3666, 4230, 4266.

Menno Singers, Kitchener: 3006, 4503.

Mennonite A Cappella Chorus: 3046.

Mennonite Aid Union: 551, 556, 1067, 1804, 3313.

Mennonite Archives of Ontario: 143, 150, 154, 157, 551.

Mennonite Benefit Association, Inc.: 3313.

Mennonite Bible School, Kitchener: 1180, 3395.

Mennonite Board of Colonization, Rosthern, Saskatchewan: 1628.

Mennonite Board of Missions and Charities: 3365.

Mennonite Brethren Church, Breslau: 3627.

Mennonite Brethren Church, Conestogo: 3608.

Mennonite Brethren Church, Hespeler: 616, 4285.

Mennonite Brethren Church, Kitchener: 1577, 3275.

Mennonite Brethren Church, New Dundee: 2535, 4485, 4495, 4499.

Mennonite Brethren in Christ: 263, 534, 555, 602, 811, 1261, 1637, 2878, 3143, 3256, 3275, 3285, 3315, 3328, 3331, 3355, 3373, 3377, 3381, 3382, 3383, 3783, 3864.

Mennonite Brethren in Christ Publishing Co.: 85, 3328.

Mennonite Central Committee: 515, 547, 549, 550, 551, 598, 602, 626, 1448, 1678, 3275, 3301, 3365, 3395, 3774, 3783, 3864.

Mennonite Conference of Eastern Canada: 551, 626.

Mennonite Conference of Ontario: 550, 551, 588, 3259, 3346, 3396.

Mennonite Conference of Ontario and Quebec: 626, 3358.

Mennonite Credit Union: 551, 1816.

Mennonite Economic Development Associates: 3301.

Mennonite Historical Society: 143, 150, 157, 551, 552, 598, 1238, 1346, 3864, 3918, 3947, 3952, 4503.

Mennonite Mission Board of Ontario: 3268.

Mennonite Society of Waterloo Township: 2809.

Mennonite Woman's Missionary Society: 3365.

Mennonitische Bruedergemeinde: 671, 672.

Mercantile Fire Insurance Co.: 37, 333, 1260, 1824, 1850, 4136, 4525.

Mercey Brothers: 4217.

Merchant's Rubber Co., Berlin: 316, 1459, 1580, 1581, 1853, 1855, 2023.

Merchant's Rubber Co., Kitchener: 326, 1186, 1838, 1903, 1924, 2012, 3739.

Merchants Bank, Ayr: 1720.

Merchants Bank, Berlin: 1168, 2053, 4374, 4380.

Merchants Bank, Galt: 37, 4179, 4237, 4246, 4251, 4255, 4263.

Merchants Button Co., Waterloo: 1914.

Merchants Casualty Co., Waterloo: 1684, 4412, 4422.

Merchants Printing Co., Kitchener: 1071.

Merlene's Beauty Salon, Elmira: 4217.

Merlin Machine Company Ltd, Kitchener: 4354.

Merner and Jansen Co., Elmira: 2001.

Merner Block, Berlin: 1530, 4298.

Merner-Bricker Foundries, Waterloo: 1531, 4525.

Merrick's China Hall, Berlin: 4374.

Messiah Lutheran Church, Waterloo: 3616.

Met-Craft Industries Ltd, Waterloo: 1703.

Metal Shingle and Siding Co., Preston: 1334, 1862, 2276, 2277, 2278, 4395.

Church: 4490, 4495.

New Dundee Co-operative Creamery Ltd: 1966, 2480, 3847, 4490, 4495, 4496, 4499, 4502.

New Dundee Community Centre: 4497, 4502.

New Dundee Community Park: 4490, 4495.

New Dundee Continuation School: 2535, 2770, 2782, 3955, 4495.

New Dundee Farmers' Institute: 4490, 4495.

New Dundee Fire Brigade: 4490, 4495, 4499.

New Dundee Fire Hall: 2535.

New Dundee Flour Mills: 1998, 4490, 4495, 4502.

New Dundee Glee Club: 4490.

New Dundee Harness Shop: 4495, 4496, 4499.

New Dundee High School: 4490, 4495.

New Dundee Library: 2992.

New Dundee Library Board: 2992.

New Dundee Literary and Debating Society: 4490.

New Dundee Lutheran Church: 157, 4490, 4495.

New Dundee Methodist Church: 4485, 4495.

New Dundee Mills: 3869.

New Dundee Musical Society Band: 4490, 4495.

New Dundee Old Boys' Reunion 1907: 4495.

New Dundee Optimist Club: 4502.

New Dundee Post Office: 4490, 4495, 4499.

New Dundee Public Library: 1238, 2971, 2977, 4490, 4495.

New Dundee Public Library Board: 1556, 2971, 4495.

New Dundee Rural Telephone Co.: 2077, 2081, 4490, 4495, 4499.

New Dundee Union Cemetery: 157, 414, 4490, 4495.

New Dundee Union Cemetery Board: 414, 2570.

New Dundee United Brethren Church: 157, 1191, 4490, 4495.

New Dundee United Missionary Church: 4490, 4495.

New Dundee Women's Institute: 1182, 3209, 3365, 3842, 3847, 3848, 3852, 4487, 4490, 4495, 4497, 4499, 4502.

New Hamburg Band: 4095.

New Hamburg Baptist Church: 4386, 4499.

New Hamburg Board of Trade: 328, 3727, 4095.

New Hamburg Brewery: 1861, 1983, 4386, 4499.

New Hamburg Brick and Tileyard: 4382.

New Hamburg Cenotaph: 4094, 4095.

New Hamburg Conservative Mennonite Church: 3276, 3277.

New Hamburg Evangelical Sunday School: 4385, 4386.

New Hamburg Fall Fair: 1674, 3855.

New Hamburg Fire Department: 2480, 3950, 4386.

New Hamburg Firehall: 2529.

New Hamburg Hydro Office: 2557, 4386.

New Hamburg Independent: 85, 105, 113, 119, 157, 1992, 2480, 4383, 4386, 4387, 4499, 4503.

New Hamburg Infantry Company: 4079, 4111, 4386.

New Hamburg Manufacturing Co.: 2021.

New Hamburg Memorial Community Centre: 3727.

New Hamburg Militia: 3894, 3895, 4382.

New Hamburg Musical Association: 4382.

New Hamburg Planing Mills: 1, 4386.

New Hamburg Planning Board: 328.

New Hamburg Police Department: 4016.

New Hamburg Poultry Association: 4382.

New Hamburg Public Library: 143, 2969, 2977, 4382, 4385, 4386.

New Hamburg Public Library Board: 4382.

New Hamburg Public School: 2767, 2782, 2824, 4382, 4386, 4387, 4388.

New Hamburg Public School Board: 217, 1530, 1533, 2767, 4382, 4487.

New Hamburg Public Utilities Commission: 328.

New Hamburg Railway Station: 4386, 4388.

New Hamburg Reformed Mennonite Cemetery: 415.

New Hamburg Skating Rink: 2767, 4386.

New Hamburg Stationary Store: 1992.

New Hamburg Steam Lager Brewery: 1983.

New Hamburg Town Council: 328, 3974, 3989, 4025, 4095, 4382, 4386.

New Hamburg Town Hall: 2529, 4383, 4499.

New Hamburg Village Council: 328, 1531, 1533, 1534, 3974, 4025, 4386, 4388.

New Hamburg Wagon Works: 1530, 1531, 1532, 4386.

New Hamburg Women's Institute: 1182, 2480, 2530, 3842, 3852, 4095, 4386, 4499.

New Hope Cemetery, Hespeler: 444.

New Hope Circuit: 3644.

New Hope Masonic Lodge, Hespeler: 1183, 1184, 4271, 4273, 4275, 4276.

New Hope Memorial Chapel, Hespeler: 4273, 4276.

New Massey Hall, Toronto: 3050.

New Royal Hotel, Galt: 1822, 4246, 4252.

Newborn Mennonite Cemetery, Woolwich Township: 416.

Newlands and Co., Galt: 332, 908, 1662, 1671, 1950, 1956, 1961, 2005, 2864, 4237, 4246, 4255, 4258, 4263.

Niagara District Court: 1324.

Niagara Power Movement: 4380, 4521, 4525.

Nichol, Wallace Displays Ltd, Galt: 4261.

Nicholson's Tavern, Blair: 4462.

Nith Valley Cheese Factory, Haysville: 1936, 4486.

Nith Valley Creamery, Haysville: 1936, 4486.

Nith Valley Mennonite Church Cemetery, Wilmot Township: 417.

Nith Valley Mennonite Church, Wilmot Township: 417, 530.

Nithvale Chair Factory: 875, 877.

Nithvale Flour and Oatmeal Mills, Ayr: 37, 1740, 4180.

Non-Resistant Relief Organization: 3399, 3783, 3864.

Nordhauser, C.G. and Co, button manufacturers, Berlin: 1165.

Norris and Lockhart, Galt: 4080.

North American Hotel, Preston: 814, 1850, 2153, 4237, 4255, 4390.

North American Hotel, St Clements:

Preston: 4395.

Smyth Bros, Berlin: 1403, 1650, 4380.

Snider Flour Milling Co., St Jacobs: 149, 294, 313, 1942, 2007, 2379, 2441, 4512, 4525, 4529.

Snider Lumber Co., Gravenhurst: 1657, 4525.

Snider Pioneer Memorial: 1089.

Snider's Bottling Co., Kitchener: 1983.

Snider's Mill, Waterloo: 13, 294, 1651, 1653, 1656, 1860, 1922, 1965, 4407, 4413, 4414, 4422.

Snyder Bros. Furniture, Elmira: 4217.

Snyder Desk Co., Waterloo: 1652, 4412.

Snyder Drug Store, Waterloo: 1184.

Snyder Furniture Warehouse, Elmira: 2534.

Snyder-Hahn Building, Waterloo: 2434.

Snyder Mennonite Church, Bloomingdale: 3259, 3275, 3316, 3328, 3355, 3367, 3391, 4449.

Snyder Roos and Co., Waterloo: 333, 1660.

Snyder Transport, Baden: 516, 4499.

Snyderdale Farms Ltd: 1773.

Snyders Ltd, Waterloo: 13, 1659, 1660.

Social Democratic Party: 4146.

Social Planning Council of Kitchener-Waterloo: 4027.

Society for German-American Studies: 632.

Society for the Propagation of the Gospel: 1248, 3469.

Society of Mennonites and Tunkers: 188, 3273.

Solar Mould Plastics Ltd, Preston: 1425.

Solarview Systems Inc., Elmira: 4225.

Soldiers' Insurance Commission of Waterloo County: 1558.

Soldiers' Memorial Home, Galt: 4082.

Soldiers' Monument, Ayr: 4180.

Soldiers' Settlement Board, Galt: 1866.

Solid Leather Show Co. Ltd, Preston: 4396.

Solomon Sauder Men's Wear, Kitchener: 2196.

Sons of England Benefit Society: 4082, 4246.

Sons of England Lodge: 1558, 4246.

Sons of Scotland: 4246.

South Peel Mennonite Cemetery: 369.

South Water Street Baptist Church, Galt: 3412.

South Waterloo Agricultural Society: 78, 143, 1185, 1216, 1217, 1218, 1302, 1365, 1510, 1549, 3825, 3841, 3847, 4212, 4251.

South Waterloo District Women's Institute: 3842, 3847, 3848.

South Waterloo/Edgar Insurance Brokers Ltd, Galt: 332.

South Waterloo Farmers' Institutes: 3770.

South Waterloo Junior Chamber of Commerce: 3766.

South Waterloo Liberal Association: 857, 1217, 1218.

South Waterloo Medical Society: 3790.

South Waterloo Memorial Hospital: 332, 553, 1184, 1334, 4059, 4261.

South Waterloo Naval Veterans: 3734.

South Waterloo Reform Association: 1619, 1620, 2536.

South Waterloo School for Retarded Children: 1185.

South Waterloo Society for the Prevention of Cruelty to Animals: 143.

South Waterloo Terminal Warehouse, Galt: 4261.

Southwood Secondary School, Galt: 2782, 3955.

Sovereign Bank of Canada, Berlin: 1.

Sovereign Bank of Canada, New Dundee: 4490, 4499.

Sovereign Bank of Canada, St Jacobs: 1, 4521.

Spae-Naur Inc., Kitchener: 2289.

Speedsville Mill: 809, 1165, 1294, 1975, 3082, 4285, 4451, 4452.

Spencer Dalton's Drug Store, Galt: 2425.

Spiers' Oatmeal Mill, Galt: 4246.

Sporting Chronicle: 4380.

Sportsman's Hall: 2172.

Spring Brewery, Waterloo: 1983.

Spring Creek Hotel: 2085.

Springstead Knitting Co., Galt: 1950.

Spruce Hedge Farms Ltd: 1773.

SS Waterman: 3707.

St Agatha Community Centre: 4499.

St Agatha Mennonite Cemetery: 476, 1046.

St Agatha Mennonite Church: 871,

924, 1046, 3176, 3259, 3275, 3334.

St Agatha Orphanage: 1329, 2480, 3428, 3429, 3432, 3440, 3441, 3444, 3455, 4030, 4499.

St Agatha Parish School: 2782, 4499.

St Agatha Roman Catholic Cemetery: 157, 1034, 3076, 3123, 3130, 3444.

St Agatha Roman Catholic Church: 143, 157, 671, 2944, 3076, 3104, 3428, 3440, 3441, 3444, 3949, 4499, 4504.

St Agnes Elementary School, Waterloo: 333, 2780, 2782.

St Agnes Roman Catholic Church, Waterloo: 2781, 3428.

St Aidan's Anglican Church, Elmira: 1647, 4217.

St Aloysius Roman Catholic Church, Kitchener: 3428.

St Ambrose's Roman Catholic Church, Galt: 698, 3428, 3433.

St Ambrose's Separate School, Galt: 3433.

St Andrew's Cemetery, Galt: 413.

St Andrew's Church of Scotland, Galt: 157, 3652, 4212, 4229.

St Andrew's Mission, Galt: 1505.

St Andrew's Presbyterian Church, Berlin: 143, 157, 1509, 1523, 1526, 1544, 1675, 3685, 4299, 4377, 4380.

St Andrew's Presbyterian Church, Galt: 8, 144, 157, 332, 1224, 1281, 1315, 1505, 3412, 3652, 3654, 3659, 3663, 3665, 3666, 3671, 3680, 3682, 3684, 3690, 3908, 4248, 4266.

St Andrew's Presbyterian Church Hall, Winterbourne: 2807.

St Andrew's Presbyterian Church, Hawkesville: 157, 4473, 4477, 4478.

St Andrew's Presbyterian Church, Hespeler: 157, 1183, 1184, 2425, 2477, 3664, 3675, 4278, 4280, 4282, 4285.

St Andrew's Presbyterian Church, Kitchener: 1266, 1286, 1289, 1508, 1525, 1645, 1725, 3631, 3632, 3656, 3685, 3691, 3693, 4011, 4084.

St Andrew's Presbyterian Church, Linwood: 4478.

St Andrew's Presbyterian Church, Winterbourne: 3669, 3683, 4526.

St Andrew's Presbyterian Women's Missionary Society, Kitchener:

Ultrametal Ltd, Elmira: 4225.

Uncle Tom's Cabin, Bridgeport: 2172, 2179, 2613, 4190, 4193, 4195, 4197.

Union Bank, Berlin: 4374, 4380.

Union Bank, Galt: 4255.

Union Bank, New Dundee: 4490, 4495, 4499.

Union Baseball Club, Galt: 4258.

Union Bus Line, Berlin: 2053.

Union Cemetery Association, New Dundee: 157, 3251.

Union Church, Hagey's Crossing: 3232.

Union Church, Hawkesville: 4477.

Union Church, Hespeler: 2760, 3232.

Union Church of Old Prussia: 1244, 3535.

Union Church, Wellesley: 3705.

Union Foundry, Waterloo: 37, 2001, 4412.

Union Gas: 168.

Union Hotel, Bridgeport: 4190, 4195, 4196, 4197.

Union Hotel, Elmira: 37, 2172, 3050, 4221, 4222.

Union Hotel, Galt: 3751.

Union Hotel, Hawkesville: 37.

Union Meeting House, Waterloo Township: 275, 3402.

Union Mills, Waterloo: 1, 29, 333, 829, 1640, 1850, 1851, 1922, 1940, 1941, 4412.

Union Presbyterian Church, Galt: 3651, 3652, 3665.

Union Star Cheese Factory, St Agatha: 1936.

Uniroyal Chemical, Elmira: 1647, 1920, 2022, 4217, 4225.

Uniroyal Goodrich Canada: 326, 2023, 2026, 4348, 4354, 4362.

United Brethren Church, Berlin: 157, 1264, 3631, 3632, 4377, 4380.

United Brethren Church, Bloomingdale: 3256, 3499.

United Brethren Church, Breslau: 2518, 3382, 4428.

United Brethren Church, Doon: 755.

United Brethren Church, Freeport: 2, 3492, 4450.

United Brethren Church, Hawkesville: 448, 3256, 4473, 4477.

United Brethren Church, Mannheim: 4499.

United Brethren Church, New Dundee: 3382, 4495, 4496, 4499.

United Brethren Church, Waterloo: 4422.

United Brethren Church, West Montrose: 157, 3256, 3485.

United Brethren in Christ: 1639.

United Church of Canada: 3505.

United Empire Bank of Canada, Galt: 4255.

United Farmers of Ontario: 3760, 3770, 4163.

United Lutheran Church Men: 3525.

United Male Singing Society of Berlin, Waterloo and Bridgeport: 671, 672, 4380.

United Mennonite Church, Waterloo: 590, 591, 604, 1455, 3266, 3275.

United Missionary Church: 2877, 2878, 3315, 3337, 3391, 3864, 4276.

United Packinghouse Workers of America: 1949.

United Presbyterian Church, Galt: 157, 376, 857, 3651, 3652, 3667, 3908, 4246, 4263.

United Presbyterian Church of North America: 3688, 3689.

United Rubber Workers of America: 143, 326, 1838, 1839, 1857, 1875, 1894, 1924, 2012, 4112.

United Steel Workers of America, Galt Branch: 1875, 1927.

Universal Lightning Rod Co., Hespeler: 1186, 4283, 4284, 4286.

University of Guelph: 2502.

University of Guelph Library: 155.

University of St Jerome's College: 2916.

University of Waterloo: 3, 11, 314, 326, 333, 516, 1435, 1436, 1449, 1737, 2026, 2393, 2394, 2415, 2456, 2464, 2509, 2510, 2526, 2598, 2601, 2656, 2781, 2782, 2868, 2869, 2870, 2871, 2881, 2882, 2883, 2885, 2886, 2887, 2891, 2892, 2893, 2894, 2895, 2897, 2900, 2904, 2905, 2906, 2911, 2912, 2913, 2915, 2916, 2917, 2918, 2920, 2922, 2923, 2926, 2927, 2929, 2931, 2970, 3043, 3053, 3137, 3537, 3948, 4135, 4416.

University of Waterloo Archives: 143, 157.

University of Waterloo Art Gallery: 2607, 3102.

University of Waterloo Library: 134, 135.

University of Waterloo Library, Doris Lewis Rare Book Room: 126, 127, 129, 130, 143.

University of Western Ontario: 2888, 2899, 2904, 2921, 3525.

Upper Canada Bible Society: 1252, 3627.

Urban Trustees Association: 2777.

Vacumax Ltd, Elmira: 4225.

Valentine and Martin Ltd, Waterloo: 1514, 1687, 1871.

Valentine Wahn's Foundry: 149.

Valhalla Inn, Kitchener: 4315, 4347, 4354.

Van Dresser, Waterloo: 333.

Varnicolour Paint and Chemical Co., Elmira: 4217, 4225.

Varnum Inn, Ebytown: 3100.

Veitchcroft Gallery: 1501.

Venetian Liquor Emporium, Galt: 4253.

Vesper Singers: 3898.

Veteran's Club House, Galt: 4233.

Vetter Shoes, Kitchener: 2014.

Vickerman Mill, Preston: 2425.

Victor Comptometer Ltd, Galt: 4261.

Victoria School, Berlin: 2747, 2782, 2818, 2843, 2851, 4365, 4370, 4380.

Victoria School, Galt: 2782, 2786, 4233, 4246, 4252, 4263, 4264.

Victoria School, Kitchener: 2391, 2699, 2747, 2782, 2789, 2851, 2852, 4107, 4370, 4380.

Victoria Wheel Works, Galt: 1619, 1620, 1722, 1740, 1851, 4230, 4237, 4246, 4253, 4263.

Victorian Order of Nurses: 3773.

Victorian Order of Nurses, Galt: 143, 3771.

Victorian Order of Nurses, Hespeler: 143, 4279, 4290.

Victorian Order of Nurses, Kitchener: 143, 4311, 4380.

Victorian Order of Nurses, Preston: 143, 1296, 1334, 1436.

Victorian Order of Nurses, Waterloo: 143, 1282.

Vince's Food Market, Elmira: 4217, 4225.

Vincent Farm Equipment, Galt: 4261.

Vogel and Wirching, Preston: 1983.

Vogt Hall, Elmira: 3030, 4225.

Voisin's Garage, St Clements: 4474.

Waterloo Historical Society: 5, 13, 27, 29, 83, 85, 132, 139, 143, 157, 212, 220, 249, 301, 355, 430, 539, 552, 559, 569, 671, 672, 1001, 1180, 1184, 1187, 1192, 1194, 1215, 1216, 1217, 1218, 1219, 1236, 1238, 1254, 1258, 1261, 1275, 1278, 1282, 1288, 1289, 1290, 1303, 1304, 1305, 1312, 1317, 1318, 1322, 1327, 1336, 1340, 1342, 1343, 1344, 1345, 1346, 1370, 1378, 1379, 1381, 1382, 1419, 1431, 1437, 1449, 1465, 1474, 1493, 1516, 1554, 1556, 1557, 1602, 1605, 1615, 1623, 1629, 1661, 1663, 1670, 1671, 1672, 1679, 1680, 1686, 1694, 1704, 1706, 1712, 1740, 1758, 1984, 2055, 2056, 2387, 2401, 2441, 2473, 2493, 2521, 2566, 2585, 2589, 2847, 2959, 2960, 2983, 2993, 3181, 3230, 3232, 3387, 3712, 3861, 3862, 3863, 3866, 3867, 3868, 3869, 3870, 3871, 3872, 3873, 3874, 3875, 3876, 3877, 3879, 3880, 3881, 3882, 3883, 3884, 3886, 3887, 3889, 3892, 3894, 3895, 3901, 3902, 3903, 3904, 3906, 3907, 3910, 3913, 3916, 3917, 3918, 3919, 3923, 3924, 3927, 3928, 3930, 3932, 3933, 3935, 3936, 3937, 3939, 3941, 3942, 3944, 3945, 3946, 3951, 3953, 3954, 3956, 3957, 3958, 3959, 3960, 3961, 3962, 3963, 3964, 3965, 3966, 3967, 3968, 4080, 4136, 4212, 4356, 4380, 4384.

Waterloo Hook and Ladder Co.: 2560, 4412.

Waterloo Horticultural Society: 3767, 3788, 3851, 3853, 4078, 4412, 4414.

Waterloo Hotel: 2451, 3892, 4412.

Waterloo House, Galt: 4253.

Waterloo Infantry Company: 4079, 4111.

Waterloo IODE, St Quentin Chapter: 333, 1191, 3773, 4082, 4412, 4422.

Waterloo Junction Railway: 1654, 2001, 2054, 2069, 2070, 4412, 4517, 4525.

Waterloo-Kitchener United Mennonite Church: 929, 1456, 3291, 3292, 3304.

Waterloo LACAC: 143, 157, 1288, 2389, 2433, 2434, 2460, 2461, 2462, 2463, 2565.

Waterloo Land Stewardship Committee: 1216.

Waterloo Lawn Bowling Club: 3738.

Waterloo Liedertafel: 671, 672, 3016,3054, 4412, 4414, 4422.

Waterloo Lions Club: 3892.

Waterloo Lions Memorial Pool, Waterloo Park: 4078.

Waterloo Lutheran Seminary: 3, 333, 671, 672, 2615, 2616, 2881, 2888, 2889, 2904, 2909, 2921, 2924, 2925, 3513, 3515, 3521, 3525, 3529, 3532, 3558, 3564, 3613, 3616, 4356, 4412.

Waterloo Lutheran Seminary Auxiliary: 3525.

Waterloo Lutheran Seminary, Faculty of Arts: 2904.

Waterloo Lutheran University: 197, 225, 333, 516, 1185, 1193, 1423, 1737, 2781, 2782, 2866, 2867, 2868, 2873, 2875, 2876, 2881, 2888, 2889, 2890, 2896, 2897, 2898, 2902, 2911, 2914, 2919, 2921, 2928, 2930, 2990, 3038, 3401, 3525, 3535, 4014, 4161, 4412.

Waterloo Lutheran University, Clara Conrad Hall: 2904.

Waterloo Maennerchor: 333.

Waterloo Malting Co.: 1861.

Waterloo Manufacturing Co.: 1, 13, 29, 333, 671, 672, 1307, 1530, 1531, 1574, 1651, 1653, 1654, 1657, 1660, 1703, 1737, 1787, 1855, 1857, 1859, 1871, 1891, 2001, 2021, 2292, 2293, 2294, 2451, 2552, 3951, 4402, 4412, 4413, 4422, 4517, 4525.

Waterloo Mechanics' Institute: 2782, 3002, 3780, 4412, 4422.

Waterloo Memorial Arena: 2581, 3722, 3736, 3755, 4414.

Waterloo Mennonite Brethren Church: 3252, 3317.

Waterloo Mennonite Church: 626, 3316, 3365.

Waterloo Metal Stamping Co.: 2166, 3036, 4370.

Waterloo Methodist Church: 1, 4082.

Waterloo Microsystems Inc., Waterloo: 2869.

Waterloo Municipal Telephone Co.: 2077.

Waterloo Music Company: 983, 1737, 2166, 2189, 3013, 3014, 3035, 3036, 3043, 3054, 4412.

Waterloo Musical Society: 3, 333, 981, 1321, 1587, 1704, 3016, 3036, 3045, 3052, 3767, 4078, 4356, 4407, 4412, 4422.

Waterloo Musical Society Band: 1, 10, 13, 671, 672, 1682, 3016, 3034, 3035, 3036, 3039, 3040, 3042, 3043, 3044, 3045, 3053, 3054, 3754, 4109, 4414.

Waterloo Mutual Fire Insurance Co.: 13, 22, 29, 143, 671, 672, 1168, 1262, 1384, 1500, 1501, 1535, 1643, 1651, 1660, 1666, 1668, 1699, 1706, 1824, 1830, 1850, 1851, 2055, 3892, 4011, 4136, 4318, 4402, 4412, 4414, 4521.

Waterloo North Land Registry Office: 143, 157, 256, 4010, 4013.

Waterloo-Oxford District High School: 2731, 2824, 4387, 4490, 4499, 4503.

Waterloo Plains Farmers' Club: 3847.

Waterloo Police Force: 4014.

Waterloo Post Office: 1918, 2095, 2818, 3874, 4356, 4411, 4412.

Waterloo Public Library: 1, 13, 143, 157, 2204, 2434, 2604, 2969, 2976, 2991, 3001, 3002, 3003, 3004, 4082, 4422.

Waterloo Public Library Board: 1672, 3001, 3003, 3004.

Waterloo Public School: 1282, 1451, 1621, 1659, 1918, 2546, 2782, 2885, 4299, 4407, 4412, 4414, 4415.

Waterloo Public School Board: 1542, 1668, 1684, 1730, 2780.

Waterloo Public Utilities Commission: 1181, 1957, 4023, 4407, 4412.

Waterloo Railway Station: 2451.

Waterloo Reform Association: 1693, 1696.

Waterloo Reformers' Gazette: 105, 120.

Waterloo Regiment, Kitchener: 4084.

Waterloo Region Lung Association: 1448.

Waterloo Region Roman Catholic Separate School Board: 143, 2815.

Waterloo Regional Credit Union: 333.

Waterloo Regional Development Council: 1732.

Waterloo Regional Health Unit: 143.

Waterloo Regional Heritage Foundation: 1318, 2389, 2500, 2566, 2570, 2588, 3914, 3918,

3919, 3920, 3921, 3946, 4362.

Waterloo Regional Library: 143, 2988.

Waterloo Regional Municipal Council: 4001.

Waterloo Regional Police Force: 143, 4014.

Waterloo Regional Project: 132, 3961.

Waterloo Regional Review Commission: 4156.

Waterloo Reunion, 1895: 4078.

Waterloo Saugeen Railway: 2128.

Waterloo Sentinel: 85, 105, 124.

Waterloo Separate School: 1, 13, 2782.

Waterloo Separate School Board: 1186, 1221, 1545, 2780.

Waterloo Shirt Co.: 13.

Waterloo Shoddy Mills: 1220.

Waterloo Siskins: 333, 3722.

Waterloo South District Women's Institute: 3852.

Waterloo South Land Registry Office: 143, 157.

Waterloo-South Wellington Area Planning and Development Technical Co-ordinating Committee: 3997.

Waterloo Spinning Mills: 2026.

Waterloo Spring Co.: 13, 1307.

Waterloo Square: 2001.

Waterloo Stockyards: 2123, 2205.

Waterloo Taxi: 2562.

Waterloo Tennis Club: 3722, 3733, 4078, 4412.

Waterloo Tigers: 333, 3722.

Waterloo Town Council: 316, 333, 1167, 1221, 1222, 1330, 1428, 1439, 1447, 1543, 1660, 1666, 1672, 1699, 1855, 1857, 2615, 2616, 3974, 4023, 4025, 4109, 4124, 4161, 4412, 4421.

Waterloo Town Hall: 1, 13, 333, 1918, 2490, 4017, 4298, 4356, 4407, 4411, 4412.

Waterloo Town Planning Commission: 1542, 2673.

Waterloo Township Council: 326, 493, 1178, 1747, 2172, 2495, 3974, 3989, 4427, 4457, 4459, 4460.

Waterloo Township Hall: 1389, 2453, 2495, 3563, 3631, 3927, 4461.

Waterloo Township Plowmen's Association: 3847, 3848.

Waterloo Township Board of Health: 4459.

Waterloo Township Roads and Bridges Committee: 2114.

Waterloo Township, S.S.#1, Blair: 2780, 2817, 2818, 2827, 3408, 4435, 4454, 4456.

Waterloo Township, S.S.#2, Strasburg: 2590, 2817, 4264, 4433.

Waterloo Township, S.S.#3, Plains: 2817, 4433.

Waterloo Township, S.S.#4, O'Loane's: 2818, 4429.

Waterloo Township, S.S.#4, Pine Grove: 956, 2813, 2817.

Waterloo Township, S.S.#5, Berlin: 2818, 2843, 4380.

Waterloo Township, S.S.#5, Centreville: 2782, 2817, 2818, 4426, 4429.

Waterloo Township, S.S.#6, Natchez: 2817.

Waterloo Township, S.S.#7, Williamsburg: 840, 2817, 4433.

Waterloo Township, S.S.#8, Elmdale (Snider's Road): 2715, 2817, 2828, 2829, 4430.

Waterloo Township, S.S.#9, Rummelhardt: 2801, 2817.

Waterloo Township, S.S.#10, Erbsville: 2745, 2782, 2817, 2847.

Waterloo Township, S.S.#11, Bridgeport: 1448, 2782, 2817, 4192, 4193, 4194, 4195, 4197.

Waterloo Township, S.S.#12, Bloomingdale: 813, 1611, 2782, 2817, 3741, 4190, 4449.

Waterloo Township, S.S.#13, New Germany: 3428, 3451, 3467, 4443, 4464, 4465.

Waterloo Township, S.S.#14, Shantz Station: 2817, 4434.

Waterloo Township, S.S.#15, Riverbank: 2728, 2736, 2782, 2817, 2825, 2995, 2999, 3365.

Waterloo Township, S.S.#16, Kossuth: 2817, 4436.

Waterloo Township, S.S.#17, Vance: 1755, 2817, 4436.

Waterloo Township, S.S.#18, Lexington: 2771, 2817, 4441.

Waterloo Township, S.S.#19, Clearview: 593, 2725, 2736, 2760, 2761, 2762, 2764, 2817.

Waterloo Township, S.S.#19, Pine Bush: 593, 2717, 2736, 2763, 2765, 3904.

Waterloo Township, S.S.#19, Union Church School: 2762, 2766.

Waterloo Township, S.S.#20, Maple Grove: 803, 2103, 2711, 2774, 2775, 2806, 2817, 2825, 3770.

Waterloo Township, S.S.#22, English Settlement: 2817.

Waterloo Township, S.S.#23, Nine Pines: 2817.

Waterloo Township, S.S.#24, Breslau: 1726, 2782, 2817, 4428.

Waterloo Township, S.S.#25, Bearinger's: 1448, 2817.

Waterloo Township, S.S.#27, Doon: 2700, 2717, 2817, 3056, 4423, 4429, 4454.

Waterloo Township, S.S.#29, Mackenzie King: 2772.

Waterloo Township, U.S.S.#28, Victoria: 2817, 4449.

Waterloo Trust and Savings Co.: 10, 143, 326, 333, 762, 1181, 1257, 1438, 1439, 1522, 1546, 1645, 1796, 1815, 1827, 1828, 1831, 1832, 1857, 2522, 3816, 4370, 4380, 4396, 4407, 4412, 4422.

Waterloo Turnverein: 671, 672, 1295, 3029, 4412.

Waterloo University College: 3525.

Waterloo Urban Renewal Committee: 2625.

Waterloo Village Council: 316, 1666, 3053, 3974, 4025, 4412, 4421.

Waterloo Water and Light Commission: 1221, 1309, 1439, 1835, 1970, 3040, 4023.

Waterloo Waterworks Co.: 4023, 4078, 4412, 4422.

Waterloo-Wellington Airport: 2042, 2133, 3818, 4261, 4396.

Waterloo, Wellington and Georgian Bay Railway Co.: 1270.

Waterloo, Wellington and Lake Huron Railway: 2054.

Waterloo-Wellington County Amputation Society: 4136.

Waterloo Wellington Flying Club: 3818.

Waterloo Wood Products: 1937.

Waterloo Woollen Manufacturing Co.: 1082, 1543, 4412.

Waterloo/Woolwich Townships, Union S.S.#21, Martin's: 1448, 2782, 2827.

Waterloo Young Men's Club: 1187, 1502, 4412.

Waterlot Restaurant, New Hamburg: 2480, 4384, 4388.

Watson and Malcolm, Galt: 4237.

Watson Woolen Mill, Doon: 2385.

Wean-McKay of Canada Ltd, Galt: 4261.

Weaver's Hotel, Berlin: 2055, 4380.

Weber and Erb, Elmira: 1710.

Weber Building, Kitchener: 4036.

Weber Carriage Works, New Dundee: 4490, 4495.

Weber Concrete Tile Ltd, Breslau: 1162.

Weber Hardware Co., Kitchener: 2295, 4315, 4347, 4380.

Weber Mennonite Cemetery, Kitchener: 491.

Weber Mennonite Church, Strasburg: 1119, 3275, 3316, 3384.

Weber's Building Supplies, New Dundee: 4495, 4499.

Weber's Grocery Store, Elmira: 4217.

Weber Street Mennonite Church, Kitchener: 626, 3259.

Weichel Hardware, Elmira: 1700.

Weichel Hardware, Waterloo: 4136.

Weichel Home Hardware, Elmira: 2410.

Wellesley Agricultural Grounds: 4466.

Wellesley Agricultural Works: 1740, 4466.

Wellesley Amish Mennonite Cemetery: 492.

Wellesley Amish Mennonite Congregation: 990, 1118, 3275.

Wellesley and District Agricultural Society: 1936.

Wellesley and North Easthope Agricultural Society: 1574, 2512, 3825, 4478.

Wellesley Apple Butter and Cheese Festival: 4479.

Wellesley Bank: 951.

Wellesley Baptist Church: 3413.

Wellesley Beachy Amish Congregation: 577.

Wellesley Cheese and Butter Company: 1936.

Wellesley Cheese Company: 2015.

Wellesley Community Hall: 4466, 4484.

Wellesley Emporium of Fashion: 2440.

Wellesley Farm Products Ltd (division of J.M. Schneider Ltd): 1936.

Wellesley Hotel: 2440, 4466, 4478.

Wellesley-Kitchener Coach Lines: 2080.

Wellesley LACAC: 143, 157, 1844, 2389, 2440, 2512, 4479.

Wellesley Maple Leaf: 85, 125, 157, 3895, 4478, 4484.

Wellesley Mennonite Congregation: 3259, 3342.

Wellesley Mill: 4472.

Wellesley Mill End Store: 951.

Wellesley Municipal Telephone Co.: 2077, 2081, 2136.

Wellesley Orphanage: 4478.

Wellesley Police Village: 3974.

Wellesley Post Office: 2095, 2515, 3898, 3926, 4478.

Wellesley Shirt Factory: 951.

Wellesley Swedenborgian Church: 2440, 2441, 4466, 4478, 4484.

Wellesley Town Band: 2480, 4478.

Wellesley Township Council: 143, 1178, 2495, 2566, 3974, 3989, 4473, 4478, 4482.

Wellesley Township Hall, Crosshill: 2425, 2441, 2495, 2566, 2589, 3918, 4470, 4478, 4484.

Wellesley Township Historical Society: 143, 157, 1422, 1936, 2480.

Wellesley Township Separate School Board: 2769.

Wellesley Township Board of Health: 4040.

Wellesley Township, S.S.#1, Moser's: 2814, 2817, 4040, 4478.

Wellesley Township, S.S.#3, Ninth/Eighteenth Line (Miller's): 2814, 2817, 4478.

Wellesley Township, S.S.#4, Linwood: 2814, 2817, 4470, 4478.

Wellesley Township, S.S.#5, Gless': 4478.

Wellesley Township, S.S.#6, Fifth Line West Section (Kelly's): 2814, 2817, 4478.

Wellesley Township, S.S.#7, Kingwood (Jausi's): 2814, 2817, 4478.

Wellesley Township, S.S.#8, Freeborn: 2814, 2817, 4478.

Wellesley Township, S.S.#9: 4040.

Wellesley Township, S.S.#10, Bamberg: 1033, 2814, 2817.

Wellesley Township, S.S.#11, Heidelberg: 2437, 2814, 2817, 4478.

Wellesley Township, S.S.#13, Hawkesville: 2814, 2817, 4470, 4473, 4478.

Wellesley Township, S.S.#14, Bricker's/Union: 2814, 2817, 4478.

Wellesley Township, S.S.#15, Beechvale: 2814, 2817, 4470, 4478.

Wellesley Township, S.S.#16, Wellesley: 1422, 2814, 2817, 4478, 4479.

Wellesley Township, S.S.#17, Crosshill: 2814, 2817, 4470, 4478.

Wellesley Township, S.S.#18, Red Hill: 2814, 2817, 4470, 4478.

Wellesley Township, S.S.#19, Seventh Line: 2814, 2817, 4478.

Wellesley Township, S.S.#2, Macton: 2814, 2817.

Wellesley Township, S.S.#21, Maple Grove (Hackett's): 2814, 4478.

Wellesley Township, S.S.#21, Thirteenth Line: 2817.

Wellesley Township, S.S.S.#11, St Clements: 2769, 2814, 2815, 2832, 3464, 4474.

Wellesley Township, S.S.S.#12, Macton: 2769, 2814, 2815, 4478.

Wellesley Township, S.S.S.#4, Linwood: 2814, 2815, 4470.

Wellesley Township, S.S.S.#5, Ninth Line: 2769, 2814, 2815, 3464, 4478.

Wellesley Township, S.S.S.#9, Bamberg: 2814, 2815, 3464.

Wellesley Trap-shooting Club: 4472, 4478.

Wellesley United Church: 3705, 4466, 4484.

Wellesley Village Council: 3974, 3989, 4025, 4478.

Wellesley Western Ontario Mennonite Congregation: 577.

Wellesley Women's Institute: 3789, 4484.

Wellington County Museum and Archives: 143, 157, 1943.

Wellington District Agricultural Society: 1803.

Wellington Field Naturalists' Club: 2326, 2327, 2328, 2329, 2330, 2331.

Wellington, Grey, and Bruce Railway: 4266.

Wellington Hotel, Ayr: 4198.

Wellington Institute, Berlin: 2782, 2818, 4380.

Werlich Co., Preston: 1862, 1926, 2000, 4395, 4396.

Weseloh-Goudie Ltd, Berlin: 878, 1184, 1403.

Wesley United Church, Elmira: 157, 1184, 3628.

Armstrong, Beverly: 2775.

Armstrong, David: 3665.

Armstrong, David, Mrs: 3665.

Armstrong Family: 4473.

Armstrong, Hugh: 2775.

Armstrong, James: 4079, 4255, 4506.

Armstrong, John, Rev.: 4124, 4380.

Armstrong, R.A., Rev.: 3472.

Armstrong, Rita: 1764, 2392.

Armstrong, Ross: 2774, 2775, 4452.

Armstrong, Thomas: 2775, 4014, 4266, 4380.

Armstrong, William: 3644.

Arndt, Rev.: 3620.

Arnetz, Jantz: 2440.

Arnold, A.J.: 1758.

Arnold, Allan: 4230, 4233.

Arnold, E.M.: 29, 4223.

Arnold, F.: 4278.

Arnold Family: 724.

Arnold, Florence: 4226.

Arnold, Frederick, Rev.: 3465.

Arnold, G.: 1861, 1983.

Arnold, Jacob: 3574.

Arnold, Jerome L., Rev.: 3428, 3447.

Arnold, John: 724.

Arnold, John, Rev.: 3442, 3450.

Arnold, Lawrence: 1.

Arnold, Mariah Barnes (Mrs John): 724.

Arnold, Steven: 119.

Arnold, Vincent, Mrs: 1169.

Arnott, Alexander D.: 1983.

Arnott, Frederick S.: 1895.

Arnott, W.J., Dr: 2822, 3790, 4298, 4380.

Arntfield, Thomas: 1, 85, 115, 4275, 4286.

Arruda, Manuel: 697, 698.

Arruda, Messias: 697.

Arsenault, Lawrence: 4278.

Arthaud, Emile: 725.

Arthaud Family: 725.

Arthaud, Susanna Ebersol (Mrs Emile): 725.

Arthur, Eric: 2507.

Arthur, Hugh: 3636.

Arthur, Robert, Mrs: 3636.

Ashton, Dorothea, "Sweezy": 3109.

Ashton, James: 3709.

Ashton, Ralph: 1836, 2997, 3109, 3936.

Ashton, Rev.: 3623.

Ashton, William: 2, 2502, 2506, 4253, 4435.

Asmus, William: 1974, 2767, 4388, 4488, 4499.

Asmussen, C.: 2496.

Asmussen, Lavern: 2591, 3923.

Asmussen, Nicholas: 326, 671, 672, 1196, 1201, 1205, 1210, 1483, 4117, 4121, 4136, 4355, 4374, 4380.

Asmussen, Venona: 2748.

Aspenleiter, John: 2424.

Aspie, Thomas: 690.

Aspinleiter, George: 4393.

Astor, John Jacob: 1975.

Atkinson, Albert: 4099.

Atkinson, G.D.: 1725.

Atkinson, Harry: 4058.

Atkinson, J.: 1977, 2379.

Atkinson, James: 3799.

Atkinson, John: 4015.

Atkinson, Joseph: 4014.

Atkinson, M.W.: 3499.

Atkinson, Miss: 1515.

Atkinson, Robert, Rev.: 4380.

Attridge, E.D.: 2811.

Atwood, Samuel: 2379.

Atwood, Walter: 4099.

Augsberger Family: 716.

Augustine, Albert W.: 1211.

Augustine, Caroline Margaret Barbara Breithaupt (Mrs Albert B.): 127,1169, 1211, 1273, 4067.

Augustine, Edna Kaufman (Mrs Albert W.): 1211, 1458, 1461, 3773, 3821.

Augustine, L., Miss: 2714.

Augustine, Sister M.: 2832.

Aulee, James: 4079.

Auman, George: 1795, 4222, 4513, 4521, 4524, 4530.

Auman, Nicholas: 4521.

Auman, Will: 4513, 4525.

Aussam, Henry: 690.

Austermuehl, Edward, Rev.: 3416.

Austin, E.E., Rev.: 3715.

Austin, Myrtle: 2748, 2798.

Austin, Samuel: 879, 1400, 1896.

Austin, William: 1866.

Aver, T. Marshall: 1187, 3687.

Aves Family: 4429.

Avinton, Timothy: 4079.

Awenhokwi: 187.

Awerbuck, Nahum: 3718.

Axford, Herbert, Dr: 2904, 3525.

Axt, Andrew: 3276, 3277.

Axt, Catherine Shantz: 1066.

Axt, Dorothy: 3410.

Axt Family: 822.

Ayres, Annie Wilfong (Mrs George): 4454.

Ayres, George: 1973.

Ayres, Henry W.: 727.

Ayres, Margaret: 727.

Ayres, S.H., Miss: 2748, 2818.

Baas Family: 636.

Babbick, A.G.: 333.

Babbs, George: 4102.

Babcock Family: 2085.

Babey, Stephan: 3466.

Bacchus, George, Rev.: 3492.

Bacchus, Wesley, Rev.: 3492.

Bach, Henry: 2144, 4362.

Bachert, Alice: 3365, 3390.

Bachert, Elvina Baer (Mrs William): 731.

Bachert Family: 4499.

Bachert, Gideon: 852.

Bachert, Magdalena Eby (Mrs Gideon): 852.

Bachert, Nellie: 3365.

Bachert, William: 731, 2760.

Bachman, Catharine: 804.

Bachman Family: 716.

Bachman, George: 804.

Bachman, Henry: 4371.

Bachman, Maria: 804.

Bachmann, Heinrich: 1636, 2095.

Bachus, Rev.: 3485.

Backus, C.W., Rev.: 3263.

Backus, Charles: 2179.

Backus, George: 3499.

Backus, J.B., Rev.: 3499.

Badcock, Gerald: 2116.

Bader, A.: 671, 672, 3527.

Badke, Julius, Rev.: 3525, 3608, 3620.

Baechler, Annie Bender: 3099.

Baechler, Christian: 3099.

Baechler, Earl: 2145.

Baechler, Elmer: 1936, 3923.

Baechler, Fred: 4474.

Baechler, Glenn: 3927.

Baechler, Magdalena Schrag: 1056.

Baechler, W.A.: 13, 3793, 3923, 3927.

Baedecker, Henry: 2818, 2843, 4371, 4380.

Baeder, Jacob: 1880.

Baer, Aaron: 2775.

Baer, Adeline Schmitt (Mrs Moses): 731.

Baer, Anna Pannabecher (Mrs John): 729, 730, 2760, 3402.

Baer, Benjamin: 4423.

Baer, Catherine Gingerich: 275, 555, 729, 730, 2760, 3402, 4452.

Baer, David: 729.

Bingeman, Jonas: 1773, 4448, 4449.

Bingeman, Joseph: 516, 2728, 2801, 3315, 3328, 3391, 4380.

Bingeman, Joseph E.: 4298.

Bingeman, Judith Snider (Mrs John): 761.

Bingeman, Marsahll O.: 4448.

Bingeman, Sylvia: 2714.

Bingham, Annie: 1484.

Bingham, G.W., Dr: 1165.

Bingham, Harry: 2714.

Bingham, Henry P.: 1195.

Bingham, S.H.K.: 4080.

Bingham, Sheldon: 2714.

Binning, G.: 4422.

Birchall, G.: 4080.

Bird, Adam: 1064.

Bird, Edward: 4080, 4102.

Bird, Ellen: 3713.

Bird, George: 4176.

Bird, Katharine Schwind (Mrs Adam): 1064.

Bird, Michael: 3148.

Bird, Samuel: 4221.

Birkin, E.H.: 4275.

Birky Family: 750.

Birley, C.: 4080.

Birmingham, Edward: 3175.

Birmingham, George: 3175.

Birnstihl, Adam: 1186, 3057, 3148, 4192, 4195.

Birnstihl, Emil: 3721.

Birnstihl, Emilea: 1186, 3148.

Birnstihl, Norma: 2179.

Birr, Frances: 4474.

Birsch, August: 4458.

Birss, J.H.: 2073.

Bisang, Plausius: 1983.

Bisch, Alfred: 3031.

Bisch, Carl: 4226.

Bisch, Carol: 4225.

Bisch, John: 1165, 1974, 2815.

Bish, A.E.: 4422.

Bish, E.N.: 4422.

Bish, Godfrey: 4102, 4422.

Bish, J.W.: 4422.

Bishop, E.F., Rev.: 3472.

Bishop Family: 2085, 4433, 4436.

Bishop, Mary: 2486.

Bishop, W.: 3709, 4499.

"Bismark", inmate of the Waterloo County Home c1900: 4034.

Bissett, J.M.: 4104.

Bissey, L., Rev.: 3433.

Bissinger, Andrew: 3442.

Bissinger, Andrew, Mrs: 3442.

Bissonette, T.H., Jr: 2720.

Bitsche, Ignatz: 1968.

Bitschy Family: 276, 477, 4443.

Bitschy, Philip J.: 4448.

Bitschy, Valentine: 4448.

Bittman, F.: 3808, 4392.

Bittman, John: 4250.

Bittman, Miss: 3029.

Bittmena, Frederick: 4393.

Bittorf, John, Jr: 4225.

Bittorf, John, Sr: 4225.

Bitzer, A.L.: 326, 671, 672, 1264, 1535, 2899.

Bitzer, Armin M.: 1191.

Bitzer, Conrad: 671, 672, 1168, 1201, 1264, 1535, 2179, 2706, 2714, 2756, 2818, 3545, 3815, 4067, 4114, 4195, 4376, 4380.

Bitzer, Dorothea: 2179, 4195, 4315.

Bitzer, Gottlieb: 1861, 1983, 2179, 4193, 4195, 4196, 4315.

Bitzer, Irmgard C.: 1497, 2983.

Bitzer, Wilfrid: 671, 672, 2179, 3815, 3923, 4315, 4350.

Black Family: 4188.

Black, J.: 4278.

Black, J.R.: 2811.

Black, James: 4079.

Black, John: 3668.

Black, John L.: 3668.

Black, John, Mrs: 3668.

Black, Malcolm, Dr: 1205.

Black, Mr: 4521.

Black, Theo: 4079.

Black, William: 4398.

Blackburn, F.: 4104.

Blackburn, William H.: 2714.

Blackford, John: 4506.

Blacklock, Thomas: 3751, 4266.

Blackstock, G.A.: 115.

Blackwell, John, Mrs: 2775.

Blackwood, Robert: 2818, 4392, 4422.

Blain, James: 1963, 2379, 4266.

Blain, Margaret Gillesby (Mrs Richard): 1245.

Blain, Richard: 1165, 1245, 1860, 1976, 2128, 3481, 4202, 4246, 4263, 4266.

Blair, Adam J.F.: 4437.

Blair, Charles: 1281.

Blair, F.: 4233.

Blair, H.A.: 4226.

Blair, Harold: 3030.

Blake, Charles: 3732, 3816.

Blake, Delbert: 3255.

Blake, Edward: 1722.

Blake, James: 302, 4079.

Blake, John R.: 1205, 3959, 4031, 4233, 4246.

Blaney, John: 3709, 3713.

Blank Family: 725, 950.

Blaschke, W.A.: 3660, 3681, 4454.

Blast, John: 4040.

Blatchford, John S.: 1165, 3474.

Blatchford, Mr: 3623, 4505.

Blatz, August: 1186, 2554, 2988, 2989, 4221, 4525.

Blatz, Caroline Klinck: 1186.

Blazenko, M., Rev.: 3466.

Bleam, Christian: 4388.

Bleam, Elizabeth: 1246.

Bleam Family: 4499.

Bleam, Jacob: 23.

Bleam, John: 4384.

Bleam, Jonathon: 4195.

Bleam, Philip: 256, 1128, 1976, 2096, 2097, 2135, 2379.

Bleck, Henry: 3549.

Bleich, James: 4100.

Bliehm, Esther Cressman: 4453.

Bliehm Family: 713, 719, 720, 4453, 4454.

Bliehm, Jacob: 1246, 4453.

Bliehm, Moses: 2379.

Bliehm, Philip: 308, 514, 671, 713, 720, 1246, 1882, 1977, 4453.

Blinkhorn, George: 3044.

Block Family: 713, 719, 720.

Block, Irvon: 956.

Block, Lydia Litwiller (Mrs Irvon): 956.

Block, Sam: 2385, 4454.

Blood, Granville, Sergeant-Major: 326, 4121.

Bloomfield, Frederick: 2775, 4279.

Bloomfield, George W.F.: 2120.

Bloquelle, Louis: 85.

Blow, Charles: 4217, 4225.

Blum, Carl: 3050, 4481.

Blum, Charles: 4395.

Blum, Jacob: 3782, 4478.

Blum, Mr: 4480, 4483.

Blum, Rose Roos (Mrs Charles): 983.

Blum, Wilfred: 3764, 3819, 3854.

Blundell, Douglas, Rev.: 3496.

Blundell Family: 711.

Blundell, John: 4103.

Boal, Robert: 3485.

Boatman, Leonard: 4099.

Bock, A.R.: 2120.

Bock, Althea: 2798.

Bock, Benjamin: 4499.

Bock, Cameron: 8, 2971, 4499, 4500.

Bock, Catharine Shupe: 1083, 3061, 3080.

Braithwaite, Gordon: 2179, 3620, 4192.

Brake Family: 769.

Bramm, Elizabeth Wenzel: 1934.

Bramm, George: 1934, 4315.

Bramm, Henry: 4362.

Bramm, Jack: 1934.

Bramm, John: 326, 1934, 2025, 4195, 4315, 4380.

Brand, Abraham: 4517.

Brand, D.H., Rev.: 3495.

Brand, Michael: 2704.

Brandon, Mr: 4080.

Brandt, A.: 4217.

Brandt, Alexander: 4494.

Brandt, F.C.: 1983.

Brandt Family: 4494, 4499.

Brandt, Frederick: 4422.

Brandt, John A.: 4494.

Brandt, Michael: 4499.

Brandt, Phillipine Grube (Mrs William): 892.

Brandt, William: 892.

Brandt, Yost, Rev.: 3525, 3550, 4221, 4525.

Braniff, Allan: 4099.

Braningan, Mary: 3709.

Branscombe, J.A., Rev.: 3414, 3415.

Brant, Catherine: 216.

Brant, John: 280, 2049, 2052.

Brant, Joseph: 188, 193, 213, 216, 224, 250, 256, 259, 271, 280, 282, 283, 294, 299, 300, 303, 326, 332, 333, 517, 555, 673, 1324, 1325, 1627, 1758, 3937, 4202, 4266, 4512, 4513, 4517, 4525.

Brant, Molly: 4517.

Brattan, Henry: 1796.

Braucht, Eleanor: 1334, 2050.

Brauer, Barthold: 4348, 4362.

Brauer, Mary: 4348, 4362.

Braugardt, Mrs: 4499.

Braun, Casper: 326, 2496, 2843, 3431, 3444, 4298, 4344, 4353, 4371, 4374, 4380.

Braun, Edward: 3702.

Braun Family: 249, 928, 998, 4221.

Braun, George: 928.

Braun, George, Rev.: 3495, 3496.

Braun, Hella Klassen: 3095, 3120, 3137.

Braun, Henry: 3702, 4017, 4380.

Braun, J.L., Rev.: 333, 3514, 3527, 3576, 3577, 3608, 4422.

Braun, Jacob: 998.

Braun, Jacob H.: 928.

Braun, John: 1654, 1977, 2007, 4517, 4521.

Braun, Joseph: 3185.

Braun, Kathrine Bergen (Mrs George): 928.

Braun, Lily Froese (Mrs Jacob H.): 928.

Braun, Wilhelmina Prankert: 998.

Brauns, Henry: 4255.

Bray, Florence: 1266.

Bray, George: 1205, 1266, 1535, 2983, 4362.

Bray, Jacob: 1266.

Bray, Jane: 1266.

Bray, Murray: 1266, 4348, 4362.

Brayshaw, D.: 4088, 4230, 4233, 4258.

Break, Abraham: 769.

Break, Alma: 4428.

Break, Caroline Cosens (Mrs Abraham): 769.

Break, David: 2518.

Break Family: 2518.

Break, Gideon: 4444.

Break, Jerry: 4428.

Break, Magdalena: 1639.

Breaven, J.R., Dr: 4031.

Brebeuf, Rev.: 187, 221, 249, 255, 256, 3877.

Brech, Catherine: 2518, 3314.

Brech, Elizabeth: 755.

Brech Family: 713, 719, 720, 2518, 3230, 4455, 4456.

Brech, John: 3314.

Brech, Widow: 713, 720, 769, 1200, 1308, 4448, 4449.

Breckbill, Philip: 599.

Breckenridge, Eleanor: 1401.

Breckenridge, J.C., Mrs: 1400.

Breckenridge, James: 1401.

Breedveld, Peter, Rev.: 3707.

Breek, Adam: 256.

Breek, John: 256.

Breek, Madelina: 256.

Brehler, Jacob: 4525.

Breich, O.: 4278.

Breimer Family: 915.

Breimer, Ivah: 3506.

Breithaupt, A.L.: 29, 127, 326, 671, 672, 771, 1179, 1273, 1466, 1483, 1924, 1945, 2519, 2568, 2714, 2818, 3007, 3048, 3490, 3821, 3960, 4080, 4299, 4374, 4380.

Breithaupt, Caroline C. Anthes (Mrs J.C.): 1187, 1272, 2723.

Breithaupt, Catharine Hailer (Mrs Louis): 1, 127, 326, 671, 672, 770, 771, 1269, 1273, 1277, 1278, 1691,
2019, 3495, 3893, 4047, 4380.

Breithaupt, E. Carl: 127, 1273, 1276, 1278, 1929, 2055, 2080, 2086, 4380.

Breithaupt, Emma Devitt (Mrs L.J.): 127, 129, 553, 1187, 1269, 1271, 1273, 1277, 3773, 3863, 3945, 3960, 4136.

Breithaupt, Emma Lillian: 127, 129, 1273, 3798, 4031.

Breithaupt, Evelyn L. (Mrs Parry): 127, 1169.

Breithaupt Family: 129, 243, 658, 671, 672, 681, 770, 771, 772, 773, 1167, 1211, 1268, 1272, 1273, 1275, 1276, 1277, 1863, 2006, 2019, 2519, 2669, 3504, 3506, 4143, 4320, 4324, 4325, 4327, 4360, 4370.

Breithaupt, Fred A.: 2519, 3915, 3923, 3944.

Breithaupt, Gladys: 3230.

Breithaupt, Herbert C., Rev.: 4136.

Breithaupt, J.C.: 1, 326, 671, 672, 1169, 1176, 1201, 1272, 1273, 1856, 1863, 1943, 2019, 2519, 2983, 4023, 4299, 4344, 4374, 4380.

Breithaupt, J. Edward: 1169.

Breithaupt, James: 326, 671, 672, 4148.

Breithaupt, James R.: 771, 2049, 3923.

Breithaupt, L.J.: 1, 22, 127, 129, 326, 553, 671, 672, 771, 772, 773, 828, 1168, 1176, 1187, 1201, 1269, 1271, 1273, 1274, 1277, 1811, 1833, 1851, 1857, 1863, 1879, 2019, 2080, 2421, 2495, 2714, 2818, 3007, 3493, 3502, 3815, 3823, 4023, 4056, 4067, 4070, 4114, 4117, 4121, 4123, 4136, 4149, 4292, 4299, 4318, 4362, 4370, 4374, 4380.

Breithaupt, Liborius: 1691, 1863, 2019.

Breithaupt, Louis: 249, 326, 671, 672, 771, 772, 773, 1167, 1169, 1201, 1269, 1273, 1277, 1278, 1672, 1691, 1850, 1855, 1856, 1863, 1974, 2019, 2053, 2056, 2144, 2421, 2519, 2669, 4124, 4159, 4299, 4306, 4348, 4371, 4374, 4377, 4380.

Breithaupt, Louis Orville: 22, 23, 127, 129, 326, 553, 646, 671, 672, 771, 1187, 1201, 1205, 1268, 1271,

Clark, Widow: 2700.
Clark, William: 1297, 2783.
Clark, William S.: 4015.
Clarke, A.L.G., Rev.: 3472.
Clarke, Alice: 2714.
Clarke, George H.: 4374.
Clarke, H.: 4080.
Clarke, J.D.: 3960, 4087, 4092.
Clarke, James D.: 120, 4080, 4104.
Clarke, Jeannette: 3109.
Clarke, John: 3667.
Clarke, Mrs: 3773.
Clarke, Reuben: 4014.
Clarke, Rev.: 3623.
Clarke, Thomas: 14, 259, 282, 1324, 4260.
Clarke, William: 4103, 4223.
Clarkson, John B., Rev.: 3622.
Class, Edward: 1508.
Class, Gerald: 4099.
Class, Harvey: 2149.
Claus, William, Col.: 224, 256, 282, 299, 303, 332.
Clausen, F.C., Dr: 2889, 2904, 3525.
Claussen, F.W.: 326.
Claxton, Miss: 2994.
Clay, Betty: 4225.
Clay, C.: 4103.
Clay, Gervais: 4225.
Clay, Nelson C.: 4104.
Clay, W.P.: 4263.
Claydon, Dolly: 2775.
Claydon, Donald: 2775.
Claydon, Douglas: 2775.
Claydon, Jimmy: 2775.
Clayfield, B.A.: 4422.
Clayton, James M.: 84.
Cleave, Hugh: 4080, 4102.
Cleaver, A.K., Miss: 4056.
Cleaver, Solomon, Rev.: 2840.
Cleghorn, Edward: 3154.
Cleghorn Family: 4518.
Cleghorn, H.G., Rev.: 3658, 3660, 3681, 4423, 4454.
Cleghorn, Reuben: 4518.
Cleghorn, Victoria: 4518.
Cleghorn, William G.: 326, 1298, 3813, 4121, 4123, 4164, 4374, 4380, 4518.
Cleland, Andrew W.: 1976, 4486, 4487, 4505, 4506.
Cleland, F.A., Mrs: 4177.
Clemens, A.: 1974, 3664.
Clemens, A.C.: 2992.
Clemens, Aaron: 289, 858, 1799, 1976, 2379, 2774, 2775, 4451.
Clemens, Abraham: 3, 238, 256, 332,

382, 514, 713, 720, 804, 809, 908, 978, 2379, 2760, 2761, 3097, 4274, 4286, 4393.
Clemens, Abraham C.: 553, 635, 729, 803, 806, 1233, 2971, 3232, 4451, 4455.
Clemens, Abraham D.: 4458, 4461.
Clemens, Abraham D., Mrs: 1698.
Clemens, Abraham L.: 804, 809, 3305, 3402.
Clemens, Abraham O.: 805.
Clemens, Abraham S.: 805, 809, 1165, 2775, 3314, 4395.
Clemens, Abram: 2379.
Clemens, Abram C.: 803, 3305.
Clemens, Abram S.: 3305.
Clemens, Alvin: 2180, 2570.
Clemens, Alvin C.: 4490.
Clemens, Amos: 809, 1877, 2073, 4458.
Clemens, Amos M.: 1877.
Clemens, Ann: 804, 809.
Clemens, Anna: 804.
Clemens, Catharine: 804, 809, 3232.
Clemens, Christian: 804.
Clemens, Daniel: 382.
Clemens, David: 84, 289, 1976, 4203, 4380, 4422.
Clemens, David H.: 4097.
Clemens, David S.: 2379.
Clemens, David W.: 2120.
Clemens, Edith: 2449.
Clemens, Eli: 2760, 3232.
Clemens, Elizabeth: 382, 804, 809.
Clemens, Elizabeth Bechtel Histand: 382, 1096, 1163.
Clemens, Elizabeth Strohm (Mrs Abram C.): 803.
Clemens, Esther Stauffer: 275, 382, 803, 806, 1096, 2760, 2766, 4452.
Clemens, Ewart: 2714.
Clemens Family: 275, 562, 713, 719, 720, 750, 761, 803, 805, 806, 807, 808, 810, 813, 887, 896, 2315, 3927, 4425, 4436.
Clemens, George: 2, 7, 255, 256, 270, 275, 294, 382, 519, 555, 635, 713, 720, 803, 804, 805, 806, 809, 1096, 1163, 2096, 2379, 2736, 2760, 2761, 2765, 2766, 3232, 3247, 3314, 3644, 4195, 4264, 4374, 4380, 4393, 4394, 4452, 4453, 4455, 4456.
Clemens, George, Dr: 809.
Clemens, George, Jr: 2760.
Clemens, Gerhard: 804, 809.
Clemens, Harold: 2775.

Clemens, Harold, Mrs: 2775.
Clemens, Harriet: 382.
Clemens, Harry U.: 2080.
Clemens, Heinrich: 740.
Clemens, Henry: 690, 3007, 3374, 4184, 4266.
Clemens, Henry L.: 804, 809.
Clemens, Herbert: 2775.
Clemens, I.U.: 286, 4385.
Clemens, Isaac: 18, 382, 554, 809, 2128, 2485, 2714, 2774, 2775, 2818, 2821, 3978, 4374, 4380, 4452, 4456, 4458.
Clemens, Isaac B.: 1165.
Clemens, J.: 1974.
Clemens, J. Arthur: 2775.
Clemens, J.U.: 1165, 2180, 2570, 4298, 4382, 4490, 4499.
Clemens, Jacob: 804, 809, 4380.
Clemens, Jacob E.: 1165.
Clemens, Jacob M.: 4456.
Clemens, James: 2775.
Clemens, Jesse: 891.
Clemens, Joel: 493, 553, 809, 1080, 1165, 2774, 2775, 4195, 4456, 4458.
Clemens, John: 804, 809, 4451.
Clemens, John K., Rev.: 809.
Clemens, John S.: 289, 803, 806, 1165, 1799, 2379, 2774, 2775.
Clemens, Joseph S.: 1165.
Clemens, Katie: 3767.
Clemens, Lena: 1671.
Clemens, Levi: 382, 2728.
Clemens, Levi B., Dr: 809.
Clemens, Lewis: 382.
Clemens, Lewis W.: 809.
Clemens, Lilly: 2775.
Clemens, M.B.: 896, 1165.
Clemens, Magdalena Eby (Mrs Abraham): 804, 978, 3402.
Clemens, Margaret: 809, 2775.
Clemens, Margaret Ellis (Mrs George, Jr): 2760.
Clemens, Margaret Miller (Mrs Jesse): 891.
Clemens, Maria: 1163.
Clemens, Marion: 2775.
Clemens, Martha: 809.
Clemens, Mary: 382, 804, 809, 3097.
Clemens, Mary Nice (Mrs Abraham O.): 805.
Clemens, Mervyn: 2775.
Clemens, Mima: 4264.
Clemens, Minnie: 2775.
Clemens, Miss: 673.
Clemens, Moses: 1165, 2728.

Clemens, Moses H., Rev.: 2714, 2736, 2764, 3496, 3930.

Clemens, Nancy: 2379.

Clemens, Nancy Bowman (Mrs Abram C.): 803.

Clemens, Nathan: 809, 2760, 2761.

Clemens, Norman, Mrs: 1204.

Clemens, Oliver: 809, 1163, 1671, 4435, 4437.

Clemens, Orval: 2760.

Clemens, P.J.: 4246.

Clemens, Polly: 809.

Clemens, Rachel: 1163.

Clemens, Rebecca Miller (Mrs Abraham C.): 803, 806.

Clemens, Rebecca Snyder (Mrs John S.): 803.

Clemens, Rothsay: 2775.

Clemens, Ruth: 2775.

Clemens, Sally: 809.

Clemens, Samuel: 3097.

Clemens, Sarah: 1002.

Clemens, Stouffer: 809, 2760.

Clemens, Thomas: 4526.

Clemens, Velma: 2775.

Clemens, Veronica A.: 3097.

Clemens, Veronica Bechtel (Mrs Nathan): 2760.

Clemens, W.A.: 2798.

Clemens, W. Ewart: 4097, 4104.

Clemens, W.G.H.: 1165.

Clemens, Wendell U.: 809.

Clemens, William: 382, 2760, 4264.

Clement, David Ward: 3631, 3632, 4103, 4107.

Clement, E.P.: 326, 1168, 1252, 1256, 1299, 1535, 1818, 1819, 1926, 3631, 3632, 3821, 3823, 3945, 3959, 4031, 4107, 4114, 4299, 4315, 4374, 4380.

Clement, E.W.: 1168, 4315, 4374, 4380.

Clement, Florence: 3773.

Clement, Jane E. Bowlby (Mrs E.P.): 326, 1252, 1299, 4380.

Clement, John Edwin: 1168, 4315.

Clement, Muriel Kerr (Mrs W.P.): 1200, 3773, 3815, 3857, 4327.

Clement, W.P.: 326, 1168, 1201, 1251, 1535, 2600, 3923, 4056, 4315, 4327, 4380.

Clement, Ward: 2714.

Clement, William: 3033.

Clemes, Jacob: 713, 720.

Clemes, John W.: 2120.

Clemmer, Aaron G.: 1165.

Clemmer, Abram: 964, 2760.

Clemmer, Abram C.: 4461.

Clemmer, Amos: 4428.

Clemmer, Anna Lichty (Mrs Jacob): 953.

Clemmer Family: 562, 711, 713, 719, 720, 4441.

Clemmer, Gordon: 2760.

Clemmer, Henry: 256, 713, 720, 2760, 2766, 4184.

Clemmer, Henry M.: 713, 720.

Clemmer, Jacob: 884, 953.

Clemmer, Joseph: 713, 720, 787.

Clemmer, Lydia Shantz (Mrs Abram): 964, 2760.

Clemmer, Mary Good (Mrs Jacob): 884.

Clemmer, Onias: 1777.

Clemmer, Sarah Bergey (Mrs Henry): 809, 2760, 2766.

Clerihew, Patrick: 85, 2843.

Clerihew, Philip: 2714.

Cliff, Alfred: 2379.

Cliff, C.F.: 502, 2994.

Cliff, Charles: 2379, 4286.

Cliff, George: 2379.

Clifford, Dorothy: 4474.

Clifford, Earnest: 4178.

Clifford, Frank: 4474.

Climenhaga, Anna: 2798.

Cline, Doris: 3506.

Cline, Mr: 3044, 3048.

Cline, W.H., Rev.: 3413.

Clinton, Louisa: 2447.

Clinton, William: 2447.

Clive, C.D.: 3936.

Clothilde, Sister M.: 2818, 2838, 3431, 4380.

Cluney, James: 4062, 4258.

Cluthe, Charles: 2379, 4429, 4454.

Cluthe, Jacob: 2385, 4423, 4439.

Cluthe, Lawrence: 1877, 4423, 4429.

Clutterbuck, Eugene: 4099, 4192.

Cober, A.H.: 2994.

Cober, Albert: 1001.

Cober, Alvin A., Rev.: 812.

Cober, Charles: 3770.

Cober, Eve Fisher: 812.

Cober Family: 275, 713, 719, 720, 811, 3373, 4433, 4436.

Cober, Isaac: 1186.

Cober, J.N.: 3644.

Cober, Jacob: 553, 811, 812.

Cober, Jacob, Mrs: 2760.

Cober, Jerry: 4273.

Cober, John: 553.

Cober, Nancy Holm: 812.

Cober, Nicholas, Jr: 811.

Cober, Nickolas: 812.

Cober, Peter: 811, 3320, 3328.

Cober, Peter, Rev.: 811, 812.

Cober, Simon: 3382.

Cober, Simon, Rev.: 811.

Cober, Solomon, Mrs: 4280.

Cober, W.: 4499.

Cober, W.F.: 4263.

Cochenour Family: 2085.

Cochrane, John: 3745, 4298.

Cochrane, Kenneth: 4099.

Cochrane, Robert: 877, 3745.

Cochrane, William: 2120.

Cockburn, F.C.: 1908.

Cockman, Thomas: 4230.

Cockrell, Richard: 255, 256, 287, 382, 2760.

Cockshutt, Henry: 2994.

Cockshutt, Ignatius: 282.

Cockshutt, W.F.: 1964.

Cockwell, Mr: 4505, 4506.

Codling, Edward C.: 3049.

Codling, Miss: 4450.

Cody, Canon, Rev.: 2720.

Cody, H.J.: 2714, 2777, 2862, 2863.

Coffey, Miss: 2815.

Coffman Family: 932.

Coffman, John: 2736.

Coffman, John S.: 3260, 3274, 3305, 3314, 3322, 3357, 3399.

Coffman, S.F.: 604, 3129, 3246, 3299, 3300, 3309, 3313, 3399, 3783.

Coghlin, Bruce L.: 4474.

Cohen, Jacob: 3718.

Cohoe, B.L., Rev.: 3643.

Colcleugh Family: 2085.

Colcleugh, Mr: 2379, 4188.

Cole, David: 2379, 2700, 4423.

Cole, Herman: 1165, 2470, 4423, 4454.

Cole, Isaac: 3642, 4014.

Cole, Mr: 4505.

Cole, William R.: 2379.

Coleman, E.M.: 4204.

Coleman, E.M., Mrs: 4204.

Coleman, E.T.: 2152, 2168, 2399, 4490, 4499.

Coleman, James: 1294.

Coleman, T.R.: 4080.

Coles, G.: 4521.

Coles, Gladys, Miss: 4029, 4031.

Coles, Gordon, Rev.: 4512.

Collacott, Alan A.: 4099.

Collett, Minnie: 3709.

Colley, J.W., Rev.: 3636.

Collier, Dale, Rev.: 3263.

Collings, Rev.: 3636.

Cosens Family: 769.
Cosens, Rev.: 3643, 3644, 3645.
Cosgrave, Mr: 1497.
Cosgrove, William: 1983.
Cossel, Mrs: 289.
Costello, Frank: 4348, 4362.
Cotton, V., Miss: 4413.
Cottrell, Mr: 4428.
Couch, Rev.: 3623.
Coulter Family: 4470.
Coulthard, William, Mrs: 3665.
Coumans, Camilla C.: 3861, 3928.
Courters, John: 3713.
Courtney, Jack: 4278.
Courtney, John N.: 4271, 4274, 4278.
Cousin, F.: 4505, 4506.
Cousineau, Robert: 4217.
Cousins, George: 13.
Coutts, Annie: 1165.
Coutts, Edgar N., Dr: 1178, 4029, 4031, 4056.
Coutts, Hugh H.: 2736, 2760, 2764.
Coutts, J.J.: 1165.
Coutts, James: 4079.
Coutts, William: 4079.
Coverett Family: 1003.
Cowan, Alice: 2843, 2852, 4380.
Cowan, Allen, Mrs: 3838.
Cowan, C.: 2496.
Cowan, Charles E.: 4065.
Cowan, David: 3660, 4099.
Cowan Family: 78, 235, 688, 713, 719, 720, 1773, 3908, 4199, 4212.
Cowan, G.A.: 4271, 4285.
Cowan, G., Mrs: 4278.
Cowan, Gary: 326.
Cowan, George: 3663, 4199.
Cowan, J.H.: 4056.
Cowan, J.L.: 4092.
Cowan, James: 2, 18, 332, 502, 908, 1165, 1304, 1374, 1549, 1877, 2736, 2760, 2765, 2975, 2986, 3663, 4116, 4155, 4263, 4266, 4268, 4286, 4380, 4458.
Cowan, James E.: 1773.
Cowan, James L.: 2736, 2761.
Cowan, James Roy: 1302.
Cowan, James S.: 3751.
Cowan, Jennie F. (Mrs Thomas D.): 1200, 1303, 1304, 1758, 3852, 3876, 3889, 3903, 3915, 3928, 3936, 3944, 3945, 4116, 4207.
Cowan, John: 3669.
Cowan, Laing: 1302, 4079.
Cowan, Mabel: 3771, 3852.
Cowan, Miss: 4395.
Cowan, R.K.: 13.

Cowan, Robert E.: 8, 1185, 1822, 2736, 2765.
Cowan, Thomas: 1549, 2109, 2120, 2736, 3663, 3761, 4229, 4263.
Cowan, Thomas D.: 1194, 1303, 1304, 1773.
Cowan, William: 29, 1822, 2591, 2736, 2765, 3663, 3665, 4263.
Cowan, William, Mrs: 3665.
Coward, W.A.: 4284.
Cowell, John J.: 4102.
Cowie, Katherine: 4031.
Cowling, J.P., Rev.: 3499.
Cowls, W.J.: 2829, 3800, 3892.
Cox, J.G.: 2055.
Cox, Mr: 3669.
Cox, Thomas L.: 709.
Coxson, Edward: 4499.
Coxson, Edward, Mrs: 2971.
Coyne, James H.: 1305, 1312, 3872.
Crackel Family: 2704.
Crackel, John: 3474, 4491.
Cragg, A.R., Rev.: 3892.
Cragg, H.H., Rev.: 3492, 3643.
Cragie, George: 3665.
Cragie, George, Mrs: 3665.
Craig, C.H.: 2710, 2793, 4274.
Craig, George: 4102.
Craig, James: 1877.
Craig, John: 1877, 3660.
Craig, W.: 4278.
Craig, Wallace: 4278.
Crail, James H.: 3631, 3632.
Cram, Mary Breithaupt: 4136.
Cram, Robert: 4136.
Cram, W.M.: 520, 1168, 1251, 1535, 2983, 3632, 3656, 3959, 4299, 4374.
Cram, W.M., Mrs: 3631.
Cramer, Joseph, Rev.: 3365, 3774, 3792, 3845.
Cranby, Mrs: 2085.
Crane, James F., Pte: 1932.
Cranston, Adam: 1983, 3888.
Cranston, Alexander: 2486, 3663, 3888, 4199.
Cranston Family: 458, 3888.
Cranston, J. Herbert: 1306, 1339, 4230, 4258.
Cranston, James Kersell: 1306, 3888, 4237, 4263.
Cranston, Robert: 2486, 3888, 3978, 4198, 4214.
Cranston, Robert, Mrs: 3665.
Cranwell, James: 3709.
Crarey, W., Rev.: 3470.
Crause, John: 3492.

Craven, James: 2145.
Craven, Rev.: 2975, 2986, 3433, 3442, 4246, 4275.
Cravers, Marie: 4177.
Crawford, A.W., Dr: 2720.
Crawford, Archibald: 4102.
Crawford, David: 4015.
Crawford, Edna: 3031.
Crawford Family: 4040.
Crawford, J.W.: 4422.
Crawford, Jack: 3031.
Crawford, James: 4015.
Crawford, Jennie: 3709.
Crawford, John: 4466.
Crawford, Lou: 1845.
Crawford, Mrs: 3838.
Crawford, Thomas: 4356.
Crawford, William: 3636.
Crawforth, Alma: 2712.
Cress, Alvin: 4521.
Cress, Catharine: 815, 816, 1308.
Cress, Christoph: 2484.
Cress, David: 4523.
Cress, Eliza Miles (Mrs Simon): 815.
Cress, Elizabeth Schaeffer (Mrs John): 815.
Cress, Ephraim: 815, 1085, 1308, 4512, 4521, 4524.
Cress Family: 713, 719, 720, 738, 778, 781, 797, 815, 816, 817, 970, 971, 973, 1085, 1087, 4455, 4456.
Cress, J.G.: 22, 1307.
Cress, Jacob: 816, 1308, 4524.
Cress, John: 815, 818, 4517, 4521.
Cress, Levi: 815, 1085, 4517, 4521.
Cress, Lloyd: 818.
Cress, Magdalena Eby (Mrs Jacob): 816.
Cress, Margarete: 2039.
Cress, Mary Ann Geip (Mrs Levi): 815.
Cress, Mary Maxwell (Mrs Samuel): 4454.
Cress, Noah: 4517.
Cress, Noah G.: 2151.
Cress, Peter: 4525.
Cress, Simon: 3, 275, 713, 720, 815, 816, 818, 1085, 1308, 4448, 4449, 4517, 4521, 4524.
Cress, Susan McMahon: 815, 1308.
Cressman, A.: 2073, 2704.
Cressman, A.K.: 1309, 4318.
Cressman, A.K., Mrs: 4031.
Cressman, Abner: 3335.
Cressman, Abraham: 256, 713, 720, 821, 1128, 1165, 2135, 4453, 4458.
Cressman, Adam: 820, 860, 2120.

Date, Henry M.: 4111.
Date, Samuel: 4371.
Daters, Hy: 13.
Dattels, D.R.: 1737, 3923.
Daub, Casper: 4474.
Daub Family: 4499.
Daub, Frederick: 1.
Dauberger, John: 326, 2421, 4372, 4380.
Daubin, Mr: 4428.
Daubrevile, Francis: 4461.
Daum, Leah Frey: 2538, 3095, 3098, 3122, 3145.
Dauphinee, J.S., Rev.: 3509, 3525.
Davey, F.C.P.: 2109, 2120, 4380.
Davey, J.W.: 4298.
David, Barbara Cress (Mrs John): 816.
David, John: 816.
David, L.W.T., Rev.: 4380.
Davidson, Alexander: 1315, 2120, 2714, 4195.
Davidson, Cam: 3745.
Davidson, Charles: 2074.
Davidson, Dr: 3413.
Davidson Family: 959, 3888.
Davidson, George: 2, 149, 260, 308, 326, 653, 1165, 1314, 1315, 1535, 1636, 1811, 1976, 2100, 2120, 2128, 2379, 3631, 3632, 3656, 3669, 3685, 3767, 3978, 4011, 4017, 4191, 4195, 4306, 4371, 4377, 4380, 4433, 4438, 4478, 4525.
Davidson, George, Jr: 1315, 4371.
Davidson, James: 2, 1693, 2120, 2701, 3683.
Davidson, John: 2, 1188, 1281, 1806, 1834, 2109, 2120, 2128, 2478, 3481, 3669, 3751, 4202, 4250, 4266, 4525.
Davidson, John, Mrs: 1986.
Davidson, M.B., Rev.: 1183, 1205, 2803, 3652, 3657, 3666, 3891.
Davidson, Margaret Garden (Mrs George): 1314, 1315.
Davidson, Mary: 2.
Davidson, Monty: 4006.
Davidson, N., Mrs: 1251, 3773.
Davidson, Richard, Rev.: 4178, 4182.
Davidson, Robert: 1315.
Davidson, Walter: 1740.
Davidson, William: 2, 326, 1315, 2073, 2100, 2109, 2120, 2714, 2818, 2821, 2843, 3656, 3973, 4306, 4380.
Davidson, William, Mrs: 3656.

Davies, Arthur: 4204.
Davies, William: 2557.
Davis, Charles: 3644.
Davis, Clarence W.: 3745.
Davis, Climpson: 1747.
Davis, D. Bruce: 3793.
Davis, Dixi: 4500.
Davis, E.C.: 4223.
Davis, E.W.: 2000.
Davis, Edward: 1747.
Davis, George: 4103.
Davis, James W.: 4266.
Davis, Jay: 3243.
Davis, Jesse: 3243.
Davis, Joy: 4500.
Davis, Mahlon, Mrs: 3773.
Davis, Richard: 4250.
Davis, Wesley G.: 1895.
Davis, William: 3474.
Davis, William G.: 127, 4102.
Davis, William Mahlon: 4023, 4104.
Davison, A.: 2109.
Davison, Fred B., Rev.: 3403, 3405, 3407.
Dawson, A.O.: 2242.
Dawson, Bessie: 1725, 3773.
Dawson, Esther Forbes (Mrs Richard B.): 1104.
Dawson Family: 1104.
Dawson, George W.: 75, 119, 121.
Dawson, Richard B.: 1104.
Dawson, Robert: 1770, 3917.
Dawson, William: 85, 113.
Day, Bryan: 2179.
Day, Frederick: 3644.
Day, James E.: 2850.
Day, Mira: 2481.
Day, Morrison: 4271, 4273.
Day, W.M.: 907.
Day, W. Morrison: 4274.
Dazell, John B.: 1205.
de Almeida Moniz, Marcelino: 697.
de Andrade, Sebastiao: 697.
de Britto Costa-Pinto, Sulamita: 697.
De Courcy, Joe: 2050.
De la Roche, Mazo: 1316, 1392, 3771, 3840.
de Mello Gouveia, Jose, Dr: 697.
de Mille, F.W.: 29.
de Vargas, Odilio: 697.
de Vries, Bren, Rev.: 4271, 4282.
Deacon, Joseph, Rev.: 436.
Deady, Martin: 4195.
Deal, A.E.: 4104.
Dean Family: 4473, 4499.
Deans, Isabella C.: 1193, 2736, 2764.
Deans, James: 3665.

Deans, John: 2005.
Deans, Miss: 2775.
Deans, Walter: 4266.
Deans, William: 4263.
Dear, Frank: 1937.
Dear, G.: 4080.
Dearborn, General: 1324.
Dearling, Caroline: 262.
Dearling, John: 262.
Deary Family: 2085.
Deary, James: 2766, 2818.
DeBeyer, P., Mrs: 2832.
Debor, H.W.: 671, 672.
DeBrusk, Harry: 2843, 2844.
Debus, Fred: 13, 3539, 4382.
Debus, George A.: 3815.
Debus, George M.: 1, 1879, 2818, 3041, 3759, 3897, 4121, 4149, 4299, 4370, 4371, 4374, 4380.
Decher, Philip: 2120.
Dechert, George: 4525.
Dechert, Martin: 4395.
Decker, Henry: 2167, 4499.
Decker, John: 1885, 4499.
Decker, Theodore: 4499.
Deckert, Clayton: 4478.
Deckert Family: 4476.
Dedels Family: 2518.
Dedels, Henry: 4428.
Dedels, Jacob: 4428.
Dedels, Mr: 2379.
Dedman, F.J.: 4104.
Dedman, Oliver: 4103.
Deemert, B.: 4278.
DeGuerre, Ambrose: 2720.
DeGuerre, H.W.: 4080.
Deguisne, Rev.: 3621.
Dehler, A.: 4040.
Dehler, Robert, Rev.: 2732, 3418, 3423, 3431, 4380.
Deibert, Adam: 4525.
Deichert, H.: 4382.
Deichert, Mary: 3074, 3101.
deJong, David: 119.
DeKay Family: 988.
DeKay, Jephtha: 987, 4422.
DeKay, Mary Moxley (Mrs Jephtha): 987.
DeKay, Miss: 4422.
DeKay, Mrs: 4371.
DeKay, William: 3631, 3632, 4380.
DeKleinhans, George: 3772, 3795, 4356.
Delion, August: 3050.
Delion Brothers: 100, 4221.
Delion, C.C.: 85, 3050, 4525.
Delion, F., Dr: 1171, 4380, 4483.

Delion, Fred: 85, 100, 110, 2808, 4525.

Delion, Henry: 85, 3050, 3782, 4525.

Delion, William: 85, 100, 110, 4525.

Deller, Howard F., Rev.: 3629.

Dellinger, John: 3465.

Delton, Harry Conrad: 4103.

Denges, Adam: 2496, 4298.

Dengis, Charles: 4514.

Dengis Family: 4221.

Denis-Nathan, Herbert: 1317, 1318, 2049, 2520, 3917.

Dennerlein, C.: 4392.

Dennis, G.W.: 77, 85, 121.

Dennis, Harris: 4362.

Dennis, Harry: 1937, 2144.

Dennis, James H.: 1948.

Dennis, John: 2144, 4362.

Dennison, Henry T.: 2767.

Dennison, Ross: 4104.

DeNoon, Alexander, Rev.: 479, 3689.

Denstadt, George: 4437.

Dentinger, Frank, Rev.: 2785.

Dentinger, Mary I., Mrs: 2120.

Dentinger, Norbert, Rev.: 3465.

Dentinger, Peter: 2769, 4477.

Dentinger, Simon: 3076, 3104, 3123, 3130.

Denton, Ernest: 1181.

Denyes, Walter: 4023.

Deppish, George: 4158, 4483.

deQuetteville, Carol Cook: 4426.

Derbecker, Donald S.: 2120, 4521.

Derby, John: 3076.

Derdarian, Edward: 4396.

Derdarian Family: 704.

Dereich, Jacob: 3503.

Derry, James: 2818, 2843, 4422.

Derry, Mr: 3669.

Derschel, Lucas D.: 4468.

Derstine, Clayton F., Rev.: 602, 1191, 3238, 3239, 3246, 3274, 3277, 3309, 3310, 3313, 3360, 3774, 3792, 3845, 3876, 4380.

Derstine, Mary Elizabeth Kolb (Mrs Clayton F.): 3365.

Des Jardins, Peter: 2051.

Deschene, Frederick: 4396.

Deseronto, John: 282.

Dessauer, Louis W.: 2151, 4017.

Dessler, Emmerson: 2098, 4527.

Dessler Family: 1110, 2518.

Dessler, Jacob: 4444.

Dessler, Oscar Z.: 2728.

Dettweiler Family: 4448.

Dettweiler, Isaiah: 2728.

Dettweiler, Norma: 2728.

Dettweiler, Norman: 2728.

Dettwiler, Abraham: 826, 941.

Dettwiler, Abraham K.: 826.

Dettwiler, Barbara Koch (Mrs Abraham): 826, 941.

Dettwiler, Enos, Mrs: 3243.

Dettwiler, Henry B.: 3319.

Dettwiler, Matilda Snyder (Mrs Henry B.): 3319.

Dettwiler, Reuben: 3243.

Dettwiler, Veronica Sauder (Mrs Abraham K.): 826.

Detweiler, Abel: 2700.

Detweiler, Abigail Bechtel: 739, 1319.

Detweiler, Adelaide: 1319.

Detweiler, Amanda: 1319.

Detweiler, Anna Wanner (Mrs Rudolph): 827, 2760.

Detweiler, Barbara Wenger (Mrs John W.): 827, 1137.

Detweiler, D.B.: 10, 14, 246, 279, 326, 516, 646, 671, 672, 908, 1236, 1319, 1484, 1758, 1836, 1842, 1846, 1873, 1879, 1887, 1897, 1916, 1964, 1971, 2014, 2039, 2066, 2333, 2441, 2533, 2539, 2615, 2616, 2714, 2818, 2983, 2997, 3631, 3632, 3633, 3724, 3821, 4046, 4149, 4212, 4299, 4318, 4319, 4320, 4370, 4374, 4380, 4517.

Detweiler, E.R.: 3279.

Detweiler, Elizabeth, Miss: 2983.

Detweiler, Enoch, Rev.: 275, 739, 1319, 3316, 3328, 3355, 3374.

Detweiler, Esther Ziegler: 2533.

Detweiler Family: 252, 562, 713, 719, 720, 827, 887, 911, 2533.

Detweiler, George: 3370.

Detweiler, George Franklin: 1319, 4380.

Detweiler, Hannah Schlichter: 2533.

Detweiler, Hannes: 2533.

Detweiler, Hetty Ziegler (Mrs Jacob): 942.

Detweiler, J.F., Rev.: 3279.

Detweiler, J.R.: 2120, 4203.

Detweiler, Jacob: 1, 433, 690, 942, 1637, 3316, 3374, 4435, 4437.

Detweiler, Jacob, Rev.: 275, 406, 1319, 4203.

Detweiler, Jacob Z.: 37, 1165, 2379, 2533, 2700, 3352, 4429.

Detweiler, John: 270, 690, 3374, 4435, 4437.

Detweiler, John W.: 827, 1137.

Detweiler, John Z.: 2533, 3279, 3374.

Detweiler, Joseph: 2700.

Detweiler, Magdalena Schlichter: 2533.

Detweiler, Margaret: 2983.

Detweiler, Maria: 755.

Detweiler, Mary Gottwals: 2533.

Detweiler, Milton: 1319, 4080.

Detweiler, Mr: 3669, 4525.

Detweiler, Noah B.: 1176, 1319, 1971, 3320, 3328, 3355.

Detweiler, Noah B., Mrs: 1628.

Detweiler, Rudolph: 827, 2760.

Detweiler, Rudolph W.: 827.

Detweiler, S.A., Mrs: 1183.

Detweiler, Samuel S.: 4450.

Detweiler, Susanna Bingeman (Mrs Rudolph W.): 827.

Detweiler, Susannah: 1515.

Detwiler, Abraham Z.: 493, 3352.

Detwiler, Ann: 1002.

Detwiler, E.: 2714.

Detwiler Family: 612.

Detwiler, J.B., Rev.: 625.

Detwiler, Jacob B.: 3320, 3328.

Detwiler, John D., Dr: 128, 1190.

Detwiler, Rudolph: 256, 4458.

Detzler Family: 2704, 4499.

DeVere, A.: 4278.

DeVere, G.: 4278.

Deverell Family: 869.

Devitt, A. Harvey: 22, 1321.

Devitt, A.W.: 2140, 3050.

Devitt, Almon: 1198.

Devitt, Alva E.: 828, 1321.

Devitt, Barnabas: 127, 553, 828, 829, 1078, 1080, 1165, 1201, 1358, 1368, 1953, 2179, 2379, 2406, 2565, 2567, 2609, 2730, 3872, 4191, 4192, 4195, 4404, 4405, 4422, 4461.

Devitt, Benjamin: 1, 13, 828, 1165, 1320, 1321, 2565, 2609, 3054, 4422.

Devitt, C. Morton: 1321.

Devitt, Caroline Schweitzer (Mrs Dennis): 1063.

Devitt, Dennis: 828, 829, 1063, 4461.

Devitt, E. Blake: 1320.

Devitt, Edward H.: 1321.

Devitt, Edward M.: 828, 1321.

Devitt, F., Miss: 4318.

Devitt, F.R.: 4422.

Devitt Family: 713, 719, 720, 828, 829, 2147.

Devitt, H.: 3048.

Devitt, Harvey: 828.

Devitt, Hilda: 1321.

Dolman, Elizabeth: 1693.

Dolman, George: 4525.

Dolman, William: 4079.

Dolotowitz, Paul: 710.

Dolph, Cyrus: 332, 1334, 1862, 2050, 2276, 2333, 2760, 4031, 4056, 4395, 4396, 4400.

Dolph, Cyrus, Mrs: 1296, 2050.

Dolph, Jack: 2714.

Dolph, Jennie Murdock: 1334.

Dolson, Harold: 4015.

Domm Family: 825.

Domm, George D., Rev.: 3494, 3495, 3501.

Donald, David: 4477.

Donald, Fred: 4477.

Donald, Frederick W.: 1165.

Donald, Irvine: 198.

Donald, James: 85, 115.

Donald, Marcus M.: 13, 115, 1335, 1862, 4150, 4299.

Donald, Nettie: 2748.

Donalds, Adam: 4079.

Donaldson, A.G.: 4246.

Donaldson, Arthur: 4230.

Donaldson Family: 1147.

Donaldson, Helen: 2474.

Donaldson, R. Leslie, Mrs: 2592.

Donaldson, Robert W.: 1188.

Donaldson, W.: 2056.

Doner, Michael: 787.

Donley, L., Miss: 1895.

Donnachie, J.W.: 4261.

Donnenworth, Agnes Godbolt (Mrs John): 840.

Donnenworth, Catharina Milhausner (Mrs Jacob): 840.

Donnenworth, Elizabeth Rickert (Mrs Michael): 840.

Donnenworth, Henry: 840.

Donnenworth, Jacob: 840, 1165, 2801, 4433.

Donnenworth, John: 840.

Donnenworth, Michael: 840.

Donnenworth, Susannah Gingerich (Mrs Henry): 840.

Donner Family: 716.

Donohoe, E.F.: 1336, 1895, 3772.

Donovan, Robert E.: 1909.

Dopp, Edward: 2756, 4467.

Dopp, George: 4422.

Dopp, John: 1862, 1895, 4371, 4396.

Dopp, Nicholas: 4014.

Dopp, Samuel: 2756.

Dornberger, Lambert: 4474.

Dorner, T.A., Mrs: 4258.

Dorow, Robert, Rev.: 3539.

Dorsch, A.F.: 1202.

Dorsch, A.F., Mrs: 1202.

Dorsch, F.: 4422.

Dorschel, Joseph: 3465.

Dorschel, Lukas: 945.

Dorscht, Gerald: 4099.

Doster, Carl: 851.

Doster, Leah: 2206.

Dotzenroth, Hugo: 4099.

Dotzert, Clayton: 2109, 2120, 4422.

Doud Family: 711.

Doud, Frank B.: 3636.

Doud, Wilfred: 2130, 4184.

Dougal, Rev.: 3623.

Dougall, J.: 4278.

Dougall, R.: 4278.

Dougherty, Eleanor: 1346.

Doughty, Dr: 2938.

Doughty, John, Mrs: 3665.

Douglas, Adam: 3761.

Douglas, Agnes: 1544.

Douglas, Asa: 2727, 2810.

Douglas, D.: 3944.

Douglas, David: 1402.

Douglas, Dr: 217.

Douglas, Francis: 289.

Douglas, J. MacDonald: 1909.

Douglas, Jack: 4103.

Douglas, John: 4079.

Douglas, M.L.: 3818.

Douglas, Mary: 4031.

Douglas, Robert: 3669.

Douglas, Stephanie Seagram: 908.

Douglas, T.C.: 1165, 4214.

Douglas, Thomas, Earl of Selkirk: 282.

Douglas, W.J.: 3760.

Douglas, William: 3665, 4470.

Douglass, Duncan: 3915.

Douglass Family: 4473.

Douglass, Frederick: 1639.

Douglass, William: 709.

Dover, D.B.: 4380.

Dow, James: 2818, 4513, 4524, 4525.

Dow, Jean: 2994.

Dowd, Mr: 2379.

Dowler, C.E.A.: 4088.

Dowling, Fred: 1875.

Dowling, T.J., Rev.: 3433, 3442.

Downey, S.L., Rev.: 703, 3256, 3485, 3492, 3499, 4422, 4473.

Downie, John, Rev.: 3468.

Downing, William: 3772.

Downs, Alice: 1197.

Downs, Gladys Hillis (Mrs Lorne): 3852.

Dows, William: 4525.

Dowswell, James: 4266.

Dowswell, M., Miss: 2748.

Dowswett, Clifford: 1903.

Doyle, E.A., Rev.: 118, 1194, 1337, 3433, 3434, 3863, 4088.

Draffin, W.L., Rev.: 3715.

Draimin, Charles: 4349.

Drake, Henry L.: 2700.

Draper, Harold: 4499.

Draves, Mr: 4428.

Drayton, James: 2994.

Drechsler, August: 671, 1338, 4499.

Dredge, William: 1696.

Dreger, Elizabeth: 1200, 4327.

Dreger, F.W.: 2039.

Dreger Family: 658.

Dreger, Fred: 1954, 3915.

Dreger, Fred, Mrs: 3927.

Dreisinger, Allen: 4225.

Dreisinger, Alma: 4226.

Dreisinger, Alvin, Mrs: 4226.

Dreisinger, Christian: 2443.

Dreisinger, Clara: 2443.

Dreisinger, David: 2443.

Dreisinger, Edwin: 2807.

Dreisinger Family: 2443, 4221.

Dreisinger, Nelson: 2807.

Drennan, George: 4416.

Dressler, Emerson: 1796.

Drew, Alfred H.: 4102.

Drew, Benjamin: 709.

Drexler, Anthony: 3160, 3438.

Drexler, Sebastian: 3160, 3438.

Driesbach, John, Rev.: 275.

Drinkwater, Harry: 4102.

Drown, Bernice F.: 2117.

Druar, John: 2769.

Druck Family: 3029.

Drudge, Barbara Shirk (Mrs Benjamin): 1078.

Drudge, Benjamin: 1078, 4441.

Drudge, Lewis: 3839.

Drummond, George M.: 4099.

Drummond, James: 2424.

Drury, E.C.: 2067.

Drury, W. Herbert: 1205.

Dryden, Agnes Kennedy (Mrs Thomas): 842, 843.

Dryden, Andrew: 841, 842, 843, 844, 3663, 4214.

Dryden, Charlotte Green (Mrs Walter K.): 842.

Dryden, Elizabeth Kennedy (Mrs Andrew): 843.

Dryden Family: 841, 842, 843, 844, 2591, 4212.

Dryden, James: 841, 842, 844, 2783.

2775.

Eaton, Nelson: 2760.

Eaton, R.: 3702, 4278.

Eaton, Wesley: 2736.

Eatough, Helen: 3773.

Ebel, Frieda, Mrs: 2549, 3608.

Ebel, Henry W.: 2549.

Ebel, Jacob: 2120, 4426.

Ebel, May: 2549, 3110.

Ebenau, Wilhelm: 1636, 4371.

Eberle, K.: 2234.

Eberly, Anna: 3127.

Ebersohl, Christian: 725, 950, 4524.

Ebersohl, Susanna Neuhauser Blank (Mrs Christian): 725.

Ebersole Family: 716, 725, 3143.

Ebert, Charles: 84, 3813.

Ebert, Dr: 635, 1171.

Ebert, George: 4422.

Eberwein-Braendle, Rosina: 1843.

Ebner, Rev.: 664, 930, 3421, 3448, 4499.

Eby, Aaron: 852, 3312.

Eby, Abraham: 348, 1358, 1369, 4195, 4196, 4525.

Eby, Absalom: 1953, 4515.

Eby, Ada: 3031, 4380.

Eby, Aden: 845, 1347, 3907, 3968.

Eby, Alexander: 249, 4080.

Eby, Alexander, Mrs: 2818.

Eby, Alexander Ralph: 249, 909, 3631, 4080, 4102.

Eby, Allan: 2818, 3633, 3930, 3933, 3956, 4067.

Eby, Amanda: 1515.

Eby, Amos: 3328.

Eby, Ananias: 2812.

Eby, Angeline Baer (Mrs David): 731, 852.

Eby, Barbara: 852, 1002, 1612.

Eby, Barbara Wenger (Mrs George): 852.

Eby, Benjamin: 3, 4, 7, 8, 9, 18, 23, 83, 84, 130, 145, 246, 249, 268, 275, 282, 292, 294, 308, 326, 333, 383, 514, 516, 517, 521, 526, 532, 534, 537, 538, 539, 542, 543, 553, 583, 610, 611, 613, 614, 615, 624, 628, 635, 646, 649, 669, 671, 672, 673, 713, 720, 787, 788, 793, 845, 846, 848, 849, 851, 1034, 1128, 1347, 1348, 1349, 1350, 1351, 1353, 1355, 1356, 1357, 1358, 1359, 1369, 1563, 1564, 1612, 1637, 1640, 1697, 1698, 2097, 2441, 2491, 2586, 2738, 2766, 2782, 2818, 2843, 3078, 3121,

3128, 3137, 3143, 3230, 3232, 3237, 3238, 3239, 3254, 3257, 3273, 3287, 3289, 3310, 3311, 3312, 3313, 3316, 3319, 3323, 3324, 3326, 3348, 3355, 3360, 3363, 3374, 3383, 3391, 3394, 3402, 3870, 3872, 3889, 3928, 4080, 4143, 4191, 4195, 4318, 4319, 4327, 4371, 4372, 4374, 4377, 4380, 4404, 4405, 4422, 4428, 4446, 4455, 4456, 4513, 4517, 4525.

Eby, Benjamin B.: 392, 987.

Eby, Benjamin E.: 1358.

Eby, Catharine: 846, 1698.

Eby, Catharine Bricker (Mrs Benjamin): 1349.

Eby, Catherine Clemens (Mrs Christian): 978.

Eby, Charles: 846.

Eby, Christian: 255, 256, 275, 628, 846, 851, 1213, 1347, 1354, 1636, 1637, 2025, 2073, 2491, 3167, 3170, 3184, 3186, 3238, 3239, 3254, 3273, 3287, 3859, 4380, 4461, 4525.

Eby, Clayton: 2760.

Eby, Cyrus D.: 2018.

Eby, Cyrus K.: 2018.

Eby, Daniel: 3, 275, 333, 731, 848, 852, 987, 1358, 1612, 2379, 4191, 4380, 4521, 4525.

Eby, David: 275, 462, 848, 849, 852, 1358, 2505, 2801, 3329, 4380, 4525.

Eby, David B.: 852, 2801, 4422.

Eby, Delilah Moxley (Mrs Daniel): 987.

Eby, Dilman: 852.

Eby, Dwight: 845.

Eby, Edgar: 1515.

Eby, Edwin: 4499.

Eby, Elgin: 852, 4094, 4104.

Eby, Elias: 85, 517, 553, 846, 1078, 1080, 1352, 1358, 1636, 1637, 2120, 2125, 2379, 2406, 2609, 2766, 2818, 2843, 3238, 3322, 3380, 3870, 4191, 4380, 4422.

Eby, Elias B.: 800.

Eby, Elizabeth: 750, 845, 3097, 3121, 3122, 3238, 4078, 4080.

Eby, Elizabeth Bechtel (Mrs David): 1358.

Eby, Elizabeth Brech (Mrs John): 3312.

Eby, Elizabeth Cressman (Mrs Benjamin E.): 1358.

Eby, Elsie Hewitt (Mrs Gordon): 978, 3128.

Eby, Enoch: 852, 1181, 1922, 2379, 2581, 2803.

Eby, Ephraim: 4192, 4197.

Eby, Esther Kraft (Mrs Moses): 852.

Eby, Esther Shantz (Mrs Moses E.): 1070.

Eby, Eva M.: 2714.

Eby, Ezra E.: 4, 27, 139, 252, 256, 268, 382, 517, 533, 610, 612, 671, 672, 673, 846, 1165, 1359, 1611, 1698, 1984, 2493, 2756, 2818, 3230, 3312, 4192, 4193, 4380, 4517.

Eby Family: 268, 275, 277, 555, 562, 612, 713, 719, 720, 800, 816, 845, 847, 848, 849, 850, 852, 861, 909, 910, 978, 988, 1137, 1139, 1354, 1358, 1359, 2829, 4221, 4455, 4494.

Eby, Floyd: 1823.

Eby, George: 255, 256, 275, 307, 308, 671, 713, 720, 846, 848, 852, 1084, 1128, 1213, 1353, 1358, 1612, 1628, 4011, 4380, 4385, 4480, 4513, 4517, 4523, 4524, 4525.

Eby, George W.: 3, 85, 106, 1706, 2379, 2446, 4422, 4517, 4521, 4525.

Eby, Gordon: 978, 1189, 1347, 1354, 4374, 4428.

Eby, Grant E.: 4448.

Eby, Henry: 9, 83, 84, 85, 94, 109, 258, 326, 607, 610, 611, 635, 673, 846, 1358, 1366, 1562, 2818, 2821, 2843, 3310, 3326, 3348, 3870, 3873, 3893, 3897, 4053, 4371, 4380.

Eby, Henry B.: 1563, 4448, 4449, 4525.

Eby, Herman: 3631, 3632.

Eby, Hiram: 852.

Eby, Ida Newman (Mrs Hiram): 852.

Eby, Ion: 1349, 1350.

Eby, Isaac: 249, 275, 846, 851, 978, 1353, 1358, 3128, 3960, 4080.

Eby, Isaac M.: 1350.

Eby, Isaac S.: 3134.

Eby, Isabelle Myers: 851.

Eby, Isadore E.: 1165.

Eby, Isaiah: 840, 845, 4433.

Eby, Jacob: 3, 333, 1347, 1358, 2379, 4136, 4461, 4521, 4523.

Eby, Jacob B.: 1078, 1165, 4195, 4458.

Gofton, Marjorie Cook (Mrs Russell): 3852.

Gofton, R.H.: 4149, 4374.

Gofton, Robert G.: 1165.

Gohn, H.M.: 2798.

Goldie, A. Gibson: 1169.

Goldie, A.R.: 878, 1169, 1400, 1401, 1522, 1806, 1909, 2777, 3982, 4031, 4088.

Goldie, A.R., Mrs: 3773.

Goldie, David: 878, 879, 880, 1400, 1401, 1402, 1693, 1896, 1976, 2379, 2536, 3650, 4079, 4176, 4177, 4181.

Goldie, E.C.: 4080.

Goldie, Eleanor: 1401.

Goldie, Elizabeth: 878, 1400, 1401, 1402.

Goldie Family: 879, 880, 881, 1524, 2429, 2536, 2591, 4178, 4187, 4188, 4212.

Goldie, Geils: 1402.

Goldie, Gilbert: 1402.

Goldie, Grace Wilson: 1169.

Goldie, Isabella Easton (Mrs David): 879, 880, 2536.

Goldie, James: 878, 1294, 1400, 1401, 1402, 1520, 1524, 1896.

Goldie, Jane: 878, 1400, 1402.

Goldie, Janet: 1402.

Goldie, John: 266, 308, 878, 879, 881, 1169, 1399, 1400, 1401, 1402, 1521, 1524, 1896, 1976, 1984, 2379, 2536, 3665, 3745, 4023, 4177, 4189.

Goldie, John G.: 1169.

Goldie, John, Jr: 878, 1400, 1401, 1896, 1909, 2536.

Goldie, Lincoln: 1400.

Goldie, Margaret: 1400, 1401.

Goldie, Margaret Smith: 878, 879, 1169, 1399, 1400, 1401, 1402.

Goldie, Mary: 1169, 1400, 1402, 1524.

Goldie, Nora Gibson: 1169.

Goldie, Rebecca: 1401.

Goldie, Roswell: 1400, 1402.

Goldie, William: 879, 1400, 1401, 1896, 4079.

Goldschmidt Family: 716, 3364.

Goldschmidt, Jacob: 517.

Goldschmidt, Joseph: 514, 521, 556, 598, 599, 1050, 3364, 4499.

Goldsworthy, R.D.: 2014.

Goldsworthy, Robert: 1971.

Gole, Carl: 4448.

Gole Family: 713, 719, 720.

Gole, Herbert: 1796.

Gole, Leander: 2093, 2167.

Gole, Oscar, Mrs: 2612, 3712.

Gole, Solomon: 4444.

Gole, Solomon S.: 3627, 4017.

Goleff, Samuel A.: 2179, 4315.

Golubski, Ray, Rev.: 3437, 3820.

Gonder, Albert: 4450.

Gonder, M.D.: 1639.

Gonder, Mina: 2812, 4450.

Gonder, Paul: 2775.

Gonder, Rebekah: 1639.

Gonder, Stanley: 2775.

Good, Aaron: 4435.

Good, Abner: 1777, 4521.

Good, Abraham: 882, 884.

Good, Alice Brubacher: 3774.

Good, Allan: 2167.

Good, Amos: 295, 884.

Good, Angeline Schmidt (Mrs Jeremiah): 882.

Good, Barbara Shantz (Mrs Abraham): 882.

Good, C.N., Rev.: 1191, 3278, 3378, 3968.

Good, Carmen: 4521.

Good, Christian: 884.

Good, Cranson: 2704.

Good, Daniel: 882, 4524.

Good, David: 2550.

Good, Della: 2446.

Good, E.H.: 1.

Good, Edward: 552, 3336, 3927.

Good, Eleanor High: 3170, 3271, 3295.

Good, Eli: 882, 3316.

Good, Elizabeth Martin (Mrs Daniel): 882.

Good, Elizabeth Schmitt (Mrs Simeon): 882.

Good, Elizabeth Snyder (Mrs Jonas): 882.

Good, Eva Stahl (Mrs Samuel): 883.

Good Family: 353, 562, 713, 719, 720, 882, 883, 884, 885, 1048, 1123, 1125, 4437, 4454.

Good, George: 2446, 4517, 4521.

Good, Henry: 884, 3320.

Good, Howard, Rev.: 3402.

Good, Ina: 4454.

Good, Ira: 3923.

Good, J.A.: 3772.

Good, J., Dr: 1171, 3007, 4525.

Good, J.R.: 4428, 4444.

Good, Jacob: 4521.

Good, Jacob G.: 2120.

Good, Jennie: 2828, 2829, 4454.

Good, Jeremiah: 882, 3335.

Good, Joanna Martin (Mrs Menno): 884.

Good, Joel: 1, 883, 1165, 2446, 2484, 4078, 4422, 4461, 4521, 4525.

Good, John: 713, 720, 883.

Good, Jonas: 882.

Good, Jonathan: 1358, 2818, 4422.

Good, Joseph: 4422, 4461.

Good, Joseph, Dr: 883.

Good, Karl: 4454.

Good, L., Miss: 2828.

Good, Lollie: 4454.

Good, M.R.: 3923.

Good, Magdalena Baumann (Mrs John): 883.

Good, Mamie: 2828, 2829, 4454.

Good, Mary Schmitt (Mrs Samuel): 882.

Good, Menno: 884, 885.

Good, Milton: 1179, 1678, 1845, 1853, 3837.

Good, Murray: 4521.

Good, Nancy Cressman (Mrs Eli): 882.

Good, Naomi Shantz (Mrs Joseph): 3365.

Good, Nelson: 1179, 1845, 4380.

Good, Newton, Mrs: 4441.

Good, Noah: 884.

Good, Norman: 1955, 2446, 4521.

Good, Olive: 3271.

Good, Oscar: 2446, 4512, 4521.

Good, Peter: 884, 4380.

Good, Polly Cline (Mrs Howard): 3402.

Good, Raymond: 4521.

Good, Samuel: 882, 883, 2379, 4521.

Good, Simeon: 882.

Good, Sylvester: 2446, 4521.

Good, Vera: 2728.

Good, Viola M.: 3361.

Good, Viola S.: 3365.

Goodacre, James: 4104.

Goodall Family: 886.

Goodall, George: 2591.

Goodall, J. Ross, Rev.: 3774, 3845.

Goodall, James: 2130.

Goodall, John: 2727, 3663.

Goodall, Martin: 3774.

Goodall, Shirley: 3774.

Goodall, William: 3663.

Goodfellow, Andrew: 3745.

Goodfellow, Oliver: 3665.

Goodger, W.D., Rev.: 1718, 3695.

Gooding, R.J., Mrs: 4088.

Gooding, William: 4506.

Goodman, Kenneth: 2767, 4079,

Green, H.M.: 1165.
Green, J.G.: 85, 125.
Green, J.W.: 4423, 4478.
Green, J.W., Mrs: 3773.
Green, John: 256, 2103, 4498, 4506.
Green, Lucinda Shupe (Mrs Wheeler): 1083.
Green, Robert, Rev.: 3623.
Green, William: 4096.
Greene, Edward: 4053.
Greene, W.A.: 1, 333, 2056, 2714, 2818, 4380.
Greenwood, John: 1165, 4466.
Gregor, David: 4433.
Gregory, W.H.: 4080.
Gremm, Catherine Otterbein (Mrs Conrad): 1000.
Gremm, Conrad: 1000.
Gremm, Henry: 4040.
Grenzebach, J.H, Rev.: 3496, 3503, 4512, 4521.
Gresman, John: 4525.
Gress, Elizabeth, "Midwife Gress": 4228.
Gress Family: 4212.
Gress, G.: 1974, 4255, 4395.
Gress, George: 4058.
Greulich, Anthony: 2167.
Greulich, Joseph: 2167.
Greulich, Wilfred: 2167.
Greunawald, William: 1899.
Greutzner, G.A.: 4031, 4280.
Grey, Jane: 1334.
Greyerbiehl, Anna Schmidt (Mrs John): 3431, 3444.
Greyerbiehl, John: 37, 2801, 2815, 3431, 3444.
Greyerbiehl, Joseph: 2769, 4468, 4474.
Greyerbiehl, P.B.: 4474.
Grier, Wyly: 2777.
Grieser Family: 716.
Grieve, John: 2727.
Grieve, Ruth V., Mrs: 2120.
Grieves, A.: 4499.
Griffin Family: 1112.
Griffin, G.B., Rev.: 3715.
Griffin, H.: 13, 1182, 4080, 4183.
Griffin, J.J.: 2056.
Griffin, Peter: 2596.
Griffin, William, Rev.: 3622, 3695.
Griffith, Enos: 4214.
Griffiths, F.M.: 4086, 4089, 4258.
Grigg, B.W.N.: 13.
Grigg, L.H.: 2909.
Griggs, Gordon, Rev.: 3681.
Grill, Carl: 2424.

Grill, Charles: 2424, 4277, 4278.
Grill, Henry: 2424.
Grill, Norman: 4104.
Grills, William: 3761.
Grimm, Carmen: 4031.
Grimm, Moses: 2760.
Grimmer Family: 2704, 4491.
Grimmer, Rena Twiss (Mrs James H.): 3852.
Grimwood, William: 3681.
Grischow, Noah C.: 2120.
Gritz, Henry: 1165.
Grobe, F.: 4395.
Grody Family: 713, 719, 720.
Groff, Abraham: 889, 890, 1165.
Groff, Amos: 889.
Groff, Andrew: 275, 516, 553, 713, 720, 889, 1976, 2379, 2441, 4458, 4517.
Groff, Andrew, Jr: 553.
Groff, Annie Huber (Mrs Andrew): 889.
Groff, C.: 3656, 4380.
Groff, Ephraim: 553.
Groff Family: 252, 713, 719, 720, 889, 890, 4212, 4433.
Groff, Frank: 2746.
Groff, George: 4499.
Groff, Henry: 1165, 4513.
Groff, Irvin: 3183.
Groff, Isaac: 553.
Groff, J.B.: 1773.
Groff, Jacob: 889, 1213, 1356, 3306, 3323.
Groff, Jacob E.: 889.
Groff, John: 256, 4517, 4525.
Groff, Levi: 889, 4441.
Groff, Mary: 3074, 3101.
Groff, Mary Eby (Mrs Abraham): 889.
Groff, Moses: 2704.
Groff, O.S.: 2775.
Groff, Samuel: 553, 3633.
Groh, Aaron: 553, 3644.
Groh, Almeda: 2736.
Groh, Anson: 616, 2736, 2760, 2765, 3271, 3305, 3904, 4428, 4452.
Groh, Anson, Mrs: 2766.
Groh, Beth (Mrs Orville): 2760.
Groh, C.T.: 13, 1984, 2736, 2760, 2761, 2765, 3770.
Groh, Christian: 2760.
Groh, Conrad: 1967.
Groh, Cora Gingrich (Mrs Harold): 3271, 3365.
Groh, Daniel: 2775.
Groh, David: 2718.

Groh, Della: 234, 2736, 2775.
Groh, Edwin: 3770.
Groh, Eldon: 2775.
Groh, Elizabeth Bechtel (Mrs Jonathan): 2760.
Groh, Elizabeth Witmer (Mrs Michael): 275, 1153, 2760, 2761.
Groh Family: 234, 275, 636, 713, 719, 720, 729, 891, 1152, 1153.
Groh, Harold, Rev.: 593, 729, 2718, 3242, 3367, 3387.
Groh, Herbert: 593, 1698, 2725, 2760.
Groh, Howard: 2736, 2760, 2761, 3770, 3809, 4461.
Groh, I.W., Rev.: 3499.
Groh, Isaac: 20, 554, 1165, 1166, 2114, 2736, 2760, 2765, 3232, 3492, 4286, 4456.
Groh, Ivan: 593, 729, 1571, 2078, 2760, 4264.
Groh, J.D.: 1165, 1967, 2120.
Groh, Jacob: 256, 827, 2760, 2761, 2766.
Groh, John: 234, 256, 275, 276, 289, 891, 1153, 2736, 2760, 2761, 2766, 3232, 3492, 3870, 3904, 4286, 4450, 4456.
Groh, John, Mrs: 2766.
Groh, John W.: 2736, 2760, 2763, 2764.
Groh, Jonathan: 2760.
Groh, L.: 4278.
Groh, Mabel: 3361, 3365.
Groh, Mary Wanner (Mrs Isaac): 2760, 2766, 3232.
Groh, Melvin S.: 382.
Groh, Melvin S., Mrs: 2760.
Groh, Michael: 255, 256, 275, 555, 671, 713, 720, 1153, 2760, 2761, 4455, 4456.
Groh, Nancy Detweiler (Mrs Jacob): 827, 2760, 2766.
Groh, Norman: 2760.
Groh, Norman, Mrs: 3232.
Groh, Orville: 2736, 2760, 3770.
Groh, Oscar: 729.
Groh, Susannah Wanner: 234, 275, 891, 1153, 2760, 3232.
Groh, Sylvanus: 2801, 3007.
Groh, Sylvester: 2728.
Groh, W.: 4278.
Groome Family: 1014.
Grose, Sharon Salm: 3761.
Gross, Audrey: 2039.
Gross, D., Jr: 4298.
Gross, David: 114, 326, 1201, 1406, 1484, 1884, 2039, 4121, 4128,

4441.
Hendrick. C.A.: 4517.
Hendrick, Samuel: 4193, 4195.
Hendrick, W.B.: 4517.
Hendry, Charles: 2, 18, 37, 1429, 1430, 1819, 2120, 2128, 2436, 2548, 2549, 3702, 3978, 4034, 4073, 4371, 4380, 4513, 4523, 4524, 4525.
Hendry, Charles, Mrs: 3702.
Hendry, Sarah Washburn (Mrs William): 1430.
Hendry, William: 1165, 1429, 1430, 1805, 1818, 2120, 2459, 2550, 3702, 3767, 4023, 4056, 4067, 4318, 4371, 4380, 4422.
Henheffer, Joseph: 2700.
Henhoefer, Dr: 4428.
Henhoeffer Family: 1778, 2815, 4433.
Henhoeffer, Leopold: 1868, 4433.
Henkel, Henry L., Rev.: 3525, 3612.
Hennig, S.: 671, 672.
Henning Brothers: 1321.
Henning, Joseph: 1165, 4392.
Henning, M., Mrs: 4395.
Henning, Michael: 1165.
Henrich, W.S., Rev.: 3496.
Henrich, Wilfred: 4014.
Henry, Bernice: 3271.
Henry, G.M.: 4277.
Henry, George: 191.
Henry, George S., Hon.: 2776.
Henry, R.D., Mrs: 3852.
Henry, Robert: 1932.
Henry, William: 4458.
Henselwood, Howard: 3049.
Henselwood, Lydia Scott: 3636.
Henshelwood, Peter: 4014, 4015.
Hensius, J.: 3048.
Hensler, Andrew: 3377.
Hensler Family: 716.
Hentschel, Elsie Seifert: 4478.
Hepburn, Leila M.: 3773.
Hepburn, Thomas: 2720.
Hepburn, W.D.: 1165.
Hepworth, John: 4438.
Herber, Ernestine: 3106.
Herber Family: 1773, 4499.
Herber, Johannes: 3552.
Herber, John: 13, 1773, 4499.
Herber, Martha: 3574.
Herbert, A.W., Rev.: 4454.
Herbert, Bill: 120.
Herborn, L.: 4193.
Herbst Family: 1047.
Herbst, Mary: 1791.
Herd, David: 3709.

Hergert, Casper: 4525.
Hergott, Albert: 3054.
Hergott, Aloyes: 4478.
Hergott, Bill: 4474.
Hergott, Edwin C.: 4474.
Hergott, Elias: 2769.
Hergott, Enoch: 2769.
Hergott Family: 959.
Hergott, George M.: 4422.
Hergott, Gerard: 4100.
Hergott, Henry: 4474.
Hergott, Jonas: 2769.
Hergott, Joseph: 4040.
Hergott, Noah: 4478.
Hergott, Norbert: 2769, 2832.
Hergott, Patricia: 2166.
Hergott, Peter: 2769, 2815.
Hergott, W.N., "Bert": 4099.
Hergott, Wilfred: 2769.
Heric, Victor: 2136, 4474.
Herlan, Frank, Rev.: 2421, 3494, 3495, 3496, 3503.
Herman, Cameron: 2775.
Herman, Larry: 2775.
Herman, Ronald: 2775.
Herman, Shirley: 2775.
Hermann, J.G.: 681.
Herner Family: 713, 719, 720, 4499.
Herner, Frederick: 256, 275, 2533, 4433.
Herner, H.: 1879.
Herner, S.S.: 1165, 2818, 2971, 2992, 4499.
Herner, Samuel: 1128, 2117.
Hernie, Steve: 3799.
Heron, H.: 4196.
Herres, Balentine: 4525.
Herres, J.K.: 4009.
Herres, Simon: 2732, 2756.
Herrfort, A.K.: 619.
Herrfort, Andrew: 906, 1165.
Herrfort, Anna Sommer: 906.
Herrfort, Esther: 3145.
Herrfort, Lydia: 3145.
Herrfort, Mary: 3145.
Herrfort, Sarah: 3145.
Herrgott, Aloyes: 3175.
Herrgott, Annie: 2801.
Herrgott, Elias: 1165.
Herrgott, Henry: 2801.
Herrgott, Herbert: 4478.
Herrgott, Jacob: 2801.
Herrgott, Ludwig: 2801.
Herrgott, Matilda: 2801.
Herrgott, Nathaniel: 3175.
Herridge, William, Rev.: 2840, 2845.
Herrington, John C.: 4422.

Herriot, David: 4214.
Herriot Family: 4204.
Herriot, William: 185, 250, 1431, 2353, 2356.
Herriott, David, Mrs: 4204.
Herris, Valentine: 4517.
Herrle Family: 1773.
Herrle, Howard: 1773.
Herrop, Hugh: 4473.
Hershey, Benjamin: 255, 256, 671, 1358, 1612, 2586, 4380.
Hershey, Christian: 294.
Hershey Family: 932.
Hershey, Jacob: 255, 256, 1358, 4380.
Hershey, Sydney, Rev.: 3499.
Herteis, Dennis: 4474.
Herteis, Joseph: 4474.
Hertel, Harman: 2813.
Hertel, Henry: 3569.
Hertel, Isaac: 4435.
Hertel, John: 3054.
Hertel, Michael: 4474.
Herter, Berneice Rudy (Mrs Jack): 4441.
Hertfelder, William: 2818, 2822, 4299, 4380.
Hertling, William: 4422.
Hertz, Amandus: 3050, 4220.
Hertz, Dina: 4371.
Hertz, Freido: 3050.
Hertz, M., Mrs: 1594.
Hertz, William: 4371.
Hertzberger, David: 4100.
Herz, Max: 3544.
Herzog, August: 2769.
Herzog, William O.: 2396, 4474.
Hesch, John: 2030.
Heslop, Bert: 4061.
Hespeler, Anna Barbara: 908.
Hespeler, Anna Wick, "Babette": 908.
Hespeler, Charles: 908.
Hespeler, Charlotte: 671, 672, 745, 908.
Hespeler, Eliza Knoth (Mrs Jacob): 908, 3773.
Hespeler Family: 4268.
Hespeler, Ferdinanda: 908, 1292.
Hespeler, George: 18, 908, 1233, 1292, 2994, 4058, 4079, 4271, 4286.
Hespeler, Jacob: 2, 3, 13, 18, 22, 249, 292, 308, 332, 635, 656, 671, 672, 806, 809, 907, 908, 1256, 1292, 1293, 1453, 1583, 1865, 1918, 1932, 1975, 1976, 1986, 2005, 2010, 2073, 2097, 2109, 2120, 2121, 2128, 2379, 3537, 3637,

3767, 3869, 3894, 3973, 4017, 4058, 4150, 4255, 4271, 4274, 4275, 4277, 4282, 4286, 4374, 4380, 4390, 4391, 4392, 4393, 4394, 4455.

Hespeler, Jacob, Jr: 908.

Hespeler, John G.: 908.

Hespeler, Laura: 908.

Hespeler, Louise: 908.

Hespeler, Marie: 908.

Hespeler, Mary Keatchie: 908.

Hespeler, Mina: 908.

Hespeler, Sophie Taylor: 908.

Hespeler, Stephanie: 908.

Hespeler, Wilhelmina: 908, 1292.

Hespeler, William: 249, 333, 536, 537, 572, 671, 672, 907, 908, 1292, 1631, 1637, 2843, 3537, 3892.

Hess, Albert, Dr: 671, 672.

Hess, Deborah: 256.

Hess, Elizabeth: 256.

Hess, George: 326.

Hess, Isabella: 256.

Hess, J.G., Dr: 4499.

Hess, John H.: 3238, 3239, 3309, 3310.

Hesse, Irvin: 3623.

Hesse, Jergen: 2179.

Hesse, John: 13, 4094.

Hesse, Julius: 1257.

Hesse, Lina: 1257.

Hessel, Francis: 2769.

Hessenaur, C.P.: 4474.

Hessenaur, Howard W.: 2289.

Hessenaur, John: 4299.

Hetherington, Earle F.: 3049.

Hett, Alice: 1433.

Hett, Casper: 79, 85, 122, 1453, 4380, 4461.

Hett, Dorothy: 979.

Hett, Dorothy Miller: 4426.

Hett, Elisabeth: 3551.

Hett, Henry: 3032, 4380.

Hett, J.E., Dr: 326, 602, 671, 672, 851, 1201, 1205, 1432, 1433, 2503, 2818, 2822, 2951, 3702, 3759, 3815, 3959, 4061, 4121, 4128, 4132, 4136, 4146, 4164, 4298, 4299, 4371, 4374, 4380.

Hett, James: 979.

Hett, John B.: 1432, 3551, 4014, 4380.

Hett, Laverne: 3044.

Heubach, R.: 4527.

Heuman, Carl: 1895.

Heveron, James: 85, 124.

Hewer, Mabel Prong (Mrs Frank): 4273.

Hewetson, A. Russell: 127.

Hewetson, Rosa Melvina Breithaupt (Mrs A. Russell): 1273.

Hewetson, Vera: 127.

Hewitt, Albert S.: 3631, 3632.

Hewitt, Ann Hamilton (Mrs Elisha): 817.

Hewitt, Catharine Benner (Mrs Elisha Jr): 817.

Hewitt, Elisha: 817, 1084, 1752, 3485, 3669, 4517, 4525, 4526.

Hewitt, Elisha, Jr: 817.

Hewitt, Elspet Meldrum (Mrs Elisha): 817.

Hewitt, Ephraim: 817.

Hewitt Family: 817, 978, 4483.

Hewitt, Frederick: 978.

Hewitt, George: 4480, 4481, 4483.

Hewitt, Hiram: 2812.

Hewitt, Jane Wright (Mrs Ephraim): 817.

Hewitt, Margaret Donaldson (Mrs Peter): 817.

Hewitt, Peter: 817.

Hewitt, Rachel Cress (Mrs Elisha): 817, 1308, 3485.

Hewitt, Richard: 3818.

Heyd, Jacob: 3775.

Hibbard, Ashley: 1993.

Hibner, Daniel: 22, 326, 1201, 1434, 1508, 1855, 1856, 2373, 4067, 4157, 4158, 4299, 4374, 4375, 4380.

Hibner Family: 249.

Hichcock, Mr and Mrs: 2179.

Hickey, Rev.: 3470, 3474, 3476.

Hicks, F.M.: 3636.

Hicks, John: 1871, 4014.

Hicks, Philip: 4014.

Hicks, Thomas, Rev.: 1281, 3470, 3474.

Hickson, George: 3936.

Hickson, Robert: 4099.

Hiebert, P.C.: 3783.

Hiebert, Victor: 3317.

Hieronymous Family: 4499.

Hiestand Family: 932.

Hiestand, Henry: 275, 3493, 3495, 4380.

Hiestand, J.: 4461.

Hiestand, Kinget: 804.

Higgins, Allona Eby (Mrs S. Keith): 845.

Higgins Family: 4473.

Higgs, Ann: 1200.

High, Ephraim, Mrs: 1188.

High Family: 911.

High, Henry: 548.

High, John: 911.

High, Mary Ann Detweiler (Mrs Samuel K.): 911.

High, Norman: 516, 1435, 1678, 2908.

High, Samuel K.: 911.

Highton, Elsie: 1932.

Hilborn, A.: 2828, 2829, 2992.

Hilborn, Aaron: 4454.

Hilborn, Aaron W.: 2843, 4230, 4233.

Hilborn, Albert: 1937.

Hilborn, Alger: 4436.

Hilborn, Amos: 1910, 1998, 2379, 2971, 3869, 4437, 4497, 4499.

Hilborn, Bill: 4477.

Hilborn, Caroline Witmer: 1153, 3082.

Hilborn, Clarence: 2535, 2703.

Hilborn, David: 1437.

Hilborn, Emanuel: 2120.

Hilborn Family: 713, 719, 720, 909, 910, 1984, 2623, 4490, 4496, 4499.

Hilborn, "Fat": 3183.

Hilborn, Florence: 2775.

Hilborn, Francis: 2760, 2775, 4452.

Hilborn, Franklin: 909.

Hilborn, G.V.: 1437, 2485, 2609, 3889, 3945, 4380.

Hilborn, Gordon: 2760.

Hilborn, Harry, Dr: 4454.

Hilborn, Henry C.: 1165, 2163, 2232, 4362.

Hilborn, Hugh: 1437.

Hilborn, Isaac: 3772.

Hilborn, Ivan: 1998, 2399, 2971, 4497, 4499.

Hilborn, Ivan M.: 1910, 2081, 4499.

Hilborn, J.: 255, 256, 2774.

Hilborn, J.B.: 4483.

Hilborn, Jacob: 1153, 2379, 3232, 4435, 4437.

Hilborn, James: 2775.

Hilborn, Jesse: 256, 555, 2097, 2533, 3082.

Hilborn, John: 2135, 3232, 3247, 3305, 3643.

Hilborn, Joseph: 909, 2379, 4435, 4437, 4454.

Hilborn, Joseph M.: 909.

Hilborn, Joseph, Mrs: 1191.

Hilborn, Joshua: 4477.

Hilborn, Maria Erb (Mrs Joseph M.): 909.

Hilborn, Miriam: 2971, 4487, 4499.

Peter): 275.

Holm, W.: 3644.

Holman, P.L., Miss: 1571.

Holme, William: 282.

Holmes, Allan: 120, 2041, 4088.

Holmes, Edwin, Rev.: 3644.

Holmes, Ernie: 2869.

Holmes, Gordon: 3713.

Holmes, T.W., Mrs: 4088.

Holmeshaw, H.: 4104.

Holowaty, Joseph: 3466.

Holst, Albert: 2705.

Holst, Delton: 3371.

Holst, Delton, Mrs: 3371.

Holst, Jacob, Mrs: 4499.

Holt Family: 4470.

Holt, Mary Grattan, Lady: 4478.

Holtby, Matthew, Rev.: 3669, 4525.

Holtzman, H., Rev.: 4512, 4521.

Holtzwarth, Barbara Schwind (Mrs George): 1064.

Holtzwarth, George: 1064.

Holwell, Frederick: 1, 1165, 2109, 2120, 2495, 4374, 4499, 4510.

Holwell, M.E., Miss: 2109, 2120.

Holzer, John, Rev.: 671, 672, 1115, 1441, 3428, 3433, 4464, 4465.

Holzmueller, Leopold: 2732, 3419, 3467.

Holzworth, Edna: 4225.

Homem, Fatima: 697.

Homewood Family: 2085.

Homuth, C.T., Rev.: 3378.

Homuth, John: 3808.

Homuth, Karl: 13, 1169, 1205, 3525, 4136, 4155, 4166, 4167, 4183, 4230, 4233, 4279, 4396.

Homuth, Minnie Rahn: 1169.

Homuth, Otto: 332, 1169, 2000, 4228, 4255, 4395, 4396.

Honderich, Abram: 556, 1754.

Honderich, Barbara: 4499.

Honderich, Cameron: 1754, 1773.

Honderich, Christian: 598, 1754, 1775, 4499.

Honderich, Cora Hostetler: 4499.

Honderich, Earl: 1754, 4499.

Honderich, Emerson: 1773, 4499.

Honderich Family: 716, 874, 1773, 4499.

Honderich, Floyd: 1754.

Honderich, John: 556, 1754.

Honderich, Robert W.: 4094, 4099.

Honey, S.L.: 4255.

Honsberger, Abraham: 4031.

Honsberger, Enock: 1891.

Honsberger Family: 252, 713, 719, 720.

Honsberger, Gordon McK.: 1442, 4031, 4112.

Honsberger, Gordon McK., Mrs: 3936.

Honsberger, J.F., Dr: 326, 851, 1442, 2714, 2818, 3631, 3632, 3633, 3759, 3960, 4029, 4031, 4056, 4114, 4121, 4128, 4132, 4136, 4146, 4157, 4158, 4299, 4371, 4374, 4380.

Honsberger, Katherine: 1442.

Honsberger, Russell: 4168.

Honsberger, Valentine: 1442.

Honsberger, William: 4192.

Honsinger Family: 4473.

Hontzberger, Martin: 256.

Hood, Adam: 2975, 3663, 3671, 4250, 4266.

Hood, James: 4250.

Hooker, William: 1402.

Hooper, H.: 4422.

Hooper, Harry: 4422.

Hooper, S.R.: 4422.

Hoover, Christian: 256, 3134.

Hoover, Eileen: 1725.

Hoover Family: 961.

Hope, Andrew: 4079.

Hope Family: 4188.

Hope, Helen: 3660.

Hope, Peter: 4079.

Hope, Thomas: 4079.

Hope, William: 1007, 2700.

Hopfen, Mr: 3551.

Hopkins, Alfred B.: 84, 2818, 2843.

Hopkins, Caleb: 3977, 4134, 4144.

Hopkins, Mr: 4521.

Hopp, Kenneth: 3936.

Hopp, Louis: 2039.

Hopper, David: 2148.

Hopps, Vernon, Mrs: 4261.

Hopton, A.W.: 3793.

Horn, Mr: 2704.

Hornby, Mr: 2828, 2829.

Horner, A., Miss: 3031.

Horner, S.: 4278.

Horning, Abraham: 256.

Horning, Peter: 255, 256, 307, 555, 3711, 4191.

Horst, Aaron: 916.

Horst, Alice: 3243.

Horst, Allen: 2814.

Horst, Amos: 941.

Horst, Angeline Snyder: 941.

Horst, Annie Weber (Mrs Daniel): 916.

Horst, Daniel: 916, 3096.

Horst, Daniel W.: 916.

Horst, David: 3062, 3066, 3096, 3099, 3143, 3148, 4524.

Horst, David B.: 3057.

Horst, David, Mrs: 3243.

Horst, Elias: 916.

Horst Family: 562, 713, 719, 720, 1123, 1125, 1443.

Horst, Fern Dettweiler: 3258.

Horst, George: 916.

Horst, Isaac: 3096.

Horst, Isaac R.: 2092.

Horst, John: 3096.

Horst, Joseph: 3499.

Horst, Leah: 3096.

Horst, Magdalena: 916, 3096.

Horst, Margaret Lorentz (Mrs Elias): 916.

Horst, Mary Ann Bowman (Mrs Daniel W.): 916.

Horst, Mary Martin: 3096.

Horst, MaryAnn Martin (Mrs Samuel W.): 916.

Horst, Menno: 3096.

Horst, Osiah: 916, 3258, 3309, 4499.

Horst, Samuel: 713, 720, 916, 2092, 3096.

Horst, Samuel R.: 1443.

Horst, Samuel W.: 916.

Horst, Susannah: 3067, 3096.

Horst, Tilman: 1796.

Hortenberger, Gregory: 3, 4517, 4521.

Horton, Anthony S.: 3001.

Horton, S.A.: 2581.

Hortop, Bessie: 2711, 2775.

Hortop, J.A.: 4435.

Hortop, James: 2000, 2401.

Hortop, William: 3644.

Hosie, Frieda H., Mrs: 2120, 4429.

Hosie, James W.: 2120.

Hossfeld, Margaret, Miss: 2801.

Hossie, Alexander: 3438.

Hossie, Orville P, Rev.: 3633, 3649.

Hostetler, Alberta Laschinger (Mrs Lafayette): 991.

Hostetler, Charity: 3127.

Hostetler, Daniel: 1165.

Hostetler, Donald: 4499.

Hostetler, Earl: 2773.

Hostetler, Emma: 3376.

Hostetler Family: 713, 719, 720, 917, 918, 2704.

Hostetler, Henry: 4040.

Hostetler, Isaac: 1165.

Hostetler, John: 4499.

Hostetler, Joseph: 2773.

Hostetler, L.: 4094, 4382.

Hymmen, Eric: 4136.
Hymmen Family: 1850.
Hymmen, Heather: 4136.
Hymmen, Henry: 3007, 3048, 4298, 4374, 4380.
Hymmen, Kieth: 326, 671, 672, 1737, 2651, 3799, 3927, 4023, 4136.
Hymmen, Lorna: 4136.
Hymmen, Peter: 326, 1930, 2496, 3759, 4380.
Hymmen, Ruth Iredale: 4136.
Hymmen, Ward: 4136.
Hynd, Allan: 4099.
Hyndman, Maggie: 2748, 2818, 4380.
Hynes, D.J.: 2798, 3915.
Hysinger, David: 3919.
Hysinger, David, Mrs: 3919.

Ibach, Franz: 4393.
Ibbott, Thomas Hargreaves, Rev.: 3256, 3485, 3499, 4473.
Idlington, John: 4392, 4393.
Idlington, Peter: 2114, 3664.
Idlington, Walter: 1165, 2775.
Illing, F.H: 4299, 4374.
Illingworth, Annie Ferguson: 4486.
Illingworth Family: 4498.
Illingworth, Margaret: 1184.
Illingworth, William: 3470, 3474, 4486, 4499, 4506.
Imhoff Family: 716.
Imlay, Alexander: 3669.
Imrie, Andrew, Rev.: 3406, 3407, 3416.
Ineson, Allen: 4099.
Ingall, Lincoln W.H.: 1909.
Ingham, George: 4226.
Ingle, Martha: 2138.
Ingle, Oliver: 2138.
Ingles, Luman: 2438, 2457.
Inglis, David, Rev.: 3660.
Inglis Family: 4436.
Inglis, Walter, Rev.: 3668, 3686, 3695, 3745, 4178.
Ingram, A.E.W., Rev.: 4280.
Inns, T.H., Rev.: 3479.
Intschert, Michael: 662.
Iredale, Charles: 1190, 3923.
Iredale, Charles, Mrs: 3923.
Iredale, Dorothy: 3923.
Iredale, William: 4396.
Ireland, John: 1179, 4079.
Ireland, Urquhart: 1932.
Irschick, Leon E., Rev.: 3512, 3547.
Irven, John: 4099.
Irvin, Norman: 3750.

Irvine, S.P., Rev.: 3472.
Irving, Emilius: 326, 2128.
Irving, George, Rev.: 3668, 3686, 3695.
Irving, Guy Emilius: 2840.
Irwin, J.M.: 4237.
Irwin, Nellie: 3773.
Irwin, Richard: 4266.
Irwin, William A.: 2083.
Isaac, Henry, Rev.: 1165, 3292.
Isbach, Adam: 3978.
Iseler, T.A., Rev.: 2899, 3598.
Isenhauer Family: 4221.
Isenhauer, George: 4525.
Isley, T.H.: 8, 1796, 3927, 3936, 3968, 4428.
Isley, Theo M., Mrs: 1773.
Israel, August: 1165.
Israel, Carl: 84, 4393.
Israel, Edward: 2807.
Israel, Elizabeth: 752.
Israel, Elizabeth Schweitzer (Mrs Michael): 1063.
Israel Family: 998.
Israel, George: 175, 2379, 4433.
Israel, Marie: 2807.
Israel, Michael: 1063, 1165.
Itter, Peter: 4034.
Itter, Peter, Mrs: 4034.
Iturbi, Jose: 1725.
Iutzi, Daniel S.: 3340.
Iutzi Family: 3340.
Iutzi, Mary Schrag (Mrs Michael): 1055, 1056.
Iutzi, Michael: 1055, 1056.

Jacklin, Maxine: 2801.
Jackman, D.S.: 2818.
Jackman, John S.: 2818.
Jackson, Agnes: 4031.
Jackson, Alexander, Rev.: 2714, 3655, 3662, 3663, 3671.
Jackson, Earl: 2458.
Jackson, Fred: 2989.
Jackson, Frederick, Rev.: 3496.
Jackson, G.: 4299.
Jackson, Geneva, Miss: 3773, 3857.
Jackson, Garth: 3499.
Jackson, H.F.J.: 908, 1252, 1535, 1811, 1812, 1833, 2055, 2379, 2446, 2714, 2818, 2857, 3468, 3894, 4124, 4191, 4318, 4371, 4372, 4380, 4517, 4521.
Jackson, H.F.J., Mrs: 1252.
Jackson, Isabella: 1204, 2055.
Jackson, James: 308, 1453, 1720,

2109, 2120, 4188, 4212, 4480.
Jackson, R.: 4221.
Jackson, Robert A., Rev.: 3662, 3663.
Jackson, Samuel W.: 2055.
Jackson, Stanley: 4282.
Jackson, Walter G.: 2458.
Jackson, William: 709, 3030, 4250.
Jacky, Luella: 4499.
Jacky, Sylvester: 1773.
Jacob, Donald: 4500.
Jacob, Keith: 4500.
Jacob, Kevin: 4500.
Jacobi, A.G., Rev.: 3525, 3532, 3537, 3563, 3583, 3613.
Jacobi, Daniel: 1967.
Jacobi, Herman: 1772.
Jacobi, John: 1967, 3080, 4422.
Jacobi, Philip: 1833.
Jacobi, Yost: 4525.
Jacobs, Charles: 2767.
Jacobs, George: 2030.
Jacobs, Helen: 3936.
Jacobs, Miss: 3029.
Jacques, Mr: 4158, 4390.
Jaeck Family: 477.
Jaeckel, Adam: 4371.
Jaeger, Henry: 3551, 4380.
Jaehle, Michael: 4371.
Jaffray, Agnes Jackson (Mrs William): 1452, 1453.
Jaffray, Amy Robsart: 1453, 3048.
Jaffray, Clive T.: 1453, 2714.
Jaffray, Edward: 1451.
Jaffray, Edward G.: 1453.
Jaffray Family: 1452, 4212.
Jaffray, George: 104, 1165, 1451, 1453, 1722, 4040.
Jaffray, Henry: 104, 1451, 1453, 3888.
Jaffray, J.P.: 85, 120, 1306, 1339, 1451, 1453, 1833, 1984, 2041, 3772, 3888, 3930, 4023, 4088, 4233, 4245, 4258, 4318, 4356.
Jaffray, John: 1453.
Jaffray, K.F., Miss: 1183, 2041, 2720, 2862, 2863, 4031.
Jaffray, Margaret: 1453.
Jaffray, Peter: 7, 83, 85, 104, 120, 1452, 1453, 2041, 2846, 3481, 3872, 4125, 4240, 4255.
Jaffray, R.M.: 85, 120, 1453.
Jaffray, Richard: 18, 1165, 1451, 1453, 1722, 3888, 4246, 4250.
Jaffray, Robert: 1451, 2714, 3888.
Jaffray, William: 79, 85, 104, 122, 123, 653, 1201, 1452, 1453, 1628, 1637, 2039, 2100, 2109, 2120,

4510.

Kaiser, Augustus: 2732, 2815, 3973.

Kaiser, Catherine, Mrs: 2120.

Kaiser, Christian: 4203.

Kaiser, Elisabetha Bohme: 930.

Kaiser, F., Rev.: 3416, 3656, 4380.

Kaiser Family: 930.

Kaiser, Frederick: 4438.

Kaiser, John: 37, 4380.

Kaiser, Joseph: 2120.

Kaiser, Karl: 3444.

Kaiser, Louis M.: 308, 1183, 1457, 3905, 4087, 4203.

Kaiser, Mrs: 1234.

Kaiser, Peter: 2732, 2815, 4380.

Kaiser, Ward L., Rev.: 3506.

Kaiser, William: 3032, 3044, 3048, 3050, 3815.

Kajsiewicz, Jerome, Rev.: 3453, 3454, 3455, 3458, 3460.

Kalbfleisch, C.: 931, 3045, 4017.

Kalbfleisch, E.: 4499.

Kalbfleisch, Eckhard: 4458.

Kalbfleisch Family: 658, 757, 931, 1129, 4499.

Kalbfleisch, George: 931, 4195.

Kalbfleisch, Harold: 3903, 4099.

Kalbfleisch, Henry: 931.

Kalbfleisch, Herbert Karl: 83, 633, 2909.

Kalbfleisch, Jacob: 1824.

Kalbfleisch, Joachim: 85, 110, 333, 931, 1545, 4422.

Kalbfleisch, John: 931.

Kalbfleisch, L.H., Rev.: 3518, 3525, 3546, 3566.

Kalbfleisch, Louis: 1895.

Kalbfleisch, Reinhardt: 931.

Kalbfleisch, Salome Poth (Mrs John): 1010.

Kale, George: 3050.

Kaljas, Anna: 1200.

Kaminska, Larry: 4467.

Kanagy, Margaret Elizabeth Brown (Mrs S.M.): 3365.

Kanagy, S.M., Rev.: 3242, 3270, 3365.

Kane, Benjamin: 4428.

Kanmacher, George: 4395.

Kannel, C. von: 4392.

Kannengieser, J.F.: 4371.

Kannmacher, C.: 4392.

Kapches, Mima: 1968.

Kappas, Conrad: 4040, 4474.

Kappes, Adolph, Rev.: 3520, 3525, 3527, 3573, 4512, 4521.

Kappes, Conrad: 2769.

Kapron, John: 4100.

Karch, Charles: 3569, 4274, 4286.

Karch, H.W.: 4286.

Karcher, Donald R.: 1773, 4448.

Karges, Fred: 4429.

Karges, George: 1195.

Karidas, Mary: 4362.

Karidas, Paul: 4362.

Karidas, Steven: 4362.

Karidas, Tom: 4362.

Karn, Philip: 851, 4044.

Kartechner, William: 4118.

Karweil Family: 4454.

Kastner Family: 3029.

Katzenmeier, Beatrice: 4382.

Kaufman, A.R.: 23, 133, 326, 334, 616, 671, 672, 1458, 1459, 1460, 1461, 1463, 1838, 1839, 1853, 1855, 1924, 1945, 2010, 2012, 2097, 2153, 2184, 2333, 2600, 2615, 2616, 2617, 2672, 2714, 3506, 3513, 3821, 3823, 3923, 4067, 4140, 4374, 4380.

Kaufman, A.R., Mrs: 3773.

Kaufman, Alfred: 4499.

Kaufman, Beth Hall: 1463.

Kaufman, Carl: 3506.

Kaufman, Edna D.: 1460, 3821.

Kaufman, Emma: 1200, 1458, 1460, 1461, 1462, 3821, 4380.

Kaufman Family: 658, 672, 713, 717, 719, 720, 932, 1129, 1139, 1211, 1458, 1459, 1462, 3504, 3506, 4325, 4499.

Kaufman, Fred: 1936.

Kaufman, H.W.: 85, 125, 4101.

Kaufman, Jacob: 249, 326, 671, 672, 1459, 1460, 1461, 1463, 1580, 1853, 1855, 1856, 1924, 1926, 1945, 1974, 3487, 3495, 3821, 4022, 4023, 4056, 4067, 4299, 4348, 4370, 4374, 4377, 4380.

Kaufman, Jean Hutton: 1463.

Kaufman, John R.: 13, 4422.

Kaufman, M.R.: 2153, 3923.

Kaufman, Mary Ratz (Mrs Jacob): 1458, 1459, 1460, 1461, 1463, 3495, 3769, 3821, 3822, 4022, 4031, 4056, 4380.

Kaufman, Meyer: 677.

Kaufman, Milton: 1459, 1460, 1461.

Kaufman, Nora: 3031.

Kaufman, Ray: 1936.

Kaufman, Solomon: 2547, 2550, 4525.

Kaufman, William: 1463, 4099.

Kauk, Ferdinand: 4435.

Kauth, C.R., Rev.: 3496.

Kavelman, Herman: 414, 2081, 2180,

2399, 2570, 2971, 3183, 3574, 4490, 4495, 4496, 4499.

Kavelman, Neil: 4014.

Kay, Adam L.: 4015.

Kay, Alexander: 4079.

Kay, Bill: 1937.

Kay Family: 1976.

Kay, Grace: 2803.

Kay, Hugh: 4079.

Kay, Isaac: 4435.

Kay, James: 3663, 4079.

Kay, Jean: 4043.

Kay, John: 2128, 3663, 4079, 4250.

Kay, R.D.: 4237.

Kay, Robert: 2701, 4079.

Kay, Thomas H.: 1187, 1895.

Kay, W.G.: 4395.

Kay, William: 1741, 2379, 4438.

Kayler, K.D.: 4290.

Kayser, C.C.F.: 664.

Kayser, John: 4371.

Kayser, Mr: 4371.

Keachie, James: 4204.

Keachie, K., Miss: 4088.

Keachie, Margaret E.: 4008, 4015.

Keachie, Thomas: 4263.

Keagie, John: 256.

Keating, E.H.: 1964.

Keefer, Angela: 1664.

Keefer, M.W.: 1759, 2506, 2520, 3923.

Keefer, Peter: 1664.

Keefer, Wilks: 2392.

Keegan Family: 3465.

Keeler, Dr: 2399.

Keeler, William J.: 4275.

Keen, A.E.: 4080.

Keen, C.M., Rev.: 3416.

Keeny, Barbara: 256.

Keffer, Barbara: 3910.

Keffer, E.M.: 3644.

Keffer, Ernest R.: 4102.

Keffer, Frank M.: 4102.

Keffer, James: 4278.

Keffer, N.A., Rev.: 2899, 3512, 3525, 3547, 3609.

Keffer, O.M.: 3044.

Keffer, Solomon, Mrs: 4280.

Keffer, Wellington: 2994, 3644.

Kegel, John: 4371.

Kehl Family: 869.

Kehl, John: 3310.

Kehl, Robert: 3050.

Kehl, Sandy: 3099.

Kehr, Jacob, Rev.: 3495, 3503.

Keil, F.: 3040.

Keinzle, Mr: 4512.

Keith, Ann: 3660.

King, Agnes: 1217.
King, Arthur: 2090.
King, C.: 4278.
King, George, Mrs: 2090.
King, H.: 2880.
King, Isabella Mackenzie (Mrs John): 1466, 1468, 1470, 2413, 4136.
King, Janie: 3723.
King, Jennie: 2748.
King, John: 326, 653, 1168, 1300, 1466, 1467, 1468, 1470, 1535, 2413, 2714, 2740, 2781, 3666, 3815, 4136, 4318, 4380, 4422.
King, John A., Dr: 1205.
King, John Barnes: 2090, 2120.
King, John M., Rev.: 3665.
King, Leonard: 4104.
King, Leslie, Rev.: 1404, 3667.
King, Mary H.: 1191.
King, Matthew: 3663.
King, W.C.J.: 4070.
King, W.L. Mackenzie: 3, 22, 297, 326, 541, 1433, 1466, 1469, 1470, 1501, 1535, 1699, 2090, 2092, 2382, 2388, 2413, 2414, 2441, 2495, 2604, 2710, 2714, 2772, 2801, 2950, 4031, 4119, 4136, 4146, 4157, 4158, 4225, 4318, 4356, 4370, 4374, 4380, 4414, 4426, 4478.
Kingsborough, Samuel: 3650.
Kingsley, Alfred: 4099.
Kinnaird, William: 4214.
Kinsey, Abraham: 1877.
Kinsey, Dilman: 255, 256, 713, 720, 809, 3097, 4374, 4380, 4455, 4456.
Kinsey Family: 252, 713, 719, 720, 933, 4437.
Kinsey, George: 4454.
Kinsey, Jacob L.: 2700.
Kinsey, Joseph: 2385, 2700.
Kinsey, Mrs: 2073.
Kinsey, William: 3660.
Kinsie, Anna: 755.
Kinsie, Henry: 1165.
Kinsie, Maurice: 1185, 2728.
Kinsie, Moses: 1165.
Kinsie, Samuel: 755.
Kinsie, Simon: 4456.
Kinsinger Family: 716.
Kinsky, Johanna Evangelista, Sister: 3451.
Kinsman, Hiram: 1975, 1986, 2005, 4393, 4394.
Kinton, Jerrine Wells: 3109, 3110.
Kintsing, Jacob: 933.
Kinzel, Amelia Milatz (Mrs Joseph):

977.
Kinzel, Joseph: 977.
Kinzel, W.: 4278.
Kinzie, A.D.: 1.
Kinzie, Abraham: 4429.
Kinzie, Anna High (Mrs Jacob L.): 911.
Kinzie, Barbara Biehn: 934, 935, 4429.
Kinzie, Clarence: 1186.
Kinzie, Dilman: 275, 409, 519, 555, 934, 935, 4429.
Kinzie, Eileen: 3390.
Kinzie, Elizabeth Moxley (Mrs John): 934, 987.
Kinzie, Ephraim: 4396.
Kinzie Family: 711, 911, 934, 935, 4453.
Kinzie, Hannah Mitchell (Mrs William): 934.
Kinzie, Harry L.: 2392, 2401.
Kinzie, Jacob: 4429.
Kinzie, Jacob L.: 911.
Kinzie, James A.: 934.
Kinzie, John: 934, 987, 4429.
Kinzie, John M.: 934.
Kinzie, Joseph: 1, 4439.
Kinzie, Lenora Wilbee (Mrs John M.): 934.
Kinzie, Mena, "Minnie": 1175.
Kinzie, Oliver: 1471, 3631, 3633.
Kinzie, Simon: 1162, 4444.
Kinzie, Stanley: 4429.
Kinzie, Susie: 4429.
Kinzie, William: 934.
Kinzinger Family: 713, 719, 720.
Kipfer, Ephraim: 1099.
Kipfer, Nurias: 2829.
Kipfer, Orville: 2829.
Kipp, Robert: 2090.
Kirby, David D.: 2179, 4315.
Kirby, Edna: 3773.
Kirby, J.B.: 2756, 3821.
Kirby, Lillian A.: 1725.
Kirchhofer, J.L., Rev.: 3525, 3552, 3553, 3621.
Kirchner, Valentine: 1165, 2120.
Kirk, Sidney: 4233.
Kirke, C.: 4422.
Kirkland, Jack: 1899.
Kirkland, Thomas: 1287.
Kirkness, I.M.: 2748.
Kirkness, Mary Anne: 2987, 2988, 2989.
Kirkpatrick, Charles: 4499.
Kirkpatrick, James: 3751.
Kirkpatrick, Mrs: 2085.

Kirkpatrick, T.C., Dr: 286, 1065, 2767, 4385.
Kirkwall Family: 4188, 4202.
Kirkwood, D.: 4031.
Kirkwood, M.W.: 8, 2122, 4280, 4435.
Kirmis, J., Rev.: 3507, 3519.
Kirsch, Johannes: 3527.
Kirschel, Fred: 2712, 3050.
Kirwan, Dominic, Rev.: 2785.
Kissner, D.: 2829.
Kissner, Fred: 4315, 4474.
Kissner, Marjorie: 2829.
Kitchen Family: 2704.
Kitchen, Lulu: 3713.
Kitchen, Phyllis: 436.
Kitchen, Russell B.: 4452.
Kitlowski, Joseph: 3448.
Kittle, Dominick: 4195.
Kittle Family: 2815.
Kittle, Jerome: 4474.
Klaehn, J.C.: 2899.
Klaehn, Norman: 4014.
Klager, Fraser: 4278.
Klager, G.C.: 4278.
Klager, Gordon: 1908, 3675, 4278.
Klager, J.E.: 4275.
Klassen, A.P.: 3291.
Klassen, Connie: 4499.
Klassen, Ernest: 2775.
Klassen, Helene Zacharias: 3120, 3137, 3146.
Klassen, Jacob: 3146.
Klassen, Peter, Rev.: 3291.
Klassen, Wilhelm: 3146.
Kleeberger, Nicholas: 2179, 4195, 4315.
Kleeman, W.: 3815.
Kleim, Charles: 4422.
Klein, Andrew: 3160, 3438.
Klein, Catherine: 3438.
Klein, Dr: 4056.
Klein Family: 249, 477, 4499.
Klein, Frank A.: 13.
Klein, George: 4371.
Klein, John: 671, 672, 2128, 2818, 2843, 3160, 3442, 4306, 4380.
Klein, Joseph: 3718.
Klein, Joseph, Mrs: 3718.
Klein, Judge: 2714, 3438.
Klein, L.: 4487.
Klein, Mr: 2843.
Klein, Nicholas: 475, 481.
Klein, Roy: 3839.
Klein, Sam: 3718.
Klein, Stanley: 4225.
Klein, William: 37, 1974.
Kleine, Siegfried: 4499.

Kopas, Dan: 3102.
Kopas, Kasindro McCloy: 1519.
Kopf, Ernst: 682.
Koplin, William: 4456.
Kopp, Alan: 4225.
Korchensky, F.: 4278.
Korman, Michael: 1861, 1983.
Kormann Family: 477.
Kormann, Ignace: 4524.
Korol, Walter: 3466.
Kosinski, John, Rev.: 3442.
Kostigian Family: 704.
Kousal, Mathew: 8, 3109.
Kovacs, Stephen: 2090.
Kowalski, Albert: 2503, 3917.
Kowalski, John, Mrs: 2612, 3712.
Kowalski, L. John: 2503.
Kraehling, Catherine: 2801.
Kraehling, Edwin: 4499.
Kraehling, J.: 2801, 4474.
Kraemer, Clarence: 2815.
Kraemer Family: 943.
Kraemer, George: 943, 2769, 4474.
Kraemer, Jacob: 4371, 4380.
Kraemer, Jim: 3102, 3109.
Kraemer, Johanna Spetz (Mrs
    George): 943.
Kraemer, John: 4467.
Kraemer, Raymond, Rev.: 4521.
Krafft, Philip: 4014.
Kraft, Aaron: 1165, 1651, 1656, 1922.
Kraft, Allen: 4448, 4449.
Kraft, Anna Shirk (Mrs William):
    1078.
Kraft, D.: 4395.
Kraft, Earl: 3712.
Kraft Family: 713, 719, 720, 769.
Kraft, George: 2179, 3711, 3712,
    4195.
Kraft, Henry: 671, 713, 720, 1141.
Kraft, Isaac: 4461.
Kraft, John: 4458.
Kraft, Moses: 1165, 4192, 4193, 4195.
Kraft, Ralph: 3923.
Kraft, Solomon: 4192, 4195.
Kraft, Solomon B.: 1165.
Kraft, William: 1078.
Kramer, C.A., Rev.: 3507, 3519.
Kramer Family: 717.
Kramer, Jacob: 4371.
Kramer, Phyllis: 3126.
Kramer, Raymond, Rev.: 4512.
Kramer, Rudolph: 2039.
Kramp, Edward: 1796.
Kramp Family: 1773.
Kramp, Howard: 1773, 1796.
Kramp, Louis: 1948.

Kramp, Wilhelmina: 3612.
Krampf, Philip: 2073.
Krampien, Mr: 4450.
Kranz, Annie: 1484.
Kranz, C.R.: 1201, 4422.
Kranz, Carl: 249, 635, 1484, 1485,
    1525, 1550, 1672, 2818, 4029,
    4031, 4136, 4299, 4374, 4380.
Kranz, Carl W.C.: 4380.
Kranz, Catherine Seip (Mrs Hugo):
    1484, 1486.
Kranz, Charles: 2714, 4158.
Kranz Family: 658, 1485.
Kranz, Hugo: 18, 20, 23, 249, 326,
    635, 671, 672, 1165, 1166, 1201,
    1252, 1260, 1484, 1485, 1486,
    1535, 1551, 1604, 1811, 1812,
    1833, 1934, 2100, 2179, 2706,
    2710, 2714, 2818, 2821, 3815,
    3977, 4073, 4079, 4136, 4191,
    4299, 4306, 4374, 4380, 4517,
    4525.
Krapler, John: 4483.
Kratz, Ann: 804.
Kratz, Valentine: 548, 804.
Kratzmeier, Hubert: 752, 2588.
Krauel, Delton: 2090.
Kraus, Christopher: 2145, 4487, 4499.
Kraus, F.A.: 1165, 4382.
Kraus, Gustaph: 752.
Kraus, Michael: 1427, 2026.
Kraus, Michael, Rev.: 4271.
Krause, Carla: 3142, 4225.
Krauter, John: 4524.
Krauth, C.F., Rev.: 3414, 3415, 3499.
Kreason, Charles: 2700.
Kreason, Frank: 4058.
Krebs, Mr: 4494.
Kreh, Daniel: 3495.
Krehbiel Family: 716, 717.
Krehbill, Jacob: 3306, 3323.
Kreig, Jack: 4276.
Kreitz, John H.: 2120.
Kreitz, Joseph P.: 2120.
Kreitzer, H.J.: 4080.
Kremer, Albert, Mrs: 4397.
Kress, Charles: 1983.
Kress, Christopher: 1165, 1861, 1983,
    2184, 4228, 4356, 4393, 4394,
    4395.
Kress Family: 1035, 3048.
Kress, Frederick: 2818, 2822, 3032,
    4299.
Kress, Henry: 3054.
Kress, Jacob: 2505, 3551.
Kress, W.F.: 4395.
Kress, Wayne: 2829.

Kress, Wilbur: 2184.
Kressler, John: 308, 2120, 4480,
    4523, 4524.
Kreuen, Catharine: 333.
Kreutzer, Elisabeth: 3551.
Kreutzer, Heinrich: 3551.
Kreutziger, Bernhard, Rev.: 3320.
Kreutzinger, Charles: 1, 37, 1165,
    1974.
Kreutzweiser, John: 3620, 4191.
Kreutzwisser, Michael: 3620, 4193.
Kribs, Aaron: 238, 4286.
Kribs, Arthur: 1862.
Kribs, Elizabeth Pannebecker (Mrs
    Lewis): 1001.
Kribs Family: 249, 4273.
Kribs, George A.: 2994.
Kribs, Lewis: 20, 242, 729, 1001,
    1165, 1166, 1292, 1974, 2379,
    2424, 2760, 3655, 3663, 3664,
    4011, 4034, 4271, 4274, 4277,
    4286, 4374, 4456.
Kribs, William A.: 1, 13, 29, 809,
    2379, 2994, 3978, 4011, 4271,
    4275, 4280, 4282, 4283, 4286.
Krieg Family: 636.
Krieger, August: 2775.
Krieger, Herbert: 1796, 2775.
Kriesel, Adie: 2971.
Kriesel, Bert: 2168, 4490, 4499.
Kriesel Family: 712.
Kriesel, Jacob: 2180, 2570, 4490.
Kriesel, K.A., Rev.: 3523, 3544, 3562.
Kriesel, Nellie: 2971.
Kriesel, William: 2168, 4490, 4499.
Krikorian Family: 704.
Krinel, Nellie: 2992.
Krismanich, Peter: 2144, 4348, 4362.
Kritikus, Dr: 631.
Kroeger, Francis, Mrs: 4207.
Kroetsch Family: 37, 1844, 2815,
    4478, 4480, 4481, 4483.
Kroetsch, Frank: 2635.
Kroetsch, George: 2379.
Kroetsch, J.L.: 1165, 1811, 1833,
    2120, 2769, 4040, 4474, 4478.
Kroetsch, J.R.: 4474.
Kroetsch, John: 943, 2379, 3442.
Kroetsch, Mary Ann Spetz (Mrs
    John): 943.
Kroeze, H., Rev.: 3707.
Krogman, Carl J.: 2120.
Kronis, Moishe H.: 3718.
Kronis, Moishe H., Mrs: 3718.
Kronis, Mr: 3718.
Kropf, Anna Nafziger (Mrs Henry):
    3364.

Large, Melvin: 2798.

Lasby, Marshall: 2760.

Laschinger, Adam: 947.

Laschinger, Charles: 2989.

Laschinger, Edmund H.: 947.

Laschinger Family: 947, 948.

Laschinger, Jacob: 947, 991, 2109, 2120, 2767, 3491.

Laschinger, Johanna C. Krause (Mrs Jacob): 947.

Laschinger, Joseph: 947, 2767, 4385.

Laschinger, Mary Merner (Mrs Joseph): 947.

Laschinger, Miss: 2712.

Laschinger, Russell H.: 947.

Laschinger, S.: 2712, 2988, 2989, 4223, 4525.

Laschinger, Sarah E. Nash (Mrs Jacob): 947, 991.

Laschinger, Wilfrid: 4094, 4104.

Lash, Greta: 3773.

Lash, John, Mrs: 4008.

Lashbrook, Vera: 2041.

Lashinger Family: 4494.

Lashinger, Irvin: 4494.

Lassel, James: 3818.

Lassere, Henri: 127.

Lassert, Charles: 1165.

Lassert, William: 3180.

Last, G.: 4080.

Lathorn, John: 1165.

Latsch, Ferdinand: 2120, 4426.

Latsch, Ferdinand, Mrs: 1698.

Latsch, George: 4467.

Latschar Family: 4499.

Latschar, Isaac: 4499.

Latschaw, Abraham: 1358, 3057, 3058, 3063, 3064, 3069, 3070, 3078, 3083, 3098, 3121, 3143, 3148.

Latschaw Family: 713, 719, 720.

Latschaw, Isaac: 1063, 3813.

Lattimer, Walter: 119.

Lauber, Catherine: 783.

Lauber Family: 477, 4443.

Lauber, Joseph: 4464.

Lauber, Oscar: 1495.

Lauer, Martin: 3503.

Laufhuber, George, Rev.: 2782, 2818, 2838, 3423, 3424, 3428, 3431, 3442, 3448, 3454, 3465, 4380.

Laurason, John: 4266.

Laurence, G.: 4278.

Laurence, Hugh: 150.

Laurence, T.: 4278.

Laurie, Lee, Dr: 4178.

Laury, Preston A., Rev.: 2889, 2909,

3525, 3537.

Lausie, Eugene, Rev.: 2769, 3433.

Lautemann, G.G.: 4396.

Lautenschlager, Arthur: 4499.

Lautenschlager, August: 4499.

Lautenschlager, Earl: 2714, 2821.

Lautenschlager, Ed: 3183.

Lautenschlager Family: 658, 949, 1010, 1496, 1773, 4360, 4494, 4499.

Lautenschlager, Frederick: 4490.

Lautenschlager, Harold: 2480.

Lautenschlager, Irvin: 2120.

Lautenschlager, Isaac: 659.

Lautenschlager, Isaac S.: 1063.

Lautenschlager, John: 1, 2151, 2480, 4382.

Lautenschlager, Mary Ann (Mrs Isaac S.): 1063.

Lautenschlager, P.S.: 1496, 1811, 1833, 1971, 4299, 4374, 4380.

Lautenschlager, Philipp: 326, 332, 333, 661, 671, 672, 1010, 1358, 1911, 3414, 3415, 4496, 4499.

Lautenschlager, S.S., Rev.: 2714, 4380.

Lautenschlager, Theodore: 3519.

Lautenschlager, Welland: 3519.

Lautenslager, James: 4014.

Lauz, Carl, Rev.: 3442.

Lavell, Alfred, Dr: 4178.

Lavell, Charles, Rev.: 3622.

Lavelle, Ethel: 1281.

Lavender, Bert: 4102.

Lavergne, Andrew, Rev.: 1244.

Lavery, Helen: 1197.

Lavery, Katherine Burke: 4467.

Lavery, Meredith: 4467.

Lavery, William: 1197.

Lavin, Peter: 4250.

Law, E.: 4233.

Law, James: 3669.

Law, William: 1371, 2151.

Lawless, John, Rev.: 4464.

Lawrason, John: 4214.

Lawrason, Mr: 4392.

Lawrason, Samuel: 4102.

Lawrason, William: 4400.

Lawrence, George: 4104.

Lawrence, George H.: 4178, 4187.

Lawrence, Jessie: 2775.

Lawrence, John: 3908.

Lawrence, M., Miss: 2828, 2829.

Lawrence, Patricia: 3818.

Lawrence, T., Mrs: 4088.

Lawrence, Thomas: 4104.

Lawrie, Alexander: 3668.

Lawrie, Alexander, Mrs: 3668.

Lawson, Alex: 4006.

Lawson, Frank, Rev.: 703, 3656, 3685.

Lawson, James, Rev.: 4271, 4282.

Lawson, Peter, "Holy Pete": 2103.

Lawson, Samuel: 3709.

Lawson, William: 709.

Lawton, C.W.: 121.

Laycock, G.S.: 2994.

Layman, Archibald: 3709.

Lazarus, Mr: 2766, 2818.

Lean, Mary: 3769.

Leard, James: 4499.

Learn, A.B.: 2147.

Learn, A.B., Mrs: 1977.

Leatham, D.B.: 2745.

Leathorne Family: 2704, 3623.

Leavine, S.F., Dr: 8, 326, 1182, 1891, 1954, 3915, 4023, 4067, 4112, 4117, 4359.

Leavitt, Charles: 326, 2615, 2616.

Lebold, Barbara: 1118.

Lebold, Barbara Roth (Mrs Christian): 950.

Lebold, Christian: 950.

Lebold, Daniel: 950, 1106, 3368.

Lebold, Elizabeth Albrecht (Mrs Christian, Jr): 950.

Lebold Family: 725, 950, 1118.

Lebold, Jacob: 725, 950.

Lebold, John: 950.

Lebold, Katherine Streicher (Mrs Daniel): 950.

Lebold, Katie Leis (Mrs Elmer): 951.

Lebold, Magdalena Blank (Mrs Jacob): 725, 950.

Lebold, Mary Bender (Mrs John): 950.

Lebold, Mary Schwartzentruber (Mrs Jacob): 950.

Lebold, Mary Streicher (Mrs Christian, Jr): 950.

Lechscheidt, Paul: 682.

Lederach, Elizabeth: 804.

Lederman, B.: 4499.

Lederman, Charles: 1948, 2117.

Lederman, Katherine: 2704.

Lederman, Sangster, Dr: 1188.

Lee, Anna A.: 2818.

Lee, E.: 4088.

Lee Family: 458, 4199.

Lee, Frank: 4104.

Lee, George: 2975, 2986, 4266.

Lee, Grace, Miss: 458.

Lee, James: 1722, 4246, 4266.

Lee, John: 78, 3761, 4102, 4266.

Lovett, James H.: 1693.
Lovett, Robert E.: 1693, 1696, 4178.
Lovett, William, Dr: 37.
Lowder, J.: 4088.
Lowe, Arthur H.: 1895.
Lowe, Douglas: 4099.
Lowe, Eleanor: 2769, 2815.
Lowe, J.E.: 4422.
Lowe, John J., Rev.: 1505, 3690, 4289.
Lowell, C.: 1165.
Lowell, Charles: 4298.
Lowell, F.: 4253, 4306.
Lowell Family: 4513, 4514.
Lowell, Francis: 4212, 4266.
Lowell, Percy: 4102.
Lowell, Richard: 4250.
Lowery, Dr: 3689, 4250.
Lowes, G.A., Rev.: 3410.
Lowes, Miss: 4299.
Lucas, C.J., Rev.: 3525, 3550, 3605.
Luce Family: 4188, 4202.
Luckhardt, Beatrice Katzenmeier (Mrs Roy C.): 1190, 3852.
Luckhardt, E.D.: 4384.
Luckhardt, John P.: 1974.
Luckhardt, Lorne: 1796.
Luckhardt, Roy C.: 4385.
Luckhart, Nelson: 749.
Lucky, Bert: 4102.
Ludgate, James: 3709.
Ludolph, Albert: 4433.
Ludwig, Albert: 4477.
Ludwig, C.: 3415.
Ludwig, Carl: 3608.
Ludwig, Charles: 4477.
Ludwig, Daniel: 3770.
Ludwig, H.: 4422.
Ludwig, Jacob: 2775.
Ludwig, Roy Frank: 4099.
Ludwig, W.D.: 1.
Ludwig, William: 3030.
Lueck, Gustav: 677.
Luetkehoelter, Henry W., Rev.: 3513.
Luft, Fred: 1506.
Luft, H.: 1861, 1983, 2557, 4040, 4499.
Luft, M., Mrs: 2530, 4499.
Luft, Milton: 4499.
Lugger, Maud: 3713.
Lugibihl, John: 579.
Lumena, Sister M.: 2832.
Lumsden, J.M.: 4056.
Lund, Henry: 264, 514.
Lundy, Allan: 2098.
Lundy, Allan, Mrs: 2098.
Lundy, Dorita: 1404.

Lundy, Isaac: 1404.
Lundy, J.R., Dr: 1316, 1404, 1688, 3790, 4400.
Lundy, Kezia: 1404.
Lundy, Louisa: 2593.
Lundy, Lydia Eck: 1404.
Lungein, Mr: 4494.
Lutz, Charles: 2120.
Lutz, Daniel: 256, 4380, 4422.
Lutz, Dr: 1705.
Lutz Family: 713, 719, 720.
Lutz, George: 4371.
Lutz, Henry: 308, 4450.
Lutz, Jacob: 1747, 2766, 2818, 4017, 4195, 4422.
Lutz, Morris C.: 332, 2128, 2474, 2478, 2592, 2986, 3671, 3978, 4015, 4125, 4202, 4242, 4265, 4266.
Lutz, William H.: 1165, 2055, 2122, 2720, 4056, 4246, 4253.
Lynch, M.E.: 2714.
Lynn, J.E., Mrs: 22, 3485, 3857.
Lynn, J.E., Rev.: 3669, 3945, 4499.
Lynn, Lida: 1725.
Lyons, A.: 4278.
Lyons, Abraham: 275.
Lyons, Mary Biehn (Mrs Abraham): 275.
Lyons, Polly: 256.
Lyons, Thomas R.: 4102.
Lytle, Samuel: 1519.

Maas, Claus: 4371, 4380.
Maas, J.: 1926, 4371.
Maas, Mr: 1984.
Maass, C.C.J., Rev.: 671, 672, 2947, 3512, 3525, 3550, 3605, 3609.
MacAllister, J.S.E.: 1909.
Macartney, J.: 4088.
Macauley, A.C.: 4080.
Macauley, W.H.: 4080.
MacCallum, J.P.: 4103.
MacCartney, J.W.: 4233.
MacDonald, A.R.: 4099.
MacDonald, C.C., Rev.: 3687.
Macdonald, Cameron: 1020.
Macdonald, D.S., Rev.: 3478.
MacDonald, David: 4225.
MacDonald, Donald: 4485.
Macdonald Family: 4508.
Macdonald, Grant, Rev.: 3513.
Macdonald, John A.: 1722, 4214.
MacDonald, K.J., Rev.: 3667, 3687.
MacDonald, L.J., Rev.: 4088.
MacDonald, Margaret: 2712.

MacDonald, Mary: 2734.
MacDonald, Randy: 4049.
MacDonald, W., Rev.: 3414, 3415.
Macdonald, W. Ross: 2910.
MacDonell, Hugh, Dr: 1184.
MacDonell, John: 4099.
MacDonnell, Elizabeth Thomson (Mrs George): 3852.
MacEachern, N.: 2780, 2781.
MacFarlane, Percy R.: 4217, 4226.
MacGachen, Frederick S.: 1824.
MacGeorge, David, "Old Mac": 2734, 2777, 2862, 2863, 2955, 2956, 2957, 2959, 3652, 4255.
MacGillivray, R.A.: 22, 1508.
MacGovern, Thomas: 2760.
Macgregor, Alexander: 1165, 2128, 3663.
MacGregor, C.J.: 2742, 2781, 3014.
MacGregor, Charles: 2780, 3049.
MacGregor, Walter: 1548.
MacIntosh, Edith: 4168, 4327.
MacIntyre, Malcolm: 2810.
Mack, Alexander: 3373.
MacKay, Crissie: 2828, 2829.
MacKay, Donald: 1.
MacKay, Gordon: 4348, 4362.
MacKay, Gordon, Jr: 4362.
MacKay, J.C.: 4473.
MacKay, "Nibs": 2701.
Mackean, William: 689.
MacKendrick, H.F., Dr: 1205, 1845, 4230, 4258, 4263.
MacKendrick, J.N.: 1180, 1404, 1806, 2379, 2720, 2777, 3732, 3960, 4088, 4246.
MacKendrick, J.N., Mrs: 3773.
MacKendrick, Norah: 3773.
Mackenzie, Alexander: 1722, 3977.
MacKenzie, Alexander, Mrs: 3665.
MacKenzie, Joe: 1894.
MacKenzie, Lyle: 1895.
MacKenzie, Malcolm, Rev.: 3481, 3660.
MacKenzie, N.D.: 4080, 4087.
Mackenzie, Thomas H.: 4423.
MacKenzie, William: 479, 690, 3689, 4202, 4214, 4250.
Mackenzie, William Lyon: 1470, 3977, 4212, 4266, 4380.
Mackie, Alexander: 2714, 3656, 3669, 4525.
Mackie Family: 4220, 4221, 4513.
Mackie, George: 2447, 3669.
Mackie, J.J.: 4124.
Mackie, James: 3669.
Mackie, James A., Mrs: 2714.

Mehl Family: 716.

Mehnert, Martin: 3815.

Meier, Anthony: 2484.

Meier, Ferdinand: 119.

Meier, Joseph, Jr: 2484.

Meikleham, Ian: 2143.

Meikleham, R.W.: 2143, 4080, 4081, 4088.

Meikleham, Robert I.: 2143.

Meikleham, William: 4499.

Meilke, E.F.: 3959.

Meinhold, Ernst, Rev.: 3512, 3547, 3612.

Meinke, August: 4380.

Meinzinger, Cecile, Mrs: 2829.

Meinzinger, Joseph: 8, 326, 1186, 1201, 1871, 1875, 1891, 1949, 4023, 4067, 4112, 4117, 4118, 4136, 4143, 4343, 4344.

Meisel, Edward, Mrs: 4193.

Meisel, Jacob: 276, 4499.

Meisel, Ralph: 4448.

Meisel, William: 2167, 4467.

Meisner, Christian: 1574, 3815.

Meisner, John L.: 2818, 2822, 3815, 4299.

Meisner, Louis: 3815.

Meldrum, Alexander: 4525.

Meldrum, Alice: 3650.

Meldrum, Norman W., Dr: 4178.

Meldrum, Will: 2989, 3745.

Melitzer Family: 4526.

Melitzer, Harvey: 2098.

Melitzer, Mel: 4225.

Melitzer, Roy: 2807.

Mellish, Fred: 1834, 2975, 4237.

Mellish, Henry, Rev.: 3470, 3474.

Mellish, Mrs: 3470.

Mellish, William: 2517, 3976.

Melvin, Albert, "Slack": 1937.

Melvin, D., Mrs: 4088.

Melvin, Robert: 1, 1818.

Menary, William M.: 4102.

Menger, E.W.: 3960, 4080.

Menger, George: 4525.

Menger, J.: 4521.

Menger, William: 2548.

Menhennick, T.A.: 4263.

Mensch, Jacob: 3322.

Mercer, A.W.: 4233.

Mercer, Rebecca: 3713.

Merkel, Henry: 3180.

Merkel, Irvin: 1862.

Merklinger, M.: 3544.

Merlau, Conrad: 1165.

Merlau Family: 1773.

Merlau, Henry P.: 1773.

Merner, Absalom: 1, 1530, 1531, 1654, 1855, 2001, 3821, 4225, 4404, 4405, 4422, 4525.

Merner, Albert Edward: 1808, 4094, 4103.

Merner, Ammon: 1530, 1861, 1880, 1983, 2001.

Merner, Anna: 976.

Merner, Barbara: 976.

Merner, C.: 1165.

Merner, Caroline: 4031.

Merner, Christian: 976, 2379, 4382, 4491.

Merner, Dorothy Willson: 1149.

Merner, Edward: 2767.

Merner, Ellen Fletcher: 1530.

Merner, F.: 1165, 1974.

Merner Family: 583, 947, 948, 976.

Merner, Frederick: 976, 1530, 1531, 1532, 1974, 2379, 4385, 4388, 4487.

Merner, Gottlieb: 976.

Merner, Gwer: 947.

Merner, Henry L., Rev.: 3645.

Merner, Hilda: 1321.

Merner, Jacob: 947, 976, 1530, 3674, 4491.

Merner, John: 976.

Merner, Levi: 4491.

Merner, Mabel Melinda: 1725.

Merner, Maria Ann: 976, 2001.

Merner, Mary Ann Grasser (Mrs Samuel): 1530, 1531, 1534.

Merner, Miss: 4485.

Merner, Nora: 1433.

Merner, Ross: 4499.

Merner, Samuel: 18, 20, 85, 109, 119, 276, 286, 671, 672, 681, 976, 1165, 1166, 1500, 1530, 1531, 1533, 1534, 1808, 1811, 1833, 1992, 2001, 2021, 2379, 2767, 3465, 3476, 3977, 4155, 4160, 4298, 4380, 4384, 4385, 4387, 4388, 4487, 4498, 4499.

Merner, Simpson: 1165, 1530, 1531, 2021.

Merner, Sulam: 1530.

Merner, Susan Schluchter: 947, 976, 1530.

Meroni, Jacob: 3465.

Merrett, Brian: 3100.

Merrick, Louis D.: 1195, 4299.

Merriett, Mr: 2818.

Merrilees, James: 3656, 4525.

Merritt, Harvey, Rev.: 1205, 3410.

Merritt, James Budd, Dr: 4179.

Merritt, R.N.: 1178, 1381, 2710, 2714, 2821, 4380.

Merritt, William H.: 282.

Mertz, John: 4040.

Messer, Georg: 682.

Messerschmidt, Erich: 3815.

Messett, Ralph: 3631.

Messett, Rollie: 4102.

Messinger, Jacob: 4473.

Messmore, Joseph, Rev.: 3636.

Messner, A.: 2120.

Messner, Columban, Rev.: 930, 2769, 2815, 3422, 3428, 3442, 3454, 3464, 4474, 4478, 4483.

Messner Family: 477.

Messner, John: 2120.

Messner, Martin: 4079, 4371.

Metcalfe, Janet: 2723, 2802, 2818, 2843, 2844, 4318, 4380.

Metcalfe, M., Rev.: 3499.

Metcalfe, William: 3628, 4298, 4380.

Mett, Christian: 3097.

Metz, Abram: 3259.

Metz, Donald: 4099.

Metz, Elvira: 2166.

Metz, William: 3620.

Metzdorf, Carl: 2745.

Metzger, A.: 8, 2899.

Metzger, Aaron: 8.

Metzger, Abe: 2745.

Metzger, Anna Barbara: 1729.

Metzger Family: 4499.

Metzger, J.F.: 2801, 4220, 4221, 4422, 4513, 4525.

Metzger, Lloyd: 4441.

Metzger, Martha: 3243.

Metzger, Mr: 4521.

Metzger, Rev.: 3525, 3552, 3553, 3621.

Metzger, Vern: 1844.

Metzger, Wesley: 2481.

Metzler, Edgar J.: 3238, 3239, 3310.

Metzler, John: 256.

Meyer, A.E.: 2728.

Meyer, Abraham: 548.

Meyer, Adam S.: 2769.

Meyer, Alexander: 1574, 4466.

Meyer, Allexius: 4483.

Meyer, Annette M.: 10, 4414.

Meyer, Annie: 2728.

Meyer, Anthony: 2769, 3465, 4474.

Meyer, Bert: 4474.

Meyer, Casper: 4040.

Meyer, Catherine Brenneman (Mrs John): 3364.

Meyer, Charles: 4428, 4490.

Meyer, Charles, Rev.: 2850, 3418, 3423.

3815, 3903, 4011, 4158, 4298, 4299, 4315, 4318, 4374, 4380.

Motz, John E.: 1546, 1824, 2600, 3923, 4031, 4315.

Motz, John, Mrs: 3461.

Motz, Mary: 1545.

Motz, Paul J.: 2600, 4315.

Motz, Philip: 4079.

Motz, Rose Huck: 1546.

Motz, W.J.: 82, 83, 85, 326, 671, 672, 1346, 1545, 1546, 1810, 1895, 2714, 2756, 2850, 2983, 3815, 3902, 3903, 3945, 3949, 3959, 4056, 4299, 4315, 4374, 4380.

Mowat, H.A.: 4080.

Mowat, James: 4371, 4380.

Mowat, James Gordon, "Moses Oates": 1165, 2714.

Mowat, John: 2714, 4429.

Mowat, Oliver: 1544, 1693, 1722, 2574, 2710.

Mowatt, Alexander H.: 3656.

Moxley Family: 382, 988, 4371.

Moxley, Mary Erb (Mrs William): 987.

Moxley, Mr: 1792.

Moxley, Mrs: 713, 720.

Moxley, Orlando H.: 987.

Moxley, Samuel: 326, 987, 4380.

Moxley, William: 256, 987.

Moyer, A.: 2120.

Moyer, A.C.: 1, 13.

Moyer, Abraham: 713, 720, 1547, 4444, 4461.

Moyer, Abraham H.: 713, 720.

Moyer, Adelaide: 1319.

Moyer, Barney: 4521.

Moyer, Benjamin Weber: 3082, 3181, 3741.

Moyer, Bernhardt: 815.

Moyer, C.E.: 37, 81, 326, 1974, 2714, 4380.

Moyer, Catharine Schiedel (Mrs Henry): 1045.

Moyer, Christian: 579.

Moyer, D.H.: 1640.

Moyer, Dilman: 348, 1793.

Moyer, Dilman G.: 1165.

Moyer, Donald: 2775.

Moyer, Edwin: 2775.

Moyer, Ella: 2775.

Moyer, Elmer, Rev.: 3320.

Moyer, Elton: 2775.

Moyer, Esther Weber (Mrs Isaac): 989.

Moyer Family: 225, 252, 524, 562, 712, 713, 719, 720, 813, 973, 989,

1547, 4360, 4443.

Moyer, Floyd: 2482.

Moyer, Frank, Rev.: 3627.

Moyer, Fred: 1974, 4521.

Moyer, Fritz: 964.

Moyer, H.A.: 3960, 4080.

Moyer, Henry: 713, 720, 1045, 1547.

Moyer, Herbert: 2775.

Moyer, Isaac: 23, 326, 989, 3082, 3627, 3645.

Moyer, Isaac M., Rev.: 3314, 3644.

Moyer, John: 973, 1936, 2128, 3722, 4499.

Moyer, John George: 2120.

Moyer, Joseph: 3438.

Moyer, L. Clare: 1182.

Moyer, Larry: 2775.

Moyer, Lydia Wismer (Mrs Samuel S.): 1547.

Moyer, Magdalena Houser (Mrs Samuel): 989.

Moyer, Maggie: 3181, 3741.

Moyer, Margaret: 2482.

Moyer, Marlene: 2775.

Moyer, Mary: 4477.

Moyer, Milton: 2775.

Moyer, Morgan: 2828, 2829.

Moyer, Moses: 37, 1165, 2109, 2120, 2379, 4428.

Moyer, Noah: 2711, 2775.

Moyer, P.E.W.: 1, 18, 80, 83, 85, 90, 110, 122, 123, 326, 1165, 1467, 1739, 1811, 1833, 1855, 1856, 2039, 2714, 2731, 2740, 2780, 2818, 2821, 2843, 2983, 3631, 3632, 3633, 4023, 4292, 4315, 4352, 4374, 4380.

Moyer, Peter: 4499.

Moyer, Philip: 3314.

Moyer, Rachel Cress (Mrs Bernhardt): 815.

Moyer, Rachel Cress (Mrs John): 973.

Moyer, Rosalie: 2775.

Moyer, S.: 4395.

Moyer, S.N., Rev.: 3496.

Moyer, Samuel: 989, 2801, 3870.

Moyer, Samuel S.: 1165, 1547, 1636, 1637, 2812, 3322.

Moyer, Sarah Snider (Mrs Isaac): 989.

Moyer, Simon: 4428, 4525.

Moyer, Susannah E.: 1652.

Moyer, Sylvester: 1165, 2818, 3671, 4155, 4263, 4395.

Moyer, William: 26, 308, 326, 664, 2379, 2470, 3631, 3632, 4371,

4380, 4441, 4461, 4525.

Muckle, Jimmy: 4253.

Muder, Elizabeth Peppler (Mrs Friederich): 1004.

Muder, Friederich: 1004.

Mudge, Abel: 308, 1976, 2379, 2441, 4182, 4184, 4185, 4187, 4188, 4202, 4212.

Mudge, B.H.: 4483.

Mudge, Louis: 1, 4188.

Muegge Family: 2745.

Mueller, Adolph: 85, 102, 110, 671, 672, 1300, 1381, 1382, 2441, 2706, 2710, 2714, 2793, 2818, 2821, 2983, 3815, 4056, 4067, 4380, 4429.

Mueller, Berthold, Rev.: 119, 3609.

Mueller, Carl: 4070.

Mueller, Charles: 1, 915, 1857, 1868, 1994, 4380, 4422.

Mueller, Charles J.: 1, 1994.

Mueller Family: 477.

Mueller, Frederick: 1955, 1968.

Mueller, Frieda: 3815.

Mueller, Harvey: 4491.

Mueller, Henry: 3767.

Mueller, Hilda: 2704, 4499.

Mueller, J. Charles: 333, 1868, 2889.

Mueller, John: 4193, 4461.

Mueller, Joseph: 4299.

Mueller, Karl: 671, 672, 2983, 3815, 4299, 4380.

Mueller, Kurt: 326.

Mueller, P.B., Rev.: 3525, 3537.

Mueller, Rosa: 3431.

Muenzinger, J.N., Rev.: 2947.

Muir, Cassie: 4439.

Muir, George: 4100.

Muir, Henry: 4422.

Muir, J.M.: 4477.

Muir, J.W.: 3767.

Muir, James: 4437.

Muir, John: 4473.

Muir, Matthew: 4079.

Muir, Mr: 3669.

Muir, Rev.: 689.

Mulhern, D.: 3413.

Mulheron, J.J.: 4195.

Mulherron, T.: 4422.

Mulhn, M.: 2736.

Mulholland, Alice: 1573.

Mulholland, Bill: 3050.

Mulkerson, Mr: 4192, 4193.

Mullan, J.A., Rev.: 3669.

Muller, F.: 4392.

Mullet, A.E.: 3640.

Mullet Family: 716.

Proctor, A.D., Dr: 4029, 4031, 4081.
Prokop, Edward: 4099.
Prong, Carl: 4436.
Prong Family: 4436.
Prong, Percy: 4436.
Prosser, W.E., Rev.: 4271.
Proudfoot, George: 1165, 4458.
Proudfoot, J.: 4395.
Proudfoot, William, Rev.: 571.
Proudlove, Maria: 1198.
Proudlove, Mr: 4371.
Prudham, J.H.: 8, 4233.
Pruefer, Helmut, Rev.: 671, 672.
Pruefer, Ida: 671.
Prueter, H.J.: 2852, 4380.
Pryer, Mr: 279.
Puddicombe, A.B.: 4499.
Puddicombe, A., Miss: 3470.
Puddicombe Family: 4491, 4508.
Puddicombe, Henry: 520, 3470, 3474, 4498, 4506, 4525.
Puddicombe, Hilda Quinton: 4486.
Puddicombe, Johanna Balkwell: 3476, 4486.
Puddicombe, Mary: 3470.
Puddicombe, Max: 3470, 4499.
Puddicombe, Miss: 3470.
Puddicombe, Reg: 3194, 4486, 4499, 4506.
Puddicombe, Robert: 2120, 3470, 3474.
Puddicombe, Robert B.: 1165.
Puddicombe, Roy M.: 4486.
Puddicombe, Sara Walker: 4486.
Puddicombe, Thomas: 1165, 3470.
Puddicombe, Thomas B.: 2120, 4486.
Puddicombe, Thomas B., Mrs: 3470.
Puddicombe, William: 2798, 3470, 3474, 3476, 4486, 4498, 4499, 4505, 4506.
Pugh, F.H.: 2714, 2821.
Pugsley, E., Mrs: 22.
Pugsley, Edmund: 1567, 2714, 2818.
Pugsley, Hugh: 1567.
Pugsley, Janet Lever: 1567.
Puisaye, Count de: 283.
Pullam, Arthur: 4280.
Pullen, Kenneth: 2775.
Purdy, J.H.: 4233.
Purdy, John: 1866.
Purdy, John A.: 1205, 4230.
Pursh, Frederick: 1400.
Pursh, George Frederick: 1402.
Purvis, Mrs: 3773.
Purzer, F.X.: 4422.
Putnam, Kenneth: 4044.
Putnam, Robert T.: 2033.

Puttock, David: 816.
Puttock, G.: 4080.
Puttock, Veronica Cress (Mrs David): 816.
Pym, A.E.: 4422.
Pym, J.H.: 4422.
Pyne, Dr: 2720.
Pyne, R.A.: 2818.

Quance, Noah: 2720.
Quarrie, William: 1165, 2109, 2120, 2128, 3663, 4255.
Quarry, Andrew: 3669.
Quarry, William: 2478.
Quast, Edgar: 4099.
Quehen, Eugenie: 1725.
Quehl, Henry: 4474.
Quentin, Albert P., Mrs: 3631, 3632.
Quentin, Albert P., Rev.: 3631, 3632, 3633.
Querin, Fred: 2179, 4192.
Querin, Norma: 2179.
Quickfall, A.C.: 1, 29, 1568.
Quickfall, Annie: 1198.
Quickfall, Charles: 1198.
Quickfall, Edith Shoemaker (Mrs A.C.): 1568.
Quickfall Family: 713, 719, 720, 1084, 1792, 4441.
Quickfall, George: 1198.
Quickfall, Hannah Martinson: 1198, 1953.
Quickfall, Leah Groff (Mrs R.M.): 1198.
Quickfall, Richard: 20, 1165, 1198, 1792, 2379, 4422.
Quickfall, Thomas: 20, 1165, 1198, 1953, 1976, 2379, 4515, 4525.
Quickfall, Walthy: 1198.
Quinlan, Ted: 4225.
Quinn, Leo M.: 1186.
Quiring, Magdalena: 671.
Quiring, Peter: 671, 672.
Quirk, Thomas M.: 4230.
Quirmbach, Albert, Rev.: 2714.
Quirmbach, Charles: 3029, 4014, 4380, 4437.
Quirmbach, Herman: 2714.

Rabb, L.S., Miss: 4382, 4499.
Rabb, S., Miss: 1200.
Rabe, Clarence: 1796.
Raber Family: 716.
Rachar, Cal: 4225.
Raddatz Family: 1129, 4499.

Raddatz, Gladys V., Mrs: 2120.
Radford, J.H., Dr: 1, 29, 1688, 2465, 2975, 2986, 4031, 4062, 4233, 4246, 4299.
Radigan, Edward: 1974, 2975, 2986, 4237, 4263.
Radtke, Carl: 4099.
Rae, Ann Dryden: 841.
Rae, Isabel: 2703.
Rae, John: 2743.
Rae, Mary Ann Dryden (Mrs William): 842, 843.
Rae, Nancy: 1190.
Rae, William: 842, 843.
Rafters, Marie: 2815.
Ragueneau, Rev.: 187.
Rahman, Charles: 2736.
Rahman, John: 2760.
Rahmann Family: 636.
Rahn, Andrew: 1983.
Rahn, Clara: 4217.
Rahn, Dorothy: 752.
Rahn, George: 2801.
Rahn, Robert: 4099.
Rahn, William: 2484.
Raich, Wilhelm: 664.
Raikes, Robert: 3387.
Railton, Richard, Rev.: 1205.
Raines Family: 1931.
Raisig, J.M.: 4422.
Rajewski, Michael: 3820.
Ralby, W.B., Rev.: 3519.
Rally, W.B.: 2767.
Rally, William, Rev.: 3470, 3474, 3476.
Ramore, Dominick: 4250, 4266.
Ramsay, D.S.: 4278.
Ramsay, D.S., Mrs: 4278.
Ramsay Family: 915, 4204.
Ramsay, J.D.: 2797, 2994, 3664, 4255, 4275, 4277, 4278, 4280, 4282, 4286.
Ramsay, Linda: 4474.
Ramsay, Robert D.: 2120.
Ramsay, Scott: 3675.
Ramseyer, Ada: 4499.
Ramseyer, Anna Litwiller (Mrs Peter K.): 955.
Ramseyer Family: 716, 1046.
Ramseyer, Nancy: 3365, 4499.
Ramseyer, Peter K.: 955.
Ramthun, F., Rev.: 3574.
Randall, Barbara: 1515.
Randall, Caroline: 2055.
Randall Family: 4436, 4499.
Randall, George: 1, 13, 18, 333, 1165, 1855, 1860, 1865, 1956, 1974,

Rieder, T.H.: 326, 1581, 1853, 1855, 1857, 1924, 1945, 2207, 2208, 3870, 4374, 4380.

Riedstra, Dick: 3050.

Riedstra, Maria: 3050.

Riegel, Jacob: 3494.

Riegelman, Frederick: 3029, 4371.

Riegert, E.R., Rev.: 3553, 3621.

Riehl, John C.: 3592.

Riehle, August: 4525.

Riener, C.: 3048.

Riener, Earl Edward: 4380.

Riener, Edward R.: 1446.

Riener, Mathias: 3815, 4371, 4380.

Ries, Eckhart: 4524, 4525.

Ries Family: 717, 1773.

Ries, William: 1773.

Riest, Terry: 2775.

Rietkirk, Alie, Mrs: 2801.

Rife, Abraham: 256.

Rife, Alexander: 1862.

Rife, Arnold: 1796, 3371, 3761.

Rife, Arnold, Mrs: 3371, 3936.

Rife, Chester: 4278.

Rife, David: 908, 1001, 1022, 1165, 1583, 2760, 3644, 3645, 4271, 4274, 4277, 4282, 4286.

Rife, David, Sr: 1583, 3644.

Rife, E.E.: 2736.

Rife, Edward: 2736.

Rife, Elizabeth: 1583.

Rife, Elizabeth Saddler (Mrs William): 4278.

Rife, Ephraim E.: 2764.

Rife Family: 713, 719, 720, 1022, 4282.

Rife, George W.: 2994, 3644, 4275.

Rife, Herbert: 1862.

Rife, Mary Pannebecker (Mrs David): 2760.

Rife, Mary Pannebecker (Mrs David, Jr): 1001.

Rife, Ophelia Lochead (Mrs David): 1022, 1182, 1583, 3644.

Rife, Samuel: 9, 256, 1583.

Rife, William A.: 1189.

Riley, Charles Herbert: 4103.

Ringel, Gordon: 4396.

Ringenberger Family: 716.

Ringle, P.R.: 2818.

Ringle, Phillip: 4374.

Ringler Family: 713, 719, 720, 797, 4380, 4455, 4456, 4499.

Ringler, Hannah Buehler (Mrs Samuel): 797.

Ringler, Henry: 275.

Ringler, Samuel: 797.

Rinner, George: 85, 1992.

Rirgert, E.R., Rev.: 3552.

Risdale, William: 4079.

Rise, John: 256.

Riser, Catherine Jantzi (Mrs Christian): 924.

Riser, Christian: 924.

Riser Family: 924.

Risk, George: 1165.

Risley, Mr: 4390.

Ritchert, A.E.: 2120.

Ritchie, Alexander, Rev.: 3668, 3686, 3695.

Ritchie, C.L.: 4499.

Ritchie, Carl: 2798.

Rittenhaus Family: 4, 2818.

Rittenhaus, Mr: 1358, 2780, 4456.

Rittenhouse, Abraham F.: 3259.

Rittenhouse, Freeman: 3319.

Rittenhouse, John F.: 3259.

Rittenhouse, Samuel: 2718.

Ritter, Alfred: 4527.

Ritter, Arthur: 3499.

Ritter, Catherine Beisel (Mrs Jacob): 1023.

Ritter, Catherine Eix (Mrs Valentine): 1023.

Ritter, Daniel: 1023.

Ritter, Elizabeth Knechtel (Mrs Philip): 1023.

Ritter, Elizabeth Korell (Mrs William): 1023.

Ritter, Elmer: 1773, 2098.

Ritter, Elmer, Mrs: 2098.

Ritter Family: 1023, 1773.

Ritter, Henry: 1023.

Ritter, Ida K., Mrs: 2120.

Ritter, Jacob: 1023.

Ritter, John: 1023.

Ritter, Magdalena Eix (Mrs John): 1023.

Ritter, Margaret Lanz (Mrs Philip): 1023.

Ritter, Melinda Stroh (Mrs Daniel): 1023.

Ritter, Philip: 1023, 3527, 4040.

Ritter, Philipina Mattusch (Mrs Henry): 1023.

Ritter, Valentine: 1023.

Ritter, William: 1023.

Rittershaus, Charles: 3042.

Rittershaus, O.: 3034, 3042.

Rittinger, Friedrich: 83, 85, 109, 112, 249, 635, 644, 664, 671, 672, 675, 1545, 1585, 2818, 2843, 4011, 4318, 4380, 4422.

Rittinger, Herman: 83, 2756.

Rittinger, John: 85, 673, 675, 3192, 4299.

Rittinger, John A.: 82, 109, 110, 112, 644, 646, 663, 671, 672, 1545, 1584, 1585, 1586, 2714, 2756, 3190, 3815, 3945, 4080, 4374.

Rittinger, William: 83.

Ritz, Betty: 4499.

Ritz, Charles: 119.

Ritz, Clara: 119.

Ritz, Daniel: 13, 85, 113, 119, 1992, 2558, 4382, 4499.

Ritz, Daniel E.: 85, 113, 1992.

Ritz, E.O.: 29, 1181, 2193.

Ritz, Elena, Mrs: 3524.

Ritz, Ernst: 328, 552, 1065, 1968, 1992, 2558, 4384, 4499.

Ritz Family: 2480.

Ritz, Henry: 2558, 4261.

Ritz, J.H.E.: 2631.

Ritz, Jacob: 85, 109, 119, 892, 1165, 1992, 4388, 4499.

Ritz, John: 1992.

Ritz, Lillie: 3511.

Ritz, Lorne W.: 85, 113, 119, 1992, 2558.

Ritz, Otto: 119, 1992, 2558.

Ritz, Richard: 119, 1992.

Ritz, Shirley: 2798.

Ritz, Tillie: 119.

Ritz, William F.: 1992.

Ritzer, John: 1, 4422.

Rivers, Gray, Rev.: 3643.

Roadhouse, S.M., Rev.: 3622, 3643.

Roat Family: 713, 719, 720, 4454.

Roat, John: 2163, 4306, 4380.

Roat, John, Mrs: 4371.

Roat, John S.: 461, 2714, 2730, 2818, 2843, 3702, 4195, 4380, 4461.

Roat, John S., Mrs: 3702.

Roat, Sarah: 461.

Robarts, John: 4225.

Robb, G.W.: 2714.

Robb, George: 4422.

Robb, Sophia: 1204.

Robb, William: 3660.

Robbins, W.A., Rev.: 3499.

Robert, Arnie: 1885.

Roberts, Amanda: 3709.

Roberts, C.S., Rev.: 2899, 3512, 3514, 3525, 3534, 3577, 4422.

Roberts, D.A.: 1796, 3892, 4410.

Roberts, E.F.: 4023.

Roberts, E. Llewelyn, Rev.: 3479, 4454.

Roberts, Fred, Rev.: 3506, 3623, 3634.

Rothman, Herman: 4044.
Rothwell, Benjamin: 4371, 4422.
Rothwell, Wilhelmina: 2714.
Rothwell, William: 3636.
Rott, George: 3499.
Rott, Mr: 2379.
Rottenburg, Baron de: 2505.
Rounds, H.C.: 4080, 4104.
Rouse, Gordon: 332, 2592, 3734.
Rousseau, John Baptiste: 188, 224, 250, 252, 256, 258, 271, 282, 287, 521, 555, 4134, 4391, 4448, 4449, 4456, 4517.
Routley, F.S.: 2056, 4080.
Routley, Frank, Mrs: 3773.
Row, Lula A.: 2807.
Rowe, Ernest J.: 4080, 4102.
Rowe, F.W.: 4422.
Rowe, Robert: 1165.
Rowell, Margaret: 2566, 4416.
Rowell, N.W.: 631.
Rowell, Robert: 2566.
Rowland, J.A.: 4223.
Roy, Alexander: 3656, 3795, 4380.
Roy, Flora: 3941.
Roy, James, Rev.: 3751.
Roy, Michael: 119.
Roy, Simon: 3795, 4079, 4371.
Rozell, Samuel: 4099.
Rubincam, Milton: 1554.
Ruby, A.: 239.
Ruby, Adam: 1165, 2818, 2843, 3701, 3702, 3703, 4380, 4458.
Ruby, Adam J.: 2828, 2829, 3702.
Ruby, Adam, Mrs: 3702.
Ruby, Albert: 2600.
Ruby, Barbara Baechler (Mrs John): 1032.
Ruby, Brian: 2600, 4315.
Ruby, Catherine Lebold (Mrs Joseph R.): 950, 1032.
Ruby, Charles: 1818, 2714, 2818, 3048, 3767, 3960.
Ruby, Charles A.: 3037, 3041, 3702, 4380.
Ruby, Charles A., Mrs: 3702.
Ruby, Christian: 1032.
Ruby, D.C.: 2801.
Ruby, Daniel: 256, 1032.
Ruby, David, Mrs: 3952.
Ruby, Eli: 1032.
Ruby, Emanuel: 2767, 2828, 2829, 4422.
Ruby Family: 932, 1032, 1157, 2829.
Ruby, H.H.: 2798.
Ruby, Jacob: 1032.
Ruby, John: 1032.

Ruby, Joseph: 1032.
Ruby, Joseph R.: 950, 1032.
Ruby, Leonard: 2600, 4315.
Ruby, Magdalena Roth (Mrs Joseph): 1032.
Ruby, Nicklas: 1032.
Ruby, S.R.: 4499.
Ruby, Samuel: 1032.
Ruby, William H.: 4441.
Rudd, Henry: 4433.
Rude, Darlene H.: 2120.
Rudel, Mary: 2179.
Rudell, A.E.: 3664, 4080, 4121, 4374.
Rudell, C.X.P.: 2424.
Rudell Family: 713, 719, 720, 3543.
Rudell, John: 3644.
Rudell, Mrs: 3773.
Rudisuela, Dwight: 4225.
Rudisuela, Helen: 2987, 2988.
Rudisuela, Willard, Mrs: 4226.
Rudolf, Martin: 2, 85, 91, 92, 106, 109, 110, 112, 294, 664, 671, 672, 1992, 2808, 2818, 2843, 4255, 4388.
Rudow, Arthur: 4104.
Rudow, Bertha: 3839.
Rudy, Adam: 493.
Rudy, Barbara Lichty (Mrs George): 953.
Rudy, Barbara Rosenburger: 1033.
Rudy, Carl J., Rev.: 3260, 3314.
Rudy, Clarence: 4451.
Rudy, Daniel: 1033, 4458.
Rudy, David: 3837.
Rudy Family: 711, 713, 719, 720, 800, 1033, 2562, 3335, 3613.
Rudy, George: 953, 4458.
Rudy, Howard: 1796.
Rudy, Jacob: 1017.
Rudy, Norma I.: 3837.
Rudy, Wilfred: 2728.
Rudy, William: 1033.
Rueffer Family: 4494, 4499.
Rueffer, Frederic: 1187.
Ruehl, John: 4521.
Ruettinger, Daniel: 4525.
Ruf, Adolph: 4362.
Ruf, Emil: 4362.
Ruff, Martin: 4474.
Ruggle, A.J.: 2148, 2149, 4525.
Ruggle, Dorothy Koch: 2149.
Ruggle, Edward: 2149.
Ruggle, Edward W.: 2120.
Ruggle Family: 2459, 4515.
Ruggle, Frank: 2149.
Ruggle, Johann Anton: 2149.
Ruggle, Louisa Kistler: 2149.

Ruggle, Louise: 2149.
Ruggle, Luise: 2149.
Ruggle, Robert: 2149.
Ruggle, Robert W.: 2120.
Ruggle, Theopil: 2149.
Ruler Family: 4470.
Rumball, Charles: 3474.
Rumble, Tom: 4521.
Rummel, Frederick: 4371, 4499.
Rummelhardt, Anastasia: 1034, 4447.
Rummelhardt, Francis: 1034.
Rummelhardt, Franz Joseph: 1034, 4446.
Rummelhardt, Jacques Antoine: 1034.
Rumpel, Ada Hilborn (Mrs Oscar): 1592, 3773.
Rumpel, David: 4315.
Rumpel Family: 249, 671, 672.
Rumpel, George: 326, 671, 672, 1201, 1590, 1591, 1811, 1833, 1855, 1856, 1857, 3041, 3044, 3048, 3559, 3815, 4047, 4070, 4127, 4292, 4299, 4315, 4374, 4380.
Rumpel, Hilda: 1836.
Rumpel, John W.: 4315.
Rumpel, Minna Hartman (Mrs George): 326, 671, 672, 1590, 1591, 4067, 4380.
Rumpel, Oscar: 671, 672, 1315, 1592, 2818, 3029, 4031, 4100, 4315, 4374.
Rumpel, Walter: 1593, 1703, 4315.
Runciman, Robert: 4506.
Runge, Edna, Miss: 2801.
Runimen, Samuel: 2025.
Runstedler, Bernard: 4278.
Runstedler, Gilbert: 1773.
Runstedler, J.: 4278.
Runstedler, John: 4225.
Runstedler, Joseph: 2084, 4470.
Runstettler, Anne E., Miss: 2120.
Rupert, A., Dr: 4454.
Rupp, H.: 1983.
Rupp, Lorenzo: 1983.
Ruppel, Agnes J.: 2481.
Ruppel, Arthur: 1594.
Ruppel, Bruce: 4225.
Ruppel, C. Percy: 1595.
Ruppel, Carl: 4525.
Ruppel, Caroline Cress: 1594.
Ruppel, Casper: 2410, 2481, 4221, 4525.
Ruppel, Charles: 4221.
Ruppel, Earl: 4099.
Ruppel, F.C.: 4223.
Ruppel Family: 249, 1035, 1595,

4220.

Ruppel, Flora: 1594.

Ruppel, Gene, Mrs: 367.

Ruppel, George: 1595, 1948, 2234, 3050, 4525.

Ruppel, George, Mrs: 1689.

Ruppel, Harold: 4217.

Ruppel, Henry: 4525.

Ruppel, John: 1035, 1594, 1595, 1811, 1833, 2109, 2484, 3531, 3782, 4220, 4221, 4222, 4225, 4525.

Ruppel, John H.: 13, 1569, 1594, 1595, 2116, 3030, 3050, 4217, 4525.

Ruppel, John R.: 2410, 2481.

Ruppel, John S.: 3050.

Ruppel, John, Sr: 2116, 2120.

Ruppel, Lauretta: 1594.

Ruppel, Lillian: 1594.

Ruppel, Louis: 1594.

Ruppel, Mary Huehn (Mrs John): 1035.

Ruppel, Mr: 1974.

Ruppel, Murray: 1595, 3050, 3549.

Ruppel, Nettie: 1594.

Ruppel, Norman: 1594, 1595, 3031, 3050.

Ruppel, Oscar: 1595, 2116, 3050, 4525.

Ruppel, Oscar, Mrs: 3549.

Ruppel, Percy: 1594, 3031, 3050.

Ruppel, R.R.: 2481, 4221.

Ruppel, Rosetta: 1594.

Ruppel, Russel: 4226.

Ruppel, Russel, Mrs: 4226.

Ruppel, Walter: 1594.

Rush, Eby: 1835, 1970, 3936.

Rush, Elisha: 436.

Rush, Esther: 436.

Rush Family: 4499.

Rush, John: 436.

Russ, C.: 4278.

Russ, Frank H.: 1184, 3644.

Russ, Wallace: 2050.

Russ, Wallace, Mrs: 2050.

Russell, Alexander: 3044, 4079.

Russell, Dorothy, Mrs: 3917.

Russell, James: 4240.

Russell, John: 3976.

Russell, John, Rev.: 3689, 4470.

Russell, Peter: 188, 256, 299, 303.

Russell, Peter, Hon.: 4517, 4525.

Rust, C.H.: 4376.

Ruston, Hilda: 3109, 3154.

Ruth, Edward: 4223, 4515.

Ruth Family: 1058.

Ruth, Jacob: 1165, 2149, 3442, 4515.

Ruth, Jacob, Mrs: 3442.

Ruth, Jerome A., Rev.: 3447.

Ruth, Joseph: 358, 3442.

Rutherford, C.W.: 2120.

Rutherford Family: 1036, 1773, 3908, 4212, 4499.

Rutherford, George: 4079.

Rutherford, George W.: 1773.

Rutherford, H.: 4080.

Rutherford, J.: 4080, 4203.

Rutherford, J.K.: 2783.

Rutherford, J. Thomas: 1036.

Rutherford, Janet: 1036.

Rutherford, Jenny Cairns (Mrs T.W.): 3852.

Rutherford, John H.: 1036.

Rutherford, T.A.: 2777, 3641, 4230.

Rutherford, T.A., Mrs: 3641.

Rutherford, T.V., Rev.: 3499.

Rutherford, T.W.: 3816.

Rutherford, Thomas: 3663.

Rutherford, Thomas, Mrs: 3665.

Rutherford, W.C.: 2783.

Rutherford, W.C., Mrs: 1773, 2783.

Rutherford, William H.: 3663.

Ruthig, Emma: 3674.

Ruthig, Isabell: 4499.

Ruthig, John: 3674.

Ruthig, Mr: 4387.

Ruthig, Philippina: 3674.

Ruthig, W.A.: 2820.

Rutledge, Garth G.: 2120.

Rutledge, Sylvester: 3709.

Rutledge, William: 4278.

Ruvenacht Family: 716.

Ruxton, William: 4525.

Ryan, Daisy: 1197.

Ryan, Eva M.: 2714.

Ryan Family: 1773, 4476.

Ryan, Gerald: 1773.

Ryan, Jeremiah, Rev.: 3433, 3442.

Ryan, Mr: 4080, 4480.

Ryan, W.L., Rev.: 4474.

Ryder, William: 4044.

Ryerson, Egerton, Dr: 2, 671, 672, 2705, 2714, 2782, 2805, 2808.

Ryerson, William, Rev.: 3631, 3632, 3633.

Rymal, Elizabeth: 256.

Rymal, George: 3636.

Saabas, H., Rev.: 3574.

Sabine, Jane, Mrs: 2840, 2845.

Sachs, Adam: 3569.

Sachs, Henry, "Hank": 4289.

Saddler, Doris: 4225.

Saddler, Norma: 4225.

Saddler, Robert: 4451.

Saddler, William: 4263.

Sadler, Harry: 2798.

Saer, John: 4481, 4483.

Sage, C.H., Rev.: 3625.

Sagehorn, Herman, Rev.: 3525, 3551, 3559, 3612.

Sala, Edward, Rev.: 3437.

Salinger, J., Rev.: 3527.

Sallans, Jim: 2030.

Sallinger, Rev.: 3518, 3546, 3566, 3608, 4221, 4512, 4521, 4525.

Salts, John: 250.

Saltsman, Max: 2592, 4165, 4166, 4167, 4228, 4279.

Saltzberger Family: 713, 719, 720.

Saltzberger, John Philip: 275, 759.

Saltzberger, Mary Biehn: 1, 13.

Saltzberger, Mr: 4487.

Saltzberger, Philip: 256.

Saltzberger, Veronica Gingrich: 275.

Saltzberry, Alva: 2030.

Saltzberry, Douglas: 4490, 4499.

Saltzberry, Russel: 4094.

Salyerds, E.B.: 1862, 4395.

Salyerds, Isaac: 671, 672, 1840, 2379, 3813, 4391, 4392, 4393, 4394.

Salyerds, Susannah: 3097.

Salzman, F.: 3519.

Salzman Family: 4499.

Salzman, Joseph: 956.

Salzman, Veronica Litwiller (Mrs Joseph): 956.

Samborski, Joseph, Rev.: 3437.

Sampson, Theophilus: 4230, 4240.

Samuel, Frederick: 2484.

Sanborn, William: 4458.

Sander, Juergen H., Rev.: 2947.

Sanderl, Simon, Rev.: 671, 3428, 3433, 3442, 3448, 3464, 3467, 4464.

Sanders, Mr: 877.

Sanderson, A.: 2760.

Sanderson, A.E.: 1, 29.

Sanderson, Benjamin: 1936.

Sanderson Family: 3623.

Sanderson, Francis: 1165.

Sanderson, James: 1185, 1370, 2995, 2999, 3000, 3889, 4150.

Sanderson, John: 3474.

Sanderson, Rev.: 3492.

Sanderson, William: 4396.

Sandford, William: 3709.

Sandrock, Arthur W.: 1796, 3585, 3614, 3793, 3898, 3950, 4315,

4448, 4449.

Schneider, Magdalena B.: 1091.

Schneider, Maria Erb (Mrs Jacob): 275.

Schneider, Martin: 2769, 4474, 4483.

Schneider, Mary: 1611, 1612, 2586.

Schneider, Mary Bauman (Mrs Joseph E.): 1091.

Schneider, Moses E.: 1612, 2586.

Schneider, Moses S.: 4448.

Schneider, N.C.: 1509, 1610, 2015, 2234, 2714, 3702, 3923, 4136.

Schneider, Nancy: 1611, 3893.

Schneider, Nicolaus: 4422.

Schneider, Norman: 326, 671, 672, 1191, 1608, 1609, 1703, 1919, 1949, 2004, 2258, 2829, 3818, 3860, 4080, 4359, 4380.

Schneider, Norman, Mrs: 4327.

Schneider, Peter: 671, 672, 1089.

Schneider, Peter, Rev.: 1115, 3422, 3428, 3433, 3442, 3444, 3448, 3465, 3467, 4464, 4465, 4474, 4478, 4499.

Schneider, Priscilla Dresch: 1661.

Schneider, Samuel B.: 1612, 1628, 2025, 2586, 3946, 4371, 4380.

Schneider, Sara: 1612, 2537, 2586.

Schneider, Theobold: 3503.

Schneider, Veronica: 1612, 2586.

Schneider, William: 1608.

Schneller, Edna Bradley (Mrs W.J.): 3852.

Schneller, W.J.: 1613, 1796, 2376, 3044, 3917, 4499.

Schnerich, John: 1213.

Schnerich, John, Mrs: 1213.

Schneuker, C.: 2030, 4371.

Schneuker, Charles: 2151.

Schnieder, J., Rev.: 2947, 3514, 3525, 3527, 3576, 3577, 3608.

Schnurr, Aaron: 2573.

Schnurr, Albert: 2573.

Schnurr Family: 477, 2608, 4472.

Schnurr, Grant: 2573.

Schnurr, John: 1974, 2573, 4470.

Schnurr, Margrita Eberwine: 2573.

Schoch Family: 1129.

Schoen Family: 835.

Schoenau, William Albert: 4422.

Schoenich, H.: 2234.

Schoenke, John: 616.

Schoenke, John, Mrs: 616.

Schoerg, Elizabeth: 252, 755.

Schoerg, John: 252, 612, 755.

Schoerg, Joseph: 2, 4, 249, 250, 252, 256, 265, 271, 282, 326, 519, 526,

542, 543, 612, 613, 614, 671, 672, 720, 755, 758, 759, 1208, 1240, 1241, 2051, 2096, 2130, 3275, 3383, 3930, 3933, 3936, 4080, 4380, 4433, 4435, 4437, 4450, 4455.

Schoerg, Maria: 787.

Schoerg, Samuel: 4080.

Schofield, Charles: 1975, 4286.

Schofield, J. Harper: 1466, 1725, 3633, 3923, 4348, 4362.

Schofield, J.W., Rev.: 3485, 3492, 3499.

Schofield, James: 2700, 4252.

Schofield, Jonathan: 1865, 1932, 1956, 1975, 2005, 4286.

Schofield, M.C.: 149, 333, 2055, 2501, 4388.

Schofield, Mr: 1922, 3669, 4499, 4521.

Schohn Family: 477.

Scholl, Helwig: 4371.

Scholtes, Walter: 3815.

Scholz, Gerald, Rev.: 3562.

Schondelmeyer, John: 1, 2033.

Schooley, Mr: 2701.

Schopp, Mr: 3029.

Schoppel, Ingo: 1737.

Schörg, Joseph: 713.

Schorten, Emma: 2050.

Schorten, J.F.H., Rev.: 2899, 3525.

Schrader, S.E., Rev.: 85, 3495.

Schrag, Catherine Zehr (Mrs Jacob): 1055, 1056.

Schrag, Christian: 1056.

Schrag, Daniel: 1056.

Schrag, Elizabeth Gingerich (Mrs Daniel): 1056.

Schrag Family: 717, 1055, 1056, 2705.

Schrag, Jacob: 1055, 1056.

Schrag, John: 1055.

Schrag, Joseph: 1055.

Schrag, Magdalena Steinman (Mrs Daniel): 1056.

Schrag, P., Miss: 2843.

Schrag, Veronica Kennel (Mrs Christian): 1055, 1056.

Schramm, Frederick: 1281.

Schrank, Charles: 4474.

Schrank, George: 4474.

Schreiber, Walter H.: 29.

Schreiter, A.G.: 326, 1614, 4348, 4374.

Schreiter, Armand: 1614, 4315.

Schreiter, H.C.: 1614, 4031.

Schreiter, Stanley W.: 1614, 2714,

4103.

Schreiter, Willard M.: 3923, 4348.

Schroder Family: 713, 719, 720.

Schroeder, A. Rev.: 3673, 3674.

Schroeder, C., Rev.: 3512, 3525, 3547, 3550, 3605.

Schroeder, Charles: 4422.

Schroeder, Leonard: 4136.

Schroer, Henry: 4225.

Schrumm, John: 1862.

Schrumm, May Reist (Mrs J.): 4396.

Schuch, E.W.: 3037, 3042.

Schuelke, Rev.: 3620.

Schuett, Anna: 2807.

Schuett, Charles: 4513.

Schuett, Clarence: 2098, 2807.

Schuett Family: 477.

Schuh, Heinrich: 275, 526, 3097.

Schuler, Albert W.J., Mrs: 3040.

Schuler, Frances: 3444.

Schuler, Thëodore: 4104.

Schuler, Wendall, Rev.: 2704, 2731, 2767, 2808, 3525, 3609, 4388, 4499.

Schuler, Wendlin: 930, 4494, 4499.

Schuller, F. Xavier: 863.

Schuller, Margaret Fischer (Mrs F. Xavier): 863.

Schult, Paul A., Rev.: 4384.

Schulte, Angeline Pequegnat (Mrs Benjamin): 1006.

Schulte, D., Rev.: 4124, 4380.

Schulte, John, Rev.: 3468.

Schulte, Rev.: 3519.

Schulter, Christian: 2482.

Schultheis Family: 380.

Schultheiss, John: 119.

Schultz, A.: 4278.

Schultz, A.R., Rev.: 3518, 3525, 3546, 3566, 3620, 4512, 4521, 4525.

Schultz, Anna C. Schenk (Mrs John): 1043.

Schultz, Annie: 1535.

Schultz, Annie Nafziger: 1057.

Schultz, B.: 3531.

Schultz, B., Mrs: 1594.

Schultz, Beatrice Schultz (Mrs Samuel N.): 3365.

Schultz, Benjamin: 3549.

Schultz, C.M.: 2109, 2120, 3644, 4275, 4277, 4280.

Schultz, Catherine Litwiller (Mrs John E.): 955.

Schultz, Daniel, Rev.: 3328.

Schultz, E.A., Rev.: 3514, 3576, 3577.

Schultz, Emil: 3180.

Schultz, Erich: 1244, 1615, 2806,

Shantz, Jesse, Mrs: 4441.
Shantz, John: 860, 2039, 2379, 2829, 3128, 3287, 3316.
Shantz, John B.: 1165, 1636, 1637.
Shantz, John C.: 1070.
Shantz, John D.: 3259.
Shantz, John, Mrs: 2715, 2829.
Shantz, John S.: 2493.
Shantz, John Y.: 4458.
Shantz, Jonas: 2379, 2731, 4499.
Shantz, Jonas C.: 1066.
Shantz, Joseph: 3, 787, 1163, 2379, 3079, 4286, 4456, 4461.
Shantz, Joseph, Jr: 2379.
Shantz, Joseph S.: 2379, 2774, 2775, 4451.
Shantz, Joseph S., Mrs: 1698.
Shantz, Joseph Y.: 1, 624, 1067, 1096, 1936, 2379, 2705, 2818, 3335, 4371, 4486.
Shantz, Joshua Y.: 1067, 2705, 3371.
Shantz, Kenneth: 3336.
Shantz, L.R.: 3923.
Shantz, Laura: 580, 4225.
Shantz, Leah Musselman (Mrs Menno S.): 3319.
Shantz, Leighton: 2120.
Shantz, Leroy: 3774.
Shantz, Lester: 3770.
Shantz, Levi: 1066, 3099, 4441, 4499.
Shantz, Lloyd E.: 4448.
Shantz, Lloyd S.: 1796, 4441.
Shantz, Lorena: 4008, 4014.
Shantz, Loretta: 1200.
Shantz, Lorne: 1074.
Shantz, Louisa Baer (Mrs Ervin B.): 731.
Shantz, Lucinda: 1636.
Shantz, Luella Kinsie (Mrs Amsy): 1070.
Shantz, Lydia Ann (Mrs Uzziah): 820.
Shantz, Lydia Martin (Mrs Henry): 3374.
Shantz, M.B.: 4380.
Shantz, Magdalena: 1066, 1070, 1073, 2801.
Shantz, Manasseh: 4499.
Shantz, Mariah Shantz Shantz (Mrs Cleason): 3361.
Shantz, Mariette Gimbel (Mrs Edmund): 1075.
Shantz, Marilyn: 2801.
Shantz, Marjorie: 3402.
Shantz, Mary: 1068, 1637, 2493, 3128, 3238, 4428.
Shantz, Mary Ann Hostetler (Mrs

Solomon): 1067.
Shantz, Mary Ann Shantz (Mrs Wendal): 1163.
Shantz, Mary Biehn (Mrs Aaron): 1067.
Shantz, Mary Jean: 2829.
Shantz, Mary Nahrgang (Mrs Daniel): 1067.
Shantz, Mary Snyder (Mrs John C.): 1070.
Shantz, Mary Weber (Mrs Daniel): 1075.
Shantz, Maryann Dettweiler (Mrs Titus S.): 1070.
Shantz, Melvin: 602.
Shantz, Menno: 3046.
Shantz, Menno M.: 4444.
Shantz, Menno S.: 2095, 2801, 3319.
Shantz, Merle: 1223, 2760, 2775, 3242, 3299, 3309.
Shantz, Mervin: 2760.
Shantz, Milo: 322, 324, 516, 3301, 4225, 4499.
Shantz, Minerva: 1758, 3150.
Shantz, Miss: 2801.
Shantz, Moses: 1040, 1066, 1165, 1187, 1628, 1631, 1636, 1637, 2039.
Shantz, Moses H.: 3374.
Shantz, Mr: 4428, 4525.
Shantz, Myra Snyder (Mrs Benjamin): 3402.
Shantz, Nancy Brubacher (Mrs Jacob Y.): 1631, 1636.
Shantz, Nelson G.: 1195, 1632.
Shantz, Nelson, Mrs: 1190.
Shantz, Noah: 4458.
Shantz, Noah M.: 4448.
Shantz, Noah S.: 517, 518, 1066, 1067, 1163, 2493, 2705.
Shantz, Noah W.: 1075.
Shantz, Norman S.: 1070.
Shantz, Nyal: 4499.
Shantz, Olive: 2971.
Shantz, Orvie: 2538, 3099, 3121, 3122.
Shantz, Orvie, Mrs: 3138.
Shantz, Orville: 2807.
Shantz, Pauline: 4225.
Shantz, Peggy: 2775.
Shantz, Peter E.: 1, 29, 635, 1233, 1633, 1698, 1808, 2278, 2280, 3808, 4199, 4393, 4394, 4395.
Shantz, Peter E., Mrs: 809.
Shantz, R.: 233.
Shantz, Rachel Shantz (Mrs Noah W.): 1075.

Shantz, Ralph: 1613, 2435, 3247, 4491.
Shantz, Reuben: 1796, 2760.
Shantz, Robert F.: 2120, 4086, 4089, 4092.
Shantz, Ross: 516, 4499.
Shantz, S.A.: 3927.
Shantz, S.E.: 1, 3631, 3632, 4456.
Shantz, S.S., Rev.: 1072, 3378.
Shantz, Salina: 3365.
Shantz, Samuel: 1165, 1633, 2073, 2128, 2828, 2829, 4199, 4458.
Shantz, Samuel Y.: 308, 1165, 2101, 2120.
Shantz, Sara: 1612.
Shantz, Sarah: 1636.
Shantz, Sarah Shuh (Mrs Jacob Y.): 1631.
Shantz, Selina Shirk (Mrs Walter C.): 1078.
Shantz, Sidney: 1698.
Shantz, Sidney S.: 3320, 3328.
Shantz, Simon: 1163, 3097, 3134.
Shantz, Solomon: 1067, 1163.
Shantz, Stanley S.: 1895.
Shantz, Stephen: 2775.
Shantz, Susanna Cassel: 580.
Shantz, Susanna Groh: 2760, 3402.
Shantz, Susannah: 1636, 3121, 3137, 3365.
Shantz, Susannah Cassel (Mrs Noah S.): 517, 1067, 3365, 4487.
Shantz, Susannah Schneider: 1075, 1611.
Shantz, Sydney S., Mrs: 1185.
Shantz, Tilman S.: 1165, 4456.
Shantz, Titus: 2493.
Shantz, Titus S.: 1070.
Shantz, U.B., Dr: 1205.
Shantz, Uzziah: 820.
Shantz, Veronica Weber: 1636, 1698.
Shantz, W.W.: 2294.
Shantz, Walter C.: 518, 1078, 2705, 2731, 4499.
Shantz, Ward M.: 1796, 2878, 3278, 3391.
Shantz, Wendal: 1163, 1879.
Shantz, Wendel E.: 1698.
Shantz, Wendel S.: 1066, 1698, 4499.
Shantz, William A., Rev.: 3328.
Shantz, Willie: 4441.
Shantz, Willis B.: 2109, 2120, 4192.
Sharbach, Joseph: 1417, 4458.
Sharbach, Mary: 1417.
Sharp, Henry: 4429.
Sharp, Marilyn Dickhout (Mrs Thomas): 3852.

Veitch, George M.: 2120.

Veitch, Harris: 1501, 4499.

Veitch, James, Jr: 2120.

Veitch, Jean Henderson: 4433.

Veitch, Lawrence: 4100.

Veitch, Ross W.: 2109, 2120.

Veitch, Thomas: 4079.

Veitch, William: 13, 1165, 2098, 2448, 2743, 2766, 2818, 3669, 3936, 4214, 4229, 4266, 4513, 4524, 4525.

Veitch, William, Mrs: 2098.

Veitel, Dora: 2547.

Veitel, Henry: 4474.

Veitel, Norman W.: 2547.

Venema, Alvin, Rev.: 3707.

Venton, Alexander: 276, 289.

Venton, Emma: 2775.

Venton, George: 2775.

Venton, Maggie: 2775.

Verkler Family: 716.

Vetter, A.: 4017.

Vetter, A., Mrs: 3620.

Vice, A.H.: 29, 4223.

Vickerman, Fred: 2379, 2774, 2775, 4452.

Vickerman, Mary: 2775.

Vickerman, Thomas G.: 2379, 2774, 2775, 4452.

Vickerman, Tillie Sauder: 2774, 2775.

Vickers, Grace: 3713.

Viedenheimer, Clayton: 4099.

Viedenheimer, Louis: 4474.

Viges, Albert: 4104.

Villaume, William J.: 1737, 2904.

Villemaire, Mervyn: 4168.

Vincent, Abraham: 1369.

Vincent, Margaret: 1369.

Vincent, Michael: 1369.

Vincent, Rachel: 1369.

Vingoe, J.W.: 1737.

Vivian, Rev.: 3470.

Vockrodt, A., Rev.: 3574.

Voege, Herman C., Rev.: 3539.

Voegele Family: 477.

Voegtle, Oliver: 2557.

Voelker, Andrew: 4525.

Voelker, Dr: 2562.

Voelker, Henry: 4525.

Voelker, Max, Rev.: 3525, 3550, 3609.

Voelker, Valentine: 4221.

Voelkner, A.W., Mrs: 2039.

Voelzing, E.: 4521.

Vogelei, Nicholas: 3574.

Vogelsang, Edith: 2039.

Vogelsang, Emil: 326, 1165, 1628, 1636, 1637, 1855, 1860, 1884, 1914, 1974, 2039, 2599, 4377, 4380.

Vogt, A.S., Dr: 4132.

Vogt, Augustus: 671, 672, 1689, 1725, 3016, 3030, 3050, 3525, 3537, 3546, 4227.

Vogt Family: 249, 477, 1035.

Vogt, George: 1689, 1974, 3030, 3050, 3525, 3546, 4221.

Vogt, George, Dr: 1689.

Vogt, John E.: 1195, 3592.

Vogt, Joseph: 2769, 2815.

Vogt, Marianna Zingg: 1689.

Vogt, O.H.: 29, 3923.

Vogt, O.H., Mrs: 3923.

Vogt, Oscar: 1689, 2438.

Vogt, Peter: 4371.

Voisin, Catherine Meyer (Mrs Joseph): 1114.

Voisin, Catherine Susz (Mrs Joseph): 1114.

Voisin, Edward: 2769, 4428, 4474.

Voisin, Elmer: 4474.

Voisin Family: 1113, 1114.

Voisin, Harold: 4474.

Voisin, Jerome: 4474.

Voisin, Joseph: 1114, 2815.

Voisin, Joseph X.: 1114, 2769.

Voisin, Julia: 1231.

Voisin, Margaretha Meyer (Mrs Peter): 1114.

Voisin, Mary Lehnhardt (Mrs Joseph X.): 1114.

Voisin, Monica Kohler Miller (Mrs Joseph): 1114.

Voisin, Peter: 1114.

Volick, V.N., Rev.: 3478, 3623.

Volker, H.A.: 2015, 2234.

Volkery, Adam: 2424.

Voll, Carl: 2815.

Voll, Henry A.: 895.

Voll, John: 4040.

Voll, Louisa Hahn (Mrs Henry A.): 895.

Vondrau, C.: 4392.

Voss, M.E., Rev.: 3512, 3547, 3574.

Voth, Henry H.: 1678.

Wachsmuth, Fredricka: 2443.

Wachsmuth, William: 2443, 4221, 4525.

Wackett, Edgar: 4080.

Waddell, George: 4422.

Waddell, H.: 4103.

Waddell, Joseph: 4465.

Waddell, R.H., Rev.: 3622.

Waddie, Geordie, "Whiskey Geordie": 1306, 4258.

Wade, Arthur: 4104.

Wade, Donald E.: 4217, 4226.

Wade, Emma: 1190.

Wadel, Stephen: 3444.

Waden, Stephen: 2732.

Waechter, A., Rev.: 1115, 3422, 3431, 3442, 3465.

Waechter, Amelia Crossin (Mrs Lorentz): 1115.

Waechter, Andrew: 1115.

Waechter Family: 1115, 1116.

Waechter, George: 2769.

Waechter, Lorentz: 1115.

Waechter, Mary Thomassing (Mrs Theobald): 1115.

Waechter, Stephen: 1115.

Waechter, Theobald: 1115.

Waechter, Theresa Forwell (Mrs Andrew): 1115.

Waelchli, F.E., Rev.: 2707, 2709, 2818, 3696, 3697, 3701, 3703, 4380, 4454.

Wafer, Thomas: 4104.

Waghorne, Jean: 2717, 3744.

Waghorne, Mary: 3744.

Wagler, Anne Marie Wagler (Mrs Christian): 1117.

Wagler, Barbara: 3099.

Wagler, Catherine Erb (Mrs David): 1118.

Wagler, Cecil: 4491, 4499.

Wagler, Christian: 556, 1117.

Wagler, Christian L.: 1118.

Wagler, David: 1118, 1184, 3230, 4318.

Wagler, Elton: 4499.

Wagler Family: 946, 1117, 1118, 4478.

Wagler, Isaac: 1118.

Wagler, Jacob: 1118, 3369.

Wagler, Jacob L.: 1118.

Wagler, John: 1118, 3368.

Wagler, Joseph: 1059.

Wagler, Mary Gerber (Mrs Daniel): 1118.

Wagler, Mary Schwartzentruber (Mrs Jacob L.): 1118.

Wagler, Mary Schwartzentruber (Mrs Joseph): 1059.

Wagler, Mary Zehr (Mrs Christian L.): 1118.

Wagler, Michael: 1118, 1184, 3230.

Wagler, Nancy: 1118.

Wagler, Noah: 1118.

Wagler, Rev.: 3492.

Wagler, Veronica Roth (Mrs Noah): 1118.

Wagley, George: 804.

Wagner, Adam: 3032.

Wagner, Allan: 3839.

Wagner, Anselm: 249, 635, 1967, 2818, 4053, 4371, 4380.

Wagner, Anthony: 4521.

Wagner, Bartholomew: 4466, 4499.

Wagner, Bertha: 2179.

Wagner, Carl: 2090, 3530.

Wagner, Catherine L. (Mrs David): 1139.

Wagner, Christina: 2179.

Wagner, David: 1139.

Wagner Family: 537, 1691, 2704, 4499.

Wagner, George: 2179.

Wagner, George, Jr: 2179.

Wagner, Gordon: 1691.

Wagner, Harold: 1197, 2780, 3915, 4416.

Wagner, Harold, Mrs: 1442.

Wagner, Harold W.: 1466, 2781.

Wagner, Henry: 127.

Wagner, Herman: 2179, 4315.

Wagner, J.: 1974.

Wagner, Jacob: 894.

Wagner, Jacob, Rev.: 326, 1691, 2019, 3495, 3503, 4380.

Wagner, Jerome: 4499.

Wagner, John: 1165, 2179, 3936, 4136, 4221, 4371, 4524.

Wagner, Jonas: 4515.

Wagner, Joseph: 1690, 1967, 4044, 4079, 4388.

Wagner, L.H., Rev.: 1691, 2714, 3493, 3495, 3496, 4380.

Wagner, Margaret Hailer: 1691, 2019.

Wagner, N.: 4299.

Wagner, Noah: 2039.

Wagner, Norman: 197.

Wagner, P.A.: 13, 2807, 4478, 4480.

Wagner, Peter: 13, 2820.

Wagner, Robert: 4148, 4168.

Wagner, Sara: 127.

Wagner, Stanley A.: 1773, 2435, 4486.

Wagner, T.D.: 2909.

Wagner, V.Z.: 2379.

Wagner, Waldemar: 4499.

Wagstaff, Bob: 2050.

Wahl, Andrew: 4521.

Wahl, B.G.: 1974.

Wahl, Elmer: 2033.

Wahl, H.: 3620.

Wahl, Henry, Jr: 1165.

Wahl, Jacob: 2972.

Wahlbaum, Herman, Rev.: 3527.

Wahling, Miss: 2815.

Wahn, Valentine: 2, 249, 635, 908, 1233, 3808, 4390, 4392, 4393, 4394.

Waind, Richard M.: 4448.

Wait, Eliza: 2818, 2843.

Wait, P., Miss: 2813.

Wake, E.G.: 2126.

Wake, G.E.: 4271.

Wake, G.E., "Ted": 4276, 4279.

Wake, Ted: 1932.

Walbaum, Herman, Rev.: 3574, 3608.

Walcot, John: 256, 382, 2760, 2761, 3232.

Walden, J.W., Dr: 1165, 1171, 1535, 1667, 1818, 1820, 4073, 4422.

Walden, William: 4017.

Walder, Harry: 2153.

Walder, Henry: 1165, 2120, 2184, 4468.

Walder, Robert: 2153, 2184.

Waldie, Geordie: 4230.

Waldie, James: 690.

Waldron, Dr: 2396, 4034.

Waldron, John: 896.

Waldron, W.G., Rev.: 3643.

Walker, Alexander: 2550.

Walker, Annie: 3470.

Walker Brothers: 4199, 4525.

Walker, C.E.: 4299.

Walker, Catherine Hymmen Brighton (Mrs Gottlieb): 742.

Walker, Clara: 3470.

Walker, Clinton T.: 1281, 3470.

Walker, Clinton Tye: 4094, 4103, 4486.

Walker, David: 3745, 4221.

Walker, Dorothy: 2798, 4486.

Walker, Edith: 1258.

Walker, Edmund: 1258, 1689.

Walker Family: 742, 2704, 4498.

Walker, Frances Tye: 4486.

Walker, Franklin A.: 2853.

Walker, Fred: 3194, 4486.

Walker, George: 4195.

Walker, Gottlieb: 742.

Walker, Harvey: 3709.

Walker, Henry, Mrs: 1281, 3470.

Walker, I.M.: 2728.

Walker, Isabella: 1230.

Walker, J.A., Rev.: 3623.

Walker, James: 4193.

Walker, John: 830, 1953, 4015, 4513, 4515, 4524, 4530.

Walker, John W.: 2788, 4104.

Walker, L.: 4499.

Walker, M.T., Rev.: 3499.

Walker, Maria Illingworth: 4486.

Walker, Marjory: 4486.

Walker, Mary: 2705, 4486.

Walker, May, Miss: 2149.

Walker, Mr: 3413.

Walker, Murial: 2728.

Walker, Murray: 4521.

Walker, R.C., Mrs: 3922.

Walker, Robert: 332.

Walker, S.J.: 4196.

Walker, T.G.: 3470.

Walker, Thomas: 3, 2438, 2457, 2458, 3470, 3474, 4221, 4486, 4506, 4523, 4524.

Walker, Thomas, Mrs: 3470.

Walker, Tom: 1281.

Walker, W.H.: 3054, 4103, 4422.

Walker, W.T.: 4263.

Walker, William: 199, 4079, 4473, 4478.

Walker, William J., Rev.: 1165, 3485, 3662, 3663.

Walker, William, Rev.: 3643.

Walker, William Wallace: 2120.

Wall, Abraham: 616.

Wall, Anna: 616.

Wall, Tina: 616.

Wallace, Agnes: 3636.

Wallace, Alan: 2030.

Wallace, Alice: 2049, 2704, 4499.

Wallace, B.: 2128.

Wallace Family: 2854, 4199.

Wallace, Frederick: 4499.

Wallace, Hugh: 3663, 3751, 4266.

Wallace, Hugh, Mrs: 4423.

Wallace, James: 1165, 2030.

Wallace, John: 1967, 3650, 3660, 3751.

Wallace, John W.: 4517.

Wallace, Munzo: 4079.

Wallace, Robert: 1664, 3732, 3750, 3751, 4266, 4499.

Wallace, Ruby, Miss: 2983.

Wallace, Thomas: 2975.

Wallace, W.G.: 2840, 2845, 2854.

Wallace, William: 250, 275, 282, 539, 1358, 1752, 2448, 2553, 2986, 3663, 4229, 4512, 4513, 4514, 4517, 4521, 4523, 4524, 4525.

Wallace, William, Mrs: 3636.

Walley, Percy: 4080, 4102.

Wallis, William: 4422.

Walmsley, D.L., Dr: 1165, 1705, 2714, 4221.

Walmsley Family: 2829.

Walmsley, John: 3702, 4380.

Walper, Abel: 2163, 4380.

Walper, C.H.: 2163, 3029, 4315, 4380.

Walper, J.: 4278.

Walper, Ora: 1185, 2714, 3100, 3109.

Walsh, A., Rev.: 3278, 3378.

Walsh, James P.: 2179, 4192.

Walter, Alexander, Rev.: 3431.

Walter, Alois: 2704, 4499.

Walter Family: 249, 2815.

Walter, Ferdinand: 18, 37, 308, 1165, 2120, 4014, 4040, 4299, 4374, 4468, 4478, 4480, 4483.

Walter, Frank: 2769, 2832.

Walter, Hermann, Rev.: 671, 672.

Walter, Jacob: 4422, 4524.

Walter, John: 128, 326, 1692, 2801, 4136, 4422.

Walter, John, Jr: 1692.

Walters, Bob: 4474.

Walters, Dr: 1281, 4299.

Waltner Family: 717.

Walton, William: 1197.

Waltz, Jacob: 4509.

Waltz, John: 1967.

Wambold, A., Rev.: 3316.

Wambold, H.E.: 3923.

Wambold, Isaac A.: 3314, 3396.

Wamboldt, Abraham: 553, 2760.

Wamboldt, Hannah Wanner (Mrs Abraham): 2760.

Wamboldt, Isaac, Rev.: 2760.

Wanklyn, Geneva, Miss: 2983.

Wanless, G.A.: 4298.

Wanless, George: 4299.

Wanless, John: 2736, 4195, 4422.

Wanner, Anna Mosser (Mrs Henry): 2760.

Wanner, Catharine Strycker: 891.

Wanner Family: 713, 719, 720, 1094, 2097, 3270, 4436, 4521.

Wanner, Hannah: 2760, 2774, 2775.

Wanner, Henry: 256, 264, 275, 514, 553, 713, 720, 2760, 2774, 2775, 3232, 3271, 4458.

Wanner, Henry, Jr: 2760.

Wanner, John: 256.

Wanner, Louis: 4525.

Wanner, Myrum: 2704, 3183.

Wanner, Nancy Clemens (Mrs Henry): 2760.

Wanner, Nancy Mosser: 3097.

Wanner, Neil: 4497.

Wanner, Tobias: 256, 891, 1557, 2760, 2766, 2818, 4429.

Ward Family: 813.

Ward, George: 3636, 4371.

Ward, H.: 2828, 2829.

Ward, J.G.: 3799.

Ward, James Frederick: 2714, 4103, 4356.

Ward, James, Rev.: 3470, 3474.

Ward, John: 3636.

Ward, Mary E., Mrs: 2120.

Warden, J.W.: 4103.

Warden, T.W., Dr: 4062.

Wardlaw, James S., Dr: 1404, 2720, 2777, 4031, 4062, 4263.

Wardlaw, John: 2005.

Waring, J. Arthur, Rev.: 3479.

Warkentin, Bernard: 1628, 1637.

Warkentin, Marvin, Rev.: 3317.

Warneke, Alexander, Rev.: 3417.

Warner, Bert: 1970.

Warner, C.M: 4080.

Warner, Charles: 4103.

Warner Family: 1083, 4436.

Warner, Henry: 4388.

Warner, Lewis, Rev.: 3622.

Warner, Mr: 3945.

Warnholz, Jerome: 4099.

Warnke, Rev.: 3518, 3546, 3566, 4512, 4521, 4525.

Warnock, Adam: 2, 332, 908, 1806, 1900, 1956, 2005, 2720, 3481, 3688, 4246, 4266.

Warnock, Amelia: 16, 1200, 2959.

Warnock, Annie: 3771.

Warnock, C.R.H.: 29, 908, 1806, 3481, 4230, 4246.

Warnock, C.R.H., Mrs: 3481, 3838, 4233.

Warnock, Daisy Nesbitt: 908.

Warnock, E.G.: 908, 1190, 1900, 4031.

Warnock, James: 2, 908, 1851, 1900, 3665, 4253, 4266.

Warnock, James A.: 908.

Warnock, James B.: 908.

Warnock, James E.: 908.

Warnock, James G.: 1900.

Warnock, John: 908, 1900, 3751, 4266.

Warnock, Stephanie Hespeler (Mrs Adam): 908, 3838.

Warren, A.D.: 3410.

Warren, F.B.: 3770.

Warren, Greta: 4278.

Warren, Ivan: 4104.

Warren, John E.: 2994, 3644.

Warren, Suzanne: 4226.

Warrender, W.K.: 2364.

Washburn, C., Mrs: 3773.

Washburn, Cameron: 4099.

Washburn, D.: 4275.

Washburn, E.B.: 3636.

Washburn, James: 2736.

Washburn, James W.: 1181, 1201, 4112.

Washburn, John S.: 2765.

Washburn, M.: 4275.

Washburn, R.G.: 4080.

Washburn, Robert: 4103.

Washburn, Stephen: 4079, 4525.

Wass, Rev.: 3643.

Waters, Arthur, Rev.: 1370.

Waters, Bob: 4225.

Waters, John: 256, 2728.

Waters, Jonathan: 3644.

Watherson, Mary: 691.

Watherson, William: 691.

Watkins, Thomas: 4204.

Watson, Alfred E.: 1693, 2379, 4176.

Watson, Alfred W.: 1189, 4178.

Watson, Anna Maria: 1693.

Watson, Annie McGirr (Mrs Thomas): 3852.

Watson, Archibald: 1693, 4079.

Watson, Charles F.: 2692.

Watson, Charles Jerome: 1693.

Watson, Elizabeth: 1693, 1694.

Watson, Elizabeth Dolman: 1693, 1694, 3852.

Watson, Emily Barbara Ure: 1693.

Watson Family: 1758, 2260, 4178, 4212, 4454, 4477.

Watson, Graham: 4423.

Watson, Harriet: 1693.

Watson, Harvey, Mrs: 4226.

Watson, Homer: 3, 8, 11, 128, 332, 502, 671, 672, 1421, 1501, 1758, 1877, 2097, 2304, 2333, 2441, 2470, 2607, 2789, 2959, 3056, 3087, 3089, 3090, 3091, 3105, 3107, 3108, 3111, 3112, 3113, 3154, 3156, 3159, 3161, 4080, 4227, 4230, 4423, 4429, 4439, 4454.

Watson, Irving: 4429, 4439.

Watson, J.: 4278.

Watson, James: 276, 2379, 2470, 2727, 3663, 3709, 4429.

Watson, James G.: 121.

Watson, James Hilman: 1693.

Watson, Jennie: 1693.

Watson, Jessie: 1693.

Watson, John: 295, 1693, 1694, 1695, 1696, 1740, 1741, 1787, 1811, 1833, 1877, 1923, 1937, 1974, 2021, 2260, 2261, 2429, 3728, 3745, 4181, 4185, 4188, 4202,

4423.
Watson, John G.: 1693, 2109, 2120.
Watson, John R.: 1466.
Watson, John W.: 2109, 2120.
Watson, Johnnie: 4225.
Watson, Jude: 4429.
Watson, Margaret: 1693.
Watson, Margaret Dorothy: 1693.
Watson, Margaret Ure: 1693, 4178.
Watson, Mary: 1693.
Watson, Mary Urie: 1200, 1693, 1694, 1695, 1696.
Watson, Mrs: 2700.
Watson, Nellie: 4080.
Watson, Norman, Rev.: 3719.
Watson, Peter: 1983.
Watson, Phoebe: 2470, 2789, 3090, 3105, 3112, 3113, 4423, 4429, 4439, 4454.
Watson, Ransford: 3090, 4423, 4429, 4456, 4458.
Watson, Robert: 1693, 4079.
Watson, Roxanna Bechtel (Mrs Homer): 3090, 3112, 4423.
Watson, Susannah: 3090.
Watson, T.H.: 3816.
Watson, Thomas: 4477.
Watson, Tillie: 2116.
Watson, Wiley: 2118.
Watson, William: 276, 4438.
Watson, William Dolman: 1693, 2021, 3650.
Watson, William James: 3090.
Watt, F.J.: 4087.
Watts, Eli: 4102.
Watts, H.W., Rev.: 3623.
Watts, J.O., Rev.: 3499, 4422.
Waugh, Annie: 2748.
Waugh, D.B.: 2801.
Waugh, D.H.: 1165.
Waugh, David H.: 3828.
Waugh, F.W.: 1712.
Waugh, Grace: 2748.
Waugh, John: 2736, 2763.
Waugh, Margaret Jane: 3828.
Waugh, Mr: 4521.
Waugh, Samuel A.: 3828.
Weaver, Abraham: 256.
Weaver, Amos: 4450.
Weaver, Benjamin: 256.
Weaver, Daniel: 1163.
Weaver, Finlay: 2714.
Weaver, George: 4429.
Weaver, Henry: 255, 256.
Weaver, Isaac: 333, 1922, 2128, 4356, 4380, 4422.
Weaver, Jacob: 2163, 3632, 4380,

4450.
Weaver, Jacob B.: 2812, 3631.
Weaver, Jacob B., Mrs: 3773.
Weaver, John: 514, 4454.
Weaver, Joseph: 4521, 4525.
Weaver, Joseph S.: 4525.
Weaver, L.E.: 1184, 1865, 2994, 4031, 4271, 4274.
Weaver, L.E., Mrs: 4031.
Weaver, Lester H.: 1001.
Weaver, Lizzie: 4521.
Weaver, Menno B.: 3319.
Weaver, Miss: 2983, 3048.
Weaver, Moses: 2812, 4450.
Weaver, Oscar: 2139.
Weaver, Ralph: 2714.
Weaver, Ralph L.: 3631, 4080, 4104.
Weaver, S.S.: 4220, 4525.
Weaver, Samuel: 2549, 4220, 4521, 4523, 4525.
Weaver, Samuel S.: 2482, 4380, 4525.
Weaver, Wesley: 2807.
Weaver, William: 2700.
Weaver, William H.: 1001, 1975, 2714, 2720, 2994, 3664, 3923, 4275.
Weaver, Yada: 4031.
Webb, D.E., Rev.: 3734.
Webb, J.H., Dr: 1, 333, 1165, 4031, 4078, 4422.
Webb, J.H., Mrs: 3773.
Webb, R.J.M.: 3767.
Weber, A.B.: 1796.
Weber, A.C.: 149, 3238.
Weber, Aaron: 1119, 1165, 1943, 1953, 2098, 3050, 4441, 4513, 4524, 4527.
Weber, Abraham: 3, 7, 252, 275, 326, 713, 720, 1120, 1128, 1185, 1256, 1358, 1612, 1628, 1640, 2051, 3893, 3911, 4377, 4380, 4405.
Weber, Abraham C.: 1128, 1256, 1356, 3239, 3254, 3274, 4380.
Weber, Abram: 4371.
Weber, Adah Frances Burkholder (Mrs Noah): 3365.
Weber, Adam: 1124.
Weber, Allan: 1773, 2807.
Weber, Amos: 1165, 4422.
Weber, Andrew: 20, 1086, 1165, 4193, 4195.
Weber, Andrew E.: 1698.
Weber, Angus: 8, 616, 1758, 1790, 2098, 2807.
Weber, Angus, Mrs: 2098.
Weber, Anna: 671, 672, 3062, 3063, 3064, 3066, 3069, 3070, 3077,

3078, 3083, 3085, 3095, 3115, 3121, 3126, 3132, 3134, 3137, 3143, 3146, 3148.
Weber, Anna Hershey: 1128.
Weber, Anna Martin (Mrs Daniel H.): 1120.
Weber, Anna Martin (Mrs Samuel): 3121.
Weber, Anthony: 1124, 2731.
Weber, Barbara Brubacher Martin Weber (Mrs Noah M.): 3365.
Weber, Barbara Horst (Mrs Moses M.): 1122.
Weber, Benjamin: 256, 1120, 1128, 1187, 1358, 4461.
Weber, Bruce: 1796, 1954, 3044, 3923.
Weber, Carl J.: 1124.
Weber, Carl N.: 2159, 2899, 3923, 4047, 4067, 4148, 4315, 4380.
Weber, Caroline: 2457.
Weber, Catherine Eby (Mrs David): 1358.
Weber, Charles: 1165.
Weber, Christian B.: 1124.
Weber, Christian S.: 2120, 4524, 4530.
Weber, Christopher: 1124, 4474, 4513.
Weber, Clarence H.: 2554.
Weber, Clayton H.: 1773.
Weber, Cleason Frey: 2120.
Weber, Daniel: 713, 720, 740, 1124, 1128, 1569, 2093, 2097, 3146, 3406, 3414, 3416, 4195, 4380.
Weber, Daniel H.: 1120.
Weber, Daniel L.: 2379.
Weber, Daniel M.: 1126.
Weber, David: 846, 1119, 1128, 1358, 1698, 2379, 2470, 3384, 4371, 4380, 4456, 4458, 4461.
Weber, Donald: 326, 1796, 1954, 3936, 4332, 4359.
Weber, Donald, Mrs: 4359.
Weber, Doris: 2728, 3269.
Weber, E. Bruce: 1128.
Weber, E.O.: 22, 326, 1508, 1862, 2714, 4380.
Weber, Edwin: 1569, 1698, 1844, 3243.
Weber, Eileen: 2457.
Weber, Elam: 3372, 4473.
Weber, Elias: 3254, 3298, 3316.
Weber, Elias E.: 392, 3242, 3314, 3316.

Michael): 1699, 1700.

Weichel, Michael: 1, 326, 1165, 1699, 1700, 2410, 3031, 3050, 4225, 4525.

Weichel, Minnie Kaitting: 1700, 4136.

Weichel, Olive Hughes: 2116, 4136.

Weichel, Oscar William: 671, 672, 1192, 1595, 2109, 2116, 2120, 3839, 3923, 4136, 4217.

Weichel, Ross: 2116, 4136.

Weichel, W.O.: 3525.

Weichel, William: 3050, 3782.

Weichel, William G.: 1, 13, 29, 326, 333, 631, 671, 672, 1176, 1201, 1699, 1700, 2495, 2850, 3040, 3525, 3536, 3537, 3618, 3959, 4031, 4087, 4117, 4119, 4121, 4128, 4132, 4136, 4146, 4149, 4158, 4164, 4374, 4422, 4525.

Weicher, Fred: 2728.

Weicker, Catherine Zinkan (Mrs John): 1131, 1132, 1133.

Weicker, Dorothy: 3849.

Weicker, Emma Jungblut (Mrs William): 1134.

Weicker Family: 711, 1130, 1131, 1132, 1133, 1134.

Weicker, Florence: 1134, 4327.

Weicker, John: 1131, 1132, 1133.

Weicker, Samuel: 1133, 1134, 3590.

Weicker, W.J.L.: 1134.

Weicker, William: 1134.

Weickert, Werner: 3182.

Weidenhammer, Andrew: 1, 13, 85, 98, 124, 2818, 4422.

Weidenhammer, Christian: 4221.

Weidenhammer, Christopher: 4483.

Weidenhammer, Frederick J., Dr: 4473, 4477.

Weidenhammer, George, Rev.: 3527, 3608, 3620, 4512, 4521.

Weidenhammer, W.B.: 2714, 3782.

Weidman, Martin: 4428.

Weihe, William: 3660, 4458.

Weiler, A.A.: 1811, 1833.

Weiler, Andrew: 4464, 4465.

Weiler, Anthony, Rev.: 1, 1701, 2732, 2756, 3422, 3431, 3442, 3460, 3462, 3465, 4380.

Weiler, Armand: 835.

Weiler, Dorothea: 4499.

Weiler Family: 1, 477, 2385, 3177, 4443.

Weiler, Frances X.: 4464.

Weiler, H.E.: 13.

Weiler, Ignatius: 3076, 4464.

Weiler, Jacob: 3076.

Weiler, Joseph: 4464.

Weiler, Leander: 3076, 3152.

Weiler, Michael, Rev.: 1701.

Weiler, Mrs: 13.

Weiler, Regina Roehmer: 1701.

Weiler, Russel: 4100.

Weinbruch, W., Rev.: 85.

Weinert, Herbert: 2451.

Weinstein, Harry: 326.

Weinstein, Robert: 4100.

Weir, Adam: 3665.

Weir, Aggie: 2775.

Weir, Alexander: 2783.

Weir, David: 4079.

Weir, George: 3709.

Weir, J.D.: 2818, 2843, 4380.

Weir, J.J.A.: 1196, 1535, 2983, 3737, 3960, 4374.

Weir, J., Mrs: 2783.

Weir, John, Mrs: 2783.

Weir, Richard: 2783.

Weir, Robert: 4104.

Weir, Samuel: 4079.

Weir, Thomas: 2775.

Weir, W., Mrs: 2783.

Weir, William: 2783.

Weis, George: 4525.

Weis, John: 4525.

Weischer, Gertrude: 2815.

Weishar, Andrew: 1135.

Weishar Family: 1135.

Weishar, Margaretha Zinger (Mrs Andrew): 1135.

Weismueller, Heinrich: 4461.

Weiss, Clarence J., Rev.: 3447.

Weiss, James: 899.

Weiss, Lerch: 4436.

Weiss, Milton: 2030.

Weitzel, Bill: 3050.

Weitzel Family: 658, 4220.

Weitzel, G.: 1569.

Weitzel, Henry: 4225.

Weitzel, John: 3050.

Weitzel, Michael: 4525.

Weitzel, Nicholas: 4221.

Welbaum, Rev.: 3620.

Welch, Albert: 4102.

Welch, Helena: 3055.

Welch, Jim: 2869.

Welhausen, John: 4043.

Welker, A.H.: 1864, 2714.

Welker, Alex: 1702, 1703, 1845, 1857, 2013.

Welker, Charles: 1174.

Welker, Charles, Mrs: 1174.

Welker, F.E.: 4521.

Welker, Frank: 4512.

Welker, Franklin E.: 1192.

Welland, F.J.: 4080.

Welland, J.F.: 4103.

Wellein, John: 37, 1974, 2983, 3620, 4195.

Wellein, Mr: 4192.

Wellein, Richard: 4099.

Welles, Elisha: 282.

Wellhauser Family: 477.

Wellhauser, Matthew: 2769, 2815.

Welliver, Chester: 4477, 4483.

Welliver Family: 4477.

Wells, Cecil: 3911.

Wells, Clayton W., Dr: 1704, 2780, 3054, 3110, 3754, 3874.

Wells, Edith: 2714.

Wells, James: 2379.

Wells, T. Hughes: 4422.

Wells, Walter, Dr: 1, 13, 333, 1704, 1808, 1922, 3054, 4078, 4422.

Wells, William: 3665.

Welsch, John: 229.

Welsh, E.: 4499.

Welsh Family: 4436, 4499.

Welsh, Gordon: 1822.

Welsh, James: 3660.

Welsman, Frank: 1725.

Welz, F.W.: 3.

Welz, John: 4521.

Welz, T.W.: 4521.

Wendling Family: 477, 837, 838, 839.

Wendling, Joseph: 671, 672, 839, 4380, 4458, 4464.

Wendling, Magdalena Beingesser (Mrs Joseph): 839.

Wendt, Gustave: 1948.

Wenger, A.D.: 3314.

Wenger, Daniel: 805, 1165.

Wenger, Donald: 3258, 4499.

Wenger, Elisabeth: 3097.

Wenger, Elizabeth Zimmerman (Mrs Joseph): 1137.

Wenger Family: 1136, 1137.

Wenger, Isaac: 4221, 4525.

Wenger, John: 3355.

Wenger, Jonas: 2481, 2484, 2554.

Wenger, Joseph: 1137, 4525.

Wenger, Martin: 2481, 2482, 2484, 2554.

Wenger, Peter: 4380, 4525.

Wenger, Ruth Hackman: 3258.

Wenger, Widow: 713, 720.

Wengest, George: 2179.

Wenz, Jacob: 4525.

Wenzel Family: 4499.

Wenzel, Helen: 1932.

Weppler, Alice: 4226.

Zinck, Frederick, Rev.: 3582.

Zing, John: 4393.

Zinger, Albert: 655, 3177, 3927.

Zinger, Albert, Rev.: 1, 1195, 1728, 2732, 2756, 2818, 2850, 2983, 3418, 3431, 3442, 3450, 3959, 4374, 4380.

Zinger, Andrew W.: 4464.

Zinger, C.H.: 1165.

Zinger, Chrysostum: 1135, 4380, 4524.

Zinger Family: 276, 477, 1773, 2815, 3467, 4443.

Zinger, George: 2120.

Zinger, H.J.: 3945.

Zinger, John: 3444.

Zinger, Joseph: 1165, 4464.

Zinger, Joseph A.: 1773, 3815, 4464.

Zinger, Louisa Motz: 1545.

Zinger, W.J.: 3959.

Zinger, Wilfred: 1773.

Zinkan, Mr: 4525.

Zinkann Family: 835.

Zinkann, Henry: 4517.

Zinkann, John: 4040, 4195, 4385, 4499.

Zinkann, Miss: 4371.

Zinken, Emma, Mrs: 2120.

Zinken, H.: 3620.

Zinken, Helen: 1933.

Zinken, John H.: 2120.

Zinken, Lorne: 4490, 4499.

Zinn, Anna C. Doerbecker (Mrs Johann Heinrich): 836.

Zinn, Johann Heinrich: 836.

Zinn, Milton: 4497.

Zirwus, Mathias: 4483.

Zoeger, Chris: 4494.

Zoeger, Christoph: 18, 4374, 4487, 4488, 4499, 4510.

Zoeger, Henry: 4483.

Zoeger, John: 419, 1165, 1574, 2109, 2120, 2128, 2440, 2608, 4466, 4472, 4478, 4480, 4481, 4483.

Zoeger, John, Jr: 4468.

Zoeger, Julianne F. Siegmund (Mrs John): 4472.

Zoeger, Louis: 4499.

Zoeller, Austin S.: 1773.

Zoeller, Daniel: 1165.

Zoeller, Henry: 1, 1165, 4499.

Zoeller, Margaret Sudden (Mrs Austin S.): 3852.

Zoeller, Noah: 3054, 4499.

Zoeller, Valentine: 13, 4499.

Zoellner, Anna, Miss: 4422.

Zoellner, Emma: 3041.

Zoellner, H.A.: 1, 333, 671, 672, 3034, 3042, 3815, 4299, 4422.

Zoellner, Herman T.: 3016, 3041, 3192.

Zoellner, M., Miss: 2714, 2818, 3048, 3631, 3632, 4380.

Zoellner, T.A.: 4380.

Zoellner, Theodore: 326, 646, 671, 672, 1338, 3034, 3037, 3048, 3815, 4067, 4299, 4422.

Zoller Family: 1773.

Zryd, Anna Barbara: 1729.

Zryd Family: 289.

Zryd, Gustave: 1729.

Zryd, John: 37, 1729, 1974, 2994, 3569, 4271, 4277, 4282.

Zryd, Joseph: 276, 4286, 4393, 4437.

Zryd, Oscar: 29, 1729.

Zuber, Carl: 4380.

Zuber, Caroline: 2447.

Zuber, Charles: 1773.

Zuber Family: 477.

Zuber, George: 4380.

Zuber, Jacob: 2447.

Zuber, Joe, Sr: 1737, 3923.

Zuber, Joseph: 1, 326, 2177, 2388, 2447, 3423, 4298.

Zuber, Joseph A.: 4315.

Zuber, Joseph Charles: 4315.

Zuber, Joseph R.: 3793, 4315.

Zuelch, John: 1165.

Zug Family: 1163, 1164.

Zukerman, Stan: 4315.

Zurbrigg, David: 4491.

Zurbrigg, Emmelia: 4491.

Zurbrigg, Gilgean: 4491.

Zurbrigg, Jacob: 2379.

Zurbrigg, Margrette Wettlaufer: 4491.

Zurbrigg, Norman H., Rev.: 3506.

Zurbrigg, Samuel H.: 4491.

Zurbrigg, T., Miss: 2798.

Zurbrigg, William: 4491.

Zurbuchen, John: 4491.

Zurnacioglu, Max Metin: 4474.

Zwalder Family: 725.

Zwick, Florence Brown: 1730.

Zwick, Frank F., Dr: 1730.